AMERICAN HISTORY

Connecting with the Past |FIFTEENTH EDITION

ALAN BRINKLEY
Columbia University

Reinforced Binding | *What does it mean?*

Since high schools frequently adopt for several years, it is important that a textbook can withstand the wear and tear of usage by multiple students. To ensure durability, McGraw-Hill has elected to manufacture this textbook with a reinforced binding.

Mc
Graw
Hill
Education

AMERICAN HISTORY: CONNECTING WITH THE PAST, 15E AP Edition
Alan Brinkley

Published by McGraw-Hill Education, 2 Penn Plaza, New York, NY 10121. Copyright © 2015 by McGraw-Hill Education. All rights reserved. Printed in the United States of America. Previous editions © 2012, 2009, and 2007. No part of this publication may be reproduced or distributed in any form or by any means, or stored in a database or retrieval system, without the prior written consent of McGraw-Hill Education, including, but not limited to, in any network or other electronic storage or transmission, or broadcast for distance learning.

Some ancillaries, including electronic and print components, may not be available to customers outside the United States.

This book is printed on acid-free paper.

5 6 7 8 9 0 DOW/DOW 1 0 9 8 7 6 5

ISBN 978-0-02-136299-8
MHID 0-02-136299-8

Senior Vice President, Products & Markets: *Kurt L. Strand*
Vice President, General Manager, Products & Markets: *Michael Ryan*
Vice President, Content Design & Delivery: *Kimberly Meriwether David*
Managing Director: *Gina Boedeker*
Brand Manager: *Laura Wilk*
Director, Product Development: *Meghan Campbell*
Executive Marketing Manager: *Stacy Best Ruel*
Marketing Manager: *April Cole*
Director of Development: *Rhona Robbin*
Digital Product Analyst: *John Brady*
Director, Content Production: *Terri Schiesl*
Production Manager: *Marianne Musni*
Content Project Manager: *Emily Kline*
Buyer: *Laura M. Fuller*
Design: *David Hash*
Content Licensing Specialists: *Carolyn Burger, Michelle Whitaker, Dianna Dausener*
Cover Image: *© Smithsonian Institution/Corbis*
Compositor: *Aptara®, Inc.*
Typeface: *9.5/12 That Book*
Printer: *R. R. Donnelley*

Library of Congress Cataloging-in-Publication Data

Brinkley, Alan.
   American history : connecting with the past / Alan Brinkley.–Fifteenth edition.
      pages cm
   Includes bibliographical references and index.
   ISBN 978-0-02-136299-8 (alkaline paper)–ISBN 0-02-136299-8 (alkaline paper)
1. United States–History–Textbooks.   I. Title.
   E178.1.B826 2014
   973–dc23   2014021721

www.mheducation.com

McGraw Hill Education

AP advantage

THE formula for improving AP exam scores. Follow these 3 steps to earn a 5!

McGraw-Hill

ONboard
AP* U.S. HISTORY

AP* Course Prep
NEWLY UPDATED for the Course Redesign!

ONBoard™ for AP U.S. History is a series of self-paced, online, interactive modules that help students master the historical thinking skills and content necessary to be successful in AP U.S. History coursework and on the AP Exam. Research-based and developed with AP teaching experts, *ONBoard™* covers ALL of the new historical thinking skills, including periodization and contextualization, crafting historical arguments from historical evidence, interpreting primary and secondary sources, historical causation, and patterns of continuity and change over time. Students self-check to ensure comprehension while the pre-test and comprehensive final assessment helps teachers identify skill and knowledge gaps.

connect plus+

AP* Course Support

Connect Plus is a robust, web-based assignment and assessment platform that helps students to better connect with coursework, teachers, and important concepts they will need to know for success now and in the future. It houses NEW AP Test Banks for each Exam question type, for each historical time period to provide students additional practice answering AP-style questions. *Connect Plus* also houses LearnSmart's adaptive study tool and SmartBook's adaptive reading experience for this new edition of *American History*.

McGraw-Hill

SCOREboard
AP* U.S. HISTORY

AP* Test Prep
NEWLY UPDATED for the Course Redesign!

SCOREboard™ AP U.S. History is the first Advanced Placement Exam Preparation solution that truly adapts to each student's learning needs, delivering personalized learning and mini-lessons to ensure student comprehension as they prepare in the weeks and months leading up to the AP Exam. *SCOREBoard™* is an online, personalized learning plan with an adaptive, focused content review and four complete AP Practice Exams. Students learn at their own pace and set their study schedules. A comprehensive reporting system provides feedback to both students and teachers.

MHEonline.com

CONTENTS

7 | THE JEFFERSONIAN ERA 180

8 | VARIETIES OF AMERICAN NATIONALISM 214

9 | JACKSONIAN AMERICA 229

10 | AMERICA'S ECONOMIC REVOLUTION 254

11 | COTTON, SLAVERY, AND THE OLD SOUTH 293

15 RECONSTRUCTION AND THE NEW SOUTH 399

16 THE CONQUEST OF THE FAR WEST 430

20 THE PROGRESSIVES   551

21 AMERICA AND THE GREAT WAR   583

23 **THE GREAT DEPRESSION** 639

24 THE NEW DEAL 661

25 THE GLOBAL CRISIS, 1921–1941 686

26 AMERICA IN A WORLD AT WAR 704

30 THE CRISIS OF AUTHORITY 807

31 FROM THE "AGE OF LIMITS" TO THE AGE OF REAGAN 837

32 THE AGE OF GLOBALIZATION   856

WHY do so many people take an interest in history? It is, I think, because we know that we are the products of the past–that everything we know, everything we see, and everything we imagine is rooted in our history. It is not surprising that there have been historians throughout almost all of recorded time. It is only natural that we are interested in what the past was like. Whether we study academic history or not, we all are connected to the past.

Americans have always had a love of their own history. It is a daunting task to attempt to convey the long and remarkable story of America in a single book, but that is what this volume attempts to do. The subtitle of this book, "Connecting with the Past," describes this edition's focus on encouraging readers to be aware of the ways in which our everyday experiences are rooted in our history.

Like any history, this book is a product of its time. It reflects the views of the past that historians continue to develop. A comparable book published decades from now will likely seem as different from this one as this book appears different from histories written a generation or more ago. The writing of history changes constantly–not, of course, because the past changes, but because of shifts in the way historians, and the publics they serve, ask and answer questions about the past.

There have always been critics of changes in historical understanding. Many people argue that history is a collection of facts and should not be subject to "interpretation" or "revision." But historians insist that history is not and cannot be simply a collection of facts. They are only the beginning of historical understanding. It is up to the writers and readers of history to try to interpret the evidence before them; and in doing so, they will inevitably bring to the task their own questions, concerns, and experiences.

Our history examines the experience of the many different peoples and ideas that have shaped American society. But it also requires us to understand that the United States is a nation whose people share many things: a common political system, a connection to an integrated national (and now international) economy, and a familiarity with a shared and enormously powerful mass culture. To understand the American past, it is necessary to understand both the forces that divide Americans and the forces that draw them together.

It is not only the writing of history that changes with time–the tools and technologies through which information is delivered change as well. Created as an integral part of the content of this fifteenth edition are an array of valuable learning resources that will aid instructors in teaching and students in learning about American history. These resources include:

- Smartbook®–an online version of this book that adapts to each student's reading experience by offering self-quizzing and highlighting material that the student is struggling with.
- Connect History®–homework and quizzing exercises including map understanding, primary source analysis, image exploration, key terms, and review and writing questions.
- Insight®–a first-of-its-kind analytics tool for Connect assignments that provides instructors with vital information about how students are performing and which assignments are the most effective.
- Interactive maps–more than thirty maps in the ebook and Connect can be manipulated by students to encourage better geographical understanding.
- Critical Missions®–an activity that immerses students in pivotal moments in history. As students study primary sources and maps, they advise a key historical figure on an issue of vital importance–for example, should President Truman drop the atomic bomb on Japan?
- A Primary Source Primer–a video exercise with multiple-choice questions teaches students the importance of primary sources and how to analyze them. This online "Introduction to Primary Sources" is designed for use at the beginning of the course, to save valuable class time.

In addition to content and scholarship updates throughout, we have added 4 new "Consider the Source" boxed features that explore the topics of family time; wartime oratory; black history; and race, gender, and military service. Our concluding chapter, "The Age of Globalization," now brings *American History* up-to-date through the summer of 2014 and includes coverage of the 2008 financial crisis, the rise of the Tea Party, the 2012 election, the Affordable Care Act, and the ongoing federal gridlock.

I am grateful to many people for their help on this book–especially the people at McGraw-Hill who have supported and sustained this book so well for many years. I am grateful to Laura Wilk, Rhona Robbin, Art Pomponio, April Cole, Stacy Ruel, Emily Kline, and Carrie Burger. I am grateful, too, to Deborah Bull for her help with photographs. I also appreciate the many suggestions I have received from students over the last several years, as well as the reviews provided by a group of talented scholars and teachers.

Alan Brinkley
Columbia University
New York, NY

3 | SOCIETY AND CULTURE IN PROVINCIAL AMERICA

LIFE IN THE AMERICAN COLONIES This colored engraving shows the domestic life of Americans during the eighteenth century. Depicted are family members at work in their cozy surroundings. Their industriousness is shown to be a singular virtue of the era.
(© Bettmann/Corbis)

AP
HISTORICAL THINKING

1. **Comparison** Compare the patterns of family life and women's roles (including social attitudes towards women) in each of the colonial regions.

2. **Historical Causation** What are the reasons for differing economic systems in each of the colonial regions and explain the impact of those systems on each region's social structure.

3. **Comparison** Compare the physical settlement patterns of each of the colonial regions and analyze the reasons for and the consequences of those patterns in the development of the colonial societies.

4. **Historical Argumentation** Analyze the relative importance of natural population increase vs. immigration in the development of colonial society.

5. **Contextualization** Identify the impact of technology, science, and education on political, social, and economic developments in each colonial region.

6. **Patterns of Continuity and Change over Time** How did the lives of African slaves change over the course of the first century of slavery in North America?

7. **Contextualization** Describe the intellectual culture of colonial America, as expressed in literature, philosophy, science, education, and law, and identify any regional differences.

8. **Patterns of Continuity and Change over Time** Describe the changes in sources of immigration from Europe and the settlement patterns of the different groups.

Key Concept Correlations

Analyze the ways the historical developments you learn about in this chapter connect to the following AP Key Concepts.

1.2 European overseas expansion resulted in the Columbian Exchange, a series of interactions and adaptations among societies across the Atlantic.

2.1 Differences in imperial goals, cultures, and the North American environments that different empires confronted led Europeans to develop diverse patterns of colonization.

2.2 European colonization efforts in North America stimulated intercultural contact and intensified conflict between the various groups of colonizers and native peoples.

2.3 The increasing political, economic, and cultural exchanges within the "Atlantic World" had a profound impact on the development of colonial societies in North America.

3.2 In the late 18th century, new experiments with democratic ideas and republican forms of government, as well as other new religious, economic, and cultural ideas, challenged traditional imperial systems across the Atlantic World.

Thematic Learning Objectives

WXT-1, 2, 4; PEO-1, 5; WOR-1, 2; ENV-2, 4; ID-1, 4, 5; POL-1; CUL-1, 4

Historical Thinking guided study helps students begin to view the key concepts through the lens of historical thinking skills.

Extensive coverage of the new AP US History **Thematic Learning Objectives** guides students as they put historical events into the context of overarching themes.

Chapter-level **Key Concept** correlations ensure proper focus by students and teachers.

Through **Connecting Concepts**, students' attention is focused on the most important AP Key Concepts presented in the chapter. Students are also encouraged to connect concepts among many chapters to discover the historical "Big Picture."

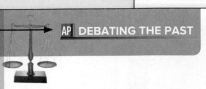

AP DEBATING THE PAST

THE ORIGINS OF SLAVERY

THE debate among historians over how and why white Americans created a system of slave labor in the seventeenth century—and how and why they determined that people of African descent and no others should populate that system—has been a long and unusually heated one. At its center is the question of whether slavery was a result of white racism or whether slavery created racism.

In 1950, Oscar and Mary Handlin published an influential article, "Origins of the Southern Labor System," comparing slavery to other systems of "unfreedom" in the colonies. What differentiated slavery from other conditions of servitude, they argued, was that it was restricted to people of African descent, it was permanent, and it passed from one generation to the next. The unique characteristics of slavery, the Handlins maintained, were part of an effort by colonial legislatures to increase the available labor force. White laborers needed an incentive to come to America; black laborers, forcibly imported from Africa, did not. The distinction between the conditions of white workers and the conditions of black workers was, therefore, based on legal and economic motives, not on racism. Racism emerged to justify slavery; it did not cause slavery.

Winthrop D. Jordan was one of a number of historians who later challenged the Handlins' thesis and argued that white racism, more than economic interests, produced African slavery. In *White Over Black* (1968) and other works, Jordan argued that Europeans had long viewed people of color—and black Africans in particular—as inferior beings appropriate for serving whites. Those attitudes migrated with white Europeans to the New World, and white racism shaped the treatment of Africans in America—and the nature of the slave labor system—from the beginning.

George Fredrickson echoed Jordan's emphasis on racism as an independent factor reinforcing slavery; but unlike Jordan, he argued that racism did not precede slavery. "The treatment of blacks," he wrote, "engendered a cultural and psycho-social racism that after a certain point took on a life of its own. . . . Racism, although the child of slavery, not only outlived its parent but grew stronger and more independent after slavery's demise."

In *Black Majority* (1974), a study of seventeenth-century South Carolina, Peter Wood moved the debate away from racism and back toward social and economic conditions. Wood demonstrated that blacks and whites often worked together on relatively equal terms in the early years of settlement. But as rice cultivation expanded, finding white laborers willing to do the arduous work became more difficult. The forcible importation of African workers and the creation of a system of permanent bondage was a response to a growing demand for labor and to fears among whites that without slavery a black labor force would be difficult to control.

Edmund Morgan argued similarly in *American Slavery, American Freedom* (1975) that the southern labor system was at first relatively flexible and later grew more rigid. In colonial Virginia, he claimed, white settlers did not at first intend to create a system of permanent bondage. But as the tobacco economy grew and created a high demand for cheap labor, white landowners began to feel uneasy about their dependence on a large group of dependent white workers, since such workers were difficult to recruit and control. Thus slavery was less a result of racism than of the desire of white landowners to find a reliable and stable labor force.

In *The Making of New World Slavery* (1996), Robin Blackburn argued that while race was a factor in allowing whites to justify to themselves the enslavement of Africans, the real reasons for slavery were hardheaded economic decisions by ambitious entrepreneurs, who realized early on that a slave-labor system in the labor-intensive agricultural world of the American South and the Caribbean was more profitable than a free-labor system. Slavery served the interests of a powerful combination of groups: planters, merchants, governments, industrialists, and consumers.

Race may have been a rationale for slavery, allowing planters and traders to justify to themselves the terrible human costs of the system. But the most important reason for the system was not just racism, but the pursuit of profit—and the success of the system in producing it. Blackburn concluded that slavery was not an antiquated remnant of an older world but, rather, a recognizably modern labor system that, however ugly, served the needs of an emerging market economy. ●

AP HISTORICAL ARGUMENTATION AND INTERPRETATION

Questions assume cumulative content knowledge from this chapter and previous chapters.

1. Identify three differing historical arguments regarding how and why white American colonists created a slave labor system. For each, describe one piece of historical evidence that supports the argument.
2. If you were writing a history of the origins of slavery in colonial America, identify three events or developments you would research, which you believe are of such significance that they are essential to telling the story.
3. With which historian's interpretation do you most agree? Explain why, supporting your argument with historical evidence.

The first African laborers arrived in English North America before 1620, and as English seamen began to establish themselves in the slave trade, the flow of Africans to the colonies gradually increased. But North America was always a much less important market for Africans than were other parts of the New World, especially the Caribbean islands and Brazil, whose labor-intensive sugar economies created an especially large demand for slaves. Less than 5 percent of the Africans imported to the Americas went directly to the English colonies on the mainland. Most blacks who ended up in what became the United States spent time first in the West Indies. Not until the 1670s did traders start importing blacks directly from Africa to North America. Even then, however, the flow remained small for a time, mainly because a single group, the Royal African Company of England, maintained a monopoly on trade in the mainland colonies and managed as a result to keep prices high and supplies low.

A turning point in the history of the African population in North America came in the mid-1690s, when the Royal African Company's monopoly was finally broken. With the trade now opened to English and colonial merchants on a competitive basis, prices fell and the number of Africans arriving in North America rapidly increased. By the end of the seventeenth century, only about one in ten of the residents of the colonies were Africans (about 25,000 in all). But because Africans were so heavily concentrated in a few southern colonies, they were already beginning to outnumber Europeans in some areas. The high ratio of men to women among African immigrants (there were perhaps two males to one female in most areas) retarded the natural increase of the black population. But in the Chesapeake at least, more new slaves were being born by 1700 than were being imported from Africa. In South Carolina, by contrast, the difficult conditions of rice

GROWING SLAVE POPULATION

culture—South Carolina, for example, where the number of [new ar]rivals swelled more quickly than anywhere else—blacks lived and worked together for a time on terms of relative equality. Some blacks were treated much like white hired servants, and some were freed after a fixed servitude. A few Africans themselves became landowners, and some apparently owned slaves of their own.

[In the] early eighteenth century, however, a rigid distinction [had] become established between black and white. (See the Past," above.) Masters were contractually obliged [to free w]hite servants after a fixed term of servitude. There [was no su]ch necessity to free black workers, and the assump[tion was] spread that blacks would remain in service perma[nently. A]nother incentive for making the status of Africans [perma]nent that the children of slaves provided white landown[ers a] self-perpetuating labor force.

72

73

Through a series of 24 **Debating the Past** features, students have the opportunity to analyze historiography, and to interpret historical arguments and evidence.

Guided questions embolden students to **interpret the arguments** of some well-known historians, with an emphasis on **historical evidence**, **periodization**, and **contextualization**.

Students and teachers connect events in the Atlantic World and beyond to fully interpret the new AP US History Theme of **America in the World** through this series of 16 parallel features.

Higher-order thinking questions encourage students to use **Historical Thinking Skills** to interpret historical information.

THE FIRST GLOBAL WAR WOR-1

THE French and Indian War in North America was only a small part of a much larger conflict. Known in Europe as the Seven Years' War it was one of the longest, most widespread, and most important wars in modern history. "Ministers in this country, where every part of the World affects us, in some way or another, should consider the whole Globe," the Duke of Newcastle wrote in Britain in 1758, reflecting the international achievements and war aims of the British in the mid-eighteenth century. Two centuries later, Winston Churchill the former British prime minister, wrote of the Seven Years' War as the first "World War."

In North America, the war was a result of tensions along the frontiers of the British Empire, but a larger war resulted from conflicts among the great powers in the 1750s with what historians have called a "diplomatic revolution." Well-established alliances between Britain and the Austro-Hungarian Empire, and between France and Prussia, collapsed, replaced by new alliances that set Britain and Prussia against France and Austria. The instability that these changing alliances produced helped speed the European nations toward war. The one thing that did not change was the continuing rivalry between Britain and France.

The Austrian-British alliance collapsed because Austria suffered a series of significant defeats at the hands of the Prussians. To the British government, these failures suggested that the Austro-Hungarian Empire was now too weak to help Britain balance French power. As a result, Britain sought new partnerships with the rising powers of northern Germany, Austria's enemies. Seeking protection from the power of their former British allies, the Austrians allied with France. Russia, concerned about the Austro-Hungarian Empire's possible dominance in central Europe, allied with Britain and Prussia.

The tensions that these complicated realignments created eventually led to war (just as the complicated alliances in Europe in the early twentieth century helped produce World War I). The European part of the war was a result of the continuing conflict between Prussia and Austria and the effect of those wars on the allies of both. The Seven Years' War soon spread across much of the world, engaging not only most of the great powers in Europe, from England to Russia, but also the emerging colonial world—India, West Africa, the Caribbean, and the Philippines—as the powerful British navy worked to strip France, and eventually Spain, of their valuable colonial holdings.

Like most modern conflicts, the Seven Years' War was a struggle for economic power. Colonial possessions, many European nations believed, were critical to their future wealth, well worth fighting for. The war's outcome affected not only the future of America, but also the distribution of power through much of the world. It destroyed the French navy and much of the French Empire, and it elevated Great Britain to undisputed preeminence among colonial powers—especially when, at the conclusion of the war, India and all of eastern North America fell firmly under English control. The war also reorganized the balance of power in Europe, with Britain now preeminent among the great powers and Prussia (later to become the core of modern Germany) rapidly rising in wealth and military power.

The Seven Years' War was not only one of the first great colonial wars; it was also one of the last great wars of religion. It extended the dominance of Protestantism in Europe. In what is now Canada, the war replaced French with British rule and thus Catholic with Protestant rule. The Vatican, no longer a military power itself, had relied on the great Catholic empires—Spain, France, and Austria-Hungary—as bulwarks of the Vatican's power and influence. The shift of power toward Protestant governments in Europe and North America weakened the Catholic Church and reduced its geopolitical influence.

The conclusion of the Seven Years' War strengthened Britain and Germany and weakened France. But it did not provide any lasting solution to the rivalries among the great colonial powers. In North America, a dozen years after the end of the war, the American Revolution—the origins of which were in many ways a direct result of the Seven Years' War—stripped the British Empire of one of its most important and valuable colonial appendages. By the time the American Revolution came to an end, the French Revolution had sparked another lengthy period of war, culminating in the Napoleonic Wars of the early nineteenth century, which once again redrew the map of Europe and, for a while, the world. ●

UNDERSTAND, ANALYZE, AND EVALUATE

1. How did the Seven Years' War change the balance of power among the nations of Europe? Who gained and who lost in the war?
2. What effect did the war's outcome have on the European colonies in North America?
3. Why is the Seven Years' War described as "one of the most important wars in modern history"?

THE SEVEN YEARS' WAR was one of the first great colonial conflicts. This etching shows a fireworks display at the Hôtel de Ville in Paris on February 10, 1763, to celebrate the end of the hostilities. (© The Granger Collection, New York)

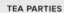

AP CONSIDER THE SOURCE

TEA PARTIES

THE BOSTON Tea Party of 1773 was a revolt against "taxation without representation." The poem "Tea, Destroyed by Indians" celebrates the action of the Boston Tea Party, expresses the colonists' resentments and complaints against the distant London government, and calls upon Boston patriots to continue to resist British actions.

The twenty-first-century Tea Party movement became prominent in 2009. Although not an official political party, members tend to endorse Republican candidates. The modern Tea Party move[ment]... years ago, a[nd]... Party: hostili[ty]... (imposed by... really take p[lace]... rary taxation...

Alan Brinkley's document pairings in the 14 **Consider the Source** features are perfectly placed to allow students to make connections to events throughout American history.

BOSTON TEA PAR[TY]

TEA, DESTROYED BY INDIA[NS]

Poem honoring the Boston Tea Par[ty]

CHORUS:

Bostonian's SONS keep up your Courage g[ood]
Or Dye, like Martyrs, in fair Free-born Blo[od]

YE GLORIOUS SONS OF FREEDOM, bra[ve]
That has flood forth–fair LIBERTY to hol[d]
Though you were INDIANS, come from
Like MEN you acted–not like savage M[en]

CHORUS

Our LIBERTY, and LIFE is now invaded,
And FREEDOM's brightest Charms are d[...]
But, we will STAND–and think it noble
To DART the man that dare oppress the[e]

CHORUS

How grand the Scene!–(No Tyrant shall [...]
The TEA is sunk in spite of all our foes.
A NOBLE SIGHT–to see th' accursed TE[A]
Mingled with MUD–and ever for to be;
For KING and PRINCE shall know that w[...]

TEA PARTY MOVEMENT—2010

Although the Tea Party movement has no centralized leadership, one organization that claims to be the "official" home of the American Tea Party movement is TeaParty.org. A description and set of core beliefs provided by this organization appear below.

TEAPARTY.ORG DESCRIPTION AND CORE BELIEFS

What Is the Tea Party?
The Tea Party is a grassroots movement that calls awareness to any issue that challenges the security, sovereignty, or domestic tranquility of our beloved nation, the United States of America.

From our founding, the Tea Party is the voice of the true owners of the United States, WE THE PEOPLE.

Many claim to be the founders of this movement–however, it was the brave souls of the men and women in 1773, known today as the Boston Tea Party, who dared defy the greatest military might on earth.

We are the beneficiaries of their courage. By joining the Tea Party, you are taking a stand for our nation. You will be upholding the grand principles set forth in the U.S. Constitution and Bill of Rights.

Non-negotiable core beliefs
Illegal Aliens Are Here Illegally.
Pro-Domestic Employment Is Indispensable.
Stronger Military Is Essential.
Special Interests Eliminated.
Gun Ownership Is Sacred.
Government Must Be Downsized.
National Budget Must Be Balanced.
Deficit Spending Will End.
Bail-Out and Stimulus Plans Are Illegal.
Reduce Personal Income Taxes A Must.
Reduce Business Income Taxes Is Mandatory.
Political Offices Available To Average Citizens.
Intrusive Government Stopped.
English As Core Language Is Required.
Traditional Family Values Are Encouraged.
Common Sense Constitutional.
Conservative Self-Governance.

Source: Tea Party/1773 Tea Party

AP TEST PRACTICE

Questions assume cumulative content knowledge from this chapter and previous chapters.

1. The poem reflects the influence of which philosophical ideas?
   (A) Religious conservatism
   (B) Ideals of religious toleration
   (C) Enlightenment
   (D) British parliamentary system

2. Which common political question is being alluded to by both the poem and the document?
   (A) Degree of authority of centralized power
   (B) Legitimacy of Parliamentary power
   (C) The extent of private property rights
   (D) Commercial regulation

3. The poem and document best share which of the following regarding the audience being addressed?
   (A) Grassroots movement
   (B) Intellectual elites
   (C) Women
   (D) Politicians

Using the documents as stimuli, **NEW AP-style multiple choice questions** match the rigor and complexity required for the new AP US History Exam.

authorities in England try to impose the common law and the statutes of the realm upon the provinces. By then, it was already too late. Although the American legal system adopted most of the essential elements of the English system, including such ancient rights as trial by jury, significant differences had already become well established. Pleading and court procedures were simpler in America than in England, and punishments were different. Instead of the gallows or prison, colonists more commonly resorted to the whipping post, the branding iron, the stocks, and (for "gossipy" women) the ducking stool. In a labor-scarce society, it was not in the interests of communities to execute or incarcerate potential workers. Crimes were redefined. In England, a printed attack on a public official, whether true or false, was considered libelous. In the 1734-1735 trial of the New York publisher John Peter Zenger, who was powerfully defended by the Philadelphia lawyer Andrew Hamilton, the courts ruled that criticisms of the government were not libelous if factually true–a verdict that removed some restrictions on the freedom of the press: there was a subtle but decisive transformation in legal philosophy. Some colonists came to think of law as a reflection of the divine will; others saw it as a result of the natural order. In neither case did they consider it an expression of the power of an earthly sovereign.

Even more significant for the future of the relationship between the colonies and England were important differences between the American and British political systems. Because the

COLONIAL GOVERNMENTS royal government was so far away, Americans created a group of institutions of their own that gave them–in reality, if not in theory–a

large measure of self-government. In most colonies, local communities grew accustomed to running their own affairs with minimal interference from higher authorities. Communities also expected to maintain strict control over their delegates to the colonial assemblies, and those assemblies came to exercise many of the powers that Parliament exercised in England (even though in theory Parliament remained the ultimate authority in America). Provincial governors appointed by the Crown had broad powers on paper, but in fact their influence was sharply limited. They lacked control over appointments and contracts; such influence resided largely in England or with local colonial leaders. They could never be certain of their tenure in office; because governorships were patronage appointments, a governor could be removed any time his patron in England lost favor. And in many cases, governors were not even familiar with the colonies they were meant to govern. Some governors were native-born Americans, but most were Englishmen who came to the colonies for the first time to assume their offices. The result of all this was that the focus of politics in the colonies became a local one. The provincial governments became accustomed to acting more or less independently of Parliament, and a set of assumptions and expectations about the rights of the colonists began to take hold in America that policymakers in England did not share. These differences caused few problems before the 1740s, because the British did little to exert the authority they believed they possessed. But when, beginning ... attempting to tigh... a great imperial cr...

AP CONNECTING THEMES

Chapter 3 discussed the development of colonial society in each of the colonial regions. You should be able to compare and contrast the colonial regions in terms of the role of women, class structure, and social mobility. Particularly important are the reasons for and consequences of a forced labor system. You should also keep in mind similarities and differences in governmental structures, economic systems, and culture throughout the colonies, including the impact of science, technology, and education on each colonial region. Finally, be able to explain the reasons for and sources of population growth in the colonies.

The following themes have a heightened importance in Chapter 3. You should now be able to do the following for each listed theme:

Identity: Identify the factors that led to distinct colonial regional identities. Identify how differing roles for women affected their identity.

Work, exchange, ...
science, and educ...
colonial regions. Ex...
growth of the instit...
Peopling: Identif...
the development ...
systems.
Politics and pow...
conflict between c...
colonial governme...
America in the ...
colonial economy...
relationships amon...
Ideas, beliefs, an...
differences in ideas...
beliefs, and cultur...
regional differences...

People, places, and events in the **AP Suggested Study** section can be used as evidence to support student answers to the new Short Answer and Long Essay questions.

Each chapter closes with **Connecting Themes** which summarizes the major AP themes discussed. Targeted thematic instruction ensures close connection with the AP Themes' overarching questions.

AP SUGGESTED STUDY

PEOPLE/PLACES/EVENTS As you study these items, think about how they demonstrate or relate to key concepts and historical themes from this chapter and previous chapters.

COTTON MATHER 94	INDENTURED SERVITUDE 66	MIDDLE PASSAGE 71
COVENANT 85	INDIGO 78	PRIMOGENITURE 86
ENLIGHTENMENT IDEALS 89	JEREMIAD 90	SAUGUS IRONWORKS 79
GEORGE WHITEFIELD 94	JOHN AND CHARLES WESLEY 90	SCOTS-IRISH 76
GREAT AWAKENING 90	JOHN LOCKE 92	SLAVE CODES 74
GULLAH 84	JOHN PETER ZENGER 96	STONO REBELLION 85
HUGUENOTS 75	JONATHAN EDWARDS 91	TRIANGULAR TRADE 80

AP TEST PRACTICE

Questions assume cumulative content knowledge from this chapter and previous chapters.

MULTIPLE CHOICE Use the images "A 'Dame School' Primer" and "Benjamin Franklin on Electricity" from pages 94-95 and your knowledge of U.S. history to answer questions 1-2.

1. Which is best supported by the two artifacts, regarding cultural values in the North American English colonies by the early to mid-18th century?

   (A) Education was valued solely as a means to advance theology.

   (B) Almost all intellectuals in the colonies began to reject traditional religious values.

   (C) Enlightenment influences were in strict conflict with traditional religious values.

   (D) Traditional religiosity intermingled with Enlightenment influences.

2. Which best explains how values reflected by the artifacts might have influenced future American colonial conflict with Great Britain?

   (A) The greater literacy rates in the colonies undermined reverence for British authority and culture.

   (B) Value placed on education, combined with Enlightenment ideas of the role of human reason in improving society, led to greater public engagement in politics.

   (C) The spread of Enlightenment ideas threatening traditional religious values led to social anxiety, spreading a culture of discontent.

   (D) Greater literacy rates and the spread of secular knowledge promoted greater class distinctions.

SHORT ANSWER Use your knowledge of U.S. history to answer questions 3-5.

3. Answer a, b, and c.
   a) Briefly explain ONE example of how the growth of colonial economies affected relationships among nations within the "Atlantic World."

   b) Briefly explain a SECOND example of how the growth of colonial economies affected relationships among nations within the "Atlantic World."

   c) Briefly explain ONE example of how interactions within the "Atlantic World" promoted Anglicization in the British colonies in North America.

4. Answer a, b, and c.
   a) Briefly explain ONE example of regional differences in the patterns of family life and attitudes toward women in the English colonies in 17th and early 18th centuries.

   b) Briefly explain ONE example of how changes in science and technology in the 17th and early 18th centuries affected regional development within the British colonies.

   c) Briefly explain ONE example of how free and forced migration affected regional development within the British colonies in the 17th and early 18th centuries.

5. Using the painting on page 82, answer a, b, and c.
   a) What does the painting suggest about the nature of the North American colonies' cultural relationship with England during the early to mid-18th century?

   b) Provide ONE example that could be used to support that view.

   c) Provide ONE example that could be used to refute that view.

LONG ESSAY Develop a thoughtful and thorough historical argument that answers the question below. Begin your essay with a thesis statement and support it with relevant historical evidence.

6. Some historians have argued that the intellectual and social culture of British colonial America did not greatly diverge from the intellectual and social life of England. Support, modify, or refute this interpretation, providing specific evidence to justify your answer.

AP Test Practice for each chapter gives students the opportunity to answer the New AP Exam-style multiple choice, short-answer, and long-essay questions. The complexity matches the rigor of the revised AP US History Exam.

AP TEACHING RESOURCES

Also available for AP United States History courses with this AP edition of *American History: Connecting with the Past*

ONBoard™ for AP United States History has been updated for the new redesigned course! *ONboard* is a series of self-paced, online, interactive modules that help students master the historical thinking skills and content necessary to be successful in AP U.S. History coursework and on the AP Exam. Research-based and developed with AP teaching experts, *ONBoard™* features animations and interactive activities. The redesigned content covers **ALL of the new AP Historical Thinking Skills**, including **periodization and contextualization, synthesis, interpreting primary sources, comparison, historical causation, continuity and change over time, and historical evidence**. Students self-check to ensure comprehension while the pre-test and comprehensive final assessment helps teachers identify skill and knowledge gaps.

ConnectPlus is a robust, web-based assignment and assessment platform that gives students the means to better connect with coursework, teachers, and important concepts they will need to know for success now and in the future. It houses our new **AP U.S. History Question Banks specific to the new course redesign** that give students additional practice answering all of the new AP Exam-style questions. *ConnectPlus* also features the LearnSmart adaptive study tool and the SmartBook adaptive reading experience specifically developed for the 15th edition help students quickly hone in on important content.

SCOREboard™ AP United States History has been updated for the new redesigned course! *SCOREboard* is the first Advanced Placement Exam Preparation solution that truly adapts to each student's learning needs, delivering personalized learning and mini-lessons to ensure student comprehension as they prepare in the weeks and months leading up to the AP Exam. *SCORE-Board™* is an online, personalized learning plan with an adaptive, focused content review and four complete AP Practice Exams in the New Exam Format. Students learn at their own pace and set their study schedules. A comprehensive reporting system provides feedback to both students and teachers.

McGraw-Hill Tegrity™ *Tegrity* captures lessons, lectures, and skills in a searchable format for use in traditional, hybrid, "flipped classes," and online courses. Its personalized learning features make study time efficient, and its ability to affordably scale brings this benefit to every student on campus. Patented search technology and real-time LMS integrations make *Tegrity* the market-leading solution and service.

With **McGraw-Hill Create™, you can create and tailor the course you want to teach.** With *McGraw-Hill Create,* create.mheducation.com, you can easily rearrange chapters, combine material from other content sources, and quickly upload content you have written, like your course syllabus or teaching notes, or arrange your book to fit your teaching style.

ConnectED e-Book This downloadable, digital version of *American History: Connecting with the Past* merges media and assessments with the text narrative to engage students, offers powerful and instant search capability, and helps students manage notes, highlights and bookmarks all in one place.

Available on this AP edition's Online Learning Center (OLC) at: *mheonline.com/brinkleyAP15*

AP Teacher's Manual by William Shelton and John R. Struck Developed specifically to help AP United States teachers seamlessly transition to the new curriculum, this resource provides a pacing guide; connections between chapter content and key AP concepts and themes; essential terms; historical thinking skills activities; and a series of discussion questions, short answer questions, and essay questions that help teachers assess full student comprehension. By using the manual teachers will find clear and direct ways to pace their course, to illustrate key concepts and thematic learning skills, and to teach students how to "think like historians" by understanding the historical thinking skills.

AP Key Concept Correlation and AP Thematic Learning Objective Correlations These resources correlate book content to specific AP concepts and themes to help teachers target critical content and prepare students for the AP exam.

ABOUT THE AP UNITED STATES HISTORY COURSE

Course Themes and Structure

This Advanced Placement Course is meant to replicate a college-level introductory United States History Survey Course and thus give you the skills and knowledge for more specialized courses in American History. While there are an infinite variety of ways to present an AP Course, there are certain things that everyone should get out of their course. These include an understanding of the chronological framework of American History, especially an understanding of how events and trends are related, rather than simply memorizing a collection of facts and dates. In addition, you should come out of an AP Course with certain skills, including the ability to critically analyze both primary and secondary sources; to develop a thesis or argument and support it with concrete historical evidence; and to understand the major interpretive frameworks that historians have used to explain the American past.

The College Board and the Educational Testing Service, which administer the AP Exam, survey over 100 college and university instructors across the country to get a sense of what is being taught in introductory college survey courses. A Test Development Committee, which consists of three college or university professors and three high school teachers, uses this information to create an examination that reflects the experience that most undergraduate students receive. It is administered in early May. The AP United States History (APUSH) Exam is then scored by a group of thousands of AP high school teachers, and college and university professors who serve as AP Exam Readers. These teachers gather for a fun-filled, action-packed week in early June and receive training in how to score the exams and then spend the rest of the week reading and scoring your essays.

The College Board introduced seven themes to help prepare you for the AP Exam. These include the following (1) Identity, (2) Work, Exchange, and Technology, (3) Peopling, (4) Politics and Power, (5) America in the World, (6) Environment and Geography, Human and Physical, and (7) Ideas, Beliefs, and Culture. Student familiarity with these themes is essential for scoring well on the exam since they provide the basis for both multiple choice and essay questions. Below is a brief description of each. A fuller discussion of these themes can be found on AP Central.

Themes

Identity: This theme focuses on a sense of belonging to a particular group of people. That might entail a sense of belonging to a nation or to a particular group within a nation (i.e. being American, being Southern, being American Indian). Students should be able to explain the continuity and change of identities over time (i.e. What did it mean to be an American during the American Revolution? What did it mean to be an American during the Red Scare?).

Work, Exchange, and Technology: This theme focuses on the development of the agricultural, commercial, and manufacturing elements of the American economy. Students should examine the degree to which and ways in which government has interacted with the economic system and the results of that interaction. Students should also be able to explain the relationship between business and labor in various time periods and should be able to examine how work has impacted various classes of society, racial and ethnic groups, and men and women.

Peopling: This theme deals with demographics and the movement of people to, from, and within the United States. Students should be able to explain the rise of the institution of slavery, important waves of immigration in different time periods, and the American response to those influxes of immigrants. Students should be able to explain the impact of immigrant populations on the culture of the United States, and the causes and effects of internal migration, and the ease or difficulty of various immigrants groups in assimilating into American society.

Politics and Power: This theme focuses on the role of federal, state, and local governments in facilitating either continuity or change in American society. This includes conflict over the power of the federal government versus the power of states and power struggles within the branches of the federal government. Students must be able to explain the causes and results of the rise of various party systems in different eras of American history.

America in the World: This theme is designed to get students to focus on United States involvement in the world and the impact of world affairs on the United States. Students should examine the competition for territory, resources, and ideological influence among nation states in various time periods and the role of the United States in that contest. Students should also focus on how U.S. military, economic, and foreign policy initiatives have affected the world and domestic affairs.

Environment and Geography - Human and Physical: Students should focus on how the geography, climate and the environment have advanced and limited human actions in America. This theme also requires students to explore the exploitation, protection, and management of the natural environment. Students should also focus on how perceptions of the human and physical environment have changed over time.

Ideas, Beliefs, and Culture: This theme explores how ideas, beliefs, and culture have played a role in shaping American thought. Students should consider how moral, religious, philosophical, and scientific beliefs have led to continuity and conflict in American society and the intermingling of these with political, economic, and social thought over time.

Historical Thinking Skills

The redesigned AP U.S. History course and exam also emphasizes the development and use of historical thinking skills. It is imperative that student understand what is entailed in each of these skills since questions on the exam will require students to respond using a particular historical thinking skill. The historical thinking skills designed by the College Board include:

Historical Causation: Historical thinking requires that students be able to analyze cause/effect relationships, both long and short term. As the course progresses student should become proficient in analyzing multi-causation and multi-effect, understanding the complexity of history.

Patterns of Continuity and Change Over Time: Historical thinking requires students to examine historical trends and recognize connections between seemingly disparate facts to support an argument of change or continuity. When questions ask students to examine continuity and change they must analyze both to get credit.

Periodization: Students need to develop an understanding of how and why historians block off different time periods and indicate critical turning points in American history. Turning points may vary according to what a historian sees as most significant. Students should develop their own logical sense of turning points in U.S. History and be able to support their choice by citing specific evidence or trends. They should also realize and understand why some historians might see a different turning point than the one a student chooses.

Comparison: Historical thinking involves the ability to compare and contrast different time periods, geographic regions, and societies. Students need to be able to see both similarities and differences within a given time period and between different time periods. Students should be able to compare and contrast each of the seven themes throughout the course of U.S. history.

Contextualization: Historical thinking requires that student be able to connect historical events to other events going on in the same time period. Students should also be able to connect events to broader regional, national, and international events to provide a context for the specific circumstance they are examining.

Historical Argumentation: Historical thinking requires students to be able to frame and/or answer a question and to construct a logical and coherent argument to support a particular position. Such arguments require an analytical thesis, relevant historical evidence, and analysis of how and why that evidence supports the thesis. Students should also be able to describe, analyze, and evaluate contradictory evidence or arguments of other historians.

Appropriate Use of Relevant Historic Evidence: Historical thinking involves the ability to describe and evaluate evidence from a variety of primary and secondary sources. Students must be able to identify and realize the importance of the author, place and time, purpose, audience, reason, main idea, and significance of documents they may use to support an argument. Critical for the AP exam, students must be able to draw conclusions and make inferences from documents and explain how and why that information supports their argument. Historical thinking also involves the ability to understand a document's point of view and the reasons for that point of view.

Interpretation: Historical thinking involves the ability to critically examine and evaluate evidence to construct different interpretations of the past. Interpretation also involves an understanding how historians weigh evidence and come to radically different interpretations of the same event or time period.

Synthesis: Historical thinking involves the ability to utilize all of the historical thinking skills discussed above to develop meaningful and persuasive new interpretations of the past. Synthesis involves the ability to utilize evidence from primary and secondary sources that both supports and challenges a particular interpretation. Synthesis also involves the ability to connect events from one time period to those of another time period.

ABOUT THE AP UNITED STATES HISTORY EXAM

There are four sections to the Advanced Placement United States History Examination: a multiple-choice section, a short answer section, a document based question, and a long essay.

Section	Question Type	Number of Questions	Timing	Percentage of Total Exam Score
I	Part A: Multiple choice questions	55 Questions	55 Minutes	40%
I	Part B: Short-answer questions	4 Questions	45 Minutes	20%
II	Part A: Document-based question	1 Question	60 Minutes	25%
II	Part B: Long essay question	1 Question (Chosen from a pair)	35 Minutes	15%

Breakdown of Coverage by Periods

The AP U.S. History course has been divided into nine distinct time periods. Students should reflect on why historians might view the breaks between these periods as turning points in U.S. history. Below is a breakdown of course coverage and exam emphasis for each of these time periods.

Table 1: Breakdown of the AP United States History Exam

Time periods	Approximate Percentage of Instructional Time	Approximate Percentage of Coverage on the AP U.S. History Exam
1491-1607	5%	5%
1607-1754	10%	45%
1754-1800	12%	
1800-1848	10%	
1844-1877	13%	
1865-1898	13%	45%
1890-1945	17%	
1945-1980	15%	
1980-present	5%	5%

Understanding the Format

Multiple-Choice Questions

There are 55 multiple-choice questions with four answer choices (A-D). Only one answer choice is correct for each question and there is no penalty for guessing incorrectly. Students are given 55 minutes to complete this section. The multiple choice questions are stimulus-based, which means that a primary or secondary source will be provided followed by between one and five questions based on that stimulus. Multiple choice questions will emphasize the seven themes that guide the course.

Short Answer Questions

The short answer section of the exam will examine the themes that make up the learning objectives for the course. There will be four short answer questions that all students must answer with forty-five minutes being allowed for the writing of all four answers (roughly twelve minutes for each question). At least two of the short answer questions will offer students an element of choice to allow student to write about what they know best. All short answer questions will test student use of historical thinking skills to respond to primary or secondary sources. There will be a finite amount of space in which student answer must be contained and no credit will be given for writing outside of this finite area. Student answers must be in complete sentences (bulleted answers will not receive credit), but a thesis statement is not required. Students must be extremely careful to follow the directions and explicitly answer the question they are asked.

Document Based Question (DBQ)

The DBQ requires students to analyze and interpret primary source documents then use the documents, as well as outside information, to support a well-developed thesis statement that directly answers the question, takes a position, establishes categories, and gives direction to those categories. Thesis statements that that simply restate the prompt as a statement will not receive credit. DBQs will contain between five and seven primary source documents and will be scored on a 0-7 scale using an analytic rubric.

The key elements of the rubric are:

0-1 point Thesis statement.

0-3 points Analysis of documents as follows:

> **0-1 point** Gives a plausible analysis of a majority of documents and explicitly uses that information to support the thesis statement.

> **0-1 point** Examines at least one of the following for the majority of documents:
> - Intended audience
> - Purpose
> - Historical context and/or
> - The author's point of view

> **0-1 point** Examines at least one of the following for all or all but one of the documents:
> - Intended audience
> - Purpose
> - Historical context and/or
> - The author's point of view

0-1 point Uses outside information not included in the documents to support the thesis.

0-1 point Contextualization: Explicitly connects historical phenomena to broader historical events.

Long Essay

Students will have the choice of answering one of two long essay questions. Both essays will test the same historical thinking skill. The long essay is designed to measure a student's ability to use historical thinking skills through the demonstration of thesis development, organized presentation of historical argument, and evidence given to support the argument. While a few questions in the multiple-choice and short essay sections may include information in Periods 1 and 9, neither the DBQ nor the long essay questions will deal exclusively with timeframes of either Period 1 or Period 9.

Grading of the AP Exam

Colleges and universities often grant credits equivalent to that which is offered for their introductory United States History survey course to those students who successfully complete the AP Exam. The criteria for receiving credit vary widely from institution to institution and you should find out from each college and university you plan to apply to what their standards are. You may also choose to have your scores sent to colleges and universities to which you are applying. The AP Exam is scored on the following 5-point scale: 5 is "extremely well qualified"; 4 is "well qualified"; 3 is "qualified"; 2 is "possibly qualified; 1 is "no recommendation."

AP KEY CONCEPT CORRELATION

HISTORICAL PERIODS, KEY CONCEPTS, SUPPORTING CONCEPTS, AND HISTORICAL DEVELOPMENT	KEY PAGES IN BRINKLEY
PERIOD 1: 1491–1607 On a North American continent controlled by American Indians, contact among the peoples of Europe, the Americas, and West Africa created a new world.	
Key Concept 1.1: Before the arrival of Europeans, native populations in North America developed a wide variety of social, political, and economic structures based in part on interactions with the environment and each other.	
1.1.I. As settlers migrated and settled across the vast expanse of North America over time, they developed quite different and increasingly complex societies by adapting to and transforming their diverse environments. (PEO-1) (ENV-1) (ENV-2)	1-27, 29-32
Key Concept 1.2: European overseas expansion resulted in the Columbian Exchange, a series of interactions and adaptations among societies across the Atlantic.	
1.2.I. The arrival of Europeans in the Western Hemisphere in the 15th and 16th centuries triggered extensive demographic and social changes on both sides of the Atlantic. (PEO-4) (PEO-5) (ENV-1) (WXT-1) (WXT-4) (WOR-1)	12-21, 29-32
1.2.II. European expansion into the Western Hemisphere caused intense social/religious, political, and economic competition in Europe and the promotion of empire building. (ENV-1) (ENV-4) (WXT-1) (WOR-1) (POL-1)	7-27, 30
Key Concept 1.3: Contacts among American Indians, Africans, and Europeans challenged the worldviews of each group.	
1.3.I. European overseas expansion and sustained contacts with Africans and American Indians dramatically altered European views of social, political, and economic relationships among and between white and nonwhite peoples. (CUL-1)	9-21, 29-32, 38-39, 41-42. 46-49
1.3.II. Native peoples and Africans in the Americas strove to maintain their political and cultural autonomy in the face of European challenges to their independence and core beliefs. (ID-4) (POL-1) (CUL-1) (ENV-2)	12-21, 54-56
PERIOD 2: 1607–1754 Europeans and American Indians maneuvered and fought for dominance, control, and security in North America, and distinctive colonial and native societies emerged.	
Key Concept 2.1: Differences in imperial goals, cultures, and the North American environments that different empires confronted led Europeans to develop diverse patterns of colonization.	
2.1.I. Seventeenth-century Spanish, French, Dutch, and British colonizers embraced different social and economic goals, cultural assumptions, and folkways, resulting in varied models of colonization. (WXT-2) (PEO-1) (WOR-1) (ENV-4)	12-18, 21-27, 29-32, 35-45, 49-63, 65-96, 101-102
2.1.II. The British-American system of slavery developed out of the economic, demographic, and geographic characteristics of the British-controlled regions of the New World. (WOR-1) (WXT-4) (ID-4) (POL-1) (CUL-1)	55-56, 68, 71-74, 83-85
2.1.III. Along with other factors, environmental and geographical variations, including climate and natural resources, contributed to regional differences in what would become the British colonies. (WXT-2) (WXT-4) (ENV-2) (ID-5) (PEO-5) (CUL-4)	35-63, 66-74, 76-89
Key Concept 2.2: European colonization efforts in North America stimulated intercultural contact and intensified conflict between the various groups of colonizers and native peoples.	
2.2.I. Competition over resources between European rivals led to conflict within and between North American colonial possessions and American Indians. (WXT-1) (PEO-1) (WOR-1) (POL-1) (ENV-1)	17-20, 38-39, 42, 46-49, 53-63, 101-107
2.2.II. Clashes between European and American Indian social and economic values caused changes in both cultures. (ID-4) (WXT-1) (PEO-4) (PEO-5) (POL-1) (CUL-1)	17-20, 38-39, 46-49, 56-60, 101-102
Key Concept 2.3: The increasing political, economic, and cultural exchanges within the "Atlantic World" had a profound impact on the development of colonial societies in North America.	
2.3.I. "Atlantic World" commercial, religious, philosophical, and political interactions among Europeans, Africans, and American native peoples stimulated economic growth, expanded social networks, and reshaped labor systems. (WXT-1) (WXT-4) (WOR-1) (WOR-2) (CUL-4)	21, 46-49, 54-60, 63, 66-68, 71-74, 80-85, 89-96
2.3.II. Britain's desire to maintain a viable North American empire in the face of growing internal challenges and external competition inspired efforts to strengthen its imperial control, stimulating increasing resistance from colonists who had grown accustomed to a large measure of autonomy. (WOR-1) (WOR-2) (ID-1) (CUL-4)	62-63, 89-96, 99-103
PERIOD 3: 1754–1800 British imperial attempts to reassert control over its colonies and the colonial reaction to these attempts produced a new American republic, along with struggles over the new nation's social, political, and economic identity.	
Key Concept 3.1: Britain's victory over France in the imperial struggle for North America led to new conflicts among the British government, the North American colonists, and American Indians, culminating in the creation of a new nation, the United States.	
3.1.I. Throughout the second half of the 18th century, various American Indian groups repeatedly evaluated and adjusted their alliances with Europeans, other tribes, and the new U.S. government. (ID-4) (POL-1) (ENV-2) (ENV-4) (CUL-1)	56-60, 101-102, 138-139, 146-147, 155, 172-173

HISTORICAL PERIODS, KEY CONCEPTS, SUPPORTING CONCEPTS, AND HISTORICAL DEVELOPMENT	KEY PAGES IN BRINKLEY
3.1.II. During and after the imperial struggles of the mid-18th century, new pressures began to unite the British colonies against perceived and real constraints on their economic activities and political rights, sparking a colonial independence movement and war with Britain. (ID-1) (WXT-1) (POL-1) (WOR-1) (CUL-2) (CUL-4)	99-100, 107-126, 129-148
3.1.III. In response to domestic and international tensions, the new United States debated and formulated foreign policy initiatives and asserted an international presence. (WOR-5) (POL-2)	139-140, 153-155, 173-176
Key Concept 3.2: In the late 18th century, new experiments with democratic ideas and republican forms of government, as well as other new religious, economic, and cultural ideas, challenged traditional imperial systems across the Atlantic World.	
3.2.I. During the 18th century, new ideas about politics and society led to debates about religion and governance, and ultimately inspired experiments with new governmental structures. (ID-1) (POL-5) (WOR-2) (CUL-4)	89-96, 116-117, 129-131, 150-155
3.2.II. After experiencing the limitations of the Articles of Confederation, American political leaders wrote a new Constitution based on the principles of federalism and separation of powers, crafted a Bill of Rights, and continued their debates about the proper balance between liberty and order. (WXT-6) (POL-5) (WOR-5)	155-156, 160-177
3.2.III. While the new governments continued to limit rights to some groups, ideas promoting self-government and personal liberty reverberated around the world. (ID-4) (WOR-2) (POL-5) (CUL-2)	141-48, 150-151, 166-167
Key Concept 3.3: Migration within North America, cooperative interaction, and competition for resources raised questions about boundaries and policies, intensified conflicts among peoples and nations, and led to contests over the creation of a multiethnic, multiracial national identity.	
3.3.I. As migrants streamed westward from the British colonies along the Atlantic seaboard, interactions among different groups that would continue under an independent United States resulted in competition for resources, shifting alliances, and cultural blending. (ID-5) (ID-6) (PEO-5) (POL-1) (WOR-1) (WOR-5)	56-59, 109-112, 138-139, 146-147, 155-156, 172-173,
3.3.II. The policies of the United States that encouraged western migration and the orderly incorporation of new territories into the nation both extended republican institutions and intensified conflicts among American Indians and Europeans in the trans-Appalachian West. (POL-1) (PEO-4) (WOR-5)	153-155, 172-174
3.3.III. New voices for national identity challenged tendencies to cling to regional identities, contributing to the emergence of distinctly American cultural expressions. (ID-5) (WXT-2) (WXT-4) (POL-2) (CUL-2) (ENV-3)	169-172, 148, 181-184
PERIOD 4: 1800–1848 The new republic struggled to define and extend democratic ideals in the face of rapid economic, territorial, and demographic changes.	
Key Concept 4.1: The United States developed the world's first modern mass democracy and celebrated a new national culture, while Americans sought to define the nation's democratic ideals and to reform its institutions to match them.	
4.1.I. The nation's transformation to a more participatory democracy was accompanied by continued debates over federal power, the relationship between the federal government and the states, the authority of different branches of the federal government, and the rights and responsibilities of individual citizens. (POL-2) (POL-5) (POL-6) (ID-5)	169-172, 174-178, 195-197, 210, 220-228, 230-238, 244-249, 317
4.1.II. Concurrent with an increasing international exchange of goods and ideas, larger numbers of Americans began struggling with how to match democratic political ideals to political institutions and social realities. (CUL-2) (POL-3) (POL-6) (WOR-2)	185-188, 232-233, 238-242, 259-262, 263 (illus.), 282-287, 303-313, 317-335, 358
4.1.III. While Americans celebrated their nation's progress toward a unified new national culture that blended Old World forms with New World ideas, various groups of the nation's inhabitants developed distinctive cultures of their own. (ID-1) (ID-2) (ID-5) (CUL-2) (CUL-5)	224, 238-242, 279-290, 298-313, 315-337
Key Concept 4.2: Developments in technology, agriculture, and commerce precipitated profound changes in U.S. settlement patterns, regional identities, gender and family relations, political power, and distribution of consumer goods.	
4.2.I. A global market and communications revolution, influencing and influenced by technological innovations, led to dramatic shifts in the nature of agriculture and manufacturing. (WXT-2) (WXT-5)	188-192, 262-279, 288-290
4.2.II. Regional economic specialization, especially the demands of cultivating southern cotton, shaped settlement patterns and the national and international economy. (PEO-2) (PEO-3) (WXT-2) (WXT-5) (WXT-6)	215-220, 238-242, 243-246, 262-279, 288-290, 294-313
4.2.III. The economic changes caused by the market revolution had significant effects on migration patterns, gender and family relations, and the distribution of political power. (WXT-2) (WXT-7) (PEO-2) (PEO-3) (ID-5) (ID-6)	212-218, 235-238, 242-249, 262-290, 294-311
Key Concept 4.3: U.S. interest in increasing foreign trade, expanding its national borders, and isolating itself from European conflicts shaped the nation's foreign policy and spurred government and private initiatives.	

HISTORICAL PERIODS, KEY CONCEPTS, SUPPORTING CONCEPTS, AND HISTORICAL DEVELOPMENT	KEY PAGES IN BRINKLEY
4.3.I. Struggling to create an independent global presence, U.S. policymakers sought to dominate the North American continent and to promote its foreign trade. (WOR-5) (WOR-6)	203-212, 218-222, 225-226, 238-242, 249-251, 326-327, 340-350
4.3.II. Various American groups and individuals initiated, championed, and/or resisted the expansion of territory and/or government powers. (WOR-6) (POL-6)	205-210, 218-224, 236-238
4.3.III. The American acquisition of lands in the West gave rise to a contest over the extension of slavery into the western territories as well as a series of attempts at national compromise. (ENV-3) (POL-6)	218-219, 222-223, 294-295, 342, 346-350
PERIOD 5: 1844–1877 As the nation expanded and its population grew, regional tensions, especially over slavery, led to a civil war — the course and aftermath of which transformed American society.	
Key Concept 5.1: The United States became more connected with the world as it pursued an expansionist foreign policy in the Western Hemisphere and emerged as the destination for many migrants from other countries.	
5.1.I. Enthusiasm for U.S. territorial expansion, fueled by economic and national security interests and supported by claims of U.S. racial and cultural superiority, resulted in war, the opening of new markets, acquisition of new territory, and increased ideological conflicts. (ID-2) (WXT-2) (WOR-5) (WOR-6) (ENV-3) (ENV-4)	320-321, 326-327, 340-344, 346-362
5.1.II. Westward expansion, migration to and within the United States, and the end of slavery reshaped North American boundaries and caused conflicts over American cultural identities, citizenship, and the question of extending and protecting rights for various groups of U.S. inhabitants. (ID-6) (WXT-6) (PEO-2) (PEO-5) (PEO-6) (POL-6)	256-262, 263 (illus.), 278, 320-321, 351-352, 431-453
Key Concept 5.2: Intensified by expansion and deepening regional divisions, debates over slavery and other economic, cultural, and political issues led the nation into civil war.	
5.2.I. The institution of slavery and its attendant ideological debates, along with regional economic and demographic changes, territorial expansion in the 1840s and 1850s, and cultural differences between the North and the South, all intensified sectionalism. (ID-5) (POL-3) (POL-5) (POL-6) (CUL-2) (CUL-6)	235-238, 266-290, 294-313, 330-336, 357-358, 420-421
5.2.II. Repeated attempts at political compromise failed to calm tensions over slavery and often made sectional tensions worse, breaking down the trust between sectional leaders and culminating in the bitter election of 1860, followed by the secession of southern states. (POL-2) (POL-6) (PEO-5) (ID-5)	351-362, 365-366
Key Concept 5.3: The Union victory in the Civil War and the contested Reconstruction of the South settled the issues of slavery and secession, but left unresolved many questions about the power of the federal government and citizenship rights.	
5.3.I. The North's greater manpower and industrial resources, its leadership, and the decision for emancipation eventually led to the Union military victory over the Confederacy in the devastating Civil War. (POL-5) (CUL-2) (ENV-3)	366-397
5.3.II. The Civil War and Reconstruction altered power relationships between the states and the federal government and among the executive, legislative, and judicial branches, ending slavery and the notion of a divisible union, but leaving unresolved questions of relative power and largely unchanged social and economic patterns. (POL-5) (POL-6) (ID-5)	400-412, 414-428
5.3.III. The constitutional changes of the Reconstruction period embodied a Northern idea of American identity and national purpose and led to conflicts over new definitions of citizenship, particularly regarding the rights of African Americans, women, and other minorities. (ID-2) (POL-6)	414-428
PERIOD 6: 1865–1898 The transformation of the United States from an agricultural to an increasingly industrialized and urbanized society brought about significant economic, political, diplomatic, social, environmental, and cultural changes.	
Key Concept 6.1: The rise of big business in the United States encouraged massive migrations and urbanization, sparked government and popular efforts to reshape the U.S. economy and environment, and renewed debates over U.S. national identity.	
6.1.I. Large-scale production—accompanied by massive technological change, expanding international communication networks, and pro-growth government policies—fueled the development of a "Gilded Age" marked by an emphasis on consumption, marketing, and business consolidation. (WXT-3) (WXT-6) (WOR-3) (CUL-3) (CUL-5)	418-422, 436, 463-475, 531-548, 494-495, 531-548
6.1.II. As leaders of big business and their allies in government aimed to create a unified industrialized nation, they were challenged in different ways by demographic issues, regional differences, and labor movements. (WXT-5) (WXT-6) (WXT-7) (PEO-6) (ID-5)	409-412, 417-421, 475-484, 487-490
6.1.III. Westward migration, new systems of farming and transportation, and economic instability led to political and popular conflicts. (ENV-5) (WXT-5) (WXT-7) (POL-3) (PEO-3) (PEO-5)	452-456, 497-500, 520-531, 572-573
Key Concept 6.2: The emergence of an industrial culture in the United States led to both greater opportunities for, and restrictions on, immigrants, minorities, and women.	

HISTORICAL PERIODS, KEY CONCEPTS, SUPPORTING CONCEPTS, AND HISTORICAL DEVELOPMENT	KEY PAGES IN BRINKLEY
6.2.I. International and internal migrations increased both urban and rural populations, but gender, racial, ethnic, religious, and socioeconomic inequalities abounded, inspiring some reformers to attempt to address these inequities. (ID-6) (PEO-2) (PEO-3) (PEO-6) (POL-3)	434-437, 476-478, 487-500, 556-560, 567
6.2.II. As transcontinental railroads were completed, bringing more settlers west, U.S. military actions, the destruction of the buffalo, the confinement of American Indians to reservations, and assimilationist policies reduced the number of American Indians and threatened native culture and identity. (PEO-4) (ENV-5) (POL-6)	355-356, 431-456
Key Concept 6.3: The "Gilded Age" witnessed new cultural and intellectual movements in tandem with political debates over economic and social policies.	
6.3.I. Gilded Age politics were intimately tied to big business and focused nationally on economic issues—tariffs, currency, corporate expansion, and laissez-faire economic policy—that engendered numerous calls for reform. (POL-6)	412-413, 422-428, 434-437, 492-494, 515-531
6.3.II. New cultural and intellectual movements both buttressed and challenged the social order of the Gilded Age. (ID-2) (CUL-3) (CUL-5) (CUL-6)	377-378, 421-422, 437, 467-475, 552-554
PERIOD 7: 1890–1945 An increasingly pluralistic United States faced profound domestic and global challenges, debated the proper degree of government activism, and sought to define its international role.	
Key Concept 7.1: Governmental, political, and social organizations struggled to address the effects of large-scale industrialization, economic uncertainty, and related social changes such as urbanization and mass migration.	
7.1.I. The continued growth and consolidation of large corporations transformed American society and the nation's economy, promoting urbanization and economic growth, even as business cycle fluctuations became increasingly severe. (WOR-3) (ID-7) (WXT-3) (WXT-5) (POL-3)	459-467, 475-478, 487-500, 553-556, 570-574-581, 598, 615-627, 630-631, 639-660, 662-684
7.1.II. Progressive reformers responded to economic instability, social inequality, and political corruption by calling for government intervention in the economy, expanded democracy, greater social justice, and conservation of natural resources. (WXT-6) (WXT-7) (WXT-8) (POL-3) (ENV-5) (CUL-5)	502, 552-581
7.1.III. National, state, and local reformers responded to economic upheavals, laissez-faire capitalism, and the Great Depression by transforming the United States into a limited welfare state. (WXT-8) (POL-2) (POL-4) (ID-3) (CUL-5)	662-684
Key Concept 7.2: A revolution in communications and transportation technology helped to create a new mass culture and spread "modern" values and ideas, even as cultural conflicts between groups increased under the pressure of migration, world wars, and economic distress.	
7.2.I. New technologies led to social transformations that improved the standard of living for many, while contributing to increased political and cultural conflicts. (ID-6) (ID-8) (WXT-3) (WXT-5) (CUL-3) (CUL-6) (CUL-7)	459-463, 508-509, 598, 606-611, 615-638, 649-654
7.2.II. The global ramifications of World War I and wartime patriotism and xenophobia, combined with social tensions created by increased international migration, resulted in legislation restricting immigration from Asia and from southern and eastern Europe. (ID-6) (WOR-4) (PEO-2) (PEO-6) (PEO-7) (POL-7) (WXT-6)	568, 599-603, 606-611, 631-634, 716
7.2.III. Economic dislocations, social pressures, and the economic growth spurred by World Wars I and II led to a greater degree of migration within the United States, as well as migration to the United States from elsewhere in the Western Hemisphere. (ID-6) (ID-8) (PEO-3) (WOR-4)	565-566, 598, 645-648, 712, 716
Key Concept 7.3: Global conflicts over resources, territories, and ideologies renewed debates over the nation's values and its role in the world while simultaneously propelling the United States into a dominant international military, political, cultural, and economic position.	
7.3.I. Many Americans began to advocate overseas expansionism in the late 19th century, leading to new territorial ambitions and acquisitions in the Western Hemisphere and the Pacific. (WOR-6) (WOR-7) (ENV-5) (POL-6)	531-549, 584-589, 603-606, 690-699
7.3.II. World War I and its aftermath intensified debates about the nation's role in the world and how best to achieve national security and pursue American interests. (WOR-4) (WOR-7) (ID-3) (POL-6)	589-591, 603-606, 611, 687-702
7.3.III. The involvement of the United States in World War II, while opposed by most Americans prior to the attack on Pearl Harbor, vaulted the United States into global political and military prominence, and transformed both American society and the relationship between the United States and the rest of the world. (WOR-4) (WOR-7) (ID-3) (ID-6) (POL-5)	699, 704-730, 732-741
PERIOD 8: 1945–1980 After World War II, the United States grappled with prosperity and unfamiliar international responsibilities, while struggling to live up to its ideals.	
Key Concept 8.1: The United States responded to an uncertain and unstable postwar world by asserting and attempting to defend a position of global leadership, with far-reaching domestic and international consequences.	
8.1.I. After World War II, the United States sought to stem the growth of Communist military power and ideological influence, create a stable global economy, and build an international security system. (WOR-4) (WOR-7) (WOR-8)	733-741, 744-747, 775-779, 792-800, 819-828

HISTORICAL PERIODS, KEY CONCEPTS, SUPPORTING CONCEPTS, AND HISTORICAL DEVELOPMENT	KEY PAGES IN BRINKLEY
8.1.II. As the United States focused on containing communism, it faced increasingly complex foreign policy issues, including decolonization, shifting international alignments and regional conflicts, and global economic and environmental changes. (ENV-5) (WOR-3) (WOR-7) (WOR-8)	747-750, 775-779, 792-793, 824-825, 827-828, 831, 867-868
8.1.III. Cold War policies led to continued public debates over the power of the federal government, acceptable means for pursuing international and domestic goals, and the proper balance between liberty and order. (ID-3) (POL-7) (WOR-4) (CUL-5)	736-741, 745-746, 747-750, 775-779, 792-800, 825-826, 827-828
Key Concept 8.2: Liberalism, based on anticommunism abroad and a firm belief in the efficacy of governmental and especially federal power to achieve social goals at home, reached its apex in the mid-1960s and generated a variety of political and cultural responses.	
8.2.I. Seeking to fulfill Reconstruction-era promises, civil rights activists and political leaders achieved some legal and political successes in ending segregation, although progress toward equality was slow and halting. (ID-8) (POL-3) (POL-4) (POL-7)	772-774, 786-791
8.2.II. Stirred by a growing awareness of inequalities in American society and by the African American civil rights movement, activists also addressed issues of identity and social justice, such as gender/sexuality and ethnicity. (POL-3) (ID-8)	770, 784-786, 813-821, 828, 870-871
8.2.III. As many liberal principles came to dominate postwar politics and court decisions, liberalism came under attack from the left as well as from resurgent conservative movements. (POL-2) (POL-5) (POL-7)	782-791, 804-805, 808-821, 828-829, 841-846
Key Concept 8.3: Postwar economic, demographic, and technological changes had a far-reaching impact on American society, politics, and the environment.	
8.3.I. Rapid economic and social changes in American society fostered a sense of optimism in the postwar years, as well as underlying concerns about how these changes were affecting American values. (WXT-3) (WXT-5) (CUL-5) (CUL-6) (CUL-7) (PEO-3)	754-779, 804-805, 808-813, 841-845
8.3.II. As federal programs expanded and economic growth reshaped American society, many sought greater access to prosperity even as critics began to question the burgeoning use of natural resources. (ID-6) (PEO-2) (PEO-3) (PEO-7) (ENV-5) (WXT-8)	759, 762-766, 771, 785, 816-817, 821-823, 842, 865 (illus.)
8.3.III. New demographic and social issues led to significant political and moral debates that sharply divided the nation. (ID-7) (POL-5) (CUL-6) (CUL-7)	764, 768-769, 808-813, 818-821, 828-835, 841-846
PERIOD 9: 1980–Present As the United States transitioned to a new century filled with challenges and possibilities, it experienced renewed ideological and cultural debates, sought to redefine its foreign policy, and adapted to economic globalization and revolutionary changes in science and technology.	
Key Concept 9.1: A new conservatism grew to prominence in U.S. culture and politics, defending traditional social values and rejecting liberal views about the role of government.	
9.1.I. Reduced public faith in the government's ability to solve social and economic problems, the growth of religious fundamentalism, and the dissemination of neoconservative thought all combined to invigorate conservatism. (POL-3)	824-835, 841-847, 857-858, 866-872
9.1.II. Conservatives achieved some of their political and policy goals, but their success was limited by the enduring popularity and institutional strength of some government programs and public support for cultural trends of recent decades. (WXT-8) (POL-4)	844-848, 851-852, 860, 875-876
Key Concept 9.2: The end of the Cold War and new challenges to U.S. leadership in the world forced the nation to redefine its foreign policy and global role.	
9.2.I. The Reagan administration pursued a reinvigorated anti-Communist and interventionist foreign policy that set the tone for later administrations. (WOR-7) (WOR-8)	848-853
9.2.II. Following the attacks of September 11, 2001, U.S. foreign policy and military involvement focused on a war on terrorism, which also generated debates about domestic security and civil rights. (POL-7) (WOR-7) (WOR-8)	870-880
Key Concept 9.3: Moving into the 21st century, the nation continued to experience challenges stemming from social, economic, and demographic changes.	
9.3.I. The increasing integration of the U.S. into the world economy was accompanied by economic instability and major policy, social, and environmental challenges. (WXT-3) (WXT-7) (WOR-3) (ENV-5) (CUL-7)	846-848, 852-855, 857, 861-866, 867-870
9.3.II. The U.S. population continued to undergo significant demographic shifts that had profound cultural and political consequences. (ID-6) (ID-7) (PEO-2) (PEO-3) (PEO-7)	841-846, 863-867

TO THE AP STUDENT

THE redesigned exam focuses on nine historical thinking skills and seven themes. It is imperative that you are absolutely familiar with historical thinking skills and what each of them means. Similarly, you must be absolutely certain that you know the seven themes that the course is centered around and what they really mean. There will be some terminology that you are unfamiliar with and you must, with the help of your instructor, internalize these terms. You and your teacher have access to the entire content outline around which all multiple choice, short answer, DBQs, and long essay questions are based at apcentral.com.

The course is based around nine historical thinking skills. Simply put, these historical thinking skills require you to be able to do the following:

Historical causation: Understand both short and long term causes and effects and multiple cause/effect relationships.

Patterns of continuity and change over time: Be able to identify both major changes and things which remain unchanged within and between different historical time periods.

Periodization: Understand why different historians divide U.S. history into discreet time periods and why certain times represent a distinctive turning point in U.S. history.

Comparison: Be able to discuss both similarity and differences both within and between different time periods.

Contextualization: Be able to connect a particular event, theme, or mindset, to a broader understanding of how it fits into the story of the development of the United States.

Historical argumentation: Be able to construct a logical argument using relevant historical information to support a particular interpretation or point of view.

Appropriate use of historical evidence: Be able to use relevant historical evidence to support an argument by showing how and why that evidence explicitly supports a particular historical interpretation or point of view.

Interpretation: Be able to construct and understand different interpretations of historical events and/or time periods, using relevant historical evidence to support that interpretation.

Synthesis: Be able to construct and support a particular interpretation of history using all of the above historical thinking skill and be able to connect that argument to different historical time periods and geographic regions.

The course also requires you to know and think about seven historical themes in each of the nine distinct time periods. The "AP Connecting Concepts" chapter introductions help you focus on events and ideas related to the Key Concepts that are covered in each chapter. Similarly, the end of each chapter features an "AP Connecting Themes" summary, to help you connect events within and across chapters thematically, all according to the new AP United States History framework. Good luck in your course. –*Warren Hierl*

The purpose of the **Sample Supporting Evidence** sections found at the end of each chapter is to alert the student to historical events, issues, documents, people, and places, which the student might study for use as supporting historical evidence when answering short answer and long-essay questions in the AP exam. Although the focus of the AP exam is now on historical thinking skills, it still maintains the expectation that students' written responses be grounded with historically accurate evidence. History is written with reference to specific historical events and so, too, then is the expectation for student responses on the AP exam.

Gone, however, is the expectation of a broad, expansive and comprehensive lexicon of issues, events, and people throughout every era and period of American history. In its place is a more focused expectation that students know some specific microcosms of larger events and trends. This section will provide some examples of this type of targeted approach.

–*Christopher Averill*

A special thanks to our esteemed group of AP United States History consultants who have provided such excellent support and expertise as we prepared for the redesigned course and our new AP Edition.

Christopher A. Averill, Cosby High School, Midlothian, Virginia–AP Edition frontmatter, glossary, and chapter Supporting Evidence

Warren Hierl, Winston-Salem/Forsyth County Schools, North Carolina– AP Edition frontmatter and chapter content

Robert Naeher, Emma Willard School, Troy, New York–AP correlations and AP test banks

William A. Shelton, Trinity Valley School, Fort Worth, Texas–AP Teacher Manual

John R. Struck, Thomas Jefferson High School for Science and Technology, Fairfax County, Virginia–AP Teacher Manual and AP test banks

1 THE COLLISION OF CULTURES

FIRST ENCOUNTERS WITH NATIVE AMERICANS This 1505 engraving is one of the earliest European images of the way Native Americans lived in the early Americas. It also represents some of the ways in which white Europeans would view the people they called Indians for many generations. Native Americans here were portrayed by Europeans as exotic savages, whose sexuality was not contained within stable families and whose savagery was evidenced in their practice of eating the flesh of their slain enemies. In the background are the ships that have brought the European visitors who recorded these images. (© North Wind Picture Archives)

AP

HISTORICAL THINKING

1. **Comparison** Compare the regional differences among Native Americans before the arrival of Europeans.

2. **Comparison** How did patterns of settlement differ among the Spanish, English, French, and Dutch immigrants?

3. **Historical Causation** What were the causes and effects of the beginning of importation of African slaves into the Americas?

4. **Periodization** Within the context of the time period, what was the impact of mercantilism on the European colonization of North America?

5. **Historical Causation** Identify the positive and negative impact of the Columbian Exchange on both European and native populations in North America.

Key Concept Correlations

Analyze the ways the historical developments you learn about in this chapter connect to the following AP Key Concepts.

1.1 Before the arrival of Europeans, native populations in North America developed a wide variety of social, political, and economic structures based in part on interactions with the environment and each other.

1.2 European overseas expansion resulted in the Columbian Exchange, a series of interactions and adaptations among societies across the Atlantic.

1.3 Contacts among American Indians, Africans, and Europeans challenged the worldviews of each group.

2.1 Differences in imperial goals, cultures, and the North American environments that different empires confronted led Europeans to develop diverse patterns of colonization.

2.2 European colonization efforts in North America stimulated intercultural contact and intensified conflict between the various groups of colonizers and native peoples.

Thematic Learning Objectives
PEO-1, 4, 5; ENV-1, 2, 4; WXT-1, 4; WOR-1; POL-1; CUL-1; ID-4

AP CONNECTING CONCEPTS

CHAPTER 1 deals with native civilizations prior to and immediately after European contact. In your reading, you should focus on the ways in which these civilizations interacted with each other prior to European contact as well as the geographical and environmental factors that led to distinct differences in American Indian societies of the different regions. Then look to relate the positive and negative consequences of the Columbian Exchange following the arrival of the Europeans. It is extremely important that you focus on changes brought about by these conflicts in both American Indian and European culture. You should also consider the similarities and difference between the major European colonizing nations regarding their respective interactions with native peoples, the political and economic structures established within their colonies, their motives for settlement, and the influence of religion on each of these aspects. As you read, evaluate the following concepts:

- A wide variety of political, economic, and social structures existed among American Indians.
- Environmental factors influenced American Indian society prior to and after European contact.
- Environmental factors led to varied regional differences among American Indians.
- The Columbian Exchange led to epidemic diseases, racially mixed populations, and the exchange of technology and foodstuffs.
- European socio-religious, political, and economic competition led to conflict in establishing New World colonies among European powers.
- American Indian resistance and conflict resulted from contact with European peoples.

AMERICA BEFORE COLUMBUS

We still know relatively little about the first peoples in the Americas. What we do know comes from scattered archaeological discoveries—new evidence from artifacts that have survived over many millennia.

THE PEOPLES OF THE PRECONTACT AMERICAS

For many decades, scholars believed that all early migrations into the Americas came from humans crossing an ancient land bridge over the Bering Strait into what is now Alaska, approximately 11,000 years ago. These migrants then traveled from the glacial north, through an unfrozen corridor between two great ice sheets, until they reached the nonglacial lands to the south. The migrations were prob-

THE "CLOVIS" PEOPLE

ably a result of the development of new stone tools—spears and other hunting implements—with which migrating people could pursue the large animals that regularly crossed between Asia and North America. All of these land-based migrants are thought to have come from a Mongolian stock related to that of modern-day Siberia. They are known to scholars as the "Clovis" people, named for a town in New Mexico.

The Clovis people established one of the first civilizations in the Americas. Archaeologists believe that they lived about 13,000 years ago. They were among the first people to make tools and to eat other animals. The Clovis are believed to have migrated from Siberia across the Bering land bridge into Alaska. From there, they moved southward to warmer regions, including New Mexico.

More recent archaeological evidence, however, suggests that not all the early migrants came across the Bering Strait. Some migrants from Asia appear to have settled as far south as Chile and

ARCHAEOLOGISTS AND POPULATION DIVERSITY

Peru even before people began moving into North America by land. This suggests that these first South Americans may have come not by land but by sea, using boats. Other discoveries on other continents made clear that migrants had traveled by water much earlier to populate Japan, Australia, and other areas of the Pacific. Those discoveries suggest that migrants were capable of making long ocean voyages—long enough to bring them to the American coasts.

This new evidence suggests that the early population of the Americas was much more diverse and more scattered than scholars used to believe. Some people came to the Americas from farther south in Asia than Mongolia—perhaps Polynesia and Japan. Recent DNA evidence has identified what may have been yet another population group that, unlike most other American groups, does not seem to have Asian characteristics. Thus it is also possible that, thousands of years before Columbus, there may have been some migration from Europe or Africa. Most Indians in the Americas today share relatively similar characteristics, and those characteristics link them to modern Siberians and Mongolians. But that does not prove that Mongolian migrants were the only immigrants to the Americas. It suggests, rather, that Mongolian migrants eventually came to dominate and perhaps eliminate earlier population groups.

The "Archaic" period is a scholarly term for the history of humans in America during a period of about 5,000 years beginning around 8000 BCE. In the first part of this period, most

THE "ARCHAIC" PERIOD

humans continued to support themselves through hunting and gathering, using the same stone tools that earlier Americans had brought with them from Asia. Some of the largest animals that the earliest humans in America once hunted became extinct during the Archaic period. But archaic people continued to hunt with spears in the area later known as the Great Plains of North America who, then as centuries later, pursued bison (also known as buffalo). Bows and arrows were unknown in most of North America until 400–500 CE.

Later in the Archaic period, population groups also began to develop new tools to perform work. Among them were nets and hooks for fishing, traps for smaller animals, and baskets for gathering berries, nuts, seeds, and other plants. Later, some groups began to farm. Through much of the Americas, the most important farm crop was corn, but many agricultural communities also grew other crops such as beans and squash. In agricultural areas, the first sedentary settlements slowly began to form, creating the basis for larger civilizations.

THE GROWTH OF CIVILIZATIONS: THE SOUTH

The most elaborate early civilizations emerged south of what is now the United States—in South and Central America and in what is now Mexico. In Peru, the Incas created the largest empire in the Americas. They began as a small tribe in the mountainous region of Cuzco, in the early fifteenth century—spurred by a powerful leader, Pachacuti (whose name meant "world shaker"). His empire stretched along almost 2,000 miles of western South America. It was an empire created as much by persuasion as by force. Pachacuti's agents fanned out around the region and explained the benefits of the empire to people in the areas the Incas hoped to control. Most local leaders eventually allied themselves with the Incas. The empire was sustained by innovative administrative systems and by the creation of a large network of paved roads.

Another great civilization emerged from the so-called Meso-Americans, the peoples of what is now Mexico and much of Central America. Organized societies emerged in these regions as early as 10,000 BCE, and the first truly complex society in the Americas—of the Olmec people—began in approximately 1000 BCE. A more sophisticated culture emerged beginning around 800 CE in parts of Central America and in the Yucatán peninsula of Mexico, in an area known as Maya. Mayan civilization developed a written language, a numerical system similar to the Arabic, an accurate calendar, an advanced agricultural system, and important trade routes into other areas of the continents.

Gradually, the societies of the Mayan regions were followed by other Meso-American tribes. They became known collectively (and somewhat inaccurately) as the Aztec. They called themselves Mexica, a name that eventually came to describe people of a number of different tribes. In about 1300 CE, the Mexica established a city, which they named Tenochtitlán, on a large island in a lake in central Mexico, the site of present-day Mexico City. The Mexica soon incorporated the peoples of other tribes into their society as well. It became by far the greatest city ever created in the Americas to that point, with a population as high as 100,000 by 1500, connected to water supplies from across the region by aqueducts. The residents of Tenochtitlán also created large and impressive public buildings, schools that all male children attended, an organized military, a medical system, and a slave workforce drawn from conquered tribes. They gradually established their dominance over almost all of central Mexico, and beyond, through a system of tribute (a heavy tax paid in crops, cloth, or animals) enforced by military power. The peoples ruled by the Mexica maintained a significant element of independence nevertheless, and many of them always considered the Mexica to be tyrannical rulers, but too powerful to resist.

Like other Meso-American societies, the Mexica developed a religion based on a belief in human sacrifice. Unlike earlier societies in the Americas, whose sacrifices to the gods emphasized blood-letting and other mostly nonfatal techniques, the Mexica also believed that the gods could be satisfied by being fed the living hearts of humans. But the Mexica also believed that the gods could be satisfied only by being fed the living hearts of humans. As a result, they sacrificed people—largely prisoners captured in combat—on a scale unknown in other American civilizations.

The Meso-American civilizations were for many centuries the center of civilized life in North and Central America—the hub of culture and trade. Disease and disunity made it difficult for them to survive the European invasions. But they were, nevertheless, very great civilizations—all the more impressive because they lacked some of the crucial technologies that Asian and European societies had long employed. As late as the sixteenth century CE, no American society had yet developed wheeled vehicles.

THE CIVILIZATIONS OF THE NORTH

The peoples north of Mexico—in the lands that became the United States and Canada—did not develop empires as large or political systems as elaborate as those of the Incas, Mayas,

NORTH AMERICAN MIGRATIONS This map tracks some of the early migrations into, and within, North America in the centuries preceding contact with Europe. The map shows the now-vanished land bridge between Siberia and Alaska over which thousands, perhaps millions, of migrating people passed into the Americas. It also shows the locations of some of the earliest settlements in North America.

• *What role did the extended glacial field in what is now Canada have on residential patterns in the ancient American world?*

and Mexica. They built complex civilizations of great variety that subsisted on hunting, gathering, and fishing. The Eskimos

COMPLEX AND VARIED CIVILIZATIONS

of the Arctic Circle fished and hunted seals; their civilization spanned thousands of miles of largely frozen land, which they traversed by dogsled. The big-game hunters of the northern forests led nomadic lives based on pursuit of moose and caribou. The tribes of the Pacific Northwest, whose principal occupation was salmon fishing,

created substantial permanent settlements along the coast and engaged in constant and often violent competition with one another for access to natural resources.

Another group of tribes spread through more arid regions of the Far West and developed successful communities—many of them quite wealthy and densely populated—based on fishing, hunting small game, and gathering. Other societies in America were primarily agricultural. Among the most elaborate were those in the Southwest. The people of that region built large

HOW THE EARLY NORTH AMERICANS LIVED This map shows the various ways in which the native tribes of North America supported themselves before the arrival of European civilization. Like most precommercial peoples, the native Americans survived largely on the resources available in their immediate surroundings. Note, for example, the reliance on the products of the sea of the tribes along the northern coastlines of the continent, and the way in which tribes in relatively inhospitable climates in the North—where agriculture was difficult—relied on hunting large game. Most native Americans were farmers.

• *What different kinds of farming would have emerged in the very different climates of the agricultural regions shown on this map?*

irrigation systems to allow farming on their relatively dry land. They constructed substantial towns that became centers of trade, crafts, and religious and civic ritual. Their densely populated settlements at Chaco Canyon and elsewhere consisted of stone and adobe terraced structures, known today as pueblos, many of which resembled the large apartment buildings of later eras in size and design. In the Great Plains region, too, most tribes were engaged in sedentary farming (corn and other grains) and lived in permanent settlements, although there were some small nomadic tribes that subsisted by hunting buffalo. (Only in the eighteenth century, after Europeans had introduced the horse to North America, did buffalo hunting begin to support a large population in the region; at that point, many once-sedentary farmers left the land to pursue the great migratory buffalo herds.)

The eastern third of what is now the United States–much of it covered with forests and inhabited by people who have

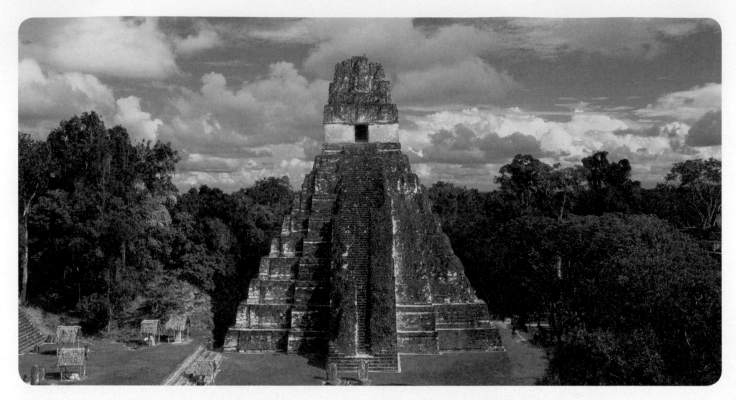

MAYAN TEMPLE, TIKAL Tikal was the largest city in what was then the vast Mayan Empire. It extended through what is now Mexico, Guatemala, and Belize. The temple shown here was built before 800 CE and was one of many pyramids created by the Mayas. Only a few of these pyramids still survive. (© M.L. Sinibaldi/Corbis)

thus become known as the Woodland Indians—had the greatest food resources of any region of the continent. Many tribes lived there, and most of them engaged in farming, hunting, gathering, and fishing. In the South there were substantial permanent settlements and large trading networks based on corn and other grains grown in the rich lands of the Mississippi River valley. Among the major cities that emerged as a result of trade was Cahokia (near present-day St. Louis), which at its peak in 1200 CE had a population of about 10,000 and contained a great complex of large earthen mounds.

The agricultural societies of the Northeast were more nomadic than those in other regions. Much of the land in the region was less fertile than other regions because farming was newer and less established. Most tribes combined farming with hunting. Farming techniques in the Northeast were usually designed to exploit the land quickly rather than to develop permanent settlements. Natives often cleared the land by setting forest fires or cutting into trees to kill them. They then planted crops—corn, beans, squash, pumpkins, and others—among the dead or blackened trunks. After a few years, when the land became exhausted or the filth from a settlement began to accumulate, they moved on and established themselves elsewhere. In some parts of eastern North America, villages dispersed every winter and families foraged in the wilderness until warm weather returned; those who survived then reassembled to begin farming again.

Many of the tribes living east of the Mississippi River were linked together loosely by common linguistic roots. The

MOBILE SOCIETIES

largest of the language groups was the Algonquian, which dominated the Atlantic seaboard from Canada to Virginia. Another important language group was the Iroquoian, centered in what is now upstate New York. The Iroquois included at least five distinct northern "nations"—the Seneca, Cayuga, Onondaga,

MAYAN MONKEY-MAN SCRIBAL GOD The Mayas believed in hundreds of different gods, and they attempted to personify many of them in various artifacts such as the one depicted on the bowl shown here, which dates from 900–1100 CE. The monkey gods were believed to be twins who took the form of monkeys after being lured into a tree from which they could not descend. According to legend, they abandoned their loincloths, which then became tails, which they then used to move more effectively up and down trees. The monkey-men were the patrons of writing, dancing, and art. (© Collection of the Lowe Art Museum, University of Miami, Gift of the Institute of Maya Studies/The Bridgeman Art Library)

CAHOKIA An artist's rendition of the city of Cahokia circa 1100 CE. Its great earthen mounds, constructed by the Cahokia Indians near present-day St. Louis, have endured into modern times as part of the Missouri landscape. (Courtesy of Cahokia Mounds State Historic Site, Collinsville, Illinois. Painting by William R. Iseminger)

Oneida, and Mohawk—and had links as well with the Cherokees and the Tuscaroras farther south, in the Carolinas and Georgia. The third-largest language group—the Muskogean—included the tribes in the southernmost region of the eastern seaboard: the Chickasaws, Choctaws, Creeks, and Seminoles. Alliances among the various Indian societies (even among those with common languages) were fragile, since the peoples of the Americas did not think of themselves as members of a single civilization.

TRIBAL CULTURES

The enormous diversity of economic, social, and political structures among the North American Indians makes large generalizations about their cultures difficult. In the last centuries before the arrival of Europeans, however, Native Americans—like peoples in other areas of the world—were experiencing an agricultural revolution. In all regions of the United States, tribes were becoming more sedentary and were developing new sources of food, clothing, and shelter. Most regions were experiencing significant population growth. Virtually all were developing the sorts of elaborate social customs and rituals that only stationary societies can produce. Religion was as important to Indian society as it was to most other cultures, and it was usually closely bound up with the natural world on which the tribes depended. Native Americans worshiped many gods, whom they associated with crops, game, forests, rivers, and other elements of nature. Some tribes created elaborate, brightly colored totems as part of their religious ritual; most staged large festivals on such important occasions as harvests or major hunts.

AGRICULTURAL REVOLUTION

As in other parts of the world, the societies of North America tended to divide tasks according to gender. All tribes assigned women the jobs of caring for children, preparing meals, and gathering certain foods. But the allocation of other tasks varied from one society to another. Some tribal groups (notably the Pueblos of the Southwest) reserved farming tasks almost entirely for men. Among others (including the Algonquins, the Iroquois, and the Muskogees), women tended the fields, while men engaged in hunting, warfare, or clearing land. Iroquois women and children were often left alone for extended periods while men were away hunting or fighting battles. As a result, women tended to control the social and economic organization of the settlements and played powerful roles within families.

EUROPE LOOKS WESTWARD

Europeans were almost entirely unaware of the existence of the Americas before the fifteenth century. A few early wanderers—Leif Eriksson, an eleventh-century Norse seaman, and perhaps others—had glimpsed parts of the New World and had demonstrated that Europeans were capable of crossing the ocean to reach it. But even if their discoveries had become common knowledge (and they had not), there would have been little incentive for others to follow. Europe in the Middle Ages (roughly 500–1500 CE) was not an adventurous civilization. Divided into innumerable small duchies and kingdoms, Europe had an overwhelmingly provincial outlook. Subsistence agriculture predominated, and commerce was limited; few merchants looked beyond the boundaries of their own regions. The Roman Catholic Church exercised a measure of spiritual authority over most of the continent, and the Holy Roman Empire provided at least a nominal political center. Even so, real power was widely dispersed; only rarely could a single leader launch a great venture. Gradually, however, conditions in Europe changed so that by the late fifteenth century, interest in overseas exploration had grown.

AP DEBATING THE PAST

WHY DO HISTORIANS SO OFTEN DIFFER?

EARLY in the twentieth century, when the professional study of history was still relatively new, many historians believed that questions about the past could be answered with the same certainty and precision that questions in more-scientific fields could be answered. By sifting through available records, using precise methods of research and analysis, and producing careful, closely argued accounts of the past, they believed they could create definitive histories that would survive without controversy. Scholars who adhered to this view believed

GEORGE BANCROFT (© Corbis)

PAULINE MAIER (© Charles Maier. Courtesy of the Maier family)

COMMERCE AND NATIONALISM

Two important and related changes provided the first incentive for Europeans to look toward new lands. One was a result of the significant population growth in fifteenth-century Europe. The Black Death, a catastrophic epidemic of the bubonic plague that began in Constantinople in 1347, had decimated Europe, killing

A REAWAKENING OF COMMERCE (according to some estimates) more than a third of the people of the continent and debilitating its already-limited economy. But a century and a half later, the population had rebounded. With that growth came a rise in land values, a reawakening of commerce, and a general increase in prosperity. Affluent landlords became eager to purchase goods from distant regions, and a new merchant class emerged to meet their demand. As trade increased, and as advances in navigation and shipbuilding made long-distance sea travel more feasible, interest in developing new markets, finding new products, and opening new trade routes rapidly increased.

Paralleling the rise of commerce in Europe, and in part responsible for it, was the rise of new governments that were more united and powerful than the feeble political entities of the feudal past. In the western areas of Europe, the authority of the distant pope and the even more distant Holy Roman Emperor was necessarily weak. As a result, strong new monarchs emerged and created centralized nation-states, with national courts, national armies, and—perhaps most important—national tax systems. As these ambitious kings and queens consolidated their power and increased their wealth, they became eager to enhance the commercial growth of their nations.

CENTRALIZED NATION-STATES

Ever since the early fourteenth century, when Marco Polo and other adventurers had returned from Asia bearing exotic goods (spices, fabrics, dyes) and exotic tales, Europeans who hoped for commercial glory had dreamed of trade with the East. For two centuries, that trade had been limited by the difficulties of the long, arduous overland journey to the Asian that real knowledge can be derived only from direct, scientific observation of clear "facts". They were known as "positivists."

A vigorous debate continues to this day over whether historical research can or should be truly objective. Almost no historian any longer accepts the "positivist" claim that history could ever be an exact science. Disagreement about the past is, in fact, at the heart of the effort to understand history. Critics of contemporary historical scholarship often denounce the way historians are constantly revising earlier interpretations. Some denounce the act of interpretation itself. History, they claim, is "what happened," and historians should "stick to the facts."

Historians, however, continue to differ with one another both because the "facts" are seldom as straightforward as their critics claim and because facts by themselves mean almost nothing without an effort to assign meaning to them. Some historical "facts," of course, are not in dispute. Everyone agrees, for example, that the Japanese bombed Pearl Harbor on December 7, 1941, and that Abraham Lincoln was elected president in 1860. But many other "facts" are much harder to determine—among them, for example, the question of how large the American population was before the arrival of Columbus, which is discussed in this chapter. How many slaves resisted slavery? This sounds like a reasonably straightforward question, but it is almost impossible to answer with any certainty—because the records of slave resistance are spotty and the definition of "resistance" is a matter of considerable dispute.

Even when a set of facts is clear and straightforward, historians disagree—sometimes quite radically—over what they mean. Those disagreements can be the result of political and ideological disagreements. Some of the most vigorous debates in recent decades have been between scholars who believe that economic interests and class divisions are the key to understanding the past, and those who believe that ideas and culture are at least as important as material interests. Whites and people of color, men and women, people from the American South and people from the North, young people and older people: these and many other points of difference find their way into scholarly disagreements. Debates can also occur over differences in methodology—between those who believe that quantitative studies can answer important historical questions and those who believe that other methods come closer to the truth.

Most of all historical interpretation changes in response to the time in which it is written. Historians may strive to be "objective" in their work, but no one can be entirely free from the assumptions and concerns of the present. In the 1950s, the omnipresent shadow of the Cold War had a profound effect on the way most historians viewed the past. In the 1960s, concerns about racial justice and disillusionment with the Vietnam War altered the way many historians viewed the past. Those events introduced a much more critical tone to scholarship and turned the attention of scholars away from politics and government and toward the study of society and culture.

Many areas of scholarship in recent decades are embroiled in a profound debate over whether there is such a thing as "truth." The world, some scholars argue, is simply a series of "narratives" constructed by people who view life in very different and often highly personal ways. "Truth" does not really exist. Everything is a product of interpretation. Not many historians embrace such radical ideas; most would agree that interpretations, to be of any value, must rest on a solid foundation of observable facts. But historians do recognize that even the most compelling facts are subject to many different interpretations and that the process of understanding the past is a forever continuing—and forever contested—process. ●

AP HISTORICAL ARGUMENTATION AND INTERPRETATION

1. Identify three arguments made regarding the issue of historical objectivity.
2. Explain at least two factors that influence historians when they are writing a historical account.
3. Take a position on the following statement: There is value to differing historical interpretations of "events." Provide examples to support your position.

courts. But in the fourteenth century, as the maritime capabilities of several western European societies increased and as Muslim societies seized control of the eastern routes to Asia, there began to be serious talk of finding a faster, safer sea route to Asia. Such dreams found a receptive audience in the courts of the new monarchs. By the late fifteenth century, some of them were ready to finance daring voyages of exploration.

The first to do so were the Portuguese. They were the preeminent maritime power in the fifteenth century, in large part because of the work of one man, Prince Henry the Navigator.

PRINCE HENRY THE NAVIGATOR Henry's own principal interest was not in finding a sea route to Asia, but in exploring the western coast of Africa. He dreamed of establishing a Christian empire there to aid in his country's wars against the Moors of northern Africa; and he hoped to find new stores of gold. The explorations he began did not fulfill his own hopes, but they ultimately led farther than he had dreamed. Some of Henry's mariners went as far south as Cape Verde, on Africa's west coast. In 1486 (six years after Henry's death), Bartholomeu Dias rounded the southern tip of Africa (the Cape of Good Hope); and in 1497-1498 Vasco da Gama proceeded all the way around the cape to India. In 1500, the next fleet bound for India, under the command of Pedro Cabral, was blown westward off its southerly course and happened upon the coast of Brazil. But by then another man, in the service of another country, had already encountered the New World.

CHRISTOPHER COLUMBUS

Christopher Columbus, who was born and reared in Genoa, Italy, obtained most of his early seafaring experience in the service of the Portuguese. As a young man, he became intrigued with the possibility, already under discussion in many seafaring circles, of reaching Asia by going not east but west. Columbus's hopes rested on several basic misconceptions. He believed that the world was far smaller than it actually is.

THE AMERICAN POPULATION BEFORE COLUMBUS

NO one knows how many people lived in the Americas in the centuries before Columbus. But scholars and other researchers have spent more than a century and have written many thousands of pages debating the question nevertheless. Interest in this question survives, despite the near impossibility of answering it. The debate over the pre-Columbian population is closely connected to the much larger debate over the consequences of European settlement of the Western Hemisphere.

Throughout the nineteenth century, Native Americans spoke often of the great days before Columbus when there were many more people in their tribes. They drew from their own rich tradition of oral history handed down through storytelling from one generation to another. The painter and ethnographer George Catlin spent much time among the tribes in the 1830s painting portraits of a race that he feared was "fast passing to extinction". He listened to these oral legends and estimated that there had been 16 million Indians in North America before the Europeans came. Other white Americans dismissed such claims as preposterous, insisting that Indian civilization was far too primitive to have been able to sustain so large a population.

In 1928, James Mooney, an ethnologist at the Smithsonian Institution, drew from early accounts of soldiers and missionaries in the sixteenth century. He came up with the implausibly precise figure of 1.15 million natives who lived north of Mexico in the early sixteenth century. That was a larger figure than nineteenth-century writers had suggested, but still much smaller than the Indians themselves claimed. A few years later, the anthropologist Alfred Kroeber used many of Mooney's methods

PUEBLO VILLAGE (© C. McIntyre/PhotoLink/Getty Images RF)

and come up with an estimate of the population of the entire Western Hemisphere—considerably larger than Mooney's, but much lower than Catlin's. He concluded in

IROQUOIS WOMEN This 1734 French engraving shows Iroquois women at work in a settlement somewhere in what is now upstate New York. In the foreground, women are cooking. Others are working in the fields. Men spent much of their time hunting and fighting battles, leaving the women to govern and dominate the internal lives of the villages. Property in Iroquois society was inherited through the mother, and women occupied positions of great authority within the tribes. (Library of Congress)

He also believed that the Asian continent extended farther eastward than it actually does. He assumed, therefore, that the Atlantic was narrow enough to be crossed on a relatively brief voyage. It did not occur to him that anything lay to the west between Europe and Asia.

Columbus failed to win support for his plan in Portugal, so he turned to Spain. The Spaniards were not yet as advanced a maritime people as the Portuguese, but they were at least as energetic and ambitious. And in the fifteenth century, the marriage of Spain's two most powerful regional rulers, Ferdinand of Aragon and Isabella of Castile, had produced the strongest monarchy in Europe. Like other young monarchies, Spain soon grew eager to demonstrate its strength by sponsoring new commercial ventures.

Columbus appealed to Queen Isabella for support for his proposed westward voyage. In 1492, Isabella agreed to Columbus's request. Commanding ninety men and three ships—the *Niña*, the *Pinta*, and the *Santa María*—Columbus left Spain in August 1492 and sailed west into the Atlantic on what he

1934 that there were 8.4 million people in the Americas in 1492, half in North America and half in the Caribbean and South America.

These low early estimates reflected an assumption that the arrival of the Europeans did not much reduce the native population. But in the 1960s and 1970s, scholars discovered that the early tribes had been catastrophically decimated by European plagues not long after the arrival of Columbus—meaning that the numbers Europeans observed even in the late 1500s were already dramatically smaller than the numbers in 1492. Drawing on early work by anthropologists and others who discovered evidence of widespread deaths by disease, historians William McNeill in 1976 and Alfred Crosby a decade later, as well as other scholars, produced powerful accounts of the near extinction of some tribes and the dramatic depopulation of others in a pestilential catastrophe with few parallels in history. Almost all scholars now accept that much, perhaps most, of the native population was wiped out by disease—smallpox, measles, tuberculosis, and other plagues imported from Europe.

Henry Dobyns, an anthropologist who was one of the earliest scholars to challenge the early, low estimates, claimed in 1966 that in 1492 there were between 10 and 12 million people north of Mexico and between 90 and 112 million in all of the Americas. No subsequent scholar has made so high a claim, but most estimates that followed have been much closer to Dobyns's than to Kroeber's. The geographer William M. Denevan, for example, argued in 1976 that the American population in 1492 was around 55 million and that the population north of Mexico was under 4 million. Those are among the lowest of modern estimates, but still dramatically higher than the nineteenth-century numbers.

The vehemence with which scholars have debated these figures is not just because it is very difficult to determine population size. It is also because the debate over the population is part of the debate over whether the arrival of Columbus—and the millions of Europeans who followed him—was a great advance in the history of civilization or an unparalleled catastrophe that exterminated a large and flourishing native population. How to balance the many achievements of European civilization in the New World after 1492 against the terrible destruction of native peoples that accompanied it is, in the end, less a historical question, perhaps, than a moral one.   ●

AP HISTORICAL ARGUMENTATION AND INTERPRETATION

1. Identify at least two historical estimates of the pre-Columbian population and the methods used to make them. For each estimate, provide one problem with the method used, which might lead to a questioning of the estimate.

2. Identify a discovery, which can be viewed as a turning point, or significant event, in the debate over the pre-Columbian population. How did this discovery change the debate?

3. Consider this statement: The arrival of Columbus to the Western World was a great advance. If the pre-Columbian population were zero, how do you view this statement. If the pre-Columbian population were 100 million, how do you view this statement? If the pre-Columbian population were 50 million, how do you view this statement?

4. If you were writing a history of European colonization in North America, how would you change the questions you would want to explore, if the pre-Columbian population were found to be 100 million and not zero? Explain.

thought was a straight course for Japan. Ten weeks later, he sighted land and assumed he had reached his target. In fact,

COLUMBUS'S FIRST VOYAGE

he had landed on an island in the Bahamas. When he pushed on and encountered Cuba, he assumed he had reached China. He returned to Spain in triumph, bringing with him several captured natives as evidence of his achievement. (He called the natives "Indians" because he believed they were from the East Indies in the Pacific.)

But Columbus had not, of course, encountered the court of the great khan in China or the fabled wealth of the Indies. A year later, therefore, he tried again, this time with a much larger expedition. As before, he headed into the Caribbean, discovering several other islands and leaving a small and short-lived colony on Hispaniola. On a third voyage, in 1498, he finally reached the mainland and cruised along the northern coast of South America. When he passed the mouth of the Orinoco River (in present-day Venezuela), he concluded for the first time that what he had discovered was not an island off the coast of China, as he had assumed, but a separate continent; such a large freshwater stream, he realized, could emerge only from a large body of land. Still, he remained convinced that Asia was only a short distance away. And although he failed in his efforts to sail around the northeastern coast of South America to the Indies (he was blocked by the Isthmus of

Panama), he returned to Spain believing that he had explored at least the fringes of the Far East. He continued to believe that for the rest of his life.

Columbus's celebrated accomplishments made him a popular hero for a time, but he later died in obscurity. When Europeans at last gave a name to the New World, they ignored him. The distinction went instead to a Florentine merchant, Amerigo Vespucci, a member of a later Portuguese expedition to the New World who wrote a series of vivid descriptions of the lands he had visited and who recognized the Americas as new continents.

Columbus has been celebrated for centuries as the "Admiral of the Ocean Sea" and as a representative of the new, secular, scientific impulses of Renaissance Europe. But Columbus was also a deeply religious man, even something of a mystic. His voyages were inspired as much by his conviction that he was fulfilling a

RELIGIOUS MOTIVES FOR EXPLORATION

divine mission as by his interest in geography and trade. A strong believer in biblical prophecies, he came to see himself as a man destined to advance the coming of the millennium. "God made me the messenger of the new heaven and the new earth," Columbus wrote near the end of his life, "and he showed me the spot where to find it." A similar combination of worldly and religious passions lay behind many subsequent efforts at exploration and settlement of the New World.

THE INDIAN VILLAGE OF SECOTON (C. 1585), BY JOHN WHITE John White created this illustration of life among the Eastern Woodland Indians in coastal North Carolina. It shows the diversified agriculture practiced by the natives: squash, tobacco, and three varieties of corn. The hunters shown in nearby woods suggest another element of the native economy. At bottom right, Indians perform a religious ritual, which White described as "strange gestures and songs." (© Private Collection /The Bridgeman Art Library)

CHRISTOPHER COLUMBUS This oil painting by Frederick Kemmelmeyer (1801/1805), *First Landing of Christopher Columbus*, depicts Columbus and his crew in a somewhat idealized fashion. The artist's perspective shows the Europeans as larger and more powerful than the Native population they encounter. (Courtesy National Gallery of Art, Washington)

but his expedition went on to complete the first known circumnavigation of the globe (1519-1522). By 1550, Spaniards had explored the coasts of North America as far north as Oregon in the west and Labrador in the east, as well as some of the interior regions of the continent.

THE CONQUISTADORES

In time, Spanish explorers in the New World stopped thinking of America simply as an obstacle to their search for a route to the East. They began instead to consider it a possible source of wealth rivaling and even surpassing the original Indies. On the basis of Columbus's discoveries, the Spanish claimed for themselves the whole of the New World, except for a piece of it (today's Brazil) that was reserved by a papal decree for the Portuguese. By the mid-sixteenth century, the Spanish were well on their way to establishing a substantial American empire.

The first Spanish colonists, whom Columbus brought on his second voyage, settled on the islands of the Caribbean, where they tried to enslave the Indians and find gold. They had little luck in either effort. But then, in 1518, Hernando Cortés led a small military expedition of about 600 men into Mexico. Cortés had been a Spanish government official in Cuba for fourteen years and to that point had achieved little success.

CORTÉS CONQUERS THE AZTECS But when he heard stories of great treasures in Mexico, he decided to go in search of them. He met strong and resourceful resistance from the Aztecs and their powerful emperor, Montezuma. But Cortés and his army had, unknowingly, unleashed an assault on the Aztecs far more devastating than military attack: they had exposed the natives to smallpox during an early and relatively peaceful visit to Tenochtitlán. A smallpox epidemic decimated the population and made it possible for the Spanish to triumph in

Partly as a result of Columbus's initiative, Spain began to devote greater resources and energy to maritime exploration and gradually replaced Portugal as the leading seafaring nation. The Spaniard Vasco de Balboa fought his way across the Isthmus of Panama in 1513. He became the first known European to gaze westward upon the great ocean that separated the Americas from China and the Indies. Seeking access

FERDINAND MAGELLAN to that ocean, Ferdinand Magellan, a Portuguese in the employ of the Spanish, found the strait that now bears his name at the southern end of South America. He struggled through the stormy narrows and into the ocean (so calm by contrast that he christened it the "Pacific"), then proceeded to the Philippines. There Magellan died in a conflict with the natives,

EUROPEAN EXPLORATION AND CONQUEST, 1492–1583 This map shows the many voyages of exploration and conquest of North America launched by Europeans in the late fifteenth and sixteenth centuries. Note how Columbus and the Spanish explorers who followed him tended to move quickly into the lands of Mexico, the Caribbean, and Central and South America, while the English and French explored the northern territories of North America.

• *What factors might have led these various nations to explore and colonize these different areas of the New World?*

THE MEXICANS STRIKE BACK In this vivid scene from the Duran Codex, Mexican artists illustrate a rare moment in which Mexican warriors gained the upper hand over the Spanish invaders. Driven back by native fighters, the Spanish have taken refuge in a room in the royal palace in Tenochtitlán while brightly attired Mexican warriors besiege them. Although the Mexicans gained a temporary advantage in this battle, the drawing illustrates one of the reasons for their inability to withstand the Spanish in the longer term. The Spanish soldiers are armed with rifles and crossbows, while the Indians carry only spears and shields. (© Biblioteca Nacional, Madrid, Spain/The Bridgeman Art Library)

their second attempt at conquest. The Spanish believed that the epidemic was a vindication of their efforts. When the Christians were exhausted from war, one follower of Cortés

PIZARRO IN PERU A European artist depicted Pizarro's arrival on the coast of Peru in the early 1530s, where he was greeted by crowds of hostile Indians. By 1538, Pizarro had conquered the empire of the Incas. (Library of Congress)

said at the time, "God saw fit to send the Indians smallpox." Through his ruthless suppression of the surviving natives, Cortés established a lasting reputation as the most brutal of the Spanish *conquistadores* (conquerors).

The news that silver was to be found in Mexico attracted the attention of other Spaniards. From the island colonies and from Spain itself, a wave of conquistadores descended on the mainland in search of fortune. Francisco Pizarro, who conquered Peru (1532–1538) and revealed to Europeans the wealth of the Incas, opened the way for other advances into South America. His onetime deputy Hernando de Soto, in a futile search for gold, silver, and jewels, led several expeditions (1539–1541) through Florida west into the continent and became the first white man known to have crossed the Mississippi River. Francisco Coronado traveled north from Mexico (1540–1542) into what is now New Mexico in a similarly fruitless search for gold and jewels; in the process, he helped open the Southwest of what is now the United States to Spanish settlement.

The story of the Spanish warriors is one of great military daring and achievement. It is also a story of great brutality and greed—a story that would be repeated time and again over centuries of European conquest of the Americas. The conquistadores in some areas almost exterminated the native populations through a combination of warfare and disease.

BRUTALITY AND GREED

DE SOTO IN NORTH AMERICA This gruesome drawing portrays Spanish troops under Hernando de Soto massacring a group of Mobile Indians in what is now Alabama, in the winter of 1540–1541. De Soto had been governor of Cuba, but in 1539 he sailed to Florida with 600 troops and for the next several years traveled through large areas of what would later become the southern United States until he died of fever in 1542. Here, as elsewhere, his troops dealt with the Indian tribes they encountered along the way with unrestrained brutality. (Rare Books and Special Collections, Library of Congress)

SPANISH AMERICA

Lured by dreams of treasure, Spanish explorers, conquistadores, and colonists established a vast empire for Spain in the New World. The history of the Spanish Empire spanned three distinct periods. The first was the age of discovery and exploration–beginning with Columbus and continuing through the first two decades of the sixteenth century. The second was the age of the conquest, in which Spanish military forces (aided by the diseases they unleashed) established their dominion over the lands once ruled by natives. The third phase began in the 1570s, when new Spanish laws–the Ordinances of Discovery–banned the most brutal military conquests. From that point on, the Spanish expanded their presence in America through colonization.

ORDINANCES OF DISCOVERY

The first Spaniards to arrive in the New World, the conquistadores, had been interested in only one thing: getting rich. And in that they were fabulously successful. For 300 years, beginning in the sixteenth century, the mines in Spanish America yielded more than ten times as much gold and silver as the rest of the world's mines put together. These riches made Spain the wealthiest and most powerful nation for a time.

After the first wave of conquest, however, most Spanish settlers in America traveled to the New World for other reasons. Many went in hopes of creating a profitable agricultural economy. Unlike the conquistadores, who left little but destruction behind them, these settlers helped establish elements of European civilization in America that permanently altered both the landscape and the social structure.

Another important force for colonization was the Catholic Church. Ferdinand and Isabella, in establishing Spain's claim to most of the Americas from Mexico south, bowed to the wishes of the Church and established the requirement that Catholicism be the only religion of the new territories. Spain abided by that condition. Although the Spanish founded commercial and military centers in the sixteenth century, another common form of settlement by the early seventeenth century was the Catholic mission. Missions had commercial lives. But their primary purpose, at least at first, was converting natives to Catholicism. There were usually military garrisons connected to the missions, to protect the Europeans from hostile natives. *Presidios* (military bases) often grew up nearby to provide additional protection.

Aztec Empire at the time of Spanish Conquest

Inca Empire at the time of Spanish Conquest

Colonial boundaries and provincial names are for the late 18th century

OUTPOSTS ON THE NORTHERN FRONTIER OF NEW SPAIN
(Not simultaneous; through the 18th century)

† Missions

■ Forts (Sometimes with missions)

⬟ Settlements

LOUISIANA
(Spanish 1763-1800)

UNITED STATES
(from 1776)

San Francisco (1776)
Monterey (1770)
San Luis Obispo (1772)
Los Angeles (1781)
San Juan Capistrano (1776)
San Diego de Alcala (1769)
Tucson (1709)

Taos (1609)
Santa Fe (1607)

SPANISH FLORIDA
(to 1819)

St. Augustine (1565)

Gulf of Mexico

Rio Grande

Bahamas
(to Britain 1646)

VICEROYALTY OF

La Habana (1515)

Tampico

Cuba (1492)

Culiacán (1531)

Yucatán Peninsula

Santiago (1514)

Espanola (1492)

Puerto Rico (1502)

Mexico City (Tenochtitlán) (1325)
Veracruz (1519)

NEW SPAIN

Jamaica
(to Britain 1655)

HAITI
(French after 1697)

Santo Domingo (1496)

Guatemala (1519)

Caribbean Sea

PACIFIC OCEAN

Panama (1519)

Caracas (1567)

Orinoco R.

Trinidad (1498)

SURINAM
(Dutch)
(1625)

FRENCH GUIANA
(1626)

Santa Fe de Bogotá (1538)

VICEROYALTY OF NEW GRANADA

Quito (1534)

Guayaquil (1535)

Amazon R.

PORTUGUESE BRAZIL

Cuidad de los Reyes (Lima) (1535)

Cuzco (1535)

VICEROYALTY OF NEW CASTILLA
(Peru)

La Paz (1548)

VICEROYALTY OF LA PLATA

Rio de Janeiro (1567)

São Paulo (1554)

Valparaiso (1544)

Santiago (1541)

Parana R.

ATLANTIC OCEAN

Montevideo (1724)

Buenos Aires (1580)

Rio de la Plata

0   1000 mi

0   1000   2000 km

SPANISH AMERICA From the time of Columbus's initial voyage in 1492 until the mid-nineteenth century, Spain was the dominant colonial power in the New World. From the southern regions of South America to the northern regions of the Pacific Northwest, Spain controlled one of the world's largest empires. Note how much of the Spanish Empire was simply grafted upon the earlier empires of native peoples—the Incas in what is today Chile and Peru, and the Aztecs across much of the rest of South America, Mexico, and the Southwest of what is now the United States.

• *What characteristics of Spanish colonization would account for Spain's preference for already-settled regions?*

Indeed, after the era of the conquistadores came to a close in the 1540s, the missionary impulse became one of the most important motives for European emigration to America. Priests or friars accompanied almost all colonizing ventures. Through their zealous work, the gospel of the Catholic Church ultimately extended throughout South and Central America, Mexico, and into the South and Southwest of the present United States.

CATHOLIC MISSIONS

NORTHERN OUTPOSTS

The Spanish fort established in 1565 at St. Augustine, Florida, became the first permanent European settlement in what is now the United States. It served as a military outpost, an administrative center for Franciscan missionaries, and a headquarters for unsuccessful campaigns against North American natives that were ultimately abandoned. But it did not mark the beginning of a substantial effort at colonization in the region.

ST. AUGUSTINE

A more substantial colonizing venture began thirty years later in the Southwest. In 1598, Don Juan de Oñate traveled north from Mexico with a party of 500 men. He claimed for Spain some of the lands of the Pueblo Indians that Coronado had passed through over fifty years before. The Spanish migrants established a colony in what is now New Mexico, modeled roughly on those the Spanish had created farther south. Oñate distributed *encomiendas* to the Spanish settlers. They were licenses to exact labor and tribute from the natives in specific areas (a system first used in dealing with the Moors in Spain). The Spanish demanded tribute from the local Indians (and at times commandeered them as laborers). Spanish colonists founded Santa Fe in 1609.

Oñate's harsh treatment of the natives (who greatly outnumbered the small Spanish population) threatened the stability of the new colony and led to his removal as governor in 1606. Over time, relations between the Spanish and the Pueblos improved. Substantial numbers of Pueblos converted to Christianity under the influence of Spanish missionaries. Others entered into important trading relationships with the Spanish. The colony remained precarious nevertheless because of the danger from Apache and Navajo raiders, who threatened the Spanish and Pueblos alike. Even so, the New Mexico settlement continued to grow. By 1680, there were over 2,000 Spanish colonists living among about 30,000 Pueblos. The economic heart of the colony was not the gold and precious metals the early Spanish explorers had tried in vain to find. It was cattle and sheep, raised on the *ranchos* that stretched out around the small towns Spanish settlers established.

In 1680, the colony was nearly destroyed when the Pueblos rose in revolt. In the 1660s and 1670s, the Spanish priests and the colonial government, which was closely tied to the missionaries, launched efforts to suppress tribal rituals that Europeans considered incompatible with Christianity. The discontent among the natives at this suppression survived for decades. More important as a cause of the Pueblo revolt of 1680, however, was a major drought and a series of raids by

PUEBLO REVOLT OF 1680

neighboring Apache tribes. The instability these events produced sparked the uprising. An Indian religious leader named Pope led an uprising that killed hundreds of European settlers (including twenty-one priests), captured Santa Fe, and drove the Spanish temporarily from the region. But twelve years later the Spanish returned, resumed seizing Pueblo lands, and crushed a last revolt in 1696.

Spanish exploitation of the Pueblos did not end. But after the revolts, many Spanish colonists realized that they could not prosper in New Mexico if they remained constantly in conflict with a native population that greatly outnumbered them. They tried to solve the problem in two ways. On the one hand, the Spanish intensified their efforts to assimilate the Indians–baptizing Indian children at birth and enforcing observance of Catholic rituals. On the other hand, they now permitted the Pueblos to own land. They stopped commandeering Indian labor, they replaced the encomienda system with a less demanding and oppressive one, and they tacitly tolerated the practice of tribal religious rituals.

These efforts were at least partially successful. After a while, there was significant intermarriage between Europeans and Indians. Increasingly, the Pueblos came to consider the Spanish their allies in the continuing battles with the Apaches and Navajos. By 1750, the Spanish population had grown modestly to about 4,000. The Pueblo population had declined (through disease, war, and migration) to about 13,000, less than half what it had been in 1680. New Mexico had by then become a reasonably stable, but still weak and isolated, outpost of the Spanish Empire.

THE EMPIRE AT HIGH TIDE

By the end of the sixteenth century, the Spanish Empire had become one of the largest in the history of the world. It included the islands of the Caribbean and the coastal areas of South America that had been the first targets of the Spanish expeditions. It extended to Mexico and southern North America, where a second wave of colonizers had established outposts. Most of all, the empire spread southward and westward into the vast landmass of South America–the areas that are now Chile, Argentina, and Peru. In 1580, when the Spanish and Portuguese monarchies temporarily united, Brazil came under Spanish jurisdiction as well.

SPAIN'S VAST EMPIRE

It was, however, a colonial empire very different from the one the English would establish in North America beginning in the early seventeenth century. The earliest Spanish ventures in the New World had been largely independent of the throne. But by the end of the sixteenth century, the monarchy had extended its authority directly into the governance of local communities. Colonists had few opportunities to establish political institutions independent of Spain. There was also a significant economic difference between the Spanish Empire and the later British one. The Spanish were far more successful than the British would be in extracting great surface wealth–gold and silver–from their American colonies. But they concentrated less energy on making agriculture and commerce

GOLD IN THE AMERICAS Spanish conquistadors and settlers were wildly successful in their acquisition of gold in the Americas. For three hundred years, beginning in the sixteenth century, mines in America produced more than ten times as much gold and silver as the rest of the world's production put together. This image shows how the Spaniards enslaved Natives to do the hard work of mining gold. (© North Wind Picture Archives/Alamy)

profitable in their colonies. The strict commercial policies of the Spanish government (policies that the British Empire was never strong enough to impose on their colonies to the north) made things worse. To enforce the collection of duties and to provide protection against pirates, the government established

RIGID ROYAL CONTROL

rigid and restrictive regulations that required all trade with the colonies to go through a single Spanish port and only a few colonial ports, in fleets making but two voyages a year. The system stifled economic development of the Spanish areas of the New World.

There was also an important difference between the character of the population in the Spanish Empire and that of the colonies to the north. Almost from the beginning, the English, Dutch, and French colonies in North America concentrated on establishing permanent settlement and family life in the New World. The Europeans in North America reproduced rapidly after their first difficult years and in time came to outnumber the natives. The Spanish, by contrast, ruled their empire but did not people it. In the first century of settlement, fewer than 250,000 settlers in the Spanish colonies were from Spain itself or from any other European country. Only about 200,000 more arrived in the first half of the seventeenth century. Some additional settlers came from various outposts of Spanish civilization in the Atlantic–the Azores, the Cape Verde Islands, and elsewhere; but even with these other sources, the number of European settlers in Spanish America remained very small

relative to the native population. Despite the ravages of disease and war, the vast majority of the population of the Spanish

A COLLISION OF CULTURES

Empire continued to consist of natives. The Spanish, in other words, imposed a small ruling class upon a much larger existing population; they did not create a self-contained European society in the New World as the English would attempt to do in North America.

BIOLOGICAL AND CULTURAL EXCHANGES

The lines separating the races in the Spanish Empire gradually grew less distinct than they would be in the English colonies to the north. European and native cultures never entirely merged in the Spanish colonies. Indeed, significant differences remain today between European and Indian cultures throughout South and Central America.

Europeans would not have been exploring the Americas at all without their early contacts with the natives. From them,

INCREASING LEVELS OF EXCHANGE

they first learned of the rich deposits of gold and silver. After that, the history of the Americas became one of increasing levels of exchanges–some beneficial, some catastrophic–among different peoples and cultures.

The first and most profound result of this exchange was the importation of European diseases to the New World. It would be difficult to exaggerate the consequences of the exposure of

Native Americans to such illnesses as influenza, measles, chicken pox, mumps, typhus, and above all smallpox–diseases to which Europeans had over time developed at least a partial immunity but to which Native Americans were tragically vulnerable. Millions died. (See "Debating the Past," pp. 8–9.)

Native groups inhabiting some of the large Caribbean islands and some areas of Mexico were virtually extinct within fifty years of their first contact with whites. On Hispaniola–where the Dominican Republic and Haiti are today and where Columbus landed and established a small, short-lived colony in the 1490s–the native population quickly declined from

DEMOGRAPHIC CATASTROPHE

approximately 1 million to about 500. In the Mayan areas of Mexico, as much as 95 percent of the population perished within a few years of their first contact with the Spanish. Some groups fared better than others; some of the tribes north of Mexico, whose contact with European settlers came later and less intimately, were spared the worst of the epidemics. But most areas of the New World experienced a demographic catastrophe at least as grave as, and in many places far worse than, the Black Death that had killed at least a third of the population of Europe two centuries before.

The decimation of native populations in the southern regions of the Americas was not, however, purely a result of this inadvertent exposure to infection. It was also a result of

DELIBERATE SUBJUGATION AND EXTERMINATION

the conquistadores' deliberate policy of subjugation and extermination. Their brutality was in part a reflection of the ruthlessness with which Europeans waged war in all parts of the world. It was also a result of their conviction that the natives were "savages"–uncivilized peoples whom they considered somehow not fully human.

Not all aspects of the exchange were so disastrous to the natives. The Europeans introduced important new crops to America (among them sugar and bananas), domestic livestock (cattle, pigs, and sheep), and perhaps most significantly the horse, which had disappeared from the Western Hemisphere in the Ice Age and now returned aboard Spanish ships in the sixteenth century. The Europeans imported these things for their own use. But Indian tribes soon learned to cultivate the new crops, and European livestock proliferated rapidly and spread widely among natives. In the past, most tribes had possessed no domesticated animals other than dogs. The horse, in particular, became central to the lives of many natives and transformed their societies.

The exchange was at least as important (and far more beneficial) to the Europeans. In both North and South America, the arriving white peoples learned new agricultural techniques from the natives, techniques often better adapted to the character of the new land than those they had brought with them from Europe. They discovered new crops, above all maize (corn), which became an important staple among the settlers.

NEW CROPS AND AGRICULTURAL TECHNIQUES

Columbus took corn back to Europe from his first trip to America, and it soon spread through much of Europe as well. Such American foods as squash, pumpkins, beans, sweet potatoes, tomatoes, peppers, and potatoes also found their way back to Europe and in the process revolutionized European agriculture. Agricultural discoveries ultimately proved more important to the future of Europe than the gold and silver the conquistadores valued so highly.

In South America, Central America, and Mexico, societies emerged in which Europeans and natives lived in intimate, if unequal, contact with one another. As a result, Indians adopted many features of European civilization. Many natives gradually came to learn Spanish or Portuguese, but in the process they created a range of dialects, combining the European languages with their own. European missionaries–through both persuasion and coercion–spread Catholicism through most areas of the Spanish Empire. But native Christians tended to connect the new creed with features of their old religions, creating a hybrid of faiths that were, while essentially Christian, nevertheless distinctively American.

Colonial officials were expected to take their wives with them to America, but among the ordinary settlers–the majority–European men outnumbered European women by at least ten to one. Not surprisingly, therefore, the Spanish immigrants had substantial sexual contact with native women. Intermarriage became frequent,

SMALLPOX AMONG THE INDIANS Far more devastating to the Indians of America than the military ventures of Europeans were deadly diseases carried to the New World by invaders from the Old World. Natives had developed no immunity to the infectious diseases of Europe, and they died by the hundreds of thousands from such epidemics as measles, influenza, and (as depicted here by a European artist) smallpox. (© Dorling Kindersley/ Getty Images) and before long the population of the colonies came to be dominated (numerically, at least) by people of mixed race, or *mestizos*. Through much of the Spanish Empire an elaborate racial hierarchy developed, with the Spanish at the top, natives

A COMPLEX RACIAL HIERARCHY at the bottom, and people of mixed races in between. Racial categories, however, were much more fluid than the Spanish wanted to believe and did not long remain fixed. Over time, the wealth and influence of a family often came to define its place in the "racial" hierarchy more decisively than race itself. Eventually, a successful or powerful person could become "Spanish" regardless of his or her actual ancestry.

Natives were the principal labor source for the Europeans. Virtually all the commercial, agricultural, and mining enterprises of the Spanish and Portuguese colonists depended on an Indian workforce. Different labor systems emerged in different areas of the Spanish Empire. In some places, Indians were sold into slavery. More often, colonists used a wage system closely related, but not identical, to slavery, by which Indians were forced to work in the mines and on the planta-

VARIED LABOR SYSTEMS tions for fixed periods, unable to leave without the consent of their employers. Such workforces survived in some areas of the South American mainland for many centuries. So great was the need for native labor that European settlers were less interested in acquiring land than they were in gaining control over Indian villages, which could become a source of labor.

Even so, the native population could not meet all the labor needs of the colonists—particularly since the native population had declined (and in some places virtually vanished) because of disease and war. As early as 1502, therefore, European settlers began importing slaves from Africa.

AFRICA AND AMERICA

Most of the African men and women who were forcibly taken to America came from a large region in west Africa below the Sahara Desert, known as Guinea. It was the home of a wide variety of peoples and cultures. Since over half of all the new arrivals in the New World between 1500 and 1800 were Africans, those cultures greatly affected the character of American civilization. Europeans and white Americans came to portray African society as primitive and uncivilized (in part to justify the enslavement of Africa's people). But most Africans were civilized peoples with well-developed economies and political systems.

Humans began settling in west Africa at least 10,000 years ago. By the fifteenth century CE, they had developed exten-

GHANA AND MALI sive civilizations and complex political systems. The residents of upper Guinea had substantial commercial contact with the Mediterranean world—trading ivory, gold, and slaves for finished goods. Largely as a result, they became early converts to Islam. After the collapse of the ancient kingdom of Ghana

around 1100 CE, the even larger empire of Mali emerged and survived well into the fifteenth century. Its great city, Timbuktu, became fabled as a trading center and a seat of education.

Africans farther south were more isolated from Europe and the Mediterranean. They were also more politically fragmented. The central social unit in much of the south was the village, which usually consisted of members of an extended family group. Some groups of villages united in small kingdoms—among them Benin, Congo, and Songhay. But no

BENIN, CONGO AND SONGHAY large empires emerged in the south comparable to the Ghana and Mali kingdoms farther north. Nevertheless, these southern societies also developed extensive trade—in woven fabrics, ceramics, and wooden and iron goods, as well as crops and livestock—both among themselves and, to a lesser degree, with the outside world.

The African civilizations naturally developed economies that reflected the climates and resources of their lands. In upper Guinea, fishing and rice cultivation, supplemented by the extensive trade with Mediterranean lands, were the foundation of the economy. Farther south, Africans grew wheat and other food crops, raised livestock, and fished. There were some nomadic tribes in the interior, which subsisted largely on hunting and gathering and developed less elaborate social systems. But most Africans were sedentary people, linked by elaborate political, economic, and familial relationships.

SCULPTURE OF DJENNÉ Many of the Africans forcibly exported from their homes to America in the seventeenth and eighteenth centuries were natives of Mali, the seat of an ancient east African civilization. This terra cotta sculpture, discovered in the 1940s, dates from between 600 and 900 years ago. It portrays a prisoner who most likely represented an African enslaved by the Malis. ("Seated Prisoner," 11th/16th Century, Mande, Founders Society Purchase, Robert H. Tannahill Foundation Fund. Photograph © 2014 The Detroit Institute of the Arts/ The Bridgeman Art Library)

Like many Native American societies, but unlike those in Europe, African societies tended to be matrilineal—which means that people traced their heredity through, and inherited property from, their mothers rather than their fathers. When a couple married, the husband left his own family to join the family of his wife. Like most other peoples, Africans divided work by gender, but the nature of that division varied greatly from place to place. Women played a major role, often the dominant role,

MATRILINEAL SOCIETIES in trade; in many areas they were the principal farmers (while the men hunted, fished, and raised livestock); and everywhere, they managed child care and food preparation. Most tribes also divided political power by gender, with men choosing leaders and systems for managing what they defined as male affairs and women choosing parallel leaders to handle female matters. Tribal chiefs generally were men (although in some places there was a female counterpart), but the position customarily passed down not to the chief's son but to the son of the chief's eldest sister. African societies, in short, were characterized by a greater degree of sexual equality than those of most other parts of the world at the time.

In those areas of west Africa where indigenous religions had survived the spread of Islam (which included most of the lands south of the empire of Mali), people worshiped many gods, whom they associated with various aspects of the natural world and whose spirits they believed lived in trees, rocks, forests, and streams. Most Africans also developed forms of ancestor worship and took great care in tracing family lineage; the most revered priests (who were often also important social and political leaders as well) were generally the oldest people in the tribe.

African societies had elaborate systems of social ranks (or hierarchies). Small elites of priests and nobles stood at the top. Most people belonged to a large middle group of farmers, traders, crafts workers, and others. At the bottom of society were slaves—men and women who were put into bondage after being captured in wars or because of criminal behavior or unpaid debts. Slavery in Africa was not usually permanent; people were generally placed in bondage for a fixed period and in the meantime retained certain legal protections (including the right to marry). Their children, moreover, did not inherit their parents' condition of bondage.

The African slave trade began long before the European migration to the New World. As early as the eighth century CE, west Africans began selling slaves to traders from the Mediterranean. They were responding to a demand from affluent families who wanted black men and women as domestic servants. They were also responding to more-general labor shortages in some areas of Europe and North Africa. When Portuguese sailors began exploring the coast of Africa in the fifteenth century, they too bought slaves—usually criminals and people captured in war—and took them back to Portugal, where there was a small but steady demand. By the 1500s, people from the Guinea region had moved into much of sub-Saharan Africa and traded gold, ivory, pepper, and many other precious commodities.

In the sixteenth century, however, the market for slaves grew dramatically as a result of the rising European demand for sugarcane. The small areas of sugar cultivation in the Mediterranean were proving inadequate, and production soon moved to the island of Madeira off the African coast, which became a Portuguese colony. Not long after that, it moved to the Caribbean islands and Brazil. Sugar was a labor-intensive crop, and the demand for workers in these new areas increased rapidly. European slave traders responded to that demand by increasing the recruitment of workers from along the coast of

GROWTH OF THE AFRICAN SLAVE TRADE west Africa (and from some areas of east Africa as well). As the demand increased, African kingdoms warred with one another in an effort to capture potential slaves to exchange for European goods. At first the slave traders were overwhelmingly Portuguese and, to a lesser extent, Spanish. By the seventeenth century, the Dutch had won control of most of the slave market. In the eighteenth century, the English dominated it. (Despite some false claims, Jews were never significantly involved in the slave trade.) By 1700, slavery had begun to spread well beyond its original locations in the Caribbean and South America and into the English colonies to the north.

THE ARRIVAL OF THE ENGLISH

England's first documented contact with the New World came only five years after Spain's. In 1497, John Cabot (like Columbus, a native of Genoa) sailed to the northeastern coast of North America on an expedition sponsored by King Henry VII. Other English navigators continued Cabot's unsuccessful search for a northwest passage through the New World to the Orient. They explored other areas of North America

JOHN CABOT during the sixteenth century. But even though England claimed dominion over the lands its explorers surveyed, nearly a century passed before the English made any serious efforts to establish colonies there. Like other European nations, England had to experience an internal transformation before it could begin settling new lands. That transformation occurred in the sixteenth century.

THE COMMERCIAL INCENTIVE

Part of the attraction of the New World to the English was its newness, its contrast to their own troubled land. America seemed a place where human settlement could start anew, where a perfect society could be created without the flaws and inequities of the Old World. Such dreams began to emerge in England only a few years after Columbus's voyages. They found classic expression in Sir Thomas More's *Utopia* (published in Latin in 1516, translated into English thirty-five years later), which described a mythical and nearly perfect society

THE ATLANTIC CONTEXT OF EARLY AMERICAN HISTORY WOR-2

MOST Americans understand that in the twenty-first century our nation has become intimately bound up with the rest of the world—that we live in a time that is often called the "age of globalization." But globalization long preceded our own time, and historians have recently come to recognize that the "New World" of seventeenth- and eighteenth-century America was part of a vast network of connections that has become known as the "Atlantic World."

The idea of an "Atlantic World" rests in part on the obvious connections between western Europe and the Spanish, British, French, and Dutch colonies in North and South America. The massive European emigration to the Americas beginning in the sixteenth century, the defeat and devastation of native populations, the creation of European agricultural and urban settlements, and the imposition of imperial regulations on trade, commerce, landowning, and political life—all of these forces reveal the influence of Old World imperialism on the history of the New World.

Although some Europeans traveled to the New World to escape oppression or to search for adventure, the great majority of European emigrants were in search of economic opportunity. Not surprisingly, therefore, the European settlements in the Americas were almost from the start connected to Europe through the growth of commerce between them. The commercial relationship between America and Europe was responsible not just for the growth of trade, but also for the increases in migration over time—as the demand for labor in the New World drew more and more settlers from the Old World. Commerce was also the principal reason for the rise of slavery in the Americas, and for the growth of the slave trade between European America and Africa. The Atlantic World, in other words, included not just Europe and the Americas, but Africa as well.

Religion was another force binding together the Atlantic World. The vast majority of people of European descent were Christians, and most of them maintained important religious ties to Europe. Catholics, of course, were part of a hierarchical church based in Rome and maintained close ties with the Vatican. But the Protestant faiths that predominated in North America were linked to their European counterparts as well. New religious ideas and movements spread back and forth across the Atlantic with astonishing speed. Great revivals that began in Europe moved quickly to America. The "Great Awakening" of the mid-eighteenth century, for example, began in Britain and traveled to America in large part through the efforts of the English evangelist George Whitefield. American evangelists later carried religious ideas from the New World back to the Old.

The early history of European America was also closely bound up with the intellectual life of Europe. The Enlightenment—the cluster of ideas that emerged in Europe in the seventeenth and eighteenth centuries emphasizing the power of human reason—moved quickly to the Americas, producing considerable intellectual ferment throughout the New World, but particularly in the British colonies in North America and the Caribbean. Many of the ideas that lay behind the American Revolution were products of British and French philosophy that had traveled across the Atlantic. The reinterpretation of those ideas by Americans to help justify their drive to independence—by, among others, Thomas Paine—moved back across the Atlantic to Europe and helped to inspire the French Revolution. Scientific and technological knowledge—another product of the Enlightenment—moved rapidly back and forth across the Atlantic. Americans borrowed industrial technology from Britain. Europe acquired much of its early knowledge of electricity from experiments done in America. But the Enlightenment was only one part of the continuing intellectual connections within the Atlantic World, connections that spread artistic, scholarly, and political ideas widely through the lands bordering the ocean.

on an imaginary island supposedly discovered by a companion of Amerigo Vespucci in the waters of the New World.

More's picture of an ideal community was, among other things, a comment on the social and economic ills of the England of his own time. The people of Tudor England suffered from frequent and costly European wars, from almost constant religious strife, and above all from a harsh economic transformation of the countryside. Because the worldwide demand for wool was growing rapidly, many landowners were finding it profitable to convert their land from fields for crops to pastures for sheep. The result was a significant growth in the wool trade. But that meant land worked at one time by agricultural serfs and later by rent–paying tenant farmers was steadily enclosed for sheep runs and taken away from the farmers. Thousands of evicted tenants roamed the countryside in gangs, begging from (and at times robbing) the more fortunate householders through whose communities they passed.

THE ENCLOSURE MOVEMENT

The government passed various laws designed to halt enclosures, relieve the worthy poor, and compel the able-bodied or "sturdy beggars" to work. Such laws had little effect. The enclosure movement continued unabated, and few of the dislocated farmers could find reemployment in raising sheep or manufacturing wool. By removing land from cultivation, the enclosure movement also limited England's ability to feed its rising population, which grew from 3 million in 1485 to 4 million in 1603. Because of both the dislocation of farmers and the restriction of the food supply, therefore, England had a serious problem of surplus population.

Amid this growing distress, a rising class of merchant capitalists was prospering from the expansion of foreign trade. At first, England had exported little except raw wool; but new merchant capitalists helped create a domestic cloth industry that allowed them to begin marketing finished goods at home and abroad. At first, most exporters did business almost entirely as individuals. In time, however, some merchants joined forces and formed chartered companies. Each such enterprise operated

(© The Granger Collection, New York)

Instead of thinking of the early history of what became the United States simply as the story of the growth of thirteen small colonies along the Atlantic seaboard of North America, the idea of the "Atlantic World" encourages us to think of early American history as a vast pattern of exchanges and interactions—trade, migration, religious and intellectual exchange, and many other relationships—among all the societies bordering the Atlantic: western Europe, western Africa, the Caribbean, and North and South America. ●

UNDERSTAND, ANALYZE, AND EVALUATE

1. What was the Atlantic World?
2. What has led historians to begin studying the idea of an Atlantic World?
3. Does studying American history in an Atlantic World context broaden or distort our understanding of American history?

on the basis of a charter acquired from the monarch, which gave the company a monopoly for trading in a particular region. Among the first of these were the Muscovy Company (1555),

CHARTERED COMPANIES

the Levant Company (1581), the Barbary Company (1585), the Guinea Company (1588), and the East India Company (1600). Investors in these companies often made fantastic profits from the exchange of English manufactures, especially woolens, for exotic goods; and they felt a powerful urge to continue the expansion of their profitable trade.

Central to this drive was the emergence of a new concept of economic life known as mercantilism, which was gaining favor throughout Europe. Mercantilism rested on the assumption that the nation as a whole, not the individuals within it, was the principal actor in the economy. The goal of economic activity should be to increase the nation's total wealth. Mercantilists believed that the world's wealth was finite. One person or nation could grow rich only at the expense of another. A nation's economic health depended, therefore, on

extracting as much wealth as possible from foreign lands and exporting as little wealth as possible from home.

The principles of mercantilism guided the economic policies of virtually all the European nation-states in the sixteenth and seventeenth centuries. Mercantilism greatly enhanced the position of the new merchant capitalists, whose overseas ventures were thought to benefit the entire nation and to be worthy of government assistance. It also increased competition among nations. Every European state was trying to find

MERCANTILISM

markets for its exports while trying to limit its imports. One result was the increased attractiveness of acquiring colonies, which could become the source of goods that a country might otherwise have to buy from other nations.

In England, the mercantilistic program thrived at first on the basis of the flourishing wool trade with the European continent and, particularly, with the great cloth market in Antwerp. Beginning in the 1550s, however, that glutted market collapsed, and English merchants found themselves obliged to look elsewhere for overseas trade. The establishment of colonies seemed to be a ready answer to that and other problems. Richard Hakluyt, an Oxford clergyman and the outstanding English propagandist for colonization, argued that colonies would not only create new markets for English goods, but they would also help alleviate poverty and unemployment by

RICHARD HAKLUYT'S ARGUMENT FOR COLONIES

siphoning off the surplus population. For the poor who remained in England "idly to the annoy of the whole state," there would be new work as a result

of the prosperity the colonies would create. Perhaps most important, colonial commerce would allow England to acquire products from its own new territories for which the nation had previously been dependent on foreign rivals—products such as lumber, naval stores, and, above all, silver and gold.

THE RELIGIOUS INCENTIVE

In addition to these economic motives for colonization, there were religious ones, rooted in the events of the European and English Reformations. The Protestant Reformation began in Germany in 1517, when Martin Luther openly challenged some of the basic practices and beliefs of the Roman Catholic Church—until then, the supreme religious authority and also one of the strongest political authorities throughout western Europe. Luther, an Augustinian monk and ordained priest, challenged the Catholic belief that salvation could be achieved through good works or through loyalty (or payments) to the Church itself. He denied the Church's claim that God communicated to the world through the pope and the clergy. The Bible, not the church, was the authentic voice of God, Luther claimed, and salvation was to be found not through "works" or through the formal practice of religion, but through faith alone. Luther's challenge quickly won him a wide following among ordinary men and women in northern Europe. He himself insisted that he was not revolting against the Church, that his purpose was to reform it from within. But when the pope

EUROPE AND WEST AFRICA IN THE FIFTEENTH CENTURY Exploration of North and South America was in part an outgrowth of earlier European trade in the Eastern Hemisphere. Europeans delivered cloth and other manufactures to northern Africa; then camels carried the cargoes across the Sahara to cities such as Timbuktu, Gao, and Djenné. There they loaded gold, ivory, and kola nuts for return to the Mediterranean. Africans also traded with Asia to obtain cloth, porcelain, and spices.

• *What areas of trade were most important to the early interaction between Africa and the Americas?*

excommunicated him in 1520, Luther defied him and began to lead his followers out of the Catholic Church entirely. A schism within European Christianity had begun that was never to be healed.

As the spirit of the Reformation spread rapidly throughout Europe, other dissidents began offering alternatives to orthodox Catholicism. The French theologian John Calvin was, after Luther, the most influential reformer and went even further than Luther had in rejecting the Catholic belief that human institutions could affect an individual's prospects for salvation. Calvin introduced the doctrine of predestination. God "elected" some people to be saved and condemned others to damnation; each person's destiny was determined before birth, and no one could change that predetermined fate. But while individuals could not alter their destinies, they could strive to know them. Calvinists believed that the way people led their lives might reveal to them their chances of salvation. A wicked or useless

DOCTRINE OF PREDESTINATION existence would be a sign of damnation; saintliness, diligence, and success could be signs of grace. Calvinism created anxieties among its followers, to be sure; but it also produced a strong incentive to lead virtuous, productive lives. The new creed spread rapidly throughout northern Europe and produced (among other groups) the Huguenots in France and the Puritans in England.

The English Reformation was very different from the Protestant Reformation. It occurred more because of a political dispute between the king and the pope than as a result of doctrinal revolts. In 1529, King Henry VIII became angered by the pope's refusal to grant him a divorce from his Spanish wife (who had failed to bear him the son he desperately wanted). In response, he broke England's ties with the Catholic Church

THE ENGLISH REFORMATION and established himself as the head of the Christian faith in his country. He made relatively few other changes in English Christianity, however, and after his death the survival of Protestantism remained in doubt for a time. When Henry's Catholic daughter Mary ascended the throne, she quickly restored England's allegiance to Rome and harshly persecuted those who refused to return to the Catholic fold. Many Protestants were executed (the origin of the queen's enduring nickname, "Bloody Mary"); others fled to the European continent, where they came into contact with the most radical ideas of the Reformation. Mary died in 1558, and her half-sister, Elizabeth, became England's sovereign. Elizabeth once again severed the nation's connection with the Catholic Church (and, along with it, an alliance with Spain that Mary had forged).

The Church of England, as the official religion was now known, satisfied the political objectives of the queen, but it failed to satisfy the religious desires of many English Christians. Catholics continued to assert allegiance to the pope. More important, many Protestants believed that the "reformation" did not create enough changes in theology. The most ardent Protestants became known as "Puritans," because they hoped to "purify" the church.

JOHN CALVIN Next to Martin Luther, John Calvin was the most important figure of the European Reformation. His belief in predestination was central to the Puritan faith of early New England. (© Bettmann/Corbis)

Some Puritans took genuinely radical positions. They were known as Separatists, and they were determined to worship as they pleased in their own independent congregations. That flew in the face of English law—which outlawed unauthorized religious meetings, required all subjects to attend

PURITAN SEPARATISTS regular Anglican services, and levied taxes to support the established church. The radicalism of the Separatists was visible in their rejection of prevailing assumptions about the proper religious roles of women. Many Separatist sects, perhaps most prominently the Quakers, permitted women to serve as preachers, which would have been impossible in the established church.

Most Puritans resisted separatism. Still, their demands were by no means modest. They wanted to simplify Anglican forms of worship. They wanted to reduce the power of the bishops, who were appointed by the Crown and who were, in many cases, openly corrupt and highly extravagant. Perhaps above all they wanted to reform the local clergy, many of them greedy, uneducated men with little interest in (or knowledge of) theology.

Puritan discontent, already festering, grew rapidly after the death of Elizabeth, the last of the Tudors, and the accession to

MERCANTILISM AND COLONIAL COMMERCE WOR-1

FOR more than two centuries, the economic life of Europe and its growing colonial possessions (the North American colonies among them) was shaped by a theory known as mercantilism. The actual application of mercantilism differed from country to country and empire to empire. But virtually all versions of mercantilism shared a belief in the economic importance of colonies to the health of the colonizing nations. As a result, mercantilism helped spur the growth of European empires around the world.

In one sense, mercantilism was a highly nationalist, as opposed to a global, theory. It rested on the conviction that the nation (not the individual) was at the center of economic life and that each nation should work to maximize its own share of the finite wealth for which all nations were competing. A gain for France, mercantilism taught, was in effect a loss for Britain or Spain. Thus, it encouraged each nation to work for itself and to attempt to weaken its rivals. But mercantilism was also a global force. What made it so was not the modern notion of the value of international economic growth but, rather, the belief that each nation must search for its own sources of trade and raw materials around the world. Every European state was trying to find markets for its exports, which would bring wealth into the nation, while trying to limit imports, which would transfer wealth to others. (Most of these central mercantilist tenets would eventually be overturned in Adam Smith's 1776 tract, *The Wealth of Nations*, which instead advocated free trade among nations and individual self-interest over national largesse as the route to increasing global—and thus national—wealth.)

In a mercantilist economy, colonies were critical to a nation's economic well-being. They served both as providers of raw materials and as markets for finished goods. Colonies, mercantilism taught, should trade only with their mother nation, and the direction of wealth should flow only in one direction, toward the center of the empire. Naval power became an integral part of the mercantilist idea. Only by controlling the sea lanes between the colonies and the homeland could a nation preserve its favorable balance of trade.

Despite the common assumptions underlying all forms of mercantilism, the system took many different forms, often depending on whether colonial merchants or state bureaucrats drove the economic discussion. In England, Spain, and the Netherlands, mercantilism was closely identified with the emerging middle class, who stood to profit personally from the increased trade. (Hence the term "mercantilism," from merchant.) In France and Germany, on the other hand, state officials rather than private citizens laid more of the groundwork for mercantilism principles. In France, mercantilism was often known as "Colbertism," after its primary proponent, Jean-Baptiste Colbert, foreign minister under Louis XIV. In Germany, the theory was known as "cameralism," for the *Kammer*, or royal treasury.

The Trades Increase

AS concerning SHIPS, It is that which everyone knoweth and can say: They are our *Weapons*; They are our *Armaments*; They are our *Strength*; They are our *Pleasures*; They are our *Defence*; They are our *Profit*. The *Subject* by them is made rich, the *Kingdom* through them, strong. The *Prince* in them is mighty, in a word: By them in manner, we live, the Kingdom is, the King Reigneth.

—From an English Pamphlet [*circa* 1681].

MERCANTILISM "The Trades Increase, as Concerning Ships" is a hand-colored woodprint depicting the vibrant state of late-seventeenth-century British mercantilism. The extended caption beneath the print acknowledges how British trade stands as a cornerstone of the British economy and a primary source of strength for the monarchy. (© North Wind Pictures Archive/Image Works)

In its early years, mercantilism was closely associated with "bullionism," which is the theory that only gold and silver defined a nation's wealth. As such, the early Spanish colonies of the New World, in particular, emphasized the procurement of gold, silver, and other precious metals for the mother nation. (English colonies such as Jamestown were founded in part with the same intention, but they were much less successful at finding precious metals.) But even when gold and silver were scarce, colonies could still provide other important resources for the imperial capitals—for example, fur, timber, sugar, tobacco, and slaves.

The theory of mercantilism taught that wealth creation was a zero-sum game: there was a fixed amount of wealth in the world, and any wealth a nation acquired was, in effect, taken away from some other nation. As a result, mercantilists believed that nations should heavily regulate the economic affairs of their colonies. One good example of this was England's passage of the Navigation Acts in the 1660s, laws that sharply restricted colonial trade with anyone else but England. But England was not alone in passing such restrictions. Spain took equally definitive control over its colonial economies, passing similarly intensive regulation and insisting until 1720 that all colonial trade pass through the port of Seville.

Still, naval vessels could not be everywhere at once. And despite the many laws restricting colonial economies to their home nations, many colonial merchants around the world struck up trade with their nonaffiliated neighbors when possible. The French, Spanish, and Dutch West Indies in particular became the site of a thriving intercolonial trade that was not, for all intent and purposes, legal according to mercantilist doctrine. Indeed, so many traders from so many countries violated mercantile laws in the eighteenth century, and so many of them amassed great profits in the process, the mercantilist system gradually began to unravel. By the time of the American Revolution, in part a result of the colonists' resistance to mercantilist policies, the patterns of global trade were already moving toward the less-regulated trading patterns of the modern capitalist world. ●

UNDERSTAND, ANALYZE, AND EVALUATE

1. What effect did mercantilism have on colonial economies? Did the effects differ according to which European nation owned the colony?
2. How did mercantilism contribute to power rivalries among the European nations?
3. Mercantilism as a nation's driving economic force has largely given way to economic globalization, that is, the increased interdependence of nations' economies. Why do you think this is so?

the throne of James I, a Scotsman and the first of the Stuarts, in 1603. James believed kings ruled by divine right, and he felt

PURITAN DISCONTENT

no obligation to compromise with his opponents. He quickly antagonized the Puritans, a group that included most of the rising businessmen, by resorting to arbitrary taxation, by favoring English Catholics in granting charters and other favors, and by supporting "high church" forms of ceremony. By the early seventeenth century, some religious nonconformists were beginning to look for places of refuge outside the kingdom. Along with the other economic and social incentives for colonization, such religious discontent helped turn England's gaze to distant lands.

THE ENGLISH IN IRELAND

England's first experience with colonization came not in the New World, but in a land separated from Britain only by a narrow stretch of sea: Ireland. The English had long laid claim to the island and had for many years maintained small settlements in the area around Dublin. Only in the second half of the sixteenth century, however, did serious efforts at large-scale colonization begin. During the 1560s and 1570s,

ELIZABETH I This is the Kitchener Portrait of Queen Elizabeth I (1533–1603) painted by an unknown artist in the English style. In this portrait, the artist conveys Elizabeth as she was seen by many of her contemporaries: a strong, confident ruler, richly dressed, presiding over an ambitious, increasingly prosperous, and expansionist state. (Private Collection /© Mallett Gallery, London, UK / The Bridgeman Art Library)

THE DOCKS OF BRISTOL, ENGLAND By the eighteenth century, when this scene was painted, Bristol had become one of the principal English ports serving the so-called triangular trade among the American colonies, the West Indies, and Africa. The lucrativeness of that trade is evident in the bustle and obvious prosperity of the town. Even earlier, however, Bristol was an important port of embarkation for the thousands of English settlers migrating to the New World. (*Docks and Quay*. English School (18th Century). City of Bristol Museum and Art Gallery/The Bridgeman Art Library, London)

would-be colonists moved through Ireland, capturing territory and attempting to subdue the native population. In the process they developed many of the assumptions that would guide later English colonists in America.

The most important of these assumptions was that the native population of Ireland–approximately 1 million people, loyal to the Catholic Church, with their own language (Gaelic) and their own culture–was a collection of wild,

SUBJUGATION OF IRELAND

vicious, and ignorant "savages." The Irish lived in ways the English considered crude and wasteful ("like beasts"), and they fought back against the intruders with a ferocity that the English considered barbaric. Such people could not be tamed, the English concluded. They certainly could not be assimilated into English society. They must, therefore, be suppressed, isolated, and if necessary destroyed. Eventually, they might be "civilized," but only after they were thoroughly subordinated.

Whatever barbarities the Irish may have inflicted on the colonizers, the English more than matched them in return. Sir Humphrey Gilbert, who was later to establish the first British colony in the New World (an unsuccessful venture in Newfoundland), served for a time as governor of one Irish district and suppressed native rebellions with extraordinary viciousness. Gilbert was an educated and supposedly civilized man. But he considered the natives less than human and therefore not entitled to whatever decencies civilized people reserved for their treatment of one another. As a result, he managed to justify, both to himself and to others, such atrocities as beheading Irish soldiers after they were killed in battle. Gilbert himself, Sir Walter Raleigh, Sir Richard Grenville, and others active in Ireland in the mid-sixteenth century derived from their experiences there an outlook they would take to America, where they made similarly vicious efforts to subdue and subjugate the natives.

The Irish experience led the English to another important (and related) assumption about colonization: that English settlements in distant lands must retain a rigid separation from the native populations. In Ireland, English colonizers estab-

THE PLANTATION MODEL

lished what they called "plantations," transplantations of English society in a foreign land. Unlike the Spanish in America, the English in Ireland did not try simply to rule a subdued native population; they tried to build a separate society, peopled with emigrants from England itself. The new society would exist within a "pale of settlement," an area physically separated from the natives. That concept, too, they would take with them to the New World, even though in Ireland, as later in America, the separation of peoples and the preservation of "pure" English culture proved impossible.

THE FRENCH AND THE DUTCH IN AMERICA

English settlers in North America, unlike those in Ireland, would encounter not only natives but also other Europeans who were, like them, driven by mercantilist ideas to establish economic outposts abroad. To the south and southwest was the Spanish Empire. Spanish ships continued to threaten English settlements along the coast for years. But except for Mexico and scattered outposts such as those in Florida and New Mexico, the Spanish made little serious effort to colonize North America.

England's more formidable North American rivals in the early sixteenth century were the French. France founded its first permanent settlement in America at Quebec in 1608, less than a year after the English started their first colony at Jamestown. The French colony's population grew very slowly. Few French Catholics felt any inclination to leave their homeland, and French Protestants who might have wished to emigrate were excluded from the colony. The French, however, exercised an influence in the New World disproportionate to their numbers, largely because of their relationships with Native Americans. Unlike the English, who for many years hugged the coastline and traded with the Indians of the interior through intermediaries, the French forged close, direct ties with natives deep inside the continent. French Jesuit missionaries were among the first to penetrate Indian societies, and they established some of the first contacts between the two peoples. More important still were

COUREURS DE BOIS

the *coureurs de bois*–adventurous fur traders and trappers–who also moved far into the wilderness and developed an extensive trade that became one of the underpinnings of the French colonial economy.

The fur trade was, in fact, more an Indian than a French enterprise. The *coureurs de bois* were, in many ways, little more than agents for the Algonquins and the Hurons, who were the principal fur traders among the Indians of the region and from whom the French purchased their pelts. The French traders were able to function only to the degree that they could form partnerships with the Indians. Successful partnerships often resulted from their ability to become a part of native society, living among the Indians and at times marrying Indian women. The fur trade helped open the way for the

THE "RESTITUTION" OF NEW AMSTERDAM This is a detail from an elaborate engraving created to celebrate the "Restitutio" (or return) of New Amsterdam to the Dutch in 1673. England had captured New Amsterdam in 1664 and made claim to the entire province of New Netherland. But in 1672, war broke out between England and the Netherlands, and the Dutch recaptured their lost province. In celebration of that event, this heroic picture of the Dutch fleet in New York was created for sale in the Netherlands. Early in 1674, at the conclusion of the war, the Dutch returned the colony to England. (© Gilder Lehrman Collection, New York, USA / The Bridgeman Art Library)

other elements of the French presence in North America–the agricultural estates (or *seigneuries*) along the St. Lawrence River, the development of trade and military centers at Quebec and Montreal, and the creation of an alliance with the Algonquins and others–that enabled the French to compete with the more numerous British in the contest for control of North America. That alliance also brought the French into conflict with the Iroquois, the Algonquins' ancient enemies, who assumed the central role in the English fur trade. An early result of these tensions was a 1609 attack led by Samuel de Champlain, the founder of Quebec, on a band of Mohawks, apparently at the instigation of his Algonquin trading partners.

The Dutch, too, were establishing a presence in North America. The Netherlands had won its independence from Spain in the early seventeenth century and had become one of the leading trading nations of the world. Its merchant fleet was larger than England's, and its traders were active not only in Europe but also in Africa, Asia, and–increasingly–America. In 1609, an English explorer in the employ of the Dutch, Henry

HENRY HUDSON

Hudson, sailed up the river that was to be named for him in what is now New York State. Because the river was so wide, he believed for a time that he had found the long-sought water route through the continent to the Pacific. He was wrong, of course, but his explorations led to a Dutch claim on territory in America and to the establishment of a permanent Dutch presence in the New World.

For more than a decade after Hudson's voyage, the Dutch maintained an active trade in furs in and around present-day New York. In 1624, the Dutch West India Company established a series of permanent trading posts on the Hudson, Delaware, and Connecticut Rivers. The company actively

NEW AMSTERDAM

encouraged settlement of the region–not just from Holland itself, but also from such other parts of northern Europe as Germany, Sweden, and Finland. It transported whole families to the New World and granted vast feudal estates to landlords (known as "patroons") on condition that they bring still more immigrants to America. The result was the colony of New Netherland and its principal town, New Amsterdam, on Manhattan Island. Its population, diverse as it was, remained relatively small; the colony was only loosely united, with chronically weak leadership.

THE FIRST ENGLISH SETTLEMENTS

The first enduring English settlement in the New World was established at Jamestown, in Virginia, in 1607. But for nearly thirty years before that, English merchants and adventurers had been engaged in a series of failed efforts to create colonies in America. Through much of the sixteenth century, the English had mixed feelings about the New World. They knew of its existence, and they were intrigued by its possibilities. Under the leadership of Elizabeth I, they were developing a powerful sense of nationalism that encouraged dreams of

expansion. At the same time, however, England was leery of Spain, which remained the dominant force in America and, it seemed, the dominant naval power in Europe.

But much changed in the 1570s and 1580s. English "sea dogs" such as Sir Francis Drake staged successful raids on Spanish merchant ships and built confidence in England's ability to challenge Spanish sea power. More important was the attempted

THE SPANISH ARMADA

invasion of England in 1588. Philip II, the powerful Spanish king, had recently united his nation with Portugal. He was now determined to end England's challenges to Spanish commercial supremacy and to bring the English back into the Catholic Church. He assembled one of the largest military fleets in the history of warfare–known to history as the "Spanish Armada"–to carry his troops across the English Channel and into England itself. Philip's bold venture turned into a fiasco when the smaller English fleet dispersed the Armada and, in a single stroke, ended Spain's domination of the Atlantic. The English now felt much freer to establish themselves in the New World.

The pioneers of English colonization were Sir Humphrey Gilbert and his half-brother Sir Walter Raleigh–both friends of Queen Elizabeth and both veterans of the earlier colonial efforts in Ireland. In 1578, Gilbert obtained from Elizabeth a patent granting him the exclusive right for six years "to inhabit and possess at his choice all remote and heathen lands not in the actual possession of any Christian prince."

After numerous setbacks, Gilbert led an expedition to

GILBERT'S EXPEDITION TO NEWFOUNDLAND

Newfoundland in 1583 and took possession of it in the queen's name. He proceeded southward along the coast, looking for a good place to build a military outpost that might eventually grow into a profitable colony. But a storm sank his ship, and he was lost at sea.

ROANOKE

Raleigh was undeterred by Gilbert's misfortune. The next year, he secured from Elizabeth a six-year grant similar to Gilbert's and sent a small group of men on an expedition to explore the North American coast. They returned with two captive Indians and glowing reports of what they had seen. They were particularly enthusiastic about an island the natives called Roanoke and about the area of the mainland just beyond it (in what is now North Carolina). Raleigh asked the queen for permission to name the entire region "Virginia" in honor of Elizabeth, "the Virgin Queen." But while Elizabeth granted the permission, she did not offer the financial assistance Raleigh had hoped his flattery would produce. So he turned to private investors to finance another expedition.

In 1585 Raleigh recruited his cousin, Sir Richard Grenville, to lead a group of men (most of them from the English plantations in Ireland) to Roanoke to establish a colony. Grenville

THE FIRST ROANOKE COLONY

deposited the settlers on the island, remained long enough to antagonize the natives by razing an Indian village as retaliation for a minor theft, and

ROANOKE A drawing by one of the English colonists in the ill-fated Roanoke expedition of 1585 became the basis for this engraving by Theodor de Bry, published in England in 1590. A small European ship carrying settlers approaches the island of Roanoke, at left. The wreckage of several larger vessels farther out to sea and the presence of Indian settlements on the mainland and on Roanoke itself suggest some of the perils the settlers encountered. (© The Gallery Collection/Corbis)

returned to England. The following spring, Sir Francis Drake unexpectedly arrived in Roanoke. With supplies and reinforcements from England long overdue, the beleaguered colonists boarded Drake's ships and left.

Raleigh tried again in 1587, sending an expedition carrying ninety-one men, seventeen women (two of them pregnant), and nine children—the nucleus, he hoped, of a viable "plantation." The settlers landed on Roanoke and attempted to take up where the first group of colonists had left off. (Shortly after arriving, one of the women—the daughter of the commander of the expedition, John White—gave birth to a daughter, Virginia Dare, the first American-born child of English parents.) White returned to England after several weeks (leaving his daughter and granddaughter behind) in search of supplies and additional settlers; he hoped to return in a few months. But the hostilities with Spain intervened, and White did not return to the island for three years. When he did, in 1590, he found the island deserted, with no clue to the settlers' fate other than the cryptic inscription "Croatoan" carved on a post. Some historians have argued that the

colonists were slaughtered by the Indians in retaliation for Grenville's hostilities. Others have contended that they left their settlement and joined native society, ultimately becoming entirely assimilated. But no conclusive solution to the mystery of the "Lost Colony" has ever been found.

The Roanoke mystery marked the end of Sir Walter Raleigh's involvement in English colonization of the New World. In 1603, when James I succeeded Elizabeth to the throne, Raleigh was accused of plotting against the king, stripped of his monopoly, and imprisoned for more than a decade. Finally (after being released for one last ill-fated maritime expedition), he was executed by the king in 1618. No later colonizer would receive grants of land in the New World as vast or undefined as those Raleigh and Gilbert had acquired. But despite the discouraging example of these early experiences, the colonizing impulse remained alive.

In the first years of the seventeenth century, a group of London merchants to whom Raleigh had assigned his charter rights decided to renew the attempt at colonization in Virginia. A rival group of merchants, from Plymouth and other West

Country towns, were also interested in American ventures and were sponsoring voyages of exploration farther north, up to Newfoundland, where West Country fishermen had been going for many years. In 1606 James I issued a new

NEW COLONIAL CHARTERS

charter, which divided America between the two groups. The London group got the exclusive right to colonize in the south, and the Plymouth merchants received the same right in the north. Through their efforts, the first enduring English colonies were planted in America.

AP CONNECTING THEMES

Chapter 1 has discussed the interaction of native peoples in the Western Hemisphere prior to and just after the arrival of Europeans. The chapter also included a discussion of the impact of the environment in shaping native populations and cultures and subsequent changes to the environment brought on by European contact. The motives for colonization among the major European powers and how their relationship with American Indians and slavery differed were also discussed. It is important to understand how and why European contact with native populations changed the lives and perceptions of each group.

The following themes have a heightened importance in Chapter 1. You should now be able to do the following for each listed theme:

Work, exchange, and technology: Identify the products and consequences of the Columbian Exchange.

Peopling: Identify patterns of movement of American Indians prior to and after European contact. Analyze the impact of migration, disease, and warfare on the American Indian population.

America in the world: Explain how exchange of commodities influenced the origin and development of British North American colonies.

Environment and geography: Explain how the introduction of plants, technology, and animals altered the environment of North American and its impact on American Indians. Discuss how the environment lead to distinct regional groups prior to and after European contact.

Ideas, beliefs, and culture: Explain intergroup relationships between Europeans, Africans, and Native Americans.

AP SUGGESTED STUDY

PEOPLE/PLACES/EVENTS As you study these items, think about how they demonstrate or relate to key concepts and historical themes from this chapter.

AFRICAN SLAVE TRADE 21
ALGONQUIAN 7
ATLANTIC WORLD 22
BIOLOGICAL AND CULTURAL CHANGES 18
CAHOKIA 6
CATHOLIC MISSIONS (SPANISH) 17
CHARTER COMPANIES 23
CHRISTOPHER COLUMBUS 9
CONQUISTADORES 12
CORN (MAIZE) CULTIVATION 5
COUREURS DE BOIS 29

DON JUAN DE ONATE 17
ENCOMIENDA 17
FUR TRADE 29
HENRY HUDSON 30
IROQUOIS 6
JAMESTOWN 30
MATRILINEAL 21
MERCANTILISM 23
MESO-AMERICANS 3
MESTIZOS 20
PUEBLO REVOLT 17

PURITANS 25
RACIAL HIERARCHY 20
ROANOKE 30
SAMUEL DE CHAMPLAIN 30
SEPARATISTS 25
SIR WALTER RALEIGH 28
SMALLPOX 19
TENOCHTITLAN 3
WOODLAND INDIANS 6

AP TEST PRACTICE

MULTIPLE CHOICE Use the excerpt below and your knowledge of U.S. history to answer questions 1–3.

"... on the said 18th day of the month of December, 1681, for the judicial proceedings and inquiry which must be made in this new reduction and pacification and in order to learn of all the motives, reasons, circumstances, designs, and other supports which the treacherous apostate rebels against the royal crown of his Majesty had and may have at present for the conspiracy, alliance, and rebellion which they executed, apostatizing from the holy faith, forsaking royal obedience, burning images and temples, killing atrociously priests, soldiers, women, and children, taking possession of all the things pertaining to divine worship, of haciendas, and of everything in the kingdom that they could, returning to the blind idolatry and superstitions of their ancient days, his lordship caused to appear before him an Indian of the Tegua nation who said his name is Juan, that he is a native of the pueblo of Tesuque, and is married."

–Spanish colonial government record of judicial proceedings regarding Pueblo Indian revolt, 1681

1. The excerpt best provides evidence of which issue being deeply troubling for Native Americans regarding the colonizing efforts of Europeans in the 17th century?

   (A) Intermarriage between the Native Americans and the Europeans

   (B) Suppression of Native American beliefs and culture

   (C) Introduction by the Europeans of new agricultural techniques

   (D) The value system of the Europeans

2. The excerpt most suggests that, in their colonization of the Western Hemisphere, the European colonists believed

   (A) in their cultural superiority

   (B) in the knowledge of Native Americans

   (C) that their European political systems would not translate effectively into the political systems already existing in the Western Hemisphere

   (D) the different cultures of the Native American groups should be respected

3. The excerpt provides evidence for which of the following regarding motives of Europeans in their conquest of the Americas in the 16th and 17th centuries?

   (A) Spreading Christianity

   (B) Exploring non-western European cultures

   (C) Pursuing trade

   (D) Discovering gold and silver

SHORT ANSWER Use your knowledge of U.S. history to answer questions 4–6.

4. Answer a, b, and c.

   a) Briefly explain ONE example of how the environment shaped the social or cultural aspect of a North American Indian group.

   b) Briefly explain ONE example of how the environment shaped the political or economic structure of a North American Indian group.

   c) Briefly explain ONE example of a cultural exchange before the arrival of the Europeans, affecting the cultural development of an American Indian group.

5. Answer a, b, and c.

   a) Briefly explain ONE example of how American Indian societies in the 15th and 16th centuries were affected during the Columbian Exchange.

   b) Briefly explain a SECOND example of how American Indian societies in the 15th and 16th centuries were affected during the Columbian Exchange.

   c) Briefly explain ONE example of how the Columbian Exchange affected the European population in the 15th and 16th centuries.

6. Answer a, b, c

   a) Briefly explain ONE example of how Europeans sought to change American Indian beliefs and world views.

   b) Briefly explain ONE example of how American Indians resisted European attempts to change their beliefs and world views.

   c) Briefly explain ONE example of how Europeans justified their treatment of American Indians.

LONG ESSAY Develop a thoughtful and thorough historical argument that answers the question below. Begin your essay with a thesis statement and support it with relevant historical evidence.

7. Some historians have argued that European expansion into the Western Hemisphere in the 15th and 16th centuries was a great advancement for human civilization. Support, modify, or refute this interpretation, providing specific evidence to justify your answer.

2 | TRANSPLANTATIONS AND BORDERLANDS

THE FORT AT JAMESTOWN The Jamestown settlement was beset with difficulties from its first days, and it was many decades before it became a stable and successful town. In the early days, the colonists suffered from the climate, the lack of food, and the spread of disease. They also struggled with the growing hostility of the neighboring Indians. This painting, made almost 150 years after the colony at Jamestown was first settled, conveys a cooperative relationship between the Native Americans and the Europeans who are seen here engaging in trade. (© MPI/Getty Images)

AP

HISTORICAL THINKING

1. **Comparison** Compare the political, economic, and social patterns of settlement and expansion in the Chesapeake region with those in the New England region.

2. **Historical Causation** For each of the colonial regions, explain the factors that promoted stability and those that undermined stability.

3. **Historical Argumentation** How did the pre-occupation of the British government on its own internal and European affairs affect the development of the British North American colonies?

4. **Contextualization** Discuss specific attempts by the British government to increase control over the colonies and assess the success of those efforts.

5. **Comparison** Analyze the impact of differing labor systems on the societal development of the New England, Middle, and Southern colonies.

6. **Comparison** Analyze the impact of religion on the political, economic and social aspects of the three colonial regions.

7. **Periodization** Trace the colonists' relations with the Native Americans and identify significant events which helped define these relations and any changes in relations.

Key Concept Correlations

Analyze the ways the historical developments you learn about in this chapter connect to the following AP Key Concepts.

1.2 European overseas expansion resulted in the Columbian Exchange, a series of interactions and adaptations among societies across the Atlantic.

1.3 Contacts among American Indians, Africans, and Europeans challenged the worldviews of each group.

2.1 Differences in imperial goals, cultures, and the North American environments that different empires confronted led Europeans to develop diverse patterns of colonization.

2.2 European colonization efforts in North America stimulated intercultural contact and intensified conflict between the various groups of colonizers and native peoples.

2.3 The increasing political, economic, and cultural exchanges within the "Atlantic World" had a profound impact on the development of colonial societies in North America.

3.3 Migration within North America, cooperative interaction, and competition for resources raised questions about boundaries and policies, intensified conflicts among peoples and nations, and led to contests over the creation of a multiethnic, multiracial national identity.

Thematic Learning Objectives

WXT-1, 2, 4; PEO-1, 4, 5; WOR-1, 2, 5; ID-4, 5, 6; ENV-1, 2, 4; POL-1

CHAPTER 2 deals with the settlement and development of the British North American colonies. You should pay particular attention to the similarities and differences that develop in each of the colonial regions as a result of motives for settlement, geographic and environmental factors, and the religious and ethnic make-up of the regions. Also, focus on disputes between the colonists and American Indians (both in the British colonies and the Spanish colonies), the intra-colonial disputes between the tidewater and the backcountry, and conflicting interests between British colonists and the interests of other European powers. To understand this period, the impact of the development of the American economy on colonial-British relations is essential. As you read, evaluate the following ideas:

- The abundance of free or cheap land necessitated the development of various labor systems to make the land productive.
- Distinct regional identities developed throughout the British North American colonies as a result of differing motives for settlement, geographic and environmental factors, and ethnic and religious differences.
- Increasing distrust between the British colonies and the home country intensified over time, leading to periodic attempts by Great Britain to increase imperial control over the colonies.
- Spanish colonization in the Southwest differed greatly from British possession on the Atlantic coast.
- Significant clashes between American Indians and European colonizers continued throughout the colonial period.
- The growth of the American economy led to ever strengthening ties and increased inter-dependence throughout the Atlantic World.

THE EARLY CHESAPEAKE

Once James I had issued his 1606 charters, the London Company moved quickly and decisively to launch a colonizing expedition headed for Virginia. A party of 144 men aboard three ships, the *Godspeed*, the *Discovery*, and the *Susan Constant*, set sail for America in 1607.

COLONISTS AND NATIVES

Only 104 men survived the journey. They reached the American coast in the spring of 1607, sailed into the Chesapeake and up a river they named the James, establishing their colony, Jamestown, on a peninsula. They chose this setting because they believed it would provide

EARLY PROBLEMS security from the natives. But they chose poorly: the site was low and swampy and surrounded by thick woods. The results could hardly have been more disastrous. The colonists were vulnerable to local diseases, particularly malaria, which was especially virulent along the marshes.

Other problems were to a large degree of the colonists' own making. They focused less on growing food and building community than on a futile search for gold. Community building was impossible because they had brought no women with them. Thus they had no real households and no real stakes in their settlement.

That the colonies survived at all was a result of the neighboring Indians teaching the colonists how to live in their new land. The natives showed the colonists their agricultural technologies, which were better adapted to the soil and climate of Virginia than the agricultural traditions the English settlers had brought with them. The natives were settled farmers whose villages were surrounded by neatly ordered fields on which they grew a variety of crops including beans, pumpkins, and above all maize (corn), which was easy to cultivate and generated large yields. The English also learned the advantages of growing beans alongside corn to enrich the soil. And they also began to combine foods they grew with food they hunted and fished. From the Indians, the English learned how to build canoes, which were good for navigating the

THE ENGLISH COME TO THE AMERICAS
Jamestown was the first English settlement in the Americas. Supported by the London Company, it was established in 1607. (© Peter Newark Pictures/Bridgeman Art Library)

local streams. Without what they learned from the natives, the early settlers would not have survived. Despite this help, the settlers often expressed hostilities toward the natives believing that English civilization was superior to that of these "savages."

Jamestown remained a tiny colony for more than a decade. The natives were far more powerful than the English for years. Coastal Virginia had numerous tribes: the Algonquins, Sioux, and Iroquois, which were all part of the Powhatan Confederacy, named after the great chief who controlled a large area near the coasts. What the English called Virginia, the natives called Tsenacommacah.

Within a few months of settling in Virginia, only 38 men of the original 144 were alive, the rest killed by disease and famine. These men owed their survival to the help provided by the Indians and to the leadership of Captain John Smith, who at age 27 was already a famous world traveler. Smith imposed work and order on the settlement and created a shaky relationship with the natives (sometimes negotiating for food and at other times stealing it).

REORGANIZATION AND EXPANSION

As Jamestown struggled to survive, the London Company (now renamed the Virginia Company) was already dreaming of bigger things. In 1609, it obtained a new charter from the king, which increased its power and enlarged its territory. It offered stock in the company to planters who were willing to migrate at their own expense. And it provided free passage to Virginia for poorer people who would agree to serve the company for seven years. In the spring of 1609, two years after the first arrival of the English, a fleet of nine vessels was dispatched to Jamestown with approximately 600 people, including some women and children.

Nevertheless, disaster followed. One of the Virginia-bound ships was lost at sea in a hurricane. Another ran aground in the Bermuda Islands and was unable to sail again for months.

THE STARVING TIME

Many of the new settlers succumbed to fevers before winter came. The winter of 1609–1610 was especially severe, a period known as the "starving time." By then the natives realized that the colonists were a threat to their civilization and stopped them from moving farther inland into Indian lands. Barricaded within a small palisade and unable to hunt or cultivate food, the colonists lived on what they could find: "dogs, cats, rats, snakes, toadstools, horsehides," and even "the corpses of dead men," as one survivor recalled. When the migrants who had run aground in Bermuda finally arrived in Jamestown the following May, they found only 60 emaciated people still alive. The new arrivals took the survivors onto their ship and sailed for England. But as the refugees proceeded down the James, they met an English ship coming up the river–part of a fleet bringing supplies and the colonies' first governor, Lord De La Warr. The departing settlers agreed to return to Jamestown. New relief expeditions soon began to arrive and the fort began to thrive.

New settlements began lining the river above and below Jamestown. There settlers discovered tobacco, which was for them a new crop that was already popular among the Spanish colonies to the south. In 1612, the Jamestown planter John Rolfe began cultivating the crop in Virginia. Soon other planters in the area followed. Tobacco was the first profitable crop in the new colony for the settlers, and it encouraged tobacco planters to move farther inland deeper into the natives' farmlands.

DE LA WARR'S HARSH DISCIPLINE

De La Warr and his successors (Sir Thomas Dale and Sir Thomas Gates) imposed a harsh and rigid discipline on the colony: they organized settlers into work

TOBACCO PLANT This 1622 woodcut, later hand-colored, represents the tobacco plant cultivated by English settlers in Virginia in the early seventeenth century after John Rolfe introduced it to the colonists. On the right is an image of a man smoking the plant through a very large pipe. (© Getty Images)

THE GROWTH OF THE CHESAPEAKE, 1607–1750 This map shows the political forms of European settlement in the region of the Chesapeake Bay in the seventeenth and early eighteenth centuries. Note the several different kinds of colonial enterprises: the royal colony of Virginia, controlled directly by the English Crown after the failure of the early commercial enterprises there; and the proprietary regions of Maryland, northern Virginia, and North Carolina, which were under the control of powerful English aristocrats.

⁕ Did these political differences have any significant effect on the economic activities of the various Chesapeake colonies?

gangs, and they sentenced offenders to be flogged, hanged, or broken on the wheel. But this communal system of labor did not function effectively for long. Settlers often evaded work. Governor Dale soon concluded that the colony would fare better if the colonists had personal incentives to work. He began to permit the private ownership and cultivation of land. Landowners would repay the company with part-time work and contributions of grain to its storehouses.

Under the leadership of these first, harsh governors, Virginia was not always a happy place. But it survived and even expanded. New settlements began lining the river above and below Jamestown. The expansion was partly a result of the order and discipline the governors at times managed to impose. It was partly a product of increased military assaults on the local Indian tribes, which provided protection for the new settlements. But it also occurred because the colonists had at last discovered a marketable crop: tobacco.

TOBACCO

Europeans had become aware of tobacco soon after Columbus's first return from the West Indies, where he had seen the Cuban natives smoking small cigars *(tabacos)*, which they inserted in the nostril. By the early seventeenth century, tobacco from the Spanish colonies was already in wide use in Europe. Some critics denounced it as a poisonous weed, the cause of many diseases. King James I himself led the attack with "A Counterblaste to Tobacco" (1604), in which he urged his people not to imitate "the barbarous and beastly manners of the wild, godless, and slavish Indians, especially in so vile and stinking a custom." Other critics were concerned because England's tobacco purchases from the Spanish colonies meant a drain of English gold to the Spanish importers. Still, the demand for tobacco soared.

Then in 1612, the Jamestown planter John Rolfe began to experiment in Virginia with a harsh strain of tobacco that local Indians had been growing for years. He produced crops of high quality and found ready buyers in England. **EMERGENCE OF THE TOBACCO ECONOMY** Tobacco cultivation quickly spread up and down the James. The character of this tobacco economy–its profitability, its uncertainty, its land and labor demands–transformed Chesapeake society in fundamental ways.

Of most immediate importance was that tobacco cultivation required territorial expansion. Tobacco growers needed large areas of farmland to grow their crops; and because tobacco exhausted the soil after only a few years, the demand for land increased even more. English farmers began establishing plantations deeper and deeper in the interior, moving from the center of European settlement at Jamestown into the territory the natives considered their own.

EXPANSION

Even the discovery of tobacco cultivation was not enough to help the Virginia Company. By 1616, there were still no profits, only land and debts. Nevertheless, the promoters continued to hope that the tobacco trade would allow them finally to turn the corner. In 1618, they launched a last great campaign to attract settlers and make the colony profitable.

Part of that campaign was an effort to recruit new settlers and workers to the colony. The company called it the "headright" system. Headrights were fifty-acre grants of land, which new settlers could acquire in a variety of ways. Those who already lived in the colony received 100 acres apiece. Each new settler received a single headright for himself or herself. This system encouraged family groups to migrate together, since the more family members traveled to America, the larger the landholding the family would receive. In addition, anyone (new settler or old) who paid for the passage of other immigrants to Virginia would receive an additional headright for each new arrival—thus, the company hoped, inducing the prosperous to import new laborers to America. Some colonists were able to assemble sizable plantations with the combined headrights they received for their families and their servants. In return, they contributed a small quitrent (one shilling a year for each headright) to the company.

THE HEADRIGHT SYSTEM

The company added other incentives as well. To diversify the colonial economy, it transported ironworkers and other skilled craftsmen to Virginia. In 1619, it sent 100 Englishwomen to the colony (which was still overwhelmingly male) to become the wives of male colonists. (The women were purchased for 120 pounds of tobacco. Their status was somewhere between indentured servants and free people, depending on the goodwill—or lack of it—of their husbands.) The company promised the colonists the full rights of Englishmen (as provided in the original charter of 1606), an end to the strict and arbitrary rule of the communal years, and even a share in self-government. On July 30, 1619, in the Jamestown church, delegates from the various communities met as the House of Burgesses. It was the first meeting of an elected legislature within what was to become the United States.

A month later, another event in Virginia established a very different but no less momentous precedent. As John Rolfe recorded, "about the latter end of August" a Dutch ship brought in "20 and odd Negroes." The status and fate of these first Africans in the English colonies remains obscure. There is some reason to believe that the colonists did not consider them slaves, that they thought of them as servants to be held for a term of years and then freed, like the white servants with whom the planters were already familiar. For a time, moreover, the use of black labor remained limited. Although Africans continued to trickle steadily into the colony, planters continued to prefer European indentured servants until at least the 1670s, when white servants began to become scarce and expensive. But whether or not anyone realized it at the time, the small group of black people who arrived in 1619 marked a first step toward the enslavement of Africans within what was to be the American republic.

The expansion of the colony was able to proceed only because of effective suppression of local Indians who resisted the expanding English presence. For two years, Sir Thomas Dale led unrelenting assaults against the Powhatan Indians and in the process kidnapped the great chief Powhatan's daughter Pocahontas. When Powhatan refused to ransom her, she converted to Christianity and in 1614 married John Rolfe. (Pocahontas accompanied her husband back to England, where, as a Christian convert and a gracious woman, she stirred interest in projects to "civilize" the Indians. She died while abroad.) At that point, Powhatan ceased his attacks on the English in the face of overwhelming odds. But after his death several years later, his brother, Opechancanough, became head of the native confederacy. Recognizing that the position of his tribe was rapidly deteriorating, he resumed the effort to defend tribal lands from European encroachments. On a March morning in 1622, tribesmen called on the white settlements as if to offer goods for sale, then suddenly attacked. Not until 347 whites of both sexes and all ages lay dead or dying were the Indian warriors finally forced to retreat. The surviving English struck back mercilessly at the Indians and turned back the threat for a time. Only after Opechancanough failed in another uprising in 1644 did the Powhatans finally cease to challenge the eastern regions of the colony.

SUPPRESSION OF THE POWHATAN INDIANS

By then the Virginia Company in London was defunct. The company had poured all its funds into its profitless Jamestown venture and, in the aftermath of the 1622 Indian uprising, faced imminent bankruptcy. In 1624, James I revoked the company's charter, and the colony came under the control of the Crown. It would remain so until 1776.

DEMISE OF THE VIRGINIA COMPANY

EXCHANGES OF AGRICULTURAL TECHNOLOGY

The hostility of the early English settlers toward their Indian neighbors was in part a result of their conviction that their own civilization was greatly superior to that of the natives—and above all that they were more technologically advanced. The English, after all, had great oceangoing vessels, muskets and other advanced implements of weaponry, and many other tools that the Indians had not developed. Indeed, when John Smith and other early Jamestown residents grew frustrated at their inability to find gold and other precious commodities, they often blamed their failure on the backwardness of the natives.

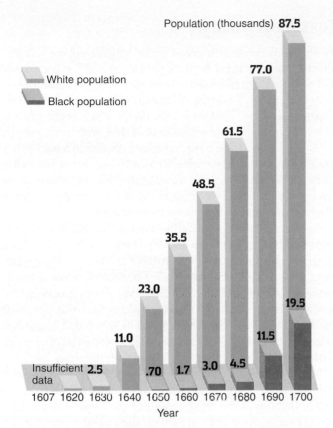

Population (thousands) **87.5**

White population

Black population

77.0

61.5

48.5

35.5

23.0

19.5

11.0

Insufficient **2.5** .70 1.7 **3.0** **4.5** **11.5**
data

1607 1620 1630 1640 1650 1660 1670 1680 1690 1700

Year

THE NON-INDIAN POPULATION OF THE CHESAPEAKE, 1607–1700 This graph shows the rapid growth of the population of the Chesapeake during its first century of European settlement. Note the dramatic increases in the first half of the century and the somewhat slower increase in the later decades. If the forcibly imported slave population were not counted in the last two decades of the century, the non-Indian population would not have grown at all.

• *What impact did the growth of African slavery have on the rate of immigration by Europeans?*

Yet the survival of Jamestown was, in the end, largely a result of agricultural technologies developed by Indians and

INDIAN AGRICULTURAL TECHNIQUES

borrowed from them by the English. Native agriculture was far better adapted to the soil and climate of Virginia than were the agricultural traditions the English

settlers brought with them. The Indians of Virginia had built successful farms with neatly ordered fields in which grew a variety of crops, some previously unknown to the English. Some of the Indian farmlands stretched over hundreds of acres and supported substantial populations.

The English settlers did not adopt all the Indian agricultural techniques. Natives cleared fields not, as the English did, by cutting down and uprooting all the trees. Instead, they killed trees in place by "girdling" them (that is, making deep incisions around the base) in the areas in which they planted or by setting fire to their roots; and they planted crops not in long, straight rows, but in curving patterns around the dead tree trunks. But in other respects, the English learned a great deal from the Indians about how to grow food in North America. In particular, they quickly recognized the great value of corn, which proved

to be easier to cultivate and to produce much greater yields than any of the European grains the English had known at home. Corn was also attractive to the settlers because its stalks could be a source of sugar and because it spoiled less easily than other grains. The English also learned the advantages of growing beans alongside corn to enrich the soil.

MARYLAND AND THE CALVERTS

Maryland was founded under circumstances very different from those of Virginia, but it nonetheless developed in ways markedly similar to those of its neighbor to the south. The new colony was the dream of George Calvert, the first Lord Baltimore, a recent convert to Catholicism and a shrewd businessman. Calvert envisioned establishing a colony both as a great speculative venture in real estate and as a retreat for English Catholics, many of whom felt oppressed by the Anglican establishment at home. He died before he could receive a charter from the king. But in 1632, his son Cecilius, the second Lord Baltimore, received a charter remarkable not only for the extent of the territory it granted him—an area that encompassed parts of what are now Pennsylvania, Delaware, and Virginia, in addition to present-day Maryland—

PROPRIETARY RULE

but also for the powers it bestowed on him. He and his heirs were to hold their province as "true and absolute lords and

proprietaries," and were to acknowledge the sovereignty of the king only by paying an annual fee to the Crown.

Lord Baltimore named one of his brothers, Leonard Calvert, governor and sent him with another brother to oversee the settlement of the province. In March 1634, two ships—the *Ark* and the *Dove*—bearing 200 to 300 passengers entered the Potomac River and turned into one of its eastern tributaries. On a high and dry bluff, these first arrivals laid out the village of St. Mary's (named, diplomatically, for the queen). The neighboring Indians, who were more worried about rival tribes in the region than they were about the new arrivals, befriended the settlers, provided them with temporary shelter, sold them land, and supplied them with corn. Unlike the Virginians, the early Marylanders experienced no Indian assaults, no plagues, no starving time.

The Calverts had invested heavily in their American possessions, and they needed to attract many settlers to make the effort profitable. As a result, they had to encourage the immigration of Protestants as well as their fellow English Catholics, who were both relatively few in number (about 2 percent of

RELIGIOUS TOLERATION

the population of England) and generally reluctant to emigrate. The Protestant settlers (mostly Anglicans) outnumbered the

Catholics from the start, and the Calverts quickly realized that Catholics would always be a minority in the colony. They prudently adopted a policy of religious toleration. To appease the non-Catholic majority, Calvert appointed a Protestant as governor in 1648. A year later, he sent from England the draft of an "Act Concerning Religion," or the Toleration Act, which assured freedom of worship to all Christians.

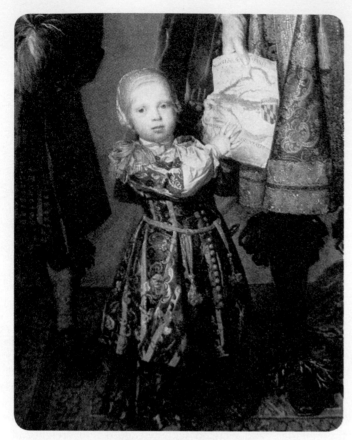

THE MARYLAND PROPRIETOR, C. 1670 In a detail of a portrait by the court painter to King Charles II, the young Cecilius Calvert reaches for a map of Maryland. His grandfather and namesake, the second Lord Baltimore (1606–1675), holds it out to him. George Calvert, the father of the elder Cecilius, began negotiations to win a royal charter for Maryland; his son completed them in 1632 and became the first proprietor of the colony. He published the map shown here in 1635 as part of an effort to attract settlers to the colony. By the time this portrait was painted, Lord Baltimore's son, Charles, was governor of Maryland. The boy Cecilius, the heir apparent, died in 1681 before he could assume his title. (© Peter Newark Pictures/Bridgeman Art Library)

Nevertheless, politics in Maryland remained plagued for years by tensions between the Catholic minority (which included the proprietor) and the Protestant majority. Zealous Jesuits and crusading Puritans frightened and antagonized their opponents with their efforts to establish the dominance of their own religion. At one point, the Protestant majority barred Catholics from voting and repealed the Toleration Act. There was frequent violence, and in 1655 a civil war temporarily unseated the proprietary government and replaced it with one dominated by Protestants.

By 1640, a severe labor shortage in the colony had forced a change in the land grant procedure; and Maryland, like Virginia, adopted a "headright" system—a grant of 100 acres to each male settler, another 100 for his wife and each servant, and 50 for each of his children. Like Virginia, Maryland became a center of tobacco cultivation; and as in Virginia, planters worked their land with the aid, first, of indentured servants imported from England and then, beginning late in the seventeenth century, with slaves imported from Africa.

TURBULENT VIRGINIA

By the mid-seventeenth century, the Virginia colony had survived its early disasters. Both its population and the complexity and profitability of its economy were increasing. It was also growing more politically contentious, as emerging factions within the province began to compete for the favor of the government. Perhaps the most important dispute involved policy toward the natives. As settlement moved west, farther into Indian lands, border conflicts grew increasingly frequent. Much of the tension within English Virginia in the late seventeenth century revolved around how to respond to those conflicts.

VIRGINIA'S WESTWARD EXPANSION

Sir William Berkeley arrived in Virginia in 1642 at the age of thirty-six, having been appointed governor by King Charles I. With but one interruption, he remained in control of the government until the 1670s. Berkeley was a popular governor at first as he sent explorers across the Blue Ridge Mountains to open up the western interior of Virginia. He organized the force that put down the 1644 Indian uprising. The defeated Indians ceded a large area of land to the English. In return, Berkeley agreed to prohibit white settlement west of a line he negotiated with the tribes.

This attempt to protect Indian territory—like many such attempts later in American history—was a failure from the start, largely because of the rapid growth of the Virginia population. Oliver Cromwell's victory in 1649 in the English Civil War (see p. 49) and the flight of many of his defeated opponents to the colony contributed to what was already a substantial population increase. Between 1640 and 1650, Virginia's population doubled from 8,000 to 16,000. By 1660, it had more than doubled again, to 40,000. As the choice lands along the tidewater became scarce, new arrivals and indentured servants completing their terms or escaping from their masters pressed westward into the piedmont. By 1652, English settlers had established three counties in the territory promised to the Indians. Unsurprisingly, there were frequent clashes between natives and whites.

By the 1660s, Berkeley had gradually become an autocrat in the colony. When the first burgesses were elected in 1619, all men aged seventeen or older were entitled to vote. By 1670, the vote was restricted to landowners, and elections were rare. The same burgesses, loyal and subservient to the governor, remained in office year after year. Each county continued to have only two representatives, even though some of the new counties of the interior contained many more people than the older ones of the tidewater area. Thus the more recent settlers in the "backcountry" were underrepresented or (if living in areas not yet formally organized as counties) not represented.

BERKELEY'S AUTOCRATIC RULE

Representation in the backcountry was not the only source of turbulence in Virginia. The system of indentured servants also played a role. The system of indentured servants also played a role. By the 1670s, many young men had finished their term as indentures and found themselves without a home or money. Many of them moved around the colony working, begging, or stealing. They would soon become a factor in what became known as Bacon's Rebellion.

BACON'S REBELLION

In 1676, backcountry unrest and political rivalries combined to create a major conflict. Nathaniel Bacon, a wealthy young graduate of Cambridge University, arrived in Virginia in 1673. He purchased a substantial farm in the west and won a seat on the governor's council. He established himself, in other words, as a member of the backcountry gentry.

But the new and influential western landowners were soon squabbling with the leaders of the tidewater region in the east. **BACKCOUNTRY GRIEVANCES** They disagreed on many issues but, above all, on policies toward the natives. The backcountry settlements were in constant danger of attack from Indians, because many of them had been established on lands reserved for the tribes by treaty. White settlers in western Virginia had long resented the governor's attempts to hold the line of settlement steady so as to avoid antagonizing the natives.

Bacon, an aristocratic man with great political ambitions, had additional reasons for unhappiness with Berkeley. He resented his exclusion from the inner circle of the governor's council (the so-called Green Spring group, whose members enjoyed special access to patronage). Bacon also fumed about Berkeley's refusal to allow him a piece of the Indian fur trade. He was developing grievances that made him a natural leader of an opposing faction.

Bloody events thrust him into that role. In 1675, some Doeg Indians–angry about the European intrusions into their lands–raided a western plantation and killed a white servant. Bands of local whites struck back angrily and haphazardly, attacking not only the small Doeg tribe but the powerful Susquehannock as well. The Indians responded with more raids on plantations and killed many more white settlers. As the fighting escalated, Bacon and other concerned landholders–unhappy with the governor's cautious response to their demand for help–defied Berkeley and struck out on their own against the Indians. Berkeley proclaimed him and his men rebels. At that point, what had started as an unauthorized assault on the Indians became a military challenge to the colonial government, a conflict known as Bacon's Rebellion. It was the largest and most powerful insurrection against established authority in the history of the colonies, one that would not be surpassed until the Revolution.

Twice, Bacon led his army east to Jamestown. The first time, he won a temporary pardon from the governor; the second time, after the governor reneged on the agreement, he burned the city and drove the governor into exile. In the midst of widespread social turmoil throughout the colony, Bacon stood on the verge of taking command of Virginia. Instead, he died suddenly of dysentery; and Berkeley, his position bolstered by the arrival of British troops, soon managed to regain control. In 1677, the Indians (aware of their inability to defeat the white forces militarily) reluctantly signed a new treaty that opened additional lands to white settlement.

Bacon's Rebellion was significant for several reasons. It was part of the continuing struggle to define the boundary between Indian and white lands in Virginia; it showed how unwilling the English settlers were to abide by earlier agreements with the natives, and how unwilling the Indians were to tolerate further white movement into their territory. It **SIGNIFICANCE OF BACON'S REBELLION** revealed the bitterness of the competition between eastern and western landowners. But it also revealed something that Bacon himself had never intended to unleash: the potential for instability in the colony's large population of free, landless men. These men–most of them former indentured servants, propertyless, unemployed, with no real prospects–had formed the bulk of Bacon's constituency during the rebellion. They had become a large, unstable, floating population eager above all for access to land. Bacon had for a time maintained his popularity among them by exploiting their hatred of Indians. Gradually, however, he found himself unintentionally leading a movement that reflected the animosity of these landless men toward the landed gentry of which Bacon himself was a part.

One result was that landed people in both eastern and western Virginia began to recognize a common interest in preventing social unrest from the former indentures. That was one of several reasons that they turned increasingly to the African slave trade to fulfill their need for labor. Enslaved blacks might pose dangers too, but the events of 1676 persuaded many colonists that the perils of importing a large white subordinate class were even greater.

THE GROWTH OF NEW ENGLAND

The first enduring settlement in New England–the second in English America–resulted from the discontent of a congregation of Puritan Separatists in England. For years, Separatists had been periodically imprisoned and even executed for defying the government and the Church of England; **RELIGIOUS REPRESSION** some of them, as a result, began to contemplate leaving England permanently in search of freedom to worship as they wished–even though Puritans did not believe in religious freedom for all others.

PLYMOUTH PLANTATION

It was illegal to leave England without the consent of the king. In 1608, however, a congregation of Separatists from the hamlet of Scrooby began emigrating quietly, a few at a time, to Leyden, Holland, where they could worship without interference. They were, however, barred from the Dutch craft guilds and had to work at unskilled and poorly paid jobs. They were also troubled by the effects of the tolerant atmosphere of Dutch society, which threatened their dream of a close-knit Christian community. As a result, some of the Separatists decided to move again, this time across the Atlantic, where they hoped to create the kind of community they wanted and where they could spread "the gospel of the Kingdom of Christ in those remote parts of the world."

Leaders of the Scrooby group obtained permission from the Virginia Company to settle in British America. From the king, they received informal assurances that he would "not molest them, provided they carried themselves peaceably." (This was a historic concession by the Crown, for it opened British America to settlement not only by the Scrooby group but by other dissenting Protestants as well.) Several English merchants agreed to advance the necessary funds in exchange for a share in the profits of the settlement at the end of seven years.

The migrating Puritans "knew they were pilgrims" even before they left Holland, their leader and historian, William Bradford, later wrote. In September 1620 they left the port of Plymouth, on the English coast, in the *Mayflower* with thirty-five "saints" (Puritan Separatists) and sixty-seven "strangers" (people who were not full members of the Puritan church) aboard. By the time they sighted land in November, it was too late in the year to go on. Their original destination was probably the mouth of the Hudson River, in what is now New York. But they found themselves instead on Cape Cod. After exploring the region for a while, they chose a site for their settlement just north of the cape, an area Captain John Smith had named "Plymouth" (after the English port from which the Puritans had sailed) during an exploratory journey some years before. Plymouth lay outside the London Company's territory, and the settlers realized they had no legal basis for settling there. As a

THE MAYFLOWER COMPACT
result, forty-one male passengers signed a document, the Mayflower Compact, which established a civil government and proclaimed their allegiance to the king. Then, on December 21, 1620, the immigrants, called Pilgrims, stepped ashore at Plymouth Rock.

They settled on cleared land that had once been an Indian village until, three years earlier, a mysterious epidemic–known as "the plague" and probably brought by earlier European explorers–had swept through the region and substantially depopulated it. The Pilgrims' first winter was a difficult one; half the colonists perished from malnutrition, disease, and exposure. Still, the colony survived.

Bradford became the governor at Plymouth, an office he would hold for more than twenty years. Despite the death of his wife, and many other losses, he managed his plantation for many years.

Like the Spanish and Portuguese colonists in the southern regions of the Americas, the Pilgrims (and other future English colonists) brought more to the New World than people and ideas. They also made profound changes in the natural landscape of New England. A smallpox epidemic caused by English carriers almost eliminated the Indian population in the areas around Plymouth in the early 1630s. The English demand for furs, animal skins, and meat greatly depleted the number of wild animals in the areas around Plymouth, one reason colonists worked so hard to develop stocks of domestic animals such as horses, cattle, sheep, and hogs. The Pilgrims and later English settlers also introduced new crops (wheat, barley, oats, and others), while incorporating many native foods (among

them corn, potatoes, and peas) into their own diets–and eventually exporting them back to England and the rest of Europe. Gradually, colonial society imposed a European pattern onto the American landscape, as the settlers fenced in pastures, meadows, orchards, and fields for cultivation.

The Pilgrims' experience with the Indians was, for a time, very different from the experiences of the early English settlers farther south. That was in part because the remaining natives in the region–their numbers thinned by disease–were significantly weaker than their southern neighbors and realized they had to get along with the Europeans. In the end, the survival and growth of the colony depended crucially on the assistance they received from natives. Important Indian friends–Squanto and Samoset, among others–showed them how to gather seafood, cultivate corn, and hunt local animals.

RELATIONS WITH THE INDIANS
Squanto, a Pawtuxet who earlier in his life had been captured by an English explorer and taken to Europe, spoke English and was particularly helpful to the settlers in forming an alliance with the local Wampanoags, under Chief Massasoit. After the first harvest, in 1621, the settlers marked the alliance by inviting the Indians to join them in an October festival, the first Thanksgiving.

But the good relationship between the settlers and the local Indians did not last. Thirteen years after the Pilgrims' arrival, a devastating smallpox epidemic–a result of contact with English settlers–wiped out much of the Indian population around Plymouth.

The Pilgrims could not hope to create rich farms on the sandy, marshy soil, and their early fishing efforts produced no profits. In 1622 the military officer Miles Standish, one of the leaders of the colony, established a semi-military regime to impose discipline on the settlers. Eventually the Pilgrims began to grow enough corn and other crops to provide them with a modest trading surplus. They also developed a small fur trade with the Abenaki Indians of Maine. From time to time new colonists arrived from England, and in a decade the population reached 300.

The people of "Plymouth Plantation," as they called their settlement, chose William Bradford again and again to be their

WILLIAM BRADFORD
governor. As early as 1621, he persuaded the Council for New England (the successor to the old Plymouth Company, which had charter rights to the territory) to give them legal permission to live there. He ended the communal labor plan Standish had helped create, distributed land among the families, and thus, as he explained it, made "all hands very industrious." He and a group of fellow "undertakers" took over the colony's debt to its original financiers in England and, with earnings from the fur trade, finally paid it off–even though the financiers had repeatedly cheated them and had failed to send them promised supplies.

The Pilgrims were always a poor community. As late as the 1640s, they had only one plow among them. But they clung to the belief that God had put them in the New World to live as a truly Christian community; and they were content to live their lives in what they considered godly ways.

At times, they spoke of serving as a model for other Christians. Governor Bradford wrote in retrospect: "As one small candle may light a thousand, so the light here kindled hath shone to many, yea in some sort to our whole nation." But the Pilgrims were less committed to grand designs, less concerned about how they were viewed by others, than were the Puritans who settled the larger and more ambitious English colonies to their north.

THE PURITAN EXPERIMENT

Turbulent events in England in the 1620s (combined with the example of the Plymouth colony) created strong interest in colonization among other groups of Puritans. King James I had been creating serious tensions for years between himself and Parliament through his effort to claim the divine right of kings and by his harsh, repressive policies toward the Puritans. The situation worsened after his death in 1625, when he was succeeded by his son, Charles I. By favoring Roman Catholicism and trying to destroy religious nonconformity, Charles I started the nation down the road that in the 1640s would lead to civil war. The Puritans were particular targets of Charles's policies. Some were imprisoned for their beliefs, and many began to consider the climate of England intolerable. The king's disbanding of Parliament in 1629 (it was not to be recalled until 1640) ensured that there would be no political solution to the Puritans' problems.

In the midst of this political and social turmoil, a group of Puritan merchants began organizing a new enterprise designed

MASSACHUSETTS BAY COMPANY

to take advantage of opportunities in America. At first their interest was largely an economic one. They obtained a grant of land in New England for most of the area now comprising Massachusetts and New Hampshire; they acquired a charter from Charles I (who was evidently unaware that they were Puritans) allowing them to create the Massachusetts Bay Company and to establish a colony in the New World; and they bought equipment and supplies from a defunct fishing and trading company that had attempted (and failed) to establish a profitable enterprise in North America earlier. In 1629, they were ready to dispatch a substantial group of settlers to New England.

Among the members of the Massachusetts Bay Company, however, were a number of Puritans who saw the enterprise as something more than a business venture. They began to consider emigrating themselves and creating a haven for Puritans in New England. Members of this faction met secretly in Cambridge in the summer of 1629 and agreed to buy out the other investors and move en masse to America.

As governor, the new owners of the company chose John Winthrop, an affluent, university-educated gentleman with

JOHN WINTHROP

a deep piety and a forceful character. Winthrop had been instrumental in organizing the migration, and he commanded the expedition that sailed for New England in 1630: seventeen ships and 1,000 people (who were, unlike the earlier

migrants to Virginia, mostly family groups). It was the largest single migration of its kind in the seventeenth century. Winthrop carried with him the charter of the Massachusetts Bay Company, which meant that the colonists would be responsible to no company officials in England, only to themselves.

The Massachusetts migration quickly produced several different new settlements. The port of Boston, at the mouth of the Charles River, became the company's headquarters and the colony's capital. But in the course of the next decade, colonists moved into a number of other new towns in eastern Massachusetts: Charlestown, Newtown (later renamed Cambridge), Roxbury, Dorchester, Watertown, Ipswich, Concord, Sudbury, and others.

The Massachusetts Bay Company soon transformed itself into a colonial government. According to the original company charter, the eight stockholders (or "freemen") were to meet as a general court to choose officers and adopt rules for the corporation. But eventually the definition of "freemen" changed to include all male citizens, not just the stockholders. John Winthrop dominated colonial politics just as he had dominated the original corporation, but after 1634 he and most other officers of the colony had to face election each year.

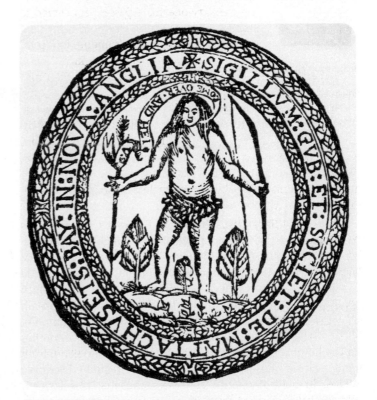

COLONIAL CURRENCY This seal was created in 1690 by the Massachusetts Bay Company to validate the paper "bills of credit" with which colonists conducted many financial transactions. Paper money met considerable resistance at first. Many people doubted its value and would not accept it, preferring instead the Spanish silver coins that were in wide circulation. Gradually, however, a shortage of silver required increasing reliance on this and other paper devices. The seal shows an Indian saying "Come over and help us," which represents the English belief in the superiority of white European society. (© Bettmann/Corbis)

PORTRAIT OF A BOSTON WOMAN Anne Pollard, a member of the original Winthrop expedition to Boston, was 100 years old when this portrait was painted in 1721. In 1643, thirteen years after her arrival in Massachusetts, she married a Boston innkeeper with whom she had 13 children. After her husband's death in 1679, she continued to manage the tavern on her own. When she died in 1725, at the age of 104, she left 130 direct descendants. The artist who painted this early portrait is unknown, but is assumed to be an American working in the primitive style common in New England before the arrival in 1729 of the first academically trained portraitists from England. (© Massachusetts Historical Society, Boston, MA, USA/ The Bridgeman Art Library)

Unlike the Separatist founders of Plymouth, the founders of Massachusetts had no intention of breaking from the Church of England. Yet, if they continued to feel any real attachment to the Anglican establishment, they gave little

THE CONGREGATIONAL CHURCH

sign of it. In every town, the community church had (in the words of the prominent minister John Cotton) "complete liberty to stand alone," unlike churches in the highly centralized Anglican structure in England. Each congregation chose its own minister and regulated its own affairs. In both Plymouth and Massachusetts, this form of parish organization eventually became known as the Congregational Church.

The Puritans, although nominally members of the Anglican Church, were in fact worshipers of a very different faith. They did not accept the authority of either the Roman Catholic hierarchy or the Church of England. They did not

follow traditional ceremonial worship and did not receive sacraments from priests. They learned, instead, from reading the Bible and from listening to ministers who spoke from their own knowledge and belief, not from the orthodoxies of traditional institutional faith. They accepted the doctrines of John Calvin's vision that everyone was destined at birth for either salvation or damnation—that nothing in people's earthly life could change their fate after death. But living a good and productive life might be a sign of salvation. Puritans not only sought salvation. They also sought freedom—not the kind of freedom Americans understand today, but the right to worship without interference from England or from established churches. That did not mean that they were free to behave as they liked; the community expected obedience to authority. But authority was based largely within the community itself and monitored by its members. It did not come from England or from centralized institutions in America.

The Massachusetts Puritans were not grim or joyless, as many observers would later portray them. They were, however, serious and pious. They strove to lead useful, conscientious lives of thrift and hard work, and they honored material success as evidence of God's favor. "We here enjoy God and Jesus Christ," Winthrop wrote to his wife soon after his arrival; "is this not enough?" He and the other Massachusetts founders believed they were founding a holy commonwealth—a "city upon a hill"—that could serve as a model for the rest of the New World.

If Massachusetts was to become a beacon to other emigrants, it had first to maintain its own "holiness." Ministers

A THEOCRATIC SOCIETY

had no formal political power, but they exerted great influence on church members, who were the only people who could vote or hold office. The government in turn protected the ministers, taxed the people (members and nonmembers alike) to support the church, and enforced the law requiring attendance at services. Dissidents had no more freedom of worship in America than the Puritans themselves had had in England. Colonial Massachusetts was in many ways a "theocracy," a society in which the line between the church and the state was hard to see.

Like other new settlements, the Massachusetts Bay colony had early difficulties. During their first winter, an unusually severe one, nearly a third of the colonists died; others left in the spring. But more rapidly than Jamestown or Plymouth, the colony grew and prospered. The Pilgrims and neighboring Indians helped with food and advice. Affluent incoming settlers brought needed tools and other goods, which they exchanged for the cattle, corn, and other produce of the established colonists and the natives. The large number of family groups in the colony (in sharp contrast to the early years at Jamestown) helped ensure a feeling of commitment to the community and a sense of order among the settlers. It also allowed the population to reproduce itself more rapidly. The strong religious and political hierarchy ensured a measure of social stability.

THE EXPANSION OF NEW ENGLAND

As the population grew, more and more people arrived in Massachusetts who were not Puritan "saints" and hence could

GROWING RELIGIOUS DISSENT

not vote. Newcomers had a choice of conforming to the religious practices of the colony or leaving. Many left, helping to begin a process that would spread settlement throughout present-day New England and beyond.

The Connecticut Valley, about 100 miles west of the edge of European settlement around Boston, began attracting English families as early as the 1630s. The valley appealed in particular to Thomas Hooker, a minister of Newtown (Cambridge), who defied the Massachusetts government in 1635 and led his congregation through the wilds to establish the town of Hartford. Four years later, the people of Hartford and of two other towns established a colonial government of their own and adopted a constitution known as the Fundamental Orders of Connecticut.

Another Connecticut colony, the project of a Puritan minister and a wealthy merchant from England, grew up around New Haven on the Connecticut coast. It reflected impatience with what its founders considered increasing religious laxity in Massachusetts. The Fundamental Articles of New Haven (1639) established a religious government even stricter than that in Boston. New Haven remained independent until 1662, when a royal charter combined it with Hartford to create the colony of Connecticut.

Rhode Island had its origins in the religious and political dissent of Roger Williams, an engaging but controversial young minister who lived for a time in Salem, Massachusetts. Even John Winthrop, who considered Williams a heretic, called him

ROGER WILLIAMS

a "sweet and amiable" man, and William Bradford described him as "a man godly and zealous." But he was, Bradford added, "very unsettled in judgment." Williams, a confirmed Separatist, argued that the Massachusetts church should abandon all allegiance to the Church of England. More disturbing to the clergy, he called for a complete separation of church and state—to protect the church from the corruption of the secular world. The colonial government, alarmed at this challenge to its spiritual authority, banished him. During the bitter winter of 1635–1636, Williams took refuge with Narragansett tribesmen; the following spring he bought a tract of land from them and, with a few followers, created the town of Providence on it. Other communities of dissidents followed him to what became Rhode Island, and in 1644 Williams obtained a charter from Parliament permitting him to establish a government. Rhode Island's government gave no support to the church and allowed "liberty in religious concernments." For a time, it was the only colony in which members of all faiths (including Jews) could worship without interference.

An even greater challenge to the established order in Massachusetts Bay emerged in the person of Anne Hutchinson, an intelligent and charismatic woman from a substantial Boston family. Hutchinson had come to Massachusetts with her husband in 1634. She antagonized the leaders of the colony by arguing vehemently that the members of the Massachusetts clergy who were not among the "elect"–that is, had not undergone a conversion experience–had no right to spiritual office. Over time, she claimed that many clergy—among them her own uninspiring minister—were among the non-elect and had no right to exercise authority over their congregations. She eventually charged that all the ministers in Massachusetts–save community leader John Cotton and her own bother-in-law–were not among the elect. Alongside such teachings (which her critics called "Antinomianism," from the

ANNE HUTCHINSON

Greek word meaning "hostile to the law"), Hutchinson also created alarm by affronting prevailing assumptions about the proper role of women in Puritan society. She was not a retiring, deferential wife and mother, but a powerful religious figure in her own right.

Hutchinson developed a large following among women, to whom she offered an active role in religious affairs. She also attracted support from merchants, young men, and dissidents of many sorts who resented the oppressive character of the colonial government. As her influence grew, the Massachusetts leadership mobilized to stop her. Hutchinson's followers were numerous and influential enough to prevent Winthrop's reelection as governor in 1636, but the next year he returned to office and put her on trial for heresy. Hutchinson embarrassed her accusers by displaying a remarkable knowledge of theology; but because she continued to defy clerical authority (and because she claimed she had herself communicated directly with the Holy Spirit–a violation of the Puritan belief that the age of such revelations had passed), she was convicted of sedition and banished as "a woman not fit for our society." Her unorthodox views had challenged both religious belief and social order in Puritan Massachusetts. With her family and some of her followers, she moved to Rhode Island and then into New Netherland (later New York), where in 1643 she died during an Indian uprising.

Alarmed by Hutchinson's heresy, male clergy began to restrict further the already-limited public activities of women within congregations. As a result, many of Hutchinson's followers began to migrate out of Massachusetts Bay, especially to New Hampshire and Maine.

Colonies had been established there in 1629 when two English proprietors, Captain John Mason and Sir Ferdinando Gorges, had received a grant from the Council for New

NEW HAMPSHIRE AND MAINE

England and divided it along the Piscataqua River to create two separate provinces. But despite their lavish promotional efforts, few settlers had moved into these northern regions until the religious disruptions in Massachusetts Bay. In 1639, John Wheelwright, a disciple of Anne Hutchinson, led some of his fellow dissenters to Exeter, New Hampshire. Other groups—of both dissenting and orthodox Puritans—soon followed. New Hampshire became a separate colony in 1679. Maine remained a part of Massachusetts until 1820.

THE GROWTH OF NEW ENGLAND, 1620–1750 The European settlement of New England, as this map reveals, traces its origins primarily to two small settlements on the Atlantic coast. The first was the Pilgrim settlement at Plymouth, which began in 1620 and spread out through Cape Cod, southern Massachusetts, and the islands of Martha's Vineyard and Nantucket. The second, much larger settlement began in Boston in 1630 and spread rapidly through western Massachusetts, north into New Hampshire and Maine, and south into Connecticut.

• *Why did the settlers of Massachusetts Bay expand more rapidly and expansively than those of Plymouth?*

SETTLERS AND NATIVES

By the mid-1630s, the native population, small to begin with, had been almost extinguished by the European epidemics. The surviving Indians sold much of their land to the English (a great boost to settlement, since much of it had already been cleared). Some natives–known as "praying Indians"–even converted to Christianity and joined Puritan communities.

Indians provided crucial assistance to the early settlers as they tried to adapt to the new land. Whites learned from

IMPORTANCE OF INDIAN ASSISTANCE

the natives about vital local food crops: corn, beans, pumpkins, and potatoes. They also learned such crucial agricultural techniques as annual burning for fertilization and planting beans to replenish exhausted soil. Natives also served as important trading partners to European immigrants, particularly in the creation of the thriving North American fur trade. They were an important

market for such manufactured goods as iron pots, blankets, metal-tipped arrows, eventually guns and rifles, and (often tragically) alcohol. Indeed, commerce with the Indians was responsible for the creation of some of the first great fortunes in British North America and for the emergence of wealthy families who would exercise influence in the colonies (and later the nation) for many generations.

But as in other areas of white settlement, there were also conflicts; and the early peaceful relations between whites and Indians did not last. Tensions soon developed as a result of the white colonists' continuing appetite for land. The expanding white demand for land was also a result of a change in the colonists' agrarian economy. As wild animals began to disappear from overhunting, colonists began to concentrate more and more on raising domesticated animals: cattle, sheep, hogs, horses, and others. As the herds expanded, so did the colonists' need for new land. As a result, the colonists moved steadily into territories such as the Connecticut

Valley where they came into conflict with natives who were more numerous and more powerful than those along the Massachusetts coast.

The character of those conflicts—and the brutality with which whites assaulted their Indian foes— changed Puritan attitudes toward the natives. At first, many white New Englanders had looked at the Indians with a slightly condescending admiration. Before long, however, they came to view them primarily as "heathens" and "savages," and hence as a constant threat to the existence of a godly community in the New World. Some Puritans believed the solution to the Indian "problem" was to "civilize" the natives by converting them to Christianity and European ways, and some English missionaries had modest success in producing converts. One such missionary, John Eliot, even translated the Bible into an Algonquian language. Other Puritans, however, envisioned a harsher "solution": displacing or, if that failed, exterminating the natives.

SHIFTING ATTITUDES

To the natives, the threat from the English was very direct. European settlers were penetrating deeper and deeper into the interior, seizing land, clearing forests, driving away much of the wild game on which the tribes depended for food. English farmers often let their livestock run wild, and the animals frequently destroyed natives' crops. Land and food shortages exacerbated the drastic Indian population decline that had begun as a result of epidemic diseases. There had been more than 100,000 Indians in New England at the beginning of the seventeenth century; by 1675, only 10,000 remained. This decline created despair among New England natives. It drove some Indians to alcoholism and others to conversion to Christianity. But it drove others to war.

THE PEQUOT WAR, KING PHILIP'S WAR, AND THE TECHNOLOGY OF BATTLE

The first major conflict came in 1637, when hostilities broke out between English settlers in the Connecticut Valley and the Pequot Indians of the region as a result of competition over trade with the Dutch in New Netherland and friction over land. In what became known as the Pequot War, English settlers allied with the Mohegan and Narragansett Indians (rivals of the Pequots). The greatest savagery in the conflict was the work of the English. In the bloodiest act of the war, white raiders under Captain John Mason marched against a palisaded Pequot stronghold and set it afire. Hundreds of Indians either burned to death in the flaming

THE PEQUOT WAR

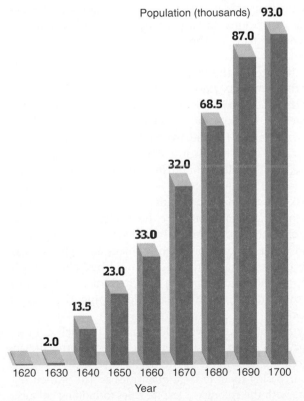

Population (thousands) **93.0**

THE NON-INDIAN POPULATION OF NEW ENGLAND, 1620–1700 As in the Chesapeake colonies, the European population of New England grew very rapidly after settlement began in 1620. The most rapid rate of growth, unsurprisingly, came in the first thirty years, when even a modest wave of immigraton could double or triple the small existing population. But the largest numbers of new immigrants arrived between 1650 and 1680.

• *What events in England in those years might have led to increased emigration to America in that period?*

ANNE HUTCHINSON PREACHING IN HER HOUSE IN BOSTON Anne Hutchinson was alarming to many of Boston's religious leaders not only because she openly challenged the authority of the clergy, but also because she implicitly challenged norms of female behavior in Puritan society. (© Bettmann/Corbis)

stockade or were killed as they attempted to escape. Those who survived were hunted down, captured, and sold as slaves. The Pequot tribe was almost wiped out.

The most prolonged and deadly encounter between whites and Indians in the seventeenth century began in 1675, a conflict that the English would remember for generations as King Philip's War. As in the earlier Pequot War in Connecticut, an Indian tribe—in this case the Wampanoags, under the leadership of a chief-

KING PHILIP'S WAR

tain known to the white settlers as King Philip and among his own people as Metacomet—rose up to resist the English. The Wampanoags had not always been hostile to the settlers; indeed, Metacomet's grandfather had once forged an alliance with the English, and Metacomet himself was well acquainted with the colonists. But by the 1670s, he had become convinced that only armed resistance could protect the Wampanoags from English incursions into their lands and, more immediately, from the efforts by the colonial governments to impose English law on them. (A court in Plymouth had recently tried and hanged several Wampanoags for murdering a member of their own tribe.)

For three years, the natives—well organized and armed with guns—terrorized a string of Massachusetts towns, destroying twenty of them and causing the deaths of as many as a thousand people (including at least one-sixteenth of the white males in the colony). The war greatly weakened both the society and economy of Massachusetts. But, in 1676, the white settlers fought back and gradually prevailed. They received critical aid from the Mohawks, longtime rivals of the Wampanoags, and guides, spies, and soldiers recruited from among the so-called praying Indians (Christian converts) of the region. While white militiamen attacked Indian villages and destroyed native food supplies, a group of Mohawks ambushed, shot, and killed Metacomet, then bore his severed head to Boston to present to the colonial leaders. After that, the fragile alliance that Metacomet had managed to forge among local tribes collapsed. Europeans were soon able to crush the uprising. Some Wampanoag leaders were executed; others were sold into slavery in the West Indies. The Wampanoags and their allies, their populations depleted and their natural resources reduced, were now powerless to resist the English.

Yet these victories by the white colonists did not end the danger to their settlements. Other Indians in other tribes survived and were still capable of attacking English settlements. The New England settlers also faced competition from the natives and also from the Dutch and the French, who claimed the territory on which some of the outlying settlements were established. The French, in particular,

A PEQUOT VILLAGE DESTROYED An English artist drew this view of a fortified Pequot village in Connecticut surrounded by English soldiers and their allies from other tribes during the Pequot War in 1637. The invaders massacred more than 600 residents of the settlement. (The Library of Congress (LC-USZ62-32055))

posed a constant threat to the English through their alliance with the Algonquins. In later years, the French would join forces with Indians in their attacks on the New England frontier.

The character of the Pequot War, King Philip's War, and many other conflicts between natives and settlers in the years that followed was crucially affected by earlier exchanges of technology between the English and the tribes. In particular, the Indians made effective use of a new

FLINTLOCK MUSKET

weapon introduced to New England by Miles Standish and others: the flintlock rifle. It replaced the earlier staple of colonial musketry, the matchlock rifle, which proved too heavy, cumbersome, and inaccurate to be useful in the kind of combat characteristic of Anglo-Indian struggles. The matchlock had to be steadied on a fixed object and ignited with a match before firing; the flintlock could be held up without support and fired without a match. (Indians using bows and arrows often outmatched settlers using the clumsy matchlocks.)

Many English settlers were slow to give up their cumbersome matchlocks for the lighter flintlocks. But the Indians recognized the advantages of the newer rifles right away and began purchasing them in large quantities as part of their regular trade with the colonists. Despite rules forbidding colonists to instruct natives on how to use and repair the weapons, the natives learned to handle the rifles, and even to repair them, very effectively on their own. They even built a substantial forge for shaping and repairing rifle parts. In King Philip's War, the very high casualties on both sides were a result of the use of these more advanced rifles.

Indians also used more traditional military technologies in their conflicts with the English–especially the construction of forts. The Narragansetts, allies of the Wampanoags in King Philip's War, built an enormous fort in the Great Swamp of Rhode Island in 1675, which became the site of one of the bloodiest battles of the war before English attackers burned it down. After that, a band of Narragansetts set out to build a large stone fort, with the help of a member of the tribe who had learned masonry while working with the English. When English soldiers discovered the stone fort in 1676, after the end of King Philip's War, they killed most of its occupants and destroyed it. In the end, the technological skills of the Indians (both those they borrowed from the English and those they drew from their own traditions) proved no match for the overwhelming advantages of the English settlers in both numbers and firepower.

THE RESTORATION COLONIES

By the end of the 1630s, English settlers had established six significant colonies in the New World: Virginia, Massachusetts, Maryland, Connecticut, Rhode Island, and New Hampshire. (Maine remained officially part of Massachusetts until after the American Revolution.) But for nearly thirty years after Lord Baltimore received the charter for Maryland in 1632, the English government launched no additional colonial ventures. It was preoccupied with troubles of its own at home.

THE ENGLISH CIVIL WAR

England's problems had begun during the rule of James I, who

ORIGINS

attracted widespread opposition before he died in 1625. James, however, did not openly challenge Parliament. His son, Charles I, was not so prudent. He dissolved Parliament in 1629 and began ruling as an absolute monarch, steadily alienating a growing number of his subjects–especially the members of the powerful Puritan community. Finally, desperately in need of money, Charles called Parliament back into session and asked it to levy new taxes. But he antagonized the members by dismissing them again twice in two years. In 1642, some of them organized a military challenge to the king, thus launching the English Civil War.

The conflict between the Cavaliers (the supporters of the king) and the Roundheads (the forces of Parliament, who were mostly Puritans) lasted seven years. Finally, in 1649, the Roundheads defeated the king's forces, captured Charles himself, and–in an action that horrified not only much of continental Europe at the time but also future generations of English men and women–beheaded the monarch. To replace him, they elevated the stern Roundhead leader Oliver Cromwell to the position of "protector," from which he ruled for the next nine years. When Cromwell died in 1658, his son and heir proved unable to maintain his authority. Two years later, King Charles II, son of the beheaded monarch, returned from exile and claimed the throne.

Charles II faced some of the same problems as his father, mostly because of the belief held by many that secretly he was a Roman Catholic. The king supported religious toleration, which, to the dismay of many Protestants, allowed Catholicism in England once again. The Parliament refused to agree, and prudently Charles did not fight them for the right of Catholics to worship openly. He did, however, make a private agreement with Louis XIV of France that he would become Catholic, which he did only on his deathbed. His son James II continued to face many of the same difficulties.

Among the many results of the Stuart Restoration–the

NEW PROPRIETARY COLONIES

return of Charles II, a member of the Stuart royal family–was the resumption of colonization in America. Charles II quickly began to reward faithful courtiers with grants of land in the New World; and in the twenty-five years of his reign, he issued charters for four additional colonies: Carolina, New York, New Jersey, and Pennsylvania. The new colonies were all proprietary ventures (modeled on Maryland rather than on Virginia and Massachusetts), thus exposing an important change in the nature of American settlement. No longer were private companies interested in launching colonies, realizing at last that there were no quick profits to be had in the New World. The goal of the new colonies was not so much quick commercial success as permanent settlements that would provide proprietors with land and power.

THE CAROLINAS

Carolina (a name derived from the Latinate form of "Charles") was, like Maryland, carved in part from the original Virginia grant. Charles II awarded the territory to a group of eight court favorites, all prominent politicians already active in colonial affairs. In successive charters issued in 1663 and 1665, the eight proprietors received joint title to a vast territory stretching south to the Florida peninsula and west to the Pacific Ocean. Like Lord Baltimore, they received almost kingly powers over their grant.

Also like Lord Baltimore, they expected to profit as landlords and land speculators. They reserved large estates for themselves, and they proposed to sell or give away the rest in smaller tracts (using a headright system similar to those in Virginia and Maryland) and to collect annual payments ("quitrents") from the settlers. Although committed Anglicans themselves, they welcomed any settlers they could get. The charter of the colony guaranteed religious freedom to everyone who would worship as a Christian. The proprietors also promised a

INCENTIVES FOR SETTLEMENT

measure of political freedom; laws were to be made by a representative assembly. With these incentives, they hoped to attract settlers from the existing American colonies and thus to avoid the expense of financing expeditions from England.

Their initial efforts failed dismally, and some of the original proprietors gave up. But one man–Anthony Ashley Cooper, soon to become the Earl of Shaftesbury–persisted. Cooper convinced his partners to finance migrations to Carolina from

CHARLES TOWN, SOUTH CAROLINA This map, drawn on deerskin by an Indian chief around 1730, illustrates the close juxtaposition of the ordered English settlement in Charles Town, South Carolina, seen on the left, and the more fluid Indian settlements near the town, on the right. It also illustrates the way in which southeastern Indians understood political relations as a series of linked circles. (© Getty Images)

England. In the spring of 1670, the first of these expeditions—a party of 300—set out from England. Only 100 people survived the difficult voyage; those who did established a settlement in the Port Royal area of the Carolina coast. Ten years later they founded a city at the junction of the Ashley and Cooper Rivers, which in 1690 became the colonial capital. They called it Charles Town. (It was later renamed Charleston.)

The Earl of Shaftesbury, troubled by the instability in England, wanted a planned and well-ordered community. With the aid of the English philosopher John Locke, he drew up the Fundamental Constitution for Carolina in 1669, which created an elaborate system of land distribution and an elaborately designed social order. In fact, however, Carolina developed along lines quite different from the utopian vision of Shaftesbury and Locke. For one thing, the colony was never united in anything more than name. The northern and southern regions remained socially and economically distinct from one another. The northern settlers were mainly backwoods

FUNDAMENTAL CONSTITUTION FOR CAROLINA

farmers, isolated from the outside world, scratching out a meager existence through subsistence agriculture. They developed no important aristocracy and for many years imported virtually no African slaves. In the south, fertile lands and the good harbor at Charles Town promoted a prosperous economy and an aristocratic society. Settlements grew up rapidly along the Ashley and Cooper Rivers, and colonists established a flourishing trade in corn, lumber, cattle, pork, and (beginning in the 1690s) rice—which was to become the colony's principal commercial crop. Traders from the interior used Charles Town to market furs and hides they had acquired from Indian trading partners; some also marketed Indian slaves, generally natives captured by rival tribes and sold to the white traders.

Southern Carolina very early developed close ties to the large (and now overpopulated) English colony on the island of Barbados. For many years, Barbados was Carolina's most important trading partner. During the first ten years of settlement, most of the new settlers in Carolina were Barbadians, some of whom arrived with large groups of African workers and established themselves quickly as substantial landlords. African slavery had taken root on Barbados earlier than in any of the mainland colonies (see pp. 54-56); and the white Caribbean migrants–tough, uncompromising profit seekers– established a similar slave-based plantation society in Carolina. The proprietors, four of whom had a financial interest in the African slave trade, also encouraged the importation of Africans.

For several decades, Carolina remained one of the most unstable English colonies in America. There were tensions between the small farmers of the Albemarle region in the north and the wealthy planters in the south. There were conflicts between the rich Barbadians in southern Carolina and **NORTH AND SOUTH CAROLINA** the smaller landowners around them. After Lord Shaftesbury's death, the proprietors proved unable to establish order, and in 1719 the colonists seized control of the colony from them. Ten years later, the king divided the region into two royal colonies, North and South Carolina.

NEW NETHERLAND, NEW YORK, AND NEW JERSEY

In 1664, one year after he issued the Carolina charter, Charles II granted to his brother James, the Duke of York, all the territory lying between the Connecticut and Delaware Rivers. But much of the territory included in the grant was already claimed by the Dutch, who had established substantial settlements at New Amsterdam and other strategic points beginning in 1624.

The growing conflict between the English and the Dutch in America was part of a larger commercial rivalry between the two nations throughout the world. But the English particularly resented the Dutch presence in America, because it served as a wedge between the northern and southern English colonies and because it provided bases for Dutch smugglers evading English customs laws. And so in 1664, an English fleet under the command of Richard Nicolls sailed into the lightly defended port of New Amsterdam and extracted a surrender from its unpopular Dutch governor, **CAPTURE OF NEW AMSTERDAM** Peter Stuyvesant, who had failed to mobilize resistance to the invasion. Under the Articles of Capitulation, the Dutch colony surrendered to the British in return for assurances that the Dutch settlers would not be displaced. In 1673, the Dutch briefly reconquered New Amsterdam. But they lost it for good in 1674.

James, the Duke of York, his title to New Netherland now clear, renamed the colony New York and prepared to govern

NEW AMSTERDAM The small Dutch settlement on Manhattan Island, known before 1664 as New Amsterdam, fell to the English in 1664. This painting shows buildings clustered at the southern tip of the island, which remained the center of what would become New York City until the nineteenth century. (© Bettmann/Corbis)

a colony of extraordinary diversity. New York contained not only Dutch and English, but Scandinavians, Germans, French, Africans (imported as slaves by the Dutch West India Company), and members of several different Indian tribes. There were, of course, many different religious faiths among these groups. James made no effort to impose his own Roman Catholicism on the colony. Like other proprietors before him, he remained in England and delegated powers to a governor and a council. But he provided for no representative assembly in New York perhaps because a parliament had executed his own father, Charles I. The laws did, however, establish local governments and guarantee religious toleration. Nevertheless, there were immediate tensions over the distribution of power in the colony. The great Dutch "patroons" (large landowners) survived with their economic and political power largely intact. James granted large estates as well to some of his own political supporters in an effort to create a class of influential landowners loyal to him. Power in the colony thus remained widely and unequally dispersed—among wealthy English landlords, Dutch patroons, fur traders (who forged important alliances with the Iroquois), and the Duke of York's political appointees. Like Carolina, New York would for many years be a highly fractious society.

It was also a growing and generally prosperous colony. By 1685, when the Duke of York ascended the English throne as James II, New York contained approximately 30,000 people, about four times as many as when James had received his grant twenty years before. Most of them still lived within the Hudson Valley, close to the river itself, with the largest settlement at its mouth, in the town of New York (formerly New Amsterdam).

Originally, James's claims in America extended south of the Hudson to the Delaware **ESTABLISHMENT OF NEW JERSEY** Valley and beyond. But shortly after receiving his charter, James gave a large portion of that land to a pair of political allies, Sir John Berkeley and Sir George Carteret, both of whom were also Carolina proprietors. Carteret named the territory New Jersey, after the island in the English Channel on which he had been born. In 1702, after nearly a decade of political squabbling and economic profitlessness, the proprietors ceded control of the territory back to the Crown and New Jersey became a royal colony.

Like New York (from which much of the population had come), New Jersey was a place of enormous ethnic and religious diversity. But unlike New York, New Jersey developed no important class of large landowners; most of its residents remained small farmers. Nor did New Jersey (which, unlike New York, had no natural harbor) produce any single major city.

THE QUAKER COLONIES

Pennsylvania, like Massachusetts, was born out of the efforts of dissenting English Protestants to find a home for their own **THE SOCIETY OF FRIENDS** religion and their own distinctive social order. The Society of Friends (also known as "Quakers") originated in mid-seventeenth-century England and grew into an important force as a result of the preachings of George Fox, a Nottingham shoemaker, and Margaret Fell. Their followers came to be known as Quakers because Fox urged them to "tremble at the name of the Lord." Unlike the Puritans, Quakers rejected the concepts of predestination and original sin. All people had divinity within themselves (an "Inner Light," which could guide them along the path of righteousness), and all who cultivated that divinity could attain salvation. Also unlike the Puritans, Quakers granted women a position within the church generally equal to that of men. Women and men alike could become preachers and define church doctrine, an equality symbolized by the longtime partnership between Fox and Fell.

Of all the Protestant sectarians of the time, the Quakers were the most anarchistic and democratic. They had no church government, only periodic meetings of representatives from congregations. They had no paid clergy, and in their worship they spoke up one by one as the spirit moved them. Disregarding distinctions of gender and class, they addressed one another with the terms "thee" and "thou," words then

A QUAKER MEETING Egbert van Heemskerck the Elder (c. 1635–1704) was a painter from Haarlem, in the Netherlands, who worked in England from about 1675 until his death. His subject matter, familiar to the Dutch but new to English viewers of his time, features ordinary people in comic or everyday scenes. In this undated oil painting, van Heemskerck shows a gathering of Quakers. Because the Society of Friends, as the Quakers were formally known, believed that all people were equal in the eyes of God, they appointed no ministers and imposed no formal structure on their religious services. *(Private Collection /© Johnny Van Haeften Ltd., London /The Bridgeman Art Library)*

commonly used in other parts of English society only in speaking to servants and social inferiors. And as confirmed pacifists, they refused to fight in wars. The Quakers were unpopular enough in England as a result of these beliefs and practices. They increased their unpopularity by occasionally breaking up other religious groups at worship. Many were jailed.

As a result, like the Puritans before them, the Quakers looked to America for asylum. A few went to New England. But except in Rhode Island, they were greeted there with fines, whippings, and banishment; three men and a woman who refused to leave were put to death. Others migrated to northern Carolina, where they became the fastest-growing religious community in the region. They were soon influential in colonial politics. But many Quakers wanted a colony of their own. As a despised sect, they had little chance of getting the necessary royal grant without the aid of someone influential at court. But fortunately for Fox and his followers, a number of wealthy and prominent men had become attracted to the faith. One of them was William Penn—the son of an admiral in the Royal Navy who was a landlord of valuable Irish estates. He had received the gentleman's education expected of a person of his standing, but he resisted his father in moving to untraditional religions. Converted to the doctrine of the Inner Light, the younger Penn became an evangelist for Quakerism. With George Fox, he visited the European continent and found Quakers there who, like Quakers in England, longed to emigrate to the New World. He set out to find a place for them to go.

WILLIAM PENN

Penn turned his attention first to New Jersey and soon became an owner and proprietor of part of the colony. But in 1681, after the death of his father, Penn inherited his father's Irish lands and also his father's claim to a large debt from the king. Charles II, short of cash, paid the debt with a grant of territory between New York and Maryland—an area larger than England and Wales combined and which (unknown to him) contained more valuable soil and minerals than any other province of English America. Penn would have virtually total authority within the province. At the king's insistence, the territory was named Pennsylvania, after Penn's late father.

Like most proprietors, Penn wanted Pennsylvania to be profitable for him and his family. And so he set out to attract settlers from throughout Europe through informative and honest advertising in several languages. Pennsylvania soon became the best known of all the colonies among ordinary people in England and on the European continent, and also the most cosmopolitan. Settlers flocked to the province from throughout Europe, joining several hundred Swedes and Finns who had been living in a small trading colony—New Sweden—established in 1638 at the mouth of the Delaware River. But the colony was never profitable for Penn and his descendants. Indeed, Penn himself, near the end of his life, was imprisoned in England for debt and died in poverty in 1718.

Penn was more than a mere real estate promoter, however, and he sought to create in Pennsylvania what he called a holy experiment. In 1682, he sailed to America and supervised the laying out of a city between the Delaware and Schuylkill Rivers, which he named Philadelphia ("Brotherly Love"). With its rectangular streets, like those of Charles Town, Philadelphia helped set the pattern for most later cities in America. Penn believed, as had Roger Williams, that the land belonged to the Indians, and he was careful to see that they were reimbursed for it, as well as to see that they were not debauched by the fur traders' alcohol. Indians respected Penn as an honest white man, and during his lifetime the colony had no major conflicts with the natives. More than any other English colony, Pennsylvania prospered from the outset (even if its proprietor did not), because of Penn's successful recruitment of emigrants, his thoughtful planning, and the region's mild climate and fertile soil.

PENNSYLVANIA FOUNDED

Penn maintained good relations with the Indians owing to his religious beliefs. Quakerism was against participation in war or violence of any kind and held that all people, whatever their background, were capable of becoming Christian. Penn worked to respect the natives and their culture. He recognized Indians' claims to the land in the province and was usually scrupulous in reimbursing them for their land. In later years, however, the relationships between the English residents of Pennsylvania and the natives were not always peaceful.

By the late 1690s, some residents of Pennsylvania were beginning to resist the nearly absolute power of the proprietor. Southern residents in particular complained that the government in Philadelphia was unresponsive to their needs. As a result, a substantial opposition emerged to challenge Penn. Pressure from these groups grew to the point that in 1701, shortly before he departed for England for the last time, Penn agreed to a Charter of Liberties for the colony. The charter established a representative assembly (consisting, alone among the English colonies, of only one house), which greatly limited the authority of the proprietor. The charter also permitted "the lower counties" of the colony to establish their own representative assembly. The three counties did so in 1703 and, as a result, became a separate colony: Delaware—although until the American Revolution, it had the same governor as Pennsylvania.

CHARTER OF LIBERTIES

BORDERLANDS AND MIDDLE GROUNDS

The English colonies along the Atlantic seaboard of North America eventually united, expanded, and became the beginnings of a great nation. But in the seventeenth and early eighteenth centuries, they were small, frail settlements surrounded by other, competing societies. The British Empire in North America was, in fact, much smaller and weaker than the great Spanish Empire to the south, and not clearly stronger than the enormous French Empire to the north.

The continuing contest for control of North America, and the complex interactions among the diverse peoples populating the continent, were most clearly visible in areas

MAKING MOLASSES IN BARBADOS African slaves, who constituted the vast majority of the population of the flourishing sugar-producing island of Barbados, work here in a sugar mill grinding sugarcane and then boiling it to produce refined sugar, molasses, and—after a later distillation process not pictured here—rum. (© Giraudon/Bridgeman Art Library)

around the borders of English settlement—the Caribbean and along the northern, southern, and western borders of the coastal colonies.

THE CARIBBEAN ISLANDS

Throughout the first half of the seventeenth century, the most important destination for English immigrants was not the main-

THE ENGLISH CARIBBEAN

land, but rather the islands of the Caribbean and the northern way station of Bermuda. More than half the English migrants to the New World in those years settled on these islands. The island societies had close ties to English North America from the beginning and influenced the development of the mainland colonies in several ways. But they were also surrounded by, and sometimes imperiled by, outposts of the Spanish Empire.

Before the arrival of Europeans, most of the Caribbean islands had substantial native populations–the Arawaks, the Caribs, and

IMPERIAL CONFLICT

the Ciboney. But beginning with Christopher Columbus's first visit in 1492, and accelerating after the Spanish established their first colony on Hispaniola in 1496, the native population was all but wiped out by European epidemics. Indians were never a significant factor in European settlement of the Caribbean. Indeed, by the time significant European settlement of the islands began, many were almost entirely deserted.

The Spanish Empire claimed title to all the islands in the Caribbean, but there was substantial Spanish settlement only on the largest of them: Cuba, Hispaniola, and Puerto Rico. English, French, and Dutch traders began settling on some of the smaller islands early in the sixteenth century, although these weak colonies were always vulnerable to Spanish attack. After Spain and the Netherlands went to war in 1621 (distracting the Spanish navy and leaving the English in the Caribbean relatively unmolested), the pace of English colonization increased. By midcentury, there were several substantial English settlements on the islands, the most important of them on Antigua, St. Kitts, Jamaica, and Barbados. Even so, through the seventeenth century, the English settlements in the Caribbean were the targets of almost constant attacks and invasions by the Spanish, the Portuguese, the French, the Dutch, and the remaining Indians of the region. The world of the Caribbean was a violent and turbulent place.

The Caribbean colonies built their economies on raising crops for export. In the early years, English settlers experimented unsuccessfully with tobacco and cotton. But they soon discovered that the most lucrative crop was sugar, for which there was a substantial and growing market in Europe. Sugarcane could also be distilled into rum, for which there was a booming market abroad. Within a decade of the introduction of sugar cultivation to the West Indies, planters were devoting almost all of their land to sugarcane. In their appetite for more

THE SEVENTEENTH-CENTURY CARIBBEAN At the same time that European powers were expanding their colonial presence on the mainland of the American continents, they were also establishing colonies in the islands of the Caribbean. In some cases, these islands were even more important to the Atlantic economy than many of the mainland possessions, particularly the large, heavily populated sugar-growing islands (among them Jamaica and Barbados), in which the majority of the population consisted of African slaves.

• *What role did the Caribbean islands play in the spread of slavery in North America?*

land for sugarcane, they cut down forests and destroyed the natural habitats of many animals, which greatly reduced the amount of land available for growing food.

Because sugar was a labor-intensive crop, and because the remnant of the native population was too small to provide a
Sugar and Slavery
workforce, English planters soon found it necessary to import laborers. As in the Chesapeake, they began by bringing indentured servants from England. But the arduous work discouraged white laborers; many found it impossible to adapt to the harsh tropical climate so different from that of England. By midcentury, therefore, the English planters in the Caribbean (like the Spanish colonists who preceded them) were relying more and more on an enslaved African workforce, which soon substantially outnumbered them.

On Barbados and other islands where a flourishing sugar economy developed, the English planters were a tough, aggressive, and ambitious breed. Some of them grew enormously wealthy; and since their livelihoods depended on their workforces, they expanded and solidified the system of African slavery there remarkably quickly. By the late seventeenth century, there were four times as many African slaves as there were white settlers. By then the West Indies had ceased to be an attractive destination for ordinary English immigrants; most now went to the colonies on the North American mainland instead.

MASTERS AND SLAVES IN THE CARIBBEAN

A small, mostly wealthy white population and a large African population held in bondage made for a potentially explosive combination. As in other English colonies in the New World in which Africans came to outnumber Europeans, whites in the Caribbean grew fearful of slave revolts. They had good
Slave Revolts
reason, for there were at least seven major slave revolts in the islands, more than the English colonies of North America experienced in their entire history as slave societies. As a result, white planters monitored

their labor forces closely and often harshly. Beginning in the 1660s, all the islands enacted legal codes to regulate relations between masters and slaves and to give white people absolute authority over Africans. A master could even murder a slave with virtual impunity.

There was little either in the law or in the character of the economy to compel planters to pay much attention to the welfare of their workers. Many white slaveowners concluded that it was cheaper to buy new slaves periodically than to protect the well-being of those they already owned, and it was not uncommon for masters to work their slaves to death. Few African workers survived more than a decade in the brutal Caribbean working environment–they either were sold to planters in North America or died. Even whites, who worked far less hard than did the slaves, often succumbed to the harsh climate; most died before the age of forty–often from tropical diseases to which they had no immunity.

Establishing a stable society and culture was extremely difficult for people living in such harsh and even deadly conditions. Many of the whites were principally interested in getting rich and had no long-term commitment to the islands.

UNSTABLE SOCIETIES Those who could returned to England with their fortunes and left their estates in the hands of overseers. A large proportion of the European settlers were single men, many of whom either died or left the islands at a young age. Those who remained, many of them common white farmers and laborers living in extreme poverty, were too poor to contribute to the development of the society. With few white women on the islands and little intermarriage between blacks and whites, Europeans in the Caribbean lacked many of the institutions that gave stability to the North American settlements: church, family, community.

Africans in the Caribbean faced even greater difficulties, of course, but they managed to create a world of their own despite the hardships. They started families (although many of them were broken up by death or the slave trade); they sustained African religious and social traditions (and showed little interest in Christianity); and within the rigidly controlled world of the sugar plantations, they established patterns of resistance.

The Caribbean settlements were connected to the North American colonies in many ways. They were an important part

CONNECTION TO BRITISH NORTH AMERICA of the Atlantic trading world in which many Americans became involved–a source of sugar and rum and a market for goods made in the mainland colonies and in England. They were the principal source of African slaves for the mainland colonies; well over half the slaves in North America came from the islands, not directly from Africa. And because Caribbean planters established an elaborate plantation system earlier than planters in North America, they provided models that many mainland people consciously or unconsciously copied. In the American South, too, planters grew wealthy at the expense of poor whites and, above all, of African slaves.

THE SOUTHWESTERN BORDERLANDS

By the end of the seventeenth century, the Spanish Empire had established only a small presence in the regions that became the United States. In Mexico and regions farther south, however, the Spanish had established a sophisticated and impressive empire. Their capital, Mexico City, was the most dazzling metropolis in the Americas. The Spanish residents, numbering well over a million, enjoyed much greater prosperity than all but a few English settlers in North America.

The principal Spanish colonies north of Mexico–Florida, Texas, New Mexico, Arizona, and California–attracted religious

SPAIN'S NORTHERN COLONIES minorities, Catholic missionaries, independent ranchers fleeing the heavy hand of imperial authority, and Spanish troops defending the northern flank of the empire. These colonies remained weak and peripheral parts of the great empire to their south.

New Mexico was the most prosperous and populous of these Spanish outposts. Once the Spanish quelled the Pueblo revolt there in 1680 (see p. 17), they worked effectively with the natives of the region to develop a flourishing agriculture. By the early nineteenth century, New Mexico had a non-Indian population of over 10,000–the largest European settlement west of the Mississippi and north of Mexico–and it was steadily expanding through the region. But New Mexico was prosperous only when compared to other borderlands. Its residents were far less successful than the Spanish in Mexico and other more densely settled regions.

The Spanish began to colonize California once they realized that other Europeans–among them English merchants and French and Russian trappers–were beginning to estab-

CALIFORNIA lish a presence in the region. Formal Spanish settlement of California began in the 1760s, when the governor of Baja California was ordered to create outposts of the empire farther north. Soon a string of missions, forts (or *presidios*), and trading communities were springing up along the Pacific coast, beginning with San Diego and Monterey in 1769 and eventually San Francisco (1776), Los Angeles (1781), and Santa Barbara (1786). As in other areas of European settlement, the arrival of the Spanish in California (and the diseases they imported) had a devastating effect on the native population. Approximately 65,000 at the time of the first Spanish settlements, by 1820 it had declined by two-thirds. As the new settlements spread, however, the Spanish insisted that the remaining natives convert to Catholicism. That explains the centrality of missions in almost all the major Spanish outposts in California. But the Spanish colonists were also intent on creating a prosperous agricultural economy, and they enlisted Indian laborers to help them do so. California's Indians had no choice but to accede to the demands of the Spanish, although there were frequent revolts by natives against the harsh conditions imposed upon them. Already decimated by disease, the tribes now declined further as a result of malnutrition and overwork at the hands of the Spanish missions.

In the late seventeenth and early eighteenth centuries, the Spanish considered the greatest threat to the northern borders of their empire to be the growing ambitions of the French. In the 1680s, French explorers traveled down the Mississippi Valley to the mouth of the river and claimed the lands they had traversed for their king, Louis XIV. They called the territory Louisiana. Fearful of French incursions farther west, and unsettled by the nomadic Indians driven into the territory by the French, the Spanish began to fortify their claim to Texas by establishing new forts, missions, and settlements there, including San Fernando (later San Antonio) in 1731. The region that is now Arizona was also becoming increasingly tied to the Spanish Empire. Northern Arizona was a part of the New Mexico colony and was governed from Santa Fe. The rest of Arizona (from Phoenix south) was controlled by the Mexican region of Sonora. As in California, much of the impetus for these settlements came from Catholic missionaries (in this case Jesuits), eager to convert the natives to Catholicism. But the missionary project met with little success. Unlike the sedentary Pueblos around Santa Fe, the Arizona natives were nomadic peoples, unlikely to settle down or to Christianize, frequently at war with rival tribes, and—like natives elsewhere—tragically vulnerable to smallpox, measles, and other imported diseases. As in California, epidemics reduced the native population of Arizona by two-thirds in the early eighteenth century.

Although peripheral to the great Spanish Empire to the south, the Spanish colonies in the Southwest nevertheless helped create enduring societies very unlike those being established by the English along the Atlantic seaboard. The Spanish colonies were committed not to displacing the native populations but, rather, to enlisting them. They sought to convert them to Catholicism, to recruit them (sometimes forcibly) as agricultural workers, and to cultivate them as trading partners. The Spanish did not consider the natives to be their equals, certainly, and they did not treat them very well. But neither did they consider them merely as obstacles to their own designs, as many English settlers along the Atlantic seaboard did.

IMPORTANCE OF THE SPANISH BORDERLANDS

THE SOUTHEASTERN BORDERLANDS

A more direct challenge to English ambitions in North America was the Spanish presence in the southeastern areas of what is now the United States. After the establishment of the Spanish claim to Florida in the 1560s (see p. 17), missionaries and traders began moving northward into Georgia and westward into what is now known as the panhandle. Some ambitious Spaniards began to dream of expanding their empire still farther north, into what became the Carolinas, and perhaps beyond. The founding of Jamestown in 1607 replaced those dreams with fears. The English colonies, they believed, could threaten their existing settlements in Florida and Georgia. As a result, the Spanish built forts in both regions to defend themselves against the slowly increasing English presence there. Throughout the eighteenth century, the area between the Carolinas and Florida was the site of continuing tension, and frequent conflict, between the Spanish and the English—and, to a lesser degree, between the Spanish and the French, who were threatening their northwestern borders with settlements in Louisiana and in what is now Alabama.

There was no formal war between England and Spain in these years, but that did not dampen the hostilities in the Southeast. English pirates continually harassed the Spanish settlements and, in 1668, sacked St. Augustine. Both sides in this conflict sought to make use of the native tribes. The English encouraged Indians in Florida to rise up against the Spanish missions. The Spanish, for their part, offered freedom to African slaves owned by Carolina settlers if they agreed to convert to Catholicism. About 100 Africans accepted the offer, and the Spanish later organized some of them into a military regiment to defend the northern border of New Spain. The English correctly viewed the Spanish recruitment of their slaves as an effort to undermine their economy. By the early eighteenth century, the constant fighting in the region had driven almost all the Spanish settlers out of Florida. The dwindling Spanish presence became almost entirely confined to St. Augustine on the Atlantic coast to Pensacola on the Gulf Coast, and to the modest colonies that surrounded the forts there. Because they were so few and so weak, they came to rely—far more than most British did—on natives and Africans and intermarried frequently with them.

HOSTILITIES IN THE SOUTHEAST

Eventually, after more than a century of conflict in the southeastern borderlands, the English prevailed—acquiring Florida in the aftermath of the Seven Years' War (known in America as the French and Indian War; see pp. 103–107) and rapidly populating it with settlers from their colonies to the north. Before that point, however, protecting the southern boundary of the British Empire in North America was a continual concern to the English and contributed in crucial ways to the founding of the colony of Georgia.

THE FOUNDING OF GEORGIA

Georgia was unique in its origins. Its founders were a group of unpaid trustees led by General James Oglethorpe, a member of Parliament and military hero. They were interested in economic success, but they were driven primarily by military and philanthropic motives. They wanted to erect a military barrier against the Spanish lands on the southern border of English America, and they wanted to provide a refuge for the impoverished, a place where English men and women without prospects at home could begin anew.

JAMES OGLETHORPE'S VISION

The need for a military buffer between South Carolina and the Spanish settlements in Florida was particularly urgent in the first years of the eighteenth century. In a 1676 treaty, Spain had recognized England's title to lands already occupied by English settlers. But conflict between the two colonizing powers had continued. In 1686, a force of Indians and Creoles from Florida, directed by Spanish agents, attacked and

AP DEBATING THE PAST

NATIVE AMERICANS AND THE "MIDDLE GROUND"

FOR many generations, historians chronicling the westward movement of European settlement in North America incorporated Native Americans into the story largely as weak and inconvenient obstacles swept aside by the inevitable progress of "civilization." Indians were presented either as murderous savages or as relatively docile allies of white people, but rarely as important actors of their own. Francis Parkman, the great nineteenth-century American historian, described Indians as a civilization "crushed" and "scorned" by the march of European powers in the New World. Many subsequent historians departed little from his assessment.

Challenges to this traditional view have come from many more-recent historians—among them, Gary Nash in *Red, White, and Black* (1974) and Ramón Gutiérrez in *When Jesus Came, the Corn Mothers Went Away* (1991). They, and other scholars, rejected the optimistic, progressive view of white triumph over adversity and presented, instead, a picture of conquest that affected both the conqueror and the conquered and did not bring to an end their influence on one another.

A new, more recent view of the relationship between the peoples of the Old and New Worlds sees Native Americans and Euro-Americans as uneasy partners in the shaping of a new society in which, for a time at least, both were a vital part. In *The Middle Ground* (1991), Richard White examined the culture of the Great Lakes region in the eighteenth century, in which Algonquin Indians created complex trading and political relationships with French, English, and American settlers and travelers in the region. In this "borderland" between the growing European settlements in the East and the still largely intact Indian civilizations farther west, a new kind of hybrid society emerged in which many cultures intermingled. In *Into the American Woods* (1999), James Merrell examined the world of negotiators and go-betweens along the western Pennsylvania frontier in the seventeenth and eighteenth centuries. Like White, he emphasized the complicated blend of European and Native American diplomatic rituals that allowed both groups to conduct business, make treaties, and keep the peace.

Daniel Richter extended the idea of a "middle ground" further in *The Ordeal of the Longhouse* (1992) and *Facing East from Indian Country* (2001). Richter demonstrates that the Iroquois

Confederacy was an active participant in the power relationships in the Hudson River basin. In his later book, he tells the story of European colonization from the Native American perspective, revealing how western myths of "first contact" such as the story of John Smith and Pocahontas look entirely different when seen through the eyes of Native Americans, who remained in many ways the more powerful of the two societies in the seventeenth century.

How did these important collaborations collapse? What happened to the "middle ground"? Over time, the delicate partnerships along the frontiers of white settlement gave way to the sheer numbers of Europeans (and, in some places, Africans) who moved westward. Joyce Chaplin in *Subject Matter* (2001) argued as well that Old World Americans at first admired the natives as a kind of natural nobility until European diseases ravaged the tribes, helping strengthen the Europeans' sense of superiority that had been a part of their view of Indians from the beginning. In *The Name of War* (1998), Jill Lepore described how the violence of King Philip's War in seventeenth-century New England helped transform English views of the tribes both because of the white victory over the Indians and because of their success in turning this victory into a

---

destroyed an outlying South Carolina settlement south of the treaty line. And when hostilities broke out again between Spain and England in 1701 (known in England as Queen Anne's War and on the Continent as the War of the Spanish Succession), the fighting renewed in America as well.

Oglethorpe, a veteran of Queen Anne's War, was keenly aware of the military advantages of an English colony south of the Carolinas. Yet his interest in settlement rested even more on his philanthropic commitments. As head of a parliamentary committee investigating English prisons, he had grown appalled by the plight of honest debtors dying in confinement. Such prisoners, and other poor people in danger of succumbing to a similar fate, could, he believed, become the farmer-soldiers of the new colony in America.

In 1732, King George II granted Oglethorpe and his fellow trustees control of the land between the Savannah and

GENERAL JAMES OGLETHORPE Oglethorpe was one of the founders of the English colony of Georgia. He and his followers established the colony to stand as a military buffer between South Carolina and the Spanish settlements in Florida. They also wanted a refuge for British men and women without economic prospects in England. (© Stock Montage/Getty Images)

seriously chronicling this story in the late nineteenth century, the Indian tribes had indeed become the defeated, helpless "obstacles" that they portrayed. But for generations before, the relationship between white Americans and Native Americans was a much less unequal one than it would later become. ●

AP | HISTORICAL ARGUMENTATION AND INTERPRETATION

Questions assume cumulative content knowledge from this chapter and previous chapters.

1. Identify three camps of historical views regarding the relationship between Native Americans and the European settlers. Name a historian representative of each view, and provide one piece of historical evidence that supports the view.
2. Offer a circumstance, or factor, surrounding one or more of these historians, which might have influenced the historian's perspective.
3. If you were writing a history of European settlement in North America, name an event, which you would consider significant, such that it is a turning point in the relationship between Native Americans and European settlers. Explain.

TRADING PARTNERS *Ralph Hamor Visits Powhatan with a Proposal* is an etching by Theodor de Bry (1528–1598) showing how Europeans and Native Americans sometimes made economic deals for mutual gain. (© Virginia Historical Society, Richmond, Virginia, USA / The Bridgeman Art Library)

rationale for the moral superiority of Europeans by portraying the Indians as brutal, uncivilized people. (In reality, the Europeans had used as much "savagery" against the natives as the natives had used against them.) As the pressures of white settlement grew, as the Indian populations weakened as a result of disease and war, and as the relationship between the tribes and the European settlers grew increasingly unequal, the cultural "middle ground" that for many decades characterized much of the contact between the Old and New Worlds gradually disappeared. By the time historians began

---

Altamaha Rivers. Their colonization policies reflected the vital military purposes of the colony. They limited the size of land-

GEORGIA'S MILITARY RATIONALE

holdings to make the settlement compact and easier to defend against Spanish and Indian attacks. They excluded Africans, free or slave; Oglethorpe feared slave labor would produce internal revolts and that disaffected slaves might turn to the Spanish as allies. The trustees prohibited rum (both because Oglethorpe disapproved of it on moral grounds and because the trustees feared its effects on the natives). They strictly regulated trade with the Indians, again to limit the possibility of wartime insurrection. They also excluded Catholics for fear they might collude with their core-ligionists in the Spanish colonies to the south.

Oglethorpe himself led the first colonial expedition to Georgia, which built a fortified town at the mouth of the Savannah River in 1733 and later constructed additional forts south of the Altamaha. In the end, only a few debtors were released from jail and sent to Georgia. Instead, the trustees brought hundreds of impoverished tradesmen and artisans from England and Scotland and many religious refugees from

Switzerland and Germany. Among the immigrants was a small group of Jews. English settlers made up a lower proportion of the European population of Georgia than of any other English colony.

The strict rules governing life in the new colony stifled its early development and ensured the failure of Oglethorpe's vision. Settlers in Georgia–many of whom were engaged in labor-intensive agriculture–needed a workforce as much as those in other southern colonies. Almost from the start they began demanding the right to buy slaves. Some opposed the restrictions on the size of individual property holdings. Many resented the nearly absolute political power of Oglethorpe and the trustees. As a result, newcomers to the region generally preferred to settle in South Carolina, where there were fewer restrictive laws.

Oglethorpe (whom some residents of Georgia began calling "our perpetual dictator") at first bitterly resisted the demands of the settlers for social and political reform. Over time, however, he wearied of the conflict in the colony and grew frustrated at its failure to grow. He also suffered military disappointments, such as a 1740 assault on the Spanish outpost at St. Augustine, Florida, which ended in failure. Oglethorpe, now disillusioned with his American venture, began to loosen his grip. Even before the 1740 defeat, the trustees had removed the limitation on

TRANSFORMATION OF GEORGIA

individual landholdings. In 1750, they removed the ban on slavery. A year later they ended the prohibition of rum and returned control of the colony to the king, who immediately permitted the summoning of a representative assembly. Georgia continued to grow more slowly than the other southern colonies, but in other ways it now developed along lines roughly similar to those of South Carolina. By 1770, there were over 20,000 non-Indian residents of the colony, nearly half of them African slaves.

MIDDLE GROUNDS

The struggle for the North American continent was, of course, not just one among competing European empires. It was also a contest between the new European immigrants and the native populations.

In some parts of the British Empire–Virginia and New England, for example–English settlers quickly established their dominance, subjugating and displacing most natives until they had established societies that were dominated almost entirely by Europeans. But elsewhere the balance of

CONFLICT AND ACCOMMODATION

power remained far more precarious. Along the western borders of English settlement, in particular, Europeans and Indians lived together in regions in which neither side was able to establish clear dominance. In these "middle grounds," as they have been called, the two populations–despite frequent conflicts–carved out ways of living together, with each side making concessions to the other. Here the Europeans found themselves obliged to adapt to tribal expectations at least as much as the Indians had to adapt to European ones.

To the Indians, the European migrants were both menacing and appealing. The Indians feared the power of these strange people: their guns, their rifles, their forts. But they also wanted the French and British settlers to behave like "fathers"–to help them mediate their own internal disputes, to offer them gifts, to help them moderate their conflicts. Europeans came from a world in which the formal institutional and military power of a nation or empire governed relationships between societies. But the natives had no understanding of the modern notion of a "nation" and thought much more in terms of ceremony and kinship. Gradually, Europeans learned to fulfill at least some of their expectations.

In the seventeenth century, before many English settlers had entered the interior of the continent, the French were particularly adept at creating mutually beneficial relationships with the tribes. They welcomed the chance to form close relationships

MUTUALLY BENEFICIAL RELATIONS

with–even to marry within–the tribes. They also recognized the importance of treating tribal chiefs with respect and channeling gifts and tributes through them. But by the mid-eighteenth century, French influence in the interior was in decline, and British settlers gradually became

the dominant European group in the "middle grounds." It took the British a considerable time to learn the lessons the French had long ago absorbed–that simple commands and raw force were much less effective in creating a workable relationship with the tribes than were gifts and ceremonies and mediation. Eventually they did so, and in large western regions–especially those around the Great Lakes–they established a precarious peace with the tribes that lasted for several decades.

But as the British and (after 1776) American presence in the region grew, the balance of power between Europeans and natives shifted. Newer settlers had difficulty adapting to the complex rituals of gift-giving and mediation that the earlier migrants had developed. The stability of the relationship between the Indians and whites deteriorated. By the early

THE SHIFTING BALANCE

nineteenth century, the "middle grounds" had collapsed, replaced by a European world in which Indians were ruthlessly subjugated and eventually removed. Nevertheless, it is important to recognize that for a considerable period of early American history, the story of the relationship between whites and Indians was not simply a story of conquest and subjugation, but also–in some regions–a story of a difficult but stable accommodation and mutual adaptation. The Indians were not simply victims in the story of the growth of European settlement in North America. They were also important actors, sometimes obstructing and sometimes facilitating the development of the new societies.

THE EVOLUTION OF THE BRITISH EMPIRE

The English colonies in America had originated as separate projects, and for the most part they grew up independent of one another. But by the mid-seventeenth century, the growing commercial success of the colonial ventures was producing pressure in England for a more rational, uniform structure to the empire.

THE DRIVE FOR REORGANIZATION

Imperial reorganization, many people in England claimed, would increase the profitability of the colonies and the power of the English government to supervise them. Above all, it would contribute to the success of the mercantile system, the foundation of the English economy. Colonies would provide a market for England's manufactured goods and a source for raw materials it could not produce at home, thus increasing the total wealth of the nation. But for the new possessions truly to promote mercantilist goals, England would have to exclude foreigners (as Spain had done) from its colonial trade. According to mercantil-

MERCANTILISM

ist theory, any wealth flowing to another nation could come only at the expense of England itself. Hence the British government sought to monopolize trade relations with its colonies.

A View of Savanah as it stood the 29th of March 1734

To the Hon.ble the Trustees for establishing the Colony of Georgia in America.
This View of the Town of Savanah is humbly dedicated by their Honours
Obliged and most Obedient Servant.
vve. de Savanah dans la Georgie.   Peter Gordon.

1. The stairs going up.
2. M.r Oglethorpes Tent.
3. The Crane & Bell.
4. The Tabernacle & Court House.
5. The publick Mill.
6. The House for Strangers.
7. The publick Oven.
8. The draw Well.

9. The Lott for the Church.
10. The publick Stores.
11. The Fort.
12. The Beaconage House.
13. The Pallisadoes.
14. The Guard House and Battery of Cannon.
15. Hutchinsons Island.

SAVANNAH IN 1734 This early view of the English settlement at Savannah by an English artist shows the intensely orderly character of Georgia in the early moments of European settlement there. As the colony grew, its residents gradually abandoned the rigid plan created by Georgia's founders. (© Historic Map Works/Getty Images)

In theory, the mercantile system offered benefits to the colonies as well by providing them with a ready market for the raw materials they produced and a source for the manufactured goods they did not. But some colonial goods were not suitable for export to England, which produced wheat, flour, and fish and had no interest in obtaining them from America. Colonists also found it more profitable at times to trade with the Spanish, French, or Dutch even in goods that England did import. Thus, a considerable trade soon developed between the English colonies and non-English markets.

For a time, the English government made no serious efforts to restrict this challenge to the principles of mercantilism. But gradually London began passing laws to regulate colonial trade. During Oliver Cromwell's "Protectorate," in 1650 and 1651, Parliament passed laws to keep Dutch ships out of the English colonies. After the Restoration, the government of Charles II adopted three Navigation Acts

THE NAVIGATION ACTS

designed to regulate colonial commerce even more strictly. The first of them, in 1660, closed the colonies to all trade except that carried in English ships. This law also required the colonists to export certain items, among them tobacco, only to England or English possessions. The second act, in 1663, provided that all goods being shipped from Europe to the colonies had to pass through England on the way; that would make it possible for England to tax them. The third act, in 1673, was a response to the widespread evasion of the first two laws by the colonial shippers, who frequently left port claiming to be heading for another English colony but then sailed to a foreign port. It imposed duties on the coastal trade among the English colonies, and it provided for the appointment of customs officials to enforce the Navigation Acts. These acts formed the legal basis of England's mercantile system in America for a century.

The system created by the Navigation Acts had obvious advantages for England. But it had some advantages for the colonists as well. By restricting all trade to British ships, the laws encouraged the colonists (who were themselves legally British subjects) to create an important shipbuilding industry of their own. And because the English wanted to import as many goods as possible from their own colonies (as opposed to importing them from rival nations), they encouraged—and at times subsidized—the development of American production of goods they needed, among them iron, silk, and lumber. Despite the bitter complaints the laws provoked in America in the late seventeenth century, and the bitter conflicts they would help to provoke decades later, the system of the Navigation Acts served the interests of the British and the Americans alike reasonably well through most of the eighteenth century.

THE DOMINION OF NEW ENGLAND

Enforcement of the Navigation Acts required not only the stationing of customs officials in America, but also the establishment of an agency in England to oversee colonial affairs. In 1679, Charles II attempted to increase his control over Massachusetts (which behaved at times as if its leaders considered it an independent nation) by stripping the colony of its authority over New Hampshire and chartering a separate, royal colony there whose governor he would himself appoint. Five years later, after the Massachusetts General Court defied instructions from Parliament to enforce the Navigation Acts, Charles revoked the Massachusetts corporate charter and made it a royal colony.

Charles II's brother and successor, James II, who came to the throne in 1685, went much further. In 1686, he created a single Dominion of New England, which combined the government of Massachusetts with the governments of the rest of the New England colonies and, in 1688, with those of New York and New Jersey as well. He eliminated the existing assemblies within the new Dominion and appointed a single governor, Sir Edmund Andros, to supervise the entire

SIR EDMUND ANDROS region from Boston. Andros was an able administrator but a stern and tactless man; his rigid enforcement of the Navigation Acts, his brusque dismissal of the colonists' claims to the "rights of Englishmen," and his crude and arbitrary tactics made him highly unpopular. He was particularly despised in Massachusetts, where he tried to strengthen the Anglican Church.

THE "GLORIOUS REVOLUTION"

James II, unlike his father, was openly Catholic. Not only that, he made powerful enemies as he appointed his fellow Catholics to high offices. The restoration of Catholicism led to fears among Protestants that the pope would soon overtake England and that the king would defer to him. At the same time, James II tried to control Parliament and the courts to make himself an absolute monarch. By 1688, the

opposition to the king was so great that the Parliament voted to force James II from the throne. James didn't resist giving up the crown, remembering his grandfather's execution. He eventually left the country and spent the rest of his life in France. His daughter, Mary II, and her husband, William of Orange of the Netherlands—both Protestants—replaced James II to reign jointly. No Catholic monarch has reigned since. This bloodless coup came to be known as the "Glorious Revolution."

When Bostonians heard of the overthrow of James II, they moved quickly to unseat his unpopular viceroy in New England. Andros managed to escape an angry mob, but he was arrested and imprisoned as he sought to flee the city dressed as a woman. The new sovereigns in England chose not to

END OF THE DOMINION contest the toppling of Andros and quickly acquiesced in what the colonists had, in effect, already done: abolishing the Dominion of New England and restoring separate colonial governments. They did not, however, accede to all the colonists' desires. In 1691, they combined Massachusetts with Plymouth and made it a royal colony. The new charter restored the General Court (Massachusetts's legislature), but it gave the Crown the right to appoint the governor. It also replaced church membership with property ownership as the basis for voting and officeholding and required the Puritan leaders of the colony to tolerate Anglican worship.

Andros had been governing New York through a lieutenant governor, Captain Francis Nicholson, who enjoyed the support of the wealthy merchants and fur traders of the province—the same groups who had dominated the colony for years. Other, less favored colonists—farmers, mechanics, small traders, and shopkeepers—had a long accumulation of grievances against both Nicholson and his allies. The leader of the New York dissidents was Jacob Leisler, a German immigrant and a prosperous merchant who had married into a prominent Dutch family but had never won acceptance as one of the colony's ruling class. Much like Nathaniel Bacon in Virginia, the ambitious Leisler resented his exclusion and eagerly grasped the opportunity to challenge the colonial elite. In May 1689, when news of the Glorious Revolution in England and the fall of Andros in Boston reached New York, Leisler raised a militia, captured the city fort, drove Nicholson into exile, and proclaimed himself the new head of government in New York. For two years, he tried in vain to stabilize his power in the colony amid fierce factional rivalry. In 1691, when William and Mary appointed a new governor, Leisler briefly resisted this challenge to his authority. Although he soon yielded, his hesitation allowed his many political enemies to charge him with treason. He and one of his sons-in-law were hanged, drawn, and quartered. Fierce rivalry between what became known as the "Leislerians" and the "anti-Leislerians" dominated the politics of New York for many years thereafter.

In Maryland, many people erroneously assumed when they heard news of the Glorious Revolution that their proprietor,

JOHN COODE'S REBELLION the Catholic Lord Baltimore, who was living in England, had sided with the Catholic James II and opposed William and Mary. So in 1689, an old opponent of the proprietor's government, John Coode, started a new revolt, which drove out Lord Baltimore's officials in the name of Protestantism. Through an elected convention, his supporters chose a committee to run the government and petitioned the Crown for a charter as a royal colony. In 1691, William and Mary complied, stripping the proprietor of his authority. The colonial assembly established the Church of England as the colony's official religion and forbade Catholics to hold public office, to vote, or even to practice their religion in public. Maryland became a proprietary colony again in 1715, but only after the fifth Lord Baltimore joined the Anglican Church.

As a result of the Glorious Revolution, the colonies revived their representative assemblies and successfully thwarted the plan for colonial unification. In the process, they legitimized the idea that the colonists had some rights within the empire, that the English government needed to consider their views in making policies that affected them. But the Glorious Revolution in America was not, as many Americans would later come to believe, a clear demonstration of American resolve to govern itself or a clear victory for colonial self-rule. In New York and Maryland, in particular, the uprisings had more to do with local factional and religious divisions than with any larger vision of the nature of the empire. And while the insurgencies did succeed in eliminating the short-lived Dominion of New England, their ultimate results were governments that increased the Crown's potential authority in many ways. As the first century of English settlement in America came to its end and as colonists celebrated their victories over arbitrary British rule, they were becoming more a part of the imperial system than ever before.

AP CONNECTING THEMES

Chapter 2 discussed the settlement of each of the thirteen British colonies. It is particularly important that you be able to place each of the colonies in the colonial region in which they belong. You should be able to compare and contrast the colonial regions in terms of motives for settlement, religious influence, economic structure, political structure, and social structure. The reasons for American economic development and its impact on relations between these colonies and Great Britain are particularity important. You should also keep in mind the causes and results of intra-colonial conflicts, disputes between British colonies and other European colonizers, and conflict between Europeans colonists and American Indians.

The following themes have heightened importance in Chapter 2. You should now be able to do the following for each listed theme:

Identity: Identify how contact between Europeans, Africans, and American Indians altered perceptions of identity among each group. Identify the factors that led to distinct regional identities among the British North American colonists.

Work, exchange, and technology: Explain the reasons for and the consequences of the development of different regional labor systems in colonial America.

Peopling: Identify the characteristics of people who settled in various colonial regions and the impact those characteristics had on the development of those regions.

Politics and power: Identify the political structures of different colonial regions and analyze the reasons for their development and the challenges they faced over time.

America in the world: Explain how the growth of the colonial economy created both continuity and change in relationships among the nations of the Atlantic World.

Environment and geography: Explain how the environment and geography influenced the development of distinct colonial regions.

Ideas, beliefs, and culture: Explain how the ideas, beliefs, and cultures of colonists influenced the development of regional differences.

AP SUGGESTED STUDY

PEOPLE/PLACES/EVENTS As you study these items, think about how they demonstrate or relate to key concepts and historical themes from this chapter and previous chapters.

AP TEST PRACTICE

Questions assume cumulative content knowledge from this chapter and previous chapters.

MULTIPLE CHOICE Use the illustration on page 54 and your knowledge of U.S. history to answer questions 1-2.

1. What does the illustration mostly suggest about the nature of processing sugarcane in the mid-17th century?

    (A) It could be done with little work.

    (B) The white English planters shared in the physical labor.

    (C) It was labor-intensive.

    (D) Little attention was paid to the welfare of the laborers.

2. How did the economic activity portrayed in the illustration affect labor systems in the North American colonies?

    (A) Indentured servitude came to dominate as a means for labor.

    (B) Growing sugarcane migrated into the economy of the southern colonies.

    (C) It provided an early model for the plantation slave labor system.

    (D) The North American planters treated their slave laborers more gently, in reaction to the harsh practices in the Caribbean.

SHORT ANSWER Use your knowledge of U.S. history to answer questions 3-5.

3. Answer a, b, and c.

    a) Briefly explain ONE example of conflict between Native peoples and colonists in the 17th century.

    b) Briefly explain a SECOND example of conflict between Native peoples and colonists in the 17th century.

    c) Briefly explain ONE example of intra-group conflict among colonists in the 17th century.

4. Answer a, b, and c.

    a) Briefly explain ONE example of continuing contact between the Native Americans and European colonists in the 17th century.

    b) Briefly explain ONE example of how continuing contact between Native Americans and European colonists in the 17th century brought about a cultural or demographic change in one group or the other.

    c) Briefly explain ONE example of differences in how the various European nation colonizers reacted to intensified conflicts with Native Americans.

5. Answer a, b, and c.

    a) Briefly explain ONE example of diverse patterns of colonization in America among the European nations in the 17th century.

    b) Briefly explain a SECOND example of diverse patterns of colonization in America among the European nations in the 17th century.

    c) Briefly explain ONE example of differences in regional development among the British colonies.

LONG ESSAY Develop a thoughtful and thorough historical argument that answers the question below. Begin your essay with a thesis statement and support it with relevant historical evidence.

6. Some historians have argued that economic concerns were largely responsible for the differences in regional social and political development of the British colonies in the Americas. Support, modify, or refute this interpretation, providing specific evidence to justify your answer.

3 SOCIETY AND CULTURE IN PROVINCIAL AMERICA

LIFE IN THE AMERICAN COLONIES This colored engraving shows the domestic life of Americans during the eighteenth century. Depicted are family members at work in their cozy surroundings. Their industriousness is shown to be a singular virtue of the era.
(© Bettmann/Corbis)

AP

HISTORICAL THINKING

1. **Comparison** Compare the patterns of family life and women's roles (including social attitudes towards women) in each of the colonial regions.

2. **Historical Causation** What are the reasons for differing economic systems in each of the colonial regions and explain the impact of those systems on each region's social structure.

3. **Comparison** Compare the physical settlement patterns of each of the colonial regions and analyze the reasons for and the consequences of those patterns in the development of the colonial societies.

4. **Historical Argumentation** Analyze the relative importance of natural population increase vs. immigration in the development of colonial society.

5. **Contextualization** Identify the impact of technology, science, and education on political, social, and economic developments in each colonial region.

6. **Patterns of Continuity and Change over Time** How did the lives of African slaves change over the course of the first century of slavery in North America?

7. **Contextualization** Describe the intellectual culture of colonial America, as expressed in literature, philosophy, science, education, and law, and identify any regional differences.

8. **Patterns of Continuity and Change over Time** Describe the changes in sources of immigration from Europe and the settlement patterns of the different groups.

Key Concept Correlations

Analyze the ways the historical developments you learn about in this chapter connect to the following AP Key Concepts.

1.2 European overseas expansion resulted in the Columbian Exchange, a series of interactions and adaptations among societies across the Atlantic.

2.1 Differences in imperial goals, cultures, and the North American environments that different empires confronted led Europeans to develop diverse patterns of colonization.

2.2 European colonization efforts in North America stimulated intercultural contact and intensified conflict between the various groups of colonizers and native peoples.

2.3 The increasing political, economic, and cultural exchanges within the "Atlantic World" had a profound impact on the development of colonial societies in North America.

3.2 In the late 18th century, new experiments with democratic ideas and republican forms of government, as well as other new religious, economic, and cultural ideas, challenged traditional imperial systems across the Atlantic World.

Thematic Learning Objectives

WXT-1, 2, 4; PEO-1, 5; WOR-1, 2; ENV-2, 4; ID-1, 4, 5; POL-1; CUL-1, 4

CHAPTER 3 deals with the development of colonial society in the 17th and 18th centuries. You should focus on the failure of the indentured servant system to provide an adequate supply of labor and its impact on the institutionalization of slavery. Also consider how and why changes occurred in the slave system over time. Particular emphasis is placed on the role of women in colonial society, so you should be able to compare and contrast the role of women in different regions. You should also focus on the regional similarities and differences in the colonial economy and how these led to the development of different class systems in the different regions. Be aware of the differences in education, religion, social mobility, and science in the different regions and how significant those factors were in the development of each region. As you read, evaluate the following ideas:

- Economic and geographic conditions, as well as perceptions of racial superiority, led to the institutionalization of slavery in the British North American colonies.
- Distinct regional identities developed throughout the British North American colonies as a result of differing motives for settlement, geographic and environmental factors, and ethnic and religious differences.
- The roles of women varied significantly throughout different colonial regions.
- Regional differences between the colonies diminished over time and a more unified colonial culture began to emerge.
- Science, technology, and education systems led to expanding social networks and greater economic development.

THE COLONIAL POPULATION

Not until long after the beginning of European colonization did Europeans and Africans in North America outnumber the native population. But after uncertain beginnings at Jamestown and

IMMIGRATION AND NATURAL INCREASE

Plymouth, the nonnative population grew rapidly and substantially, through continued immigration and through natural increase, until by the late seventeenth century Europeans and Africans became the dominant population groups along the Atlantic coast.

A few of the early English settlers were members of the upper classes—usually the younger sons of the lesser gentry, men who stood to inherit no land at home and aspired to establish estates for themselves in America. For the most part, however, the early English population was very unaristocratic. It included some members of the emerging middle class, businessmen who migrated to America for religious or commercial reasons, or (like John Winthrop) both. But the dominant element was English laborers. Some came to the New World independently. The religious dissenters who formed the bulk of the population of early New England, for example, were men and women of modest means who arranged their own passage, brought their families with them, and established themselves immediately on their own land. But in the Chesapeake, at least three-fourths of the immigrants in the seventeenth century arrived as indentured servants.

INDENTURED SERVITUDE

The system of temporary servitude in the New World developed out of existing practices in England. Young men and women bound themselves to masters for a fixed term of servitude (usually four to five years). In return they received passage to America, food, and shelter. Upon completion of their terms of service, male indentures were supposed to receive such benefits as clothing, tools,

ORIGINS

and occasionally land; in reality, however, many left service without anything, unprepared and unequipped to begin earning a living on their own. Roughly one-fourth of the indentures in the Chesapeake were women, most of whom worked as domestic servants. Because men greatly outnumbered women in the region in the seventeenth century,

NORTH AMERICA IN 1700 This map reveals how tiny a proportion of North America was settled by Europeans in 1700, nearly a century after the first English settlements began there. The largest area of settlement was the thin fringe of colonies along the northern Atlantic seaboard. There were additional scattered settlements, almost all of them tiny, in eastern Canada, along the southern Atlantic coast, in the Mississippi Valley, and in the Southwest.

• *What accounted for the isolated colonies in noncoastal areas of North America?*

women could reasonably expect to marry when their terms of servitude expired. Male domestic servants, however, usually had no such options.

Most indentured servants came to the colonies voluntarily, but not all. Beginning as early as 1617, the English government occasionally dumped shiploads of convicts in America to be sold into servitude, although some criminals, according to Captain John Smith, "did chuse to be hanged ere they would go thither, and were." The government also sent prisoners taken in battles with the Scots and the Irish in the 1650s, as well as other groups deemed undesirable: orphans, vagrants, paupers, and those who were "lewd and dangerous." Other involuntary immigrants were neither dangerous nor indigent but were simply victims of kidnapping, or "impressment," by aggressive and unscrupulous investors and promoters.

It was not difficult to understand why the system of indentured servitude proved so appealing to colonial employers–particularly once it became clear, as it quickly did, that the Indian population could not easily be transformed into a servile workforce. The indenture system provided a means of coping with the severe labor shortage in the New World. In the Chesapeake, the head-right system (by which masters received additional land grants

for every servant they imported) offered another incentive. For the servants themselves, the attractions were not always so clear. Those who came voluntarily often did so to escape troubles in England; others came in the hope of establishing themselves on land or in trades of their own when their terms of service expired. Yet the reality often differed sharply from the hope.

Some former indentures managed to establish themselves successfully as farmers, tradespeople, or artisans. Others (mostly males) found themselves without land, without employment, without families, and without prospects. A large floating population of young single men traveled restlessly from place to place, often in groups, in search of work or land and were a potential (and at times actual) source of social unrest, particularly in the Chesapeake. Even free laborers who found employment or land and settled down with families often did not stay put for very long. The phenomenon of families simply pulling up stakes and moving to another, more promising location every several years was one of the most prominent characteristics of the colonial population.

Indentured servitude remained an important source of population growth well into the eighteenth century, but beginning

REALITIES OF INDENTURED SERVITUDE

in the 1670s the flow began to decline substantially. A decrease in the English birth rate and an increase in English prosperity reduced the pressures on many men and women who might otherwise have considered emigrating. After 1700, those who did travel to America as indentured servants generally avoided the southern colonies, where working conditions were arduous and prospects for advancement were slim, and took advantage of the better opportunities in the mid-Atlantic colonies, especially Pennsylvania and New York. In the Chesapeake, landowners themselves began to find the indenture system less attractive, in part because they were troubled by the instability that former servants created or threatened to create. That was one reason for the increasing centrality of African slavery in the southern agricultural economy.

BIRTH AND DEATH

At first, new arrivals in most colonies, whatever their background or status, could anticipate great hardship: inadequate food, frequent epidemics, and in an appalling number of cases, early death. Gradually, however, conditions improved enough to allow the non-Indian population to begin to expand. By the end of the seventeenth century, the non-Indian population in the English colonies of North America had grown to over a quarter of a million, of whom about 25 percent were Africans.

Population (thousands) **2,780**

2,148

1,594

1,171

906

629

466

251 **332**

1700 1710 1720 1730 1740 1750 1760 1770 1780
Year

THE NON-INDIAN POPULATION OF NORTH AMERICA, 1700–1780 The European population of North America grew much more dramatically in the eighteenth century than it had in the seventeenth, exceeding 2 million by 1770. But unlike in the seventeenth century, the most important reason for this expansion was natural increase (children born in America), replacing immigration from Europe.

* *Why was the natural increase so much larger than in the past?*

SERVANTS FOR SALE The *South-Carolina Gazette* of Charles Town ran this advertisement in November 1749 to announce the arrival of a group of English "indentures"—men and women who had accepted passage to America in exchange for their agreement to sell themselves as servants for a fixed period of years once they arrived. Indentures were the most common form of labor in most of the colonies during much of the seventeenth century, but by 1749 the system was already beginning to die out—replaced in the South by the enslavement of Africans. (© Charleston Library Society (Charleston, SC))

Although immigration remained for a time the greatest source of population increase, marked improvement in the reproduction rate began in New England and the mid-Atlantic colonies in the second half of the seventeenth century. After the 1650s, natural increase became the most important source of population. The New England population more than quadrupled through reproduction alone in the second half of the seventeenth century. This was less a result of **EXCEPTIONAL LONGEVITY IN NEW ENGLAND** unusual fertility (families in New England and in other regions were probably equally fertile) than of exceptional longevity. Indeed, the average life spans of residents of some areas of New England were nearly equal to those of people in the twentieth century. In the first generation of American-born colonists, according to one study, men who survived infancy lived to an average age of seventy-one, women to seventy. The next generation's life expectancy declined somewhat–to sixty-five for men who survived infancy–but remained at least ten years higher than the English equivalent and approximately twenty years higher than life expectancy in the South. Scholars disagree on the reasons for these remarkable life spans, but contributing factors probably included the cool climate and the relatively disease-free environment it produced, clean water (a stark contrast to England in these years), and the absence of large population centers that might breed epidemics.

Conditions improved much more slowly in the South. The mortality rates for whites in the Chesapeake region remained markedly higher than those elsewhere until the mid-eighteenth century (and the mortality rates for Africans higher still). Throughout the seventeenth century, the average life expectancy for white men in the region was just over forty years and, for white women, slightly less. One in four children died in infancy, and fully half died before the age of twenty. The high death rate among adults meant that only about a third of all marriages lasted more than ten years; thus those children who survived infancy often lost one or both of their parents before reaching maturity. Widows, widowers, and orphans formed a substantial proportion of the white population of the Chesapeake. The continuing ravages of disease (particularly malaria) and the prevalence of salt-contaminated water kept the death rate high in the South; only after the settlers developed immunity to the local diseases (a slow process known as "seasoning") did life expectancy increase significantly. Population growth was substantial in the region, but largely as a result of immigration.

Natural increases in the population, wherever they occurred, were largely a result of a steady improvement in the sex ratio through the seventeenth century. In the early years of settlement, more than three-quarters of the white population of the Chesapeake consisted of men. And even in New England, which from the beginning had attracted more families (and

MORE-BALANCED SEX RATIO thus more women) than the southern colonies, 60 percent of the white inhabitants in 1650 were male. Gradually, however, more women began to arrive in the colonies; and increasing birth rates, which of course produced roughly equal numbers of males and females, contributed to shifting the sex ratio as well. Not until well into the eighteenth century did the ratio begin to match that in England (where women were a slight majority), but by the late seventeenth century, the proportion of males to females in all the colonies was becoming more balanced.

MEDICINE IN THE COLONIES

The very high death rates of women who bore children illustrate the primitive nature of medical knowledge and practice in the colonies. Seventeenth- and eighteenth-century physicians had little or no understanding of infection and sterilization. As a result, many people died from infections contracted during childbirth or surgery from dirty instruments or dirty hands. Because communities were unaware of bacteria, many were plagued with infectious diseases transmitted by garbage or unclean water.

One result of the limited extent of medical knowledge was that it was relatively easy for people to enter the medical field, even without professional training. The biggest beneficiaries of

MIDWIVES this ease of access were women, who established themselves in considerable numbers as midwives. Midwives assisted women in childbirth, but they also dispensed other medical advice—usually urging their

patients to use herbs or other natural remedies. Midwives were popular because they were usually friends and neighbors of the people they treated, unlike physicians, who were few and therefore not often well known to their patients. Male doctors felt threatened by the midwives and struggled continually to drive them from the field, although they did not make substantial progress in doing so until the nineteenth century.

Midwives and doctors alike practiced medicine on the basis of the prevailing assumptions of their time, most of them derived from the theory of "humoralism" popularized by the second-century Roman physician Galen. Galen argued that the human body was governed by four "humors" that were lodged in four bodily fluids: yellow bile (or "choler"), black bile ("melancholy"), blood, and phlegm. In a healthy body, the four humors existed in balance. Illness represented an imbalance and suggested the need for removing from the body the excesses of whatever fluid was causing the imbalance. That was the rationale that lay behind the principal medical techniques of the seventeenth century: purging, expulsion, and bleeding. Bleeding was the most extreme of the treatments (and the most destructive), and it was practiced mostly by male physicians. Midwives preferred more homeopathic treatments and favored "pukes" and laxatives. The great majority of early Americans, however, had little contact with physicians, or even midwives, and sought instead to deal with illness on their own, confident that their abilities were equal to those of educated physicians—which, given the state of medical knowledge, was often true.

That seventeenth-century medicine rested so much on ideas produced 1,400 years before is evidence of how little support there was for the scientific method—which rests on experimentation and observation rather than on inherited faiths—in England and America at the time. Bleeding, for example, had been in use for hundreds of years, during which time there had been no evidence that it helped people recover from illness; indeed, if anyone had chosen to look for it, there was considerable evidence that bleeding could do great harm. But what would seem in later eras to be the simple process of testing scientific assumptions was not yet a common part of Western thought. Only with the birth of the Enlightenment in the late seventeenth century—with its faith in human reason and its belief in the capacity of individuals and societies to create better lives—would the scientific method begin to find acceptance.

WOMEN AND FAMILIES IN THE CHESAPEAKE

The importance of reproduction in the labor-scarce society of seventeenth-century America had particularly significant effects on women. The high sex ratio meant that few women remained unmarried for long. The average European woman in America

MALE AUTHORITY UNDERMINED married for the first time at twenty or twenty-one years of age, considerably earlier than in England; in some areas of the Chesapeake, the average bride was three to four years younger. In the Chesapeake, the most important factor affecting women and families remained, until at least the mid-eighteenth century, the extraordinarily high mortality rate. Under those circumstances, the traditional male-centered family structure of England–by which husbands and fathers exercised firm, even dictatorial control over the lives of their wives and children–was difficult to maintain. Because so few families remained intact for long, rigid patterns of male authority were constantly undermined. Standards of sexual behavior were also more flexible in the South than they were in England or other parts of America. Because of the large numbers of indentured servants who were forbidden to marry until their terms of service expired, premarital sexual relationships were frequent. Female servants who became pregnant before the expiration of their terms could expect harsh treatment: heavy fines, whippings if no one could pay the fines, an extra year or two of service added to their contract, and the loss of their children after weaning. Bastard children were themselves bound out as indentures at a very early age. On the other hand, a pregnant woman whose term of service expired before the birth of her child or whose partner was able to buy her remaining time from her master might expect to marry quickly. Over a third of Chesapeake marriages occurred with the bride already pregnant.

Women in the Chesapeake could anticipate a life consumed with childbearing. The average wife became pregnant every two years. Those who lived long enough bore an average of eight children apiece (up to five of whom typically died in infancy or early childhood). Since childbirth was one of the most frequent causes of female death, relatively few women survived to see all their children grow to maturity.

For all the hardships women encountered in the seventeenth-century South, they also enjoyed more power and a greater level of freedom than women in other parts of America (or than southern women in later years). Because men were plentiful and women scarce, females had considerable latitude in choosing husbands. (They also

GREATER INDEPENDENCE IN THE SOUTH often had no fathers or other male relatives nearby trying to control their choices.) Because women generally married at a much younger age than men, they often outlived their husbands (even though female life expectancy was somewhat shorter than male). Widows were often left with several children and with responsibility for managing a farm or plantation, a circumstance of enormous hardship but one that also gave them significant economic power.

Widows seldom remained unmarried for long, however. Those who had no grown sons to work the tobacco farms and plantations had particular need for male assistance, and marriage was the surest way to secure it. Since many widows married men who were themselves widowers, complex combinations of households were frequent. With numerous stepchildren, half brothers, and half sisters living together in a single household, women often had to play the role of peacemaker–a role that may have further enhanced their authority within the family.

By the early eighteenth century, the character of the Chesapeake population was beginning to change, and with it the nature of the typical family. Life expectancy was increasing; indentured servitude was in decline; and natural repro-

REVIVAL OF PATRIARCHY duction was becoming the principal source of white population increase. The sex ratio was becoming more equal. One result of these changes was that life for white people in the region became less perilous and less arduous. Another result was that

GUIDE TO THE SEASONS Among their many purposes, almanacs sought to help farmers predict weather and plan for the demands of changing seasons. This illustration, part of a "calendar" of farming images, shows a man and a woman tending fields in July, in preparation for the coming harvest.
(© American Antiquarian Society)

women lost some of the power that their small numbers had once given them. As families grew more stable, traditional patterns of male authority revived. By the mid-eighteenth century, southern families were becoming highly "patriarchal," that is, dominated by the male head of the family.

WOMEN AND FAMILIES IN NEW ENGLAND

In New England, where many more immigrants arrived with family members and where death rates declined quickly, family structure was much more stable than it was in the Chesapeake and hence much more traditional. Because the sex ratio was reasonably balanced, most men could expect to marry.

Women, however, remained in the minority; and as in the Chesapeake, they married young, began producing children early, and continued to do so well into their thirties. In contrast to the South, however, northern children were more likely to survive (the average family raised six to eight children to maturity), and families were more likely to remain intact. Fewer New England women became widows, and those who did generally lost their husbands later in life. Hence women were less often cast in roles independent of their husbands. Young women, moreover, had less control over the conditions of marriage, both because there were fewer unmarried men vying for them and because their fathers were more often alive and able to exercise control over their choice of husbands.

Among other things, increased longevity meant that, unlike in the Chesapeake (where three-fourths of all children lost at least one parent before the age of twenty-one), white parents in New England usually lived to see their children and even their grandchildren grow to maturity. Still, the lives of most New England women were nearly as consumed by childbearing and child rearing as those of women in the Chesapeake. Even women

LIFE SPANS

who lived into their sixties spent the majority of their mature years with young children in the home. The longer lives in New England also meant that parents continued to control their children far longer than did parents in the South. Although they were less likely than parents in England to "arrange" marriages for their children, few sons and daughters could choose spouses entirely independent of their parents' wishes. Men usually depended on their fathers for land—generally a prerequisite for beginning families of their own. Women needed dowries from their parents if they were to attract desirable husbands. Stricter parental supervision of children meant, too, that fewer women became pregnant before marriage than in the South (although even in Puritan New England the premarital pregnancy rate was not insubstantial—as high as 20 percent in some communities).

Puritanism placed a high value on the family, which was the principal economic and religious unit within every community. At the same time, however, Puritanism reinforced the idea of nearly absolute male authority and the assumption of female weakness and inferiority. Women were

THE PATRIARCHAL PURITAN FAMILY

expected to be modest and submissive. Such popular girls' names as Prudence, Patience, Chastity, and Comfort suggest something about Puritan expectations of female behavior. A wife was expected to devote herself to serving the needs of her husband and household.

THE BEGINNINGS OF SLAVERY IN BRITISH AMERICA

Almost from the beginning of European settlement in North America, there was a demand for African workers to supplement the always-scarce southern labor supply. The demand grew rapidly once tobacco cultivation became a staple of the Chesapeake economy. But the supply of African laborers was limited during much of the seventeenth century, because the Atlantic slave trade did not at first serve the English colonies in America. Portuguese slavers, who had dominated the trade since the sixteenth century, shipped captive men and women from the west coast of Africa to the new European colonies in South America and the Caribbean. Gradually, Dutch and French navigators joined the slave trade. But a substantial commerce in slaves grew up within the Americas, particularly between the Caribbean islands and the southern colonies of British America. By the late seventeenth century, the supply of African workers in North America was becoming plentiful.

As the commerce in slaves grew more extensive and sophisticated, it also grew more horrible. Before it ended in the nineteenth century, it was responsible for the forced immigration of as many as 11 million Africans to the New World. (Until the late eighteenth century, the number of African immigrants to the Americas was higher than that of Europeans.) Native African chieftains captured members of enemy tribes in battle, tied them together in long lines, or "coffles," and sold them in the flourishing slave marts on the African coast. Then, after some haggling on the docks between the European traders and the African suppliers, the terrified victims were packed into the dark, filthy holds of ships for the horrors of the "middle passage"–the journey to America.

THE MIDDLE PASSAGE

For weeks, sometimes even months, the African prisoners remained chained in the bowels of the slave ships. Conditions varied from one ship to another. Some captains took care to see that their potentially valuable cargo remained reasonably healthy. Others accepted the deaths of numerous Africans as inevitable and tried to cram as many as possible into their ships to ensure that enough would survive to yield a profit at journey's end. On such ships, the African prisoners were sometimes packed together in such close quarters that they were unable to stand, hardly able to breathe. Some ships supplied them with only minimal food and water. Women were often victims of rape and other sexual abuse. Those who died en route were simply thrown overboard. Upon arrival in the New World, slaves were auctioned off to white landowners and transported, frightened and bewildered, to their new homes.

THE ORIGINS OF SLAVERY

THE debate among historians over how and why white Americans created a system of slave labor in the seventeenth century—and how and why they determined that people of African descent and no others should populate that system—has been a long and unusually heated one. At its center is the question of whether slavery was a result of white racism or whether slavery created racism.

In 1950, Oscar and Mary Handlin published an influential article, "Origins of the Southern Labor System," comparing slavery to other systems of "unfreedom" in the colonies. What differentiated slavery from other conditions of servitude, they argued, was that it was restricted to people of African descent, it was permanent, and it passed from one generation to the next. The unique characteristics of slavery, the Handlins maintained, were part of an effort by colonial legislatures to increase the available labor force. White laborers needed an incentive to come to America; black laborers, forcibly imported from Africa, did not. The distinction between the conditions of white workers and the conditions of black workers was, therefore, based on legal and economic motives, not on racism. Racism emerged to justify slavery; it did not cause slavery.

Winthrop D. Jordan was one of a number of historians who later challenged the Handlins' thesis and argued that white racism, more than economic interests, produced African slavery. In *White Over Black* (1968) and other works, Jordan argued that Europeans had long viewed people of color—and black Africans in particular—as inferior beings appropriate for serving whites. Those attitudes migrated with white Europeans to the New World, and white racism shaped the treatment of Africans in America—and the nature of the slave labor system—from the beginning.

George Fredrickson echoed Jordan's emphasis on the importance of racism as an independent factor reinforcing slavery; but unlike Jordan, he argued that racism did not precede slavery. "The treatment of blacks," he wrote, "engendered a cultural and psycho-social racism that after a certain point took on a life of its own. . . . Racism, although the child of slavery, not only outlived its parent but grew stronger and more independent after slavery's demise."

In *Black Majority* (1974), a study of seventeenth-century South Carolina, Peter Wood moved the debate away from racism and back toward social and economic conditions. Wood demonstrated that blacks and whites often worked together on relatively equal terms in the early years of settlement. But as rice cultivation expanded, finding white laborers willing to do the arduous work became more

difficult. The forcible importation of African workers and the creation of a system of permanent bondage was a response to a growing demand for labor and to fears among whites that without slavery a black labor force would be difficult to control.

Edmund Morgan argued similarly in *American Slavery, American Freedom* (1975) that the southern labor system was at first relatively flexible and later grew more rigid. In colonial Virginia, he claimed, white settlers did not at first intend to create a system of permanent bondage. But as the tobacco economy grew and created a high demand for cheap labor, white landowners began to feel uneasy about their dependence on a large group of dependent white workers, since such workers were difficult to recruit and control. Thus slavery was less a result of racism than of the desire of white landowners to find a reliable and stable labor force.

In *The Making of New World Slavery* (1996), Robin Blackburn argued that while race was a factor in allowing whites to justify to themselves the enslavement of Africans, the real reasons for slavery were hardheaded economic decisions by ambitious entrepreneurs, who realized early on that a slave-labor system in the labor-intensive agricultural world of the American South and the Caribbean was more profitable than a free-labor system. Slavery served the interests of a powerful combination of groups: planters, merchants, governments, industrialists, and consumers.

Race may have been a rationale for slavery, allowing planters and traders to justify to themselves the terrible

---

The first African laborers arrived in English North America before 1620, and as English seamen began to establish themselves in the slave trade, the flow of Africans to the colonies gradually increased. But North America was always a much less important market for Africans than were other parts of the New World, especially the Caribbean islands and Brazil, whose labor-intensive sugar economies created an especially large demand for slaves. Less than 5 percent of the Africans imported to the Americas went directly to the English colonies on the mainland. Most blacks who ended up in what became the United States spent time first in the West Indies. Not until the 1670s did traders start importing blacks directly from Africa to North America. Even then, however, the flow remained small for a time, mainly because a single group, the Royal African Company of England, maintained a monopoly on trade in the mainland colonies and managed as a result to keep prices high and supplies low.

A turning point in the history of the African population in North America came in the mid-1690s, when the Royal African Company's monopoly was finally broken. With the trade now opened to English and colonial merchants on a competitive basis, prices fell and the number of Africans arriving in North America rapidly increased. By the end of the seventeenth century, only about one in ten of the residents of the colonies were Africans (about 25,000 in all). But because Africans were so heavily concentrated in a few southern colonies, they were already beginning to outnumber Europeans in some areas. The high ratio of men to women among African immigrants (there were perhaps two males to one female in most areas) retarded the natural increase of the black population. But in the Chesapeake at least, more new slaves were being born by 1700 than were being imported from Africa. In South Carolina, by contrast, the difficult conditions of rice

GROWING SLAVE POPULATION

LONDON'S VIRGINIA.

(© The Granger Collection, New York)

human costs of the system. But the most important reason for the system was not just racism, but the pursuit of profit—and the success of the system in producing it. Blackburn concluded that slavery was not an antiquated remnant of an older world but, rather, a recognizably modern labor system that, however ugly, served the needs of an emerging market economy. ●

AP HISTORICAL ARGUMENTATION AND INTERPRETATION

Questions assume cumulative content knowledge from this chapter and previous chapters.

1. Identify three differing historical arguments regarding how and why white American colonists created a slave labor system. For each, describe one piece of historical evidence that supports the argument.
2. If you were writing a history of the origins of slavery in colonial America, identify three events or developments you would research, which you believe are of such significance that they are essential to telling the story.
3. With which historian's interpretation do you most agree? Explain why, supporting your argument with historical evidence.

cultivation—and the high death rates of those who worked in the rice fields—ensured that the black population would barely be able to sustain itself through natural increase until much later.

Between 1700 and 1760, the number of Africans in the colonies increased tenfold to about a quarter of a million. A relatively small number (16,000 in 1763) lived in New England; there were slightly more (29,000) in the middle colonies. The vast majority, however, continued to live in the South. By then the flow of free white laborers to that region had all but stopped, and Africans had become securely established as the basis of the southern workforce.

It was not entirely clear at first that the status of African laborers in America would be fundamentally different from that of white indentured servants. In the rugged conditions of the seventeenth-century South, it was often difficult for Europeans and Africans to maintain strictly separate roles. In some areas—South Carolina, for example, where the number of African arrivals swelled more quickly than anywhere else—whites and blacks lived and worked together for a time on terms of relative equality. Some blacks were treated much like white hired servants, and some were freed after a fixed term of servitude. A few Africans themselves became landowners, and some apparently owned slaves of their own.

UNCERTAIN STATUS

By the early eighteenth century, however, a rigid distinction had become established between black and white. (See "Debating the Past," above.) Masters were contractually obliged to free white servants after a fixed term of servitude. There was no such necessity to free black workers, and the assumption slowly spread that blacks would remain in service permanently. Another incentive for making the status of Africans rigid was that the children of slaves provided white landowners with a self-perpetuating labor force.

White assumptions about the inferiority of people of color contributed to the growing rigidity of the system. Such assumptions came naturally to the English settlers. They had already defined themselves as a superior race in their relations with the native Indian population (and earlier in their relations with the Irish). The idea of subordinating a supposedly inferior race was, therefore, already established in the English imagination by the time substantial numbers of Africans appeared in America.

In the early eighteenth century, colonial assemblies began to pass "slave codes," limiting the rights of blacks in law and ensuring almost absolute authority to white masters. One factor, and one factor only, determined whether a person was subject to the slave codes: color. In contrast to the colonial societies of Spanish America, where people of mixed race had a different (and higher) status than

SLAVE CODES

pure Africans, English America recognized no such distinctions. Any African ancestry was enough to classify a person as black.

CHANGING SOURCES OF EUROPEAN IMMIGRATION

By the early eighteenth century, the flow of immigrants from England itself began to decline substantially–a result of better economic conditions there and of new government restrictions on emigration in the face of massive depopulation in some regions of the country. But as English immigration declined, French, German, Swiss, Irish, Welsh, Scottish, and Scandinavian immigration continued and increased.

The earliest, although not the most numerous, of these non-English European immigrants were the French Calvinists,

AFRICAN SLAVE TRADE This image is from a plate from British author Amelia Opie's poem *Black Slaves in the Hold of the Slave Ship: or How to Make Sugar*, published in London in 1826. Opie's poem depicts the life of an African who was captured by slave traders and chronicles his journey to the West Indies on a slave ship and his enforced work on the sugar plantations there. Slaves were packed like cargo for the long ocean voyage. (© Universal History Archive/UIG/The Bridgeman Art Library)

or Huguenots. A royal proclamation, the Edict of Nantes of 1598, had allowed them to become practically a state within the state in Roman Catholic France. In 1685, however, the French government revoked the edict. Soon after that,

HUGUENOTS AND PENNSYLVANIA DUTCH

Huguenots began leaving the country. About 300,000 left France in the following decades. A small proportion of them traveled to the English colonies in North America. Many German Protestants suffered similarly from the arbitrary religious policies of their rulers; and all Germans, Catholics as well as Protestants, suffered from the devastating wars with King Louis XIV of France (the "Sun King"). The Rhineland of southwestern Germany, the area known as the Palatinate, experienced particular hardships. Because it was close to France, its people were particularly exposed to slaughter and ruin at the hands of invaders. The unusually cold winter of 1708-1709 dealt a final blow to the precarious economy of the region. More than 12,000 Palatinate Germans sought refuge in England, and approximately 3,000 of them soon found their way to America. They arrived in New York and tried at first to make homes in the Mohawk Valley, only to be ousted by the powerful landlords of the region. Some of

the Germans moved farther up the Mohawk, out of reach of the patroons; but most made their way to Pennsylvania, where they received a warm welcome (and where they ultimately became known to English settlers as the "Pennsylvania Dutch," a corruption of their own word for "German": "Deutsch"). The Quaker colony became the most common destination for Germans, who came to America in growing numbers. (Among them were Moravians and Mennonites, with religious views similar in many ways to those of the Quakers.) Many German Protestants went to North Carolina as well, especially after the founding of New Bern in 1710 by a company of 600 German-speaking Swiss.

The most numerous of the newcomers were the Scots-Irish–Scottish Presbyterians who had settled in northern Ireland (in the province of Ulster) in the early seventeenth century. The Ulster colonists had prospered for a time despite the barren soil and the constant, never wholly successful, struggle to suppress the Catholic natives. But in the first years of the eighteenth century, Parliament prohibited Ulster from exporting to England the woolens and other products that had become the basis of the northern Irish economy; at the same time, the English government virtually outlawed the practice of the Presbyterian religion

THE SLAVE SHIP *BROOKES* The British slave ship *Brookes* provided this plan of its "stowage" of slaves to conform to 1798 legislation from Parliament. It illustrates vividly the terrible conditions under which slaves were shipped from Africa to the Americas—human beings squeezed into every available space like cargo for the long, dangerous passage during which many Africans died. (Library of Congress)

Population (thousands) **575**

325

150

69

28

7

3

.60

1620 1640 1660 1680 1700 1720 1740 1760 1780
Year

THE AFRICAN POPULATION OF THE BRITISH COLONIES, 1620–1780
From tiny beginnings in the seventeenth century, the African population of the British colonies grew rapidly in the eighteenth century. The growth of slavery was a result of both supply (a readily available population of African workers in the Caribbean islands) and demand (the growth of tobacco, rice, and cotton cultivation in larger areas of the South). The slave population in the colonies also increased naturally in this period at a far greater rate than in the past, largely because living conditions for African workers improved.

• *Why did slaveowners invest in better conditions for their slaves?*

in Ulster and insisted on conformity with the Anglican Church. After 1710, moreover, the long-term leases of many Scots-Irish expired; English landlords doubled and even tripled the rents. Thousands of tenants embarked for America.

Often coldly received at the colonial ports, many of the Scots-Irish pushed out to the edges of European settlement. There they occupied land without much regard for who actually claimed to own it, whether absentee whites, Indians, or the colonial governments. They were as ruthless in their displacement and

THE "PENNSYLVANIA DUTCH" This folk-art painted dish illustrates the traditional dress of the Pennsylvania Dutch. The Pennsylvania Dutch were, in fact, German immigrants, known to their neighbors as "Dutch" because that was how their native word for their nationality ("Deutsch") sounded to most English speakers. (© The Granger Collection, New York)

SCOTS-IRISH suppression of the Indians as they had been with the native Irish Catholics.

Immigrants from Scotland and southern Ireland added other elements to the colonial population in the eighteenth century. Scottish Highlanders, some of them Roman Catholics who had been defeated in rebellions in 1715 and 1745, immigrated into several colonies, North Carolina above all. Presbyterian Lowlanders, faced in Scotland with high rents in the country and unemployment in the towns, left for America in large numbers shortly before the American Revolution, joining earlier groups of Scots, who had arrived in the late seventeenth century. They became a significant influence in New Jersey and Pennsylvania and helped establish Presbyterianism as an important religion in those colonies. The Catholic Irish migrated steadily over a long period, and by the time of the Revolution they were almost as numerous as the Scots, although less conspicuous. Many of them had by then abandoned their Roman Catholic religion and with it much of their ethnic identity.

Continuing immigration and natural increase contributed to a rapid population growth in the colonies in the eighteenth century. In 1700, the non-Indian population of the colonies totaled less than 250,000; by 1775, it was over 2 million—a nearly tenfold increase. Throughout the colonial period, the non-Indian population nearly doubled every twenty-five years.

THE COLONIAL ECONOMIES

To those who remained in Europe, and even to some who settled in North America, the English colonies often appeared so small and isolated as to seem virtually at the end of the world. But from the beginning, almost all the English colonies were commercial ventures and were tied in crucial ways to other economies. They developed substantial trade with the native population of North America, with the French settlers to the north and, to a lesser extent, with Spanish colonists to the south and west. And over time they developed an even more substantial trade within the growing Atlantic economy of the sixteenth and seventeenth centuries, of which they became a critical part.

American colonists engaged in a wide range of economic pursuits. But except for a few areas in the West where the small white populations subsisted largely on the fur and skin trade with the Indians, farming dominated all areas of European and African settlement throughout the seventeenth and eighteenth centuries. Some farmers engaged in simple subsistence agriculture; but whenever possible, American farmers attempted to grow crops for the local, intercolonial, and export markets.

THE SOUTHERN ECONOMY

In the Chesapeake region, tobacco quickly became the basis of the economy. A strong European demand for the crop enabled some planters to grow enormously wealthy and at times allowed the region as a whole to prosper. But production frequently exceeded demand, and as a result the price of tobacco periodically suffered severe declines.

TOBACCO

The first major bust in the tobacco economy occurred in 1640, and the boom-and-bust pattern continued throughout the colonial period and beyond. Growing more tobacco only made the problem of overproduction worse, but Chesapeake farmers never understood that. Those planters who could afford to do so expanded their landholdings, enlarged their fields, and acquired additional laborers. After 1700, tobacco plantations employing several dozen slaves or more were common.

The staple of the economies of South Carolina and Georgia was rice. By building dams and dikes along the many tidal rivers, farmers managed to create rice paddies that could be flooded and then drained. Rice cultivation was arduous work, performed standing knee-deep in the mud of malarial swamps under a blazing sun, surrounded by insects. It was a task so difficult and unhealthful that white laborers generally refused to perform it.

IMMIGRANT GROUPS IN COLONIAL AMERICA, 1760 Even though the entire Atlantic seaboard of what is now the United States had become a series of British colonies by 1760, the population consisted of people from many nations. As this map reveals, English settlers dominated most of the regions of North America. But note the large areas of German settlement in the western Chesapeake and Pennsylvania; the swath of Dutch settlement in New York and New Jersey; the Scots-Irish areas in the western regions of the South; and the large areas in which Africans were becoming the majority of the population, even if subjugated by the white minority.

• *What aspects of the history of these colonies help explain their ethnic composition?*

As a result, planters in South Carolina and Georgia were even more dependent than those elsewhere on African slaves. It was not only because Africans could be compelled to perform difficult work that whites found them so valuable. It was also because they were much better at it. They showed from the beginning a greater resistance to malaria and other local diseases (although the impact of disease on African workers was by no means inconsiderable). And they proved more adept at the basic agricultural tasks required, in part because some of them had come from rice-producing regions of west Africa.

In the early 1740s, another staple crop contributed to the South Carolina economy: indigo. Eliza Lucas, a young Antiguan woman who managed her family's North American plantations, experimented with cultivating the West Indian plant (which was the source of a blue dye in great demand in Europe) on the mainland. She discovered that it could grow on the high ground **INDIGO** of South Carolina, which was unsuitable for rice planting, and that its harvest came while the rice was still growing. Indigo became an important complement to rice and a popular import in England.

Because of the South's early dependence on large-scale cash crops, the southern colonies developed less of a commercial or industrial economy than the colonies of the North. The trading in tobacco and rice was handled largely by merchants based in London and, later, in the northern colonies. Few cities of more than modest size developed in the South.

NORTHERN ECONOMIC AND TECHNOLOGICAL LIFE

In the North, agriculture was the single most important part of the economy. But unlike in the South, the northern colonies were less dominated by farming. The northern economy was **MORE DIVERSE ECONOMY IN THE NORTH** more diverse than the economy in the South in part because conditions for farming were less favorable there. In northern New England, in particular, colder weather and hard, rocky soil made it difficult for colonists to develop the kind of large-scale commercial farming system that southerners were creating. Conditions for agriculture were better in southern New England and the middle colonies, where the soil was fertile and the weather more temperate. New York, Pennsylvania, and the Connecticut River valley were the chief suppliers of wheat to much of New England and to parts of the South. Even there, however, a substantial commercial economy emerged alongside the agricultural one.

PREPARING TOBACCO This 1790 engraving is designed to illustrate the African origins of the enslaved workers who processed tobacco in Virginia. Their "primitive" costumes seemed to the artist, a French visitor to America, to be in keeping with the crude processes they had created for drying, rolling, and sorting tobacco. (© The Stapleton Collection/Bridgeman Art Library)

Almost every colonist engaged in a certain amount of industry at home. Occasionally these home industries provided families with surplus goods they could trade or sell. Beyond these domestic efforts, craftsmen and artisans established themselves in colonial towns as cobblers, blacksmiths, riflemakers, cabinetmakers, silversmiths, and printers. In some areas, entrepreneurs harnessed water power to run small mills for grinding grain, processing cloth, or milling lumber. And in several places, large-scale shipbuilding operations began to flourish.

The first effort to establish a significant metals industry in the colonies was an ironworks established in Saugus, Massachusetts, in the 1640s after iron ore deposits had been

SAUGUS IRONWORKS discovered in the region. Iron technology was already advancing rapidly in England, and the colonists attempted to transfer those skills to America. The Saugus works used water power to drive a bellows, which controlled the heat in a charcoal furnace. As the ore melted, it trickled down into molds or was taken in the form of simple "sow bars" to a forge to be shaped into such marketable objects as plows, hoes, axes, pots, and other tools. The Saugus works was a technological success; indeed, it could boast technological capabilities equal to those of any ironworks in Europe at the time. But it was a financial failure. It began operations in 1646; in 1668, its financial problems forced it to close its doors.

Metalworks, however, gradually became an important part of the colonial economy. The largest industrial enterprise anywhere in English North America was the ironworks of the German ironmaster Peter Hasenclever in northern New Jersey. Founded in 1764 with British capital, it employed several hundred laborers, many of them imported from ironworks in Germany. There were other, smaller ironmaking enterprises in every northern colony (with particular concentrations in Massachusetts, New Jersey, and Pennsylvania), and there were ironworks as well in several southern colonies. Even so, these and other growing industries did not become the basis for the kind of explosive industrial growth that Great Britain

COMMERCE IN NEW ENGLAND This late-eighteenth-century painting of the home, wharves, countinghouse, and fleet of a prosperous New England fisherman gives some indication of how commerce was expanding even in such relatively small places as Duxbury, Massachusetts. The owner, Joshua Winsor, was active in the mackerel and cod fishing industry. The painting—evidently an effort to celebrate Winsor's great material success and record it for posterity—was by his son-in-law, Dr. Rufus Hathaway. (© Collection American Folk Art Museum, New York. Promised gift of Ralph Esmerian. (P1.2001.53))

experienced in the late eighteenth century–in part because English parliamentary regulations such as the Iron Act of 1750 restricted metal processing in the colonies. Similar prohibitions limited the manufacture of woolens, hats, and other goods. But the biggest obstacles to industrialization in America were an inadequate labor supply, a small domestic market, and inadequate transportation facilities and energy supplies.

More important than manufacturing were industries that exploited the natural resources of the continent. By the mid-seventeenth century, the flourishing **EXTRACTIVE INDUSTRIES** fur trade of earlier years was in decline. Taking its place were lumbering, mining, and fishing, particularly in the waters off the New England coast. These industries provided commodities that could be exported to England in exchange for manufactured goods. And they helped produce the most distinctive feature of the northern economy: a thriving commercial class.

THE EXTENT AND LIMITS OF TECHNOLOGY

Despite the technological progress that was occurring in some parts of America in the seventeenth and eighteenth centuries, much of colonial society was conspicuously lacking in even very basic technologies. Up to half the farmers in the colonies were so primitively equipped that they did not even own a plow. Substantial numbers of households owned no pots or kettles for cooking. And only about half the households in the colonies owned guns or rifles–with rural people almost as unlikely to have firearms as urban people. The relatively low levels of ownership of these and other elementary tools was not because such things were difficult to make, but because most Americans remained too poor or too isolated to be able to afford them. Many households had few if any candles, because they were unable to afford candle molds or tallow (wax), or because they had no access to commercially produced candles. In the early eighteenth century, very few farmers owned wagons. Most made do with two-wheeled carts, which could be hauled by hand (or by horse) around the farm but which were not very efficient for transporting crops to market. The most commonly owned tool on American farms was the axe, which suggests how much time most farmers had to spend clearing land. But throughout the colonies, the ability of people to acquire manufactured implements lagged far behind the capacity to produce them.

Even so, few colonists were self-sufficient in the late seventeenth and early eighteenth centuries. The popular image of early American households is of people who had little **MYTH OF SELF-SUFFICIENCY** connection to the market, who grew their own food, made their own clothes, and bought little from anyone else. In fact, relatively few colonial families owned spinning wheels or looms, which suggests that most people purchased whatever yarn and cloth they needed, or could afford, from merchants. Most farmers who grew grain took it to centralized facilities for processing.

THE RISE OF COLONIAL COMMERCE

Perhaps the most remarkable feature of colonial commerce in the seventeenth century was that it was able to survive. American merchants faced such bewildering and intimidating obstacles, and lacked so many basic institutions of trade, they managed to **SHORTAGE OF CURRENCY** stay afloat only with great difficulty. There was, first, no commonly accepted medium of exchange. The colonies had almost no specie (gold or silver coins). They experimented at times with different forms of paper currency–tobacco certificates, for example, which were secured by tobacco stored in warehouses; or land certificates, secured by property. Such paper was not, however, acceptable as payment for any goods from abroad, and it was in any case ultimately outlawed by Parliament. For many years, colonial merchants had to rely on a haphazard barter system or on crude money substitutes such as beaver skins.

A second obstacle was the near impossibility of imposing order on their trade. In the fragmented, jerry-built commercial world of colonial America, no merchants could be certain that the goods they sold would be produced in sufficient quantity; nor could they be certain of finding adequate markets for them. Few channels of information existed to inform traders of what they could expect in foreign ports; vessels sometimes stayed at sea for several years, journeying from one market to another, trading one commodity for another, attempting to find some way to turn a profit. Engaged in this chaotic commerce, moreover, were an enormous number of small, fiercely competitive companies, which made the problem of stabilizing the system even more acute.

Despite these and other problems, commerce in the colonies not only survived but grew. There was an elaborate coastal trade, through which the colonies did business with one another and sold goods to the West Indies–among them rum, agricultural products, meat, and fish. The mainland colonies **TRIANGULAR TRADE** bought sugar, molasses, and slaves from the Caribbean markets in return. There was also an expanding transatlantic trade, which linked the North American colonies in an intricate network of commerce with England, continental Europe, and the west coast of Africa. This commerce has often been described, somewhat inaccurately, as the "triangular trade," suggesting a neat process: merchants carried rum and other goods from New England to Africa; exchanged their merchandise for slaves, whom they then transported to the West Indies (hence the term "middle passage" for the dreaded journey–it was the second of the three legs of the voyage); and then exchanged the slaves for sugar and molasses, which they shipped back to New England to be distilled into rum. In fact, the system was almost never so simple. The "triangular" trade in rum, slaves, and sugar was in fact part of a maze of highly diverse trade routes: between the northern and southern colonies, America and England, America and Africa, the West Indies and Europe, and other combinations.

Out of this complex and highly risky trade emerged a group of adventurous entrepreneurs who by the mid-eighteenth

THE "TRIANGULAR TRADE" This map illustrates the complex pattern of trade that fueled the colonial American economy in the seventeenth and eighteenth centuries. A simple explanation of this trade is that the American colonies exported raw materials (agricultural products, furs, and others) to Britain and Europe and imported manufactured goods in return. But while that explanation is accurate, it is not complete, largely because the Atlantic trade was not a simple exchange between America and Europe but, rather, a complex network of exchanges involving the Caribbean, Africa, and the Mediterranean. Note the important exchanges between the North American mainland and the Caribbean islands; the important trade between the American colonies and Africa; and the wide range of European and Mediterranean markets in which Americans were active. Not shown on this map, but also very important to colonial commerce, was a large coastal trade among the various regions of British North America.

• *Why did the major ports of trade emerge almost entirely in the northern colonies?*

century were beginning to constitute a distinct merchant class. Concentrated in the port cities of the North (above all, Boston, New York, and Philadelphia), they enjoyed protection

EMERGING MERCHANT CLASS

from foreign competition within the English colonies—the British Navigation Acts had excluded all non-British ships from the colonial carrying trade. They had access to a market in England for such American products as furs, timber, and ships. That did not, however, satisfy all their commercial needs. Many colonial products—fish, flour, wheat, and meat, all of which England could produce for itself—needed markets outside the British Empire. Ignoring laws restricting colonial trade to England and its possessions, many merchants

developed markets in the French, Spanish, and Dutch West Indies, where prices were often higher than in the British colonies. The profits from this illegal commerce enabled the colonies to import the manufactured goods they needed from Europe.

THE RISE OF CONSUMERISM

Among relatively affluent residents of the colonies, the growing prosperity and commercialism of British America created both new appetites and new opportunities. The result was a growing preoccupation with the consumption of material goods—and of the association of possessions with social status.

TEA PARTY IN THE TIME OF GEORGE I This painting by an unknown artist dates from the 1720s and shows a prosperous Virginian posing with a fashionable and expensive tea service, some of it from China. His eagerness to display his possessions in this way is a sign of the growing interest in the badges of refinement among colonial Americans of means in the eighteenth century. (© The Colonial Williamsburg Foundation)

The growth of eighteenth-century consumerism was partly a result of the increasing division of American societies by class. As the difference between the upper and lower classes became more glaring, people of means became more intent on demonstrating their own membership in the upper ranks of society.

GROWING CONSUMERISM The ability to purchase and display consumer goods was an important way of doing so, particularly for affluent people in cities and towns. But the growth of consumerism was also a product of the early stages of the industrial revolution. Although there was relatively little industry in America in the eighteenth century, England and Europe were making rapid advances and producing more and more affordable goods for affluent Americans to buy. The new manufacturing was dependent, of course, on customers for its products. In an increasingly commercial society, therefore, there were many people committed to promoting the purchase of consumer goods as a positive social good. Consumption also grew because of an increasing tendency among colonists to take on debt to finance purchases and because of the willingness of some merchants to offer credit.

To facilitate the new consumer appetites, merchants and traders began advertising their goods in journals and newspapers. Agents of urban merchants—the first traveling salesmen—fanned out through the countryside, attempting to interest wealthy landowners and planters in luxury goods. George and Martha Washington, for example, spent considerable time and money ordering elegant furnishings for their home at Mount Vernon, goods that were shipped to them mostly from England and Europe.

Things that had once been considered expensive luxuries gradually became commonplace necessities—among them tea, household linens, glassware, manufactured cutlery, crockery, and furniture, and many others.

SOCIAL CONSEQUENCES Another result of consumerism was the association of material goods—of the quality of a person's home and possessions and clothing, for example—with virtue and "refinement." The ideal of the cultivated "gentleman" and the gracious "lady" became increasingly powerful throughout the colonies in the eighteenth century. That meant striving to become educated and "refined"—"gentlemanly" or "ladylike" in speech and behavior. Americans read books on manners and fashion. They bought magazines about London society. They also commissioned portraits of themselves and their families, devoted large portions of their homes to entertainment, built shelves and cases in which they could display fashionable possessions, constructed formal gardens, and lavished attention on their wardrobes and hairstyles.

The growing importance of consumption and refinement was visible in public spaces as well. Eighteenth-century cities—in America as in England and Europe—began to plan their growth to ensure that there would be elegant and gracious public squares, parks, and boulevards. In the past, social interaction in American communities had largely been between neighbors and relatives, or at most among members of church congregations. Now that a wider "society" was emerging within cities, it became important to create not just private but also public stages for social display.

PATTERNS OF SOCIETY

Although there were sharp social distinctions in the colonies, the deeply entrenched class system of England failed to reproduce itself in America. In England, land was scarce and the population large.

SOCIAL MOBILITY The relatively small number of people who owned property had power over the great majority who did not; the imbalance between land and population became a foundation of the English economy and the cornerstone of its class system.

In early America, the opposite was true. Land was abundant, and people were scarce. Aristocracies emerged in America, to be sure. But they tended to rely less on landownership than on control of a substantial workforce, and they were generally less secure and less powerful than their English counterparts. Far more than in England, there were opportunities in America for social mobility–both up and down.

THE PLANTATION

The plantation defined a distinctive way of life for many white and black southerners that would survive, in varying forms, until the Civil War. The first plantations emerged in the early settlements of Virginia and Maryland, once tobacco became the economic basis of the Chesapeake.

Some plantations were enormous–much like some of the great estates of England. The Maryland plantation of Charles Carroll of Carrollton, reputedly the wealthiest man in the colonies, covered 40,000 acres and contained 285 slaves. On the whole, however, seventeenth-century colonial plantations were rough and relatively small estates. In the early days in Virginia, most plantations were crude clearings where landowners and indentured servants worked side by side in conditions so rugged that death was an everyday occurrence. Even in later years, when the death rate declined and the landholdings became more established, plantation workforces seldom exceeded thirty people.

The economy of the plantation, like all agricultural economies, was precarious. In good years, successful growers could earn great profits and expand their operations. But since they could not control their markets, even the largest planters were constantly at risk. When prices for their crops fell–as tobacco prices did, for example, in the 1660s–they faced ruin.

VAGARIES OF THE PLANTATION ECONOMY

Because plantations were sometimes far from cities and towns–which were relatively few in the South–they tended to become self-contained communities. Residents lived in close proximity to one another in a cluster of buildings that included the "great house" of the planter (a house that was usually far from great), the service buildings, the barns, and the cabins of the slaves. Wealthier planters often created something approaching a full town on their plantations, with a school (for white children only), a chapel, and a large population. Smaller planters lived more modestly, but still in a relatively self-sufficient world. In some parts of the South, for example, the region around Charleston, South Carolina, planters often divided their time between the city and their nearby plantations.

On the larger plantations, the presence of a substantial slave workforce altered not only the economic but also the family lives of the planter class. The wives of plantation owners, unlike the wives of small farmers, could rely on servants to perform ordinary household chores. They could thus devote more time to their husbands and children than people in poorer parts of colonial society. But there were also frequent sexual liaisons between their husbands or sons and black women of the slave community. Southern white women generally learned to pretend not to notice these relationships, but they were almost certainly a source of anxiety and resentment. Black women, naturally, had even greater cause to resent such liaisons.

Southern society was highly stratified. Within given areas, great landowners controlled not only the lives of those who worked on their own plantations. Wealthy planters also shaped the livelihoods of small farmers, who could not effectively compete with the wealthy planters and thus depended on them to market crops and receive credit. Small farmers, working modest plots of land with few or no slaves to help them, formed the majority of the southern agrarian

STRATIFIED SOUTHERN SOCIETY

AFRICAN POPULATION AS A PROPORTION OF TOTAL POPULATION, C. 1775 This map illustrates the parts of the colonies in which slaves made up a large proportion of the population—in some areas, a majority. The densest African population was in Tidewater Virginia, but there were black majorities as well in South Carolina and parts of North Carolina. The slave population was smallest in the western regions of the southern colonies and in the area north of the Chesapeake, although there remained a significant African population in parts of New Jersey and New York (some slave, some free).

• *What explains the dense concentrations of slaves in certain areas of the South?*

Percent of Population That Was Black Per County/Colony in 1775
- 61 to 71%
- 51 to 60%
- 31 to 50%
- 11 to 30%
- 0.1 to 10%

MULBERRY PLANTATION, 1770 This painting of a rice plantation in South Carolina is unusual in placing the slave quarters in the forefront of the picture. The steep roofs of the slave cabins, which were built by the slaves themselves, reflected African architectural styles. The high roofs helped keep the cabins cool by allowing the heat to rise into the rafters. The master's house and adjacent chapel, built in conventional European style, are in the background. (View of Mulberry, House and Street, 1805, by Thomas Coram (American, 1756–1811), Oil on paper. © Image Gibbes Museum of Art/Carolina Art Association, (1968.18.01))

population, but it was the planters who dominated the southern agrarian economy. Most landowners lived in rough cabins or houses, with their servants or slaves nearby. Few landowners lived in anything resembling aristocratic splendor.

PLANTATION SLAVERY

African slaves, of course, lived very differently than white planters. On the smaller farms with only a handful of slaves, there was not always a rigid social separation between whites and blacks. But by the mid-eighteenth century, over three-fourths of all blacks lived on plantations of at least ten slaves; nearly half lived in communities of fifty slaves or more. In these larger establishments, Africans developed a society and culture of their own—influenced by their white masters, to be sure, but also partly independent of them.

Although whites seldom encouraged formal marriages among slaves, Africans themselves developed an elaborate family structure. This became possible beginning in the eighteenth century as a result of the increased life expectancy of slaves, the gradual equalization of the sex ratio, and the growth of the population through natural increase. Slaves attempted to construct nuclear families, and they managed at times to build stable households, even to work together growing their own food in gardens provided by their masters. But such

efforts were in constant jeopardy. Any family member could be sold at any time to another planter, even to one in another colony. As a result, the black family developed in ways different from its white counterpart. Africans placed special emphasis on extended kinship networks, even creating surrogate "relatives" for those who were separated from their own families. They adapted themselves, in short, to difficult conditions over which they had limited control.

African workers also developed languages of their own. In South Carolina, for example, the early slaves communicated with one another in Gullah, a hybrid of English and

SLAVE CULTURE

African tongues, which enabled them to engage in conversations their white masters could not understand. There emerged, too, a distinctive slave religion, which blended Christianity with African folklore.

Nevertheless, slave society was heavily tied to white society. African house servants, for example, at times lived in what was, by the standards of slavery, great luxury; but they were also isolated from their own community and under constant surveillance from whites. Black women were often subjected to unwanted sexual advances from owners and overseers and hence to bearing mulatto children, who were rarely recognized by their white fathers but generally accepted as members of the slave community. On some plantations, African workers received kindness and even affection from their masters and mistresses and displayed genuine devotion in return. On others, they encountered physical brutality and occasionally even sadism, against which they were powerless.

There were occasional acts of individual resistance by slaves against harsh masters, and at least twice during the colonial period there were actual slave rebellions. In the most import-

STONO REBELLION

ant such revolt, the so-called Stono Rebellion in South Carolina in 1739, about 100 Africans rose up, seized weapons, killed several whites, and attempted to escape south to Florida. Whites quickly crushed the uprising and executed most participants. The most frequent form of resistance was simply running away, but for most slaves that provided no real solution either. There was nowhere to go.

Most slaves, male and female, worked as field hands (with women also shouldering the additional burdens of cooking and child rearing). On the larger plantations that aspired to

genuine self-sufficiency, some slaves learned trades and crafts: blacksmithing, carpentry, shoemaking, spinning, weaving, sewing, midwifery, and others. These skilled craftsmen and craftswomen were at times hired out to other planters. Some set up their own establishments in towns or cities and shared their profits with their owners. On occasion, they were able to buy their freedom. There was a small free black population living in southern cities by the time of the Revolution.

THE PURITAN COMMUNITY

A very different form of community emerged in Puritan New England, but one that was also distinctively American. The characteristic social unit in New England was not the isolated

PATTERNS OF SETTLEMENT

farm, but the town. Each new settlement drew up a "covenant" among its members, binding all residents in a religious and social commitment to unity and harmony. Some such settlements consisted of people who had emigrated to America

THE NEW ENGLAND TOWN: SUDBURY, MASSACHUSETTS, 17TH CENTURY Just as the plantation was a characteristic social form in the southern colonies, the town was the most common social unit in New England. This map shows the organization of Sudbury, Massachusetts, a town west of Boston, in the early years in the seventeenth century. Note the location of the houses, which are grouped mostly together around a shared pasture (or "commons") and near the church. Note, too, the outlying fields, which were divided among residents of the town, even though they were often not connected to the land on which they lived. The gray areas of the map illustrate the holdings of a single resident of Sudbury, John Goodnow, whose house was on the common, but whose lands were scattered over a number of areas of Sudbury. (Based on: Sumner Chilton Powell, *Puritan Village: The Formation of a New England Town.* Copyright © 1963 by Wesleyan University.)

• *What aspects of New England life might help explain the clustering of residences at the center of the town?*

together (occasionally entire Puritan congregations who had traveled to the New World as a group).

The structure of the towns reflected the spirit of the covenant. Colonists laid out a village, with houses and a meetinghouse arranged around a central pasture, or "common." They also divided up the outlying fields and woodlands of the town among the residents; the size and location of a family's field depended on the family's numbers, wealth, and social station. But wherever their lands might lie, families generally lived in the village with their neighbors close by, reinforcing the strong sense of community.

Once established, a town was generally able to run its own affairs with little interference from the colonial government.

PURITAN DEMOCRACY
Residents held a yearly "town meeting" to decide important questions and to choose a group of "selectmen," who governed until the next meeting. Only adult males were permitted to participate in the meeting. But even among them, important social distinctions remained, the most crucial of which was membership in the church. Only those residents who could give evidence of grace, of being among the elect (the "visible saints") confident of salvation as a result of a conversion experience, were admitted to full membership. Residents who had not experienced "conversion" could participate in the church through what was known as the "halfway covenant."

The English system of primogeniture—the passing of all inherited property to the firstborn son—did not take root in New England. Instead, a father divided his lands among all his sons. His control of this inheritance was one of the most effective means of exercising power over the male members of his family. Often a son would reach his late twenties before his father would allow him to move into his own household and work his own land. Even then, sons would usually continue to live in close proximity to their fathers. Young women were generally more mobile than their brothers, since they did not stand to inherit land; their dowries and their inheritances consisted instead of movable objects (furniture, household goods, occasionally money or precious objects) and thus did not tie them to a particular place.

As the years passed and the communities grew, the tight-knit social structure of the Puritans experienced strains. This was partly because of the increasing commercialization of New England society. But it was also a result of other pressures that developed even within purely agricultural communities, pressures that were a result primarily of population growth.

As towns grew larger, residents tended to cultivate lands farther and farther from the community center. Some farmers

POPULATION PRESSURE
moved out of the town center to be nearer their lands and thus began to find themselves far away from the church. Outlying residents would often apply for permission to build a church of their own, which was usually the first step toward creation of a new town. Such applications were frequently the occasion for bitter quarrels between the original townspeople and those who proposed to break away.

The dispersion of communities was a result of the practice of distributing land through the patriarchal family structure. In the first generations, fathers generally controlled enough land to satisfy the needs of all their sons. After several generations, however, when such lands were being subdivided for the third or fourth time, there was often too little to go around, particularly in communities surrounded by other towns, with no room to expand outward, forcing younger residents to break off and move elsewhere—at times far away—to form towns of their own where land was more plentiful.

Even within the family, economic necessity often undermined the patriarchal model to which most Puritans, in theory at least, subscribed. It was not only the sons who needed their fathers (as a source of land and wealth); fathers needed their

GENERATIONAL INTERDEPENDENCE
sons, as well as their wives and daughters, as a source of labor to keep the farm and the household functioning. Thus, while in theory men had nearly dictatorial control over their wives and children, in reality relationships were contractual, with the authority of husbands and fathers limited by economic necessity (and, of course, bonds of affection).

THE WITCHCRAFT PHENOMENON

By the late seventeenth century, growth and diversity had begun to undermine the cohesiveness of many New England communities. At times, such tensions could produce bizarre and disastrous events. One example was the widespread hysteria in the 1680s and 1690s over supposed witchcraft in New England.

The most famous outbreak (although by no means the only one) was in Salem, Massachusetts, where adolescent girls

SALEM WITCH TRIALS
began to exhibit strange behavior and leveled accusations of witchcraft against several West Indian servants steeped in voodoo lore. The hysteria they produced spread throughout the town, and before it was over, hundreds of people (most of them women) were accused of witchcraft. As the crisis in Salem grew, accusations shifted from marginal women like the West Indians to prominent and substantial people. Nineteen residents of Salem were put to death before the trials ended in 1692; the girls who had been the original accusers later recanted and admitted that they had made up the story.

The Salem experience was only one of many. Accusations of witchcraft spread through many New England towns in the early 1690s (and indeed had emerged periodically in Puritan society for many years before). Research into the background of accused witches reveals that most were middle-aged women, often widowed, with few or no children. Many accused witches were of low social position, were often involved in domestic conflicts, had frequently been accused of other crimes, and were considered abrasive by their neighbors. Others were women who, through inheritance or enterprise, had come into possession of substantial land and property on their own and hence also challenged the gender norms of the community. Puritan society had little tolerance for

SALEM WITCH TRIALS In his painting *The Trial of George Jacobs, Fifth August 1692*, Tompkins Harrison Matteson (1813–1884) depicts the trial of George Jacobs, who was accused by his granddaughter of practicing witchcraft. At his trial, Jacobs failed to recite the Lord's Prayer—a failure that was interpreted as evidence of his status as sorcerer. He was found guilty and hanged on August 19, 1692. (© Peabody Essex Museum, Salem, Massachusetts, USA/The Bridgeman Art Library)

"independent" women. That so many "witches" were women who were not securely lodged within a male-dominated family structure (and that many seemed openly to defy the passive, submissive norms society had created for them) suggests that tensions over gender roles played a substantial role in generating the crisis.

Above all, however, the witchcraft controversies were a reflection of the highly religious character of these societies. New Englanders believed in the power of Satan and his ability to assert his power in the world. Belief in witchcraft was not a marginal superstition, rejected by the mainstream. It was a common feature of Puritan religious conviction.

CITIES

To call the commercial centers that emerged along the Atlantic coast in the eighteenth century "cities" would be to strain the modern definition of that word. Even the largest colonial community was scarcely bigger than a modern small town. Yet, by the standards of the eighteenth century, cities

GROWTH OF COLONIAL CITIES

did indeed exist in America. By the 1770s the two largest ports–Philadelphia and New York–had populations of 28,000 and 25,000, respectively, which made them larger than most English urban centers. Boston (16,000), Charles Town (later Charleston), South Carolina (12,000), and Newport, Rhode Island (11,000), were also substantial communities by the standards of the day.

Colonial cities served as trading centers for the farmers of their regions and as marts for international trade. Their leaders were generally merchants who had acquired substantial estates. Disparities of wealth were features of almost all communities in America, but in cities they seemed particularly glaring. Moving beside the wealthy merchants were numerous minor tradesmen, workers, and indigents who lived in crowded and often filthy conditions. More than in any other

WEALTH DISTRIBUTION IN COLONIAL CITIES, 1687–1771 Although the gap between rich and poor in colonial America was not as large as it would become in the nineteenth and twentieth centuries, the rise of commerce in the early eighteenth century did produce increasing inequality. This chart shows the distribution of wealth in three important commercial cities—Boston, Philadelphia, and New York. The upper pie charts show the distribution of wealth in the late seventeenth century, and the lower charts show how that distribution had changed by the mid- or late eighteenth century. Note the heavy concentration of wealth in the top 10 percent of the population in the seventeenth century, and the even heavier concentration of wealth in Boston and Philadelphia in the eighteenth century. In New York, by contrast, wealth distribution became slightly more equal between 1695 and 1730, because of the breaking up of the great Dutch estates once the colony came under the control of the British. In later years, New York would show the same pattern of growing inequality that Boston and Philadelphia experienced.

• *What aspects of colonial commerce helped concentrate so much wealth in the hands of a relatively small group?*

area of colonial life (except, of course, in the relationship between masters and slaves), social distinctions were real and visible in urban areas.

Cities were also the centers of much of what industry there was in the colonies, such as ironworks and distilleries for turning imported molasses into exportable rum. And they were the locations of the most advanced schools, the most sophisti-cated cultural activities, and shops where imported goods could be bought. In addition, they were communities with peculiarly urban social problems: crime, vice, pollution, epidemics, traffic. Unlike smaller towns, cities were required to establish elaborate governments. They set up constables' offices and fire departments. They devel-oped systems for supporting the urban poor, whose numbers grew steadily and became especially large in times of eco-nomic crisis.

COMMERCIAL AND CULTURAL IMPORTANCE

Cities were also particularly vulnerable to fluctuations in trade. When a market for a particular product became glut-ted and prices fell, the effects on merchants and other resi-dents could be severe. In the countryside, the impact of economic instability was generally more muted than in cities.

Farmers were still somewhat independent from the larger world of the markets.

Of particular importance for the political future of the colonies, cities became places where new ideas could circu-late and be discussed. Because there were printers, it was possible to have regular newspapers. Books and other publi-cations from abroad introduced new intellectual influences. And the taverns and coffeehouses of cities provided forums in which people could gather and debate the issues of the day. It was not surprising that when the revolutionary crisis began to build in the 1760s and 1770s, it was first visible in the cities.

INEQUALITY

New England, for all its belief in community and liberty, was far from an egalitarian society. "Some must be rich and some poor," John Winthrop wrote early in the seventeenth century, and his prediction perhaps exceeded his expectations. Wealthy families and socially distinguished ones (which were usually the same people) had privileges and rights that were not available to poor citizens. Elites were called "ladies" and "gentleman," while people in the lower levels of society were known as "goodman" or "goodwife." Elites were given the best seats in their churches and had the most influence over the parish. Men had more power than women. Servants had few rights. The church itself taught that inequality reflected God's intention.

In cities, such economic stratification was significant—although, unlike in later eras, the ranks of the richest were the largest group in the population and, in Boston in the eighteenth century, the majority. That was partly because wealthy people were more likely than poor people to move to cities and participate in commerce. In the agricultural countryside, many fewer people accumulated significant wealth.

AWAKENINGS AND ENLIGHTENMENTS

Two powerful forces were competing in American intellectual life in the eighteenth century. One was the traditional outlook of the sixteenth and seventeenth centuries, with its emphasis on a personal God, intimately involved with the world, keeping watch over individual lives. The other was the new spirit of the Enlightenment, a movement sweeping both Europe and America, which stressed the importance of science and human reason. The old views supported such phenomena as the belief in witchcraft, and they placed great value on a stern moral code in which intellect was less important than faith. The Enlightenment, by contrast, suggested that people had substantial control over their own lives and the course of their societies, that the world could be explained and therefore could be structured along rational scientific lines. Much of the intellectual climate of colonial America (and long after) was shaped by the tension between these two impulses.

The Pattern of Religions

Religious toleration flourished in many parts of America to a degree unmatched in any European nation, not because

Roots of Religious Toleration

Americans deliberately sought to produce it but because conditions virtually required it. Settlers in America brought with them so many different religious practices that it proved difficult to impose a single religious code on any large area.

The Church of England was established as the official faith in Virginia, Maryland, New York, the Carolinas, and Georgia. But with few exceptions, the laws establishing the Church of England as the official colonial religion were largely ignored. Even in New England, where the Puritans had originally believed that they were all part of a single faith, there was a growing tendency in the eighteenth century for different congregations to affiliate with different denominations, especially Congregationalism and Presbyterianism. In parts of New York and New Jersey, Dutch settlers had established their own Calvinist denomination, Dutch Reformed, which survived after

SINNERS IN HELL, 1744 This mid-eighteenth-century religious image illustrates both the fears and prejudices of many colonial Christians. The idyllic city of Sion, in the center of the drawing, is threatened on all sides by forces of evil, which include images not just of Satan and sin, but also of some of the perceived enemies of Protestants—the Catholic Church (symbolized by the image of the pope) and Islam (symbolized by Turks). (© The Granger Collection, New York)

the colonies became part of the British Empire. American Baptists (considered to have been introduced to Americans by Roger Williams) developed a great variety of sects. All Baptists shared the belief that rebaptism, usually by total immersion, was necessary when believers reached maturity. But while some Baptists remained Calvinists (believers in predestination), others came to believe in salvation by free will.

Protestants extended toleration to one another more readily than they did to Roman Catholics. Many Protestants in

Anti-Catholicism

America, like many in England, feared and hated the pope. New Englanders, in particular, viewed their Catholic neighbors in New France (Canada) not only as commercial and military rivals but also as dangerous agents of Rome. In most of the English colonies,

THE WITCHCRAFT TRIALS

THE witchcraft trials of the 1690s—which began in Salem, Massachusetts, and spread to other areas of New England—have been the stuff of popular legend for centuries. They have also engaged the interest of generations of historians, who have tried to explain why these seventeenth-century Americans became so committed to the belief that some of their own neighbors were agents of Satan. Although there have been many explanations of the witchcraft phenomenon, some of the most important in recent decades have focused on the central place of women in the story.

Through the first half of the twentieth century, most historians dismissed the witchcraft trials as "hysteria," prompted by the intolerance and rigidity of Puritan society. This interpretation informed perhaps the most prominent popular portrayal of witchcraft in the twentieth century: Arthur Miller's play *The Crucible,* first produced in 1953, which was clearly an effort to use the Salem trials as a comment on the great anticommunist frenzy of his own time. But at almost the same time, the renowned scholar of Puritanism Perry Miller argued in a series of important studies that belief in witchcraft was not a product of hysteria or intolerance but, rather, a widely shared part of the religious worldview of the seventeenth century. To the Puritans, witchcraft seemed not only plausible, but scientifically rational as well.

A new wave of interpretation of witchcraft began in the 1970s, with the publication of *Salem Possessed* (1976), by Paul Boyer and Stephen Nissenbaum. Their examination of the town records of Salem in the 1690s led them to conclude that the witchcraft controversy there was a product of class tensions between the poor, marginal residents of one part of Salem and the wealthy, privileged residents of another. These social tensions, which could not find easy expression on their own terms, led some poor Salemites to lash out at their rich neighbors by charging them, or their servants, with witchcraft. A few years later, John Demos, in *Entertaining Satan* (1983), examined witchcraft accusations in a larger area of New England and similarly portrayed them as products of displaced anger about social and economic grievances that could not be expressed otherwise. Demos provided a far more complex picture of the nature of these grievances than had Boyer and Nissenbaum but, like them, saw witchcraft as a symptom of a persistent set of social and psychological tensions.

At about the same time, however, a number of scholars were beginning to look at witchcraft through the scholarly lens of gender. Carol Karlsen's *The Devil in the Shape of a Woman* (1987) demonstrated

---

however, Roman Catholics were too few to cause serious conflict. They were most numerous in Maryland, and even there they numbered no more than 3,000. Perhaps for that reason they suffered their worst persecution in that colony. After the overthrow of the original proprietors in 1691, Catholics in Maryland not only lost their political rights but also were forbidden to hold religious services except in private houses.

Jews in provincial America totaled no more than about 2,000 at any time. The largest community lived in New York City. Smaller groups settled in Newport and Charles Town, and there were scattered Jewish families in all the colonies. Nowhere could they vote or hold office. Only in Rhode Island could they practice their religion openly.

By the beginning of the eighteenth century, some Americans were growing troubled by the apparent decline in religious piety in their society. The movement of the population westward and the wide scattering of settlements had caused many communities to lose touch with organized religion. The rise of commercial prosperity created a secular outlook in urban areas. The progress of science and free thought in Europe–and the importation of Enlightenment ideas to America–caused at least some colonists to doubt traditional religious beliefs.

Concerns about weakening piety surfaced as early as the 1660s in New England, where the Puritan oligarchy warned of a decline in the power of the church. Sabbath after Sabbath, ministers preached sermons of

JEREMIADS

despair (known as "jeremiads"), deploring the signs of waning piety. By the standards of other societies or other eras, the Puritan faith remained remarkably strong. But New Englanders measured their faith by their own standards, and to them the "declension" of religious piety seemed a serious problem.

THE GREAT AWAKENING

By the early eighteenth century, concerns about declining piety and growing secularism were emerging in other regions and among members of other faiths. The result was the first major American revival: the Great Awakening.

The Great Awakening began in earnest in the 1730s, reached its climax in the 1740s, and brought a new spirit of religious fervor to the colonies. The revival had particular appeal to women (who constituted the majority of converts) and to younger sons of the third or fourth generation of settlers–those who stood to inherit the least land and who faced the most uncertain futures. The rhetoric of the revival emphasized the potential for every person to break away from the constraints of the past and start anew in his or her relationship with God. Such beliefs may have reflected the desires of many people to break away from their families or communities and start a new life.

Powerful evangelists from England helped spread the revival. John and Charles Wesley, the founders of Methodism, visited Georgia and other colonies in the 1730s. George through intensive scrutiny of records across New England that a disproportionate number of those accused of witchcraft were property-owning widows or unmarried women—in other words, women who did not fit comfortably into the normal pattern of male-dominated families. Karlsen concluded that such women were vulnerable to these accusations because they seemed threatening to people (including many women) who were accustomed to women as subordinate members of the community.

Mary Beth Norton's *In the Devil's Snare* (2002) placed the witchcraft trials in the context of other events of their time—particularly in the terrifying upheavals and dislocations that the Indian wars of the late seventeenth century created in Puritan communities. In the face of this crisis, in which refugees from King William's War were fleeing towns destroyed by the Indians and flooding Salem and other eastern towns, fear and social instability helped create a more-than-normal readiness to connect aberrant behavior (such as the actions of unusually independent or eccentric women) to supernatural causes. The result was a wave of witchcraft accusations that

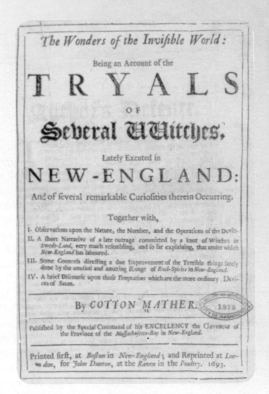

(The Library of Congress (LC-USZ62-51641))

ultimately led to the execution of at least twenty people, mostly women. ●

HISTORICAL ARGUMENTATION AND INTERPRETATION

Questions assume cumulative content knowledge from this chapter and previous chapters.

1. Briefly describe how historical interpretations of the witchcraft trials of the New England colonies in the 17th century have changed over time. Identify the different scholarly "lenses" through which the historical phenomenon (ie. the witchcraft trials) has been viewed.
2. More fully describe the interpretations of three of the historians discussed, and offer one piece of historical evidence supporting that interpretation.
3. With which historical interpretation do you tend to agree? Explain why, using historical evidence.

Whitefield, a powerful open-air preacher and for a time an associate of the Wesleys, made several evangelizing tours through the colonies and drew tremendous crowds. But the outstanding preacher of the Great Awakening was the New England Congregationalist Jonathan Edwards, a deeply orthodox Puritan but a highly original theologian. From his pulpit in Northampton, Massachusetts, Edwards attacked the new doctrines of easy salvation for all. He preached anew the traditional Puritan ideas of the absolute sovereignty of God, predestination, and salvation by God's grace alone. His vivid descriptions of hell could terrify his listeners.

The Great Awakening led to the division of congregations between "New Light" revivalists and "Old Light" traditionalists. It also affected areas of society outside the churches. Some of

OLD LIGHTS AND NEW LIGHTS

the revivalists denounced book learning as a hindrance to salvation, and some communities repudiated secular education. But other evangelists saw education as a means of furthering religion, and they founded or led schools for the training of New Light ministers.

THE ENLIGHTENMENT

The Great Awakening caused one great upheaval in the culture of the colonies. The Enlightenment, a very different—and in many ways competing—phenomenon, caused another.

The Enlightenment was largely the product of some of the great scientific and intellectual discoveries in seventeenth-century Europe. As scientists and other thinkers discovered natural laws that they believed regulated the workings of nature, they came to celebrate the power of human reason and scientific inquiry. Enlightenment thinkers argued that reason, not just faith, could create progress and advance knowledge. They argued that humans had a moral sense on which they could rely to tell the difference between right and wrong—that they did not need always to turn to God for guidance in making decisions. They insisted that men and women could, through the power of their own reason, move civilization to ever-greater heights.

In celebrating reason, the Enlightenment slowly helped undermine the power of traditional authority—something the Great Awakening did as well. But unlike the Great Awakening, the Enlightenment encouraged men and women to look to themselves—not to God—for guidance as to how to live their

TRADITIONAL AUTHORITY CHALLENGED

lives and to shape society. Enlightenment thought, with its emphasis on human rationality, encouraged a new emphasis on education and a heightened interest in politics and government (for through governments, the believers in reason argued, society had its best chance of bettering itself). Most Enlightenment figures did not challenge religion and insisted that rational inquiry would support, not undermine,

PATTERNS OF POPULAR CULTURE

COLONIAL ALMANACS

BOOKS were scarce and expensive in colonial America, and many families owned only one: the Bible. But starting very early in the life of the English colonies, men and women had another important source of information: almanacs, the most popular nonreligious literature in early America.

Almanacs first appeared in America in 1638 or 1639 when printers in Cambridge, Massachusetts, began publishing the *Philomath Almanac*, which combined an elaborate calendar of religious holidays with information about astronomy, astrology, and other popular interests. By the 1680s, the *Farmer's Almanac*, a heavily illustrated publication that added medical advice, practical wisdom, navigational information, and humor, began to rival the *Philomath*. Through a combination of superstition, popular folklore, and astronomical (and astrological) devices, the *Farmer's Almanac* also predicted weather patterns throughout the year, crop yields, and many other things. Almanac predictions were notoriously unreliable, but many people relied on them nevertheless.

By 1700, there were dozens, perhaps hundreds, of almanacs circulating throughout the colonies and even in the sparsely settled lands to the west and north. The most popular almanacs sold tens of thousands of copies every year. Most families had at least one, and many had several. "It is easy to prove," one almanac writer claimed in the mid-eighteenth century, "that no book we read (except the Bible) is so much valued and so serviceable to the community." America was a multilingual society, and although most almanacs were in English, some appeared in French, Dutch, Hebrew, Norwegian, Spanish, German, and various Indian languages. For five years just after the Revolution, Benjamin Banneker of Maryland was the only African American almanac writer, publishing a book that occasionally included harsh commentary on slavery and the slave trade.

The best-known almanac in the colonies in the years before the American Revolution was *Poor Richard's Almanack*, published in Philadelphia by Benjamin Franklin under the pseudonym Richard Saunders. "I endeavor'd to make it both entertaining and useful," Franklin later wrote in his autobiography. "And observing that it was generally read, . . . I consider'd it as a proper vehicle for conveying instruction among the common people, who bought scarcely any other books." In issue after issue, Franklin accompanied his calendars, astronomical information, and other standard almanac fare with "proverbial sentences, chiefly such as inculcated industry and frugality." Poor Richard's many sayings became among the most familiar passages in America. Franklin was among many writers who used the almanac to promote the new scientific discoveries of his time and to try to discredit what he considered the backward superstitions standing in the way of knowledge.

Almanacs were the only widely read publications in America that contained popular humor, and they are one of the best sources today for understanding what early Americans considered funny. Not unlike later generations, they delighted in humor that ridiculed the high and mighty (aristocrats, lawyers, clergymen, politicians), made fun of relationships between men and women, and expressed stereotypes about racial and ethnic groups. In the 1760s and 1770s, almanac humor was often used to disguise political ideas, in the way it ridiculed British officials and American Tories. During the war itself, humorous anecdotes about military officers and political leaders reflected the uneasy views of Americans about the long and difficult struggle.

During and after the Revolution, much almanac humor consisted of admiring anecdotes about the man who was by then perhaps the most famous and beloved man in

---

Christianity. But they challenged the notion of some religious groups that the answer to all questions about human society should, or could, come directly from God.

In the early seventeenth century, Enlightenment ideas in America were largely borrowed from abroad—from such earlier giants as Francis Bacon and John Locke, and from more contemporary Enlightenment thinkers in England and Scotland. Few Americans had yet made important contributions of their own to the new age of science and reason. Later, however, such Americans as Benjamin Franklin, Thomas Jefferson, Thomas Paine, and James Madison made their own contributions to the Enlightenment tradition.

EDUCATION

Even before Enlightenment ideas became common in America, colonists had placed a high value on education, despite the difficulties they confronted in gaining access to it. Some families tried to teach their children to read and write at home, although the heavy burden of work in most agricultural households limited the time available for schooling. In Massachusetts, a 1647 law required every town to support a public school, and while many communities failed to comply, a modest network of educational establishments emerged as a result. Elsewhere, the Quakers and other sects operated church schools. And in some communities, widows or unmarried women conducted "dame schools" by holding private classes in their homes. In cities, master craftsmen set up evening schools for their apprentices; at least a hundred such schools appeared between 1723 and 1770.

Only a relatively small number of children received education beyond the primary level; but white male Americans, at least, achieved a high degree of literacy. By the time of the Revolution, well over half of all white men could read and write, a rate substantially higher than in most European countries. The large number of colonists who could read helped create a market for the first widely circulated publications in America other than the Bible: almanacs (see "Patterns of Popular Culture," above). The literacy rate of women lagged behind that of men until the nineteenth century; and while opportunities for education beyond primary school were scarce for males, they were almost nonexistent for females. Nevertheless, in their early years

HIGH WHITE LITERACY RATES

Kind Katharine to her husband kiss'd these words,
'Mine own sweet Will, how dearly I love thee!
If true (quoth Will) the World no such affords,
And that its true I durst his warrant be;
For ne'er heard I of Woman good or ill,
But always loved best, her own sweet Will.

POOR RICHARD'S ALMANACK This page from a 1757 edition of Poor Richard's Almanack illustrates the wide range of material that almanacs presented to their readers—an uplifting poem, a calendar of holidays and weather predictions, and such scattered pieces of advice and wisdom as "A rich rogue is like a fat hog, who never does good till as dead as a log." (© Fotosearch/Getty Images)

TOWN AND COUNTRY-MAN'S ALMANACK As the population of colonial cities and towns grew, almanacs—originally targeted mainly at farmers—began to make explicit appeal to townspeople as well. (© Universal Images Group/Getty Images)

America—Poor Richard himself, Benjamin Franklin. Much less reverential, and probably funnier to readers, was the often-ribald ethnic and racial humor in almanacs. In *Beer's Almanac* of 1801, an Irishman boasted that he had owned a large estate in Ireland before leaving for America. Why, he was asked, had he left it to come to the United States? "Ah," he replied, "It was indeed under a small encumbrance; for another man's land lay right a top of it."

Almanacs remained enormously popular throughout the nineteenth century, and some are still published today. But they had their greatest influence in the early years of European settlement when, for thousands of Americans, they were virtually the only source of printed information available. "A good Almanac," the printer Isaac Briggs wrote in 1798, in a preface to one of his own, "is, like iron, far more valuable (although much less valued) than gold, if we estimate its value by its absolute usefulness to the common purposes of life." ●

UNDERSTAND, ANALYZE, AND EVALUATE

1. Why were almanacs so popular in colonial America?
2. What can almanacs tell us about life in colonial America?
3. The *Farmer's Almanac* is still popular today, distributing more than 4 million copies a year. Why do you think it continues to be popular?

colonial girls often received the same home-based education as boys, and their literacy rate too was substantially higher than that of their European counterparts. African slaves had virtually no access to education. Occasionally a master or mistress would teach slave children to read and write, but they had few real incentives to do so. Indeed, as the slave system became firmly entrenched, strong social (and ultimately legal) sanctions developed to discourage any efforts to promote black literacy, lest it encourage slaves to question their station. Indians, too, remained largely outside the white educational system—to a large degree by choice; most tribes preferred to educate their children in their own way. But some white missionaries and philanthropists established schools for Native Americans and helped create a small but significant population of Indians literate in spoken and written English.

Nowhere was the intermingling of the influences of traditional religiosity and the new spirit of the Enlightenment clearer than in the colleges and universities that grew up in colonial America. Of the six colleges in operation by 1763, all but two were founded by religious groups primarily for the training of preachers. Yet in almost all, the influences of the new scientific, rational approach to knowledge could be felt. Harvard, the first American college, was established in 1636 by the General Court (legislature) of Massachusetts at the behest of Puritan theologians, who wanted to create a training center for ministers. The college was named for a Charlestown minister, John Harvard, who had died and left his library and half his estate to the college. Decades later, in 1693, William and Mary College (named for the English king and queen) was established in Williamsburg, Virginia, by Anglicans; like Harvard, it was conceived as an academy to train clergymen. In 1701, conservative Congregationalists, dissatisfied with what they considered the growing religious liberalism of Harvard, founded Yale (named for one of its first benefactors, Elihu Yale) in New Haven, Connecticut. Out of the Great Awakening emerged the College of New Jersey, founded in 1746 and known later as Princeton (after the town in which it is located). One of its first presidents was Jonathan Edwards.

Despite the religious basis of these colleges, students at most of them could derive something of a secular education from the curricula, which included not only theology, but logic, ethics,

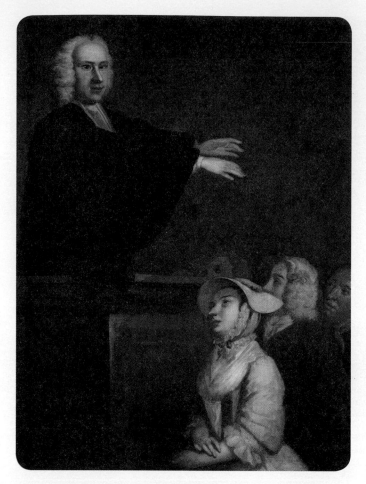

GEORGE WHITEFIELD Whitefield succeeded John Wesley as leader of the Calvinist Methodists in Oxford, England. Like Wesley, he was a major force in promoting religious revivalism in both England and America. He made his first missionary journey to the New World in 1738 and returned in the mid-1740s for a celebrated journey through the colonies that helped spark the Great Awakening. (© Francis G. Mayer/Corbis)

A "DAME SCHOOL" PRIMER More than the residents of any other region of North America (and far more than those of most of Europe), the New England colonists strove to educate their children and achieved perhaps the highest level of literacy in the world. Throughout the region, young children attended institutions known as "dame schools" (because the teachers were almost always women) and learned from primers like this one. Puritan education emphasized both basic skills (the alphabet and reading) and moral and religious precepts, as this sample page suggests. (© American Antiquarian Society)

physics, geometry, astronomy, rhetoric, Latin, Hebrew, and Greek as well. From the beginning, Harvard attempted not only to provide an educated ministry but also to "advance learning and perpetuate it to posterity." Members of the Harvard faculty made strenuous efforts to desseminate new scientific ideas—particularly the ideas of Copernican astronomy—to a larger public, often publishing their ideas in popular almanacs. By doing so, they hoped to stamp out popular belief in astrology, which they considered pagan superstition.

LIBERAL CURRICULA

King's College, founded in New York in 1754 and later renamed Columbia, was even more devoted to the spread of secular knowledge. Although it was founded in part by the Anglican Trinity Church in New York, it had no theological faculty and was interdenominational from the start. The Academy and College of Philadelphia, which became the University of Pennsylvania, was a completely secular institution, founded in 1755 by a group of laymen under the inspiration of Benjamin Franklin. It offered courses in utilitarian subjects—mechanics, chemistry, agriculture, government, commerce, and modern languages—as well as in the liberal arts. It also became the site of the first medical school in British America, founded in 1765.

THE SPREAD OF SCIENCE

The clearest indication of the spreading influence of the Enlightenment in America was an increasing interest in scientific knowledge. Most of the early colleges established chairs in the natural sciences and introduced some of the advanced scientific theories of Europe, including Copernican astronomy and Newtonian physics, to their students.

But the most vigorous promotion of science in these years occurred outside the colleges, through the private efforts of amateurs and the activities of scientific societies. Leading merchants, planters, and even theologians became corresponding members of the Royal Society of London, the leading English scientific organization. Benjamin Franklin, the most celebrated amateur scientist in America, won international fame through his experimental proof of the nature of lightning and electricity and his invention of the lightning rod. His 1752 demonstration, using a kite, of his theory that lightning and electricity were the same was widely celebrated in the colonies.

The high value that influential Americans were beginning to place on scientific knowledge was clearly demonstrated by the most daring and controversial scientific experiment of the eighteenth century: inoculation against smallpox. The Puritan theologian Cotton Mather heard, reportedly from his own slave, of the practice of deliberately infecting people with mild cases of smallpox in order to immunize them against the deadly disease. He learned, too, that experiments in inoculation were being conducted, with some success, in England. Mather was not,

SMALLPOX INOCULATION

BENJAMIN FRANKLIN ON ELECTRICITY The discovery of electricity was one of the great scientific events of the eighteenth century, even though large-scale practical use of electrical energy emerged much later. Benjamin Franklin was one of the first Americans, and certainly the most famous one, to experiment with electricity. This is the frontispiece for a book, originally published in 1750 in Philadelphia, that describes his "experiments and observations." The pages shown here are from the London edition, which appeared in 1774. (© Getty Images)

certainly, a wholly committed scientist. He continued to believe that disease was a punishment for sin. Yet, despite strong opposition from many of his neighbors, he urged inoculation on his fellow Bostonians during an epidemic in the 1720s. The results confirmed the effectiveness of the technique. Other theologians (including Jonathan Edwards) took up the cause, along with many physicians. By the mid-eighteenth century, inoculation had become a common medical procedure in America.

CONCEPTS OF LAW AND POLITICS

In seventeenth- and eighteenth-century law and politics, as in other parts of their lives, Americans of European descent believed that they were re-creating in the New World the practices and institutions of the Old. But as in other areas, they managed to create something very different.

Changes in the law in America resulted in part from the scarcity of English-trained lawyers, who were almost unknown in the colonies **COLONIAL LEGAL SYSTEM** until after 1700. Not until well into the eighteenth century did

The ducking stool was a common punishment for scolds in all the American colonies, save in New England.

PUNISHMENT IN NEW ENGLAND New England communities prescribed a wide range of punishments for misconduct and crime in the seventeenth and eighteenth centuries. Among the more common punishments were public humiliations—placing offenders in stocks, forcing them to wear badges of shame, or, as in this woodcut, publicly ducking them in a stream or pond to create both discomfort and embarrassment. (© Fotosearch/Getty Images) authorities in England try to impose the common law and the statutes of the realm upon the provinces. By then, it was already too late. Although the American legal system adopted most of the essential elements of the English system, including such ancient rights as trial by jury, significant differences had already become well established. Pleading and court procedures were simpler in America than in England, and punishments were different. Instead of the gallows or prison, colonists more commonly resorted to the whipping post, the branding iron, the stocks, and (for "gossipy" women) the ducking stool. In a labor-scarce society, it was not in the interests of communities to execute or incarcerate potential workers. Crimes were redefined. In England, a printed attack on a public official, whether true or false, was considered libelous. In the 1734–1735 trial of the New York publisher John Peter Zenger, who was powerfully defended by the Philadelphia lawyer Andrew Hamilton, the courts ruled that criticisms of the government were not libelous if factually true—a verdict that removed some restrictions on the freedom of the press: there was a subtle but decisive transformation in legal philosophy. Some colonists came to think of law as a reflection of the divine will; others saw it as a result of the natural order. In neither case did they consider it an expression of the power of an earthly sovereign.

Even more significant for the future of the relationship between the colonies and England were important differences between the American and British political systems. Because the

COLONIAL GOVERNMENTS royal government was so far away, Americans created a group of institutions of their own that gave them—in reality, if not in theory—a

large measure of self-government. In most colonies, local communities grew accustomed to running their own affairs with minimal interference from higher authorities. Communities also expected to maintain strict control over their delegates to the colonial assemblies, and those assemblies came to exercise many of the powers that Parliament exercised in England (even though in theory Parliament remained the ultimate authority in America). Provincial governors appointed by the Crown had broad powers on paper, but in fact their influence was sharply limited. They lacked control over appointments and contracts; such influence resided largely in England or with local colonial leaders. They could never be certain of their tenure in office; because governorships were patronage appointments, a governor could be removed any time his patron in England lost favor. And in many cases, governors were not even familiar with the colonies they were meant to govern. Some governors were native-born Americans, but most were Englishmen who came to the colonies for the first time to assume their offices. The result of all this was that the focus of politics in the colonies became a local one. The provincial governments became accustomed to acting more or less independently of Parliament, and a set of assumptions and expectations about the rights of the colonists began to take hold in America that policymakers in England did not share. These differences caused few problems before the 1760s, because the British did little to exert the authority they believed they possessed. But when, beginning in 1763, the English government began attempting to tighten its control over the American colonies, a great imperial crisis developed.

AP CONNECTING THEMES

Chapter 3 discussed the development of colonial society in each of the colonial regions. You should be able to compare and contrast the colonial regions in terms of the role of women, class structure, and social mobility. Particularly important are the reasons for and consequences of a forced labor system. You should also keep in mind similarities and differences in governmental structures, economic systems, and culture throughout the colonies, including the impact of science, technology, and education on each colonial region. Finally, be able to explain the reasons for and sources of population growth in the colonies.

The following themes have a heightened importance in Chapter 3. You should now be able to do the following for each listed theme:

Identity: Identify the factors that led to distinct colonial regional identities. Identify how differing roles for women affected their identity.

Work, exchange, and technology: Explain how technology, science, and education affected the economies of various colonial regions. Explain the reason for and consequences of the growth of the institution of slavery.

Peopling: Identify the impact of free and forced migration on the development of regional cultural, economic, and social systems.

Politics and power: Analyze the impact of cooperation and conflict between different social groups on the formation of colonial governments.

America in the World: Explain how the growth of the colonial economy created both continuity and change in relationships among the nations of the Atlantic World.

Ideas, beliefs, and cultures: Analyze the reasons for regional differences in ideas, beliefs, and culture. Explain how the ideas, beliefs, and cultures of colonists influenced the development of regional differences.

AP SUGGESTED STUDY

PEOPLE/PLACES/EVENTS As you study these items, think about how they demonstrate or relate to key concepts and historical themes from this chapter and previous chapters.

AP TEST PRACTICE

Questions assume cumulative content knowledge from this chapter and previous chapters.

MULTIPLE CHOICE Use the images "A 'Dame School' Primer" and "Benjamin Franklin on Electricity" from pages 94-95 and your knowledge of U.S. history to answer questions 1-2.

1. Which is best supported by the two artifacts, regarding cultural values in the North American English colonies by the early to mid-18th century?

   (A) Education was valued solely as a means to advance theology

   (B) Almost all intellectuals in the colonies began to reject traditional religious values.

   (C) Enlightenment influences were in strict conflict with traditional religious values.

   (D) Traditional religiosity intermingled with Enlightenment influences.

2. Which best explains how values reflected by the artifacts might have influenced future American colonial conflict with Great Britain?

   (A) The greater literacy rates in the colonies undermined reverence for British authority and culture.

   (B) Value placed on education, combined with Enlightenment ideas of the role of human reason in improving society, led to greater public engagement in politics.

   (C) The spread of Enlightenment ideas threatening traditional religious values led to social anxiety, spreading a culture of discontent.

   (D) Greater literacy rates and the spread of secular knowledge promoted greater class distinctions.

SHORT ANSWER Use your knowledge of U.S. history to answer questions 3-5.

3. Answer a, b, and c.

   a) Briefly explain ONE example of how the growth of colonial economies affected relationships among nations within the "Atlantic World."

   b) Briefly explain a SECOND example of how the growth of colonial economies affected relationships among nations within the "Atlantic World."

   c) Briefly explain ONE example of how interactions within the "Atlantic World" promoted Anglicization in the British colonies in North America.

4. Answer a, b, and c.

   a) Briefly explain ONE example of regional differences in the patterns of family life and attitudes toward women in the English colonies in 17th and early 18th centuries.

   b) Briefly explain ONE example of how changes in science and technology in the 17th and early 18th centuries affected regional development within the British colonies.

   c) Briefly explain ONE example of how free and forced migration affected regional development within the British colonies in the 17th and early 18th centuries.

5. Using the painting on page 82, answer a, b, and c.

   a) What does the painting suggest about the nature of the North American colonies' cultural relationship with England during the early to mid-18th century?

   b) Provide ONE example that could be used to support that view.

   c) Provide ONE example that could be used to refute that view.

LONG ESSAY Develop a thoughtful and thorough historical argument that answers the question below. Begin your essay with a thesis statement and support it with relevant historical evidence.

6. Some historians have argued that the intellectual and social culture of British colonial America did not greatly diverge from the intellectual and social life of England. Support, modify, or refute this interpretation, providing specific evidence to justify your answer.

4 | THE EMPIRE IN TRANSITION

LA DESTRUCTION DE LA STATUE ROYALE A NOUVELLE YORCK.

Die Zerstorung der Koniglichen Bild Saule zu Neu Yorck | La Destruction de la Statue royale a Nouvelle Yorck

TOPPLING GEORGE III
In the immediate aftermath of the Declaration of Independence, patriots in New York pulled down a statue of King George III from its pedestal in the center of the city. Among those pulling down the statue were a number of African Americans—both free blacks and slaves. This print is a French illustration of the event, with captions in both French and German. (The Library of Congress (ppmsca-17521))

AP

HISTORICAL THINKING

1. **Contextualization** In which ways did the Seven Years' War change the balance of power in North America and throughout the world?

2. **Historical Argumentation** To what degree and in which ways did British attempts to reassert control over the colonies contribute to the colonial revolt?

3. **Periodization** Explain the chronological sequence of British acts intended to increase imperial control over the colonies and the colonist's reaction to those attempts.

4. **Appropriate Use of Relevant Historical Evidence** Describe the influence of philosophical principles on the American Revolution.

5. **Contextualization** Explain the reason for discontent among backcountry colonists and the manifestations of that discontent.

6. **Contextualization** Explain the position of American Indian tribes in the French and Indian War and assess why they took that position.

Key Concept Correlations

Analyze the ways the historical developments you learn about in this chapter connect to the following AP Key Concepts.

2.2 European colonization efforts in North America stimulated intercultural contact and intensified conflict between the various groups of colonizers and native peoples.

2.3 The increasing political, economic, and cultural exchanges within the "Atlantic World" had a profound impact on the development of colonial societies in North America.

3.1 Britain's victory over France in the imperial struggle for North America led to new conflicts among the British government, the North American colonists, and American Indians, culminating in the creation of a new nation, the United States.

3.2 In the late 18th century, new experiments with democratic ideas and republican forms of government, as well as other new religious, economic, and cultural ideas, challenged traditional imperial systems across the Atlantic World.

3.3 Migration within North America, cooperative interaction, and competition for resources raised questions about boundaries and policies, intensified conflicts among peoples and nations, and led to contests over the creation of a multiethnic, multiracial national identity.

Thematic Learning Objectives

ID-1, 4, 5; POL-1, 2; ENV-1, 2, 4; WXT-1, 2, 6; CUL-1, 2, 4; WOR-1, 2

CHAPTER 4 deals with the French and Indian War, which is a part of the Seven Years' War, and its impact on the relationship between Great Britain and the colonies. The war brought to the forefront colonial noncompliance with the mercantile system and the British perception of how the colonies should be behaving. Also, saddled with a huge debt from the Seven Years' War, the British government looked to the colonies for revenue. You should focus on specific British attempts to increase imperial control over the colonies and the colonial reaction to those attempts. You should also take note of the philosophical principles influencing the colonists as well as the discontent among the colonists themselves and the consequences of that discontent. Finally, it is important to understand the reasons for shifting alliances between American Indians and the colonists and Great Britain. As you read, evaluate the following ideas:

- American Indians continuously adjusted their alliances with European powers during the 18th century.
- British attempts to assert control over the colonies led to organized, violent resistance.
- The Enlightenment and the First Great Awakening led to new experiments in democratic and republican forms of government and led to increased questioning of authority.

LOOSENING TIES

After the Glorious Revolution of 1688 in England and the collapse of the Dominion of New England in America, the English government (which became the British government after 1707, when a union of England and Scotland created Great Britain) made no serious or sustained effort to tighten its control over the colonies for over seventy years. During those years, an increasing number of colonies were brought under the direct control of the king. New Jersey in 1702, North and South Carolina in 1729, Georgia in 1754—all became royal colonies, bringing the total to eight; in all of them, the king had the power to appoint the governors and other colonial officials. During those years, Parliament also passed new laws supplementing the original Navigation Acts and strengthening the mercantilist program—laws restricting colonial manufactures, prohibiting paper currency, and regulating trade. On the whole, however, the British government remained uncertain and divided about the extent to which it ought to interfere in colonial affairs. The colonies were left, within broad limits, to go their separate ways.

A TRADITION OF NEGLECT

In the fifty years after the Glorious Revolution, the British Parliament established a growing supremacy over the king. During the reigns of George I (1714-1727) and George II (1727-1760),

GROWING POWER OF PARLIAMENT both of whom were German born and unaccustomed to English ways, the prime minister and his cabinet ministers began to become the nation's real executives. They held their positions not by the king's favor but by their ability to control a majority in Parliament.

These parliamentary leaders were less inclined than the seventeenth-century monarchs had been to try to tighten imperial organization. They depended heavily on the support of the great merchants and landholders, most of whom feared that any such experiments would require large expenditures, increase taxes, and diminish the profits they were earning from the colonial trade. The first of the modern prime ministers, Robert Walpole, deliberately refrained from strict enforcement of the Navigation Acts, believing that relaxed trading restrictions would stimulate commerce.

Meanwhile, the day-to-day administration of colonial affairs remained decentralized and inefficient. There was no colonial office in London. The nearest equivalent was the Board of Trade and Plantations, established in 1696—a mere advisory body that had little role in any actual decisions. Real authority rested in the Privy Council (the central administrative agency for the government as a whole), the admiralty, and the treasury. But those agencies were responsible for administering

DECENTRALIZED COLONIAL ADMINISTRATION laws at home as well as overseas; none could concentrate on colonial affairs. To complicate matters further, there was considerable overlapping and confusion of authority among the departments.

Few of the London officials, moreover, had ever visited America; few knew very much about conditions there. What information they did gather came in large part from agents sent to England by the colonial assemblies to lobby for American interests. These agents, naturally, did nothing to encourage interference with colonial affairs. (The best known of them, Benjamin Franklin, represented not only his own colony, Pennsylvania, but also Georgia, New Jersey, and Massachusetts.)

It was not only the weakness of administrative authority in London and the policy of neglect that weakened England's hold on the colonies. It was also the character of the royal officials in America–among them the governors, the collectors of customs, and naval officers. Some of these officeholders were able and intelligent; most were not. Appointments generally came as the result of bribery or favoritism, not as a reward for merit. Many appointees remained in England and, with part of their salaries, hired substitutes to take their places in America. Such deputies received paltry wages and thus faced great temptations to augment their incomes with bribes. Few resisted the temptation. Customs collectors, for example, routinely waived duties on goods when merchants paid them to do so. Even honest and well-paid officials usually found it expedient, if they wanted to get along with their neighbors, to yield to the colonists' resistance to trade restrictions.

Resistance to imperial authority centered in the colonial legislatures. By the 1750s, the American assemblies had claimed the right to levy taxes, make appropriations, approve appointments, and pass laws for their respective colonies.

POWERFUL COLONIAL LEGISLATURES Their legislation was subject to veto by the governor or the Privy Council. But the assemblies had leverage over the governor through their control of the colonial budget, and they could circumvent the Privy Council by repassing disallowed laws in slightly altered form. The assemblies came to look upon themselves as little parliaments, each practically as sovereign within its colony as Parliament itself was in England.

THE COLONIES DIVIDED

Despite their frequent resistance to the authority of London, the colonists continued to think of themselves as loyal English subjects. In many respects, in fact, they felt stronger ties to England than they did to one another. "Fire and water," an English traveler wrote, "are not more heterogeneous than the different colonies in North America." New Englanders and Virginians viewed each other as something close to foreigners. A Connecticut man denounced the merchants of New York for their "frauds and unfair practices," while a New Yorker condemned Connecticut because of the "low craft

AN APPEAL FOR COLONIAL UNITY This sketch, one of the first American editorial cartoons, appeared in Benjamin Franklin's Philadelphia newspaper, the *Pennsylvania Gazette*, on May 9, 1754. It was meant to illustrate the need for intercolonial unity and, in particular, for the adoption of Franklin's Albany Plan. (The Library of Congress (LC-USZC4-5315))

and cunning so incident to the people of that country." Only an accident of geography, it seemed, connected these disparate societies to one another.

Yet, for all their differences, the colonies could scarcely avoid forging connections with one another. The growth of the colonial population produced an almost continuous line of settlement along the seacoast and led to the gradual construction of roads and the rise of intercolonial trade. The colonial postal service helped increase communication. In 1691, it had operated only from Massachusetts to New York and Pennsylvania. In 1711, it extended to New Hampshire in the North; in 1732, to Virginia in the South; and ultimately, all the way to Georgia.

Still, the colonists were loath to cooperate even when, in 1754, they faced a common threat from their old rivals, the

ALBANY PLAN French, and France's Indian allies. A conference of colonial leaders–with delegates from Pennsylvania, Maryland, New York, and New England–was meeting in Albany in that year to negotiate a treaty with the Iroquois, as the British government had advised the colonists to do. The delegates stayed on to talk about forming a colonial federation for defense against the Indians. Benjamin Franklin proposed, and the delegates tentatively approved, a plan by which Parliament would set up in America "one general government" for all the colonies (except Georgia and Nova Scotia). Each colony would "retain its present constitution," but would grant to the new general government such powers as the authority to govern all relations with the Indians. The central government would have a "president general" appointed and paid by the king (just as colonial governors were) and a legislature (a "grand council") elected by the colonial assemblies.

War with the French and Indians was already beginning when this Albany Plan was presented to the colonial assemblies. None approved it. "Everyone cries, a union is necessary," Franklin wrote to the Massachusetts governor, "but when they come to the manner and form of the union, their weak noodles are perfectly distracted."

THE STRUGGLE FOR
THE CONTINENT

In the late 1750s and early 1760s, a great war raged through North America, changing forever the balance of power both on the continent and throughout much of the world. The war in America was part of a titanic struggle between England and France for dominance in world trade and naval power. The British victory in that struggle, known in Europe as the Seven Years' War, rearranged global power and cemented England's role as the world's great commercial and imperial nation. It also cemented its control of most of the settled regions of North America.

In America, however, the conflict was the final stage in a long battle among the three principal powers in northeastern North America: the English, the French, and the Iroquois. For more than a century prior to the conflict known in America as the French and Indian War, these three groups had maintained an uneasy balance of power. The events of the 1750s upset that balance, produced a prolonged and open conflict, and established a precarious dominance for the English societies throughout the region.

AN UNEASY BALANCE OF POWER

The French and Indian War was important to the English colonists in America for another reason as well. By bringing the Americans into closer contact with British authority than ever before, it raised to the surface some of the underlying tensions in the colonial relationship.

NEW FRANCE AND THE IROQUOIS NATION

The French and the English had coexisted peacefully in North America for nearly a century. But by the 1750s, religious and commercial tensions began to produce new conflicts. The crisis began in part because of the expansion of the French presence in America in the late seventeenth century—a result of Louis XIV's search for national unity and increased world power. The lucrative fur trade drew immigrant French peasants deeper into the wilderness, while missionary zeal drew large numbers of French Jesuits into the interior in search of potential converts. The bottomlands of the Mississippi River valley attracted French farmers discouraged by the short growing season in Canada.

NEW SOURCES OF CONFLICT

By the mid-seventeenth century, the French Empire in America comprised a vast territory. Louis Joliet and Father Jacques Marquette, French explorers of the 1670s, journeyed together by canoe from Green Bay on Lake Michigan as far south as the junction of the Arkansas and Mississippi Rivers. A year later, René-Robert Cavelier, Sieur de La Salle, began the explorations that in 1682 took him to the delta of the Mississippi, where he claimed the surrounding country for France and named it Louisiana in the king's honor. Subsequent traders and missionaries wandered to the southwest as far as the Rio Grande; and the explorer Pierre Gaultier de Varennes,

Sieur de La Vérendrye, pushed westward in 1743 from Lake Superior to a point within sight of the Rocky Mountains. The French had by then revealed the outlines of, and laid claim to, almost the whole continental interior.

To secure their hold on these enormous claims, they founded a string of widely separated communities, fortresses, missions, and trading posts. Fort Louis-bourg, on Cape Breton Island, guarded the approach to the Gulf of St. Lawrence. Would-be feudal lords established large estates (*seigneuries*) along the banks of the St. Lawrence River; and on a high bluff above the river stood the fortified city of Quebec, the center of the French Empire in America. To the south was Montreal, and to the west Sault Sainte Marie and Detroit. On the lower Mississippi emerged plantations much like those in the southern colonies of English America, worked by black slaves and owned by "Creoles" (white immigrants of French descent). New Orleans, founded in 1718 to service the French plantation economy, soon was as big as some of the larger cities of the Atlantic seaboard; Biloxi and Mobile to the east completed the string of French settlement.

FRANCE'S NORTH AMERICAN EMPIRE

But the French were not, of course, alone in the continental interior. They shared their territories with a large and powerful Indian population–in regions now often labeled the "middle grounds" (see p. 60)–and their relations with the natives were crucial to the shaping of their empire. They also shared the interior with a growing number of English traders and settlers, who had been moving beyond the confines of the colonial boundaries in the East. Both the French and the English were aware that the battle for control of North America would be determined in part by which group could best win the allegiance of native tribes–as trading partners and, at times, as military allies. The Indians, for their part, were principally concerned with protecting their independence. Whatever alignments they formed with the European societies growing up around them were generally marriages of convenience, determined by which group offered the most attractive terms.

The English–with their more advanced commercial economy–could usually offer the Indians better and more plentiful goods. But the French offered something that was often more important: tolerance. Unlike the English settlers, most of whom tried to impose their own social norms on the Native Americans they encountered, the French settlers in the interior generally adjusted their own behavior to Indian patterns. French fur traders frequently married Indian women and adopted tribal ways. Jesuit missionaries interacted comfortably with the natives and converted them to Catholicism by the thousands without challenging most of their social customs. By the mid-eighteenth century, therefore, the French had better and closer relations with most of the tribes of the interior than did the English.

The most powerful native group, however, had a different relationship with the French. The Iroquois Confederacy–the five Indian nations (Mohawk, Seneca, Cayuga, Onondaga, and Oneida) that had formed a defensive alliance in the fifteenth century–had been the most powerful tribal presence in the Northeast since the 1640s, when they had fought–and **THE IROQUOIS CONFEDERACY** won–a bitter war against the Hurons. Once their major competitors were largely gone from the region, the Iroquois forged an important commercial relationship with the English and Dutch along the eastern seaboard–although they continued to trade with the French as well. Indeed, the key to the success of the Iroquois in maintaining their independence was that they avoided too close a relationship with either group and astutely played the French and the English against each other. As a result, they managed to maintain an uneasy balance of power in the Great Lakes region and beyond.

The principal area of conflict among these many groups was the Ohio Valley. The French claimed it. Several competing Indian tribes (many of them refugees from lands farther east, driven into the valley by the English expansion) lived there. English settlement was expanding into it. And the Iroquois were trying to establish a presence there as traders. With so many competing groups jostling for influence, the Ohio Valley quickly became a potential battleground.

ANGLO-FRENCH CONFLICTS

As long as England and France remained at peace in Europe, and as long as the precarious balance in the North American interior survived, the tensions among the English, French, and Iroquois remained mild. But after the Glorious Revolution in England, the English throne passed to one of Louis XIV's **EUROPEAN SEEDS OF CONFLICT** principal enemies, William III, who was also the stadholder (chief magistrate) of the Netherlands and who had long opposed French expansionism. William's successor, Queen Anne (the daughter of James II), ascended the throne in 1702 and carried on the struggle against France and its new ally, Spain. The result was a series of Anglo-French wars that continued intermittently in Europe for nearly eighty years.

The wars had important repercussions in America. King William's War (1689-1697) produced a few, indecisive clashes between the English and French in northern New England. Queen Anne's War, which began in 1701 and continued for nearly twelve years, generated substantial conflicts: border fighting with the Spaniards in the South as well as with the

THE SIEGE OF LOUISBOURG, 1758 The fortress of Louisbourg, on Cape Breton Island in Nova Scotia, was one of the principal French outposts in eastern Canada during the French and Indian War. It took a British fleet of 157 ships nearly two months to force the French garrison to surrender. "We had not had our Batteries against the Town above a Week," wrote a British soldier after the victory, "tho we were ashore Seven Weeks; the Badness of the Country prevented our Approaches. It was necessary to make Roads for the Cannon, which was a great Labour, and some Loss of Men; but the spirits the Army was in is capable of doing any Thing." (© The New Brunswick Museum, Saint John, NB)

French and their Indian allies in the North. The Treaty of Utrecht, which brought the conflict to a close in 1713, transferred substantial areas of French territory in North America to the English, including Acadia (Nova Scotia) and Newfoundland. Two decades later, European rivalries led to still more conflicts in America. Disputes over British trading rights in the Spanish colonies produced a war between England and Spain and led to clashes between the British in Georgia and the Spaniards in Florida. (It was in the context of this conflict that the last English colony in America, Georgia, was founded in 1733; see pp. 57-60.) The Anglo-Spanish conflict soon merged with a much larger European war, in which England and France lined up on opposite sides of a territorial dispute between Frederick the Great of Prussia and Maria Theresa of Austria. The English colonists in America were soon drawn into the struggle, which they called King George's War; and between 1744 and 1748, they engaged in a series of conflicts with the French. New Englanders captured the French bastion at Louisbourg on Cape Breton Island; but the peace treaty that finally ended the conflict forced them (in bitter disappointment) to abandon it.

In the aftermath of King George's War, relations among the English, French, and Iroquois in North America quickly deteriorated. The Iroquois (in what in retrospect appears a major blunder) began to grant trading concessions in the interior to English merchants. In the context of the already tense Anglo-French relationship in America, the decision to side with the British set in motion a chain of events disastrous for the Iroquois Confederacy. The French feared that the English were using the concessions as a first step toward expansion into French lands (which to some extent they were). They began in 1749 to construct new fortresses in the Ohio Valley. The English interpreted the French activity as a threat to their western settlements. They protested and began making military preparations and building fortresses of their own. The balance of power that the Iroquois had striven to maintain for so long rapidly disintegrated, and the five Indian nations allied themselves with the British and assumed an essentially passive role in the conflict that followed.

For the next five years, tensions between the English and the French increased. In the summer of 1754, the governor of Virginia sent a militia force (under the command of an inexperienced young colonel, George Washington) into the

FORT NECESSITY — Ohio Valley to challenge French expansion. Washington built a crude stockade (Fort Necessity) not far from the larger French outpost, Fort Duquesne, on the site of what is now Pittsburgh. After the Virginians staged an unsuccessful attack on a French detachment, the French countered with an assault on Fort Necessity, trapping Washington and his soldiers inside. After a third of them died in the fighting, Washington surrendered.

That clash marked the beginning of what became the French and Indian War, the American part of the much larger Seven Years' War that spread through Europe at the same time. It was the climactic event in the long Anglo-French struggle for empire.

THE GREAT WAR FOR THE EMPIRE

The French and Indian War lasted nearly nine years, and it proceeded in three distinct phases. The first phase lasted from the Fort Necessity debacle in 1754 until the expansion of the war to Europe in 1756. It was primarily a North American conflict, which the English colonists managed largely on their own.

The British provided modest assistance during this period, but they provided it so ineptly that it had little impact on the

BRADDOCK DEFEATED — struggle. The British fleet failed to prevent the landing of large French reinforcements in Canada; and the newly appointed commander in chief of the British army in America, General Edward Braddock, failed miserably in a major effort in the summer of 1755 to retake the crucial site at the forks of the Ohio River where Washington had lost the battle at Fort Necessity. A French and Indian ambush a few miles from the fort left Braddock dead and his remaining forces in disarray.

The local colonial forces, meanwhile, were preoccupied with defending themselves against raids on their western settlements by the Indians of the Ohio Valley. Virtually all of the tribes (except the Iroquois) were now allied with the French, having interpreted the defeat of the Virginians at Fort Duquesne as evidence of British weakness. Even the Iroquois, who were nominally allied with the British, remained fearful of antagonizing the French. They engaged in few hostilities and launched no offensive into Canada, even though they had, under heavy English pressure, declared war on the French. By late 1755, many English settlers along the frontier had withdrawn to the east of the Allegheny Mountains to escape the hostilities.

The second phase of the struggle began in 1756, when the governments of France and England formally opened hostilities and a truly international conflict (the Seven Years' War) began. In Europe, the war was marked by a realignment within the complex system of alliances. France allied with its former enemy, Austria; England joined France's former ally, Prussia. The fighting now spread to the West Indies, India, and Europe. But the principal struggle remained the one in North America, where so far England had suffered nothing but frustration and defeat.

Beginning in 1757, William Pitt, the English secretary of state (and future prime minister), began to transform the war

WILLIAM PITT TAKES CHARGE — effort in America by bringing it for the first time fully under British control. Pitt himself began planning military strategy for the North American conflict, appointing military commanders, and issuing orders to the colonists. Military recruitment had slowed dramatically in America after the defeat of Braddock. To replenish the army, British commanders began forcibly enlisting colonists (a practice known as "impressment"). Officers also began to seize supplies and equipment from local farmers and tradesmen and compelled colonists to offer shelter to British troops—all generally without compensation. The Americans had long ago become accustomed to running their own affairs and had been fighting for over two years without

THE FIRST GLOBAL WAR WOR-1

THE French and Indian War in North America was only a small part of a much larger conflict. Known in Europe as the Seven Years' War it was one of the longest, most widespread, and most important wars in modern history. "Ministers in this country, where every part of the World affects us, in some way or another, should consider the whole Globe," the Duke of Newcastle wrote in Britain in 1758, reflecting the international achievements and war aims of the British in the mid-eighteenth century. Two centuries later, Winston Churchill, the former British prime minister, wrote of the Seven Years' War as the first "World War."

In North America, the war was a result of tensions along the frontiers of the British Empire, but a larger war resulted from conflicts among the great powers in Europe. It began in the 1750s with what historians have called a "diplomatic revolution." Well-established alliances between Britain and the Austro-Hungarian Empire, and between France and Prussia, collapsed, replaced by new alliances that set Britain and Prussia against France and Austria. The instability that these changing alliances produced helped speed the European nations toward war. The one thing that did not change was the continuing rivalry between Britain and France.

The Austrian-British alliance collapsed because Austria suffered a series of significant defeats at the hands of the Prussians. To the British government, these failures suggested that the Austro-Hungarian Empire was now too weak to help Britain balance French power. As a result, Britain sought new partnerships with the rising powers of northern Germany, Austria's enemies. Seeking protection from the power of their former British allies, the Austrians allied with France. Russia, concerned about the Austro-Hungarian Empire's possible dominance in central Europe, allied with Britain and Prussia.

The tensions that these complicated realignments created eventually led to war (just as the complicated alliances in Europe in the early twentieth century helped produce World War I). The European part of the war was a result of the continuing conflict between Prussia and Austria and the effect of those wars on the allies of both. The Seven Years' War soon spread across much of the world, engaging not only most of the great powers in Europe, from England to Russia, but also the emerging

THE SEVEN YEARS' WAR was one of the first great colonial conflicts. This etching shows a fireworks display at the Hôtel de Ville in Paris on February 10,1763, to celebrate the end of the hostilities. (© The Granger Collection, New York)

colonial world—India, West Africa, the Caribbean, and the Philippines—as the powerful British navy worked to strip France, and eventually Spain, of their valuable colonial holdings.

Like most modern conflicts, the Seven Years' War was a struggle for economic power. Colonial possessions, many European nations believed, were critical to their future wealth, well worth fighting for. The war's outcome affected not only the future of America, but also the distribution of power through much of the world. It destroyed the French navy and much of the French Empire, and it elevated Great Britain to undisputed preeminence among colonial powers—especially when, at the conclusion of the war, India and all of eastern North America fell firmly under English control. The war also reorganized the balance of power in Europe, with Britain now preeminent among the great powers and Prussia (later to become the core of modern Germany) rapidly rising in wealth and military power.

The Seven Years' War was not only one of the first great colonial wars; it was also one of the last great wars of religion. It extended the dominance of Protestantism in Europe. In what is now Canada, the war replaced French with British rule and thus Catholic with Protestant rule. The Vatican, no longer a military power itself, had relied on the great Catholic empires—Spain, France, and Austria-Hungary—as bulwarks of the Vatican's power and influence. The shift of power toward Protestant governments in Europe and North America weakened the Catholic Church and reduced its geopolitical influence.

The conclusion of the Seven Years' War strengthened Britain and Germany and weakened France. But it did not provide any lasting solution to the rivalries among the great colonial powers. In North America, a dozen years after the end of the war, the American Revolution—the origins of which were in many ways a direct result of the Seven Years' War—stripped the British Empire of one of its most important and valuable colonial appendages. By the time the American Revolution came to an end, the French Revolution had sparked another lengthy period of war, culminating in the Napoleonic Wars of the early nineteenth century, which once again redrew the map of Europe and, for a while, the world. ●

UNDERSTAND, ANALYZE, AND EVALUATE

1. How did the Seven Years' War change the balance of power among the nations of Europe? Who gained and who lost in the war?
2. What effect did the war's outcome have on the European colonies in North America?
3. Why is the Seven Years' War described as "one of the most important wars in modern history"?

much assistance or direction from the British. They resented these new impositions and firmly resisted them—at times, as in a 1757 riot in New York City, violently. By early 1758, the friction between the British authorities and the colonists was threatening to bring the war effort to a halt.

Beginning in 1758, therefore, Pitt initiated the third and final phase of the war by relaxing many of the policies that Americans found oppressive. He agreed to reimburse the colonists for all supplies requisitioned by the army. He returned control over military recruitment to the colonial assemblies (which resulted in an immediate and dramatic increase in enlistments). And he dispatched large numbers of additional troops to America.

Finally, the tide of battle began to turn in England's favor. The French had always been outnumbered by the British colonists; after 1756, the French colonies suffered as well from a series of poor harvests. As a result, they were unable to sustain their early military successes. By mid-1758, the British regulars (who did the bulk of the fighting) and the colonial militias were seizing one French stronghold after another.

SIEGE OF QUEBEC Two brilliant English generals, Jeffrey Amherst and James Wolfe, captured the fortress at Louisbourg in July 1758; a few months later Fort Duquesne fell without a fight. The next year, at the end of a siege of Quebec, supposedly impregnable atop its towering cliff, the army of General James Wolfe struggled up a hidden ravine under cover of darkness, surprised the larger forces of the

WILLIAM PITT THE ELDER This dedication on the cover of the Bickerstaff *Boston Almanac* in 1772 honors the British statesman who voiced his support for the American colonialists in the years leading to the Revolution. (© Corbis)

Marquis de Montcalm, and defeated them in a battle in which both commanders died. The dramatic fall of Quebec on September 13, 1759, marked the beginning of the end of the American phase of the war. A year later, in September 1760, the French army formally surrendered to Amherst in Montreal.

Not all aspects of the struggle were as romantic as Wolfe's dramatic assault on Quebec. The British resorted at times to such brutal military expedients as population dispersal. In Nova Scotia, for example, they uprooted several thousand French inhabitants, whom they suspected of disloyalty, and scattered them throughout the English colonies. (Some of these Acadians eventually made their way to Louisiana, where they became the ancestors of the present-day Cajuns.) Elsewhere, English and colonial troops inflicted even worse atrocities on the Indian allies of the French–for example, offering "scalp bounties" to those who could bring back evidence of having killed a native. The French and their Indian allies retaliated, and hundreds of families along the English frontier perished in brutal raids on their settlements.

Peace finally came after the accession of George III to the British throne and the resignation of Pitt, who, unlike the new king, wanted to continue hostilities. The British achieved most of Pitt's aims nevertheless in the Peace of **PEACE OF PARIS** Paris, signed in 1763. Under its terms, the French ceded to Great Britain some of their West Indian islands and most of their colonies in India. They also transferred Canada and all other French territory east of the Mississippi, except New Orleans, to Great Britain. They ceded New Orleans and their claims west of the Mississippi to Spain, thus surrendering all title to the mainland of North America.

The French and Indian War had profound effects on the British Empire and the American colonies. It greatly expanded England's territorial claims in the New World. At the same time, it greatly enlarged Britain's debt; financing the vast war had been a major drain on the treasury. It also generated substantial resentment toward the Americans among British

THE SEVEN YEARS' WAR After Washington's surrender and Braddock's defeat in the Pennsylvania backcountry, the British and French waged their final contest for supremacy in North America in northern New York and New France. But the rivalry for empire between France and Britain was worldwide, with naval superiority providing the needed edge to Britain.

leaders, many of whom were contemptuous of the colonists for what they considered American military ineptitude during the war. They were angry as well that the colonists had made so few financial contributions to a struggle waged largely for American benefit; they were particularly bitter that some colonial merchants had been selling food and other goods to the French in the West Indies throughout the conflict. All these factors combined to persuade many English leaders that a major reorganization of the empire, giving London increased authority over the colonies, would be necessary in the aftermath of the war.

The war had an equally profound but very different effect on the American colonists. It forced them, for the first time, to act in concert against a common foe. The friction of 1756–1757 over British requisition and impressment policies, and the 1758 return of authority to the colonial assemblies,

CONSEQUENCES OF THE SEVEN YEARS' WAR

established an important precedent in the minds of the colonists: it seemed to confirm the illegitimacy of English interference in local affairs. For thousands of Americans–the men who served in the colonial armed forces–the war was an important socializing experience. The colonial troops, unlike the British regiments, generally viewed themselves as part of a "people's army." The relationship of soldiers to their units was, the soldiers believed, in some measure voluntary; their army was a communal, not a coercive or hierarchical, organization. The contrast with the British regulars, whom the colonists widely resented for their arrogance and arbitrary use of power, was striking; and in later years, the memory of that contrast helped to shape the American response to British imperial policies.

For the Indians of the Ohio Valley, the third major party in the French and Indian War, the British victory was disastrous. Those tribes that had allied themselves with the French had earned the enmity of the victorious English. The Iroquois Confederacy, which had allied with Britain, fared only slightly better. English officials saw the passivity of the Iroquois during the war (a result of their effort to hedge their bets and avoid antagonizing the French) as evidence of duplicity. In the aftermath of the peace settlement, the Iroquois alliance with the British quickly unraveled, and the Iroquois Confederacy itself began to crumble from within. The Iroquois nations would continue to contest the English for control of the Ohio Valley for another fifty years; but increasingly divided and increasingly outnumbered, they would seldom again be in a position to deal with their white rivals on terms of military or political equality.

THE NEW IMPERIALISM

With the treaty of 1763, England found itself at peace for the first time in more than fifty years. But saddled with enormous debts and responsible for vast new lands in the New World, the imperial government could not long avoid expanding its involvement in its colonies.

BURDENS OF EMPIRE

The experience of the French and Indian War suggested that such increased involvement would not be easy to achieve. Not only had the colonists proved so resistant to British control that Pitt had been forced to relax his policies in 1758, but the colonial assemblies had continued after that to respond to British needs slowly and grudgingly. Unwilling to be taxed by Parliament to support the war effort, the colonists were generally reluctant to tax themselves as well. Defiance of imperial trade regulations and other British demands continued, and even increased, through the last years of the war.

The problems of managing the empire became more difficult after 1763 because of a basic shift in Britain's imperial design. In the past, the English had viewed their colonial

COMMERCIAL VERSUS TERRITORIAL IMPERIALISTS

empire primarily in terms of trade; they had opposed acquisition of territory for its own sake. But by the mid-eighteenth century, a growing number of English and American leaders (including William Pitt and Benjamin Franklin) were beginning to argue that land itself was of value to the empire–because of the population it could support, the taxes it could produce, and the imperial splendor it would confer. The debate between the old commercial imperialists and the new territorial ones came to a head at the conclusion of the French and Indian War. The mercantilists wanted England to return Canada to France in exchange for Guadeloupe, the most commercially valuable of the French "sugar islands" in the West Indies. The territorialists, however, prevailed. The acquisition of the French territories in North America was a victory for, among others, Benjamin Franklin, who had long argued that the American people would need these vast spaces to accommodate their rapid and, he believed, limitless growth.

With the territorial annexations of 1763, the area of the British Empire was suddenly twice as great as it had been, and the problems of governing it were thus considerably more complex. Some British officials argued that the empire should restrain rapid settlement in the western territories. To allow Europeans to move into the new lands too quickly, they warned, would run the risk of stirring up costly conflicts with the Indians. Restricting settlement would also keep the land available for hunting and trapping.

Many colonists wanted to see the new territories opened for immediate development, but they disagreed among themselves about who should control the western lands. Colonial governments made fervent, and often conflicting, claims of jurisdiction. Other colonists argued that control should remain in England, and that the territories should be considered entirely new colonies, unlinked to the existing settlements. There were, in short, a host of problems and pressures that the British could not ignore.

At the same time, the government in London was running out of options in its effort to find a way to deal with its staggering war debt. Landlords and merchants in England itself were objecting strenuously to increases in what they already considered

THE THIRTEEN COLONIES IN 1763 This map is a close-up of the thirteen colonies at the end of the Seven Years' War. It shows the line of settlement established by the Proclamation of 1763 (the red line), as well as the extent of actual settlement in that year (the blue line). Note that in the middle colonies (North Carolina, Virginia, Maryland, and southern Pennsylvania), settlement had already reached the red line—and in one small area of western Pennsylvania moved beyond it—by the time of the Proclamation of 1763. Note also the string of forts established beyond the Proclamation line.

• How do the forts help to explain the efforts of the British to restrict settlement? And how does the extent of actual settlement help explain why it was so difficult for the British to enforce their restrictions?

excessively high taxes. The necessity of stationing significant numbers of British troops on the Indian border after 1763 was adding even more to the cost of defending the American settlements. And the half-hearted response of the colonial assemblies to the war effort had suggested that in its search for revenue, England could not rely on any cooperation from the colonial governments. Only a system of taxation administered by London, the leaders of the empire believed, could effectively meet England's needs.

BRITAIN'S STAGGERING WAR DEBT

At this crucial moment in Anglo-American relations, with the imperial system in desperate need of redefinition, George III became king in 1760 on the death of his grandfather. He brought two particularly unfortunate qualities to the office.

First, he was determined, unlike his two predecessors, to be an active and responsible monarch. In part because of pressure from his ambitious mother, he removed from power the long-standing and stable coalition of Whigs, who had (under Pitt and others) governed the empire for much of the century and whom the new king mistrusted. In their place, he created a new coalition of his own through patronage and bribes and gained an uneasy control of Parliament. The new ministries that emerged as a result of these changes were unstable, each lasting in office only about two years.

Second, the king had serious intellectual and psychological limitations that compounded his political difficulties. He suffered, apparently, from a rare disease that produced intermittent bouts of insanity. (Indeed, in the last years of his long reign he was, according to most accounts, deranged, confined to the palace and unable to perform any official functions.) Yet, even when George III was lucid and rational, which in the 1760s and 1770s was most of the time, he was painfully immature (he was only twenty-two when he ascended the throne) and insecure—striving constantly to prove his fitness for his position but time and again finding himself ill equipped to handle the challenges he seized for

GEORGE III'S SHORTCOMINGS

himself. The king's personality, therefore, contributed to both the instability and the intransigence of the British government during these critical years.

More immediately responsible for the problems that soon emerged with the colonies, however, was George Grenville, whom the king made prime minister in 1763. Grenville did not share his brother-in-law William Pitt's sympathy with the American point of view. He agreed instead with the prevailing opinion within Britain that the colonists had been too long indulged and that they should be compelled to obey the laws and to pay a part of the cost of defending and administering the empire. He promptly began trying to impose a new system of control upon what had been a loose collection of colonial possessions in America.

THE BRITISH AND THE TRIBES

The western problem was the most urgent. With the departure of the French, settlers and traders from the English colonies moved immediately into the upper Ohio Valley. The Indians of the region objected to this intrusion, and an alliance of tribes, under the Ottawa chieftain Pontiac, struck back. To prevent an escalation of the fighting that might threaten western trade, the British government issued a ruling—the Proclamation of 1763—forbidding settlers to advance beyond a line drawn along the Appalachian Mountains.

The Proclamation of 1763 was appealing to the British for several reasons. It would allow London, rather than the provincial

PROCLAMATION OF 1763

governments and their land-hungry constituents, to control the westward movement of the white population. Hence, westward expansion would proceed in an orderly manner, and conflicts with the tribes, which were both militarily costly and dangerous to trade, might be limited. Slower western settlement would also slow the population exodus from the coastal colonies, where England's most important markets and investments were. And it would reserve opportunities for land speculation and fur trading for English rather than colonial entrepreneurs.

Although the tribes were not enthusiastic about the Proclamation, which required them to cede still more land to the white settlers, many tribal groups supported the agreement as the best bargain available to them. The Cherokee, in particular, worked actively to hasten the drawing of the boundary, hoping to end white encroachments. Relations between the western tribes and the British improved in some areas after the Proclamation, partly as a result of the work of the Indian superintendents the British appointed. John Stuart was in charge of Indian affairs in the southern colonies, and Sir William Johnson in the northern ones. Both were sympathetic to Native American needs and lived among the tribes; Johnson married a Mohawk woman, Mary Brant, who was later to play an important role in the American Revolution.

In the end, however, the Proclamation of 1763 failed to meet even the modest expectations of the Native Americans. It had some effect in limiting colonial land speculation in the West and

GEORGE III George III was twenty-two years old when he ascended the throne in 1760, and for many years almost all portraits of him were highly formal, with the king dressed in elaborate ceremonial robes. This less formal painting dates from much later in his reign, after he had begun to suffer from the mental disorders that eventually consumed him. After 1810, he was blind and permanently deranged, barred from all official business by the Regency Act of 1811. His son (later King George IV) served as regent in those years until he became king after his father's death in 1820. (© The Granger Collection, New York)

in controlling the fur trade, but on the crucial point of the line of settlement it was ineffective. White settlers continued to

WHITE ENCROACHMENT

swarm across the boundary and to claim lands farther and farther into the Ohio Valley. The British authorities tried repeatedly to establish limits to the expansion but continually failed to prevent the white colonists from pushing the line of settlement still farther west.

THE COLONIAL RESPONSE

The Grenville ministry soon moved to increase its authority in the colonies in more direct ways. Regular British troops, London announced, would now be stationed permanently in America; and under the Mutiny Act of 1765 the colonists were required to assist in provisioning and maintaining the army. Ships of the British navy were assigned to patrol American waters and search for smugglers. The customs service was reorganized and enlarged. Royal officials were ordered to take up their colonial posts in person instead of sending substitutes. Colonial manufacturing was to be restricted so that it would not compete with the rapidly expanding industry of Great Britain.

The Sugar Act of 1764, designed in part to eliminate the illegal sugar trade between the continental colonies and the French and Spanish West Indies, strengthened enforce-

SUGAR, CURRENCY, AND STAMP ACTS

ment of the duty on sugar (while lowering the duty on molasses, further damaging the market for sugar grown in the colonies). It also established new vice-admiralty courts in America to try accused smugglers—thus depriving them of the benefit of sympathetic local juries. The Currency Act of 1764 required the colonial assemblies to stop issuing paper money (a widespread practice during the war) and to retire on schedule all the paper money already in circulation. Most momentous of all, the Stamp Act of 1765 imposed a tax on most printed documents in the colonies: newspapers, almanacs, pamphlets, deeds, wills, licenses.

The new imperial program was an effort to reapply to the colonies the old principles of mercantilism. And in some ways, it proved highly effective. British officials were soon collecting more than ten times as much annual revenue from America as before 1763. But the new policies created many more problems than they solved.

The colonists may have resented the new imperial regulations, but at first they found it difficult to resist them effectively. Americans continued to harbor as many grievances against one another as against the authorities in London. Often, the conflicts centered around tensions between the

PAXTON BOYS

established societies of the Atlantic coast and the "backcountry" farther west, whose residents often felt isolated from, and underrepresented in, the colonial governments. These western settlers sometimes felt resentful because they lived closer to the worlds of the Indian tribes than the societies of the East. In

1763, for example, a band of people from western Pennsylvania known as the "Paxton Boys" descended on Philadelphia with demands for relief from colonial (not British) taxes and for money to help them defend themselves against Indians; the colonial government averted bloodshed only by making concessions to them.

In 1771, a small-scale civil war broke out as a result of the so-called Regulator movement in North Carolina. The

REGULATOR MOVEMENT

Regulators were farmers of the Carolina upcountry who organized in opposition to the high taxes that local sheriffs (appointed by the colonial governor) collected. The western counties were badly underrepresented in the colonial assembly, and the Regulators failed to win redress of their grievances there. Finally, they armed themselves and began resisting tax collections by force. To suppress the revolt, Governor William Tryon raised an army of militiamen, mostly from the eastern counties, who defeated a band of 2,000 Regulators in the Battle of Alamance. Nine on each side were killed, and many others were wounded. Afterward, six Regulators were hanged for treason.

The bloodshed was exceptional, but bitter conflicts within the colonies were not. After 1763, however, the new policies of the British government began to create common grievances among virtually all colonists that to some degree counterbalanced these internal divisions.

Indeed, there was something in the Grenville program to antagonize everyone. Northern merchants believed they would suffer from restraints on commerce, closing opportunities for manufacturing, and increased taxes. Settlers in the northern backcountry resented the closing of the West to land speculation and fur trading. Southern planters, in debt to English merchants, feared having to pay additional taxes and losing their ability to ease their debts by speculating in western land. Professionals—ministers, lawyers, professors, and others—depended on merchants and planters for their livelihood and thus shared their concerns about the effects of English law. Small farmers, the largest group in the colonies, believed they would suffer from increased taxes and from the abolition of paper money, which had enabled them to pay their loans. Workers in towns opposed the restraints on manufacturing.

The new restrictions came, moreover, at the beginning of an economic depression. The British government, by pouring

POSTWAR DEPRESSION

money into the colonies to finance the fighting, had stimulated a wartime boom. When the flow of funds stopped after the peace in 1763, an economic bust followed. The imperial policies would, many colonists feared, doom them to permanent economic stagnation and a declining standard of living.

In reality, most Americans soon found ways to live with (or circumvent) the new British policies. The American economy was not, in fact, being destroyed. But economic anxieties were rising in the colonies nevertheless, and they created a growing sense of unease.

Whatever the economic consequences of the British government's programs, the political consequences were—in the

NORTH AMERICA IN 1763 The victory of the English over the French in the Seven Years' War (or, as it was known in America, the French and Indian War) reshaped the map of colonial North America. Britain gained a vast new territory, formerly controlled by France—Canada, and a large area west of the Mississippi River—thus more than doubling the size of the British Empire in America. French possessions in the New World dwindled to a few islands in the Caribbean. Spain continued to control a substantial empire in the North American interior. The red line along the western borders of the English colonies represents the line of settlement established by Britain in 1763. White settlers were not permitted to move beyond that line.

• *Why did the British wish to restrict settlement of the western lands?*

eyes of the colonists–far worse. Perhaps nowhere else in the late-eighteenth-century world did so large a proportion of the people take an active interest in public affairs. That was partly because Anglo-Americans were deeply attached to broad powers of self-government; and the colonists were determined to protect those powers. The keys to self-government, they believed, were the provincial assemblies; and the key to the power of the provincial assemblies was their long-established

POLITICAL CONSEQUENCES OF THE GRENVILLE PROGRAM

right to give or withhold appropriations for the colonial governments, a right the British were now challenging. Home rule, therefore, was not something new and different that the colonists were striving to attain, but something old and familiar that they desired to keep. The movement to resist the new imperial policies, a movement for which many would ultimately

THE PAXTON EXPEDITION. Inscribed to the Author of the FARCE. by HD.

PREPARING TO MEET THE PAXTON BOYS The "Paxton Boys" were residents of western Pennsylvania who were declared outlaws by the assembly in Philadelphia after they launched an unauthorized attack on neighboring Conestoga Indians. Instead of surrendering, they armed themselves and marched on Philadelphia. This engraving satirizes the haphazard military preparations in the city for the expected invasion. An accompanying poem, expressing the contempt some colonists felt toward the urbanized, pacifist Quakers of Philadelphia, commented: "To kill the Paxtonians, they then did Advance, With Guns on their Shoulders, but how did they Prance." Benjamin Franklin finally persuaded the Paxton rebels not to attack in return for greater representation in the legislature. (© Fotosearch/Getty Images)

fight and die, was at the same time democratic and conservative. It was a movement to conserve liberties Americans believed they already possessed.

STIRRINGS OF REVOLT

By the mid-1760s, a hardening of positions had begun in both England and America that would bring the colonies into increasing conflict with the mother country. The victorious war for empire had given the colonists a heightened sense of their own importance and a renewed commitment to protecting their political autonomy. But it had also given the British a strengthened belief in the need to tighten administration of the empire and use the colonies as a source of revenue. The result was a series of events that, more rapidly than anyone had imagined, shattered the British Empire in America.

THE STAMP ACT CRISIS

Even if he had tried, Prime Minister Grenville could not have devised a better method for antagonizing and unifying the colonies than the Stamp Act of 1765. The Sugar Act of a year earlier had affected few people other than the New

EFFECTS OF THE STAMP ACT

England merchants. But the new tax fell on all Americans, and it evoked particular opposition from some of the most powerful members of the population. Merchants and lawyers were obliged to buy stamps for ships' papers and legal documents. Tavern owners, often the political leaders of their neighborhoods, were required to buy stamps for their licenses. Printers—the most influential group in distributing information and ideas in colonial society—had to buy stamps for their newspapers and other publications.

The actual economic burdens of the Stamp Act were relatively light; the stamps were not expensive. What made the law offensive to the colonists was the precedent it seemed to set. In the past, Americans had rationalized the taxes and duties on colonial trade as measures to regulate commerce, not raise money. Some Americans had even managed to persuade themselves that the Sugar Act, which was in fact designed primarily to raise money, was not fundamentally different from the traditional imperial duties. The Stamp Act, however, they could interpret in only one way: it was a direct attempt by England to raise revenue in the colonies without the consent of the colonial assemblies. If this new tax passed without resistance, the door would be open for more burdensome taxation in the future.

Few colonists believed that they could do anything more than grumble and buy the stamps—until the Virginia House of

THE ALTERNATIVES OF WILLIAM BURG In the aftermath of the Boston Tea Party and in response to the Coercive Acts Great Britain enacted to punish the colonists, the First Continental Congress called on Americans to boycott British goods until the acts were repealed. In this drawing, a prosperous Virginia merchant is seen signing a pledge to honor the nonimportation agreement—not surprising, given the alternative, visible in the background of the picture: tar and feathers hanging from a post labeled "A Cure for the Refractory." (© The Colonial Williamsburg Foundation)

Burgesses sounded what one colonist called a "trumpet of sedition" that aroused Americans to action almost everywhere. The "trumpet" was the collective voice of a group of young Virginia aristocrats. They hoped, among other things, to challenge the power of tidewater planters who (in alliance with the royal governor) dominated Virginia politics. Foremost among the malcontents was Patrick Henry, who had already achieved fame for his fiery oratory and his occasional defiance of British authority. Henry made a dramatic speech to the House of Burgesses in May 1765, concluding with a vague prediction that if present policies were not revised, George III, like earlier tyrants, might lose his head. There were shocked cries of "Treason!" and, according to one witness, an immediate apology from Henry (although many years later he was quoted as having made the defiant reply: "If this be treason, make the most of it").

Henry introduced a set of resolutions declaring that Americans possessed the same rights as the English, especially the right to be taxed only by their own representatives; that Virginians should pay no taxes except those voted by the Virginia assembly; and that anyone advocating the right of

VIRGINIA RESOLVES

Parliament to tax Virginians should be deemed an enemy of the colony. The House of Burgesses defeated the most extreme of Henry's resolutions. All of them, however, were printed and circulated as the "Virginia Resolves" (creating an impression in other colonies that the people of Virginia were more militant than they actually were).

In Massachusetts at about the same time, James Otis persuaded his fellow members of the colonial assembly to call an intercolonial congress for action against the new tax. In October 1765, the Stamp Act Congress met in New York with delegates from nine colonies and decided to petition the king and the two houses of Parliament. Their petition conceded that Americans owed to Parliament "all due subordination," but it denied that the colonies could rightfully be taxed except through their own provincial assemblies.

Meanwhile, in several colonial cities, crowds began taking the law into their own hands. During the summer of 1765, serious riots broke out up and down the coast, the largest of them in Boston. Men belonging to the newly organized Sons of Liberty terrorized stamp agents and burned the stamps. The agents, themselves Americans, hastily resigned; and the sale of stamps in the continental colonies ceased. In Boston, a crowd also attacked such pro-British "aristocrats" as the lieutenant governor, Thomas Hutchinson (who had privately opposed passage of the Stamp Act but who, as an officer of the crown, felt obliged to support it once it became law). The protesters pillaged Hutchinson's elegant house and virtually destroyed it.

SONS OF LIBERTY

The Stamp Act crisis was a dangerous moment in the relationship between the colonies and the British government. But the crisis subsided, largely because England backed down. The authorities in London changed their attitude not because of the colonists' defiance but because of economic pressure. Even before the Stamp Act, many New Englanders had stopped buying English goods to protest the Sugar Act of 1764. Now the colonial boycott spread, and the Sons of Liberty intimidated colonists who were reluctant to participate in it. The merchants of England, feeling the loss of much of their colonial market, begged Parliament to repeal the Stamp Act, and stories of unemployment, poverty, and discontent arose from English seaports and manufacturing towns.

The Marquis of Rockingham, who succeeded Grenville as prime minister in July 1765, tried to appease both the English merchants and the American colonists, and he finally convinced the king to kill the Stamp Act. On March 18, 1766, Parliament repealed it. Rockingham's opponents were strong and vociferous, and they insisted that unless England compelled the colonists to obey the Stamp Act, they would soon cease to obey any laws of Parliament. So, on the same day, to satisfy such critics, Parliament passed the Declaratory Act, asserting Parliament's authority over the colonies "in all cases whatsoever." In their rejoicing over the repeal of the Stamp Act, most Americans paid little attention to this sweeping declaration of power.

PARLIAMENT RETREATS

INTERNAL REBELLIONS

The conflicts with Britain were not the only uprisings emerging in the turbulent years of the 1760s. In addition to the Stamp Act crisis and other challenges to London, there were internal rebellions that had their roots in the class system in New York and New England. In the Hudson Valley in New York, great estates had grown up, whose owners had rented their land to small farmers. The revolutionary fervor of the time led many of these tenants to demand ownership of the land they worked. To emphasize their determination, they stopped paying rents. The challenge to landownership soon failed. But other challenges to landownership continued in other colonies. In Vermont, which still was governed by New York, insurgent farmers challenged landowners (many of them the same owners whom tenants had challenged on the Hudson) by taking up arms and demanding ownership of the land they

"THE TORY'S DAY OF JUDGMENT" A mob of American Patriots hoists a Loyalist neighbor up a flagpole in this woodcut, which is obviously sympathetic to the victim. The crowd is shown as fat, rowdy, and drunken. Public humiliations of Tories were not infrequent during the war. More common, however, was seizure of their property. (Library of Congress)

worked. Ethan Allen (later a hero of the Revolutionary War and himself a land speculator) took up the cause of the Green Mountain farmers and accused the landowners of trying to "enslave a free people." Allen eventually succeeded in making Vermont into a separate state, which broke up some of the large estates.

THE TOWNSHEND PROGRAM

The reaction in England to the Rockingham government's policy of appeasement was less enthusiastic than it was in America. English landlords, a powerful political force, angrily protested that the government had "sacrificed the landed gentlemen to the interests of traders and colonists." They feared that backing down from taxing the colonies would lead the government to increase taxes on them. The king finally bowed to their pressure and dismissed the Rockingham ministry. To replace it, he called upon the aging but still powerful William Pitt to form a government. Pitt had been a strong critic of the Stamp Act and had a reputation in America as a friend of the colonists. Once in office, however, Pitt (now Lord Chatham) was so hobbled by gout and at times so incapacitated by mental illness that the actual leadership of his administration fell to the chancellor of the exchequer, Charles Townshend—a brilliant, flamboyant, and at times reckless politician known to his contemporaries variously as "the Weathercock" and "Champagne Charlie."

Among Townshend's first challenges was dealing with the continuing American grievances against Parliament, now

MUTINY ACT most notably the Mutiny (or Quartering) Act of 1765, which required the colonists to provide quarters and supplies for the British troops in America. The British considered this a reasonable requirement. The troops were stationed in North America to protect the colonists from Indian or French attack and to defend the frontiers; lodging the troops in coastal cities was simply a way to reduce the costs to England of supplying them. To the colonists, however, the law was another assault on their liberties.

They did not so much object to quartering the troops or providing them with supplies; they had been doing that voluntarily ever since the last years of the French and Indian War. They resented that these contributions were now mandatory, and they considered it another form of taxation without consent. The Massachusetts Assembly refused to vote the mandated supplies to the troops. The New York Assembly soon did likewise, posing an even greater challenge to imperial authority, since the army headquarters were in New York City.

To enforce the law and to try again to raise revenues in the colonies, Townshend steered two inflammatory measures through Parliament in 1767. The first disbanded the New

INTERNAL AND EXTERNAL TAXES York Assembly until the colonists agreed to obey the Mutiny Act. (By singling out New York, Townshend thought he would avoid Grenville's mistake of arousing all the colonies at once.) The second levied new taxes (known as the Townshend Duties) on various goods imported to the colonies from England—lead, paint, paper, and tea. The colonists could not logically object to taxation of this kind, Townshend reasoned, because it met standards they themselves had accepted. Benjamin Franklin, as a colonial agent in London trying to prevent the passage of the Stamp Act, had long ago argued for the distinction between "internal" and "external" taxes and had denounced the stamp duties as internal taxation. Townshend himself had considered the distinction laughable; but he was nevertheless imposing duties on what he believed were clearly external transactions.

Yet Townshend's efforts to satisfy colonial grievances were to no avail. He might call them external taxes, but they were no more acceptable to colonial merchants than the Stamp Act. Their purpose, Americans believed, was the same as that of the Stamp Act: to raise revenue from the colonists without their consent. And the suspension of the New York Assembly, far from isolating New York, aroused the resentment of all the colonies. They considered this assault on the rights of one provincial government a precedent for the annihilation of the rights of all of them.

The Massachusetts Assembly took the lead in opposing the new measures by circulating a letter to all the colonial governments urging them to stand up against every tax, external or internal, imposed by Parliament. At first, the circular evoked little response in some of the legislatures (and ran into strong opposition in Pennsylvania's). Then Lord Hillsborough, secretary of state for the colonies, issued a circular letter of his own from London in which he warned that assemblies endorsing the Massachusetts letter would be dissolved. Massachusetts defiantly reaffirmed its support for the circular. (The vote in the Assembly was 92 to 17, and for a time "ninety-two" became a patriotic rallying cry throughout British America.) The other colonies, including Pennsylvania, promptly rallied to the support of Massachusetts.

In addition to his other unpopular measures, Townshend tried to strengthen enforcement of commercial regulations in the colonies by, among other things, establishing a new board of customs commissioners in America. Townshend hoped the new board would stop the rampant corruption in the colonial customs houses, and to some extent his hopes were fulfilled. The new commissioners ended smuggling in Boston, their headquarters, although smugglers continued to carry on a busy trade in other colonial seaports.

The Boston merchants—accustomed to loose enforcement of the Navigation Acts and doubly aggrieved now that the new commission was diverting the lucrative smuggling trade—were **COLONIAL BOYCOTTS** indignant and took the lead in organizing another boycott. In 1768, the merchants of Philadelphia and New York joined them in a nonimportation agreement, and later some southern merchants and planters also agreed to cooperate. Colonists boycotted British goods subject to the Townshend Duties; and throughout the colonies, American homespun and other domestic products became fashionable overnight, while English luxuries fell from favor.

Late in 1767, Charles Townshend suddenly died—before the consequences of his ill-conceived program had become fully apparent. The question of dealing with colonial resistance to the Townshend Duties fell, therefore, to the new prime minister, Lord North. Hoping to break the nonimportation agreement and divide the colonists, Lord North secured the repeal of all the Townshend Duties except the tax on tea in March 1770.

THE BOSTON MASSACRE

The withdrawal of the Townshend Duties never had a chance to pacify colonial opinion. Before news of the repeal reached America, an event in Massachusetts raised colonial resentment **COMPETITION FOR SCARCE EMPLOYMENT** to a new level of intensity. The colonists' harassment of the new customs commissioners in Boston had grown so intense that the British government had placed four regiments of regular troops inside the city. The presence of the "redcoats" was a constant affront to the colonists' sense of their independence and a constant reminder of what they considered British oppression. In addition, British soldiers, poorly paid and poorly treated by the army, wanted jobs in their off-duty hours; and they competed with local workers in an already tight market. Clashes between them were frequent.

On the night of March 5, 1770, a few days after a particularly intense skirmish between workers at a ship-rigging factory and British soldiers who were trying to find work there, a crowd of dockworkers, "liberty boys," and others began pelting the sentries at the customs house with rocks and snowballs. Hastily, Captain Thomas Preston of the British regiment lined up several of his men in front of the building to protect it. There was some scuffling; one of the soldiers was knocked down; and in the midst of it all, apparently, several British soldiers fired into the crowd, killing five people (among them a mulatto sailor, Crispus Attucks).

This murky incident, almost certainly the result of panic and confusion, was quickly transformed by local resistance leaders into the "Boston Massacre"—a graphic symbol of British oppression and brutality. The victims became popular martyrs; the event became the subject of many lurid (and inaccurate) accounts. A famous engraving by Paul Revere, widely reproduced and circulated, falsely portrayed the "massacre" as a carefully organized, calculated assault on a peaceful crowd. A jury of Massachusetts colonists found two British soldiers guilty of manslaughter and acquitted six others. Colonial pamphlets and newspapers, however, convinced many Americans that all of the soldiers were guilty of official murder. Year after year, resistance leaders marked the anniversary of the massacre with demonstrations and speeches.

The leading figure in fomenting public outrage over the Boston Massacre was Samuel Adams, the most effective radical in the colonies. Adams (a distant cousin of John Adams,

THE BOSTON MASSACRE (1770), BY PAUL REVERE This is one of many sensationalized engravings, by Revere and others, of the conflict between British troops and Boston laborers that became important propaganda documents for the Patriot cause in the 1770s. Among the victims of the massacre listed by Revere was Crispus Attucks, probably the first black man to die in the struggle for American independence. (Library of Congress)

second president of the United States) was born in 1722 and

SAMUEL ADAMS

was thus somewhat older than other leaders of colonial protest. As a member of an earlier generation with strong ties to New England's Puritan past, he was particularly inclined to view public events in stern moral terms. A failure in business, he became an unflagging voice expressing outrage at British oppression. England, he argued, had become a morass of sin and corruption; only in America did public virtue survive. He spoke frequently at Boston town meetings; and as one unpopular English policy followed another—the Townshend Duties, the placement of customs commissioners in Boston, the stationing of British troops in the city (with its violent results)—his message attracted increasing support. In 1772, he proposed the creation of a "committee of correspondence" in Boston to publicize the grievances against England throughout the colony. He became its first head. Other colonies followed Massachusetts's lead, and a loose network of political organizations grew up that kept the spirit of dissent alive through the 1770s.

THE PHILOSOPHY OF REVOLT

A superficial calm settled on the colonies for approximately three years after the Boston Massacre. But the crises of the 1760s had helped arouse enduring ideological challenges to England and had produced powerful instruments for publicizing colonial grievances. Gradually a political outlook gained a following in America that would ultimately serve to justify revolt.

The ideas that would support the Revolution emerged from many sources. Some were drawn from religious (particularly Puritan) sources or from the political experiences of the colonies. Others came from abroad. Most important, perhaps, were the "radical" ideas of those in Great Britain who stood in opposition to their government. Some were Scots, who considered the English state tyrannical. Others were embittered "country Whigs," who felt excluded from power and considered the existing political system corrupt and oppressive. Drawing from some of the great philosophical minds of earlier generations—most notably John Locke—these English dissidents framed a powerful argument against their government.

Central to this emerging ideology was a new concept of what government should be. Because humans were inherently corrupt and selfish, government was necessary to protect individuals from the evil in one another. But because any government was run by corruptible people, the people needed safeguards against its possible abuses of power. Most people in both England and America had long considered the English constitution the best system ever devised to meet these necessities. By distributing power among the three elements of society—the monarchy, the aristocracy, and the common people—the English political system ensured that no individual or group could exercise authority unchecked by another. Yet, by the mid-seventeenth century, dissidents in both England and America had become convinced that the constitution was in danger. A single center of power—the king and his ministers—was becoming so powerful that it could not be effectively checked. The system, the dissidents believed, was becoming a corrupt and dangerous tyranny.

ENGLAND'S BALANCED CONSTITUTION

Such arguments found little sympathy in most of England. The English constitution was not a written document or a fixed set of unchangeable rules. It was a general sense of the "way things are done," and most people in England were willing to accept changes in it. Americans, by contrast, drew from their experience with colonial charters, in which the shape and powers of government were permanently inscribed on paper. They resisted the idea of a flexible, changing set of basic principles.

One basic principle, Americans believed, was the right of people to be taxed only with their own consent—a belief that gradually took shape in the widely repeated slogan "No taxation without representation." This clamor about "representation" made little sense to the English. According to

"THE CRUEL FATE OF THE LOYALISTS" This British cartoon, published near the end of the American Revolution, shows three Indians, representing American revolutionaries, murdering six Loyalists: four by hanging, one by scalping, and one—appealing to Fate—about to be killed by an axe-wielding native. By using Indians to represent Anglo-American soldiers, the British were trying to equate the presumed savagery of Native Americans with the behavior of the revolutionaries. (The Library of Congress (LC-USZ62-1540))

English constitutional theory, members of Parliament did not represent individuals or particular geographic areas. Instead, each member represented the interests of the whole nation and indeed the whole empire, no matter where the member came from. The many boroughs of England that had no representative in Parliament, the whole of Ireland, and the colonies thousands of miles away—all were thus represented in the Parliament at London, even though they elected no representatives of their own. This was the theory of "virtual" representation. But Americans, drawing from their experiences with their town meetings and their colonial assemblies, believed in "actual" representation: every community was entitled to its own representative, elected by the people of that community and directly responsible to them. Since the colonists had none of their own representatives in Parliament, it followed that they were not represented there. Instead, Americans believed that the colonial assemblies played the same role within the colonies that Parliament did within England. The British Empire, the Americans began to argue, was a sort of federation of commonwealths, each with its own legislative body, all tied together by common loyalty to the king.

Such ideas illustrated a fundamental difference of opinion between England and America over the nature of sovereignty—over the question of where ultimate power lay. By arguing that Parliament had the right to legislate for England and for the empire as a whole, but that only the provincial assemblies could legislate for the individual colonies, Americans were in effect arguing for a division of sovereignty. Parliament would be sovereign in some matters; the assemblies would be sovereign in others. To the British, such an argument was absurd. In any system of government

VIRTUAL VERSUS ACTUAL REPRESENTATION

there must be a single, ultimate authority. And since the empire was, in their view, a single, undivided unit, there could be only one authority within it: the English government of king and Parliament.

THE TEA EXCITEMENT

The relatively calm first years of the 1770s disguised a growing sense of resentment at the increasingly heavy-handed British enforcement of the Navigation Acts. The customs commissioners, who remained in the colonies despite the repeal of the Townshend Duties, were mostly clumsy, intrusive, and arrogant officials. They harassed colonial merchants and seamen constantly with petty restrictions, and they also enriched themselves through graft and illegal seizures of merchandise.

Colonists also kept revolutionary sentiment alive through writing and talking. Dissenting leaflets, pamphlets, and books circulated widely through the colonies. In towns and

REVOLUTIONARY DISCOURSE cities, men gathered in churches, schools, town squares, and above all in taverns (see "Patterns of Popular Culture," pp. 122-123) to discuss politics and express their growing disenchantment with English policy. The rise of revolutionary ideology was not simply a result of the ideas of intellectuals. It was also a product of a social process by which ordinary people heard, discussed, and absorbed new ideas.

The popular anger lying just beneath the surface was also visible in occasional acts of rebellion. At one point, colonists seized a British revenue ship on the lower Delaware River. And in 1772, angry residents of Rhode Island boarded the British

schooner *Gaspée*, set it afire, and sank it in Narragansett Bay. The British response to the *Gaspée* affair further inflamed American opinion. Instead of putting the accused attackers on trial in colonial courts, the British sent a special commission to America with power to send the defendants back to England for trial.

What finally revived the revolutionary fervor of the 1760s, however, was a new act of Parliament—one that the English government had expected to be relatively uncontroversial. It involved the business of selling tea. In 1773, Britain's East India Company (which had an official monopoly on trade with the Far East) was on the verge of bankruptcy and sitting on large stocks of tea that it could not sell in England. In an effort to save the company, the government passed the Tea Act of 1773, which gave the company the right to export its merchandise directly to the colonies without paying any of the navigation taxes that were imposed on the colonial merchants, who had traditionally served as the middlemen in such transactions. With these privileges, the East India Company could undersell American merchants and monopolize the colonial tea trade.

The Tea Act angered many colonists for several reasons. First, it enraged influential colonial merchants, who feared being replaced and bankrupted by a powerful monopoly. The East India Company's decision to grant franchises to certain American merchants for the sale of its tea created further

THE TEA ACT resentments among those excluded from this lucrative trade. More important, however, the Tea Act revived American passions about the issue of taxation without representation. The law provided no new tax on tea. But it exempted the East India Company from having to pay the normal customs duties. That put

Monday Morning December 27, 1773.

THE TEA-SHIP being arrived, every Inhabitant, who wishes to preserve the Liberty of America, is desired to meet at the STATE-HOUSE, This Morning, precisely at TEN o'Clock, to advise what is best to be done on this alarming Crisis.

FAC-SIMILE OF THE PROCLAMATION ABOUT THE TEA-SHIP.

To the PUBLIC.

THE Sense of the City relative to the Landing the India Company's Tea, being signified to Captain Lockyer, by the Committee, nevertheless, it is the Desire of a Number of the Citizens, that at his Departure from hence, he should see, with his own Eyes, their Detestation of the Measures pursued by the Ministry and the India Company, to enslave this Country. This will be declared by the Convention of the People at his Departure from this City; which will be on next Saturday Morning, about nine o'Clock, when no Doubt, every Friend to this Country will attend. The Bells will give the Notice about an Hour before he embarks from Murray's Wharf.

By Order of the COMMITTEE.

NEW YORK, APRIL 21st, 1774.

THE BOSTON TEA PARTY The artist Ramberg produced this wash drawing of the Boston Tea Party in 1773. A handbill in a Philadelphia newspaper ten days later and another distributed in New York the following April illustrate how quickly the spirit of resistance spread to other colonies. (*Left:* © The Granger Collection, New York; *Top Right:* Private Collection/
© Peter Newark American Pictures/The Bridgeman Art Library; *Bottom Right:* © Bettmann/Corbis)

colonial merchants at a grave competitive disadvantage. British Prime Minister Lord North assumed that most colonists would welcome the new law because it would reduce the price of tea to consumers by removing the middlemen. But resistance leaders in America argued that it was another insidious example of the results of an unconstitutional tax. Many colonists responded by boycotting tea.

The boycott was an important event in the history of colonial resistance. Unlike earlier protests, most of which had involved small numbers of people, the boycott mobilized large segments of the population. It also helped link the colonies in a common experience of mass popular protest. Particularly important to the movement were the activities of colonial women, who were among the principal consumers of tea and now became leaders of the effort to boycott it.

Women had played a significant role in resistance activities from the beginning. Several women (most prominently Mercy Otis Warren) had been important in writing the dissident literature—in Warren's case, satirical plays—that did much to fan colonial resentments in the 1760s. Women had participated actively in anti-British riots and crowd activities in the 1760s; they had formed an informal organization—the Daughters of Liberty—that occasionally mocked their male counterparts as insufficiently militant. Now, as the sentiment for a boycott grew, some women mobilized as never before, determined (as the Daughters of Liberty had written) "that rather than Freedom, we'll part with our Tea."

In the last weeks of 1773, with strong popular support, leaders in various colonies made plans to prevent the East India Company from landing its cargoes in colonial ports. In Philadelphia and New York City, determined colonists kept the tea from leaving the company's ships. In Charles Town, they stored it in a public warehouse. In Boston, after failing to turn

BOSTON TEA PARTY

back the three ships in the harbor, local Patriots staged a spectacular drama. On the evening of December 16, 1773, three companies of fifty men each, masquerading as Mohawks, passed through a tremendous crowd of spectators (which served to protect them from official interference), went aboard the three ships, broke open the tea chests, and heaved them into the harbor. As the electrifying news of the Boston "tea party" spread, other seaports followed the example and staged similar acts of resistance.

When the Bostonians refused to pay for the property they had destroyed, George III and Lord North decided on a policy of coercion, to be applied only against Massachusetts—the chief center of resistance. In four acts of 1774, Parliament closed the port of Boston, drastically reduced colonial self-government, permitted royal officers to be tried in other colonies or in England when accused of crimes, and provided for the quartering of troops in the colonists' barns and empty houses.

Parliament followed these Coercive Acts—or, as they were more widely known in America, Intolerable Acts—with the

COERCIVE ACTS

Quebec Act, which was separate from them in origin and quite different in purpose. Its object was to provide a civil government for the

PAYING THE EXCISEMAN This eighteenth-century satirical drawing by a British artist depicts Bostonians forcing tea down the throat of a customs official, whom they have tarred and feathered. In the background, colonists are dumping tea into the harbor (presumably a representation of the 1773 Boston Tea Party); and on the tree at right is a symbol of the Stamp Act, which the colonists had defied eight years earlier. (© GL Archive/Alamy)

French-speaking Roman Catholic inhabitants of Canada and the Illinois country. The law extended the boundaries of Quebec to include the French communities between the Ohio and Mississippi Rivers. It also granted political rights to Roman Catholics and recognized the legality of the Roman Catholic Church within the enlarged province. In many ways it was a tolerant and long-overdue piece of legislation. But in the inflamed atmosphere of the time, many people in the thirteen English-speaking colonies considered it a threat. They were already alarmed by rumors that the Church of England was scheming to appoint a bishop for America who would impose Anglican authority on all the various sects. Since the line between the Church of England and the Church of Rome had always seemed to many Americans dangerously thin, the passage of the Quebec Act convinced some of them that a plot was afoot in London to subject Americans to the tyranny of the pope. Those interested in western lands, moreover, believed that the act would hinder westward expansion.

The Coercive Acts, far from isolating Massachusetts, made it a martyr to residents of other colonies and sparked new resistance up and down the coast. Colonial

CONSEQUENCES

legislatures passed a series of resolves

AP CONSIDER THE SOURCE

TEA PARTIES

THE BOSTON Tea Party of 1773 was a revolt against "taxation without representation." The poem "Tea, Destroyed by Indians" celebrates the action of the Boston Tea Party, expresses the colonists' resentments and complaints against the distant London government, and calls upon Boston patriots to continue to resist British actions.

The twenty-first-century Tea Party movement became prominent in 2009. Although not an official political party, members tend to endorse Republican candidates. The modern Tea Party movement has borrowed its name from the Boston event that took place over 200 years ago, and has picked up some (although not all) of the ideas of the 1773 Boston Tea Party: hostility to distant authority (London then, Washington now) and resentment of taxes (imposed by Britain then, and by Washington now). Although taxation in our time does not really take place "without representation," today's Tea Partiers certainly feel that contemporary taxation is as illegitimate as the Bostonians felt it was in 1773.

BOSTON TEA PARTY—1773

TEA, DESTROYED BY INDIANS

Poem honoring the Boston Tea Party, Dec. 1773

CHORUS:

Bostonian's SONS keep up your Courage good,
Or Dye, like Martyrs, in fair Free-born Blood.

YE GLORIOUS SONS OF FREEDOM, brave and bold,
That has flood forth–fair LIBERTY to hold;
Though you were INDIANS, come from distant shores,
Like MEN you acted–not like savage Moors.

CHORUS

Our LIBERTY, and LIFE is now invaded,
And FREEDOM's brightest Charms are darkly shaded;
But, we will STAND–and think it noble mirth,
To DART the man that dare oppress the Earth.

CHORUS

How grand the Scene!–(No Tyrant shall oppose)
The TEA is sunk in spite of all our foes.
A NOBLE SIGHT–to see th' accursed TEA
Mingled with MUD–and ever for to be;
For KING and PRINCE shall know that we are FREE.

CHORUS

Must we be still– and live on Blood-bought Ground,
And not oppose the Tyrants cursed found?
We Scorn the thought–our views are well refin'd
We Scorn those slavish shackles of the Mind,
"We've Souls that were not made to be confin'd."

CHORUS

Could our Fore-fathers rise from their cold Graves,
And view their Land, with all their Children SLAVES;
What would they say! how would their Spirits rend,
And, Thunder-strucken, to their Graves descend.

CHORUS

Let us with hearts of steel now stand the task,
Throw off all darksome ways, nor wear a Mask.
Oh! may our noble Zeal support our frame,
And brand all Tyrants with eternal SHAME.

CHORUS

Bostonian's SONS keep up your Courage good,
And sink all Tyrants in their GUILTY BLOOD.

Source: www.masshist.org

TEA PARTY MOVEMENT—2010

Although the Tea Party movement has no centralized leadership, one organization that claims to be the "official" home of the American Tea Party movement is TeaParty.org. A description and set of core beliefs provided by this organization appear below.

TeaParty.org Description and Core Beliefs

What Is the Tea Party?

The Tea Party is a grassroots movement that calls awareness to any issue that challenges the security, sovereignty, or domestic tranquility of our beloved nation, the United States of America.

From our founding, the Tea Party is the voice of the true owners of the United States, WE THE PEOPLE.

Many claim to be the founders of this movement—however, it was the brave souls of the men and women in 1773, known today as the Boston Tea Party, who dared defy the greatest military might on earth.

We are the beneficiaries of their courage. By joining the Tea Party, you are taking a stand for our nation. You will be upholding the grand principles set forth in the U.S. Constitution and Bill of Rights.

Non-negotiable core beliefs

Illegal Aliens Are Here Illegally.
Pro-Domestic Employment Is Indispensable.
Stronger Military Is Essential.
Special Interests Eliminated.
Gun Ownership Is Sacred.
Government Must Be Downsized.
National Budget Must Be Balanced.
Deficit Spending Will End.
Bail-Out and Stimulus Plans Are Illegal.
Reduce Personal Income Taxes A Must.
Reduce Business Income Taxes Is Mandatory.
Political Offices Available To Average Citizens.
Intrusive Government Stopped.
English As Core Language Is Required.
Traditional Family Values Are Encouraged.
Common Sense Constitutional.
Conservative Self-Governance.

Source: Tea Party/1773 Tea Party

AP TEST PRACTICE

Questions assume cumulative content knowledge from this chapter and previous chapters.

1. The poem reflects the influence of which philosophical ideas?

(A) Religious conservatism

(B) Ideals of religious toleration

(C) Enlightenment

(D) British parliamentary system

2. Which common political question is being alluded to by both the poem and the document?

(A) Degree of authority of centralized power

(B) Legitimacy of Parliamentary power

(C) The extent of private property rights

(D) Commercial regulation

3. The poem and document best share which of the following regarding the audience being addressed?

(A) Grassroots movement

(B) Intellectual elites

(C) Women

(D) Politicians

TAVERNS IN REVOLUTIONARY MASSACHUSETTS

IN colonial Massachusetts, as in many other American colonies in the 1760s and 1770s, taverns (or "public houses," or "pubs," as they came to be known) were crucial to the development of popular resistance to British rule. The Puritan culture of New England created some resistance to taverns, and there were continuing efforts by reformers to regulate or close them to reduce the problems caused by "public drunkenness," "lewd behavior," and anarchy. But as the commercial life of the colonies expanded, and as increasing numbers of people began living in towns and cities, taverns became a central institution in American social life—and eventually in its political life as well.

Taverns were appealing, of course, because they provided alcoholic drinks in a culture where the craving for alcohol—and the extent of drunkenness—was very high. But taverns had other attractions as well. There were few other places where people could meet and talk openly in public, and to many colonists the life of the tavern came to seem the most democratic experience available to them. Gradually, many began to see the attacks on the public houses as efforts to increase the power of existing elites and suppress the freedoms of ordinary people. The tavern was a mostly male institution, just as politics was considered a mostly male concern. And so the fusion of male camaraderie and political discourse emerged naturally out of the tavern culture.

As the revolutionary crisis deepened, taverns and pubs became the central meeting places for discussions of the ideas that fueled resistance to British polices. Educated and uneducated men alike joined in animated discussions of events. Those who could not read—and there were many—could learn about the contents of revolutionary pamphlets from listening to tavern discussions. They could join in the discussion of the new republican ideas emerging in the Americas by participating in tavern celebrations of, for example, the anniversaries of resistance to the Stamp Act. Those anniversaries inspired elaborate toasts in public houses throughout the colonies. Such toasts were the equivalents of political speeches, and illiterate men could learn much from them about the political concepts that were circulating through the colonies.

THE SCALES OF JUSTICE This sign for a Hartford tavern promises hospitality (from "the charming Patroness") and "entertainment" as well as food and drink. (© The Connecticut Historical Society, Gift of Mrs. Morgan Brainard)

supporting Massachusetts. Women's groups throughout the colonies mobilized to extend the boycotts of British goods and to create substitutes for the tea, textiles, and other commodities they were shunning.

COOPERATION AND WAR

Revolutions do not simply happen. They need organizers and leaders. Beginning in 1765, colonial leaders developed a variety of organizations for converting popular discontent into direct action–organizations that in time formed the basis for an independent government.

NEW SOURCES OF AUTHORITY

The passage of authority from the royal government to the colonists themselves began on the local level, where the tradition of autonomy was already strong. In colony after colony, local institutions responded to the resistance movement by simply seizing authority on their own. At times, entirely new, extralegal bodies emerged semispontaneously and began to perform some of the functions of government. In Massachusetts in 1768, for example, Samuel Adams called

a convention of delegates from the towns of the colony to sit in place of the General Court, which the governor had dissolved. The Sons of Liberty, which Adams had helped organize in Massachusetts and which sprang up elsewhere as well, became another source of power. Its members at times formed disciplined bands of vigilantes who made certain that all colonists respected the boycotts and other forms of popular resistance. And in most colonies, committees of prominent citizens began meeting to perform additional political functions.

The most effective of these new groups were the committees of correspondence, which Adams had inaugurated in

FIRST CONTINENTAL CONGRESS

Massachusetts in 1772. Virginia later established the first intercolonial committees of correspondence, which made possible continuous cooperation among the colonies. Virginia also took the greatest step of all toward united action in 1774 when, after the royal governor dissolved the assembly, a special session met in the Raleigh Tavern at Williamsburg, declared that the Intolerable Acts menaced the liberties of every colony, and issued a call for a Continental Congress. Variously elected by the assemblies and by extralegal meetings, delegates from all the thirteen colonies except Georgia were present when, in September 1774, the First

TAVERNS AND POLITICS The Green Dragon Tavern is where protestors planned the Boston Tea Party. (© The Granger Collection, New York)

Taverns were important sources of information in an age before any wide distribution of newspapers. Tavernkeepers were often trusted informants and confidants to the Sons of Liberty and other activists, and they were fountains of information about the political and social turmoil of the time. Taverns were also the settings for political events. In 1770, for example, a report circulated through the taverns of Danvers, Massachusetts, about a local man who was continuing to sell tea despite the colonial boycott. The Sons of Liberty brought the seller to the Bell Tavern and persuaded him to sign a confession and apology before a crowd of defiant men.

Almost all politicians found it necessary to visit taverns in colonial Massachusetts if they wanted any real contact with the public. Samuel Adams spent considerable time in the public houses of Boston, where he sought to encourage resistance to British rule while taking care to drink moderately so as not to erode his stature as a leader. His cousin John Adams was somewhat more skeptical of taverns, more sensitive to the vices they encouraged. But he, too, recognized their political value. In taverns, he once said, "bastards, and legislatores are frequently begotten." ●

UNDERSTAND, ANALYZE, AND EVALUATE

1. Why were taverns so important in educating colonists about the relationship with Britain?
2. The tavern is described as a "mostly male institution" yet women often participated in political activities. Where might women have gathered and discussed political ideas (if not in the tavern)?
3. What gathering places today serve the same purposes that taverns did in colonial America?

RECRUITING PATRIOTS This Revolutionary War recruiting poster attracted recruits by appealing to their patriotism (asking them to defend "the liberties and independence of the United States"), their vanity (by showing the "handsome clothing" and impressive bearing of soldiers), and their greed (by offering them "a bounty of twelve dollars" and "sixty dollars a year"). (Library of Congress)

Continental Congress convened in Carpenter's Hall in Philadelphia. They made five major decisions. First, in a very close vote, they rejected a plan (proposed by Joseph Galloway of Pennsylvania) for a colonial union under British authority (much like the earlier Albany Plan). Second, they endorsed a statement of grievances, whose tortured language reflected the conflicts among the delegates between moderates and extremists. The statement seemed to concede Parliament's right to regulate colonial trade and addressed the king as "Most Gracious Sovereign"; but it also included a more extreme demand for the repeal of all the oppressive legislation passed since 1763. Third, they approved a series of resolutions, recommending, among other things, that the colonists make military preparations for defense against possible attack by the British troops in Boston. Fourth, they agreed to nonimportation, nonexportation, and nonconsumption as means of stopping all trade with Great Britain, and they formed a "Continental Association" to enforce the agreements. And fifth, when the delegates

THE BATTLES OF LEXINGTON AND CONCORD, 1775 This map shows the fabled series of events that led to the first battle of the American Revolution. On the night of April 18, 1775, Paul Revere and William Dawes rode out from Boston to warn the outlying towns of the approach of British troops. Revere was captured just west of Lexington, but Dawes escaped and returned to Boston. The next morning, British forces moved out of Boston toward Lexington, where they met armed American minutemen on the Lexington common and exchanged fire. The British dispersed the Americans in Lexington. But they next moved on to Concord, where they encountered more armed minutemen, clashed again, and were driven back toward Boston. All along their line of march, they were harassed by riflemen.

• *What impact did the Battles of Lexington and Concord (and the later Battle of Bunker Hill, also shown on this map) have on colonial sentiment toward the British?*

adjourned, they agreed to meet again the next spring, thus indicating that they considered the Continental Congress a continuing organization.

Through their representatives in Philadelphia the colonies had, in effect, reaffirmed their autonomous status within the empire and declared something close to economic war to maintain that position. The more optimistic of the Americans hoped that this economic warfare alone would win a quick and bloodless victory, but the more pessimistic had their doubts. "I expect no redress, but, on the contrary, increased resentment and double vengeance," John Adams wrote to Patrick Henry; "we must fight." And Henry replied, "By God, I am of your opinion."

During the winter, the Parliament in London debated proposals for conciliating the colonists. Lord Chatham (William Pitt), the former prime minister, urged the withdrawal of troops from America. Edmund Burke called for the repeal of the Coercive Acts. But their efforts

THE CONCILIATORY PROPOSITIONS

were in vain. Lord North finally won approval early in 1775 for a series of measures known as the Conciliatory Propositions, but they were far less conciliatory than the approaches Burke or Chatham had urged. Parliament now proposed that the colonies, instead of being taxed directly by Parliament, would tax themselves at Parliament's demand. With this offer, Lord North hoped to divide the American moderates, who he believed represented the views of the majority, from the extremist minority. But his offer was too little and too late. It did not reach America until after the first shots of war had been fired.

LEXINGTON AND CONCORD

For months, the farmers and townspeople of Massachusetts had been gathering arms and ammunition and training as "minutemen," preparing to fight on a minute's notice. The Continental Congress had approved preparations for a defensive war, and the citizen-soldiers awaited an aggressive move by the British regulars in Boston.

The Retreat

From Concord to Lexington of the Army of Wild Irish Asses Defeated by the Brave American Militia

Mr Deacon Mr Loeings Mr Mulikens Mr Bonds Houses and Barn all Plundered and Burnt on April 19th

THE BRITISH RETREAT FROM CONCORD, 1775 This American cartoon satirizes the retreat of British forces from Concord after the battle there on April 19, 1775. Patriot forces are lined up on the left, and the retreating British forces (portrayed with dog heads, perhaps because many of the soldiers were "wild" Irish) straggle off at right—some fleeing in panic, others gloating over the booty they have plundered from the burning homes above. In its crude and exaggerated way, the cartoon depicts the success of Patriot forces at the Old North Bridge in Concord in repulsing a British contingent under the command of Lord Percy. As the redcoats retreated to Lexington and then to Boston, they continued to encounter fire from colonial forces, not arrayed in battle lines as shown here, but hidden along the road. One British soldier described the nightmarish withdrawal: "We were fired on from Houses and behind Trees . . . the Country was . . . full of Hills, Woods, stone Walls . . . which the Rebels did not fail to take advantage of." (© Anne S. K. Brown Military Collection, Brown University Library)

In Boston, General Thomas Gage, commanding the British garrison, knew of the military preparations in the countryside but considered his army too small to do anything until reinforcements arrived. He resisted the advice of less cautious officers, who assured him that the Americans would never dare actually to fight, that they would back down quickly before any show of British force. Major John Pitcairn, for example, insisted that a single "small action," such as the burning of a few towns, would "set everything to rights."

GENERAL THOMAS GAGE

General Gage still hesitated when he received orders from England to arrest the rebel leaders Sam Adams and John Hancock, known to be in the vicinity of Lexington. But when Gage heard that the minutemen had stored a large supply of gunpowder in Concord (eighteen miles from Boston), he finally decided to act. On the night of April 18, 1775, he sent a detachment of about 1,000 soldiers out from Boston on the road to Lexington and Concord. He intended to surprise the colonials and seize the illegal supplies without bloodshed.

But Patriots in Boston were watching the British movements closely, and during the night two horsemen, William Dawes and Paul Revere, rode out to warn the villages and farms. When the

British troops arrived in Lexington the next day, several dozen minutemen awaited them on the town common. Shots were fired and minutemen fell; eight of them were killed and ten more wounded. Advancing to Concord, the British discovered that the Americans had hastily removed most of the powder supply, but the British burned what was left of it. All along the road from Concord back to Boston, farmers hiding behind trees, rocks, and stone fences harassed the British with continual gunfire. By the end of the day, the British had lost almost three times as many men as the Americans.

The first shots–the "shots heard round the world," as Americans later called them–had been fired. But who had fired them? According to one of the minutemen at Lexington, Major Pitcairn had shouted to the colonists on his arrival, "Disperse, ye rebels!" When the Americans ignored the command, he had given the order to fire. British officers and soldiers told a different story. They claimed that the minutemen had fired first, that only after seeing the flash of American guns had the British begun to shoot. Whatever the truth, the rebels succeeded in circulating their account well ahead of the British version, adorning it with lurid tales of British atrocities. The effect was to rally to the rebel cause thousands of colonists, north and south, who previously had had little enthusiasm for war.

Jeremy Lister, a minuteman in Lexington, wrote later: "We got all over the bay and landed on the opposite shore betwixt twelve and one O'Clock and was on our March by one, which was at first through some swamps and slips of the Sea till we got into the Road leading to Lexington soon after which the Country people begun to fire their alarm guns light their Beacons, to raise the Country. . . . To the best of my recollection about 4 oClock in the morning being the 19th of April the 5 front Compys. was ordered to Load which we did."

THE REVOLUTION BEGINS

It was not immediately clear to the British, and even to many Americans, that the skirmishes at Lexington and Concord were the first battles of a war. Many saw them as simply another example of the tensions that had been afflicting Anglo-American relations for years. But whether they recognized it at the time or not, the British and the Americans had taken a decisive step. The War for Independence had begun.

AP CONNECTING THEMES

Chapter 4 discussed the importance of the French and Indian War and its effect on subsequent relations between the colonists and Great Britain. Victory in the war left the colonists and Great Britain with substantially different perceptions of the contributions of each to the war. Saddled with debt and recognizing that the colonists were not behaving in a mercantilistic manner, the British government made various attempts to increase control over the colonies. Those attempts were resisted by many colonists, and greater colonial unity resulted as organizational structures of resistance were formed.

The following themes have a heightened importance in Chapter 4. You should now be able to do the following for each listed theme:

Identity: Explain how the escalating conflict between Great Britain and the colonists led to a redefining of American identity.
Work, Exchange, and Technology: Explain how disagreements over trade and taxation led to increased conflict between the colonists and Great Britain.
Politics and Power: Analyze the reasons for and the consequences of the struggle for political power between the colonists and Great Britain.
Ideas, Beliefs, and Culture: Explain how the conflict over taxation and representation compounded problems between the colonists and Great Britain. Describe the role philosophical principles played in the revolt of the British colonies.

AP SUGGESTED STUDY

PEOPLE/PLACES/EVENTS As you study these items, think about how they demonstrate or relate to key concepts and historical themes from this chapter and previous chapters.

ALBANY PLAN 100
BENJAMIN FRANKLIN 100
BOSTON MASSACRE 115
BOSTON TEA PARTY 119
CHARLES TOWNSHEND 114
COERCIVE ACTS (INTOLERABLE ACTS) 119
COMMITTEES OF CORRESPONDENCE 123
CREOLES 101
CURRENCY ACT 111
DAUGHTERS OF LIBERTY 119
FIRST CONTINENTAL CONGRESS 123
GEORGE GRENVILLE 109

IMPERIAL AUTHORITY 99
IMPRESSMENT 103
IROQUOIS CONFEDERACY 101
LORD NORTH 115
MERCY OTIS WARREN 119
MUTINY ACT 110
PATRICK HENRY 113
PAXTON BOYS 110
PONTIAC'S REBELLION 109
PROCLAMATION OF 1763 109
QUEBEC ACT 119
SAMUEL ADAMS 116

SEVEN YEARS' WAR (FRENCH AND INDIAN WAR) 103-107
SONS OF LIBERTY 122
STAMP ACT 111
STAMP ACT CONGRESS 113
SUGAR ACT 113
TEA ACT 118
TOWNSHEND DUTIES 115
VIRGINIA RESOLVES 113
WILLIAM PITT 103

AP TEST PRACTICE

Questions assume cumulative content knowledge from this chapter and previous chapters.

MULTIPLE CHOICE Use the map on page 108 and your knowledge of U.S. history to answer questions 1-4.

1. Which best expresses the British government's motive for establishing the boundary represented by the red line?

   (A) The British government did not want the colonists to expand into any more territory.

   (B) The British government wanted to control tensions between the coastal regions and the "backcountry."

   (C) Great Britain resolved to truly support American Indian needs.

   (D) Great Britain wanted to wrest control of colonial westward expansion from the provincial colonial governments.

2. British colonial expansion westward during the early to mid-1700s directly resulted in

   (A) restoring the mercantilistic relationship between Great Britain and the colonies

   (B) tensions between backcountry settlers and the colonial governments

   (C) colonial assemblies issuing paper money

   (D) complete control of the fur trade in North America by the British government

3. The North American colonies' response to the boundary represented by the red line most echoes the colonies' response to which earlier English government action?

   (A) The decentralization of Britain's day-to-day administration of colonial affairs in the early 1700s

   (B) The English monarch's attempts in the 17th century to establish Catholicism as England's official religion

   (C) The English government's attempts in the mid-17th century to regulate colonial commerce

   (D) The English monarch's resumption in the mid- to late 1700s of grants of land in North America to loyal courtiers

4. The colonists' general attitude toward the boundary represented by the red line parallels which colonial attitude toward American Indian rights?

   (A) In their desire for land, the colonists had little regard for treaties made with Native Americans.

   (B) The colonists' renegotiated treaties with Native Americans, before beginning to encroach on new western lands.

   (C) The colonial governments attempted to tax Native Americans for the western lands they occupied.

   (D) The colonists viewed orderly westward expansion as a means to protect natural resources.

SHORT ANSWER Use your knowledge of U.S. history to answer questions 5–8.

5. Answer a, b, and c.

   a) Briefly explain ONE example of how the Seven Years' War affected Britain's attitude and policies toward its North American colonies.

   b) Briefly explain a SECOND example of how the Seven Years' War affected Britain's attitude and policies toward its North American colonies.

   c) Briefly explain ONE example of how British colonists' attitudes toward the British government changed from

the time of the Seven Years' War to the American Revolution.

6. Answer a, b, and c.

   a) Briefly explain ONE example of how imperial competition affected colonial conflict with American Indian groups.

   b) Briefly explain a SECOND example of how imperial competition affected colonial conflict with American Indian groups.

   c) Briefly explain ONE example of the effect of the British victory in the Seven Years' War on Native American groups.

7. Answer a and b.

   a) For ONE of the areas below, identify ONE event or development regarding American Indian relations with European colonial nations. Briefly explain how that relationship affected the position of American Indians in the Seven Years' War.

   • Political

   • Economic

   • Cultural

   b) Choose a second area and explain why that perspective is not as important in analyzing the American Indians' position in the Seven Years' War.

8. Using the poster shown on page 116, answer a, b, and c.

   a) Briefly explain the point of view of the poster regarding the British colonies' relations with Great Britain between 1763 and 1775.

   b) Briefly explain ONE development in that time period, which could be used to support that point of view.

   c) Briefly explain ONE development in that time period, which could be used to challenge that point of view.

LONG ESSAY Develop a thoughtful and thorough historical argument that answers the question below. Begin your essay with a thesis statement and support it with relevant historical evidence.

9. Some historians have argued that the American Revolution was more an economic revolt than a philosophical or political revolt. Support, modify, or refute this interpretation, providing specific evidence to justify your answer.

5 | THE AMERICAN REVOLUTION

SURRENDER OF CORNWALLIS On October 19, 1781, Lord Charles Cornwallis surrendered to George Washington at Yorktown. This painting by James S. Baillie depicts the event that ended the hostilities between Britain and the United States. (© Gilder Lehrman Collection, New York, USA/The Bridgeman Art Library)

AP

HISTORICAL THINKING

1. **Patterns of Continuity and Change over Time** To what degree and in what ways did American Indians adjust to British-American conflict both during and after the revolution?

2. **Comparison** Compare and contrast the makeup of groups that supported the American Revolution and the makeup of those that opposed the revolution.

3. **Historical Argumentation** In descending order of importance, rank the factors that led to American victory in the American Revolution and defend your ranking.

4. **Contextualization** To what degree and in what ways did the American Revolution foster the further development of republican ideas of self-government, both at the national and state levels?

5. **Patterns of Continuity and Change over Time** To what degree and in what ways were the lives of African Americans and women changed by the American Revolution?

6. **Historical Argumentation** Analyze both the strengths and weaknesses of the Articles of Confederation citing specific historical evidence to support your position.

7. **Historical Causation** Analyze the reasons for and consequence of national and state policies that encouraged western migration.

Key Concept Correlations

Analyze the ways the historical developments you learn about in this chapter connect to the following AP Key Concepts.

3.1 Britain's victory over France in the imperial struggle for North America led to new conflicts among the British government, the North American colonists, and American Indians, culminating in the creation of a new nation, the United States.

3.2 In the late 18th century, new experiments with democratic ideas and republican forms of government, as well as other new religious, economic, and cultural ideas, challenged traditional imperial systems across the Atlantic World.

3.3 Migration within North America, cooperative interaction, and competition for resources raised questions about boundaries and policies, intensified conflicts among peoples and nations, and led to contests over the creation of a multiethnic, multiracial national identity.

Thematic Learning Objectives

ID-1, 4, 5, 6; WXT-1; POL-1, 2; WOR-1, 2, 5; CUL-1, 2, 4; PEO-4, 5; ENV-2, 4

CHAPTER 5 discusses the American Revolution and its immediate aftermath. You should be familiar with the three phases of the American Revolution as the war moved from north to south. Be aware of the adaptations American Indians had to make in choosing sides between the colonists and Great Britain. The American Revolution had a liberalizing effect on American society, and you should be aware of the degree of change experienced by African Americans and women. You should be able to analyze the impact of the United States moving outside of the British mercantile system and how that move required the United States to form new trading patterns with foreign nations. States rewrote their constitutions and, in so doing, reflected movement toward ideals of republican self-government enfranchising more people. It is absolutely important that you understand the concept of republican and democratic ideals. Westward migration was encouraged by both state and national governments and led to increased problems with American Indians and British and Spanish interests. You should be able to explain those problems and understand the attempts at resolution. As you read, evaluate the following ideas:

- American Indians continuously adjusted their alliances with European powers during the 18th century.
- The American colonies overcame significant obstacles to defeat Great Britain in the American Revolution.
- Ideas from the Enlightenment and the belief in republican ideas of self-government led to a transformation of political thought in the United States.
- The United States established a weak confederal system of government based on residual fears of tyranny.
- Western expansion led to continued conflict with American Indians and foreign countries.

THE STATES UNITED

Although many Americans had been anticipating a military conflict with Britain for months, even years, the actual beginning of hostilities in 1775 found the colonies generally unprepared for the enormous challenges awaiting them. America was an unformed nation, with a population less than a third as large as the 9 million of Great Britain, and with vastly inferior economic and military resources. It faced the task of mobilizing for war against the world's greatest armed power at the same time Americans were deeply divided about what they were fighting for.

DEFINING AMERICAN WAR AIMS

Three weeks after the Battles of Lexington and Concord, the Second Continental Congress met in the State House in Philadelphia, with delegates from every colony except Georgia, which sent no representative until the following autumn. The members agreed to support the war, but they disagreed, at times profoundly, about its purpose.

At one pole was a group led by the Adams cousins (John and Samuel), Richard Henry Lee of Virginia, and others, who favored complete independence from Great Britain. At the other pole was a group led by such moderates as John Dickinson of Pennsylvania, who hoped for modest reforms in the imperial relationship that would permit an early reconciliation with Great Britain. Most of the delegates tried to find some middle ground between these positions. They demonstrated their uncertainty in two very different declarations, which they adopted in quick succession. They approved one last, conciliatory appeal to the king, the "Olive Branch Petition," which the British government rejected. Then, on July 6, 1775, they adopted an antagonistic "Declaration of the Causes and Necessity of Taking Up Arms." It proclaimed that the British government had left the American people with only two alternatives: "unconditional submission to the tyranny of irritated ministers or resistance by force."

OLIVE BRANCH PETITION

The attitude of much of the public mirrored that of the Congress. At first, most Americans believed they were fighting not for independence but for a redress of grievances within the British Empire. During the first year of fighting, however, many of them began to change their minds, for several reasons. First, the costs of the war–human and financial–were so high that the original war aims began to seem too modest to justify them. Second, what lingering affection American Patriots retained for England greatly diminished when the British began trying to recruit Indians, African slaves, and foreign mercenaries (the hated Hessians) against them. Third, and most important, colonists came to believe that the British government was forcing them toward independence by rejecting the Olive Branch Petition and instead enacting a "Prohibitory Act." It closed the colonies to all overseas trade and made no concessions to American demands except an offer to pardon repentant rebels. The British enforced the Prohibitory Act with a naval blockade of colonial ports.

But the growing support for independence remained to a large degree unspoken until January 1776, when an impassioned pamphlet appeared that galvanized many Americans. It was called, simply, *Common Sense*. Its author, unmentioned on the title page, was thirty-eight-year-old Thomas Paine, who had emigrated from England to America fifteen months before.

COMMON SENSE He barely survived the transatlantic voyage to America. For much of his life he lived in poverty, and he was ostracized because he openly ridiculed Christianity. But his pamphlets influenced the developing ideals of the United States. A failure in various trades, Paine now proved a brilliant success as a Revolutionary propagandist. His *Common Sense* helped change the American outlook toward the war. Paine wanted to turn the anger of Americans away from the specific parliamentary measures they were resisting and toward what he considered the root of the problem–the English constitution itself. It was not enough, he argued, for Americans to continue blaming their problems on particular ministers, or even on Parliament. It was the king, and the system that permitted him to rule, that was to blame. It was, he argued, simple common sense for Americans to break completely with a government that could produce so corrupt a monarch as George III, a government that could inflict such brutality on its own people, a government that could drag Americans into wars in which America had no interest. The island kingdom of England was no more fit to rule the American continent, Paine claimed, than a satellite was fit to rule the sun.

THE DECISION FOR INDEPENDENCE

Common Sense sold more than 100,000 copies in its first few months. To many of its readers it was a revelation. Although sentiment for independence remained far from unanimous, support for the idea grew rapidly in the first months of 1776.

At the same time, the Continental Congress was moving slowly and tentatively toward a final break with England. It declared American ports open to the ships of all nations except Great Britain's. It entered into communication with foreign powers. It recommended to the various colonies that they establish new governments independent of the British Empire, as most already were doing. Congress also appointed a committee to draft a formal declaration of independence. On July 2, 1776, it adopted a resolution: "That these United Colonies are, and, of right, ought to be, free and independent states; that

THE DECLARATION OF INDEPENDENCE they are absolved from all allegiance to the British crown, and that all political connexion between them and the state of Great Britain is, and ought to be, totally dissolved." Two days later, on July 4, Congress approved the Declaration of Independence, which provided the formal justifications for the actions the delegates had in fact taken two days earlier.

Thomas Jefferson, a thirty-three-year-old delegate from Virginia, wrote most of the Declaration, with help from Benjamin Franklin and John Adams. As Adams later observed, Jefferson said little in the document that was new. Its power lay in the eloquence with which it expressed beliefs already widespread in America. In particular, it repeated ideas that had been voiced throughout the colonies in the preceding months in the form of at least ninety local "declarations of independence"–declarations

THOMAS PAINE Paine emigrated to America in 1774 and quickly became involved in the revolutionary circles in Philadelphia. Early in 1776, he published an anonymous pamphlet titled *Common Sense*, which called for an end to British rule in America. He served in the American army during the Revolution in New Jersey, while also writing additional tracts promoting independence. In later years, he joined the French Revolution and published *The Rights of Man* in 1791–1792. (© Corbis)

drafted up and down the coast by town meetings, artisan and militia organizations, county officials, grand juries, Sons of Liberty, and colonial assemblies. Jefferson borrowed heavily from these texts, both for the ideas he expressed and, to some extent, for the precise language he used.

The document was in two parts. In the first, the Declaration restated the familiar contract theory of John Locke: that governments were formed to protect the rights of life, liberty, and property; Jefferson gave the theory a more idealistic tone by replacing "property" with "the pursuit of happiness." In the second part, the Declaration listed the alleged crimes of the king, who, with the backing of Parliament, had violated his "contract" with the colonists and thus had forfeited all claim to their loyalty.

The Declaration's ringing endorsement of the idea that "all men are created equal"–a phrase borrowed from an earlier document by Jefferson's fellow Virginian George Mason–later helped inspire movements of liberation and reform of many kinds in the United States and abroad, among them the French Revolution's own Declaration of the Rights of Man. More immediately, the Declaration–and its bold claim that the American colonies were now a sovereign nation, "The United States of America"–led to increased foreign aid for the struggling rebels and prepared the way for France's intervention on their side. The Declaration also encouraged American Patriots, as those opposing the British called themselves, to fight on and to reject the idea of a peace that stopped short of winning independence. At the same time, it created deep divisions within American society.

RESPONSES TO INDEPENDENCE

At the news of the Declaration of Independence, crowds in Philadelphia, Boston, and other places gathered to cheer, fire guns and cannons, and ring church bells. But there were many in America who did not rejoice. Some had disapproved of the war from the beginning. Others had been willing to support it only so long as its aims did not conflict with their basic loyalty to the king. Such people were a minority, but a substantial one. They called themselves Loyalists; supporters of independence called them Tories.

In the aftermath of the Declaration of Independence, the colonies began to call themselves "states"–a reflection of their belief that each province was now in some respects a separate and sovereign entity. Even before the Declaration, colonies were beginning to operate independently of royal authority.

DIVIDED AMERICANS The Parliament in London had suspended representative government in America. That suspension did not end colonial self-government. It increased it, since the colonial assemblies continued to meet, now independent of imperial law. After the Declaration of 1776, the former colonies marked their independence by writing formal constitutions for themselves. By 1781, most of the new states had produced such constitutions, which established republican governments. Some of these constitutions survived for many decades without significant change.

At the national level, however, the process of forming a government was more halting and less successful. For a time, Americans were uncertain whether they even wanted a real national government; the Continental Congress had not been much more than a coordinating mechanism, and virtually everyone considered the individual colonies (now states) the real centers of authority. Yet fighting a war required a certain amount of central direction. Americans began almost immediately to do something they would continue to do for more than two centuries: balance the commitment to state and local autonomy against the need for some centralized authority.

In November 1777, Congress adopted the Articles of Confederation (which were not finally ratified until 1781). They did little more than confirm the weak, decentralized system already in operation. The Continental Congress **ARTICLES OF CONFEDERATION** would survive as the chief coordinating agency of the war effort. Its powers over the individual states would be very limited. Indeed, the Articles did not make it entirely clear that the Congress was to be a real government. As a result, the new nation had to fight a war for its own survival with a weak and uncertain central government, never sure of its own legitimacy.

MOBILIZING FOR WAR

The new governments of the states and the nation faced a series of overwhelming challenges: raising and organizing armies, providing them with supplies and equipment, and finding a way to pay for it all. Without access to the British markets on which the colonies had come to depend, finding necessary supplies was exceptionally difficult.

America had many gunsmiths, but they could not come close to meeting the wartime demand for guns and ammunition, let alone the demand for heavy arms. Although Congress created a government arsenal at Springfield, Massachusetts, in 1777, the Americans managed to manufacture only a small fraction of the equipment they needed. Instead, they relied heavily on weapons and matériel they were able to capture from the British. But they got most of their war supplies from European nations, mainly from France.

Financing the war proved in many ways the most nettlesome problem. Congress had no authority to levy taxes directly on the people; it had to requisition funds from the state governments. But hard money was scarce in America, and the states were little better equipped to raise it than Congress was. None of them contributed more than a small part of their expected share. Congress tried to raise money by selling long-term bonds, but few Americans could afford them and those who could generally preferred to invest in more-profitable ventures, such as privateering. In the end, the government had no choice but to issue paper money. Continental currency came from the printing presses in large and repeated batches. The states printed sizable amounts of paper currency of their own.

VOTING FOR INDEPENDENCE The Continental Congress actually voted in favor of independence from Great Britain on July 2, 1776. July 4, the date Americans now celebrate as Independence Day, is when the Congress formally ratified the Declaration of Independence. This painting by Edgar Pine-Savage re-creates the scene in Philadelphia as delegates from the various colonies made their momentous decision. (© Philadelphia History Museum at the Atwater Kent/Courtesy of Historical Society of Pennsylvania Collection,/The Bridgeman Art Library)

war. Many English authorities continued to believe that British forces were simply attempting to quell pockets of rebellion in the contentious area around Boston. Gradually, however, colonial forces took the offensive and made almost the entire territory of the American colonies a battleground.

After the British withdrawal from Concord and Lexington in April 1775, American forces besieged the army of General **BUNKER HILL** Thomas Gage in Boston. The Patriots suffered severe casualties in the Battle of Bunker Hill (actually fought on Breed's Hill) on June 17, 1775, and were ultimately driven from their position there. But they inflicted much greater losses on the enemy than the enemy inflicted on them. Indeed, the British suffered their heaviest casualties of the entire war at Bunker Hill. After the battle, the Patriots continued to tighten the siege.

By the first months of 1776, the British had concluded that Boston was not the best place from which to wage war. Not only was it in the center of the most fervently anti-British

region of the colonies, it was also tactically indefensible–a narrow neck of land, easily isolated and besieged. By late winter, in fact, Patriot forces had surrounded the city and occupied strategic positions on the heights. On March 17, 1776 (a date still celebrated in Boston as Evacuation Day), the British departed Boston for Halifax in Nova Scotia with hundreds of Loyalist refugees. Less than a year after the firing of the first shots, the Massachusetts colonists had driven the British–temporarily–from American soil.

Elsewhere, the war proceeded fitfully and inconclusively. To the south, at Moore's Creek Bridge in North Carolina, a band of Patriots crushed an uprising of Loyalists on February 27, 1776, and in the process discouraged a British plan to invade the southern states. The British had expected substantial aid from local Tories in the South; they realized now that such aid might not be as effective as they had hoped. To the north, Americans launched an invasion of Canada–hoping to remove the British threat and win the Canadians to their cause. Benedict Arnold, the

REVOLUTIONARY SOLDIERS Jean Baptiste de Verger, a nineteen-year-old French officer serving in America during the Revolution, kept a journal of his experiences illustrated with watercolors. Here he portrays four American soldiers carrying different kinds of arms: a black infantryman with a light rifle, a musketman, a rifleman, and an artilleryman. (© Anne S. K. Brown Military Collection, Brown University Library)

INVASION OF CANADA commander of a small American force, threatened Quebec in late 1775 and early 1776 after a winter march of incredible hardship. Richard Montgomery, coming to his assistance, combined his forces with Arnold's and took command of both. Montgomery died in the assault on the city; and although a wounded Arnold kept up the siege for a time, the Quebec campaign ended in frustration. Congress sent a civilian commission to Canada, headed by the seventy-year-old Benjamin Franklin. But Franklin also failed to win the allegiance of the northern colonists. Canada did not become part of the new nation.

The British evacuation of Boston in 1776 was not, therefore, so much a victory for the Americans as a reflection of changing English assumptions about the war. By the spring of 1776, it had become clear to the British that England must be prepared to fight a much larger and longer conflict. The departure of the British, therefore, signaled the beginning of a new phase in the war.

THE SECOND PHASE: THE MID-ATLANTIC REGION

The next phase of the war, which lasted from 1776 until early 1778, was when the British were in the best position to win. Indeed, had it not been for a series of blunders and misfortunes, they probably would have crushed the rebellion then. During this period the struggle became, for the most part, a traditional, conventional war. And in that, the Americans were woefully overmatched.

The British regrouped quickly after their retreat from Boston. During the summer of 1776, in the weeks immediately following the Declaration of Independence, the waters around New York City grew crowded with the most formidable military force Great Britain had ever sent abroad. Hundreds of man-of-war vessels and troopships and 32,000 disciplined soldiers arrived, under the command of the affable William Howe. Howe felt no particular hostility toward the Americans. He hoped to awe them into submission rather than fight them, and he believed that most of them, if given a chance, would show their loyalty to the king. In a meeting with commissioners from Congress, he offered them a choice between submission with royal pardon and a battle against overwhelming odds.

To oppose Howe's impressive array, Washington could muster only about 19,000 poorly armed and lightly trained soldiers, even after combining the Continental army with state militias; he had no navy at all. Even so, the Americans quickly

THE BATTLE OF GERMANTOWN The Battle of Germantown, a campaign intended by Washington to liberate Philadelphia from British occupation, took place on October 4, 1777. In this painting by Alonzo Chappel (1828–1887), *Battle of Germantown, Attack on Judge Chew's House* (1860), Washington's much larger force cannot defeat the 120 British infantrymen who barricaded themselves in the summer home of Loyalist Benjamin Chew. Twelve thousand American troops were forced to retreat into nearby Montgomery County. (© Chicago History Museum, USA/The Bridgeman Art Library)

BRITISH TAKE NEW YORK rejected Howe's offer and chose to continue the war—a decision that led inevitably to a succession of rapid defeats. The British pushed the defenders off Long Island, compelled them to abandon Manhattan, and then drove them in slow retreat over the plains of New Jersey, across the Delaware River, and into Pennsylvania.

For eighteenth-century Europeans, warfare was a seasonal activity. Fighting generally stopped in cold weather. The British settled down for the winter at various points in New Jersey, leaving an outpost of Hessians (German mercenaries) at Trenton on the Delaware River. But Washington did not sit still. On Christmas night 1776, he boldly recrossed the icy river, surprised and scattered the Hessians, and occupied the town. Then he advanced to Princeton and drove a British force from their base in the college there. But Washington was unable to hold either

Princeton or Trenton, and he finally took refuge for the rest of the winter in the hills around Morristown, New Jersey.

For their campaigns of 1777, the British devised a strategy to cut the United States in two. Howe would move north from **BRITAIN'S STRATEGY** New York City up the Hudson to Albany, while another British force would come south from Canada to meet him. One of the younger British officers, the dashing John Burgoyne, secured command of this northern force and planned a two-pronged attack along both the Mohawk and the upper Hudson approaches to Albany.

But after setting this plan in motion, Howe himself abandoned it. He decided instead to launch an assault on the rebel capital Philadelphia—an assault that would, he hoped, discourage the Patriots, rally the Loyalists, and bring the war to a speedy conclusion. He removed the bulk of his forces from

THE REVOLUTION IN THE NORTH, 1775–1776 After initial battles in and around Boston, the British forces left Massachusetts and (after a brief stay in Halifax, Canada) moved south to New York. In the meantime, American forces moved north in an effort to capture British strongholds in Montreal and Quebec, with little success.

• *Why would the British have considered New York a better base than Boston?*

New York by sea, landed at the head of the Chesapeake Bay, brushed Washington aside at the Battle of Brandywine Creek on September 11, and proceeded north to Philadelphia, which he was able to occupy with little resistance. Meanwhile, Washington, after an unsuccessful October 4 attack at Germantown (just outside Philadelphia), went into winter quarters at Valley Forge. The Continental Congress, now dislodged from its capital, reassembled at York, Pennsylvania.

Howe's move to Philadelphia left Burgoyne to carry out the campaign in the north alone. Burgoyne sent Colonel Barry St. Leger up the St. Lawrence River toward Lake Ontario and the headwaters of the Mohawk, while Burgoyne himself advanced directly down the upper Hudson Valley. He got off to a flying start. He seized Fort Ticonderoga easily and with it an enormous store of powder and supplies; this caused such dismay in Congress that the delegates removed General Philip Schuyler from command of American forces in the north and replaced him with Horatio Gates.

By the time Gates took command, Burgoyne had already experienced two staggering defeats. In one of them–at Oriskany, New York, on August 6–a Patriot band of German farmers led by Nicholas Herkimer held off a force of Indians and Tories commanded by St. Leger. That gave Benedict

Arnold time to go to the relief of Fort Stanwix and close off the Mohawk Valley to St. Leger's advance.

In the other battle–at Bennington, Vermont, on August 16– New England militiamen under the Bunker Hill veteran John Stark severely mauled a British detachment that Burgoyne had sent out to seek supplies. Short of materials, with all help cut off, Burgoyne fought several costly engagements and then withdrew to Saratoga, where Gates surrounded him. On October 17, 1777, Burgoyne ordered what was left of his army, nearly 5,000 men, to surrender to the Americans.

To the Patriots and peoples watching from around the world, the New York campaign was a remarkable victory. The British surrender at Saratoga became a major turning point in the war–above all, perhaps, because it led directly to an alliance between the United States and France.

PATRIOT VICTORY AT SARATOGA

The British failure to win the war during this period, a period in which they had overwhelming advantages, was in large part a result of their own mistakes. And in assessing them, the role of William Howe looms large. He abandoned his own most important strategic initiative–the northern campaign–leaving Burgoyne to fight alone. And even in Pennsylvania, where he chose to

BRITISH BLUNDERS

THE BATTLE OF BUNKER HILL, 1775 British troops face Patriot forces outside Boston on June 17, 1775, in the first great battle of the American Revolution. The British ultimately drove the Americans from their positions on Breed's Hill and Bunker Hill, but only after suffering enormous casualties. General Gage, the British commander, reported to his superiors in London after the battle: "These people show a spirit and conduct against us they never showed against the French." This anonymous painting reveals the array of British troops and naval support and also shows the bombardment and burning of Charles Town from artillery in Boston. (Private Collection/© Peter Newark American Pictures/Bridgeman Images)

engage the enemy, he refrained from moving in for a final attack on the weakened Continental army, even though he had several opportunities. Instead, he repeatedly allowed Washington to retreat and regroup; and he permitted the American army to spend a long winter unmolested in Valley Forge, where–weak and hungry–they might have been easy prey for a British attack. Some British critics believed that Howe did not want to win the war, that he was secretly in sympathy with the American cause. His family had close ties to the colonies, and he was linked politically to those forces within the British government that opposed the war. Others pointed to personal weaknesses: Howe's apparent alcoholism, his romantic attachment (he spent the winter of 1777-1778 in Philadelphia with his mistress when many of his advisers were urging him to move elsewhere). But the most important problem, it seems clear, was his failure to understand the nature of the war that he was fighting–or even to understand that it was truly a war.

THE IROQUOIS AND THE BRITISH

The campaign in upstate New York was not just a British defeat. It was also a setback for the ambitious efforts of several

Iroquois leaders, who had hoped to involve Indian forces in the English military effort, believing that a British victory would help stem white movement onto tribal lands. The Iroquois Confederacy had declared itself neutral in the war in 1776, but not all its members were content to remain passive in the northern campaign. Among those who worked to expand the Native American role in the war were a Mohawk brother and sister, Joseph Brant and Mary Brant. Both were people of stature within the Mohawk nation: Joseph was a celebrated warrior; Mary was a charismatic woman and the widow of Sir William Johnson, the British superintendent of Indians, who had achieved wide popularity among the tribes. The Brants persuaded their own tribe to contribute to the British cause and attracted the support of the Seneca and Cayuga as well. They played an important role in Burgoyne's unsuccessful campaigns in the north.

But the alliance was also a sign of the growing divisions within the Iroquois Confederacy. Only three of the six nations of the Confederacy supported the British. The Oneida and the Tuscarora backed the Americans; the Onondaga split into several factions. The three-century-old

DIVISIONS IN THE IROQUOIS CONFEDERACY

THE REVOLUTION IN THE MIDDLE COLONIES, 1776–1778 These maps illustrate the major campaigns of the Revolution in the middle colonies—New York, New Jersey, and Pennsylvania—between 1776 and 1778. The large map on the left shows the two prongs of the British strategy: first, a movement of British forces south from Canada into the Hudson Valley; and second, a movement of other British forces, under General William Howe, out from New York and south into New Jersey and Pennsylvania. The strategy was designed to trap the American army between the two British movements. The two smaller maps on the right show detailed pictures of some of the major battles. The upper one reveals the surprising American victory at Saratoga. The lower one shows a series of inconclusive battles between New York and Philadelphia in 1777 and 1778.

• *What movements of Howe helped thwart that plan?*

Confederacy, weakened by the aftermath of the French and Indian War, continued to unravel.

The alliance had other unhappy consequences for the Iroquois. A year after Oriskany, Indians joined British troops in a series of raids on outlying white settlements in upstate New York. Months later, Patriot forces under the command of General John Sullivan harshly retaliated, wreaking such destruction on tribal settlements that large groups of Iroquois fled north into Canada to seek refuge. Many never returned.

SECURING AID FROM ABROAD

The failure of the British to crush the Continental army in the mid-Atlantic states, combined with the stunning American victory at Saratoga, was a turning point in the war. It transformed the conflict and ushered it into a new and final phase.

Central to this transformation of the war was American success in winning support from abroad—indirectly from several European nations and directly from France. Even before the Declaration of Independence, Congress dispatched representatives to the capitals of Europe to negotiate commercial treaties with the governments there; if America was to leave the British Empire, it would need to cultivate new trading partners. Such treaties would, of course, require European governments to recognize the United States as an independent nation. John Adams called the early American representatives abroad "militia diplomats." Unlike the diplomatic regulars of Europe, they had little experience with the formal art and etiquette of Old World diplomacy. Since transatlantic communication was slow and uncertain (it took from one to three months for a message to cross the Atlantic), they had to interpret the instructions of Congress very freely and make crucial decisions entirely on their own.

MILITIA DIPLOMATS

The most promising potential ally for the United States was France. King Louis XVI, who had come to the throne in 1774, and his astute foreign minister, the Count de Vergennes, were eager to see Britain lose a crucial part of its empire. Through a series of secret bargains, facilitated by the creation of a fictional trading firm and the use of secret agents on both sides (among them the famed French dramatist Caron de Beaumarchais), France began supplying the Americans large quantities of much-needed supplies. But the French government remained reluctant to provide the United States with what it most wanted: diplomatic recognition.

Finally, Benjamin Franklin himself went to France to represent the United States. A natural diplomat, Franklin became a popular hero among the French–aristocrats and common people alike. His popularity there greatly helped the American cause. Of even greater help was the news of the American victory at Saratoga, which arrived in London on December 2, 1777, and in Paris two days later. On February 6, 1778–in part to forestall a British peace offensive that Vergennes feared might persuade the Americans to abandon the war–France formally recognized the United States as a sovereign nation and laid the groundwork for greatly expanded assistance to the American war effort.

France's intervention made the war an international conflict. In the course of the next two years, France, Spain, and the **PIVOTAL FRENCH AID** Netherlands all drifted into another general war with Great Britain in Europe, and all contributed both directly and indirectly to the ultimate American victory. But France was America's truly indispensable ally. Not only did it furnish the new nation with most of its money and munitions; it also provided a navy and an expeditionary force that proved invaluable in the decisive phase of the Revolutionary conflict.

THE FINAL PHASE: THE SOUTH

The last phase of the military struggle in America was very different from either of the first two. The British government had never been fully united behind the war; after the defeat at Saratoga and the intervention of the French, it imposed new limits on its commitment to the conflict. Instead of a full-scale military struggle against the American army, therefore, the British decided to try to enlist the support of those elements of the American population–a majority, they continued to believe–who were still loyal to the Crown; in other words, they would work to undermine the Revolution from within. Since the British believed Loyalist sentiment was strongest in the southern colonies (despite their earlier failure to enlist Loyalist support in North Carolina), the main focus of their effort shifted there; and so it was in the South, for the most part, that the final stages of the war occurred.

The new British strategy was a dismal failure. British forces spent three years (from 1778 to 1781) moving through the South, fighting small battles and large, and attempting to neutralize the territory through which they traveled. All such efforts ended in frustration. The British badly overestimated the extent of Loyalist sentiment. There were many Tories in Georgia and the Carolinas, some of them disgruntled members of the Regulator movement. But there were also many more Patriots than the British had believed. In Virginia, support for independence was as fervent as in Massachusetts. And even in the lower South, Loyalists often refused to aid the British because they feared reprisals from the Patriots around them. The British also harmed their own cause by encouraging southern slaves to desert their owners in return for promises of emancipation. Many slaves (perhaps 5 percent of the total) took advantage of this offer, despite the great difficulty of doing so. But white southerners were aghast; and even many who might otherwise have been inclined to support the Crown now joined the Patriot side, which posed no such threat to slavery. The British also faced severe logistical problems in the South. Patriot forces could move at will throughout the region, living off the resources of the countryside, blending in with the civilian population and leaving the British unable to distinguish friend from foe. The British, by contrast, suffered all the disadvantages of an army in hostile territory.

It was this phase of the conflict that made the war truly "revolutionary"–not only because it introduced a new kind of combat, but also because it had the effect of mobilizing and politicizing large groups of the population who had previously remained aloof from the struggle. With the war expanding into previously isolated communities, with many civilians forced to involve themselves whether they liked it or not, the political climate of the United States grew more heated than ever. And support for independence, far from being crushed as the British had hoped, greatly increased.

That was the context in which the important military encounters of the last years of the war occurred. In the North, where significant numbers of British troops remained, the fighting settled into a relatively quiet stalemate. Sir Henry **REVOLUTIONARY CONSEQUENCES OF THE SOUTHERN CAMPAIGN** Clinton replaced the hapless William Howe in 1778 and moved what had been Howe's army from Philadelphia back to New York City. There the British troops stayed for more than a year, with Washington using his army to keep watch around them. The American forces in New York did so little fighting in this period that Washington sent some troops west to fight hostile Indians who had been attacking white settlers. In that same winter, George Rogers Clark, under orders from the state of Virginia–not from either Washington or Congress–led a daring expedition over the mountains and captured settlements in the Illinois country from the British and their Indian allies.

During this period of relative calm, General Benedict Arnold shocked the American forces–and Washington in particular–by becoming a traitor. Arnold had been one of the early heroes of the war, but now, convinced that the American cause was hopeless, he conspired with British agents to betray the Patriot

THE REVOLUTION IN THE SOUTH, 1778–1781 The final phase of the American Revolution occurred largely in the South, which the British thought would be a more receptive region for their troops. This map reveals the many, scattered military efforts of the British and the Americans in those years, none of them conclusive. It also shows the final chapter of the Revolution around the Chesapeake Bay and the James River.

• *What errors led the British to their surrender at Yorktown?*

stronghold at West Point on the Hudson River. The scheme unraveled before Arnold could complete it, and he fled to the safety of the British camp, where he spent the rest of the war.

In the meantime, decisive fighting was in progress in the South. The British did have some significant military successes during this period. On December 29, 1778, they captured Savannah, on the coast of Georgia; and on May 12, 1780, they took the port of Charles Town, South Carolina. They also inspired some Loyalists to take up arms and advance with them into the interior. But although the British were able to win conventional battles, they were constantly harassed as

they moved through the countryside by Patriot guerrillas led by such resourceful fighters as Thomas Sumter, Andrew Pickens, and Francis Marion, the "Swamp Fox."

Moving inland to Camden, South Carolina, Lord Cornwallis (Clinton's choice as British commander in the South) met and crushed a Patriot force under Horatio Gates on August 16, 1780. Congress recalled Gates, and Washington gave the southern command to Nathanael Greene, a Quaker and a former blacksmith from Rhode Island and probably the ablest of all the American generals of the time next to Washington.

NATHANAEL GREENE

THE BRITISH ON THE HUDSON, 1776 In one of the largest troop movements of the Revolution, English commanders sent 13,000 British and Hessian troops up the Hudson River to drive George Washington and his Patriot army from strongholds in the palisades above the river. The British took nearly 3,000 prisoners when the Patriots surrendered on November 16, 1776. Thomas Davies painted this watercolor of the British landing at the time. (© Fotosearch/Getty Images)

Even before Greene joined the southern army, the tide of battle began to turn against Cornwallis. At King's Mountain (near the North Carolina–South Carolina border) on October 7, 1780, a band of Patriot riflemen from the backwoods killed, wounded, or captured an entire force of 1,100 New York and South Carolina Tories that Cornwallis was using as auxiliaries. Once Greene arrived, he confused and exasperated Cornwallis further by dividing the American forces into small, fast-moving contingents and refraining from a showdown in open battle. One of the contingents inflicted what Cornwallis admitted was "a very unexpected and severe blow" at Cowpens on January 17, 1781. Finally, after receiving reinforcements, Greene combined all his forces and maneuvered to meet the British on ground of his own choosing, at Guilford Court House, North Carolina. After a hard-fought battle there on March 15, 1781, Greene withdrew from the field; but Cornwallis had lost so many men that he decided at last to abandon the Carolina campaign.

Cornwallis withdrew to the port town of Wilmington, North Carolina, to receive supplies being sent to him by sea; later he moved north to launch raids in the interior of Virginia.

But Clinton, concerned for the army's safety, ordered him to take up a position on the peninsula between the York and James Rivers and wait for ships to carry his troops to New York City or Charles Town. So Cornwallis retreated to Yorktown and began to build fortifications there.

George Washington–along with Count Jean Baptiste de Rochambeau, commander of the French expeditionary force in America, and Admiral François Joseph Paul de Grasse, commander of the French fleet in American waters–set out to trap

YORKTOWN

Cornwallis at Yorktown. Washington and Rochambeau marched a French-American army from New York City to join other French forces under Lafayette in Virginia, while de Grasse sailed with additional troops for Chesapeake Bay and the York River. These joint operations, perfectly timed and executed, caught Cornwallis between land and sea. After a few shows of resistance, he capitulated on October 17, 1781 (four years to the day after the surrender of Burgoyne at Saratoga). Two days later, as a military band played the old tune "The World Turn'd Upside Down," Cornwallis, claiming to be ill, sent a deputy who formally surrendered the British army of more than 7,000 men.

Except for a few skirmishes, the fighting was now over; but the United States had not yet won the war. British forces continued to hold the seaports of Savannah, Charles Town, Wilmington, and New York City. Before long, a British fleet met and defeated Admiral de Grasse's fleet in the West Indies, ending Washington's hopes for further French naval assistance. For more than a year, although there was no significant further combat between British and American forces, it remained possible that the war might resume and the struggle for independence might still be lost.

WINNING THE PEACE

Cornwallis's defeat provoked outcries in England against continuing the war. Lord North resigned as prime minister; Lord Shelburne emerged from the political wreckage to succeed him; and British emissaries appeared in France to talk informally with the American diplomats in Paris. The three American principals were Benjamin Franklin, John Adams, and John Jay.

The Americans were under instructions to cooperate fully with France in their negotiations with England. But Vergennes insisted that France could not agree to any settlement of the war with England until its ally Spain had achieved its principal war aim: winning back Gibraltar from the British. There was no real prospect of that happening soon, and the Americans began to fear that the alliance with France might keep them at war indefinitely. As a result, Franklin, Jay, and Adams began proceeding on their own, without informing Vergennes, and signed a preliminary treaty with Great Britain on November 30, 1782. Franklin, in the meantime, skillfully pacified Vergennes and avoided an immediate rift in the French-American alliance.

The British and Americans reached a final settlement–the Treaty of Paris–on September 3, 1783, when both Spain and France agreed to end hostilities. It was, on the whole, remark-

TREATY OF
PARIS

ably favorable to the United States in granting a clear-cut recognition of its independence and a generous, though ambiguous, cession of territory–from the southern boundary of Canada to the northern boundary of Florida and from the Atlantic to the Mississippi. With good reason, Americans celebrated in the fall of 1783 as the last of the British occupation forces embarked from New York and General Washington, at the head of his troops, rode triumphantly into the city.

WAR AND SOCIETY

Historians have long debated whether the American Revolution was a social as well as a political revolution. Some have argued that the colonists were struggling not only over the question of home rule, but also over "who should rule at home." Others claim that domestic social and economic concerns had little to do with the conflict. (See "Debating the Past," pp. 132-133.) Whatever the motivations of Americans, however, there can

be little doubt that the War for Independence had important effects on the nature of American society.

LOYALISTS AND MINORITIES

The losers in the American Revolution included not only the British but also American Loyalists. There is no way to be sure how many Americans remained loyal to England during the Revolution, but it is clear that there were many–at least a fifth (and some historians estimate as much as a third) of the white population. Their motivations were varied. Some were officeholders in the imperial government, who stood to lose their positions as a result of the Revolution. Others were merchants engaged in trade closely tied to the imperial system. (Most merchants, however, supported the Revolution.) Still others were people who lived in relative isolation and had not been exposed to the wave of discontent that had turned so many Americans against Britain. There were cultural and ethnic minorities who feared that an independent America would not offer them sufficient protection. There were settled, cautious people who feared social instability. And there were those who, expecting the British to win the war, were simply currying favor with the anticipated victors.

What happened to these men and women during the war was a turbulent and at times tragic story. Hounded by Patriots in their communities, harassed by legislative and

THE LOYALISTS'
PLIGHT

judicial actions, the position of many Loyalists became intolerable. Up to 100,000 fled the country. Those who could afford to moved to England, where many lived in difficult and lonely exile. Thomas Hutchinson, who was a wealthy businessman, historian, and loyalist of the king, served in the Massachusetts government for many years as lieutenant governor and from 1758 to 1774 as governor. He was a polarizing figure; and as the Revolution began, his Boston mansion was ransacked during protests against the Stamp Acts. After being replaced as governor in May 1774 by General Thomas Gage, Hutchinson left Boston and moved first to Canada and then to England.

Loyalists of modest means moved to Canada, establishing the first English-speaking community in the province of Quebec. Some returned to America after the war and, as the earlier passions and resentments faded, managed to reenter the life of the nation. Others remained abroad for the rest of their lives.

Most Loyalists were people of average means, but a substantial minority consisted of men and women of wealth. They left behind large estates and vacated important positions of social and economic leadership. Even some who remained in the country saw their property confiscated and their positions forfeited. The result was new opportunities for Patriots to acquire land and influence, a situation that produced significant social changes in many communities.

It would be an exaggeration, however, to claim that the departure of the Loyalists was responsible for anything approaching a social revolution or that the Revolution created a general assault on the wealthy and powerful in America. When the war

THE AGE OF REVOLUTIONS WOR-2

THE American Revolution was a result of specific tensions and conflicts between Britain and its North American colonies. But it was also a part, and a cause, of what historians have come to call an "age of revolutions" that spread through much of the Western world in the late eighteenth and early nineteenth centuries.

The modern idea of revolution—the overturning of old systems and regimes and the creation of new ones—was largely a product of the ideas of the Enlightenment. Among those ideas was the

notion of popular sovereignty, articulated by the English philosopher John Locke and others. Locke argued that political authority did not derive from the divine right of kings or the inherited authority of aristocracies but, rather, from the consent of the governed. A related Enlightenment idea was the concept of individual freedom, which challenged the traditional belief that governments had the right to prescribe the way people act, speak, and even think. Champions of individual freedom in the eighteenth century—among them the French philosopher Voltaire—advocated religious toleration and freedom of thought and expression. The Swiss-French Enlightenment theorist Jean-Jacques Rousseau helped spread the idea of political and legal equality for all people—the end of special privileges for aristocrats and elites, the right of all citizens to participate in the formation of policies and laws.

The American Revolution was the first and in many ways the most influential of the Enlightenment-derived uprisings against established orders. It served as an inspiration to people in other lands who were trying to find a way to oppose unpopular regimes. In 1789, a little over a decade after the beginning of the American Revolution, revolution began in France. The monarchy was abolished (and the king and queen publicly executed in 1793), the authority of the Catholic Church was challenged and greatly weakened, and at the peak of revolutionary chaos during the Jacobin period (1793–1794), more than 40,000 suspected enemies of the revolution were executed and hundreds of thousands of others imprisoned. The most radical phase of the revolution came to an end in 1799, when Napoleon Bonaparte, a young general, seized power and began to build a new French empire. But France's *ancien régime* of king and aristocracy never wholly revived.

The American and French Revolutions helped inspire uprisings in many other parts of the Atlantic world.

STORMING THE BASTILLE This painting portrays the storming of the great Parisian fortress and prison, the Bastille, on July 14, 1789. The Bastille was a despised symbol of royal tyranny to many of the French, because of the arbitrarily arrested and imprisoned people who were sent there. The July assault was designed to release the prisoners, but in fact the revolutionaries found only seven people in the vast fortress. Even so, the capture of the Bastille—which marked one of the first moments in which ordinary Frenchmen joined the Revolution—became one of the great moments in modern French history. The anniversary of the event, "Bastille Day," remains the French national holiday. (© Musee de la Ville de Paris, Musee Carnavalet, Paris, France/The Bridgeman Art Library)

ended, those who had been wealthy at its beginning were, for the most part, still wealthy at the end. Most of those who had wielded social and political influence continued to wield it.

The war had a significant effect on other minorities as well, and on certain religious groups in particular. No sect suffered more than the Anglicans, many of whom were Loyalists. In Virginia and Maryland, where the colonial governments had recognized Anglicanism as the official religion and had imposed a tax for its maintenance, the new Revolutionary regimes disestablished the Anglican Church and

WEAKENING OF THE ANGLICAN CHURCH

eliminated the subsidy. By the time the fighting ended, many Anglican parishes no longer had clergymen, for there were few ministers to take the place of those who had died or who had left the country as Loyalist refugees. Anglicanism survived in America, but the losses during the Revolution permanently weakened it. The Revolution also weakened the Quakers in Pennsylvania and elsewhere. They incurred widespread unpopularity because of their pacifism, which destroyed much of the social and political prestige they had once enjoyed.

While the war was weakening the Anglicans and the Quakers, it was strengthening the position of the Roman

In 1791, a major slave uprising began in Haiti and soon attracted more than 100,000 rebels. The slave army defeated both the white settlers of the island and the French colonial armies sent to quell their rebellion. Under the leadership of General Toussaint L'Ouverture, they began to agitate for independence, which they obtained on January 1, 1804, a few months after Toussaint's death.

Revolution spread next into the Spanish and Portuguese colonies in the Americas, particularly among the so-called Creoles, people of European ancestry born in the Americas. In the late eighteenth century, they began to resist the authority of colonial officials sent from Spain and Portugal and to demand a greater say in governing their own lands. Napoleon's invasion of Spain and Portugal in 1807 weakened the ability of the European regimes to sustain authority over their American colonies. In the years that followed, revolutions swept through much of Latin America. Mexico became an independent nation in 1821, and provinces of Central America that had once been part of Mexico (Guatemala, El Salvador, Honduras, Nicaragua, and Costa Rica) established their independence three years later. Simón Bolívar, modeling his efforts on those of George Washington, led a great revolutionary movement that won independence for Brazil in 1822 and also helped lead revolutionary campaigns in Venezuela, Ecuador, and Peru—all of which won their independence in the 1820s. Across the Atlantic, Greek patriots—drawing from the examples of other revolutionary nations—launched a movement to win their independence from the Ottoman Empire, which finally succeeded in 1830.

The age of revolutions left many new, independent nations in its wake. It did not, however, succeed in establishing the ideals of popular sovereignty, individual freedom, and political equality in all the nations it affected. Slavery survived in the United States and in many areas of Latin America. New forms of aristocracy and even monarchy emerged in France, Mexico, Brazil, and elsewhere. Women—many of whom had hoped the revolutionary age would win new rights for them—made few legal or political gains in this era. But the ideals that the revolutionary era introduced to the Western world continued to shape the histories of nations throughout the nineteenth century and beyond. ●

UNDERSTAND, ANALYZE, AND EVALUATE

1. How did the American Revolution influence the French Revolution?
2. What other nations were affected by the example of the American Revolution?
3. What was the significance of the revolution in Haiti, and how much attention did it get in other nations?

Catholic Church. On the advice of Charles Carroll of Carrollton, a Maryland statesman and Catholic lay leader, most American

STRENGTHENING OF THE CATHOLIC CHURCH

Catholics supported the Patriot cause during the war. The French alliance brought Catholic troops and chaplains to the country, and the gratitude with which most Americans greeted them did much to erode old and bitter hostilities toward Catholics. The Catholic Church did not greatly increase its numbers as a result of the Revolution, but it did gain considerable strength as an institution. Not long after the end of the war, the Vatican provided the United States with its own Catholic hierarchy. (Until then, Catholic bishops in Europe had controlled the American church.) Father John Carroll (also of Maryland) was named head of Catholic missions in America in 1784 and, in 1789, the first American bishop. In 1808 he became archbishop of Baltimore.

THE WAR AND SLAVERY

For the largest of America's minorities—the African American population—the war had limited, but nevertheless profound, significance. For some, it meant freedom, because many slaves took advantage of the British presence in the South in the final years of the war to escape. The British enabled many of them to leave the country—not so much as any principled commitment to emancipation, but more as a way of disrupting the American war effort. In South Carolina, for example, nearly a third of all slaves defected during the war. Africans had constituted over 60 percent of the population in 1770; by 1790, that figure had declined to about 44 percent.

For other African Americans, the Revolution meant an increased exposure to the concept, although seldom to the reality, of liberty. Most black Americans could not read, but few

AFRICAN AMERICAN DESIRE FOR FREEDOM

could avoid the new and exciting ideas circulating through the towns and cities and even at times on the plantations. The results included incidents in several communities in which African Americans engaged in open resistance to white control. In Charles Town, South Carolina, for example, Thomas Jeremiah, a free black, was executed in 1775 after Patriot leaders accused him of conspiring to smuggle British guns to South Carolina slaves. The Revolution also produced some eloquent efforts by black writers (mostly in the North) to articulate its lessons for their people. "Liberty is a jewel which was handed Down to man from the cabinet of heaven," the black New Englander Lemuel Hayes wrote in 1776. "Even an African has Equally good a right to his Liberty in common with Englishmen. . . . Shall a man's Couler Be the Decisive Criterion wherby to Judg of his natural right?"

That was one reason why in South Carolina and Georgia—where slaves constituted half or more of the population—there was great ambivalence about the Revolution. Slaveowners opposed British efforts to emancipate their slaves, but they also feared that the Revolution itself would foment slave rebellions. The same fears helped prevent English colonists in the Caribbean islands (who were far more greatly outnumbered by African slaves) from joining with the continental Americans in the revolt against Britain. In much of the North, the combination of Revolutionary sentiment and evangelical Christian fervor helped spread antislavery sentiments widely through society. But in the South, white support for slavery survived. Southern churches rejected the antislavery ideas of the North and worked instead to develop a rationale for slavery—in part by reinforcing ideas about white superiority, in part by encouraging slaveowners to make slavery more humane.

As in so many other periods of American history, the Revolution exposed the continuing tension between the nation's commitment to liberty and its commitment to slavery. To people in our time, and even to some people in Revolutionary times, it seems obvious that liberty and slavery are incompatible. But to many white Americans in the eighteenth century, especially in the South, that did not seem obvious. Many white southerners believed, in fact, that enslaving Africans—whom they considered inferior and unfit for citizenship—was the best way to ensure liberty for white people. They feared the impact

TENSION BETWEEN LIBERTY AND SLAVERY

of free black people living alongside whites. They also feared that without slaves, it would be necessary to recruit a servile white workforce in the South, and that the resulting inequalities would jeopardize the survival of liberty. One of the ironies of the American Revolution, therefore, was that white Americans were fighting both to secure freedom for themselves and to preserve slavery for others.

NATIVE AMERICANS AND THE REVOLUTION

Most Indians viewed the American Revolution with considerable uncertainty. The American Patriots tried to persuade them to remain neutral in the conflict, which they described as a "family quarrel" between the colonists and Britain that had nothing to do with the tribes.

But in fact a great deal was at stake for Native Americans in the American Revolution. During the colonial period, the British government struggled for many years to restrain the growth of white migration into the Indian lands west of the Appalachian Mountains. Such efforts were mostly unsuccessful. The white colonists, the royal governor of Virginia wrote, "do not conceive that the government has any right to forbid taking possession of a vast tract of country." But the British believed that the government did have a right to protect the lands of the Indians—not because of benevolence, but because of their desire to avoid further battles with the tribes, especially on land that had been promised to the Indians.

Once the Revolutionary War began, the role of the Indians became of critical significance to both sides of the conflict. For the American Patriots, among the goals of battle for independence was their right to expand into the western lands, at the expense of the Indians. Some of the most eminent figures in the new nation were themselves land speculators in the west, among them George Washington, and many such men had long complained about the Proclamation of 1763, which had forbidden white movement into tribal lands. Other colonial grievances against the British included the recruitment of Indians to join the Royal Army. In fact, both sides tried to recruit Indians to help them.

In the western Carolinas and Virginia, a Cherokee faction led by Dragging Canoe attacked outlying white settlements in the summer of 1776. Patriot militias responded with overwhelming force, ravaging Cherokee lands and forcing Dragging Canoe and many of his followers to flee west across the

Tennessee River. Those Cherokees who remained behind agreed to a new treaty by which they gave up still more land. Not all Native American military efforts were so unsuccessful. Some Iroquois, despite the setbacks at Oriskany, continued to wage war against white Americans in the West and caused widespread destruction in large agricultural areas of New York and Pennsylvania—areas whose crops were of crucial importance to the Patriot cause. And although the retaliating United States armies inflicted heavy losses on the Indians, the attacks continued throughout the war.

In the end, however, the Revolution generally weakened the position of Native Americans in several ways. The Patriot victory increased the white demand for western lands; many American whites associated restrictions on settlement with British oppression and expected the new nation to remove the obstacles. At the same time, white attitudes toward the tribes, seldom friendly in the best of times, took a turn for

TAKING SIDES

the worse. Many whites deeply resented the assistance the Mohawk and other Indian nations had given the British and insisted on treating them as conquered people. Others adopted a paternalistic

JOSEPH BRANT, CHIEF OF THE MOHAWKS George Romney painted this portrait, *Joseph Brant, Chief of the Mohawks, 1742–1807,* to depict the Mohawk leader who led four of the six Iroquois nations against the American forces in support of the British. He achieved a formidable reputation after participating in the Battle of Oriskany and a raid against the fortified village of Cherry Valley, New York. (© National Gallery of Canada, Ottawa, Ontario, Canada/The Bridgeman Art Library)

view of the tribes that was only slightly less dangerous to them. Thomas Jefferson, for example, came to view the Native Americans as "noble savages" uncivilized in their present state but redeemable if they were willing to adapt to the norms of white society.

Among the tribes themselves, the Revolution both revealed and increased the deep divisions that made it difficult for them to form a common front to resist the growing power of whites. In 1774, for example, the Shawnee Indians

GROWING
DIVISIONS
AMONG THE
INDIANS

in western Virginia had attempted to lead an uprising against white settlers moving into the lands that would later become Kentucky. They attracted virtually no allies and (in a conflict known as Lord Dunmore's War) were defeated by the colonial militia and forced to cede more land to white settlers. And the Iroquois, whose power had been eroding since the end of the French and Indian War, were similarly unable to act in unison in the Revolution.

Bands of Native Americans continued to launch raids against white settlers on the frontier. White militias, often using such raids as pretexts, continued to attack Indian tribes who stood in the way of expansion. Perhaps the most vicious massacre of the era occurred in 1782, after the British surrender, when white militias slaughtered a peaceful band of Delaware Indians at Gnadenhuetten in Ohio. They claimed to be retaliating for the killing of a white family several days before, but few white settlers believed this band of Delaware (who were both Christian converts and pacifists) had played any role in the earlier attack. The white soldiers killed ninety-six people, including many women and children. Such massacres did not become the norm of Indian-white relations. But they did reveal how little the Revolution had done to settle the basic conflict between the two peoples.

The triumph of the American patriots in the Revolution contributed to the ultimate defeat of the Indian tribes. To white Americans, independence meant, among other things, their right to move aggressively into the western lands, despite the opposition of the Indians. To the Indians, American independence was "the greatest blow that could have been dealt us," one tribal leader warned.

WOMEN'S RIGHTS AND WOMEN'S ROLES

The long Revolutionary War, which touched the lives of people in almost every region, naturally had a significant effect on American women. The departure of so many men to fight in the Patriot armies left wives, mothers, sisters, and daughters in charge of farms and businesses. Other women whose husbands or fathers went off to war did not have even a farm or shop to fall back on. Many cities and towns developed significant populations of impoverished women, who on occasion led popular protests against price increases. On a few occasions, hungry women rioted and looted for food. Elsewhere (in New Jersey and on Staten Island), women launched attacks on occupying

British troops, whom they were required to house and feed at considerable expense.

Not all women, however, stayed behind when the men went off to war. Sometimes by choice, but more often out of economic necessity or because they had been driven from

WOMEN OF
THE ARMY

their homes by the enemy (and by the smallpox and dysentery the British army carried with it), women flocked in increasing numbers to the camps of the Patriot armies to join their male relatives. George Washington looked askance at these female "camp followers," convinced that they were disruptive and distracting (even though his own wife, Martha, spent the winter of 1778-1779 with him at Valley Forge). Other officers were even more hostile, voicing complaints that reflected a high level of anxiety over this seeming violation of traditional gender roles (and also, perhaps, over the generally lower-class backgrounds of the camp women). One described them in decidedly hostile terms: "their hair falling, their brows beady with the heat, their belongings slung over one shoulder, chattering and yelling in sluttish shrills as they went." In fact, however, the women were of significant value to the new army. It had not yet developed an adequate system of supply and auxiliary services, and it profited greatly from the presence of women, who increased army morale and performed such necessary tasks as cooking, laundry, and nursing.

But female activity did not always remain restricted to "women's" tasks. In the rough environment of the camps, traditional gender distinctions proved difficult to maintain. Considerable numbers of women became involved, at least intermittently, in combat—including the legendary Molly Pitcher (so named because she carried pitchers of water to soldiers on the battlefield). She watched her husband fall during one encounter and immediately took his place at a field gun. A few women even disguised themselves as men so as to be able to fight.

After the war, of course, the soldiers and the female camp followers returned home. The experience of combat had little visible impact on how society (or on how women themselves) defined female roles in peacetime. The Revolution did, however, call certain assumptions about women into question in other ways. The emphasis on liberty and the "rights of man" led some women to begin to question their position in society as well. "By the way," Abigail Adams wrote to her husband, John Adams, in 1776, "in the new code of laws which I suppose it will be necessary for you to make, I desire you would remember the ladies and be more generous and favorable to them than your ancestors."

Adams was calling for a very modest expansion of women's rights. She wanted new protections against abusive and tyrannical men. A few women, however, went further. Judith Sargent Murray, one of the leading essayists of the late eighteenth century, wrote in 1779 that women's minds were as good as men's and that girls as well as boys therefore deserved access to education.

Some political leaders—among them Benjamin Franklin and Benjamin Rush—also voiced support for the education of women and for other feminist reforms. Yale students in the 1780s debated the question "Whether women ought to

CALLS FOR WOMEN'S RIGHTS

be admitted into the magistracy and government of empires and republics." And there was for a time wide discussion of the future role of women in a new republic that had broken with so many other traditions already. But few concrete reforms became either law or common social practice.

In colonial society, under the doctrines of English common law, an unmarried woman had some legal rights (to own property, to enter contracts, and others), but a married woman had virtually no rights. She could own no property and earn no independent wages; everything she owned and everything she earned belonged to her husband. She had no legal authority over her children; the father was, in the eyes of the law, the autocrat of the family. Because a married woman had no property rights, she could not engage in any legal transactions (buying or selling, suing or being sued, writing wills). She could not vote. Nor could she obtain a divorce in most states; that, too, was a right reserved mostly for men, although in much of the South men could not obtain divorces either. These restrictions were what Abigail Adams (who herself enjoyed a successful marriage) was describing when she appealed to her husband not to put "such unlimited power into the hands of the Husbands."

The Revolution did little to change any of these legal customs. In some states, it did become easier for women to obtain divorces. And in New Jersey, women obtained the right to vote (although that right was repealed in 1807). Otherwise, there were few advances and some setbacks—including widows' loss of the right to regain their dowries from their husbands' estates. That change left many widows without any means of support and was one of the reasons for the increased agitation for female education: such women needed a way to support themselves.

The Revolution, in other words, far from challenging the patriarchal structure of American society, actually confirmed and strengthened it. Few American women challenged the belief that they occupied a special sphere distinct from that of men. Most accepted that their place remained in the family. Nevertheless, the Revolutionary experience did contribute to a subtle but important alteration of women's roles. In the past, they had often been little better than servants in their husbands' homes. But the Revolution encouraged people of both genders to reevaluate the contribution of women to the family and the society.

One reason for this was a reevaluation of American life during and after the Revolutionary struggle. As the republic

THE BRITISH INFANTRY The world's greatest military power raised its armies in almost haphazard fashion. Command of a British regiment was a favor to well-positioned gentlemen, who received a cash reward for every man they enlisted. With that incentive, they were hardly picky, and the foot soldiers of the British army were mostly men who could be persuaded (or tricked) into enlisting through a combination of liquor and cash. Even so, the rough-and-ready quality of the British infantry made them good soldiers on the whole. This drawing portrays a British encampment during the American Revolution. As with the colonial armies, the British troops attracted women, seen at left, some of whom served as "camp followers," doing chores to help the soldiers. The soldiers themselves wore highly ornamental uniforms that were in many ways very impractical. To keep himself properly groomed and attired could take a soldier up to three hours a day. (© Anne S. K. Brown Military Collection, Brown University Library)

searched for a cultural identity for itself, it began to place additional value on the role of women as mothers. The new nation

A STRENGTHENED PATRIARCHAL STRUCTURE

was, many Americans liked to believe, producing a new kind of citizen, steeped in the principles of liberty. Mothers had a particularly important task, therefore, in instructing their children in the virtues the republican citizenry was expected now to possess. Wives were still far from equal partners in marriage, but their ideas, interests, and domestic roles received increased respect from many men.

THE WAR ECONOMY

Inevitably, the Revolution produced important changes in the structure of the American economy. After more than a century of dependence on the British imperial system, American trade suddenly found itself on its own. No longer did it have the protection of the great British navy; on the contrary, English ships now attempted to drive American vessels from the seas. No longer did American merchants have access to the markets of the empire; those markets were now hostile ports—including, of course, the most important source of American trade: England itself.

Yet, while the Revolution disrupted traditional economic patterns, in the long run it strengthened the American economy. Well before the war was over, American ships had learned to evade the British navy with light, fast, easily maneuverable vessels. Indeed, the Yankees began to prey on British commerce with hundreds of privateers. For many shipowners, privateering proved to be more profitable than ordinary peacetime trade. More important in the long run, the end of imperial restrictions on American shipping opened up enormous

new areas of trade to the nation. Enterprising merchants in New England and elsewhere began to develop new commerce in the Caribbean and in South America. By the mid-1780s, American merchants were developing an important new pattern of trade with Asia; and by the end of that decade, Yankee ships were regularly sailing from the eastern seaboard around Cape Horn to the Pacific coast of North America, there exchanging manufactured goods for hides and furs, and then proceeding across the Pacific to barter for goods in China. There was also a substantial increase in trade among the American states.

When English imports to America were cut off—first by the prewar boycott, then by the war itself—there were desperate

NEW PATTERNS OF TRADE

efforts throughout the states to stimulate domestic manufacturing of certain necessities. No great industrial expansion resulted, but there were several signs of the economic growth that was to come in the next century. Americans began to make their own cloth—"homespun," which became both patriotic and fashionable—to replace now-unobtainable British fabrics. It would be some time before a large domestic textile industry would emerge, but the nation was never again to rely exclusively on foreign sources for its cloth. There was, of course, pressure to build factories for the manufacture of guns and ammunition. And there was a growing general awareness that America need not forever be dependent on other nations for manufactured goods.

The war stopped well short of revolutionizing the American economy; not until the nineteenth century would that begin to occur. But it did serve to release a wide range of entrepreneurial energies that, despite the temporary dislocations, encouraged growth and diversification.

BANNER OF THE SOCIETY OF PEWTERERS Members of the American Society of Pewterers carried this patriotic banner when they marched in a New York City parade in July 1788. Its inscription celebrates the adoption of the new federal Constitution and predicts a future of prosperity and freedom in "Columbia's Land." The banner also suggests the growing importance of American manufacturing, which had received an important boost during the Revolution when British imports became unavailable. (© Collection of the New-York Historical Society, USA/The Bridgeman Art Library International)

150 · CHAPTER 5

THE CREATION OF STATE GOVERNMENTS

At the same time that Americans were struggling to win their independence on the battlefield, they were also struggling to create new institutions of government to replace the British system they had repudiated. That struggle continued for more than fifteen years, but its most important phase occurred during the war itself, at the state level.

THE ASSUMPTIONS OF REPUBLICANISM

If Americans agreed on nothing else when they began to build new governments for themselves, they agreed that those governments would be republican. To them, that meant a political system in which all power came from the people, rather than from some supreme authority (such as a king). The success of such a government depended on the nature of its citizenry.

IMPORTANCE OF CIVIC VIRTUE — If the population consisted of sturdy, independent property owners imbued with civic virtue, then the republic could survive. If it consisted of a few powerful aristocrats and a great mass of dependent workers, then it would be in danger. From the beginning, therefore, the ideal of the small freeholder (the independent landowner) was basic to American political ideology.

Another crucial part of that ideology was the concept of equality. The Declaration of Independence had given voice to that idea in its most ringing phrase: "All men are created equal." It was a belief that stood in direct contrast to the old European assumption of an inherited aristocracy. The innate talents and energies of individuals, not their positions at birth, would determine their roles in society. Some people would inevitably be wealthier and more powerful than others. But all people would have to earn their success. There would be no equality of condition, but there would be equality of opportunity.

In reality, of course, the United States was never a nation in which all citizens were independent property holders. From the beginning, there was a sizable dependent labor force. White laborers enjoyed some of the privileges of citizenship.

PERSISTENT INEQUALITY — Black workers were allowed virtually none. American women remained both politically and economically subordinate. Native Americans were systematically exploited and displaced. Nor was there ever full equality of opportunity. American society was more open and more fluid than the societies of most European nations, but the condition of a person's birth was almost always a crucial determinant of success.

Nevertheless, in embracing the assumptions of republicanism, Americans were adopting a powerful, even revolutionary, ideology, and their experiment in statecraft became a model for many other countries. It made the United States for a time the most admired and studied nation on earth.

THE FIRST STATE CONSTITUTIONS

The first and perhaps most basic decision about the character of government was that the constitutions were to be written down, because Americans believed the

WRITTEN CONSTITUTIONS AND STRONG LEGISLATURES — vagueness of England's unwritten constitution had produced corruption. The second decision was that the power of the executive, which Americans believed had grown too great in England, must be limited. Pennsylvania eliminated the executive altogether. Most other states inserted provisions that limited the power of governors to make appointments and veto legislation. Most states also prevented governors from dismissing the legislature. Most important, every state forbade the governor or any other executive officer from holding a seat in the legislature, thus ensuring that, unlike in England, the executive and legislative branches of government would remain wholly separate.

But the new constitutions did not embrace direct popular rule. In Georgia and Pennsylvania, the legislature consisted of one popularly elected house. But in every other state, there was an upper and a lower chamber, and in most cases, the upper chamber was designed to represent the "higher orders" of society. There were property requirements for voters—some modest, some substantial—in all states.

REVISING STATE GOVERNMENTS

By the late 1770s, many Americans were growing concerned about the apparent divisiveness and instability of their new state governments. Most states were having trouble accomplishing anything. Many believed the problem was one of too much democracy. As a result, most of the states began to revise their constitutions to limit popular power. Massachusetts, which waited until 1780 to ratify its first constitution, was the first to act on the new concerns.

Two changes in particular differentiated the Massachusetts and later constitutions from the earlier ones. The first was a change in the process of constitution writing itself. Most of the first documents had been written by state legislatures and thus could easily be amended (or violated) by them. Massachusetts and, later, other states sought a way to protect the constitutions from ordinary politics and created the constitutional convention: a special assembly of the people that would meet only for the purpose of writing the constitution and that would never (except under extraordinary circumstances) meet again.

The second change was a significant strengthening of the executive, a reaction to what many Americans believed was the instability of the original state governments that had weak governors. The 1780 Massachusetts constitution made

SHIFT TO STRONG EXECUTIVES — the governor one of the strongest in any state. He was to be elected directly by the people; he was to have a fixed salary (in other words, he would not be dependent on the goodwill of the legislature each year for his wages); he would have significant appointment powers and a veto over legislation. Other states followed. Those with weak or nonexistent upper houses strengthened or created them. Most increased the powers of the governor. Pennsylvania, which had no executive at first, now produced a strong one. By the late 1780s, almost every state had either revised its constitution or drawn up a new one in an effort to produce stability in government.

TOLERATION AND SLAVERY

The states moved far in the direction of complete religious freedom. Most Americans continued to believe that religion should play some role in government, but they did not wish to give special powers to any particular denomination. The privileges that churches had once enjoyed were now largely stripped away. In 1786, Virginia enacted the Statute of Religious Liberty, written by Thomas Jefferson, which called for the complete separation of church and state.

STATUTE OF RELIGIOUS LIBERTY

More difficult to resolve was the question of slavery. In areas where slavery was already weak–in New England, where there had never been many slaves, and in Pennsylvania, where the Quakers opposed slavery–it was abolished relatively early. Even in the South, there were some pressures to amend or even eliminate the institution; every state but South Carolina and Georgia prohibited further importation of slaves from abroad, and South Carolina banned the slave trade during the war. Virginia passed a law encouraging manumission (the freeing of slaves).

Nevertheless, slavery survived in all the southern and border states. There were several reasons: racist assumptions among whites about the inferiority of blacks; the enormous economic investments many white southerners had in their slaves; and the inability of even such men as Washington and Jefferson, who had moral misgivings about slavery, to envision any alternative to it. If slavery were abolished, what would happen to the black people in America? Few whites believed blacks could be integrated into American society as equals. In maintaining slavery, Jefferson once remarked, Americans were holding a "wolf by the ears." However unappealing it was to hold on to it, letting go would be even worse.

A FREE BLACK MAN John Singleton Copley, the great American portraitist of the Revolutionary age, painted this picture of a young African American in 1777–1978. He was probably a worker on New England fishing boats who appeared in another Copley painting *(Watson and the Shark)*. It is one of a small number of portrayals of the free blacks in the North in this era, and one of even a smaller number that portrays them realistically and seriously. *(Head of a Negro, 1777–1778. By John Singleton Copley. Oil on canvas, 53.3 × 41.3 cm. Founders Society Purchase, Gibbs-Williams Fund. Photograph © Detroit Institute of Arts, USA/The Bridgeman Art Library)*

THE SEARCH FOR A NATIONAL GOVERNMENT

Americans were much quicker to agree on state institutions than they were on the structure of their national government. At first, most believed that the central government should remain a relatively weak and unimportant force and that each state would be virtually a sovereign nation. It was in response to such ideas that the Articles of Confederation emerged.

THE CONFEDERATION

The Articles of Confederation, which the Continental Congress had adopted in 1777, provided for a national government much like the one already in place. Congress wrote for ratification of the Articles: "Permit us, then, earnestly to recommend these articles to the immediate and dispassionate attention of the legislatures of the respective states. Let them be candidly reviewed under a sense of the difficulty of combining in one system the various sentiments and interests of a continent divided into so many sovereign and independent communities, under a conviction of the absolute necessity of uniting all our councils and all our strengths, to maintain and defend our common liberties."

Under the Articles, Congress remained the central–indeed the only–institution of national authority. Its powers expanded to give it authority to conduct wars and foreign relations and to appropriate, borrow, and issue money. But it did not have power to regulate trade, draft troops, or levy taxes directly on the people. For troops and taxes, it had to make formal

LIMITED POWER OF THE NATIONAL GOVERNMENT

requests to the state legislatures, which could—and often did—refuse them. There was no separate executive; the "president of the United States" was merely the presiding officer at the sessions of Congress. Each state had a single vote in Congress, and at least nine of the states had to approve the admission of a new state. All thirteen state legislatures had to approve any amendment of the Articles.

During the process of ratifying the Articles of Confederation (which required approval by all thirteen states), broad disagreements over the plan became evident. The small states had insisted on equal state representation, but the larger states wanted representation to be based on population. The smaller states prevailed on that issue. More important, the states claiming western lands wished to keep them, but the rest of the

states demanded that all such territory be turned over to the national government. New York and Virginia had to give up their western claims before the Articles were finally approved. They went into effect in 1781.

The Confederation, which existed from 1781 until 1789, was not a complete failure, but it was far from a success. It lacked adequate powers to deal with interstate issues or to enforce its will on the states, and it had little stature in the eyes of the world.

DIPLOMATIC FAILURES

Evidence of the low esteem in which the rest of the world held the Confederation was its difficulty in

POSTWAR DISPUTES WITH BRITAIN AND SPAIN

persuading Great Britain (and to a lesser extent Spain) to live up to the terms of the peace treaty of 1783.

The British had promised to evacuate American territory, but British forces continued to occupy

THE CONFLICT OVER WESTERN LANDS The American victory in the Revolution transformed the colonies into "states" within a new nation whose central government claimed at least some sovereignty over the individual units. An early conflict between national and state power took place over the state claims to western lands—claims established during the colonial period. This map shows the extensive western lands claimed by most of the original thirteen colonies to land in the West, and it illustrates the shifting nature of those claims over time—as colonies and then states transferred land to one another. The new national government gradually persuaded the states to give it control of the western lands, and in 1784 and 1785 it issued ordinances governing the process of settling those lands.

• Why did the national government consider it important for the states to give up their claim to these territories?

a string of frontier posts along the Great Lakes within the United States. Nor did the British honor their agreement to make restitution to slaveowners whose slaves the British army had confiscated. There were also disputes over the boundaries of the new nation. Americans wanted full access to British markets; England, however, placed sharp restrictions on that access.

In 1784, Congress sent John Adams as minister to London to resolve these differences, but Adams made no headway with the English, who were never sure whether he represented a single nation or thirteen different ones. Throughout the 1780s, the British government refused even to send a diplomatic minister to the American capital.

THE CONFEDERATION AND THE NORTHWEST

The Confederation's most important accomplishment was its resolution of controversies over the western lands. When the Revolution began, only a few thousand whites lived west of the Appalachian mountains; but by 1790 their numbers had increased to 120,000. The Confederation had to find a way to include these new settlements in the political structure of the nation. The landed states began to yield their western claims to the national government in 1781, and by 1784 the Confederation controlled enough land to permit Congress to begin making policy for the western lands.

THE TREATY OF GREENVILLE ON AUGUST 3, 1795 This painting, from the American School of painting, depicts the Treaty of Greenville ending the Northeast Indian War in the Ohio Country. In exchange for $20,000 worth of various goods such as blankets, utensils, and domesticated animals, the United States acquired large parts of Ohio, tracts of what would soon become Chicago, and the Fort Detroit area. (© Chicago History Museum, USA/The Bridgeman Art Library)

THE ORDINANCES OF 1784 AND 1785

The Ordinance of 1784, based on a proposal by Thomas Jefferson, divided the western territory into ten self-governing districts, each of which could petition Congress for statehood when its population equaled the number of free inhabitants of the smallest existing state. The provision reflected the desire of the Revolutionary generation to avoid creating second-class citizens in subordinate territories. Then, in the Ordinance of 1785, Congress created a system for surveying and selling the western lands. The territory north of the Ohio River was to be surveyed and marked off into neat rectangular townships, each divided into thirty-six identical sections. In every township, four sections were to be set aside for the United States; the revenue from the sale of one of the other sections was to support creation of a public school. Sections were to be sold at auction for no less than one dollar an acre.

Among the many important results of the Ordinance of 1785 was the establishment of an enduring pattern of dividing up land for human use. Many such systems have emerged throughout history. Some have relied on natural boundaries (rivers, mountains, and other topographical features). Some have reflected informal claims of landlords over vast but vaguely defined territories. Some have rested on random allocations of acres, to be determined by individual landholders. But many

THE GRID

Enlightenment thinkers began in the eighteenth century to imagine more precise, even mathematical, forms of land distribution, which required both careful surveying and a clear method for defining boundaries. The result was the method applied in 1785 in the Northwest Territory, which came to be known as "the grid"–the division of land into carefully measured and evenly divided squares or rectangles. This pattern of land distribution eventually became the norm for much of the land west of the Appalachians. It also became a model for the organization of many towns and cities, which distributed land in geometrical patterns within rectangular grids defined by streets. Although older land-distribution systems survive within the United States, the grid has become the most common form by which Americans impose human ownership and use on the landscape.

NORTHWEST ORDINANCE

The original ordinances were highly favorable to land speculators and less so to ordinary settlers, many of whom could not afford the price of the land. Congress compounded the problem by selling much of the best land to the Ohio and Scioto land companies before making it available to anyone else. Criticism of these policies led to the passage in 1787 of another law governing western settlement–legislation that became known as the "Northwest Ordinance." The 1787 Ordinance abandoned the ten districts established in 1784 and created a single Northwest Territory out of the lands

The Seven Ranges First Area Survey
GEOGRAPHER'S LINE (BASE LINE)

7th Range | 6th Range | 5th Range | 4th Range | 3rd Range | 2nd Range | 1st Range

Little Muskingum R. — *Ohio River*

VIRGINIA / PENNSYLVANIA

Lake Erie

NORTHWEST TERRITORY — PA.

OHIO (1803)

INDIANA · Cincinnati

KENTUCKY (1792)

VIRGINIA

* Four sections reserved for subsequent sales

Section 16 reserved for school funds

One Section = 640 acres (1 mile square)
A Half section = 320 acres
B Quarter section = 160 acres
C Half-quarter section = 80 acres
D & E Quarter-quarter section = 40 acres

One township (six miles square)

36	30	24	18	12	6
35	29*	23	17	11*	5
34	28	22	16	10	4
33	27	21	15	9	3
32	26*	20	14	8*	2
31	25	19	13	7	1

6 miles

1 mile

LAND SURVEY: ORDINANCE OF 1785 In the Ordinance of 1785, the Congress established a new system for surveying and selling western lands. These maps illustrate the way in which the lands were divided in an area of Ohio. Note the highly geometrical grid pattern that the ordinance imposed on these lands. Each of the squares in the map on the left was subdivided into 36 sections, as illustrated in the map at the lower right.

• Why was this grid pattern so appealing to the planners of the western lands?

north of the Ohio; the territory could eventually be divided into between three and five territories. It also specified a population of 60,000 as a minimum for statehood, guaranteed freedom of religion and the right to trial by jury to residents of the Northwest, and prohibited slavery throughout the territory.

The western lands south of the Ohio River received less attention from Congress, and development was more chaotic there. The region that became Kentucky and Tennessee developed rapidly in the late 1770s, and in the 1780s speculators and settlers began setting up governments and asking for recognition as states. The Confederation was never able to successfully resolve the conflicting claims in that region.

INDIANS AND THE WESTERN LANDS

On paper at least, the western land policies of the Confederation created a system that brought order and stability to the process of white settlement in the Northwest. But in reality, order and stability came slowly and at great cost, because much of the land the Confederation was neatly subdividing and offering for sale consisted of territory claimed by the Indians of the region. Congress tried to resolve that problem in 1784, 1785, and 1786 by persuading Iroquois, Choctaw, Chickasaw, and Cherokee leaders to sign treaties ceding substantial western lands in the North and South to the United States. But those agreements proved ineffective. In 1786, the leadership of the Iroquois Confederacy repudiated the treaty it had signed two years earlier and threatened to attack white settlements in the disputed lands. Other tribes had never accepted the treaties affecting them and continued to resist white movement into their lands.

Violence between whites and Indians on the Northwest frontier reached a crescendo in the early 1790s. In 1790 and again in 1791, a group of tribes led by the famed Miami warrior Little Turtle defeated United States

BATTLE OF FALLEN TIMBERS forces in two major battles near what is now the western border of Ohio; in the second of those battles, on November 4, 1791, 630 white Americans died in fighting at the Wabash River (the greatest military victory Indians had ever or would ever again achieve in their battles with whites). Efforts to negotiate a settlement failed because of the Miami's insistence that no treaty was possible unless it forbade white settlement west of the Ohio River. Negotiations did not resume until after General Anthony Wayne led 4,000 soldiers into the Ohio Valley in 1794 and defeated the Indians in the Battle of Fallen Timbers.

A year later, the Miami signed the Treaty of Greenville, ceding substantial new lands to the United States (which was now operating under the Constitution of 1789) in exchange for a formal acknowledgment of their claim to the territory they had managed to retain. In doing so, the United States was affirming that Indian lands could be ceded only by the tribes themselves. That hard-won assurance, however, proved a frail

protection against the pressure of white expansion westward in later years.

DEBTS, TAXES, AND DANIEL SHAYS

The postwar depression, which lasted from 1784 to 1787,

POSTWAR DEPRESSION increased the perennial American problem of an inadequate money supply, a problem that weighed particularly heavily on debtors. In dealing with this problem, Congress most clearly demonstrated its weakness.

The Confederation itself had an enormous outstanding debt that it had accumulated at home and abroad during the Revolutionary War. It had few means with which to pay it, having no power to tax. It could only make requisitions of the states, and it received only about one-sixth of the money it requisitioned. The fragile new nation was faced with the grim prospect of defaulting on its obligations.

This alarming possibility brought to the fore a group of leaders who would play a crucial role in the shaping of the

LITTLE TURTLE Little Turtle led the Miami confederacy in its wars with the United States in what is now Ohio and Indiana in the early 1790s. For a time he seemed almost invincible, but in 1794 Little Turtle was defeated in the Battle of Fallen Timbers. In this sketch (a rough copy of a painting attributed to Gilbert Stuart), Little Turtle wears a medal bearing the likeness of George Washington, awarded him by the United States after the signing of the Treaty of Greenville. (© The Granger Collection, New York)

DANIEL SHAYS AND JOB SHATTUCK Shays and Shattuck were the principal leaders of the 1786 uprising by poor farmers in Massachusetts demanding relief from their indebtedness. Shattuck led an insurrection in the east, which collapsed when he was captured on November 30. Shays organized the rebellion in the west, which continued until the state militia dispersed the rebels in late February 1787. The following year, state authorities pardoned Shays; even before that, the legislature responded to the rebellion by providing some relief to the impoverished farmers. These drawings are part of a hostile account of the rebellion published in 1787 in a Boston almanac. (© The Granger Collection, New York)

republic for several decades. Committed nationalists, they sought ways to increase the powers of the central government and to meet its financial obligations. Robert Morris, the head of the Confederation's treasury; Alexander Hamilton, his young

POLITICAL DISPUTES OVER ECONOMIC ISSUES

protégé; James Madison of Virginia; and others called for a "continental impost"—a 5 percent duty on imported goods to be levied by Congress and used to fund the debt. Many Americans, however, feared that the impost plan would concentrate too much financial power in the hands of Morris and his allies in Philadelphia. Congress failed to approve the impost in 1781 and again in 1783. Angry and discouraged, the nationalists largely withdrew from any active involvement in the Confederation.

The states had war debts, too, and they generally relied on increased taxation to pay them. But poor farmers, already burdened by debt and now burdened again by new taxes, considered such policies unfair, even tyrannical. They demanded that the state governments issue paper currency to increase the money supply and make it easier for them to meet their obligations. Resentment was especially high among farmers in New England, who felt that the states were squeezing them to enrich already wealthy bondholders in Boston and other towns.

Throughout the late 1780s, therefore, mobs of distressed farmers rioted periodically in various parts of New England. Dissidents in the Connecticut Valley and the Berkshire Hills of Massachusetts, many of them Revolutionary veterans, ral-

SHAYS'S REBELLION

lied behind Daniel Shays, a former captain in the Continental army. Shays issued a set of demands that included paper money, tax relief, a moratorium on debts, the relocation of the state capital from Boston to the interior, and the abolition of imprisonment for debt. During the summer of 1786, the Shaysites concentrated on preventing the collection of debts, private or public, and used force to keep courts from sitting and sheriffs from selling confiscated property. In Boston, members of the legislature, including Samuel Adams, denounced Shays and his men as rebels and traitors. When winter came, the rebels advanced on Springfield, hoping to seize weapons from the arsenal there. An army of state militiamen, financed by a loan from wealthy merchants, set out from Boston to confront them. In January 1787, this army met Shays's band and dispersed his ragged troops.

As a military enterprise, Shays's Rebellion was a failure, although it produced some concessions to the aggrieved farmers. Shays and his lieutenants, at first sentenced to death, were later pardoned, and Massachusetts offered the protesters some tax relief and a postponement of debt payments. The rebellion had more important consequences for the future of the United States, however, for it added urgency to a movement already gathering support throughout the new nation–the movement to produce a new, national constitution.

AP CONNECTING THEMES

Chapter 5 discussed the political, economic, and social consequences of the American Revolution. You should focus on divisions in American society at the outset of the war and how those divisions changed what it was to be called an American. The revolution also resulted in westward migration that ultimately led to new challenges for the country. Particularly important are the relations with foreign countries that the American Revolution brought about. It is essential that you understand how the political structure of the United States was changed by independence, both at the national and state level.

The following themes have heightened importance in Chapter 5. You should now be able to do the following for each listed theme:

Identity: Explain how economic, political, and social factors created regional identities in the United States.

Peopling: Analyze the factors that encouraged western migration and the consequences of that migration.

America and the World: Explain how the American Revolution and its aftermath altered relations between the United States and foreign countries.

Ideas, Beliefs, and Culture: Explain how Enlightenment ideas and the belief in republican principles of self-government manifested themselves during and after the American Revolution.

AP SUGGESTED STUDY

PEOPLE/PLACES/EVENTS As you study these items, think about how they demonstrate or relate to key concepts and historical themes from this chapter and previous chapters.

AP TEST PRACTICE

Questions assume cumulative content knowledge from this chapter and previous chapters.

MULTIPLE CHOICE Use the excerpts below and your knowledge of U.S. history to answer questions 1-4.

"In order to gain a clear and just idea of the design and end of government, let us suppose a small number of persons settled in some sequestered part of the earth, unconnected with the rest, they will then represent the first peopling of any country, or of the world. In this state of natural liberty, society will be their first thought. A thousand motives will excite them thereto, the strength of one man is so unequal to his wants, and his mind so unfitted for perpetual solitude, that he is soon obliged to seek assistance and relief of another, who in his turn requires the same. Four or five united would be able to raise a tolerable dwelling in the midst of a wilderness, but one man might labour out of the common period of life without accomplishing any thing. . . ."

"Some convenient tree will afford them a State-House, under the branches of which, the whole colony may assemble to deliberate on public matters. . . . In this first parliament every man, by natural right, will have a seat.

But as the colony increases, the public concerns will increase likewise, and the distance at which the members may be separated, will render it too inconvenient for all of them to meet on every occasion as at first, when their number was small, their habitations near, and the public concerns few and trifling. This will point out the convenience of their consenting to leave the legislative part to be managed by a select number chosen from the whole body, who are supposed to have the same concerns at stake which those who appointed them, and who will act in the same manner as the whole body would act, were they present. If the colony continues increasing, it will become necessary to augment the number of the representatives, and that the interest of every part of the colony may be attended to, it will be found best to divide the whole into convenient parts, each part sending its proper number. . . ."

—From the pamphlet *Common Sense* published by Thomas Paine, 1776

"To understand political power right, and derive it from its original, we must consider, what state all men are naturally in, and that is, a state of perfect freedom to order their actions, and dispose of their possessions and persons, as they think fit, within the bounds of the law of nature, without asking leave, or depending upon the will of any other man.

. . . But though this be a state of liberty, yet it is not a state of licence. . . . The state of nature has a law of nature to govern it, which obliges every one: and reason, which is that law, teaches all mankind, who will but consult it, that being all equal and independent, no one ought to harm another in his life, health, liberty, or possessions. . . ."

—John Locke, *Second Treatise of Government*, published in 1690

1. Paine is echoing from Locke the tying of which principle to the foundation for government that would most support revolt from Great Britain?

   (A) That humans were naturally virtuous, and so government was not necessary

   (B) That humans need to form societies for survival

   (C) The natural state of equality among humans

   (D) That monarchs arise due to the inability of humans to refrain from harming one another

2. Which Enlightenment value is best demonstrated by the excerpts?

   (A) The idea that humans are not solitary creatures

   (B) The love of nature

   (C) The idea of humans being blessed creatures

   (D) The belief in human reason

3. The American colonists embraced which idea being implied in both excerpts regarding the purpose of government?

   (A) That the purpose of government was to preserve individual liberty

   (B) That the purpose of government was to ensure that individual labor benefited the entire community

   (C) That the purpose of government was to ensure that the rewards of labor were shared according to individual talent

   (D) That the purpose of government was not to interfere with individual freedom

4. How does Paine's version of representative government differ from the traditional British parliamentary view of representative government?

   (A) Representatives to government represent the interests of their locality

   (B) Representatives to government represent the entirety of the nation

   (C) Representatives to government should represent citizens according to social class

   (D) Those demonstrating greater talent should have more representation in government

SHORT ANSWER Use your knowledge of U.S. history to answer questions 5–6.

5. Answer a, b, and c.

   a) Briefly explain ONE example of conflict that arose during the process of ratifying the Articles of Confederation.

   b) Briefly explain ONE example of a weakness or failure of the Articles of Confederation.

   c) Briefly explain ONE example of a success achieved by the Confederation government.

6. Answer a, b, and c.

   a) Briefly explain a significant effect of the American Revolution on ONE of the following groups.
      • Women
      • African Americans
      • Native Americans

   b) Provide an example of an event or development to support your explanation.

   c) Provide an example of an event or development that could be used to challenge your explanation.

LONG ESSAY Develop a thoughtful and thorough historical argument that answers the questions below. Begin your essay with a thesis statement and support it with relevant historical evidence.

7. To what extent was the political, social, and economic position of Native Americans affected by the Revolutionary War? Include in your analysis the perspective of at least two of the following groups: the British, American colonists, Native Americans.

8. Some historians have argued that it was the success of the American Revolution that led to a series of revolutions across the world, notably in France and Haiti. Support, refute, or modify this assertion, providing specific evidence to justify your answer.

6 | THE CONSTITUTION AND THE NEW REPUBLIC

THE AMERICAN STAR Frederick Kemmelmeyer painted this tribute to George Washington sometime in the 1790s. It was one of many efforts by artists and others to create an iconography for the new republic. (Private Collection/photo © Boltin Picture Library/The Bridgeman Art Library)

AP

HISTORICAL THINKING

1. **Historical Causation** What were the major compromises necessary for the U.S. Constitution to successfully get through the convention and ratification process?

2. **Comparison** Compare and contrast the beliefs of the Federalists and the Republicans in the 1790s.

3. **Contextualization** To what degree and in what ways did the Constitution overcome the weaknesses of the Articles of Confederation?

4. **Historical Argumentation** Analyze the foreign policy issues facing the nation in the 1790s and evaluate the relative success of the United States in dealing with those problems.

5. **Contextualization** Analyze the reasons for and the reaction to attempts to limit personal liberty during the administration of John Adams.

6. **Periodization** To what degree was the election of 1800 a turning point in United States history? Defend your position.

7. **Appropriate Use of Relevant Historical Evidence** Analyze the degree to which and the ways in which the U.S. Constitution can be subject to varying interpretations.

Key Concept Correlations

Analyze the ways the historical developments you learn about in this chapter connect to the following AP Key Concepts.

3.1 Britain's victory over France in the imperial struggle for North America led to new conflicts among the British government, the North American colonists, and American Indians, culminating in the creation of a new nation, the United States.

3.2 In the late 18th century, new experiments with democratic ideas and republican forms of government, as well as other new religious, economic, and cultural ideas, challenged traditional imperial systems across the Atlantic World.

3.3 Migration within North America, cooperative interaction, and competition for resources raised questions about boundaries and policies, intensified conflicts among peoples and nations, and led to contests over the creation of a multiethnic, multiracial national identity.

4.1 The United States developed the world's first modern mass democracy and celebrated a new national culture, while Americans sought to define the nation's democratic ideals and to reform its institutions to match them.

Thematic Learning Objectives

WOR-2, 5; POL-1, 2, 5, 6; ID-1, 5, 6; PEO-4, 5; ENV-3

CHAPTER 6 discusses the writing of the U.S. Constitution and the compromises necessary to secure ratification. Importantly, it focuses on the development of the first American party system, consisting of Federalists and Republicans. You should be certain to focus on the beliefs of Alexander Hamilton and Thomas Jefferson. It is very important that you understand how the parties differed, particularly with their views on how powerful the national government should be. The new government faced problems with westerners, American Indians, and foreign nations on which you should focus, including treaties that resolved differences with both Great Britain and Spain. The tradition of American neutrality grew out of this period, but the French Revolution ultimately led to conflict with France. That conflict resulted in suppression of personal liberties that would become a recurring theme during wars in which the United States was involved. Lastly, think about why the presidential election of 1800 would become a turning point in American history in the minds of many historians. As you read, evaluate the following concepts:

- American Indians continuously adjusted their alliances with European powers during the 18th century.
- The presence of European powers on the borders of the United States forced the United States to safeguard its territory and defend its commercial interests diplomatically and militarily.
- Ideas from the Enlightenment and the belief in republican ideas of self-government led to a transformation of political thought in the United States with the ratification of the Constitution.
- Dissatisfaction with the Articles of Confederation led to the writing of the Constitution and the creation of a stronger central government.
- The Constitution was based on the idea of federalism, which divided power between the states and the national government.

FRAMING A NEW GOVERNMENT

So unpopular and ineffectual had the Confederation Congress become by the mid-1780s that it began to lead an almost waiflike existence. In 1783, its members timidly withdrew from Philadelphia to escape from the clamor of army veterans demanding back pay. They took refuge for a while in

A WEAK CENTRAL GOVERNMENT

Princeton, New Jersey, then moved to Annapolis, and in 1785 settled in New York. Through all of this, the delegates were often conspicuous largely by their absence. Only with great difficulty did Congress secure a quorum to ratify the treaty with Great Britain ending the Revolutionary War. Eighteen members, representing only eight states, voted on the Confederation's most important piece of legislation, the Northwest Ordinance. In the meantime, a major public debate was beginning over the future of the Confederation.

ADVOCATES OF CENTRALIZATION

Weak and unpopular though the Confederation was, it had for a time satisfied a great many—probably a majority—of the people. They believed they had fought the Revolutionary War to avert the danger of what they considered remote and tyrannical authority; now they wanted to keep political power centered in the states, where they could carefully and closely control it.

But during the 1780s, some of the wealthiest and most powerful groups in the country began to clamor for a more genuinely national government capable of dealing with the nation's problems—

SUPPORTERS OF A STRONG NATIONAL GOVERNMENT

particularly the economic problems that most directly afflicted them. Some military men, many of them members of the exclusive and hereditary Society of the Cincinnati (formed by Revolutionary army officers in 1783), were disgruntled at the refusal of Congress to fund their pensions. They began aspiring to influence and invigorate the national government; some even envisioned a form of military dictatorship and flirted briefly (in 1783, in the so-called Newburgh Conspiracy) with a

GEORGE WASHINGTON AT MOUNT VERNON Washington was in his first term as president in 1790 when an anonymous folk artist painted this view of his home at Mount Vernon, Virginia. Washington appears in uniform, along with members of his family, on the lawn. After he retired from office in 1797, Washington returned happily to his plantation and spent the two years before his death in 1799 "amusing myself in agricultural and rural pursuits." He also played host to an endless stream of visitors from throughout the country and Europe. (Courtesy, National Gallery of Art, Washington)

direct challenge to Congress, until George Washington intervened and blocked the potential rebellion.

American manufacturers—the artisans and "mechanics" of the nation's cities and towns—wanted to replace the various state tariffs with a uniformly high national duty. Merchants and shippers wanted to replace the thirteen different (and largely ineffective) state commercial policies with a single, national one. Land speculators wanted the "Indian menace" finally removed from their western tracts. People who were owed money wanted to stop the states from issuing paper money, which would lower the value of what they received in payment. Investors in Confederation securities wanted the government to fund the debt and thus enhance the value of their securities. Large property owners looked for protection from the threat of mobs, a threat that seemed particularly menacing in light of such episodes as Shays's Rebellion. This fear of disorder and violence expressed a tension between the resolute defense of individual rights, which was a core principle of the Revolution and found reflection in the Bill of Rights (p. 168), and the public concern for safety and security, which the occasional chaos of the Confederation period had reinforced. Frequent conflicts between liberty and order became, and remain, a central feature of American democracy.

By 1786, these diverse demands had grown so powerful that the issue was no longer whether the Confederation should be changed but how drastic the changes should be. Even the defenders of the existing system reluctantly came to agree that the government needed strengthening at its weakest point—its lack of power to tax.

The most resourceful of the reformers was Alexander Hamilton, political genius, New York lawyer, onetime military aide to General Washington, and illegitimate son of a Scottish merchant in the West Indies. From the beginning, Hamilton had been unhappy with the Articles of Confederation and the weak central government they had created. He now called for a national convention to overhaul the entire document. He found an important ally in James Madison of Virginia, who persuaded the Virginia legislature to convene an interstate conference on commercial questions. Only five states sent delegates to the meeting, held in Annapolis, Maryland, in 1786; but the delegates approved a proposal drafted by Hamilton (who was representing New York) recommending that Congress call a convention of special delegates from all the states to gather in Philadelphia the next year and consider ways to "render the constitution of the Federal government adequate to the exigencies of the union."

ALEXANDER HAMILTON

At that moment, in 1786, there seemed little possibility that the Philadelphia convention would attract any more interest than the meeting at Annapolis had attracted. Only by winning the support of George Washington, the centralizers believed,

CONSIDERATIONS

ON THE

SOCIETY OR ORDER

OF

CINCINNATI;

LATELY INSTITUTED

By the Major-Generals, Brigadier-Generals, and other Officers of the AMERICAN ARMY.

PROVING THAT IT CREATES

A RACE OF HEREDITARY PATRICIANS,

OR

NOBILITY.

INTERSPERSED WITH REMARKS

On its CONSEQUENCES to the FREEDOM and HAPPINESS of the REPUBLIC.

Addressed to the PEOPLE of SOUTH-CAROLINA, and their REPRESENTATIVES.

By CASSIUS. Burke

Supposed to be written by ÆDANUS BURKE, Esquire, one of the Chief Justices of the State of South-Carolina.

Blow ye the Trumpet in Zion.   The BIBLE.

PHILADELPHIA:

Printed and Sold by ROBERT BELL, in Third-Street.
Price, one-sixth of a Dollar. M,DCC,LXXXIII.

A BROADSIDE AGAINST "NOBILITY" This 1783 pamphlet was one of many expressions of the broad democratic sentiment that the Revolution unleashed in American society. The Society of the Cincinnati was an organization created shortly after the Revolution by men who had served as high-ranking officers in the Patriot army. To many Americans, however, the society—membership in which was to be hereditary—looked suspiciously like the inherited aristocracies of England. This pamphlet, printed in Philadelphia but intended for South Carolinians, warns of the dangers the society supposedly posed to the "Freedom and Happiness of the Republic." (© Fotosearch/Getty Images)

could they hope to prevail. But Washington at first showed little interest in joining the cause. Then, early in 1787, the news of Shays's Rebellion spread throughout the nation. Thomas Jefferson, then the American minister in Paris, was not alarmed. "I hold," he confided in a letter to James Madison, "that a little rebellion, now and then, is a good thing, and as necessary in the political world as storms in the physical." But Washington took the news less calmly. In May, he left his home at Mount Vernon in Virginia for the Constitutional Convention in Philadelphia. His support gave the meeting immediate credibility.

A DIVIDED CONVENTION

Fifty-five men, representing all the states except Rhode Island, attended one or more sessions of the convention that sat in the Philadelphia State House from May to September 1787. These "Founding Fathers," as they would later become known, were relatively young; their average age was forty-four, and only one delegate (Benjamin Franklin, then eighty-one) was of advanced age. They were well educated by the standards of their time.

THE FOUNDING FATHERS Most represented the great propertied interests of the country, and many feared what one of them called the "turbulence and follies" of democracy. Yet all were also products of the American Revolution and retained the Revolutionary suspicion of concentrated power.

The convention unanimously chose Washington to preside over its sessions and then closed its business to the public and the press. The members then ruled that each state delegation would have a single vote. Major decisions would not require unanimity, as they did in Congress, but only a simple majority. Virginia, the most populous state, sent the best-prepared delegation to Philadelphia. James Madison (thirty-six years old) was its intellectual leader. He had devised a detailed plan for a new "national" government, and the Virginians used it to control the agenda from the moment the convention began.

Edmund Randolph of Virginia began the discussion by proposing that "a national government ought to be established, consisting of a supreme Legislative, Executive, and Judiciary." Despite its vagueness, it was a drastic proposal. It called for the creation of a government very different from the existing

THE VIRGINIA PLAN Confederation, which, among other things, had no executive branch. But so committed were the delegates to fundamental reform that they approved this resolution after only perfunctory debate. Then Randolph introduced the details of Madison's plan. The Virginia Plan (as it came to be known) called for a new national legislature consisting of two houses. In the lower house, the states would be represented in proportion to their population; thus the largest state (Virginia) would have about ten times as many representatives as the smallest (Delaware). Members of the upper house were to be elected by the lower house under no rigid system of representation; thus some of the smaller states might at times have no members in the upper house.

The proposal aroused immediate opposition among delegates from Delaware, New Jersey, and other small states. Some responded by arguing that Congress had called the convention "for the sole and express purpose of revising the Articles of Confederation" and had no authority to do more than that. Eventually, however, William Paterson of New Jersey submitted a substantive alternative to the Virginia Plan, a proposal for a "federal" as opposed to a "national" government. The New Jersey Plan would preserve the existing one-house legislature, in which each state had equal representation, but it gave Congress expanded powers to tax and to regulate commerce. The delegates voted to table Paterson's proposal, but not without taking note of the substantial support for it among small-state representatives.

The Virginia Plan remained the basis for discussion. But its supporters realized they would have to make concessions to the small states if the convention was ever to reach a general agreement. They soon conceded an important point by agreeing to permit the members of the upper house to be elected by the state legislatures rather than by the lower house of the national legislature. Thus each state would always have at least one member in the upper house.

But many questions remained. Would the states be equally represented in the upper house, or would the large states have more members than the small ones? Would slaves (who could

SMALL STATES VERSUS LARGE STATES

not vote) be counted as part of the population in determining the size of a state's representation in Congress, or were they to be considered simple property? Delegates from states with large and apparently permanent slave populations–especially those from South Carolina–wanted to have it both ways. They argued that slaves should be considered persons in determining representation. But they wanted slaves to be considered property if the new government were to levy taxes on each state on the basis of population. Representatives from states where slavery had disappeared or was expected soon to disappear argued that slaves should be included in calculating taxation but not representation. No one argued seriously for giving slaves citizenship or the right to vote.

COMPROMISE

The delegates bickered for weeks. By the end of June, as both temperature and tempers rose to uncomfortable heights, the

THE GREAT COMPROMISE

convention seemed in danger of collapsing. Benjamin Franklin, who remained a calm voice of conciliation through the summer,

"THE GRAND CONVENTION" The engraver John Norman created this imagined view of the Constitutional Convention in 1787 for the *Weatherwise's Federal Almanack*, whose title suggested its pro-Constitution political leanings. Norman was familiar with the interior of the hall in Philadelphia where the convention took place, which gave this engraving a sense of reality—even though Norman never attended a session of the convention. (© Hall of Representatives, Washington, D.C./The Bridgeman Art Library)

THE MEANING OF THE CONSTITUTION

THE constitution has inspired debate from the moment it was drafted. Some people argue that the Constitution is a flexible document intended to evolve in response to society's evolution. Others argue that it has a fixed meaning, rooted in the "original intent" of the framers, and that to move beyond that is to deny its value.

Historians, too, disagree about why the Constitution was written and what it meant. To some scholars, the creation of the federal system was an effort to preserve the ideals of the Revolution and to create a strong national government capable of exercising real authority. To others, the Constitution was an effort to protect the economic interests of existing elites, even at the cost of betraying the principles of the Revolution. To still others, the Constitution was designed to protect individual freedom and to limit the power of the federal government.

The first influential exponent of the heroic view of the Constitution as the culmination of the Revolution was John Fiske. In *The Critical Period of American History* (1888), Fiske described the many problems that beset the nation under the Articles of Confederation: economic difficulties, the weakness and ineptitude of the new national government, threats from abroad, interstate jealousies, and widespread lawlessness. Only the timely adoption of the Constitution, Fiske claimed, saved the young republic from disaster.

In *An Economic Interpretation of the Constitution of the United States* (1913), Charles A. Beard challenged Fiske's view. According to Beard, the 1780s had been a "critical period" primarily for conservative businessmen who feared that the decentralized political structure of the republic imperiled their financial position. Such men, he claimed, wanted a government able to promote industry and trade, protect private property, and make good the public debt—much of which was owed to them. The Constitution was, Beard claimed, "an economic document drawn with superb skill by men whose property interests were immediately at stake" and who won its ratification over the opposition of a majority of the people.

A series of powerful challenges to Beard's thesis emerged in the 1950s, as many scholars began to argue that the Constitution was not an effort to preserve property but, rather, an enlightened effort to ensure stability and order. Examining the debate between the Federalists and the Antifederalists, Forrest McDonald, in *We the People* (1958), concluded that there was no consistent relationship between wealth and property and support for the Constitution. Instead, opinion on the new system was far more likely to reflect local and regional interests. The cumulative effect of these challenges greatly weakened Beard's argument; few historians any longer accepted his thesis without reservation.

warned that if they failed, the delegates would "become a reproach and by-word down to future ages. And what is worse, mankind may hereafter, from this unfortunate instance, despair of establishing governments by human wisdom, and leave it to chance, war and conquest." Partly because of Franklin's soothing presence, the delegates refused to give up.

Finally, on July 2, the convention agreed to create a "grand committee," with a single delegate from each state (and with Franklin as chairman), to resolve the disagreements. The committee produced a proposal that became the basis of the "Great Compromise." Its most important achievement was resolving the difficult problem of representation. The proposal called for a legislature in which the states would be represented in the lower house on the basis of population. Each slave would count as three-fifths of a free person in determining the basis for both representation and direct taxation. (The three-fifths formula was based on the false assumption that a slave was three-fifths as productive as a free worker and thus contributed only three-fifths as much wealth to the state.) The committee proposed that in the upper house, the states should be represented equally with two members apiece. The proposal broke the deadlock. On July 16, 1787, the convention voted to accept the compromise.

Over the next few weeks, the convention agreed to another important compromise on the explosive issue of slavery. The representatives of the southern states feared that the power to regulate trade might interfere with their agrarian economy, which relied heavily on sales abroad, and with slavery. In response, the convention agreed that the new legislature would not be permitted to tax exports; Congress would also be forbidden to impose a duty of more than $10 a head on imported slaves, and it would have no authority to stop the slave trade for twenty years. To those delegates who viewed the continued existence of slavery as an affront to the principles of the new nation, this was a large and difficult concession. They agreed to it because they feared that without it the Constitution would fail.

The convention chose to ignore differences of opinion it was unable to resolve, leaving important questions alive that would surface again in later years. The Constitution provided no definition of citizenship. Most important was the absence of a list of individual rights, which would restrain the powers of the national government in the way that bills of rights restrained the state governments. Madison opposed the idea, arguing that specifying rights that were reserved to the people would, in effect, limit those rights. Other delegates, however, feared that without such protections the national government might abuse its new authority.

THE CONSTITUTION OF 1787

Many people contributed to the creation of the American Constitution, but the single most important of them was

In the 1960s, a new group of scholars began to revive an economic interpretation of the Constitution—one that differed from Beard's in important ways but that nevertheless emphasized social and economic factors as motives for supporting the federal system. Jackson Turner Main argued, in *The Anti-federalists* (1961), that supporters of the Constitution were "cosmopolitan commercialists," eager to advance the economic development of the nation; the Antifederalists, by contrast, were "agrarian localists," fearful of centralization. Gordon Wood, in *The Creation of the American Republic* (1969), suggested that the debate over the state constitutions in the 1770s and 1780s reflected profound social divisions and that those same divisions helped shape the argument over the federal Constitution. The Federalists, Wood suggested, were largely traditional aristocrats deeply concerned over the instability of life under the Articles of Confederation and particularly alarmed by the decline in popular deference toward social elites. The creation of the Constitution, Wood argued, was part of a larger search to create a legitimate political leadership based on the existing social hierarchy.

Historians have continued to examine the question of "intent." Did the framers intend a strong, centralized political system; or did they intend to create a decentralized system with a heavy emphasis on individual rights? The answer, according to Jack Rakove in *Original Meanings* (1996) and *Revolutionaries* (2010), is both—and many other things as well. The Constitution, Rakove argues, was the result of a long and vigorous debate through which the views of many different groups found their way into the document. James Madison, a strong nationalist, believed that only a powerful central government could preserve stability in a large nation. Alexander Hamilton also saw the Constitution as a way to protect order and property and to defend the nation against the dangers of too much liberty. But if Madison and Hamilton feared too much liberty, they also feared too little. And that made them receptive to the vigorous demands of the "Antifederalists" for protections of individual rights, which culminated in the Bill of Rights. The Constitution is not, Rakove argues, "infinitely malleable." But neither does it have a fixed meaning that can be a reliable guide to how we interpret it today. ●

AP HISTORICAL ARGUMENTATION AND INTERPRETATION

Questions assume cumulative content knowledge from this chapter and previous chapters.

1. Identify three broad schools of historical interpretation concerning the writing of the U.S. Constitution and the development of U.S. federalism. For each, identify a historian and describe his or her argument. For each of these arguments, describe one piece of historical evidence that supports it and one that refutes it.

2. If you were writing a history of the Constitution from an economic lens, around which factors might you construct your interpretation? If you were writing from a political philosophy lens, around which factors might you construct your interpretation?

3. With which historical interpretation do you most agree? Explain why, using historical evidence.

JAMES MADISON

James Madison—the most creative political thinker of his generation. Perhaps Madison's most important achievement was in helping resolve two important philosophical questions that had served as obstacles to the creation of an effective national government: the question of sovereignty and the question of limiting power.

THE QUESTION OF SOVEREIGNTY

The question of sovereignty had been one of the chief sources of friction between the colonies and Great Britain, and it continued to trouble Americans as they attempted to create their own government. How could both the national government and the state governments exercise sovereignty at the same time? Where did ultimate sovereignty lie? The answer, Madison and his contemporaries decided, was that all power, at all levels of government, flowed ultimately from the people. Thus neither the federal government nor the state governments were truly sovereign. All of them derived their authority from below. The opening phrase of the Constitution (devised by Gouverneur Morris) was "We the people of the United States"—an expression of the belief that the new government derived its power not from the states but from its citizens.

Resolving the problem of sovereignty made possible one of the distinctive features of the Constitution—its distribution of powers between the national and state governments.

It was, Madison wrote at the time, "in strictness, neither a national nor a federal Constitution, but a composition of both." The Constitution and the government it created were to be the "supreme law" of the land; no state would have the authority to defy it. The federal government was to have broad powers, including the power to tax, to regulate commerce, to control the currency, and to pass such laws as would be "necessary and proper" for carrying out its other responsibilities. Gone was the stipulation of the Articles that "each State shall retain every power, jurisdiction, and right not expressly delegated to the United States in Congress assembled." On the other hand, the Constitution accepted the existence of separate states and left important powers in their hands.

In addition to solving the question of sovereignty, the Constitution produced a solution to a problem troubling to Americans: the problem of concentrated authority. Nothing so frightened the leaders of the new nation as the prospect of creating a tyrannical government. That fear had been one of the chief obstacles to the creation of a national government. Drawing from the ideas of the French philosopher Baron de Montesquieu, most Americans had long believed that the best way to avoid tyranny was to keep government close to the people. A republic, they thought, must remain confined to a small area. A large nation would breed corruption and despotism because the rulers would be so distant from most of the people that there would be no way to control them. In the first years of the new American nation, these assumptions had led to the belief that the individual states must remain sovereign and that a strong national government would be dangerous.

Madison, however, helped break the grip of these assumptions by arguing that a large republic would be less, not more, likely to produce tyranny, because it would contain so many different factions that no single group would ever be able to dominate it. (In this, he drew from–among other sources–the

SEPARATION OF POWERS

Scottish philosopher David Hume.) This idea of many centers of power "checking each other" and preventing any single, despotic authority made possible the idea of a large republic and also helped shape the internal structure of the federal government. The Constitution's most distinctive feature was its "separation of powers" within the government, its creation of "checks and balances" among the legislative, executive, and judicial branches. The array of forces within the government would constantly compete with (and often frustrate) one another. Congress would have two chambers, the Senate and the House of Representatives, each with members elected in a different way and for different terms, and each checking the other, since both would have to agree before any law could be passed. The president would have the power to veto acts of Congress. The federal courts would have protection from both the executive and the legislature because judges and justices, once appointed by the president and confirmed by the Senate, would serve for life.

The "federal" structure of the government, which divided power between the states and the nation, and the system of "checks and balances," which divided power among various elements within the national government, were designed to protect the United States from the kind of despotism Americans believed had emerged in England. But they were also designed to protect the nation from another kind of despotism, perhaps equally menacing: the tyranny of the people. Fear of the "mob," of an "excess of democracy," was at least as important to the framers of the Constitution as fear of a single tyrant. Shays's Rebellion had been only one example, they believed, of what could happen if a nation did not defend itself against the unchecked exercise of popular will. Thus, in the new government, only the members of the House of Representatives would be elected directly by the people. Senators, the president, and federal judges would be insulated in varying degrees from the public.

On September 17, 1787, thirty-nine delegates signed the Constitution, doubtless sharing the feelings that Benjamin Franklin expressed at the end: "Thus I consent, Sir, to this Constitution, because I expect no better, and because I am not sure it is not the best."

THE LIMITS OF THE CONSTITUTION

The Constitution of 1789 was a document that established a democratic republic for white people, mostly white men. Indians and African Americans, the two largest population groups sharing the lands of the United States with Anglo-Americans, enjoyed virtually none of the rights and privileges provided to the white population. Native Americans had at least the semblance of a legal status within the nation, through treaties that assured them lands that would be theirs forever. But most of these treaties did not survive for long, and the Indians found themselves driven farther and farther west with little of the protection that the government had promised them.

Among the white leaders of the United States, there were eminent figures who believed Indians could join the republic as citizens. Jefferson was among them, believing that Indians could be taught the ways of "civilization." Jefferson, and other Americans with good intentions, sought to teach the Indians to live as white Americans did. Efforts to teach them Anglo farming methods were based on sedentary farms that relied on men doing the farming and women caring for the home. Indians had no interest in such ways and preferred to retain their traditional cultures. Their repudiation of white civilization contributed to the erosion of support among white Americans. Indians were not granted citizenship of the United States until the 1920s.

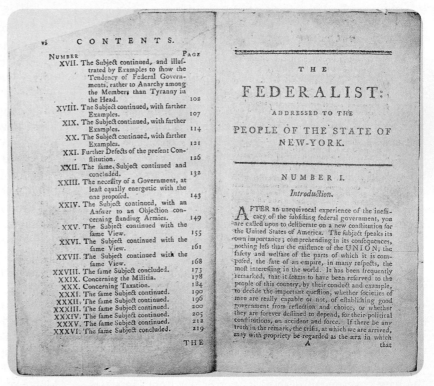

FEDERALIST #1 *The Federalist Papers,* gathered here in a book distributed to the people of New York, began as essays, letters, and articles published in newspapers throughout America during the debate over the Constitution. Its authors—James Madison, Alexander Hamilton, and John Jay—were defenders of the new Constitution and wrote these essays to explain its value and importance. They remain today one of the most important American contributions to political theory. (© The Granger Collection, New York)

Far more removed from the guarantees of the Constitution were African American slaves, who were given virtually none of the rights and protections that the new government provided to white people. They were, one southern official noted, not "constituent members of our society." The French-Canadian writer Hector St. John de Crèvecoeur, who after the Revolution settled in the United States, wrote a famous book, *Letters from an American Farmer*, in 1782. In it, he posed what became a famous question: "What then is the American, this new man?" Crèvecoeur answered his own question by noting that "individuals of all nations" would become "melted" into a common citizenry. But he too saw no room for African Americans in the community of the "new man." Indeed, among the first laws passed by the new United States under the Constitution was the Naturalization Act of 1790, which helped legalize the stream of immigrants coming into the country and allowed them to become citizens. But it defined citizenry as a status available only to white people. Even free black people were barred from citizenship.

Jefferson, who had briefly tried without result to give Indians a legal status within the new nation, had no such aspirations for African Americans. He was an uneasy defender of slavery, worrying about excluding "a whole race of men" from the natural rights that Jefferson himself had done so much to promote. But he could never accept the idea that black men and black women could attain the level of knowledge and intelligence of white people. Jefferson's long romantic relationship with a black woman, Sally Hemmings, did nothing to change his mind. Hemmings was a light-skinned woman who was a slave on Jefferson's plantation in Virginia. Jefferson lived with her after the death of his wife and fathered several of her children. But his intimate relationship with the Hemmings family did not ultimately change his postion on slavery. Unlike George Washington, who stipulated that his slaves be freed after his death, Jefferson (deeply in debt) required his heirs to sell his slaves after he died (after liberating the Hemmings family). Not until the end of the Civil War were black men and black women eligible to live as citizens in the United States, and even then with only partial rights until a century later.

FEDERALISTS AND ANTIFEDERALISTS

The delegates at Philadelphia had greatly exceeded their instructions from Congress and the states. Instead of making simple revisions to the Articles of Confederation, they had produced a plan for a completely different form of government. They feared, therefore, that the Constitution might never be ratified under the rules of the Articles of Confederation, which required unanimous approval by the state legislatures. So the convention changed the rules. The Constitution specified that the new government would come into existence among the ratifying states when any nine of the thirteen had ratified it. The delegates recommended to Congress that special state conventions, not state legislatures, consider the document.

They were required to vote "yes" or "no" on the document. They could make no changes until after the Constitution was ratified by the required number of states, at which point the Constitution's amendment process could be used (as it was for the Bill of Rights).

The old Confederation Congress, now overshadowed by the events in Philadelphia, passively accepted the Constitutional Convention's work and submitted it to the states for approval. All the state legislatures except Rhode Island's elected delegates to ratifying conventions, most of which began meeting by early 1788. Even before the ratifying conventions convened, however, a great national debate on the new Constitution had begun–in the state legislatures, in mass meetings, in the columns of newspapers, and in ordinary conversations. Occasionally, passions rose to the point that opposing factions came to blows. In at least one place–Albany, New York–such clashes resulted in injuries and death.

Supporters of the Constitution had a number of advantages. They were better organized than their opponents, and they had the support of the two most eminent men in America, Franklin and Washington. And they seized

THE FEDERALIST PAPERS an appealing label for themselves: "Federalists"–the term that opponents of centralization had once used to describe themselves–thus implying that they were less committed to a "nationalist" government than in fact they were. The Federalists also had the support of the ablest political philosophers of their time: Alexander Hamilton, James Madison, and John Jay. Those three men, under the joint pseudonym "Publius," wrote a series of essays–widely published in newspapers throughout the nation–explaining the meaning and virtues of the Constitution. They did so in an effort to counter the powerful arguments that those opposed to the Constitution–those who became known as the Antifederalists–were making. Without a powerful defense of the new Constitution, they feared, the Antifederalists might succeed in several crucial states, most notably in New York. The essays were later issued as a book, and they are known today as *The Federalist Papers*. They are among the most important American contributions to political theory.

The Federalists called their critics "Antifederalists," implying that their rivals had nothing to offer except opposition

THE ANTIFEDERALISTS and chaos. But the Antifederalists had serious and intelligent arguments of their own. They presented themselves as the defenders of the true principles of the Revolution. The Constitution, they believed, would betray those principles by establishing a strong, potentially tyrannical, center of power in the new national government. The "federal" government, they claimed, would increase taxes, obliterate the states, wield dictatorial powers, favor the "well born" over the common people, and put an end to individual liberty. But their biggest complaint was that the Constitution lacked a bill of rights, a concern that revealed one of the most important sources of their opposition: a basic mistrust of human nature and of the capacity of human beings to wield power. The Antifederalists argued that any government that centralized authority would inevitably produce despotism. Their demand for a bill of rights was a product of this belief: no government could be trusted to protect the liberties of its citizens; only by enumerating the natural rights of the people could there be any assurance that those rights would be preserved.

At its heart, then, the debate between the Federalists and the Antifederalists was a battle between two fears. The Federalists were afraid, above all, of disorder, anarchy, chaos; they feared the unchecked power of the masses, and they sought in the Constitution to create a government that would function at some distance from popular passions. The

DEBATING THE CONSTITUTION

Antifederalists were not anarchists; they too recognized the need for an effective government. But they were much more concerned about the dangers of concentrated power than about the dangers of popular will. They opposed the Constitution for some of the same reasons the Federalists supported it: because it placed obstacles between the people and the exercise of power.

Despite the Antifederalist efforts, ratification proceeded quickly (although not without occasional difficulty) during the winter of 1787-1788. The Delaware convention was the first to act, when it ratified the Constitution unanimously. The New Jersey and Georgia conventions did the same. In the larger states of Pennsylvania and Massachusetts, the Antifederalists put up a determined struggle but lost in the final vote. New Hampshire ratified the document in June 1788–the ninth state to do so. It was now theoretically possible for the Constitution to go into effect.

A new government could not hope to flourish, however, without the participation of Virginia and New York, the two most populous states, whose conventions remained closely divided. By the end of June, first Virginia and then New York had consented to the Constitution by narrow margins. The New York convention yielded to expediency–even some of the most staunchly Antifederalist delegates feared that the state's commercial interests would suffer if, once the other states gathered under the "New Roof," New York were to remain outside. Massachusetts, Virginia, and New York all ratified, on the assumption that a bill of rights would be added to the Constitution. The North Carolina convention adjourned without taking action, waiting to see what happened to the amendments. Rhode Island, whose leaders had opposed the Constitution almost from the start, did not even call a convention to consider ratification.

COMPLETING THE STRUCTURE

The first elections under the Constitution took place in the early months of 1789. Almost all the newly elected congressmen and senators had favored ratification, and many had served as delegates to the Philadelphia convention. There was never any real doubt about who would be the first president. George Washington had presided at the Constitutional Convention, and many delegates who had favored ratification did so only because they expected him to preside over the new government as well. Washington received the votes of all the presidential electors. John Adams, a leading Federalist, became vice president. After a journey from Mount Vernon marked by elaborate celebrations along the way, Washington was inaugurated in New York–the national capital for the time being–on April 30, 1789.

The first Congress served in many ways almost as a continuation of the Constitutional Convention, because its principal responsibility was filling in the various gaps in the Constitution.

THE BILL OF RIGHTS

Its most important task was drafting a bill of rights. By early 1789, even Madison had come to agree that some sort of bill of rights was essential to legitimize the new government in the eyes of its opponents. Congress approved twelve amendments on September 25, 1789; ten of them were ratified by the states by the end of 1791. What we know as the Bill of Rights is these first ten amendments to the Constitution. Nine of them placed limitations on Congress by forbidding it to infringe on certain basic rights: freedom of religion, speech, and the press; immunity from arbitrary arrest; trial by jury; and others. The Tenth Amendment reserved to the states all powers except those specifically withheld from them or delegated to the federal government.

On the subject of the federal courts, the Constitution said only: "The judicial power of the United States shall be vested in one Supreme Court, and in such inferior courts as the Congress may from time to time ordain and establish." It was left to Congress to determine the number of Supreme Court judges to be appointed and the kinds of lower courts to be organized. In the Judiciary Act of 1789, Congress provided for a Supreme Court of six members, with a chief justice and five associate justices; thirteen district courts with one judge apiece; and three circuit courts of appeal, each to consist of one of the district judges sitting with two of the Supreme Court justices. In the same act, Congress gave the Supreme Court the power to make the final decision in cases involving the constitutionality of state laws.

The Constitution referred indirectly to executive departments but did not specify what or how many there should be. The first Congress created three such departments–state, trea-

THE CABINET

sury, and war–and also established the offices of the attorney general and the postmaster general. To the office of secretary of the treasury, Washington appointed Alexander Hamilton of New York, who at age thirty-two was an acknowledged expert in public finance. For secretary of war he chose a Massachusetts Federalist, General Henry Knox. As attorney general he named Edmund Randolph of Virginia, sponsor of the plan on which the Constitution had been based. As secretary of state he chose another Virginian, Thomas Jefferson, who had recently served as minister to France.

FEDERALISTS AND REPUBLICANS

The resolution of these initial issues, however, did not resolve the deep disagreements about the nature of the new government. On the contrary, for the first twelve years under the Constitution, American politics was characterized by a level of acrimony seldom matched in any period since. The framers of the Constitution had dealt with many disagreements not by solving them but by papering them over with a series of vague compromises; as a result, the conflicts survived to plague the new government.

At the heart of the controversies of the 1790s was the same basic difference in philosophy that had been at the heart of the debate over the Constitution. On one side stood a powerful group that believed America required a strong, national gov-

COMPETING VISIONS

ernment: that the country's mission was to become a genuine nation-state, with centralized authority, a complex commercial economy, and a proud standing in world affairs. On the other side stood another group—a minority at first, but one that gained strength during the decade—that envisioned a far weaker central government. American society should not, this group believed, aspire to be highly commercial or urban. It should remain predominantly rural and agrarian, and it should have a central government of modest size and powers that would leave most power in the hands of the states and the people. The centralizers became known as the Federalists and gravitated to the leadership of Alexander Hamilton. Their opponents took the name Republicans and gathered under the leadership of James Madison and Thomas Jefferson.

HAMILTON AND THE FEDERALISTS

For twelve years, control of the new government remained firmly in the hands of the Federalists. That was in part because George Washington had always envisioned a strong national government and as president had quietly supported those who were attempting to create one. His enormous prestige throughout the nation was one of the Federalists' greatest assets. But Washington also believed that the presidency should remain above political controversies, and so he avoided any personal involvement in the deliberations of Congress. As a result, the dominant figure in his administration became his talented secretary of the treasury, Alexander Hamilton, who exerted more influence on domestic and foreign policy than anyone else both during his term of office and, to an almost equal extent, after his resignation in 1794.

Of all the national leaders of his time, Hamilton was one of the most aristocratic in personal tastes and political philosophy—ironically, perhaps, since his own origins as an illegitimate child in the Caribbean had been so humble. Far from embracing the republican ideals of the virtue of the people, he believed that a stable and effective government

ALEXANDER HAMILTON As President George Washington's secretary of the Treasury, Alexander Hamilton exerted enormous influence in both domestic and foreign affairs. Hamilton favored the establishment of an enlightened ruling class to govern the new nation. His plans for the new federal government to assume existing public debt and to establish a national bank were part of his vision of a powerful nation with a vigorous and independent commercial economy, a robust industrial sector, and a dynamic role in world economic affairs. (© De Agostini Picture Library/The Bridgeman Art Library)

required an enlightened ruling class. Thus the new government needed the support of the wealthy and powerful; and to get that support, it needed to give those elites a stake in its

ASSUMING THE DEBT

success. Hamilton proposed, therefore, that the new government take responsibility for the existing public debt. Many of the miscellaneous, uncertain, depreciated certificates of indebtedness that the old Congress had issued during and after the Revolution were now in the hands of wealthy speculators; the government should call them in and exchange them for uniform, interest-bearing bonds, payable at definite dates. (This policy was known as "funding" the debt.) He also recommended that the federal government "assume" (or take over) the debts the states had accumulated during the Revolution; this assumption policy would encourage state as well as federal bondholders to look to the central government for eventual payment. Hamilton did not, in other words, envision paying off and thus eliminating the debt. He wanted instead to create a large and permanent national debt, with new bonds being issued as old ones were paid off. The result, he believed, would be that creditors–the wealthy classes most likely to lend money to the government–would have a permanent stake in seeing the government survive.

Hamilton also wanted to create a national bank. At the time, there were only a few banks in the country, located principally in Boston, Philadelphia, and New York City. A new, national bank would help fill the void that the absence of a well-developed banking system had created. It would provide loans and currency to businesses. It would give the government a safe place to deposit federal funds. It would help collect taxes and disburse the government's expenditures. The bank would be chartered by the federal government, would have a monopoly of the government's own banking business, and would be controlled by directors, of whom one-fifth would be appointed by the government. It would provide a stable center to the nation's small and feeble banking system.

The funding and assumption of debts would require new sources of revenue, since the government would now have to pay interest on the loans it was accepting. Up to now, most government revenues had come from the sale of public lands in the West. Hamilton proposed two new

HAMILTON'S REPORT ON MANUFACTURING

kinds of taxes. One was an excise to be paid by distillers of alcoholic liquors, a tax that would fall most heavily on the whiskey distillers of the backcountry, especially in Pennsylvania, Virginia, and North Carolina–small farmers who converted part of their corn and rye crop into whiskey. The other was a tariff on imports, which not only would raise revenue but also would protect American manufacturing from foreign competition. In his famous "Report on Manufactures" of 1791, Hamilton laid out a grand scheme for stimulating the growth of industry in the United States and wrote glowingly of the advantages to the nation of a healthy manufacturing base.

The Federalists, in short, offered more than a vision of how to stabilize the new government. They offered a vision of the sort of nation America should become–a nation with a wealthy, enlightened ruling class, a vigorous, independent commercial economy, and a thriving industrial sector; a nation able to play a prominent role in world economic affairs.

ENACTING THE FEDERALIST PROGRAM

Few members of Congress objected to Hamilton's plan for funding the national debt, but many did oppose his proposal to accept the debt "at par," that is, at face value. The old certificates had been issued to merchants and farmers in payment for

DEBATING HAMILTON'S PROGRAM

war supplies during the Revolution, or to officers and soldiers of the Revolutionary army in payment for their services. But many of these original holders had sold their bonds during the hard times of the 1780s to speculators, who had bought them at a fraction of their face value. Many

members of Congress believed that if the federal government was to assume responsibility for these bonds, some of them should be returned to the original purchasers. James Madison, now a representative from Virginia, proposed dividing the federally funded bonds between the original purchasers and the speculators. But Hamilton's allies insisted that such a plan was impractical and that the honor of the government required that it pay the bondholders themselves, not the original lenders who had sold their bonds of their own accord. Congress finally passed the funding bill Hamilton wanted.

Hamilton's proposal that the federal government assume the state debts encountered greater difficulty. His opponents argued that if the federal government took over the state debts, the people of states with few debts would have to pay taxes to service the larger debts of other states. Hamilton and his supporters struck a bargain with the Virginians to win passage of the bill.

The deal involved the location of the national capital. The capital had moved from New York City back to Philadelphia in

LOCATION OF THE CAPITAL

1790. But the Virginians wanted a new capital near them in the South. Hamilton met with Thomas Jefferson and agreed over dinner to provide northern support for placing the capital in the South in exchange for Virginia's votes for the assumption bill. The bargain called for the construction of a new capital city on the banks of the Potomac River, which divided Virginia and Maryland, on land to be selected by Washington himself. The government would move there by the beginning of the new century.

Hamilton argued that creation of a national bank was compatible with the intent of the Constitution, even though the

BANK OF THE UNITED STATES

document did not explicitly authorize it. But Madison, Jefferson, Randolph, and others argued that Congress should exercise no powers that the Constitution had not clearly assigned it. Nevertheless, both the House and the Senate finally agreed to Hamilton's bill. Washington displayed some uncertainty about its legality at first, but he finally signed it. The Bank of the United States began operations in 1791, under a charter that granted it the right to continue for twenty years.

Once enacted, Hamilton's program had many of the effects he had intended and won the support of influential segments of the population. It quickly restored public credit; the bonds of the United States were soon selling at home and abroad at prices even above their face value. Speculators (among them many members of Congress) reaped large profits as a result. Manufacturers profited from the tariffs, and merchants in the seaports benefited from the new banking system.

Small farmers, who formed the vast majority of the population, complained that they had to bear a disproportionate tax burden. Not only did they have to pay property taxes to their state governments, but they bore the brunt of the excise tax on distilleries that Hamilton had initiated. They also opposed a 1792 tariff, also promoted by Hamilton. Many Americans came to believe that the Federalist program served the interests not of the people but of small, wealthy elites. Partly as a result, an organized political opposition arose.

THE REPUBLICAN OPPOSITION

The Constitution had made no reference to political parties, and the omission was not an oversight. Most of the framers–George Washington in particular–believed that organized parties were dangerous and should be avoided. Disagreement on particular issues was inevitable, but most of the founders believed that such disagreements need not and should not lead to the formation of permanent factions. "The public good is disregarded in the conflicts of rival parties," Madison wrote in *The Federalist Papers*, Number 10, perhaps the most influential of all the essays, "and . . . measures are too often decided, not according to the rules of justice and the rights of the minor party, but by the superior force of an interested and overbearing majority."

Yet, within just a few years after ratification of the Constitution, Madison and others became convinced that Hamilton and his followers had become just such an "interested and overbearing majority." The Hamiltonians, Madison and others agreed, had worked to establish a national network of influence that embodied all the worst features of a party. The Federalists had used their control over appointments and the awarding of government franchises to reward their supporters and win additional allies. They had encouraged the formation of local associations–largely aristocratic in nature–to strengthen their standing in local communities. They were doing many of the same things, their opponents believed, that the corrupt British governments of the early eighteenth century had done.

ESTABLISHMENT OF THE FEDERALIST PARTY

Because the Federalists appeared to be creating a menacing and tyrannical structure of power, their opponents believed that there was no alternative but to organize a vigorous opposition. The result was the emergence of an alternative political organization, which called itself the Republican Party. (This first "Republican" Party is not an ancestor of the modern Republican Party, which was born in the 1850s.) By the late 1790s, the Republicans were going to even greater lengths than the Federalists to create an apparatus of partisan influence. In every state they formed committees, societies, and caucuses. Republican groups corresponded with one another across state lines. They banded together to influence state and local elections. And they justified their actions by claiming that they and they alone represented the true interests of the nation–that they were fighting to defend the people against a corrupt conspiracy by the Federalists. Just as Hamilton believed that the network of supporters he was creating represented the only legitimate interest group in the nation, so the Republicans believed that their party organization represented the best interests of the people. Neither side was willing to admit that it was acting as a party; neither would concede the right of the other to exist. This institutionalized factionalism is known to scholars as the "first party system."

FORMATION OF THE REPUBLICAN PARTY

THE JEFFERSONIAN IDYLL American artists in the early nineteenth century were drawn to tranquil rural scenes, symbolic of the Jeffersonian vision of a nation of small, independent farmers. By 1822, when Francis Alexander painted this pastoral landscape of "Ralph Wheelock's Farm," the simple agrarian republic it depicts was already being transformed by rapid economic growth. (Courtesy, National Gallery of Art, Washington)

From the beginning, the preeminent figures among the Republicans were Thomas Jefferson and James Madison. Indeed, the two men were such intimate collaborators with such similar political philosophies that it is sometimes difficult to distinguish the contributions of one from those of the other. But Jefferson, the more charismatic personality of the two, gradually emerged as the most prominent spokesman for the Republicans. Jefferson considered himself a farmer. (He was, in fact, a substantial planter; but he had spent little time in recent years at his estate in Virginia.) He believed in an agrarian republic, most of whose citizens would be sturdy, independent farmer-citizens tilling their own soil.

Jefferson did not scorn commercial activity; he assumed farmers would market their crops in the national and even international markets. Nor did he oppose industry; he believed the United States should develop some manufacturing capacity. But he was suspicious of large cities, feared urban mobs as "sores upon the body politic," and opposed the development of an advanced industrial economy because it would, he feared, increase the number of propertyless workers packed in cities. In short, Jefferson envisioned a decentralized society, dominated by small property owners engaged largely in agrarian activities.

The difference between the Federalist and Republican social philosophies was visible in, among other things, reactions to the

DIFFERENCES OVER THE FRENCH REVOLUTION

French Revolution. As that revolution grew increasingly radical in the 1790s, with its attacks on organized religion, the overthrow of the monarchy, and eventually the execution of the king and queen, the Federalists expressed horror. But the Republicans generally applauded the democratic, antiaristocratic spirit they believed the French Revolution embodied. Some even imitated the French radicals (the Jacobins) by cutting their hair short, wearing pantaloons, and addressing one another as "Citizen" and "Citizeness."

Although both parties had supporters in all parts of the country and among all classes, there were regional and economic differences. The Federalists were most numerous in the commercial centers of the Northeast and in such southern seaports as Charleston; the Republicans were most numerous in the rural areas of the South and the West.

As the 1792 presidential election—the nation's second—approached, both Jefferson and Hamilton urged Washington to run for another term. The president reluctantly agreed. But while most Americans considered Washington above the partisan battle, he was actually much more in sympathy with the Federalists than with the Republicans. And during his presidency, Hamilton remained the dominant figure in government.

ESTABLISHING NATIONAL SOVEREIGNTY

The Federalists consolidated their position—and for a time attracted wide public support for the new national government—by dealing effectively with two problems the old Confederation had been unable fully to resolve. They helped stabilize the nation's western lands, and they strengthened America's international position.

SECURING THE FRONTIER

Despite the Northwest Ordinance, the Confederation Congress had largely failed to tie the outlying western areas of the country firmly to the government. Farmers in western Massachusetts had risen in revolt; settlers in Vermont, Kentucky, and Tennessee had toyed with the idea of separating from the Union. The new government under the Constitution inherited these problems.

In 1794, farmers in western Pennsylvania raised a major challenge to federal authority when they refused to pay a whiskey excise tax and began terrorizing the tax collectors (much as colonists had done at the time of the Stamp Act). But the federal government did not leave settlement of the so-called Whiskey Rebellion to Pennsylvania, as the

WHISKEY REBELLION

Confederation Congress had left Shays's Rebellion to Massachusetts. At Hamilton's urging, Washington called out the militias of three states, raised an army of nearly 15,000 (a larger force than he had commanded against the British during most of the Revolution), and personally led the troops into Pennsylvania. As the militiamen approached Pittsburgh, the center of the resistance, the rebellion quickly collapsed.

The federal government won the allegiance of the whiskey rebels by intimidating them. It won the loyalties of other frontier people by accepting their territories as new states in the Union. The last of the original thirteen colonies joined the Union once the Bill of Rights had been appended to the Constitution—North Carolina in 1789 and Rhode Island in 1790. Then Vermont, which had had its own state government since the Revolution, became the fourteenth state in 1791 after New York and New Hampshire finally agreed to give up their claims to it. Next came Kentucky, in 1792, when Virginia gave up its claim to that region. After North Carolina finally ceded its western lands to the Union, Tennessee became first a territory and, in 1796, a state.

NATIVE AMERICANS AND THE NEW NATION

The new government faced a greater challenge, also inherited from the Confederation, in the more distant areas of the Northwest and the Southwest, where Indians (occasionally in alliance with the British and Spanish) fought to retain tribal lands that the U.S. government claimed for itself. The ordinances of 1784–1787 had produced a series of border conflicts with Indian tribes resisting white settlement in what they considered their lands. Although the United States eventually defeated virtually every Indian challenge (if often at great cost), it was clear that the larger question of who was to control the lands of the West—the United States or the Indian nations—remained unanswered.

These clashes revealed another issue the Constitution had done little to resolve: the place of the Indian nations within the new federal structure. The Constitution barely mentioned Native Americans. Article I excluded "Indians not taxed" from

INDIANS AND THE CONSTITUTION

being counted in the population totals that determined the number of seats states would receive in the House of Representatives; and it gave Congress the power to "regulate Commerce with foreign Nations, and among the several States, and with the Indian tribes." Article VI bound the new government to respect treaties negotiated by the Confederation, most of which had been with the tribes. But none of this did much to clarify the precise legal standing of Indians or Indian nations within the United States.

On the one hand, the Constitution seemed to recognize the existence of the tribes as legal entities. On the other hand, it made clear that they were not "foreign Nations" (in the same sense that European countries were); nor were their members citizens of the United States. The tribes received no direct representation in the new government. Above all, the Constitution did not address the major issue that would govern relations between whites and Indians: land. Indian nations lived within the boundaries of the United States, yet they claimed (and the white government at times agreed) that they had some measure of sovereignty within their own lands. But neither the Constitution nor common law offered any clear guide to the rights of a "nation within a nation" or to the precise nature of tribal sovereignty, which ultimately depended on control of land. Thus the relationship between the tribes and the United States remained to be determined by a series of treaties, agreements, and judicial decisions in a process that has continued for more than 200 years.

MAINTAINING NEUTRALITY

Not until 1791–eight years after the end of the Revolution– did Great Britain send a minister to the United States, and then only because Madison and the Republicans were threatening to place special trade restrictions on British ships. That was one of many symbols of the difficulty the new government had in establishing its legitimacy in the eyes of the British. Another crisis in Anglo-American relations emerged in 1793 when the new French government, created by the Revolution of 1789, went to war with Great Britain and its allies. Both the president and Congress took steps to establish American neutrality in that conflict. But the neutrality quickly encountered severe tests.

The first challenge to American neutrality came from revolutionary France and its first diplomatic representative to America, the brash and youthful Edmond Genet. Instead of landing at Philadelphia and presenting himself immediately to the president, Genet disembarked at Charleston. There he made plans to use American ports to outfit French warships,

CITIZEN GENET

encouraged American shipowners to serve as French privateers, and commissioned the aging George Rogers Clark to lead a military expedition against Spanish lands to the south. (Spain was at the time an ally of Great Britain and an enemy of France.) In all of this, Genet was brazenly ignoring Washington's policies and flagrantly violating the Neutrality Act. His conduct infuriated Washington (who provided "Citizen Genet," as he was known, with an icy reception in Philadelphia) and the Federalists; it also embarrassed all but the most ardent admirers of the French Revolution among the Republicans. Washington eventually demanded that the French government recall him, but by then Genet's party was out of power in France. (The president granted him political asylum in the United States, and he settled with his American wife on a Long Island farm.) The neutrality policy had survived its first serious test.

A second and even greater challenge came from Great Britain. Early in 1794, the Royal Navy began seizing hundreds of American ships engaged in trade in the French West Indies,

A COMMENT ON THE WHISKEY REBELLION Although Thomas Jefferson and other Republicans claimed to welcome occasional popular uprisings, the Federalists were horrified by such insurgencies as Shays's Rebellion in Massachusetts and, later, the Whiskey Rebellion in Pennsylvania. This Federalist cartoon portrays the rebels as demons who pursue and eventually hang an unfortunate "exciseman" (tax collector), who has confiscated two kegs of rum. (© Philadelphia History Museum at the Atwater Kent,/ The Bridgeman Art Library)

outraging public opinion in the United States. Anti-British feeling rose still higher at the report that the governor general of Canada had delivered a warlike speech to the Indians on the northwestern frontier encouraging them to challenge U.S. dominance there. Hamilton was deeply concerned. War would mean an end to imports from England, and most of the revenue for maintaining his financial system came from duties on those imports.

JAY'S TREATY AND PINCKNEY'S TREATY

This was, Hamilton believed, no time for ordinary diplomacy. He did not trust the State Department to reach a settlement with Britain. Jefferson had resigned as secretary of state in 1793 to devote more time to his political activities, but his successor, Edmund Randolph, was even more ardently pro-French than Jefferson had been. So Hamilton persuaded Washington to name a special commissioner to England: John Jay, chief justice of the United States Supreme Court and a staunch New York Federalist. Jay was instructed to secure compensation for the recent British assaults on American shipping, to demand withdrawal of British forces from the frontier posts, and to negotiate a new commercial treaty.

The long and complex treaty Jay negotiated in 1794 failed to achieve these goals. But it was not without merit. It settled the conflict with Britain and helped prevent what had seemed likely to become a war between the two nations. It established

JAY'S TREATY undisputed American sovereignty over the entire Northwest. And it produced a reasonably satisfactory commercial relationship with Britain, whose trade was important to the United States. Nevertheless, when the terms became public in America, there were bitter public denunciations of it for having failed to extract enough promises from the British. Jay was burned in effigy in various parts of the country. Opponents of the treaty–nearly all the Republicans and even some Federalists, encouraged by agents of France–went to extraordinary lengths to defeat it in the Senate. The American minister to France, James Monroe, and even the secretary of state, Edmund Randolph, joined the desperate attempt to prevent ratification. But in the end the Senate ratified what was by then known as Jay's Treaty.

Among other things, the treaty made possible a settlement of America's conflict with the Spanish, because it raised fears in Spain that the British and the Americans might now join

PINCKNEY'S TREATY together to challenge Spanish possessions in North America. When Thomas Pinckney arrived in Spain as a special negotiator, he had no difficulty in gaining nearly everything the United States had sought from the Spaniards for more than a decade. Under Pinckney's Treaty (signed in 1795), Spain recognized the right of Americans to navigate the Mississippi to its mouth and to deposit goods at New Orleans for reloading on oceangoing ships; agreed to fix the northern boundary of Florida where Americans always had insisted it should be, along the 31st parallel; and required Spanish authorities to prevent the Indians in Florida from launching raids across the border.

THE DOWNFALL OF THE FEDERALISTS

The Federalists' impressive triumphs did not ensure their continued dominance in the national government. On the contrary, success seemed to produce problems of its own–problems that led to their downfall.

Since almost all Americans in the 1790s agreed that there was no place in a stable republic for an organized opposition, the emergence of the Republicans as powerful contenders for popular favor seemed to the Federalists a grave threat to national stability. Beginning in the late 1790s, when international perils confronted the government as well, the Federalists could not resist the temptation to move forcefully against the opposition. Facing what they believed was a stark choice between respecting individual liberties and preserving stability, the Federalists chose stability. The result was political disaster. After 1796, the Federalists never won another election. The popular respect for the institutions of the federal government, which they had worked so hard to

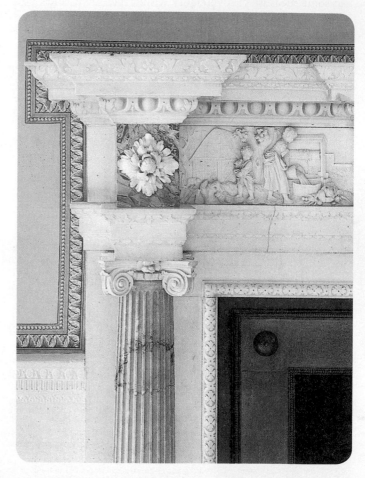

MOUNT VERNON George and Martha Washington lavished enormous attention on their home at Mount Vernon, importing materials and workmen from Europe to create a house that they hoped would rival some of the elegant country homes of England. Like many wealthy planters and merchants of their time, they strove to bring refinement and gentility to their lives. (© Paul G. Rocheleau)

produce among the people, survived. But the Federalists themselves gradually vanished as an effective political force.

THE ELECTION OF 1796

Despite strong pressure from his many admirers to run for a third term as president, George Washington insisted on retiring from office in 1797. In his Farewell Address to the American people (actually a long letter, composed in part by Hamilton and published in a Philadelphia newsletter), he reacted sharply to the Republicans. His reference to the "insidi-

WASHINGTON'S FAREWELL ADDRESS

ous wiles of foreign influence" was not just an abstract warning against international entanglements; it was also a specific denunciation of those Republicans who had been conspiring with the French to frustrate the Federalist diplomatic program.

With Washington out of the running, no obstacle remained to an open expression of the partisan rivalries that had been building over the previous eight years. Jefferson was the uncontested candidate of the Republicans in 1796. The Federalists faced a more difficult choice. Hamilton, the personification of Federalism, had created too many enemies to be a

JOHN ADAMS John Adams's illustrious career as Revolutionary leader, diplomat, and president marked the beginning of four generations of public distinction among members of his family. His son, John Quincy Adams, served as secretary of state and president. His grandson, Charles Francis Adams, was one of the great diplomats of the Civil War era. His great-grandson, Henry Adams, was one of America's most distinguished historians and writers. (Courtesy National Gallery of Art, Washington, D.C.)

credible candidate. So Vice President John Adams, who had been directly associated with none of the unpopular Federalist measures, became his party's nominee for president.

The Federalists were still clearly the dominant party, and there was little doubt of their ability to win a majority of the presidential electors. But without Washington to mediate, they fell victim to fierce factional rivalries that almost led to their undoing. Hamilton and many other Federalists (especially in the South) were not reconciled to Adams's candidacy and favored his running mate, Thomas Pinckney, instead. And when, as expected, the Federalists elected a majority of the presidential electors, some of these Pinckney supporters declined to vote for Adams; he managed to defeat Jefferson by only three electoral votes. Because a still-larger number of Adams's supporters declined to vote for Pinckney, Jefferson finished second in the balloting and became vice president. (Until the Twelfth Amendment was adopted in 1804, the Constitution provided for the candidate receiving the second highest number of electoral votes to become vice president—hence the awkward result of men from different parties serving in the nation's two highest elected offices.)

Adams thus assumed the presidency under unhappy circumstances. He presided over a divided party, which faced a

DIVIDED FEDERALISTS

strong and resourceful Republican opposition committed to its extinction. Adams was not even the dominant figure in his own party; Hamilton remained the most influential Federalist, and Adams was never able to challenge him effectively. The new president was one of the country's most accomplished and talented diplomats, but he had few skills as a politician. Austere, rigid, aloof, he had little talent at conciliating differences, soliciting support, or inspiring enthusiasm. He was a man of enormous, indeed intimidating, rectitude, and he seemed to assume that his own virtue and the correctness of his positions would be enough to sustain him.

THE QUASI WAR WITH FRANCE

American relations with Great Britain and Spain improved as a result of Jay's and Pinckney's Treaties. But the nation's relations with revolutionary France quickly deteriorated. French vessels captured American ships on the high seas and at times imprisoned the crews. When the South Carolina Federalist Charles Cotesworth Pinckney, brother of Thomas Pinckney, arrived in France, the government refused to receive him as the official representative of the United States.

Some of President Adams's advisers favored war, most notably Secretary of State Thomas Pickering, a stern New Englander who detested France. But Hamilton recommended conciliation, and Adams agreed. In an effort to stabilize relations, Adams appointed a bipartisan commission—consisting of Charles Cotesworth Pinckney, the recently rejected minister; John Marshall, a Virginia Federalist, later chief justice of the Supreme Court; and Elbridge Gerry, a Massachusetts Republican but a friend of the president—to negotiate with France. When the Americans arrived in Paris in 1797, three

---

agents of the French foreign minister, Prince Talleyrand, demanded a loan for France and a bribe for French officials before any negotiations could begin. Pinckney responded: "No! No! Not a sixpence!"

When Adams heard of the incident, he sent a message to Congress denouncing the French insults and urging preparations for war. He then turned the report of the American commissioners over to Congress, after deleting the names of the three French agents and designating them only as "Messrs. X, Y, and Z." When the report was published, it created widespread popular outrage at France's actions and strong support for the Federalists' response. For nearly two years after the "XYZ Affair," as it became known, the United States found itself engaged in an undeclared war with France.

THE XYZ AFFAIR

Adams persuaded Congress to cut off all trade with France and to authorize American vessels to capture French armed ships on the high seas. In 1798, Congress created a Department of the Navy and appropriated money for the construction of new warships. The navy soon won a number of duels with French vessels and captured eighty-five ships, including armed merchantmen. The United States also began cooperating closely with the British and became an ally of Britain in the war with France.

THE QUASI WAR

In the end, France chose to conciliate the United States before the conflict grew. Adams sent another commission to Paris in 1800, and the new French government (headed now by "first consul" Napoleon Bonaparte) agreed to a treaty with the United States that canceled the old agreement of 1778 and established new commercial arrangements. As a result, the "quasi war" came to a reasonably peaceful end.

REPRESSION AND PROTEST

The conflict with France helped the Federalists increase their majorities in Congress in 1798. Armed with this new strength, they began to consider ways to silence the Republican opposition. The result was some of the most controversial legislation in American history: the Alien and Sedition Acts.

ALIEN AND SEDITION ACTS

The Alien Act placed new obstacles in the way of foreigners who wished to become American citizens, and it strengthened the president's hand in dealing with aliens. The Sedition Act allowed the government to prosecute those who engaged in "sedition" against the government. In theory, only libelous or treasonous activities were subject to prosecution; but since such activities were open to widely varying definitions, the law made it possible for the federal government to stifle almost any opposition. The Republicans interpreted the new laws as part of a Federalist campaign to destroy them and fought back.

President Adams signed the new laws but was cautious in implementing them. He did not deport any aliens, and he prevented the government from launching a major crusade

THE XYZ AFFAIR The sensational "XYZ Affair" of 1798 is the subject of this American political cartoon. The five-headed figure in the center represents the Directory of the French government; he is demanding "money, money, money" from the three diplomats at left who were in Paris representing the United States. The monster at the top right is operating a guillotine—a symbol of the violence and terror of the later stages of the French Revolution. (© The Granger Collection, New York)

against the Republicans. But the legislation had a significant repressive effect nevertheless. The Alien Act helped discourage immigration and encouraged some foreigners already in the country to leave. And the administration made use of the Sedition Act to arrest and convict ten men, most of them Republican newspaper editors whose only crime had been to criticize the Federalists in government.

Republican leaders pinned their hopes for a reversal of the Alien and Sedition Acts on the state legislatures. (The Supreme

VIRGINIA AND KENTUCKY RESOLUTIONS

Court had not yet established its sole right to nullify congressional legislation, and there were many Republican leaders who believed that the states had that power too.) The Republicans laid out a theory for state action in two sets of resolutions in 1798-1799, one written (anonymously) by Jefferson and adopted by the Kentucky legislature and the other drafted by Madison and approved by the Virginia legislature. The Virginia and Kentucky Resolutions, as they were known, used the ideas of John Locke to argue that the federal government had been formed by a "compact" or contract among the states and possessed only certain delegated powers. Whenever the federal government exercised any undelegated powers, its acts were "unauthoritative, void, and of no force." If the parties to the contract, the states, decided that the central government had exceeded those powers, the Kentucky Resolution claimed, they had the right to "nullify" the appropriate laws. (Such claims emerged again in the South in the decades before the Civil War.)

The Republicans did not win wide support for nullification; only Virginia and Kentucky declared the congressional statutes void. The Republicans did, however, succeed in elevating their dispute with the Federalists to the level of a national crisis. By the late 1790s, the entire nation was deeply and bitterly divided politically. State legislatures at times resembled battlegrounds. Even the United States Congress was plagued with violent disagreements. In one celebrated incident in the chamber of the House of Representatives, Matthew Lyon, a Republican from Vermont, responded to an insult from Roger Griswold, a Federalist from Connecticut, by spitting in Griswold's face. Griswold attacked Lyon with his cane. Lyon fought back with a pair of fire tongs, and the two men ended up wrestling on the floor.

THE "REVOLUTION" OF 1800

These bitter controversies shaped the 1800 presidential election. Adams and Jefferson were again the opposing candidates. But the

THE ELECTION OF 1800

campaign of 1800 was very different from the one preceding it. Indeed, it may have been the ugliest in American history. Adams and Jefferson themselves displayed reasonable dignity, but their supporters showed no such restraint. The Federalists accused Jefferson of being a dangerous radical and his followers of being wild men who, if they came to power, would bring on a reign of terror comparable to that of the French Revolution. The Republicans portrayed Adams as a tyrant conspiring to become king, and they accused the Federalists of plotting to subvert human liberty and impose slavery on the people. There was considerable personal invective as well. For example, it was during this campaign that the story of Jefferson's romantic involvement with a slave woman on his plantation was first widely aired. (Recent DNA evidence has proven that the story was true.)

The election was close, and the crucial contest was in New York. There, Aaron Burr had mobilized an organization of Revolutionary War veterans, the Tammany Society, to serve as

CONGRESSIONAL BRAWLERS This cartoon lampoons a celebrated fight on the floor of the House of Representatives in 1798 between Matthew Lyon, a Republican from Vermont, and Roger Griswold, a Federalist from Connecticut. The conflict began when Griswold insulted Lyon by attacking his military record in the Revolutionary War. Lyon replied by spitting in Griswold's face. Two weeks later, Griswold attacked Lyon with his cane, and Lyon seized a pair of fire tongs and fought back. That later scene is depicted (and ridiculed) here. Other members of Congress are portrayed as enjoying the spectacle. On the wall is a picture titled "Royal Sport," showing animals fighting. (The Library of Congress (LC-DIG-ppmsca -31832))

a Republican political machine. And through Tammany's efforts, the Republicans carried the city by a large majority and, with it, the state. Jefferson was, apparently, elected.

But an unexpected complication soon jeopardized the Republican victory. The Constitution called for each elector to "vote by ballot for two persons." The normal practice was for an elector to cast one vote for his party's presidential candidate and another for the vice presidential candidate. To avoid a tie between Jefferson and Aaron Burr (the Republican vice presidential candidate), the Republicans had intended for one elector to refrain from voting for Burr. But the plan went awry. When the votes were counted, Jefferson and Burr each had 73. No candidate had a majority. According to the Constitution, the House of Representatives had to choose between the two leading candidates when no one had a majority; in this case, that meant deciding between Jefferson and Burr. Each state delegation would cast a single vote.

The new Congress, elected in 1800 with a Republican majority, was not to convene until after the inauguration of the president, so it was the Federalist Congress that had to decide the question. Some Federalists hoped to use the situation to salvage the election for their party; others wanted to strike a bargain with Burr and elect him. But after a long deadlock, several leading Federalists, most prominent among them Alexander Hamilton, concluded that Burr (whom many suspected of hav-ing engineered the deadlock in the first place) was too unreliable to trust with the presidency. On the thirty-sixth ballot, Jefferson was elected.

After the election of 1800, the only branch of the federal government left in Federalist hands was the judiciary. The Adams administration spent its last months in office taking steps to make the party's hold on the courts secure. By the Judiciary Act of **THE JUDICIARY ACT OF 1801** 1801, passed by the lame duck Congress, the Federalists reduced the number of Supreme Court justiceships by one but greatly increased the number of federal judgeships as a whole. Adams quickly appointed Federalists to the newly created positions. Indeed, there were charges that he stayed up until midnight on his last day in office to finish signing the new judges' commissions. These officeholders became known as the "midnight appointments."

Even so, the Republicans viewed their victory, incorrectly, as almost complete. The nation, they believed, had been saved from tyranny. A new era could now begin, one in which the true principles on which America had been founded would once again govern the land. The exuberance with which the victors viewed the future—and the importance they attributed to the Federalists' defeat—was evident in the phrase Jefferson later used to describe his election: the "Revolution of 1800." It remained to be seen how revolutionary it would really be.

AP CONNECTING THEMES

Chapter 6 discussed the political, economic, and social consequences of the American Revolution. You should focus on divisions in American society at the outset of the war and how those divisions changed what it was to be called an American. The revolution also resulted in westward migration that ultimately led to new challenges for the country. Particularly important are the relations with foreign countries that the American Revolution brought about. It is essential that you understand how the political structure of the United States was changed by the winning of its independence, both at the national and state level.

The following themes have a heightened importance in Chapter 6. You should now be able to do the following for each listed theme:

Identity: Explain how disagreements in politics led to questions about what it meant to be an American.
Peopling: Analyze the factors that encouraged western migration and the consequences of that migration.
Politics and Power: Explain the reasons for the development of political parties in the United States and how their beliefs differed.
America and the World: Explain how American trade, policies of neutrality, and westward expansion led to conflict with a variety of different European countries.
Ideas, Beliefs, and Culture: Explain how Enlightenment ideas and the belief in republican principles of self-government manifested themselves during and after the writing of the Constitution.

AP SUGGESTED STUDY

PEOPLE/PLACES/EVENTS As you study these items, think about how they demonstrate key concepts and historical themes from this chapter and previous chapters.

AP TEST PRACTICE

Questions assume cumulative content knowledge from this chapter and previous chapters.

MULTIPLE CHOICE Use the cartoon on page 177 and your knowledge of U.S. history to answer questions 1-3.

1. What was an issue of contention in the 1790s, which contributed to the state of politics as depicted in the cartoon?
   (A) Failure of the Constitution to address the status of Native Americans
   (B) Relations with revolutionary France
   (C) Border conflicts with Native Americans in the Northwest Territory
   (D) The rise of political parties

2. The major difference in philosophical outlook between the two political parties battling in the cartoon was regarding
   (A) the process of selling lands in the Northwest Territory
   (B) the issue of slavery in the Northwest Territory
   (C) the strength of the national government
   (D) the source of power for the government of the newly-independent U.S.

3. The point of view of the cartoon reinforces what perspective about political parties in the late 18th century?
   (A) Organized political parties are dangerous in that the public good is often ignored in the rivalry between the parties
   (B) Political parties are necessary to allow all political differences to surface for public scrutiny
   (C) The existence of organized political parties leads to heated disagreements over issues.
   (D) Conflicts arising from party politics demeans the stature of Congress

SHORT ANSWER Use your knowledge of U.S. history to answer questions 4-6.

4. Using the painting from page 171, answer a, b, and c.
   a) Briefly explain three characteristics of the ideal republic, represented in the painting, which a contingent of American leaders envisioned in the years immediately following the revolution.
   b) Briefly explain ONE development in the period from 1780 to 1800, which serves as an example of the vision being implemented.
   c) Briefly explain ONE development in the period from 1780 to 1800, which challenged implementation of that vision.

5. Answer a, b, and c.
   a) Briefly explain why ONE of the following options most clearly marks the beginning of the formation of political parties in America.
      • The revising of the Articles of Confederation (1786)
      • Ratification of the U.S. Constitution (1788)
      • Creation of a national bank (1791)
   b) Provide a specific historical example that supports your explanation above.
   c) Briefly explain why one of the other options is not as useful to mark the beginning of the formation of political parties in America.

6. Answer a, b, and c.
   a) Briefly explain ONE example of problems faced by the U.S. in the 1790s due to foreign interference.
   b) Briefly explain a SECOND example of problems faced by the U.S. in the 1790s due to foreign interference.
   c) Briefly explain ONE example of diplomatic success in foreign policy achieved by American political leaders in the 1790s.

LONG ESSAY Develop a thoughtful and thorough historical argument that answers the question below. Begin your essay with a thesis statement and support it with relevant historical evidence.

7. Some historians have argued that the presidential election of 1800 was a turning point in U.S. history. Support, refute, or modify this interpretation, providing specific evidence to justify your answer.

7 | THE JEFFERSONIAN ERA

THE BURNING OF WASHINGTON This dramatic engraving somewhat exaggerates the extent of the blazes in Washington when the British occupied the city in August 1814. But the invaders did set fire to the Capitol, the White House, and other public buildings in retaliation for the American burning and looting of the Canadian capital at York. (© The Granger Collection, New Yrok)

AP

HISTORICAL THINKING

1. **Contextualization** Identify and explain, using specific evidence, how the debate over the power of the national government versus states' rights intensified.

2. **Comparison** Compare and contrast the economic and social systems of the northern, southern, and western regions.

3. **Patterns of Continuity and Change over Time** To what degree and in what ways did the First Industrial Revolution alter the labor force and family relationships in the United States?

4. **Historical Argumentation** Analyze the foreign policy issues facing the nation between 1800 and 1820 and evaluate the relative success of the United States in dealing with them.

5. **Patterns of Continuity and Change over Time** Analyze cultural and religious changes that occurred between 1800 and 1820 and evaluate the consequences of those changes.

6. **Historical Interpretation** To what degree did the United States enter into a war with Great Britain over the issue of freedom of the seas and neutral rights, as opposed to other motives?

7. **Contextualization** Analyze the degree to which and the ways in which the transportation revolution brought economic and social changes to the United States.

Key Concept Correlations

Analyze the ways the historical developments you learn about in this chapter connect to the following AP Key Concepts.

3.3 Migration within North America, cooperative interaction, and competition for resources raised questions about boundaries and policies, intensified conflicts among peoples and nations, and led to contests over the creation of a multiethnic, multiracial national identity.

4.1 The United States developed the world's first modern mass democracy and celebrated a new national culture, while Americans sought to define the nation's democratic ideals and to reform its institutions to match them.

4.2 Developments in technology, agriculture, and commerce precipitated profound changes in U.S. settlement patterns, regional identities, gender and family relations, political power, and distribution of consumer goods.

4.3 U.S. interest in increasing foreign trade, expanding its national borders, and isolating itself from European conflicts shaped the nation's foreign policy and spurred government and private initiatives.

Thematic Learning Objectives

CUL-2; ENV-3; POL-2, 3, 5, 6; ID-5; WOR-2, 6; WXT-2, 4, 5; PEO-4, 5

CHAPTER 7 discusses the growth of education, culture, and religion in the United States during the Jeffersonian era. Particular attention should be given to the impact of the Second Great Awakening on American society. Also important is the development of the First Industrial Revolution in conjunction with improved transportation and the effects of both on American society. Attempts to expand U.S. territory westward led to renewed conflict with American Indians and plots to separate western lands from the United States. The chapter also examines continuing debate over the power of the national government relative to that of the states. Close attention should be given to the impact of the Napoleonic Wars on the United States and how the United States eventually went to war with Britain. Be familiar with the consequences of the war, the subsequent peace, and its impact on regional rifts. As you read, evaluate the following concepts:

- There was continuing debate over the power of the national government versus states' rights.
- The economic and social systems of the north, south, and west became more pronounced and slavery, more entrenched.
- The Second Great Awakening believed in the perfectibility of man and, thus, was a catalyst for many reform movements.
- Americans attempted to develop a culture of their own—free from the domination of European constraints.
- The Napoleonic Wars led to increased confrontation with France and Britain and eventually led to the War of 1812.
- Advances in technology promoted the development of the First Industrial Revolution and an increasing market economy, which altered family and gender relationships, as well as migration patterns of groups of people.
- Improved transportation systems allowed for greater access to natural resources, markets, and western lands.
- The United States doubled its size and sought to dominate the North American continent by military, diplomatic, and demographic means.

THE RISE OF CULTURAL NATIONALISM

In many respects, American cultural life in the early nineteenth century seemed to reflect the Republican vision of the nation's future. Opportunities for education increased; the nation's literary and artistic life began to free itself from European influences; and American religion began to confront and adjust to the spread of Enlightenment rationalism. In other respects, however, the new culture was posing a serious challenge to Republican ideals.

PATTERNS OF EDUCATION

Central to the Republican vision of America was the concept of a virtuous and enlightened citizenry. Jefferson himself called emphatically for a national "crusade against ignorance." Republicans

IMPORTANCE OF A VIRTUOUS CITIZENRY believed, therefore, in the establishment of a nationwide system of public schools to create the educated electorate they believed a republic required. All white male citizens (the nation's prospective voters) should, they argued, receive free education.

Some states endorsed the principle of public education for all in the early years of the republic, but none actually created a working system of free schools. A Massachusetts law of 1789 reaffirmed the colonial laws by which each town was obligated to support a school, but there was little enforcement. In Virginia, the state legislature ignored Jefferson's call for universal elementary education and for advanced education for the gifted. As late as 1815, not a single state had a comprehensive public school system.

Instead, schooling became primarily the responsibility of private institutions, most of which were open only to those who could afford to pay for them. In the South and in the mid-Atlantic states, religious groups ran most of the schools. In New England and elsewhere, private academies were usually secular, many of them modeled on schools founded by the Phillips family at Andover, Massachusetts, in 1778, and at Exeter, New Hampshire, three years later. By 1815, there were thirty such private secondary schools in Massachusetts, thirty-seven in New York, and several dozen more scattered throughout the country. Many were frankly aristocratic in outlook, training their students to become members of the nation's elite. There were a few schools open to the poor offering education that was clearly inferior to that provided at exclusive schools.

PRIVATE SCHOOLING

Private secondary schools such as those in New England, and even many public schools, accepted only male students. Yet the early nineteenth century did see some important advances in female education.

In the eighteenth century, women received very little education of any kind, and the female illiteracy rate at the time of the Revolution was very high–at least 50 percent. At the same time, however, Americans had begun to place a new value on the contribution of the "republican mother" to the training of the new generation. That raised an important question: If mothers remained ignorant, how could they raise their children to be enlightened? Beginning as early as the 1770s and accelerating thereafter, such concerns led to the creation of a network of female academies throughout the nation (usually for the daughters of affluent families). In 1789, Massachusetts required that its public schools serve females as well as males. Other states, although not all, soon followed.

NEW EDUCATIONAL OPPORTUNITIES FOR WOMEN

Most white men, at least, assumed that female education should serve only to make women better wives and mothers. Women therefore had no need for advanced or professional training; there was no reason for colleges and universities to make space for female students. Some women, however, aspired to more. In 1784, Judith Sargent Murray published an essay defending women's rights to education, a defense set in terms very different from those used by most men. Men and women were equal in intellect and potential, Murray argued. Women, therefore, should have precisely the same educational opportunities as men. Moreover, they should have opportunities to earn their own living, to establish a role for themselves in society apart from their husbands and families. Murray's ideas became an inspiration to later generations of women, but during most of her own lifetime (1751–1820) they attracted little support.

Reformers who believed in the power of education to reform and redeem ignorant and "backward" people spurred a

A SEMINARY FOR WOMEN Educational opportunities for women were scarce in the early nineteenth century, but by the 1820s a number of seminaries were created for young ladies, mostly affluent students. The watercolor on silk is by an unknown artist and portrays two women studying geography. (© The Granger Collection, New York)

growing interest in Indian education. Because Jefferson and his followers liked to think of Native Americans as "noble savages" (uncivilized but, unlike their view of African Americans, not necessarily innately inferior), they hoped that schooling the Indians in white culture would tame and "uplift" the tribes. Although white governments did little to promote Indian education, missionaries and mission schools proliferated among the tribes.

INDIAN EDUCATION

Almost no white people in the early nineteenth century believed that there was a need to educate African Americans, almost all of whom were still slaves. In a few northern states, some free black children attended segregated schools. In the South, slaveowners generally tried to prevent their black workers from learning to read or write, fearful that knowledge would make them unhappy with their condition. Some African Americans managed to acquire some education despite these obstacles, by teaching themselves and their own children. But the numbers of literate slaves remained very small.

Higher education was much less widely available than education at lower levels, despite Republican hopes for a wide dispersion of advanced knowledge. (Jefferson founded the University of Virginia to promote that ideal.) The number of colleges and universities in America grew from nine at the start of the Revolution to twenty-two by 1800 and continued to increase thereafter. None of the new schools, however, was truly public. Even those established by state legislatures (in Georgia, North Carolina, Vermont, Ohio, and South Carolina, for example) relied on private contributions and on tuition fees. Scarcely more than one white man in a thousand (and no women, blacks, or Indians) had access to

HIGHER EDUCATION

college education, and those few who did attend universities were almost without exception members of prosperous, propertied families.

The education that the colleges provided was exceedingly limited—narrow training in the classics and a few other areas and intensive work in theology. Indeed, the clergy was the only profession for which college training was generally a prerequisite. A few institutions attempted to provide their students advanced education in other fields. The College of William and Mary in Virginia, the University of Pennsylvania, and Columbia College in New York all created law schools before 1800, but most lawyers continued to train for their profession simply by apprenticing themselves to practicing attorneys.

MEDICINE AND SCIENCE

The University of Pennsylvania created the first American medical school in the eighteenth century. In the early nineteenth century, however, most doctors studied medicine by working with an established practitioner. Some American physicians believed in applying new scientific methods to medicine and struggled against age-old prejudices and superstitions. Efforts to teach anatomy, for example, encountered strong public hostility because of the dissection of cadavers that the study required. Municipal authorities had no understanding of medical science and almost no idea of what to do in the face of the severe epidemics that so often swept their populations; only slowly did they respond to the warnings of, among others, Benjamin Rush, a pioneering Philadelphia physician, that lack of adequate sanitation programs was to blame for disease.

Individual patients often had more to fear from their doctors than from their illnesses. Even the leading advocates of scientific medicine often embraced useless and dangerous

BENJAMIN RUSH

treatments. Benjamin Rush, for example, was an advocate of the new and supposedly scientific techniques of bleeding and purging, and many of his patients died. George Washington's death in 1799 was probably less a result of the minor throat infection that had afflicted him than of his physicians' efforts to cure him by bleeding and purging.

The medical profession also used its newfound commitment to the "scientific" method to justify expanding its own role to kinds of care that had traditionally been outside its domain. Most childbirths, for example, had been attended by female midwives. In the early nineteenth century, physicians began to handle deliveries themselves and to demand restrictions on the

DECLINE OF MIDWIFERY

role of midwives. Among the results of that change was a narrowing of opportunities for women (midwifery was an important female occupation) and a restriction of access to childbirth care for poor mothers (who could have afforded midwives, but who could not pay the higher physicians' fees).

Education and professional training in the early republic—in medicine and in many other fields—thus fell far short of the Jeffersonian vision. Indeed, efforts to promote education and increase professionalism often had the effect of strengthening existing elites rather than eroding them.

CULTURAL ASPIRATIONS IN THE NEW NATION

Many Americans in the Jeffersonian era may have repudiated the Federalist belief in political and economic centralization,

ESTABLISHMENT OF A NATIONAL CULTURE

but most embraced another form of nationalism with great fervor. Having won political independence from Europe, they aspired now to a form of cultural independence.

THE PENNSYLVANIA HOSPITAL The ideas of the Enlightenment spread through American culture in the eighteenth and nineteenth centuries and strengthened the belief that every individual was a divine being and could be redeemed from even the most miserable condition. Hospitals and asylums—such as this institution in Pennsylvania—began to emerge to provide settings for the redemption of the poor, the ill, and the deviant. (© Archive Photos/Getty Images)

In the process, they dreamed of an American literary and artistic life that would rival the greatest achievements of Europe. As a popular "Poem on the Rising Glory of America" had predicted as early as 1772, Americans believed that their "happy land" was destined to become the "seat of empire" and the "final stage" of civilization, with "glorious works of high invention and of wond'rous art." The United States, another eighteenth-century writer had proclaimed, would serve as "the last and greatest theatre for the improvement of mankind."

Such nationalism found expression, among other places, in early American schoolbooks. The Massachusetts geographer Jedidiah Morse, author of *Geography Made Easy* (1784), said the country must have its own textbooks to prevent the aristocratic ideas of England from infecting the people. The Connecticut schoolmaster and lawyer Noah Webster argued similarly that American students should be educated as patriots, their minds filled with nationalistic, American thoughts.

To encourage a distinctive American culture and help unify the new nation, Webster insisted on a simplified and Americanized system of spelling—"honor" instead of "honour," for example. His *American Spelling Book*, first published in 1783 and commonly known as the "blue-backed speller," eventually sold over 100 million copies, to become the **NOAH WEBSTER** best-selling book (except for the Bible) in the history of American publishing. In addition, his school dictionary, issued in 1806, was republished in many editions and was eventually enlarged to become (in 1828) *An American Dictionary of the English Language*. His speller and his dictionary established a national standard of words and usages.

Those Americans who aspired to create a more elevated national literary life faced a number of obstacles. There was a large potential audience for a national literature—a substantial reading public, created in part by the wide circulation of newspapers and political pamphlets during the Revolution. But there were few opportunities for would-be American authors to get their work before the public. Printers preferred to publish popular works by English writers (for which they had to pay no royalties); magazine publishers filled their pages largely with items clipped from British periodicals. Only those American writers willing to pay the cost and bear the risk of publishing their own works could compete for public attention.

Even so, a growing number of American authors struggled to create a strong native literature so that, as the poet Joel Barlow wrote, "true ideas of glory may be implanted in the minds of men here, to take the place of the false and destructive ones that have degraded the species in other countries." Barlow himself, one of a group of Connecticut writers known as the "Hartford Wits," published an epic poem, *The Columbiad*, in 1807, in an effort to convey the special character of American civilization. The acclaim it received helped to encourage other native writers.

Among the most ambitious was the Philadelphian Charles Brockden Brown. Like many Americans, he was attracted to the relatively new literary form of the novel, which had become popular in England in the late eighteenth century and had been successfully imported to America. But Brown sought to do more than simply imitate the English forms; he tried to use his novels to give voice to distinctively American themes, to convey the "soaring passions and intellectual energy" of the new nation. His obsession with originality led him to produce a body of work characterized by a fascination with horror and deviant behavior. Perhaps as a result, his novels failed to develop a large popular following.

Much more successful was Washington Irving, a resident of New York State who won wide acclaim for his satirical histories of early American life and his powerful fables of **WASHINGTON IRVING** society in the New World. His popular folktales, recounting the adventures of such American rustics as Ichabod Crane and Rip Van Winkle, made him the widely acknowledged leader of American literary life in his era and one of the few writers of that time whose works would continue to be read by later generations.

Perhaps the most influential works by American authors in the early republic were not poems, novels, or stories, but works of history that glorified the nation's past. Mercy Otis Warren, who had been an influential playwright and agitator during the 1770s, continued her literary efforts with a three-volume *History of the Revolution*, published in 1805 and emphasizing the heroism of the American struggle. Mason Weems, an Anglican clergyman, published a eulogistic *Life of Washington* in 1806, which became one of the best-selling books of the era. Weems had little interest in historical accuracy. He portrayed the aristocratic former president as a homespun man possessing simple republican virtues. (He also invented, among other things, the famous story of Washington and the cherry tree.) History, like literature, was serving as a vehicle for instilling a sense of nationalism in the American people.

RELIGIOUS SKEPTICISM

The American Revolution weakened traditional forms of religious practice by detaching churches from government and by elevating ideas of individual liberty and reason. By the 1790s, only a small proportion of white Americans (perhaps as few as 10 percent) were members of formal churches, and ministers were complaining often about the "decay of vital piety." Religious traditionalists were particularly alarmed about the emergence of new, "rational" theologies that reflected modern, scientific attitudes and de-emphasized the role of God in the world.

Some Americans, including Jefferson and Franklin, embraced "deism," which had originated among Enlightenment philosophers in France. Deists accepted the existence of God, but considered God a remote being who, after having created the universe, had withdrawn from direct involvement with the human race **DEISM** and its sins. Books and articles attacking religious "superstitions" attracted wide readerships and provoked much discussion, among them Thomas Paine's *The Age of Reason*, published in parts between 1794 and 1796. Paine once declared that Christianity was the "strangest religion ever set up," for "it committed a murder upon Jesus in order to redeem mankind from the sin of eating an apple."

Religious skepticism also produced the philosophies of "universalism" and "unitarianism," which emerged at first as dissenting views within the New England Congregational Church. Disciples of these new ideas rejected the Calvinist belief in predestination, arguing that salvation was available to all. They rejected, too, the idea of the Trinity. Jesus was only a great religious teacher, they claimed, not the Son of God. So wide was the gulf between these dissenters and the Congregationalist establishment that it finally became a permanent schism. James Murray (who later married Judith Sargent Murray) founded the Universalist Church as a separate denomination in Gloucester, Massachusetts, in 1779; the Unitarian Church was established in Boston three years later.

Some Americans believed that the spread of rationalism marked the end of traditional, evangelistic religion in the new nation. But quite the contrary was true. In fact, most Americans continued to hold strong religious beliefs. What had declined was their commitment to organized churches and denominations, which many considered too formal and traditional for their own zealous religious faith. Deism, Universalism, Unitarianism, and other "rational" religions seemed more powerful than they actually were because for a time traditional evangelicals were confused and disorganized. But beginning in 1801, traditional religion staged a dramatic comeback in the form of a wave of revivalism known as the Second Great Awakening.

THE SECOND GREAT AWAKENING

The origins of the Second Great Awakening lay in the efforts of conservative theologians of the 1790s to fight the spread of religious rationalism, and to encourage church establishments to revitalize their organizations.

Leaders of several different denominations participated in the evangelizing efforts that drove the revival. Presbyterians tried to arouse the faithful on the western fringe of white settlement, and conservatives in the church denounced New Light dissenters (people who had altered their religious views to make them more compatible with the world of scientific rationalism). Methodism, which John Wesley had founded in England, spread to America in the 1770s and became a formal denomination in 1784 under the leadership of Francis Asbury. Authoritarian and hierarchical in structure, the Methodist Church sent itinerant preachers throughout the nation to win recruits; it soon became the fastest-growing denomination in America. Almost as successful were the Baptists, who were themselves relatively new to America; they found an especially fervent following in the South.

By 1800, the revivalist energies of all these denominations were combining to create the greatest surge of evangelical fervor since the first Great Awakening sixty years before. Beginning among Presbyterians in several eastern colleges (most notably at Yale, under the leadership of President Timothy Dwight), the new awakening

CANE RIDGE

soon spread rapidly throughout the country, reaching its greatest heights in the western regions. In only a few years, a large proportion of the American people were mobilized by the movement, and membership in those churches embracing the revival—most prominently the Methodists, the Baptists, and the Presbyterians—was mushrooming. At Cane Ridge, Kentucky, in the summer of 1801, a group of evangelical ministers presided over the nation's first "camp meeting"—an extraordinary revival that lasted several days and impressed all who saw it with its size (some estimated that 25,000 people attended) and its fervor. Such events became common in subsequent years, as the Methodists in particular came to rely on them as a way to "harvest" new members. The Methodist circuit-riding preacher Peter Cartwright won national fame as he traveled from region to region exhorting his listeners to embrace the church. Even Cartwright, however, was often unprepared for the results of his efforts—a religious frenzy that at times produced convulsions, fits, rolling in the dirt, and twitching "holy jerks."

The message of the Second Great Awakening was not entirely consistent, but its basic thrust was clear: individuals must readmit God and Christ into their daily lives, must embrace a fervent, active piety, and must reject the skeptical rationalism that threatened traditional beliefs. Even so, the wave of revivalism did not serve to restore the religious ideas of the past. Few of the revivalist denominations any longer accepted the idea of predestination; and the belief that a person could affect his or her own destiny added intensity to the individual's search for salvation. The Awakening, in short, combined a more active piety with a belief in God as an active force in the world whose grace could be attained through faith and good works.

The Second Great Awakening also accelerated the growth of different sects and denominations. It helped create a broad

MESSAGE OF THE SECOND GREAT AWAKENING

popular acceptance of the idea that men and women could belong to different Protestant churches and still be committed to essentially the same Christian faith. Finally, the new evangelicalism—by spreading religious fervor into every area of the nation—provided a vehicle for establishing a sense of order and social stability in communities still searching for an identity.

One of the most striking features of the Second Great Awakening was the preponderance of women (particularly young women) within it. One reason for this was that women were more numerous in certain regions than men. Adventurous young men often struck out on their own and moved west; women, for the most part, had no such options. Their marriage prospects thus diminished and their futures plagued with uncertainty, some women discovered in religion a foundation on which to build their lives. But even where there was no shortage of men, women flocked to the revivals in enormous numbers, which suggests that they were responding to their changing economic roles as well. The movement of industrial work out of the home (where women had often contributed to the family economy through spinning and weaving) and into the factory—a process making rapid strides in the early nineteenth century (see pp. 192-193)—deprived

RELIGIOUS REVIVALS

Camp (or revival) meetings were popular among some evangelical Christians in America as early as 1800. By the 1820s, there were approximately 1,000 meetings a year, most of them in the South and West. Estimated attendance at some of the larger meetings was as large as 25,000 people.

Today, there are many "megachurches" throughout the United States. Although opinions vary on what constitutes a "megachurch," the Hartford Institute on Religious Research lists these characteristics: (1) 2,000 or more persons in attendance at weekly worship; (2) a charismatic, authoritative senior minister; (3) a very active seven-day-a-week congregational community; (4) a multitude of social and outreach ministries; and (5) a complex differentiated organizational structure. By this definition, there are more than 1,200 megachurches in the United States, most of them located in Sunbelt states, especially California, Texas, Georgia, and Florida.

The two images that follow, the first a lithograph dated 1837 and the second a photograph of a modern megachurch, suggest both comparisons and contrasts between the two religious movements.

CAMP MEETINGS—1837

METHODIST CAMP MEETING, 1837. (© The Granger Collection, New York)

MEGACHURCHES—2010

LAKEWOOD CHURCH IN HOUSTON, TEXAS Pastor Joel Osteen preaches each week to some 25,000 people in attendance and thousands more on television. (© Timothy Fadek/Corbis)

AP TEST PRACTICE

Questions assume cumulative content knowledge from this chapter and previous chapters.

1. The illustration of the camp meeting best suggests which of the following regarding a feature of the Second Great Awakening?

    (A) Most participants were not fervent supporters.

    (B) Large numbers of women were a part of the movement.

    (C) Men's leadership roles were limited.

    (D) Attendees of camps in the wilderness faced attacks by Native Americans.

2. What central belief of the Second Great Awakening is best supported by the illustration?

    (A) That organized religious practice should be highly ritualistic and formal

    (B) That prayer was the only means to personal salvation

    (C) That salvation was predestined to a select few

    (D) The role of personal action in achieving salvation

3. The illustration and photograph best offer a link concerning which aspect of American democratic ideals?

    (A) A belief in the power of the individual vs. power stemming from hereditary privilege

    (B) A belief that people have a responsibility to their communities

    (C) A belief that Americans should serve as a role model for the world

    (D) A belief that old European customs should not be a part of American democracy.

older women, in particular, of one of their most important social roles. Religious enthusiasm helped compensate for the losses and adjustments these transitions produced; it also provided access to a new range of activities associated with the churches–charitable societies ministering to orphans and the poor, missionary organizations, and others–in which women came to play important roles.

Although revivalism was most widespread within white society, it penetrated other cultures as well. In some areas of

AFRICAN AMERICANS AND THE REVIVALS
the country, revivals were open to people of all races, and many African Americans not only attended but eagerly embraced the new religious fervor as well. Out of these revivals, in fact, emerged a substantial group of black preachers, who became important figures within the slave community. Some of them translated the apparently egalitarian religious message of the Second Great Awakening–that salvation was available to all–into a similarly egalitarian message for blacks in the present world. Out of black revival meetings in Virginia arose an elaborate plan in 1800 (devised by Gabriel Prosser, the brother of an African American preacher) for a slave rebellion and attack on Richmond. The plan was discovered and the rebellion forestalled by whites, but revivalism continued to stir racial unrest in the South.

The spirit of revivalism was also particularly strong in these years among Native Americans, although very different from revivalism in white or black society. It drew heavily from earlier tribal experiences. In the 1760s, the Delaware prophet Neolin had sparked a widespread revival in the Old Northwest with a message combining Christian and Indian imagery and bringing to Native American religion a vision of a personal God, intimately involved in the affairs of man. Neolin had also called for Indians to rise up in defense of their lands and had denounced the growth of trade and other relationships with white civilization. His vehement statements had helped stimulate the Indian military efforts of 1763 and beyond.

The dislocations and military defeats Indians suffered in the aftermath of the American Revolution created a sense of crisis

INDIANS AND THE SECOND GREAT AWAKENING
among many of the eastern tribes in particular; as a result, the 1790s and early 1800s became another era of Indian religious fervor and prophecy. Presbyterian and Baptist missionaries were active among the southern tribes and sparked a great wave of conversions. The most important revivalism came from the efforts of another great prophet: Handsome Lake, a Seneca whose seemingly miraculous "rebirth" after years of alcoholism helped give him a special stature within his tribe. Handsome Lake, like Neolin before him, called for a revival of traditional Indian ways. (He claimed to have met Jesus, who instructed him to "tell your people they will become lost when they follow the ways of the white man.") Handsome Lake's message spread through the scattered Iroquois communities and inspired many Indians to give up whiskey, gambling, and other destructive customs derived from white society.

But the revival did not, in fact, lead to a true restoration of traditional Iroquois culture. Instead, Handsome Lake encouraged Christian missionaries to become active within the tribes, and he urged Iroquois men to abandon their roles as hunters (partly because so much of their hunting land had been seized by whites) and become sedentary farmers instead. Iroquois women, who had traditionally done the farming, were to move into more-domestic roles. When some women resisted the change, Handsome Lake denounced them as witches. He demanded confessions from them and killed some of those who refused.

The Second Great Awakening also had important effects on those Americans who did not accept its teachings. The rational

FREETHINKERS
"freethinkers," whose skeptical philosophies had helped produce the revivals, were in many ways victims of the new religious fervor. They did not disappear after 1800, but their influence rapidly declined, and for many years they remained a small and defensive minority within American Christianity. Instead, the dominant religious characteristic of the new nation became a fervent evangelicalism, which would survive into the mid-nineteenth century and beyond.

STIRRINGS OF INDUSTRIALISM

Despite the hopes of Jefferson and his followers that the United States would remain a simple agrarian republic, the nation took its first, tentative steps in these years toward its transformation into an urban, industrial society.

TECHNOLOGY IN AMERICA

Americans imported some of these technological advances from England. (See "America in the World," pp. 192-193.) The British government attempted to protect the nation's manufacturing preeminence by preventing the export of textile machinery or the emigration of skilled mechanics. Despite such efforts, immigrants arrived in the United States with advanced knowledge of English technology, eager to introduce the new machines to America. Samuel Slater, for example, used the knowledge he had acquired before leaving England to build a spinning mill for the Quaker merchant Moses Brown in Pawtucket, Rhode Island, in 1790. It was the first modern factory in America.

America in the early nineteenth century also produced several important inventors of its own. Among them was Oliver Evans of Delaware, who devised a number of ingenious new machines: an automated flour mill, a card-making machine, and others. He made several important improvements in the steam engine, and in 1795 he published America's first textbook of mechanical engineering: *The Young Mill-Wright's and Miller's Guide.* His own flour mill, which began operations in 1787, required only two men to operate: one of them emptying a bag of wheat into the

THE COTTON GIN Eli Whitney's cotton gin revolutionized the cotton economy of the South by making the processing of short-staple cotton simple and economical. With the device, a single operator could clean as much cotton in a few hours as a group of workers had once needed a whole day to do. (Private Collection/© J. T. Vintage/The Bridgeman Art Library)

machinery, another putting the lid on the barrels of flour and rolling them away.

Even more influential for the future of the nation were the inventions of the Massachusetts-born, Yale-educated Eli Whitney, who revolutionized both cotton production and weapons manufacturing. The growth of the textile industry in England had created an enormous demand for cotton, a demand that planters in the American South were finding impossible to meet. Their greatest obstacle was separating the seeds from cotton fiber—a difficult and time-consuming process that was essential before cotton could be sold. Long-staple, or Sea Island, cotton, with its smooth black seeds and long fibers, was easy to clean, but it grew successfully only along the Atlantic coast or on the offshore islands of Georgia and South Carolina. There was not nearly enough of it to satisfy the demand. Short-staple cotton, by contrast, could grow inland through vast areas of the South. But its sticky green seeds were extremely difficult to remove. A skilled worker could clean no more than a few pounds a day by hand. Then, in 1793, Whitney, who was working at the time as a tutor on

ELI WHITNEY'S COTTON GIN the Georgia plantation of General Nathanael Greene's widow, invented a machine that performed the arduous task quickly and efficiently. It was dubbed the cotton gin ("gin" was an abbreviation for "engine"), and it transformed the life of the South.

Mechanically, the gin was very simple. A toothed roller caught the fibers of the cotton boll and pulled them between the wires of a grating. The grating caught the seeds while a revolving brush removed the lint from the roller's teeth. With the device, a single operator could clean as much cotton in a few hours as a group of workers had once needed a whole day to do. The results were profound. Soon cotton growing spread into the upland South and beyond, and within a decade total crop production increased eightfold.

African American slavery, which with the decline of tobacco production some had considered a dwindling institution, regained its importance, expanded, and became more firmly fixed upon the South.

The cotton gin not only changed the economy of the South, it also helped transform the North. The large supply of

THE COTTON GIN'S IMPACT ON THE NORTH domestically produced fiber was a strong incentive to entrepreneurs in New England and elsewhere to develop an American textile industry. Few northern states could hope to thrive on the basis of agriculture alone; by learning to turn cotton into yarn and thread, plantation owners could become industrially prosperous instead. The manufacturing preeminence of the North, which emerged with the development of the textile industry in the 1820s and 1830s, helped drive a wedge between the nation's two most populous regions—one becoming increasingly industrial, the other more firmly bound to agriculture.

Whitney also made a major contribution to the development of modern warfare and in the process made a contribution to other industrial techniques. During the two years of undeclared war with France (1798 and 1799), Americans were deeply troubled by their lack of sufficient armaments for the expected hostilities. Production of muskets—each carefully handcrafted by a skilled gunsmith—was discouragingly slow. Whitney devised a machine to make each part of a gun according to an exact pattern. Tasks could thus be divided among several workers, and one laborer could quickly assemble a weapon out of parts made by several others. Before long, manufacturers of sewing machines, clocks, and many other complicated products were using the same system.

The new technological advances were relatively isolated phenomena during the early years of the nineteenth century. Not until at least the 1840s did the nation begin to develop a true manufacturing economy. But the inventions of this period were crucial in making the eventual transformation possible.

TRANSPORTATION INNOVATIONS

One of the prerequisites for industrialization is an efficient system for transporting raw materials to factories and finished goods to markets. The United States had no such system in the early years of the republic. But work was under way that would ultimately remove the transportation obstacle.

There were several ways to solve the problem of the small American market. One was to look for customers overseas, and American merchants continued their efforts to do that. Among the first acts of the new Congress when it met in 1789 were two tariff bills giving preference to American ships in American ports, helping to stimulate an expansion of domestic shipping. More important—indeed the principal reason for the growth

RAPID GROWTH OF AMERICAN SHIPPING of American trade in this period—was the outbreak of war in Europe in the 1790s, allowing Yankee merchant vessels to take over most of the carrying trade between

PAWTUCKET BRIDGE AND FALLS One reason for the growth of the textile industry in New England in the early nineteenth century was that there were many sources of water power in the region to run the machinery in the factories. That was certainly the case with Slater's Mill, one of the first American textile factories. It was located in Pawtucket, Rhode Island, alongside a powerful waterfall, demonstrating the critical importance of water power to early American industry. (© Bettmann/Corbis)

Europe and the Western Hemisphere. As early as 1793, the young republic had a merchant marine and a foreign trade larger than those of any country except England. In proportion to its population, the United States had more ships and international commerce than any other country. Between 1789 and 1810, the total tonnage of American vessels engaged in overseas traffic rose from less than 125,000 to nearly 1 million. American ships had carried only 30 percent of the country's exports in 1789; they were carrying over 90 percent in 1810. The figures for American ships carrying imports increased even more dramatically, from 17.5 percent to 90 percent in the same period.

Another solution to the problem of limited markets was to develop new markets at home, by improving transportation between the states and into the interior of the continent. In river transportation, a new era began with the development of the steamboat. A number of inventors began experimenting with steam-powered craft in the late eighteenth century; John Fitch exhibited a forty-five-foot vessel with paddles operated by steam to some of the delegates at the Constitutional Convention in 1787. But the real breakthrough was Oliver Evans's development of a high-pressure engine, lighter and more efficient than James Watt's, which made steam more

feasible for powering boats (and, eventually, locomotives) as well as mill machinery.

The inventor Robert Fulton and the promoter Robert R. Livingston were principally responsible for perfecting the steamboat and bringing it to the attention of the nation. Their *Clermont*, equipped with paddle wheels and an English-built

ROBERT FULTON'S STEAMBOAT

engine, sailed up the Hudson in the summer of 1807, demonstrating the practicability of steam navigation (even though it took the ship thirty hours to go 150 miles). In 1811, a partner of Livingston's, Nicholas J. Roosevelt (a remote ancestor of Theodore Roosevelt), introduced the steamboat to the West by sending the *New Orleans* from Pittsburgh down the Ohio and Mississippi. The next year, this vessel began a profitable career of service between New Orleans and Natchez.

Meanwhile, what was to become known as the "turnpike

THE TURNPIKE ERA

era" had begun. In 1792, a corporation constructed a toll road running the sixty miles from Philadelphia to Lancaster, Pennsylvania, with a hard-packed surface of crushed rock. This venture proved so successful that several other companies laid out similar turnpikes (so named from the kind of tollgate

Wdd delᵗ   J. Stoner sculp
AMERICAN STAGE WAGGON.
Published Dec. 21 1798 by I. Stockdale, Piccadilly.

AMERICAN STAGE WAGGON This image of a stagecoach, by J. Stoner, shows how roads were beginning to link the disparate regions of early-nineteenth-century America. (© Corbis)

frequently used) from other cities to neighboring towns. Since the turnpikes had to produce profits for the companies that built them, construction costs had to be low enough and the prospective traffic heavy enough to ensure an early and ample return. As a result, these roads, radiating from eastern cities, ran comparatively short distances and through densely settled areas. No private operators were willing to build similar highways over the mountains and into the less populated interior. State governments and the federal government eventually had to finance them.

THE RISING CITIES

Despite all the changes and all the advances, America in the early nineteenth century remained an overwhelmingly rural and agrarian nation. Only 3 percent of the non-Indian population lived in towns of more than 8,000 at the time of the second census, in 1800. Ten percent lived west of the Appalachian Mountains, far from what urban centers there were. Much of the country remained a wilderness. Even the nation's largest cities could not begin to compare, either in size or in cultural sophistication, with such European capitals as London and Paris.

Yet here too there were signs of change. The leading American cities might not yet have become world capitals, but they were large and complex enough to rival the important secondary cities of Europe. Philadelphia, with 70,000 residents, and New York, with 60,000, were becoming major centers of commerce and learning. The cities were also developing a distinctively urban culture. So too were the next-largest cities of the new nation: Baltimore (26,000 in 1800), Boston (24,000), and Charleston (20,000).

People living in towns and cities lived differently than the vast majority of Americans who continued to work as farmers. **URBAN LIFE** Among other things, urban life produced affluence, and affluent people sought amenities

THE GLOBAL INDUSTRIAL REVOLUTION WOR-3

THE tentative stirrings of industrial activity in the United States in the early nineteenth century were part of a vast movement that over the course of the century transformed much of the globe. Historians differ over precisely when the industrial revolution began, but it is clear that by the end of the eighteenth century it was well under way in many parts of the world. By the beginning of the twentieth century, industrialization had transformed the societies of Britain, most of continental Europe, Japan, and the United States.

For Americans, the industrial revolution was largely a result of the rapid changes in Great Britain, the nation with which they had the closest relations. Britain was the first nation to develop significant industrial capacity. The factory system took root in England in the late eighteenth century, revolutionizing the manufacture of cotton thread and cloth. One invention followed another in quick succession. Improvements in weaving drove improvements in spinning, and these changes created a demand for new devices for carding (combing and straightening the fibers for the spinner). Water, wind, and animal power continued to be important in the textile industry; but more important was the emergence of steam power—which proliferated after the appearance of James Watt's advanced steam engine (patented in 1769). England's textile industry quickly became the most profitable in the world, and it helped encourage comparable advances in other fields of manufacturing as well. Despite the efforts of the British government to prevent the export of English industrial technology, knowledge of the new machines reached other nations quickly, usually through the emigration of people who had learned the technology in British factories.

America benefited the most from English technology, because it received more immigrants from Great Britain than from any other country. But English technology spread quickly to the nations of continental Europe as well. In Japan, the sudden intrusion of American and European traders helped cause the so-called Meiji reforms of the 1880s and 1890s, which launched a period of rapid industrialization there.

Industrialization changed not just the world's economies, but also its societies. First in England, and then in Europe, America, and Japan, social systems underwent wrenching changes. Hundreds of thousands, and eventually millions, of men and women moved from rural areas into cities to work in factories, where they experienced both the benefits and the costs of industrialization. Many of those who moved from farm to factory experienced some improvement in nutrition and other material circumstances, even in their health. But there were psychological costs to being suddenly uprooted from one way of life and thrust into another, fundamentally different one. Little in most workers' prior experience had prepared them for the nature of industrial labor. The routinized, rigidly scheduled work of the urban factory contrasted sharply with the varying, seasonal work pattern of the rural economy. Industrial workers experienced, too, a fundamental change in their relationship

THE ENGLISH CANAL AGE Industrialization in England contributed, as it did in America, to the building of new transportation facilities to serve the growing commercial markets of the new economy. Among the most popular such facilities were canals, among them the Regent's Canal in London, pictured here in the 1820s. (© Guildhall Library, Corporation of London, UK/The Bridgeman Art Library)

that would not have entered the imaginings of any but the wealthiest farmers. They sought increasing elegance and refinement in their homes, their grounds, and their dress. They also looked for diversions—music, theater, dancing, and, for many people, one of the most popular entertainments of all, horse racing. (See "Patterns of Popular Culture," pp. 196-197.)

Much remained to be done before this small and still half-formed nation would become a complex modern society. It was still possible in the early nineteenth century to believe that those changes might not ever occur. But forces were already at work that, in time, would lastingly transform the United States.

JEFFERSON THE PRESIDENT

Privately, Thomas Jefferson may well have considered his victory over John Adams in 1800 to be what he later termed it: a revolution "as real . . . as that of 1776." Publicly, however, with their employers. Unlike rural landlords and local aristocrats, factory owners and managers—the new class of industrial capitalists, many of them accumulating unprecedented wealth—were usually remote and inaccessible. They dealt with their workers impersonally, and the result was a growing schism between the two classes—each lacking access to or understanding of the other. Working men and women throughout the globe began thinking of themselves as a distinct class, with common goals and interests. Their efforts simultaneously to adjust to their new way of life and to resist its most damaging aspects sometimes created great social turbulence. Battles between workers and employers became a characteristic feature of industrial life throughout the world.

Life in industrial nations changed at every level. Populations in industrial countries grew rapidly, and people began to live longer. At the same time, industrial cities began to produce great increases in pollution, crime, and—until modern sanitation systems emerged—infectious disease. Around the industrial world, middle classes expanded and came to dominate the economy (although not always the culture or the politics) of their nations.

Not since the agricultural revolution thousands of years earlier, when many humans had turned from hunting to farming for sustenance, had there been an economic change of a magnitude comparable to that of the industrial revolution. Centuries of traditions, social patterns, and cultural and religious assumptions were challenged and often shattered. The social and economic consequences of industrialism were complex and profound, and they continue today to shape the nature of global society. ●

UNDERSTAND, ANALYZE, AND EVALUATE

1. Why did the British government attempt to prevent the export of Britain's industrial technology?
2. Was the industrial revolution truly a global revolution? Why or why not?
3. Some observers have compared the information technology developments of the late twentieth century to those of the industrial revolution. Are the changes that have resulted from the high-tech developments of the late twentieth century as profound as those resulting from the industrial revolution? In what way might the high-tech advances be considered a "revolution"? What have been the social and economic consequences of these advances?

he was restrained and conciliatory as he assumed office, attempting to minimize the differences between the two parties and to calm the passions that the bitter campaign had aroused. "We are all republicans, we are all federalists," he said in his inaugural address. And during his eight years in office, he did much to prove those words correct. There was no complete repudiation of Federalist policies, no true "revolution." Indeed, at times Jefferson seemed to outdo the Federalists at their own work—most notably in overseeing a remarkable expansion of the territory of the United States.

THE FEDERAL CITY AND THE "PEOPLE'S PRESIDENT"

The newly founded national capital was the city of Washington. The French architect Pierre L'Enfant had designed the capital

THE NEW CAPITAL CITY

on a grand scale, with broad avenues radiating out from the uncompleted Capitol building, set on one of the area's highest hills. Washington was, many Americans believed, to become the Paris of the United States.

In reality, however, throughout Jefferson's presidency—and indeed through most of the nineteenth century—Washington remained little more than a provincial village. Although the population increased steadily from the 3,200 counted in the 1800 census, it never rivaled that of New York, Philadelphia, or the other major cities of the nation. The city remained a raw, inhospitable community with few public buildings of any consequence. Members of Congress viewed Washington not as a home but as a place to visit briefly during sessions of the legislature and leave as quickly as possible. Most lived in a cluster of simple boardinghouses in the vicinity of the Capitol. It was not unusual for a member of Congress to resign his seat in the midst of a session to return home if he had an opportunity to accept the more prestigious post of member of his state legislature.

Jefferson set out as president to act in a spirit of democratic simplicity in keeping with the frontierlike character of the unfinished federal city. He was a wealthy and aristocratic planter by background, the owner of more than 100 slaves, and a man of rare cultivation and sophistication; but he conveyed to the public an image of plain, almost crude disdain for pretension. He walked like an ordinary citizen to and from his inauguration at the Capitol. In the presidential mansion, which had not yet acquired the name "White House," he disregarded the courtly etiquette of his predecessors (in part, no doubt, because as a widower he had no First Lady to take charge of social affairs). At state dinners, he let his guests scramble pell-mell for places at the table. He did not always bother to dress up, once prompting the fastidious British ambassador to complain of being received by the president in coat and pantaloons that were "indicative of utter slovenliness and indifference to appearances."

Yet Jefferson managed nevertheless to impress most of those who knew him. He was a brilliant conversationalist, a gifted writer, and one of the nation's most intelligent and creative men, with perhaps a wider range of interests and accomplishments than any public figure in American history. In addition to politics and diplomacy, he was an active architect, educator, inventor, scientific farmer, and philosopher-scientist.

Jefferson was, above all, a shrewd and practical politician. On the one hand, he went to great lengths to eliminate the

JEFFERSON THE POLITICIAN

aura of majesty surrounding the presidency that he believed his predecessors had created. At the same time, however, Jefferson worked hard to exert influence as the leader of his

NORTH AMERICA IN 1800 This map illustrates how substantially the non-Indian settlement of British North America (much of it by 1800 the United States) had expanded since 1700. On p. 67, a similar map shows a tiny fringe of settlement along the Atlantic seaboard. Note the new areas of settlement here: west of the original thirteen colonies—including, in Kentucky, an area that reaches almost to the Mississippi River. Significant settlements are also now visible along the Gulf Coast, especially in the territory around New Orleans. Scattered non-Indian settlements are visible in the Southwest and along the coast of California, as well as in southern Canada (where the settlements were largely forts).

• *How does this map help explain the spread of settlement south from Pittsburgh into western Virginia and Kentucky?*

WASHINGTON, D.C., IN THE EARLY NINETEENTH CENTURY The nation's capital moved from New York City to Washington, D.C., in 1800, into a new city designed on a grand scale by the French planner Pierre L'Enfant. But in the early eighteenth century, it remained little more than a village on a marshy tract of land, with hot, humid summers. This map shows the location of the principal government buildings in the early republic, and also the sites of the homes of members of the executive and legislative branches. Note how the homes of executive officials mostly clustered around the White House and the Treasury, while those of legislators mainly clustered around the Capitol.

• *How did the geography of the city help shape the relationship between the executive and legislative branches?*

THE JEFFERSONIAN ERA • 195

party, giving direction to Republicans in Congress by quiet and sometimes even devious means. Although the Republicans had objected strenuously to the efforts of their Federalist predecessors to build a network of influence through patronage, Jefferson, too, used his powers of appointment as an effective political weapon. By the end of his first term about half the government jobs, and by the end of his second term practically all of them, were in the hands of loyal Republicans.

When Jefferson ran for reelection in 1804, he won overwhelmingly. The Federalist presidential nominee, Charles C. Pinckney, could not even carry most of the party's New England strongholds. Jefferson won 162 electoral votes to Pinckney's 14, and the Republican majorities in both houses of Congress increased.

DOLLARS AND SHIPS

Under Washington and Adams, the Republicans believed, the government had been needlessly extravagant. Yearly federal expenditures had almost tripled between 1793 and 1800. Hamilton had, as he had intended, increased the public debt and created an extensive system of internal taxation, including the hated whiskey excise tax.

The Jefferson administration moved deliberately to reverse the trend. In 1802, it persuaded Congress to abolish all internal taxes, leaving customs duties and the sale of western lands as the only sources of revenue for the government. Meanwhile, Secretary of the Treasury Albert Gallatin drastically reduced government spending, cutting the already small staffs of the executive departments to minuscule levels. Although Jefferson was unable to retire the entire national debt, as he had hoped, he did cut it almost in half (from $83 million to $45 million) during his presidency.

LIMITING THE FEDERAL GOVERNMENT

Jefferson also scaled down the armed forces. He reduced the army of 4,000 men to 2,500. He cut the navy from twenty-five ships to seven and reduced the number of officers and sailors accordingly. Anything but the smallest of standing armies, he argued, might menace civil liberties and civilian control of government. And a large navy, he feared, might promote overseas commerce, which Jefferson believed should remain secondary to agriculture. Yet Jefferson was not a pacifist. At the same time that he was reducing the size of the army and navy, he was helping to establish the United States Military Academy at West Point, founded in 1802. And when trouble began brewing overseas, he began again to build up the fleet.

Such trouble appeared first in the Mediterranean, off the coast of northern Africa. For years the Barbary states of North Africa–Morocco, Algiers, Tunis, and Tripoli (now part of Libya)–had been demanding protection money from all nations whose ships sailed the Mediterranean. Even Great Britain gave regular contributions to the Barbary pirates. During the 1780s and 1790s the

CHALLENGING THE BARBARY PIRATES

United States agreed to treaties providing for annual tribute to the Barbary states, but Jefferson was reluctant to continue this policy of appeasement. "Tribute or war is the usual alternative of these Barbary pirates," he said. "Why not build a navy and decide on war?"

In 1801, the pasha (leader) of Tripoli forced Jefferson's hand. Unsatisfied by the American response to his extortionate demands, he ordered the flagpole of the American consulate chopped down–a symbolic declaration of war. Jefferson responded cautiously, building up the American fleet in the region over the next several years. Finally, in 1805, the United States reached an agreement with the pasha that ended American payments of tribute to Tripoli but required the United States to pay a substantial (and humiliating) ransom of $60,000 for the release of American prisoners seized by Barbary pirates.

CONFLICT WITH THE COURTS

Having won control of the executive and legislative branches of government, the Republicans looked with suspicion on the judiciary, which remained largely in the hands of Federalist judges. Soon after Jefferson's first inauguration, his followers in Congress launched an attack on this last preserve of the opposition. Their first step was the repeal of the Judiciary Act of 1801, thus eliminating the judgeships to which Adams had made his "midnight appointments."

The debate over the courts led to one of the most important judicial decisions in the history of the nation. Federalists had long maintained that the Supreme Court had the authority to nullify acts of Congress (although the Constitution said nothing specifically to support the claim), and the Court itself had actually exercised the power of judicial review in 1796 when it upheld the validity of a law passed by the legislature. But the Court's authority in this area would not be secure, it was clear, until it actually declared a congressional act unconstitutional.

JUDICIAL REVIEW

In 1803, in the case of *Marbury v. Madison*, it did so. William Marbury, one of Adams's "midnight appointments," had been named a justice of the peace in the District of Columbia. But his commission, although signed and sealed, had not been delivered to him before Adams left office. Once Jefferson became president, the new secretary of state, James Madison, was responsible for transmitting appointments. He had refused to hand over the commission to Marbury. Marbury appealed to the Supreme Court for an order directing Madison to perform his official duty. In its historic ruling, the Court found that Marbury had a right to his commission but that the Court had no authority to order Madison to deliver it. On the surface, therefore, the decision was a victory for the administration. But of much greater importance than the relatively insignificant matter of Marbury's commission was the Court's reasoning in the decision.

MARBURY V. MADISON

The original Judiciary Act of 1789 had given the Court the power to compel executive officials to act in such matters as

HORSE RACING IN EARLY AMERICA

INFORMAL horse racing began in North America almost as soon as Europeans settled the English colonies. Formal racing followed quickly. The first race track in North America—New Market (named for a popular race course in England)—was established in 1665 near the site of present-day Garden City, on Long Island in New York. Tracks quickly developed wide appeal, and soon horse racing had spread up and down the Atlantic coast. By the time of the American Revolution, it had become popular in almost every colony

OAKLAND HOUSE AND RACE COURSE This 1840 painting by Robert Brammer and August A. Von Smith portrays men and women flocking to an early race course in Louisville, Kentucky, which provided entertainment to affluent white southerners. (*Oakland House and Race Course, Louisville, 1840.* By Robert Brammer and August A. Von Smith. © Collection of The Speed Art Museum, Louisville, Kentucky. Purchase, Museum Art fund, 56.19)

and was moving as well into the newly settled areas of the Southwest. Andrew Jackson was a founder of the first racing track in Nashville, Tennessee, in the early nineteenth century. Kentucky—whose native bluegrass was early recognized as ideal for grazing horses—had eight tracks by 1800.

Like almost everything else in the life of early America, the world of horse racing was bounded by lines of class and race. For many years, it was considered the exclusive preserve of "gentlemen," so much so that in 1674 a court in Virginia fined James Bullocke, a tailor, for proposing a race, "it being contrary to Law for a Labourer to make a race, being a sport only for Gentlemen." But while white aristocrats retained control of racing, they were not the only people who participated in it. Southern aristocrats often trained young male slaves as jockeys for their horses, just as northern horse owners employed the services of free blacks as riders. In the North and the South, African Americans eventually emerged as some of the most talented and experienced trainers of racing horses. And despite social and legal pressures, free blacks and poor whites often staged their own informal races.

Racing also began early to reflect the growing sectional rivalry between the North and the South. In 1824, the Union Race Course on Long Island established an astounding $24,000 purse for a race between two famous thoroughbreds: American Eclipse (from the

---

the delivery of commissions, and it was on that basis that Marbury had filed his suit. But the Court ruled that Congress had exceeded its authority in creating that statute: that the Constitution had defined the powers of the judiciary and that the legislature had no right to expand them. The relevant section of the 1789 act was therefore void. In seeming to deny its own authority, the Court was in fact radically enlarging it. The justices had repudiated a relatively minor power (the power to force the delivery of a commission) by asserting a vastly greater one (the power to nullify an act of Congress).

JOHN MARSHALL

The chief justice of the United States at the time of the ruling was John Marshall, one of the towering figures in the history of American law. A leading Federalist and prominent Virginia lawyer, he had served John Adams as secretary of state. (It had been Marshall, ironically, who had neglected to deliver Marbury's commission in the closing hours of the administration.) In 1801, just before leaving office, Adams had appointed him chief justice, and almost immediately Marshall established himself as the dominant figure on the Court, shaping all its most important rulings—including, of course, *Marbury v. Madison.*

Through a succession of Republican administrations, he established the judiciary as a branch of government coequal with the executive and the legislature—a position that the founders of the republic had never clearly indicated it should occupy.

Jefferson recognized the threat that an assertive judiciary could pose to his policies. Even while the *Marbury* case was still pending, he was preparing for a renewed assault on this last Federalist stronghold. He urged Congress to impeach obstructive judges, and Congress attempted to oblige him. The Republicans successfully removed from office a district judge, John Pickering of New Hampshire (on the perhaps specious grounds that he was insane and thus unfit for office). They later targeted a justice of the Supreme Court itself: Justice Samuel Chase, a highly partisan Federalist. Chase had certainly been injudicious; he had, for example,

IMPEACHMENT OF SAMUEL CHASE

THE ECLIPSE-HENRY MATCH RACE "Match races" between famous horses were a popular feature of early-nineteenth-century horse racing. This famous 1823 race on Long Island, New York, pitted prize-winning horses from the North and the South against one another. American Eclipse, the northern entry, won. (Private Collection)

North) and Sir Henry (from the South). American Eclipse won two of the three heats, but a southern racehorse prevailed in another such celebrated contest in 1836. These intersectional races, which drew enormous crowds and created tremendous publicity, continued into the 1850s, until the North-South rivalry began to take a deadly form.

Horse racing remained popular after the Civil War, but two developments changed its character considerably. One was the successful effort to drive African Americans out of the sport. At least until the 1890s, black jockeys and trainers remained central to racing. At the first Kentucky Derby, in 1875, fourteen of the fifteen horses had African American riders. One black man, Isaac Murphy, won a remarkable 44 percent of all races in which he rode, including three Kentucky Derbys. Gradually, however, the same social dynamics that enforced racial segregation in so many other areas of American life penetrated racing as well. By the beginning of the twentieth century, white jockeys and organized jockey clubs had driven almost all black riders and many black trainers out of the sport.

The second change was the introduction of formalized betting to the sport. In the late nineteenth century, race tracks began creating betting systems to lure customers to the races. At the same time that the breeding of racehorses was moving into the hands of enormously wealthy families, the audience for racing was becoming increasingly working class and lower middle class. The people who now came to tracks were mostly white men, and some white women, lured to the races not by a love of horses—which were coming to play a less central role in their everyday lives—but by the usually futile hope of quick and easy riches through gambling. ●

UNDERSTAND, ANALYZE, AND EVALUATE

1. Why do you think horse racing was such a popular spectator sport in early America? Why has it continued to be popular?
2. How did changes in the sport of horse racing reflect similar changes in American society?
3. Is horse racing still a sport "bounded by lines of class and race"? What other spectator sports were or are similarly bounded?

delivered stridently partisan speeches from the bench. But he had committed no crime. Some Republicans argued, however, that impeachment was not merely a criminal proceeding. Congress could properly impeach a judge for political reasons— for obstructing the other branches of the government and disregarding the will of the people.

At Jefferson's urging, the House impeached Chase and sent him to trial before the Senate early in 1805. But Republican leaders were unable to get the necessary two-thirds vote for conviction in the Senate. Chase's acquittal helped establish that impeachment would not become a routine political weapon, that something more than partisan disagreement should have to underlie the process, a precedent that Congress only occasionally violated in future years. Marshall remained secure in his position as chief justice. And the judiciary survived as a powerful force within the government—more often than not ruling on behalf of the centralizing, expansionary policies that the Republicans had hoped to reverse.

DOUBLING THE NATIONAL DOMAIN

In the same year that Jefferson became president of the United States, Napoleon Bonaparte made himself ruler of France with the title of first consul. In the year that Jefferson was reelected, Napoleon named himself emperor. The two men had little in common. Yet for a time they were of great help to each other in international politics—until Napoleon's ambitions moved from Europe to America and created conflict and estrangement.

JEFFERSON AND NAPOLEON

Having failed in a grandiose plan to seize India from the British Empire, Napoleon turned his imperial ambitions in a new direction: he began to dream of restoring French power in the New World. The territory east of the Mississippi, which France

THOMAS JEFFERSON This 1805 portrait by the noted American painter Rembrandt Peale shows Jefferson at the beginning of his second term as president. It also conveys (through the simplicity of dress and the slightly unkempt hair) the image of democratic simplicity that Jefferson liked to project. (© Collection of the New-York Historical Society, USA/The Bridgeman Art Library)

JEFFERSON THE ARCHITECT Among his many accomplishments, Thomas Jefferson was a gifted architect. This rotunda is the centerpiece of the central campus of the University of Virginia, which Jefferson designed near the end of his life. Earlier, he designed his own home near Charlottesville, Monticello; and his proposal for a president's mansion in Washington, D.C., placed second in a blind competition. (© The Granger Collection, New York)

had ceded to Great Britain in 1763, was now mostly part of the United States and lost to France forever. But Napoleon wanted to regain the lands west of the Mississippi, which now belonged to Spain, over which Napoleon now exercised strong influence. Under the secret Treaty of San Ildefonso of 1800 between the French and the Spanish, France regained title to Louisiana, which included almost the whole of the Mississippi Valley to the west of the river, plus New Orleans near its mouth. The Louisiana Territory would, Napoleon hoped, become the heart of a great French empire in America.

Also part of Napoleon's empire in the New World were the sugar-rich and strategically valuable West Indian islands that still belonged to France—Guadeloupe, Martinique, and above all Santo Domingo. But unrest among the Caribbean slaves posed a threat to Napoleon's hopes for the islands. Africans in Santo Domingo (inspired by the French Revolution) revolted and cre-

TOUSSAINT L'OUVERTURE

ated a republic of their own, under the remarkable black leader Toussaint L'Ouverture. Taking advantage of a truce in his war with England, Napoleon sent an army to the West Indies. It temporarily crushed the insurrection and restored French authority; but the incident was an early sign of the problems Napoleon would have in realizing his ambitions in America.

Jefferson was unaware at first of Napoleon's imperial ambitions in America, and for a time he pursued a foreign policy that reflected his well-known admiration for France. He appointed as American minister to Paris the ardently pro-French Robert R. Livingston. He worked to secure ratification of the Franco-American settlement of 1800 and began observing the terms of the treaty even before it was ratified. The Adams administration had joined with the British in recognizing and supporting the rebel regime of Toussaint L'Ouverture in Santo Domingo; Jefferson assured the French minister in Washington that the American people, especially those of the slaveholding states, did not approve of the black revolutionary, who they thought was setting a bad example for their own slaves. He even implied that the United States might join with France in putting down the rebellion (although nothing ever came of the suggestion). Jefferson began to reconsider his position toward France, however, when he heard rumors of the secret transfer of Louisiana.

Jefferson was even more alarmed when, in the fall of 1802, he learned that the Spanish intendant at New Orleans (who still governed the city, since the French had not yet taken formal possession of the region) had announced a disturbing new regulation. American ships sailing the Mississippi River had for many years been accustomed to depositing their cargoes in New Orleans for transfer to oceangoing vessels. The intendant now forbade the practice—even though Spain had guaranteed Americans that right in the Pinckney Treaty of 1795—thus effectively closing the lower Mississippi to American shippers.

Westerners demanded that the federal government do something to reopen the river. The president faced a dilemma. If he yielded to the frontier clamor and tried to change the policy by force, he would run the risk of a major war with

WEST POINT Creating a professional military was an important task for the leaders of the early republic. Without an army, they realized, it would be difficult for the United States to win respect in the world. The establishment in 1802 of the United States Military Academy at West Point (whose parade ground is pictured here) was, therefore, an important event in the early history of the republic. (© West Point Museum Collections, United States Military Academy)

France. If he ignored the westerners' demands, he might lose political support. But Jefferson saw another solution. He instructed Robert Livingston, the American ambassador in Paris, to negotiate the purchase of New Orleans. Livingston, on his own authority, proposed that the French sell the United States the vast western part of Louisiana as well.

In the meantime, Jefferson persuaded Congress to appropriate funds for an expansion of the army and the construction of a river fleet, and he deliberately gave the impression that American forces might soon descend on New Orleans and that the United States might form an alliance with Great Britain if the problems with France were not resolved. Perhaps that was why Napoleon suddenly decided to accept Livingston's proposal and offer the United States the entire Louisiana Territory.

NAPOLEON'S OFFER

Napoleon had good reasons for the decision. His plans for an American empire had already gone seriously awry. That was partly because a yellow fever epidemic had wiped out much of the French army in the New World. But it was also because the expeditionary force Napoleon sent to take possession of Louisiana had been frozen into a Dutch harbor through the winter of 1802–1803. By the time the harbor thawed in the spring of 1803, Napoleon was preparing for a renewed war in Europe. He would not, he realized, have the resources now to secure an American empire.

THE LOUISIANA PURCHASE

Faced with Napoleon's startling proposal, Livingston and James Monroe, whom Jefferson had sent to Paris to assist in the negotiations, had to decide first whether they should even consider making a treaty for the purchase of the entire Louisiana Territory, since they had not been authorized by their government to do so. But fearful that Napoleon might withdraw the offer, they decided to proceed without further instructions from home. After some haggling over the price, Livingston and Monroe signed the agreement on April 30, 1803.

By the terms of the treaty, the United States was to pay a total of 80 million francs ($15 million) to the French government. The United States was also to grant certain exclusive commercial privileges to France in the port of New Orleans and was to incorporate the residents of Louisiana into the Union with the same rights and privileges as other citizens. The boundaries of the purchase were not clearly defined; the treaty simply specified that Louisiana would occupy the "same extent" as it had when France and Spain had owned it.

EXPLORING THE LOUISIANA PURCHASE, 1804–1807 When Jefferson purchased the Louisiana Territory from France in 1803, he doubled the size of the nation. But few Americans knew what they had bought. The Lewis and Clark expedition set out in 1804 to investigate the new territories, and this map shows their route, along with that of another inveterate explorer, Zebulon Pike. Note the vast distances the two parties covered (including, in both cases, a great deal of land outside the Louisiana Purchase). Note, too, how much of this enormous territory lay outside the orbit of even these ambitious explorations.

• *How did the American public react to the addition of these new territories?*

In Washington, the president was both pleased and embarrassed when he received the treaty. He was pleased with the terms of the bargain but uncertain whether the United States had authority to accept it, since he had always insisted that the federal government could rightfully exercise only those powers explicitly assigned to it. Nowhere did the Constitution say anything about the acquisition of new territory. But Jefferson's advisers persuaded him that his treaty-making power under the Constitution would justify the purchase of Louisiana. The president finally agreed, trusting, as he said, "that the good sense of our country will correct the evil of loose construction when it shall produce ill effects." The Republican Congress promptly approved the treaty and appropriated

JEFFERSON'S QUANDARY

money to implement its provisions. Finally, late in 1803, the French assumed formal control of Louisiana from Spain just long enough to turn the territory over to General James Wilkinson, the commissioner of the United States.

The government organized the Louisiana Territory much as it had organized the Northwest Territory, with the assumption that its various territories would eventually become states. The first of these was admitted to the Union as the state of Louisiana in 1812.

LEWIS AND CLARK EXPLORE THE WEST

Meanwhile, several ambitious explorations were revealing the geography of the far-flung new territory to white Americans,

THE EXPLORATIONS OF LEWIS AND CLARK This map was drawn by William Clark while on his famous journey with Meriwether Lewis through the territory the United States had acquired in the Louisiana Purchase—and beyond. It shows the portages around the "Great Falls" of the Columbia River. (© The Granger Collection, New York)

few of whom had ever ventured much beyond the Mississippi River. In 1803, even before Napoleon's offer to sell Louisiana, Jefferson helped plan an expedition that was to cross the continent to the Pacific Ocean, gather geographic facts, and investigate prospects for trade with the Indians. He named as its leader his private secretary and Virginia neighbor, the thirty-three-year-old Meriwether Lewis, a veteran of Indian wars skilled in the ways of the wilderness. Lewis chose as a colleague the twenty-nine-year-old William Clark, who–like George Rogers Clark, his older brother–was an experienced frontiersman and Indian fighter. In the spring of 1804, Lewis and Clark, with a company of four dozen men, started up the Missouri River from St. Louis. With a Shoshone woman, Sacajawea, as their guide, they eventually crossed the Rocky Mountains, descended the Snake and Columbia Rivers, and in the late autumn of 1805 camped on the Pacific coast. In September 1806, they were back in St. Louis with elaborate records of the geography and the Indian civilizations they had observed along the way, and a lengthy diary recounting their experiences.

While Lewis and Clark were still on their journey, Jefferson dispatched other explorers to other parts of the Louisiana Territory. Lieutenant Zebulon Montgomery Pike, twenty-six

ZEBULON PIKE years old, led an expedition in the fall of 1805 from St. Louis into the upper Mississippi Valley. In the summer of 1806, he set out again up the valley of the Arkansas River and into what later became Colorado, where he encountered (but failed in his attempt to climb) the peak that now bears his name. His account of his western travels created an enduring (and inaccurate) impression among many Americans in the East that the land between the Missouri River and the Rockies was an uninhabitable, uncultivable desert.

THE BURR CONSPIRACY

Jefferson's triumphant reelection in 1804 suggested that most of the nation approved the new territorial acquisition. But some New England Federalists raged against it. They realized that the more the West grew and the more new states joined the Union, the less power the Federalists and their region

ESSEX JUNTO would retain. In Massachusetts, a group of the most extreme Federalists, known as the "Essex Junto," concluded that the only recourse for New England was to secede from the Union and form a separate "Northern Confederacy." If this confederacy was to have any hope for lasting success, the Federalists believed, it would have to include New York and New Jersey as well. But the leading Federalist in New York, Alexander Hamilton, refused to support the secessionist scheme. "Dismemberment of our empire," he wrote, "will be a clear sacrifice of great positive advantages without any counterbalancing good, administering no relief to our real disease, which is democracy."

Federalists in New York then turned to Hamilton's greatest political rival: Vice President Aaron Burr. He was a politician without prospects in his own party. Jefferson had never forgiven him for the 1800 election deadlock.

HAMILTON AND BURR Burr accepted a Federalist proposal that he become their candidate for governor of New York in 1804, and there were rumors (unsupported by any evidence) that he had also agreed to support the Federalist plans for secession. Hamilton accused Burr of plotting treason and made numerous private remarks, widely reported in the press, about Burr's "despicable" character. When Burr lost the New York election, he blamed his defeat on Hamilton's malevolence. "These things must have an end," Burr wrote. He challenged Hamilton to a duel.

Dueling had by then already fallen into some disrepute in America, but many people still considered it a legitimate institution for settling matters of "honor." Hamilton feared that refusing Burr's challenge would brand him a coward. And so, on a July morning in 1804, the two men met at Weehawken, New Jersey. Hamilton was mortally wounded; he died the next day.

The resourceful and charismatic Burr was now a political outcast who had to flee New York to avoid an indictment for murder. But he found new outlets for his ambitions in the West. Even before the duel, he had begun corresponding with prominent white settlers in the Southwest, especially with General James Wilkinson, now governor of the Louisiana Territory. Burr and Wilkinson hoped to lead an expedition that would capture Mexico from the Spanish. "Mexico glitters in all our eyes," Burr wrote; "the word is all we wait for." But there were also rumors that they wanted to separate the Southwest from the United States and create a western empire that Burr would rule. There is little evidence to support them.

Whether the rumors were true or not, many of Burr's opponents–including, ultimately, Jefferson himself–chose to believe them. When Burr led a group of armed followers down the Ohio River by boat in 1806, disturbing reports flowed into Washington. The most alarming was from Wilkinson. He had suddenly turned against Burr and now informed the president that treason was afoot and that an attack on New Orleans was imminent. Jefferson ordered Burr and his men arrested as traitors. Burr was brought to Richmond for trial. Determined to win a conviction, Jefferson carefully managed the government's

NEW ORLEANS IN 1803 Because of its location near the mouth of the Mississippi River, New Orleans was the principal port of western North America in the early nineteenth century. Through it, western farmers shipped their produce to markets in the East and Europe. This 1803 painting celebrates the American acquisition of the city from France as part of the Louisiana Purchase. (© Chicago History Museum, USA/The Bridgeman Art Library)

case from Washington. But Chief Justice Marshall, presiding over the trial on circuit duty, limited the evidence the government could present and defined the charge in such a way that the jury had little choice but to acquit Burr.

The Burr "conspiracy" was in part the story of a single man's soaring ambitions and flamboyant personality. But it was also a symbol of the larger perils still facing the new nation. With a central government that remained deliberately weak, with vast tracts of land only nominally controlled by the United States, with ambitious political leaders willing, if necessary, to circumvent normal channels in their search for power, the legitimacy of the federal government, and indeed the existence of the United States as a stable and united nation, remained to be fully established.

EXPANSION AND WAR

Two very different conflicts were taking shape in the later years of Thomas Jefferson's presidency that would, together, draw the United States into a difficult and frustrating war. One was the continuing tension in Europe, which in 1803 escalated

THE NAPOLEONIC WARS

once again into a full-scale conflict (the Napoleonic Wars). As the fighting escalated, both the British and the French took steps to prevent the United States from trading with (and thus assisting) the other.

The other conflict was in North America, a result of the ceaseless westward expansion of white settlement, which was now stretching to the Mississippi River and beyond, colliding again with Native American populations committed to protecting their lands and their trade from intruders. In both the North and the South, the threatened tribes mobilized to resist white encroachments. They began as well to forge connections with British forces in Canada and Spanish forces in Florida. The Indian conflict on land therefore became intertwined with the European conflict on the seas and ultimately helped cause the War of 1812, an unpopular conflict with ambiguous results.

CONFLICT ON THE SEAS

The early nineteenth century saw a dramatic expansion of American shipping in the Atlantic. Britain retained significant naval superiority, but the British merchant marine was preoccupied with commerce in Europe and Asia and devoted little energy to trade with America. Thus the United States stepped effectively into the void and developed one of the most important merchant marines in the world, which soon controlled a large proportion of the trade between Europe and the West Indies.

In 1805, at the Battle of Trafalgar, a British fleet virtually destroyed what was left of the French navy. Because France could no longer challenge the British at sea, Napoleon now chose to pressure England through economic rather than naval means. He announced the creation of what he called the "Continental System." It was designed to close the European continent to British trade. The British government replied to Napoleon's decrees by establishing through a series of "orders in council"—a blockade of the European coast. It required that any goods being shipped to Napoleon's Europe be carried either in British vessels or in neutral vessels stopping at British ports—precisely what Napoleon's policies forbade.

American ships were caught between Napoleon's decrees and Britain's orders in council. If they sailed directly for the European continent, they risked being captured by the British navy; if they sailed by way of a British port, they risked seizure by the French. Both of the warring powers were violating America's rights as a neutral nation. But most

AMERICA'S PREDICAMENT

Americans considered the British, with their greater sea power, the worse offender. British ships pounced on Yankee merchantmen all over the ocean. Particularly infuriating to Americans, British vessels stopped United States ships on the high seas and seized sailors off the decks, making them victims of "impressment."

IMPRESSMENT

The British navy—with its floggings, low pay, and terrible shipboard conditions—was known as a "floating hell" to its sailors. Few volunteered. Most had to be "impressed" (forced) into the service. At every opportunity they deserted. By 1807, many of these deserters had joined the American merchant marine or the American navy. To check this loss of vital manpower, the British claimed the right to stop and search American merchant ships (although at first not naval vessels) and reimpress deserters. They did not claim the right to take native-born Americans, but they did claim the right to seize naturalized Americans born on British soil. In practice, the British navy often made no such distinctions, impressing British deserters and native-born Americans alike into service.

In the summer of 1807, the British went to more provocative extremes in an incident involving a vessel of the American navy. Sailing from Norfolk, with several alleged deserters from the

CHESAPEAKE-LEOPARD INCIDENT

British navy among the crew, the American naval frigate *Chesapeake* encountered the British ship *Leopard*. When the American commander, James Barron, refused to allow the British to search the *Chesapeake*, the *Leopard* opened fire.

IMPORTANT

AND

LUMINOUS COMMUNICATION

ON THE

SUBJECT OF THE

IMPRESSMENT OF AMERICAN AND FOREIGN

SEAMEN

AND OTHER PERSONS.

IT has become manifest to every attentive observer, that the early and continued aggressions of Great Britain on our persons, our property, and our rights, imperiously demand a firm stand—an effectual, though calm system of measures of arrestation. For this purpose, it is our duty to make ourselves completely masters of the great truths and arguments by which our rights have been elucidated, supported and maintained.

On the 17th of January, 1806, the President of the United States communicated to Congress an extract from a dispatch of James Madison Esq. our secretary of state, to James Monroe Esq. our minister in London, which contains many facts highly important, and observations and arguments perfectly satisfactory and conclusive against "*impressments* of seamen and passengers, whether Foreign or American, on board of our vessels." The republication of that document at this crisis will at once display some of the reasons on which the government has probably declined to sanction the recent draught of a treaty with Great Britain, and will elucidate the ground on which the question of *the impressment of persons*, both native and alien, has been rested by our administration.

Extract of a letter from the Secretary of State to James Monroe Esq. dated 5th January, 1804.

We consider a neutral flag, on the high seas, as a safeguard to those sailing under it. Great Britain, on the contrary, asserts a right to search for, and seize her own subjects ; and un-

RESISTING THE IMPRESSMENT OF SAILORS On January 5, 1804, Secretary of State James Madison wrote this public letter to James Monroe on the unlawful impressment of American sailors by the British Royal Navy. The practice of boarding US ships and taking away sailors deemed by the British to be deserters from their navy came to a climax with the Chesapeake-Leopard Incident. (© The Granger Collection, New York)

Barron had no choice but to surrender, and a boarding party from the *Leopard* dragged four men off the American frigate.

When news of the *Chesapeake-Leopard* incident reached the United States, there was great popular clamor for revenge. If Congress had been in session, it might have declared war. But Jefferson and Madison tried to maintain the peace. Jefferson expelled all British warships from American waters to lessen the likelihood of future incidents. Then he sent instructions to his minister in England, James Monroe, to demand that the British government renounce impressment. The British government disavowed the action of the officer responsible for the *Chesapeake-Leopard* incident and recalled him; it offered compensation for those killed and wounded in the incident;

and it promised to return three of the captured sailors (one of the original four had been hanged). But the British refused to renounce impressment.

"PEACEABLE COERCION"

In an effort to prevent future incidents that might bring the nation again to the brink of war, Congress enacted a drastic measure known as "the Embargo." It became one of the most controversial political issues of its time. The Embargo prohib-

THE EMBARGO ited American ships from leaving the United States for any foreign port anywhere in the world. The law was widely evaded, but it was effective enough to create a serious depression through most of the nation. Hardest hit were the merchants and shipowners of the Northeast, most of them Federalists.

The election of 1808 came in the midst of the Embargo-(1807) induced depression. James Madison, Jefferson's secretary of state

and political ally, won the presidency. But the Embargo was clearly a growing political liability, and Jefferson decided to back down. A few days before leaving office, he approved a bill ending his experiment with what he called "peaceable coercion."

To replace the Embargo, Congress passed the Non-Intercourse Act just before Madison took office. The new law

NON-INTERCOURSE ACT reopened trade with all nations but Great Britain and France. A year later, in 1810, Congress allowed the Non-Intercourse Act to expire and replaced it with Macon's Bill No. 2, which conditionally reopened free commercial relations with Britain and France. Napoleon announced that France would no longer interfere with American shipping, and Madison announced that an embargo against Great Britain alone would automatically go into effect early in 1811 unless Britain renounced its restrictions on American shipping. The British government repealed its blockade of Europe. But the repeal came too late to prevent war.

STRUGGLING WITH THE EMBARGO This cartoon lampoons the U.S. Embargo against Britain in 1807, a decision that created much economic hardship for many people. The word "Ograbme" (a common nickname for a snapping turtle) is "embargo" spelled backward. It shows a struggling merchant wrestling with the results of the Embargo. It was an effort to prevent the United States from being drawn into the wars between Britain and France. But the Embargo, which continued until 1812, not only hurt the American economy but also helped draw the nation into the War of 1812. (© The Granger Collection, New York)

THE "INDIAN PROBLEM" AND THE BRITISH

The 1807 war crisis following the *Chesapeake-Leopard* incident revived the conflict between Indians and white Americans.

WILLIAM HENRY HARRISON

Two important (and very different) leaders emerged to oppose one another in the conflict: William Henry Harrison and Tecumseh.

The Virginia-born Harrison, already a veteran Indian fighter at age twenty-six, became a congressional delegate from the Northwest Territory in 1799. He was a committed advocate of growth and development in the western lands, and he was largely responsible for the passage in 1800 of the so-called Harrison Land Law, which enabled white settlers to acquire farms from the public domain on much easier terms than before.

In 1801, Jefferson appointed Harrison governor of the Indiana Territory to administer the president's proposed solution to the "Indian problem." Jefferson offered the Native Americans a choice: they could convert themselves into set-

JEFFERSON'S OFFER

tled farmers and assimilate—become a part of white society; or they could migrate to the west of the Mississippi. In either case, they would have to give up their claims to tribal lands in the Northwest.

THE INDIAN RESPONSE TO WHITE ENCROACHMENT With land cessions and white western migration placing increased pressure on Indian cultures after 1790, news of the Prophet's revival fell on eager ears. It spread especially quickly northward along the shores of Lake Michigan and westward along Lake Superior and the interior of Wisconsin. Following the Battle of Tippecanoe, Tecumseh eclipsed the Prophet as the major leader of Indian resistance, but his trips south to forge political alliance met with less success.

Jefferson considered the assimilation policy a benign alternative to continuing conflict between Indians and white settlers, a conflict he assumed the tribes were destined to lose. But to the tribes, the new policy seemed far from benign, especially given the bludgeonlike efficiency with which Harrison set out to implement it. He played one tribe against another and used threats, bribes, trickery, and whatever other tactics he felt would help him conclude treaties. In the first decade of the nineteenth century, the number of western Americans who had settled east of the Appalachians had grown to more than 500,000–a population far larger than that of the Native Americans. It was becoming almost inevitable, as a result, that the tribes would face ever-growing pressure to move out of the way of the rapidly growing white settlements.

By 1807, the United States had extracted from reluctant tribal leaders treaty rights to eastern Michigan, southern Indiana, and most of Illinois. Meanwhile, in the Southwest, white Americans were taking millions of acres from other tribes in Georgia, Tennessee, and Mississippi. The Indians wanted to resist, but the separate tribes were helpless by themselves against the power of the United States. They might have accepted their fate passively but for the emergence of two new factors.

One factor was the policy of the British authorities in Canada. After the *Chesapeake-Leopard* incident and the surge of anti-British feeling throughout the United States, the British colonial authorities began to expect an American invasion of Canada and took measures for their own defense. Among those measures were efforts to renew friendship with the Indians and provide them with increased supplies.

TECUMSEH AND THE PROPHET

The second, and more important, factor intensifying the border conflict was the rise of two remarkable Native American leaders, who together helped create an age of religious fervor and prophecy. One was Tenskwatawa, a charismatic religious leader and orator known as "the Prophet." He had experienced a mystical awakening in the process of recovering from alcoholism. Having freed himself from what he considered the evil effects of white culture, he began to speak to his people of the superior virtues of Indian civilization and the sinfulness and corruption of the white world. In the process, he inspired a religious revival that spread through numerous tribes and helped unite them. Like Neolin before him, and like his contemporary to the east, Handsome Lake, Tenskwatawa demonstrated the power of religious leaders to mobilize Indians behind political and military objectives. The Prophet's headquarters at the confluence of Tippecanoe Creek and the Wabash River (known as Prophetstown) became a sacred place for people of many tribes and attracted thousands of Indians from throughout the Midwest. Out of their common religious experiences, they began to consider joint political and military efforts as well. Tenskwatawa advocated an Indian society entirely separate from that of white Americans and a culture rooted in tribal tradition. The effort to trade with the Anglos and to borrow from their culture would, he argued, lead to the death of Indian ways.

THE PROPHET'S MESSAGE

Tecumseh–the chief of the Shawnees called by his tribe "the Shooting Star"–was in many ways even more militant than his brother. "Where today are the Pequot?" he thundered. "Where are . . . the other powerful tribes of our people? They have vanished before the avarice and oppression of the white man." And he warned of his tribe's extermination if they did not take action against the white Americans moving into their lands.

Tecumseh understood, as few other Indian leaders had, that only through united action could the tribes hope to resist the advance of white civilization. Beginning in 1809, after tribes in Indiana had ceded vast lands to the United States, he set out to

TECUMSEH Tecumseh's efforts to unite the tribes of the Mississippi Valley against further white encroachments on their lands led him ultimately into an alliance with the British after the Battle of Tippecanoe in 1811. In the War of 1812, he was commissioned a brigadier general by the British and fought against the United States in the Battle of the Thames. (© Parks Canada Agency - Fort Malden NHS)

JAMES AND DOLLEY MADISON James Madison may have been the most brilliant of the early leaders of the republic, but he was also one of the most serious and humorless, as this grim portrait suggests. His wife (born Dolley Payne in North Carolina and raised a Quaker in Virginia) was twenty-six when she married the forty-three-year-old Madison in 1794. Her charm and social grace made her one of her husband's greatest political assets. She acted as hostess for Thomas Jefferson, a widower, while her husband was secretary of state. And she presided over a lively social life during her eight years in the White House as First Lady. (Both © Collection of the New-York Historical Society, USA/The Bridgeman Art Library)

unite all the Indians of the Mississippi Valley, north and south.

TECUMSEH'S STRATEGY Together, he promised, they would halt white expansion, recover "the whole Northwest, and make the Ohio River the boundary between the United States and the Indian country. He maintained that Harrison and others, by negotiating treaties with individual tribes, had obtained no real title to land. The land belonged to all the tribes; none of them could rightfully cede any of it without the consent of the others.

In 1811, Tecumseh left Prophetstown and traveled down the Mississippi to visit the tribes of the South, hoping to persuade them to join the alliance. During his absence, Harrison camped near Prophetstown with 1,000 soldiers. On November 7, 1811, he provoked a battle. The white forces suffered losses as heavy as those of the natives, but Harrison drove off the

BATTLE OF TIPPECANOE Indians and burned the town. The Battle of Tippecanoe (named for the creek near the fighting) disillusioned many of the Prophet's followers, who had believed that his magic would protect them. Tecumseh returned to find the confederacy in disarray. But there were still many warriors eager for combat, and by the spring of 1812 they were raiding white settlements and terrifying white settlers.

The bloodshed along the western borders was largely a result of the Indians' own initiative, but Britain's agents in Canada had encouraged and helped supply the uprising. To Harrison and most white residents of the regions, there seemed only one way to make the West safe for Americans: drive the British out of Canada and annex that province to the United States.

FLORIDA AND WAR FEVER

While white "frontiersmen" in the North demanded the conquest of Canada, those in the South wanted the United States to acquire Spanish Florida, a territory that included the present state of Florida and the southern areas of what are now Alabama, Mississippi, and Louisiana. The territory was a continuing threat to whites in the southern United States. Slaves escaped across the Florida border; Indians launched frequent raids north into white settlements from Florida. But white southerners also coveted Florida because through it ran rivers that could provide residents of the Southwest with access to valuable ports on the Gulf of Mexico.

In 1810, American settlers in West Florida (an area that is part of Mississippi and Louisiana today) seized the Spanish fort at Baton Rouge and asked the federal government to annex the captured territory to the United States. President Madison happily agreed and then began planning to get the rest of Florida, too. The desire for Florida became yet another motivation for war with Britain. Spain was Britain's ally, and a war with Britain might provide a pretext for taking Spanish territory.

By 1812, war fever was growing on both the northern and southern borders of the United States. In the congressional elections of 1810, voters from these regions elected a large number of representatives of both parties eager for war with Britain. They became known as the "war hawks." Some of them were ardent nationalists fired by passion for territorial expansion—among them two men who would play a great role **WAR HAWKS** in national politics for much of the next four decades: Henry Clay of Kentucky and John C. Calhoun of South Carolina. Others were men impassioned in their defense of Republican values. Together, they formed a powerful coalition in favor of war.

Clay became Speaker of the House in 1811, and he filled committees with those who shared his eagerness for war. He appointed Calhoun to the crucial Committee on Foreign Affairs, and both men began agitating for the conquest of Canada. Madison still hoped for peace. But he shared the concerns of other Republicans about the dangers to American trade, and he was losing control of Congress. On June 18, 1812, he gave in to the pressure and approved a declaration of war against Britain.

THE WAR OF 1812

Preoccupied with their struggle against Napoleon in Europe, the British were not eager for a conflict with the United States. Even after the Americans declared war, Britain largely ignored them for a time. But in the fall of 1812, Napoleon launched a catastrophic campaign against Russia that left his army in disarray and his power in Europe diminished. By late 1813, with the French Empire on its way to final defeat, Britain was able to turn its military attention to America.

BATTLES WITH THE TRIBES

Americans entered the War of 1812 with great enthusiasm, but events on the battlefield soon cooled their ardor. In the summer of 1812, American forces invaded Canada through Detroit. They soon had to retreat back to Detroit and in August surrendered the fort there. Other invasion efforts also failed. In the meantime, Fort Dearborn (Chicago) fell before an Indian attack.

Things went only slightly better for the United States on the seas. At first, American frigates won some spectacular victories over British warships, and American privateers destroyed or captured many British merchant ships, occasionally braving the coastal waters of the British **EARLY DEFEATS** Isles themselves and burning vessels within sight of the shore. But by 1813, the British navy—now less

preoccupied with Napoleon—was counterattacking effectively, driving the American frigates to cover and imposing a blockade on the United States.

The United States did, however, achieve significant early military successes on the Great Lakes. First, the Americans took command of Lake Ontario, which permitted them to raid and burn York (now Toronto), the capital of Canada. American forces then seized control of Lake Erie, mainly through the **PUT-IN-BAY** work of the youthful Oliver Hazard Perry, who engaged and dispersed a British fleet at Put-in-Bay on September 10, 1813. This made possible another invasion of Canada by way of Detroit, which Americans could now reach easily by water. William Henry Harrison, the American commander in the West, pushed up the Thames River into upper Canada and, on October 5, 1813, won a victory notable for the death of Tecumseh, who was serving as a brigadier general in the British army. The Battle of the Thames weakened and disheartened the Native Americans of the Northwest and greatly diminished their ability to defend their claims to the region.

In the meantime, another white military leader was striking an even harder blow at the tribes of the Southwest. The Creeks, whom Tecumseh had aroused on a visit to the South and whom the Spanish had supplied with weapons, had been attacking white settlers near the Florida border. Andrew Jackson, a wealthy Tennessee planter and a general in the state militia, temporarily abandoned plans for an invasion of Florida and set off in pursuit of them. On March 27, 1814, in the Battle of Horseshoe Bend, Jackson's men took terrible revenge on the Indians—slaughtering women and children along with warriors—and broke the resistance of the Creeks. The tribe agreed to cede most of its lands to the United States and retreated westward, farther into the interior. The battle also won Jackson a commission as a major general in the United States Army. In that capacity he led his men farther south into Florida and, on November 7, 1814, seized the Spanish fort at Pensacola.

BATTLES WITH THE BRITISH

The victories over the tribes were not enough for the United States to win the war. After the surrender of Napoleon in 1814, **THE BRITISH INVASION** England prepared to invade the United States. A British armada sailed up the Patuxent River from Chesapeake Bay and landed an army that marched a short distance overland to Bladensburg, on the outskirts of Washington, where it dispersed a poorly trained force of American militiamen. On August 24, 1814, the British troops entered Washington and set fire to several public buildings, including the White House, in retaliation for the earlier American burning of the Canadian capital at York. This was the low point of American fortunes in the war.

Leaving Washington in partial ruins, the British army proceeded up the bay toward Baltimore. But Baltimore harbor, guarded by Fort McHenry, was prepared. To block the

THE WAR OF 1812 This map illustrates the military maneuvers of the British and the Americans during the War of 1812. It shows all the theaters of the war, from New Orleans to southern Canada, the extended land and water battle along the Canadian border and in the Great Lakes, and the fighting around Washington and Baltimore. Note how in all these theaters there are about the same number of British and American victories.

• *What finally brought this inconclusive war to an end?*

approaching fleet, the American garrison had sunk several ships to clog the entry to the harbor, thus forcing the British to bombard the fort from a distance.

Through the night of September 13, Francis Scott Key, a Washington lawyer who was on board one of the British ships trying to secure the release of an American prisoner, watched the bombardment. The next morning, "by the dawn's early light," he could see the flag on the fort still flying; he recorded his pride in the moment by scribbling a poem–"The Star-Spangled Banner"–on the back of an envelope. The British withdrew from Baltimore, and Key's words were soon set to

the tune of an old English drinking song. In 1931, "The Star-Spangled Banner" became the official national anthem.

Meanwhile, American forces repelled another British invasion in northern New York at the Battle of Plattsburgh, on September 11, 1814, which turned back a much larger British naval and land force and secured the northern border of the United States. In the South, a formidable array of battle-hardened British veterans, fresh from the campaign against the French in Spain, landed below New Orleans and prepared to advance north up the Mississippi. Awaiting the British was

BATTLE OF NEW ORLEANS

Andrew Jackson with a motley collection of Tennesseans, Kentuckians, Creoles, blacks, pirates, and regular army troops behind earthen fortifications. On January 8, 1815, the British advanced, but their exposed forces were no match for Jackson's well-protected men. After the Americans had repulsed several waves of attackers, the British finally retreated, leaving behind 700 dead (including their commander, Sir Edward Pakenham), 1,400 wounded, and 500 prisoners. Jackson's losses were 8 killed and 13 wounded. Only later did news reach North America that the United States and Britain had signed a peace treaty several weeks before the Battle of New Orleans.

THE REVOLT OF NEW ENGLAND

With a few notable exceptions, such as the Battles of Put-in-Bay and New Orleans, the military operations of the United States between 1812 and 1815 consisted of a series of humiliating failures. As a result, the American government faced increasing popular opposition as the contest dragged on. In New England, opposition both to the war and to the Republican government that was waging it was so extreme that some Federalists celebrated British victories. In Congress, in the meantime, the Republicans had persistent trouble with the Federalist opposition, led by a young congressman from New Hampshire, Daniel Webster, who missed no opportunity to embarrass the administration.

By now the Federalists were a minority in the country as a whole, but they were still the majority party in New England. Some of them began to dream again of creating a separate nation in that region, which they could dominate and in which they could escape what they saw as the tyranny of slaveholders and backwoodsmen. Talk of secession revived and reached a climax in the winter of 1814–1815.

On December 15, 1814, delegates from the New England states met in Hartford, Connecticut, to discuss their grievances. Those who favored secession at the Hartford Convention were outnumbered by a comparatively moderate majority. But while the convention's report only hinted at secession, it reasserted the right of nullification and proposed seven amendments to the Constitution (presumably as the condition of New England's remaining in the Union)—amendments designed to protect New England from the growing influence of the South and the West.

HARTFORD CONVENTION

Because the war was going badly and the government was becoming desperate, the New Englanders assumed that the Republicans would have to agree to their demands. Soon after the convention adjourned, however, the news of Jackson's smashing victory at New Orleans reached the cities of the Northeast. A day or two later, reports arrived from abroad of a negotiated peace. In the euphoria of this apparent triumph, the Hartford Convention and the Federalists came to seem futile, irrelevant, even treasonable. The failure of the secession effort was a virtual death blow to the Federalist Party.

THE PEACE SETTLEMENT

Peace talks between the United States and Britain had begun even before fighting in the War of 1812 began. John Quincy Adams, Henry Clay, and Albert Gallatin led the American delegation.

In the negotiations, the Americans gave up their demand for a British renunciation of impressment and for the cession of Canada to the United States. The British abandoned their call for

TREATY OF GHENT

THE BOMBARDMENT OF FORT MCHENRY The British bombardment of Fort McHenry in Baltimore harbor in September 1814 was of modest importance to the outcome of the War of 1812. It is remembered as the occasion for Francis Scott Key to write his poem "The Star-Spangled Banner," which recorded his sentiments at seeing an American flag still flying over the fort "by the dawn's early light." (The Library of Congress)

A VIEW of the BOMBARDMENT of Fort McHenry, near Baltimore, by the British fleet taken from the Observatory under the Command of Admirals Cochrane & Cockburn on the morning of the 13th of Sept 1814 which lasted 24 hours, & thrown from 1500 to 1800 shells in the Night attempted to land by forcing a passage up the ferry branch but were repulsed with great loss.

ATTACKING THE FEDERALISTS A Republican cartoonist derided the secession efforts of New England Federalists at the Hartford Convention in this cartoon. It portrays timid men representing Massachusetts, Connecticut, and Rhode Island preparing to leap into the arms of George III. (The Library of Congress)

the creation of an Indian buffer state in the Northwest. The negotiators referred other disputes to arbitration. Hastily drawn up, a treaty was signed on Christmas Eve 1814. It was named the Treaty of Ghent after the Dutch city in which it was signed.

Other settlements followed the Treaty of Ghent and contributed to a long-term improvement in Anglo-American rela-

RUSH-BAGOT AGREEMENT

tions. A commercial treaty in 1815 gave Americans the right to trade freely with England and much of the British Empire. The Rush-Bagot agreement of 1817 provided for mutual disarmament on the Great Lakes; eventually (although not until 1872) the Canadian-American boundary became the longest "unguarded frontier" in the world.

For the other parties to the War of 1812, the Indian tribes east of the Mississippi, the Treaty of Ghent was of no lasting value. It required the United States to restore to the tribes lands seized by white Americans in the fighting, but those provisions were never enforced. Ultimately, the war was another disastrous blow to the capacity of Native Americans to resist white expansion. Tecumseh, their most important leader, was dead. The British, their most important allies, were gone from the Northwest. The alliance that Tecumseh and the Prophet had forged was in disarray. And the end of the war spurred a great new drive by white settlers deeper into the West, into land the Indians were less than ever able to defend.

AP CONNECTING THEMES

Chapter 7 discussed a myriad of different themes. Particularly important are the regional political, economic, and social divisions that seemed to be widening as a result of land acquisition, the transportation revolution, and the First Industrial Revolution. You should also focus on the impact of that

revolution on the American workforce and family relationships in the United States. Be familiar with the land acquisitions of the United States during this period and the consequences of that physical growth. Finally, the expanding economic presence on the world stage led to hostile encounters with both the French and the British as the United States attempted to maintain neutrality and protect its trade.

The following themes have a heightened importance in Chapter 7. You should now be able to do the following for each listed theme:

Work, Exchange and Technology: Analyze the impact of the First Industrial Revolution and the development of a national market economy on the economic, political, and social aspects of American life.

Peopling: Analyze the factors that encouraged western migration and the consequences of that migration.

Politics and Power: Explain the issues involved in the dissolution of the first American party system.

America and the World: Explain how American trade and neutrality and westward expansion led to conflict with a variety of European countries.

Environment and Geography: Explain the impact of territorial acquisition on migration, political power, and foreign relations in the United States.

Ideas, Beliefs, and Culture: Explain how Enlightenment ideas and the belief in the perfectibility of man influenced the development of American culture and society.

AP SUGGESTED STUDY

PEOPLE/PLACES/EVENTS As you study these items, think about how they demonstrate or relate to key concepts and historical themes from this chapter and previous chapters.

AARON BURR 201
AMERICAN SHIPPING 189
CAMP MEETINGS 186
CANE RIDGE 185
DEISM 184
ELI WHITNEY 189
EMBARGO ACT 204
HANDSOME LAKE 206
HARTFORD CONVENTION 210
IMPRESSMENT 203
INDUSTRIALISM 188

JOHN MARSHALL 196
JUDICIAL REVIEW 195
JUDITH SARGENT MURRAY 182
LOUISIANA PURCHASE 199
MARBURY VS. MADISON 195
MERCY OTIS WARREN 184
NEOLIN 188
NEW LIGHT DISSENTERS 185
NOAH WEBSTER 184
ROBERT FULTON 190
SAMUEL SLATER 188

SECOND GREAT AWAKENING 185
TECUMSEH 206
THE EMBARGO 204
THE PROPHET (TENSKWATAWA) 206
TOUSSAINT L'OUVERTURE 198
WAR HAWKS 208
WAR OF 1812 208
WASHINGTON IRVING 184
WILLIAM HENRY HARRISON 208

AP TEST PRACTICE

Questions assume cumulative content knowledge from this chapter and previous chapters.

MULTIPLE CHOICE Use the painting on page 190 and your knowledge of U.S. history to answer questions 1–2.

1. How did developments like that depicted in the painting most directly affect regionalism between the North and the South in the early 1800s?

   (A) Northern states began to diversify into industrial manufacturing.

   (B) Transportation systems became important.

   (C) The British government tried to restrict importation of technology to the U.S.

   (D) The southern states began to rely more heavily on machinery for processing cotton.

2. How did the economic development illustrated in the painting promote national economic ties in the early 19th century?

   (A) The increased demand for cotton led the North to embrace the slave trade.

   (B) Southern cotton provided the raw material for the growing textile factories in the North.

   (C) The southern states began to industrialize rapidly, along with the North.

   (D) The North and South became more culturally unified in their competition with the British textile industry.

SHORT ANSWER Use your knowledge of U.S. history to answer questions 3–6.

3. Answer a, b, and c.

   a) Briefly explain why ONE of the following technological developments can best be considered a turning point in the history of regionalism between the North and the South in the U.S.?

   • Steam engine

   • Invention of a new machine for cleaning short-staple cotton

   • Textile machinery based on technology imported from England

   b) Describe a development or example to support your explanation.

c) Briefly explain why one of the other options is not as useful to serve as a turning point in the history of regionalism between the North and the South in the U.S.

4. Answer a, b, and c.

a) Briefly explain ONE example of how Native Americans leveraged relations among Americans and other major European powers in efforts to maintain their tribal lands.

b) Briefly explain a SECOND example of how Native Americans leveraged relations among Americans and other major European powers in efforts to maintain their tribal lands.

c) Briefly explain ONE example of how conflict among the major European imperial powers led to territorial expansion of the newly formed U.S.

5. Answer a, b, and c.

a) Briefly explain ONE example of how the Enlightenment influenced American culture in the late 18th and early 19th centuries.

b) Briefly explain ONE example of how religion influenced American culture in the late 18th and early 19th centuries.

c) Briefly explain ONE example of the influence of the Enlightenment or religious developments on Native American or African American groups in the late 18th and early 19th centuries.

6. Answer a, b, and c.

a) Briefly explain why ONE of the following options was most responsible for a lasting change in American cultural identity between 1800 and 1820.

- Education
- Science and medicine
- Transportation

b) Provide ONE example or development to support your explanation.

c) Briefly explain why ONE of the other options is not as useful to illustrate a lasting change in American cultural identity.

LONG ESSAY Develop a thoughtful and thorough historical argument that answers the questions below. Begin your essay with a thesis statement and support it with relevant historical evidence.

7. Some historians have argued that the technological advances and governmental policies established during the Jefferson presidency did little to create a national market economy. Support, modify, or refute this assertion, providing specific evidence to justify your answer.

8. To what extent did the Louisiana Purchase further deepen regional conflict in the United States? Use historical evidence to support your argument.

8 | VARIETIES OF AMERICAN NATIONALISM

CELEBRATING THE NATION Celebrations of Independence Day, like this one in New York City, became major festive events throughout the United States in the early nineteenth century, a sign of rising American Nationalism.
(© North Wind Picture Archives/Alamy)

AP

HISTORICAL THINKING

1. **Contextualization** Identify and explain the ways in which the Marshall Court attempted to increase the power of the federal government at the expense of the states.

2. **Patterns of Continuity and Change over Time** Explain how the American System represented a change in the economic structure of the American economy.

3. **Historical Interpretation** To what degree was the period shortly after 1812 through the early 1820s a time of exceptional political unity?

4. **Contextualization** Identify and explain the factors that led to the demise of the first era of political parties.

5. **Contextualization** Analyze the ways in which westward migration intensified conflict over slavery.

Key Concept Correlations

Analyze the ways the historical developments you learn about in this chapter connect to the following AP Key Concepts.

3.3 Migration within North America, cooperative interaction, and competition for resources raised questions about boundaries and policies, intensified conflicts among peoples and nations, and led to contests over the creation of a multiethnic, multiracial national identity.

4.1 The United States developed the world's first modern mass democracy and celebrated a new national culture, while Americans sought to define the nation's democratic ideals and to reform its institutions to match them.

4.2 Developments in technology, agriculture, and commerce precipitated profound changes in U.S. settlement patterns, regional identities, gender and family relations, political power, and distribution of consumer goods.

4.3 U.S. interest in increasing foreign trade, expanding its national borders, and isolating itself from European conflicts shaped the nation's foreign policy and spurred government and private initiatives.

Thematic Learning Objectives

WXT-2, 4, 5, 6; POL-2, 5, 6; ID-1, 2, 5; CUL-2, 5; PEO-2, 3; WOR-5, 6, ENV-3

CHAPTER 8 discusses the rise of American nationalism following the War of 1812. Examine how this nationalism took the form of attempts to develop a unified national economy, such as the American System, and the impact such efforts had on both the economic development of the United States as well as the intensification of regional differences. Also important is the expanding exploration of the Far West and the impact it had on westward migration. Particular attention should be paid to the expansion of slavery into the territories and compromise solutions that provided a temporary remedy for the issue. Be aware that the Marshall Court attempted to strengthen the power of the national government in various rulings and the impact of that attempt on regional controversy. Also, be able to explain foreign policy initiatives undertaken following the War of 1812. As you read, evaluate the following concepts:

- The Supreme Court under Chief Justice John Marshall asserted federal power over state laws.
- The American System of Henry Clay sought to establish a more unified national market economy through the creation of a Second Bank of the United States and enactment of a protective tariff and federally funded internal improvements.
- Improved transportation aided in the movement of goods and people.
- Improved transportation systems allowed for greater access to natural resources, markets, and western lands.
- Trade and trapping became important in the Far West, leading to a better understanding of the environment.
- The United States sought dominance over not only the North American continent, but sought to extend its influence into Latin America with the Monroe Doctrine.
- The geographic growth of the United States led to controversy over the expansion of slavery into new territories and increased conflict with American Indians.

BUILDING A NATIONAL MARKET

The end of the War of 1812 allowed the United States to resume the economic growth and territorial expansion that had characterized the first decade of the nineteenth century. A vigorous postwar boom led to a disastrous bust in 1819. Brief though it was, the collapse was evidence that the United States continued to lack some of the basic institutions necessary to sustain long-term growth. In the years to follow, there were strenuous efforts to introduce stability to the expanding economy.

BANKING, CURRENCY, AND PROTECTION

The War of 1812 may have stimulated the growth of manufacturing by cutting off imports, but it also produced chaos in shipping and banking, and it exposed dramatically the inadequacy of the existing transportation and financial systems. The aftermath of the war, therefore, saw the emergence of a series of political issues connected with national economic development.

POSTWAR ISSUES

The wartime experience underlined the need for another national bank. After the expiration of the first Bank of the United States's charter in 1811, a large number of state banks had begun operations. They issued vast quantities of bank notes but did not always retain enough reserves of gold or silver to redeem the notes on demand. The notes passed from hand to hand more or less as money, but their actual value depended on the reputation of the bank that issued them. Thus there was a wide variety of notes, of widely differing value, in circulation at the same time. The result was a confusion that made honest business difficult and counterfeiting easy.

Congress dealt with the currency problem by chartering a second Bank of the United States in 1816. It was essentially the same institution Hamilton had founded in 1791 except that it had

AN EARLY MILL IN NEW ENGLAND This early folk painting of about 1814 shows the small town of East Chelmsford, Massachusetts—still primarily agrarian, with its rural houses, open fields, and grazing livestock, but with a small textile mill already operating along the stream, at right. A little more than a decade later, the town had been transformed into a major manufacturing center and renamed for the family that owned the mills: Lowell. (*Part of the Town of Chelmsford.* By Miss Warren. Abby Aldrich Rockefeller Folk Art Museum, Colonial Williamsburg Foundation, Williamsburg, VA) (© Abby Aldrich Rockefeller Folk Art Museum, The Colonial Williamsburg Foundation, Willliamsburg, VA)

SECOND BANK OF THE UNITED STATES

more capital than its predecessor. The national bank could not forbid state banks to issue currency, but its size and power enabled it to dominate the state banks. It could compel them to issue only sound notes or risk being forced out of business.

Congress also acted to promote the already burgeoning manufacturing sector of the nation's economy. Manufactured goods had been so scarce during the conflict that, even with comparatively unskilled labor and inexperienced management, new factories could start operations virtually assured of quick profits.

The American textile industry experienced a particularly dramatic growth. Between 1807 and 1815, the total number of cotton spindles increased more than fifteen-fold, from 8,000 to

GROWTH OF THE TEXTILE INDUSTRY

130,000. Until 1814, the textile factories—most of them in New England—produced only yarn and thread; families operating hand-looms at home did the actual weaving of cloth. Then the Boston merchant Francis Cabot Lowell, after examining textile machinery in England, developed a power loom that was better than its English counterpart. In 1813, Lowell organized the Boston Manufacturing Company and, at Waltham, Massachusetts, founded the first mill in America to carry on spinning and weaving under a single roof. Lowell's company was an important step in revolutionizing American

manufacturing and in shaping the character of the early industrial workforce.

But the end of the war suddenly dimmed the prospects for American industry. British ships–determined to recapture their lost markets–swarmed into American ports and unloaded cargoes of manufactured goods, many priced below cost. As one English leader explained to Parliament, it was "well worth while to incur a loss upon the first exportation, in order, by the glut, to stifle in the cradle those rising manufactures in the United States." The "infant industries" cried out for protection against these tactics, arguing that they needed time to grow strong enough to withstand the foreign competition.

In 1816, protectionists in Congress won passage of a tariff law that effectively limited competition from abroad on a wide range of items, the most important of which was cotton

A PROTECTIVE TARIFF

cloth. There were objections from agricultural interests, who would have to pay higher prices for manufactured goods as a result. But the nationalist dream of creating an important American industrial economy prevailed.

TRANSPORTATION

The nation's most pressing economic need in the aftermath of the war was for a better transportation system. Without one, manufacturers would not have access to the raw materials they needed or to domestic markets. So an old

AMERICAN IMPORTS AND EXPORTS, 1790–1820 This chart shows the pattern of goods imported to and exported from the United States—the level of foreign trade, and the balance between goods bought and goods sold. Americans were heavily dependent on Britain and Europe for "finished" or "manufactured" goods in these years; and as you can see, imports grew as rapidly as, and often even more rapidly than, exports. Note how the nation's disputes with European powers depressed both exports and imports from about 1808 to 1814.

• *How does this chart help explain Congress's passage of a protective tariff law in 1816?*

debate resumed: Should the federal government help to finance roads and other "internal improvements"?

The idea of using government funds to finance road building was not new. When Ohio entered the Union in 1803, the federal government agreed that part of the proceeds from the government's sale of public lands should finance road construction. In 1807, Jefferson's secretary of the treasury, Albert Gallatin, proposed that revenues from the Ohio land sales should help finance a National Road from the Potomac River to the Ohio River. Both Congress and the president approved. After many delays, construction of the National Road finally began in 1811 at Cumberland, Maryland, on the Potomac; and by 1818, this

GOVERNMENT-FUNDED ROADS highway—with a crushed stone surface and massive stone bridges—ran as far as Wheeling, Virginia, on the Ohio River. Meanwhile, the state of Pennsylvania gave $100,000 to a private company to extend the Lancaster pike westward to Pittsburgh. Over both of these roads a heavy traffic soon moved: stagecoaches, Conestoga wagons, private carriages, and other vehicles, as well as droves of cattle. Despite high tolls, the roads made transportation costs across the mountains lower than ever before. Manufactures,

particularly textiles, moved from the Atlantic seaboard to the Ohio Valley in unprecedented quantities.

At the same time, on the rivers and the Great Lakes, steam-powered shipping was expanding rapidly. The development of steamboat lines was already well under way before the War of 1812, thanks to the technological advances introduced by Robert Fulton and others. The war had retarded expansion for a

STEAMBOATS time, but by 1816, river steamers were beginning to journey up and down the Mississippi to the Ohio River, and up the Ohio as far as Pittsburgh. Within a few years, steamboats were carrying far more cargo on the Mississippi than all the earlier forms of river transport—flatboats, barges, and others—combined. They stimulated the agricultural economy of the West and the South, by providing much readier access to markets at greatly reduced cost. And they enabled eastern manufacturers to send their finished goods west.

Despite the progress with steamboats and turnpikes, there remained serious gaps in the nation's transportation network, as the War of 1812 had shown. Once the British blockade cut off Atlantic shipping, the coastal roads became choked by the unaccustomed volume of north-south traffic. Long lines of wagons

STEAMBOATS ON THE HUDSON Inventor Robert Fulton developed an engine that could propel a boat from Manhattan to Albany, a distance of about 150 miles, in thirty two hours. His steam-powered vessels, first built in 1807, were the first large and reliable enough to be commercially valuable. (Photo © Tarker/The Bridgeman Art Library)

waited for a chance to use the ferries that were still the only means of crossing most rivers. Oxcarts, pressed into emergency service, took six or seven weeks to go from Philadelphia to Charleston. In some areas there were serious shortages of goods that normally traveled by sea, and prices rose to new heights. Rice cost three times as much in New York as in Charleston, flour three times as much in Boston as in Richmond–all because of the difficulty of transportation. There were military consequences, too. On the northern and western frontiers, the absence of good roads had frustrated American campaigns.

In 1815, with this wartime experience in mind, President Madison called the attention of Congress to the "great importance of establishing throughout our country the roads and canals which can be best executed under the national authority," and suggested that a constitutional amendment would resolve any doubts about Congress's authority to provide for their construction. Representative John C. Calhoun promptly introduced a bill that would have used the funds owed the government by the Bank of the United States to finance internal improvements. "Let us, then, bind the republic together with a perfect system of roads and canals," Calhoun urged. "Let us conquer space."

Congress passed Calhoun's internal improvements bill, but President Madison, on his last day in office (March 3, 1817), vetoed it. He supported the purpose of the bill, he explained,

VETOING INTERNAL IMPROVEMENTS but he still believed that Congress lacked authority to fund the improvements without a constitutional amendment. It remained for state governments and private enterprise to undertake the tremendous task of building the transportation network necessary for the growing American economy.

EXPANDING WESTWARD

One reason for the growing interest in internal improvements was the sudden and dramatic surge in westward expansion in the years following the War of 1812. "Old America seems to be breaking up and moving westward," wrote an English observer at the time. By the time of the census of 1820, white settlers had pushed well beyond the Mississippi River, and the population of the western regions was increasing more rapidly than that of the nation as a whole. Almost one of every four white Americans lived west of the Appalachians in 1820; ten years before, only one in seven had resided there.

THE GREAT MIGRATIONS

The westward movement of the white American population was one of the most important developments of the nineteenth century. It had a profound effect on

REASONS FOR WESTWARD EXPANSION the nation's economy, bringing vast new regions into the emerging capitalist system. It had great political ramifications, which ultimately became a major factor in the coming of the Civil War. And like earlier movements west, it thrust peoples

of different cultures and traditions into intimate (and often disastrous) association with one another.

There were several important reasons for this expansion. The pressures driving white Americans out of the East came in part from the continued growth of the nation's population–both through natural increase and through immigration. Between 1800 and 1820, the population nearly doubled–from 5.3 million to 9.6 million. The growth of cities absorbed some of that increase, but most Americans were still farmers. The agricultural lands of the East were by now largely occupied, and some of them were exhausted. In the South, the spread of the plantation system, and of a slave labor force, limited opportunities for new settlers.

At the same time, the West itself was becoming increasingly attractive to white settlers. The War of 1812 had helped diminish (although it did not wholly eliminate) one of the traditional deterrents to western expansion: Native American opposition. And in the aftermath of the war, the federal government continued its policy of pushing the remaining tribes farther and farther west. A series of treaties in 1815 wrested more land from the Indians. In the meantime, the government was erecting a chain

THE FACTOR SYSTEM of stockaded forts along the Great Lakes and the Mississippi to protect the frontier. It also created a "factor" system, by which government factors (or agents) supplied the tribes with goods at cost. This not only worked to drive Canadian traders out of the region; it also helped create a situation of dependency on the factors that made Native Americans easier to control.

Now that fertile lands were secure for white settlement, migrants from throughout the East flocked to the Old Northwest (now called the Midwest). The Ohio and Monongahela Rivers were the main routes westward, until the completion of the Erie Canal in 1825. Once on the Ohio, the migrants floated downstream on flatboats bearing all their possessions, then left the river (often at Cincinnati, which was becoming one of the region's–and the nation's–principal cities) and pressed on overland with wagons, handcarts, packhorses, cattle, and hogs.

THE PLANTATION SYSTEM IN THE SOUTHWEST

In the Southwest, the new agricultural economy emerged along different lines. The principal attraction was cotton. The cotton lands in the uplands of the Old South had lost much of their fertility through overplanting and erosion. But the market for cotton continued to grow, so there was no lack of ambitious farmers seeking fresh soil in a climate suitable for the crop. In the Southwest, there were vast tracts of land appropriate for growing cotton. They included what would become known as the Black Belt of central Alabama and Mississippi, a large region with a dark, productive soil of rotted limestone.

The growth of southern settlement spread cotton, plantations, and slavery. The first arrivals in an uncultivated region were usually small farmers who made

COTTON AND THE EXPANSION OF SLAVERY rough clearings in the forest. But wealthier planters soon followed. They bought up cleared or partially cleared land, and the original settlers moved farther west and started over again.

FORT SNELLING This is an 1838 sketch of Fort Snelling (at the juncture of the Minnesota and Mississippi Rivers), containing instructions for reaching it from St. Louis. It was one of a string of fortifications built along the western edge of European settlement along the Great Lakes and the upper Mississippi in the first three decades of the nineteenth century. The forts were designed to protect the new white communities from hostile Indians. Fort Snelling stands today in Minnesota as a "living history" site. ("Fort Snelling from the East." Smithsonian Institution Archives. Record Unit 7290, Carl Andreas Geyer Journal, 1838. Negative # SA-861.)

The large planters made the westward journey in a style quite different from that of the first pioneers. Over the alternately dusty and muddy roads came great caravans consisting of herds of livestock, wagonloads of household goods, long lines of slaves, and—at the rear—the planter's family riding in carriages. Success in the wilderness was by no means ensured, even for the wealthiest settlers. But many planters soon expanded small clearings into vast cotton fields. They replaced the cabins of the early pioneers with sumptuous log dwellings and ultimately with imposing mansions that symbolized the emergence of a newly wealthy class. In later years, these western planters would assume the airs of a long-standing aristocracy. But by the time of the Civil War, few planter families in the Southwest had been there for more than one or two generations.

The rapid growth of the Northwest and Southwest resulted in the admission of four new states to the Union in the immediate aftermath of the War of 1812: Indiana in 1816, Mississippi in 1817, Illinois in 1818, and Alabama in 1819.

TRADE AND TRAPPING IN THE FAR WEST

Not many Anglo-Americans had much knowledge of or interest in the far western areas of the continent. But a significant trade nevertheless developed between these far western regions and the United States beginning early in the nineteenth century and growing steadily for decades.

Mexico, which controlled Texas, California, and much of the rest of the Southwest, won its independence from Spain in 1821. Almost immediately, it opened its northern territories to trade with the United States. American traders poured into the region—overland into Texas and New Mexico, by sea into California. Merchants from the United States quickly displaced both Indian and Mexican traders who had previously dominated trade. A steady traffic of commercial wagon trains was moving back and forth along the Santa Fe Trail between Missouri and New Mexico.

Fur traders created a wholly new commerce with the West. Before the War of 1812, John Jacob Astor's American

ASTOR'S AMERICAN FUR COMPANY

Fur Company had established Astoria as a trading post at the mouth of the Columbia River in Oregon. But when the war came, Astor sold his suddenly imperiled interests to the Northwestern Fur Company, a British concern operating out of Canada. After the war, Astor centered his operations in the Great Lakes area and eventually extended them westward to the Rockies. Other companies carried on operations up the Missouri and its tributaries and into the Rocky Mountains.

At first, fur traders did most of their business by purchasing pelts from the Indians. But increasingly, white trappers entered the region and began to hunt beaver on their own. Substantial numbers of Anglo-Americans and French Canadians moved deep into the Great Lakes region and beyond to join the Iroquois and other Indians in pursuit of furs.

As the trappers, or "mountain men," moved west from the Great Lakes region, they began to establish themselves in what is now Utah and in parts of New Mexico. In 1822, Andrew Henry and William Ashley founded the Rocky Mountain Fur Company and recruited white trappers to move permanently into the Rockies in search of furs, which were becoming increasingly scarce farther east. Henry and Ashley dispatched supplies annually to their trappers in exchange for furs and skins. The arrival of the supply train became the occasion for a gathering of scores of mountain men, some of whom lived much of the year in considerable isolation.

But however isolated their daily lives, these mountain men were closely bound up with the expanding market economy

THE FUR TRADE AND THE MARKET ECONOMY

of the United States. Some were employees of the Rocky Mountain Fur Company (or some other, similar enterprise), earning a salary in return for providing a steady supply of furs. Others were nominally independent but relied on the companies for credit; they were almost always in debt and hence economically bound to the companies. Some trapped entirely on their own and simply sold their furs for cash, but they too depended on merchants from the East for their livelihoods. And it was to those merchants that the bulk of the profits from the trade flowed.

Many trappers and mountain men lived peacefully and successfully with the Native Americans and Mexicans whose

RENDEZVOUS, 1837 The annual gathering of fur trappers and traders was a major event in the lives of the lonely men who made their livelihoods gathering furs. It was also a meeting of representatives of the many cultures that mingled in the Far West, among them Anglo-Americans, French Canadians, and those of Spanish origins. (© Walters Art Museum, Baltimore, USA/The Bridgeman Art Library)

lands they shared. Perhaps two-thirds of the white trappers married women of Indian or Spanish backgrounds while living in the West. But white-Indian relations were not always friendly or peaceful. Jedediah S. Smith, a trapper who became an Ashley partner, led a series of forays deep into Mexican territory that ended in disastrous battles with the Mojaves and other tribes. Four years after an 1827 expedition to Oregon in which sixteen members of his party of twenty had died, Smith set out for New Mexico and was killed by Comanches, who took the weapons he was carrying and sold them to Mexican settlers.

EASTERN IMAGES OF THE WEST

Americans in the East were only dimly aware of the world the trappers were entering and helping to reshape. Smith and others became the source of dramatic (and often exaggerated) popular stories. But few trappers themselves wrote of their lives.

More important in increasing eastern awareness of the West were explorers, many of them dispatched by the U.S. government with instructions to chart the territories they visited. In

STEPHEN
LONG'S
EXPEDITION

1819 and 1820, Stephen H. Long led nineteen soldiers on a journey up the Platte and South Platte Rivers through what is now Nebraska and eastern Colorado, and then returned eastward along the Arkansas River through what is

now Kansas. He wrote an influential report on his trip, including an assessment of the region's potential for future settlement and development that echoed the dismissive conclusions of Zebulon Pike fifteen years before. On the published map of his expedition, he labeled the Great Plains the "Great American Desert."

THE "ERA OF GOOD FEELINGS"

The expansion of the economy, the growth of white settlement and trade in the West, the creation of new states—all reflected the rising spirit of nationalism that was permeating the United States in the years following the War of 1812. That spirit found reflection for a time in the character of national politics.

THE END OF THE FIRST PARTY SYSTEM

Ever since 1800, the presidency seemed to have been the special possession of Virginians. After two terms in office, Jefferson chose his secretary of state, James Madison of Virginia, to succeed him, and after two more terms, Madison secured the presidential nomination for his secretary of state, James Monroe,

THE VIRGINIA
DYNASTY

also of Virginia. Many in the North were expressing impatience with the so-called Virginia Dynasty, but the Republicans had no difficulty electing their candidate in the listless campaign of

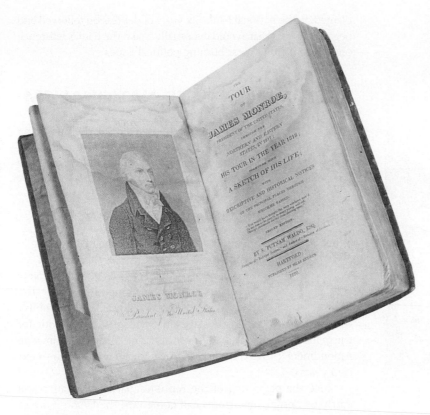

THE TRIUMPHANT TOUR OF JAMES MONROE After James Monroe's enormously successful tour of the northern and eastern states in 1818, midway through his first term as president, there was widespread self-congratulation through much of the United States for the apparent political unity that had gripped the nation. Only a few years earlier, the Northeast had been the bastion of Federalist Party opposition to the Republican governments of the early nineteenth century. At one point, some Federalist leaders had even proposed secession from the United States. But now a Virginia Republican president had been greeted as a hero in the former Federalist strongholds. This book, published in 1820 (when Monroe ran virtually unopposed for reelection), is an account of the president's triumphant tour and a short account of his life—an early version of the now-familiar campaign biography. (© Collection of David J. and Janice L. Frent)

1816. Monroe received 183 ballots in the electoral college; his Federalist opponent, Rufus King of New York, received only 34—from Massachusetts, Connecticut, and Delaware.

Monroe was sixty-one years old when he became president. In the course of his long career, he had served as a soldier in the Revolution, as a diplomat, and most recently as a cabinet officer. He entered office under what seemed to be remarkably favorable circumstances. With the decline of the Federalists, his party faced no serious opposition. With the conclusion of the War of 1812, the nation faced no important international threats. American politicians had dreamed since the first days of the republic of a time in which partisan divisions and factional disputes might come to an end. In the prosperous postwar years, Monroe attempted to use his office to realize that dream.

He made that clear, above all, in the selection of his cabinet. For secretary of state, he chose the New Englander and former Federalist John Quincy Adams. Jefferson, Madison, and Monroe had all served as secretary of state before becoming president; Adams, therefore, immediately became the heir apparent, suggesting that the "Virginia Dynasty" would soon come to an end. Speaker of the House Henry Clay declined an offer to be secretary of war, so Monroe named John C. Calhoun instead. In

his other appointments, too, Monroe took pains to include both northerners and southerners, easterners and westerners, Federalists and Republicans.

Soon after his inauguration, Monroe did what no president since Washington had done: he made a good-

MONROE'S GOODWILL TOUR

will tour through the country. In New England, so recently the scene of rabid Federalist discontent, he was greeted everywhere with enthusiastic demonstrations. The *Columbian Centinel*, a Federalist newspaper in Boston, commenting on the "Presidential Jubilee" in that city, observed that an "era of good feelings" had arrived. And on the surface, at least, the years of Monroe's presidency did appear to be an "era of good feelings." In 1820, Monroe was reelected without opposition. For all practical purposes, the Federalist Party had now ceased to exist.

JOHN QUINCY ADAMS AND FLORIDA

Like his father, the second president, John Quincy Adams had spent much of his life in diplomatic service. Even before becoming secretary of state, he had become one of the great diplomats in American history. He was also a committed nationalist, and he considered his most important task to be the promotion of American expansion.

Adams's first challenge as secretary of state was Florida. The United States had already annexed West Florida, but that claim remained in dispute. Most Americans believed the nation should gain possession of the entire peninsula. In 1817, Adams began negotiations with the Spanish minister, Luis de Onís, in hopes of resolving the dispute and gaining the entire territory for the United States.

In the meantime, events were taking their own course in Florida. Andrew Jackson, now in command of American troops along the Florida frontier, had orders from

THE SEMINOLE WAR

Secretary of War Calhoun to "adopt the necessary measures" to stop continuing raids on American territory by Seminole Indians south of the Florida border. Jackson used those orders as an excuse to invade Florida, seize the Spanish forts at St. Marks and Pensacola, and order the hanging of two British subjects on the charge of supplying and inciting the Indians. The operation became known as the Seminole War.

Instead of condemning Jackson's raid, Adams urged the government to assume responsibility for it. The United States, he told the Spanish, had the right under international law to defend itself against threats from across its borders. Since Spain was unwilling or unable to curb those threats, America had simply done what was necessary. Jackson's raid demonstrated to the Spanish that the United States could easily take Florida by force. Adams implied that the nation might consider doing so.

Onís realized, therefore, that he had little choice but to come to terms with the Americans. Under the provisions of

SEMINOLE DANCE This 1838 drawing by a U.S. military officer portrays a dance by Seminole Indians near Fort Butler in Florida. It was made in the midst of the prolonged Second Seminole War, which ended in 1842 with the removal of most of the tribe from Florida to reservations west of the Mississippi. (© Huntington Library (HM 4021)/SuperStock)

ADAMS-ONÍS TREATY the Adams-Onís Treaty of 1819, Spain ceded all of Florida to the United States and gave up as well its claim to territory north of the 42nd parallel in the Pacific Northwest. In return, the American government gave up its claims to Texas.

THE PANIC OF 1819

But the Monroe administration had little time to revel in its diplomatic successes, for the nation was falling victim to a serious economic crisis: the Panic of 1819. It followed a period of high foreign demand for American farm goods and thus of exceptionally high prices for American farmers (all as a result of the disruption of European agriculture caused by the Napoleonic Wars). The rising prices for farm goods had stimulated a land boom in the western United States. Fueled by speculative investments, land prices soared.

The availability of easy credit to settlers and speculators–from the government (under the land acts of 1800 and 1804), from state banks and wildcat banks, even for a time from the rechartered Bank of the United States–fueled the land boom. Beginning BOOM AND BUST in 1819, however, new management at the national bank began tightening credit, calling in loans, and foreclosing mortgages. This precipitated a series of failures by state banks. The result was a financial panic, which many Americans, particularly those in the West,

blamed on the national bank. Six years of depression followed and began a process that would eventually make the Bank's existence one of the nation's most burning political issues.

SECTIONALISM AND NATIONALISM

For a brief but alarming moment in 1819-1820, the increasing differences between the North and the South threatened the unity of the United States–until the Missouri Compromise temporarily averted a sectional crisis.

THE MISSOURI COMPROMISE

When Missouri applied for admission to the Union as a state in 1819, slavery was already well established there. Even so, TALLMADGE AMENDMENT Representative James Tallmadge Jr. of New York proposed an amendment to the Missouri statehood bill that would prohibit the further introduction of slaves into Missouri and provide for the gradual emancipation of those already there. The Tallmadge Amendment provoked a controversy that raged for the next two years.

Since the beginning of the republic, partly by chance and partly by design, new states had come into the Union more or less in pairs, one from the North, another from the South. In 1819, there were eleven free states and eleven slave states; the admission of Missouri as a free state would upset that balance and increase the political power of the North over the South. Hence the controversy over slavery and freedom in Missouri.

Complicating the Missouri question was the application of Maine (previously the northern part of Massachusetts) for MISSOURI COMPROMISE admission as a new (and free) state. Speaker of the House Henry Clay informed northern members that if they blocked Missouri from entering the Union as a slave state, southerners would block the admission of Maine. But Maine ultimately offered a way out of the impasse, as the Senate agreed to combine the Maine and Missouri proposals into a single bill. Maine would be admitted as a free state, Missouri as a slave state. Then Senator Jesse B. Thomas of Illinois proposed an amendment prohibiting slavery in the rest of the Louisiana Purchase territory north of the southern boundary of Missouri (the 36°30' parallel). Congress adopted the Thomas Amendment.

Nationalists in both North and South hailed this settlement–which became known as the Missouri Compromise–as a happy resolution of a danger to the Union. But the debate over the bill had revealed a strong undercurrent of sectionalism that was competing with–although at the moment failing to derail–the powerful tides of nationalism.

MARSHALL AND THE COURT

John Marshall served as chief justice of the United States from 1801 to 1835, and he dominated the Court more fully than anyone else before or since. More than anyone but the framers

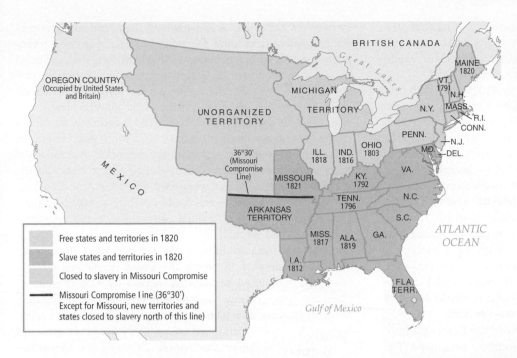

THE MISSOURI COMPROMISE, 1820 This map illustrates the way the Missouri Compromise proposed to settle the controversy over slavery in the new western territories of the United States. The compromise rested on the virtually simultaneous admission of Missouri and Maine to the Union, one a slave state and the other a free one. Note the red line extending beyond the southern border of Missouri, which in theory established a permanent boundary between areas in which slavery could be established and areas where it was banned.

• *What precipitated the Missouri Compromise?*

themselves, he molded the development of the Constitution: strengthening the judicial branch at the expense of the executive and legislative branches, increasing the power of the federal government at the expense of the states, and advancing the interests of the propertied and commercial classes.

Committed to promoting commerce, the Marshall Court staunchly defended the inviolability of contracts. In *Fletcher v. Peck* (1810), which arose out of a series of notorious land frauds in Georgia, Marshall held that a land grant was a valid contract and could not be repealed even if corruption was involved.

Dartmouth College v. Woodward (1819) further expanded the meaning of the contract clause of the Constitution. Having

DARTMOUTH COLLEGE V. WOODWARD

gained control of the New Hampshire state government, Republicans tried to revise Dartmouth College's charter (granted by King George III in 1769) to convert the private college into a state university. Daniel Webster, a Dartmouth graduate and brilliant orator, argued the college's case. The Dartmouth charter, he insisted, was a contract, protected by the same doctrine that the Court had already upheld in *Fletcher v. Peck*. Then, according to legend, he brought some of the justices to tears with an irrelevant passage that concluded: "It is, sir, . . . a small college. And yet there are those who love it." The Court ruled for Dartmouth. The decision placed important restrictions on the ability of state governments to control corporations.

In overturning the act of the legislature and the decisions of the New Hampshire courts, the justices also implicitly claimed for themselves the right to override the decisions of state courts. But advocates of states' rights, especially in the South, continued to challenge the Supreme Court's right to do so. In *Cohens v. Virginia* (1821), Marshall explicitly affirmed the constitutionality of federal review of state court decisions. The

JOHN MARSHALL The imposing figure in this image is John Marshall, the most important chief justice of the Supreme Court in American history. A former secretary of state, Marshall served as chief justice from 1801 until his death in 1835 at the age of eighty. Such was the power of his intellect and personality that he dominated his fellow justices throughout that period, regardless of their previous party affiliations or legal ideologies. Marshall established the independence of the Court, gave it a reputation for nonpartisan integrity, and established its powers, which were only vaguely defined by the Constitution. (© Archive Photos/Getty Images)

states had given up part of their sovereignty in ratifying the Constitution, he explained, and their courts must submit to federal jurisdiction; otherwise, the federal government would be powerless "at the feet of every state in the Union."

Meanwhile, in *McCulloch v. Maryland* (1819), Marshall confirmed the "implied powers" of Congress by upholding the

CONFIRMING IMPLIED POWERS

constitutionality of the Bank of the United States. The Bank had become so unpopular in the South and the West that several of the states tried to drive branches out of business by outright prohibition or by confiscatory taxes. This case presented two constitutional questions: Could Congress charter a bank? And if so, could individual states ban it or tax it? Daniel Webster, one of the Bank's attorneys, argued that establishing such an institution came within the "necessary and proper" clause of the Constitution and that the power to tax involved a "power to destroy." If the states could tax the Bank at all, Webster said, they could "tax it to death." Marshall adopted Webster's words in deciding for the Bank.

In the case of *Gibbons v. Ogden* (1824), the Court strengthened Congress's power to regulate interstate commerce. The state of New York had indirectly granted Aaron Ogden the business of carrying passengers across the river between New York and New Jersey. But Thomas Gibbons, with a license granted under an act of Congress, began competing with Ogden for the ferry traffic. Ogden brought suit against him and won in the New York courts. Gibbons appealed to the Supreme Court. The most important question facing the justices was whether Congress's power to give Gibbons a license to operate his ferry superseded the state of New York's power to grant Ogden a monopoly. Marshall claimed that the power of Congress to regulate interstate commerce (which, he said, included navigation) was "complete in itself" and might be "exercised to its utmost extent." Ogden's state-granted monopoly, therefore, was void.

The decisions of the Marshall Court established the primacy of the federal government over the states in regulating the

ESTABLISHING FEDERAL PRIMACY

economy and opened the way for an increased federal role in promoting economic growth. They protected corporations and other private economic institutions from local government interference. They were, in short, highly nationalistic decisions, designed to promote the growth of a strong, unified, and economically developed United States.

THE COURT AND THE TRIBES

The nationalist inclinations of the Marshall Court were visible as well in a series of decisions concerning the legal status of Indian tribes within the United States. But these decisions did not simply affirm the supremacy of the United States; they also carved out a distinctive position for Native Americans within the constitutional structure.

The first of the crucial Indian decisions was in the case of *Johnson v. McIntosh* (1823). Leaders of the Illinois and

Pinakeshaw tribes had sold parcels of their land to a group of white settlers (including Johnson) but later signed a treaty with the federal government ceding territory that included those same parcels to the United States. The government proceeded to grant homestead rights to new white settlers (among them McIntosh) on the land claimed by Johnson. The Court was asked to decide which claim had precedence. Marshall's ruling, not surprisingly, favored the United States. But in explaining it, he offered a preliminary definition of the place of Indians within the nation. The tribes had a basic right to their tribal lands, he said, that preceded all other American law. Individual American citizens could not buy or take land from the tribes; only the federal government–the supreme authority–could do that.

Even more important was the Court's 1832 decision in *Worcester v. Georgia*, in which the Court invalidated Georgia laws that attempted to regulate access by U.S. citizens to Cherokee country. Only the federal government could do that, Marshall claimed, thus taking another important step in consol-

WORCESTER V. GEORGIA

idating federal authority over the states (and over the tribes). In doing so, he further defined the nature of the Indian nations. The tribes, he explained, were sovereign entities in much the same way Georgia was a sovereign entity– "distinct political communities, having territorial boundaries within which their authority is exclusive." In defending the power of the federal government, he was also affirming, indeed expanding, the rights of the tribes to remain free from the authority of state governments.

The Marshall decisions, therefore, did what the Constitution itself had not done: they defined a place for Indian tribes within the American political system. The tribes had basic property rights. They were sovereign entities not subject to the authority of state governments. But the federal government, like a "guardian" governing its "ward," had ultimate authority over tribal affairs–even if that authority was, according to the Court, limited by the government's obligation to protect Indian welfare. These provisions were seldom enough to defend Indians from the steady westward march of white civilization, but they formed the basis of what few legal protections they had.

THE LATIN AMERICAN REVOLUTION AND THE MONROE DOCTRINE

Americans looking southward in the years following the War of 1812 beheld a gigantic spectacle: the Spanish Empire in its death

REVOLUTION IN LATIN AMERICA

throes, a whole continent in revolt, new nations in the making. Already the United States had developed a profitable trade with Latin America and was rivaling Great Britain as the principal trading nation there. Many Americans believed the success of the anti-Spanish revolutions would further strengthen America's position in the region.

In 1815, the United States proclaimed neutrality in the wars between Spain and its rebellious colonies, implying a partial recognition of the rebels' status as nations. Moreover, the United States sold ships and supplies to the revolutionaries, a clear indication that it was not genuinely neutral but was trying to help the insurgents. Finally, in 1822, President Monroe established diplomatic relations with five new nations–La Plata (later Argentina), Chile, Peru, Colombia, and Mexico–making the United States the first country to recognize them.

In 1823, Monroe went further and announced a policy that would ultimately be known (beginning some thirty years later) as the "Monroe Doctrine," even though it was primarily the

THE MONROE DOCTRINE

work of John Quincy Adams. "The American continents," Monroe declared, ". . . are henceforth not to be considered as subjects for future colonization by any European powers." The United States would consider any foreign challenge to the sovereignty of existing American nations an unfriendly act. At the same time, he proclaimed, "Our policy in regard to Europe . . . is not to interfere in the internal concerns of any of its powers."

The Monroe Doctrine emerged directly out of America's relations with Europe in the 1820s. Many Americans feared that

AMERICAN FEARS

Spain's European allies (notably France) would assist Spain in an effort to retake its lost empire. Even more troubling to Adams (and many other Americans) was the fear that Great Britain had designs on Cuba. Adams wanted to keep Cuba in Spanish hands until it fell (as he believed it ultimately would) to the Americans.

The Monroe Doctrine had few immediate effects, but it was important as an expression of the growing spirit of nationalism in the United States in the 1820s. And it established the idea of the United States as the dominant power in the Western Hemisphere.

THE MONROE DOCTRINE On December 2, 1823, President James Monroe delivered his seventh annual message to Congress. In it, he outlined an important part of his foreign policy that subsequently became known as the "Monroe Doctrine." Monroe declared that henceforth any attempt by a European power to colonize any part of the "American continents" would be viewed as an "unfriendly act" toward the United States. (© Everett Collection Historical/Alamy)

THE REVIVAL OF OPPOSITION

After 1816, the Federalist Party offered no presidential candidate and soon ceased to exist as a national political force. The Republican Party (which considered itself not a party but an organization representing the whole of the population) was the only organized force in national politics.

By the late 1820s, however, partisan divisions were emerging once again. In some respects, the division mirrored the schism that had produced the first party system in the 1790s.

NEW POLITICAL DIVISIONS

The Republicans had in many ways come to resemble the early Federalist regimes in their promotion of economic growth and centralization. And the opposition, like the opposition in the 1790s, objected to the federal government's expanding role in the economy. There was, however, a crucial difference. At the

CHEROKEE LEADER SEQUOYAH Sequoyah (who also used the name George Guess) was a mixed-blood Cherokee who translated his tribe's language into writing through an elaborate syllabary (equivalent to an alphabet) of his own invention, pictured here. He opposed Indian assimilation into white society and saw the preservation of the Cherokee language as a way to protect the culture of his tribe. He moved to Arkansas in the 1820s and became a chief of the western Cherokee tribes. (© Hulton Archive/Getty Images)

beginning of the century, the opponents of centralization had also often been opponents of economic growth. Now, in the 1820s, the controversy involved not whether but how the nation should continue to expand.

THE "CORRUPT BARGAIN"

Until 1820, when the Federalist Party effectively ceased operations and James Monroe ran for reelection unopposed, presidential candidates were nominated by caucuses of the two parties in Congress. But in the presidential election of 1824, "King Caucus" was overthrown. The Republican caucus nominated William H. Crawford of Georgia, the secretary of the treasury and the favorite of the extreme states' rights faction of the party. But other candidates received nominations from state legislatures and won endorsements from irregular mass meetings throughout the country.

END OF THE CAUCUS SYSTEM

One of them was Secretary of State John Quincy Adams, who held the office that was the traditional stepping-stone to the presidency. But as he himself ruefully understood, he was a man of cold and forbidding manners, with little popular appeal. Another contender was Henry Clay, the Speaker of the House. He had a devoted personal following and a definite and coherent program: the "American System," which proposed creating a great home market for factory and farm producers by raising the protective tariff, strengthening the national bank, and financing internal improvements. Andrew Jackson, the fourth major candidate, had no significant political record–even though he had served briefly as a representative in Congress and was now a new member of the U.S. Senate. But he was a military hero and had the help of shrewd political allies from his home state of Tennessee.

Jackson received more popular and electoral votes than any other candidate, but not a majority. He had 99 electoral votes to Adams's 84, Crawford's 41, and Clay's 37. The Twelfth Amendment to the Constitution (passed in the aftermath of the contested 1800 election) required the House of Representatives to choose among the three candidates with the largest numbers of electoral votes. Crawford was by then seriously ill and not a plausible candidate. Clay was out of the running, but he was in a strong position to influence the result.

ELECTION OF 1824

Jackson was Clay's most formidable political rival in the West, so Clay supported Adams, in part because, alone among the candidates, Adams was an ardent nationalist and a likely supporter of the American System. With Clay's endorsement, Adams won election in the House.

The Jacksonians believed their large popular and electoral pluralities entitled their candidate to the presidency, and they were enraged when he lost. But they grew angrier still when Adams named Clay his secretary of state. The State Department was the well-established route to the presidency, and Adams thus appeared to be naming Clay as his own successor. The outrage the Jacksonians expressed at what they called a "corrupt bargain" haunted Adams throughout his presidency.

JOHN QUINCY ADAMS This photograph of the former president was taken shortly before his death in 1848 at the age of eighty—almost twenty years after he had left the White House—when he was serving as a congressman from Massachusetts. During his years as president, he was—as he had been throughout his life—an intensely disciplined and hardworking man. He rose at four in the morning and made a long entry in his diary for the previous day. He wrote so much that his right hand at times became paralyzed with writer's cramp, so he taught himself to write with his left hand as well. (© Hulton Archive/Getty Images)

THE SECOND PRESIDENT ADAMS

Throughout Adams's term in the White House, the political bitterness arising from the "corrupt bargain" charges thoroughly frustrated his policies. Adams proposed an ambitiously nationalist program reminiscent of Clay's American System. But Jacksonians in Congress blocked most of it.

Adams also experienced diplomatic frustrations. He appointed delegates to an international conference that the Venezuelan liberator, Simón Bolívar, had called in Panama in 1826. But Haiti was one of the participating nations, and southerners in Congress opposed the idea of white Americans mingling with the black delegates. Congress delayed approving the Panama mission so long that the American delegation did not arrive until after the conference was over.

Adams also lost a contest with the state of Georgia, which wished to remove the remaining Creek and Cherokee Indians from the state to gain additional soil for cotton planters. The

U.S. government, in a 1791 treaty, had guaranteed that land to the Creeks; but in 1825, white Georgians had extracted a new treaty from William McIntosh, the leader of one faction in the tribe and a longtime advocate of Indian cooperation with the United States. Adams believed the new treaty had no legal force, since McIntosh clearly did not represent the wishes of the tribe; and he refused to enforce the treaty, setting up a direct conflict between the president and the state. The governor of Georgia defied the president and proceeded with plans for Indian removal. Adams found no way to stop him.

Even more damaging to the administration was its support for a new tariff on imported goods in 1828. This measure orig-

TARIFF OF ABOMINATIONS

inated with the demands of Massachusetts and Rhode Island woolen manufacturers, who complained that the British were dumping textiles on the American market at artificially low prices. But to win support from middle and western states, the administration had to accept duties on other items. In the process, it antagonized the original New England supporters of the bill; the benefits of protecting their manufactured goods from foreign competition now had to be weighed against the prospects of having to pay more for raw materials. Adams signed the bill, earning the animosity of southerners, who cursed it as the "tariff of abominations."

JACKSON TRIUMPHANT

By the time of the 1828 presidential election, a new two-party system had begun to emerge out of the divisions among the Republicans. On one side stood the supporters of John Quincy Adams, who called themselves the National Republicans and who supported the economic nationalism of the preceding years. Opposing them were the followers of Andrew Jackson, who took the name Democratic Republicans and who called for an assault on privilege and a widening of opportunity. Adams attracted the support of most of the remaining Federalists; Jackson appealed to a broad coalition that opposed the "economic aristocracy."

But issues seemed to count for little in the end, as the campaign degenerated into a war of personal invective. The Jacksonians charged that Adams as president had been guilty of gross waste and extravagance and had used public funds to buy gambling devices (a chess set and a billiard table) for the White House. Adams's supporters hurled even worse accusations at Jackson. They called him a murderer and distributed a "coffin handbill," which listed, within coffin-shaped outlines, the names of militiamen whom Jackson was said to have shot in cold blood during the War of 1812. (The men had been

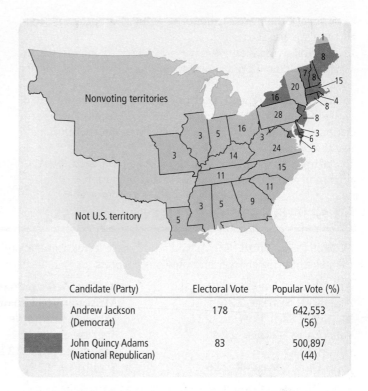

THE ELECTION OF 1828 As this map shows, Andrew Jackson's victory over John Quincy Adams was one of the most decisive in American history for a challenger facing an incumbent president.

• *What accounts for this decisive repudiation of President Adams?*

Candidate (Party)	Electoral Vote	Popular Vote (%)
Andrew Jackson (Democrat)	178	642,553 (56)
John Quincy Adams (National Republican)	83	500,897 (44)

deserters who were legally executed after sentence by a court-martial.) And they called his wife a bigamist. Jackson had married his beloved Rachel at a time when the pair incorrectly believed her first husband had divorced her. (When Jackson's wife first read of the accusations against her shortly after the election, she collapsed and, a few weeks later, died; not without reason, Jackson blamed his opponents for her death.)

Jackson's victory was decisive, but sectional. He won 56 percent of the popular vote and an electoral majority of 178

JACKSON TRIUMPHAN

votes to 83. Adams swept virtually all of New England and showed significant strength in the mid-Atlantic region. Nevertheless, the Jacksonians considered their victory as complete and as important as Jefferson's in 1800. Once again, the forces of privilege had been driven from Washington. Once again, a champion of democracy would occupy the White House and restore liberty to the people and to the economy. America had entered, some Jacksonians claimed, a new era of democracy, the "age of the common man."

AP CONNECTING THEMES

Chapter 8 continued the discussion of the growth of American nationalism during the period. The chapter also examined the exploration of the Far West in making the American people more aware of the extent and character of the newly added territories. You should, in conjunction with Chapter 7, continue to look at the factors that led to the dissolution of the

first American party system and how intensifying regional differences played a role in its demise. Particularly important is the discussion of the Missouri Compromise and the broader issue of the expansion of slavery into the new territories. Pay close attention to foreign policy of the time period—focusing on territorial acquisition, resolution of outstanding problems with Great Britain, and attempts to reduce European influence in Latin America.

The following themes have a heightened importance in Chapter 8. You should now be able to do the following for each listed theme:

Work, Exchange and Technology: Analyze the impact of the First Industrial Revolution and the development of a national market economy on the economic, political, and social aspects of American life.

Peopling: Analyze the factors that encouraged western migration and the consequences of that migration.

Politics and Power: Explain the issues involved in the dissolution of the first American party system and how those issues were tied to distinct regional differences in the United States.

America and the World: Explain attempts the United States made to resolve lingering issues with foreign countries and to extend its influence into Latin America.

Environment and Geography: Explain the push and pull factors that led Americans to migrate westward.

Ideas, Beliefs, and Culture: Explain the degree to which American nationalism conflicted with American regionalism.

AP SUGGESTED STUDY

PEOPLE/PLACES/EVENTS As you study these items, think about how they demonstrate or relate to key concepts and historical themes from this chapter and previous chapters.

ADAMS-ONÍS TREATY 222
AMERICAN SYSTEM 226
FRANCIS CABOT LOWELL 216
GIBBONS VS. OGDEN 224
HENRY CLAY 226
JOHN QUINCY ADAMS 226

MCCULLOCH VS. MARYLAND 224
MISSOURI COMPROMISE 222
MONROE DOCTRINE 225
SECTIONALISM 222
SEMINOLE WAR 221
SEQUOYAH 225

STEPHEN H. LONG 220
TALLMADGE AMENDMENT 222
TRANSPORTATION IMPROVEMENTS
WORCESTER VS. GEORGIA 224

AP TEST PRACTICE

Questions assume cumulative content knowledge from this chapter and previous chapters.

MULTIPLE CHOICE Use the painting on page 216 and your knowledge of U.S. history to answer questions 1–2.

1. Developments such as that depicted in the painting affected the American economy in the early 1800s by

   (A) decreasing the desire for imported goods in America

   (B) sharply increasing labor costs

   (C) growing the desire and need for access to domestic and international markets

   (D) restricting American shipping overseas

2. What important national political debate recurred in the early 1800s regarding economic growth in relation to developments like that depicted in the painting?

   (A) The role of women in the workforce

   (B) The breaking of land treaties with Native American groups

   (C) The power of the national government to control the currency

   (D) The question of the national government's constitutional powers

SHORT ANSWER Use your knowledge of U.S. history to answer questions 3–4.

3. Answer a, b, and c.

   a) Briefly explain ONE example of how the U.S. Supreme Court in the early 1800s asserted federal power over that of states.

   b) Briefly explain a SECOND example of how the U.S. Supreme Court in the early 1800s asserted federal power over that of states.

   c) Briefly explain ONE example of a how the U.S. Supreme Court in the early 1800s defined national sovereignty over Native Americans.

4. Answer a, b, and c.

   a) Briefly explain ONE example of dramatic regional economic growth in the early 1800s.

   b) Briefly explain a SECOND example of dramatic regional economic growth in the early 1800s.

   c) Briefly explain ONE example of a Congressional action and the regional responses to these actions.

LONG ESSAY Develop a thoughtful and thorough historical argument that answers the question below. Begin your essay with a thesis statement and support it with relevant historical evidence.

5. Some historians have described the decade following 1812 as the "Era of Good Feelings." Support, modify, or refute this interpretation, providing specific evidence to justify your answer.

9 ⎪ JACKSONIAN AMERICA

THE VERDICT OF THE PEOPLE (1855), BY GEORGE CALEB BINGHAM This scene of an election-day gathering is peopled almost entirely by white men. Women and African Americans were barred from voting, but political rights expanded substantially in the 1830s and 1840s among white males.
(© Courtesy of The Saint Louis Art Museum)

AP

HISTORICAL THINKING

1. **Historical Argumentation** To what degree and in what ways did the political system become more democratic during the 1820s to the 1840s?

2. **Contextualization** Explain how ideas like those of Henry Clay's American System contributed to increased sectional tension.

3. **Comparison** Compare and contrast the beliefs of the Democratic Party with those of the Whig Party.

4. **Patterns of Continuity and Change over Time** To what degree and in what ways was the Whig Party reflective of the old Federalist Party, in terms of agenda and constituency?

5. **Appropriate Use of Relevant Historical Evidence** To what degree and in what ways was the power of the presidency increased between 1828 and 1836?

6. **Interpretation** To what degree did the actions of Andrew Jackson during his presidency between 1828 and 1836 threaten separation of powers among the three branches of the federal government?

Key Concept Correlations

Analyze the ways the historical developments you learn about in this chapter connect to the following AP Key Concepts.

4.1 The United States developed the world's first modern mass democracy and celebrated a new national culture, while Americans sought to define the nation's democratic ideals and to reform its institutions to match them.

4.2 Developments in technology, agriculture, and commerce precipitated profound changes in U.S. settlement patterns, regional identities, gender and family relations, political power, and distribution of consumer goods.

4.3 U.S. interest in increasing foreign trade, expanding its national borders, and isolating itself from European conflicts shaped the nation's foreign policy and spurred government and private initiatives.

5.1 The United States became more connected with the world as it pursued an expansionist foreign policy in the Western Hemisphere and emerged as the destination for many migrants from other countries.

Thematic Learning Objectives

POL-2, 3, 5, 6; ID-1, 2, 5, 6; WXT-2; CUL-2, 5; WOR-2, 5, 6; WXT-2, 7; PEO-2, 3; ENV-3, 4

AP CONNECTING CONCEPTS

CHAPTER 9 discusses rise of democracy during the Jacksonian Era, focusing on how citizens were encouraged to participate in the democratic process. You should focus on the rise of the Second American Party System and the beliefs of both the Whigs and the Democrats. Also, examine the ideas of Henry Clay's American System and its impact on national economic development as well as its effects of intensifying regional differences and challenges to federal authority. Chapter 9 also explains in depth the increased intensity of sectional debate over the power of the federal government versus states' rights. Be aware of the impact that Andrew Jackson had on the concept of the separation of powers within the federal government. As you read, evaluate the following concepts:

- The Jacksonian Era saw the emergence of the Second American Party System, with the Democrats and Whigs being the two major parties.
- The political system became much more democratic during the Jacksonian Era.
- Debate over the power of the federal government versus states' rights flared into a direct challenge to federal authority economically and politically.
- The American System of Henry Clay sought to establish a national market economy, but resulted in increased sectional tension.
- In their desire for land, whites continued to encroach into American Indian lands, which ultimately led to the removal of eastern tribes, including the "five civilized tribes," to west of the Mississippi River.
- Improved transportation systems allowed for greater access to natural resources, markets, and western lands.
- Regional economic and social differences led to greater sectional controversy.

THE RISE OF MASS POLITICS

On March 4, 1829, an unprecedented throng–thousands of Americans from all regions of the country, including farmers, laborers, and others of modest social rank–crowded before the Capitol in Washington, D.C., to witness the inauguration of Andrew Jackson. After the ceremonies, the boisterous crowd poured down Pennsylvania Avenue, following their hero to the White House. There, at a public reception open to all, they filled the state rooms to overflowing, trampling one another, soiling the carpets, ruining elegantly upholstered sofas and chairs in their eagerness to shake the new president's hand. "It was a proud day for the people," wrote Amos Kendall, one of Jackson's closest political associates. "General Jackson is their own President." To other observers, however, the scene was less appealing. Justice of the Supreme Court Joseph Story, a friend and colleague of John Marshall, looked on the inaugural levee, as it was called, and remarked with disgust: "The reign of King 'Mob' seems triumphant."

JACKSON'S INAUGURATION

THE EMERGENCE OF ANDREW JACKSON

Jackson, one of the most powerful presidents of the nineteenth century, was born in 1767 to modest parents. They had moved from Ireland two years before Andrew was born in a small village in the Carolinas. At the age of thirteen, he was captured by the British during the American Revolution. When Jackson refused to clean the boots of a British officer, the officer cut Jackson with a sword, leaving him with scars and an enduring hatred of the British. As he became older, Jackson received only sporadic education and worked in various shops and on farms. As a young man, he studied law and was admitted to the bar.

Most of Jackson's early legal work involved disputed land-claims of which he soon tired. He was elected as a delegate to the Tennessee constitutional convention in 1796 and, later that same year, became a U.S. congressman. In 1797, he went on to become a U.S. senator but resigned within a year. In 1798, he was appointed a judge of the Tennessee Supreme Court, a position he held until 1804.

Gradually, Jackson prospered as planter and merchant. He also bought slaves to help his growing plantation. In 1804, he acquired an elegant home, the Hermitage, a large plantation in Davidson County, near Nashville. In time, he had one of the largest plantations in the state with up to 300 slaves.

Jackson joined the Tennessee militia in 1801 and in the next year was elected major general. He fought Indians in Alabama and Georgia. In the War of 1812, he fought against Britain. When the British threatened New Orleans, Jackson took command. In the Battle of New Orleans, his soldiers won a decisive victory over the British that ensured New Orleans would be part of the United States. He developed the reputation for being as "tough as old hickory" and thus earned the nickname "Old Hickory." Jackson left the war with many people calling for him to run for president of the United States.

EXPANDING DEMOCRACY

What some have called the "age of Jackson" did not much advance the cause of economic equality. The distribution of wealth and property in America was little different at the end of the Jacksonian era than it had been at the start. But it did mark a transformation of American politics that widely extended to new groups the right to vote.

Until the 1820s, relatively few Americans had been permitted to vote. Most states restricted the franchise to white males

BROADENING THE FRANCHISE who were property owners or taxpayers or both, effectively barring an enormous number of the less affluent from the voting rolls. But beginning even before Jackson's election, the rules governing voting began to expand. Changes came first in Ohio and other new states of the West, which, on joining the Union, adopted constitutions that guaranteed all adult white males the right to vote and gave all voters the right to hold public office. Older states, concerned about the loss of their population to the West and thinking that extending the franchise might encourage some residents to stay, began to grant similar political rights to their citizens, dropping or reducing their property ownership or taxpaying requirements. Eventually, every state democratized its electorate to some degree, although some much later and less fully than others.

Change provoked resistance, and at times the democratic trend fell short of the aims of the radical reformers, as when Massachusetts held its constitutional convention in 1820. Reform-minded delegates complained that in the Massachusetts government the rich were better represented than the poor, both because of restrictions on voting and officeholding and because of a peculiar system by which members of the state senate represented property rather than simply people. But Daniel Webster, one of the conservative delegates, opposed democratic changes on the grounds that "power naturally and necessarily follows property" and that "property as such should have its weight and influence in political arrangement." Webster and the rest of the conservatives could not prevent the reform of the rules for representation in the state senate; nor could they prevent elimination of the property requirement

ANDREW JACKSON This stern portrait suggests something of the fierce determination that characterized Andrew Jackson's military and political careers. Shattered by the death of his wife a few weeks after his election as president—a death he blamed (not without reason) on the attacks his political opponents had leveled at her—he entered office with a steely determination to live by his own principles and give no quarter to his adversaries. (© Collection of the New-York Historical Society, USA/The Bridgeman Art Library)

for voting. But, to the dismay of the radicals, the new constitution required that every voter be a taxpayer and that the governor be the owner of considerable real estate.

More often, however, the forces of democratization prevailed in the states. In the New York convention of 1821, for example, conservatives led by James Kent insisted that a taxpaying requirement for suffrage was not enough and that, at least in the election of state senators, the property qualification should survive. But reformers, citing the Declaration of Independence, maintained that life, liberty, and the pursuit of happiness, not property, were the main concerns of society and government. The property qualification was abolished.

The wave of state reforms was generally peaceful, but in Rhode Island democratization efforts created considerable instability. The Rhode Island constitution (still basically the old colonial charter) barred more than half the adult males of the state from voting. The conservative legislature, chosen by this restricted electorate, consistently blocked all efforts at reform. In 1840, the lawyer and activist Thomas W. Dorr and a group of

THE DORR REBELLION his followers formed a "People's Party," held a convention, drafted a new constitution, and submitted it to a popular vote. It was overwhelmingly approved. The existing legislature, however,

Percentage

26.9 · 57.6 · 55.4 · 57.8 · 80.2 · 78.9 · 72.7 · 69.6 · 78.9 · 81.2

1824 1828 1832 1836 1840 1844 1848 1852 1856 1860
Year

PARTICIPATION IN PRESIDENTIAL ELECTIONS, 1824–1860 This chart reveals the remarkable increase in popular participation in presidential elections in the years after 1824. Participation almost doubled between 1824 and 1828, and it increased substantially again beginning in 1840 and continuing through and beyond the Civil War.

• *What accounts for this dramatic expansion of the electorate? Who remained outside the voting population in these years?*

refused to accept the Dorr document and submitted a new constitution of its own to the voters. It was narrowly defeated. The Dorrites, in the meantime, had begun to set up a new government, under their own constitution, with Dorr as governor; and so, in 1842, two governments were claiming legitimacy in Rhode Island. The old state government proclaimed that Dorr and his followers were rebels and began to imprison them. Meanwhile, the Dorrites made a brief and ineffectual effort to capture the state arsenal. The Dorr Rebellion, as it was known, quickly failed. Dorr himself surrendered and was briefly imprisoned. But the episode helped pressure the old guard to draft a new constitution, which greatly expanded the suffrage.

The democratization process was far from complete. In much of the South, election laws continued to favor the planters and politicians of the older counties and to limit the influence of newly settled western areas. Slaves, of course, were disenfranchised by definition; they were not considered citizens and were believed to have no legal or political rights. Free blacks could vote nowhere in the South and hardly anywhere in the North. Pennsylvania, in fact, amended its state constitution in 1838 to strip African Americans of the right to vote they had previously enjoyed. In no state could women vote. Nowhere was the ballot secret, and often voters had to cast a spoken vote rather than a written one, which meant that political bosses could, and often did, bribe and intimidate them.

THE DORR REBELLION The democratic sentiments that swept much of the nation in the 1830s and 1840s led to, among many other events, the Dorr Rebellion (as its opponents termed it) in Rhode Island. Thomas Dorr was one of many Rhode Islanders who denounced the state's constitution, which limited voting rights to a small group of property owners known as "freeholders." (Encyclopaedia Britannica/© UIG/The Bridgeman Art Library)

Despite the persisting limitations, however, the number of voters increased far more rapidly than did the population as a whole. Indeed, one of the most striking political trends of the early nineteenth century was the change in the method of choosing presidential electors and the dramatic increase in popular participation in the process. In 1800, the legislature had chosen the presidential electors in ten of the states, and the people in only six. By 1828, electors were chosen by popular vote in every state but South Carolina. In the presidential election of 1824, less than 27 percent of adult white males had voted. In the election of 1828, the figure rose to 58 percent, and in 1840 to 80 percent.

DEMOCRATIC REFORMS

TOCQUEVILLE AND *DEMOCRACY IN AMERICA*

The rapid growth of the electorate—and the emergence of political parties—were among the most striking events of the early nineteenth century. As the right to vote spread widely in these years, it came to be the mark of freedom and democracy. One of the most important commentaries on this extraordinary moment in American life was a book by a French aristocrat, Alexis de Tocqueville. He spent two years in the United States in the 1830s watching the dramatic political changes in the age of

... he first who attracts the eye, the first in enlightenment, in power and in happiness, is the white man, the European, man par excellence; below him appear the Negro and the Indian. These two unfortunate races have neither birth, nor face, nor language, nor mores in common; only their misfortunes look alike. Both occupy an equally inferior position in the country that they inhabit; both experience the effects of tyranny; and if their miseries are different, they can accuse the same author for them.

Tocqueville's book helped spread the idea of American democracy into France and other European nations. Only later did it become widely read and studied in the United States as a remarkable portrait of the emerging democracy of the United States.

THE LEGITIMIZATION OF PARTY

The high level of voter participation was only partly the result of an expanded electorate. It was also the result of a growing interest in politics and a strengthening of party organization and, perhaps equally important, party loyalty. Although party competition was part of American politics almost from the beginning of the republic, acceptance of the idea of party was not. For more than thirty years, most Americans who had opinions about the nature of government considered parties evils to be avoided and thought the nation should seek a broad consensus in which permanent factional lines would not exist. But in the 1820s and 1830s, those assumptions gave way to a new view: that permanent, institutionalized parties were a desirable part of the political process, that indeed they were essential to democracy.

The elevation of the idea of party occurred first at the state level, most prominently in New York State. There Martin Van Buren led a dissident political faction (known as the "Bucktails" or the "Albany Regency"). In the years after the War of 1812, this group began to challenge the established political leadership–led by the aristocratic governor De Witt Clinton–that had dominated the state for years. Factional rivalries were not new, of course. But the nature of Van Buren's challenge was. Refuting the traditional view of a political party as undemocratic, they argued that only an institutionalized party, based in the populace at large, could ensure genuine democracy. The alternative was the sort of closed elite that Clinton had created. In the new kind of party the Bucktails proposed, ideological commitments would be less important than loyalty to the party itself. Preservation of the party as an institution–through the use of favors, rewards, and patronage–would be the principal goal of the leadership. Above all, for a party to survive, it must have a permanent opposition. Competing parties would give each political faction a sense of purpose; they would force politicians to remain continually attuned to the will of the people; and they would check and balance each other in much the same way that the different branches of government checked and balanced one another.

By the late 1820s, this new idea of party was spreading beyond New York. The election of Jackson in 1828, the result of a popular movement that seemed to stand apart from the usual political elites, seemed further to legitimize the idea of

ALEXIS DE TOCQUEVILLE Renowned French printmaker and lithographer Honoré Daumier created this caricature of Alexis de Tocqueville in 1849. Tocqueville, also a Frenchman, traveled throughout the United States for two years in the 1830s witnessing the extraordinary growth of the U.S. electorate. In his famous book *Democracy in America*, he examined and analyzed the political, cultural, and social life of the United States. His work strongly influenced how many in France and the rest of Europe would understand the young country's experience of its emerging democracy. (© Sterling and Francine Clark Art Institute, Williamstown, Massachusetts, USA/The Bridgeman Art Library)

Andrew Jackson. The French government had requested him to make a study of American prisons, which were thought to be more humane and effective institutions than prisons in Europe. But Tocqueville quickly went far beyond the study of prisons and wrote a classic study of American life, titled *Democracy in America*. Tocqueville examined not just the politics of the United States, but also the daily lives of many groups of Americans and their cultures, their associations, and their visions of democracy. In France in the early decades of the nineteenth century, the fruits of democracy were largely restricted to landowners and aristocrats. But Tocqueville recognized that traditional aristocracies were rapidly fading in America and that new elites could rise and fall no matter what their backgrounds.

Tocqueville also realized that the rising democracy of America had many limits. Democracy was a powerful, visible force in the lives of most white men. Few women could vote, although some shared the democratic ethos through their families. For many other Americans, democracy was a distant hope. Tocqueville wrote of the limits of equality and democracy:

THE SECOND PARTY SYSTEM

THE "AGE OF JACKSON"

TO many Americans in the 1820s and 1830s, Andrew Jackson was a champion of democracy, a symbol of a spirit of anti-elitism and egalitarianism that was sweeping American life. In the twentieth and twenty-first centuries, however, historians have disagreed sharply not only in their assessments of Jackson himself, but also in their portrayal of American society in his era.

The "progressive" historians of the early twentieth century tended to see the politics of Jackson and his supporters as a forerunner of their own generation's battles against economic privilege and political corruption. Frederick Jackson Turner encouraged scholars to see Jacksonianism as the product of the democratic West: a protest by the people of the frontier against the conservative aristocracy of the East, which they believed restricted their own freedom and opportunity. Jackson represented those who wanted to make government responsive to the will of the people rather than to the power of special interests. The culmination of this progressive interpretation of Jacksonianism was the publication in 1945 of Arthur M. Schlesinger Jr.'s *The Age of Jackson*. Less interested in the regional basis of Jacksonianism than Turner's disciples had been, Schlesinger argued that Jacksonian democracy was an effort "to control the power of the capitalist groups, mainly Eastern, for the benefit of non-capitalist groups, farmers and laboring men, East, West, and South." He portrayed Jacksonianism as an early version of modern reform efforts to "restrain the power of the business community."

Richard Hofstadter, in an influential essay in his 1948 book *The American Political Tradition*, sharply disagreed. Jackson, he argued, was the spokesman of rising entrepreneurs—aspiring businessmen who saw the road to opportunity blocked by the monopolistic power of eastern

(The Library of Congress (3g06446u))

party as a popular, democratic institution. "Parties of some sort must exist," said a New York newspaper. "'Tis in the nature and genius of our government." Finally, in the 1830s, a fully formed two-party system began to operate at the national level, with each party committed to its own existence as an institution and willing to accept the legitimacy of its opposition. The anti-Jackson forces began to call themselves Whigs. Jackson's followers called themselves Democrats (no longer Democratic Republicans), thus giving a permanent name to what is now the nation's oldest political party.

"PRESIDENT OF THE COMMON MAN"

Unlike Thomas Jefferson, Jackson was no democratic philosopher. The Democratic Party, much less than Jefferson's Republicans, embraced no clear or uniform ideological position. But Jackson himself did embrace a distinct, if simple, theory of democracy. It should offer "equal protection and equal benefits" to all its white male citizens and favor no region or class over another. In practice, that meant an assault on what Jackson and his associates considered the citadels of the eastern aristocracy and an effort to extend opportunities to the rising classes of the West and the South. It also meant a firm commitment to the continuing subjugation of African Americans and Indians (and, although for different reasons, women), for the Jacksonians believed that only by keeping these "dangerous" elements from

the body politic could the white-male democracy they valued be preserved.

Jackson's first targets were the entrenched officeholders in the federal government, many of whom had been in place for a generation or more. Official duties, he believed, could be made "so plain and simple that men of intelligence may readily qualify themselves for their performance." Offices belonged to the people, he argued, not to the entrenched officeholders. Or, as one of his henchmen, William L. Marcy of New York, cynically put it, "To the victors belong the spoils."

In the end, Jackson removed a total of no more than one-fifth of the federal officeholders during his eight years in office, many **THE SPOILS SYSTEM** of them less for partisan reasons than because they had misused government funds or engaged in other corruption. Proportionally, Jackson dismissed no more jobholders than Jefferson had dismissed during his presidency. But by embracing the philosophy of the "spoils system," a system already well entrenched in a number of state governments, the Jackson administration helped make the right of elected officials to appoint their own followers to public office an established feature of American politics.

Jackson's supporters also worked to transform the process by which presidential candidates won their party's nomination. They had long resented the congressional caucus, a process they believed favored entrenched elites. Jackson himself had avoided the caucus process in 1828. In 1832, the aristocrats. The Jacksonian leaders were less sympathetic to the aspirations of those below them than they were to the destruction of obstacles to their own success. Bray Hammond, writing in 1957, argued similarly that the Jacksonian cause was "one of enterpriser against capitalist." Other historians saw Jacksonianism less as a democratic reform movement than as a nostalgic effort to restore a lost (and largely imagined) past. In *The Jacksonian Persuasion* (1957), Marvin Meyer argued that Jackson and his followers looked with misgivings on the new industrial society emerging around them and yearned instead for a restoration of the agrarian, republican virtues of an earlier time.

In the 1960s, historians examining the Jacksonian era began looking less at Jackson himself and more at the nature of American society in the early nineteenth century. Lee Benson's *The Concept of Jacksonian Democracy* (1961) used quantitative methods to demonstrate the role of religion and ethnicity in determining political divisions in the 1830s. Edward Pessen's *Jacksonian America* (1969) portrayed the Jacksonian era as an increasingly stratified society. This inclination to look more closely at society than at formal "Jacksonianism" continued into the late twentieth and early twenty-first centuries. Sean Wilentz, in *Chants Democratic* (1984) and in *The Rise of American Democracy* (2005), examined the rise in the 1820s of powerful movements among ordinary citizens, who were attracted less to Jackson than to the notion of popular democracy.

Gradually, this attention to Jacksonian-era society has led to reassessments of Jackson himself and the nature of his regime. In *Fathers and Children: Andrew Jackson and the Subjugation of the American Indian* (1975), Michael Rogin portrays Jackson as a leader of a new American revolution, not against British tyranny but against those who challenged the ability of white men to control the continent. Alexander Saxton, in *The Rise and Fall of the White Republic* (1990), makes the related point that "Jacksonian democracy" was explicitly a white man's democracy that rested on the subjugation of women, slaves, and Indians. But the portrayal of Jackson as a champion of the common man has not vanished from scholarly life. The leading Jackson biographer of the postwar era, Robert V. Remini, has noted the flaws in Jackson's concept of democracy; but within the context of his time, Remini claims, Jackson was a genuine "man of the people." ●

AP HISTORICAL ARGUMENTATION AND INTERPRETATION

Questions assume cumulative content knowledge from this chapter and previous chapters.

1. How has the historical debate regarding Jacksonian democracy changed over the years?
2. Identify the different arguments of four historians discussed and describe one piece of historical evidence that supports and one that refutes each argument.
3. With which historical argument do you most agree? Explain why using historical evidence.

president's followers staged a national party convention to renominate him for the presidency—one year after the Anti-Masons (see p. 245) became the first party to hold such a meeting. In later generations, some Americans would see the party convention as a source of corruption and political exclusivity. But those who created it in the 1830s considered it a great triumph for democracy. Through the convention, they believed, power would arise directly from the people, not from aristocratic political institutions such as the caucus.

LIMITED NATURE OF DEMOCRATIC REFORM The "spoils" system and the political convention did serve to limit the power of two entrenched elites—permanent officeholders and the exclusive party caucus. Yet neither really transferred power to the people. Appointments to office almost always went to prominent political allies of the president and his associates. Delegates to national conventions were less often common men than members of local party organizations. Political opportunity within the party was expanding, but much less so than Jacksonian rhetoric suggested.

"OUR FEDERAL UNION"

Jackson's commitment to extending power beyond entrenched elites led him to want to reduce the functions of the federal government. The concentration of power in Washington, he believed, restricted opportunity to people with political connections. But Jackson also believed in forceful presidential leadership and was strongly committed to the preservation of the Union. Thus, at the same time that Jackson was promoting an economic program to reduce the power of the national government, he was asserting the supremacy of the Union in the face of a potent challenge. For no sooner had he entered office than his own vice president—John C. Calhoun—began to champion a controversial (and, in Jackson's view, dangerous) constitutional theory: nullification.

CALHOUN AND NULLIFICATION

Calhoun was forty-six years old in 1828, with a distinguished past and an apparently promising future. But the smoldering issue of the tariff created a dilemma for him. Once he had been an outspoken protectionist and had strongly supported the tariff of 1816. But by the late 1820s, many South Carolinians had come to believe that the "tariff of abominations" was responsible for the stagnation of the state's economy—even though the stagnation was largely a result of the exhaustion of South Carolina's farmland, which could no longer compete effectively with the newly opened fertile lands of the Southwest. Some exasperated Carolinians were ready to consider a drastic remedy—secession.

JOHN C. CALHOUN This photograph, by Mathew Brady, captured Calhoun toward the end of his life, when he was torn between his real commitment to the ideals of the Union and his equally fervent commitment to the interests of the South. The younger generation of southern leaders, who would dominate the politics of the region in the 1850s, were less idealistic and more purely sectional in their views. (The Library of Congress)

Calhoun's future political hopes rested on how he met this challenge in his home state. He did so by developing a

CALHOUN'S THEORY OF NULLIFICATION

theory that he believed offered a moderate alternative to secession: the theory of nullification. Drawing from the ideas of Madison and Jefferson and their Virginia and Kentucky Resolutions of 1798-1799 and citing the Tenth Amendment to the Constitution, Calhoun argued that since the federal government was a creation of the states, the states—not the courts or Congress—were the final arbiters of the constitutionality of federal laws. If a state concluded that Congress had passed an unconstitutional law, then it could hold a special convention and declare the federal law null and void within the state. The nullification doctrine—and the idea of using it to nullify the 1828 tariff—quickly attracted broad support in South Carolina. But it did nothing to help Calhoun's standing within the new administration, in part because he had a powerful rival in Martin Van Buren.

THE RISE OF VAN BUREN

Van Buren was about the same age as Calhoun and equally ambitious. He had won election to the governorship of New

York in 1828 and then resigned in 1829 when Jackson appointed him secretary of state. Alone among the figures in the

MARTIN VAN BUREN'S GROWING INFLUENCE

Jackson administration, Van Buren soon established himself as a member both of the official cabinet and of the president's unofficial circle of political allies, known as the "Kitchen Cabinet" (which included such Democratic newspaper editors as Isaac Hill of New Hampshire and Amos Kendall and Francis P. Blair of Kentucky). Van Buren's influence with the president was unmatched and grew stronger still as a result of a quarrel over etiquette that drove a wedge between the president and Calhoun.

Peggy O'Neale was the attractive daughter of a Washington tavernkeeper with whom both Andrew Jackson and his friend John H. Eaton had taken lodgings while serving as senators from Tennessee. O'Neale was married, but rumors circulated in Washington in the mid-1820s that she and the unmarried Senator Eaton were having an affair. O'Neale's husband died in 1828, and she and Eaton were soon married. A few weeks later, Jackson named Eaton secretary of war and thus made the new Mrs. Eaton a cabinet wife. The rest of the administration wives, led by Mrs. Calhoun, refused to receive her socially. Jackson (remembering the effects of public slander directed against his own late wife) was furious and demanded that the members of the cabinet accept her into their social world. Calhoun, under pressure from his wife, refused. Van Buren, a widower, befriended the Eatons and thus ingratiated himself with Jackson. By 1831, partly as a result of the Peggy Eaton affair, Jackson had chosen Van Buren to succeed him in the White House, apparently ending Calhoun's dreams of the presidency.

THE WEBSTER-HAYNE DEBATE

In January 1830, as the controversy over nullification grew more intense, a great debate occurred in the U.S. Senate over another sectional controversy. In the midst of a routine debate over federal policy toward western lands, a senator from Connecticut suggested that all land sales and surveys in the west be temporarily discontinued so as to slow the growth of slavery. Robert Y. Hayne, a young senator from South Carolina, responded, charging that slowing down the growth of the West was a way for the East to retain its political and economic power. Although he had no real interest in western lands, he hoped his stance would attract support from westerners in Congress for South Carolina's drive to lower the tariff. Both the South and the West, he argued, were victims of the tyranny of the Northeast. He hinted that the two regions might combine to defend themselves against that tyranny.

Daniel Webster, now a senator from Massachusetts and a nationalistic Whig, attacked Hayne the next day, and through him Calhoun, for what he considered their challenge to the integrity of the Union. He was, in fact, challenging Hayne to a debate not on public lands and the tariff but on the issue of states' rights versus national power. Hayne, coached by Calhoun,

MARTIN VAN BUREN As leader of the so-called Albany Regency in New York in the 1820s, Van Buren helped create one of the first modern party organizations in the United States. Later, as Andrew Jackson's secretary of state and (after 1832) vice president, he helped bring party politics to the national level. In 1840, when he ran for reelection to the presidency, he lost to William Henry Harrison, whose Whig Party made effective use of many of the techniques of mass politics that Van Buren himself had pioneered. (The Library of Congress)

DANIEL WEBSTER The great Civil War photographer Mathew Brady took this portrait of Daniel Webster shortly before Webster's death in 1852. It conveys something of Webster's intensity of purpose—an intensity that was perhaps most famously visible in his dramatic 1830 debate with South Carolina senator Robert Y. Hayne. In his response to Hayne, he spoke words that became a rallying cry in the North: "Liberty and Union, now and forever, one and inseparable." During his long political career, Webster was one of the giants of American politics, a man of much greater stature than many of the presidents who were his contemporaries. (The Library of Congress)

responded with a defense of the theory of nullification. Webster then spent two full afternoons delivering what became known as his "Second Reply to Hayne," a speech that northerners quoted and revered for years to come. He concluded with the ringing appeal "Liberty and Union, now and forever, one and inseparable!"

STATES' RIGHTS VERSUS NATIONAL POWER

Both sides now waited to hear what President Jackson thought of the argument. The answer became clear at the annual Democratic Party banquet in honor of Thomas Jefferson. After dinner, guests delivered a series of toasts. The president arrived with a written text in which he had underscored certain words: "Our Federal Union–It must be preserved." While he spoke, he looked directly at Calhoun. The diminutive Van Buren, who stood on his chair to see better, thought he saw Calhoun's hand shake and a trickle of wine run down his glass as he responded to the president's toast with his

own: "The Union, next to our liberty most dear." The two most important figures in government had drawn sharp lines between themselves.

THE NULLIFICATION CRISIS

In 1832, finally, the controversy over nullification produced a crisis. A congressional tariff bill was passed that offered South Carolinians no relief from the 1828 "tariff of abominations." Almost immediately, the legislature summoned a state convention, which voted to nullify the tariffs of 1828 and 1832 and to forbid the collection of duties within the state. At the same time, South Carolina elected Hayne to serve as governor and Calhoun (who resigned as vice president) to replace Hayne as senator.

Jackson insisted that nullification was treason and that those implementing it were traitors. He strengthened the federal forts in South Carolina and ordered a warship and several revenue ships to Charleston. When Congress convened early in 1833, Jackson proposed a force bill authorizing the president to use the military to see that acts of Congress were obeyed. Violence seemed a real possibility.

NEW YORK HARBOR This aquatint, by W. J. Bennett (after the painting by John William Hill) shows Manhattan viewed from Brooklyn Heights around 1836. By this time, overseas traders had increasingly directed their business to New York, leaving much less opportunity for other cities, especially those in the South. (© The Granger Collection, New York)

Calhoun faced a predicament as he took his place in the Senate. Not a single state had come to South Carolina's support. Even South Carolina itself was divided and could not hope to prevail in a showdown with the federal government. But the timely intervention of Henry Clay, newly elected to the Senate, averted a crisis. Clay devised a compromise by which the tariff would be lowered gradually so that, by 1842, it would reach approximately the same level as in 1816. The compromise and the force bill were passed on the same day, March 1, 1833. Jackson signed them both. In South Carolina, the convention reassembled and repealed its nullification of the tariffs. Calhoun and his followers claimed a victory for nullification, which had, they insisted, forced the revision of the tariff. But the episode made clear that no state could defy the federal government alone.

COMPROMISE

THE REMOVAL OF THE INDIANS

There had never been any doubt about Andrew Jackson's attitude toward the Indian tribes that continued to live in the eastern states and territories of the United States. He wanted them to move west, beyond the Mississippi, out of the way of expanding white settlement. Jackson's antipathy toward the Native Americans had a special intensity because of his own earlier experiences leading military campaigns against tribes along the southern border. But in most respects, his views were little different from those of most other white Americans.

WHITE ATTITUDES TOWARD THE TRIBES

In the eighteenth century, many white Americans had considered the Indians "noble savages," peoples without real civilization but with an inherent dignity that made civilization possible among them. By the first decades of the nineteenth century, this vaguely paternalistic attitude (the attitude of Thomas Jefferson, among others) was giving way to a more hostile one, particularly among the whites in the western states and territories whom Jackson came to represent. Such whites were coming to view Native Americans simply as "savages," not only uncivilized but uncivilizable. Whites, they believed, should not be expected to live in close proximity to the tribes.

CHANGING ATTITUDES TOWARD THE INDIANS

White westerners favored removal as well because they feared that continued contact between the expanding white settlements and the Indians would produce endless conflict and violence. Most of all, however, they favored Indian removal because of their own insatiable desire for territory. The tribes possessed valuable land in the path of expanding white settlement. White Americans wanted it.

THE BLACK HAWK WAR

In the Old Northwest, the long process of expelling the woodland Indians culminated in a last battle in 1831–1832, between white settlers in Illinois and an alliance of Sauk (or Sac) and Fox Indians under the fabled and now aged warrior Black Hawk. An earlier treaty had ceded tribal lands in Illinois to the United States; but Black Hawk and his followers refused to recognize the legality of the agreement, which a rival tribal faction had signed. Hungry and resentful, a thousand of them crossed the river and reoccupied vacant lands in Illinois. White settlers in the region feared that the resettlement was the beginning of a substantial invasion, and they assembled the Illinois state militia and federal troops to repel the "invaders."

The Black Hawk War, as it became known, was notable chiefly for the viciousness of the white military efforts. White

SAUK AND FOX INDIANS DEFEATED

leaders in western Illinois vowed to exterminate the "bandit collection of Indians" and attacked them even when Black Hawk attempted to surrender. The Sauks and Foxes, defeated and starving, retreated across the Mississippi into Iowa. White troops (and some bands of Sioux whom they encouraged to join the chase) pursued them as they fled and

BLACK HAWK AND WHIRLING THUNDER After his defeat by white settlers in Illinois in 1832, the famed Sauk warrior Black Hawk and his son Whirling Thunder were captured and sent on a tour of the East by Andrew Jackson, displayed to the public as trophies of war. They showed such dignity through the ordeal that much of the white public quickly began to sympathize with them. This portrait, by John Wesley Jarvis, was painted on the tour's final stop, in New York City. Black Hawk wears the European-style suit, while Whirling Thunder wears native costume to emphasize his commitment to his tribal roots. Soon thereafter, Black Hawk returned to his tribe, wrote a celebrated autobiography, and died in 1838. (© The Granger Collection, New York)

slaughtered most of them. United States troops captured Black Hawk himself and sent him on a tour of the East, where Andrew Jackson was one of many curious whites who arranged to meet him. (Abraham Lincoln served as a captain of the militia, but saw no action, in the Black Hawk War; Jefferson Davis was a lieutenant in the regular army.)

THE "FIVE CIVILIZED TRIBES"

More troubling to the government in the 1830s were the tribes remaining in the South. In western Georgia, Alabama,

AGRARIAN TRIBES OF THE SOUTH

Mississippi, and Florida lived what were known as the "Five Civilized Tribes" the Cherokee, Creek, Seminole, Chickasaw, and Choctaw—most of whom had established settled agricultural societies with successful economies. The Cherokees in Georgia had formed a particularly stable and sophisticated culture, with their own written language and a formal constitution (adopted in 1827) that created an independent Cherokee Nation. They were more closely tied to their lands than many of the nomadic tribes to the north.

Even some whites argued that the Cherokees, unlike other tribes, should be allowed to retain their eastern lands, since they had become such a "civilized" society and had, under pressure from missionaries and government agents, given up many of their traditional ways. Cherokee men had once been chiefly hunters and had left farming mainly to women. By now the men had given up most of their hunting and (like most white men) took over the farming themselves; Cherokee women, also like their white counterparts, restricted themselves largely to domestic tasks.

The federal government worked steadily to negotiate treaties with the southern Indians that would remove them to the West

REMOVAL ACT

and open their lands for white settlement. But the negotiating process did not proceed fast enough to satisfy the region's whites. The state of Georgia's independent effort to dislodge the Creeks, over the objection of President Adams, was one example of this impatience. That same impatience became evident early in Jackson's administration, when the legislatures in Georgia, Alabama, and Mississippi began passing laws to regulate the tribes remaining in their states. They received assistance in these efforts from Congress, which in 1830 passed the Removal Act (with Jackson's approval) to appropriate money to finance federal negotiations with the southern tribes aimed at relocating them to the West. The president quickly dispatched federal officials to negotiate nearly a hundred new treaties with the remaining tribes. Thus the southern tribes faced a combination of pressures from both the state and federal governments. Most tribes were too weak to resist, and they ceded their lands in return for token payments. Some, however, balked.

In Georgia, the Cherokees tried to stop the white encroachments (which were actively encouraged by Jackson) by appealing to the Supreme Court. The Court's decisions in *Cherokee Nation v. Georgia* and *Worcester v. Georgia* in 1831 and 1832 (see p. 224) seemed at least partially to vindicate the tribe. But Jackson's longtime hostility toward Native Americans left him with little sympathy for the Cherokees and little patience with the Court. He was eager to retain the support of white southerners and westerners in the increasingly bitter partisan battles in which his administration was becoming engaged. When the chief justice announced the decision in *Worcester v. Georgia*, Jackson reportedly responded with contempt. "John Marshall has made his decision," he was reported to have said. "Now let him enforce it." The decision was not enforced.

In 1835, the federal government extracted a treaty from a minority faction of the Cherokees, none of them a chosen rep-

CHEROKEE RESISTANCE

resentative of the Cherokee Nation. The treaty ceded the tribe's land to Georgia in return for $5 million and a reservation west of the Mississippi. The great majority of the 17,000 Cherokees did not recognize the treaty as legitimate and refused to leave their homes. But Jackson would not be thwarted. He sent an army of 7,000 under General Winfield Scott to round them up and drive them westward at bayonet point.

TRAILS OF TEARS

About 1,000 Cherokees fled across the state line to North Carolina, where the federal government eventually provided a

CHEROKEE REMOVAL

small reservation for them in the Smoky Mountains, which survives today. But most of the rest made the long, forced trek to "Indian Territory" (which later became Oklahoma) beginning in the winter of 1838. Along the way, a Kentuckian observed: "Even aged females, apparently nearly ready to drop in the grave, were travelling with heavy burdens attached to their backs, sometimes on frozen ground and sometimes on muddy streets, with no covering for their feet."

Thousands, perhaps an eighth or more of the emigrés, perished before or soon after reaching their unwanted destination.

INDIAN REMOVAL

In the harsh new reservations in which they were now forced to live, the survivors never forgot the hard journey. They called their route "The Trail Where They Cried," the Trail of Tears. Jackson claimed that the "remnant of that ill-fated race" was now "beyond the reach of injury or oppression," apparently trying to convince himself or others that he had supported removal as a way to protect the tribes.

The Cherokees were not alone in experiencing the hardships of the Trail of Tears. Between 1830 and 1838, virtually all the "Five Civilized Tribes" were expelled from the southern states and forced to relocate in the new Indian Territory, which

THE EXPULSION OF THE TRIBES, 1830–1835 Andrew Jackson was famous well before he became president for his military exploits against the tribes. Once in the White House, he ensured that few Indians would remain in the southern states of the nation, now that white settlement was increasing there. The result was a series of dramatic "removals" of Indian tribes out of their traditional lands and into new territories west of the Mississippi—mostly in Oklahoma. Note the very long distance many of these tribes had to travel.

• *Why was the route of the Cherokees, shown in the upper portion of the map, known as the "Trail of Tears"?*

Congress had officially created by the Indian Intercourse Act of 1834. The Choctaws of Mississippi and western Alabama were the first to make the trek, beginning in 1830. The army moved out the Creeks of eastern Alabama and western Georgia in 1836. The Chickasaws in northern Mississippi began the long march westward a year later, and the Cherokees, finally, a year after that. The government thought the Indian Territory was safely distant from existing white settlements and consisted of land that most whites considered undesirable. It had the additional advantage, the government believed, of being on the eastern edge of what earlier white explorers had christened the "Great American Desert," land unfit for habitation. It seemed unlikely that whites would ever seek to settle along the western borders of the Indian Territory; and thus the prospect of whites surrounding the reservation and producing further conflict seemed remote.

Only the Seminoles in Florida managed to resist the pressures to relocate, and even their success was limited. Like other tribes, the Seminoles had agreed under pressure to a settlement (the 1832–1833 treaties of Payne's Landing), by which they ceded their lands to the government and agreed to move to Indian Territory within three years. Most did move west, but a substantial minority, under the leadership of the chieftain Osceola, refused to leave and staged an uprising beginning in 1835 to defend their lands. (Joining the Seminoles in their struggle was a group of runaway black slaves who had been living with the tribe.) The Seminole War dragged on for years. Jackson sent troops to Florida, but the Seminoles with their African American associates were masters of guerrilla warfare in

THE SEMINOLE WAR the jungly Everglades. Even after Osceola had been treacherously captured by white troops while under a flag of truce and had died in prison; even after white troops had engaged in a systematic campaign of extermination against the resisting Indians and their black allies; even after 1,500 white soldiers had died and the federal government had spent $20 million on the struggle—even then, followers of Osceola remained in Florida. Finally, in 1842, the government abandoned the war. By then, many of the Seminoles had been either killed or forced westward. But the relocation of the Seminoles, unlike the relocation of most of the other tribes, was never complete.

THE MEANING OF REMOVAL

By the end of the 1830s, almost all the important Indian societies east of the Mississippi had been removed to the West. The tribes had ceded over 100 million acres of eastern land to the federal government; they had received in return about $68 million and 32 million acres in the far less hospitable lands west of the Mississippi between the Missouri and Red Rivers. There they lived, divided by tribe into a series of carefully defined reservations, in a territory surrounded by a string of United States forts to keep them in (and to keep most whites out), in a region whose climate and topography bore little relation to anything they had known before. Eventually, even this forlorn enclave would face incursions from white civilization.

What were the alternatives to the removal of the eastern Indians? There was probably never any realistic possibility that the government could stop white expansion westward. White people had already been penetrating the West for nearly two centuries, and such penetrations were certain to continue. But did that expansion really require removal?

There were, in theory at least, several alternatives to the brutal removal policy. There were many examples in the West of

ALTERNATIVES TO REMOVAL white settlers and native tribes living side by side and creating a shared (if not necessarily equal) world. In the pueblos of New Mexico,

THE REMOVAL OF INDIANS FROM GEORGIA On April 24, 1831, Georgia issued an agreement to document the forced removal of Native Americans from the state. This policy forced thousands of Native Americans from their traditional tribal lands to new "reservations" west of the Mississippi River. The Cherokees were among the first tribes forced to move. The conditions of this forced displacement were harsh and many people died, prompting survivors to call the route they had traveled the "Trail of Tears." (Private Collection/© Peter Newark American Pictures/The Bridgeman Art Library)

in the fur trading posts of the Pacific Northwest, in parts of Texas and California, settlers from Mexico, Canada, and the United States had created societies in which Indians and whites were in intimate contact with each other. Even during the famous Lewis and Clark expedition, white explorers had lived with western Indians on terms of such intimacy that many of them contracted venereal disease from Indian sexual partners. Sometimes these close contacts between whites and Indians were beneficial to both sides, even reasonably equal. Sometimes they were cruel and exploitive. But the early multiracial societies of the West did not separate whites and Indians. They demonstrated ways in which the two cultures could interact, each shaping the other.

By the mid-nineteenth century, however, white Americans had adopted a different model as they contemplated westward expansion. Much as the early British settlers along the Atlantic coast had established "plantations," from which natives were, in theory, to be excluded, so the westward-moving whites of later years came to imagine the territories they were entering as virgin land, with no preexisting civilization. Native Americans, they believed, could not be partners—either equal or subordinate—in the creation of new societies in the West. They were obstacles, to be removed and, as far as possible, isolated. Indians, Andrew Jackson once said, had "neither the intelligence, the industry, the moral habits, nor the desire of improvement" to be fit partners in the project of extending white civilization westward. By dismissing Native American cultures in that way, white Americans justified to themselves a series of harsh policies that they believed (incorrectly) would make the West theirs alone.

JACKSON AND THE BANK WAR

Jackson was quite willing to use federal power against rebellious states and Indian tribes. On economic issues, however, he was consistently opposed to concentrating power either in the federal government or in powerful and, in his view, aristocratic institutions associated with it. An early example of his skeptical view of federal power was his 1830 veto of a congressional

JACKSON'S OPPOSITION TO CONCENTRATED POWER
measure providing a subsidy to the proposed Maysville Road in Kentucky. The bill was unconstitutional, Jackson argued, because the road in question lay entirely within Kentucky and was not, therefore, a part of "interstate commerce." But the bill was also unwise, he believed, because it committed the government to what Jackson considered extravagant expenditures.

Jackson's opposition to federal power and aristocratic privilege lay behind the most celebrated episode of his presidency: the war against the Bank of the United States.

BIDDLE'S INSTITUTION

The Bank of the United States in the 1830s was a mighty institution, and it is not surprising that it would attract Jackson's wrath. Its stately headquarters in Philadelphia seemed to

NICHOLAS BIDDLE
symbolize its haughty image of itself. It had branches in twenty-nine other cities, making it the most powerful and far-flung financial institution in the nation. By law, the Bank was the only place that the federal government could deposit its own funds; the government, in turn, owned one-fifth of the Bank's stock. The Bank did a tremendous business in general banking. It provided credit to growing enterprises; it issued bank notes, which served as a dependable medium of exchange throughout the country; and it exercised a restraining effect on the less well-managed state banks. Nicholas Biddle, who served as president of the Bank from 1823 on, had done much to put the institution on a sound and prosperous basis. Nevertheless, Andrew Jackson was determined to destroy it.

Opposition to the Bank came from two very different groups: the "soft-money" faction and the "hard-money" faction. Advocates of soft money—people who wanted more currency in circulation and believed that issuing bank notes unsupported by gold and silver was the best way to circulate more currency—consisted largely of state bankers and their allies.

HARD AND SOFT MONEY
They objected to the Bank of the United States because it restrained the state banks from issuing notes freely. The hard-money people believed that gold and silver were the only basis for money. They condemned all banks that issued bank notes, including the Bank of the United States. The soft-money advocates were believers in rapid economic growth and speculation; the hard-money forces embraced older ideas of "public virtue" and looked with suspicion on expansion and speculation.

Jackson supported the hard-money position. Many years before, he had been involved in some grandiose land and commercial speculations based on paper credit. His business had failed in the Panic of 1797, and he had fallen deeply into debt. After that, he was suspicious of all banks and all paper currency. But as president he was also sensitive to the complaints of his many soft-money supporters in the West and the South. He made it clear that he would not favor renewing the charter of the Bank of the United States, which was due to expire in 1836.

A Philadelphia aristocrat unaccustomed to politics, Biddle nevertheless began granting financial favors to influential men who he thought might help him preserve the Bank. In particular, he turned to Daniel Webster and cultivated a close personal friendship with him. He named Webster the Bank's legal counsel and director of its Boston branch; Webster was also a frequent, heavy borrower from the Bank. He helped Biddle win the support of other important figures, among them Henry Clay.

Clay, Webster, and other advisers persuaded Biddle to apply to Congress in 1832 for a bill to renew the Bank's charter. That was four years ahead of the date the original charter was scheduled to expire. But forcing a vote now would allow the Bank to become a major issue in the 1832 national elections. Congress

JACKSON'S VETO
passed the recharter bill; Jackson, predictably, vetoed it; and the Bank's supporters in

Denouncing the [...]
to themselves as [...]
tionally worked [...]
gence of the W[...]
political parties [...]
System" began w[...]

DEMOCRATS [...]

The two parties [...]
ophies, in their [...]
leaders. But the [...]
approached the [...]

Democrats in [...]
expanding econo[...]

DEMOCRATS' EMPHASIS ON OPPORTUNITY

ing the Union, v[...]
dynamic econon[...]
centers of corru[...]
well address, the [...]
planter, the farm[...]
their success de[...]
which artificial [...]
Among the mos [...]
Locofocos, mainl[...]
fessionals in the [...]
perhaps even vi[...]
advance of anyth[...]

The political [...]
was very differe[...]

WHIGS' CALL FOR ECONOMIC UNION

rial progress ent[...]
were cautious a[...]
territorial growt[...]
America was of [...]
rising to world [...]
power. Thus, wh[...]
lation establishir[...]
institutions, Wh[...]

The Whigs [...]
merchants and r[...]
planters of the S[...]
ment and the st[...]
ambitious farme[...]
usually migrants[...]
improvements, e[...]
The Democrats [...]
and the working[...]
suspicious of inc[...]
with southern r[...]

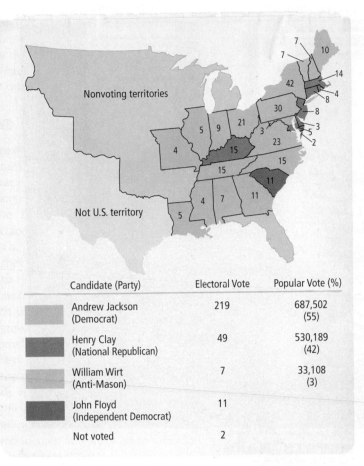

THE ELECTION OF 1832 Jackson's reelection victory in 1832 was almost as decisive as his earlier victory in 1828.

• *What changes are visible in party loyalties since the previous election?*

Congress failed to override the veto. Just as Clay had hoped, the 1832 campaign now centered on the future of the Bank.

Clay ran for president that year as the unanimous choice of the National Republicans, who held a nominating convention in Baltimore late in 1831. But the Bank War failed to provide him with the winning issue for which he had hoped. Jackson, with Van Buren as his running mate, overwhelmingly defeated Clay (and several minor party candidates) with 55 percent of the popular vote and 219 electoral votes (more than four times as many as Clay received). These results were a defeat not only for Clay, but also for Biddle.

THE "MONSTER" DESTROYED

Jackson was now more determined than ever to destroy the "monster" Bank as quickly as possible. He could not legally abolish the institution before the expiration of its charter. Instead, he tried to weaken it. He decided to remove the government's deposits from the Bank. His secretary of the treasury believed that such an action would destabilize the financial system and refused to give the order. Jackson fired him and

REMOVAL OF GOVERNMENT DEPOSITS

appointed a new one. When the new secretary similarly balked, Jackson fired him too and named a third, more compliant secretary: Attorney General Roger B. Taney, his close friend and loyal ally. Taney began placing the government's deposits not in the Bank of the United States, as it had in the past, but in a number of state banks (which Jackson's enemies called "pet banks").

Nicholas Biddle, whom Jacksonians derisively called "Czar Nicholas," did not give in without a fight. "This worthy President," he wrote sarcastically, "thinks that because he has scalped Indians and imprisoned Judges, he is to have his way with the Bank. He is mistaken." When the administration began to transfer funds directly from the Bank of the United States to the pet banks (as opposed to the initial practice of simply depositing new funds in those banks), Biddle called in loans and raised interest rates, explaining that without the government deposits the Bank's resources were stretched too thin. He realized his actions were likely to cause financial distress. He hoped a short recession would persuade Congress to recharter the Bank. "Nothing but the evidence of suffering," he told a colleague, would "produce any effect in Congress." By now, the struggle had become not just a conflict over policy and principle, but also a bitter personal battle between two proud men—both of them acting recklessly in an effort to humiliate and defeat the other.

As financial conditions worsened in the winter of 1833–1834, supporters of the Bank blamed Jackson's policies for the recession. They organized meetings around the country and sent petitions to Washington urging a rechartering of the Bank. But the Jacksonians blamed the recession on Biddle and refused to budge. When distressed citizens appealed to the president for help, he dismissively answered, "Go to Biddle."

Finally, Biddle contracted credit too far even for his own allies in the business community, who began to fear that in his effort to save his own bank he was threatening their interests. Some of them did "go to Biddle." A group of New York and Boston merchants protested. To appease the business community, Biddle at last reversed himself and began to grant credit in abundance and on reasonable terms. His vacillating and unpopular tactics ended his chances of winning a recharter of the Bank.

Jackson had won a considerable political victory. But when the Bank of the United States died in 1836, the country lost a valuable, albeit flawed, financial institution and was left with a fragmented and chronically unstable banking system that would plague the economy for more than a century.

JACKSON VICTORIOUS

THE TANEY COURT

In the aftermath of the Bank War, Jackson moved against the most powerful institution of economic nationalism of all: the Supreme Court. In 1835, when John Marshall died, the president appointed as the new chief justice his trusted ally Roger B. Taney. Taney did not bring a sharp break in constitutional interpretation, but he gradually helped modify Marshall's vigorous nationalism.

Perhaps the clearest indication of the new judicial mood was the celebrated case of *Charles River Bridge v. Warren Bridge* reliance on rich men for financial support, and his excessive and often embarrassing fondness for brandy prevented him from developing enough of a national constituency to win him the office he so desperately wanted. John C. Calhoun, the third member of the Great Triumvirate, never considered himself a true Whig, and his identification with the nullification controversy in effect disqualified him from national leadership in any case. But he had tremendous strength in the South, supported a national bank, and shared with Clay and Webster a strong animosity toward Andrew Jackson.

The problems that emerged from this divided leadership became particularly clear in 1836. The Democrats were united

ELECTION OF 1836

behind Andrew Jackson's personal choice for president, Martin Van Buren. The Whigs could not agree on a single candidate. Instead, they ran several candidates, hoping to profit from the regional strength of each. Webster represented the party in New England; Hugh Lawson White of Tennessee ran in the South; and the former Indian fighter and hero of the War of 1812, William Henry Harrison, from Ohio, was the candidate in the middle states and the West. Party leaders hoped the three candidates

together might draw enough votes from Van Buren to prevent his getting a majority and throw the election to the House of Representatives, where the Whigs might be able to elect one of their own leaders. In the end, however, Van Buren won easily, with 170 electoral votes to 124 for all his opponents combined.

VAN BUREN AND THE PANIC OF 1837

Andrew Jackson retired from public life in 1837, beloved by most Americans. Martin Van Buren was very different from his predecessor and far less fortunate. He was never able to match Jackson's personal popularity, and his administration encountered economic difficulties that devastated the Democrats and helped the Whigs.

Van Buren's success in the 1836 election was a result in part of a nationwide economic boom that was reaching its height in that year. Canal and railroad builders were at a peak of activity. Prices were rising, money was plentiful, and credit was easy as banks increased their loans and notes with little regard to their reserves of cash. The land business, in particular, was booming. Between 1835 and 1837, the government sold nearly 40 million acres of public land, nearly three-fourths of it to speculators, who purchased large tracts in hopes of reselling them at a profit. These land sales, along with revenues the government received from the tariff of 1833, created a series of substantial federal budget surpluses and made possible a steady reduction of the national debt (something Jackson had always advocated). From 1835 to 1837, the government for the first and only time in its history was out of debt, with a substantial surplus in the Treasury.

Congress and the administration now faced the question of what to do with the Treasury surplus. Reducing the tariff was not an option, since no one wanted to raise that thorny issue again. Instead, support grew for returning the federal surplus to

DISTRIBUTION ACT

the states. In 1836, Congress passed a "distribution" act requiring the federal government to pay its surplus funds to the states each year in four quarterly installments as interest-free, unsecured loans. No one expected the "loans" to be repaid. The states spent the money quickly, mainly to encourage construction of highways, railroads, and canals. The distribution of the surplus thus gave further stimulus to the economic boom.

Congress did nothing to check the speculative fever, with which many congressmen themselves were badly infected. Webster, for one, was buying up thousands of acres in the West. But Jackson, always suspicious of paper currency, was unhappy that the government was selling good land and receiving in return various state bank notes worth no more than the credit of the issuing bank.

In 1836, not long before leaving office, he issued a presidential order, the "specie circular." It provided that in payment for public lands the government would accept only gold or silver coins or currency securely backed by gold or silver. Jackson was right to fear the speculative fever but wrong in thinking the specie circular would cure it. On the contrary, it produced a financial panic that began in the first months of

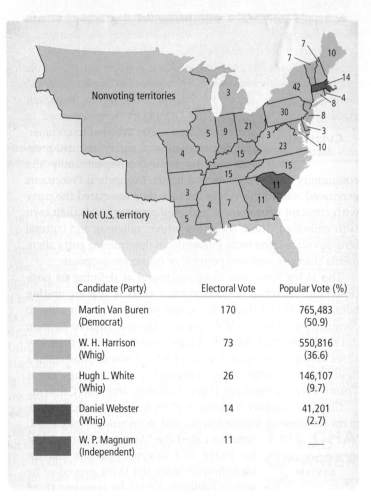

Candidate (Party)	Electoral Vote	Popular Vote (%)
Martin Van Buren (Democrat)	170	765,483 (50.9)
W. H. Harrison (Whig)	73	550,816 (36.6)
Hugh L. White (Whig)	26	146,107 (9.7)
Daniel Webster (Whig)	14	41,201 (2.7)
W. P. Magnum (Independent)	11	—

THE ELECTION OF 1836 Martin Van Buren, who had served as vice president and secretary of state for Andrew Jackson, was the Democratic candidate for president in 1836. His connection to the revered Jackson helped him easily defeat his Whig opponent, William Henry Harrison. Four years later, the same two men contested the presidency, but that time it was Harrison who won.

"THE DOWN
corrupt support

CHARLES
BRIDG
WARREN

Cambridge
state to op
anteed it a
had applie
second, co
free–greatl
The firs
charter the
and noted
case and ot
abrogate co
majority on
award the
maintained,
that took p
A state, the
if such acti
community

"THE TIMES," 1837 This savage caricature of the economic troubles besetting the United States in 1837 illustrates, among other things, popular resentment of the hard-money orthodoxies of the time. A sign on the Custom House reads: "All bonds must be paid in Specie." Next door, the bank announces: "No specie payments made here." Women and children are shown begging in the street, while unemployed workers stand shoeless in front of signs advertising loans and "grand schemes." (© Museum of the City of New York, USA/The Bridgeman Art Library)

PANIC OF 1837 Van Buren's presidency. Hundreds of banks and businesses failed. Unemployment grew. Bread riots broke out in some of the larger cities. Prices fell, especially the price of land. Many railroad and canal projects failed. Several of the debt-burdened state governments ceased to pay interest on their bonds, and a few repudiated their debts, at least temporarily. It was the worst depression in American history to that point, and it lasted for five years. It was a political catastrophe for Van Buren and the Democrats.

Both parties bore some responsibility for the panic. But the depression was only partly a result of American policies. England and western Europe were facing panics of their own, which caused European (and especially English) investors to withdraw funds from America, putting an added strain on American banks. A succession of crop failures on American farms reduced the purchasing power of farmers and required increased imports of food, which sent more money out of the country. But whatever its actual causes, the Panic of 1837 occurred during a Democratic administration, and the Democrats paid the political price for it. The Van Buren administration, which strongly opposed government intervention in the economy, did little to fight the depression. Some of the steps it took—borrowing money to pay government debts and

accepting only specie for payment of taxes—may have made things worse. Van Buren did succeed in establishing a ten-hour workday on all federal projects, by presidential order, but he had only a few legislative achievements.

The most important and controversial of them was the creation of a new financial system to replace the Bank of the United States. Under Van Buren's plan, known as the "independent treasury" or "subtreasury" system, the government would **INDEPENDENT TREASURY** place its funds in an independent treasury at Washington and in subtreasuries in other cities. No private banks would have the government's money or name to use as a basis for speculation; the government and the banks would be "divorced."

Van Buren called a special session of Congress in 1837 to consider the proposal, which failed in the House. In 1840, the last year of Van Buren's presidency, the administration finally succeeded in driving the measure through both houses of Congress.

THE LOG CABIN CAMPAIGN

As the campaign of 1840 approached, the Whigs realized that they would have to settle on one candidate for president this time if they were to have any hope of winning. As a result, they held their first national nominating convention in Harrisburg, Pennsylvania, in December 1839. Passing over the controversial Henry Clay, who had expected the nomination, the convention chose William Henry Harrison and, for vice president, John Tyler of Virginia. Harrison was a descendant of the Virginia aristocracy but had spent his adult life in the Northwest. He was a renowned soldier, a famous Indian fighter, and a popular national figure. The Democrats nominated Van Buren. But because they were not much more united than the Whigs, they failed to nominate a vice presidential candidate, leaving the choice of that office to the electors.

The 1840 campaign was the first in which the new popular "penny press" carried news of the candidates to a large audience of workers and tradespeople. It also illustrated how fully the concept of party competition, the subordination of ideology to immediate political needs, had established itself in America. The Whigs represented the affluent elements of the population, and they favored government policies that would aid business. But they presented themselves in 1840 as the party of the common people. So, of course, did the

NEW TECHNIQUES OF POLITICAL CAMPAIGNING

Democrats. Both parties used the same techniques of mass voter appeal, the same evocation of simple, rustic values. What mattered now was not the philosophical purity of the party but its ability to win votes. The Whig campaign was particularly effective in portraying William Henry Harrison, a wealthy member of the frontier elite with a considerable estate, as a simple man of the people who loved log cabins and hard cider. They accused Van Buren of being an aloof aristocrat who used cologne, drank champagne, and ate from gold plates. The Democrats had no defense against the combination of these campaign techniques and the effects of the depression. Harrison won the election with 234 electoral votes to 60 for Van Buren and with a popular vote majority of 53 percent.

THE FRUSTRATION OF THE WHIGS

Despite their decisive victory, the Whigs found their four years in power frustrating and divisive. In large part, that was because their popular new president, "Old Tippecanoe," William Henry Harrison, died of pneumonia one month after taking office. Vice President Tyler succeeded him. Control of the administration thus fell to a man with whom the Whig party leadership had weak ties. Harrison had generally deferred

HARRISON AND REFORM This hand-colored engraving was made for a brass brooch during the 1840 presidential campaign and served the same purposes that modern campaign buttons do. It conveys Harrison's presumably humble beginnings in a log cabin. In reality, Harrison was a wealthy, aristocratic man; but the unpopularity of the aristocratic airs of his opponent, President Martin Van Buren, persuaded the Whig Party that it would be good political strategy to portray Harrison as a humble "man of the people." (© David J. & Janice L. Frent Collection/Corbis)

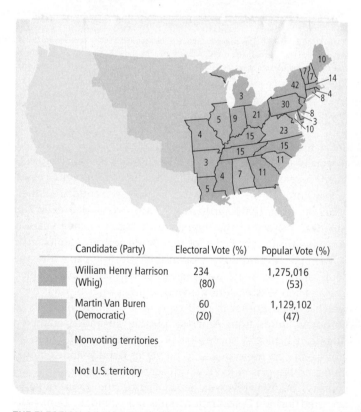

Candidate (Party)	Electoral Vote (%)	Popular Vote (%)
William Henry Harrison (Whig)	234 (80)	1,275,016 (53)
Martin Van Buren (Democratic)	60 (20)	1,129,102 (47)
Nonvoting territories		
Not U.S. territory		

THE ELECTION OF 1840 President Martin Van Buren was defeated in 1840 despite his close relationship to the popular former president, Andrew Jackson. Van Buren, unlike Jackson, was president during a sharp economic recession. And even though his opponent, William Henry Harrison, was a wealthy frontier aristocrat, the Whig Party effectively portrayed him as a humble man of the people, a contrast to what they claimed was Van Buren's extravagance and elitism.

A BEAUTIFUL GOBLET OF WHITE·HOUSE CHAMPAGNE

AN UGLY *MUG* OF LOG·CABIN HARD CIDER

AN ATTACK ON VAN BUREN This "pull card," made during the 1840 presidential campaign, which Van Buren lost to William Henry Harrison, satirizes the president as an aristocratic dandy. The card displays Van Buren grinning while he drinks champagne in the White House. Pulling a tab on the card changes his champagne glass to a mug of hard cider (with Harrison's initials on it) and changes his expression from delight to revulsion. (© The Granger Collection, New York)

to Henry Clay and Daniel Webster, whom he named secretary of state. Under Tyler, things quickly changed.

Tyler was a former Democrat who had left the party in reaction to what he considered Jackson's excessively egalitarian program and imperious methods. But there were still signs of his Democratic past in his approach to public policy. The president did agree to bills abolishing Van Buren's independent treasury system and raising tariff rates. But he refused to support Clay's attempt to recharter a Bank of the United States. And he vetoed several internal improvement bills that Clay and other congressional Whigs sponsored. Finally, a conference of congressional Whigs read Tyler out of the party. Every cabinet member but Webster resigned; five former Democrats took their places. When Webster, too, left the cabinet, Tyler appointed Calhoun, who had rejoined the Democratic Party, to replace him.

WHIGS BREAK WITH TYLER

A new political alignment was emerging. Tyler and a small band of conservative southern Whigs were preparing to rejoin the Democrats. Joining the "common man's party" of Jackson and Van Buren was a faction with decidedly aristocratic political ideas, who thought that government had an obligation to protect and even expand the institution of slavery, and who believed in states' rights with almost fanatical devotion.

WHIG DIPLOMACY

In the midst of these domestic controversies, a series of incidents in the late 1830s brought Great Britain and the United States once again to the brink of war. Residents of the eastern provinces of Canada launched a rebellion against the British colonial government in 1837, and some of the rebels chartered an American steamship, the *Caroline*, to ship supplies across

PATTERNS OF
POPULAR CULTURE

THE PENNY PRESS

ON September 3, 1833, a small newspaper appeared in New York City for the first time: the *New York Sun*, published by a young former apprentice from Massachusetts named Benjamin Day. Four pages long, it contained mostly trivial local news, with particular emphasis on sex, crime, and violence.

It sold for a penny, launching a new age in the history of American journalism, the age of the "penny press."

Before the advent of the penny press, newspapers in America were far too expensive for most ordinary citizens to buy. But several important changes in the business of journalism and the character of American society paved the way for Benjamin Day and others to challenge the established press. New technologies—the steam-powered cylinder printing press, new machines for making paper, railroads and canals for distributing issues to a larger market—made it possible to publish newspapers inexpensively and to sell them widely. A rising popular literacy rate, a result in part of the spread of public education, created a bigger reading public.

The penny press was also a response to the changing culture of the 1820s and 1830s. The spread of an urban, market economy contributed to the growth of the penny press by drawing a large population of workers, artisans, and clerks into large cities, where they became an important

market for the new papers. The spirit of democracy—symbolized by the popularity of Andrew Jackson and the rising numbers of white male voters across the country—helped create an appetite for journalism that spoke to and for "the people." Hence Benjamin Day's slogan for his new paper: "It Shines for ALL." The *Sun* and papers like it were committed to feeding the appetites of the people of modest means, who constituted most of their readership. "Human interest stories" helped solidify their hold on the working public. Condescending stories about poor black men and women—ridiculing their subjects' illiteracy and their accents—were also popular among these papers' virtually all-white readership.

Within six months of its first issue, the *Sun* had the largest circulation in New York—8,000 readers, more than twice the number of its nearest competitors. James Gordon Bennett's *New York Herald*, which began publication in 1835, soon surpassed the *Sun* in popularity with its lively combination of sensationalism and local gossip and with its aggressive pursuit of national and international stories. The *Herald* pioneered a "letters to the editor" column, was the first paper to have regular reviews of books and the arts, and launched the first daily sports section. By 1860, its circulation of more than 77,000 was the largest of any daily newspaper in the world.

THE NEW YORK *SUN* This 1834 front page of *The Sun*, which had begun publication a year earlier, contains advertisements, human interest stories, a description of a slave auction in Charleston, S.C., and homespun advice: "Life is short. The poor pittance of several years is not worth being a villain for." (© Collection of the New-York Historical Society)

---

the Niagara River to them from New York. British authorities in Canada seized the *Caroline* and burned it, killing one American in the process. The British government refused either to disavow the attack or to provide compensation for it, and resentment in the United States ran high. But the British soon had reasons for anger as well. Authorities in New York,

THE *CAROLINE* AFFAIR

attempting to exploit the *Caroline* affair, arrested a Canadian named Alexander McLeod and charged him with the murder of the American who had died in the incident. The British government, expressing majestic rage, insisted that McLeod could not be accused of murder because he had acted under official orders. The foreign secretary, the bellicose Lord Palmerston, demanded McLeod's release and threatened that his execution would bring "immediate and frightful" war.

Webster as secretary of state did not think McLeod was worth a war, but he was powerless to release him. The prisoner was under New York jurisdiction and had to be tried in the state courts, a peculiarity of American jurisprudence that the

British did not seem to understand. A New York jury did what Webster could not: it defused the crisis by acquitting McLeod.

At the same time, tensions flared over the boundary between Canada and Maine, which had been in dispute since

AROOSTOOK WAR

the Treaty of 1783. In 1838, groups of Americans and Canadians, mostly lumberjacks, began moving into the Aroostook River region in the disputed area, precipitating a violent brawl between the two groups that became known as the "Aroostook War."

Several years later, there were yet more Anglo-American problems. In 1841, an American ship, the *Creole*, sailed from Virginia for New Orleans with more than 100 slaves aboard. En route the slaves mutinied, took possession of the ship, and took it to the Bahamas. British officials there declared the slaves free, and the English government refused to overrule them. Many Americans, especially southerners, were furious.

At this critical juncture, a new government eager to reduce the tensions with the United States came to power in Great

THE LEXINGTON BLOWS! This image in the *New York Sun* was one of the first examples of large and (in this case at least) lurid illustration in the daily press. This dramatic picture depicts an event that took place on the Long Island Sound in 1840. (The Library of Congress (LC-USZ62-2527))

The newspapers of the penny press initiated the process of turning journalism into a profession. They were the first to pay their reporters and the first to rely heavily on advertisements, often devoting up to half their space to paid advertising. They tended to be sensationalist and opinionated, but they were often also aggressive in uncovering serious and important news—in police stations, courts, jails, streets, and private homes as well as in city halls, state capitals, Washington, D.C., and the world. ●

UNDERSTAND, ANALYZE, AND EVALUATE

1. How were the penny press newspapers a product of the Jacksonian era?
2. Before the advent of the penny press, newspapers in America were aimed at a much narrower audience. Some published mainly business news, and others worked to advance the aims of a political party. What nationally circulated newspapers and other media today continue this tradition?
3. What characteristics of penny press newspapers are still common in newspapers today? In what other contemporary news media do you see these same (or similar) elements?

Not all the new penny papers were as sensationalist as the *Sun* and the *Herald*. Both the *Philadelphia Public Ledger* and the *Baltimore Sun,* founded in 1836 and 1837 respectively, strove to provide serious coverage of the news. The *Baltimore Sun* even developed a Washington bureau, the first of the penny papers to do so. The *New York Tribune,* founded in 1841 by Horace Greeley, prided itself on serious reporting and commentary, all of it tinged with a conspicuous sympathy for socialism and for the aspirations of working people. As serious as the *Tribune,* but more sober and self-consciously "objective" in its reportage, was the *New York Times,* which Henry Raymond founded in 1851. "We do not mean to write as if we were in a passion—unless that shall really be the case," the *Times* huffily proclaimed in its first issue, in an obvious reference to Greeley and his impassioned reportage; "and we shall make it a point to get into a passion as rarely as possible."

Britain. In the spring of 1842, it sent Lord Ashburton, an admirer of America, to negotiate an agreement on the Maine boundary and other matters. The result of his negotiations with Secretary of State Webster and representatives from Maine and Massachusetts was the Webster-Ashburton Treaty of 1842. Its terms established a firm northern boundary between the United States and Canada along the Maine–New Brunswick border that survives to this day; the new border gave the United States a bit more than half of the previously disputed territory. Other, smaller provisions placated Maine and Massachusetts and protected critical trade routes in both the northern United States and southern Canada. In a separate exchange of notes, Ashburton eased the memory of the *Caroline* and *Creole* affairs by expressing regret and promising no future "officious interference" with American ships.

WEBSTER-ASHBURTON TREATY

During the Tyler administration, the United States established its first diplomatic relations with China. In 1842,

TREATY OF WANG HYA

Britain forced China to open certain ports to foreign trade. Eager to share the new privileges, American mercantile interests persuaded Tyler and Congress to send a commissioner–Caleb Cushing–to China to negotiate a treaty giving the United States some part in the China trade. In the Treaty of Wang Hya, concluded in 1844, Cushing secured most-favored-nation provisions giving Americans the same privileges as the English. He also won for Americans the right of "extraterritoriality"–the right of Americans accused of crimes in China to be tried by American, not Chinese, officials. In the next ten years, American trade with China steadily increased.

In their diplomatic efforts, at least, the Whigs were able to secure some important successes. But by the end of the Tyler administration, the party could look back on few other victories. In the election of 1844, the Whigs lost the White House. They were to win only one more national election in their history.

AP CONNECTING THEMES

Chapter 9 explored the reasons for and the manifestation of rising political participation by the common man. Extremely important are the reasons for the emergence of a Second American Party System, consisting of Whigs and Democrats. Be able to discuss the beliefs and constituencies of both parties. You should also focus on rising sectional tension and the specific challenges to the authority of the federal government by the states. The chapter also discussed the theory behind, and the use of, nullification as a political tool. Additionally, be able to analyze challenges Jackson posed to the concept of separation of powers within the federal government.

The following themes have heightened importance in Chapter 9. You should now be able to do the following for each listed theme:

Identity: Analyze the threats to American nationalism posed by increased sectional tension.

Peopling: Analyze the factors that encouraged western migration and the consequences of that migration.

Politics and Power: Explain the issues involved in the rise of the Second American Party System.

Environment and Geography: Explain the push and pull factors that led Americans to migrate westward.

Ideas, Beliefs, and Culture: Explain the theory of nullification and opposing views on the nature of the Union.

AP SUGGESTED STUDY

PEOPLE/PLACES/EVENTS As you study these items, think about how they demonstrate or relate to key concepts and historical themes from this chapter and previous chapters.

ANDREW JACKSON 230	INDIAN TERRITORY 240	SEMINOLE WAR 241
ANTI-MASONRY 245	JOHN C. CALHOUN 246	SPECIE CIRCULAR 246
AROOSTOOK WAR 250	JOHN TYLER 248	SPOILS SYSTEM 234
BANK WAR 242	MARTIN VAN BUREN 233	TRAIL OF TEARS 240
CAROLINE AFFAIR 250	NICHOLAS BIDDLE 242	WEBSTER-ASHBURTON TREATY 251
DANIEL WEBSTER 231	NULLIFICATION 235	WEBSTER-HAYNE DEBATE 236
DEMOCRATS 234	PANIC OF 1837 246	WHIGS 234
DORR REBELLION 231	REMOVAL ACT 239	WILLIAM HENRY HARRISON 246
"FIVE CIVILIZED TRIBES" 239	ROGER B. TANEY 243	

AP TEST PRACTICE

Questions assume cumulative content knowledge from this chapter and previous chapters.

MULTIPLE CHOICE Use the political cartoon on page 244 and your knowledge of U.S. history to answer questions 1–4.

1. Which group would least agree with the event being depicted in the cartoon?

   (A) Democratic-Republicans of the late 18th century

   (B) Whigs

   (C) Anti-federalists

   (D) Those in the 1830s who wanted bank notes to be issued more freely

2. Which regions of the U.S. in the early 1800s would most have supported the action being shown in the cartoon?

   (A) The North and West

   (B) The North and South

   (C) The East and South

   (D) The South and West

3. What was the significance of the event depicted in the cartoon for those in the early 1800s who supported such action?

   (A) It meant a weakening of the power of those whom they considered the "Eastern aristocratic elite."

   (B) It meant a significant weakening of the power of state governments.

   (C) It meant that state banks could no longer issue paper money at will and at any amounts, which had led to instability in the banking system and, hence, economic instability.

   (D) It demonstrated the increasing strength of the presidency.

4. Those in the early 1800s who would have supported the action depicted in the cartoon would more likely have also supported

(A) The American System

(B) Improvements to existing national infrastructure

(C) Rapid industrialization

(D) Unfettered westward expansion

SHORT ANSWER Use your knowledge of U.S. history to answer questions 5–7.

5. Answer a, b, and c.

a) Briefly explain ONE example of sectional tensions in the early 1800s, which threatened American nationalism.

b) Briefly explain a SECOND example of sectional tensions in the early 1800s, which threatened American nationalism.

c) Briefly explain ONE example of federal government action that enforced its powers over that of states.

6. Answer a, b, and c.

a) Briefly explain why ONE of the following options best demonstrates the historical interpretation that democracy in America was expanded in the 1820s and 1830s.

- Permanent institutionalization of the political party system (1836)

- Non-renewal of the charter for the national bank (1836)

- Government policies supporting rapid westward expansion (1830)

b) Provide an example of an event or development to support your explanation.

c) Briefly explain why one of the other options is not as useful as evidence that democracy in America expanded in the time of the 1820s and 1830s.

7. Using the map on page 240, answer a, b, and c.

a) Briefly explain ONE example of Native American resistance in the 1830s or 1840s to events like that shown in the map.

b) Briefly explain ONE example demonstrating the economic motivations of white settlers in the 1830s or 1840s in supporting policies such as that shown on the map.

c) Briefly explain ONE example of cultural adaptation by Native Americans in the 1830s or 1840s, reflecting their experience with white Americans.

LONG ESSAY Develop a thoughtful and thorough historical argument that answers the question below. Begin your essay with a thesis statement and support it with relevant historical evidence.

8. Analyze the extent to which the debate over federal power vs. states' power influenced the institutionalization in the early 1800s of the political party system in the United States.

10 | AMERICA'S ECONOMIC REVOLUTION

THE LOWELL MILLS Fifteen years earlier, Lowell, Massachusetts, had been a small farming village known as East Chelmsford. By the 1840s, when Fitzhugh Lane painted *The Middlesex Company Woolen Mills,* the town had become one of the most famous manufacturing centers in America and a magnet for visitors from around the world. Lane's painting shows female workers, who dominated the labor force in Lowell, entering the factory. (© American Textile History Museum)

AP

HISTORICAL THINKING

1. **Historical Causation** Analyze the reasons for rapid population growth in the United States and the consequence of that growth.

2. **Contextualization** Explain how transportation innovations further isolated the South from other regions of the United States.

3. **Comparison** Compare and contrast the agricultural focus of each of the regions of the United States.

4. **Historical Causation** To what degree and in what ways did the early industrial revolution change the labor force, gender roles, and social mobility?

5. **Contextualization** Analyze the degree to which the factory system, transportation revolution, and agricultural revolution complemented each other and led to concentrated areas of population.

6. **Historical Argumentation** Analyze the degree to which development of the factory system further isolated the South and set the stage for increased sectional tension?

Key Concept Correlations

Analyze the ways the historical developments you learn about in this chapter connect to the following AP Key Concepts.

3.3 Migration within North America, cooperative interaction, and competition for resources raised questions about boundaries and policies, intensified conflicts among peoples and nations, and led to contests over the creation of a multiethnic, multiracial national identity.

4.1 The United States developed the world's first modern mass democracy and celebrated a new national culture, while Americans sought to define the nation's democratic ideals and to reform its institutions to match them.

4.2 Developments in technology, agriculture, and commerce precipitated profound changes in U.S. settlement patterns, regional identities, gender and family relations, political power, and distribution of consumer goods.

5.1 The United States became more connected with the world as it pursued an expansionist foreign policy in the Western Hemisphere and emerged as the destination for many migrants from other countries.

5.2 Intensified by expansion and deepening regional divisions, debates over slavery and other economic, cultural, and political issues led the nation into civil war.

Thematic Learning Objectives

CUL-2, 5, 6; POL-2, 3, 6; WOR-2, 5, 6; ID-1, 2, 5, 6; WXT-2, 4, 5, 6, 7; PEO-2, 3, 6; ENV-3, 4

CHAPTER 10 discusses demographic changes as the United States population grew rapidly. Increased immigration led to rising nativist sentiment and significant changes in the nature of the American workforce. Particularly important to keep in mind as you read are the reactions of Americans to Irish and German immigration. Also important are the growing economic and social links between the Northeast and Northwest (now considered the Midwest) brought about by transportation links and commercial links, and how those growing links led to further isolation with the South, politically and economically. You should also focus on how the factory system, combined with the agricultural, business, technological, and transportation revolutions, led to urbanization, the growing disparity between rich and poor, and the emergence of a significant middle class. Additionally, the chapter focuses on the changing role of women in an increasingly industrial society and the emergence of the "cult of domesticity." Lastly you should also focus on the differences in the type of agriculture pursued in each of the different regions. As you read, evaluate the following ideas:

- Industrialization increased sectional differences, which led to varied expectations on the role of government in the economy.
- Increasing advanced technology and industrialization led to a rapidly expanding middle class, while also increasing the disparity of wealth between the rich and poor.
- Improvements in transportation systems tied the Northeast and Northwest more closely together, both economically and socially.
- The agricultural and transportation revolutions improved mobility of the American people and enriched diets and allowed settlement in growing urban industrial areas.
- The factory system led to the need for an increased labor supply that was increasingly met by native-born women and immigrants.
- Industrialization and the factory system transformed gender and family roles, and increased the separation between home and the workplace.
- Natural population growth was aided by increasing immigration from Europe, which led to rising nativist sentiment.

THE CHANGING AMERICAN POPULATION

The American industrial revolution was a result of many factors. Before it could occur, the United States needed a population large enough both to grow its own food and to provide a surplus workforce for an industrial economy. It needed a transportation and communications system capable of sustaining commerce over a large geographic area. It needed the technology to permit manufacturing on a large scale. And it needed systems of business organization capable of managing large industrial enterprises. By 1860, the northern regions of the nation had acquired at least the beginnings of all those things.

THE AMERICAN POPULATION, 1820–1840

Three trends characterized the American population between 1820 and 1840, all of them contributing in various ways to economic growth. The population was increasing rapidly; much of it was moving from the countryside into the industrializing cities of the Northeast and Northwest; and much of it was migrating westward.

The American population had stood at only 4 million in 1790. By 1820, it had reached 10 million; by 1830, nearly 13 million; and by 1840, 17 million. The United States was growing much more rapidly in population than Britain or Europe. One reason for this substantial population growth was improvements in public health. The number and ferocity of epidemics (such as the great cholera plague of 1832)–which had periodically decimated urban and even rural populations in America–slowly declined, as did the nation's mortality rate. The population increase was also a

Population (millions)

Year	Population
1620	.005
1650	.05
1680	.15
1710	.35
1740	.90
1770	2.15
1800	5.30
1830	12.90
1860	31.50

POPULATION GROWTH, 1620–1860 From its tiny beginnings in the seventeenth century, the American population grew rapidly and dramatically so that by 1860—with more than 31 million people—the United States was one of the most populous countries in the world.

• *How did this growing population contribute to the nation's economic transformation?*

Total immigration during five-year periods (in thousands)

Year	Total
1821–1825	41
1826–1830	103
1831–1835	203
1836–1840	347

IMMIGRATION, 1821–1840 Among the sources of the nation's growing population in the nineteenth century was rapidly increasing immigration. This graph shows how rapidly immigration to the United States increased in the 1820s and 1830s. The 347,000 immigrants in the second half of the 1830s were almost nine times the number in the first half of the 1820s.

• *Where did most of these new immigrants settle?*

REASONS FOR POPULATION INCREASE result of a high birth rate. In 1840, white women bore an average of 6.14 children each, a decline from the very high rates of the eighteenth century but still substantial enough to produce rapid population increases, particularly since a larger proportion of children could expect to grow to adulthood than had been the case a generation or two earlier.

Immigration, choked off by wars in Europe and economic crises in America, contributed little to the American population in the first three decades of the nineteenth century but rapidly revived beginning in the 1830s. Of the total 1830 population of nearly 13 million, the foreign-born numbered fewer than 500,000. But the number of immigrants climbed by 60,000 in 1832 and nearly 80,000 in 1837. Reduced transportation costs and increasing economic opportunities helped stimulate the immigration boom, as did deteriorating economic conditions in some areas of Europe. The migrations introduced new groups to the United States. In particular, the number of immigrants arriving from the southern counties of Ireland began to grow, marking the beginning of a tremendous influx of Irish Catholics that would continue through the three decades before the Civil War.

Much of this new European immigration flowed into the rapidly growing cities of the Northeast. But urban growth was a result of substantial internal migration as well. As the agricultural regions of New England and other areas grew less profitable, more and more people picked up stakes and moved–some to more promising agricultural regions in the West, but many to eastern cities. In 1790, one person in thirty had lived in a city (defined as a community of 8,000 or more); in 1820, one in twenty; and in 1840, one in twelve.

The rise of New York City was particularly dramatic. By 1810, it was the largest city in the United States. That was partly a result of its superior natural harbor. It was also a result of the Erie Canal (completed in 1825), which gave the city unrivaled access to the interior, and of liberal state laws that made the city attractive for both foreign and domestic commerce.

IMMIGRATION AND URBAN GROWTH, 1840–1860

The growth of cities accelerated even more dramatically between 1840 and 1860. The population of New York, for example, rose from 312,000 to 805,000. **RAPID URBANIZATION** (New York's population would have numbered 1.2 million in 1860 if Brooklyn, which was then a separate municipality, had been included in the total.) Philadelphia's population grew over the same twenty-year period from 220,000 to 565,000; Boston's from 93,000 to

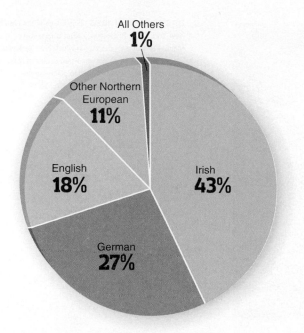

SOURCES OF IMMIGRATION, 1820–1840 This pie chart shows where the large numbers of immigrants portrayed in the previous chart came from. Note the very large number of Irish immigrants.

• *Why were the Irish among the most likely immigrant groups to become part of the industrial workforce?*

177,000. By 1860, 26 percent of the population of the free states was living in towns (places of 2,500 people or more) or cities (8,000 people or more), up from 14 percent in 1840. That percentage was even higher for the industrializing states of the Northeast. (In the South, by contrast, the increase of urban residents was only from 6 percent in 1840 to 10 percent in 1860.)

The booming agricultural economy of the western regions of the nation produced significant urban growth as well. Between 1820 and 1840, communities that had once been small western villages or trading posts became major cities: St. Louis, Pittsburgh, Cincinnati, Louisville. All of them benefited from strategic positions on the Mississippi River or one of its major tributaries. All of them became centers of the growing carrying trade that connected the farmers of the Midwest with New Orleans and, through it, the cities of the Northeast. After 1830, however, substantial shipping began from the Mississippi River to the Great Lakes, creating major new urban centers that gradually superseded the river ports. Among them were Buffalo, Detroit, Milwaukee, Cleveland, and most important—Chicago.

The enlarged urban population was in part a reflection of the growth of the national population as a whole, which rose by more than a third—from 23 million to over 31 million—in the decade of the 1850s alone. By 1860, the American population was larger than Britain's and quickly approaching that of France and

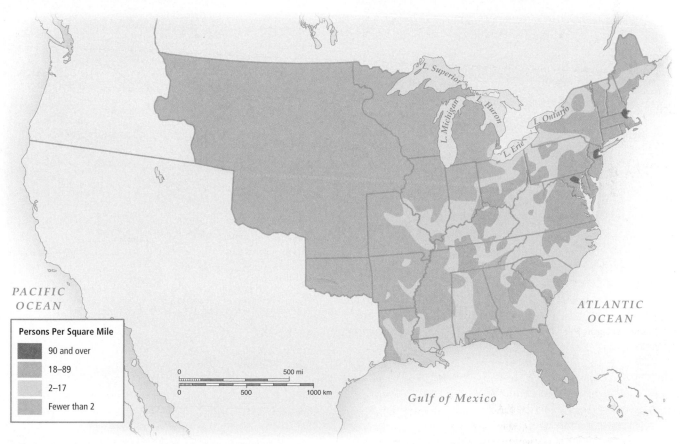

AMERICAN POPULATION DENSITY, 1820 The population of the United States in 1820 was still overwhelmingly rural and agrarian and was still concentrated largely in the original thirteen states, although settlement was growing in the Ohio River valley to the west. Note how few areas of the country were populated really densely: a small area in northeastern Massachusetts, the area around New York City, and the area in Maryland adjoining Baltimore.

• *What accounts for the density in these areas?*

BROADWAY IN 1836 This image of the area of New York City's Broadway in what is now lower Manhattan suggests the way in which New York was becoming an increasingly important center of trade and commerce—and a densely urban place—in the 1830s. (© The Granger Collection, New York)

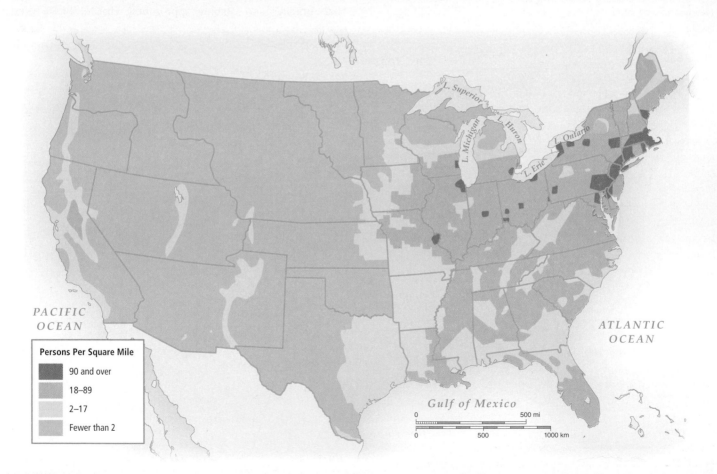

Persons Per Square Mile

- 90 and over
- 18–89
- 2–17
- Fewer than 2

AMERICAN POPULATION DENSITY, 1860 By 1860, the population of the United States had spread much more evenly across the entire country. Communities that had once been small trading posts emerged as major cities. Among them were St. Louis, Pittsburgh, Cincinnati, and Louisville. In the meantime, the Erie Canal had opened up a large and prosperous market area for New York City. Note the larger and more numerous areas of dense population, including many in the Midwest.

• *What accounts for the growing population density in some areas of the South?*

Germany. Urban growth was also a result of the increasing flow of people into cities from the farms of the Northeast. Immigration from abroad continued to increase as well. Between 1840 and 1850, more than 1.5 million Europeans moved to America, three

SURGING IMMIGRATION times the number of arrivals in the 1830s. Still greater numbers arrived in the 1850s–over 2.5 million. Almost half the residents of New York City in the 1850s were recent immigrants. In St. Louis, Chicago, and Milwaukee, the foreign-born outnumbered those of native birth. Few immigrants settled in the South. Only 500,000 lived in the slave states in 1860, and a third of these were concentrated in Missouri, mostly in St. Louis.

The newcomers came from many different countries and regions: England, France, Italy, Scandinavia, Poland, and Holland.

GERMAN AND IRISH IMMIGRANTS But the overwhelming majority came from Ireland and Germany. In 1850, the Irish constituted approximately 45 percent and the Germans over 20 percent of the foreign-born in America. By 1860, there were more than 1.5 million Irish-born and approximately 1 million German-born people in the United States. In Germany, the economic dislocations of the industrial revolution had caused widespread poverty, and the collapse of the liberal revolution there in 1848 also persuaded many Germans to emigrate. In Ireland, the oppressiveness and unpopularity of English rule drove many people out. But even more important was the greatest disaster in Ireland's history: a catastrophic failure of the potato crop (and other food crops) that caused the devastating "potato famine" of 1845-1849. Nearly a million people died of starvation and disease. Well over a million more emigrated to the United States.

The great majority of Irish immigrants settled in the eastern cities, where they swelled the ranks of unskilled labor. Most German immigrants moved on to the Northwest, where they became farmers or went into business in the western towns. One reason for the difference was wealth: German immigrants generally arrived with at least some money; the Irish had practically none. Another important reason was gender. Most German immigrants were members of family groups or were single men, for whom movement to the agricultural frontier was both possible and attractive. Many Irish immigrants were young, single women, for whom movement west was much less plausible. They were more likely to stay in the eastern cities, where factory and domestic work was available.

THE RISE OF NATIVISM

Some native-born Americans welcomed the new immigration, which provided a large supply of cheap labor that they believed would help keep wage rates low. Land speculators and others with investments in the sparsely populated West hoped that immigrants would move into the region and help expand the population, and thus the market for land and goods, there. Political leaders in western states and territories wanted the immigrants to swell their population, which would increase the political influence of the region. Wisconsin, for example, permitted foreign-born residents to become voters as soon as they had

declared their intention of seeking citizenship and had resided in the state for a year; other western states soon followed its lead. In eastern cities, too, urban political organizations eagerly courted immigrant voters, hoping to enhance their own political strength.

Other Americans, however, viewed the growing foreign-born population with alarm. Their fears led to the rise of what is known as "nativism," a defense of native-born people and a hostility to the foreign-born, usually combined with a desire to stop or slow immigration. The emerging nativism took many forms. Some of it was a result of simple racism. Many nativists (conveniently overlooking their own immigrant heritage) argued that the new immigrants were inherently inferior to older-stock Americans. Some viewed them with the same contempt and prejudice–and the same low estimate of their potential abilities–with which they viewed African Americans and Indians. Many nativists avoided racist arguments but argued nevertheless that the newcomers were socially unfit to live alongside people of older stock, that they did not bring with them sufficient standards of civilization. Evidence for that, they claimed, was the wretched urban and sometimes rural slums in which they lived. (Many nativists seemed to assume that such wretchedness was something immigrants chose, rather than the result of their extreme poverty.) Others–especially workers–complained that because foreigners were willing to work for low wages, they were stealing jobs from the native labor force. Protestants, observing the success of Irish Catholics in establishing footholds

Total immigration during five-year periods (in millions)

1,748

1,283

850

430

1841–1845 1846–1850 1851–1855 1856–1860
Year

IMMIGRATION, 1841–1860 Immigration continued to increase in the forty years before the Civil War. This chart illustrates the much higher levels of growth than in the previous forty years. The low point in this era was the first half of the 1840s, in which 430,000 new immigrants entered the United States. That was significantly higher than the largest number of the previous twenty years. In the early 1850s, the number of immigrants grew to nearly 2 million. (© Comstock Images/Alamy)

• *What events in Europe contributed to this increase in immigration?*

AP CONSIDER THE SOURCE

NATIVISM AND ANTI-IMMIGRATION SENTIMENT

ANTI-IMMIGRATION SENTIMENT AND NATIVISM HAVE LONG BEEN PRESENT IN THE NATION, as indicated by the first two items below: an 1852 broadside announcing publication of The *American Patriot,* a nativist newspaper, and a cartoon from 1850. The broadside issues a dire warning: "Already the enemies of our dearest institutions, like the foreign spies in the Trojan horse of old, are within our gates. They are disgorging themselves upon us, at the rate of Hundreds of Thousands Every Year! They aim at nothing short of conquest and supremacy over us."

Fast-forward to April 2010 when Arizona Senate Bill 1070 was signed into law by Governor Jan Brewer. Provisions of the law include the right of law enforcement agents to ask for a person's immigration documents during routine stops and a mandate that any illegal immigrant convicted of a crime or misdemeanor be turned over to federal immigration agents. Critics claim that the law is a product of nativism and anti-immigration sentiment directed specifically at those of Hispanic origin, which will result in persecution of both legal and undocumented immigrants. See the excerpt on p. 261.

ANTI-IMMIGRATION SENTIMENT—1850/1852

(Historicus, Inc.)

ARIZONA SENATE BILL 1070—2010

AP TEST PRACTICE

Questions assume cumulative content knowledge from this chapter and previous chapters.

1. Both the broadside and cartoon from the 1850s and the excerpt of the 2010 Arizona law—particularly section E—demonstrate what commonality in the anti-immigrant attitudes from both time periods?

   (A) Anti-immigrant attitudes in both time periods were solely based on economic issues.

   (B) Anti-immigrant attitudes in both time periods carried a strong racial component.

   (C) Anti-immigrant attitudes in both time periods revolved around voting rights.

   (D) Anti-immigrant attitudes in both time periods stemmed from religious differences.

2. Both the broadside and cartoon from the 1850s and the excerpt from the Arizona law most suggest which bias regarding their view of the immigrants they are targeting?

   (A) The immigrants are gentle folk, but are paupers.

   (B) The immigrants bring new economic opportunities.

   (C) The immigrants take away economic opportunities from American citizens.

   (D) The immigrants are criminal or deceptive.

Notwithstanding any other law, a law enforcement agency may securely transport an alien who is unlawfully present in the United States and who is in the agency's custody to a federal facility in this state or to any other point of transfer into federal custody that is outside the jurisdiction of the law enforcement agency.

E. A law enforcement officer, without a warrant, may arrest a person if the officer has probable cause to believe that the person has committed any public offense that makes the person removable from the United States.

F. Except as provided in federal law, officials or agencies of this state and counties, cities, towns and other political subdivisions of this state may not be prohibited or in any way be restricted from sending, receiving or maintaining information relating to the immigration status of any individual or exchanging that information with any other federal, state or local governmental entity for the following official purposes:

1. Determining eligibility for any public benefit, service or license provided by any federal, state, local or other political subdivision of this state.

2. Verifying any claim of residence or domicile if determination of residence or domicile is required under the laws of this state or a judicial order issued pursuant to a civil or criminal proceeding in this state.

3. Confirming the identity of any person who is detained.

4. If the person is an alien, determining whether the person is in compliance with the federal registration laws prescribed by Title II, Chapter 7 of the Federal Immigration and Nationality Act.

Source: State of Arizona Senate Bill 1070, 2010.

in urban politics, warned that the Catholic Church and the pope were gaining a foothold in American government. Whig politicians were outraged because so many of the newcomers voted Democratic. Others complained that the immigrants corrupted politics by selling their votes. Many older-stock Americans of both parties feared that immigrants would bring new, radical ideas into national life.

Out of these tensions and prejudices emerged a number of new secret societies created to combat what nativists had come to call the "alien menace." Most of them originated in the

NATIVE AMERICAN PARTY

Northeast. Some later spread to the West and even to the South. The first of these, the Native American Association, began agitating against immigration in 1837. In 1845, nativists held a convention in Philadelphia and formed the Native American Party (unaware that the term they used to describe themselves would one day become a common label for American Indians). Many of the nativist groups combined in 1850 to form the Supreme Order of the Star-Spangled Banner. It endorsed a list of demands that included banning Catholics or the foreign-born from holding public office, more-restrictive naturalization laws, and literacy tests for voting. The order adopted a strict code of secrecy, which included the secret password, used in lodges across the country, "I know nothing." Ultimately, members of the movement became known as the "Know-Nothings."

Gradually, the Know-Nothings turned their attention to party politics, and after the election of 1852 they created a new political organization that they called the American Party. In the East, the new organization scored an immediate and astonishing success in the elections of 1854: the Know-Nothings cast a large vote in

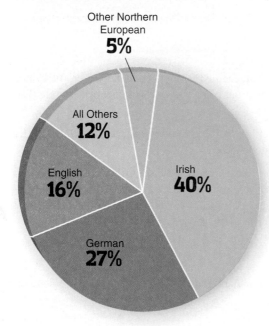

SOURCES OF IMMIGRATION, 1840–1860 Although the extent of immigration increased dramatically in the two decades after 1840, the sources of it remained remarkably stable. Note how closely the distribution of immigrant groups portrayed in this pie chart parallels that in the similar chart for the 1820–1840 period on p. 257.

* *What were some of the differences between what German and Irish immigrants did once they arrived in America?*

THE LAMENT OF THE IRISH EMIGRANT This poem, written by Helen Selina Blackwood and set to music by William R. Dempster captures the painful time in Ireland during the potato famine from the mid 1840s to the early 1850s. During this period an estimated 1 million people died of starvation and another million emigrated, many to the United States. The protagonist of the poem sings of his grief from having lost his wife and his promise to remember her in the new land. (The Library of Congress [LC-USZ62-41030])

THE KNOW-NOTHINGS

Pennsylvania and New York and won control of the state government in Massachusetts. Elsewhere, the progress of the Know-Nothings was modest. Western members of the party, because of the presence of many German voters in the area, found it expedient not to oppose naturalized Protestants. After 1854, the strength of the Know-Nothings declined.

TRANSPORTATION, COMMUNICATIONS, AND TECHNOLOGY

Just as the industrial revolution needed a growing population, it also required an efficient system of transportation and communications. Such a system was essential in creating regional, national, and ultimately international markets. Progress in this area required not just significant investment, but also important advances in technological knowledge.

The Canal Age

From 1790 until the 1820s, the so-called turnpike era, Americans had relied largely on roads for internal transportation. But in a country as large as the United States was becoming, roads alone (and the mostly horse-drawn vehicles that used them) were not adequate for the nation's expanding needs. And so, in the 1820s and 1830s, Americans began to turn to other means of transportation as well.

The larger rivers, especially the Mississippi and the Ohio, had been important transportation routes for years, but most of the traffic on them consisted of flat barges—little more than rafts—that floated downstream laden with cargo and were broken up at the end of their journeys because they could not navigate back upstream. To return north, shippers had to send goods by land or by agonizingly slow upstream vessels that sometimes took up to four months to travel the length of the Mississippi.

These rivers became vastly more important by the 1820s, as **STEAMBOATS** steamboats grew in number and improved in design. The new riverboats carried the corn and wheat of northwestern farmers and the cotton and tobacco of southwestern planters to New Orleans in a fraction of the time of the old barges. From New Orleans, oceangoing ships

KNOW-NOTHING SOAP This illustrated advertising label for soap manufactured in Boston alludes to the Know Nothing or nativist movement. The Indians depicted in the foreground and the teepees and camp in the background symbolize the movement's prejudice against foreigners. (The Library of Congress [LC-USZCN4-182])

THE ERIE CANAL This lithograph suggests something of the enormous engineering challenges faced by the builders of the Erie Canal. This picture shows a deep cutting at Lockport, New York. The canal was completed in 1825 and connected New York to the Great Lakes via the Hudson River. (© The Granger Collection, New York)

took the cargoes on to eastern ports. Steamboats also developed a significant passenger traffic, and companies built increasingly lavish vessels to compete for this lucrative trade.

But neither the farmers of the West nor the merchants of the East were wholly satisfied with this pattern of trade. Farmers would pay less to transport their goods (and eastern consumers would pay less to consume them) if they could ship them directly eastward to market, rather than by the roundabout river-sea route; and northeastern merchants, too, could sell larger quantities of their manufactured goods if they could transport their merchandise more directly and economically to the West. New highways across the mountains provided a partial solution to the problem. But the costs of hauling goods overland, although lower than before, were still too high for anything except the most compact and valuable merchandise. The thoughts of some merchants and entrepreneurs began, therefore, to turn to an alternative: canals.

A team of four horses could haul one and a half tons of goods eighteen miles a day on the turnpikes. But the same four horses, walking along the "towpaths" next to canals while yoked to barges, could draw a boatload of a hundred tons twenty-four miles a day. By the 1820s, the economic advantages of canals had

ECONOMIC ADVANTAGES OF CANALS

generated a booming interest in expanding the water routes to the West. Canal building was too expensive for private enterprise, and the job of digging canals fell largely to the states. The ambitious state governments of the Northeast took the lead in constructing them. New York was the first to act. It had the natural advantage of a good land route between the Hudson River and Lake Erie through the only real break in the Appalachian chain. But the engineering tasks were still imposing. The distance was more than 350 miles, several times the length of any of the existing canals in America. The route was interrupted by high ridges and a wilderness of woods. After a long public debate over whether the scheme was practical, canal advocates prevailed when De Witt Clinton, a late but ardent convert to the cause, became governor in 1817. Digging began on July 4, 1817.

The building of the Erie Canal was the greatest construction project the United States had ever undertaken. The canal itself was simple: a ditch forty feet wide and four feet deep, with

THE ERIE CANAL

towpaths along the banks. But hundreds of difficult cuts and fills, some of them enormous, were required to enable the canal to pass through hills and over valleys; stone aqueducts were

CANALS IN THE NORTHEAST, 1823–1860 The great success of the Erie Canal, which opened in 1825, inspired decades of energetic canal building in many areas of the United States, as this map illustrates. But none of the new canals had anything like the impact of the original Erie Canal, and thus none of New York City's competitors—among them Baltimore, Philadelphia, and Boston—were able to displace it as the nation's leading commercial center.

• *What form of transportation ultimately displaced the canals?*

necessary to carry it across streams; and eighty-eight locks, of heavy masonry with great wooden gates, were needed to permit ascents and descents. The Erie Canal was not just an engineering triumph, but an immediate financial success as well. It opened in October 1825, amid elaborate ceremonies and celebrations, and traffic was soon so heavy that within about seven years tolls had repaid the entire cost of construction. By providing a route to the Great Lakes, the canal gave New York City direct access to Chicago and the growing markets of the West. New York City could now compete with (and increasingly replace) New Orleans as a destination for agricultural goods (particularly wheat) and other products of the West, and as a source for manufactured goods to be sold in the region.

The system of water transportation–and the primacy of New York City–extended farther when the states of Ohio and Indiana, inspired by the success of the Erie Canal, provided water connections between Lake Erie and the Ohio River. These canals helped connect them by an inland water route all the way to New York, although it was still necessary to transfer cargoes several times between canal, lake, and river craft. One of the immediate results of these new transportation routes was increased white settlement in the Northwest, because canals made it easier for migrants to make the westward journey and to ship their goods back to eastern markets.

Rival cities along the Atlantic seaboard took alarm at the prospect of New York's acquiring so vast a hinterland. But they had limited success in catching up. Boston, its way to the Hudson River blocked by the Berkshire Mountains, did not even try to connect itself to the West by canal; its hinterland would remain confined largely to New England. Philadelphia and Baltimore had the still more formidable Allegheny Mountains to contend with. They made a serious effort at canal building, nevertheless, but with discouraging results. Pennsylvania's effort ended in an expensive failure. Maryland constructed part of the Chesapeake and Ohio Canal beginning in 1828, but completed only the stretch between Washington, D.C., and Cumberland, Maryland, and thus never crossed the mountains. In the South, Richmond and Charleston also aspired to build water routes to the Ohio Valley, but never completed them.

In the end, canals did not provide a satisfactory route to the West for any of New York's rivals. Some cities, however, saw their opportunity in a different and newer means of transportation. Even before the canal age had reached its height, the era of the railroad was already beginning.

The Early Railroads

Eventually, railroads became the primary transportation system for the United States, and they remained so until the construction of the interstate highway system in the midtwentieth century.

Railroads emerged from a combination of technological and entrepreneurial innovations. The technological breakthroughs

TECHNOLOGICAL BASIS OF THE RAILROAD

included the invention of tracks, the creation of steam-powered locomotives, and the development of railroad cars that could serve as public carriers of passengers and freight. By 1804, both English and American inventors had experimented with steam engines for propelling land vehicles. In 1820, John Stevens ran a locomotive and cars around a circular track on his New Jersey estate. And in 1825, the Stockton and Darlington Railroad in England opened a short length of track and became the first line to carry general traffic.

American entrepreneurs, especially in those northeastern cities that sought better communication with the West, quickly grew interested in the English experiment. The first company to begin actual operations was the Baltimore and Ohio, which opened a thirteen-mile stretch of track in 1830. In New York, the Mohawk and Hudson began running trains along the sixteen miles between Schenectady and Albany in 1831. By 1836, more than a thousand miles of track had been laid in eleven states.

But there was not yet a true railroad system. Even the longest of the lines was comparatively short in the 1830s, and most of them served simply to connect water routes, not to link one railroad to another. Even when two lines did connect, the tracks often differed in gauge (width), so that cars from one line often could not fit onto the tracks of another.

RACING ON THE RAILROAD Peter Cooper, who in later years was best known as a philanthropist and as the founder of the Cooper Union in New York City, was also a successful iron manufacturer. Cooper designed and built the first steam-powered locomotive in America in 1830 for the Baltimore and Ohio Railroad. On August 28 of that year, he raced his locomotive (the Tom Thumb) against a horse-drawn railroad car. This sketch depicts the moment when Cooper's engine overtook the horsecar. (© Universal Images Group/Getty Images)

Schedules were erratic, and wrecks were frequent. But railroads made some important advances in the 1830s and 1840s. The introduction of heavier iron rails improved the roadbeds. Steam locomotives became more flexible and powerful. Redesigned passenger cars became stabler, more comfortable, and larger.

Railroads and canals were soon competing bitterly. For a time, the Chesapeake and Ohio Canal Company blocked the advance of the Baltimore and Ohio Railroad through the narrow gorge of the upper Potomac, which it controlled; and the state of New York prohibited railroads from hauling freight in competition with the Erie Canal and its branches. But railroads had so many advantages that when they were able to compete freely with other forms of transportation they almost always prevailed.

COMPETITION BETWEEN RAILROADS AND CANALS

THE TRIUMPH OF THE RAILS

After 1840, railroads gradually supplanted canals and all other modes of transport. In 1840, there were 2,818 miles of railroad tracks in the United States; by 1850, there were 9,021. An unparalleled burst of railroad construction followed in the 1850s, tripling the amount of trackage in just ten years. The most comprehensive and efficient system was in the Northeast, which had twice as much trackage per square mile as the Northwest and four times as much as the South. But the expansion of the rails left no region untouched. Railroads were even reaching west of the Mississippi, which was spanned at several points by great iron bridges. One line ran from Hannibal to St. Joseph on the Missouri River, and another was under construction between St. Louis and Kansas City.

An important change in railroad development was the trend toward the consolidation of short lines into longer lines (known as "trunk lines"). By 1853, four major railroad trunk lines had crossed the Appalachian Mountains to connect the Northeast with the Northwest. The New York Central and the New York and Erie gave New York City access to the Lake Erie ports. The Pennsylvania railroad linked Philadelphia and Pittsburgh, and the Baltimore and Ohio connected Baltimore with the Ohio River at Wheeling. From the terminals of these lines, other railroads into the interior touched the Mississippi River at eight points. Chicago became the rail center of the West, served by fifteen lines and more than a hundred daily trains. The appearance of the great trunk lines tended to divert traffic from the main water routes–the Erie Canal and the Mississippi River. By lessening the dependence of the West on the Mississippi, the railroads helped weaken further the connection between the Northwest and the South.

CONSOLIDATION

Capital to finance the railroad boom came from many sources. Private American investors provided part of the necessary funding, and railroad companies borrowed large sums from abroad. But local governments–states, counties, cities, towns–also often contributed capital, because they were eager to have railroads serve them. The railroads obtained substantial additional assistance from the federal government in the form of public land grants. In 1850, Senator Stephen A. Douglas of Illinois and other railroad-minded politicians persuaded Congress to grant federal lands to aid the Illinois Central, which was building from Chicago toward the Gulf of Mexico. Other states and their railroad promoters demanded the same privileges, and by 1860, Congress had allotted over 30 million acres to eleven states to assist railroad construction.

INNOVATIONS IN COMMUNICATIONS AND JOURNALISM

Critical to the railroads was an important innovation in communications: the magnetic telegraph. Telegraph lines extended along the tracks, connecting one station with another and aiding the scheduling and routing of trains. But the telegraph also permitted instant communication between distant cities, tying the nation together as never before. At the same time, it helped reinforce the schism between the North and the South. Like railroads, telegraph lines were far more extensive in the North than in the South, and they helped similarly to link the North to the Northwest (and thus to separate the Northwest further from the South).

THE TELEGRAPH

The telegraph burst into American life in 1844, when Samuel F. B. Morse, after several years of experimentation, succeeded in transmitting from Baltimore to Washington, D.C., the news of James K. Polk's nomination for the presidency. The relatively low cost of constructing wire systems made the Morse telegraph system seem the ideal answer to the problems of long-distance communication. By 1860, more than 50,000 miles of wire connected most parts of the country; and a year later, the Pacific telegraph, with 3,595 miles of wire, opened between New York City and San Francisco. By then, nearly all the independent lines had joined in one organization, the Western Union Telegraph Company.

New forms of journalism also drew communities into a common communications system. In 1846, Richard Hoe invented the steam cylinder rotary press, making it possible to print newspapers rapidly and cheaply. The development of the telegraph, together with the introduction of the rotary press, made possible much speedier collection and distribution of news than ever before. In 1846, newspaper publishers from around the nation formed the Associated Press to promote cooperative news gathering by wire; no longer did they have to depend on the cumbersome exchange of newspapers for out-of-town reports.

THE ASSOCIATED PRESS

Major metropolitan newspapers began to appear in the larger cities of the Northeast. In New York alone, there were Horace Greeley's *Tribune*, James Gordon Bennett's *Herald*, Henry J. Raymond's *Times*, and others. All gave serious attention to national and even international events and had substantial circulations beyond the city.

In the long run, journalism would become an important unifying factor in American life. In the 1840s and 1850s, however, the rise of the new journalism helped to feed sectional discord. Most of the major magazines and newspapers were in

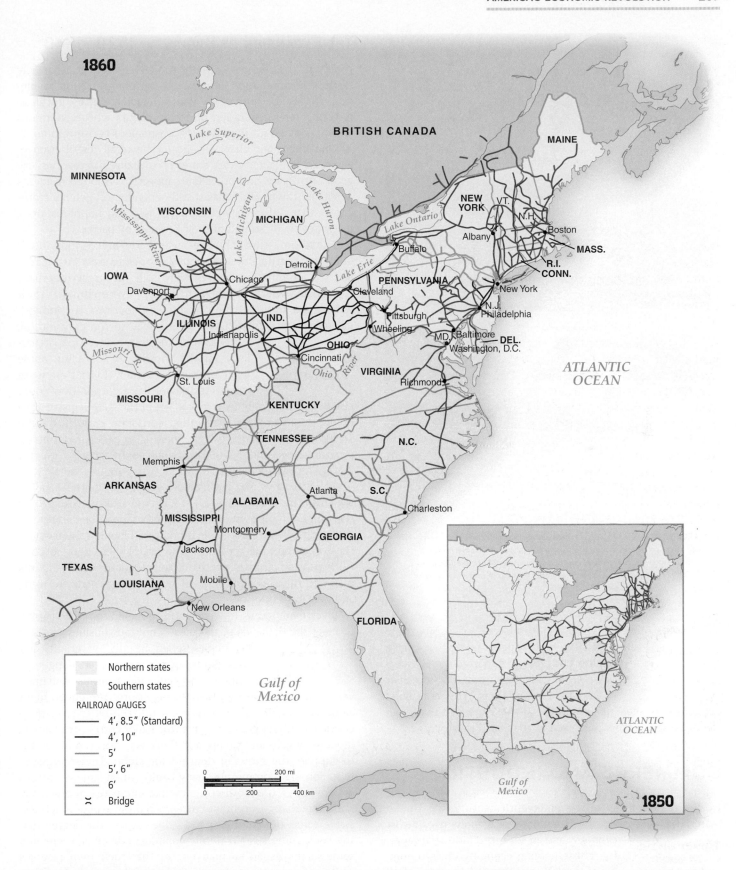

RAILROAD GROWTH, 1850–1860 These two maps illustrate the dramatic growth in the extent of American railroads in the 1850s. Note the particularly extensive increase in mileage in the upper Midwest (known at the time as the Northwest). Note too the relatively smaller increase in railroad mileage in the South. Railroads forged a close economic relationship between the upper Midwest and the Northeast, and weakened the Midwest's relationship to the South.

• *How did the growth of railroads in the North contribute to the South's growing sense of insecurity within the Union?*

THE TELEGRAPH The telegraph provided rapid communication across the country—and eventually across oceans—for the first time. Samuel F. B. Morse was one of a number of nineteenth-century inventors who helped create the telegraph, but Morse was the most commercially successful of the rivals, hence his greater reputation than others who helped create it. (The Library of Congress [LCUSZC4-5040])

THE EXPANSION OF BUSINESS, 1820–1840

American business grew rapidly in the 1820s and 1830s, partly because of population growth and the transportation revolution, but also because of the daring, imagination, and ruthlessness of a new generation of entrepreneurs whose enormous wealth allowed for lifestyles of "conspicuous consumption."

One important change came in the retail distribution of goods. In the larger cities, stores specializing in groceries, dry goods, hardware, and other lines appeared, although residents of smaller towns and villages still depended on general stores (stores that did not specialize). In these less populous areas, many people did much of their business by barter.

The organization of business was also changing. Individuals or limited partnerships continued to operate most businesses, and the dominating figures were still the great merchant capitalists, who generally had sole ownership of their enterprises. In some larger businesses, however, the individual merchant capitalist was giving way to the corporation.

ADVANTAGES OF THE CORPORATION Corporations began to develop particularly rapidly in the 1830s, when some legal obstacles to their formation were removed. Previously, a corporation could obtain a charter only by a special act of the state legislature—a cumbersome process that stifled corporate growth. By the 1830s, however, states were beginning to pass general incorporation laws, under which a group could secure a charter merely by paying a fee.

The new laws also permitted a system of limited liability, which meant that individual stockholders risked losing only the value of their own investment if a corporation should fail, and that they were not liable (as they had been in the past) for the corporation's larger losses. The rise of these new corporations made possible the accumulation of much greater amounts of capital and hence made possible much larger manufacturing and business enterprises.

Investment alone, however, still provided too little capital to meet the demands of the most ambitious businesses. Such **INADEQUATE CREDIT** businesses relied heavily on credit, and their borrowing often created dangerous instability. Credit mechanisms remained very crude in the early nineteenth century. The government alone could issue official currency, but the official currency consisted only of gold and silver (or paper certificates backed literally by gold and silver), and there was thus too little of it to support the growing demand for credit. Under pressure from corporate promoters, many banks issued large quantities of bank notes—unofficial currency that circulated in much the same way that government currency did but was of much less stable value. But the notes had value only to the degree that the bank could sustain public confidence in their value; and some banks issued so many notes that their own reserves could not cover them. As a result, bank failures were frequent, and bank deposits were often insecure. The difficulty of obtaining credit for business investment remained, therefore, an impediment to economic growth.

the North, reinforcing the South's sense of subjugation. **FUELING SECTIONAL DISCORD** Southern newspapers tended to have smaller budgets and reported largely local news. Few had any impact outside their immediate communities. The combined circulation of the *Tribune* and the *Herald* exceeded that of all the daily newspapers published in the South put together.

COMMERCE AND INDUSTRY

By the middle years of the nineteenth century, the United States had developed the beginnings of a modern capitalist **IMPACT OF THE MARKET ECONOMY** economy and an advanced industrial capacity. This emerging economy created enormous wealth and changed the face of all areas of the nation. But it did not, of course, affect everyone equally. Some classes and regions benefited from the economic development far more than others.

THE EMERGENCE OF THE FACTORY

The most profound economic development in mid-nineteenth-century America was the rise of the factory. Before the War of 1812, most of what manufacturing there was in the United States took place within private households or in small, individually operated workshops. Men and women built or made products by hand, or with simple machines such as hand-operated looms. Gradually, however, improved technology and increasing demand produced a fundamental change. It came first in the New England textile industry. There, entrepreneurs were beginning to make use of new and larger machines driven by water power that allowed them to bring textile operations together under a single roof. This factory system, as it came to be known, spread rapidly in the 1820s and began to make serious inroads into the old home-based system of spinning thread and weaving cloth.

Factories also penetrated the shoe industry, concentrated in eastern Massachusetts. Shoes were still largely handmade,

TRANSFORMATION OF THE SHOE INDUSTRY but manufacturers were beginning to employ workers who specialized in one or another of the various tasks involved in production. Some factories began producing large numbers of identical shoes in ungraded sizes and without distinction as to rights and lefts. By the 1830s, factory production was spreading from textiles and shoes into other industries and from New England to other areas of the Northeast.

Between 1840 and 1860, American industry experienced even more dramatic growth as the factory system spread rapidly. In 1840, the total value of manufactured goods produced in the United States stood at $483 million; ten years later the figure had climbed to over $1 billion; and in 1860 it reached close to $2 billion. For the first time, the value of manufactured goods was approximately equal to that of agricultural products.

Of the approximately 140,000 manufacturing establishments in the country in 1860, 74,000 were located in the

THE INDUSTRIAL NORTHEAST Northeast. The Northeast plants were so large that the region produced more than two-thirds of the nation's manufactured goods. Of the 1,311,000 workers in manufacturing in the United States, about 938,000 were employed in the mills and factories of New England and the mid-Atlantic states.

ADVANCES IN TECHNOLOGY

Even the most highly developed industries were still immature by later standards. American cotton manufacturers, for example, produced goods of coarse grade; fine items continued to come from England. But machine technology advanced more rapidly in the United States in the mid-nineteenth century than in any other country in the world. The American economy was growing so rapidly that the rewards of technological innovation were very great. Change was so rapid, in fact, that some manufacturers built their new machinery out of wood; by the time the wood wore out, they reasoned, improved

CARGO IN CHICAGO This engraving of cargo ships docked in the Chicago River illustrates the rapid growth of the city in the 1850s as it was becoming the great trading center of the central part of the United States. (© Archive Photos/Getty Image)

technology would have made the machine obsolete. By the beginning of the 1830s, American technology had become so advanced–particularly in textile manufacturing–that industrialists in Britain and Europe were beginning to travel to the United States to learn new techniques, instead of the other way around.

The manufacturing of machine tools–the tools used to make machinery parts–was an important contribution to manufacturing. The government supported much of the research and development of machine tools, often in connection with supplying the military. For example, a government armory in Springfield, Massachusetts, developed two important tools–the turret lathe (used for cutting screws and other metal parts) and the universal milling machine (which replaced the hand chiseling of complicated parts and dies)–early in the nineteenth century. The precision grinding machine (which became critical to, among other things, the construction of sewing machines) was designed in the 1850s to help the United States Army produce standardized rifle parts. The federal armories such as those at Springfield and Harpers Ferry, Virginia, became the breeding ground for many technological discoveries, and a magnet for craftsmen and factory owners looking for ideas that could be useful to them. By the 1840s, the machine tools used in the factories of the Northeast were already better than those in most European factories.

INTERCHANGEABLE PARTS Interchangeable parts, which Eli Whitney and Simeon North had tried to introduce into gun factories, now found their way into many industries. Eventually, interchangeability would revolutionize watch and clock making, the manufacturing of locomotives and steam engines, and the making of many farm tools. It would also help make possible such newer devices as bicycles, sewing machines, typewriters, cash registers, and eventually the automobile.

Industrialization was also profiting from the introduction of new sources of energy. Coal was replacing wood and water power as fuel for many factories. The production of coal, most of it mined around Pittsburgh in western Pennsylvania, leaped from 50,000 tons in 1820 to 14 million tons in 1860. The new power source made it possible to locate mills away from running streams and thus permitted industry to expand still more widely.

TECHNOLOGICAL INNOVATIONS The great technological advances in American industry owed much to American inventors, as the patent records of the time make clear. In 1830, the number of inventions patented was 544; by 1850, the figure had risen to 993; and in 1860, it stood at 4,778. In 1839, Charles Goodyear, a New England hardware merchant, discovered a method of vulcanizing rubber (treating it to give it greater strength and elasticity); by 1860, his process had found over 500 uses and had helped create a major American rubber industry. In 1846, Elias Howe of Massachusetts constructed a sewing machine; Isaac Singer made improvements on it, and the Howe-Singer machine was soon being used in the manufacture of ready-to-wear clothing.

For all the technological innovations that characterized the early factory system, most American industry remained dependent on the most traditional source of power: water. In the 1820s and 1830s, water power remained the most important source of power for manufacturing. The first important factory towns in New England–Lawrence, Lowell, and others–emerged where they did because of the natural waterfalls that could be channeled to provide power for the mills built along their banks. This sometimes required factories to close for periods in the winter when rivers were frozen. That was one reason factory owners began to look for alternative forms of energy that could be used throughout the year, which led them by the late 1830s to rely more and more on steam and other transportable forms of energy that could be fueled by wood, coal, or (later) petroleum.

MEN AND WOMEN AT WORK

However sophisticated industrial firms became technologically and administratively, manufacturers still relied above all on a supply of labor. In the 1820s and 1830s, factory labor came primarily from the native-born population. After 1840, the growing immigrant population became the most important new source of workers.

RECRUITING A NATIVE WORKFORCE

Recruiting a labor force was not an easy task in the early years of the factory system. Ninety percent of Americans in the 1820s still lived and worked on farms, and many urban residents were skilled artisans–independent crafts workers who owned and managed their own shops as small businessmen; they were not likely to flock to factory jobs. The available unskilled workers were not numerous enough to form a reservoir from which the new industries could draw.

The beginnings of an industrial labor supply came instead from the transformation of American agriculture in the nineteenth century. The opening of vast, fertile new farmlands in

TRANSFORMATION OF AMERICAN AGRICULTURE the Midwest, the improvement of transportation systems, the development of new farm machinery–all combined to increase food production dramatically. New farming methods were also less labor-intensive than the old ones; the number of workers required to produce large crops in the West was much smaller than the number required to produce smaller crops in the less fertile Northeast. No longer did each region have to feed itself entirely from its own farms; it could import food from other regions. As as result, farmers and their families began to abandon some of the relatively unprofitable farming areas of the East. In the Northeast, especially in New England, where poor land had always placed harsh limits on farm productivity, rural people began leaving the land to work in the factories.

Two systems of recruitment emerged to bring this new labor supply to the expanding textile mills. One, common in the mid-Atlantic states (especially in such major manufacturing centers as New York City and Philadelphia), brought whole families from the farm to the mill. Parents tended looms alongside their children, some of whom were no more than four or five years old. The second system, common in Massachusetts, enlisted young women, mostly farmers' daughters in their late teens and early twenties. It was known as the Lowell or Waltham System, after the factory towns in which it first emerged. Many of these women worked for several years in the factories, saved their wages, and returned home to marry and raise children. Others married men they met in the factories or in town and remained part of the industrial world, but often stopped working in the mills to take up domestic roles instead.

Labor conditions in these early years of the factory system were significantly better than those in English industry, better too than they would ultimately become in much of the United States. The employment of young children created undeniable hardships. But the misery was not as great as in European factories, since working children in America usually remained under the supervision of their parents. In England, by contrast, asylum authorities often hired out orphans to factory owners who showed little concern for their welfare and kept them in something close to slavery.

Even more different from the European labor pattern was the "Lowell System," which relied heavily, indeed almost exclusively, on young unmarried women.

THE LOWELL SYSTEM In England and other areas of industrial Europe, the conditions of work for women were often horrifyingly bad. A British parliamentary investigation revealed, for example, that women workers in the coal mines endured unimaginably wretched conditions. Some had to crawl on their hands and knees, naked and filthy, through cramped, narrow tunnels, pulling heavy coal carts behind them. It was little wonder that English visitors to America considered the Lowell mills a female paradise by contrast. The Lowell workers lived in clean boardinghouses and dormitories, which the factory owners maintained for them. They were well fed and carefully supervised. Because many New Englanders considered the employment of women to be vaguely immoral, the factory owners placed great emphasis on maintaining a proper environment for their employees, enforcing strict curfews and requiring regular church attendance. Employers quickly dismissed women suspected of immoral conduct. Wages for the Lowell workers were generous by the standards of the time. The women even found time to write and publish a monthly magazine, the *Lowell Offering*.

Yet even these relatively well-treated workers often found the transition from farm life to factory work difficult, even traumatic. Uprooted from everything familiar, forced to live

WOMEN WORKERS among strangers in a regimented environment, many women suffered from severe loneliness and disorientation. Still more had difficulty adjusting to the nature of factory work—the repetition of fixed tasks hour after hour, day after day. That the women had to labor from sunrise to sunset was not in itself a new experience; many of them had worked similarly long days on the farm. But that they now had to spend those days performing tedious, unvarying chores, and that their schedules did not change from week to week or season to season, made the adjustment to factory work especially painful. But however uncomfortable women may have found factory work, they had few other options. They were barred from such manual labor as construction or from work as sailors or on the docks. Most of society considered it unthinkable

RULES FOR EMPLOYEES

STRICT RULES GOVERNED THE WORKING LIFE OF THE YOUNG WOMEN who worked in the textile mills in Lowell, Massachusetts, in the first half of the nineteenth century. Equally strict rules regulated their time away from work (what little leisure time they enjoyed) in the company-supervised boardinghouses in which they lived. The excerpts from the *Handbook to Lowell* from 1848 that follow suggest the tight supervision under which the Lowell mill girls worked and lived.

Many companies today publish employee handbooks that provide information about employee responsibilities, including working hours and days, and expectations of employee performance. They may also outline employee benefits, such as compensation, vacation policies, and medical benefits. Some companies issue formal rules of conduct and ethics by which their employees must abide. The example from the Simpson Manufacturing Company, which makes building products, provides an interesting comparison to the Lowell guidelines.

HANDBOOK TO LOWELL—1848

HANDBOOK TO LOWELL

Factory Rules

REGULATIONS TO BE OBSERVED by all persons employed in the factories of the Hamilton Manufacturing Company. The overseers are to be always in their rooms at the starting of the mill, and not absent unnecessarily during working hours. They are to see that all those employed in their rooms are in their places in due season, and keep a correct account of their time and work. They may grant leave of absence to those employed under them, when they have spare hands to supply their places and not otherwise, except in cases of absolute necessity.

All persons in the employ of the Hamilton Manufacturing Company are to observe the regulations of the room where they are employed. They are not to be absent from their work without the consent of the overseer, except in cases of sickness, and then they are to send him word of the cause of their absence. They are to board in one of the houses of the company and give information at the counting room, where they board, when they begin, or, whenever they change their boarding place; and are to observe the regulations of their boarding-house.

Those intending to leave the employment of the company are to give at least two weeks' notice thereof to their overseer.

All persons entering into the employment of the company are considered as engaged for twelve months, and those who leave sooner, or do not comply with all these regulations, will not be entitled to a regular discharge.

The company will not employ anyone who is habitually absent from public worship on the Sabbath, or known to be guilty of immorality.

A physician will attend once in every month at the counting-room, to vaccinate all who may need it, free of expense.

Anyone who shall take from the mills or the yard, any yarn, cloth or other article belonging to the company will be considered guilty of stealing and be liable to prosecution.

Payment will be made monthly, including board and wages. The accounts will be made up to the last Saturday but one in every month, and paid in the course of the following week.

These regulations are considered part of the contract, with which all persons entering into the employment of the Hamilton Manufacturing Company, engage to comply.

Boarding House Rules

REGULATIONS FOR THE BOARDING-HOUSES of the Hamilton Manufacturing Company. The tenants of the boarding-houses are not to board, or permit any part of their houses to be occupied by any person, except those in the employ of the company, without special permission.

They will be considered answerable for any improper conduct in their houses, and are not to permit their boarders to have company at unseasonable hours.

The doors must be closed at ten o'clock in the evening, and no person admitted after that time, without some reasonable excuse.

The keepers of the boarding-houses must give an account of the number, names and employment of their boarders, when required, and report the names of such as are guilty of any improper conduct, or are not in the regular habit of attending public worship.

The buildings, and yards about them, must be kept clean and in good order; and if they are injured, otherwise than from ordinary use, all necessary repairs will be made, and charged to the occupant.

The sidewalks, also, in front of the houses, must be kept clean, and free from snow, which must be removed from them immediately after it has ceased falling; if neglected, it will be removed by the company at the expense of the tenant.

It is desirable that the families of those who live in the houses, as well as the boarders, who have not had the kine pox, should be vaccinated, which will be done at the expense of the company, for such as wish it.

Some suitable chamber in the house must be reserved, and appropriated for the use of the sick, so that others may not be under the necessity of sleeping in the same room.

JOHN AVERY, Agent.

Source: The Handbook to Lowell (1848)

SIMPSON MANUFACTURING CODE OF CONDUCT—2011

SIMPSON MANUFACTURING: CODE OF BUSINESS CONDUCT AND ETHICS

November 1, 2011

At Simpson Manufacturing Co., Inc. and its subsidiaries (Company), we expect that all of our employees, officers and directors will treat each other, our customers, and our suppliers with goodwill, trust, and respect. As a Company, we value honesty, high ethical standards and compliance with laws, rules and regulations

The following provides guidance on the application of these principles:

Compliance with laws, rules and regulations

...

Accounting Requirements: Follow the accepted rules and controls required by the U.S. Securities and Exchange Commission (SEC), Financial Accounting Standards Board (FASB), and New York Stock Exchange (NYSE). For additional information on these rules and controls, contact the Company's Chief Financial Officer.

Equal Employment Opportunity (EEO) and Discrimination Laws: It continues to be the practice of the Company to employ positive business and personnel practices designed to ensure the full realization of equal employment opportunity. Further, we expect all employees to accomplish their work in a businesslike manner with a concern for the well-being of their co-workers. Harassment of any employee by any other employee is prohibited, regardless of their working relationship. Any employee who experiences harassment should bring it to the attention of his/her supervisor or branch manager. If the employee is not satisfied that the matter has been appropriately addressed, the employee should feel free to contact the President of Simpson Strong-Tie or the President of Simpson Manufacturing.

Securities Laws: All employees of the Company are prohibited from transacting in the Company's securities, for themselves, family members, friends or any other person, while in the possession of material, nonpublic (inside) information concerning the Company. In addition employees must not give inside information to anyone. Inside information is information that the Company has not made public about any Company activities, such as earnings estimates, the commencement or outcome of litigation, mergers and acquisitions, or any other information that could affect the Company's fortunes and therefore the price of the stock. For more detailed information, please refer to Insider Trading Policies and Procedures, available from the Company's Chief Financial Officer.

Antitrust Laws: We do not discuss our prices with our competitors. We do not enter into illegal agreements or engage in illegal practices in restraint of trade. For additional information on antitrust laws, contact the President of Simpson Strong-Tie or the President of Simpson Manufacturing.

Anti Corruption Laws: Our officers, directors, employees and agents are expected to comply with all U.S. and foreign laws while conducting business outside the United States, including, but not limited to, the United States Foreign Corrupt Practices Act ("FCPA").

Health and safety

The Company seeks to provide a clean, safe and healthy place to work. All employees are expected to observe all safety rules and practices and to follow instructions concerning safe work practices.

Record keeping and reporting of information

All records and reported information must be accurate, complete, honest and timely.

Conflicts of interest

Every employee, officer and director, is expected to make decisions in the best interest of the Company and not for personal gain. A conflict of interest can arise when an employee, officer or director takes action or has a personal interest that may make it difficult to perform his or her work for the Company objectively and effectively. This may include outside business interests, outside employment, outside investments and business relationships with friends or relatives that could cause a conflict of interest. Employees, officers and directors should report potential conflicts of interest and are prohibited from taking for themselves personally opportunities that are discovered or may be available through the use of the Company's property, information or position. Employees are prohibited from accepting meals, entertainment, travel, gratuities, merchandise or promotional material that could influence objectivity in making business decisions. Employees are generally prohibited from accepting any such item worth more than $50. Certain business events may require an employee's participation in excess of this amount. These must be approved by their supervisor.

Fair dealing

Employees, officers and directors should endeavor to deal fairly with the Company's customers and suppliers and each other. No one should take unfair advantage of anyone else through manipulation or misrepresentation of material facts.

Quality

Products that meet our quality standards are essential to our success. Everyone in the Company is responsible for product quality and must be committed to ensuring the effectiveness of the Quality Management System. For more information on the Company's Quality Principles, please see your supervisor.

Protection and proper use of Company assets

All employees, officers and directors should protect the Company's assets and ensure their efficient use.

Confidentiality

Employees, officers and directors should maintain the confidentiality of information entrusted to them by the Company, its customers, and its vendors and suppliers, except when disclosure is authorized or legally mandated. Confidential information includes all non-public information.

Encouraging the reporting of any illegal or unethical behavior

Many areas of the law, such as securities and antitrust, are very complicated. The Company encourages employees to talk to supervisors, managers or other appropriate personnel when in doubt about the best course of action in a particular situation. Additionally, employees should report violations of laws, rules, regulations or the Code of Business Conduct and Ethics to the President of the Company or the subsidiary or an ombudsman appointed for this purpose. There will be no retaliation against anyone who presents this type of information in good faith.

Waiver of the Code of Business Conduct and Ethics

There will be no waivers to the Code of Business Conduct and Ethics.

AP TEST PRACTICE

Questions assume cumulative content knowledge from this chapter and previous chapters.

1. The difference in the nature of the content from the Lowell handbook from that of the Simpson guidelines best indicates which of the following regarding attitudes toward the workers in the textile mills of Lowell?

   (A) The textile workers were given greater personal freedom during the workday.

   (B) The textile workers were treated in a much more paternalistic manner.

   (C) The textile workers were looked upon with suspicion and distrust.

   (D) Professionalism was not expected of the textile workers.

2. What does the difference between the documents in the kinds of issues addressed best suggest about big business in the 19th century versus that in the 21st century?

   (A) Business in the 19th century contended with fewer government regulations.

   (B) Business in the 19th century had greater expectations for worker conduct.

   (C) Business in the 19th century faced more government regulations.

   (D) Issues of ethics were of greater concern to business in the 19th century.

3. Which of the following best describes a commonality between the two documents?

   (A) The purpose of both documents is to recruit employees.

   (B) The purpose of both documents is, ultimately, to protect the company.

   (C) The purpose of both documents is to ensure the well-being of its employees.

   (D) The purpose of both documents is to, ultimately, ensure employee morality.

LOWELL, MASSACHUSETTS, 1832 Lowell was one of the leading manufacturing centers of New England in the 1830s, and one of the largest textile centers in America. Lowell relied heavily on women workers. Company owners—in deference to popular uneasiness about women working outside the home—created a paternalistic system of boardinghouses for them, where they could be carefully supervised. This map shows the clusters of boardinghouses adjacent to groups of factories. Note how concentrated the manufacturing center of the town was, and how the transportation system (rail and water) served the factories. Note also the many churches, which women workers were usually required to attend.

• *What happened to this labor system in the 1840s and 1850s?*

for women to travel the country alone, as many men did, in search of opportunities. Work in the mills was in many cases the only alternative to returning to farms that could no longer support them.

The paternalistic factory system of Lowell did not, in any case, survive for long. In the competitive textile market as it developed in the 1830s and 1840s–a market prey to the booms

DECLINE OF THE LOWELL SYSTEM

and busts that afflicted the American economy as a whole–manufacturers found it difficult to maintain the high living standards and the attractive working conditions with which they had begun. Wages declined; the hours of work lengthened; the conditions of the boardinghouses deteriorated as the buildings decayed and overcrowding increased.

In 1834, mill workers in Lowell organized a union–the Factory Girls Association–which staged a strike to protest a 25 percent wage cut. Two years later, the association struck again–against a rent increase in the boardinghouses. Both strikes failed, and a recession in 1837 virtually destroyed the organization. Eight years later the Lowell women, led by the militant Sarah Bagley, created the Female Labor Reform

Association and began demanding a ten-hour day (some women worked twelve-hour shifts) and for improvements in conditions in the mills. The new association not only made demands of management; it also turned to state government and asked for legislative investigation of conditions in the mills. By then, however, the character of the factory workforce was changing again. The young women who had worked in the mills were gradually moving into other occupations–teaching or domestic service–or they got married. And textile manufacturers were turning to a less contentious labor supply: immigrants.

THE IMMIGRANT WORKFORCE

The rapidly increasing supply of immigrant workers after 1840 was a boon to manufacturers and other entrepreneurs. At last they had access to a source of labor that was both large and inexpensive. These new workers, because of their vast numbers and unfamiliarity with their new country, had less leverage than the women they at times displaced. As a result, they often encountered far worse working conditions. Construction

FOUR WOMEN WEAVERS This tintype shows four young women employed in the textile factories of Lowell, Massachusetts. Neatly dressed in matching uniforms, they conveyed the image the factory managers wanted the public to absorb: that women could work in the mills and still be protected from the rough-and-tumble world of industrialization. (© American Textile History Museum, Lowell, MA)

profitably and efficiently. By the mid-1840s, the town of Lowell—once a model for foreign visitors of enlightened industrial development—had become a squalid slum. Similarly miserable working-class neighborhoods were emerging in other northeastern cities.

Conditions were still not as bad as in most factory towns in England and Europe, but in almost all industrial areas, factories themselves were becoming large, noisy, unsanitary, and **HARSH WORK CONDITIONS** often dangerous places to work. The average workday was extending to twelve, often fourteen hours. Wages were declining, so that even skilled male workers could hope to earn only from $4 to $10 per week, while unskilled laborers were likely to earn only about $1 to $6 per week. Women and children, whatever their skills, also earned less than most men.

THE FACTORY SYSTEM AND THE ARTISAN TRADITION

It was not only the mill workers who suffered from the transition to the modern factory system. It was also the skilled artisans whose trades the factories were displacing. The artisan tradition was as much a part of the older, republican vision of America as the tradition of sturdy, independent, yeoman farmers. Independent craftsmen considered themselves embodiments of the American ideal; they clung to a vision of economic life that was in some ways very different from what the new capitalist class was promoting. Skilled artisans valued their independence; they also valued the stability and relative equality within their economic world.

The factory system threatened that world with obsolescence. **DE-SKILLING** Some artisans made successful transitions into small-scale industry. But others found themselves unable to compete with the new factory-made goods that sold for a fraction of the artisans' prices. In the face of this competition from industrial capitalists, craftsmen began early in the nineteenth century to form organizations—workingmen's political parties and the first American labor unions—to protect their endangered positions and to resist the new economic order. As early as the 1790s, printers and cordwainers (makers of high-quality boots and shoes) took the lead. Members of other skilled trades—carpenters, joiners, masons, plasterers, hatters, and shipbuilders—felt similarly vulnerable.

In such cities as Philadelphia, Baltimore, Boston, and New York, the skilled workers of each craft formed societies for **NATIONAL TRADE UNIONS** mutual aid. During the 1820s and 1830s, the craft societies began to combine on a city-wide basis and set up central organizations known as trade unions. With the widening of markets, the

gangs, made up increasingly of Irish immigrants, performed the **ECONOMIC ADVANTAGES OF IMMIGRANT LABOR** heavy, unskilled work on turnpikes, canals, and railroads under often intolerable conditions. Because most of these workers had no marketable skills and because of native prejudice against them, they received wages so low (and so intermittently, since the work was seasonal and uncertain) that they generally did not earn enough to support their families in even minimal comfort. Many of them lived in flimsy shanties, in grim conditions that endangered the health of their families (and reinforced native prejudices toward the "shanty Irish").

The arrival of Irish workers accelerated the deterioration of working conditions in New England. There was far less social pressure on owners to provide a decent environment for Irish workers than there had been for native women. Employers began paying piece rates (wages tied to how much a worker produced) rather than a daily wage and employed other devices to speed up production and use the labor force more economies of cities were interconnected, so workers soon realized there were advantages in joining forces. They established national unions or federations of local ones. In 1834, delegates from six cities founded the National Trades' Union; and in 1836, the printers and the cordwainers set up their own national craft unions.

This early craft union movement fared poorly. Labor leaders struggled against the handicap of hostile laws and hostile courts. The common law, as interpreted by the courts in the industrial states, viewed a combination among workers as an illegal conspiracy. The Panic of 1837, a dramatic financial collapse that produced a severe recession, weakened the movement further.

FIGHTING FOR CONTROL

Workers at all levels of the emerging industrial economy attempted to improve their lots. They tried, with little success, to persuade state legislatures to pass laws setting a maximum workday. Two states–New Hampshire in 1847 and Pennsylvania in 1848–passed ten-hour laws, limiting the workday unless the workers agreed to an "express contract" calling for more time on the job. Such measures were virtually without impact, however, because employers could simply require prospective employees to sign the "express contract" as a condition of hiring. Three states–Massachusetts, New Hampshire, and Pennsylvania–passed laws regulating child labor. But again, the results were minimal. The laws simply limited the workday to ten hours for children unless their parents agreed to something longer; employers had little difficulty persuading parents to consent to additional hours.

Perhaps the greatest legal victory of industrial workers came in Massachusetts in 1842, when the supreme court of the state, in *Commonwealth v. Hunt*, declared that unions were lawful organizations and that the strike was a lawful weapon. Other state courts gradually accepted the principles of the Massachusetts decision. On the whole, however, the union movement of the 1840s and 1850s remained generally ineffective. Some workers were reluctant to think of themselves as members of a permanent laboring force and resisted joining unions. But even those unions that did manage to recruit significant numbers of industrial workers were usually not large enough or strong enough to stage strikes, and even less frequently strong enough to win them.

Artisans and skilled workers, despite their setbacks in the 1830s, had somewhat greater success than did factory workers. But their unions often had more in common with preindustrial guilds than with modern labor organizations. In most cases, their primary purpose was to protect the favored position of their members in the labor force by restricting admission to the skilled trades. The organizing effort that had floundered in the 1830s revived impressively in the 1850s. Among the new organizations skilled workers created were the National Typographical Union, founded in 1852, the Stone

COMMONWEALTH v. HUNT

Cutters in 1853, the Hat Finishers in 1854, and the Molders and the Machinists, both in 1859.

Virtually all the early craft unions excluded women, even though female workers were numerous in almost every industry and craft. As a result, women began establishing their own protective unions by the 1850s, often with the support of middle-class female reformers. Like the male craft unions, the female protective unions had little power in dealing with employers. They did, however, serve an important role as mutual-aid societies for women workers.

FEMALE PROTECTIVE UNIONS

Despite these persistent efforts at organization and protest, the American working class in the 1840s and 1850s was notable for its relatively modest power. In England, workers were becoming a powerful, united, and often violent economic and political force. They were creating widespread social turmoil and helping to transform the nation's political structure. In America, nothing of the sort happened. Many factors combined to inhibit the growth of effective labor resistance. Among the most important was the flood of immigrant laborers into the country. The newcomers were usually willing to work for lower wages than native workers. Because they were so numerous, manufacturers had little difficulty replacing disgruntled or striking workers with eager immigrants. Ethnic divisions and tensions–both between natives and immigrants and among the various immigrant groups themselves–often led workers to channel their resentments into internal bickering rather than into their shared grievances against employers. There was, too, the sheer strength of the industrial capitalists, who had not only economic but also political and social power and could usually triumph over even the most militant challenges.

AMERICA'S DIVIDED WORKING CLASS

"FREE LABOR"

Despite the many obstacles and challenges that faced northern workers in the first half of the nineteenth century, nothing was more important than the idea of personal freedom. Most workers had hard lives, but they were proud of their personal freedoms and considered themselves what some people called the "sovereign individual"–people who could, at least in theory, make choices and change their lives.

Modern notions of freedom are much more robust than those of the early nineteenth century, when only a few men (and no women) were able to vote; when workers were sometimes bound to their employers for years; when husbands subjugated their wives and when, of course, millions of African Americans were living with almost no freedom. But even in the early years of American history, the belief in the freedom of the individual was strong. In the North in particular, personal liberty was growing exponentially for more and more Americans. By the mid-nineteenth century, most white Americans identified themselves as free individuals, no matter what their occupations or means.

Some of the great philosophers of nineteenth-century America argued that the "independency of the individual" required free people to escape from the market economy and find freedom in solitude and the wonders of nature—as Henry David Thoreau tried to do in his famous retreat to live alone in a cabin on Walden Pond in Concord, Massachusetts (see p. 318). But for most Americans, the opportunities for solitude and communion with nature were slim. For most northern workers, freedom meant the absence of slavery. It meant that they could leave jobs they did not want, move to new areas of the country, and seek opportunities to change their lives. Their material circumstances were sometimes far worse than those of many slaves in the South. Still, they believed that their lives were better than those who lacked freedom. And when the great debate over slavery began in the 1840s and 1850s, northern laborers—however bad their own lots—abhorred slavery, both because it was the antithesis of freedom and because they feared that slavery threatened the jobs of free laborers.

Not only slaves were denied the freedom that most Americans valued. The more than 200,000 free black men and women living in the North (and a few in the South) remained ineligible to vote and were not considered legal citizens. Many of the free blacks in the North were people who had been skilled crafts workers as slaves and who bought or were given their freedom. But their lots were in many ways worse than when they were working in the South. In the northern cities to which many free blacks moved, there were many white craftsmen already who saw black workers as rivals. Most free blacks worked in menial jobs and as domestic servants.

PATTERNS OF INDUSTRIAL SOCIETY

The industrial revolution made the United States—and particularly its more economically developed regions—dramatically wealthier almost every year. It was also making society more unequal, and it transformed social relationships and everyday life at almost every level—from the workplace to the family.

THE RICH AND THE POOR

The commercial and industrial growth of the United States greatly elevated the average income of the American people. But this increasing wealth was being distributed highly unequally. Substantial groups of the population shared hardly at all in the economic growth: slaves, Indians, landless farmers, and many of the unskilled workers on the fringes of the manufacturing system. But even among the rest of the population, disparities of income were marked. Wealth had always been unequally distributed in the United States, to be sure. Even in the era of the Revolution, according to some estimates, 45 percent of the wealth was concentrated in

INCREASING INEQUALITY IN WEALTH

the hands of about 10 percent of the population. But by the mid-nineteenth century, that concentration had become far more pronounced. In Boston in 1845, for example, 4 percent of the citizens are estimated to have owned more than 65 percent of the wealth; in Philadelphia in 1860, 1 percent of the population possessed more than half the wealth. Among the American people overall in 1860, according to scholarly estimates, 5 percent of the families possessed more than 50 percent of the wealth.

There had been wealthy classes in America almost from the beginning of European settlement. But the extent and character of wealth were changing in response to the commercial revolution of the mid-nineteenth century. Merchants and industrialists were accumulating enormous fortunes; and because there was now a significant number of rich people living in cities, a distinctive culture of wealth began to emerge. In large cities, people of great wealth gathered together in neighborhoods of great opulence. They founded clubs and developed elaborate social rituals. They looked increasingly for ways to display their wealth—in the great mansions they built, the showy carriages in which they rode, the lavish household goods they accumulated, the clothes they wore, the elegant social establishments they patronized. New York City, which had more wealthy families than anywhere else, developed a particularly elaborate high society.

POVERTY IN NEW YORK CITY This wood engraving from 1869 shows "squatters" and their dilapidated shanties. This group of extremely poor people lived on hilly land near New York City's new Central Park, an urban retreat designed for the city's wealthier classes. Compare the circumstances of these homeless people with those of the aristocrats shown in the picture on page 280. (© The Granger Collection, New York)

CENTRAL PARK To affluent New Yorkers, the construction of the city's great Central Park was important because it provided them with an elegant setting for their daily carriage rides—an activity ostensibly designed to expose the riders to fresh air but that was really an occasion for them to display their finery to their neighbors. (© Private Collection/The Bridgeman Art Library)

New Yorkers in 1857 were trying to make the city as important as London and Paris. To achieve this goal, they decided to build a great park that would impart elegance to the city and draw New Yorkers to the upper part of the city where new real estate was available. Two great landscape architects—Frederick Law Olmsted and Calvert Vaux—developed a vast part of Manhattan, displacing people from their houses in the process. The result was one of the largest parks

CENTRAL PARK in America. Olmsted called Central Park a place of "great importance as the first real park in this country." Designed with hills, lakes, paths, bridges, and elegant buildings, it began as a place for wealthy New Yorkers, but very soon became important to almost everyone in the city.

There was also a significant population of genuinely desti-

THE URBAN POOR tute people emerging in the growing urban centers of the nation. These were people who were not merely poor, in the sense of having to struggle to sustain themselves–most Americans were poor in that sense. They were almost entirely without resources, often homeless, dependent on charity or crime or both for survival.

Some of these "paupers," as contemporaries called them, were recent immigrants who had failed to find work or to adjust to life in the New World. Some were widows and orphans, stripped of the family structures that allowed most working-class Americans to survive. Some were people suffering from alcoholism or mental illness, unable to work. Others were victims of native prejudice–barred from all but the most menial employment because of race or ethnicity. The Irish were particular victims of such prejudice.

Among the worst off were free blacks. African American communities in antebellum northern cities were small by later standards, but most major urban areas had significant

AFRICAN AMERICAN POVERTY black populations. Some of these African Americans were descendants of families that had lived in the North for generations. Others were former slaves who had escaped from the South or been released by their masters or had bought their freedom; some former slaves, once free, then worked to buy the freedom of relatives left behind. In material terms, at least, life was not always much better for them in the North than it had been in slavery. Most had access only to very menial jobs, which usually paid too little to allow workers to support their families or educate their children; in bad times, many had access to no jobs at all. In most parts of the North, blacks could not vote, could not attend public schools, indeed could not use any of the public services available to white residents. Still, most blacks preferred life in the North, however arduous, to life in the South because it permitted them at least some level of freedom.

SOCIAL MOBILITY

One might expect the contrasts between conspicuous wealth and conspicuous poverty in antebellum America to have encouraged more class conflict than actually occurred. But a number of factors operated to limit resentments. For one thing, however much the relative economic position of American workers may have been declining, the absolute living standard of most laborers was improving. Life, in material terms at least, was usually better for factory workers than it had been on the farms or in the European societies from which they had migrated. They ate better, they were often better clothed and housed, and they had greater access to consumer goods.

SOCIAL MOBILITY There was also a significant amount of mobility within the working class, which helped to limit discontent. Opportunities for social mobility, for working one's way up the economic ladder, were relatively modest. A few workers did manage to move from poverty to riches by dint of work, ingenuity, and luck—a very small number, but enough to support the dreams of those who watched them. And a much larger number of workers managed to move at least one notch up the ladder—for example, becoming in the course of a lifetime a skilled, rather than an unskilled, laborer. Such people could envision their children and grandchildren moving up even further.

More common than social mobility was geographic mobility, which was even more extensive in the United States than in Europe, where it was considerable. America had a huge expanse of uncultivated land in the West, much of it open for settlement for the first time in the 1840s and 1850s. Some workers saved money, bought land, and moved west to farm it. The historian Frederick Jackson Turner later referred to the availability of western lands as a "safety valve" for discontent, a basic explanation for the relative lack of social conflict in the antebellum United States. But few urban workers, and even fewer poor ones, could afford to make such a move or had the expertise to know how to work land even if they could. Much more common was the movement of laborers from one industrial town to another. Restless, questing, sometimes hopeful, sometimes despairing, these frequently moving people were often the victims of layoffs, looking for better opportunities elsewhere. Their searches may seldom have led to a marked improvement in their circumstances, but the rootlessness of this large segment of the workforce—one of the most distressed segments—made effective organization and protest difficult.

There was, finally, another "safety valve" for working-class discontent: politics. Economic opportunity may not have greatly expanded in the nineteenth century, but opportunities to participate in politics did. And to many white, male working people, access to the ballot seemed to offer a way to help guide their society and to feel like a significant part of their communities.

MIDDLE-CLASS LIFE

For all the visibility of the very rich and the very poor in antebellum society, the fastest-growing group in America was the middle class. The expansion of the middle class was in part a result of the growth of the industrial economy and the increasing commercial life that accompanied it. Economic development opened many more opportunities for people to **RAPIDLY EXPANDING MIDDLE CLASS** own or work in businesses, to own shops, to engage in trade, to enter professions, and to administer organizations. In earlier times, when ownership of land had been the only real basis of wealth, society had been divided between people with little or no land (people Europeans generally called peasants) and a landed gentry (which in Europe usually meant an inherited aristocracy). Once commerce and industry became a source of wealth, these rigid distinctions broke down, and many people who did not own land could become prosperous by providing valuable services to the new economy or by owning capital other than land.

Middle-class life in the years before the Civil War rapidly established itself as the most influential cultural form of urban America. Middle-class families lived in solid and often substantial homes, which, like the wealthy, they tended to own. Workers and artisans were increasingly becoming renters—a relatively new phenomenon in American cities that spread widely in the early nineteenth century.

Middle-class women tended to remain in the home and care for the children and the household, although increasingly they were also able to hire servants—usually young, unmarried immigrant women who put in long hours of arduous work for very little money. One of the aspirations of middle-class women in an age when doing the family's laundry could take an entire day was to escape from some of the drudgery of housework.

New household inventions altered, and greatly improved, the character of life in middle-class homes. Perhaps the most **NEW HOUSEHOLD INVENTIONS** important was the invention of the cast-iron stove, which began to replace fireplaces as the principal vehicle for cooking and also as an important source of heat. These wood- or coal-burning devices were hot, clumsy, and dirty by the standards of the twenty-first century; but compared to the inconvenience and danger of cooking on an open hearth, they seemed a great luxury. Stoves gave cooks more control over the preparation of food and allowed them to cook several things at once.

Middle-class diets were changing rapidly in the antebellum years, and not just because of the wider range of cooking the stove made possible. The expansion and diversification of American agriculture, and the ability of farmers to ship goods to urban markets by rail from distant regions, greatly increased the variety of food available in cities. Fruits and vegetables were difficult to ship over long distances in an age with little refrigeration, but families had access to a greater variety of meats, grains, and dairy products than they had had in the past. A few households acquired iceboxes in the years before the Civil War, and the sight of wagons delivering large chunks of ice to wealthy and middle-class homes began to become a familiar part of urban life. Iceboxes allowed their owners to keep fresh meat and dairy products for as long as several days without spoilage. Most families, however, did not yet have any kind of refrigeration. Preserving food for them meant curing meat with salt and preserving fruits in sugar. Diets were generally much heavier and starchier than they are today, and middle-class people tended to be considerably stouter than would be fashionable in the twenty-first century.

Middle-class homes came to differentiate themselves from those of workers and artisans in other ways as well. They

GROWING CLASS DISTINCTIONS

were more elaborately decorated and furnished, with household goods made available for the first time through factory production. Houses that had once had bare walls and floors now had carpeting, wallpaper, and curtains. The spare, simple styles of eighteenth-century homes gave way to the much more elaborate, even baroque household styles of the early Victorian era—styles increasingly characterized by crowded, even cluttered rooms, dark colors, lush fabrics, and heavy furniture and draperies. Middle-class homes also became larger. It became less common for children to share beds and less common for all family members to sleep in the same room. Parlors and dining rooms separate from the kitchen—once a luxury reserved largely for the wealthy—became the norm for the middle class as well. Some urban middle-class homes had indoor plumbing and indoor toilets by the 1850s—a significant advance over the outdoor wells and privies that had been virtually universal only a few years earlier (and that remained common among working-class people).

THE CHANGING FAMILY

The new industrializing society of the northern regions of the United States produced profound changes in the nature and function of the family. At the heart of the transformation was the movement of families from farms to urban areas, where jobs, not land, were the most valued commodities. The patriarchal system of the countryside, whereby fathers controlled their children's futures by controlling the distribution of land to them, could not survive the move to a city or town. Sons and daughters were much more likely to leave the family in search of work than they had been in the rural world.

Another important change was the shift of income-earning work out of the home and into the shop, mill, or factory. In the early decades of the nineteenth century (and for many years before that), the family had been the principal unit of economic activity. Family farms, family shops, and family industries were the norm throughout most of the United States. Men, women, and children worked together, sharing tasks and jointly earning the income that sustained the family. But as farming spread to the fertile lands of the Northwest and

DECLINING ECONOMIC ROLE OF THE FAMILY

as the size and profitability of farms expanded, agricultural work became more commercialized. Farm owners in need of labor began to rely less on their families (which often were not large enough to satisfy the demand) and more on hired male workers. These farmhands performed many of the tasks that on smaller farms had once been the jobs of the women and children of the family. As a result, farm women tended to work increasingly at domestic tasks—cooking, sewing, gardening, and dairying—a development that spared them from some heavy labor but that also removed them from the principal income-producing activities of the farm. (See Chapter 11 for a discussion of family relations in the agrarian South.)

In the industrial economy of the rapidly growing cities, there was an even more significant decline in the traditional economic function of the family. The urban household became less important as a center of production. Instead, most income earners left home each day to work elsewhere. A sharp distinction began to emerge between the public world of the workplace—the world of commerce and industry—and the private world of the family. The world of the family was now more often dominated not by production, but by housekeeping, child rearing, and other primarily domestic concerns. It was also a world dominated by women.

Accompanying (and perhaps in part caused by) the changing economic function of the family was

FALLING BIRTH RATES

a decline in the birth rate. In 1800, the average American woman could be expected to give birth to approximately seven children during her childbearing years. By 1860, the average woman bore five children. The birth rate fell most quickly in urban areas and among middle-class women. Mid-nineteenth-century Americans had access to some birth-control devices, which undoubtedly contributed in part to the change. There was also a significant rise in abortions, which remained legal in some states until after the Civil War and which, according to some estimates, may have terminated as many as 20 percent of all pregnancies in the 1850s. But the most important cause of the declining birth rate was changes in sexual behavior—including increased abstinence.

WOMEN AND THE "CULT OF DOMESTICITY"

The emerging distinction between the public and private worlds, between the workplace and the home, led to increasingly sharp distinctions between the social roles of men and women. Those distinctions affected not only factory workers and farmers, but members of the growing middle class as well. There had, of course, always been important differences between

PASTORAL AMERICA, 1848 This painting by the American artist Edward Hicks suggests the degree to which Americans continued to admire the "Peaceable Kingdom" (the name of another, more famous Hicks work) of the agrarian world. Hicks titled this work *An Indian Summer View of the Farm w. Stock of James C. Cornell of Northampton Bucks County Pennsylvania. That Took the Premium in the Agricultural Society, October the 12, 1848.* It portrays the diversified farming of a prosperous Pennsylvania family, shown here in the foreground with their cattle, sheep, and workhorses. In the background stretches a field ready for plowing and another ready for harvesting. (Courtesy National Gallery of Art, Washington)

the male and female spheres in American society. Women had long been denied many legal and political rights enjoyed by men; within the family, the husband and father had traditionally ruled, and the wife and mother had generally bowed to his demands and desires. It had long been practically impossible for most women to obtain divorces, although divorces initiated by men were often easier to arrange. (Men were also far more likely than women to win custody of children in case of a divorce.) In most states, husbands retained almost absolute authority over both the property and persons of their wives. Wife beating was illegal in only a few areas, and the law did not acknowledge that rape could occur within marriage. Women traditionally had very little access to the worlds of business or politics. Indeed, in most communities custom dictated that women never speak in public before audiences that included men.

Most women also had much less access to education than men, a situation that survived into the mid-nineteenth cen-

FEMALE EDUCATION

tury. Although they were encouraged to attend school at the elementary level, they were strongly discouraged–and in most cases effectively barred–from pursuing higher education.

Oberlin in Ohio became the first college in America to accept female students; it permitted four to enroll in 1837, despite criticism that coeducation was a rash experiment approximating free love. Oberlin authorities were confident that "the mutual influence of the sexes upon each other is decidedly happy in the cultivation of both mind & manners." But few other institutions shared their views. Coeducation remained extraordinarily rare until long after the Civil War; and only a very few women's colleges–such as Mount Holyoke, founded in Massachusetts by Mary Lyon in 1837–emerged.

No longer income producers, middle-class women became guardians of the "domestic virtues." Their role as mothers,

NEW ROLES FOR WOMEN

entrusted with the nurturing of the young, seemed more central to the family than it had in the past. And their role as wives–as companions and helpers to their husbands–grew more important as well. Middle-class women also became more important as consumers. They learned to place a high value on keeping a clean, comfortable, and well-appointed home, on entertaining, and on dressing elegantly and stylishly.

AP CONSIDER THE SOURCE

FAMILY TIME

HOW A FAMILY SPENDS TIME TOGETHER has been a favorite subject of artists for centuries. Studying where families gather, how they celebrate, and how they interact and communicate when relaxing or playing is a powerful way to gather information about conventional roles of mothers, fathers, extended family members, children, and sometimes servants.

The two images following are separated by 172 years yet strive to tell a similar story about family life. The first image, of a parlor in antebellum Philadelphia, appeared in *Godey's Lady's Book* in May 1842. Focused on the lives of better-off white women, *Godey's Lady's Book* featured advice columns on fashion, manners, home decoration, and child rearing. The second, by photographer Eric Audras, is set in present-day America. Audras, who chronicles the joys and struggles of modern families, has a keen eye for catching what fascinates parents and children today.

Much is communicated in the small details of each composition: the style of dress, the type of activities being pursued, and the spatial organization of family members. When such details are collectively analyzed, they tell us about the evolution of family life in America.

FAMILY TIME—1842

FAMILY DEVOTION-MORNING (© Archive Photos/Getty Images)

FAMILY TIME—2013

(© ONOKY/Getty Images (RF))

AP TEST PRACTICE

Questions assume cumulative content knowledge from this chapter and previous chapters.

1. What does the illustration from *Godey's Lady's Book* most suggest about the value of reading as a leisure activity—at least for middle class families—in the first half of the 19th century?

   (A) Reading was one among a great variety of leisure activities highly valued.

   (B) Reading was not highly valued, as only the father is reading in the illustration.

   (C) Reading was given high importance, as the father, who is central in the illustration, is prominently shown reading to an attentive family.

   (D) Books were mostly used as decorative items to display social status.

2. What does the difference in the ways that the pursuit of leisure activity is shown and the spatial organization of the family members in both images most suggest about family life in the first half of the 19th century, compared to family life of today?

   (A) Family life in the early half of the 19th century was less patriarchal.

   (B) Family life in the early half of the 19th century was more patriarchal.

   (C) Children had greater independence within the family, in the early half of the 19th century.

   (D) Family life in the early half of the 19th century was matriarchal.

3. What does the difference in the activities of the parents in both images best suggest about middle-class, domestic gender roles in the first half of the 19th century, compared to middle-class, domestic gender roles of today?

   (A) The gender roles within domestic life were much more distinct in the 19th century.

   (B) In the 19th century, both genders shared equally in the domestic roles.

   (C) The distinction between domestic gender roles was less sharp in the 19th century.

   (D) There was less formality in gender roles in the 19th century.

4. What does the illustration from *Godey's Lady Book* most suggest about the ideal of women in the 19th century?

   (A) Expectations of women to direct the social life within the family became more prominent.

   (B) Women were increasingly expected to display independence.

   (C) The role of women as nurturers became more prominent.

   (D) The role of women as nurturers became less important.

NATHAN HAWLEY AND FAMILY Nathan Hawley, seated at center in this 1801 painting, was typical of many early-nineteenth-century fathers in having a very large family. Nine members are visible here. Hawley at the time was the warden of the Albany County jail in New York, and the painting was by William Wilkie, one of the inmates there. The painting suggests that Hawley was a man of modest but not great means. His family is fashionably dressed, and there are paintings on the walls—signs of style and affluence. But the house is very simply furnished, without drapes for the windows, with a simple painted floor cloth in the front room, and a bare floor in the back. (*Nathan Hawley and Family;* William Wilkie ca.1801. Albany, New York. Watercolor on paper; 15 3/4″ × 20″. Signed lower right: *William Wilkie fecit;* inscribed in lower margin: *NATHAN HAWLEY and FAMILY, Nov*ʳ*. 3*ᵈ*. 1801.* © Albany Institute of History and Art Purchase 1951.58)

Occupying their own "separate sphere," some women began to develop a distinctive female culture. Friendships among women became increasingly intense; women began to form

WOMEN'S SEPARATE SPHERE

their own social networks (and, ultimately, to form female clubs and associations that were of great importance to the advancement of various reforms). A distinctive feminine literature began to emerge to meet the demands of middle-class women. There were women's magazines, of which the most prominent was *Godey's Lady's Book,* edited after 1837 by Sarah Hale. The magazine scrupulously avoided dealing with public controversies or political issues and focused instead on fashions, shopping and homemaking advice, and other purely domestic concerns. Politics and religion were inappropriate for the magazine, Hale explained in 1841, because "other subjects are more important for our sex and more proper for our sphere."

By the standards of a later era, the increasing isolation of women from the public world seems to be a form of oppression and discrimination. And it is true that few men considered women fit for business, politics, or the professions. On the other hand, most middle-class men—and many middle-class women as well—considered the new female sphere a vehicle

for expressing special qualities that made women in some ways superior to men. Women were to be the custodians of

BENEFITS AND COSTS

morality and benevolence, just as the home—shaped by the influence of women—was to be a refuge from the harsh, competitive world of the marketplace. It was women's responsibility to provide religious and moral instruction to their children and to counterbalance the acquisitive, secular impulses of their husbands. Thus the "cult of domesticity," as some scholars have called it, brought both benefits and costs to middle-class women. It allowed them to live lives of greater material comfort than in the past, and it placed a higher value on their "female virtues" and on their roles as wife and mother. At the same time, it left women increasingly detached from the public world, with few outlets for their other interests and energies.

The costs of that detachment were particularly clear among unmarried women of the middle class. By the 1840s, the ideology of domesticity had grown so powerful that few genteel women would any longer consider working (as many had in the past) in shops or mills, and few employers would consider hiring them. But unmarried women nevertheless required some income-producing activity. They had few choices. Some could become teachers or nurses, professions that seemed to call for the same female qualities that made women important within the home; and both of those professions began in the 1840s and 1850s to attract significant numbers of women, although not until the Civil War did females begin to dominate them. Otherwise, unmarried females were largely dependent on the generosity of relatives or hired as governesses for children or companions for widows and other women.

Middle-class people gradually came to consider work by women outside the household to be unseemly, something

WORKING-CLASS WOMEN

characteristic of the lower classes—as indeed it was. But working-class women could not afford to stay home and cultivate the "domestic virtues." They had to produce income for their families. They continued to work in factories and mills, but under conditions far worse than those that the original, more "respectable" women workers had once enjoyed. They also frequently found employment in middle-class homes. Domestic service became one of the most frequent sources of female employment. In other words, now that production had moved outside the household, women who needed to earn money had to move outside their own households to do so.

LEISURE ACTIVITIES

Leisure time was scarce for all but the wealthiest Americans in the mid-nineteenth century. Most people worked long hours. Saturday was a normal working day. Vacations—paid or unpaid—were rare. For most people, Sunday was the only respite from work and was generally reserved for religion and rest. Almost no commercial establishments did any business on Sunday, and even within the home many families frowned upon playing games or engaging in other kinds of entertainment on the Sabbath. For working-class and middle-class people, therefore, holidays took on a special importance. That was one reason for the strikingly elaborate Fourth of July celebrations throughout the country. The celebrations were not just expressions of patriotism. They were also a way of enjoying one of the few holidays from work available to virtually all Americans.

In rural America, where most people still lived, the erratic pattern of farmwork gave many people some relief from the relentless work schedules of city residents. For urban people, however, leisure was something to be seized in what few free moments they had. Men gravitated to taverns for drinking, talking, and game-playing. Women gathered in one another's homes for conversation or card games or to share work on such household tasks as sewing. For educated people, whose numbers were rapidly expanding, reading became one of the principal leisure activities. Newspapers and magazines proliferated rapidly, and books—novels, histories, autobiographies, biographies, travelogues, and others—became staples of affluent homes. Women were particularly avid readers, and women writers created a new genre of fiction specifically for females—

the "sentimental novel," which often offered idealized visions of women's lives and romances (see p. 336).

There was also a vigorous culture of public leisure, even if many families had to struggle to find time or means to participate in it. In larger cities, theaters were becoming increasingly popular; and while some of them catered to particular

MINSTREL SHOWS

social groups, others attracted audiences that crossed class lines. Wealthy people, middle-class people, workers and their families: all could sometimes be found watching a performance of Shakespeare or a melodrama based on a popular novel or an American myth. Minstrel shows—in which white actors mimicked (and ridiculed) African American culture—became increasingly popular (see p. 420). Public sporting events—boxing, horse racing, cockfighting (already becoming controversial), and others—often attracted considerable crowds. Baseball—not yet organized into professional leagues—was beginning to attract large crowds when played in city parks or fields on the edges of towns (see p. 384). A particularly exciting event in many communities was the arrival of the circus—a traveling entertainment with roots in the Middle Ages that continued to entertain, delight, and bamboozle children and adults alike.

Popular tastes in public spectacle tended toward the bizarre and the fantastic. Most men and women lived in a constricted world of familiar things. Relatively few people traveled; and in the absence of film, radio, television, or even much photography, they hungered for visions of unusual phenomena that contrasted with their normal experiences. People going to the theater or the circus or the museum wanted to see things that amazed and even frightened them. Perhaps the most celebrated provider of such experiences

P. T. BARNUM

was the famous and unscrupulous showman P. T. Barnum, who opened the American Museum in New York City in 1842—not a showcase for art or nature, but a great freak show populated by midgets (the most famous named Tom Thumb), Siamese twins, magicians, and ventriloquists. Barnum was a genius in publicizing his ventures with garish posters and elaborate newspaper announcements. Only later, in the 1870s, did he launch the famous circus for which he is still best remembered. But he was always a pioneer in exploiting public tastes for the wild and exotic.

One of the ways Barnum tried to draw visitors to his museum was by engaging lecturers. He did so because he understood that the lecture was one of the most popular forms of entertainment in nineteenth-century America. Men and women flocked in enormous numbers to lyceums, churches, schools, and auditoriums to hear lecturers explain the latest advances in science, to describe their visits to exotic places, to provide vivid historical narratives, or to rail against the evils of alcohol or slavery. Messages of social uplift and reform attracted rapt audiences, particularly among women eager for guidance as they adjusted to the often jarring changes in the character of family life in the industrializing world.

P. T. BARNUM AND TOM THUMB P. T. Barnum, circus producer, next to a table on which stands Charles Stratton, a little person who came to be known as General Tom Thumb. Hoping to capitalize on the popular fascination with the bizarre and the fantastic, Barnum hired Stratton at the age of five to tour the country with his circus. Stratton sang, danced, and impersonated famous people such as Napoleon Bonaparte. (© Corbis)

THE AGRICULTURAL NORTH

Even in the rapidly urbanizing and industrializing Northeast, and more so in what nineteenth-century Americans called the Northwest (and what Americans today call the Midwest), most people remained tied to the agricultural world. But agriculture,

RISE OF COMMERCIAL AGRICULTURE

like industry and commerce, was becoming increasingly a part of the new capitalist economy, linked to the national and international market. Where agriculture could not compete in this new commercial world, it declined. Where it could compete, it simultaneously flourished and changed.

NORTHEASTERN AGRICULTURE

The story of agriculture in the Northeast after 1840 is one of decline and transformation. The reason for the decline was simple: the farmers of the section could no longer compete with the new and richer soil of the Northwest. Centers of production were gradually shifting westward for many of the farm goods that had in the past been most important to northeastern agriculture: wheat, corn, grapes, cattle, sheep, and hogs.

Some eastern farmers responded to these changes by moving west themselves and establishing new farms. Still others moved to mill towns and became laborers. Some farmers, how-

TRUCK FARMING IN THE NORTHEAST

ever, remained on the land and managed to hold their own. As the eastern urban centers increased in population, many farmers turned to the task of supplying food to

nearby cities; they raised vegetables (truck farming) or fruit and sold it in local towns. New York, for example, led all other states in apple production.

The rise of cities also stimulated the rise of profitable dairy farming. Approximately half the dairy products of the country were produced in the East; most of the rest came from the West, where Ohio was the leading dairy state. Partly because of the expansion of the dairy industry, the Northeast led other sections in the production of hay. New York was the leading hay state in the nation; Pennsylvania and New England grew large crops as well. The Northeast also exceeded other areas in producing potatoes.

But while agriculture in the region remained an important part of the economy, it was steadily becoming less important than the industrial growth of the Northeast itself. As a result, the rural population in many parts of the Northeast continued to decline.

THE OLD NORTHWEST

There was some industry in the states of the Northwest, more than in the South; and in the two decades before the Civil War, the region experienced steady industrial growth. By 1860, it had 36,785 manufacturing establishments employing 209,909 workers. There was a flourishing industrial and commercial area along the shore of Lake Erie, with Cleveland at its center. Another manufacturing region was in the Ohio River

INDUSTRIALIZATION IN THE OLD NORTHWEST

valley; the meatpacking city of Cincinnati was its nucleus. Farther west, the rising city of Chicago, destined to become the great metropolis

of the region, was emerging as the national center of the agricultural machinery and meatpacking industries.

Most of the major industrial activities of the West either served agriculture (as in the case of farm machinery) or relied on agricultural products (as in flour milling, meatpacking, whiskey distilling, and the making of leather goods). As this suggests, industry was much less important in the Northwest than farming.

Some areas of the Northwest were not yet dominated by whites. Indians remained the most numerous inhabitants of much of the upper third of the Great Lakes states until after the Civil War. In those areas, hunting and fishing, along with some sedentary agriculture, remained the principal economic activities of both whites and Native Americans. But the tribes did not become integrated into the new commercialized economy that was emerging elsewhere in the Northwest.

For the white (and occasionally black) settlers who populated the lands farther south, the Northwest was primarily an agricultural region. Its rich and plentiful lands made farming a lucrative and expanding activity there, in contrast to the declining agrarian Northeast. Thus the typical citizen of the Northwest was not an industrial worker or poor, marginal farmer, but the owner of a reasonably prosperous family farm. The average size of western farms was 200 acres, the majority owned by the people who worked them.

Rising farm prices around the world provided a strong incentive for these western farmers to engage in commercial agriculture. That usually meant concentrating on a single crop for market (corn, wheat, cattle, sheep, hogs, and others). In the early years of white settlement in the Northwest, farm prices rose because of the debilitation of European agriculture in the

AGRICULTURAL SPECIALIZATION aftermath of the Napoleonic Wars and the growing urban population (and hence the growing demand for food) of industrializing areas of Europe. The Northwest, with good water routes on the Mississippi for getting its crops to oceangoing vessels, profited from this international trade.

But industrialization, in both the United States and Europe, provided the greatest boost to agriculture. With the growth of factories and cities in the Northeast, the domestic market for farm goods increased dramatically. The growing national and worldwide demand for farm products resulted in steadily rising farm prices. For most farmers, the 1840s and early 1850s were years of increasing prosperity.

To meet the increasing demand for its farm products, residents of the Northwest worked strenuously, and often frantically, to increase their productive capacities. Many tried to take advantage of the large areas of still-uncultivated land and to enlarge the area of white settlement during the 1840s. By 1850, the growing western population was moving into the prairie regions both east and west of the Mississippi: into areas of Indiana, Michigan, Illinois, Missouri, Iowa, and Minnesota. Residents cleared forest lands or made use of fields the Indians had cleared many years earlier. And they began to develop a timber industry to make use of the forests that remained. Wheat was the staple crop of the region, but other crops—corn, potatoes, and oats—and livestock were also important.

The Northwest increased production not only by expanding the area of settlement, but also by adopting new agricultural technologies that greatly reduced the labor necessary for producing a crop and slowed the exhaustion of

NEW AGRICULTURAL TECHNOLOGIES the region's rich soil. Farmers began to cultivate new varieties of seed, notably Mediterranean wheat, which was hardier

CYRUS McCORMICK'S AUTOMATIC REAPER Cyrus McCormick invented an automatic reaper in 1831 and had it patented in 1834. The machine, drawn by a horse, cut wheat, corn, or other crops and left it lying in swaths in the field where farmworkers would gather it up and store it in stacks. The reaper allowed one worker to harvest as much wheat in a day as five could harvest using earlier methods. (© Hulton Archive/Getty Images)

than the native type; and they imported better breeds of animals, such as hogs and sheep from England and Spain, to take the place of native stock. Most important were improved tools and farm machines, which American inventors and manufacturers produced in rapidly increasing numbers. During the 1840s, more-efficient grain drills, harrows, mowers, and hay rakes came into wide use. The cast-iron plow, an earlier innovation, remained popular because its parts could be replaced when broken. An even better tool appeared in 1847, when John Deere established at Moline, Illinois, a factory to manufacture steel plows, which were more durable than those made of iron.

Two new machines heralded a coming revolution in grain production. The most important was the automatic reaper,

McCORMICK REAPER the invention of Cyrus H. McCormick of Virginia. The reaper enabled one worker to harvest as much wheat (or any other small grain) in a day as five could harvest using older methods. McCormick, who had patented his device in 1834, established a factory at Chicago, in the heart of the grain belt, in 1847. By 1860, more than 100,000 reapers were in use on western farms. Almost as important to the grain grower was the thresher—a machine that separated the grain from the wheat stalks. Threshers appeared in large numbers after 1840. Before that, farmers generally flailed grain by hand (seven bushels a day was a good average for a farm) or used farm animals to tread it (twenty bushels a day on the average). A threshing machine, such as those manufactured by the Jerome I. Case factory in Racine, Wisconsin, could thresh twenty-five bushels or more in an hour.

The Northwest considered itself the most democratic section of the country. But its democracy was based on a defense of economic freedom and the rights of property—a white, middle-class vision of democracy that was becoming common in many other parts of the country as well. Abraham Lincoln, an Illinois Whig, voiced the economic opinions of many of the people of his section. "I take it that it is best for all to leave each man free to acquire property as fast as he can," said Lincoln. "Some will get wealthy. I don't believe in a law to prevent a man from getting rich; it would do more harm than good. . . . When one starts poor, as most do in the race of life, free society is such that he knows he can better his condition; he knows that there is no fixed condition of labor for his whole life."

RURAL LIFE

Life for farming people was very different from life in towns and cities. It also varied greatly from one farming region to another. In the more densely populated farm areas east of the Appalachians and in the easternmost areas of the Northwest, farmers were usually part of vibrant communities and made extensive use of the institutions of those communities–the churches, schools, stores, and taverns. As white settlement moved farther west, farmers became isolated and had to struggle to find any occasions for contact with people outside their own families.

Religion drew farm communities together perhaps more than any other force, particularly since so many farm areas were populated by people of common ethnic (and therefore religious) backgrounds. Town or village churches were popular meeting places, for both services and social events–most of them dominated by women. Even in areas with no organized churches, farm families–and,

IMPORTANCE OF RELIGION IN RURAL COMMUNITIES

again, women in particular–gathered in one another's homes for prayer meetings, Bible readings, and other religious activities. Weddings, baptisms, and funerals also brought communities together in celebration or mourning.

But religion was only one of many reasons for interaction. Farm people joined together frequently to share tasks that a single family would have difficulty performing on its own; festive barn raisings were among the most frequent. Women prepared large suppers while the men worked on the barn and the children played. Large numbers of families also gathered together at harvest time to help bring in crops, husk corn, or thresh wheat. Women came together to share domestic tasks as well, holding "bees" in which groups of women joined together to make quilts, baked goods, preserves, and other products.

But despite the many social gatherings farm families managed to create, they lived in a world with much less contact with popular culture and public social life than people who lived in towns and cities. Rural people, often even more than urban ones, treasured their links to the outside world–letters from relatives and friends in distant places, newspapers and magazines from cities they had never seen, catalogs advertising merchandise that their local stores never had. Yet many also valued their separation from urban culture and cherished the relative autonomy that farm life gave them. One reason many rural Americans looked back nostalgically on country life once they moved to the city was that they sensed that in the urban world they did not have as much control over the patterns of their daily lives as they had once known.

AP CONNECTING THEMES

Chapter 10 examined the reasons for and consequences of rapid population growth in the United States. Increased immigration brought changes to the labor force and to American society in general, including to regional identities. Chapter 10 also examined how the agricultural and transportation revolutions complemented the rise of the American factory system, discussing the ways in which the rise of the factory system affected society. Especially affected were the labor force, economic growth, and social systems, including changing family and gender roles, growing inequities in the distribution of wealth, growth of urban areas, and cultural concepts, such as leisure time. Women, both working and middle class, experienced changes in social roles and expectations. Importantly, review the chapter for the continuing development of the national market economy and its impact on growing sectionalism.

The following themes have heightened importance in Chapter 10. You should now be able to do the following for each listed theme:

Identity: Analyze the impact of Irish and German immigration on notions of American identity.

Work, Exchange, and Technology: Analyze the impact of technological innovations on the labor force, class distinctions, and social mobility.

Peopling: Explain the reasons for and consequences of rapid population growth in the United States.

Politics and Power: Explain how movement toward a national market economy and the factory system led to political divisions and increased sectional tension.

Environment and Geography: Explain the impact of the natural environment on the development of regional political and economic identities.

Ideas, Beliefs, and Culture: Analyze how the role of women changed as America moved closer to an urban-based industrial society.

AP SUGGESTED STUDY

PEOPLE/PLACES/EVENTS As you study these items, think about how they demonstrate or relate to key concepts and historical themes from this chapter and previous chapters.

AP TEST PRACTICE

Questions assume cumulative content knowledge from this chapter and previous chapters.

MULTIPLE CHOICE Use the map on page 276 and your knowledge of U.S. history to answer questions 1-4.

1. Which factor exhibited by this map explains why manufacturing began in New England in the early 1800's?
   (A) An existing complex system of railroads for transportation of goods
   (B) Large numbers of laborers already available in urban areas
   (C) Abundant sources of water power
   (D) The Puritan ethos of industriousness and social order centered around the town meeting house

2. Which of the following most contributed to the decline of systems like those depicted in the map?
   (A) Social objections to women in the labor force
   (B) Increasing immigration to the U.S.
   (C) Harsh working conditions
   (D) Growth of trade unions

3. What was the socioeconomic background of many of the factory workers in systems like those depicted in the map?
   (A) Newly-arrived Dutch immigrants
   (B) Native American women, who were Christian converts
   (C) Young women from rural areas of the Northeast, where farming was more difficult
   (D) Recently-arrived, young Irish immigrant women

4. Which of the following developments most directly contributed to the availability of an initial workforce for systems like those shown in the map?
   (A) Dramatic increase in German and Irish immigration
   (B) Dramatic increase in food production capability in American agriculture

(C) Dramatic increase in transportation infrastructure
(D) The development of interchangeable parts in factory production of goods

MULTIPLE CHOICE Use the broadside and cartoon found on pages 260-261 to answer questions 5-6.

5. The broadside offers strong evidence that a major thrust of nativist sentiment against immigrants in the early to mid-19th century was
   (A) Strongly anti-Protestant
   (B) Strongly anti-British
   (C) Strongly anti-Chinese
   (D) Strongly anti-Catholic

6. Which of the following best describes what the broadside and cartoon suggest about the tone and nature of nativist sentiments in the first half of the 19th century?
   (A) Alarmist and that immigrants were threatening American democracy
   (B) Not taken very seriously and that immigrants weren't true threats
   (C) Fever-pitched, in which the nativist movement was posing a serious threat to U.S. foreign relations
   (D) Relatively low-key, but that immigrants were corrupt and vulgar

SHORT ANSWER Use your knowledge of U.S. history to answer questions 7-11.

7. Using the graphs on pages 257 and 262, answer a, b, and c.
   a) Briefly explain a reaction of Americans to the immigration patterns depicted in the graphs.
   b) Briefly explain ONE development in the period 1820-1860 that supports your answer in part a.

c) Briefly explain ONE development in the period 1820–1860 that serves as a counter-example to your answer in part a.

8. Answer a, b, and c.

a) Briefly explain ONE example of how technological development extended markets for the U.S. economy in the early- to mid-1800s.

b) Briefly explain ONE example of how technological development in the early- to mid-1800s increased efficiency in production of goods.

c) Briefly explain ONE example of how changes in business practices in the early- to mid-1800s accelerated the market economy.

9. Answer a, b, and c.

a) For one of the areas below, identify ONE historical development and briefly explain how this development affected regionalism in the U.S. by the mid-19th century.

   • Immigration
   • Technology
   • Westward expansion

b) For the same area, identify a SECOND historical development and explain how this development affected regionalism in the U.S. by the mid-19th century.

c) Choose a second area and explain why that area did not play as important a role in regional development in the U.S. by the mid-19th century.

10. Using the painting on page 283, answer a, b, and c.

a) Briefly explain the perspective about American life in the mid-19th century expressed in the painting.

b) Briefly explain ONE development in the period between 1820 and 1860 that could be used to support this view.

c) Briefly explain ONE development in the period between 1820 and 1860 that could be used to challenge this view.

11. Answer a, b, and c.

a) Briefly explain ONE example of how the increasing market economy shaped social class structure in the U.S. by the mid- to late 1800s.

b) Briefly explain ONE example of how the increasing market economy shaped family life in the U.S. by the mid- to late 1800s.

c) Briefly explain ONE example of how the increasing market economy shaped women's roles in the U.S. by the mid- to late 1800s.

LONG ESSAY For each question below, develop a thoughtful and thorough historical argument that answers the question. Begin each essay with a thesis statement and support it with relevant historical evidence.

12. Analyze to what extent technological developments affected the roles of women and the perceptions of womanhood in the mid-1800s.

13. To what extent were government policies responsible for the creation of a national and international market economy during the early to mid-1800s?

11 | COTTON, SLAVERY, AND THE OLD SOUTH

THE OLD PLANTATION This painting, by an unidentified folk artist of the early nineteenth century, suggests the importance of music in the lives of plantation slaves in America. The banjo, which the black musician at right is playing, was originally an African instrument. (© The Granger Colletion, New York)

AP

HISTORICAL THINKING

1. **Contextualization** Analyze the impact of "King Cotton" (particularly, the cultivation of short-staple cotton) on the development of political, economic, and social systems in the South.

2. **Contextualization** Explain the factors that led to an alliance between poor whites and planters in the American South.

3. **Comparison** Compare and contrast gender roles in white and in slave society.

4. **Comparison** Compare and contrast the agricultural focus of each of the regions of the United States.

5. **Synthesis** Explain why Southerners came to defend slavery as a positive good rather than a necessary evil.

6. **Historical Argumentation** Analyze the ways in which slave society and culture both resisted and accommodated the institution.

7. **Contextualization** Analyze the degree to which development of the factory system further isolated the South and set the stage for increased sectional tension.

Key Concept Correlations

Analyze the ways the historical developments you learn about in this chapter connect to the following AP Key Concepts.

4.1 The United States developed the world's first modern mass democracy and celebrated a new national culture, while Americans sought to define the nation's democratic ideals and to reform its institutions to match them.

4.2 Developments in technology, agriculture, and commerce precipitated profound changes in U.S. settlement patterns, regional identities, gender and family relations, political power, and distribution of consumer goods.

4.3 U.S. interest in increasing foreign trade, expanding its national borders, and isolating itself from European conflicts shaped the nation's foreign policy and spurred government and private initiatives.

5.2 Intensified by expansion and deepening regional divisions, debates over slavery and other economic, cultural, and political issues led the nation into civil war.

Thematic Learning Objectives

ID-1, 5, 6; CUL-2, 5, 6; PEO-2, 3; WXT-2, 5, 6, 7; ENV-3; POL-5, 6

CHAPTER 11 discusses southern society and the impact of slavery and cotton on its development. It looks at the structure and gender roles of both white and slave society in the South. It pays particular attention to the development of a class structure in white society and the relationship between those classes. The chapter also focuses on the nature of slavery, development of slave culture, and resistance to the institution. As you read, evaluate the following ideas:

- The South remained politically, culturally, and ideologically different from other regions of the United States, despite certain economic ties between the South and the North.
- Free and enslaved African Americans developed a distinct society and created networks of support for each other.
- White southerners began to view slavery as a "positive good" (apologist's view) rather than a "necessary evil."
- White southerners developed a distinct social structure, emphasizing pride and honor.
- The South remained in a semi-colonial status to the North.
- There were significant differences in the labor systems of the North and South.
- Enslaved African Americans developed various means of resistance to the institution of slavery.
- The cotton economy and slavery shaped the political, economic, and social development of the South.

THE COTTON ECONOMY

The most important economic development in the mid-nineteenth-century South was the shift of economic power from the "upper South" (the original southern states along the Atlantic coast) to the "lower South" (the expanding agricultural regions in the new states of the Southwest). That shift reflected above all the growing dominance of cotton in the southern economy.

THE RISE OF KING COTTON

Much of the upper South continued in the nineteenth century to rely, as it always had, on the cultivation of tobacco. But the market for that crop was notoriously unstable. Tobacco prices were

DECLINE OF THE TOBACCO ECONOMY

subject to frequent depressions, including a prolonged one that began in the 1820s and extended into the 1850s. Tobacco also rapidly exhausted the land on which it grew; it was difficult for most growers to remain in business in the same place for very long. By the 1830s, therefore, many farmers in the old tobacco-growing regions of Virginia, Maryland, and North Carolina were shifting to other crops—notably wheat—while the center of tobacco cultivation was moving westward, into the Piedmont area.

The southern regions of the coastal South—South Carolina, Georgia, and parts of Florida—continued to rely on the cultivation of rice, a more stable and lucrative crop than tobacco. Rice, however, demanded substantial irrigation and needed an exceptionally long growing season (nine months), so cultivation of that staple remained restricted to a relatively small area. Sugar growers along the Gulf Coast, similarly, enjoyed a reasonably profitable market for their crop. But sugar cultivation required intensive (and debilitating) labor and a long growing time. Only relatively wealthy planters could afford to engage in it, and they faced major competition from the great sugar plantations of the Caribbean. Sugar cultivation, therefore, did not spread much beyond a small area in southern Louisiana and eastern Texas. Long-staple (Sea Island) cotton was another lucrative crop, but like rice and sugar, it could grow only in a limited area—the coastal regions of the Southeast.

The decline of the tobacco economy in the upper South, and the limits of the sugar, rice, and long-staple cotton economies farther south, might have forced the region to shift its attention in

SHORT-STAPLE COTTON

the nineteenth century to other nonagricultural pursuits, had it not been for the growing importance of a new product that soon overshadowed all else: short-staple cotton. This was a hardier and coarser strain of cotton that could grow successfully in a variety of climates and in a variety of soils. It was harder to process than the

THE NEW ORLEANS COTTON EXCHANGE Edgar Degas, the French impressionist, painted this scene of cotton traders examining samples in the New Orleans cotton exchange in 1873. By this time the cotton trade was producing less impressive profits than those that had made it the driving force of the booming southern economy of the 1850s. Degas's mother came from a Creole family of cotton brokers in New Orleans, and two of the artist's brothers (depicted here reading a newspaper and leaning against a window) joined the business in America. (Musee des Beaux-Arts, Pau, France/© Giraudon/The Bridgeman Art Library)

long-staple variety; its seeds were more difficult to remove from the fiber. But the 1793 invention of the cotton gin (see p. 189) had largely solved that problem.

Demand for cotton was growing rapidly. The growth of the textile industry in Britain in the 1820s and 1830s, and in New England in the 1840s and 1850s, created an enormous new demand for the crop. As a result, ambitious men and women rapidly moved into previously uncultivated lands—many of them newly open to planter settlement after the relocation of the tribes in the 1820s and 1830s—to establish new cotton-growing regions.

Beginning in the 1820s, therefore, cotton production spread rapidly. From the western areas of South Carolina and Georgia, production moved steadily westward—first into Alabama and Mississippi, then into northern Louisiana, Texas, and Arkansas. By the 1850s, cotton had become the linchpin of the southern economy. In 1820, the South had produced about 500,000 bales of cotton. By 1850 it was producing nearly 3 million bales a year, and by 1860 nearly 5 million. There were periodic fluctuations in cotton prices, resulting generally from overproduction; peri-

SPREAD OF COTTON PRODUCTION

ods of boom frequently gave way to abrupt busts. But the cotton economy continued to grow, even if in fits and starts. By the time of the Civil War, cotton constituted nearly two-thirds of the total export trade of the United States and was bringing in nearly $200 million a year. The annual value of the rice crop, in contrast, was $2 million. It was little wonder that southern politicians now proclaimed: "Cotton is king!"

Cotton production dominated the more recently settled areas of what came to be known as the "lower South" (or, in a later era, the "Deep South"). Many people began to call this region the "Cotton Kingdom." Settlement of the area resembled in some ways the rush of gold seekers to a new strike. The prospect of tremendous profits from growing cotton drew white settlers to the lower South by the thousands. Some were wealthy planters from the older states who transferred their assets and slaves to a cotton plantation. Most were small slaveholders or slaveless farmers who hoped to move into the planter class.

A similar shift, if an involuntary one, occurred in the slave population. Between 1820 and 1860, the number of slaves in

EXPANSION OF SLAVERY

Alabama leaped from 41,000 to 435,000, and in Mississippi from 32,000 to 436,000. In the same period, the increase in Virginia was only from 425,000 to 490,000. Between 1840 and 1860, according to some estimates, 410,000 slaves moved from the upper South to the cotton states—either accompanying masters who were themselves migrating to the Southwest or (more often) sold to planters already there. Indeed, the sale of slaves to the Southwest became an important economic activity in the upper South and helped the troubled planters of that region compensate for the declining value of their crops.

SOUTHERN TRADE AND INDUSTRY

In the face of this booming agricultural expansion, other forms of economic activity developed slowly in the South. The busi-

WEAK MANUFACTURING SECTOR

ness classes of the region—the manufacturers and merchants—were not unimportant. There was growing activity in flour milling and in textile and iron manufacturing, particularly in the upper South. The Tredegar Iron Works in Richmond, for example, compared favorably with the best iron mills in the Northeast. But industry remained an insignificant force in comparison with the agricultural economy. The total value of southern textile manufactures in 1860 was $4.5 million—a threefold increase over the value of those goods twenty years before, but only about 2 percent of the value of the raw cotton exported that year.

To the degree that the South developed a nonfarm commercial sector, it was largely to serve the needs of the plantation economy. Particularly important were the brokers, or "factors," who marketed the planters' crops. These merchants tended to live in such towns as New Orleans, Charleston, Mobile, and Savannah, where they worked to find buyers for cotton and other crops and where they purchased goods for the planters they served. The South had only a very rudimentary financial system, and the factors often also served the planters as bankers, providing them with credit. Planters frequently accumulated substantial debts, particularly during periods when cotton prices were in decline; and the southern merchant-bankers thus became figures of considerable influence and importance in the region. There were also substantial groups of professional people in the South—lawyers, editors,

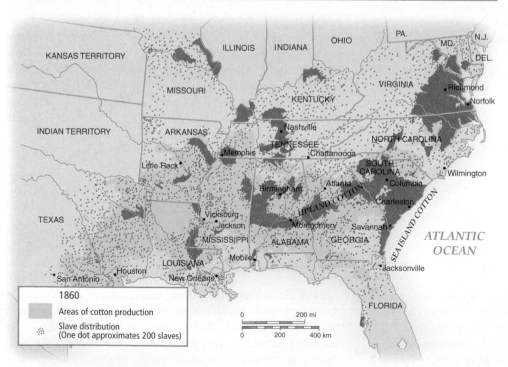

SLAVERY AND COTTON IN THE SOUTH, 1820 AND 1860 These two maps show the remarkable spread of cotton cultivation in the South in the decades before the Civil War. Both maps show the areas of cotton cultivation (the green-colored areas) as well as areas with large slave populations (the brown-dotted areas). Note how in the top map, which represents 1820, cotton production is concentrated largely in the East, with a few areas scattered among Alabama, Mississippi, Louisiana, and Tennessee. Slavery is most concentrated along the Georgia and South Carolina coast, areas in which long-staple cotton was grown, with only a few other areas of highly dense slave populations. By 1860, the South had changed dramatically. Cotton production had spread throughout the lower South, from Texas to northern Florida, and slavery had moved with it. Slavery was also much denser in the tobacco-growing regions of Virginia and North Carolina, which had also grown.

• *How did this economic shift affect the white South's commitment to slavery?*

doctors, and others. In most parts of the region, however, they too were closely tied to and dependent on the plantation economy. However important manufacturers, merchants, and professionals might have been to southern society, they were relatively unimportant in comparison with the manufacturers, merchants, and professionals of the North, on whom southerners were coming more and more (and increasingly unhappily) to depend.

The primitive character of the region's banking system matched a lack of development in other basic services and structures

INADEQUATE REGIONAL TRANSPORTATION SYSTEM

necessary for industrial development. Perhaps most notable was the South's inadequate transportation system. In the North in the antebellum period, enormous sums were invested in roads, canals, and above all railroads to knit the region together into an integrated market. In the South there were no such investments. Canals were almost nonexistent; most roads were crude and unsuitable for heavy transport; and railroads, although they expanded substantially in the 1840s and 1850s,

failed to tie the region together effectively. Such towns as Charleston, Atlanta, Savannah, and Norfolk had direct connections with Memphis, and thus with the Northwest; and Richmond was connected, via the Virginia Central, with the Memphis and Charleston Railroad. In addition, several independent lines furnished a continuous connection between the Ohio River and New Orleans. Most of the South, however, remained unconnected to the national railroad system. Most lines in the region were short and local. The principal means of transportation was water. Planters generally shipped their crops to market along rivers or by sea; most manufacturing was in or near port towns.

Perceptive southerners recognized the economic subordination of their region to the North. "From the rattle with which the nurse tickles the ear of the child born in the South to the shroud that covers the cold form of the dead, everything comes to us from the North." the Arkansas journalist Albert Pike lamented. Perhaps the most prominent advocate of southern economic independence was James B. D. De Bow, a resident of New Orleans. He published a magazine advocating

PLANTATIONS IN LOUISIANA, 1858 This map provides a detailed view of plantation lands along a stretch of the Mississippi River between New Orleans and Baton Rouge, Louisiana. Note the long, narrow shapes of these landholdings—known as "long lots." This system was designed to give as many planters as possible frontage on the river, which they needed to transport their crops to market and to receive goods in return. The river also deposited rich soil on the lands near its banks, which made cultivation of crops easier. Note how towns, stores, and churches all are near the riverbank, so planters and others living on plantations nearby could reach them easily by boat.

• *How is this landscape different from that of the newly opened federal lands in the West?*

southern commercial and agricultural expansion, *De Bow's Review*, which survived from its founding in 1846 until 1880.

DE BOW'S REVIEW

De Bow made his journal into a tireless advocate of southern economic independence from the North, warning constantly of the dangers of the "colonial" relationship between the sections. One writer noted in the pages of his magazine: "I think it would be safe to estimate the amount which is lost to us annually by our vassalage to the North at $100,000,000. Great God!" Yet *De Bow's Review* was itself evidence of the dependency of the South on the North. It was printed in New York, because no New Orleans printer had facilities adequate for the task; it was filled with advertisements from northern manufacturing firms; and its circulation was always modest in comparison with those of northern publications. In Charleston, for example, it sold an average of 173 copies per issue; *Harper's Magazine* of New York, in contrast, regularly sold 1,500 copies to South Carolinians.

SOURCES OF SOUTHERN DIFFERENCE

Despite this growing concern about the region's "colonial dependency," the South made few serious efforts to build an economy that might challenge its dependency. An important question about antebellum southern history, therefore, is why the region did so little to develop a larger industrial and commercial economy of its own. Why did it remain so different from the North?

Part of the reason was the great profitability of the South's agricultural system, particularly of cotton production. In the Northeast, many people had turned to manufacturing as the agricultural economy of the region declined. In the South,

REASONS FOR COLONIAL DEPENDENCY

the agricultural economy was booming, and ambitious people eager to profit from the emerging capitalist economy had little left for other investments. Some historians have suggested that the southern climate—with its long, hot, steamy summers—was less suitable for industrial development than the climate of the North. Still others have claimed that southern work habits (perhaps a reflection of the debilitating effects of the climate) impeded industrialization; some white southerners appeared—at least to many northern observers—not to work very hard, to lack the strong work ethic that fueled northern economic development.

But the southern failure to create a flourishing commercial or industrial economy was also in part the result of a set of values distinctive to the South that discouraged the growth of cities and industry. Many white southerners liked to think of them-

THE CAVALIER IMAGE

selves as representatives of a special way of life based on traditional values of chivalry, leisure, and elegance. White southerners were, they argued, "cavaliers"—people happily free from the base, acquisitive instincts of the "yankees" to their north. Southern white people were, they believed, more concerned with a refined and gracious way of life than with rapid growth and development. Appealing as the "cavalier" image was to southern whites, however, it conformed to the reality of southern society in very limited ways.

WHITE SOCIETY IN THE SOUTH

Only a small minority of southern whites owned slaves. In 1850, when the total white population of the South was over 6 million, the number of slaveholders was only 347,525. In 1860, when the white population was just above 8 million, the number of slaveholders had risen to only 383,637. These figures are somewhat misleading, since each slaveholder was normally the head of a family averaging five members. But even with all members of slaveowning families included in the figures, those owning slaves still amounted to perhaps no more than one-quarter of the white population. And of the minority of whites holding slaves, only a small proportion owned them in substantial numbers.

THE PLANTER CLASS

How, then, did the South come to be seen—both by the outside world and by many southerners themselves—as a society dom-

PLANTER ARISTOCRACY

inated by great plantations and wealthy landowning planters? In large part, it was because the planter aristocracy—the cotton magnates, the sugar, rice, and tobacco nabobs, the whites who owned at least forty or fifty slaves and 800 or more acres—exercised power and influence far in excess of their numbers. They stood at the apex of society, determining the political, economic, and even social life of their region. Enriched by vast annual incomes, dwelling in palatial homes, surrounded by broad acres and many black servants, they became a class to which all other southerners deferred. The wealthiest planters also maintained homes in towns or cities and spent several months of the year there, engaged in a glittering social life. Others traveled widely, especially to Europe, as an antidote to the isolation of plantation life. And many used their plantations to host opulent social events.

White southerners liked to compare their planter class to the old upper classes of England and Europe: true aristocracies, long entrenched. In fact, however, the southern upper class was in most cases not at all similar to the landed aristocracies of the Old World. In some areas of the upper South—the Tidewater region of Virginia, for example—some of the great aristocrats were indeed people whose families had occupied positions of wealth and power for generations. In most of the South, however, a long-standing landed aristocracy, although central to the "cavalier" image, was largely a myth. Even the most important planters in the cotton-growing areas of the South were, typically, new to their wealth and power. As late as the 1850s, many of the great landowners in the lower South were still first-generation settlers, who had arrived with only modest resources, struggled for years to clear land and develop a plantation in what was at first a rugged wilderness, and only recently had started to live in the comfort and luxury for which they became famous. Large areas of the "Old South" (as Americans later called the South of the pre–Civil War era) had been settled and cultivated for less than two decades at the time of the Civil War.

Nor was the world of the planter nearly as leisured and genteel as the "cavalier" myth would suggest. Growing staple crops was a business that was in its own way just as competitive and just as

PLANTATION MANAGEMENT

risky as the industrial enterprises of the North. Planters had to supervise their operations carefully if they hoped to make a profit. They were, in many respects, just as much competitive capitalists as the industrialists of the North whose lifestyles they claimed to hold in contempt. Even many affluent planters lived modestly, their wealth so heavily invested in land and slaves that there was little left for personal comfort. And white planters, even some substantial ones, tended to move frequently as new and presumably more-productive areas opened up to cultivation.

Indeed, it may have been the very newness and precariousness of the plantation way of life, and the differences between the reality of that life and the image of it, that made many southern planters determined to portray themselves as genteel aristocrats. Having struggled so hard to reach and maintain their positions, they were all the more determined to defend them. Perhaps that was why the defense of slavery and of the South's "rights" was stronger in the new, booming regions of the lower South and weaker in the more established and less flourishing areas of the Tidewater.

Wealthy southern whites sustained their image of themselves as aristocrats in many ways. They avoided such "coarse"

ARISTOCRATIC VALUES

occupations as trade and commerce; those who did not become planters often gravitated toward the military, a "suitable" career for men raised in a culture in which medieval knights (as portrayed in the novels of Walter Scott) were a powerful and popular image. The aristocratic ideal also found reflection in the definition of a special role for southern white women.

A GEORGIA PLANTATION This map of the Hopeton Plantation in Georgia shows both how much plantations were connected to the national and world markets, and how much they tried to be self-sufficient. Note the large areas of land devoted to growing cotton, rice, and sugarcane, all of them crops for the market. Note also the many crops grown for the local market or for consumption by residents of the plantation—potatoes, vegetables, corn, and others. The top left of the map shows the distribution of living quarters, with slaves' quarters grouped together very near the owner's residence.

• *Why would a plantation in this part of the South be so much more diversified in the market crops it raised than the cotton plantations in the Mississippi Delta?*
• *Why would planters want their slaves living nearby? Why might slaves be unhappy about being so close to their owners?*

"HONOR"

Above all, perhaps, white males adopted an elaborate code of chivalry, which obligated them to defend their "honor," often through dueling–which survived in the South long after it had largely vanished in the North. Southern white males placed enormous stock in conventional forms of courtesy and respect in their dealings with one another–perhaps to distance themselves from the cruelty and disrespect that were so fundamental to the slave system they controlled. Violations of such forms often brought what seemed to outsiders a disproportionately heated and even violent response.

The idea of honor in the South was only partly connected to the idea of ethical behavior and bravery. It was also tied to the importance among white males of the public appearance of dignity and authority–of saving face in the presence of others. Anything that seemed to challenge the dignity, social station, or "manhood" of a white southern male might be the occasion for a challenge to duel, or at least for a stern public rebuke. When the South Carolina congressman Preston Brooks strode into the chamber of the United States Senate and savagely beat Senator Charles Sumner of Massachusetts with a cane to retaliate for what he considered an insult to a relative, he was acting wholly in accord with the idea of southern honor. In the North, he was reviled as a savage. In the South, he became a popular hero. But Brooks was only the most public example of a code

CULT OF HONOR

of behavior that many white southern men followed. Avenging insults was a social necessity in many parts of southern society, and avenging insults to white southern women was perhaps the most important obligation of a white southern "gentleman."

THE "SOUTHERN LADY"

In some respects, affluent white women in the South occupied roles very similar to those of middle-class white women in the North. Their lives generally centered in the home, where they served as companions to and hostesses for their husbands and as nurturing mothers for their children. Even less frequently than in the North did "genteel" southern white women engage in public activities or find income-producing employment.

But the life of the "southern lady" was also in many ways

SUBORDINATE STATUS OF WOMEN

very different from that of her northern counterpart. For one thing, the cult of honor in the region meant in theory that southern white men gave particular importance to

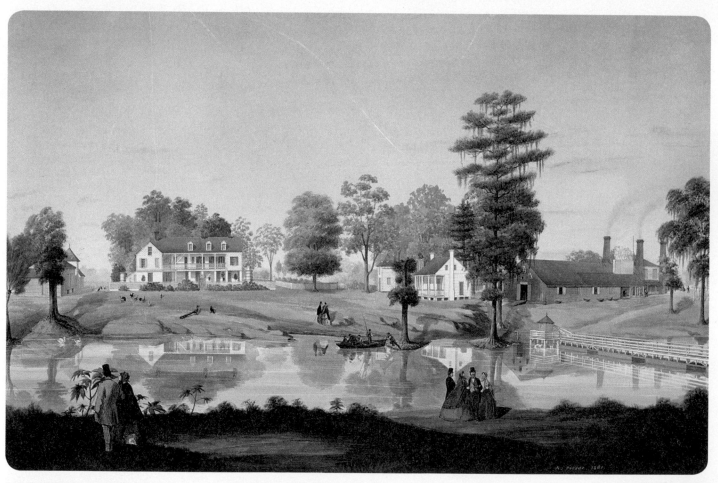

THE OLIVIER PLANTATION In this watercolor on paper, Adrien Persac (1823–1873) places the main house of this sugar plantation on the left with additional dwellings towards the right, on the east bank of the Bayou Teche, an important waterway in Louisiana. Also on the right, he depicts the sugar house and a floating pontoon bridge. The artist represents the self-consciously elegant life of the planter and his family. (© Louisiana State Museum, USA/Bridgeman Images)

the "defense" of women. In practice, this generally meant that white men were even more dominant and white women even more subordinate in southern culture than they were in the North. George Fitzhugh, one of the South's most important social theorists, wrote in the 1850s: "Women, like children, have but one right, and that is the right to protection. The right to protection involves the obligation to obey."

More important in determining the role of southern white women, however, were the social and economic realities in which they lived. The vast majority of females in the region lived on farms, isolated from people outside their own families, with virtually no access to the "public world" and thus few opportunities to look beyond their roles as wives and mothers. Because the family was the principal economic unit on most farms, the dominance of husbands and fathers over wives and children was even greater than in those northern families in which income producing activities had moved out of the home and into the factory or office. For many white women, living on farms of modest size meant a fuller engagement in the economic life of the family than was becoming typical for middle-class women in the North. These women engaged in spinning, weaving, and other production; they participated in agricultural tasks; they helped supervise the slave workforce. On some of the larger plantations, however, even these limited roles were sometimes considered unsuitable for white women; and the "plantation mistress" became, in some cases, more an ornament for her husband than an active part of the economy or the society.

Southern white women also had less access to education than their northern counterparts. Nearly a quarter of all white women over twenty were completely illiterate; relatively few women had more than a rudimentary exposure to schooling. Even wealthy planters were not interested in extensive schooling for their daughters. The few female "academies" in the South trained women primarily to be suitable wives.

CLEAR STARCHING IN LOUISIANA This 1837 etching by Auguste Hervieu offers a strikingly unromanticized view of plantation women in the South. The white plantation mistress, soberly dressed, speaks harshly to two black household servants, presumably criticizing the way they are doing the laundry. The slaves cower, carefully hiding whatever resentment they might feel behind a submissive pose. Nothing in this picture suggests anything like the kind of ease and luxury often associated with plantation life in popular mythology at the time and since. (*The Life and Adventures of Jonathan Jefferson Whitlaw*, by Frances Trollope, 1836)

Southern white women had other special burdens as well. The southern white birth rate remained nearly 20 percent higher than that of the nation as a whole, and infant mortality in the region remained higher than elsewhere; nearly half the children born in the South in 1860 died before they reached five years of age. The slave-labor system had a mixed impact on white women. It helped spare many of them from certain kinds of arduous labor, but it also threatened their relationships with their husbands. Male slaveowners had frequent sexual relationships with the female slaves on their plantations; the children of those unions became part of the plantation labor force and served as a constant reminder to white women of their husbands' infidelity. Black women (and men) were obviously the most important victims of such practices. But white women suffered too.

OTHER BURDENS

A few southern white women rebelled against their roles and against the prevailing assumptions of their region. Some became outspoken abolitionists and joined northerners in the crusade to abolish slavery. Some agitated for other reforms within the South itself. Most white women, however, found few outlets for whatever discontent they may have felt with their lives. Instead, they generally convinced themselves of the benefits of their position and—even more fervently than southern white men—defended the special virtues of the southern way of life. Upper-class white women in the South were particularly energetic in defending the class lines that separated them from poorer whites.

THE PLAIN FOLK

The typical white southerner was not a great planter and slave-holder, but a modest yeoman farmer. Some of these "plain folk," as they have become known, owned a few slaves, with whom they worked and lived far more closely than did the larger planters. Most (in fact, three-quarters of all white families) owned no slaves. Some plain folk, most of whom owned their own land, devoted themselves largely to subsistence farming; others grew cotton or other crops for the market, but usually could not produce enough to allow them to expand their operations or even get out of debt. During the 1850s, the number of nonslaveholding landowners increased much faster than the number of slaveholding landowners. While there were occasional examples of poor farmers moving into the ranks of the planter class, such cases were rare. Most yeomen knew that they had little prospect of substantially bettering their lot.

One reason was the southern educational system, which provided poor whites with few opportunities to learn and thus limited their chances of advancement. For the sons of wealthy planters, the region provided ample opportunities to gain an education. In 1860 there were 260 southern colleges and universities, public and private, with 25,000 students enrolled in them, or more than half the total number of students in the United States. But universities were within the reach of only the upper class. The elementary and secondary schools of the South were not only fewer but also inferior to those of the Northeast (although not much worse than the crude

LIMITED EDUCATIONAL OPPORTUNITIES

schools of the Northwest), and a higher proportion of whites were illiterate than in other parts of the country.

That a majority of the South's white population consisted of modest farmers largely excluded from the dominant plantation society raises another important question about the antebellum South. Why did the plain folk have so little power in the public world of the Old South? Why did they not oppose the aristocratic social system in which they shared so little? Why did they not resent the system of slavery, from which they generally did not benefit?

Some nonslaveowning whites did oppose the planter elite, but for the most part in limited ways and in a relatively few, isolated areas. These were southern highlanders, the "hill people," who lived in the Appalachian ranges east of the Mississippi, in the Ozarks to the west of the river, and in other "hill country" or "backcountry" areas cut off from the commercial world of the plantation system. Of all southern whites, they were the most isolated from the mainstream of the region's life. They practiced a simple form of subsistence agriculture, owned practically no slaves, and had a proud sense of seclusion. They were, in most respects, unconnected to the new commercial economy that dominated the great cotton-planting region of the South. They produced almost no surplus for the market, had little access to money, and often bartered for the goods they could not grow themselves.

HILL PEOPLE

To such men and women, slavery was unattractive for many of the same reasons it was unappealing to workers and small farmers in the North: because it threatened their sense of their own independence. Hill country farmers lived in a society defined by individual personal freedom and unusual isolation from modern notions of property. They also held to older political ideals, which for many included the ideal of fervent loyalty to the nation.

Such whites frequently expressed animosity toward the planter aristocracy of the other regions of the South. The mountain region was the only part of the South to defy the trend toward sectional conformity, and the only part to resist the movement toward secession when it finally developed. Even during the Civil War, many hill country southerners refused to support the Confederacy; some even fought for the Union.

Far greater in number, however, were the nonslaveowning whites who lived in the midst of the plantation system. Many, perhaps most of them, accepted that system because they were tied to it in important ways. Small farmers depended on the local plantation aristocracy for many things: access to cotton gins, markets for their modest crops and their livestock, credit or other financial assistance. In many areas, there were also extensive kinship networks linking lower- and upper-class whites. The poorest resident of a county might be a cousin of the richest aristocrat. Together, these mutual ties helped mute what might otherwise have been pronounced class tensions.

CLOSE RELATIONS WITH THE PLANTATION ARISTOCRACY

Small farmers felt tied to the plantation society in other ways as well. For white men, at least, the South was an unusually democratic society, in that participation in politics—both through voting and through attending campaign meetings and barbecues—was even more widespread than in the North, where participation was also high. Just as political participation gave workers in the North a sense of connection to the social order, so it did for farmers in the South—although officeholders in the South, even more than in the North, were almost always members of the region's elites. In the 1850s, moreover, the boom in the cotton economy allowed many small farmers to improve their economic fortunes. Some bought more land, became slaveowners, and moved into at least the fringes of plantation society. Others simply felt more secure in their positions as independent yeomen and hence more likely to embrace the fierce regional loyalty that was spreading throughout the white South in these years.

Small farmers, even more than great planters, were also committed to a traditional, male-dominated family structure. Their household-centered economies required the participation of all family members and, they believed, a stable system of gender relations to ensure order and stability. Men were the unquestioned masters of their homes; women and children, who were both family and workforce, were firmly under the master's control. As the northern attack on slavery increased in the 1840s and 1850s, it was easy for such farmers to believe—and easy for ministers, politicians, and other propagandists for slavery to persuade them—that an assault on one hierarchical system (slavery) would open the way to an assault on another such system (patriarchy).

COMMITMENT TO PATERNALISM

There were other white southerners, however, who did not share in the plantation economy in even limited ways and yet continued to accept its premises. These were the members of a particularly degraded class—numbering perhaps a half million in 1850—known to other classes variously and demeaningly as "crackers," "sand hillers," or "poor white trash" (a phrase used as a chapter title in Harriet Beecher Stowe's *Uncle Tom's Cabin*). Occupying the infertile lands of the pine barrens, the red hills, and the swamps, they lived in miserable cabins amid genuine destitution. Many owned no land (or owned land on which nothing could be grown) and supported themselves by foraging or hunting. Others worked as common laborers for their neighbors, although the slave system limited their opportunities. Their degradation resulted partly from dietary deficiencies and disease. Some resorted at times to eating clay (hence the tendency of affluent whites to refer to them disparagingly as "clay eaters"); and they suffered from pellagra, hookworm, and malaria. Planters and small farmers alike held them in contempt. They formed a true underclass. In some material respects, their plight was worse than that of the African American slaves (who themselves often looked down on the poor whites).

Yet, even among these southerners—the true outcasts of white society in the region—there was no real opposition to the plantation system or slavery. In part, undoubtedly, this was because these men and women were so benumbed by poverty that they had little strength to protest. But their relative passivity resulted also from perhaps the single greatest unifying factor among the southern white population, the one force that was most responsible for reducing tensions among the various classes: their perception of race. However poor and miserable these white southerners were, they could still

LIMITED CLASS CONFLICT

consider themselves members of a ruling race; they could still look down on the black population of the region and feel a bond with their fellow whites born of a determination to maintain their racial supremacy. As Frederick Law Olmsted, a northerner who visited the South and chronicled southern society in the 1850s, wrote: "From childhood, the one thing in their condition which has made life valuable to the mass of whites has been that the niggers are yet their inferiors."

SLAVERY: THE "PECULIAR INSTITUTION"

White southerners often referred to slavery as the "peculiar institution." By that they meant not that the institution was odd, but that it was distinctive, special. The description was apt, for American slavery was indeed distinctive. The South in the mid-nineteenth century was the only area in the Western world—except for Brazil, Cuba, and Puerto Rico—where slavery still existed. Slavery, more than any other single factor, isolated the South from the rest of American society. And as that isolation increased, so did the commitment of southerners to defend the institution.

Within the South itself, the institution of slavery had paradoxical results. On the one hand, it isolated blacks from whites, drawing a sharp and inviolable racial line dividing one group of southerners from another. As a result, African Americans under slavery began to develop a society and culture of their own, one unrelated to the white civilization around them. On the other hand, slavery created a unique bond between blacks and whites—masters and slaves—in the South. The two groups may have maintained separate spheres, but each sphere was deeply influenced by, indeed dependent on, the other.

VARIETIES OF SLAVERY

Slavery was an institution established and regulated in detail by law. The slave codes of the southern states forbade slaves to hold property, to leave their masters' premises without permission, to be out after dark, to congregate with other slaves except at church, to carry firearms, or to strike a white person, even in self-defense. The codes of some states prohibited whites

LEGAL BASIS OF SLAVERY from teaching slaves to read or write and denied slaves the right to testify in court against white people. The laws contained no provisions to legalize slave marriages or divorces. If an owner killed a slave while punishing him, the act was generally not considered a crime. Slaves, however, faced the death penalty for killing or even resisting a white person and for inciting revolt. The codes also contained extraordinarily rigid provisions for defining a person's race. Anyone with even a trace of African ancestry was defined as black. And anyone even rumored to possess any such trace was presumed to be black unless he or she could prove otherwise—which was, of course, almost impossible to do.

These and dozens of other restrictions might seem to suggest that slaves lived under a uniformly harsh and dismal regime. Had the laws been rigidly enforced, that might have been the case. In fact, however, enforcement was spotty and uneven. Some slaves did acquire property, did learn to read and write, and did assemble with other slaves, in spite of laws to the contrary. Although the major slave offenses generally fell under the jurisdiction of the courts (and thus of the slave codes), white owners handled most transgressions and inflicted

REALITY OF SLAVERY widely varying punishments. In other words, despite the rigid provisions of law, there was in reality considerable variety within the slave system. Some blacks lived in almost prisonlike conditions, rigidly and harshly controlled by their masters. Many (probably most) others enjoyed some flexibility and (at least in comparison to the regimen prescribed by law) a significant degree of autonomy.

Most masters possessed very few slaves, and their experience with (and image of) slavery was a reflection of the special nature of slavery on the small farm. White farmers with few slaves generally supervised their workers directly and often worked closely alongside them. On such farms, blacks and whites developed a form of intimacy unknown on larger plantations. The paternal relationship between such masters and their slaves could, like relationships between fathers and children, be warm and affectionate. It could also be tyrannical and cruel. In either case, it was a relationship based on the relative powerlessness of the slaves.

Although the majority of slaveowners were small farmers, the majority of slaves lived on plantations of medium or large size, with sizable slave workforces. Substantial planters often hired overseers and even assistant overseers to represent them. "Head drivers," trusted and responsible slaves often assisted by several subdrivers, acted under the overseer as foremen.

Larger planters generally used one of two methods of assigning slave labor. One was the task system (most common

TASK AND GANG SYSTEMS in rice culture), under which slaves were assigned a particular task in the morning, for example, hoeing one acre; after completing the job, they were free for the rest of the day. The other, far more common, was the gang system (employed on the cotton, sugar, and tobacco plantations), under which slaves were simply divided into groups, each of them directed by a driver, and compelled to work for as many hours as the overseer considered a reasonable workday.

LIFE UNDER SLAVERY

Slaves generally received at least enough necessities to enable them to live and work. Their masters usually furnished them with an adequate, if mostly coarse, diet, consisting mainly of cornmeal, salt pork, molasses, and on special occasions fresh meat or poultry. Many slaves cultivated gardens for their own use. They received cheap clothing and shoes. They lived in crude cabins, called slave quarters, usually clustered in a complex near the master's house. The plantation mistress or a doctor retained by the owner provided some medical care; but slave women themselves—as "healers" and midwives, or simply as mothers—were the more important source.

WAVING FROM THE SHORE This image, from the mid-1800s, depicts slaves picking cotton along a riverbank. They are waving to men sitting on bales as they ride the barge on route to the market. (© Archive Photos/Getty Images)

Slaves worked hard, beginning with light tasks as children. Their workdays were longest at harvest time. Slave women worked particularly hard. They generally labored in the fields with the men, and they assumed as well the crucial chores traditionally reserved for women–cooking, cleaning, and child rearing. Because slave families were often divided, with husbands and fathers frequently living on neighboring plantations (or, at times, sold to plantation owners far away), black women often found themselves acting in effect as single parents. Within the slave family, therefore, women had special burdens but also a special authority.

SPECIAL POSITION OF WOMEN

Slaves were, as a group, much less healthy than southern whites. After 1808, when the international slave trade became illegal in America, the proportion of blacks to whites steadily declined. In 1820, there was one African American to every four whites; in 1840, one to every five. The slower increase of the black population was a result of its comparatively high death rate. Slave mothers had large families, but the enforced poverty in which virtually all African Americans lived ensured that fewer of their children would survive to adulthood than the children of white parents. Even

HIGH SLAVE MORTALITY RATES

those who did survive typically died at a younger age than the average white person.

Even so, according to some scholars, the actual material conditions of slavery may have been better than those of some northern factory workers and better than those of both peasants and industrial workers in much of nineteenth-century Europe. The conditions of American slaves were certainly less severe than those of slaves in the Caribbean and South America crops, which required more arduous labor. Sugar production in the Caribbean islands, in particular, involved extraordinarily backbreaking work and a high risk of fatal tropical diseases. Caribbean and South American planters continued to use the African slave trade well into the nineteenth century to replenish their labor supply, so they had less incentive than American planters (who no longer had access to that trade) to protect their existing laborers. Growing cotton, the principal activity for most slaves in the United States, was much less debilitating than growing sugar; and planters had strong economic incentives to maintain a healthy slave population. One result of this was that America became the only country where a slave population actually increased through natural reproduction (although it grew much more slowly than the white population).

Most masters did make some effort to preserve the health—and thus the usefulness—of their slaves. One example was the frequent practice of protecting slave children from hard work until early adolescence. Masters believed that doing so would make young slaves more loyal and would also ensure better health as adults. Another example was the use of hired labor, when available, for the most unhealthy or dangerous tasks. A traveler in Louisiana noted, for example, that Irishmen were employed to clear malarial swamps and to handle cotton bales at the bottom of chutes extending from the river bluff down to a boat landing. If an Irish worker died of disease or in an accident, a master could hire another for a dollar a day or less. But a master would lose an investment of perhaps $1,000 or more if a prime field hand died. Still, cruel masters might forget their pocketbooks in the heat of anger. Slaves were often left to the discipline of overseers, who had less of an economic stake in their well-being; overseers were paid in proportion to the amount of work they could get out of the slaves they supervised.

Household servants had a somewhat easier life—physically at least—than did field hands. On a small plantation, the same slaves might do both field work and housework. But on a large **HOUSE SLAVES** estate, there would generally be a separate domestic staff: nursemaids, housemaids, cooks, butlers, coachmen. These people lived close to the master and his family, eating the leftovers from the family table and in some cases even sleeping in the "big house." Between the

blacks and whites of such households affectionate, almost familial relationships might sometimes develop. More often, however, house servants resented their isolation from their fellow slaves and the lack of privacy that came with living in such close proximity to the master's family. Among other things, that proximity meant that their transgressions were more visible than those of field hands, and so they received punishments more often than did other slaves. When emancipation came after the Civil War, it was often the house servants who were the first to leave the plantations of their former owners.

Female household servants were especially vulnerable to sexual abuse by their masters and white overseers, who **SEXUAL ABUSE** sometimes pressured them into supposedly consensual sexual relationships and sometimes raped them. In addition to unwanted sexual attention from white men, female slaves often received vindictive treatment from white women. Plantation mistresses naturally resented the sexual liaisons between their husbands and female slaves. Punishing their husbands was not usually possible, so they often punished the slaves instead—with arbitrary beatings, increased workloads, and various forms of psychological torment.

SLAVERY IN THE CITIES

The conditions of slavery in the cities differed significantly from those in the countryside. On relatively isolated plantations, slaves had little contact with free blacks and lower-class whites, and masters maintained direct and effective control; a deep and seemingly unbridgeable chasm yawned between slavery and freedom. In the city, however, a master often could not supervise his slaves closely and at the same time use them profitably. Even if they slept at night in carefully watched backyard barracks, slaves moved about during the day alone, performing errands of various kinds. Thus urban slaves gained numerous opportunities to mingle with free blacks and with whites. In the cities, the line between slavery and freedom became increasingly indistinct.

There was a considerable market in the South for common laborers, particularly since, unlike in the North, there were few **AUTONOMY OF URBAN SLAVES** European immigrants to perform menial chores. Even the poorest whites tended to prefer working on farms to doing ordinary labor, and so masters often hired out slaves for such tasks. Slaves on contract worked in mining and lumbering (often far from cities); but others worked on the docks and on construction sites, drove wagons, and performed other unskilled jobs in cities and towns. Slave women and children worked in the region's few textile mills. Particularly skilled workers such as blacksmiths or carpenters were also often hired out.

Many white southerners considered slavery to be incompatible with city life, and as southern cities grew the number of slaves in them declined, relatively if not absolutely. Fearing conspiracies and insurrections, many urban slaveowners sold off much of their male property to the countryside. The remaining black women outnumbered black men. The same cities also had more white men than women—a situation that

NURSING THE MASTER'S CHILD This photograph shows a black slave woman caring for a white child. The image was taken in Arkansas in 1855. Black women typically cared for white children on plantations, sometimes with great affection and sometimes—as this photograph may suggest—dutifully and without enthusiasm. (The Library of Congress (LC-USZC4-5251))

THE CHARACTER OF SLAVERY

NO issue in American history has produced a richer literature or a more spirited debate than the nature of American slavery. The debate began even before the Civil War, when abolitionists strove to expose slavery to the world as a brutal, dehumanizing institution, while southern defenders of slavery tried to depict it as a benevolent, paternalistic system. But by the late nineteenth century, as historian David Blight noted in *Race and Reunion* (2002), with white Americans eager for sectional conciliation, both northern and southern chroniclers of slavery began to accept a romanticized and unthreatening picture of the Old South and its "peculiar institution."

The first major scholarly examination of slavery was Ulrich B. Phillips's *American Negro Slavery* (1918), which portrayed slavery as an essentially benign institution in which kindly masters looked after submissive, childlike, and generally contented African Americans. Phillips's apologia for slavery remained the authoritative work on the subject for nearly thirty years.

Challenges to Phillips began to emerge in the 1940s, as concern about racial injustice increasingly engaged the attention of white Americans. In 1941, Melville J. Herskovits challenged Phillips's contention that black Americans retained little of their African cultural inheritance. In 1943, Herbert Aptheker published a chronicle of slave revolts as a way of refuting Phillips's claim that blacks were submissive and content.

A somewhat different challenge to Phillips emerged in the 1950s from historians who emphasized the brutality of the institution. Kenneth Stampp's *The Peculiar Institution* (1956) and Stanley Elkins's *Slavery* (1959) described a labor system that did serious physical and psychological damage to its victims. Stampp, and especially Elkins, portrayed slavery as something like a prison, in which men and women had no space in which to develop their own social and cultural lives.

In the 1970s, new scholarship on slavery focused on slaves' striking success in building a culture of their own despite their enslavement. John Blassingame in 1973 argued that "the most remarkable aspect of the whole process of enslavement is the extent to which the American-born slaves were able to retain their ancestors' culture." Herbert Gutman, in *The Black Family in Slavery and Freedom* (1976), challenged the prevailing belief that slavery had weakened and even destroyed the African American family. On the contrary, he argued, the black family survived slavery with impressive strength. Eugene Genovese's *Roll, Jordan, Roll* (1974) and other works revealed how African Americans manipulated the paternalist assumptions at the heart of slavery to build a large cultural space of their own within the system where they could develop their own family life, social traditions, and religious patterns. That same year, Robert Fogel and Stanley Engerman published their controversial *Time on the Cross*, a highly quantitative study that supported some of the claims of Gutman and

helped account for the birth of many mulattoes. Even while slavery in the cities was declining, the forced segregation of urban blacks, both free and slave, from white society increased. Segregation was a means of social control intended to make up for the loosening of the discipline of slavery in urban areas.

FREE AFRICAN AMERICANS

There were about 250,000 free African Americans in the slaveholding states by the start of the Civil War, more than half of them in Virginia and Maryland. In some cases, they were slaves who had somehow earned money with which they managed to buy their own and their families' freedom, usually by developing a skill they could market independently of their masters. It was usually urban blacks, with their greater freedom of movement and activity, who could take that route. One example was Elizabeth Keckley, a slave woman who bought freedom for herself and her son with proceeds from sewing. She later became a seamstress, personal servant, and companion to Mary Todd Lincoln in the White House. But few masters had any incentive, or inclination, to give up their slaves, so this route was open to relatively few people.

Some slaves were sometimes set free by a master who had moral qualms about slavery, or by a master's will after his death—for example, the more than 400 slaves belonging to John Randolph of Roanoke, freed in 1833. From the 1830s on, however, state

TIGHTENED RESTRICTIONS ON FREE BLACKS

laws governing slavery became more rigid. That was in part a response to the fears Nat Turner's revolt (see p. 310) created among white southerners: free blacks, removed from close supervision by whites, might generate more violence and rebellion than slaves. It was also in part because the community of free blacks in southern cities was becoming larger and, to whites, more threatening—a dangerous example to blacks still in slavery. The rise of abolitionist agitation in the North—and the fear that it would inspire slaves to rebel—also persuaded southern whites to tighten their system. The new laws made it more and more difficult, and in some cases practically impossible, for owners to set free (or "manumit") their slaves; all southern states forbade free African Americans from entering. Arkansas even forced the freed slaves living there to leave.

A few free blacks (generally those on the northern fringes of the slaveholding regions) attained wealth and prominence. Some owned slaves themselves, usually relatives whom they had bought in order to ensure their ultimate emancipation. In a few cities—New Orleans, Natchez, Charleston—free black communities managed to flourish relatively unmolested by whites and with some economic stability. Most free blacks, however, lived in abject poverty, under conditions worse than those of African Americans in the North. Law or custom closed many occupations to them, forbade them to assemble without

(© The Granger Collection, New York)

Recent works by Walter Johnson and Ira Berlin mark at least a partial return to the "damage" thesis. In *Soul by Soul* (2000), a study of the New Orleans slave market, Johnson contends that for whites, purchasing slaves was a way of fulfilling the middle-class fantasy of success and independence, but for the slaves themselves the trade was destructive and dehumanizing. Ira Berlin's *Many Thousands Gone* (2000), *Generation of Captivity* (2003), and *The Making of African America* (2010) similarly emphasize the dehumanizing character of the slave market and argue that slavery was less a social system than a commodification of human beings. ●

HISTORICAL ARGUMENTATION AND INTERPRETATION

Questions assume cumulative content knowledge from this chapter and previous chapters.

1. How has the historical debate regarding the nature of slavery changed over the years?
2. Describe a societal or cultural change between the early 20th century to the mid-20th century, which affected historians' interpretations of the nature of slavery in America.
3. Describe the argument of one historian, whose interpretation regarding the nature of slavery you agree with the most. Explain why, using historical evidence to support your position. Suggest a piece of historical evidence that could be used to refute your position.

Genovese about black achievement, but that went much further in portraying slavery as a successful and reasonably humane (if ultimately immoral) system. Slave workers, they argued, were better treated and lived in greater comfort than most northern industrial workers of the same era.

Other scholarship on slavery has focused on the role of women within it. Elizabeth Fox-Genovese's *Within the Plantation Household* (1988) examined the lives of both white and black women on the plantation. Rejecting the claims of some feminist historians that black and white women shared a common female identity born of their shared subordination to men, she portrayed slave women as defined by their dual roles as members of the plantation workforce and anchors of the black family.

---

white supervision, and placed numerous other restraints on them. They were only quasi-free, but they had all the burdens of freedom: the necessity to support themselves, to find housing, to pay taxes. Yet, great as were the hardships of freedom, these blacks preferred them to slavery.

THE SLAVE TRADE

The transfer of enslaved people from one part of the South to another was one of the most important and terrible consequences of slavery. Sometimes slaves moved to the new cotton lands in

SLAVE MARKETS

the company of their original owners, who were migrating themselves. But more often, the transfer occurred through the efforts of professional slave traders. For shorter journeys slaves traveled on foot, trudging in coffles of hundreds along dusty highways. For transfers over longer distances, the traders conveyed slaves via river or ocean steamers. Central slave markets included Natchez, New Orleans, Charleston, and Mobile. In the 1840s and 1850s, healthy young field hands could fetch between $500 and $1,700, depending on the fluctuations in the market.

The domestic slave trade, essential to the growth and prosperity of the system, was one of its most horrible aspects. The trade dehumanized all who were involved in it. It separated children from their parents and parents from each other. Even families who had long been together might be broken up by

new owners in the division of the estate after an old master's death. Planters might deplore the trade, but they eased their consciences by holding traders in contempt.

The foreign slave trade was usually badly conducted, resulting in many people dying along the way. Although federal law

THE FOREIGN SLAVE TRADE

had prohibited the importation of slaves from 1808 on, some continued to be smuggled into the United States as late as the 1850s when the supply of slaves had become inadequate. At the annual southern commercial conventions, planters began to discuss the legal reopening of the trade. "If it is right to buy slaves in Virginia and carry them to New Orleans," William L. Yancey of Alabama asked his fellow delegates in 1858, "why is it not right to buy them in Cuba, Brazil, or Africa?" The convention that year voted to repeal all the laws against slave imports, but the government never acted on its proposal.

The continued smuggling was not without resistance from the slaves themselves. In 1839, a group of fifty-three slaves in Cuba took charge of the ship *Amistad* that was transporting them to another part of Cuba. Their goal was to sail back to their homeland in Africa. The slaves had no experience with sailing, and they tried to compel the crew to steer them across the Atlantic. Instead, the ship sailed up the Atlantic coast until it was captured by a ship of the United States Revenue Service. Many Americans, including President Van Buren, thought the slaves should be returned to Cuba. But at the request of a

THE BUSINESS OF SLAVERY The offices of slave dealers were familiar sights on the streets of pre–Civil War southern cities and towns. They provide testimony to the way in which slavery was not just a social system, but a business, deeply woven into the fabric of southern economic life. (The Library of Congress)

slaves were returned to Africa, with funding from American abolitionists.

Two years later, in 1841, another group of slaves revolted on board a ship and took control of it—this time an American vessel bound from Norfolk, Virginia, to New Orleans—and steered it (and its 135 slaves) to the British Bahamas, where slavery was illegal and the slaves were given sanctuary. Such shipboard revolts were rare, but they were symbols of the continued efforts by Africans to resist slavery.

SLAVE RESISTANCE

Few issues have sparked as much debate among historians as the effects of slavery on the blacks themselves. (See "Debating the Past," pp. 306–307.) Slaveowners, and many white Americans after emancipation, liked to argue that the slaves were generally content, "happy with their lot." That may have been true in some cases. But it is clear that the vast majority of southern blacks were not content with being slaves, that they yearned for freedom even though most realized there was little they could do to secure it. Evidence for that conclusion can be found, if nowhere else, from the reaction of slaves when emancipation finally came. Virtually all reacted to freedom with joy and celebration; few chose to remain in the service of the whites who had owned them before the Civil War (although most African Americans remained for many years subservient to whites in one way or another).

Rather than contented acceptance, the dominant response of blacks to slavery was a complex one: a combination of

group of abolitionists, former president John Quincy Adams went before the Supreme Court to argue that they should be freed. Adams argued that the foreign slave trade was illegal and thus the *Amistad* rebels could not be returned to slavery. The Court accepted his argument in 1841, and most of the former

REVOLT ON THE *AMISTAD* Joseph Cinquez led the revolt of African slaves on the Spanish vessel *Amistad* en route to Cuba in June 1839. Once exonerated of charges of murder and piracy, he was reported to have said, "Brothers, we have done that which we purposed, our hands are now clean for we have Striven to regain the precious heritage we received from our fathers. . . . I am resolved it is better to die than to be a white man's slave." (© Chicago History Museum, USA/The Bridgeman Art Library)

adaptation and resistance. At the extremes, slavery could produce two very different reactions, each serving as the basis for a powerful stereotype in white society. One extreme was what became known as the "Sambo"—the shuffling, grinning, head-scratching, deferential slave who acted out the role that he recognized the white world expected of him. More often than not, the "Sambo" pattern of behavior was a charade, a façade assumed in the presence of whites. The other extreme was the slave rebel—the African American who could not bring himself or herself to either acceptance or accommodation but remained forever rebellious. Actual slave revolts were extremely rare, but the knowledge that they were possible struck terror into the hearts of white southerners everywhere. In 1800, Gabriel Prosser gathered 1,000 rebellious slaves outside Richmond; but two Africans gave the plot away, and the Virginia militia stymied the uprising before it could begin. Prosser and thirty-five others were executed. In 1822, the Charleston free black Denmark Vesey and his followers—rumored to total 9,000—made preparations for

PROSSER AND TURNER REBELLIONS

revolt; but again word leaked out, and suppression and retribution followed. In 1831, Nat Turner, a slave preacher, led a band of African Americans who armed themselves with guns and axes and, on a summer night, went from house to house in Southampton County, Virginia. They killed sixty white men, women, and children before being overpowered by state and federal troops. More than a hundred blacks were executed in the aftermath. Nat Turner's was the only large-scale slave insurrection in the nineteenth-century South, but fear of slave conspiracies and renewed violence pervaded the section as long as slavery lasted.

For the most part, however, resistance to slavery took less drastic forms such as running away. A small number of slaves managed to escape to the North or to Canada, especially after sympathetic whites began organizing the so-called underground railroad to assist them in flight. But the odds against a successful escape, particularly from the Deep South, were almost impossibly high. The hazards of distance and the slaves' ignorance of geography were serious obstacles. So were the white "slave patrols," which stopped wandering blacks on sight throughout the South demanding to see travel permits. Without such a permit, slaves were presumed to be runaways and were taken captive. Slave patrols often employed bloodhounds to track African Americans who attempted to escape through the woods. Despite all the obstacles to success, however, blacks continued to run away from their masters in large numbers. Some did so repeatedly, undeterred by the whippings and other penalties inflicted on them when captured.

HARRIET TUBMAN WITH ESCAPED SLAVES Harriet Tubman (c. 1820–1913) was born into slavery in Maryland. In 1849, when her master died, she escaped to Philadelphia to avoid being sold out of state. Over the next ten years, she assisted first members of her own family and then up to 300 other slaves to escape from Maryland to freedom. During the Civil War, she served alternately as a nurse and as a spy for Union forces in South Carolina. She is shown here, on the left, with some of the slaves she had helped to free. (© Archive Photos/Getty Images)

THE SLAVES' MUSIC

FOR African Americans living as slaves on southern plantations, there was little leisure time—and little opportunity for the kinds of cultural activities that were beginning to appeal to other groups of Americans. But slaves managed nevertheless to create a culture of their own. And among its most distinctive and pervasive features was music.

Indeed, to white observers at least, nothing was more striking about slave life than the role music played within it. African Americans sang frequently, sometimes alone, more often in groups. They sang while they worked together in the fields, as they shucked corn, slaughtered hogs, or repaired fences. They sang whenever they had social gatherings—on Sundays or on the rare other holidays from work. They sang when they gathered for chores in the evenings. They sang during their religious services. And they sang with a passion, at times even an ecstasy, that was completely unfamiliar to whites—and sometimes troubling to them.

Their songs were rarely written down and often seemed entirely spontaneous; but much slave music was really derived from African and Caribbean traditions passed on through generations and from snatches of other songs the performers had heard before and from which they improvised variations. In its emotionalism, its pulsing rhythms, and its lack of conventional formal structure, it resembled nothing its white listeners had ever heard before.

Slaves sang whether or not there were any musical instruments to accompany them, but they often created instruments for themselves out of whatever materials were at hand. "Us take pieces of sheep's rib or cow's jaw or a piece of iron, with an old kettle or a hollow gourd and some horsehair to make the drum," one former slave recalled years later. "They'd take the buffalo horn and scrape it out to make the flute." When they could, they would build banjos, an instrument that had originated in Africa. Their masters sometimes gave them violins and guitars. When the setting permitted it, African Americans danced to their music—dances very different from and much more spontaneous than the formal steps that nineteenth-century whites generally learned. They also used music to accompany one of their other important cultural traditions: storytelling. Black music on the plantations took a number of forms. The most common was religious songs, the precursors of modern gospel music, which expressed—in terms that their white masters, who usually did not listen to the words very carefully, found acceptable—a faith in their eventual freedom and salvation and often spoke of Africans as a chosen people waiting for redemption. At other times, the songs would express a bitterness toward white slaveholders. The great black abolitionist Frederick Douglass remembered one:

> We raise de wheat,
> Dey gib us de corn;
> We bake de bread,
> Dey gib us de crust;
> We sif the meal,
> Dey gib us de huss;
> We peel de meat,
> Dey gib us de skin;
> And dat's de way
> Dey take us in;
> We skim de pot,
> Dey gib us de liquor,

But perhaps the most important method of resistance was simply a pattern of everyday behavior by which blacks defied their masters. That whites so often considered blacks to be lazy and shiftless suggests one means of resistance: refusal to work hard.

Some slaves stole from their masters or from neighboring whites. Some performed isolated acts of sabotage: losing or breaking tools (southern planters gradually began to buy unusually heavy hoes because so many of the lighter ones got broken) or performing tasks improperly. Many African Americans resisted by building into their normal patterns of behavior subtle methods of rebellion.

SLAVE RESISTANCE

THE CULTURE OF SLAVERY

Resistance was only part of the slave response to slavery. Another was an elaborate process of adaptation. The process did not imply contentment with bondage. It represented a recognition that there was no realistic alternative. One of the ways blacks adapted was by developing their own, separate culture, one that enabled them to sustain a sense of racial pride and unity.

LANGUAGE AND MUSIC

In many areas, slaves retained a language of their own, sometimes incorporating African speech patterns into English. Having arrived in America speaking many different African languages, the first generations of slaves had as much difficulty communicating with one another as they did with white people. To overcome these barriers, they learned a simple, common language (known to linguists as "pidgin"). It retained some African words, but it drew primarily, if selectively, from English. And while slave language grew more sophisticated as blacks spent more time in America—and as new generations grew up never having known African tongues—some features of this early pidgin survived in black speech for many generations.

PIDGIN

Music was especially important in slave society. In some ways, it was as important to African Americans as language. Most important were voices and song. Field workers often used songs to pass the time in the fields; since they sang them in the presence of whites, they usually attached relatively innocuous words to them. But African

IMPORTANCE OF SLAVE SPIRITUALS

SLAVE MUSIC This folk painting illustrates the importance of music to slaves (and at times also to their masters). The banjo in the hands of the man in the center was an instrument that originated in Africa. (Private Collection/© Peter Newark American Pictures/Bridgeman Art Library International)

And say dat's good enough for nigger.
Your butter and the fat;
Poor nigger, you can't ever get that.

To African Americans, music was a treasured avenue of escape from the hardships of slavery. It was also a vehicle through which they could express anger, resentment, and hope. Their masters generally tolerated their slaves' music—and even valued it, both because they often enjoyed listening to it and because the more intelligent understood that without this means of emotional and spiritual release, active resistance to slavery might be more frequent.

The powerful music that emerged from slavery helped shape the lives of African Americans on the plantations. It also helped lay the foundations for music that almost all Americans later embraced: gospel, blues, jazz, rhythm and blues, rock, and rap. ●

UNDERSTAND, ANALYZE, AND EVALUATE

1. Does the prominent place of music in slave culture support the thesis that slavery was essentially a benign institution?
2. The English dramatist William Congreve in *The Mourning Bride* wrote:

    Music hath charms to soothe the savage breast,
    To soften rocks, or bend a knotted oak.

    How might this quote apply to the place of music in African American slave culture?
3. What more recent musical forms continue the tradition of the slaves' religious songs or spirituals? In what way do these more recent forms serve purposes similar to the purpose of the slaves' religious songs? Does music continue to shape a distinct African American culture?

Americans also created emotionally rich and politically challenging music in the relative privacy of their religious services. It was there that the tradition of the spiritual emerged in the early nineteenth century.

AFRICAN AMERICAN RELIGION

A separate slave religion was not supposed to exist. Almost all African Americans were Christians by the early nineteenth century. Some had converted voluntarily, and some were coerced by their masters and by the Protestant missionaries who evangelized among them. Masters expected their slaves to worship under the supervision of white ministers. Indeed, autonomous black churches were banned by law; and many slaves became members of the same denominations as their owners—usually Baptist or Methodist. In the 1840s and 1850s, as slavery expanded in the South, missionary efforts increased. Vast numbers of African Americans became members of Protestant churches in those years.

Nevertheless, blacks throughout the South developed their own version of Christianity, at times incorporating into it such practices as voodoo or other polytheistic religious traditions of Africa. Or they simply bent religion to the special circumstances of bondage. Natural leaders emerging within the slave community rose to the rank of preacher.

African American religion was often more emotional than that of its white counterparts and reflected the influence of African customs and practices. Slave prayer meetings routinely involved fervent chanting, spontaneous exclamations from the congregation, and ecstatic conversion experiences. Black religion was also more joyful and affirming than that of many white denominations. And above all, African American religion emphasized the dream of freedom and deliverance. In their prayers and songs and sermons, black Christians talked and sang of the day when the Lord would "call us home," "deliver us to freedom," "take us to the Promised Land." And while their white masters generally chose to interpret such language merely as the expression of hopes for life after death, many African Americans themselves used the images of Christian salvation to express their own dream of freedom in the present world. Christian images, and biblical injunctions, were central to Gabriel Prosser, Denmark Vesey, Nat Turner, and others who planned or engaged in open resistance to slavery.

SLAVE RELIGION

In cities and towns in the South, some African Americans had their own churches, where free blacks occasionally worshiped alongside slaves. In the countryside, however, slaves usually attended the same churches as their masters–sometimes a chapel on the plantation itself, sometimes a church serving a larger farm community. Seating in such churches was usually segregated. Slaves sat in the rear or in balconies. They held their own services later, often in secret, usually at night.

THE SLAVE FAMILY

The slave family was the other crucial institution of black culture in the South. Like religion, it suffered from certain legal restrictions–most notably the lack of legal marriage. Nevertheless, what we now call the "nuclear family" consistently emerged as the dominant kinship model among African Americans.

Such families did not always operate according to white customs. Black women generally began bearing children at younger ages than most white women, often as early as age fourteen or fifteen. Slave communities did not condemn premarital pregnancy in the way white society did, and African American couples would often begin living together before marrying. It was customary, however, for couples to marry–in a ceremony involving formal vows–soon after conceiving a child. Often, marriages occurred between slaves living on neighboring plantations. Husbands and wives sometimes visited each other with the permission of their masters, but often such visits had to be in secret, at night. Family ties were no less strong than those of whites, and many slave marriages lasted throughout the course of long lifetimes.

SLAVE MARRIAGES

When marriages did not survive, it was often because of circumstances over which blacks had no control. Up to a third of all black families were broken apart by the slave trade; an average slave might expect during a lifetime to see ten or more relatives sold. And that accounted for some of the other distinctive characteristics of the black family, which adapted itself to the cruel realities of its own uncertain future. Extended kinship networks–which grew to include not only spouses and their children, but also aunts, uncles, grandparents, even distant cousins–were strong and important and often helped compensate for the breakup of nuclear families. A slave forced suddenly to move to a new area, far from his or her family, might create fictional kinship ties and become "adopted" by a family in the new community. Even so, the impulse to maintain contact with a spouse and children remained strong long after the breakup of a family. One of the most frequent causes of flight from the plantation was a slave's desire to find a husband, wife, or child who had been sent elsewhere.

IMPORTANCE OF KINSHIP NETWORKS

It was not only by breaking up families through sale that whites intruded on black family life. Black women, usually powerless to resist the sexual advances of their masters, often bore the children of whites–children whom the whites almost never recognized as their own and who were consigned to slavery from birth.

In addition to establishing social and cultural institutions of their own, slaves adapted themselves to slavery by forming complex relationships with their masters. However much blacks resented their lack of freedom, they often found it difficult to maintain an entirely hostile attitude toward their owners. Not only were they dependent on whites for the material means of existence–food, clothing, and shelter; they also often derived from their masters a sense of security and protection. There was, in short, a paternal relationship between slave and master–sometimes harsh, sometimes kindly, but almost invariably important. Paternalism, in fact, became (even if not always consciously) a vital instrument of white control. By creating a sense of mutual dependence, whites helped reduce resistance to an institution that, in essence, served only the interests of the ruling race.

PATERNAL NATURE OF SLAVERY

AP CONNECTING THEMES

Chapter 11 examined the importance of both cotton and the institution of slavery in forming a distinct regional identity in the South. It also discussed the development of a class system in white society in the South and the reasons for the existence of little class conflict in this area. The reasons for and the consequences of the lack of development of a large middle class in the South are important to remember when thinking about regional development. Also important to remember is the nature of gender roles in both white and slave society in the South. Chapter 11 also focused on specific examples that characterized the development of African American culture among both slaves and free blacks. Lastly, important to trace is the ideological shift in the idea of slavery as a "necessary evil" to a "positive good" in the minds of white southerners.

The following themes have heightened importance in Chapter 11. You should now be able to do the following for each listed theme:

Identity: Analyze the factors that led to the creation of a distinct regional identity for southern whites and the characteristics that set that society apart from other regions.

Work, Exchange, and Technology: Analyze the nature of the southern economy and its consequences in the development of southern society. Also, analyze the labor system that developed in the South and be able to compare and contrast it with that of other regions.

Politics and Power: Explain how the development of "King Cotton" and the institution of slavery led to a distinct regional political system in the South.

Environment and Geography: Explain the impact of the natural environment on the development of the South's political and economic identities.

Ideas, Beliefs, and Culture: Compare and contrast gender roles in white and slave society in the South. Also, explain the transformation of the view of the institution of slavery as a "necessary evil" to a "positive good" in the minds of white southerners.

AP SUGGESTED STUDY

PEOPLE/PLACES/EVENTS As you study these items, think about how they demonstrate or relate to key concepts and historical themes from this chapter and previous chapters.

CULT OF HONOR 300	GANG SYSTEM 303	"SAMBO" 309
DE BOW'S REVIEW 298	NAT TURNER 309	SLAVE CODES 303
DENMARK VESEY 309	PATERNALISM 302	SLAVE MUSIC 310
GABRIEL PROSSER 309	PIDGIN 310	TASK SYSTEM 303

AP TEST PRACTICE

Questions assume cumulative content knowledge from this chapter and previous chapters.

MULTIPLE CHOICE Use the map on page 296 and your knowledge of U.S. history to answer questions 1–2.

1. Which of the following can best be viewed as a highly significant event, or turning point, leading to the trends shown by the maps?

    (A) Development of agricultural technology that greatly improved the ability to process cotton

    (B) Outlawing of the international slave, leading to a greater internal trade

    (C) The South's investment in canals to improve the transportation of cotton

    (D) The trade in slaves from the old upper South to the new lower South

2. Based on the information shown in the maps and your knowledge of U.S. history so far, which conclusion about economic ties between the North and South by the 1860s can be most reasonably drawn?

    (A) A strong national banking system supported the relationship of the South's supply of cotton for manufacturing in the North.

    (B) The North helped the South develop canals to facilitate shipping of cotton to the North.

    (C) The South supplied most of the food products for the increasingly urbanized North.

    (D) The South supplied cotton for textile factories in the North.

SHORT ANSWER Use your knowledge of U.S. history to answer questions 3–5.

3. Answer a, b, and c.

    a) Briefly explain ONE example of how African Americans maintained a distinct African American culture, despite slavery.

    b) Briefly explain a SECOND example of how African Americans maintained a distinct African American culture, despite slavery.

    c) Briefly explain ONE example of the effects of the slave system on white southern culture by the mid-19th century.

4. Answer a, b, and c.

    a) For one of the areas below, identify and briefly explain ONE difference between the North and the South by the mid-19th century.

    • Cultural

    • Economic

    • Political

    b) For the same area, identify and briefly explain a SECOND difference between the North and the South by the mid-19th century.

    c) Choose a second area and explain why that area is not as important an area of concern regarding differences between the North and the South by the mid-19th century.

5. Answer a, b, and c.

    a) For one of the areas below, identify and briefly explain ONE example of the impact of the natural environment on regional identity.

    • Old Northwest (Midwest)

    • Northeast

    • South

    b) For the same area, identify and briefly explain a SECOND example of the impact of the natural environment on regional identity.

    c) Choose a second area and identify and briefly explain ONE example of the impact of the natural environment on regional identity.

LONG ESSAY Develop a thoughtful and thorough historical argument that answers the question below. Begin your essay with a thesis statement and support it with relevant historical evidence.

6. Analyze to what extent the labor systems of the North and the South differed in the United States by the mid-19th century.

12 | ANTEBELLUM CULTURE AND REFORM

GIRLS' EVENING SCHOOL (C. 1840), ANONYMOUS Schooling for women, which expanded significantly in the mid-nineteenth century, included training in domestic arts (as indicated by the sewing table at right), as well as in reading, writing, and other basic skills. (© The Granger Collection, New York)

AP

HISTORICAL THINKING

1. **Historical Argumentation** Analyze the reasons for and the success of various reform movements in the mid-19th century.

2. **Historical Argumentation** Analyze the divisions within and the impact of the abolition movement on American society.

3. **Historical Argumentation** Analyze the degree to which and ways in which reform movements led to intensified sectional conflict.

4. **Contextualization** Analyze the impact of the Second Great Awakening in inspiring various reform movements.

5. **Contextualization** To what degree and in what ways did utopian communitarianism influence American society?

Key Concept Correlations

Analyze the ways the historical developments you learn about in this chapter connect to the following AP Key Concepts.

4.1 The United States developed the world's first modern mass democracy and celebrated a new national culture, while Americans sought to define the nation's democratic ideals and to reform its institutions to match them.

4.2 Developments in technology, agriculture, and commerce precipitated profound changes in U.S. settlement patterns, regional identities, gender and family relations, political power, and distribution of consumer goods.

5.1 The United States became more connected with the world as it pursued an expansionist foreign policy in the Western Hemisphere and emerged as the destination for many migrants from other countries.

5.2 Intensified by expansion and deepening regional divisions, debates over slavery and other economic, cultural, and political issues led the nation into civil war.

Thematic Learning Objectives

CUL-2, 5, 6; POL-3, 5; WOR-2; ID-1, 2, 5, 6; WXT-6; PEO-6

CHAPTER 12 discusses the Romantic period in literature and art, sometimes called the First American Renaissance, and the interwoven influences of the Enlightenment. Also, the chapter goes into significant depth in dealing with reform movements brought about by urbanization and the Second Great Awakening. It focuses on individual reform movements, including temperance, women's rights, abolitionism, education, and prison reform. There is discussion of the reasons for utopian communitarianism and the various types of communities that developed. Particular attention is given to the abolitionist movement and the divisions within it, as well as its influence in American society. As you read, evaluate the following ideas:

- The First American Renaissance brought about an outpouring of American art and literature.
- The Second Great Awakening's belief in the perfectibility of the self led to the formation of many reform movements, having an impact into the future.
- African Americans actively participated in the abolitionist movement.
- The women's rights movement attempted to challenge traditional beliefs about gender roles.
- The South remained politically, culturally, and ideologically distinct from the other sections.
- Abolitionists, despite being a minority even in the North, intensified sectional conflict.

THE ROMANTIC IMPULSE

"In the four quarters of the globe," wrote the English wit Sydney Smith in 1820, "who reads an American book? or goes to an American play? or looks at an American picture or statue?" The

NATIONAL CULTURAL ASPIRATIONS

answer, he assumed, was obvious: no one. American intellectuals were fully aware of the low regard in which Europeans held their artistic and intellectual life. In the middle decades of the nineteenth century, they continued to work for both an elevation and a liberation of their nation's culture—for the creation of an American artistic world independent of Europe, one that would express their nation's special virtues.

At the same time, however, some of the nation's cultural leaders were beginning to strive for another kind of liberation, one that would eventually overshadow their self-conscious nationalism. That impulse—which was, ironically, largely an import from Europe—was the spirit of romanticism. In literature, philosophy, art, even in politics and economics, American intellectuals were committing themselves to the liberation of the human spirit.

NATIONALISM AND ROMANTICISM IN AMERICAN PAINTING

When Sydney Smith asked in 1820 who looked at an American painting, he was expressing the belief among European artists that they—and they alone—stood at the center of the world of art. But in the United States, many people were looking at American paintings in the antebellum era—and they were doing so not because the paintings introduced them to the great traditions of Europe, but because they believed Americans were creating important new artistic traditions.

The most important and popular American paintings of the first half of the nineteenth century set out to evoke the wonder of the nation's landscape. Unlike their European counterparts, American painters did not favor gentle scenes of carefully cultivated countrysides. They sought instead to capture the undiluted power of nature by portraying some of the nation's wildest and most spectacular areas—to evoke what many nineteenth-century people called the "sublime," the feeling of awe and wonderment and even fear of the grandeur of nature. The first great school of American painters emerged in New York. Frederic Church, Thomas Cole, Thomas Doughty, and Asher Durand—known, along with others, as the Hudson River School—painted the spectacular vistas of the rugged and still largely unsettled Hudson Valley. Like Emerson and Thoreau, whom many of the painters read and admired, they considered nature–more than civilization–the best source of wisdom and spiritual fulfillment. In portraying the Hudson Valley,

HUDSON RIVER SCHOOL

they seemed to announce that in America, unlike in Europe, "wild nature" still existed; and that America, therefore, was a nation of greater promise than the played-out lands of the Old World. Yet there was also a sense of nostalgia in many of the Hudson River paintings, an effort to preserve and cherish a kind of nature that many Americans feared was fast disappearing.

In later years, some of the Hudson River painters traveled farther west, in search of more profound spiritual experiences. They found an even more rugged and spectacular natural world. Their enormous canvases of great natural wonders–the Yosemite Valley, Yellowstone, the Rocky Mountains–touched a passionate chord among the American public. Some of the most famous of their paintings–particularly the works of Albert Bierstadt and Thomas Moran–traveled around the country attracting enormous crowds.

LITERATURE AND THE QUEST FOR LIBERATION

American readers in the first decades of the nineteenth century were relatively indifferent to the work of their nation's own writers. The most popular novelist in America in these years was the British writer Sir Walter Scott, whose swashbuckling historical novels set in eighteenth-century England and Scotland won him an impassioned readership in both Britain and America. When Americans read books written in their own country, many were likely to turn to the large number of "sentimental novels," written mostly by and for women. (See "Patterns of Popular Culture," pp. 336-337.)

But even during the heyday of Scott in the 1820s, the effort to create a distinctively American literature–which Washington Irving and others had advanced in the first decades of the century–made considerable progress with the emergence of the first great American novelist: James Fenimore Cooper. The author of more than thirty novels in the space of three decades, Cooper was known to his contemporaries as a master of adventure and suspense. What

COOPER AND THE AMERICAN WILDERNESS

most distinguished his work, however, was its evocation of the American wilderness. Cooper had grown up in central New York, at a time when the edge of white settlement was not far away; and he retained throughout his life a fascination with man's relationship to nature and with the challenges (and dangers) of America's expansion westward. His most important novels were known as the "Leatherstocking Tales." Among them were *The Last of the Mohicans* (1826) and *The Deerslayer* (1841), which explored the American frontiersman's experience with Indians, pioneers, violence, and the law.

Cooper's novels were a continuation of the early-nineteenth-century effort to produce a truly American literature. But they also served as a link to the concerns of later intellectuals. For in the "Leatherstocking Tales" could be seen not only a celebration of the American spirit and landscape but also an evocation, through the central character of Natty Bumppo, of the ideal of the independent individual with a natural inner goodness. There was also evidence of another impulse that would motivate American reform: the fear of disorder. Many of Cooper's less savory characters illustrated the vicious, grasping nature of some of the nation's western settlers and suggested a need for social discipline even in the wilderness.

Walt Whitman, the self-proclaimed poet of American democracy, became one of the most important writers of his time. He was born in 1819, on Long Island, to Quaker parents–the second of nine children. As he grew older, he worked as an

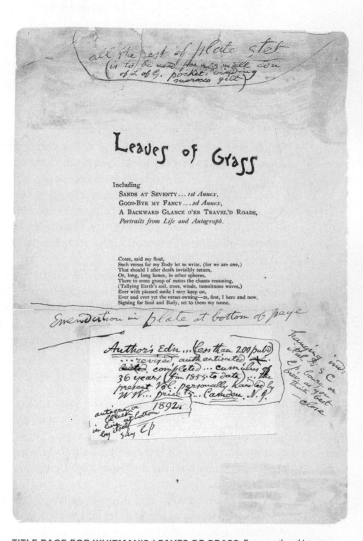

TITLE PAGE FOR WHITMAN'S *LEAVES OF GRASS* For more than thirty years after the publication of the original *Leaves of Grass* in 1855, Walt Whitman constantly revised and expanded the collection of poems and issued numerous subsequent editions. This sample title page, with notations by Whitman indicating changes and additions he wanted made, is for the final such edition, published in 1892, the year of Whitman's death. In a statement Whitman wrote to announce publication, he said that "the book *Leaves of Grass*, which he has been working on at great intervals and partially issued for the past thirty-five or forty years, is now completed. . . . Faulty as it is, he decides it is by far his special and entire self-chosen poetic utterance." (The Library of Congress)

apprentice in newspapers. At age sixteen, he moved to New York City, where he worked as a printer and later taught at several schools. After his teaching attempts, Whitman went to Huntington, New York, to found his own newspaper, the *Long Islander*, and served as its publisher, editor, pressman, and distributor and even provided home delivery. But he began to write poetry when he could and eventually left his newspaper. In 1855, he hired a printer and published a first volume of work: *Leaves of Grass*. His poems were an unrestrained celebration of democracy, of the liberation of the individual, and of the pleasures of the flesh as well as of the spirit. They also expressed Whitman's personal yearning for emotional and physical release and personal fulfillment—a yearning perhaps rooted in part in his own experience as a homosexual living in a society profoundly intolerant of unconventional sexuality. In his large body of poems, Whitman not only helped liberate verse from traditional, restrictive conventions but also helped express the soaring spirit of individualism that characterized his age.

The new literary concern with the unleashing of human emotions did not always produce such optimistic works, as the work of Herman Melville suggests. Born in New York in 1819, Melville ran away to sea as a youth and spent years sailing the world before returning home to become the greatest American novelist of his era. The most important of his novels was *Moby Dick*, published in 1851. His portrayal of Ahab, the powerful, driven captain of a whaling vessel, was a story of courage and of the strength of individual will; but it was also a tragedy of pride and revenge. Ahab's maniacal search for Moby Dick, a great white whale that had maimed him, suggested how the search for personal fulfillment and triumph could not only liberate but destroy as well. The result of Ahab's great quest was his own annihilation, reflecting Melville's conviction that the human spirit was a troubled, often self-destructive force.

HERMAN MELVILLE

Even more bleak were the works of one of the few southern writers of the time to embrace the search for the essence of the human spirit: Edgar Allan Poe. In the course of his short and unhappy life (he died in 1849 at the age of forty), Poe produced stories and poems that were primarily sad and macabre. His first book, *Tamerlane and Other Poems* (1827), received little recognition. But later works, including his most famous poem, "The Raven" (1845), established him as a major, if controversial, literary figure. Poe evoked images of individuals rising above the narrow confines of intellect and exploring the deeper world of the spirit and the emotions. Yet that world, he seemed to say, contained much pain and horror. Other American writers were contemptuous of Poe's work and his message, but he was ultimately to have a profound effect on European poets such as Baudelaire.

LITERATURE IN THE ANTEBELLUM SOUTH

Poe, however, was something of an exception in the world of southern literature. Like the North, the South experienced a literary flowering in the mid-nineteenth century, and produced writers and artists who were concerned with defining the nature of American society and the American nation. But white southerners produced very different images of what that society was and should be.

Southern novelists of the 1830s (among them Beverly Tucker, William Alexander Caruthers, and John Pendleton Kennedy), some of them writers of great talent, many of them residents of Richmond, produced historical romances or romantic eulogies of the plantation system of the upper South. In the 1840s, the southern literary capital moved to Charleston, home of the most distinguished of the region's men of letters: William Gilmore Simms. For a time, Simms's work expressed a broad nationalism that transcended his regional background, but by the 1840s he too had become a strong defender of southern institutions—especially slavery—against the encroachments of the North. There was, he believed, a unique quality to southern life that it was the duty of intellectuals to defend.

SOUTHERN ROMANTICISM

One group of southern writers, however, produced works that were more broadly American and less committed to a glorification of the peculiarities of southern life. These were writers from the fringes of plantation society, who depicted the world of the backwoods rural areas. Augustus B. Longstreet, Joseph G. Baldwin, Johnson J. Hooper, and others focused not on aristocratic "cavaliers," but on ordinary people and poor whites. Instead of romanticizing their subjects, they were deliberately and sometimes painfully realistic. And they seasoned their sketches with a robust, vulgar humor that was new to American literature. These southern realists established a tradition of American regional humor that was ultimately to find its most powerful voice in Mark Twain.

THE TRANSCENDENTALISTS

One of the outstanding expressions of the romantic impulse in America came from a group of New England writers and philosophers known as the transcendentalists. Borrowing heavily from German philosophers such as Kant, Hegel, and Schelling, and from the English writers Coleridge and Carlyle, the transcendentalists embraced a theory of the individual that rested on a distinction (first suggested by Kant) between what they called "reason" and "understanding"—words they used in ways that seem unfamiliar, even strange, to modern ears. Reason, as they defined it, had little to do with rationality. It was, rather, the individual's innate capacity to grasp beauty and truth through giving full expression to the instincts and emotions; and as such, it was the highest human faculty. Understanding, the transcendentalists argued, was the use of intellect in the narrow, artificial ways imposed by society; it involved the repression of instinct and the victory of externally imposed learning. Every person's goal, therefore, should be liberation from the confines of "understanding" and the cultivation of "reason." Each individual should strive to "transcend" the limits of the intellect and allow the emotions, the "soul," to create an "original relation to the Universe."

Transcendentalist philosophy emerged first among a small group of intellectuals centered in Concord, Massachusetts. Their leader and most eloquent voice was Ralph Waldo Emerson. A Unitarian minister in his youth, Emerson left the church in 1832 to devote himself entirely to writing and teaching the elements of transcendentalism. He was a dazzling figure to his contemporaries–a lecturer whose public appearances drew rapturous crowds; a conversationalist who drew intellectuals to his Concord home almost daily. He was the most important intellectual of his age.

RALPH WALDO EMERSON

Emerson produced a significant body of poetry, but he was most renowned for his essays and lectures. In "Nature" (1836), one of his best-known essays, Emerson wrote that in the quest for self-fulfillment, individuals should work for a communion with the natural world: "in the woods, we return to reason and faith. . . . Standing on the bare ground–my head bathed by the blithe air, and uplifted into infinite space–all mean egotism vanishes. . . . I am part and particle of God." In other essays, he was even more explicit. "Nothing is at last sacred," he wrote in "Self-Reliance" (1841), perhaps his most famous essay, "but the integrity of your own mind." The quest for self-reliance, he explained, was really a search for communion with the unity of the universe, the wholeness of God, the great spiritual force that he described as the "Oversoul." Each person's innate capacity to become, through his or her private efforts, a part of this essence was perhaps the classic expression of the romantic belief in the "divinity" of the individual.

Emerson was also a committed nationalist, an ardent proponent of American cultural independence. In a famous 1837 lecture, "The American Scholar," he boasted that "our day of dependence, our long apprenticeship to the learning of other lands, draws to a close." His belief that truth and beauty could be derived as much from instinct as from learning suggested that Americans, lacking the rich cultural heritage of European nations, could still aspire to artistic and literary greatness. Artistic and intellectual achievement need not rely on tradition and history; it could come from the instinctive creative genius of individuals. "Let the single man plant himself indomitably on his instincts and there abide," Emerson once said, "and the huge world will come round to him."

Almost as influential as Emerson was another leading Concord transcendentalist, Henry David Thoreau. Thoreau went even further than his friend Emerson in repudiating the repressive forces of society, which produced, he said, "lives of quiet desperation." Individuals should work for self-realization by resisting pressures to conform to society's expectations and responding instead to their own instincts. Thoreau's own effort to free himself–immortalized in his most famous book, *Walden* (1854)–led him to build a small cabin in the Concord woods on the edge of Walden Pond, where he lived alone for two years as simply as he could. "I went to the woods," he explained, "because I wished to live deliberately, to front only the essential facts of life, and see if I could not learn what it

had to teach, and not, when I came to die, discover that I had not lived." Living simply, Thoreau believed, was a desirable alternative to the rapidly modernizing world around him–a world, he believed, that the disruptive and intrusive railroad unhappily symbolized.

Thoreau's rejection of what he considered the artificial constraints of society extended as well to his relationship with government. In 1846, he went to jail (briefly) rather than agree to pay a poll tax. He would not, he insisted, give financial support to a government that permitted the existence of slavery. In his 1849 essay "Resistance to Civil Government," Thoreau explained his refusal by claiming that the individual's personal morality had the first claim on his or her actions, that a government which required violation of that morality had no legitimate authority. The proper response was "civil disobedience," or "passive resistance"–a public refusal to obey unjust laws.

THOREAU AND CIVIL DISOBEDIENCE

THE DEFENSE OF NATURE

The transcendentalists, and others, feared the impact of the new capitalist enthusiasms on the integrity of the natural world. "The mountains and cataracts, which were to have made poets and painters," wrote the essayist Oliver Wendell Holmes, "have been mined for anthracite and dammed for water power."

Nature was not just a setting for economic activity, as many farmers, miners, and others believed; and it was not simply a body of data to be catalogued and studied, as many scientists thought. It was the source of human inspiration–the vehicle through which individuals could best realize the truth within their own souls. Genuine spirituality, they argued, came not from formal religion but through communion with the natural world. "In wildness is the preservation of the world." Thoreau once wrote. Humans separated from nature, he believed, would lose a substantial part of their humanity.

In making such claims, the transcendentalists were among the first Americans to anticipate the environmental movement of the twentieth century. They had no scientific basis for their defense of the wilderness, no knowledge of modern ecology, little sense of the twentieth-century notion of the interconnectedness of species. But they did believe in, and articulate, an essential unity between humanity and nature–a spiritual unity, they believed, without which civilization would be impoverished. They looked at nature, they said, "with new eyes," and with those eyes they saw that "behind nature, throughout nature, spirit is present."

VISIONS OF UTOPIA

Although transcendentalism was above all an individualistic philosophy, it helped spawn the most famous of all nineteenth-century experiments in communal living: Brook Farm, which the Boston transcendentalist George Ripley established as an experimental

BROOK FARM

community in West Roxbury, Massachusetts, in 1841. There, according to Ripley, individuals would gather to create a new form of social organization. All residents would share equally in the labor of the community so that all could share too in the leisure, because leisure was the first necessity for cultivation of the self. (Ripley was one of the first Americans to attribute positive connotations to the idea of leisure; most of his contemporaries equated it with laziness and sloth.) Participation in manual labor served another purpose as well: it helped individuals bridge the gap between the world of the intellect and learning, and the world of instinct and nature. The obvious tension between the ideal of individual freedom and the demands of a communal society took their toll on Brook Farm. Many residents became disenchanted and left; when a fire destroyed the central building of the community in 1847, the experiment dissolved.

Among the original residents of Brook Farm was the writer Nathaniel Hawthorne, who expressed his disillusionment with the experiment and, to some extent, with transcendentalism in a series of notable novels. In *The Blithedale Romance* (1852), he wrote scathingly of Brook Farm itself, portraying the disastrous consequences of the experiment on the individuals who had submitted to it.

The failure of Brook Farm did not, however, prevent the formation of other experimental communities. Some borrowed, as Ripley had done, from the ideas of the French philosopher Charles Fourier, whose ideas of socialist communities organized as cooperative "phalanxes" received wide attention in America. Others drew from the ideas of the Scottish industrialist and philanthropist Robert Owen. Owen himself founded an experimental community in Indiana in 1825, which he named

NEW HARMONY New Harmony. It was to be a "Village of Cooperation," in which every resident worked and lived in total equality. The community was an economic failure, but the vision that had inspired it continued to enchant Americans. Dozens of other "Owenite" experiments began in other locations in the following years.

REDEFINING GENDER ROLES

One of the principal concerns of many of the new utopian communities (and of the new social philosophies on which they rested) was the relationship between men and women. Transcendentalism and other movements of this period fostered expressions of a kind of feminism that would not gain a secure foothold in American society until the late twentieth century.

One of those most responsible for raising issues of gender was Margaret Fuller. A leading transcendentalist and a close associate of Emerson, she suggested the important relationship between the discovery of the "self" that was so central to antebellum reform and the questioning of gender roles: "Many

MARGARET FULLER As a leading transcendentalist, Fuller argued for the important relationship between the discovery of the "self" and the questioning of the prevailing gender roles of her era. In her famous feminist work, *Women in the Nineteenth Century*, Fuller wrote, "Many women are considering within themselves what they need and what they have not." She encouraged her readers, especially women, to set aside conventional thinking about the role of women in society: "I would have Woman lay aside all thought, such as she habitually cherishes, of being taught and led by men." Fuller provided a strong voice in the redefinition of gender roles in the nineteenth century. (© Corbis)

women are considering within themselves what they need and what they have not," she wrote in a famous feminist work, *Woman in the Nineteenth Century* (1844). "I would have Woman lay aside all thought, such as she habitually cherishes, of being taught and led by men." Fuller herself, before her premature death in a shipwreck in 1850, lived a life far different from the domestic ideal of her time. She had intimate relationships with many men; became a great admirer of European socialists and a great champion of the Italian revolution of 1848, which she witnessed during travels there; and established herself as an intellectual leader whose power came in part from her perspective as a woman.

A redefinition of gender roles was crucial to one of the most enduring utopian colonies of the nineteenth century: the Oneida

REDEFINED GENDER ROLES AT THE ONEIDA COMMUNITY Community, established in 1848 in upstate New York by John Humphrey Noyes. The Oneida "Perfectionists," as residents of the community called themselves, rejected traditional notions of family and marriage. All residents, Noyes declared, were "married" to all other residents; there were no permanent conjugal ties. But Oneida was not, as its horrified critics often claimed, an experiment in "free love." It was a place where the community carefully monitored sexual behavior; where women were to be protected from unwanted childbearing; in which children were raised communally, often seeing little of their own parents. The Oneidans took special pride in what they considered the liberation of their women from the demands of male "lust" and from the traditional bonds of family.

The Shakers, even more than the Oneidans, made a redefinition of traditional sexuality and gender roles central to their society. Founded by "Mother" Ann Lee in the 1770s, the society of the Shakers survived throughout the nineteenth century and into the twentieth. (A tiny remnant survives today.) But the Shakers attracted a particularly large following in the antebellum period and established more than twenty communities throughout the Northeast and Northwest in the 1840s. They derived their name from a unique religious ritual, a sort of ecstatic dance, in which members of a congregation would "shake" themselves free of sin while performing a loud chant.

The most distinctive feature of Shakerism, however, was its commitment to complete celibacy–which meant, of course, that no one could be born to Shakerism; all Shakers had to choose the faith voluntarily. Shaker communities attracted about 6,000 members in the 1840s, more women than men; and members lived in conditions in which contact between men and women was very limited. Shakers openly endorsed the idea of sexual equality; they even embraced the idea of a God who was not clearly male or female. Within the Shaker society as a whole, it was women who exercised the most power. Mother Ann Lee was succeeded as leader of the movement by Mother Lucy Wright. Shakerism, one observer wrote in the 1840s, was a refuge from the "perversions of marriage" and "the gross abuses which drag it down."

THE SHAKERS

The Shakers were not, however, motivated only by a desire to escape the burdens of traditional gender roles. They were trying as well to create a society separated and protected from the chaos and disorder that they believed had come to characterize American life as a whole. Less interested in personal freedom than in social discipline, they were like some other dissenting religious sects and utopian communities of their time. Another example was the Amana Community, founded by German immigrants in 1843, whose members settled in Iowa in 1855 and attempted to realize Christian ideals by creating an ordered, socialist society.

THE MORMONS

Among the most important efforts to create a new and more ordered society within the old was that of the Church of Jesus Christ of Latter-Day Saints–the Mormons. Mormonism began in upstate New York as a result of the efforts of Joseph Smith, a young, energetic, but economically unsuccessful man, who had spent most of his twenty-four years moving restlessly through New England and the Northeast. Then, in 1830, he published a remarkable document–the Book of Mormon, named for the ancient prophet who he claimed had written it. It was, Smith said, a translation of a set of golden tablets he had found in the hills of New York, revealed to him by an angel of God. The Book of Mormon told the story of an ancient and successful civilization in America, peopled by one of the lost tribes of Israel who had found their

JOSEPH SMITH

way to the New World centuries before Columbus. Its members waited patiently for the appearance of the Messiah, and they were rewarded when Jesus came to America after his resurrection. Subsequent generations, however, strayed from the path of righteousness that Jesus had laid out for them. Ultimately, their civilization collapsed, and God punished the sinful by making their skin dark. These darkened people, Smith believed, were the descendants of the American Indians, although the modern tribes had no memory of their origins. But while the ancient Hebrew kingdom in America had ultimately vanished, Smith believed, its history as a righteous society could serve as a model for a new holy community in the United States.

In 1831, gathering a small group of believers around him, Smith began searching for a sanctuary for his new community of "saints," an effort that would continue unhappily for more than twenty years. Time and again, the Mormons attempted to establish their "New Jerusalem." Time and again, they met with persecution from surrounding communities suspicious of their radical religious doctrines–which included polygamy (the right of men to take several wives), a rigid form of social organization, and, particularly damaging to their image, an intense secrecy, which gave rise to wild rumors among their critics of conspiracy and depravity.

Driven from their original settlements in Independence, Missouri, and Kirtland, Ohio, the Mormons moved on to the new town of Nauvoo, Illinois, which by the early 1840s had become an imposing and economically successful community. In 1844, however, Joseph Smith was arrested, charged with treason (for allegedly conspiring against the government to win foreign support for a new Mormon colony in the Southwest), and imprisoned in Carthage, Illinois. There an angry mob attacked the jail, forced Smith from his cell, and shot and killed him. The Mormons now abandoned Nauvoo and, under the leadership of Smith's successor, Brigham Young, traveled across the desert–a society of 12,000 people, in one of the largest single group migrations in American history–and established a new community in Utah, the present Salt Lake City. There, at last, the Mormons were able to create a lasting settlement.

ESTABLISHMENT OF SALT LAKE CITY

Like other experiments in social organization of the era, Mormonism reflected a belief in human perfectibility. God had once been a man, the church taught, and thus every man or woman could aspire to become–as Joseph Smith had become–a saint. But unlike other new communities, such as the Oneidans, the Mormons did not embrace the doctrine of individual liberty. Instead, they created a highly organized, centrally directed, almost militarized social structure, a refuge against the disorder and uncertainty of the secular world. They placed particular emphasis on the structure of the family. Mormon religious rituals even included a process by which men and women went through baptism ceremonies in the name of deceased ancestors; as a result, they believed, they would be reunited with those ancestors in heaven. The intense Mormon interest in genealogy, which continues today, is a reflection of

MORMONS HEADING WEST   This lithograph, by William Henry Jackson (1843–1942), shows Mormon handcart pioneers heading west to Utah in 1850.   (Private Collection/© Peter Newark American Pictures/The Bridgeman Art Library)

this belief in the possibility of reuniting present generations with those of the past.

The original Mormons were, for the most part, men and women who felt displaced in their rapidly changing society–people left behind or troubled by the material growth and social progress of their era. In the new religion, they found genuine faith. In the society Mormonism created, they found security and order.

REMAKING SOCIETY

The simultaneous efforts to liberate the individual and impose order on a changing world also helped create a wide range of new movements to remake society–movements in which, to a striking degree, women formed the real rank and file and often the leadership as well. By the 1830s, such movements had taken the form of organized reform societies. "In no country in the world," Tocqueville had observed, "has the principle of association been more successfully used, or more unsparingly applied to a multitude of different objects, than in America."

NEW REFORM MOVEMENTS

The new organizations did indeed work on behalf of a wide range of issues: temperance; education; peace; the care of the poor, the handicapped, and the mentally ill; the treatment of criminals; the rights of women; and many more. Few eras in American history have witnessed as wide a range of reform efforts as emerged in the mid-nineteenth century. And few eras have exposed more clearly the simultaneous attraction of Americans to the ideas of personal liberty and social order.

REVIVALISM, MORALITY, AND ORDER

The philosophy of reform arose from several distinct sources. One was the optimistic vision of those who, like the transcendentalists, rejected Calvinist doctrines and preached the divinity of the individual. These included not only Emerson, Thoreau, and their followers, but also a much larger group of Americans who embraced the doctrines of Unitarianism and Universalism and absorbed European romanticism.

A second, and in many respects more important, source was Protestant revivalism—the movement that had begun with the Second Great Awakening early in the century and had, by the 1820s, evolved into a powerful force for social reform. Although the New Light revivalists were theologically far removed from the transcendentalists and Unitarians, they had come to share the optimistic belief that every individual was capable of salvation. According to Charles Grandison Finney, an evangelistic Presbyterian minister who became the most influential revival leader of the 1820s and 1830s, traditional Calvinist doctrines of predestination and individual human helplessness were both obsolete and destructive. Each person, he preached, contained within himself or herself the capacity to experience spiritual rebirth and achieve salvation. A revival of faith need not depend on a miracle from God; it could be created by individual effort.

Finney enjoyed particular success in upstate New York, where he helped launch a series of passionate revivals in towns along the Erie Canal—a region so prone to religious awakenings that it was known as the "burned-over district." It was no coincidence that the new revivalism should prove so powerful

REVIVALISM IN THE BURNED-OVER DISTRICT

there, for this region of New York was experiencing—largely as a result of the construction of the canal—a major economic transformation. And with that transformation had come changes in the social fabric so profound that many men and women felt baffled and disoriented. (It was in roughly this same area of New York that Joseph Smith first organized the Mormon church.)

In Rochester, New York, the site of his greatest success, Finney staged a series of emotionally wrenching religious meetings that aroused a large segment of the community. He had

FINNEY'S DOCTRINE OF PERSONAL REGENERATION

particular success in mobilizing women, on whom he tended to concentrate his efforts— both because women found the liberating message of revivalism particularly appealing and because, Finney discovered, they provided him with access to their male relatives. Gradually, he developed a large following among the prosperous citizens of the region. They were enjoying the economic benefits of the new commercial growth, but they were also uneasy about some of the social changes accompanying it (among them the introduction into their community of a new, undisciplined pool of transient laborers). For them, revivalism became not only a means of personal salvation but also a mandate for the reform (and control) of their society. Finney's revivalism became a call for a crusade against personal immorality. "The church," he maintained, "must take right ground on the subject of Temperance, the Moral Reform, and all the subjects of practical morality which come up for decision from time to time."

THE TEMPERANCE CRUSADE

Evangelical Protestantism added major strength to one of the most influential reform movements of the era: the crusade against drunkenness. No social vice, argued some reformers (including many of Finney's converts in cities such as Rochester), was more responsible for crime, disorder, and poverty than the excessive use of alcohol. Women, who were particularly active in the temperance movement, claimed that alcoholism placed a special burden on wives: men spent money on alcohol that their families needed for basic necessities, and drunken husbands often abused their wives and children.

In fact, alcoholism was an even more serious problem in antebellum America than it has been in the twentieth and twenty-first centuries. The supply of alcohol was growing rapidly, particularly in the West; farmers there grew more grain than they could sell in the still-limited markets in this prerailroad era, so they distilled much of it into whiskey. But in the East, too, commercial distilleries and private stills were widespread. The appetite for alcohol was growing along with the supply: in isolated western areas, where drinking provided a social pastime in small towns and helped ease the loneliness and isolation on farms; in pubs and saloons in eastern cities, where drinking was the principal leisure activity for many workers. The average male in the 1830s drank nearly three times as much alcohol as the average person does today. And

CHARLES GRANDISON FINNEY Evangelistic Presbyterian minister Charles Grandison Finney became the most influential revival leader of the 1820s and 1830s. He argued that each person contained within herself or himself the capacity to experience spiritual rebirth and achieve salvation. Finney's views on revivalist faith contrasted with earlier Calvinist doctrines of predestination and individual human helplessness. (© Bettmann/Corbis)

as that figure suggests, many people drank habitually and excessively, with bitter consequences for themselves and others. Among the many supporters of the temperance movement were people who saw it as a way to overcome their own problems with alcoholism.

Although advocates of temperance had been active since the late eighteenth century, the new reformers gave the movement an energy and influence it had never previously known. In 1826, the American Society for the Promotion of Temperance emerged as a coordinating agency among various groups; it attempted to use many of the techniques of revivalism in preaching abstinence. Then, in 1840, six reformed alcoholics in Baltimore organized the Washington Temperance Society and began to draw large crowds—in which workers (many of them attempting to overcome their own alcoholism) were heavily represented—to hear their impassioned and intriguing confessions of past sins. By then, temperance advocates had grown dramatically in numbers; more than a million people had signed a formal pledge to forgo hard liquor.

AMERICAN SOCIETY FOR THE PROMOTION OF TEMPERANCE

As the movement gained in strength, it also became divided in purpose. Some temperance advocates now urged that abstinence include not only liquor but beer and wine as well. Not everyone agreed. Some began to demand state legislation to restrict the sale and consumption of alcohol (Maine passed such a law in 1851); others insisted that temperance must rely on the conscience of the individual. Whatever their disagreements, by promoting abstinence reformers were attempting to promote the moral self-improvement of individuals. They were also trying to impose discipline on society.

The search for social discipline was particularly clear in the battle over prohibition laws, which pitted established Protestants against new Catholic immigrants, to many of whom drinking was an important social ritual and an integral part of the life of their communities. The arrival of the immigrants was profoundly disturbing to established residents of many communities, and the restriction of alcohol seemed to them a way to curb the disorder they believed the new population was creating.

CULTURAL DIVISIONS OVER ALCOHOL

HEALTH FADS AND PHRENOLOGY

For some Americans, the search for individual and social perfection led to an interest in new theories of health and knowledge. Threats to public health were critical to the sense of insecurity that underlay many reform movements, especially after the terrible cholera epidemics of the 1830s and 1840s. Cholera is a severe bacterial infection of the intestines, usually a result of consuming contaminated food or water. In the nineteenth century, long before the discovery of antibiotics, less

THE DRUNKARD'S PROGRESS This 1846 lithograph by Nathaniel Currier shows what temperance advocates argued was the inevitable consequence of alcohol consumption. Beginning with an apparently innocent "glass with a friend," the young man rises step by step to the summit of drunken revelry, then declines to desperation and suicide while his abandoned wife and child grieve. (The Library of Congress)

than half of those who contracted the disease survived. Thousands of people died of cholera during its occasional outbreaks, and in certain cities–New Orleans in 1833 and St. Louis in 1849–the effects were truly catastrophic. Nearly a quarter of the population of New Orleans died in the 1833 epidemic. Many municipalities, pressured by reformers, established city health boards to try to find solutions to the problems of epidemics. But the medical profession of the time, unaware of the nature of bacterial infections, had no answers; and the boards therefore found little to do.

Instead, many Americans turned to nonscientific theories for improving health. Affluent men and, especially, women flocked to health spas for the celebrated "water cure," which purported to improve health through immersing people in hot or cold baths or wrapping them in wet sheets. Although the water cure delivered few of the benefits its promoters promised, it did have some therapeutic value; some forms of hydrotherapy are still in use today. Other people adopted new dietary theories. Sylvester Graham, a Connecticut-born Presbyterian minister and committed reformer, won many followers with his prescriptions for eating fruits, vegetables, and bread made from coarsely ground flour–a prescription not unlike some dietary theories today–instead of meat. (The "Graham cracker" is made from a kind of flour named for him.) Graham accompanied his dietary prescriptions with moral warnings about the evils of excess and luxury.

Perhaps strangest of all to modern sensibilities was the widespread belief in the new "science" of phrenology, which appeared first in Germany and became popular in the United States beginning in the 1830s through the efforts of Orson

PHRENOLOGY

and Lorenzo Fowler, publishers of the *Phrenology Almanac*. Phrenologists argued that the shape of an individual's skull was an important indicator of his or her character and intelligence. They made elaborate measurements of bumps and indentations to calculate the size (and, they claimed, the strength) of different parts of the brain, each of which, they argued, controlled a specific kind of intelligence or behavior. For a time, phrenology seemed to many Americans an important vehicle for improving society. It provided a way of measuring an individual's fitness for various positions in life and seemed to promise an end to the arbitrary process by which people matched their talents to occupations and responsibilities. The theory is now universally believed to have no scientific value.

MEDICAL SCIENCE

In an age of rapid technological and scientific advances, the science of medicine sometimes seemed to lag behind. In part, that was because of the greater difficulty of experimentation in medicine, which required human subjects as compared to other areas of science and technology that relied on inanimate objects. In part, it was because of the character of the medical profession, which–in the absence of any significant regulation–attracted many poorly educated people and many quacks, in addition to trained physicians. Efforts to regulate the profession

"SPOUT BATH AT WARM SPRINGS" Among the many fads and theories about human health to gain currency in the 1830s and 1840s, one of the most popular was the idea that bathing in warm, sulphurous water was restorative. Visitors to "warm springs" all over the United States and Europe "took the baths," drank the foul-smelling water, and sometimes stayed for weeks as part of a combination vacation and "cure." This 1837 drawing is by Sophie Dupont, a visitor to a popular spa. She wrote to a friend that the water, "notwithstanding its odour of half spoiled eggs and its warmth, is not very nauseous to the taste." (© Courtesy of Hagley Museum and Library)

were opposed in the 1830s and 1840s by those who considered the licensing of physicians to be a form of undemocratic monopoly. The prestige of the profession, therefore, remained low, and it was for many people a career of last resort.

The biggest problem facing American medicine, however, was the absence of basic knowledge about disease. The great medical achievement of the eighteenth century–the development of a vaccination against smallpox by the English Physician Edward Jenner–came from no broad theory of infection, but from a brilliant adaptation of folk practices among country people. The development of anesthetics came not from medical doctors at first, but from a New England dentist, William Morton, who was looking for ways to help his patients endure the extraction of teeth. Beginning in 1844, Morton began experimenting with using sulphuric ether. John Warren, a Boston surgeon, soon began using ether to sedate surgical patients. Even these advances met with stiff resistance from traditional physicians, some of whom continued to believe that all medical knowledge derived from timeless truths and ancient scholars and who mistrusted innovation and experimentation. Others rejected scientific advances because of unorthodox, and untested "medical" techniques popularized by entrepreneurs, many of them charlatans.

In the absence of any broad acceptance of scientific methods and experimental practice in medicine, it was very difficult for even the most talented doctors to succeed in treating disease. Even so, halting progress toward the discovery of the germ theory did occur in antebellum America. In 1843, the

PHRENOLOGY This lithograph illustrates some of the ideas of the popular "science" of phrenology in the 1830s. Drawing from the concepts of the German writer Johann Gaspar Spurzheim, American phrenologists promoted the belief that a person's character and talents could be understood by the formation of his or her skull; that the brain was, in fact, a cluster of autonomous organs, each controlling some aspect of human thought or behavior. In this diagram, the areas of the brain that supposedly control "identity," "acquisitiveness," "secretiveness," "marvelousness," and "hope" are clearly identified. The theory has no scientific basis. (The Library of Congress)

Boston essayist, poet, and physician Oliver Wendell Holmes published his findings from a study of large numbers of cases of "puerperal fever" (septicemia in children) and concluded that the disease could be transmitted from one person to another. This discovery of contagion met with a storm of criticism, but was later vindicated by the clinical success of the Hungarian physician Ignaz Semmelweis, who noticed that the infection seemed to be spread by medical students who had been working with corpses. Once he began requiring students to wash their hands and disinfect their instruments, the infections virtually disappeared.

DISCOVERY OF CONTAGION

REFORMING EDUCATION

One of the outstanding reform movements of the mid-nineteenth century was the effort to produce a system of universal public education. As of 1830, no state yet had such a system, although some states—such as Massachusetts—had supported a limited version for many years. In the 1830s, however, interest in public education grew rapidly. It was a reflection of the new belief in the innate capacity of every person and of society's obligation to tap that capacity; but it was a reflection, too, of the desire to expose students to stable social values as a way to resist instability.

The greatest educational reformer was Horace Mann, the first secretary of the Massachusetts Board of Education, which was established in 1837. To Mann and his followers, education was the only way to "counterwork this tendency to the domination of capital and the servility of labor." The only way to protect democracy, Mann believed, was to create an educated electorate. He reorganized the Massachusetts school system, lengthened the academic year (to six months), doubled teachers' salaries (although he did nothing to eliminate the large disparities between the salaries of male and female teachers), enriched the curriculum, and introduced new methods of professional training for teachers.

Other states experienced similar expansion and development. They built new schools, created teachers' colleges, and offered large new groups of children access to education. Henry Barnard helped produce a educational system in Connecticut and Rhode Island. Pennsylvania passed a law in 1835 appropriating state funds for the support of universal education. Governor William Seward of New York extended public support of schools throughout the state in the early 1840s. By the 1850s, the principle of tax-supported elementary schools had been accepted in all the states; and all were making at least a start toward putting the principle into practice.

RAPID GROWTH OF PUBLIC EDUCATION

Yet the quality of the new education continued to vary widely. In some places—Massachusetts, for example, where Mann established the first American state-supported teachers' college in 1839 and where the first professional association of teachers was created in 1845—educators were usually capable men and women, often highly trained, and with an emerging sense of themselves as career professionals. In other areas, however, teachers were often barely literate, and limited funding for education restricted opportunities severely. In the newly settled regions of the West, where the white population was highly dispersed, many children had no access to schools. In the South, the entire black population was barred from formal education (although approximately 10 percent of the slaves achieved literacy anyway), and only about a third of all white children of school age actually enrolled in schools in 1860. In the North the percentage was 72 percent, but even there, many students attended classes only briefly and casually.

The interest in education was visible too in the growing movement to educate American Indians in the antebellum period. Some reformers held racist assumptions about the unredeemability of nonwhite peoples; but even many who accepted that idea about African Americans continued to believe that Indians could be "civilized" if only they could be taught the ways of the white world. Efforts to educate Native

Americans and encourage them to assimilate were particularly prominent in such areas of the Far West as Oregon. Substantial numbers of whites were beginning to settle there in the 1840s. Nevertheless, the great majority of Native Americans remained outside the reach of educational reform, either by choice or by circumstance or both.

Despite limitations and inequities, the achievements of **ACHIEVEMENTS OF EDUCATIONAL REFORM** the school reformers were impressive by any standard. By the beginning of the Civil War, the United States had one of the highest literacy rates of any nation: 94 percent of the population of the North and 83 percent of the white population of the South (58 percent of the total southern population).

The conflicting impulses underlying the movement for school reform were visible in some of the different educational institutions that emerged. In New England, for example, the transcendentalist Bronson Alcott established a controversial experimental school in Concord that reflected his strong belief in the importance of complete self-realization. He urged children to learn from their own inner wisdom, not from the imposition of values by the larger society. Children were to teach themselves, rather than rely on teachers.

A similar emphasis on the potential of the individual **THE BENEVOLENT EMPIRE** sparked the creation of new institutions to help the handicapped, institutions that formed part of a great network of charitable activities known as the Benevolent Empire. Among them was the Perkins School for the Blind in Boston, the first such school in America. Nothing better exemplified the romantic impulse of the era than the belief of those who founded Perkins that even society's supposedly least-favored members—the blind and otherwise handicapped—could be helped to discover inner strength and wisdom.

More typical of educational reform, however, were efforts to use schools to impose a set of social values on children—the values that reformers believed were appropriate for their new, industrializing society. These values included thrift, order, discipline, punctuality, and respect for authority. Horace Mann, for example, spoke frequently of the role of public schools in extending democracy and expanding individual opportunity. But he spoke, too, of their role in creating social order. "The unrestrained passions of men are not only homicidal, but suicidal," he said, suggesting a philosophy very different from that of Alcott and other transcendentalists, who emphasized instinct and emotion. "Train up a child in the way he should go, and when he is old he will not depart from it."

Rehabilitation

Similar impulses helped create another powerful movement of reform: the creation of "asylums" (as they now were called) for criminals and for the mentally ill. On the one hand, in advocating **THE ASYLUM MOVEMENT** prison and hospital reform, Americans were reacting to one of society's most glaring ills. Criminals of all kinds, debtors unable to pay their debts, the mentally ill, even senile paupers—all were crowded together indiscriminately into prisons and jails, which in some cases were holes in the ground; one jail in Connecticut was an abandoned mine shaft. Beginning in the 1820s, numerous states replaced these antiquated facilities with new "penitentiaries" and mental institutions designed to provide a proper environment for inmates. New York built the first penitentiary at Auburn in 1821. In Massachusetts, the social reformer Dorothea Dix began a national movement for new methods of treating the mentally ill. Imprisonment of debtors and paupers gradually disappeared, as did such traditional practices as legal public hangings.

But the creation of "asylums" for social deviants was not **PRISON REFORM** simply an effort to curb the abuses of the old system. It was also an attempt to reform and rehabilitate the inmates. New forms of rigid prison discipline were designed to rid criminals of the "laxness" that had presumably led them astray. Solitary confinement and the imposition of silence on work crews (both adopted in Pennsylvania and New York in the 1820s) were meant to give prisoners opportunities to meditate on their wrongdoings (hence the term "penitentiary": a place for individuals to cultivate penitence). Some reformers argued that the discipline of the asylum could serve as a model for other potentially disordered environments—for example, factories and schools. But penitentiaries and mental hospitals often fell victim to overcrowding, and the original reform ideal gradually faded. Many prisons ultimately degenerated into little more than warehouses for criminals, with scant emphasis on rehabilitation, which was far from the original, optimistic vision.

The "asylum" movement was not, however, restricted to criminals and people otherwise considered "unfit." The idea that a properly structured institution could prevent moral failure or rescue individuals from failure and despair helped spawn the creation of new orphanages designed as educational institutions. Such institutions, reformers believed, would provide an environment in which children who might otherwise be drawn into criminality could be trained to become useful citizens. Similar institutions emerged to provide homes for "friendless" women—women without families or homes, but otherwise "respectable," for whom the institutions might provide an opportunity to build a new life. (Such homes were in part an effort to prevent such women from turning to prostitution.) There were also new facilities for the poor: almshouses and workhouses, which created closely supervised environments for those who had failed to work their way up in society. Such an environment, reformers believed, would train them to live more productive lives.

The Indian Reservation

Some of these same beliefs underlay the emergence in the 1840s and 1850s of a new "reform" approach to the problems of Native Americans: the idea of the reservation. For several decades, the dominant thrust of U.S. policy toward the Indians

PERKINS SCHOOL FOR THE BLIND The Perkins School in Boston was the first school for the blind in the United States and was committed to the idea that the blind could be connected effectively to the world through the development of new skills, such as reading through the relatively new technique of embossed writing systems. This woodcut shows Perkins's main building in the mid-1850s, by which time the school was already over twenty years old. It continues to educate the blind today. (© Courtesy of Perkins School for the Blind, Watertown, Massachusetts)

in areas of white settlement had been relocation. The principal motive behind relocation had always been a simple one: getting the tribes out of the way of white civilization. But among some whites there had also been another, if secondary, intent: to move the Indians to a place where they would be protected from whites and allowed to develop to a point where assimilation might be possible. Even Andrew Jackson, whose animus toward Indians was legendary, once described the removals as part of the nation's "moral duty . . . to protect and if possible to preserve and perpetuate the scattered remnants of the Indian race."

It was a small step from the idea of relocation to the idea of the reservation: the idea of creating an enclosed region in which Indians would live in isolation from white society. The reservations served white economic purposes above all—moving Native Americans out of good lands that white settlers wanted. But they were also supposed to serve a reform purpose. Just as prisons, asylums, and orphanages would provide society with an opportunity to train and uplift misfits and unfortunates within white society, so the reservations might provide a way to undertake what one official called "the great work of regenerating the Indian race." Native Americans on reservations, reformers argued, would learn the ways of civilization in a protected setting.

THE EMERGENCE OF FEMINISM

The reform ferment of the antebellum period had a particular meaning for American women. They played central roles in a wide range of reform movements and a particularly important role in the movements on behalf of temperance and the abolition of slavery. In the process, they expressed their awareness of the problems that women themselves faced in a male-dominated society. The result was the creation of the first important American feminist movement, one that laid the groundwork for more than a century of agitation for women's rights.

Women in the 1830s and 1840s faced not only all the traditional restrictions imposed on members of their sex by society, but also a new set of barriers that had emerged from the doctrine of "separate spheres" and the transformation of the family. Many women who began to involve themselves in reform movements in the 1820s and 1830s came to look on

REFORM MOVEMENTS AND THE RISE OF FEMINISM

such restrictions with rising resentment. Some began to defy them. Sarah and Angelina Grimké, sisters born in South Carolina who had become active and outspoken abolitionists, ignored attacks by men who claimed that their activities were inappropriate for their sex. "Men and women were CREATED EQUAL," they argued. "They are both moral and accountable beings, and whatever is right for man to do, is right for women to do." Other reformers—Catharine Beecher, Harriet Beecher Stowe (her sister), Lucretia Mott, Elizabeth Cady Stanton, and Dorothea Dix—also chafing at the restrictions placed on them by men, similarly pressed at the boundaries of "acceptable" female behavior.

Finally, in 1840, the patience of several women snapped. A group of American female delegates arrived at a world antislavery convention in London, only to be turned away by the men who controlled the proceedings. Angered at the rejection, several of the delegates—notably Lucretia Mott and Elizabeth Cady Stanton—became convinced that their first duty as reformers should now be to elevate the status of women. Over the next several years, Mott, Stanton, Susan B. Anthony, and

THE RISE OF FEMINISM

IN THE 1840S, a group of women who had started out as abolitionists began to advocate for the rights of women. "All men and women are created equal," they declared. They argued that women should have the same opportunities as men and should no longer be restricted to the domestic sphere. This effort reached its peak at the 1848 convention in Seneca Falls, New York, where a Declaration of Sentiments was proclaimed.

Just as the women's rights movement of the nineteenth century grew out of the abolitionist movement, so the feminist movement of the twentieth century built upon the civil rights movement. The modern feminist movement often marks its beginning with the publication of Betty Friedan's *The Feminine Mystique* in 1963 and the formation of the National Organization for Women (NOW) in 1966. Despite the more than one hundred years separating the two documents that follow, the basic sentiments of the Seneca Falls Declaration bear many similarities to the ideas that have shaped feminist thinking of the twentieth and twenty-first centuries.

SENECA FALLS—1848

THE DECLARATION OF SENTIMENTS, SENECA FALLS CONVENTION, 1848

When, in the course of human events, it becomes necessary for one portion of the family of man to assume among the people of the earth a position different from that which they have hitherto occupied, but one to which the laws of nature and of nature's God entitle them, a decent respect to the opinions of mankind requires that they should declare the causes that impel them to such a course.

We hold these truths to be self-evident: that all men and women are created equal; that they are endowed by their Creator with certain inalienable rights; that among these are life, liberty, and the pursuit of happiness; that to secure these rights governments are instituted, deriving their just powers from the consent of the governed. Whenever any form of government becomes destructive of these ends, it is the right of those who suffer from it to refuse allegiance to it, and to insist upon the institution of a new government, laying its foundation on such principles, and organizing its powers in such form, as to them shall seem most likely to effect their safety and happiness. . . . Such has been the patient sufferance of the women under this government, and such is now the necessity which constrains them to demand the equal station to which they are entitled. The history of mankind is a history of repeated injuries and usurpations on the part of man toward woman, having in direct object the establishment of an absolute tyranny over her. . . .

Now, in view of this entire disfranchisement of one-half the people of this country, . . . because women do feel themselves aggrieved, oppressed, and fraudulently deprived of their most sacred rights, we insist that they have immediate admission to all the rights and privileges which belong to them as citizens of the United States.

From Elizabeth Cady Stanton, *A History of Woman Suffrage*, vol. 1 (Rochester, NY: Fowler and Wells, 1889), pp. 70–71.

NATIONAL ORGANIZATION FOR WOMEN (NOW)—1966

THE NATIONAL ORGANIZATION FOR WOMEN'S 1966 STATEMENT OF PURPOSE

We, men and women who hereby constitute ourselves as the National Organization for Women, believe that the time has come for a new movement toward true equality for all women in America, and toward a fully equal partnership of the sexes, as part of the worldwide revolution of human rights now taking place within and beyond our national borders.

The purpose of NOW is to take action to bring women into full participation in the mainstream of American society now, exercising all the privileges and responsibilities thereof in truly equal partnership with men.

We believe the time has come to . . . confront, with concrete action, the conditions that now prevent women from enjoying the equality of opportunity and freedom of choice which is their right, as individual Americans, and as human beings.

NOW is dedicated to the proposition that women, first and foremost, are human beings, who, like all other people in our society, must have the chance to develop their fullest human potential. We believe that women can achieve such equality only by accepting to the full the challenges and responsibilities they share with all other people in our society, as part of the decision-making mainstream of American political, economic and social life.

. . .

WE BELIEVE that the power of American law, and the protection guaranteed by the U.S. Constitution to the civil rights of all individuals, must be effectively applied and enforced to isolate and remove patterns of sex discrimination, to ensure equality of opportunity in employment and education, and equality of civil and political rights and responsibilities on behalf of women, as well as for Negroes and other deprived groups.

. . .

WE BELIEVE THAT women will do most to create a new image of women by acting now, and by speaking out in behalf of their own equality, freedom, and human dignity—not in pleas for special privilege, nor in enmity toward men, who are also victims of the current, half-equality between the sexes—but in an active, self-respecting partnership with men. By so doing, women will develop confidence in their own ability to determine actively, in partnership with men, the conditions of their life, their choices, their future and their society.

This Statement of Purpose was written by Betty Friedan, author of The Feminine Mystique.

Source: National Organization for Women Statement of Purpose (1966).

AP TEST PRACTICE

Questions assume cumulative content knowledge from this chapter and previous chapters.

1. Which best describes what both documents are responding to, regarding social ideals of womanhood?

   (A) The ideal that women are the keepers of American democratic principles

   (B) The ideal of the woman's "separate sphere"

   (C) The romantic ideal of the "Southern lady"

   (D) The ideal that women were highly sensitive creatures, occupying solely the realm of emotions.

2. Which of the following best describes the similarity in sentiments between the two documents?

   (A) Both assert that women need to unite to overthrow a tyrannical government.

   (B) Both assert the rights of women to vote.

   (C) Both assert the rights of women to the American democratic ideals of liberty and equal opportunity.

   (D) Both assert the rights of other disenfranchised groups.

3. Both documents most demonstrate the influence of which of the following?

   (A) 19th century Romanticism

   (B) The Enlightenment

   (C) Federalist notions of a strong union

   (D) The religious skepticism of the late 18th century

> 7
>
> FREDERICK DOUGLASS, AMY POST, CATHARINE STEBBINS, and ELIZABETH C. STANTON, and was unanimously adopted, as follows :
>
> ## DECLARATION OF SENTIMENTS.
>
> When, in the course of human events, it becomes necessary for one portion of the family of man to assume among the people of the earth a position different from that which they have hitherto occupied, but one to which the laws of nature and of nature's God entitle them, a decent respect to the opinions of mankind requires that they should declare the causes that impel them to such a course.

THE "DECLARATION OF SENTIMENTS" Frederick Douglass joined female abolitionists in signing the famous "Declaration of Sentiments" that emerged out of the Women's Rights Convention at Seneca Falls, New York, in 1848—one of the founding documents of American feminism. (The Library of Congress)

others began drawing pointed parallels between the plight of women and the plight of slaves; and in 1848, they organized a convention in Seneca Falls, New York, to discuss the question of women's rights. Out of the meeting emerged a "Declaration of Sentiments" (patterned on the 1776 Declaration of Independence), which stated that "all men and women are created equal," that women no less than men have certain inalienable rights. Their most prominent demand was for the right to vote, thus launching a movement for woman suffrage that would continue until 1920. But the document was in many ways more important for its rejection of the whole notion that men and women should be assigned separate "spheres" in society.

SENECA FALLS CONVENTION

It should not be surprising, perhaps, that many of the women involved in these feminist efforts were Quakers. Quakerism had long embraced the ideal of sexual equality and had tolerated, indeed encouraged, the emergence of women as preachers and community leaders. Women taught to expect the absence of gender-based restrictions in their own communities naturally resented the restrictions they encountered when they moved outside them. Quakers had also been among the leaders of the antislavery movement, and Quaker women played a leading role within those efforts. Of the women who drafted the Declaration of Sentiments, all but Elizabeth Cady Stanton were Quakers.

Progress toward feminist goals was limited in the antebellum years, but individual women did manage to break the social barriers to advancement. Elizabeth Blackwell, born in England, gained acceptance and fame as a physician. Her sister-in-law Antoinette Brown Blackwell became the first ordained woman minister in the United States; and another sister-in-law, Lucy Stone, took the revolutionary step of

LIMITED PROGRESS FOR WOMEN

retaining her maiden name after marriage (as did the abolitionist Angelina Grimké). Stone became a successful and influential lecturer on women's rights. Emma Willard, founder of the Troy Female Seminary in 1821, and Catharine Beecher, who founded the Hartford Female Seminary in 1823, worked on behalf of women's education. Some women expressed their feminist sentiments even in their choice of costume—by wearing a distinctive style of dress (introduced in the 1850s) that combined a short skirt with full-length pantalettes—an outfit that allowed freedom of movement without loss of modesty. Introduced by the famous actress Fanny Kemble, it came to be called the "bloomer" costume, after one of its advocates, Amelia Bloomer. (It provoked so much controversy that feminists finally abandoned it, convinced that the furor was drawing attention away from their more important demands.)

There was an irony in this rise of interest in the rights of women. Feminists benefited greatly from their association with other reform movements, most notably abolitionism; but they also suffered from them. For the demands of women were usually assigned—even by some women themselves—a secondary position to what many considered the far greater issue of the rights of slaves.

THE CRUSADE AGAINST SLAVERY

The antislavery movement was not new to the mid-nineteenth century. There had been efforts even before the Revolution to limit, and even eliminate, the institution. Those efforts had helped remove slavery from most of the North by the end of the eighteenth century and had led to the legal prohibition of the international slave trade in 1808. There were powerful antislavery movements in Europe that cried out forcefully against human bondage, perhaps most notably from Britain, where the great antislavery leader, William Wilberforce, had led the effort to abolish the slave trade, and later slavery itself, from the British Empire. But American anti-slavery sentiment remained relatively muted in the first decades after independence. Not until 1830 did it begin to gather the force that would ultimately enable it to overshadow virtually all other efforts at social reform.

EARLY OPPOSITION TO SLAVERY

In the early years of the nineteenth century, those who opposed slavery were, for the most part, a calm and genteel lot, expressing moral disapproval but engaging in few overt activities. To the extent that there was an organized antislavery movement, it centered on the concept of colonization—the effort to encourage the resettlement of African Americans in Africa or the Caribbean. In 1817, a group of prominent white Virginians organized the American Colonization Society (ACS), which worked carefully to challenge slavery without challenging property rights or southern sensibilities. The ACS proposed

AMERICAN COLONIZATION SOCIETY

a gradual manumission (or freeing) of slaves, with masters receiving compensation through funds raised by private charity or appropriated by state legislatures. The Society would then transport liberated slaves out of the country and help them to establish a new society of their own elsewhere.

The ACS was not without impact. It received some funding from private donors, some from Congress, some from the legislatures of Virginia and Maryland. And it arranged the shipment of several groups of African Americans out of the country, some of them to the west coast of Africa, where in 1830 they established the nation of Liberia (which became an independent republic in 1846–its capital, Monrovia, was named for the American president who had presided over the initial settlement).

But the ACS was in the end a negligible force. Neither private nor public funding was nearly enough to carry out the vast projects its supporters envisioned. In the space of a decade, they managed to "colonize" fewer slaves than were born in the United States in a month. No amount of funding, in fact, would have been enough; there were far too many black men and women in America in the nineteenth century to be transported to Africa by any conceivable program. And in any case, the ACS met resistance from African Americans themselves, many of whom were now three or more generations removed from Africa and had no wish to move to a land of which they knew almost nothing. (The Massachusetts free black Paul Cuffe had met similar resistance from members of his own race in the early 1800s when he proposed a colonization scheme of his own.)

FAILURE OF COLONIZATION

By 1830, in other words, the early antislavery movement was rapidly losing strength. Colonization was proving not to be a viable method of attacking the institution, particularly since the cotton boom in the Deep South was increasing the commitment of planters to their "peculiar" labor system. Those opposed to slavery had reached what appeared to be a dead end.

GARRISON AND ABOLITIONISM

At this crucial juncture, with the antislavery movement seemingly on the verge of collapse, a new figure emerged to transform it into a dramatically different phenomenon. He was William Lloyd Garrison. Born in Massachusetts in 1805, Garrison was an assistant in the 1820s to the New Jersey Quaker Benjamin Lundy, who published the leading antislavery newspaper of the time–the *Genius of Universal Emancipation*–in Baltimore. Garrison shared Lundy's abhorrence of slavery, but he soon grew impatient with his employer's moderate tone and mild proposals for reform. In 1831, therefore, he returned to Boston to found his own weekly newspaper, the *Liberator*.

GARRISON AND THE *LIBERATOR*

Garrison's simple philosophy was genuinely revolutionary. Opponents of slavery, he said, should view the institution from the point of view of the black man, not the white slaveowner. They should not, as earlier reformers had done, talk about the evil influence of slavery on white society; instead, they should talk about the damage the system did to Africans. And they should, therefore, reject "gradualism" and demand the immediate, unconditional, universal abolition of slavery. Garrison spoke with particular scorn about the advocates of colonization. They were not emancipationists, he argued; on the contrary, their real aim was to strengthen slavery by ridding the country of those African Americans who were already free. The true aim of foes of slavery, he insisted, must be to extend to African Americans all the rights of American citizenship. As startling as the drastic nature of his proposals was the relentless, uncompromising tone with which he promoted them. "I am aware," he wrote in the first issue of the *Liberator*, "that many object to the severity of my language; but is there not cause for severity? I will be as harsh as truth, and as uncompromising as justice. . . . I am in earnest–I will not equivocate–I will not excuse–I will not retreat a single inch–AND I WILL BE HEARD."

Garrison soon attracted a large group of followers throughout the North, enough to enable him to found the New England Anti-Slavery Society in 1832 and a year later, after a convention in Philadelphia, the American Anti-Slavery Society. Membership in the new organizations mushroomed. By 1835, there were more than 400 chapters of the societies; by 1838, there were 1,350 chapters, with more than 250,000 members. Antislavery sentiment was developing a strength and assertiveness greater than at any other point in the nation's past history.

AMERICAN ANTI-SLAVERY SOCIETY

BLACK ABOLITIONISTS

Abolitionism had a particular appeal to the free blacks of the North, who in 1850 numbered about 250,000, mostly concentrated in cities. They lived in conditions of poverty and oppression often worse than those of their slave counterparts in the South. An English traveler who had visited both sections of the country wrote in 1854 that he was "utterly at a loss to imagine the source of that prejudice which subsists against [African Americans] in the Northern states, a prejudice unknown in the South, where the relations between the Africans and the European [white American] are so much more intimate." This confirmed an earlier observation by the French observer Alexis de Tocqueville that "the prejudice which repels the Negroes seems to increase in proportion as they are emancipated." Northern blacks were often victimized by mob violence; they had virtually no access to education; they could vote in only a few states; and they were barred from all but the most menial of occupations. Most worked either as domestic servants or as sailors in the American merchant marine, and their wages were such that they lived in squalor. Some were kidnapped by whites and forced back into slavery.

For all their problems, however, northern blacks were aware of, and fiercely proud of, their freedom. And they remained acutely sensitive to the plight of those members of their race who remained in bondage, aware that their own position in society would remain precarious as long as slavery existed. Many in the 1830s came to support Garrison, to subscribe to his newspaper, and to sell subscriptions to it in their

FUGITIVE SLAVE LAW CONVENTION Abolitionists gathered in Cazenovia, New York, in August 1850 to consider how to respond to the law recently passed by Congress requiring northern states to return fugitive slaves to their owners. Frederick Douglass is seated just to the left of the table in this photograph of some of the participants. The gathering was unusual among abolitionist gatherings in including substantial numbers of African Americans. (From the Collection of the Madison County Historical Society, Oneida, New York)

FREE BLACKS' COMMITMENT TO ABOLITION

own communities. Indeed, the majority of the *Liberator*'s early subscribers were free African Americans.

There were also important African American leaders who expressed the aspirations of their race. One of the most militant was David Walker, a free black from Boston, who in 1829 published a harsh pamphlet: *Walker's Appeal . . . to the Colored Citizens*. In it he declared: "America is more our country than it is the whites'–we have enriched it with our blood and tears." He warned: "The whites want slaves, and want us for their slaves, but some of them will curse the day they ever saw us." Slaves should, he declared, cut their masters' throats, should "kill, or be killed!"

Most African American critics of slavery, however, were less violent in their rhetoric. Sojourner Truth, a freed black woman, spent several years involved in a strange religious cult in upstate New York. She emerged as a powerful and eloquent spokeswoman for the abolition of slavery.

The greatest African American abolitionist of all–and one

FREDERICK DOUGLASS

of the most electrifying orators of his time, black or white–was Frederick Douglass. Born a slave in Maryland, Douglass escaped to Massachusetts in 1838, became an outspoken leader of antislavery sentiment, and spent two years lecturing in England, where members of that country's vigorous antislavery movement lionized him. On his return to the United States in 1847, Douglass purchased his freedom from his Maryland owner and founded an antislavery newspaper, the *North Star*, in Rochester, New York. He achieved wide renown as well for his autobiography, *Narrative of the Life of Frederick Douglass* (1845), in which he presented a damning picture of slavery. Douglass demanded for African Americans not only freedom but full social and economic equality as well. "What, to the American slave, is your 4th of July?" Douglass harshly asked in an Independence Day speech in Rochester, New York, in 1854. "I answer: a day that reveals to him, more than all other days in the year, the gross injustice and cruelty to which he is the constant victim. . . . There is not a nation on earth guilty of practices, more shocking and bloody, than are the people of these United States at this very hour."

Black abolitionists had been active for years before Douglass emerged as a leader of their cause; they had held their first national convention in 1830. But with Douglass's leadership, they became a more influential force; and they began, too, to forge alliances with white antislavery leaders such as Garrison.

ANTI-ABOLITIONISM

Abolitionism was a powerful force, but it provoked a powerful opposition as well. Almost all white southerners, of course, looked on the movement with fear and contempt. But so too did many northern whites. Indeed, even in the North, abolitionists were never more than a small, dissenting minority.

To its critics, the abolitionist crusade was a dangerous and frightening threat to the existing social system. Some whites correctly warned that it would produce a terrible war between the sections. Others feared, also correctly, that it might lead to a great influx of free blacks into the North. The strident, outspoken abolition movement seemed to many northern whites a sign of the disorienting social changes their society was experiencing—yet another threat to stability and order. To other northerners, mostly men of business, abolition was a threat to lucrative trade with the South.

The result was an escalating wave of violence directed against abolitionists in the 1830s. When Prudence Crandall

VIOLENT REPRISALS attempted to admit several African American girls to her private school in Connecticut, local citizens had her arrested, threw filth into her well, and forced her to close down the school. A mob in Philadelphia attacked the abolitionist headquarters, the "Temple of Liberty," in 1834, burned it to the ground, and began a bloody race riot. Another mob seized Garrison on the streets of Boston in 1835 and threatened to hang him. Authorities saved him from death only by locking him in jail. Elijah Lovejoy, the editor of an abolitionist newspaper in Alton, Illinois, was a repeated victim of mob violence. Three times, angry whites

WILLIAM LLOYD GARRISON Garrison was the first member of the antislavery movement to call publicly for "immediate and complete emancipation" of slaves. That was in 1831, and for the next three decades he remained a stern and uncompromising enemy of slavery. After the Civil War, however, Garrison displayed little interest in the plight of the blacks he had tried to emancipate. Instead, he turned to women's suffrage, Indian rights, and the prohibition of alcohol. (© FPG/Getty Images)

invaded his offices and smashed his presses. Three times, Lovejoy installed new machines and began publishing again. When a mob attacked his office a fourth time, late in 1837, he tried to defend his press. The attackers set fire to the building and, as Lovejoy fled, shot and killed him.

That so many men and women continued to embrace abolitionism in the face of such vicious opposition from within their own communities suggests much about the nature of the movement. Abolitionists were not people who made their political commitments lightly or casually. They were strong-willed, passionate crusaders, displaying enormous courage and moral strength, and displaying, too, at times a level of fervor that many of their contemporaries found disturbing. Abolitionists were widely denounced, even by some who shared their aversion to slavery, as wild-eyed fanatics bent on social revolution. The anti-abolitionist mobs, in other words, were only the most violent expression of a sentiment that many other white Americans shared.

ABOLITIONISM DIVIDED

By the mid-1830s, the abolitionist crusade had become impossible to ignore. It had also begun to experience serious internal strains and divisions. One reason was the violence of the anti-abolitionists, which persuaded some members of the

MODERATES VERSUS EXTREMISTS movement that a more moderate approach was necessary. Another reason was the growing radicalism of William Lloyd Garrison, who shocked even many of his own allies (including Frederick Douglass) by attacking not only slavery but the government itself. The Constitution, he said, was "a covenant with death and an agreement with hell." The nation's churches, he claimed, were bulwarks of slavery. In 1840, finally, Garrison precipitated a formal division within the American Anti-Slavery Society by insisting that women, who had always been central to the organization's work, be permitted to participate in the movement on terms of full equality. He continued after 1840 to arouse controversy with new, more-radical stands: an extreme pacifism that rejected even defensive wars; opposition to all forms of coercion—not just slavery but prisons and asylums as well; and finally, in 1843, a call for northern disunion from the South. The nation could, Garrison suggested, purge itself of the sin of slavery by expelling the slave states from the Union.

From 1840 on, therefore, abolitionism moved in many channels and spoke with many different voices. The Garrisonians remained influential, with their uncompromising moral stance. Others operated in moderate ways, arguing that abolition could be accomplished only as the result of a long, patient, peaceful struggle—"immediate abolition gradually accomplished," as they called it. At first, such moderates depended on "moral suasion." They would appeal to the conscience of the slaveholders and convince them that their institution was sinful. When that produced no results, they turned to political action, seeking to induce the northern states and the federal government to aid the cause wherever

THE ABOLITION OF SLAVERY WOR-2, 3

THE Thirteenth Amendment to the Constitution, ratified in 1865, following the Civil War, abolished slavery in the United States. But the effort to abolish slavery did not begin or end in North America. Emancipation in the United States was part of a worldwide antislavery movement that had begun in the late eighteenth century and continued through the end of the nineteenth.

The movement to end slavery reflected the ideals of the Enlightenment, which inspired new concepts of individual freedom and political equality. As Enlightenment ideas spread throughout the Western world in the seventeenth and eighteenth centuries, introducing human rights and individual liberty to the concept of civilization, people on both sides of the Atlantic began to ask whether slavery was compatible with these new ideas. Some Enlightenment thinkers, including some of the founders of the American republic,

believed that freedom was appropriate for white people, but not for people of color. But others came to believe that all human beings had an equal claim to liberty, and their views became the basis for an escalating series of antislavery movements.

Opponents of slavery first targeted the slave trade—the vast commerce in human beings that had grown up in the seventeenth and eighteenth centuries and had come to involve large parts of Europe, Africa, the Caribbean, and North and South America. In the aftermath of the revolutions in America, France, and Haiti in the late eighteenth and early nineteenth centuries, the attack on the slave trade gained momentum. The English reformer William Wilberforce spent years attacking Britain's connection with the slave trade, arguing against it on moral and religious grounds. After the Haitian revolution, he argued as well that the continuation of slavery would create more slave revolts. In 1807, he persuaded Parliament to pass a law ending the slave trade within the entire British Empire. The British example—combined with political, economic, and military pressure from London—persuaded many other nations to make the international slave trade illegal: the United States in 1808, France in 1814, Holland in 1817, and Spain in 1845. Trading in slaves continued within countries and colonies where slavery remained legal (including the United States), and some illegal slave trading continued throughout the Atlantic world. But the sale of slaves steadily declined after 1807. The last known shipment of slaves across the Atlantic—from Africa to Cuba—occurred in 1867.

Ending the slave trade was a great deal easier than ending slavery itself. But pressure to abolish slavery grew steadily throughout the nineteenth century, with Wilberforce once more helping lead the international outcry against the institution. In Haiti, the slave revolts that began in 1791 eventually abolished not only slavery but also French rule. In some parts of South America, slavery came to an end with the overthrow of Spanish rule in the

ANTI-SLAVE MESSAGE This sampler conveys a potent anti-slave message, "Thou God Seest Me." Originally from the Bible (Genesis 16:13), this quote expresses the sentiment that the kneeling slave should be seen as a man rather than chattel. (© Wilberforce House, Hull City Museums and Art Galleries, UK/The Bridgeman Art Library)

possible. They joined the Garrisonians in helping runaway slaves find refuge in the North or in Canada through the so-called underground railroad (although their efforts were never as highly organized as the term suggests). They helped fund the legal battle over the Spanish slave vessel *Amistad*.

Later, after the Supreme Court (in *Prigg v. Pennsylvania*, 1842) ruled that states need not aid in enforcing the 1793 law requiring the return of fugitive slaves to their owners, abolitionists secured the passage of "personal liberty laws" in several northern states. These laws forbade state officials to assist

in the capture and return of runaways. Above all, the antislavery societies petitioned Congress to abolish slavery in places where the federal government had jurisdiction–in the territories and in the District of Columbia–and to prohibit the interstate slave trade. But political abolitionism had severe limits. Few members of the movement believed that Congress could constitutionally interfere with a "domestic" institution such as slavery within the individual states themselves.

The abolitionists never formed a political party. Antislavery sentiment underlay the formation in 1840 of the Liberty Party,

1820s. Simón Bolívar, the great leader of Latin American independence, considered abolishing slavery an important part of his mission. He freed those slaves who joined his armies, and he insisted on prohibitions of slavery in several of the constitutions he helped frame. In 1833, the British Parliament passed a law abolishing slavery throughout the British Empire and compensated slaveowners for freeing their slaves. France abolished slavery in its empire in 1848. In the Caribbean, Spain followed Britain in slowly eliminating slavery from its colonies. Puerto Rico abolished slavery in 1873 and Cuba became the last colony in the Caribbean to end slavery, in 1886, in the face of increasing slave resistance and the declining profitability of slave-based plantations. Brazil was the last nation in the Americas to end the system, in 1888. The Brazilian military began to turn against slavery after the valiant participation of slaves in Brazil's war with Paraguay in the late 1860s; eventually, educated Brazilian civilians began to oppose the system too, arguing that it obstructed economic and social progress.

In the United States, the power of world opinion—and the example of Wilberforce's movement in England—became an important spur to the abolitionist movement as it gained strength in the 1820s and 1830s. American abolitionism, in turn, helped reinforce the movements abroad. Frederick Douglass, the former slave turned abolitionist, became a major figure in the international antislavery movement and was a much-admired and much-sought-after speaker in England and Europe in the 1840s and 1850s. No other nation paid as terrible a price for abolishing slavery as did the United States during its Civil War, but American emancipation was nevertheless a part of a worldwide movement toward ending legalized human bondage. ●

UNDERSTAND, ANALYZE, AND EVALUATE

1. Why did opponents of slavery focus first on ending the slave trade, rather than abolishing slavery itself? Why was ending the slave trade easier than ending slavery?
2. How do William Wilberforce's arguments against slavery compare with those of the abolitionists in the United States?
3. How could a nation that declared "all men are created equal" justify slavery?

which chose the Kentucky antislavery leader James G. Birney as its presidential candidate. But this party, and its successors, never campaigned for outright abolition (an illustration of the important fact that "antislavery" and "abolitionism" were not always the same thing). They stood instead for "free soil," for keeping slavery out of the territories. Some free-soilers were concerned about the welfare of African Americans; others cared nothing about the slaves but simply wanted to keep the West a country for whites. Garrison dismissed free-soilism as "white-manism." But the free-soil position would ultimately do what abolitionism never could accomplish: attract the support of large numbers, even a majority, of the white population of the North.

The frustrations of political abolitionism drove some critics of slavery to embrace more drastic measures. A few began to advocate violence; a group of prominent abolitionists in New England, for example, funneled money and arms to John Brown to enable bloody uprisings in Kansas and Virginia (see pp. 356–357, 360). Others attempted to arouse widespread public anger through propaganda. Abolitionist descriptions of slavery–for example, Theodore Dwight Weld and Angelina Grimké's *American Slavery as It Is: Testimony of a Thousand Witnesses* (1839)–presented what the authors claimed were careful, factual pictures of slavery, but what were in fact highly polemical, often wildly distorted images.

HARRIET BEECHER STOWE

The most powerful document of abolitionist propaganda, however, was a work of fiction: Harriet Beecher Stowe's *Uncle Tom's Cabin*. It appeared first, in 1851–1852, as a serial in an antislavery weekly. Then, in 1852, it was published as a book. It rocked the nation, selling more than 300,000 copies within a year of publication, and was later issued again and again to become one of the most remarkable best-sellers in American history.

Stowe's novel emerged not just out of abolitionist politics, but also out of a popular tradition of sentimental novels written by, and largely for, women. (See "Patterns of Popular Culture," pp. 336–337) Stowe combined the emotional conventions of the sentimental novel with the political ideas of the abolition movement, and to sensational effect. Her novel, by embedding the antislavery message within a familiar and popular literary form, succeeded in bringing the message of abolitionism to an enormous new audience–not only those who read the book but also those who watched dramatizations of its story by countless theater companies throughout the nation. The novel's emotional portrayal of good, kindly slaves victimized by a cruel system; of the loyal, trusting Uncle Tom; of the vicious overseer Simon Legree (described as a New Englander so as to prevent the book from seeming to be an attack on southern whites); of the escape of the beautiful Eliza; of the heartrending death of Little Eva–all became a part of American popular legend. Reviled throughout the South, Stowe became a hero to many in the North. And in both regions, her novel helped to inflame sectional tensions to a new level of passion. Few books in American history have had so great an impact on the course of public events.

ABOLITIONISM'S ENDURING INFLUENCE

Even divided, therefore, abolitionism remained a powerful influence on the life of the nation. Only a relatively small number of people before the Civil War ever accepted the abolitionist position that slavery must be entirely eliminated in a single stroke. But the crusade that Garrison had launched, and that thousands of committed men and women kept alive for three decades, was a constant, visible reminder of how deeply the institution of slavery was dividing America.

SENTIMENTAL NOVELS

"**AMERICA** is now wholly given over to a damned mob of scribbling women," Nathaniel Hawthorne complained in 1855, "and I should have no chance of success while the public taste is occupied with their trash." Hawthorne, one of the leading novelists of his time, was complaining about the most popular form of fiction in mid-nineteenth-century America—not his own dark and serious works, but the "sentimental novel," a genre of literature written and read mostly by middle-class women.

In an age when affluent women occupied primarily domestic roles, and in which finding a favorable marriage was the most important thing many women could do to secure or improve their lots in life, the sentimental novel gave voice to both female hopes and female anxieties. The plots of sentimental novels were usually filled with character-improving problems and domestic trials, but most of them ended with the heroine securely and happily married. They were phenomenally successful, many of them selling more than 100,000 copies each—far more than almost any other books of the time.

Sentimental heroines were almost always beautiful and endowed with specifically female qualities—"all the virtues," one novelist wrote, "that are founded in the sensibility of the heart: Pity, the attribute of angels, and friendship, the balm of life, delight to dwell in the female breast." Women were highly sensitive creatures, the sentimental writers believed, incapable of disguising their feelings, and subject to fainting, mysterious illnesses, trances, and, of course, tears—things rarely expected of men. But they were also capable of a kind of nurturing love and natural sincerity that was hard to find in the predominantly male public world. In Susan Warner's *The Wide, Wide World* (1850), for example, the heroine, a young girl named Ellen Montgomery, finds herself suddenly thrust into the "wide, wide world" of male competition after her father loses his fortune. She is unable to adapt to this world, but she is saved in the end when she is taken in by wealthy relatives, who will undoubtedly prepare her for a successful marriage. They restore to her the security and comfort to which she had been born and without which she seemed unable to thrive.

Sentimental novels accepted uncritically the popular assumptions about women's special needs and desires, and they offered stirring tales of how women satisfied them. But sentimental novels were not limited to romanticized images of female fulfillment through protection and marriage. They hinted as well at the increasing role of women in reform movements. Many such books portrayed women dealing with social and moral problems—and using their highly developed female sensibilities to help other women escape from their troubles. Women were particularly suitable for such reform work, the writers implied, because they were specially gifted at helping and nurturing others.

AP CONNECTING THEMES

Chapter 12 discussed art and literature in what was one of the most prolific periods of creativity in American history and its impact on American society. Reform movements, their goals and successes at the time, also were discussed in great depth. Particularly important to the discussion were the women's rights and abolitionist movements, their origins, and their influence on American society. Additionally, the philosophical influences of the time led some Americans to build utopian communities, asserting various agendas to try to transform American society.

The following themes have heightened importance in Chapter 12. You should now be able to do the following for each listed theme:

Identity: Analyze the factors that led to the creation of distinct identities for reform movements and utopian communitarian ventures, and the degree of success each had.

Peopling: Analyze the degree to which utopian communitarianism encouraged western settlement.

Politics and Power: Explain how women and African Americans attempted to influence the political culture of the United States and the degree of success they attained in this time period.

Environment and Geography: Explain the continuing impact of the natural environment on the development of regional political and economic identities.

Ideas, Beliefs, and Culture: Explain how science and technology influenced American culture in the time period. Examine the emergence of the cultural outpouring of art and literature in the time period.

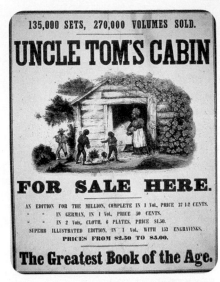

135,000 SETS, 270,000 VOLUMES SOLD.

UNCLE TOM'S CABIN

FOR SALE HERE.

AN EDITION FOR THE MILLION, COMPLETE IN 1 Vol., PRICE 37 1-2 CENTS.
"   "   IN GERMAN, IN 1 Vol., PRICE 50 CENTS.
"   "   IN 2 Vols., CLOTH, 6 PLATES, PRICE $1.50.
SUPERB ILLUSTRATED EDITION, IN 1 Vol., WITH 153 ENGRAVINGS,
PRICES FROM $2.50 TO $5.00.

The Greatest Book of the Age.

UNCLE TOM'S CABIN Uncle Tom's Cabin did much to inflame public opinion in both the North and the South in the last years before the Civil War. When Abraham Lincoln was introduced to Stowe once in the White House, he reportedly said to her: "So you are the little lady that has brought this great war." At the time, however, Stowe was equally well known as one of the most successful American writers of sentimental novels. (© Corbis)

The most famous sentimental novelist of the nineteenth century was Harriet Beecher Stowe. Most of her books—*The Minister's Wooing, My Wife and I, We and Our Neighbors,* and others—portrayed the travails and ultimate triumphs of women as they became wives, mothers, and hostesses. But Stowe was and remains best known for her 1852 antislavery novel, *Uncle Tom's Cabin,* one of the most influential books ever published in America. As a story about slavery, and about an aging black man—Uncle Tom—who is unfailingly submissive to his white masters, it is in many ways very different from her other novels. But *Uncle Tom's Cabin* is a sentimental novel, too. Stowe's critique of slavery is based on her belief in the importance of domestic values and family security. Slavery's violation of those values, and its denial of that security, is what made it so abhorrent to her. The simple, decent Uncle Tom faces many of the same dilemmas that the female heroines of other sentimental novels encounter in their struggles to find security and tranquillity in their lives.

Another way in which women were emerging from their domestic sphere was in becoming consumers of the expanding products of America's industrializing economy. The female characters in sentimental novels searched not just for love, security, and social justice; they also searched for luxury and for the pleasure of buying some favored item. Susan Warner illustrated this aspect of the culture of the sentimental novel—and the desires of the women who read them—in *The Wide, Wide World,* in her description of the young Ellen Montgomery in an elegant bookstore, buying a Bible: "Such beautiful Bibles she had never seen; she pored in ecstasy over their varieties of type and binding, and was very evidently in love with them all." ●

UNDERSTAND, ANALYZE, AND EVALUATE

1. How did the lives of the heroines of the sentimental novels compare with the lives of real women of the nineteenth century? What made them so popular?
2. How did the sentimental novels encourage women's participation in public life? Did the novels reinforce prevailing attitudes toward women or broaden the perception of women's "proper role"?
3. *Uncle Tom's Cabin* is probably one of the best-known works of American fiction. Why was this novel so much more powerful than other sentimental novels? Why has it endured?

AP SUGGESTED STUDY

PEOPLE/PLACES/EVENTS As you study these items, think about how they demonstrate or relate to key concepts and historical themes from this chapter and previous chapters.

AP TEST PRACTICE

Questions assume cumulative content knowledge from this chapter and previous chapters.

MULTIPLE CHOICE Use the lithograph on page 323 and your knowledge of U.S. history to answer questions 1–3.

1. What significant philosophical idea from the Second Great Awakening did the movement represented in the lithograph have in common with many reform movements of the mid-19th century?

   (A) The idea of the importance of a "virtuous" citizenry

   (B) The idea that every individual could achieve salvation through individual effort

   (C) The idea of predestination

   (D) The idea of women occupying a "separate sphere"

2. Which of the following most reasonably explains the drive for social order that instigated many social reform efforts in the first half of the 19th century?

   (A) The influence of the Romantic movement sweeping Europe at the time

   (B) A general popular desire for a uniquely American identity

   (C) Ideas from the Romantic movement in Europe clashing with Enlightenment ideals of reason

   (D) Social changes stemming from industrialization and the great rise in immigration

3. Which demographic group composed the largest constituent group of reformers in the first half of the 19th century?

   (A) Religious leaders

   (B) Middle-class women

   (C) Middle-class men

   (D) Abolitionists

SHORT ANSWER Use your knowledge of U.S. history to answer questions 4–6.

4. Answer a, b, and c.

   a) Briefly explain ONE example from the first half of the 19th century that demonstrates an influence of the Second Great Awakening idea of the perfectibility of the self.

   b) Briefly explain ONE example from the first half of the 19th century that demonstrates an influence of the Second Great Awakening value of individual action.

   c) Briefly explain ONE example from the first half of the 19th century that demonstrates an influence of the Romantic notion of self-liberation.

5. Answer a, b, and c.

   a) Briefly explain ONE example of how the abolitionist movement in the first half of the 19th century affected African Americans.

   b) Briefly explain ONE example of how the abolitionist movement in the first half of the 19th century affected white reformers of the era.

   c) Briefly explain ONE example of reactions of white Americans against the abolitionist movement.

6. Answer a, b, and c.

   a) Briefly explain ONE example from the first half of the 19th century of American national culture with a heavy European influence.

   b) Provide ONE piece of historical evidence to support your example in a.

   c) Briefly explain ONE example from the first half of the 19th century of a cultural ideal that was uniquely American.

LONG ESSAY Develop a thoughtful and thorough historical argument that answers the question below. Begin your essay with a thesis statement and support it with relevant historical evidence.

7. Some historians have argued that industrialization had the greatest influence on the development of reform movements in the first half of the 19th century. Support, modify, or refute this interpretation providing specific evidence to support your answer.

13 THE IMPENDING CRISIS

"BLEEDING KANSAS" The battle over the fate of slavery in Kansas was one of the most turbulent events of the 1850s. This 1855 poster invites antislavery forces to a meeting to protest the actions of the "bogus" pro-slavery territorial legislature, which had passed laws that, among other things, made it illegal to speak or write against slavery. "Squatter sovereignty" was another term for "popular sovereignty," the doctrine that gave residents of a prospective state the power to decide the fate of slavery there. (© Bettmann/Corbis)

AP

HISTORICAL THINKING

1. **Historical Argumentation** Analyze the specific attempts at compromise between the North and the South during the 1850s and their relative success.

2. **Historical Causation** Explain the factors that intensified sectional conflict during the 1850s.

3. **Interpretation** Explain the positive and negative benefits of territorial expansion during the 1840s and 1850s.

4. **Comparison** Compare and contrast the views of abolitionists and apologists.

5. **Contextualization** Explain the factors that led to the increasingly emotional debate over the extension of slavery into the territories.

6. **Historical Argumentation** Evaluate the legitimacy of the concept of Manifest Destiny and the means by which the United States acquired territory during the period.

7. **Historical Argumentation** Analyze the impact of the election of 1860 on the possibility of compromise on the issue of slavery.

Key Concept Correlations

Analyze the ways the historical developments you learn about in this chapter connect to the following AP Key Concepts.

4.3 U.S. interest in increasing foreign trade, expanding its national borders, and isolating itself from European conflicts shaped the nation's foreign policy and spurred government and private initiatives.

5.1 The United States became more connected with the world as it pursued an expansionist foreign policy in the Western Hemisphere and emerged as the destination for many migrants from other countries.

5.2 Intensified by expansion and deepening regional divisions, debates over slavery and other economic, cultural, and political issues led the nation into civil war.

Thematic Learning Objectives

WOR-5, 6; POL-2, 3, 5, 6; ID-2, 5, 6; WXT-2, 6; ENV-3, 4; PEO-2, 5, 6; CUL-2, 6

AP CONNECTING CONCEPTS

CHAPTER 13 discusses the belief in the "Manifest Destiny" of the United States to spread over the continent, and analyzes the ways in which the United States gained territory, both militarily and diplomatically. This expansion brought with it worsening sectional tensions as the issue of the extension of slavery into the new territories became more prominent due to apprehensions over changes in the balance of political power between the "slave" states and the "non-slave" states. The chapter traces specific events that led to the debate over slavery to become more emotional and, thus, making compromise less likely. This progression will take you through the Compromise of 1850, to the Kansas-Nebraska Act, to the Dred Scott case, and into the election of 1860. As you read, evaluate the following ideas:

- Territorial acquisition increased sectional tension, as opposing sides argued over the extension of slavery into new lands.
- The increasing political emotionalism of the slavery issue highlighted cultural differences between the North and South.
- Southerners began to view slavery as a "positive good" (apologist's view) rather than a "necessary evil," while abolitionists saw it as a moral wrong.
- Attempts at compromise were ultimately unsuccessful during the 1850s.
- A Third American Party system emerged as a result of conflict over the extension of slavery into new territories of the growing United States.
- Lincoln's election in 1860 on a Free Soil ideology led southern leaders to conclude that secession was their only viable option.

LOOKING WESTWARD

The United States acquired more than a million square miles of new territory in the 1840s—the greatest wave of expansion since the Louisiana Purchase nearly forty years before. By the end of the decade, the nation possessed all the territory of the present-day United States except Alaska, Hawaii, and a few relatively small areas acquired later through border adjustments. Many factors accounted for this great new wave of expansion, the most important of which were the hopes and ambitions of the many thousands of white Americans who moved into or invested in these new territories. Advocates of expansion justified their goals with a carefully articulated set of ideas—an ideology known as "Manifest Destiny," which became one of the factors driving white Americans to look to the West.

MANIFEST DESTINY

Manifest Destiny reflected both the burgeoning pride that characterized American nationalism in the mid-nineteenth century and the idealistic vision of social perfection that fueled so much of the reform energy of the time. It rested on the idea that America was destined—by God and by history—to expand its boundaries over a vast area, an area that included, but was not necessarily restricted to, the continent of North America. American expansion was not selfish, its advocates insisted; it was an altruistic attempt to extend American liberty to new realms. John L. O'Sullivan, the influential Democratic editor who gave the movement its name, wrote in 1845 that the American claim to new territory

> is by the right of our manifest destiny to overspread and to possess the whole of the continent which Providence has given us for the development of the great experiment of liberty and federative self government entrusted to us.

Manifest Destiny represented more than pride in the nation's political system. Running throughout many of the arguments for expansion was an explicitly racial justification. Throughout the 1840s, many Americans defended the idea of westward expansion by citing the superiority of the "American race"—white people of northern European origins. The "nonwhite" peoples of the territories could not be absorbed into the republican system. The Indians, the Mexicans, and others in the

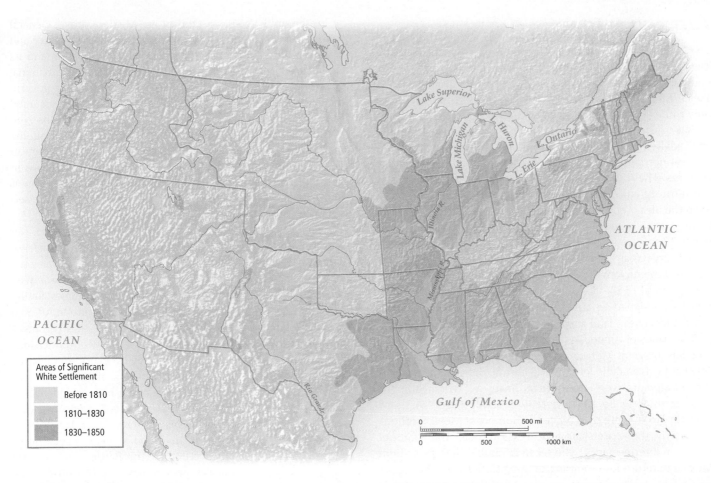

Areas of Significant
White Settlement

Before 1810

1810–1830

1830–1850

EXPANDING SETTLEMENT, 1810–1850 This map shows the dramatic expansion of the territorial boundaries of the United States in the decades after the Louisiana Purchase. By 1850, the nation had reached its present boundaries (with the exception of Alaska and Hawaii, which it acquired later). Much of this acquisition occurred in the 1840s. It also shows the spread of white settlement within the territories and states.

• *What events contributed to the annexation of new land to the United States in those years?*

RACIAL JUSTIFICATION western regions were racially unfit to be part of an "American" community, Manifest Destiny advocates insisted. Westward expansion was, therefore, a movement to spread both a political system and a racially defined society. O'Sullivan called "racial purity" (or "whiteness") the "key" to the triumph of the nation.

By the 1840s, the idea of Manifest Destiny had spread throughout the nation, publicized by the new "penny press" (inexpensive newspapers aimed at a mass audience) and fanned by the rhetoric of nationalist politicians. Advocates of Manifest Destiny disagreed, however, about how far and by what means the nation should expand. Some had relatively limited territorial goals; others envisioned a vast new "empire of liberty" that would include Canada, Mexico, Caribbean and Pacific islands, and ultimately, a few dreamed, much of the rest of the world. Some believed America should use force to achieve its expansionist goals, while others felt that the nation should expand peacefully or not at all.

Not everyone embraced the idea of Manifest Destiny. Henry Clay and other prominent politicians feared, correctly as it turned out, that territorial expansion would reopen the painful controversy over slavery and threaten the **OPPOSITION TO FURTHER EXPANSION**

stability of the Union. But their voices were barely audible over the clamor of enthusiasm for expansion in the 1840s, which began with the issues of Texas and Oregon.

THE LONE STAR FLAG Almost from the moment Texas won its independence from Mexico in 1836, it sought admission to the United States as a state. Controversies over the status of slavery in the territories prevented its admission until 1845, and so for nine years it was an independent republic. The tattered banner pictured here was one of the republic's original flags. (© The Granger Collection, New York)

AMERICANS IN TEXAS

The United States had once claimed Texas–which until the 1830s was part of the Republic of Mexico–as a part of the Louisiana Purchase, but it had renounced the claim in 1819. Twice thereafter the United States had offered to buy Texas, only to meet with indignant Mexican refusals.

But in the early 1820s, the Mexican government launched an ill-advised experiment that would eventually cause it to lose its great northern province: it encouraged American emigration to Texas. The Mexicans hoped to strengthen the economy of the territory and increase their own tax revenues. They also liked the idea of the Americans sitting between Mexican settlement and the large and sometimes militant Indian tribes to the north. They convinced themselves, too, that settlers in Texas would serve as an effective buffer against United States expansion into the region; the Americans, they thought, would soon become loyal to the Mexican government. An 1824 colonization law designed to attract American settlers promised the newcomers cheap land and a four-year exemption from taxes.

Thousands of Americans, attracted by the rich soil in Texas, took advantage of Mexico's welcome. Since much of the available land was suitable for growing cotton, the great majority of the immigrants were southerners, many of whom brought slaves with them. By 1830, there were about 7,000 Americans living in Texas, more than twice the number of Mexicans there.

Most of the settlers came to Texas through the efforts of American intermediaries, who received sizable land grants from Mexico in return for promising to bring settlers into the region.

STEPHEN AUSTIN The most successful of them was Stephen F. Austin, a young immigrant from Missouri who had established the first legal American settlement in Texas in 1822. Austin and other intermediaries were effective in recruiting American immigrants to Texas, but they also created centers of power in the region that competed with the Mexican government. In 1826, one of these American intermediaries led a revolt to establish Texas as an independent nation (which he proposed calling Fredonia). The Mexicans quickly crushed the revolt and, four years later, passed new laws barring any further American immigration into the region. They were too late. Americans kept flowing into the territory, and in 1833 Mexico dropped the futile immigration ban. By 1835 more than 30,000 Americans, white and black, had settled in Texas.

TENSIONS BETWEEN THE UNITED STATES AND MEXICO

Friction between the American settlers and the Mexican government continued to grow. It arose from the continuing ties of the immigrants to the United States, and it arose, too, from their desire to legalize slavery, which the Mexican government had made illegal in Texas in 1830. But the Americans were divided over how to address their unhappiness with Mexican rule. Austin and his followers wanted to reach a peaceful settlement that would give Texas more autonomy within the Mexican republic. Other Americans wanted to fight for independence.

In the mid-1830s, instability in Mexico drove General Antonio Lopez de Santa Anna to seize power as a dictator and impose a new, more autocratic regime on the nation and its territories. A new law increased the powers of the national government of Mexico at the expense of the state governments, a measure that Texans from the United States assumed Santa Anna was aiming specifically at them. The Mexicans even imprisoned Stephen Austin in Mexico City for a time, claiming that he was encouraging revolts among his fellow Americans in Texas. Sporadic fighting between Americans and Mexicans in Texas began in 1835 and escalated as the Mexican government sent more troops into the territory. In 1836, the American settlers defiantly proclaimed their independence from Mexico.

Santa Anna led a large army into Texas, where the American settlers were having difficulties organizing an effective defense of their new "nation." Several different factions claimed to be the legitimate government of Texas, and the rebels could not even agree on who their commanders were. Mexican forces annihilated an American garrison at the Alamo mission in San Antonio after a famous, if futile, defense by a group of Texas patriots, a group that included, among others, the renowned frontiersman and former Tennessee congressman Davy Crockett. Another garrison, at Goliad, suffered substantially the same fate when the Mexicans executed most of the force after it had surrendered. By March 1836, the rebellion appeared to have collapsed. Americans were fleeing east toward Louisiana to escape Santa Anna's army.

But General Sam Houston managed to keep a small force together. And on April 23, 1836, at the Battle of San Jacinto

SAN JACINTO (near the present-day city of Houston), he defeated the Mexican army and took Santa Anna prisoner. During the surrender, American troops killed many of the Mexican soldiers in retribution for the executions at Goliad. Santa Anna, under pressure from his captors, signed a treaty giving Texas independence. The Mexican government repudiated the treaty, and Mexican troops briefly occupied San Antonio in 1842 but were unable to win Texas back.

A number of Mexican residents of Texas (known as "Tejanos") had fought with the Americans in the revolution. But soon after Texas won its independence, their positions grew difficult. The Americans did not trust the Mexicans, fearing that they were agents of the Mexican government, and in effect drove many of them out of the new republic. Most of those who stayed had to settle for a politically and economically subordinate status within the fledgling nation.

Above all, American Texans hoped for annexation by the United States. One of the first acts of the new president of Texas, Sam Houston, was to send a delegation to Washington with an offer to join the Union. There were supporters of expansion in the United States who welcomed these overtures; indeed, expan-

OPPOSITION TO ANNEXATION sionists in the United States had been supporting and encouraging the revolt against Mexico for years. But there was also opposition. Many American northerners opposed acquiring a large new slave territory, and others opposed increasing the southern votes in Congress and in the electoral college. Unfortunately for the Texans, one of the opponents was President

AUSTIN, TEXAS, 1840 Four years after Texas declared its independence from Mexico, the new republic's capital, Austin, was still a small village, most of whose buildings were rustic cabins, as this hand-colored lithograph from the time suggests. The imposing house atop the hill at right was a notable exception. It was the residence of President Mirabeau Lamar. (© The Granger Collection, New York)

Jackson, who feared annexation might cause a dangerous sectional controversy and even a war with Mexico. He therefore did not support annexation and even delayed recognizing the new republic until 1837. Presidents Martin Van Buren and William Henry Harrison also refrained from pressing the issue during their terms of office.

Spurned by the United States, Texas cast out on its own. Its leaders sought money and support from Europe. Some of them dreamed of creating a vast southwestern nation, stretching to the Pacific, that would rival the United States—a dream that appealed to European nations eager to counter the growing power of America. England and France quickly recognized and concluded trade treaties with Texas. In response, President Tyler persuaded Texas to apply for statehood again in 1844. But when Secretary of State Calhoun presented an annexation treaty to Congress as if its only purpose were to extend slavery, northern senators rebelled and defeated it. Rejection of the treaty only spurred advocates of Manifest Destiny to greater efforts toward their goal. The Texas question quickly became the central issue in the election of 1844.

OREGON

Control of what was known as Oregon Country, in the Pacific Northwest, was another major political issue in the 1840s. Its half-million square miles included the present states of Oregon, Washington, and Idaho, parts of Montana and Wyoming, and half of British Columbia. Both Britain and the United States claimed sovereignty in the region—the British on the basis of explorations in the 1790s by George Vancouver, a naval officer; the Americans on the basis of simultaneous claims by Robert Gray, a fur trader. Unable to resolve their conflicting claims diplomatically, they agreed in an 1818 treaty to allow citizens of each country equal access to the territory. This arrangement, known as "joint occupation," continued for twenty years.

DISPUTED CLAIMS

In fact, by the time of the treaty neither Britain nor the United States had established much of a presence in Oregon Country. White settlement in the region consisted largely of American and Canadian fur traders; and the most significant white settlements were the fur trading post established by John Jacob Astor's company at Astoria and other posts built by the British Hudson's Bay Company north of the Columbia River—where residents combined fur trading with farming and recruited Indian labor to compensate for their small numbers.

But American interest in Oregon grew substantially in the 1820s and 1830s. Missionaries considered the territory an attractive target for evangelical efforts, especially after the strange appearance of four Nez Percé and Flathead Indians in St. Louis in 1831. White Americans never discovered what had brought the Indians (who spoke no English) from Oregon to Missouri, and all four died before they could find out. But some missionaries considered the visit a divinely inspired invitation to extend their efforts westward. They were also motivated by a desire to counter the Catholic missionaries from Canada, whose presence in Oregon, many settlers believed, threatened American hopes for annexation. The missionaries had little success with the tribes they attempted to convert, and some—embittered by Indian resistance to their efforts—began encouraging white emigration to the region, arguing that by repudiating Christianity the Indians had abdicated their right to the land. "When a people refuse or neglect to fill the designs of Providence, they ought not to complain of the results," said the missionary Marcus Whitman, who, with his wife, Narcissa, had established an important, if largely unsuccessful, mission among the Cayuse Indians east of the Cascade Mountains.

Significant numbers of white Americans began emigrating to Oregon in the early 1840s, and they soon substantially outnumbered the British settlers there. They also devastated much of the Indian population, in part through a measles epidemic that spread through the Cayuse. The tribe blamed the Whitman mission for the plague,

CONFLICT BETWEEN SETTLERS AND INDIANS

and in 1847 they attacked it and killed thirteen whites, including Marcus and Narcissa. But such resistance did little to stem the white immigration. By the mid-1840s, American settlements had spread up and down the Pacific coast; and the new settlers (along with advocates of Manifest Destiny in the East) were urging the U.S. government to take possession of the disputed Oregon Country.

WESTWARD MIGRATION

The migrations into Texas and Oregon were part of a larger movement that took hundreds of thousands of white and black Americans into the far western regions of the continent between 1840 and 1860. Southerners flocked mainly to Texas. But the largest number of migrants came from the Old Northwest–white men and women, and a few African Americans, who undertook arduous journeys in search of new opportunities. Most traveled in family groups, until the early 1850s, when the great California gold rush attracted many single men (see pp. 351-352). Most were relatively prosperous young people. Poor people could not afford the expensive trip, and those who wished to migrate usually had to do so by joining established families or groups as laborers–men as farm or ranch hands, women as domestic servants, teachers, or, in some cases, prostitutes. The character of the migrations varied according to the destination of the migrants. Groups headed for areas where mining or lumbering was the principal economic activity consisted mostly of men. Those heading for farming regions traveled mainly as families.

All the migrants were in search of a new life, but they harbored many different visions of what a new life would bring. Some–particularly after the discovery of gold in California in 1848–hoped for quick riches. Others planned to take advantage of the vast public lands the federal government was selling at modest prices to acquire property for farming or speculation. Still others hoped to establish themselves as merchants and serve the new white communities developing in the West. Some (among them the Mormons) were on religious missions or were attempting to escape the epidemic diseases plaguing many cities in the East. But the vast majority of migrants were looking for economic opportunities. They formed a vanguard for the expanding capitalist economy of the United States.

LIFE ON THE TRAIL

Most migrants–about 300,000 between 1840 and 1860–traveled west along the great overland trails. They generally gathered in one of several major depots in Iowa and Missouri (Independence, St. Joseph, or Council Bluffs), joined a wagon train led by hired guides, and set off with their belongings piled in covered wagons, livestock trailing behind. The major route west was the 2,000-mile Oregon Trail, which stretched from Independence across the Great Plains and through the South Pass of the Rocky Mountains. From there, migrants moved north into Oregon or south (along **OREGON TRAIL** the California Trail) to the northern California coast. Other migrations moved

WESTWARD HO! *Westward the Course of Empire Takes Its Way,* painted by Emanuel Gottlieb Leutze (1816–1868) in 1861, is a pictorial representation of Manifest Destiny. It symbolizes the belief held by many during the mid-1800s that the United States was destined by divine plan and authority for western exploration and expansion. This mural is displayed in the House of Representatives in the United States Capitol building. (Private Collection/© Peter Newark American Pictures/The Bridgeman Art Library)

along the Santa Fe Trail, southwest from Independence into New Mexico.

However they traveled, overland migrants faced considerable hardships—although the death rate for travelers was only slightly higher than the rate for the American population as a whole. The mountain and desert terrain in the later portions of the trip were particularly difficult. Most journeys lasted five or six months (from May to November), and there was always pressure to get through the Rockies before the snows began, not always an easy task given the very slow pace of most wagon trains (about fifteen miles a day). And although some migrants were moving west at least in part to escape the epidemic diseases of eastern cities, they were not immune from plagues. Thousands of people died on the trail of cholera during the great epidemic of the early 1850s.

In the years before the Civil War, fewer than 400 migrants (about one-tenth of 1 percent) died in conflicts with the tribes. In fact, Indians were usually more helpful than dangerous to the white migrants. They often served as guides through difficult terrain or aided travelers in crossing streams or herding

WESTERN TRAILS IN 1860 As settlers began the long process of exploring and establishing farms and businesses in the West, major new trails began to facilitate travel and trade between the region and the more thickly settled areas to the east. Note how many of the trails led to California and how few of them led into any of the far northern regions of United States territory. Note too the important towns and cities that grew up along these trails.

• What forms of transportation later performed the functions that these trails performed prior to the Civil War?

CROSSING THE SIERRAS A wagon train struggles across the rugged trails over the Sierra Nevada, as migrants travel in California. The image is a black-and-white photograph that was colored by paint. Only a few years later, the same trip could be achieved much easier because of the transcontinental railroad. (© The Granger Collection, New York)

livestock. They maintained an extensive trade with the white travelers in horses, clothing, and fresh food. But stories of the occasional conflicts between migrants and Indians on the trail created widespread fear among white travelers, even though more Indians than white people (and relatively few of either) died in those conflicts.

Life on the trail was obviously very different from life on a farm or in a town. But the society of the trail re-created many of the patterns of conventional American society. Families divided tasks along gender lines: the men driving and, when

LIFE ON THE TRAIL

necessary, repairing the wagons or hunting game; the women cooking, washing clothes, and caring for children. Almost everyone, male or female, walked the great majority of the time, to lighten the load for the horses drawing the wagons; and so the women, many of whose chores came at the end of the day, generally worked much harder than the men, who usually rested when the caravan halted.

Despite the traditional image of westward migrants as rugged individualists, most travelers found the journey a highly collective experience. That was partly because many expeditions consisted of groups of friends, neighbors, or relatives who had decided to pull up stakes and move west together. And it was partly because of the intensity of the experience: many weeks of difficult travel with no other human contacts except, occasionally, with Indians. Indeed, one of the most frequent causes of disaster for travelers was the breakdown of the necessarily communal character of the migratory companies. It was a rare expedition in which there were not some internal conflicts before the trip was over.

EXPANSION AND WAR

The growing number of white Americans in the lands west of the Mississippi put great pressure on the government in Washington to annex Texas, Oregon, and other territory. In the 1840s, these expansionist pressures helped push the United States into a war that—however dubious its origins— became a triumph for the advocates of Manifest Destiny.

THE DEMOCRATS AND EXPANSION

In preparing for the presidential election of 1844, the two leading candidates—Henry Clay and former president Martin Van Buren—both tried to avoid taking a stand on the controversial issue of the annexation of Texas. Sentiment for

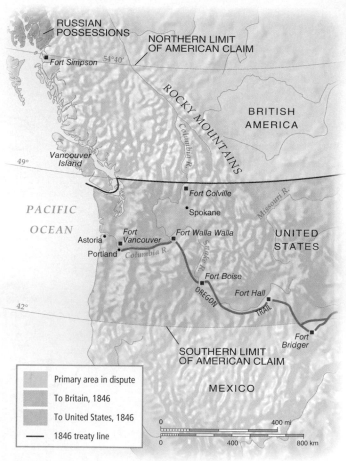

THE OREGON BOUNDARY, 1846 One of the last major boundary disputes between the United States and Great Britain involved the territory known as Oregon—the large region on the Pacific coast north of California (which in 1846 was still part of Mexico). For years, America and Britain had overlapping claims on the territory. The British claimed land as far south as the present state of Oregon, while the Americans claimed land extending well into what is now Canada. Tensions over the Oregon border at times rose to the point that many Americans were demanding war, some using the slogan "54–40 or fight," referring to the latitude of the northernmost point of the American claim.

• *How did President James K. Polk defuse the crisis?*

JAMES K. POLK expansion was mild within the Whig Party, and Clay had no difficulty securing the nomination despite his noncommittal position. But many southern Democrats supported annexation, and the party passed over Van Buren to nominate a strong supporter of annexation, the previously unheralded James K. Polk.

Polk was not as obscure as his Whig critics claimed. He had represented Tennessee in the House of Representatives for fourteen years, four of them as Speaker, and had subsequently served as governor. But by 1844, he had been out of public office—and for the most part out of the public mind—for three years. What made his victory possible was his support for the position, expressed in the Democratic platform, "that the re-occupation of Oregon and the re-annexation of Texas at the earliest practicable period are great American measures." By combining the Oregon and Texas questions, the Democrats hoped to appeal to both northern and southern expansionists. Polk carried the election by 170 electoral votes to 105, although his popular majority was less than 40,000.

Polk entered office with a clear set of goals and with plans for attaining them. John Tyler accomplished the first of Polk's goals for him. Interpreting the election returns as a mandate for the annexation of Texas, the outgoing president won congressional approval for it in February 1845. That December, Texas became a state.

Polk himself resolved the Oregon question. The British minister in Washington brusquely rejected a compromise

COMPROMISE OVER OREGON Polk offered that would establish the United States-Canadian border at the 49th parallel; he did not even refer the proposal to London. Incensed, Polk again asserted the American claim to all of Oregon. There was loose talk of war on both sides of the Atlantic—talk that in the United States often took the form of the bellicose slogan "54-40 or fight!" (a reference to where the Americans hoped to draw the northern boundary of their part of Oregon). But neither country really wanted war. Finally, the British government accepted Polk's original proposal. On June 15, 1846, the Senate approved a treaty that fixed the boundary at the 49th parallel, where it remains today.

THE SOUTHWEST AND CALIFORNIA

One of the reasons the Senate and the president had agreed so readily to the British offer to settle the Oregon question was that new tensions were emerging in the Southwest—tensions that ultimately led to a war with Mexico. As soon as the United States admitted Texas to statehood in 1845, the Mexican government broke diplomatic relations with Washington. Mexican-American relations grew still worse when a dispute developed over the boundary between Texas and Mexico. Texans claimed the Rio Grande as their western and southern border, a claim that would have added much of what is now New Mexico to Texas. Mexico, although still not conceding the loss of Texas, argued nevertheless that the border had always been the Nueces River, to the north of the Rio Grande. Polk accepted the Texas claim, and in the summer of 1845 he sent a small army under General Zachary Taylor to Texas to protect it against a possible Mexican invasion.

Part of the area in dispute was New Mexico, whose Spanish and Indian residents lived in a multiracial society that by the 1840s had endured for nearly a century and a half. In the 1820s, the Mexican government had invited American traders into the region (just as it invited American settlers into Texas), hoping to speed development of the province. And New Mexico, like Texas, began to become more American than Mexican. A flourishing commerce soon developed between Santa Fe and Independence, Missouri.

Americans were also increasing their interest in an even

AMERICAN INTERESTS IN CALIFORNIA more distant province of Mexico: California. In this vast region lived members of several western Indian tribes and perhaps 7,000 Mexicans, mostly descendants of Spanish colonists. Gradually, however, white Americans began to arrive: first maritime traders and captains of Pacific whaling ships, who stopped to barter goods or buy supplies; then merchants, who established stores, imported merchandise, and developed a profitable trade with the Mexicans and Indians; and finally pioneering farmers, who entered California from the east, by land, and settled in the Sacramento Valley. Some of these new settlers began to dream of bringing California into the United States.

SACRAMENTO IN THE 1850S The busy river port of Sacramento served the growing agricultural and mining economies of north central California in the 1850s—years in which the new state began the dramatic population growth that a century later would make it the nation's largest. (The Library of Congress (LC-USZC4-2853))

THE MEXICAN WAR, 1846–1848 Shortly after the settlement of the Oregon border dispute with Britain, the United States entered a war with Mexico over another contested border. This map shows the movement of Mexican and American troops during the fighting, which extended from the area around Santa Fe south to Mexico City and west to the coast of California. Note the American use of its naval forces to facilitate a successful assault on Mexico City, and other attacks on the coast of California. Note, too, how unsuccessful the Mexican forces were in their battles with the United States. Mexico won only one battle—a minor one at San Pasqual near San Diego—in the war.

• *How did President Polk deal with the popular clamor for the United States to annex much of present-day Mexico?*

President Polk soon came to share their dream and committed himself to acquiring both New Mexico and California for the United States. At the same time that he dispatched troops to Texas, he sent secret instructions to the commander of the Pacific naval squadron to seize the California ports if Mexico declared war. Representatives of the president quietly informed Americans in California that the United States would respond sympathetically to a revolt against Mexican authority there.

THE MEXICAN WAR

Having appeared to prepare for war, Polk turned to diplomacy and dispatched a special minister, John Slidell, to try to buy off the Mexicans. But Mexican leaders rejected Slidell's offer to purchase the disputed territories. On January 13, 1846, as soon as he heard the news, Polk ordered Taylor's army in Texas to

FAILURE OF THE SLIDELL MISSION

move across the Nueces River, where it had been stationed, to the Rio Grande. For months, the Mexicans refused to fight. But finally, according to disputed American accounts, some Mexican troops crossed the Rio Grande and attacked a unit of American soldiers. Polk now told Congress: "War exists by the act of Mexico herself." On May 13, 1846, Congress declared war by votes of 40 to 2 in the Senate and 174 to 14 in the House.

The war had many opponents in the United States. Whig critics charged from the beginning (and not without justification) that Polk had deliberately maneuvered the country into the conflict and had staged the border incident that had precipitated the declaration. Many other critics argued that the hostilities with Mexico were draining resources and attention away from the more important issue of the Pacific Northwest. Even when the United States finally reached its agreement

OPPOSITION TO THE WAR with Britain on the Oregon question, opponents claimed that Polk had settled for less than he should have because he was preoccupied with Mexico. Opposition intensified as the war continued and as the public became aware of the casualties and expense.

To others, the war was a moral crime. Ulysses Grant, then an officer in the Mexican War, called it "one of the most unjust ever waged." Abraham Lincoln criticized the war on the grounds that it gave the president too much power. "Allow the President to invade a neighboring country whenever he shall deem it necessary . . . ," he said, "and you allow him to make war at pleasure." Pacifists were particularly dismayed. Henry David Thoreau was so horrified by the war that he refused to pay taxes (which he said financed the conflict) and spent time in jail.

American forces did well against the Mexicans, but victory did not come as quickly as Polk had hoped. The president ordered Taylor to cross the Rio Grande, seize parts of northeastern Mexico, beginning with the city of Monterrey, and then march on to Mexico City itself. Taylor captured Monterrey in September 1846, but he let the Mexican garrison evacuate without pursuit. Polk now began to fear that Taylor lacked the tactical skill for the planned advance against Mexico City. He also feared that, if successful, Taylor would become a powerful political rival (as, in fact, he did).

In the meantime, Polk ordered other offensives against New Mexico and California. In the summer of 1846, a small army under Colonel Stephen W. Kearny captured Santa Fe **BEAR FLAG REVOLUTION** with no opposition. Then Kearny proceeded to California, where he joined a conflict already in progress that was being staged jointly by American settlers, a well-armed exploring party led by John C. Frémont, and the United States Navy: the so-called Bear Flag Revolution. Kearny brought the disparate American forces together under his command, and

BATTLE OF MONTEREY.
THE AMERICANS FORCING THEIR WAY TO THE MAIN PLAZA SEP. 23. 1846

THE BATTLE OF MONTERREY The Battle of Monterrey in 1846 was one of the most important conflicts of the Mexican War. Troops under the command of General Zachary Taylor defeated the Mexican forces, but not without significant American casualties. The surrender of the Mexican army on September 26 was a result of the Americans surrounding the Mexican soldiers. It was an important step in the American victory in the Mexican War. (Historicus, Inc.)

by the autumn of 1846 he had completed the conquest of California.

The United States now controlled the two territories for which it had gone to war. But Mexico still refused to concede defeat. At this point, Polk and General Winfield Scott, the commanding general of the army and its finest soldier, launched a bold new campaign. Scott assembled an army at Tampico, which the navy transported down the Mexican coast to Veracruz. With an army that never numbered more than 14,000, Scott advanced 260 miles along the Mexican National Highway toward Mexico City, kept American casualties low, and never lost a battle before finally seizing the Mexican capital. A new Mexican government took power and announced its willingness to negotiate a peace treaty.

President Polk was now unclear about his objectives. He continued to encourage those who demanded that the United States annex much of Mexico itself. At the same time, concerned about the approaching presidential election, he was growing anxious to finish the war quickly. Polk had sent a special presidential envoy, Nicholas Trist, to negotiate a

TREATY OF GUADALUPE HIDALGO

settlement. On February 2, 1848, Trist reached agreement with the new Mexican government on the Treaty of Guadalupe Hidalgo, by which Mexico agreed to cede California and New Mexico to the United States and acknowledge the Rio Grande as the boundary of Texas. In return, the United States promised to assume any financial claims its new citizens had against Mexico and to pay the Mexicans $15 million. Trist had obtained most of Polk's original demands, but he had not satisfied the new, more expansive dreams of acquiring additional territory in Mexico itself. Polk angrily claimed that Trist had violated his instructions, but he soon realized that he had no choice but to accept the treaty to silence a bitter battle growing between ardent expansionists demanding the annexation of "All Mexico!" and antislavery leaders charging that the expansionists were conspiring to extend slavery to new realms. The president submitted the Trist treaty to the Senate, which approved it by a vote of 38 to 14. The war was over, and America had gained a vast new territory. But it had also acquired a new set of troubling and divisive issues.

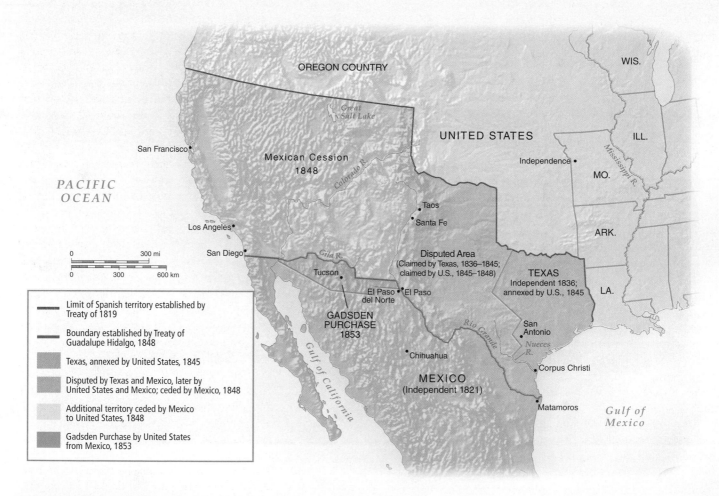

SOUTHWESTERN EXPANSION, 1845–1853 The annexation of much of what is now Texas in 1845, the much larger territorial gains won in the Mexican War in 1848, and the purchase of additional land from Mexico in 1853 completed the present continental border of the United States.

• *What great event shortly after the Mexican War contributed to a rapid settlement of California by migrants from the eastern United States?*

THE SECTIONAL DEBATE

James Polk tried to be a president whose policies transcended sectional divisions. But conciliating the sections was becoming an almost impossible task. Polk gradually earned the enmity of northerners and westerners alike, who believed his policies (particularly his enthusiasm for territorial expansion in the Southwest) favored the South at their expense.

SLAVERY AND THE TERRITORIES

In August 1846, while the Mexican War was still in progress, Polk asked Congress to appropriate $2 million for purchasing peace with Mexico. Representative David Wilmot of Pennsylvania, an antislavery Democrat, introduced an amendment to the appropriation bill prohibiting slavery in any territory acquired from Mexico. The so-called Wilmot Proviso
WILMOT PROVISO passed the House but failed in the Senate. It would be called up, debated, and voted on repeatedly for years. Southern militants, in the meantime, contended that all Americans had equal rights in the new territories, including the right to move their "property" (slaves) there.

As the sectional debate intensified, President Polk supported a proposal to extend the Missouri Compromise line through the new territories to the Pacific coast, banning
COMPETING PLANS slavery north of the line and permitting it south of the line. Other politicians supported a plan, originally known as "squatter sovereignty" and later by the more dignified phrase "popular sovereignty," which would allow the people of each territory (acting through their legislature) to decide the status of slavery there. The debate over these various proposals dragged on for many months, and the issue remained unresolved when Polk left office in 1849.

The presidential campaign of 1848 dampened the controversy for a time as both Democrats and Whigs tried to avoid the slavery question. When Polk, in poor health, declined to run again, the Democrats nominated Lewis Cass of Michigan, a dull, aging party regular. The Whigs nominated General Zachary Taylor of Louisiana, hero of the Mexican War but a man with no political experience. Opponents of slavery found the choice of candidates unsatisfying, and out of their discontent emerged the new Free-Soil Party, which drew from the existing Liberty Party and the antislavery wings of the Whig and Democratic Parties and which endorsed the Wilmot Proviso. Its candidate was former president Martin Van Buren.

Taylor won a narrow victory. But while Van Buren failed to carry a single state, he polled an impressive 291,000 votes (10 percent of the total), and the Free-Soilers elected ten members
FREE-SOIL PARTY to Congress. The emergence of the Free-Soil Party as an important political force, like the emergence of the Know-Nothing and Liberty Parties before it, signaled the inability of the existing parties to contain the political passions slavery was creating.

THE CALIFORNIA GOLD RUSH

By the time Taylor took office, the pressure to resolve the question of slavery in the far western territories had become more urgent as a result of dramatic events in California. In January 1848, James Marshall, a carpenter working on one of rancher John Sutter's sawmills, found traces of gold in the foothills of the Sierra Nevada. Sutter tried to suppress the news, fearing a gold rush would destroy his own substantial empire in the region. But by May, word of the discovery had reached San Francisco; by late summer, it had reached the east coast of the United States and much of the rest of the world. Almost immediately, hundreds of thousands of people from around the world began flocking to California in a frantic search for gold. California's non-Indian population increased nearly twentyfold in four years: from 14,000 in 1848 to over 220,000 in 1852.

The atmosphere in California at the peak of the gold rush was one of crazed excitement and greed. For a short time, San Francisco was almost completely depopulated as residents raced to the mountains to search for gold; the city's principal newspaper (which had been criticizing the gold mania) had to stop publication because it could no longer find either staff or readers. "Nothing but the introduction of insane asylums can effect a cure," one visitor remarked of the gold mania.

Most pre–gold-rush migrants to the Far West had prepared carefully before making the journey. But the gold-rush migrants
FORTY-NINERS (known as "Forty-niners") threw caution to the winds. They abandoned farms, jobs, homes, families; they piled onto ships and flooded the overland trails—many carrying only what they could pack on their backs. The overwhelming majority of the Forty-niners (perhaps 95 percent) were men, and the society they created on their arrival in California was unusually volatile because of the absence of women, children, and families.

The gold rush also attracted some of the first Chinese migrants to the western United States. News of the discoveries created great excitement in China, particularly in impoverished areas, where letters from Chinese already in California and reports from Americans visiting in China spread the word. It was, of course, extremely difficult for a poor Chinese peasant to get to America; but many young, adventurous people (mostly men) decided to go anyway—believing that they could quickly become rich and then return to China. Emigration brokers loaned many migrants money for passage to California, which the migrants would pay off out of their earnings there. The migration was almost entirely voluntary (unlike the forced movement of kidnapped "coolies" to such places as Peru and Cuba at about the same time). The Chinese in California were, therefore, free laborers and merchants, looking for gold or, more often, hoping to profit from other economic opportunities the gold boom was creating.

The gold rush created a serious labor shortage in California, as many male workers left their jobs and flocked to the gold fields. This shortage created opportunities for many people who needed work (including Chinese immigrants). It also led to an overt exploitation of Indians that resembled slavery in all

LOOKING FOR GOLD Finding gold in California was not, for the most part, a task for lone prospectors. More common were teams of people who, together, built elaborate mining technologies. As this 1852 photograph shows, the mining teams were often interracial. The white miners on the left stand conspicuously apart from the Chinese workers on the right, but both groups were essential parts of the enterprise. (© The Granger Collection, New York)

but name. White vigilantes, who called themselves "Indian hunters," were already hunting down and killing thousands of Indians before the gold rush (contributing to the process by which the Native American population of California declined from 150,000 to 30,000 between the 1850s and 1870). Now a new state law permitted the arrest of "loitering" or orphaned Indians and their assignment to a term of "indentured" labor.

INDIAN SLAVERY

The gold rush was of critical importance to the growth of California, but not for the reasons most of the migrants hoped. There was substantial gold in the hills of the Sierra Nevada, and many people got rich from it. But only a tiny fraction of the Forty-niners ever found gold, or even managed to stake a claim to land on which they could look for gold. Some disappointed migrants returned home after a while. But many stayed in California and swelled both the agricultural and urban populations of the territory. By 1856, for example, San Francisco—whose population had been 1,000 before the gold rush (and at one point declined to about 100 as people left for the mines)—was the home of over 50,000 people. By the early 1850s, California's population, which had always been diverse, had become even more so. The gold rush had attracted not just white Americans, but also Europeans, Chinese, South Americans, Mexicans, free blacks, and slaves who accompanied southern migrants. Conflicts over gold intersected with racial and ethnic tensions to make the territory an unusually turbulent place. As a result, pressure grew to create a stable and effective government. The gold rush, therefore, became another factor putting pressure on the United States to resolve the status not only of California, but of all territories—and of slavery within them—as well.

RISING SECTIONAL TENSIONS

Zachary Taylor believed statehood could become the solution to the issue of slavery in the territories. As long as the new lands remained territories, the federal government was responsible for deciding the fate of slavery within them. But once they became states, he thought, their own governments would be able to settle the slavery question. At Taylor's urging, California quickly adopted a constitution that prohibited slavery, and in December 1849 Taylor asked Congress to admit California as a free state. New Mexico, he added, should also be granted statehood as soon as it was ready and should, like California, be permitted to decide for itself what it wanted to do about slavery.

Congress balked, in part because of several other controversies concerning slavery that were complicating the debate. One was the effort of antislavery forces to abolish slavery in the District of Columbia, a movement bitterly resisted by southerners. Another was the emergence of personal liberty laws in northern states, which barred courts and police officers from helping to return runaway slaves to their owners. In response, southerners demanded a stringent law that would require northern states to return fugitive slaves to their owners. But the biggest obstacle to the president's program was the white South's fear that two new free states would be added to the northern majority. The number of free and slave states was equal in 1849–fifteen each. But the admission of California would upset the balance; and New Mexico, Oregon, and Utah might upset it further, leaving the South in a minority in the Senate, as it already was in the House.

Tempers were now rising to dangerous levels. Even many **SECTIONAL CONFLICT OVER SLAVERY IN THE TERRITORIES** otherwise moderate southern leaders were beginning to talk about secession from the Union. In the North, every state legislature but one adopted a resolution demanding the prohibition of slavery in the territories.

THE COMPROMISE OF 1850

Faced with this mounting crisis, moderates and unionists spent the winter of 1849-1850 trying to frame a great compromise. The aging Henry Clay, who was spearheading the effort, believed that no compromise could last unless it settled all the issues in dispute between the sections. As a result, he **CLAY'S PROPOSED SOLUTION** took several measures that had been proposed separately, combined them into a single piece of legislation, and presented it to the Senate on January 29, 1850. Among the bill's provisions were the admission of California as a free state; the formation of territorial governments in the rest of the lands acquired from Mexico, without restrictions on slavery; the abolition of the slave trade, but not slavery itself, in the District of Columbia; and a new, more effective fugitive slave law. These resolutions launched a debate that raged for seven months–both in Congress and throughout the nation. The debate occurred in two phases, the differences between which revealed much about how American politics was changing in the 1850s.

In the first phase of the debate, the dominant voices in Congress were those of old men—national leaders who still remembered Jefferson, Adams, and other founders—who argued for or against the compromise on the basis of broad ideals. Clay himself, seventy-three years old in 1850, appealed to shared national sentiments of nationalism. Early in March, another of the older leaders—John C. Calhoun, sixty-eight years old and so ill that he had to sit grimly in his seat while a colleague read his speech for him—joined the debate. He insisted that the North grant the South equal rights in the territories, that it agree to observe the laws concerning fugitive slaves, that it cease attacking slavery, and that it amend the Constitution to create dual presidents, one from the North and one from the South, each with a veto. Calhoun was making radical demands that had no chance of passage. But like Clay, he was offering what he considered a comprehensive, permanent solution to the sectional problem that would, he believed, save the Union. After Calhoun came the third of the elder statesmen, sixty-eight-year-old Daniel Webster, one of the great orators of his time. Still nourishing presidential ambitions, he delivered an eloquent address in the Senate, trying to rally northern moderates to support Clay's compromise.

But in July, after six months of this impassioned, nationalistic debate, Congress defeated the Clay proposal. And with that, the controversy moved into its second phase, in which a very different cast of characters predominated. Clay, ill and tired, left Washington to spend the summer resting in the mountains. Calhoun had died even before the vote in July. And Webster accepted a new appointment as secretary of state, thus removing himself from the Senate and from the debate.

In place of these leaders, a new, younger group now emerged. One spokesman was William H. Seward of New York, **NEW LEADERSHIP** forty-nine years old, a wily political operator who staunchly opposed the proposed compromise. The ideals of union were to him less important than the issue of eliminating slavery. Another was Jefferson Davis of Mississippi, forty-two years old, a representative of the new, cotton South. To him, the slavery issue was less one of principles and ideals than one of economic self-interest. Most important of all, there was Stephen A. Douglas, a thirty-seven-year-old Democratic senator from Illinois. A westerner from a rapidly growing state, he was an open spokesman for the economic needs of his section—especially for the construction of railroads. His was a career devoted not to any broad national goals but to sectional gain and personal self-promotion.

The new leaders of the Senate were able, as the old leaders had not been, to produce a compromise. One spur to the compromise was the disappearance of the most powerful obstacle to it: the president. Zachary Taylor had been adamant that only after California and possibly New Mexico were admitted as states could other measures be discussed. But on July 9, 1850, Taylor suddenly died–the victim of a violent stomach disorder. He was succeeded by Millard Fillmore of New York–a dull, handsome,

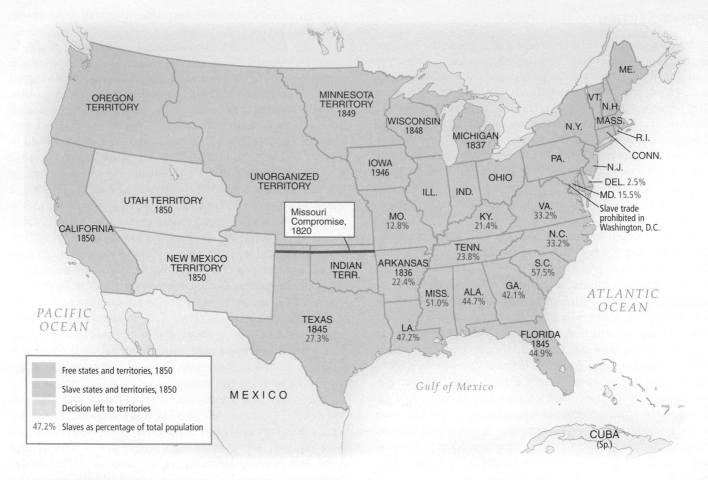

SLAVE AND FREE TERRITORIES UNDER THE COMPROMISE OF 1850 The acquisition of vast new western lands raised the question of the status of slavery in new territories organized for statehood by the United States. Tension between the North and the South on this question led in 1850 to a great compromise, forged in Congress, to settle this dispute. The compromise allowed California to join the Union as a free state and introduced the concept of "popular sovereignty" for other new territories.

• *How well did the Compromise of 1850 work?*

dignified man who understood the political importance of flexibility. He supported the compromise and used his powers of persuasion to swing northern Whigs into line.

The new leaders also benefited from their own pragmatic tactics. Douglas's first step, after the departure of Clay, was to break up the "omnibus bill" that Clay had envisioned as a great, comprehensive solution to the sectional crisis and to introduce instead a series of separate measures to be voted on one by one. Thus representatives of different sections could support those elements of the compromise they liked and oppose those they did not. Douglas also gained support with complicated backroom deals linking the compromise to such nonideological matters as the sale of government bonds and the construction of railroads. As a result of his efforts, by mid-September Congress had enacted and the president had signed all the components of the compromise.

TEMPORARY COMPROMISE

The Compromise of 1850, unlike the Missouri Compromise thirty years before, was not a product of widespread agreement on common national ideals. It was, rather, a victory of bargaining and self-interest. Still, members of Congress hailed

the measure as a triumph of statesmanship; and Millard Fillmore, signing it, called it a just settlement of the sectional problem, "in its character final and irrevocable."

THE CRISES OF THE 1850S

For a few years after the Compromise of 1850, the sectional conflict seemed briefly to have succeeded amid booming prosperity and growth. But the tensions between North and South remained, and the crisis continued to smolder until—in 1854—it once more burst into the open.

THE UNEASY TRUCE

Both major parties endorsed the Compromise of 1850 in 1852, and both nominated presidential candidates unidentified with sectional passions. The Democrats chose the obscure New Hampshire politician Franklin Pierce, and the Whigs the military hero General Winfield Scott, a man of unknown political views. But the sectional question was a divisive influence in the election anyway, and the Whigs were the principal victims. They suffered the massive defection of antislavery members angered by the party's evasiveness on the issue. Many of them flocked to the Free-Soil Party, whose antislavery presidential candidate, John P. Hale, repudiated the Compromise of 1850. The divisions among the Whigs helped produce a victory for the Democrats in 1852.

Franklin Pierce, a charming, amiable man of no particular distinction, attempted to maintain party–and national–harmony by avoiding divisive issues, particularly by avoiding the issue of

OPPOSITION TO THE FUGITIVE SLAVE ACT
slavery. But it was an unachievable goal. Northern opposition to the Fugitive Slave Act intensified quickly after 1850, when southerners began appearing in northern states to pursue people they claimed were fugitives. Mobs formed in some northern cities to prevent enforcement of the law, and several northern states also passed their own laws barring the deportation of fugitive slaves. White southerners watched with growing anger and alarm as the one element of the Compromise of 1850 that they had considered a victory seemed to become meaningless as a result of northern defiance.

"YOUNG AMERICA"

One of the ways Franklin Pierce hoped to dampen sectional controversy was through his support of a movement in the Democratic Party known as "Young America." Its adherents saw the expansion of American democracy throughout the world as a way to divert attention from the controversies over slavery. The great liberal and nationalist revolutions of 1848 in Europe stirred them to dream of a republican Europe with governments based on the model of the United States. They dreamed as well of expanding American commerce in the Pacific and acquiring new territories in the Western Hemisphere.

But efforts to extend the nation's domain could not avoid becoming entangled with the sectional crisis. Pierce had been pursuing unsuccessful diplomatic attempts to buy Cuba from Spain (efforts begun in 1848 by Polk). In 1854, however, a group

OSTEND MANIFESTO
of his envoys sent him a private document from Ostend, Belgium, making the case for seizing Cuba by force. When the Ostend Manifesto, as it became known, was leaked to the public, it enraged many antislavery northerners, who charged the administration with conspiring to bring a new slave state into the Union.

The South, for its part, opposed all efforts to acquire new territory that would not support a slave system. The kingdom of Hawaii agreed to join the United States in 1854, but the treaty died in the Senate because it contained a clause prohibiting slavery in the islands. A powerful movement to annex Canada to the United States–a movement that had the support of many Canadians eager for access to American markets–similarly foundered, at least in part because of slavery.

SLAVERY, RAILROADS, AND THE WEST

What fully revived the sectional crisis was the same issue that had produced it in the first place: slavery in the territories. By the mid-1850s, the line of substantial white settlement had moved beyond the boundaries of Missouri, Iowa, and what became Minnesota into a great expanse of plains, which many white Americans had once believed was unfit for cultivation. Now it was becoming apparent that large sections of this region were, in fact, suitable for farming and ranching. In the states of the Old Northwest, therefore, prospective settlers urged the government to open the area to them, provide territorial governments, and–despite the solemn assurance the United States had earlier given the Indians of the sanctity of their reservations–dislodge the tribes located there to make room for white settlers. There was relatively little opposition from any segment of white society to this proposed violation of Indian rights. But the interest in further settlement raised two divisive issues that gradually became entwined with each other: railroads and slavery.

As the nation expanded westward, the problem of communication between the older states and the areas west of the Mississippi River became more and more critical. As a result,

TRANSCONTINENTAL RAILROAD AND SLAVERY
broad support began to emerge for building a transcontinental railroad. The problem was where to place it– and in particular, where to locate the railroad's eastern terminus, where the line could connect with the existing rail network east of the Mississippi. Northerners favored Chicago, the rapidly growing capital of the free states of the Northwest. Southerners supported St. Louis, Memphis, or New Orleans–all located in slave states. The transcontinental railroad, in other words, had become part of the struggle between the North and the South.

Pierce's secretary of war, Jefferson Davis of Mississippi, removed one obstacle to a southern route. Surveys indicated that a railroad with a southern terminus would have to pass through an area in Mexican territory. But in 1853 Davis

GADSDEN PURCHASE
sent James Gadsden, a southern railroad builder, to Mexico, where he persuaded the Mexican government to accept $10 million in exchange for a strip of land that today comprises part of Arizona and New Mexico and that would have facilitated a southern route for the transcontinental railroad. The so-called Gadsden Purchase only accentuated the sectional rivalry.

THE KANSAS-NEBRASKA CONTROVERSY

As a senator from Illinois, a resident of Chicago, and the acknowledged leader of northwestern Democrats, Stephen A. Douglas naturally wanted the transcontinental railroad for his own city and section. He also realized the strength of the principal argument against the northern route west of the Mississippi: that it would run mostly through country with a substantial Indian population. As a result, he introduced a bill in January 1854 to organize (and thus open to white settlement) a huge new territory, known as Nebraska, west of Iowa and Missouri.

Douglas knew the South would oppose his bill because it would prepare the way for a new free state; the proposed territory was in the area of the Louisiana Purchase north of the

Missouri Compromise line (36°30´) and hence closed to slavery. In an effort to make the measure acceptable to southerners, Douglas inserted a provision that the status of slavery in the territory would be determined by the territorial legislature—that is, according to "popular sovereignty." In theory, the region could choose to open itself to slavery (although few believed it actually would). When southern Democrats demanded more, Douglas agreed to an additional clause explicitly repealing the Missouri Compromise. He **KANSAS-NEBRASKA ACT** also agreed to divide the area into two new territories—Nebraska and Kansas—instead of one. The new, second territory (Kansas) was more likely to become a slave state. In its final form the measure was known as the Kansas-Nebraska Act. President Pierce supported the bill, and after a strenuous debate, it became law in May 1854 with the unanimous support of the South and the partial support of northern Democrats.

Perhaps no piece of legislation in American history produced so many immediate, sweeping, and ominous consequences. It divided and destroyed the Whig Party, which nearly disappeared by 1856. It divided the northern Democrats (many of whom were appalled at the repeal of the Missouri Compromise, which they considered an almost sacred part of the fabric of the Union) and drove many of them from the party. Most important, it spurred the creation of a new party that was frankly sectional in composition and creed. People in **BIRTH OF THE REPUBLICAN PARTY** both major parties who opposed Douglas's bill began to call themselves Anti-Nebraska Democrats and Anti-Nebraska Whigs. In 1854, they formed a new organization and named it the Republican Party. It instantly became a major force in American politics. In the elections of that year, the Republicans won enough seats in Congress to permit them, in combination with allies among the Know-Nothings, to organize the House of Representatives.

"BLEEDING KANSAS"

Events in Kansas in the next two years increased the political turmoil in the North. White settlers from both the North and the South began moving into the territory almost immediately after the passage of the Kansas-Nebraska Act. In the spring of 1855, elections were held for a territorial legislature. There were only about 1,500 legal voters in Kansas by then, but thousands of Missourians, some traveling in armed bands into Kansas, swelled the vote to over 6,000. The result was that pro-slavery forces elected a majority to the legislature, which immediately legalized slavery. Outraged free-staters elected their own delegates to a constitutional convention, which met at Topeka and adopted a constitution excluding slavery. They then chose their own governor and legislature and petitioned Congress for statehood. President Pierce denounced them as traitors and threw the full support of the federal government behind the pro-slavery territorial legislature. A few months later a pro-slavery federal marshal assembled a large posse, consisting mostly of Missourians, to arrest the free-state leaders, who had set up their headquarters in Lawrence. The posse sacked the town, burned the "governor's" house, and destroyed several printing presses. Retribution came quickly.

Among the most fervent abolitionists in Kansas was John Brown, a fiercely committed foe of slavery who considered himself an instrument of God's will to destroy slavery. He had moved to Kansas with his sons so that they could fight to make it a free state. After the events in Lawrence, he gathered **POTAWATOMIE MASSACRE** six followers (including four of his sons) and in one night murdered five pro-slavery settlers, leaving their mutilated bodies to discourage other supporters of slavery from entering Kansas. This bloody episode, known as the Potawatomie Massacre, led to more civil strife in Kansas—irregular, guerrilla warfare conducted by armed bands, some of them more interested in

"BLEEDING KANSAS" During the bitter battles over slavery in 1856, the slave state of Missouri tried to prevent antislavery emigrants from passing through their territory en route to Kansas. Free-staters responded by organizing a large emigration through Iowa, circumventing Missouri. Those who entered Kansas by that route tended to arrive armed, some of them with large cannons—among them the one pictured here, which free-staters brought with them to Topeka that year. (© Kansas State Historical Society)

land claims or loot than in ideologies. Northerners and south-erners alike came to believe that the events in Kansas illus-trated (and were caused by) the aggressive designs of the other section. "Bleeding Kansas" became a symbol of the sectional controversy.

Another symbol soon appeared, in the United States Senate. In May 1856, Charles Sumner of Massachusetts—a militant and passionate opponent of slavery—rose to give a speech titled "The Crime Against Kansas." In it, he gave particular attention to Senator Andrew P. Butler of South Carolina, an outspoken defender of slavery. The South Carolinian was, Sumner claimed, the "Don Quixote" of slavery, having "chosen a mistress . . . who, though ugly to others, is always lovely to him, though polluted in the sight of the world, is chaste in his sight . . . the harlot slavery."

The pointedly sexual references and the viciousness of the speech enraged Butler's nephew, Preston Brooks, a member of the House of Representatives from South Carolina. Several

PRESTON BROOKS AND CHARLES SUMNER

days after the speech, Brooks approached Sumner at his desk in the Senate chamber during a recess, raised a heavy cane, and began beating him repeatedly on the head and shoulders. Sumner, trapped in his chair, rose in agony with such strength that he tore the desk from the bolts holding it to the floor. Then he collapsed, bleeding and unconscious. So severe were his injuries that he was unable to return to the Senate for four years. Throughout the North, he became a hero—a martyr to the barbarism of the South. In the South, Preston Brooks became a hero, too. Censured by the House, he resigned his seat, returned to South Carolina, and stood successfully for reelection.

THE FREE-SOIL IDEOLOGY

What had happened to produce such deep hostility between the two sections? In part, the tensions were reflections of the two sections' differing economic and territorial interests. But they were also reflections of a hardening of ideas in both North and South. As the nation expanded and political power grew more dispersed, each section became concerned with ensuring that its vision of America's future would be the dominant one.

In the North, assumptions about the proper structure of society came to center on the belief in "free soil" and "free labor." Although abolitionists generated some support for their argument that slavery was a moral evil and must be elim-inated, most white northerners came to believe that the exis-

"FREE-SOIL" IDEOLOGY

tence of slavery was dangerous not because of what it did to blacks but because of what it threatened to do to whites. At the heart of American democracy, they argued, was the right of all citizens to own property, to control their own labor, and to have access to opportunities for advancement.

According to this northern vision, the South was the

"SLAVE POWER CONSPIRACY"

antithesis of democracy—a closed, static society, in which slavery preserved an entrenched aristocracy and in which common whites had no opportunity to improve themselves. While the North was growing and prospering, the South was stagnating, rejecting the values of individualism and progress. The South was, northern free-laborites further maintained, engaged in a conspiracy to extend slavery throughout the nation and thus to destroy the openness of northern capitalism and replace it with the closed, aristo-cratic system of the South. The only solution to this "slave power conspiracy" was to fight the spread of slavery and extend the nation's democratic, free-labor ideals to all sec-tions of the country.

This ideology, which lay at the heart of the new Republican Party, also strengthened the commitment of Republicans to the Union. Since the idea of continued growth and progress was central to the free-labor vision, the prospect of dismem-berment of the nation—a diminution of America's size and eco-nomic power—was unthinkable.

ANTI-ABOLITIONIST VIOLENCE This 1838 woodcut depicts the anti-abolitionist riot in Alton, Illinois, in which Elijah P. Lovejoy, publisher of an abolitionist newspaper, was slain on November 7, 1837. The death of Lovejoy aroused the antislavery movement throughout the United States. (The Library of Congress)

THE PRO-SLAVERY ARGUMENT

In the South, in the meantime, a very different ideology—entirely incompatible with the free-labor ideology—was emerging among southern whites on the issue of slavery. It was a result of many things: the Nat Turner uprising in 1831, which terrified southern whites and made them more determined than ever to make slavery secure; the expansion of the cotton economy into the Deep South, which made slavery unprecedentedly lucrative; and the growth of the Garrisonian abolitionist movement, with its strident attacks on southern society. The popularity of Harriet Beecher Stowe's *Uncle Tom's Cabin* was perhaps the most glaring evidence of the success of those attacks, but other abolitionist writings had been antagonizing white southerners for years.

In response to these pressures, a number of white southerners produced a new intellectual defense of slavery. Professor Thomas R. Dew of the College of William and Mary helped begin that effort in 1832. Twenty years later, supporters of slavery summarized their views in an anthology titled *The Pro-Slavery Argument.* John C. Calhoun stated the essence of the case in 1837: Southerners should stop apologizing for slavery as a necessary evil and defend it as "a good–a positive good." It was good for the slaves, white southerners argued, because they enjoyed better conditions than industrial workers in the North. Slavery was good for southern society as a whole because it was the only way the two races could live together in peace. It was good for the entire country because the southern economy, based on slavery, was the key to the prosperity of the nation.

THE PRO-SLAVERY ARGUMENT

Above all, southern apologists argued, slavery was good because it served as the basis for the southern way of life–a way of life superior to any other in the United States, perhaps in the world. White southerners looking at the North saw a spirit of greed, debauchery, and instability. "The masses of the North are venal, corrupt, covetous, mean and selfish," wrote one southerner. Others wrote with horror of the factory system and the crowded, pestilential cities filled with unruly immigrants. The South, by contrast, was a stable, orderly society, operating at a slow and human pace. It was free from the feuds between capital and labor plaguing the North. It protected the welfare of its workers. And it allowed the aristocracy to enjoy a refined and accomplished cultural life. It was, in short, an ideal social order in which all elements of the population were secure and content.

The defense of slavery rested, too, on increasingly elaborate arguments about the biological inferiority of African Americans, who were, many white Southerners claimed, inherently unfit to take care of themselves, let alone exercise the rights of citizenship. And just as abolitionist arguments drew strength from Protestant theology in the North, the pro-slavery defense mobilized the Protestant clergy in the South to give the institution a religious and biblical justification.

BUCHANAN AND DEPRESSION

In this unpromising climate, the presidential campaign of 1856 began. Democratic Party leaders wanted a candidate who,

ELECTION OF 1856

unlike President Pierce, was not closely associated with the explosive question of "Bleeding Kansas." They chose James Buchanan of Pennsylvania, a reliable Democratic stalwart who as minister to England had been safely out of the country during the recent controversies. The Republicans, participating in their first presidential contest, denounced the Kansas-Nebraska Act and the expansion of slavery but also endorsed a Whiggish program of internal improvements, thus combining the idealism of antislavery with the economic aspirations of the North. As eager as the Democrats to present a safe candidate, the Republicans nominated John C. Frémont, who had made a national reputation as an explorer of the Far West and who had no political record. The Native American, or Know-Nothing, Party was beginning to break apart, but it nominated former president Millard Fillmore, who also received the endorsement of a small remnant of the Whig Party.

After a heated, even frenzied campaign, Buchanan won a narrow victory over Frémont and Fillmore. A slight shift of votes in Pennsylvania and Illinois would have elected the Republican candidate. Particularly significant was that Frémont had attracted virtually no votes in the South while outpolling all other candidates in the North. At the time of his inauguration, Buchanan was, at age sixty-five, the oldest president, except for William Henry Harrison, ever to have taken office. Whether because of age and physical infirmities or because of a fundamental weakness of character, he was a painfully timid and indecisive president at a critical moment in history.

In the year Buchanan took office, a financial panic struck the country, followed by a depression that lasted several years. In the North, the depression strengthened the Republican Party because distressed manufacturers, workers, and farmers came to believe that the hard times were the result of the unsound policies of southern-controlled Democratic administrations. They expressed their frustrations by moving into an alliance with antislavery elements and thus into the Republican Party.

THE *DRED SCOTT* DECISION

On March 6, 1857, the Supreme Court of the United States projected itself into the sectional controversy with one of the most controversial and notorious decisions in its history–its ruling in the case of *Dred Scott v. Sandford*, handed down two days after Buchanan was inaugurated. Dred Scott was a Missouri slave, once owned by an army surgeon who had taken Scott with him into Illinois and Wisconsin, where slavery was forbidden. In 1846, after the surgeon died, Scott sued his master's widow for freedom on the grounds that his residence in free territory had liberated him from slavery. The claim was well grounded in Missouri law, and in 1850 the circuit court in which Scott filed the suit declared him free. By now, John Sanford, the brother of the surgeon's widow, was claiming ownership of Scott, and he appealed the circuit court ruling to the state supreme court, which reversed the earlier decision. When Scott appealed to the federal courts, Sanford's attorneys claimed that Scott had no standing to sue because he was not a citizen, but private property.

The Supreme Court (which misspelled Sanford's name in its decision) was so divided that it was unable to issue a single ruling on the case. The thrust of the various rulings, however, was a stunning defeat for the antislavery movement. Chief Justice Roger Taney, who wrote one of the majority opinions,

TANEY'S SWEEPING OPINION declared that Scott could not bring a suit in the federal courts because he was not a citizen. African Americans had no claim to citizenship, Taney argued, and virtually no rights under the Constitution. Slaves were property, and the Fifth Amendment prohibited Congress from taking property without "due process of law." Consequently, Taney concluded, Congress possessed no authority to pass a law depriving persons of their slave property in the territories. The Missouri Compromise, therefore, had always been unconstitutional.

The ruling did nothing to challenge the right of an individual state to prohibit slavery within its borders, but the statement that the federal government was powerless to act on the issue was drastic and startling. Few judicial opinions have ever created as much controversy. Southern whites were elated: the highest tribunal in the land had sanctioned some of the most extreme southern arguments. In the North, the decision produced widespread fury and dismay. The decision, the *New York Tribune* wrote, "is entitled to just so much moral weight as would be the judgment of a majority of those congregated in any Washington bar-room." Republicans threatened that when they won control of the national government, they would reverse the decision—by "packing" the Court with new members.

DEADLOCK OVER KANSAS

President Buchanan timidly endorsed the *Dred Scott* decision. At the same time, he tried to resolve the controversy over Kansas by supporting its admission to the Union as a slave state. In response, the pro-slavery territorial legislature called an election for delegates to a constitutional convention. The free-state residents refused to participate, claiming that the legislature had discriminated against them in drawing district lines. As a result, the pro-slavery forces won control of the convention, which met in 1857 at Lecompton, framed a constitution legalizing slavery, and refused to give voters a chance to reject it. When an election for a new territorial legislature was called, the antislavery groups turned out to vote and won a majority. The new legislature promptly submitted the Lecompton constitution to the voters, who rejected it by more than 10,000 votes.

Both sides had resorted to fraud and violence, but it was clear nevertheless that a majority of the people of Kansas opposed slavery. Buchanan, however, pressured Congress to admit Kansas under the Lecompton constitution. Stephen A. Douglas and other western Democrats refused to support the president's proposal, which died in the House of Representatives. Finally, in April 1858, Congress approved a compromise:

The Lecompton constitution would be submitted to the voters of Kansas again. If it was approved, Kansas would be admitted

LECOMPTON CONSTITUTION REJECTED to the Union; if it was rejected, statehood would be postponed. Again, Kansas voters decisively rejected the Lecompton constitution. Not until the closing months of Buchanan's administration in early 1861, after several southern states had already withdrawn from the Union, did Kansas enter the Union—as a free state.

THE EMERGENCE OF LINCOLN

Given the gravity of the sectional crisis, the congressional elections of 1858 took on a special importance. Of particular note was the United States Senate election in Illinois, which pitted Stephen A. Douglas, the most prominent northern Democrat, against Abraham Lincoln, who was largely unknown outside Illinois but who quickly emerged as one of the most skillful politicians in the Republican Party.

Lincoln was a successful lawyer who had long been involved in state politics. He had served several terms in the Illinois legislature and one undistinguished term in Congress. He was

LINCOLN-DOUGLAS DEBATES not a national figure like Douglas, so he tried to increase his visibility by engaging Douglas in a series of debates. The Lincoln-Douglas debates attracted enormous crowds and received wide attention in newspapers across the country. By the time the debates ended, Lincoln's increasingly eloquent and passionate attacks on slavery had made him nationally prominent.

At the heart of the debates was a basic difference on the issue of slavery. Douglas appeared to have no moral position on the issue. "One of the reserved rights of the states," he said, "was the right to regulate the relations between master and servant, on the slavery question." But Douglas went further, endorsing what was still the dominant sentiment among whites (both North and South) of his time: "I am opposed to negro citizenship in any and every form. I believe this government was made on the white basis. I believe it was made by white men for the benefit of white men and their posterity forever." Lincoln's opposition to slavery was different. If the nation could accept that African Americans were not entitled to basic human rights, he argued, then it could accept that other groups—immigrant laborers, for example—could be deprived of rights, too. And if slavery were to extend into the western territories, he claimed, opportunities for poor white laborers to better their lots in life would be lost. The nation's future, he argued (reflecting the central idea of the Republican Party), rested on the spread of free labor.

Lincoln believed slavery was morally wrong, but he was not an abolitionist. That was in part because he could not envision an easy alternative to slavery in the areas where it already existed. He shared the prevailing view among northern whites that

LINCOLN'S POSITION African Americans were not prepared (and perhaps never would be) to live on equal terms with whites. But even while Lincoln

THE HARPERS FERRY ARSENAL John Brown's famous raid on Harpers Ferry in 1859 centered on this arsenal, from which he and his followers tried, in vain, to foment slave rebellion throughout the South. (National Park Service, Harper's Ferry. U.S. Department of the Interior/National Archives and Records Administration)

accepted the inferiority of black people, he continued to believe that they were entitled to basic rights. "I have no purpose to introduce political and social equality between the white and the black races. . . . But I hold that . . . there is no reason in the world why the negro is not entitled to all the natural rights enumerated in the Declaration of Independence, the right to life, liberty, and the pursuit of happiness. I hold that he is as much entitled to these as the white man." Lincoln and his party wanted to "arrest the further spread" of slavery–that is, prevent its expansion into the territories; but they would not directly challenge it where it already existed and would instead trust that the institution would gradually die there of its own accord.

Douglas's position satisfied his followers sufficiently to win him reelection to the Senate in 1858, but it aroused little enthusiasm and did nothing to enhance his national political ambitions. Lincoln, by contrast, lost the election but emerged with a growing following both in and beyond the state. And outside Illinois, the elections went heavily against the Democrats, who lost ground in almost every northern state. The Democratic Party retained control of the Senate but lost its majority in the House, with the result that the congressional sessions of 1858 and 1859 were bitterly deadlocked.

JOHN BROWN'S RAID

The battles in Congress, however, were overshadowed by a spectacular event that enraged and horrified the entire South and greatly hastened the rush toward disunion. In the fall of

JOHN BROWN'S RAID 1859, John Brown, the antislavery zealot whose bloody actions in Kansas had inflamed the crisis there, staged an even more dramatic episode, this time in the South itself. With private encouragement and financial aid from some prominent eastern abolitionists, he made elaborate plans to seize a mountain fortress in Virginia from which, he believed, he could foment a slave insurrection in the South. On October 16, he and a group of eighteen followers attacked and seized control of a U.S. arsenal in Harpers Ferry, Virginia. But the slave uprising Brown hoped to inspire did not occur, and he quickly found himself besieged by citizens, local militia companies, and, before long, U.S. troops under the command of Robert E. Lee. After ten of his men were killed, Brown surrendered. He was promptly tried in a Virginia court for treason against the state, found guilty, and sentenced to death. He and six of his followers were hanged.

No other single event did more than the Harpers Ferry raid to convince white southerners that they could not live safely in the Union. John Brown's raid, many southerners believed (incorrectly) had the support of the Republican Party, and it suggested to them that the North was now committed to producing a slave insurrection.

THE ELECTION OF LINCOLN

The presidential election of 1860 had the most momentous consequences of any in American history. It was also among the most complex.

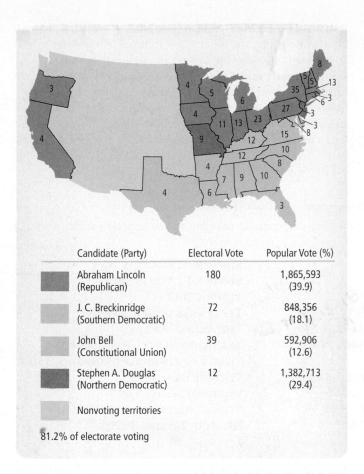

Candidate (Party)	Electoral Vote	Popular Vote (%)
Abraham Lincoln (Republican)	180	1,865,593 (39.9)
J. C. Breckinridge (Southern Democratic)	72	848,356 (18.1)
John Bell (Constitutional Union)	39	592,906 (12.6)
Stephen A. Douglas (Northern Democratic)	12	1,382,713 (29.4)
Nonvoting territories		

81.2% of electorate voting

THE ELECTION OF 1860 The stark sectional divisions that helped produce the Civil War were clearly visible in the results of the 1860 presidential election. Abraham Lincoln, the antislavery Republican candidate, won almost all of the free states. Stephen Douglas, a northern Democrat with no strong position on the issue of slavery, won only one border and one free state, and John Bell, a supporter of both slavery and union, won three border states. John Breckinridge, a strong pro-slavery southern Democrat, carried the entire Deep South. Lincoln won less than 40 percent of the popular vote but, because of the four-way division in the race, managed to win a clear majority of the electoral vote.

• *What impact did the election of Lincoln have on the sectional crisis?*

The Democratic Party was torn apart by a battle between southerners, who demanded a strong endorsement of slavery, and westerners, who supported the idea of popular sovereignty. The party convention met in April in Charleston, South Carolina.

DIVIDED DEMOCRATS When the convention endorsed popular sovereignty, delegates from eight states in the lower South walked out. The remaining delegates could not agree on a presidential candidate and finally adjourned after agreeing to meet again in Baltimore in June. The decimated convention at Baltimore nominated Stephen Douglas for president. In the meantime, disenchanted southern Democrats met in Richmond and nominated John C. Breckinridge of Kentucky. Later, a group of conservative ex-Whigs met in Baltimore to form the Constitutional Union Party, with John Bell of Tennessee as their presidential candidate. They endorsed the Union and remained silent on slavery.

The Republican leaders, in the meantime, were trying to broaden their appeal so as to attract every major interest group in the North. They warned that the South was blocking the North's economic aspirations. The platform endorsed such traditional Whig measures as a high tariff, internal improvements, a homestead bill, and a Pacific railroad to be built with federal financial assistance. It supported the right of each state to decide the status of slavery within its borders. But it also insisted that neither Congress nor territorial legislatures could legalize slavery in the territories. The Republican convention chose Abraham Lincoln as the party's presidential nominee. Lincoln was appealing because of his growing reputation for eloquence, because of his firm but moderate position on slavery, and because his relative obscurity ensured that he would have none of the drawbacks of other, more prominent (and therefore more controversial) Republicans. He was a representative of the West, a considerable asset in a race against Douglas.

In the November election, Lincoln won the presidency with a majority of the electoral votes but only about two-fifths of the fragmented popular vote. The Republicans, moreover, failed to win a majority in Congress. Even so, the election of Lincoln became the final signal to many white southerners that their position in the Union was hopeless. And within a few weeks of Lincoln's victory, the process of disunion began—a **DISUNION** process that would quickly lead to a prolonged and bloody war between two groups of Americans, each heir to more than a century of struggling toward nationhood, each now convinced that it shared no common ground with the other.

AP CONNECTING THEMES

Chapter 13 examined the concept of Manifest Destiny and the impact of territorial acquisition on intensifying sectional conflict. Expansionist government policies, including, importantly, James K. Polk's expansionist agenda, entangled the issue of slavery into debates over territorial acquisition. The Compromise of 1850 and its impact on subsequent sectional conflict, particularly in regard to the Fugitive Slave Law, was one of a series of events that would eventually lead to civil war. As part of the effort to find solutions to the issue of territorial expansion and slavery, the Kansas-Nebraska Act was introduced, but it ultimately brought about the demise of the Second Party System and the emergence of the Third American Party System. The increasing emotionalism over the issue of slavery, the growing abolitionist movement, the expression of the northerners' Free Soil ideology, and the apologists' defense of slavery polarized American society. The issue of slavery came to be the focal point for each side wanting to ensure that its view of what America should be and what American democracy meant came to dominate. As part of this struggle, the *Dred Scott* decision and the election of

1860 would become final events leading to the impending crisis of civil war.

The following themes have heightened importance in Chapter 13. You should now be able to do the following for each listed theme:

Identity: Analyze the causes and consequences of the pro-slavery and abolitionist groups' belief in their own superior moral identity.

Politics and Power: Explain how both the North and South felt threatened by the other side's ability to control the federal government and legislate against the interests of their region.

Environment and Geography: Explain the impact of territorial acquisition in intensifying sectional conflict.

Ideas, Beliefs, and Culture: Analyze the degree to which and the ways in which the shift of pro-slavery and anti-slavery forces to more extreme positions worsened the sectional crisis.

AP SUGGESTED STUDY

PEOPLE/PLACES/EVENTS As you study these items, think about how they demonstrate or relate to key concepts and historical themes from this chapter and previous chapters.

ABRAHAM LINCOLN 359	HENRY CLAY 353	STEPHEN A. DOUGLAS 353
COMPROMISE OF 1850 353	JAMES K. POLK 346	STEPHEN F. AUSTIN 342
DRED SCOTT DECISION 358	JOHN BROWN 356	TEJANOS 342
ELECTION OF 1860 360	JOHN C. CALHOUN 353	TEXAS ANNEXATION 342
FUGITIVE SLAVE ACT 355	KANSAS-NEBRASKA ACT 356	THE ALAMO 342
GOLD RUSH 351	MANIFEST DESTINY 340	TRANSCONTINENTAL RAILROAD 355
FREE-SOIL IDEOLOGY 357	MEXICAN WAR 348	TREATY OF GUADALUPE-HIDALGO 350
FREE-SOIL PARTY 351	OREGON BORDER DISPUTE 343	WILMOT PROVISO 351
GADSDEN PURCHASE 355	OREGON TRAIL 344	WINFIELD SCOTT 350
GENERAL ANTONIO LOPEZ DE SANTA ANNA 342	POPULAR SOVEREIGNTY 351	"YOUNG AMERICA" 355
	REPUBLICAN PARTY 364	ZACHARY TAYLOR 347
HARPERS FERRY 360	SAM HOUSTON 342	

AP TEST PRACTICE

Questions assume cumulative content knowledge from this chapter and previous chapters.

MULTIPLE CHOICE Use the map on page 361 and your knowledge of U.S. history to answer questions 1-2.

1. In what way does the map best demonstrate the break-up of the second party system?
   (A) The map shows the relative balance in the split between the North and the South
   (B) The map shows the division of the Democratic Party
   (C) The map demonstrates the stark sectional divisions between the regions.
   (D) The map shows the shift of California and the Oregon territory from slave states to free states.

2. What was the most immediate effect of the election outcome shown on the map?
   (A) The Compromise of 1850 was repealed.
   (B) The *Dred-Scott* decision was overturned.
   (C) Kansas was admitted into the union as free state.
   (D) Southern states began to secede.

SHORT ANSWER Use your knowledge of U.S. history to answer questions 3-6.

3. Answer a, b, and c.
   a) Briefly explain ONE example of how the South defended the institution of slavery.
   b) Briefly explain a SECOND example of how the South defended the institution of slavery.
   c) Briefly explain ONE example of arguments made in the 19th century against the institution of slavery.

4. Answer a, b, and c.
   a) Briefly explain ONE example of how territorial expansion intensified sectional conflict.
   b) Briefly explain a SECOND example of how territorial expansion intensified sectional conflict.
   c) Briefly explain ONE example of action taken by an individual, which consequences greatly contributed to the sectional conflict over slavery.

5. Answer a, b, and c.

  a) For one of the areas below, identify ONE event or historical example from the first half of the 19th century and briefly explain how this event or example contributed to intensifying section conflict.

    • Economic

    • Political

    • Cultural

  b) Choose a second area and identify ONE event or historical example from the first half of the 19th century and briefly explain how this event or example contributed to intensifying section conflict.

6. Use this excerpt and your knowledge of United States history to answer a, b, and c.

"Two factors—the expansionist pursuit of Jefferson's empire of liberty, and the extraordinary continued growth of plantation slavery thanks to the cotton revolution—upset the Democratic and Whig Parties that had formed by 1840, and hastened the growth of the antagonistic northern and southern democracies. Americans experienced the crack-up primarily as a political crisis, about whether slavery would be allowed to interfere with democratic rights—or, alternatively, whether northern tyranny would be allowed to interfere with southern democracy. Over those questions, which encompassed clashes over northern free labor and southern slavery, the political system began falling apart in the mid-1840s."

    –from *The Rise of American Democracy: Jefferson to Lincoln* by historian Sean Wilentz, 2005

  a) Briefly explain the main point of the Wilentz's historical argument.

  b) Provide ONE piece of historical evidence that is not included in the passage and explain how it supports the historian's argument.

  c) Briefly relate the historian's argument to the theme of Politics and Power.

LONG ESSAY For each question below, develop a thoughtful and thorough historical argument that answers the question. Begin your essay with a thesis statement and support it with relevant historical evidence.

7. Evaluate to what extent the concept of Manifest Destiny led to the sectional crisis that would become the Civil War.

8. Some historians have argued that the influence of philosophical ideas from the Second Great Awakening and the Enlightenment led to the sectional crisis that would lead to Civil War. Support, modify, or refute this interpretation, providing specific evidence to justify your answer.

14 | THE CIVIL WAR

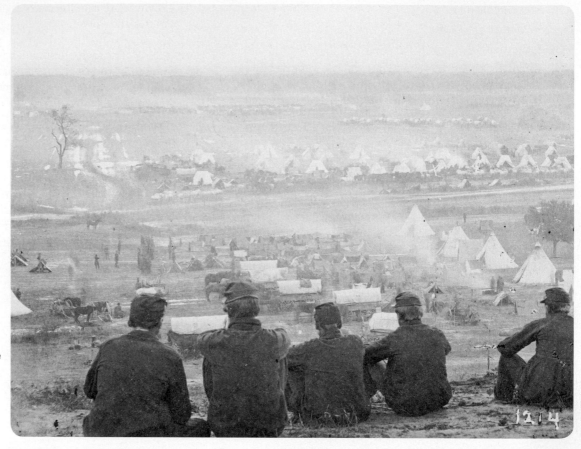

UNION SOLDIERS AT REST The Civil War was one of the bloodiest conflicts in American history. But there were many times at which the armies were not in battle. This photograph of Union soldiers was taken at a large supply base in northern Virginia in 1862— one of many sites in which soldiers spent long, idle periods. (The Library of Congress)

AP

HISTORICAL THINKING

1. **Comparison** Compare the relative advantages of the North and the South in the Civil War.

2. **Historical Argumentation** Analyze the reasons for secession and why attempts at compromise failed.

3. **Contextualization** Evaluate the degree of and reason for the suppression of Constitutional rights during the Civil War.

4. **Historical Causation** In what ways and to what degree did the Civil War alter the role of both Northern and Southern women?

5. **Comparison** Evaluate the military strategy of both the North and the South during the course of the war.

6. **Historical Argumentation** Analyze the impact of the Civil War on Northern and Southern society economically and politically.

Key Concept Correlations

Analyze the ways the historical developments you learn about in this chapter connect to the following AP Key Concepts.

5.2 Intensified by expansion and deepening regional divisions, debates over slavery and other economic, cultural, and political issues led the nation into civil war.

5.3 The Union victory in the Civil War and the contested Reconstruction of the South settled the issues of slavery and secession, but left unresolved many questions about the power of the federal government and citizenship rights.

Thematic Learning Objectives

POL-2, 5, 6; PEO-5; ID-5; CUL-2; ENV-3

CHAPTER 14 discusses the lead-in to the Civil War, the conduct of the war, and the impact of the war on Northern and Southern society. It examines the mobilization of resources, including manpower, by both the North and South. In studying the chapter, you should focus on the relative advantages that each side had at the outset of the war and the relative costs each side paid at the end of the war. Look at African American participation in the war and the problems they continued to face, even as they fought for the Union. Pay attention to how the role of Northern and Southern women changed as a result of the war. Lastly, this chapter deals in depth with the strategy and conduct of the war, and you should have a general conception of how the war progressed, paying particular attention to turning points in the war. As you read, evaluate the following ideas:

- The abolition of slavery led to a reshaping of cultural identities and concepts of citizenship.
- The Civil War brought new economic opportunities to many Americans.
- Repeated attempts at compromise failed to prevent the Civil War.
- The North's advantage in manpower, industrial capacity, and political leadership led to victory in the Civil War.
- Both the Union and the Confederacy mobilized manpower and resources to fight the Civil War.
- The Emancipation Proclamation and the Thirteenth Amendment offered new opportunities for African Americans.

THE SECESSION CRISIS

Almost as soon as the news of Abraham Lincoln's election reached the South, the militant leaders of the region–the champions of the new concept of "Southern nationalism," men known both to their contemporaries and to history as the "fire-eaters"– began to demand an end to the Union.

"SOUTHERN NATIONALISM"

THE WITHDRAWAL OF THE SOUTH

South Carolina, long the hotbed of Southern separatism, seceded first. It called a special convention, which voted unanimously on December 20, 1860, to withdraw the state from the Union. Horace Greeley of the *New York Tribune* wrote three days before secession, "We fully realize that the dilemma of the incoming administration will be a critical one. It must endeavor to uphold and enforce laws, as well against rebellious slaveholders as fugitives."

By the time Lincoln took office, six other states from the lower South–Mississippi (January 9, 1861), Florida (January 10), Alabama (January 11), Georgia (January 19), Louisiana (January 26), and Texas (February 1)–had seceded. In February 1861, representatives of the seven seceded states met at Montgomery, Alabama, and announced the formation of a new nation: the Confederate States of America. The response from the North was confused and indecisive. President James Buchanan told Congress in December 1860 that no state had the right to secede from the Union but suggested that the federal government had no authority to stop a state if it did.

ESTABLISHMENT OF THE CONFEDERACY

The seceding states immediately seized the federal property–forts, arsenals, government offices–within their boundaries. Robert Toombs, a Confederate cabinet member and general, said, "Our property has been stolen, our people murdered; felons and assassins have found sanctuary in the arms of the party which elected Mr. Lincoln. The Executive power, the last bulwark of the Constitution to defend us against these enemies of the Constitution, has been swept away, and we now stand without a shield, with bare bosoms presented to our enemies." At first they did not have sufficient military power to seize two fortified offshore military installations: Fort Sumter, on an island in the harbor of Charleston, South Carolina, garrisoned by a small force under Major Robert Anderson; and Fort Pickens, in the harbor of Pensacola, Florida. South

Carolina sent commissioners to Washington to ask for the surrender of Sumter; but Buchanan, timid though he was, refused to yield it. Indeed, in January 1861 he ordered an unarmed merchant ship to proceed to Fort Sumter with additional troops and supplies. Confederate guns on shore fired at the vessel–the first shots between North and South–and turned it back. Still, neither section was yet ready to concede that war had begun. And in Washington, efforts began once more to forge a compromise.

THE FAILURE OF COMPROMISE

Gradually, compromise forces gathered behind a proposal first submitted by Senator John J. Crittenden of Kentucky and known as the Crittenden Compromise. It called for several constitutional amendments, which would guarantee the permanent existence of slavery in the slave states and would satisfy Southern demands on such issues as fugitive slaves and slavery in the District of Columbia. But the heart of Crittenden's plan was a proposal to reestablish the Missouri Compromise line in all present and future territory of the United States: Slavery would be prohibited north of the line and permitted south of it. The remaining Southerners in the Senate seemed willing to accept the plan, but the Republicans were not. The compromise would have required the Republicans to abandon their most fundamental position: that slavery not be allowed to expand.

CRITTENDEN COMPROMISE

And so nothing had been resolved when Abraham Lincoln arrived in Washington for his inauguration–sneaking into the city in disguise on a night train to avoid assassination as he passed through the slave state of Maryland. In his inaugural address, which dealt directly with the secession crisis, Lincoln laid down several basic principles. Since the Union was older than the Constitution, no state could leave it. Acts of force or violence to support secession were insurrectionary. And the government would "hold, occupy, and possess" federal property in the seceded states–a clear reference to Fort Sumter.

FORT SUMTER

Conditions at Fort Sumter were deteriorating quickly. Union forces were running short of supplies; unless they received fresh provisions, the fort would have to be evacuated. Lincoln believed that if he surrendered Sumter, his commitment to maintaining the Union would no longer be credible. So he sent a relief expedition to the fort, carefully informing the South Carolina authorities that there would be no attempt to send troops or munitions unless the supply ships met with resistance.

The new Confederate government now faced a dilemma. Permitting the expedition to land would seem to be a tame submission to federal authority. Firing on the ships or the fort would seem (to the North at least) to be aggression. But Confederate leaders finally decided that to appear cowardly would be worse than to appear belligerent, and they ordered General P. G. T. Beauregard, commander of Confederate forces at Charleston, to take the island, by force if necessary. When Anderson refused to surrender the fort, the Confederates bombarded it for two days, April 12-13, 1861. On April 14, Anderson surrendered. The Civil War had begun.

THE WAR BEGINS

As the southern states began to secede, Abraham Lincoln spoke of American liberty: "It was not the mere matter of the separation of the Colonies from the motherland; but that sentiment in the Declaration of Independence which gave liberty, not alone to the people of this country, but, I hope, to the world, for all future time. It was that which gave promise that in due time the weight would be lifted from the shoulders of all men. This is a sentiment embodied in the Declaration of Independence. Now, my friends, can this country be saved upon that basis? If it can, I will consider myself one of the happiest men in the world, if I can help to save it. If it cannot be saved, upon that principle, it will be truly awful."

Almost immediately, Lincoln began mobilizing the North for war. And equally promptly, four more slave states seceded from the Union and joined the Confederacy: Virginia (April 17, 1861), Arkansas (May 6), North Carolina (May 20), and Tennessee (June 8). The four remaining slave states–Maryland, Delaware, Kentucky, and Missouri–cast their lot with the Union (under heavy political and even military pressure from Washington).

Was there anything that Lincoln (or those before him) could have done to settle the sectional conflict peaceably? That question has preoccupied historians for more than a century without resolution. (See "Debating the Past," pp. 372-373.) There were, of course, actions that might have prevented a war: if, for example, Northern leaders had decided to let the South withdraw in peace. The real question, however, is not what hypothetical situations might have reversed the trend toward war but whether the preponderance of forces in the nation were acting to hold the nation together or to drive it apart. And by 1861, it seems clear that in both the North and the South, sectional antagonisms–whether justified or not–had risen to such a point that the existing terms of union had become untenable.

People in both regions had come to believe that two distinct and incompatible civilizations had developed in the United States and that those civilizations were incapable of living together in peace. Ralph Waldo Emerson, speaking for much of the North, said at the time: "I do not see how a barbarous community and a civilized community can constitute one state." And a slaveowner, expressing the sentiments of much of the South, said shortly after the election of Lincoln: "These [Northern] people hate us, annoy us, and would have us assassinated by our slaves if they dared. They are a different people from us, whether better or worse, and there is no love between us. Why then continue together?"

That the North and the South had come to believe these things helped lead to secession and war. Whether these things

FORT SUMTER DURING THE BOMBARDMENT This graphic drawing shows the interior of Fort Sumter during its bombardment by Confederate forces in April 1861. Union forces faced the dual problem of heavy Confederate artillery and cannon fire, and dwindling supplies—since the Confederates had blockaded the Charleston harbor to prevent the North from resupplying the fort. (© The Granger Collection, New York)

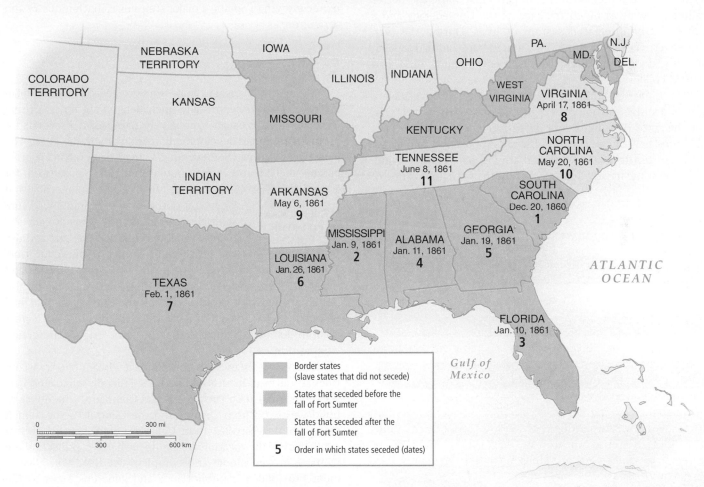

THE PROCESS OF SECESSION The election of Lincoln, the candidate of the antislavery Republican Party, to the presidency had the immediate result of inspiring many of the states in the Deep South to secede from the Union, beginning with South Carolina only a little more than a month after the November election. Other states nearer the northern border of the slaveholding region remained in the Union for a time, but the U.S. attempt to resupply Fort Sumter (and the bombardment of the fort by the new Confederate army) mobilized the upper South to secede as well. Only enormous pressure from the federal government kept the slaveholding states of Maryland, Delaware, Kentucky, and Missouri in the Union.

• *What accounted for the creation of the state of West Virginia in 1861?*

were actually true—whether the North and the South were really as different and incompatible as they thought—is another question, one that the preparations for and conduct of the war help to answer.

THE OPPOSING SIDES

As the war began, only one thing was clear: all the important material advantages lay with the North. Its population

UNION ADVANTAGES

was more than twice as large as that of the South (and nearly four times as large as the nonslave population of the South), so the Union had a much greater manpower reserve for both its armies and its workforce. The North had an advanced industrial system and was able by 1862 to manufacture almost all its own war materials. The South had almost no industry at all and, despite impressive efforts to increase its manufacturing capacity, had to rely on imports from Europe throughout the war.

In addition, the North had a much better transportation system than did the South and, in particular, more and better railroads: twice as much trackage as the Confederacy and a much better integrated system of lines. During the war, moreover, the already inferior Confederate railroad system steadily deteriorated and by the beginning of 1864 had almost collapsed.

But in the beginning the North's material advantages were not as decisive as they appear in retrospect. The South was, for the most part, fighting a defensive war on its own land and thus had the advantage of local support and familiarity with the territory. The Northern armies, on the other hand, were fighting mostly within the South, with long lines of

communications, amid hostile local populations, and with access only to the South's own inadequate transportation system. The commitment of the white population of the

SOUTHERN ADVANTAGES

South to the war was, with limited exceptions, clear and firm. In the North, opinion about the war was divided and support for it remained shaky until near the end. A major Southern victory at any one of several crucial moments might have proved decisive by breaking the North's will to continue the struggle. Finally, many Southerners believed that the dependence of the English and French textile industries on American cotton would require those nations to intervene on the side of the Confederacy.

THE MOBILIZATION OF THE NORTH

In the North, the war produced considerable discord, frustration, and suffering. But it also produced prosperity and economic growth by giving a major stimulus to both industry and agriculture.

ECONOMIC MEASURES

With Southern forces now gone from Congress, the Republican Party could exercise virtually unchallenged authority. During the war, it enacted an aggressively nationalistic program to promote economic development, particularly in the West. The Homestead Act of 1862 permitted any citizen or prospective citizen to claim 160 acres of public land and to purchase it for a small fee after living on it for five years. The Morrill Land

REPUBLICAN ECONOMIC POLICY

Grant Act of the same year transferred substantial public acreage to the state governments, which were to sell the land and use the proceeds to finance public education. This act led to the creation of many new state colleges and universities, the so-called land-grant institutions. Congress also passed a series of tariff bills that by the end of the war had raised duties to the highest level in the nation's history—a great boon to domestic industries eager for protection from foreign competition.

Congress also moved to complete the dream of a transcontinental railroad. It created two new federally chartered corporations: the Union Pacific Railroad Company, which was to build westward from Omaha, and the Central Pacific, which was to build eastward from California, settling the prewar conflict over the location of the line. The two projects were to meet in the middle and complete the link. The government provided free public lands and generous loans to the companies.

The National Bank Acts of 1863–1864 created a new national banking system. Existing or newly formed banks could join the system if they had enough capital and were willing to invest one-third of it in government securities. In

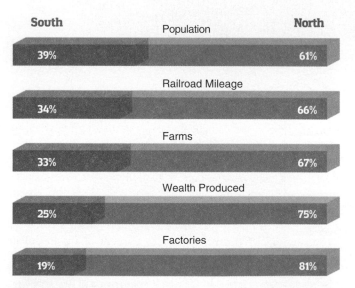

South		North
Population		
39%		61%
Railroad Mileage		
34%		66%
Farms		
33%		67%
Wealth Produced		
25%		75%
Factories		
19%		81%

UNION AND CONFEDERATE RESOURCES Virtually all the material advantages—population, manufacturing, railroads, wealth, even agriculture—lay with the North during the Civil War, as this chart shows.

• *What advantages did the South have in the conflict?*

WAR BY RAILROAD Union soldiers pose beside a mortar mounted on a railroad car in July 1864, during the siege of Petersburg, Virginia. Railroads played a critical role in the Civil War, and the superiority of the North's rail system was an important factor in its victory. It was appropriate, perhaps, that the battle for Petersburg, the last great struggle of the war, was over control of critical railroad lines. (National Archives and Records Administration)

NATIONAL BANK ACTS

return, they could issue U.S. Treasury notes as currency. The new system eliminated much of the chaos and uncertainty in the nation's currency and created a uniform system of national bank notes.

More difficult than promoting economic growth was financing the war. The government tried to do so in three ways: by levying taxes, issuing paper currency, and borrowing. Congress levied new taxes on almost all goods and services; and in 1861 the government levied an income tax for the first

FINANCING THE WAR

time, with rates that eventually rose to 10 percent on incomes above $5,000. But taxation raised only a small proportion of the funds necessary for financing the war, and strong popular resistance prevented the government from raising the rates. At least equally controversial was the printing of paper currency, or "greenbacks." The new currency was backed not by gold or silver, but simply by the good faith and credit of the government (much like today's currency). The value of the greenbacks fluctuated according to the fortunes of the Northern armies. Early in 1864, with the war effort bogged down, a greenback dollar was worth only 39 percent of a gold dollar. Even at the close of the war, it was worth only 67 percent of a gold dollar. Because of the difficulty of making purchases with this uncertain currency, the government used greenbacks sparingly. The Treasury issued only $450 million worth of paper currency–a small proportion of the cost of the war but enough to produce significant inflation.

By far the largest source of financing for the war was loans from the American people. In previous wars, the government had sold bonds only to banks and to a few wealthy investors. Now, however, the Treasury persuaded ordinary citizens to buy over $400 million worth of bonds–the first example of mass financing of a war in American history. Still, bond purchases by individuals constituted only a small part of the government's borrowing, which in the end totaled $2.6 billion. Most of the loans to finance the war came from banks and large financial interests.

RAISING THE UNION ARMIES

Over 2 million men served in the Union armed forces during the course of the Civil War. But at the beginning of 1861, the regular army of the United States consisted of only 16,000 troops, many of them stationed in the West to protect white settlers from Indians. So the Union, like the Confederacy, had to raise its army mostly from scratch. Lincoln called for an increase of 23,000 in the regular army, but the bulk of the fighting, he knew, would have to be done by volunteers in state militias. When Congress convened in July 1861, it authorized enlisting 500,000 volunteers for three-year terms (as opposed to the customary three-month terms). This voluntary system of recruitment produced adequate forces only briefly. After the first flush of enthusiasm for the war, enlistments declined. By March 1863, Congress was forced to pass a national draft law. Virtually all young adult males were eligible to be drafted; but a man could escape service by hiring someone to go in his place or by paying the government a fee of $300. Only about 46,000 men were ever actually conscripted, but the draft greatly increased voluntary enlistments.

To a people accustomed to a remote and inactive national government, conscription was strange and threatening.

DRAFT RIOTS Opposition to the law was widespread, particularly among laborers, immigrants, and Democrats opposed to the war (known as "Peace Democrats" or "Copperheads" by their opponents). Occasionally, opposition to the draft erupted into violence. Demonstrators against the draft rioted in New York City for four days in July 1863, after the first names were selected for conscription. It was among the most violent urban uprisings in American history. More than 100 people died. Irish workers were at the center of the violence. They were angry because black strikebreakers had been used against them in a recent longshoremen's strike; and they blamed African Americans generally for the war, which they thought was being fought for the benefit of slaves who would soon be competing with white workers for jobs. The rioters lynched a number of African Americans, burned down homes and businesses (mostly those of free blacks), and even destroyed an orphanage for African American children. Only the arrival of federal troops subdued the rioters.

WARTIME POLITICS

When Abraham Lincoln arrived in Washington early in 1861, many politicians–noting his lack of national experience and his folksy, unpretentious manner–considered him a minor politician from the prairies, a man whom the real leaders of his party would easily control. But the new president moved quickly to establish his own authority. He assembled a cabinet representing every faction of the Republican Party and every segment of Northern opinion–men of exceptional prestige and influence and in some cases arrogance, several of whom believed that they, not Lincoln, should be president. Lincoln moved boldly as well to use the war powers of the presidency, ignoring what he considered inconvenient parts of the Constitution

SENDING THE BOYS OFF TO WAR In this painting, *The Departure of the Seventh Regiment to the War*, by Thomas Nast, New York's Seventh Regiment parades down Broadway in April 1861, to the cheers of exuberant, patriotic throngs, shortly before departing to fight in what most people then assumed would be a brief war. Thomas Nast is better known for his famous political cartoons of the 1870s. (© The Granger Collection, New York)

because, he said, it would be foolish to lose the whole by being afraid to disregard a part. He sent troops into battle without asking Congress for a declaration of war. (Lincoln insisted on calling the conflict a domestic insurrection, which required no formal declaration of war; to ask for a declaration would, he believed, constitute implicit recognition of the Confederacy as an independent nation.) He increased the size of the regular army without receiving legislative authority to do so. He unilaterally proclaimed a naval blockade of the South.

Lincoln's greatest political problem was the widespread popular opposition to the war, mobilized by factions in the Democratic Party. The Peace Democrats feared that the agricultural Northwest was losing influence to the industrial East

WARTIME REPRESSION and that Republican nationalism was eroding states' rights. Lincoln used extraordinary methods to suppress them. He ordered military arrests of civilian dissenters and suspended the right of habeas corpus (the right of a person to be released by a judge or court from unlawful detention, as in the case of insufficient evidence). At first, Lincoln used these methods only in sensitive areas such as the border states; but in 1862, he proclaimed that all persons who discouraged enlistments or engaged in disloyal practices were subject to martial law. In all, more than 13,000 persons were arrested and imprisoned for varying periods. The most prominent Copperhead in the country—Ohio Congressman Clement L. Vallandigham—was seized by military authorities and exiled to the Confederacy after he made a speech claiming that the purpose of the war was to free the blacks and enslave the whites. Lincoln defied all efforts to curb his authority to suppress opposition, even those of the Supreme Court. When Chief Justice Taney issued a writ (*Ex parte Merryman*) requiring him to release an imprisoned Maryland secessionist leader, Lincoln simply ignored it. (After the war, in 1866, the Supreme Court ruled in *Ex parte Milligan* that military trials in areas where the civil courts existed were unconstitutional.)

Repression was not the only tool the North used to strengthen support for the war. In addition to arresting "disloyal" Northerners, Lincoln's administration used new tools of persuasion to build popular opinion in favor of the war. In addition to pro-war pamphlets, posters, speeches, and songs, the war mobilized a significant corps of photographers—organized by the renowned Mathew Brady, one of the first important photographers in American history—to take pictures of the war. The photographs that resulted from this effort—new to warfare—were among the grimmest ever made to that point, many of them displaying the vast numbers of dead on the Civil War battlefields. For some Americans, the images of death contributed to a revulsion from the war. But for most Northerners, they gave evidence of the level of sacrifice that had been made for the preservation of the Union and thus spurred the nation on to victory. (Southerners used similar propaganda in the Confederacy, although less effectively.)

The presidential election of 1864 occurred, therefore, in the midst of considerable political dissension. The Republicans had suffered heavy losses in the congressional elections of 1862, and in response leaders of the party tried to create a broad coalition of all the groups that supported the war. They called the new organization the Union Party, but in reality it was little more than the Republican Party and a small faction of War Democrats. The Union Party nominated Lincoln for another term as president and Andrew Johnson of Tennessee, a War Democrat who had opposed his state's decision to secede, for the vice presidency.

The Democrats nominated George B. McClellan, a celebrated former Union general who had been relieved of his command by Lincoln. The party adopted a platform denouncing the war and calling for a truce. McClellan repudiated that demand, but the Democrats were clearly the peace party in the campaign, trying to profit from growing war weariness and from the Union's discouraging military position in the summer of 1864.

At this crucial moment, however, several Northern military victories, particularly the capture of Atlanta, Georgia, early in

1864 ELECTION September, rejuvenated Northern morale and boosted Republican prospects. Lincoln won

HANGING A NEGRO IN CLARKSON STREET.

THE NEW YORK CITY DRAFT RIOT, 1863 Opposition to the Civil War draft was widespread in the North and in July 1863 produced a violent four-day uprising in New York City in which as many as 100 people died. The riot began on July 13 with a march by 4,000 men, mostly poor Irish laborers, who were protesting the provisions by which some wealthy people could be exempted from conscription. "Rich man's war, poor man's fight," the demonstrators cried (just as some critics of the war chanted at times in the South). Many New Yorkers also feared that the war would drive black workers north to compete for their jobs. The demonstration turned violent when officials began drawing names for the draft. The crowd burned the draft building and then split into factions. Some rioters attacked symbols of wealth such as exclusive shops and mansions. Others terrorized black neighborhoods and lynched some residents. This contemporary engraving depicts one such lynching. Only by transferring five regiments to the city from Gettysburg (less than two weeks after the great battle there) was the government able to restore order. (© The Granger Collection, New York)

THE CAUSES OF THE CIVIL WAR

IN his second inaugural address in March 1865, Abraham Lincoln looked back at the beginning of the Civil War four years earlier. "All knew," he said, that slavery "was somehow the cause of the war." Few historians doubt the basic truth of Lincoln's statement, but they have disagreed

ON TO LIBERTY This painting by Theodore Kaufmann shows a group of fugitive slaves escaping from the South in the late years of the Civil War. Thousands of former slaves crossed the Union lines, where they were given their freedom. Many of them joined the Union army. (© The Granger Collection, New York)

sharply about whether slavery was the only, or even the principal, cause of the war.

This debate began even before the war itself. In 1858, Senator William H. Seward of New York took note of two competing explanations of the sectional tensions that were then inflaming the nation. On one side, he claimed, stood those who believed the sectional hostility to be "accidental, unnecessary, the work of interested or fanatical agitators." Opposing them stood those (like Seward himself) who believed there to be "an irrepressible conflict between opposing and enduring forces."

The "irrepressible conflict" argument dominated historical discussion of the war from the 1860s to the 1920s. Because the North and the South had reached positions on the issue of slavery that were both irreconcilable and seemingly unalterable, some historians claimed, the conflict had become "inevitable." James Rhodes, in his seven-volume *History of the United States from the Compromise of 1850* . . . (1893–1900), placed greatest emphasis on the moral conflict over slavery, but he suggested as well that the struggle also reflected fundamental differences between the Northern and Southern economic systems. Charles and Mary Beard, in *The Rise of American Civilization* (2 vols., 1927), also viewed the war as an irrepressible economic, rather than moral, conflict. Ultimately, however,

reelection comfortably, with 212 electoral votes to McClellan's 21; the president carried every state except Kentucky, New Jersey, and Delaware. But Lincoln's lead in the popular vote was a modest 10 percent. Had Union victories not occurred when they did, and had Lincoln not made special arrangements to allow Union troops to vote, McClellan might have won.

THE POLITICS OF EMANCIPATION

Despite their surface unity in 1864 and their general agreement on most economic matters, the Republicans disagreed sharply on the issue of slavery. Radicals—led in Congress by such men as Representative Thaddeus Stevens of Pennsylvania and Senators Charles Sumner of Massachusetts and Benjamin Wade of Ohio—wanted to use the war to abolish slavery immediately and completely. Conservatives favored a slower, more gradual, and, they believed, less disruptive process for ending slavery. In the beginning, at least, they had the support of the president.

Despite Lincoln's cautious view of emancipation, momentum began to gather behind it early in the war. In 1861, Congress passed the Confiscation Act, which declared that all

CONFISCATION ACTS

slaves used for "insurrectionary" purposes (that is, in support of the Confederate military effort) would be considered freed. Subsequent laws in the spring of 1862 abolished slavery in Washington, D.C., and in the western territories, and compensated owners. In July 1862, the Radicals pushed through Congress the second Confiscation Act, which again declared free the slaves of persons aiding and supporting the insurrection (whether or not the slaves themselves were doing so) and which also authorized the president to employ African Americans, including freed slaves, as soldiers. As the war progressed, much of the North seemed slowly to accept emancipation as a central war aim; nothing less would justify the enormous sacrifices of the struggle, many Northerners believed. As a result, the Radicals increased their influence within the Republican Party—a development that did not go most of those who believed the Civil War to have been "irrepressible" returned to an emphasis on social and cultural factors. Allan Nevins, in *The Ordeal of the Union* (8 vols., 1947–1971), argued that the "problem of slavery" lay at the root of the cultural differences between the North and the South, but that the "fundamental assumptions, tastes, and cultural aims" of the two regions were diverging in other ways as well.

More-recent proponents of the "irrepressible conflict" argument have taken different views of the Northern and Southern positions on the conflict but have been equally insistent on the role of culture and ideology in creating them. Eric Foner, in *Free Soil, Free Labor, Free Men* (1970) and other writings, emphasized the importance of the "free-labor ideology" to Northern opponents of slavery. Most Northerners (including Abraham Lincoln), Foner claimed, opposed slavery largely because they feared it might spread to the North and threaten the position of free white laborers. Eugene Genovese, writing of Southern slaveholders in *The Political Economy of Slavery* (1965), argued that just as Northerners were becoming convinced of a Southern threat to their economic system, so Southerners believed that the North had aggressive and hostile designs on the Southern way of life. Like Foner, therefore, Genovese saw cultural differences as the source of an all but inevitable conflict.

Other historians have argued that the Civil War might have been avoided, that the differences between North and South were not so fundamental as to have necessitated war. The idea of the war as avoidable gained wide recognition among historians in the 1920s and 1930s, when a group known as the "revisionists" began to offer new accounts of the origins of the conflict. One of the leading revisionists was James G. Randall, who saw in the social and economic systems of the North and the South no differences so fundamental as to require a war. Avery Craven, another leading revisionist, argued similarly in *The Coming of the Civil War* (1942) that slave laborers were not much worse off than Northern industrial workers, that the institution was already on the road to "ultimate extinction," and that war could therefore have been averted had skillful and responsible leaders worked to produce compromise.

More-recent students of the Civil War have emphasized the role of political agitation and ethnocultural conflicts in the coming of the war. Michael Holt, in *The Political Crisis of the 1850s* (1978), emphasized the role of political parties and especially the collapse of the Second Party System, rather than the irreconcilable differences between sections, in explaining the conflict, although he avoided placing blame on any one group. Along with Paul Kleppner, Joel Silbey, and William Gienapp, Holt was one of the creators of an "ethnocultural" interpretation of the war. These scholars argue that the Civil War began in large part because the party system—the most effective instrument for containing and mediating sectional differences—collapsed in the 1850s and produced a new Republican Party that aggravated, rather than calmed, the divisions in the nation. William Gienapp, in *The Origins of the Republican Party, 1852–1856* (1987), argued that the disintegration of the party system in the early 1850s was less a result of the debate over slavery in the territories than of such ethnocultural issues as temperance and nativism. Gienapp and the other ethnoculturalists would not entirely dispute Lincoln's claim that slavery was "somehow the cause of the war." But they do challenge the arguments of Eric Foner and others that the "free labor ideal" of the North— and the challenge slavery, and its possible expansion into the territories, posed to that ideal—was the principal reason for the conflict. Slavery became important, they suggest, less because of irreconcilable differences of attitude than because of the collapse of parties and other structures that might have contained the conflict. ●

AP HISTORICAL ARGUMENTATION AND INTERPRETATION

Questions assume cumulative content knowledge from this chapter and previous chapters.

1. Describe the respective arguments made by four of the historians discussed. For each, identify one piece of historical evidence that could be used to support the argument and one piece of historical evidence that could be used to refute the argument.
2. Identify an argument examining the causes of the Civil War made through an economic lens. Identify an argument made through a cultural lens. Identify an argument made through a political lens.
3. With which argument do you most agree? Support your view, using historical evidence.

---

unnoticed by the president, who decided to seize the leadership of the rising antislavery sentiment himself.

On September 22, 1862, after the Union victory at the Battle of Antietam, the president announced his intention to use his war powers to issue an executive order freeing all slaves in the Confederacy. And on January 1, 1863, he formally signed the Emancipation Proclamation, which declared forever free slaves in all areas of the Confederacy except those already under Union control: Tennessee, western Virginia, and southern Louisiana. The proclamation did not apply to the border slave states, which had never seceded from the Union and therefore were not subject to the president's war powers. On the day of Emancipation, Ralph Waldo Emerson wrote a "Boston Hymn":

EMANCIPATION PROCLAMATION

Today unbind the captive
So only are ye unbound;
Lift up a people from the dust,
Trump of their rescue sound . . .

Pay ransom to the owner,
And fill the bag to the brim,
Who is the owner? The slave is owner,
And ever was. Pay him.

Source: English Poetry III: From Tennyson to Whitman. Vol. XLII. The Harvard Classics, edited by Charles W. Eliot (New York: P. F. Collier & Son, 1909-1914).

The immediate effect of the proclamation was limited, since it applied only to slaves still under Confederate control. But the document was of great importance nevertheless, because it clearly and irrevocably established that the war was being fought not only to preserve the Union but also to eliminate slavery. Eventually, as federal armies occupied much of the South, the proclamation became a practical reality and led directly to the freeing of thousands of slaves. Even in areas not directly affected by the proclamation, the antislavery impulse gained strength.

The U.S. government's tentative measures against slavery were not, at first, a major factor in the liberation of slaves. Instead, the

WARTIME ORATORY

THE *CAUSES* OF WARS are rather different from their *meanings*. Presidents often use wartime speeches to shape public understanding of those meanings–to articulate their visions of what wars are really about. They tend to emphasize broad principles and cherished ideals rather than more-narrow economic concerns or even national security arguments.

More than four months after the pivotal battle at Gettysburg, President Abraham Lincoln traveled there to dedicate a military cemetery. A crowd of 15,000 listened first to the famed orator Edward Everett's two-hour account of the battle. Then came Lincoln. His speech was much shorter–just over two minutes. The President touched briefly on American history before turning to the Civil War and what it meant. The Gettysburg Address is reproduced here in its entirety (the "1863" document).

Almost a hundred and fifty years later, President George W. Bush also appealed to the past in explaining the conflict of his time, the war on terrorism of the early twenty-first century. The occasion was Bush's second inaugural address, delivered in January 2005 after his victory over the Democratic nominee, John Kerry. His speech came in the middle of the ongoing wars in Iraq and Afghanistan that had been prompted by the terrorist attacks of September 11, 2001. Though the context couldn't have been more different, Bush devoted part of his address to themes similar to Lincoln's so many years before. That excerpt is included here as the "2005" document.

LINCOLN—1863

THE GETTYSBURG ADDRESS, NOVEMBER 19, 1863

Four score and seven years ago our fathers brought forth on this continent, a new nation, conceived in Liberty, and dedicated to the proposition that all men are created equal.

Now we are engaged in a great civil war, testing whether that nation, or any nation so conceived and so dedicated, can long endure. We are met on a great battle-field of that war. We have come to dedicate a portion of that field, as a final resting place for those who here gave their lives that that nation might live. It is altogether fitting and proper that we should do this.

But, in a larger sense, we can not dedicate–we can not consecrate–we can not hallow–this ground. The brave men, living and dead, who struggled here, have consecrated it, far above our poor power to add or detract. The world will little note, nor long remember what we say here, but it can never forget what they did here. It is for us the living, rather, to be dedicated here to the unfinished work which they who fought here have thus far so nobly advanced. It is rather for us to be here dedicated to the great task remaining before us–that from these honored dead we take increased devotion to that cause for which they gave the last full measure of devotion–that we here highly resolve that these dead shall not have died in vain–that this nation, under God, shall have a new birth of freedom–and that government of the people, by the people, for the people, shall not perish from the earth.

Source: abrahamlincolnonline.org

BUSH—2005

GEORGE W. BUSH'S SECOND INAUGURAL ADDRESS, JANUARY 20, 2005

We are led, by events and common sense, to one conclusion: The survival of liberty in our land increasingly depends on the success of liberty in other lands. The best hope for peace in our world is the expansion of freedom in all the world.

America's vital interests and our deepest beliefs are now one. From the day of our Founding, we have proclaimed that every man and woman on this earth has rights, and dignity, and matchless value, because they bear the image of the Maker of Heaven and earth. Across the generations we have proclaimed the imperative of self-government, because no one is fit to be a master, and no one deserves to be a slave. Advancing these ideals is the mission that created our Nation. It is the honorable achievement of our fathers. Now it is the urgent requirement of our nation's security, and the calling of our time.

So it is the policy of the United States to seek and support the growth of democratic movements and institutions in every nation and culture, with the ultimate goal of ending tyranny in our world.

This is not primarily the task of arms, though we will defend ourselves and our friends by force of arms when necessary. Freedom, by its nature, must be chosen, and defended by citizens, and sustained by the rule of law and the protection of minorities. And when the soul of a nation finally speaks, the institutions that arise may reflect customs and traditions very different from our own. America will not impose our own style of government on the unwilling. Our goal instead is to help others find their own voice, attain their own freedom, and make their own way.

Source: http://georgewbush-whitehouse.archives.gov

AP TEST PRACTICE

Questions assume cumulative content knowledge from this chapter and previous chapters.

1. Which of the following groups might most applaud Lincoln's message regarding the meaning for fighting the war?

   (A) Those who supported the formation of political parties in the early years of the nation

   (B) Those in the early 1800s who opposed a strong, national bank

   (C) Those who, at the time of the American Revolution, supported the formation of America as a confederation of states

   (D) Those who at the time of the Constitutional Convention wished to build a stronger central government

2. Which of the following best describes the common vision expressed in both documents regarding the respective war's meaning?

   (A) Ending tyranny in the world

   (B) Spread of American democracy through all the nations

   (C) Fulfillment of the American democratic ideal of individual freedom of opportunity and choice

   (D) The need for America to adopt a policy of imperialism

3. How does Bush's speech reflect his articulation about the larger meaning for the war on terrorism?

   (A) By stating that America will not impose its political and social systems on a country, but will, instead, help that country determine its own freedom

   (B) By stating that it will overthrow tyranny in the world and establish American-style democracy throughout the world

   (C) By stating that the security of America depends on the security of all nations.

   (D) By stating that America is a blessed country

war helped African Americans to liberate themselves, and they did so in increasing numbers as the war progressed. Many slaves were taken from their plantations and put to work building defenses and other chores. Once transported to the front, many of them found ways to escape across Northern lines, where they were treated as "contraband"–goods seized from people who had no right to them. They could not be returned to their masters. By 1862, the Union army often penetrated deep into the Confederacy. Almost everywhere they went, escaped slaves, often whole families, flocked to join them by the thousands. Some of them joined the Union army, others simply stayed with the troops until they could find their way to free states. When the Union captured New Orleans and much of southern Louisiana, slaves refused to work for their former masters, even though the Union occupiers had not made any provisions for liberating African Americans.

By the end of the war, slavery had been abolished in two Union slave states–Maryland and Missouri–and in three Confederate states occupied by Union forces–Tennessee, Arkansas, and Louisiana. The final step came in 1865, when Congress approved and the necessary states ratified the Thirteenth Amendment, abolishing slavery as an institution in all parts of the United States. After more than two centuries, legalized slavery finally ceased to exist in the United States.

AFRICAN AMERICANS AND THE UNION CAUSE

About 186,000 emancipated African Americans served as soldiers, sailors, and laborers for the Union forces, joining a significant number of free blacks from the North. The services of African Americans to the Union military were significant in many ways, not least because of the substantial obstacles many black men had to surmount in order to enlist.

In the first months of the war, African Americans were largely excluded from the military. A few black regiments

BLACK ENLISTMENT

eventually took shape in some of the Union-occupied areas of the Confederacy, mainly because they were a ready source of manpower in these defeated regions. But once Lincoln issued the Emancipation Proclamation, black enlistment increased rapidly and the Union military began actively to recruit African American soldiers and sailors in both the North and, where possible, the South.

Some of these men were organized into fighting units. The best known was probably the Fifty-fourth Massachusetts Infantry, which (like most black regiments) had a white commander: Robert Gould Shaw, a member of an aristocratic Boston family. Shaw and more than half his regiment died during a battle near Charleston, South Carolina, in the summer of 1863.

Most black soldiers, however, were assigned menial tasks behind the lines, such as digging trenches and transporting water. Even though fewer African Americans than whites died

MISTREATMENT OF BLACK SOLDIERS

in combat, the black mortality rate was higher than the rate for white soldiers because so many died of disease from working long, arduous hours in unsanitary conditions. Conditions for blacks and whites were unequal in other ways as well. African American soldiers were paid a third less than were white soldiers (until Congress changed the law in mid-1864). But however dangerous, onerous, or

AFRICAN AMERICAN TROOPS Although most of the black soldiers who enlisted in the Union army during the Civil War performed noncombat jobs behind the lines, there were also black combat regiments—members of one of which are pictured here—who fought with great success and valor in critical battles. (The Library of Congress)

menial the tasks black soldiers were given, most of them felt enormous pride in their service–pride they retained throughout their lives and often through the lives of their descendants. Many moved from the army into politics and other forms of leadership (in both the North and, after the war, the Reconstruction South).

Black fighting men captured by the Confederates were, unlike white prisoners, not returned to the North in exchange for Southern soldiers being returned to the South. They were sent back to their masters (if they were escaped slaves) or often executed. In 1864, Confederate soldiers killed more than 260 African Americans after capturing them in Tennessee.

THE WAR AND ECONOMIC DEVELOPMENT

The Civil War did not, as some historians used to claim, transform the North from an agrarian to an industrial society. Industrialization was already far advanced when the war began, and in some areas, the war retarded growth–by cutting manufacturers off from their Southern markets and sources of raw material, and by diverting labor and resources to military purposes.

On the whole, however, the war sped the economic development of the North. That was in part a result of the political dominance of the Republican Party and its promotion of nationalistic economic legislation. But it was also because the war itself required the expansion of certain sectors of the economy. Coal production increased by nearly 20 percent during the war. Railroad facilities improved–mainly through the adoption of a standard gauge (track width) on new lines. The loss of farm labor to the military forced many farmers to increase the mechanization of agriculture.

The war was a difficult experience for many American workers. For industrial workers, there was a substantial loss of purchasing power, as prices in the North rose by more than 70 percent during the war, while wages rose only about 40 percent. That

HARD TIMES FOR WORKERS was partly because liberalized immigration laws permitted a flood of new workers into the labor market and helped keep wages low. It was also because the increasing mechanization of production eliminated the jobs of many skilled workers. One result of these changes was a substantial increase in union membership in many industries and the creation of several national unions, for coal miners, railroad engineers, and others–organizations bitterly opposed and rigorously suppressed by employers.

WOMEN, NURSING, AND THE WAR

Responding not only to the needs of employers for additional labor, but to their own, often desperate, need for money, women found themselves, by either choice or necessity, thrust into new and often unfamiliar roles during the war. They took over positions vacated by men and worked as teachers, retail salesclerks, office workers, and mill and factory hands.

Above all, women entered nursing, a field previously dominated by men. The U.S. Sanitary Commission, an organization of civilian volunteers led by social reformer **U.S. SANITARY COMMISSION** Dorothea Dix, mobilized large numbers of female nurses to serve in field hospitals. By the end of the war, women were the dominant force in nursing; by 1900, nursing had become an almost entirely female profession. Female nurses not only cared for patients but also performed other tasks considered appropriate for women: cooking, cleaning, and laundering.

Female nurses encountered considerable resistance from male doctors, many of whom considered women too weak **TRADITIONAL GENDER ROLES REINFORCED** for medical work and who, in any case, thought it inappropriate that women were taking care of men who were strangers to them. The Sanitary Commission tried to counter such arguments by attributing to nursing

THE U.S. SANITARY COMMISSION Mathew Brady took this photograph of female nurses and Union soldiers standing before an infirmary at Brandy Station, Virginia, near Petersburg, in 1864. The infirmary was run by the U.S. Sanitary Commission, the government-supported nursing corps that became important to the medical care of wounded soldiers during the Civil War. (National Archives and Records Administration)

many of the domestic ideals that American society attributed to women's work in the home: women as nurses would play the same maternal, nurturing, instructive role they played as wives and mothers. "The right of woman to her sphere, which includes housekeeping, cooking, and nursing, has never been disputed," one Sanitary Commission official insisted. But not all women who worked for the commission were content with a purely maternal role; some challenged the dominance of men in the organization and even stood up against doctors whom they considered incompetent, increasing the resentment felt toward them by many men. In the end, though, the work of female nurses was so indispensable to the military that the complaints of male doctors were irrelevant.

Nurses, and many other women, found the war a liberating experience, in which (as one Sanitary Commission nurse later wrote) the American woman "had developed potencies and possibilities of which she had been unaware and which surprised her, as it did those who witnessed her marvelous achievement." Some women, especially those who had been committed to feminist causes earlier, came to see the war as an opportunity to win support for their own goals. Elizabeth Cady Stanton and Susan B. Anthony, who together founded the National Woman's Loyal League in 1863, worked simultaneously for the abolition of slavery and the awarding of suffrage to women. Clara Barton, who was active during the war in collecting and distributing medical supplies and who later became an important figure in the nursing profession (and a founder of the American Red Cross), said in 1888: "At the war's end, woman was at least fifty years in advance of the normal position which continued peace would have assigned her." That may have been an exaggeration; but it captured the degree to which many women looked back on the war as a crucial moment in the redefinition of female roles and in the awakening of a sense of independence and new possibilities.

Whatever nursing may have done for the status of women, it had an enormous impact on the medical profession and on the treatment of wounded soldiers during the war. The U.S. Sanitary Commission not only organized women to serve at the front; it also funneled medicine and supplies to badly overtaxed field hospitals. The commission also (as its name suggests) helped spread ideas about the importance of sanitary conditions in hospitals and clinics and probably contributed to the relative decline of death by disease in the Civil War. Nevertheless, twice as many soldiers died of diseases—malaria, dysentery, typhoid, gangrene, and others—as died in combat during the war. Even minor injuries could lead to fatal infections.

NURSING AND MEDICINE

THE MOBILIZATION OF THE SOUTH

Many Southerners boasted loudly of the differences between their new nation and the nation they had left. The differences were real. But there were also important similarities between the Union and the Confederacy, which became clear as the two sides mobilized for war: similarities in their political systems, in the methods they used for financing the war and conscripting troops, and in the way they fought.

THE CONFEDERATE GOVERNMENT

The Confederate constitution was largely identical to the Constitution of the United States, but with several significant exceptions: it explicitly acknowledged the sovereignty of the individual states (although not the right of secession), and it specifically sanctioned slavery and made its abolition (even by one of the states) practically impossible.

The constitutional convention at Montgomery named a provisional president and vice president: Jefferson Davis of Mississippi and Alexander H. Stephens of Georgia, who were later chosen by the general electorate, without opposition, for six-year terms. Davis had been a moderate secessionist before the war; Stephens had argued against secession. The Confederate government, like the Union government, was dominated throughout the war by moderate leaders. Also like the Union's, it was dominated less by the old aristocracy of the East than by the newer aristocrats of the West, of whom Davis was the most prominent example.

Davis was, in the end, an unsuccessful president. He was a reasonably able administrator and the dominating figure in his government, encountering little interference from the generally tame members of his unstable cabinet and serving as his own secretary of war. But he rarely provided genuinely national leadership. One shrewd Confederate official wrote: "All the revolutionary vigor is with the enemy. . . . With us timidity-hair splitting."

DAVIS'S LEADERSHIP

There were no formal political parties in the Confederacy, but its congressional and popular politics were rife with dissension nevertheless. Some white Southerners (and of course most African Americans who were aware of the course of events) opposed secession and war. Many white people in poorer "backcountry" and "upcountry" regions, where slavery was limited, refused to recognize the new Confederate government or to serve in the Southern army; some worked or even fought for the Union. Most white Southerners supported the war; but as in the North, many were openly critical of the government and the military, particularly as the tide of battle turned against the South and the Confederate economy decayed.

SOUTHERN DIVISIONS

MONEY AND MANPOWER

Financing the Confederate war effort was a monumental and ultimately impossible task. It involved creating a national revenue system in a society unaccustomed to significant tax burdens. It depended on a small and unstable banking system that had little capital to lend. Because most wealth in the South was invested in slaves and land, liquid assets were scarce; and the Confederacy's only gold—seized from U.S. mints located in the South—was worth only about $1 million.

The Confederate congress tried at first not to tax the people directly but to requisition funds from the individual states. Most of the states, however, were also unwilling to tax their

FUNDING PROBLEMS

citizens and paid their shares, when they paid them at all, with bonds or notes of dubious worth. In 1863, the congress enacted an income tax—which planters could pay "in kind" (as a percentage of their produce). But taxation never provided the Confederacy with much revenue; it produced only about 1 percent of the government's total income. Borrowing was not much more successful. The Confederate government issued bonds in such vast amounts that the public lost faith in them and stopped buying them. Efforts to borrow money in Europe using cotton as collateral fared no better.

As a result, the Confederacy had to pay for the war through the least stable, most destructive form of financing: paper currency, which it began issuing in 1861. By 1864, the Confederacy had issued the staggering total of $1.5 billion in paper money, more than twice what the Union had produced. And unlike

CONFEDERATE VOLUNTEERS Young Southern soldiers posed for this photograph in 1861, shortly before the First Battle of Bull Run. The Civil War was the first major military conflict in the age of photography, and it launched the careers of many of America's early photographers. (Cook Collection, © Valentine Richmond History Center)

the Union, the Confederacy did not establish a uniform currency system; the national government, states, cities, and private banks all issued their own notes, producing widespread chaos and confusion. The result was a disastrous inflation, far worse than anything the North experienced. Prices in the North rose 80 percent in the course of the war; in the South they rose 9,000 percent, with devastating effects on the South's morale.

Like the United States, the Confederacy first raised a military by calling for volunteers. And as in the North, by the end of 1861 voluntary enlistments were declining. In April 1862, there-

RAISING THE CONFEDERATE ARMY

fore, the congress enacted a Conscription Act, which subjected all white males between the ages of eighteen and thirty-five to military service for three years. As in the North, a draftee could avoid service if he furnished a substitute. But since the price of substitutes was high, the provision aroused such opposition from poorer whites that it was repealed in 1863. Even more controversial was the exemption from the draft of one white man on each plantation with twenty or more slaves, a provision that caused smaller farmers to make the same complaint some Northerners made: "It's a rich man's war but a poor man's fight." Many more white Southerners were exempted from military service than were Northerners.

Even so, conscription worked for a time. At the end of 1862, about 500,000 men were in the Confederate military. (A total of approximately 900,000 served in the course of the entire war.) That number did not include the many slave men and slave women recruited by the military to perform such services as cooking, laundry, and manual labor, hence freeing additional white manpower for fighting. After 1862, however, conscription began producing fewer men—in part because the Union had by then begun to seize large areas of the Confederacy and thus had cut off much of the population from conscription or recruitment.

Early in 1864, the government faced a critical manpower shortage. In a desperate move, the Confederate congress began trying to draft men as young as seven-

MANPOWER SHORTAGE

teen and as old as fifty. But in a nation suffering from intense war weariness, where many had concluded that defeat was inevitable, nothing could attract or retain an adequate army any longer. In 1864–1865 there were 100,000 desertions. In a frantic final attempt to raise men, the Confederate congress authorized the conscription of 300,000 slaves, but the war ended before the government could attempt this incongruous experiment.

STATES' RIGHTS VERSUS CENTRALIZATION

The greatest sources of division in the South, however, were differences of opinion over the doctrine of states' rights. States' rights had become such a cult among many white Southerners that they resisted all efforts to exert national authority, even those necessary to win the war. They restricted Davis's ability to impose martial law and suspend habeas corpus. They obstructed conscription. Recalcitrant governors such as Joseph Brown of Georgia and Zebulon M. Vance of North Carolina tried at times to keep their own troops apart from the Confederate forces and insisted on hoarding surplus supplies for their own states' militias.

Even so, the Confederate government did make substantial strides in centralizing power in the South. By the end of the war, the Confederate bureaucracy was larger than its counterpart in Washington. The central government experimented, successfully for a time, with a "food draft"–which permitted soldiers to feed themselves by seizing crops from farms in their path. The government impressed slaves, often over the objections of their owners, to work as laborers on military projects. The Confederacy seized control of the railroads and shipping; it imposed regulations on industry; it limited corporate profits. States' rights sentiment was a significant handicap, but the South nevertheless took important steps in the direction of centralization–becoming in the process increasingly like the region whose institutions it was fighting to escape.

CENTRALIZATION

ECONOMIC AND SOCIAL EFFECTS OF THE WAR

The war had a devastating effect on the economy of the South. It cut off Southern planters and producers from the markets in the North on which they had depended; it made the sale of cotton overseas much more difficult; it robbed farms and industries that did not have large slave populations of a male workforce, leaving some of them unable to function effectively. While in the North production of all goods, agricultural and industrial, increased somewhat during the war, in the South production declined by more than a third.

Most of all, perhaps, the fighting itself wreaked havoc on the Southern economy. Almost all the major battles of the war occurred within the Confederacy; both armies spent most of their time on Southern soil. As a result of the savage fighting, the South's already inadequate railroad system was nearly destroyed; much of its most valuable farmland and many of its most successful plantations were ruined by Union troops (especially in the last year of the war).

Once the Northern naval blockade became effective in 1862, the South experienced massive shortages of almost everything. The region was overwhelmingly agricultural, but since it had concentrated so single-mindedly on producing cotton and other export crops, it did not grow enough food to meet its own needs. And despite the efforts of women and slaves to keep farms functioning, the departure of white male workers seriously diminished the region's ability to keep up

ECONOMIC WOES

what food production there had been. Large numbers of doctors were conscripted to serve the needs of the military, leaving many communities without any medical care. Blacksmiths, carpenters, and other craftsmen were similarly in short supply.

As the war continued, the shortages, the inflation, and the suffering created increasing instability in Southern society. There were major food riots, some led by women, in Georgia, North Carolina, and Alabama in 1863, as well as a large demonstration in Richmond that quickly turned violent. Resistance to conscription, food impressment, and taxation increased throughout the Confederacy, as did hoarding and black-market commerce.

Despite the economic woes of the South, the war transformed Confederate society in many of the same ways that it was changing the society of the Union. The changes were particularly significant for Southern women. Because so many men left the farms and plantations to fight, the task of keeping families together and maintaining agricultural production fell increasingly to women. Slaveowners' wives often became responsible for managing large slave workforces; the wives of modest farmers learned to plow fields and harvest crops. Substantial numbers of females worked as schoolteachers or in government agencies in Richmond. Even larger numbers chose nursing, both in hospitals and in temporary facilities set up to care for wounded soldiers.

NEW ROLES FOR WOMEN

The long-range results of the war for Southern women are more difficult to measure but equally profound. The experience of the 1860s forced many women to question the prevailing Southern assumption that females were unsuited for certain activities, that they were not fit to participate actively in the public sphere. A more concrete legacy was the decimation of the male population and the creation of a major gender imbalance in the region. After the war, there were many thousands more women in the South than there were men. In Georgia, for example, women outnumbered men by 36,000 in 1870; in North Carolina by 25,000. The result, of course, was a large number of unmarried or widowed women who, both during and after the war, had to find employment–thus, by necessity rather than choice, expanding the number of acceptable roles for women in Southern society.

Even before emancipation, the war had far-reaching effects on the lives of slaves. Confederate leaders, who were more terrified of slave revolts during the war than they had been in peacetime, enforced slave codes and other regulations with particular severity. Even so, many slaves–especially those near the front–found ways to escape their masters and cross behind Union lines in search of freedom. Those who had no realistic avenue for escape seemed, to their owners at least, to be particularly resistant to authority during the war. That was in part because on many plantations, the masters and overseers for whom they were accustomed to working were away at war; they found it easier to resist the authority of the women and boys left behind to manage the farms.

ATLANTA AFTER THE BURNING General Sherman captured Atlanta on September 2, 1864, evacuated most of the population, and set fire to the city. This photograph shows the extent of the devastation. The destruction of Atlanta was the beginning of Sherman's famous "March to the Sea." It also signaled the beginning of a new kind of warfare, waged not just against opposing armies but also against the economies and even the populations of the enemy. (© Corbis)

STRATEGY AND DIPLOMACY

Militarily, the initiative in the Civil War lay mainly with the North, since it needed to destroy the Confederacy, while the South needed only to avoid defeat. Diplomatically, however, the initiative lay with the South. It needed to enlist the recognition and support of foreign governments; the Union wanted to preserve the status quo prior to the war.

THE COMMANDERS

The most important Union military commander was Abraham Lincoln, whose previous military experience consisted only

LINCOLN'S LEADERSHIP of brief service in his state militia during the Black Hawk War. Lincoln was a successful commander in chief because he realized that numbers and resources were on his side, and because he took advantage of the North's material advantages. He realized, too, that the proper objective of his armies was the destruction of the Confederate armies, not the occupation of Southern territory. It was important that Lincoln had a good grasp of strategy, because many of his generals did not. The problem of finding adequate commanders for the troops in the field plagued him throughout the first three years of the war.

From 1861 to 1864, Lincoln tried time and again to find a chief of staff capable of orchestrating the Union war effort. He turned first to General Winfield Scott, the aging hero of the Mexican War. But Scott was unprepared for the magnitude of the new conflict and retired on November 1, 1861. Lincoln replaced him with the young George B. McClellan, commander of the Union armies in the East, the Army of the Potomac; but the proud, arrogant McClellan had a wholly inadequate grasp of strategy and returned to the field in March 1862. For most of the rest of the year, Lincoln had no chief of staff. And when he finally appointed General Henry W. Halleck to the post, he found him an ineffectual strategist who left all substantive decision making to the president. Not until March 1864 did Lincoln finally find a general he trusted to command the war effort: Ulysses S. Grant, who shared Lincoln's belief in making enemy armies and resources, not enemy territory, the target of military efforts. Lincoln gave Grant a relatively free hand, but the general always submitted at least the broad outlines of his plans to the president for advance approval.

Lincoln's (and later Grant's) handling of the war effort faced constant scrutiny from the Committee on the Conduct of the War, a joint investigative committee of the two houses of Congress and the most powerful voice the legislative branch has ever had in formulating war policies. Established in December 1861 and chaired by Senator Benjamin F. Wade of Ohio, it complained constantly of the insufficient ruthlessness of Northern generals, which Radicals on the committee attributed (largely inaccurately) to a secret sympathy among the officers for slavery. The committee's efforts often seriously interfered with the conduct of the war.

Southern command arrangements centered on President Davis, who, unlike Lincoln, was a trained professional soldier. Nevertheless, he failed to create an effective command system.

ULYSSES S. GRANT One observer said of Grant (seen here posing for a photograph during the Wilderness campaign of 1864): "He habitually wears an expression as if he had determined to drive his head through a brick wall, and was about to do it." It was an apt metaphor for Grant's military philosophy, which relied on constant, unrelenting assault. One result was that Grant was willing to fight when other Northern generals held back. Another was that Grant presided over some of the worst carnage of the Civil War. (The Library of Congress)

ROBERT E. LEE Lee, who was a moderate by the standards of Southern politics in the 1850s, opposed secession and was ambivalent about slavery. But he could not bring himself to break with his region, and he left the U.S. Army to lead Confederate forces beginning in 1861. He was (and remains) the most revered of all the white Southern leaders of the Civil War. For decades after his surrender at Appomattox, Lee was a symbol to white Southerners of the "Lost Cause." (© Corbis)

Early in 1862, Davis named General Robert E. Lee as his principal military adviser. But in fact, Davis had no intention of sharing

ROBERT E. LEE control of strategy with anyone. After a few months, Lee left Richmond to command forces in the field, and for the next two years Davis planned strategy alone. In February 1864, he named General Braxton Bragg as a military adviser; but Bragg never provided much more than technical advice. Not until February 1865 did the Confederate Congress create the formal position of general in chief. Davis named Lee to the post but made clear that he expected to continue to make all basic decisions. In any case, the war ended before this last command structure had time to take shape.

At lower levels of command, men of markedly similar backgrounds controlled the war in both the North and the South. Many of the professional officers on both sides were graduates of the U.S. Military Academy at West Point and the U.S. Naval Academy at Annapolis, and thus had been trained in similar ways. Many were closely acquainted, even friendly, with their counterparts on the other side. And all were imbued with the classic, eighteenth-century models of warfare that the service

academies still taught. The most successful officers were those who, like Grant and William Tecumseh Sherman, were able to see beyond their academic training and envision a new kind of warfare in which destruction of resources was as important as battlefield tactics.

Amateur officers played an important role in both armies as commanders of volunteer regiments. In both North and South, such men were usually economic or social leaders in their communities who appointed themselves officers and rounded up troops to lead. This system was responsible for recruiting considerable numbers of men into the armies of the two nations. Only occasionally, however, did it produce officers of real ability.

THE ROLE OF SEA POWER

The Union had an overwhelming advantage in naval power, and it gave its navy two important roles in the war. One was enforcing a blockade of the Southern coast, which the president ordered on April 19, 1861. The other was assisting the Union armies in field operations.

The blockade of the South was never fully effective, but it had a major impact on the Confederacy nevertheless. The U.S.

THE UNION BLOCKADE Navy could generally keep oceangoing ships out of Confederate ports. For a time, small blockade runners continued to slip through. But gradually, federal forces tightened the blockade by seizing the ports themselves. The last important port in Confederate hands–Wilmington, North Carolina–fell to the Union early in 1865.

The Confederates made bold attempts to break the blockade with new weapons. Foremost among them was an iron-clad warship, constructed by plating with iron a former U.S. frigate, the *Merrimac*, which the Yankees had scuttled in

IRONCLADS Norfolk harbor when Virginia seceded. On March 8, 1862, the refitted *Merrimac*, renamed the *Virginia*, left Norfolk to attack a blockading squadron of wooden ships at nearby Hampton Roads. It destroyed two of the ships and scattered the rest. But the Union government had already built ironclads of its own. And one of them, the *Monitor*, arrived off the coast of Virginia only a few hours after the *Virginia*'s dramatic foray. The next day, it met the *Virginia* in the first battle between ironclad ships. Neither vessel was able to sink the other, but the *Monitor* put an end to the *Virginia*'s raids and preserved the blockade. The Confederacy experimented as well with other naval innovations, such as small torpedo boats and hand-powered submarines. But despite occasional small successes with these new weapons, the South never managed to overcome the Union's naval advantages.

As a supporter of land operations, the Union navy was particularly important in the western theater of war–the vast region between the Appalachian Mountains and the Mississippi River–where the major rivers were navigable by large vessels. The navy transported supplies and troops and joined in attacking Confederate strong points. With no significant navy of its own, the South could defend only with fixed land fortifications, which proved no match for the mobile land-and-water forces of the Union.

EUROPE AND THE DISUNITED STATES

Judah P. Benjamin, the Confederate secretary of state for most of the war, was a clever and intelligent man, but he confined most of his energy to routine administrative tasks. William Seward, his counterpart in Washington, gradually became one of the great American secretaries of state. He had invaluable assistance from Charles Francis Adams, the American minister to London, who had inherited the considerable diplomatic talents of his father, John Quincy Adams, and his grandfather, John Adams.

At the beginning of the war, the ruling classes of England and France, the two nations whose support was most crucial to both sides, were generally sympathetic to the Confederacy, for several reasons. The two nations imported much Southern cotton for their textile industries; they were eager to weaken the United States, an increasingly powerful commercial rival;

and some British and French citizens admired the supposedly aristocratic social order of the South, which they believed resembled the hierarchical structures of their own societies. But France was unwilling to take sides in the conflict unless England did so first. And in England, the government was reluctant to act because there was powerful popular support for the Union. Important English liberals such as John Bright and Richard Cobden considered the war a struggle between free and slave labor and urged their followers to support the Union cause. The politically conscious but largely unenfranchised workers in Britain expressed their sympathy for the North frequently and unmistakably–in mass meetings, in resolutions, and through their champions in Parliament. After Lincoln issued the Emancipation Proclamation, these groups worked particularly avidly for the Union.

Southern leaders hoped to counter the strength of the British antislavery forces by arguing that access to Southern

KING COTTON DIPLOMACY cotton was vital to the English and French textile industries. But this "King Cotton diplomacy," on which the Confederacy had staked so many of its hopes, failed. English manufacturers had a surplus of both raw cotton and finished goods on hand in 1861 and could withstand a temporary loss of access to American cotton. Later, as the supply of American cotton began to diminish, both England and France managed to keep some of their mills open by importing cotton from Egypt, India, and other sources. Equally important, English workers, the people most seriously threatened by the cotton shortage, did not clamor to have the blockade broken. Even most of the 500,000 English textile workers thrown out of jobs as a result of mill closings continued to support the North. In the end, therefore, no European nation offered diplomatic recognition to the Confederacy or intervened in the war. No nation wanted to antagonize the United States unless the Confederacy seemed likely to win, and the South never came close enough to victory to convince its potential allies to support it.

Even so, there was considerable tension, and on occasion near hostilities, between the United States and Britain, beginning in the first days of the war. Great Britain declared itself neutral as soon as the fighting began, followed by France and other nations. The Union government was furious: neutrality implied that the two sides to the conflict had equal stature. Leaders in Washington were insisting that the conflict was simply a domestic insurrection, not a war between two legitimate governments.

A more serious crisis, the so-called Trent affair, began in late 1861. Two Confederate diplomats, James M. Mason and John

TRENT AFFAIR Slidell, had slipped through the then-ineffective Union blockade to Havana, Cuba, where they boarded an English steamer, the *Trent*, for England. Waiting in Cuban waters was the American frigate *San Jacinto*, commanded by the impetuous Charles Wilkes. Acting without authorization, Wilkes stopped the British vessel, arrested the diplomats, and carried them in triumph to Boston. The British government demanded the release of the prisoners, reparations, and an apology. Lincoln and Seward, aware that Wilkes had violated

BASEBALL AND THE CIVIL WAR

LONG before the great urban stadiums, long before the lights and the cameras and the multimillion-dollar salaries, long before the Little Leagues and the high school and college teams, baseball was the most popular game in America. And during the Civil War, it was a treasured pastime for soldiers, and for thousands of men (and some women) behind the lines, in both North and South.

The legend that baseball was invented by Abner Doubleday, who probably never even saw the game, came from Albert G. Spalding, a patriotic sporting-goods manufacturer eager to prove that the game had purely American origins and to dispel the notion that it came from England. In fact, baseball was derived from a variety of earlier games, especially the English pastimes of cricket and rounders. American baseball took its own distinctive form beginning in the 1840s, when Alexander Cartwright, a shipping clerk, formed the New York Knickerbockers, laid out a diamond-shaped field with four bases, and declared that batters with three strikes were out and that teams with three outs were retired.

Cartwright moved west in search of gold in 1849, ultimately grew rich, and settled finally in Hawaii (where he brought the game to Americans in the Pacific). But the game did not languish in his absence. Henry Chadwick, an English-born journalist, spent much of the 1850s popularizing the game (and regularizing its rules). By 1860, baseball was being played by college students and Irish workers, by urban elites and provincial farmers, by people of all classes and ethnic groups from New England to Louisiana. It was also attracting the attention of women. Students at Vassar College formed "ladies" teams in the 1860s, and in Philadelphia, free black men formed the first of what would become a great network of African American baseball teams, the Pythians. From the beginning, they were barred from playing against most white teams.

When young men marched off to war in 1861, some took their bats and balls with them. Almost from the start of the fighting, soldiers in both armies took advantage of idle moments to lay out baseball diamonds and organize games. There were games in prison camps; games on the White House lawn (where Union soldiers were sometimes billeted); and games on battlefields that were sometimes interrupted by gunfire and cannonfire. "It is astonishing how indifferent a person can become to danger," a soldier wrote home to Ohio in 1862. "The report of musketry is heard but a very little distance from us, . . . yet over there on the other side of the road is most of our company, playing Bat Ball." After a skirmish in Texas, another Union soldier lamented that, in addition to casualties, his company had lost "the only baseball in Alexandria, Texas." Far from discouraging baseball, military commanders—and the U.S. Sanitary Commission, the Union army's medical arm—actively encouraged the game during the war. It would, they believed, help keep up the soldiers' morale.

Away from the battlefield, baseball continued to flourish. In New York City, games between local teams drew crowds of ten or twenty thousand. The National Association of Baseball Players (founded in 1859) had recruited ninety-one clubs in ten northern states by

---

maritime law and unwilling to risk war with England, stalled the negotiations until American public opinion had cooled off, then released the diplomats with an indirect apology. A second diplomatic crisis lasted for years. Unable to construct large vessels itself, the Confederacy bought six ships, known as commerce destroyers, from British shipyards. The best known of them were the *Alabama*, the *Florida*, and the *Shenandoah*. The United States protested that this sale of military equipment to a belligerent violated the laws of neutrality, and the protests became the basis, after the war, of damage claims by the United States against Great Britain.

THE AMERICAN WEST AND THE WAR

Except for Texas, which joined the Confederacy, all the western states and territories remained officially loyal to the Union—but not without controversy and conflict. Southerners and Southern sympathizers were active throughout the West. And, in some places, there was actual combat between Unionists and secessionists.

There was particularly vicious fighting in Kansas and Missouri, the scene of so much bitterness before the war. The same pro-slavery and free-state forces who had fought one another in the 1850s continued to do so, with even more deadly results. William C. Quantrill, an Ohio native who had spent much of his youth in the West, became a captain in the **GUERRILLA WAR IN THE WEST** Confederate army after he organized a band of guerrilla fighters (mostly teenage boys) with which he terrorized areas around the Kansas-Missouri border. Quantrill and his band were an exceptionally murderous group, notorious for killing almost everyone in their path. Their most infamous act was a siege of Lawrence, Kansas, during which they slaughtered 150 civilians, adults and children alike. Union troops killed Quantrill shortly after the end of the war. Union sympathizers in Kansas, organized in bands known as the Jayhawkers, were only marginally less savage, as they moved across western Missouri exacting reprisals for the actions of Quantrill and other Confederate guerrillas. One Jayhawk unit was jointly commanded by the son of John Brown and the brother of Susan B. Anthony, men who brought the fervor of abolitionists to their work. Even without a major battle, the border areas of Kansas and Missouri were among the bloodiest and most terrorized places in the United States during the Civil War.

Not long after the war began, Confederate agents tried to negotiate alliances with the Five Civilized Tribes living in Indian Territory (later Oklahoma), in hopes of recruiting their support against Union forces in the West. The Indians themselves were divided. Some wanted to support the South, both because they resented the way the U.S. government had treated them and

1865; a North Western Association of Baseball Players, organized in Chicago in 1865, indicated that the game was becoming well established in the West as well. In Brooklyn, William Cammeyer drained a skating pond on his property, built a board fence around it, and created the first enclosed baseball field in America—the Union grounds. He charged 10 cents admission. The professionalization of the game was under way.

Despite the commercialization and spectacle that became associated with baseball in the years after the Civil War, the game remained for many Americans what it was to millions of young men fighting in the most savage war in the nation's history—an American passion that at times, even if briefly, erased the barriers dividing groups from one another. "Officers and men forget, for a time, the differences in rank," a Massachusetts private wrote in 1863, "and indulge in the invigorating sport with a schoolboy's ardor." ●

BATS BEHIND BARS Baseball was a popular recreation for troops on both sides of the Civil War. This image depicts Union prisoners playing the game while incarcerated in a prison camp at Salisbury, North Carolina, in about 1863. (© Archive Photos/Getty Images)

UNDERSTAND, ANALYZE, AND EVALUATE

1. How could a competitive game of baseball erase "the barriers dividing groups from one another"?
2. The United States today is engaged in wars in Iraq and Afghanistan. Are the cultural pastimes or recreations available to the men and women fighting these wars to help relieve the stress of war and bridge the differences between the opposing sides as successful in these aims as was baseball during the Civil War? Why or why not?
3. Baseball during the Civil War crossed the lines of cultural differences between the North and the South. Does baseball today—professional or amateur—continue to cross lines of cultural differences?

because some tribal leaders were themselves slaveholders. But other Indians supported the North out of a general hostility to slavery (in both the South and their own nation).

One result of these divisions was a civil war within Indian Territory. Another was that Indian regiments fought for both the Union and the Confederacy during the war. But the tribes themselves never formally allied themselves with either side.

THE COURSE OF BATTLE

In the absence of direct intervention by the European powers, the two contestants in America were left to resolve the conflict between themselves. They did so in four long years of bloody combat that produced more carnage than any war in American history, before or since. More than 618,000 Americans died in the Civil War, far more than the 115,000 who perished in World War I or the 318,000 who died in World War II—more, indeed, than died in all other American wars combined prior to Vietnam. There were nearly 2,000 deaths for every 100,000 of population during the Civil War. In World War I, the comparable figure was 109 deaths; in World War II, 241 deaths. Massive death, and along with it massive grief, shadowed both North and South during and after the war.

HIGH CASUALTIES

Despite the gruesome cost, the Civil War has become the most romanticized and the most intently studied of all American wars. In part, that is because the conflict produced—in addition to terrible fatalities—a series of military campaigns of classic strategic interest and a series of military leaders who displayed unusual brilliance and daring.

THE TECHNOLOGY OF BATTLE

Much of what happened on the battlefield in the Civil War was a result of new technologies that transformed the nature of combat. The Civil War has often been called the first "modern" war and the first "total" war. The great conflict between the North and the South was unlike any war fought before it, and it suggested what warfare would be like in the future.

The most obvious change in the character of warfare in the 1860s was the nature of the armaments that both sides used in battle. Among the most important was the introduction of repeating weapons. Samuel Colt had patented a repeating pistol (the revolver) in 1835, but more important for military purposes was the repeating rifle, introduced in 1860 by Oliver Winchester. Also important were greatly improved cannons and artillery, a result of advances in iron and steel technology of the previous decades.

REPEATING WEAPONS

THE CONSOLIDATION OF NATIONS WOR-3, 5

THE American Civil War was an event largely rooted in conditions particular to the United States. But it was also a part of a worldwide movement in the nineteenth century to create large, consolidated nations. A commitment to preserving the Union—to consolidating, rather than dismantling, the nation—was one of the principal motives for the North's commitment to fighting a war against the seceding states. Similar efforts at expansion, consolidation, and unification were occurring in many other nations around the same time.

The consolidation of nation-states was, of course, not new to the nineteenth century. The revolutions in America and France in the late eighteenth century—and the subsequent strengthening of the French concept of nationhood under Napoleon in the early nineteenth century—inspired new nationalist enthusiasms in other parts of Europe. Nationalist sentiment also grew among peoples who shared language, culture, ethnicity, and tradition and who came to believe that a consolidated nation was the best vehicle for strengthening their common bonds.

In 1848, a wave of nationalist revolutions erupted in Italy, France, and Austria, challenging the imperial powers that many Europeans believed were subjugating national cultures. Those revolutions failed, but they helped lay the groundwork for the two most important national consolidations of nineteenth-century Europe.

One of these consolidations occurred in Germany, which was divided into numerous small, independent states in the early nineteenth century but where popular sentiment for German unification had been growing for decades. It was spurred in part by new histories of the German *Volk* (people) and by newly constructed images of German traditions, visible in such literature as the Grimms' fairy tales—an effort to record and popularize German folk traditions and make them the basis of a shared sense of a common past. In 1862, King Wilhelm I of Prussia—the leader of one of the most powerful of the scattered German states—appointed an aristocratic landowner, Otto von Bismarck, as his prime minister. Bismarck exploited the growing nationalism throughout the various German states and helped develop a strong popular base for unification. He did so in part by launching Prussian wars against Denmark, Austria, and France—wars Prussia easily won, inspiring pride in German power that extended well beyond Prussia. The Franco-Prussian War of 1870 was particularly important, because Prussia fought it to take possession of the French provinces of Alsace and Lorraine—provinces the Prussians claimed were part of the German "national community" because its people, although legally French citizens, were ethnically and linguistically German. In 1871, capitalizing on the widespread nationalist sentiment the war had created throughout the German-speaking states, Bismarck persuaded the German king to proclaim himself emperor (or *Kaiser*) of a new empire that united all German peoples except those in Austria and Switzerland.

THE UNIFICATION OF ITALY This engraving shows the Battle of Volturno, which was really a series of skirmishes that took place in September and October 1860. The main battle, between Garibaldi's volunteers and the troops of the Kingdom of the Two Sicilies, occurred on October 1. Although the immediate aftermath of the battle left Garibaldi's forces exhausted, they did go on to successfully unify Italy under King Victor Emmanuel II. (Italy © Tarker Archive/The Image Works)

These devastating advances in the effectiveness of arms and artillery changed the way soldiers in the field fought. It was now impossibly deadly to fight battles as they had been fought for centuries, with lines of infantry soldiers standing erect in the field firing volleys at their opponents until one side withdrew. Fighting in that way now produced almost inconceivable slaughter, and soldiers quickly learned that the proper position for combat was staying low to the ground and behind cover. For the first time in the history of organized warfare infantry did not fight in formation, and the battlefield became a more chaotic place. Gradually, the deadliness of the new weapons encouraged armies on both sides to spend a great deal of time building elaborate fortifications and trenches to protect themselves from enemy fire. The sieges of Vicksburg and Petersburg, the defense of Richmond, and many other sieges led to the construction of vast fortifications around

The second great European movement for national unification occurred in Italy, which had long been divided into small kingdoms, city-states, and regions controlled by the Vatican. Beginning in the early nineteenth century, Italian nationalists formed what became known as the "Young Italy" movement, under the leadership of Giuseppe Mazzini. The movement demanded an end to foreign control in Italy and the unification of the Italian people into a single nation. Peoples with common language, culture, and tradition, Mazzini believed, should be free to unite and govern themselves. More important than this growing popular nationalism as a cause of Italian unification were the efforts of powerful and ambitious leaders. The most powerful Italian state in the mid-nineteenth century was the kingdom of the Piedmont and Sardinia, in the northwestern part of the peninsula. Its king, Victor Emmanuel II, appointed his own version of Bismarck—Camillo di Cavour—as prime minister in 1852. Cavour joined forces with nationalists in other areas of Italy to drive the Spanish and the Austrians out of Italian territory. Having first won independence for northern Italy, Cavour joined forces with the southern nationalist leader Giuseppe Garibaldi, who helped win independence in the south and then agreed to a unification of the entire Italian nation under Victor Emmanuel II in 1860.

Other nations in these years were also trying to create, preserve, and strengthen nation-states. Some failed to do so—Russia, for example, despite the reform efforts of several tsars, never managed to create a stable nation-state from among its broad and diverse peoples. But others succeeded—Meiji Japan, for example, instituted a series of reforms in the 1880s and 1890s that created a powerful new Japanese nation-state.

In fighting and winning the Civil War, the nationalists of the Northern parts of the United States not only preserved the unity of their nation. They also became part of a movement toward the consolidation of national cultures and national territories that extended through many areas of the globe. ●

UNDERSTAND, ANALYZE, AND EVALUATE

1. How did the problems facing Bismarck differ from those facing Lincoln?
2. Which man—Mazzini, Cavour, or Garibaldi—in the struggle to achieve the unification of Italy most closely parallels Lincoln and the fight to preserve the Union?
3. Does Mazzini's argument—that peoples with common language, culture, and tradition should be free to unite and govern themselves—apply to the North's attempt to preserve the Union, or does it better fit the South's attempt to secede and form a separate nation?

cities and attacking armies. (They were the predecessors to the great network of trenches that became so central a part of World War I.)

Other weapons technologies were less central to the fighting of the war, but important nevertheless. There was sporadic use of the relatively new technology of hot-air balloons, employed intermittently to provide a view of enemy formations in the field. (During one battle, a Union balloonist took a

telegraph line aloft with him in his balloon and tapped out messages about troop movements to the commanders below.) Ironclad ships such as the *Merrimac* (or *Virginia*) and the *Monitor*, torpedoes, and submarine technology all suggested the dramatic changes that would soon overtake naval warfare, although none played a major role in the Civil War.

Critical to the conduct of the war, however, were two other relatively new technologies: the railroad and the telegraph. The railroad was particularly important in a war in

IMPORTANCE OF THE RAILROAD which millions of soldiers were being mobilized and transferred to the front, and in which a single field army could number as many as 250,000 men. Transporting such enormous numbers of soldiers, and the supplies necessary to sustain them, would have been almost impossible without railroads. But they also limited mobility. Railroad lines and stations are, of course, in fixed positions. Commanders, therefore, were forced to organize their campaigns around the location of the railroads whether the location was optimal or not.

The impact of the telegraph on the war was limited both by the scarcity of qualified telegraph operators and by the difficulty of bringing telegraph wires into the

THE TELEGRAPH fields where battles were being fought. The situation improved somewhat after the new U.S. Military Telegraph Corps, headed by Thomas Scott and Andrew Carnegie, trained and employed over 1,200 operators. Gradually, too, both the Union and Confederate armies learned to string telegraph wires along the routes of their troops so that field commanders were able to stay in close touch with one another during battles. Both the North and the South sent spies behind enemy lines who tried to tap the telegraph lines of their opponents and send important information back about troop movements and formations.

THE OPENING CLASHES, 1861

The Union and the Confederacy fought their first major battle of the war in northern Virginia. A Union army of over 30,000 men under the command of General Irvin McDowell was stationed just outside Washington. About thirty miles away, at the town of Manassas, was a slightly smaller Confederate army under General P. G. T. Beauregard. If the Northern army could destroy the Southern one, Union leaders believed, the war might end at once. In mid-July, McDowell marched his inexperienced troops toward Manassas. Beauregard moved his troops behind Bull Run, a small stream north of Manassas, and called for reinforcements, which reached him the day before the battle. The two armies were now approximately the same size.

On July 21, in the First Battle of Bull Run, or First Battle of Manassas, McDowell almost succeeded in dispersing the Confederate forces. But the Southerners stopped a last strong Union assault and then began a savage counterattack. The

FIRST BATTLE OF BULL RUN Union troops, exhausted after hours of hot, hard fighting, suddenly panicked. They broke ranks and retreated chaotically.

McDowell was unable to reorganize them, and he had to order a retreat to Washington–a disorderly withdrawal complicated by the presence along the route of many civilians who had ridden down from the capital, picnic baskets in hand, to watch the battle from nearby hills. The Confederates, as disorganized by victory as the Union forces were by defeat, and short of supplies and transportation, did not pursue. The battle was a severe blow to Union morale and to President Lincoln's confidence in his officers. It also dispelled the illusion that the war would be a brief one.

Elsewhere in 1861, Union forces were achieving some small but significant victories. In Missouri, rebel forces gathered **WILSON'S CREEK** behind Governor Claiborne Jackson and other state officials who wanted to secede from the Union. Nathaniel Lyon, who commanded a small regular army force in St. Louis, moved his troops into southern Missouri to face the secessionists. On August 10, at the Battle of Wilson's Creek, Lyon was defeated and killed–but not before he had seriously weakened the striking power of the Confederates. Union forces were subsequently able to hold most of the state.

Meanwhile, a Union force under George B. McClellan moved east from Ohio into western Virginia. By the end of 1861, it had "liberated" the anti-secession mountain people of the region. They created their own state government loyal to the Union and were admitted to the Union as West Virginia in 1863. The occupation of western Virginia was of limited military value, since the mountains cut the area off from the rest of Virginia. It was, however, an important symbolic victory for the North.

THE WESTERN THEATER

After the First Battle of Bull Run, military operations in the East settled into a long and frustrating stalemate. The first decisive operations in 1862 occurred in the West. Union forces were trying to seize control of the southern Mississippi River, which would divide the Confederacy and give the North easy transportation into the heart of the South. Northern soldiers advanced on the river from both the north and south, moving downriver from Kentucky and upriver from the Gulf of Mexico toward New Orleans.

In April, a Union squadron of ironclads and wooden vessels commanded by David G. Farragut gathered in the Gulf of Mexico, then smashed past weak Confederate forts near the **NEW ORLEANS CAPTURED** mouth of the Mississippi, and from there sailed up to New Orleans, which was defenseless because the Confederate high command had expected the attack to come from the north. The city surrendered on April 25–the first major Union victory and an important turning point in the war. From then on, the mouth of the Mississippi was closed to Confederate trade; and the South's largest city and most important banking center was in Union hands.

Farther north in the western theater, Confederate troops under the command of Albert Sidney Johnston were stretched out in a long defensive line centered at two forts in Tennessee, Fort Henry and Fort Donelson, on the Tennessee and Cumberland Rivers, respectively. But the forts were well behind the main Southern flanks, a fatal weakness that Union commanders recognized and exploited. Early in 1862, Ulysses S. Grant attacked Fort Henry, whose defenders, awed by the ironclad riverboats accompanying the Union army, surrendered with almost no resistance on February 6. Grant then moved both his naval and ground forces to Fort Donelson, where the Confederates put up a stronger fight but finally, on February 16, had to surrender. By cracking the Confederate center, Grant had gained control of river communications and forced Confederate forces out of Kentucky and half of Tennessee.

With about 40,000 men, Grant now advanced south along the Tennessee River to seize control of railroad lines vital to the Confederacy. From Pittsburg Landing, he marched to **SHILOH** nearby Shiloh, Tennessee, where a force almost equal to his own, commanded by Albert Sidney Johnston and P. G. T. Beauregard, caught him by surprise. The result was the Battle of Shiloh, April 6-7. In the first day's fighting (during which Johnston was killed), the Southerners drove Grant back to the river. But the next day, reinforced by 25,000 fresh troops, Grant recovered the lost ground and forced Beauregard to withdraw. After the narrow Union victory at Shiloh, Northern forces occupied Corinth, Mississippi, the hub of several important railroads, and established control of the Mississippi River as far south as Memphis.

Braxton Bragg, who succeeded Johnston as commander of the Confederate army in the West, gathered his forces at Chattanooga, in eastern Tennessee, which the Confederacy still controlled. He hoped to win back the rest of the state and then move north into Kentucky. But first he had to face a Union army (commanded by Don Carlos Buell and later William S. Rosecrans), whose assignment was to capture Chattanooga. The two armies maneuvered for advantage inconclusively in northern Tennessee and southern Kentucky for several months until they finally met, December 31-January 2, in the Battle of Murfreesboro, or Stone's River. Bragg was forced to withdraw to the south, his campaign a failure. By the end of 1862, Union forces had made considerable progress in the West. But the major conflict remained in the East, where they were having much less success.

THE VIRGINIA FRONT, 1862

Union operations were being directed in 1862 by George B. McClellan, commander of the Army of the Potomac and the most controversial general of the war. McClellan was a superb trainer of men, but he often appeared reluctant to commit his troops to battle. Opportunities for important engagements came and went, and McClellan seemed never **GEORGE McCLELLAN** to take advantage of them–claiming always that his preparations were not yet complete or that the moment was not right.

THE WAR IN THE WEST, 1861–1863 While the Union armies in Virginia were meeting with repeated frustrations, the Union armies in the West were scoring notable successes in the first two years of the war. This map shows a series of Union drives in the western Confederacy. Admiral David Farragut's ironclads led to the capture of New Orleans—a critical Confederate port—in April 1862, while forces farther north under the command of Ulysses S. Grant drove the Confederate army out of Kentucky and western Tennessee. These battles culminated in the Union victory at Shiloh, which led to Union control of the upper Mississippi River.

• *Why was control of the Mississippi so important to both sides?*

During the winter of 1861-1862, McClellan concentrated on training his army of 150,000 men near Washington. Finally, he designed a spring campaign whose purpose was to capture the Confederate capital at Richmond. But instead of heading overland directly toward Richmond, McClellan chose a complicated, roundabout route that he thought would circumvent the Confederate defenses. The navy would carry his troops down the Potomac to a peninsula east of Richmond, between the York and James Rivers. The army would approach the city from there. It became known as the Peninsular campaign.

McClellan began the campaign with only part of his army. Approximately 100,000 men accompanied him down the Potomac. Another 30,000–under General Irvin McDowell–remained behind to protect Washington. McClellan insisted that Washington was safe as long as he was threatening Richmond, and finally persuaded Lincoln to promise to send him the additional men. But before the president could do so, a Confederate army under Thomas J. ("Stonewall") Jackson changed his plans. Jackson staged a rapid march north through the Shenandoah Valley, as if he were planning to cross the Potomac and attack Washington. Alarmed, Lincoln dispatched

THE VIRGINIA THEATER, 1861–1863 Much of the fighting during the first two years of the Civil War took place in what became known as the Virginia theater—although the campaigns in this region eventually extended north into Maryland and Pennsylvania. The Union hoped for a quick victory over the newly created Confederate army. But as these maps show, the Southern forces consistently thwarted such hopes. The map at top left shows the battles of 1861 and the first half of 1862, almost all of them won by the Confederates. The map at lower left shows the last months of 1862, during which the Southerners again defeated the Union in most of their engagements—although Northern forces drove the Confederates back from Maryland in September. The map on the right shows the troop movements that led to the climactic battle of Gettysburg in 1863.

• *Why were the Union forces unable to profit more from their material advantages during these first years of the war?*

McDowell's corps to head off Jackson. In the brilliant Valley campaign of May 4–June 9, 1862, Jackson defeated two separate Union forces and slipped away before McDowell could catch him.

Meanwhile, Confederate troops under Joseph E. Johnston were attacking McClellan's advancing army outside Richmond. But in the two-day Battle of Fair Oaks, or Seven Pines (May 31–June 1), they could not repel the Union forces. Johnston, badly wounded, was replaced by Robert E. Lee, who then recalled Stonewall Jackson from the Shenandoah Valley. With a combined force of 85,000 to face McClellan's 100,000, Lee launched a new offensive, known as the Battle of the Seven Days (June 25–July 1). Lee wanted to cut McClellan off from his base on the York River and then destroy the isolated Union army. But McClellan fought his way across the peninsula and set up a new base on the James. There, with naval support, the Army of the Potomac was safe.

SEVEN PINES

McClellan was now only twenty-five miles from Richmond, with a secure line of water communications, and thus in a good position to renew the campaign. Time and again, however, he found reasons for delay. Instead of replacing McClellan with a more aggressive commander, Lincoln finally ordered the army to move to northern Virginia and join a smaller force under John Pope. The president hoped to begin a new offensive against Richmond on the direct overland route that he himself had always preferred.

As the Army of the Potomac left the peninsula by water, Lee moved north with the Army of Northern Virginia to strike Pope before McClellan could join him. Pope was as rash as McClellan was cautious, and he attacked the approaching Confederates without waiting for the arrival of all of McClellan's troops. In the ensuing Second Battle of Bull Run, or Second Battle of Manassas (August 29–30), Lee threw back the assault and routed Pope's army, which fled to Washington. With hopes for an overland campaign against Richmond now in disarray, Lincoln removed Pope from command and put McClellan in charge of all the Union forces in the region.

Lee soon went on the offensive again, heading north through western Maryland, and McClellan moved out to meet him. McClellan had the good luck to get a copy of Lee's orders, which revealed that a part of the Confederate army, under Stonewall Jackson, had separated from the rest to attack Harpers Ferry. But instead of attacking quickly before the Confederates could recombine, McClellan delayed and gave Lee time to pull most of his forces together behind Antietam Creek, near the town of Sharpsburg. There, on September 17, in the bloodiest single-day engagement of the war, McClellan's 87,000-man army repeatedly attacked Lee's force of 50,000, with enormous casualties on both sides. Six thousand soldiers died, and 17,000 sustained injuries. Late in the day, just as the Confederate line seemed ready to break, the last of Jackson's troops arrived from Harpers Ferry to reinforce it. McClellan might have

ANTIETAM

broken through with one more assault. Instead, he allowed Lee to retreat into Virginia. Technically, Antietam was a Union victory, but in reality, it was an opportunity squandered. In November, Lincoln finally removed McClellan from command for good.

McClellan's replacement, Ambrose E. Burnside, was a short-lived mediocrity. He tried to move toward Richmond by crossing the Rappahannock at Fredericksburg, the strongest defensive point on the river. There, on December 13, he launched a series of attacks against Lee, all of them bloody, all of them hopeless. After losing a large part of his army, Burnside withdrew to the north bank of the Rappahannock. He was relieved at his own request.

THE PROGRESS OF THE WAR

Why did the Union—with its much larger population and its much better transportation and technology than the Confederacy—make so little progress in the first two years of the war? Had there been a decisive and dramatic victory by either side early in the war—for example, a major victory by the Union at the First Battle of Bull Run—the conflict might have ended quickly by destroying the Confederacy's morale. But no such decisive victory occurred in the first two years of the war.

Many Northerners blamed the military stalemate on timid or incompetent Union generals, and there was some truth to that view. But the more important reason for the drawn-out conflict was that it was not a traditional war of tactics and military strategy. It was, even if the leaders of both sides were not yet fully aware of it, a war of attrition. Winning or losing battles here and there would not determine the outcome of the war. What would bring the war to a conclusion was the steady destruction of the resources that were necessary for victory. More than two bloody years of fighting was still to

THE FIRST CONNECTICUT ARTILLERY Mathew Brady's photograph shows the First Connecticut Artillery at Fort Richardson, Virginia. (The Library of Congress (LC-B8184-10601))

come. But those last years were a testimony to the slow, steady deterioration of the Confederacy's ability to maintain the war and to the consistent growth of the resources that allowed the Union armies to grow steadily stronger.

With the federal blockade growing tighter and tighter, the Confederacy found it difficult to secure food. On April 2, 1863, a Confederate soldier received a letter from Richmond from a friend. "Something very sad has just happened in Richmond," she said, "something that makes me ashamed of all my . . . hats, bonnets, gowns, stationery, books, magazines, dainty food." She saw hundreds of young women and men looking for food. "The crowd now rapidly increased and numbered, I am sure, more than a thousand women and children. It grew and grew until it reached the dignity of a mob–a bread riot. . . . While I write women and children are still standing in the streets, demanding food."

1863: Year of Decision

At the beginning of 1863, General Joseph Hooker was in command of the still formidable Army of the Potomac, whose 120,000 troops remained north of the Rappahannock, opposite Fredericksburg. But despite his reputation as a fighter (his popular nickname was "Fighting Joe"), Hooker showed little resolve as he launched his own campaign in the spring. Taking part of his army, Hooker crossed the river above Fredericksburg and moved toward the town and Lee's army. But at the last minute, he apparently lost his nerve and drew back to a defensive position in a desolate area of brush and scrub trees known as "the Wilderness." Lee had only half as many men as

BATTLE OF CHANCELLORSVILLE

Hooker did, but he boldly divided his forces for a dual assault on the Union army. In the Battle of Chancellorsville, May 1-5, Stonewall Jackson attacked the Union right and Lee himself charged the front. Hooker barely managed to escape with his army. Lee had defeated the Union objectives, but he had not destroyed the Union army. And his ablest officer, Jackson, was wounded during the battle and subsequently died of pneumonia.

While the Union forces were suffering repeated frustrations in the East, they were continuing to achieve important

VICKSBURG

victories in the West. In the spring of 1863, Ulysses S. Grant was driving at Vicksburg, Mississippi, one of the Confederacy's two remaining strongholds on the southern Mississippi River. Vicksburg was well protected, surrounded by rough country on the north and low, marshy ground on the west, and with good artillery coverage of the river itself. But in May, Grant boldly moved men and supplies–overland and by water–to an area south of the city, where the terrain was better. He then attacked Vicksburg from the rear. Six weeks later, on July 4, Vicksburg–whose residents were by then literally starving as a result of a prolonged siege–surrendered. At almost the same time, the other Confederate strong point on the river, Port Hudson, Louisiana, also surrendered–to a Union force that had moved north from New Orleans. The Union had achieved one

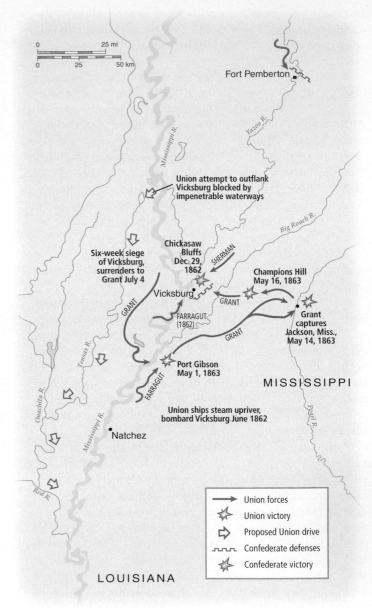

THE SIEGE OF VICKSBURG, MAY–JULY 1863 In the spring of 1863, Grant began a campaign to win control of the final piece of the Mississippi River still controlled by the Confederacy. To do that required capturing the Southern stronghold at Vicksburg—a well-defended city sitting above the river. Vicksburg's main defenses were in the North, so Grant boldly moved men and supplies around the city and attacked it from the south. Eventually, he cut off the city's access to the outside world, and after a six-week siege, its residents finally surrendered.

• *What impact did the combined victories at Vicksburg and Gettysburg have on Northern commitment to the war?*

of its basic military aims: control of the whole length of the Mississippi. The Confederacy was split in two, with Louisiana, Arkansas, and Texas cut off from the other seceded states. The victories on the Mississippi were among the great turning points of the war.

During the siege of Vicksburg, Lee proposed an invasion of Pennsylvania, which would, he argued, divert Union troops north and remove the pressure on the lower Mississippi.

GETTYSBURG, JULY 1–3, 1863 Gettysburg was the most important single battle of the Civil War. The map on the left shows the distribution of Union and Confederate forces at the beginning of the battle, July 1, after Lee had driven the Northern forces south of town. The map on the right reveals the pattern of the attacks on July 2 and 3. Note, in particular, Pickett's bold and costly charge, whose failure on July 3 was the turning point in the battle and, some chroniclers have argued, the war.

* *Why did Robert E. Lee believe that an invasion of Pennsylvania would advance the Confederate cause?*

Further, he argued, if he could win a major victory on Northern soil, England and France might come to the Confederacy's aid. The war-weary North might even quit the war before Vicksburg fell.

In June 1863, Lee moved up the Shenandoah Valley into Maryland and then entered Pennsylvania. The Union Army of the Potomac, commanded first by Hooker and then by George C. Meade, also moved north, parallel with the Confederates' movement, staying between Lee and Washington. The two armies finally encountered each other at the small town of Gettysburg, Pennsylvania. There, on July 1–3, 1863, they fought the most celebrated battle of the war.

Meade's army established a strong, well-protected position on the hills south of the town. The confident and combative

GETTYSBURG Lee attacked, even though his army was outnumbered 75,000 to 90,000. His first assault on the Union forces on Cemetery Ridge failed. A day later he ordered a second, larger effort. In what is remembered as Pickett's Charge, a force of 15,000 Confederate soldiers advanced for almost a mile across open country while being

swept by Union fire. Only about 5,000 made it up the ridge, and this remnant finally had to surrender or retreat. By now Lee had lost nearly a third of his army. On July 4, the same day as the surrender of Vicksburg, he withdrew from Gettysburg—another major turning point in the war. Never again were the weakened Confederate forces able to threaten Northern territory seriously.

Before the end of 1863, there was a third important turning point, this one in Tennessee. After occupying Chattanooga on September 9, Union forces under William Rosecrans began an unwise pursuit of Bragg's retreating Confederate forces. Bragg was waiting for them just across the Georgia line, with reinforcements from Lee's army. The two armies engaged in the Battle of Chickamauga (September 19–20), one of the few battles in which the Confederates enjoyed a numerical superiority (70,000 to 56,000). Union forces could not break the Confederate lines and retreated back to Chattanooga.

Bragg now began a siege of Chattanooga itself, seizing the heights nearby and cutting off fresh supplies to the

Union forces. Grant came to the rescue. In the Battle of Chattanooga (November 23-25), the reinforced Union army **BATTLE OF CHATTANOOGA** drove the Confederates back into Georgia. Northern troops then occupied most of eastern Tennessee. Union forces had now achieved a second important objective: control of the Tennessee River. Four of the eleven Confederate states were now effectively cut off from the Southern nation. No longer could the Confederacy hope to win independence through a decisive military victory. They could hope to win only by holding on and exhausting the Northern will to fight.

THE LAST STAGE, 1864–1865

By the beginning of 1864, Ulysses S. Grant had become general in chief of all the Union armies. At long last, President Lincoln had found a commander whom he could rely on to pursue the war doggedly and tenaciously. Grant was not a subtle strategic or tactical general; he believed in using the North's overwhelming advantage in troops and material resources to overwhelm the South. He was not afraid to absorb massive casualties as long as he was inflicting similar casualties on his opponents.

Grant planned two great offensives for 1864. In Virginia, the Army of the Potomac (technically under Meade's command, but really now under Grant's) would advance toward Richmond and **GRANT'S STRATEGY** force Lee into a decisive battle. In Georgia, the western army, under William Tecumseh Sherman, would advance east toward Atlanta and destroy the remaining Confederate force farther south, which was now under the command of Joseph E. Johnston. The northern campaign began when the Army of the Potomac, 115,000 strong, plunged into the rough, wooded Wilderness area of northwestern Virginia in pursuit of Lee's 75,000-man army. After avoiding an engagement for several weeks, Lee turned Grant back in the Battle of the Wilderness (May 5-7). But Grant was undeterred. Without stopping to rest or reorganize, he resumed his march toward Richmond. He met Lee again in the bloody, five-day Battle of Spotsylvania Court

VIRGINIA CAMPAIGNS, 1864–1865 From the Confederate defeat and retreat from Gettysburg until the end of the war, most of the eastern fighting took place in Virginia. By now, Ulysses S. Grant was commander of all Union forces and had taken over the Army of the Potomac. Although Confederate forces won a number of important battles during the Virginia campaign, the Union army grew steadily stronger and the Southern forces steadily weaker. Grant believed that the Union strategy should reflect the North's greatest advantage: its superiority in men and equipment.

• *What effect did this decision have on the level of casualties?*

MOBILE BAY, 1864 This image by Currier and Ives portrays a famous naval battle at the entrance to Mobile Bay between a Union sloop-of-war, the USS *Richmond*, part of a fleet commanded by Admiral David Farragut, and a Confederate ironclad, the CSS *Tennessee*. Although Confederate mines were scattered across the entrance to the harbor, Farragut ordered his ships into battle with the memorable command "Damn the torpedoes! Full speed ahead!" The Union forces defeated the Confederate flotilla and three weeks later captured the forts defending the harbor—thus removing from Confederate control the last port on the Gulf Coast available to the blockade runners who were attempting to supply the South's war needs. (© Archive Photos/Getty Images)

SHERMAN'S MARCH TO THE SEA, 1864–1865 While Grant was wearing Lee down in Virginia, General William Tecumseh Sherman was moving east across Georgia. After a series of battles in Tennessee and northwest Georgia, Sherman captured Atlanta and then marched unimpeded to Savannah, on the Georgia coast—deliberately devastating the towns and plantations through which his troops marched. Note that after capturing Savannah by Christmas 1864, Sherman began moving north through the Carolinas. A few days after Lee surrendered to Grant at Appomattox, Confederate forces farther south surrendered to Sherman.

• *What did Sherman believe his devastating March to the Sea would accomplish?*

House, in which 12,000 Union troops and a large but unknown number of Confederates died or were wounded. Despite the enormous losses, Grant kept moving. But victory continued to elude him.

Lee kept his army between Grant and the Confederate capital and on June 1-3 repulsed the Union forces again, just northeast of Richmond, at Cold Harbor. The month-long Wilderness campaign had cost Grant 55,000 men (killed, wounded, and captured) to Lee's 31,000. And Richmond still had not fallen.

Grant now changed his strategy. He moved his army east of Richmond, bypassing the capital altogether, and headed south toward the railroad center at Petersburg. If he could seize Petersburg, he could cut off the capital's communications with the rest of the Confederacy. But Petersburg had strong defenses; and once Lee came to the city's relief, the assault became a prolonged siege, which lasted nine months.

In Georgia, meanwhile, Sherman was facing less ferocious resistance. With 90,000 men, he confronted Confederate forces of 60,000 under Johnston, who was unwilling to risk a direct engagement. As Sherman advanced, Johnston tried to delay him by maneuvering. The two armies fought only one real battle–at Kennesaw Mountain, northwest of Atlanta, on June 27–where Johnston scored an impressive victory. Even so, he was unable to stop the Union advance toward Atlanta.

CAPTURE OF ATLANTA

President Davis replaced Johnston with the combative John B. Hood, who twice daringly attacked Sherman's army but accomplished nothing except seriously weakening his own forces. Sherman took Atlanta on September 2. News of the victory electrified the North and helped unite the previously divided Republican Party behind President Lincoln.

A young Union drummer boy, William Bircher, left an account of the burning of Atlanta. "At night we destroyed the city by fire," he wrote. "A grand and awful spectacle it presented to the beholder. . . . The heaven was one expanse of lurid fire; the air was filled with flying, burning cinders. Buildings, covering two hundred acres, were in ruins or in flames; every instant there was the sharp detonation of the smothered booming sound of exploding shells and powder concealed in the buildings, and then the sparks and flames would shoot up into the black and red roof. . . . I heard the real fine band of the Thirty-third Massachusetts playing, 'John Brown's soul goes marching on.'"

Hood now tried unsuccessfully to draw Sherman out of Atlanta by moving back up through Tennessee and threatening an invasion of the North. Sherman did not take the bait. But he did send Union troops to reinforce Nashville. In the Battle of Nashville, on December 15-16, 1864, Northern forces practically destroyed what was left of Hood's army.

Meanwhile, Sherman had left Atlanta to begin his soon-to-be-famous March to the Sea. Living off the land, destroying supplies it could not use, his army cut a sixty-mile-wide swath of desolation across Georgia. "War is all hell," Sherman had once said. By that he meant not that war is a terrible thing to

A LETTER FROM THE FRONT Charles Wellington Reed, a nineteen-year-old Union soldier who was also a talented artist, sent illustrated letters to the members of his family throughout the war. In this 1863 letter to his mother, he portrays the Ninth Massachusetts Battery leaving Centreville, Virginia, on its way to Gettysburg. Two weeks later, Reed fought in the famous battle and eventually received the Congressional Medal of Honor for his bravery there. "Such a shrieking, hissing, seathing I never dreamed was imaginable," he wrote of the fighting at the time. (Manuscript Division, The Library of Congress)

MARCH TO THE SEA

be avoided, but that it should be made as horrible and costly as possible for the opponent. He sought not only to deprive the Confederate army of war materials and railroad communications but also to break the will of the Southern people, by burning towns and plantations along his route. By December 20, he had reached Savannah, which surrendered two days later. Sherman offered it to President Lincoln as a Christmas gift. Early in 1865, having left Savannah largely undamaged, Sherman continued his destructive march northward through South Carolina. He was virtually unopposed until he was well inside North Carolina, where a small force under Johnston could do no more than cause a brief delay.

In April 1865, Grant's Army of the Potomac–still engaged in the prolonged siege at Petersburg–finally captured a vital railroad

APPOMATTOX COURT HOUSE junction southwest of the town. Without rail access to the South, cut off from other Confederate forces, Lee could no longer hope to defend Richmond. With the remnant of his army, now about 25,000 men, Lee began moving west in the forlorn hope of finding a way around the Union forces so that he could head south and link up with Johnston in North Carolina. But the Union army pursued him and blocked his escape route. Finally recognizing that further bloodshed was futile, Lee arranged to meet Grant at a private home in the small town of Appomattox Court House, Virginia. There, on April 9, he surrendered what was left of his forces. Nine days later, near Durham, North Carolina, Johnston surrendered to Sherman.

In military terms, at least, the long war was now effectively over, even though Jefferson Davis refused to accept defeat. He fled south from Richmond and was finally captured in Georgia. A few Southern diehards continued to fight, but even their resistance collapsed before long. Well before the last shot was fired, the difficult process of reuniting the shattered nation had begun.

The war ensured the permanence of the Union, but many other issues remained far from settled. What would happen to the freedmen (the term used for slaves who were now liberated)? Could the South and the North reconcile? Would the massive industrial growth in the North during the Civil War spread to the South, or would the South remain an agrarian region with much less wealth than in the North? The end of the war was the beginning of more than a generation of struggle to determine the legacy of the Civil War.

IMPACT OF THE NORTH'S VICTORY The North's victory was not just a military one. The war strengthened the North's economy, giving a spur to industry and railroad development. It greatly weakened the South's, by destroying millions of dollars of property and depleting the region's young male population. Southerners had gone to war in part because of their fears of growing Northern dominance. The war itself, ironically, confirmed and strengthened that dominance. There was no doubt by 1865 that the future of the United States lay in the growth of industry and commerce, which would occur for many years primarily outside the South.

But most of all, the Civil War was a victory for the millions of African American slaves, over whose plight the conflict had largely begun in the first place. The war produced Abraham Lincoln's epochal Emancipation Proclamation and, later, the Thirteenth Amendment to the Constitution, which abolished slavery. It also encouraged hundreds of thousands of slaves to free themselves, to desert their masters and seek refuge behind Union lines—at times to fight in the Union armies. The future of the freed slaves was not to be without challenges and hardships, but 3.5 million people who had once lived in bondage emerged from the war as free men and women.

AP CONNECTING THEMES

Chapter 14 examined the causes of the Civil War and the failure of compromise. Look back through the chapter and through the previous chapter to review the causes of the war, and consider the consequences of the war on society, both in the North and in the South. Each side had certain advantages at the beginning of the war, and this chapter examined the role of those advantages in the war's outcome. A significant event of the war was the Emancipation Proclamation, changing the motives for the war and affecting African American participation in the war effort, along with having a significant effect on both sides' goals of garnering overseas support. Lastly, Chapter 14 discussed several battles, but important to understand is the general strategies of each side and the general progression of the war.

The following themes have heightened importance in Chapter 14. You should now be able to do the following for each listed theme:

Identity: Analyze the ways in which American concepts of identity were changed during and after the war, particularly for African Americans.

Work, Exchange, and Technology: Describe how the Civil War affected the economies of both the North and the South. Analyze how the Civil War altered existing labor systems. Discuss the role the differences in regional economic development played in the causes and the outcomes of the war.

Peopling: Evaluate how the population of the United States was affected by the Civil War and by 19th century immigration.

Politics and Power: Understand the political changes brought about by the Northern victory.

Environment and Geography: Explain the impact of the Civil War on the infrastructure of the South.

Ideas, Beliefs, and Culture: Analyze the degree to which the Civil War altered perceptions of government and democratic ideals.

AP SUGGESTED STUDY

PEOPLE/PLACES/EVENTS As you study these items, think about how they demonstrate or relate to key concepts and historical themes from this chapter and previous chapters.

ABRAHAM LINCOLN 366
ANTIETAM 391
APPOMATTOX COURT HOUSE 397
BULL RUN 387

CLARA BARTON 378
EMANCIPATION PROCLAMATION 373
FORT SUMTER 366
GEORGE B. MCCLELLAN 371

GETTYSBURG 393
GETTYSBURG ADDRESS 374
GREENBACKS 369
HOMESTEAD ACT 368

AP TEST PRACTICE

Questions assume cumulative content knowledge from this chapter and previous chapters.

MULTIPLE CHOICE Use the excerpt below and your knowledge of U.S. history to answer questions 1-2.

"Since we have discerned, however, that the victory of the free north, in the war which has so sorely distressed us as well as afflicted you, will strike off the fetters of the slave, you have attracted our warm and earnest sympathy. We joyfully honor you, as the President, and the Congress with you, for many decisive steps toward practically exemplifying your belief in the words of your great founders: 'All men are created free and equal.'"

—"Address from Working Men to President Lincoln," official letter from British working men sent to Lincoln, printed in the *Manchester Guardian* (UK), January 1st, 1863

1. What development is being referred to in the letter, which could be viewed as a turning point in the Civil War?

    (A) The beginning of the Civil War

    (B) The issuing of the Emancipation Proclamation

    (C) The North's victory in a series of battles

    (D) The enlistment of African Americans to fight for the North

2. The letter best provides evidence of what outcome of the political development referenced in the letter which helped facilitate the South's defeat?

    (A) England decided to help the North by providing naval support.

    (B) Northern leaders were able to recruit Native Americans to their cause.

    (C) The Confederacy did not receive the support it was seeking from European powers.

    (D) Southern states' infrastructure began to fail.

SHORT ANSWER Use your knowledge of U.S. history to answer questions 3-5.

3. Answer a, b, and c.

    a) Briefly explain ONE example of how regional economic differences affected the outcome of the war.

    b) Briefly explain a SECOND example of how regional economic differences affected the outcome of the war.

    c) Briefly explain ONE example of how regional economic differences affected the causes of the war.

4. Answer a, b, and c.

    a) Briefly explain ONE example of the impact of the victory of the North in the Civil War.

    b) Briefly explain a SECOND example of the impact of the victory of the North in the Civil War.

    c) Briefly explain ONE example of the impact of the war on the social infrastructure of the South.

5. Answer a, b, and c.

    a) For ONE of the areas below, explain why it was the most significant in the downfall of the Confederacy.

    • Economic

    • Political

    • Cultural

    b) Provide ONE piece of historical evidence to support your contention in a.

    c) Briefly explain why ONE of the other areas was not as significant as the one you chose.

LONG ESSAY Develop a thoughtful and thorough historical argument that answers the question below. Begin your essay with a thesis statement and support it with relevant historical evidence.

6. Some historians have argued that the Civil War drastically changed perceptions of government and of American democratic ideals. Support, modify, or refute this interpretations, providing specific evidence to justify your answer.

15 | RECONSTRUCTION AND THE NEW SOUTH

THE GENIUS OF FREEDOM This 1874 lithograph portrays a series of important moments in the history of African Americans in the South during Reconstruction— among them the participation of black soldiers in the Civil War, a speech by a black representative in the North Carolina legislature, and the movement of African American workers from slavery into a system of free labor. It also portrays some of the white leaders (among them Lincoln and Charles Sumner) who had promoted the cause of the freedmen. (The Library of Congress (LC-USZ62-2247))

AP

HISTORICAL THINKING

1. **Comparison** Compare and contrast congressional and presidential Reconstruction plans.

2. **Patterns of Continuity and Change over Time** Analyze the degree of change brought to the American South as a result of Reconstruction.

3. **Contextualization** Analyze the economic, political, and social methods used to create and maintain second-class citizenship for African Americans.

4. **Historical Causation** What caused Southern Democrats to regain power, replacing Republican governments with Redeemer governments?

5. **Historical Argumentation** Analyze the degree to which the New South was really new.

6. **Contextualization** To what degree and in what ways was the Compromise of 1877 justified?

7. **Patterns of Continuity and Change over Time** To what degree did patterns of labor and land ownership change as a result of the Civil War and Reconstruction?

Key Concept Correlations

Analyze the ways the historical developments you learn about in this chapter connect to the following AP Key Concepts.

5.3 The Union victory in the Civil War and the contested Reconstruction of the South settled the issues of slavery and secession, but left unresolved many questions about the power of the federal government and citizenship rights.

6.1 The rise of big business in the United States encouraged massive migrations and urbanizations, sparked government and popular efforts to reshape the U.S. economy and environment, and renewed debates over U.S. national identity.

Thematic Learning Objectives

POL-5, 6; ID-2, 5; WXT-6, 7; PEO-6

AP CONNECTING CONCEPTS

CHAPTER 15 discusses the impact of Reconstruction on the United States in politically altering the relationship and balance of power between the three branches of the federal government. It discusses presidential and congressional plans for reconstructing the nation and analyzes the differences between the plans. African Americans experienced political opportunities during Reconstruction, and you should understand how these opportunities arose and how they gave way. Also discussed in this chapter are the scandals under President Grant and the waning commitment of Northerners to Reconstruction, which allowed Redeemer governments to displace Republican state governments in the South. As you progress through the chapter, focus on the positive and negative consequences of Reconstruction. Be attentive to the establishment of the sharecropping system and the degree to which land was redistributed. Important is the rise of the Jim Crow system and the means by which African Americans are denied their constitutional rights. Lastly, the chapter looks at ideas of some southerners for rebuilding a "New South" as well as the ending of Reconstruction with the Compromise of 1877. As you read, evaluate the following ideas:

- The abolition of slavery led to a reshaping of cultural identities and new concepts of citizenship.
- The Civil War cemented the theory of perpetual union and rejected the notion of the compact theory (that the Union was a voluntary association of states).
- While the Thirteenth, Fourteenth, and Fifteenth Amendments granted African Americans equal protection under the law, many of those rights were stripped away by rulings of the U.S. Supreme Court, segregation, and Jim Crow laws.
- Reconstruction changed very few social and economic patterns in the South.
- The sharecropping system limited the economic possibilities for many African Americans and poor whites.
- The legislative and executive branches argued over who would control Reconstruction, changing the balance of power between the two branches.
- Reconstruction had both positive and negative effects on the South.
- The constitutional changes brought about by the Civil War and Reconstruction provided the future basis for women, African American, and other minorities gaining their civil rights.

THE PROBLEMS OF PEACEMAKING

In 1865, as it became clear that the war was almost over, no one in Washington had yet formed a plan for what would happen to the defeated South. Lincoln could not negotiate a treaty with the Confederate government; he continued to insist that the Confederate government had no legal right to exist. Yet neither could he simply readmit the Southern states into the Union as if nothing had happened.

THE AFTERMATH OF WAR AND EMANCIPATION

The Civil War was a catastrophe for the South with no parallel in America's experience as a nation. Towns had been gutted, plantations burned, fields neglected, bridges and railroads destroyed.

THE DEVASTATED SOUTH — Many white Southerners, stripped of their slaves through emancipation and stripped of the capital they had invested in now-worthless Confederate bonds and currency, had almost no personal property. Many families had to rebuild their fortunes without the help of adult males, massive numbers of whom had died in the war. Some white Southerners faced starvation and homelessness.

The more than 258,000 Confederate soldiers who had died in the war constituted over 20 percent of the adult white male population of the region; thousands more returned home wounded or sick. Almost all surviving white Southerners had lost people close to them in the fighting. A cult of ritualized mourning developed throughout the region in the late 1860s, particularly

MYTH OF THE "LOST CAUSE" — among white women–many of whom wore mourning clothes (and jewelry) for two years or longer. At the same time, white Southerners began to romanticize the

RICHMOND, 1865 By the time Union forces captured Richmond in early 1865, the Confederate capital had been under siege for months and much of the city lay in ruins, as this photograph reveals. On April 4, President Lincoln, accompanied by his son Tad, visited Richmond. As he walked through the streets of the shattered city, hundreds of former slaves emerged from the rubble to watch him pass. "No triumphal march of a conqueror could have equalled in moral sublimity the humble manner in which he entered Richmond," a black soldier serving with the Union army wrote. "It was a great deliverer among the delivered. No wonder tears came to his eyes." (The Library of Congress)

"Lost Cause" and its leaders, and to look back nostalgically at the South as it had existed before the terrible disruptions of war. Such Confederate heroes as Robert E. Lee, Stonewall Jackson, and (later) Jefferson Davis were treated with extraordinary reverence, almost as religious figures. Communities throughout the South built elaborate monuments in town squares to commemorate their war dead. The tremendous sense of loss that pervaded the white South reinforced the determination of many whites to protect what remained of their now-vanished world.

If conditions were bad for many Southern whites, they were worse for most Southern blacks–the 4 million men and women emerging from bondage. Some of them had also seen service during the war–as servants to Confederate officers or as teamsters and laborers for the Southern armies. Nearly 200,000 had fought for the Union, and 38,000 had died. Others had worked as spies or scouts for Union forces in the South. Many more had flocked to the Union lines to escape slavery. Even before Emancipation, thousands of slaves in many parts of the South had taken advantage of wartime disruptions to leave their owners and move off in search of freedom. As soon as the war ended, hundreds of thousands more former slaves–young and old, healthy and sick–left their plantations. Some went in search of

family members who had been sold by their former masters. But many others had nowhere to go. Some trudged to the nearest town or city, roamed the countryside camping at night on the bare ground, or gathered around Union occupation forces, hoping for assistance. Virtually none owned any land or property. Most had no possessions except the clothes they wore.

In 1865, in short, Southern society was in vast disarray. Blacks and whites, men and women faced a future of great uncertainty. Yet all Southerners faced this future with some very clear aspirations. For both blacks and whites, Reconstruction became a struggle to define the meaning of freedom. But the former slaves and the defeated whites had very different conceptions of what freedom meant.

COMPETING NOTIONS OF FREEDOM

For African Americans, freedom meant above all an end to slavery and to all the injustices and humiliation they associated with it. But it also meant the acquisition of rights and protections that would allow them to live as free men and women in the same way white people did. "If I cannot do like a white man," one African American man told his former master, "I am not free."

A MONUMENT TO THE "LOST CAUSE" This monument in the town square of Monroe, Georgia, was typical of many such memorials erected all across the South after the Civil War. They served both to commemorate the Confederate dead and to remind white Southerners of what was by the 1870s already widely known and romanticized as the "Lost Cause." (© Lee Snider/Photo Images/Corbis)

A FREEDMEN'S BUREAU SCHOOL African American students and teachers stand outside a school for former slaves, one of many run by the Freedmen's Bureau throughout the defeated Confederacy in the first years after the war. (© Corbis)

African Americans differed with one another on how to achieve that freedom. Some demanded a redistribution of economic resources, especially land, because, as a convention of Alabama freedmen put it in a formal resolution, "The property which they hold was nearly all earned by the sweat of our brows." Others asked simply for legal equality, confident that given the same opportunities as white citizens they could advance successfully in American society. But whatever their particular demands, virtually all former slaves were united in their desire for independence from white control. Freed from slavery, blacks throughout the South began almost immediately to create autonomous African American communities. They pulled out of white-controlled churches and established their own. They created fraternal, benevolent, and mutual-aid societies. When they could, they began their own schools.

For most white Southerners, freedom meant something very different. It meant the ability to control their own destinies

FREEDOM FOR THE EX-SLAVES

without interference from the North or the federal government. And in the immediate aftermath of the war, they attempted to exercise this version of freedom by trying to restore their society to its antebellum form. Slavery had been abolished in the former Confederacy by the Emancipation Proclamation, and everywhere else (as of December 1865) by the Thirteenth Amendment. But many white planters continued a kind of slavery in an altered form by keeping black workers legally tied to the plantations. When many white Southerners fought for what they considered freedom, they were fighting above all to preserve local and regional autonomy and white supremacy.

The federal government kept troops in the South after the war to preserve order and protect the freedmen. In March 1865, Congress established the Freedmen's Bureau, an agency of the army directed by General Oliver O. Howard. The Freedmen's Bureau distributed food to millions of former slaves. It established schools staffed by missionaries and teachers who had been sent to the South by Freedmen's Aid Societies and other private and church groups in the North. It made modest efforts to settle blacks on lands of their own. (The bureau also offered considerable assistance to poor whites, many of whom were similarly destitute and homeless after the war.) But the Freedmen's Bureau was not a permanent solution. It had authority to operate for only one year; and in any case it was far too small to deal effectively with the enormous problems facing Southern society. By the time the war ended, other proposals for reconstructing the defeated South were emerging.

THE FREEDMEN'S BUREAU

ISSUES OF RECONSTRUCTION

Reconstruction was determined not just by social realities or ideals. It was also determined by partisan politics. The terms by which the Southern states rejoined the Union had important implications for both major political parties. The Republican victories in 1860 and 1864 had been a result in large part of the division of the Democratic Party and, later, the removal of the South from the electorate. Readmitting the South, leaders of both parties believed, would reunite the Democrats and weaken the Republicans. In addition, the Republican Party had taken advantage of the South's absence from Congress to pass a program of nationalistic economic legislation–railroad subsidies, protective tariffs, banking and currency reforms, and other measures to benefit Northern business leaders and industrialists. Should the Democratic Party regain power with heavy Southern support, these programs would be in jeopardy. Complicating these practical questions were emotional concerns. Many Northerners believed the South should be punished in some way for the suffering and sacrifice its rebellion had caused. Many Northerners believed, too, that the South should be transformed, made over in the North's urbanized image—its supposedly backward, feudal, undemocratic society civilized and modernized.

Even among the Republicans in Congress, there was considerable disagreement about the proper approach to Reconstruction—disagreement that reflected the same factional divisions that had created disputes over emancipation during the war. Conservatives insisted that the South accept the abolition of slavery, but proposed few other conditions for the readmission of the seceded states. The Radicals, led by Representative Thaddeus Stevens of Pennsylvania and Senator Charles Sumner of Massachusetts, urged that the civil and military leaders of the Confederacy be punished, that large numbers of Southern whites be disenfranchised, that the legal rights of former slaves be protected, and that the property of wealthy white Southerners who had aided the Confederacy be confiscated and distributed among the freedmen. Some Radicals favored granting suffrage to the former slaves. Others hesitated, since few Northern states permitted blacks to vote. Between the Radicals and the Conservatives stood a faction of uncommitted Republicans, the Moderates, who rejected the punitive goals of the Radicals but supported extracting at least some concessions from the South on African American rights.

CONSERVATIVE AND RADICAL REPUBLICANS

PLANS FOR RECONSTRUCTION

President Lincoln's sympathies lay with the Moderates and Conservatives of his party. He believed that a lenient Reconstruction policy would encourage Southern unionists and other former Whigs to join the Republican Party and would thus prevent the readmission of the South from strengthening the Democrats. More immediately, the Southern unionists could become the nucleus of new, loyal state governments in the South. Lincoln was not uninterested in the fate of the freedmen, but he was willing to defer questions about their future for the sake of rapid reunification.

Lincoln's Reconstruction plan, which he announced in December 1863, offered a general amnesty to white Southerners—other than high officials of the Confederacy—who would pledge loyalty to the government and accept the elimination of slavery. Whenever 10 percent of the number of voters in 1860 took the oath in any state, those loyal voters could set up a state government. Lincoln also hoped to extend suffrage to African Americans who were educated, owned property,

LINCOLN'S 10% PLAN

and had served in the Union army. Three Southern states—Louisiana, Arkansas, and Tennessee, all under Union occupation—reestablished loyal governments under the Lincoln formula in 1864.

The Radical Republicans were astonished at the mildness of Lincoln's program. They persuaded Congress to deny seats to representatives from the three "reconstructed" states and refused to count the electoral vote of those states in the election of 1864. But for the moment, the Radicals were uncertain about what form their own Reconstruction plan should take. Their first effort to resolve that question was the Wade-Davis Bill, passed by Congress in July 1864. It authorized the president to appoint a provisional governor for each conquered state. When a majority (not Lincoln's 10 percent) of the white males of the state pledged their allegiance to the Union, the governor could summon a state constitutional convention, whose delegates were to be elected by those who would swear (through the so-called Ironclad Oath) that they had never borne arms against the United States—another departure from Lincoln's plan. The new state constitutions would have to abolish slavery, disenfranchise Confederate civil and military leaders, and repudiate debts accumulated by the state governments during the war. After a state had met these conditions, Congress would readmit it to the Union. Like the president's proposal, the Wade-Davis Bill left up to the states the question of political rights for blacks. Congress passed the bill a few days before it adjourned in 1864, and Lincoln disposed of it with a pocket veto. His action enraged the Radical leaders, and the pragmatic Lincoln became convinced he would have to accept at least some of the Radical demands. He began to move toward a new approach to Reconstruction.

WADE-DAVIS BILL

THE DEATH OF LINCOLN

What plan Lincoln might have produced no one can say. On the night of April 14, 1865, the president and his wife attended a play at Ford's Theater in Washington. As they sat in the presidential box, John Wilkes Booth, a member of a distinguished family of actors and a zealous advocate of the Southern cause, entered the box from the rear and shot Lincoln in the head. The president was carried unconscious to a house across the street, where early the next morning, surrounded by family, friends, and political associates (among them a tearful Charles Sumner), he died.

The circumstances of Lincoln's death earned him immediate martyrdom. It also produced something close to hysteria throughout the North. There were accusations that Booth had acted as part of a great conspiracy—accusations that contained some truth. Booth did indeed have associates, one of whom stabbed and wounded Secretary of State Seward the night of the assassination, another of whom abandoned at the last moment a plan to murder Vice President Johnson. Booth himself escaped on horseback into the Virginia countryside, where, on April 26, he was cornered by Union troops and shot to

ABRAHAM LINCOLN This haunting photograph of Abraham Lincoln, showing clearly the weariness and aging that four years as a war president had created, was taken in Washington only four days before his assassination in 1865. (The Library of Congress)

death in a blazing barn. A military tribunal convicted eight other people of participating in the conspiracy (at least two of them on the basis of virtually no evidence). Four were hanged.

To many Northerners, however, the murder of the president seemed evidence of an even greater conspiracy—one masterminded and directed by the unrepentant leaders of the defeated South. Militant Republicans exploited such suspicions relentlessly for months, ensuring that Lincoln's death would help doom his plans for a relatively easy peace.

JOHNSON AND "RESTORATION"

Leadership of the Moderates and Conservatives fell to Lincoln's successor, Andrew Johnson, who was not well suited, by either circumstance or personality, for the task. A Democrat until he had joined the Union ticket with Lincoln in 1864, he became

ANDREW JOHNSON'S PERSONALITY

a Republican president at a moment when partisan passions were growing. Johnson himself was an intemperate and tactless man, filled with resentments and insecurities. He was also openly hostile to the freed slaves and unwilling to support any plans that guaranteed them civil equality or enfranchisement. He once declared, "White men alone must manage the South."

Johnson revealed his plan for Reconstruction—or "Restoration," as he preferred to call it—soon after he took office, and he implemented it during the summer of 1865, when Congress was in recess. Like Lincoln, he offered amnesty to those Southerners who would take an oath of allegiance. (High-ranking Confederate officials and any white Southerner with land worth $20,000 or more would have to apply to the president for individual pardons. Johnson, a self-made man, apparently liked the thought of the great planter aristocrats humbling themselves before him.) In most other respects, however, his plan resembled that of the Wade-Davis Bill. For each state, the president appointed a provisional governor, who was to invite qualified voters to elect delegates to a constitutional convention. Johnson did not specify how many qualified voters were necessary, but he implied that he would require a majority (as had the Wade-Davis Bill). In order to win readmission to Congress, a state had to revoke its ordinance of secession, abolish slavery, ratify the Thirteenth Amendment, and repudiate the Confederate and state war debts. The final procedure before restoration was for a state to elect a state government and send representatives to Congress.

Whereas Johnson helped white southerners to return to their land, he did little in support of the former slaves. Although freedmen had been given their liberty, holding on to it proved difficult. Many freedmen who returned to work for white planters found themselves almost like slaves again. Johnson offered no help. "Are not our rights as a free people and good citizens of the United States to be considered?" asked a petition against the president. It was a long time before freedmen truly found liberty.

By the end of 1865, all the seceded states had formed new governments–some under Lincoln's plan, some under Johnson's–and were prepared to rejoin the Union as soon as

NORTHERN ATTITUDES HARDEN

Congress recognized them. But Radical Republicans vowed not to recognize the Johnson governments, just as they had previously refused to recognize the Lincoln regimes; for by now, Northern opinion had hardened and become more hostile toward the South than it had been a year earlier when Congress passed the Wade-Davis Bill. Many Northerners were disturbed by the apparent reluctance of some delegates to the Southern conventions to abolish slavery, and by the refusal of all the conventions to grant suffrage to any blacks. They were astounded that states claiming to be "loyal" should elect prominent leaders of the recent Confederacy as state officials and representatives to Congress. Particularly hard to accept was Georgia's choice of Alexander H. Stephens, former Confederate vice president, as a United States senator.

RADICAL RECONSTRUCTION

Reconstruction under Johnson's plan–often known as "presidential Reconstruction"–continued only until Congress reconvened in December 1865. At that point, Congress refused to seat the representatives of the "restored" states and created a new Joint Committee on Reconstruction to frame a Reconstruction policy of its own. The period of "congressional," or "Radical," Reconstruction had begun.

THE BLACK CODES

Meanwhile, events in the South were driving Northern opinion in more-radical directions. Throughout the South in 1865 and early 1866, state legislatures were enacting sets of laws known as the "Black Codes," designed to give whites substantial control over former slaves. The codes authorized local officials to apprehend unemployed African Americans, fine them for vagrancy, and hire them out to private employers to satisfy the fine. Some of the codes forbade blacks to own or lease farms or to take any jobs other than as plantation workers or domestic servants.

Congress first responded to the Black Codes by passing an act extending the life of the Freedmen's Bureau and widening its powers so that it could nullify work agreements forced on freedmen under the Black Codes. Then, in April 1866, Congress passed the first Civil Rights Act, which declared African Americans to be citizens of the United States and gave the federal government power to intervene in state affairs to protect the rights of citizens. Johnson vetoed both bills, but Congress overrode him on each of them.

JOHNSON'S VETOES

THE FOURTEENTH AMENDMENT

In April 1866, the Joint Committee on Reconstruction proposed a new amendment to the Constitution, which Congress approved in early summer and sent to the states for ratification. Eventually, it became one of the most important provisions in the Constitution.

The Fourteenth Amendment offered the first constitutional definition of American citizenship: everyone born in the United States, and everyone naturalized, was automatically a citizen and entitled to all the "privileges and immunities" guaranteed by the Constitution, including equal protection of the laws by both the state and national governments. There could be no other requirements (for example, being white) for citizenship. The amendment also imposed penalties–reduction of representation in Congress and in the electoral college–on states that denied suffrage to any adult male inhabitants. (The wording reflected the prevailing view in Congress and elsewhere that the franchise was properly restricted to men.) Finally, it prohibited former members of Congress or other former federal officials who had aided the Confederacy from holding any state or federal office unless two-thirds of Congress voted to pardon them.

CITIZENSHIP FOR BLACKS

Congressional Radicals offered to readmit to the Union any state whose legislature ratified the Fourteenth Amendment. Only Tennessee did so. All the other former Confederate states, along with Delaware and Kentucky, refused, leaving the amendment temporarily without the necessary approval of three-fourths of the states.

FOURTEENTH AMENDMENT Among its provisions, the Fourteenth Amendment provided the first constitutional definition of U.S. citizenship. Everyone born in the United States, and everyone naturalized, was automatically a citizen and entitled to all the "privileges and immunities" guaranteed by the Constitution, including equal protection of the laws by both the state and national governments. This amendment also imposed penalties on states that did not extend the right to vote to all male citizens, including African American men. African American women, like all women, had to wait until 1920 and the ratification of the Nineteenth Amendment before legally entitled to vote. (© North Wind Picture Archives/Alamy)

But by now, the Radicals were growing more confident and determined. Bloody race riots in New Orleans and other Southern cities–riots in which African Americans were the principal victims–were among the events that strengthened their hand. In the 1866 congressional elections, Johnson actively campaigned for Conservative candidates, but he did his own cause more harm than good with his intemperate speeches. The voters returned an overwhelming majority of Republicans, most of them Radicals, to Congress. In the Senate, there were now 42 Republicans to 11 Democrats; in the House, 143 Republicans to 49 Democrats. (The South remained largely unrepresented in both chambers.) Congressional Republicans were now strong enough to enact a plan of their own even over the president's objections.

THE CONGRESSIONAL PLAN

The Radicals passed three Reconstruction bills early in 1867 and overrode Johnson's vetoes of all of them. These bills

THREE RECONSTRUCTION BILLS

finally established, nearly two years after the end of the war, a coherent plan for Reconstruction.

Under the congressional plan, Tennessee, which had ratified the Fourteenth Amendment, was promptly readmitted. But Congress rejected the Lincoln-Johnson governments of the other ten Confederate states and, instead, combined those states into five military districts. A military commander governed each district and had orders to register qualified voters (defined as all adult black males and those white males who had not participated in the rebellion). Once registered, voters would elect conventions to prepare new state constitutions, which had to include provisions for black suffrage. Once voters ratified the new constitutions, they could elect state governments. Congress had to approve a state's constitution, and the state legislature had to ratify the Fourteenth Amendment. Once that happened, and once enough states ratified the amendment to make it part of the Constitution, then the former Confederate states could be restored to the Union.

By 1868, seven of the ten former Confederate states (Arkansas, North Carolina, South Carolina, Louisiana, Alabama, Georgia, and Florida) had fulfilled these conditions (including ratification of the Fourteenth Amendment, which now became part of the Constitution). They were readmitted to the Union. Conservative whites held up the return of Virginia and Texas until 1869 and Mississippi until 1870. By then, Congress had added one more requirement for readmission—ratification of another constitutional amendment, the Fifteenth, which forbade the states and the federal government to deny suffrage to any citizen on account of "race, color, or previous condition of servitude."

FIFTEENTH AMENDMENT

To stop the president from interfering with their plans, the congressional Radicals passed two remarkable laws of dubious constitutionality in 1867. One, the Tenure of Office Act, forbade the president to remove civil officials, including members of his own cabinet, without the consent of the Senate. The principal purpose of the law was to protect the job of Secretary of War Edwin M. Stanton, who was cooperating with the Radicals. The other law, the Command of the Army Act, prohibited the president from issuing military orders except through the commanding general of the army (General Grant), who could not be relieved or assigned elsewhere without the consent of the Senate.

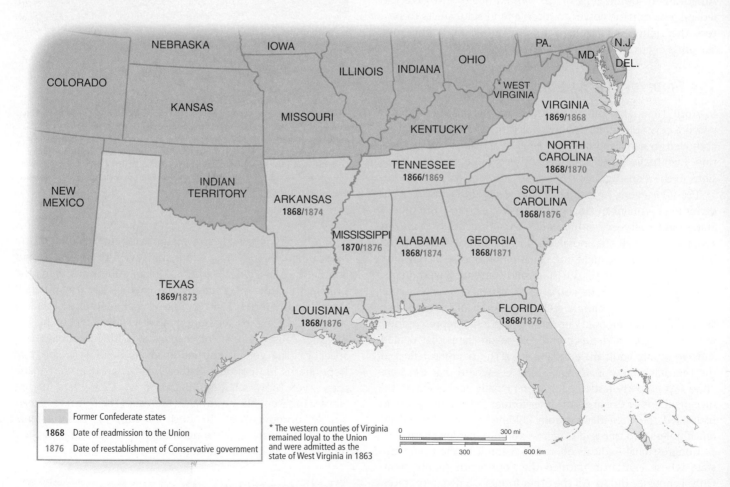

Former Confederate states
1868 Date of readmission to the Union
1876 Date of reestablishment of Conservative government

* The western counties of Virginia remained loyal to the Union and were admitted as the state of West Virginia in 1863

0   300 mi
0   300   600 km

RECONSTRUCTION, 1866–1877 This map shows the former Confederate states and provides the date when each was readmitted to the Union as well as a subsequent date when each state managed to return political power to traditional white, conservative elites—a process white Southerners liked to call "redemption."

• *What had to happen for a state to be readmitted to the Union? What had to happen before a state could experience "redemption"?*

The congressional Radicals also took action to stop the Supreme Court from interfering with their plans. In 1866, the Court had declared in the case of *Ex parte Milligan* that military tribunals were unconstitutional in places where civil courts were functioning, a decision that seemed to threaten the system of military government the Radicals were planning for the South. Radicals in Congress immediately proposed several bills that would require two-thirds of the justices to support any decision overruling a law of Congress, would deny the Court jurisdiction in Reconstruction cases, would reduce its membership to three, and would even abolish it. The justices apparently took notice. Over the next two years, the Court refused to accept jurisdiction in any cases involving Reconstruction (and the congressional bills concerning the Court never passed).

THE IMPEACHMENT OF THE PRESIDENT

President Johnson had long since ceased to be a serious obstacle to the passage of Radical legislation, but he was still the official charged with administering the Reconstruction programs. As such, the Radicals believed, he remained a serious impediment to their plans. Early in 1867, they began looking for a way to impeach him and remove him from office. Republicans found grounds for impeachment, they believed, when Johnson dismissed Secretary of War Stanton despite Congress's refusal to agree, thus deliberately violating the Tenure of Office Act in hopes of testing the law before the courts. Elated Radicals in the House quickly impeached the president and sent the case to the Senate for trial. By that time, the Radicals were determined to impeach President Johnson. "Who does not know," said Benjamin Butler, an opponent of Johnson, "that from the hour [Johnson] began these, his usurpations of power, he everywhere denounced Congress, the legality and constitutionality of its action, and defied its legitimate power."

TENURE OF OFFICE ACT

The trial before the Senate lasted throughout April and May 1868. The Radicals put heavy pressure on all the Republican senators, but the Moderates (who were losing faith in the Radical program) vacillated. On the first three charges to come to a vote, seven Republicans joined the Democrats and independents to support acquittal. The vote was 35 to 19, one short of the constitutionally required two-thirds majority. After that, the Radicals dropped the impeachment effort.

JOHNSON ACQUITTED

THE SOUTH IN RECONSTRUCTION

When white Southerners spoke bitterly in later years of the effects of Reconstruction, they referred most frequently to the governments Congress helped impose on them—

governments they claimed were both incompetent and corrupt, that saddled the region with enormous debts, and that trampled on the rights of citizens. When black Southerners and their defenders condemned Reconstruction, in contrast, they spoke of the failure of the national and state governments to go far enough to guarantee freedmen even the most elemental rights of citizenship—a failure that resulted in a harsh new system of economic subordination. (See "Debating the Past," pp. 416–417.)

THE RECONSTRUCTION GOVERNMENTS

In the ten states of the South that were reorganized under the congressional plan, approximately one-fourth of the white males were at first excluded from voting or holding office. That produced black majorities among voters in South Carolina, Mississippi, and Louisiana (states where blacks were also a majority of the population), and in Alabama and Florida (where they were not). But the government soon lifted most suffrage restrictions so that nearly all white males could vote. After that, Republicans maintained control only with the support of many Southern whites.

Critics called these Southern white Republicans "scalawags." Many were former Whigs who had never felt comfortable

THE "STRONG" GOVERNMENT 1869–1877.

THE BURDENED SOUTH This Reconstruction-era cartoon expresses the South's sense of its oppression at the hands of Northern Republicans. President Grant (whose hat bears Abraham Lincoln's initials) rides in comfort in a giant carpetbag, guarded by bayonet-wielding soldiers, as the South staggers under the burden in chains. More evidence of destruction and military occupation is visible in the background. (© The Granger Collection, New York) in the Democratic Party—some of them wealthy (or once wealthy) planters or businessmen interested in the economic development of the region. Others were farmers who lived in remote areas where there had been little or no slavery and who hoped the Republican program of internal improvements would help end their economic isolation. Despite their diverse social positions, scalawags shared a belief that the Republican Party would serve their economic interests better than the Democrats.

"SCALAWAGS"

White men from the North also served as Republican leaders in the South. Critics of Reconstruction referred to them pejoratively as "carpetbaggers," which conveyed an image of penniless adventurers who arrived with all their possessions in a carpet-bag (a common kind of cheap suitcase covered with carpeting material). In fact, most of the so-called carpetbaggers were well-educated people of middle-class origin, many of them doctors, lawyers, and teachers. Most were veterans of the Union army who looked on the South as a new frontier, more promising than the West. They had settled there at war's end as hopeful planters or as business and professional people.

"CARPETBAGGERS"

But the most numerous Republicans in the South were the black freedmen, most of whom had no previous experience in politics and who tried, therefore, to build institutions through which they could learn to exercise their power. In several states, African American voters held their own conventions to chart their future course. One such "colored convention," as Southern whites called them, assembled in Alabama in 1867 and announced: "We claim exactly the same rights, privileges and immunities as are enjoyed by white men—we

FREEDMEN

THE RIOT IN NEW ORLEANS—SIEGE AND ASSAULT OF THE CONVENTION BY THE POLICE AND CITIZENS.—Sketched by Theodore R. Davis.

NEW ORLEANS RIOT On July 30, 1866, a violent conflict took place outside the Mechanics Institute in New Orleans. Whites attacked blacks parading outside the building where a reconvened Louisiana Constitutional Convention was being held. The state's Radical Republicans had called for the Convention because they were angered by the legislature's enactment of the Black Codes that restricted the rights of African Americans to travel and work. An estimated thirty-eight people were killed and forty-six wounded, most of them African American. (© The Granger Collection, New York)

ask nothing more and will be content with nothing else." The black churches that freedmen created after emancipation also helped give unity and political self-confidence to the former slaves. African Americans played a significant role in the politics of the Reconstruction South. They served as delegates to the constitutional conventions. They held public offices of practically every kind. Between 1869 and 1901, twenty African Americans served in the U.S. House of Representatives, two in the Senate (Hiram Revels of Mississippi and Blanche K. Bruce of Mississippi). African Americans served, too, in state legislatures and in various other state offices. Southern whites complained loudly (both at the time and for generations to come) about "Negro rule" during Reconstruction, but no such thing ever actually existed in any of the states. No black man was ever elected governor of a Southern state (although Lieutenant Governor P. B. S. Pinchback briefly performed gubernatorial duties in Louisiana). African Americans never controlled any of the state legislatures, although they held a majority in the lower house in South Carolina for a short time. In the South as a whole, the percentage of black officeholders was always far lower than the percentage of blacks in the population.

The record of the Reconstruction governments is mixed. Critics at the time and since denounced them for corruption and financial extravagance, and there is some truth to both charges. Officeholders in many states enriched themselves through graft and other illicit activities. State budgets expanded to hitherto unknown totals, and state debts soared to previously undreamed-of heights. In South Carolina, for example, the public debt increased from $7 million to $29 million in eight years.

But the corruption in the South, real as it was, was hardly unique to the Reconstruction governments. Corruption was at least as rampant in the Northern states. And in both North and South, it was a result of the same thing: a rapid economic expansion of government services (and revenues) that put new strains on (and new temptations before) elected officials everywhere. The end of Reconstruction did not end corruption in Southern state governments. In many states, in fact, corruption increased.

And the state expenditures of the Reconstruction years were huge only in comparison with the meager budgets of the antebellum era. They represented an effort to provide the South with urgently needed services that antebellum governments had never offered: public education, public works programs, relief for the poor, and other costly new commitments. There were, to be sure, graft and extravagance in Reconstruction governments; there were also positive and permanent accomplishments.

EDUCATION

Perhaps the most important of those accomplishments was a dramatic improvement in the education of African Americans and white Southerners with scant learning. In the first years of Reconstruction, much of the impetus for educational reform in the South came from outside groups—from the Freedmen's Bureau, from Northern private philanthropic organizations, from many Northern women, black and white, who traveled to the South to teach in freedmen's schools—and from black Southerners themselves. Over the opposition of many Southern whites, who feared that education would give African Americans "false notions of equality," these reformers established a large network of schools for former slaves—4,000 schools by 1870, staffed by 9,000 teachers (half of them black), teaching 200,000 students (about 12 percent of the total school-age population of the freedmen). In the 1870s, Reconstruction governments also began to build a comprehensive public school system in the South. By 1876, more than half of all white children and about 40 percent of all black children were attending schools in the South. Several black "academies," offering more advanced education, also began operating. Gradually, these academies grew into an important network of black colleges and universities, which included such distinguished schools as Fisk and Atlanta Universities and Morehouse College.

Already, however, Southern education was becoming divided into two separate systems, one black and one white.

SEGREGATED SCHOOLS

Early efforts to integrate the schools of the region were a dismal failure. The Freedmen's Bureau schools, for example, were open to students of all races, but almost no whites attended them. New Orleans set up an integrated school system under the Reconstruction government; again, whites almost universally stayed away. The one federal effort to mandate school integration—the Civil Rights Act of 1875—had its provisions for educational desegregation removed before it was passed. As soon as the Republican governments of Reconstruction were replaced, the new Southern Democratic regimes quickly abandoned all efforts to promote integration.

LANDOWNERSHIP AND TENANCY

The most ambitious goal of the Freedmen's Bureau, and of some Radical Republicans in Congress, was to make Reconstruction the vehicle for a fundamental reform of

THE SOUTHERN PLANTATION BEFORE AND AFTER EMANCIPATION This map shows the distribution of lands and dwellings on the Barrow Plantation in Oglethorpe County, Georgia, before and after the emancipation of slaves at the close of the Civil War. The map on the left shows the plantation in 1861, as the war began. Like the Hopeton Plantation shown on p. 299, the Barrow Plantation was highly centralized before the war, with all slaves living together in a complex of dwellings near the master's house. Twenty years later, as the map on the right shows, the same landscape was very differently divided. Housing was now widely dispersed, as former slaves became tenants or sharecroppers and began working their own small pieces of land and living independently. Churches had sprung up away from the landowner's house as well.

• *Why did former slaves move so quickly to relocate their homes and churches away from their former masters?*

landownership in the South. The effort failed. In the last years of the war and the first years of Reconstruction, the Freedmen's Bureau did oversee the redistribution of substantial amounts of land to freedmen in a few areas–notably the Sea Islands of South Carolina and Georgia, and areas of Mississippi that had

FAILURE OF LAND REDISTRIBUTION

once belonged to the family of Jefferson Davis. By June 1865, the bureau had settled nearly 10,000 black families on their own land–most of it drawn from abandoned plantations–arousing dreams among former slaves throughout the South of "forty acres and a mule." By the end of that year, however, the experiment was already collapsing. Southern plantation owners were returning and demanding the restoration of their property, and President Johnson was supporting their demands. Despite the resistance of the Freedmen's Bureau, the government eventually returned most of the confiscated land to the original white owners.

Very few Northern Republicans believed that the federal government had the right to confiscate property. Even so, distribution of landownership in the South changed considerably in the postwar years. Among whites, there was a significant decline in landownership, from 80 percent before the war to 67 percent by the end of Reconstruction. Some whites lost their land because of unpaid debt or increased taxes; some left the marginal lands they had owned to move to more-fertile areas, where they rented.

During the same period, the number of African Americans who owned land rose from virtually none to more than 20 percent. Many black landowners acquired their property through hard work or luck or both. But some relied unwisely on assistance from white-dominated financial or philanthropic institutions. One of them was the Freedman's Bank, established in 1865 by antislavery whites in an effort to promote landownership among African Americans. They persuaded thousands of freedmen to deposit their modest savings in the bank, but then invested heavily in unsuccessful enterprises. It was ill prepared, therefore, for the national depression of the 1870s and it failed in 1874.

Still, most blacks, and a growing minority of whites, did not own their own land during Reconstruction; and some who acquired land in the 1860s had lost it by the 1890s. These

SHARECROPPING

people worked for others in one form or another. Many African American agricultural laborers–perhaps 25 percent of the total–simply worked for wages. Most, however, became tenants of white landowners–working their own plots of land and paying their landlords either a fixed rent or a share of their crop (see p. 420).

The new system was a repudiation of former slaves of the gang-labor system of the antebellum plantation, in which slaves had lived and worked together under the direction of a master. As tenants and sharecroppers, African Americans enjoyed at least a physical independence from their landlords and had the sense of working their own land, even if in most cases they could never hope to buy it. But tenantry also benefited landlords in some ways, relieving them of any responsibility for the physical well-being of their workers.

THE CROP-LIEN SYSTEM

In some respects, the postwar years were a period of remarkable economic progress for African Americans. If the material benefits they had received under slavery are calculated as income, then prewar blacks had earned about a 22 percent share of the profits of the plantation system. By the end of Reconstruction, they were earning 56 percent. Measured another way, the per capita income of Southern blacks rose 46 percent between 1857 and 1879, while the per capita income of Southern whites declined 35 percent. This represented one of the most significant redistributions of income in American history.

But these figures are somewhat misleading. While the black share of profits was increasing, the total profits of Southern agriculture were declining–a result of the dislocations

SHARECROPPERS, 1879 This painting, by Winslow Homer (1836–1910), depicts sharecroppers picking cotton. In sharecropping, a landowner permits tenants to use the land in exchange for a share of the crops produced. (© The Granger Collection, New York)

of the war and a reduction in the world market for cotton. In addition, while African Americans were earning a greater return on each hour of labor than they had under slavery, they were working fewer hours. Women and children were less likely to labor in the fields than in the past. Adult men tended to work shorter days. In all, the black labor force worked about one-third fewer hours during Reconstruction than slaves had been compelled to work under slavery—a reduction that brought the working schedule of blacks roughly into line with that of white farm laborers. Nor did the income redistribution of the postwar years lift many African Americans out of poverty. Black per capita income rose from about one-quarter of white per capita income to about one-half in the first few years after the war. And after this initial increase, it rose hardly at all.

For blacks and poor whites alike, whatever gains there might have been as a result of land and income redistribution were often overshadowed by the ravages of the crop-lien system.

Few of the traditional institutions of credit in the South—the "factors" and banks—returned after the war. In their stead

NEW SYSTEM OF CREDIT

emerged a new system of credit, centered in large part on local country stores, some of them owned by planters, others by independent merchants. Blacks and whites, landowners and tenants—all depended on these stores for such necessities as food, clothing, seed, and farm implements. And since farmers did not have the same steady cash flow as other workers, customers usually had to rely on credit from these merchants in order to purchase what they needed. Most local stores had no competition (and went to great lengt hs to ensure that things stayed that way). As a result, they were able to set interest rates as high as 50 or 60 percent. Farmers had to give the merchants a lien (or claim) on their crops as collateral for the loans (thus the term "crop-lien system"). Farmers who suffered a few bad years in a row, as often happened, could become trapped in a cycle of debt from which they could never escape.

WASH DAY ON THE PLANTATION One of the most common occupations of women recently emancipated from slavery was taking in laundry from white families who no longer had slaves as household servants. This photograph of a group of African American women illustrates how arduous a task laundry was. (The Library of Congress)

This burdensome credit system had a number of effects on the region, almost all of them unhealthy. One effect was that some former slaves who had acquired land during the early years of Reconstruction gradually lost it as they fell into debt. So, to a lesser extent, did white small landowners. Another effect was that Southern farmers became almost wholly dependent on cash crops—and most of all on cotton—because only such marketable commodities seemed to offer any possibility of escape from debt. Thus Southern agriculture, never sufficiently diversified even in the best of times, became more one-dimensional than ever. The relentless planting of cotton, moreover, was contributing to an exhaustion of the soil. The crop-lien system, in other words, was not only helping to impoverish small farmers; it was also contributing to a general decline in the Southern agricultural economy.

The African American Family in Freedom

One of the most striking features of the black response to Reconstruction was the effort to build or rebuild family structures and to protect them from the interference they had experienced under slavery. A major reason for the rapid departure of so many emancipated slaves from plantations was the desire to find lost relatives and reunite families. Thousands of African Americans wandered through the South—often over vast distances—looking for husbands, wives, children, or other relatives from whom they had been separated. In the few black newspapers that circulated in the South, there were many advertisements by people searching for information about their relatives. Former slaves rushed to have marriages, previously without legal standing, sanctified by church and law. Black families resisted living in the former slave quarters and moved instead to small cabins scattered widely across the countryside, where they could enjoy at least some privacy. Within the black family, the definition of male and female roles quickly came to resemble that within white families. Many women and children ceased working in the fields. Such work, they believed, was a badge of slavery. Instead, many women restricted themselves largely to domestic tasks—cooking, cleaning, gardening, sewing, raising children, attending to the needs of their husbands. Some black husbands refused to allow their wives to work as servants in white homes. "When I married my wife I married her to wait on me," one freedman told a former master who was attempting to hire his wife as a servant. "She got all she can do right here for me and the children."

Still, middle-class notions of domesticity were often difficult to sustain in the impoverished circumstances of most former slaves. Economic necessity required many black women to engage in income-producing activities, including activities that they and their husbands resisted: working as domestic servants, taking in laundry, or helping in the field. By the end of Reconstruction, half of all black women over the age of sixteen were working for wages. And unlike white working women, most black female income-earners were married.

CHANGING GENDER ROLES

THE GRANT ADMINISTRATION

Exhausted by the political turmoil of the Johnson administration, American voters in 1868 yearned for a strong, stable figure to guide them through the troubled years of Reconstruction. They turned trustingly to General Ulysses S. Grant, the hero of the war and, by 1868, a revered national idol.

The Soldier President

Grant could have had the nomination of either party in 1868. But believing that Republican Reconstruction policies were more popular in the North, he accepted the Republican nomination. The Democrats nominated former governor Horatio Seymour of New York. The campaign was a bitter one, and Grant's triumph was surprisingly narrow. Without the 500,000 new black Republican voters in the South, he would have had a minority of the popular vote.

U.S. GRANT

Grant entered the White House with no political experience, and his performance was clumsy and ineffectual from the start. Except for Hamilton Fish, whom Grant appointed secretary of state and who served for eight years with great distinction, most members of the cabinet were ill equipped for their tasks. Grant relied chiefly, and increasingly, on established party leaders—the group most ardently devoted to patronage. His administration used the spoils system even more blatantly than most of its predecessors, embittering reform-minded members of his party. Grant also alienated the many Northerners who were growing disillusioned with Radical Reconstruction policies, which the president continued to support. Some Republicans suspected, correctly, that there was also corruption in the Grant administration itself.

By the end of Grant's first term, therefore, members of a substantial faction of the party—who referred to themselves as Liberal Republicans—had come to oppose what they called "Grantism." In 1872, hoping to prevent Grant's reelection, they bolted the party and nominated their own presidential candidate: Horace Greeley, veteran editor and publisher of the *New York Tribune*. The Democrats, somewhat reluctantly, named Greeley their candidate as well, hoping that the alliance with the Liberals would enable them to defeat Grant. But the effort was in vain. Grant won a substantial victory, polling 286 electoral votes to Greeley's 66, and nearly 56 percent of the popular total.

LIBERAL REPUBLICANS

The Grant Scandals

During the 1872 campaign, the first of a series of political scandals came to light that would plague Grant and the Republicans for years. It involved the Crédit Mobilier construction company, which had helped build the Union Pacific Railroad. The heads of Crédit Mobilier had used their positions

CRÉDIT MOBILIER

CRÉDIT MOBILIER This political cartoon by Thomas Nast, called "The Cherubs of Crédit Mobilier," depicts the censure by the House of Representatives of Congressmen James Brooks of New York and Oakes Ames of Massachusetts for their involvement in the Crédit Mobilier scandal, one of several scandals to stain the Grant administration. (© The Granger Collection, New York)

as Union Pacific stockholders to steer large fraudulent contracts to their construction company, thus bilking the Union Pacific (and the federal government, which provided large subsidies to the railroad) of millions. To prevent investigations, the directors had given Crédit Mobilier stock to key members of Congress. In 1872, Congress launched an investigation, which revealed that some highly placed Republicans–including Schuyler Colfax, now Grant's vice president–had accepted some of the stock.

One dreary episode followed another in Grant's second term. Benjamin H. Bristow, Grant's third Treasury secretary, discovered that some of his officials and a group of distillers operating as a "whiskey ring" were cheating the government out of taxes by filing false reports. Then a House investigation revealed that William W. Belknap, secretary of war, had accepted bribes to retain an Indian post trader in office (the so-called Indian ring). Other, lesser scandals added to the growing impression that "Grantism" had brought rampant corruption to government.

THE GREENBACK QUESTION

Compounding Grant's, and the nation's, problems was a financial crisis, known as the Panic of 1873. It began with the

PANIC OF 1873 failure of a leading investment banking firm, Jay Cooke and Company, which had invested too heavily in postwar railroad building. There had been panics before–in 1819, 1837, and 1857–but this was worse than any earlier economic crisis. The depression it produced lasted four years.

Debtors now pressured the government to redeem federal war bonds with greenbacks, paper currency of the sort printed during the Civil War, which would increase the amount of money in circulation. But Grant and most Republicans wanted a "sound" currency–based solidly on gold reserves–which would favor the interests of banks and other creditors. Approximately $356 million in paper currency issued during the Civil War was still in circulation. In 1873, the Treasury issued more in response to the panic. But in 1875, Republican leaders in Congress, in an effort to crush the greenback movement for good, passed the Specie Resumption Act. It provided that after January 1, 1879, the greenback dollars, whose value constantly fluctuated, would be redeemed by the government and replaced with new certificates, firmly pegged to the price of gold. The law satisfied creditors, who had worried that debts would be repaid in paper currency of uncertain value. But "resumption" made things more difficult for debtors, because the gold-based money supply could not easily expand.

In 1875, the "greenbackers," as the inflationists were called, formed their own political organization: the National Greenback Party. It was active in the next three presidential

NATIONAL GREENBACK PARTY elections, but it failed to gain widespread support. It did, however, keep the money issue alive. The question of the proper composition of the currency was to remain one of the most controversial and enduring issues in late-nineteenth-century American politics.

REPUBLICAN DIPLOMACY

The Johnson and Grant administrations achieved their greatest successes in foreign affairs. The accomplishments were the work not of the presidents themselves, who displayed little aptitude for diplomacy, but of two outstanding secretaries of state: William H. Seward, who had served Lincoln and who remained in office until 1869; and Hamilton Fish, who served throughout the two terms of the Grant administration.

An ardent expansionist, Seward acted with as much daring as the demands of Reconstruction politics and the Republican

"SEWARD'S FOLLY" hatred of President Johnson would permit. Seward accepted a Russian offer to sell Alaska to the United States for $7.2 million, despite criticism from many Americans who considered Alaska a frozen wasteland and derided it as "Seward's Folly." In 1867, Seward also engineered the American annexation of the tiny Midway Islands, west of Hawaii.

Hamilton Fish's first major challenge was resolving the long-standing controversy with England over the American claims that the British government had violated neutrality laws during the Civil War by permitting English shipyards to

ALABAMA CLAIMS build ships (among them the *Alabama*) for the Confederacy. American demands that England pay for the damage these vessels had caused became known as the "*Alabama* claims." In 1871, after a number of failed efforts, Fish forged an agreement, the Treaty of Washington, which provided for international arbitration and in which Britain expressed regret for the "escape" of the *Alabama* from England.

THE ABANDONMENT OF RECONSTRUCTION

As the North grew increasingly preoccupied with its own political and economic problems, interest in Reconstruction began to wane. The Grant administration continued to protect Republican governments in the South, but less because of any interest in ensuring the position of freedmen than because of a desire to prevent the reemergence of a strong Democratic Party in the region. But even the presence of federal troops was not enough to prevent white Southerners from overturning the Reconstruction regimes. By the time Grant left office, Democrats had taken back (or, as white Southerners called it, "redeemed") the governments of seven of the eleven former Confederate states. For three other states—South Carolina, Louisiana, and Florida—the end of Reconstruction had to wait for the withdrawal of the last federal troops in 1876, a withdrawal that was the result of a long process of political bargaining and compromise at the national level. (One former Confederate state, Tennessee, had never been part of the Reconstruction process because it had ratified the Fourteenth Amendment and rejoined the Union in 1866.)

THE SOUTHERN STATES "REDEEMED"

In the states where whites constituted a majority—the states of the upper South—overthrowing Republican control was relatively simple. By 1872, all but a handful of Southern whites had regained suffrage. Now a clear majority of the electorate, they needed only to organize and vote for their candidates.

In other states, where African Americans were a majority or the black and white populations were almost equal, whites used intimidation and violence to undermine the Reconstruction regimes. Secret societies—the Ku Klux Klan, the Knights of the White Camellia, and others—used terrorism to frighten or physically bar blacks from voting or otherwise exercising citizenship. Paramilitary organizations—the Red Shirts and White Leagues—armed themselves to "police" elections and worked to force all white males to join the Democratic Party and to exclude all African Americans from meaningful political activity.

The Ku Klux Klan was the largest and most effective of these organizations. Formed in 1866 and led by former **KU KLUX KLAN** Confederate general Nathan Bedford Forrest, it gradually absorbed many of the smaller terrorist organizations in the South. Its leaders devised rituals, costumes, secret languages, and other airs of mystery to create a bond among its members and make the organization seem even more terrifying to those it was attempting to intimidate. The Klan's "midnight rides"—bands of men clad in white sheets and masks, their horses covered with white robes and with hooves muffled—created terror in black communities throughout the South.

Many white Southerners considered the Klan and the other secret societies and paramilitary groups proud, patriotic societies. Together such groups served, in effect, as a military force (even if a decentralized and poorly organized one) continuing the battle against Northern rule. They worked in particular to advance the interests of those with the most to gain from a restoration of white supremacy—above all the planter class and the Southern Democratic Party. Even stronger than the Klan in discouraging black political power, however, was the simple weapon of economic pressure: some planters refused to rent land to Republican blacks; storekeepers refused to extend them credit; employers refused to give them work.

THE KU KLUX KLAN ACTS

The Republican Congress tried for a time to turn back this new wave of white repression. In 1870 and 1871, it passed **ENFORCEMENT ACTS** two Enforcement Acts, also known as the Ku Klux Klan Acts, which were in many ways the most radical measures of the era. The Enforcement Acts prohibited the states from discriminating against voters on the basis of race and gave the federal government power to supersede the state courts and prosecute violations of the law. It was the first time the federal government had ever claimed the power to prosecute crimes by individuals under federal law. Federal district attorneys were now empowered to take action against conspiracies to deny African Americans such rights as voting, holding office, and serving on juries. The new laws also authorized the president to use the military to protect civil rights and to suspend the right of habeas corpus when violations of the rights seemed particularly egregious. In October 1871, President Grant used this provision of the law when he declared a "state of lawlessness" in nine counties in South Carolina and sent in federal troops to occupy the area. Hundreds of suspected Klan members were arrested; some were held for long periods without trial; some were eventually convicted under the law and sent to jail.

The Enforcement Acts were seldom used as severely as they were in South Carolina, but they were effec-**DECLINE OF THE KLAN** tive in the effort by blacks and Northern whites to weaken the Klan. By 1872, Klan violence against blacks was in decline throughout the region.

WANING NORTHERN COMMITMENT

The Ku Klux Klan Acts marked the peak of Republican commitment to enforce the new rights Reconstruction was extending to black citizens. But that commitment did not last for long. Southern blacks were gradually losing the support of many of their former backers in the North. As early as 1870, after the adoption of the Fifteenth Amendment, some northern reformers convinced themselves that their long campaign on behalf of black people was now over—that with the vote, African Americans ought to be able to take care of themselves. Over the next several years, former Radical leaders such as Charles Sumner and Horace Greeley now began calling themselves Liberals, cooperating with Democrats and, at times, outdoing even the Democrats in denouncing what they viewed as black and carpetbag misgovernment. Within the South itself, many white Republicans joined the Liberals and eventually moved into the Democratic Party.

The Panic of 1873 further undermined support for Reconstruction. The economic crisis spurred Northern industrialists and their allies to find an explanation for the poverty and instability around them. They found it in a new idea known as "Social Darwinism" (see p. 471), a harsh theory that argued that individuals who failed did so because of their

IMPACT OF SOCIAL DARWINISM

own weakness and "unfitness." Those influenced by Social Darwinism came to view the large number of unemployed vagrants in the North—and poor African Americans in the South—as irredeemable misfits. Social Darwinism also encouraged a broad critique of government intervention in social and economic life, which further weakened commitment to the Reconstruction program. Support for land redistribution, never great, and willingness to spend money from the depleted federal treasury to aid the freedmen, waned quickly after 1873. State and local governments also found themselves short of funds, and rushed to cut back on social services—which in the South meant the end of almost all services to the former slaves.

In the congressional elections of 1874, the Democrats won control of the House of Representatives for the first time since 1861. Grant took note of the changing temper of the North and made use of military force to prop up the Republican regimes that were still standing in the South. By the end of 1876, only three southern states were left in the hands of the Republicans—South Carolina, Louisiana, and Florida. In state elections that year, Democrats (after using terrorist tactics) claimed victory in all three. But the Republicans challenged the results and claimed victory as well, and they were able to remain in office because of the presence of federal troops. Without federal troops, it was now clear, the last of the Republican regimes would quickly fall.

THE COMPROMISE OF 1877

Grant had hoped to run for another term in 1876. But most Republican leaders were shaken by recent Democrat success, afraid of the scandals with which Grant was associated, and

HAYES VERSUS TILDEN

concerned about the president's declining health. Instead, they sought a candidate not associated with the problems of the Grant years, one who might entice Liberals and unite the party again. They settled on Rutherford B. Hayes of Ohio, a former Union army officer, governor, and congressman, champion of civil service reform. The Democrats united behind Samuel J. Tilden, the reform governor of New York who had been instrumental in challenging the corrupt Tweed Ring of New York City's Tammany Hall.

Although the campaign was a bitter one, there were few differences of principle between the candidates, both of whom were conservatives committed to moderate reform. The

November election produced an apparent Democratic victory. Tilden carried the South and several large Northern states, and his popular margin over Hayes was nearly 300,000 votes. But disputed returns from Louisiana, South Carolina, Florida, and Oregon, whose total electoral vote was 20, threw the election in doubt. Tilden had undisputed claim to 184 electoral votes, only one short of a majority. But Hayes could still win if he managed to receive all 20 disputed votes.

The Constitution had established no method to determine the validity of disputed returns. It was clear that the decision lay with Congress, but it was not clear with which house or through what method. (The Senate was Republican, the House, Democratic.) Members of each party naturally supported a solution that would yield them the victory.

Finally, late in January 1877, Congress tried to break the deadlock by creating a special electoral commission to judge

SPECIAL ELECTORAL COMMISSION

the disputed votes. The commission would be composed of five senators, five representatives, and five justices of the Supreme Court. The congressional delegation would consist of five Republicans and five Democrats. The Court delegation would include two Republicans, two Democrats, and an independent. But the independent seat ultimately went to a justice whose real sympathies were with the Republicans. The commission voted along straight

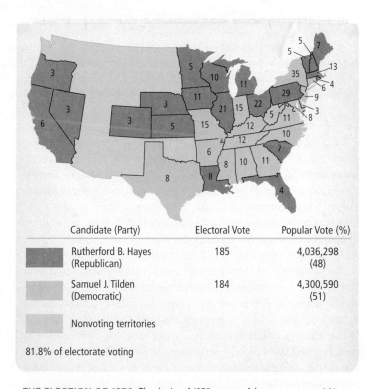

Candidate (Party)	Electoral Vote	Popular Vote (%)
Rutherford B. Hayes (Republican)	185	4,036,298 (48)
Samuel J. Tilden (Democratic)	184	4,300,590 (51)
Nonvoting territories		

81.8% of electorate voting

THE ELECTION OF 1876 The election of 1876 was one of the most controversial in American history. As in the elections of 1824, 1888, and 2000, the winner of the popular vote—Samuel J. Tilden—was not the winner of the electoral college, which he lost by one vote. The final decision as to who would be president was not made until the day before the official inauguration in March.

• How did the Republicans turn this apparent defeat into a victory?

RECONSTRUCTION

DEBATE over the nature of Reconstruction has created so much controversy over the decades that one scholar, writing in 1959, described the issue as a "dark and bloody ground." For many years, a relatively uniform and highly critical view of Reconstruction prevailed among historians. William A. Dunning offered the principal scholarly expression of this view in *Reconstruction, Political and Economic* (1907), the first major historical interpretation of Reconstruction. Dunning portrayed Reconstruction as a corrupt outrage perpetrated on the prostrate South by a vicious and vindictive group of Northern Republican Radicals. Unscrupulous carpetbaggers flooded the South to profit from the misery of the defeated region. Ignorant, illiterate blacks were thrust into positions of power for which they were entirely unfit. The Reconstruction experiment survived only because of the determination of the Republican Party to keep itself in power. Some later writers, notably Howard K. Beale, added an economic motive—to protect Northern business interests.

Dunning's interpretation shaped the views of several generations of historians and helped shape popular depictions of Reconstruction such as those expressed in the 1915 film *The Birth of a Nation* and then the 1936 book and 1939 movie *Gone with the Wind*.

The great African American scholar W. E. B. Du Bois was among the first to challenge the Dunning view. In *Black Reconstruction* (1935), Du Bois argued that Reconstruction politics in the Southern states had been an effort on the part of the masses, black and white, to create a more democratic society. The misdeeds of the Reconstruction governments, he claimed, had been greatly exaggerated, and their achievements overlooked. In the 1940s, the historians C. Vann Woodward, David Herbert Donald, Thomas B. Alexander, and others began to reexamine the Reconstruction governments in the South and to suggest that their records were not nearly as inaccurate and incomplete as most historians had previously assumed.

By the early 1960s, a new view of Reconstruction was emerging. The revisionist approach was summarized by John Hope Franklin in *Reconstruction after the Civil War* (1961) and Kenneth Stampp in *The Era of Reconstruction* (1965), who claimed that the postwar Republicans had been engaged in a genuine, if flawed, effort to solve the problem of race in the South by providing much-needed protection to the freedmen. The Reconstruction governments, for all their faults, had been bold experiments in interracial politics. The congressional Radicals were not saints, but they had displayed a genuine concern for the rights of slaves. Andrew Johnson was not a martyred defender of the Constitution, but an inept, racist politician who resisted reasonable compromise and brought the government to a crisis. African Americans had played only a small part in Reconstruction governments and had generally acquitted themselves well. The Reconstruction regimes had, in fact, brought important progress to the South, establishing the region's first public school system and other important social changes. Corruption in the South had been no worse than corruption in the North at that time. What was tragic about Reconstruction, the revisionist view claimed, was not what it did to Southern whites but, rather, what it did not do for Southern blacks. By stopping short of the reforms necessary to ensure blacks genuine equality, Reconstruction had consigned them to more than a century of injustice and discrimination.

In later years, scholars began to question the revisionist view in an attempt to draw attention to the achievements of Reconstruction. Eric Foner, in *Nothing but Freedom* (1983) and *Reconstruction: America's Unfinished Revolution* (1988), emphasized how far the former slaves moved toward freedom and independence

---

party lines, 8 to 7, awarding every disputed vote to Hayes. Congress accepted their verdict on March 2. Two days later, Hayes was inaugurated.

Behind the resolution of the deadlock, however, lay a series of elaborate compromises among leaders of both parties. When a Democratic filibuster threatened to derail the commission's report, Republican Senate leaders met secretly with Southern Democratic leaders to work out terms by which the Democrats would allow the election of Hayes. According to traditional accounts, Republicans and Southern Democrats met at Washington's Wormley Hotel. In return for a Republican pledge that Hayes would withdraw the last federal troops from the South, thus permitting the overthrow of the last Republican governments there, the Southerners agreed to abandon the filibuster.

Actually, the story behind the "Compromise of 1877" is more complex. Hayes was already on record favoring withdrawal of the troops, so Republicans needed to offer more than that if they hoped for Democratic support. The real

COMPROMISE OF 1877

agreement, the one that won over the Southern Democrats, was reached well before the Wormley meeting. As the price of their cooperation, the Southern Democrats (among them some former Whigs) exacted several pledges from the Republicans in addition to withdrawal of the troops: the appointment of at least one Southerner to the Hayes cabinet, control of federal patronage in their areas, generous internal improvements, and federal aid for the Texas and Pacific Railroad. Many powerful Southern Democrats supported industrializing their region. They believed Republican programs of federal support for business would aid the South more than the states' rights policies of the Democrats.

In his inaugural address, Hayes announced that the South's most pressing need was the restoration of "wise, honest, and peaceful local self-government"–a signal that he planned to withdraw federal troops and let white Democrats take over the state governments. That statement, and Hayes's subsequent actions, supported the widespread charges that he was

THE FREEDMEN'S BUREAU For four years after the Civil War, the Freedmen's Bureau served newly freed slaves, helping them to get housing, food, education, and other services. This image shows African American men and women waiting for rations, most of them old and sick. (© The Granger Collection, New York)

own terms and asserting their control over family life, reproduction, and work. According to Jones in *Labor of Love, Labor of Sorrow* (1985), women in particular sought the opportunity "to labor on behalf of their own families and kin within the protected spheres of household and community."

Some historians have begun to argue that Reconstruction was not restricted to the South alone. Heather Richardson, in *West from Appomattox* (2007) and *The Death of Reconstruction* (2001), shows how the entire nation changed during the Civil War and Reconstruction—with the South, perhaps, changing least of all. The age of Reconstruction was also the age of western expansion and industrialization. ●

AP HISTORICAL ARGUMENTATION AND INTERPRETATION

Questions assume cumulative content knowledge from this chapter and previous chapters.

1. Describe the respective historical interpretations of four of the historians discussed, regarding the nature of Reconstruction. For each, identify one piece of historical evidence that could be used to support the argument and one piece of historical evidence that could be used to refute the argument.
2. In the 1960s, America experienced a significant civil rights movement, particularly for African American rights. Explain in what way this civil rights movement might have encouraged historians of the time to reexamine past historical interpretations of Reconstruction.
3. With which historical argument regarding Reconstruction do you most agree? Support your view, using historical evidence.

in a short time and how large a role African Americans played in shaping Reconstruction. During Reconstruction, blacks won a certain amount of legal and political power in the South; even though they held that power only temporarily, they used it to strengthen their economic and social positions and to win a position of limited but genuine independence. Though they failed to achieve equality, they won a measure of individual and community autonomy that they used as building blocks of the freedom that emancipation alone had not guaranteed. Leon Litwack argued similarly in *Been in the Storm So Long* (1979) that former slaves used the relative latitude they enjoyed under Reconstruction to build a certain independence for themselves within Southern society. They strengthened their churches; they reunited their families; by refusing to work in the "gang-labor" system of the plantations, they forced the creation of a new labor system in which they had more control over their own lives. Writing from the perspective of women's history, Amy Dru Stanley and Jacqueline Jones have both argued that the freed slaves displayed considerable independence in constructing their households on their

paying off the South for acquiescing in his election and strengthened those who referred to him as "his Fraudulency." Hayes tried to counter such charges by projecting an image of stern public (and private) rectitude. But the election had already created such bitterness that even Hayes's promise to serve only one term could not mollify his critics.

The president and his party had hoped to build up a "new Republican" organization in the South drawn from Whiggish conservative white groups and committed to some modest

REPUBLICAN FAILURE IN THE SOUTH

acceptance of African American rights. But all such efforts failed. Although many white Southern leaders sympathized with Republican economic policies, popular resentment of Reconstruction and its attack on white supremacy was so deep that supporting the party was politically impossible. At the same time, the withdrawal of federal troops signaled that the national government was giving up its attempts to control Southern politics and to improve the lot of African Americans in Southern society.

THE LEGACIES OF RECONSTRUCTION

Reconstruction made some important contributions to the efforts of former slaves to achieve dignity and equality in American life. And it was not as disastrous an experience for Southern whites as most of them believed at the time. But Reconstruction was in the end largely a failure, for in those years the United States abandoned its first serious effort to resolve the nation's oldest and deepest social problem—the problem of race. Moreover, the experience so disappointed, disillusioned, and embittered white Americans that it would be nearly a century before they would try again in any serious way.

Why did this great assault on racial injustice not achieve more? In part, it was because of the weaknesses and errors of the people who directed it. But in greater

IDEOLOGICAL LIMITS

part, it was because attempts to produce solutions ran up against conservative obstacles so deeply embedded in the nation's life that they could not be dislodged. Veneration of the Constitution

"IS THIS A REPUBLICAN FORM OF GOVERNMENT?" The New York artist and cartoonist Thomas Nast marked the end of Reconstruction in 1876 with this biting cartoon in *Harper's Weekly*, expressing his dismay at what he considered the nation's betrayal of the former slaves, who still had not received adequate guarantees of their rights. The caption of the cartoon continued: "Is *this* protecting life, liberty, or property? Is *this* equal protection of the laws?" (The Library of Congress (LC-USZ62-116355))

sharply limited the willingness of national leaders to infringe on the rights of states and individuals. A profound respect for private property and free enterprise prevented any real assault on economic privilege in the South. Above all, perhaps, a pervasive belief among many of even the most liberal whites that African Americans were inherently inferior served as an obstacle to equality. Given the context within which Americans of the 1860s and 1870s were working, what is surprising is not that Reconstruction did so little, but that it did as much as it did.

Considering the odds confronting them, therefore, African Americans had reason for pride in the gains they made during Reconstruction. And future generations had reason for gratitude for two great charters of freedom—the Fourteenth and Fifteenth Amendments to the Constitution—which, although largely ignored at the time, would one day serve as the basis for a "Second Reconstruction" that would renew the drive to bring freedom and equality to all Americans.

THE NEW SOUTH

The agreement between southern Democrats and northern Republicans that helped settle the disputed election of 1876 was supposed to be the first step toward developing a stable, permanent Republican Party in the South. In that respect, at

least, it failed. In the years following the end of Reconstruction, white southerners established the Democratic Party as the only viable political organization for the region's whites. Even so, the South did change in the years after Reconstruction in some of the ways the framers of the Compromise of 1877 had hoped.

THE "REDEEMERS"

By the end of 1877–after the last withdrawal of federal troops–every southern state government had been "redeemed" by white Democrats. Many white southerners rejoiced at the res-

BOURBON RULE toration of what they liked to call "home rule." But in reality, political power in the region was soon more restricted than at any time since the Civil War. Once again, the South fell under the control of a powerful, conservative oligarchy, whose members were known variously as the "Redeemers" (to themselves and their supporters) or the "Bourbons" (a term for aristocrats used by some of their critics).

In a few places, this post-Reconstruction ruling class was much the same as the ruling class of the antebellum period. In Alabama, for example, the old planter elite–despite challenges from new merchant and industrial forces–retained much of its former power and continued largely to dominate the state for decades. In most areas, however, the Redeemers constituted a genuinely new ruling class. They were merchants, industrialists, railroad developers, and financiers. Some of them were former planters, some of them northern immigrants who had become absorbed into the region's life, some of them ambitious, upwardly mobile white southerners from the region's lower social tiers. They combined a commitment to "home rule" and social conservatism with a commitment to economic development.

The various Bourbon governments of the New South behaved similarly to one another. Conservatives had complained that the Reconstruction governments fostered widespread corruption, but the Redeemer regimes were even more awash in waste and fraud. (In this, they were little different from governments in every region of the country.) At the same time, virtually all the new Democratic regimes lowered taxes, reduced spending, and drastically diminished state services–including many of the most important accomplishments of Reconstruction. In one state after another, for example, state support for public school systems was reduced or eliminated. "Schools are not a necessity," an economy-conscious governor of Virginia commented.

By the late 1870s, significant dissenting groups were challenging the Bourbons: protesting the cuts in services and denouncing the commitment of the Redeemer governments to

THE READJUSTER CHALLENGE paying off the prewar and Reconstruction debts in full, at the original (usually high) rates of interest. In Virginia, for example, a vigorous "Readjuster" movement emerged, demanding that the state revise its debt payment procedures so as to make more money available for state services. In 1879, the

Readjusters won control of the legislature, and in the next few years they captured the governorship and a U.S. Senate seat. Other states produced similar movements, some of them adding demands as well for greenbacks, debt relief, and other economic reforms. (A few such independent movements included significant numbers of African Americans in their ranks, but all consisted primarily of lower-income whites.) By the mid-1880s, however, conservative southerners–largely by exploiting racial prejudice–had destroyed most of the dissenting movements.

INDUSTRIALIZATION AND THE "NEW SOUTH"

Some white southern leaders in the post-Reconstruction era hoped to see their region become the home of a vigorous industrial economy. The South had lost the war, such leaders

HENRY GRADY argued, because its economy had been unable to compete with the modernized manufacturing capacity of the North. Now the region must "out-Yankee the Yankees" and build a "New South." Henry Grady, editor of the *Atlanta Constitution,* and other prominent spokesmen for a New South seldom challenged white supremacy, but they did advocate other important changes in southern values. Above all, they promoted the virtues of thrift, industry, and progress–qualities that prewar southerners had often denounced in northern society. "We have sown towns and cities in the place of theories," Grady boasted to a New England audience in the 1880s, "and put business above politics. . . . We have fallen in love with work." But even the most fervent advocates of the New South creed were generally unwilling to break entirely with the southern past. That was evident in, among other things, the popular literature of the region. At the same time that white southern writers were extolling the virtues of industrialization in newspaper editorials and speeches, they were painting nostalgic portraits of the Old South in their literature. Few southerners advocated a literal return to the old ways, but most whites eagerly embraced romantic talk of the "Lost Cause." And they responded warmly to the local-color fiction of such writers as Joel Chandler Harris, whose folktales–the most famous being *Uncle Remus* (1880)– portrayed the slave society of the antebellum years as a harmonious world marked by engaging dialect and close emotional bonds between the races. The writer Thomas Nelson Page similarly extolled the old Virginia aristocracy. The growing popularity of minstrel shows also reflected the romanticization of the Old South (see "Patterns of Popular Culture," pp. 420–421). The white leaders of the New South, in short, faced their future with one foot still in the past.

Even so, southern industry expanded dramatically in the years after Reconstruction and became a more important part of the region's economy than ever before. Most visible was the growth in textile manufacturing, which increased ninefold in the last twenty years of the century. In the past, southern planters had usually shipped their cotton out of the region to manufacturers in the North or in Europe. Now textile factories appeared in the South itself–many of them drawn to the South from New England by the abundance of water power, the

ready supply of cheap labor, the low taxes, and the accommodating conservative governments. The tobacco-processing industry, similarly, established an important foothold in the region, largely through the work of James B. Duke of North Carolina, whose American Tobacco Company established for a time a virtual monopoly over the processing of raw tobacco into marketable materials. In the lower South, particularly in Birmingham, Alabama, the iron (and, later, steel) industry grew rapidly. By 1890, the southern iron and steel industry represented nearly a fifth of the nation's total capacity.

Railroad development increased substantially in the post-Reconstruction years–at a rate far greater than that of the nation at large. Between 1880 and 1890, trackage in the South

RAILROAD DEVELOPMENT more than doubled. And the South took a major step toward integrating its transportation system with that of the rest of the country when, in 1886, it changed the gauge (distance between the two rails) of its trackage to correspond with the standards of the North. Yet southern industry developed within strict limits, and its effects on the region were never even remotely comparable to the effects of industrialization on the North. The southern share of national manufacturing doubled in the last twenty years of the century, to 10 percent of the total. But that percentage was the same the South had claimed in 1860; the region, in other words, had done no more than regain what it had lost during the war and its aftermath. The region's per capita income increased 21 percent in the same period. But at the end of the century, average income in the South was only 40 percent of that in the North; in 1860 it had been more than 60 percent. And even in those areas where development had been most rapid–textiles, iron, railroads–much of the capital had come from the North. In effect, the South was developing a colonial economy.

The growth of industry in the South required the region to recruit a substantial industrial workforce for the first time. From the beginning, a high percentage of the factory workers (and an especially high percentage of textile workers) were women. Heavy male casualties in the Civil War had helped create a large population of unmarried women who were in dire need of employment. Factories also hired entire families, many of whom were moving into towns from failed farms. Workdays were long (often twelve hours a day) and wages were far below the northern equivalent; indeed, one of the greatest attractions of the South to industrialists was that employers were able to pay workers there as little as one-half what northern workers received.

Life in most mill towns was rigidly controlled by the owners and managers of the factories, who rigorously suppressed attempts at protest or union organization. Company stores sold goods to workers at inflated prices and issued credit at exorbitant rates (much like country stores in agrarian areas), and mill owners ensured that no competitors were able to establish themselves in the community. At the same time, however, the conditions of the mill town helped create a strong sense of community and solidarity among workers (even if they seldom translated such feelings into militancy).

THE MINSTREL SHOW

THE minstrel show was one of the most popular forms of entertainment in America in the second half of the nineteenth century. It was also a testament to the high awareness of race (and the high level of racism) in American society both before and after the Civil War. Minstrel performers were mostly white, usually disguised as black. But African American performers also formed

their own minstrel shows and transformed them into vehicles for training black entertainers and developing new forms of music and dance.

Before and during the Civil War, when minstrel shows consisted almost entirely of white performers, performers blackened their faces with cork and presented grotesque stereotypes of the slave culture of the American South. Among the most popular of the stumbling, ridiculously ignorant characters invented for these shows were such figures as "Zip Coon" and "Jim Crow" (whose name later resurfaced as a label for late-nineteenth-century segregation laws). A typical minstrel show presented a group of seventeen or more men seated in a semicircle facing the audience. The man in the center ran the show, played the straight man for the jokes of others, and led the music—lively dances and sentimental ballads played on banjos, castanets, and other instruments and sung by soloists or the entire group.

After the Civil War, white minstrels began to expand their repertoire. Drawing from the famous and successful freak shows of P. T. Barnum and other entertainment entrepreneurs, some began to include Siamese twins, bearded ladies, and even a supposedly 8-foot 2-inch "Chinese giant" in their shows. They also incorporated sex, both by including women in some shows and, even more popularly, by recruiting female impersonators. One of the most successful minstrel performers of the 1870s was Francis Leon, who delighted crowds with his female portrayal of a flamboyant "prima donna."

One reason white minstrels began to move in these new directions was that they were now facing competition from black performers, who could provide more-authentic versions of black music, dance, and humor.

MINSTRELSY AT HIGH TIDE The Primrose & West minstrel troupe—a lavish and expensive entertainment that drew large crowds in the 1800s—was one of many companies to offer this brand of entertainment to eager audiences all over the country. Although minstrelsy began with white musicians performing in blackface, the popularity of real African American minstrels encouraged the impresarios of the troupe to include groups of white and black performers alike. (The Library of Congress (LC-USZ62-2659))

Some industries, textiles for example, offered virtually no opportunities to African American workers. Others–including tobacco, iron, and lumber–did provide some employment for blacks, usually the most menial and lowest-paid positions. Some mill towns, therefore, were places where black and white culture came into close contact. That proximity contributed less to the growth of racial harmony than to the determination of white leaders to take additional measures to protect white supremacy.

At times, industrialization proceeded on the basis of no wage-paying employment. Through the "convict-lease" system, southern states leased gangs of convicted criminals to private **"CONVICT-LEASE" SYSTEM** interests as a cheap labor supply. The system exposed the convicts to brutal and at times fatal mistreatment. It paid them nothing (the leasing fees went to the states, not the workers).

And it denied employment in railroad construction and other projects to the free labor force.

TENANTS AND SHARECROPPERS

Despite significant growth in southern industry, the region remained primarily agrarian. The most important economic reality in the post-Reconstruction South, therefore, was the impoverished state of agriculture. The 1870s and 1880s saw an acceleration of the trends that had begun in the immediate postwar years: the imposition of systems of tenantry and debt peonage on much of the region; the reliance on a few cash crops rather than on a diversified agricultural system; and increasing absentee ownership of valuable farmlands (many of them purchased by merchants and industrialists who paid little

AG FIELD MINSTRELS This famous minstrel group stands in front of a huge promotional poster sometime in the late 1890s. (© Archive Photos/Getty Images)

But interest in the minstrel show did not die altogether. In 1927, Hollywood released *The Jazz Singer*, the first feature film with sound. It was about the career of a white minstrel performer, and its star was one of the most popular singers of the twentieth century: Al Jolson, whose career had begun on the blackface minstrel circuit years before. ●

They usually brought more talent to the task than white performers. The Georgia Minstrels, organized in 1865, was one of the first all-black minstrel troupes, and it had great success in attracting white audiences in the Northeast for several years. By the 1870s, touring African American minstrel groups were numerous. The black minstrels used many of the conventions of the white shows. There were dances, music, comic routines, and sentimental recitations. Some black performers even chalked their faces to make themselves look as dark as the white blackface performers with whom they were competing. Black minstrels sometimes denounced slavery (at least indirectly) and did not often speak demeaningly of the capacities of their race. But they could not entirely escape caricaturing African American life as they struggled to meet the expectations of their white audiences.

The black minstrel shows had few openly political aims. They did help develop some important forms of African American entertainment and transform them into a part of the national culture. Black minstrels introduced new forms of dance, derived from the informal traditions of slavery and black community life. They showed the "buck and wing," the "stop time," and the "Virginia essence," which established the foundations for the tap and jazz dancing of the early twentieth century. They also improvised musically and began experimenting with forms that over time contributed to the growth of ragtime, jazz, and rhythm and blues.

Eventually, black minstrelsy—like its white counterpart—evolved into other forms of theater, including the beginnings of serious black drama. At Ambrose Park in Brooklyn in the 1890s, for example, the celebrated black comedian Sam Lucas (a veteran of the minstrel circuit) starred in the play *Darkest America,* which one black newspaper later described as a "delineation of Negro life, carrying the race through all their historical phases from the plantation, into reconstruction days and finally painting our people as they are today, cultured and accomplished in the social graces, [holding] the mirror faithfully up to nature."

attention to whether the land was being properly used). During Reconstruction, perhaps a third or more of the farmers in the South were tenants; by 1900, the figure had increased to 70 percent. That was in large part the result of the crop-lien system, the system by which farmers borrowed money against their future crops and often fell deeper and deeper into debt.

Tenantry took several forms. Farmers who owned tools, equipment, and farm animals–or who had the money to buy them–usually paid an annual cash rent for their land. But many farmers (including most black ones) had no money or equipment. Landlords would supply them with land, a crude house, a few tools, seed, and sometimes a mule. In return, farmers would promise the landlord a large share of the annual crop–hence the term "sharecropping." After paying their landlords

and their local merchants (who were often the same people), sharecroppers seldom had anything left to sell on their own.

AFRICAN AMERICANS AND THE NEW SOUTH

The "New South creed" was not the property of whites alone. Many African Americans were attracted to the vision of progress and self-improvement as well. Some blacks succeeded in elevating themselves into a distinct middle class—most of them economically inferior to the white middle class, but nevertheless significant. These were former slaves (and, as the decades passed, their offspring) who managed to acquire property, build small businesses, or enter professions. A few African Americans accumulated substantial fortunes by establishing banks and

BLACK MIDDLE CLASS

FAMILY PORTRAIT This photograph of an African American family of four generations was taken in the late nineteenth century. Every member of this family was born on the plantation of J. J. Smith of Beaufort, South Carolina. The youngest members, while certainly touched by slavery, were not born into that institution. (© Corbis)

insurance companies to serve the black community. One of those was Maggie Lena, a black woman who became the first female bank president in the United States when she founded the St. Luke Penny Savings Bank in Richmond in 1903. Most middle-class blacks experienced more-modest gains by becoming doctors, lawyers, nurses, or teachers serving African American communities.

A cardinal tenet of this rising group of African Americans was that education was vital to the future of their race. With the support of northern missionary societies and, to a far lesser extent, a few southern state governments, they expanded the network of black colleges and institutes that had taken root during Reconstruction into an important educational system.

The chief spokesman for this commitment to education, and **BOOKER T. WASHINGTON** for a time the major spokesman for African Americans in the South (and beyond), was Booker T. Washington, founder and president of the Tuskegee Institute in Alabama. Born into slavery, Washington had worked his way out of poverty after acquiring an education (at Virginia's famous Hampton Institute). He urged other blacks to follow the same road to self-improvement.

Washington's message was both cautious and hopeful. African Americans should attend school, learn skills, and establish a solid footing in agriculture and the trades. Industrial, not classical, education should be their goal. They should, moreover, refine their speech, improve their dress, and adopt habits of thrift and personal cleanliness; they should, in short, adopt the standards of the white middle class. Only thus, he claimed, could they win the respect of the white population, the prerequisite for any larger social gains. African Americans should forgo agitating for political rights, he said, and concentrate on self-improvement and preparation for equality. In a famous speech **THE ATLANTA COMPROMISE** in Georgia in 1895, Washington outlined a philosophy of race relations that became widely known as the Atlanta Compromise. "The wisest among my race understand," he said, "that the agitation of questions of social equality is the extremest folly." Rather, blacks should engage in "severe and constant struggle" for economic gains; for, as he explained, "no race that has anything to contribute to the markets of the world is long in any degree ostracized." If African Americans were ever to win the rights and privileges of citizenship, they must first show that they were "prepared for the exercise of these privileges." Washington offered a powerful challenge to those whites who wanted to discourage African Americans from acquiring an education or winning any economic gains. He helped awaken the interest of a new generation to the possibilities for self-advancement through self-improvement. But his message was also an implicit promise that African Americans would not overtly challenge the system of segregation that whites were then in the process of erecting.

THE BIRTH OF JIM CROW

Few white southerners had ever accepted the idea of racial equality. That the former slaves acquired any legal and political rights at all after emancipation was in large part the result of federal support. That support all but vanished after 1877. Federal troops withdrew. Congress lost interest. And the Supreme Court effectively stripped the Fourteenth and Fifteenth Amendments of much of their significance. In the so-called civil rights cases of 1883, the Court ruled that the Fourteenth Amendment prohibited state governments from discriminating against people because of race but did not restrict private organizations or individuals from doing so. Thus railroads, hotels, theaters, and workplaces could legally practice segregation.

Eventually, the Court also validated state legislation that institutionalized the separation of the races. In *Plessy v. Ferguson* (1896), a case involving a Louisiana law that required separate **PLESSY V. FERGUSON** seating arrangements for the races on railroads, the Court held that separate accommodations did not deprive blacks of equal rights if the accommodations were equal, a decision that survived for years as part of the legal basis for segregated schools. In *Cumming v. County Board of Education* (1899), the Court ruled that laws establishing separate schools for whites were valid even if there were no comparable schools for African Americans.

Before these decisions, white southerners were working to strengthen white supremacy and to separate the races to the greatest extent possible. One illustration of this movement

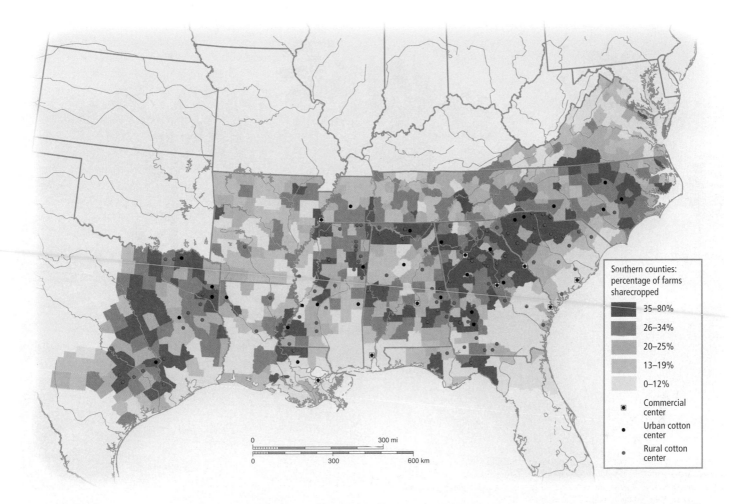

Southern counties: percentage of farms sharecropped

- 35–80%
- 26–34%
- 20–25%
- 13–19%
- 0–12%
- ◉ Commercial center
- • Urban cotton center
- • Rural cotton center

THE CROP-LIEN SYSTEM IN 1880 In the years after the Civil War, more and more southern farmers—white and black—became tenants or sharecroppers on land owned by others. This map shows the percentage of farms that were within the so-called crop lien system, the system by which people worked their lands for someone else, who had a claim (or "lien") on a part of the farmers' crops. Note the high density of sharecropping and tenant farming in the most fertile areas of the Deep South, the same areas where slaveholding had been most dominant before the Civil War.

• *How did the crop-lien system contribute to the shift in southern agriculture toward one-crop farming?*

from subordination to segregation was black voting rights. In some states, disenfranchisement had begun almost as soon as Reconstruction ended. But in other areas, black voting continued for some time after Reconstruction—largely because conservative whites believed they could control the black electorate and use it to beat back the attempts of poor white farmers to take control of the Democratic Party. In the 1890s, however, franchise restrictions became much more rigid. During those years, some small white farmers began to demand complete black disenfranchisement—both because of racial prejudice and because they objected to the black vote being used against them by the conservative planters (known as "Bourbons", see p. 418). At the same time, many members of the conservative elite began to fear that poor whites might unite politically with poor African Americans to challenge them. They too began to support further franchise restrictions.

In devising laws to disenfranchise black males, the southern states had to find ways to evade the Fifteenth Amendment, which prohibited states from denying anyone the right to vote because of race. Two devices emerged before 1900 to accomplish this goal. One was the poll tax or some form of property

RESTRICTING THE FRANCHISE

qualification; few African Americans were prosperous enough to meet such requirements. Another was the "literacy" or "understanding" test, which required voters to demonstrate an ability to read and interpret the Constitution. Even those African Americans who could read had trouble passing the difficult test white officials gave them. Such restrictions were often applied unequally. Literacy tests for whites, for example, were sometimes much easier than those for blacks. Even so, the laws affected poor white voters as well as African Americans. By the late 1890s, the black vote had decreased by 62 percent, the white vote by 26 percent. One result was that some states passed so-called grandfather laws, permitting men who could not meet the literacy and property qualifications to be enfranchised if their ancestors had voted before Reconstruction began, thus barring the descendants of slaves from the polls while allowing poor whites access to them. In many areas, however, ruling elites were quite content to see poor whites, a potential source of opposition to their power, barred from voting.

The Supreme Court proved as compliant in ruling on the disenfranchising laws as it was in dealing with the civil rights

REMEMBERING BLACK HISTORY

HOW WE REMEMBER THE PAST can tell us a great deal about our values and priorities as a nation. When these memories take official form, as in a public monument erected in a culturally significant setting, they offer a view into how Americans understood history in a particular time. What is revealed, however, is rarely a popular consensus about what individuals or events were worthy of being celebrated. Rather, the final construction and placement of any public monument typically reflects a series of tough debates between people with different views of the meaning of the past.

The two monuments pictured on the following page are among the most famous in American history in general and African American history in particular. The first is a bronze relief by Augustus Saint-Gaudens commemorating the Fifty-Fourth Massachusetts Volunteer Infantry Regiment, the first military unit composed of black soldiers raised in the North during the Civil War. At full fighting strength, with over 1000 African American men led by an all-white officer corps, the 54th became a national symbol of African American freedom. Leading the assault on July 18, 1863, against the Confederate stronghold, Fort Wagner, on Morris Island, South Carolina, it sustained heavy losses, including that of its commanding officer, Colonel Robert Shaw. Despite failing to take the fort, the black troops fought passionately and with discipline, thereby silencing critics who doubted the very ability of African Americans to stand strong in battle.

Saint-Gaudens unveiled his memorial in May 1897. Eleven feet high and 14 feet long, it depicts the 54th marching through Boston in the first leg of its journey to the battlefront. Leading the unit is Colonel Shaw, on horseback. It still sits in its original locale, at the edge of the Boston Common in the shadow of the Massachusetts State House.

The second monument is a white granite statue by Lie Yixin, a sculptor from the People's Republic of China, honoring the life of civil rights pioneer, Martin Luther King, Jr. King, a Baptist minister born in Atlanta, Georgia, who led the fight to end segregation in the South in the 1950s and 1960s. He spearheaded the drive to pass the Civil Rights Act of 1964 and the Voting Rights Act of 1965. He was assassinated in 1968.

The King statue is actually part of a larger, four-acre park dedicated to his life that sits in the southwest corner of the National Mall in Washington, D.C. The 30-foot high statue has a clear view of the Lincoln Memorial and the Jefferson Memorial and is accompanied by a 450-foot long inscription wall that bears quotes from King's most famous speeches. The King Memorial is the first dedicated to a black American on the National Mall.

MEMORIALIZING BLACK HISTORY IN 1897 Memorial to Robert Gould Shaw and the Fifty-Fourth Regiment. (© Egg Images/Alamy)

MEMORIALIZING BLACK HISTORY IN 2011 The Martin Luther King, Jr. National Memorial. (© Evan Golub/Demotix/Corbis)

Questions assume cumulative content knowledge from this chapter and previous chapters.

1. Which statement best describes what the monument from 1897 suggests about general societal attitudes towards African Americans at the turn of the 20th century in America?

   (A) Efforts of African Americans to achieve social equality came to be deeply appreciated by American society in general.

   (B) The inordinate prominence of the white officer suggests that American society still did not fully appreciate African Americans as equals.

   (C) The dominance of the number of African Americans suggests that turn-of-the-century America experienced a boom in African American population.

   (D) The placement of the African American soldiers in the background suggests that around the turn of the 20th century, American society developed great interest in viewing American history from a "black" lens.

2. How does the memorial honoring Martin Luther King, Jr. differ from the monument from 1897?

   (A) The Martin Luther King, Jr., monument suggests that African Americans have achieved social equality, due to the use of white granite.

   (B) The Martin Luther King, Jr., monument reflects less societal appreciation for African American achievement.

   (C) The Martin Luther King, Jr., monument reflects a greater appreciation by American society for African American achievement—in this case, that of Martin Luther King.

   (D) The Martin Luther King, Jr., monument suggests more than the monument from 1897 that more progress needs to be made towards racial equality.

3. In what way might the establishment of the monument from 1897 be viewed as a significant event in black history?

   (A) By offering the public a glimpse of the perspective of African Americans during the war

   (B) By the mere fact of the public memorializing of the role of African Americans in the Civil War

   (C) By revealing through public art the plight of African Americans

   (D) By reinforcing to the public the dominance of white society state and local governments in the South were generally unwilling to do: punish those responsible for lynchings.

But the substantial white opposition to lynchings stood as an exception to the general white support for suppression of African Americans. Indeed, just as in the antebellum period, the shared commitment to white supremacy helped dilute class

WHITE UNITY

animosities between poorer whites and the Bourbon oligarchies. Economic issues tended to play a secondary role to race in southern politics, distracting people from the glaring social inequalities that afflicted blacks and whites alike. The commitment to white supremacy, in short, was a burden for poor whites as well as for blacks.

AP CONNECTING THEMES

Chapter 15 examined conflicts between the North and the South over Reconstruction, as well as related conflicts within various branches of government. Important to understanding this time in U.S. history are the differences between presidential and congressional Reconstruction plans and their impact on the South. Also, important are the constitutional changes brought about in civil liberties and the political system. Reconstruction had varying degrees of success economically, politically, and socially, and views regarding this success differ. As you review the chapter, be very conscious of the means by which southern society created a segregated system that placed African Americans in a status of second-class citizenship. It is important that you understand how the sharecropping system to some degree re-enslaved African Americans. Make a determination on the degree to which you believe a New South arose after Reconstruction and think about evidence that would support your position. Finally, review the controversial election of 1877 and the provisions of the Compromise of 1877, which ended Reconstruction.

The following themes have heightened importance in Chapter 15. You should now be able to do the following for each listed theme:

Identity: Analyze the ways in which American concepts of identity were changed during and after the Civil War and Reconstruction, particularly for African Americans.

Work, Exchange, and Technology: Explain how the Civil War and Reconstruction affected the economies of both the North and the South, including existing labor systems.

Peopling: Explain how the Civil War and Reconstruction encouraged migration.

Politics and Power: Identify the political changes brought about by Reconstruction.

Environment and Geography: Explain the impact of the Civil War on the infrastructure of the South.

Ideas, Beliefs, and Culture: Explain the degree to which the Civil War and Reconstruction altered the beliefs of Northerners and Southerners concerning each other.

AP SUGGESTED STUDY

PEOPLE/PLACES/EVENTS As you study these items, think about how they demonstrate or relate to key concepts and historical themes from this chapter and previous chapters.

AP TEST PRACTICE

Questions assume cumulative content knowledge from this chapter and previous chapters.

MULTIPLE CHOICE Use the excerpt below and your knowledge of U.S. history to answer questions 1–2.

"All persons born or naturalized in the United States, and subject to the jurisdiction thereof, are citizens of the United States and of the state wherein they reside. No state shall make or enforce any law which shall abridge the privileges or immunities of citizens of the United States; nor shall any state deprive any person of life, liberty, or property, without due process of law; nor deny to any person within its jurisdiction the equal protection of the laws."

—14th Amendment to the U.S. Constitution, Section 1

1. What political struggles occurred regarding the implementation of the above amendment in the late 19th century?

   (A) Debate over the criteria for citizenship
   (B) Debate over the legal validity of the Emancipation Proclamation
   (C) Debate over the legal scope of the rights granted by the amendment
   (D) The extension of rights to newly-arrived immigrants

2. Which of the following most subverted the above amendment in the late 19th century?

   (A) Opposition to Reconstruction plans for redistribution of land
   (B) Passage of the 15th Amendment
   (C) Passage of segregation laws
   (D) Debate over industrialization of the South's economy

SHORT ANSWER Use your knowledge of U.S. history to answer questions 3–5.

3. Answer a, b, and c.
   a) Briefly explain ONE example of how partisan politics affected Reconstruction policies.
   b) Briefly explain a SECOND example of how partisan politics affected Reconstruction policies.
   c) Briefly explain ONE example of how Reconstruction policies affected partisan politics.

4. Answer a, b, and c.
   a) Briefly explain ONE example of how Southern whites strove to re-establish their regional autonomy.
   b) Briefly explain a SECOND example of how Southern whites strove to re-establish their regional autonomy.
   c) Briefly explain ONE example of a cultural, political, or economic effect of Southern whites' efforts in re-establishing their regional way of life.

5. Answer a, b, and c.
   a) Briefly explain why ONE of the following developments during Reconstruction BEST marks the beginning of African American progress between 1860 and 1900.
      • Implementation of the Emancipation Proclamation of 1863
      • Passage of the 14th amendment in 1868
      • Passage of the 15th amendment in 1870
   b) Provide ONE piece of historical evidence to support your contention.
   c) Briefly explain why ONE of the options is not as persuasive as the one you chose.

LONG ESSAY Develop a thoughtful and thorough historical argument that answers the question below. Begin your essay with a thesis statement and support it with relevant historical evidence.

6. Evaluate the extent to which Reconstruction policies contributed to maintaining continuity as well as fostering change in the economic and cultural institutions of the South before 1900.

16 | THE CONQUEST OF THE FAR WEST

**AMERICAN PROGRESS,
1872** The Brooklyn artist John Gast painted this tribute to westward expansion—an image of hardy pioneers marching toward the frontier, protected by the goddess of progress. It was designed for travel guides to encourage tourists and migrants to travel to the West. (The Library of Congress (LC-USZC4-668))

AP

HISTORICAL THINKING

1. **Patterns of Continuity and Change over Time** Analyze changing government policy toward American Indians and the reaction of tribes to that change.

2. **Contextualization** Analyze the racial, ethnic, and gender make-up of the far western frontier and the consequences of that make-up.

3. **Historical Causation** Analyze the economic, political, and social consequences of the completion of the transcontinental railroad on the Far West.

4. **Contextualization** To what degree and in what ways did federal government policy encourage westward migration

5. **Contextualization** To what degree and in what ways did the mining, cattle, and agricultural frontiers alter the western environment?

6. **Historical Causation** Analyze the reasons for farmer discontent in the trans-Mississippi West.

Key Concept Correlations

Analyze the ways the historical developments you learn about in this chapter connect to the following AP Key Concepts.

5.1 The United States became more connected with the world as it pursued an expansionist foreign policy in the Western Hemisphere and emerged as the destination for many migrants from other countries.

6.1 The rise of big business in the United States encouraged massive migrations and urbanization, sparked government and popular efforts to reshape the U.S. economy and environment, and renewed debates over U.S. national identity.

6.2 The emergence of an industrial culture in the United States led to both greater opportunities for, and restrictions on, immigrants, minorities, and women.

6.3 The "Gilded Age" witnessed new cultural and intellectual movements in tandem with political debates over economic and social policies.

Thematic Learning Objectives

WXT-2, 4, 5, 6; POL-2, 5, 6; ID-1, 2, 5; CUL-2, 5; PEO-2, 3; WOR-5, 6, ENV-3

CHAPTER 16 discusses the rise of the Far West and its increasing importance in American economic development. The varied ethnic makeup of the region led to examples of extreme racial prejudice and sometimes violence. The transcontinental railroad transformed western society economically, politically, and socially. Chapter 16 also focuses on the federal and state government's role in the encouragement of western settlement. Heavy emphasis is placed on the impact of westward expansion on the lives of native populations. Also important is the development of the mining, cattle, and agricultural industries and the impact they had on the environment and each other. Lastly, the chapter looks at the rising challenges facing western farmers as they face a world of international markets and powerful corporate institutions. As you read, evaluate the following ideas:

- Territorial acquisitions in the west opened new markets, led to claims of white racial superiority, and increased ideological conflict.
- Increased western settlement led to the transformation of the environment.
- Westward expansion led to conflicts over American identity, citizenship, and the protection of individual rights.
- The federal government encouraged western settlement through subsidizing transportation systems and offering cheap federal lands to settlers.
- Westward migration led to political and popular conflicts.
- The rise of corporate agriculture led individual farmers to organize in order to remedy their grievances.
- Completion of the transcontinental railroad threatened native culture and identity.

THE SOCIETIES OF THE FAR WEST

The Far West (or what many nineteenth-century Americans called the "Great West")–the region beyond the Mississippi River into which millions of Anglo-Americans moved in the years after the Civil War–was in fact many lands. It contained some of the most arid territory in the United States, and some of the wettest and lushest. It contained the flattest plains and the highest mountains. It contained vast treeless prairies and deserts and great forests. And it contained many peoples.

THE WESTERN TRIBES

The largest and most important western population group before the great Anglo-American migration was the Indian tribes. Some were members of eastern tribes–Cherokee, Creek, and others–who had been forcibly resettled west of the Mississippi to "Indian Territory" (later Oklahoma) and elsewhere before the Civil War. But most were members of tribes that had always lived in the West.

The western tribes had developed several forms of civilization. More than 300,000 Indians (among them the Serrano, Chumash, Pomo, Maidu, Yurok, and Chinook) had lived on the Pacific coast before the arrival of Spanish settlers. Disease and dislocation decimated the tribes, but in the mid-nineteenth century 150,000 remained–some living within the Hispanic society the Spanish and Mexican settlers had created, many still living within their own tribal communities. The Pueblos of the Southwest had long lived largely as farmers and had established permanent settlements there even before the Spanish arrived in the seventeenth century. The Pueblos grew corn; they built towns and cities of adobe houses; they practiced elaborate forms of irrigation; and they participated in trade and commerce. In the eighteenth and nineteenth centuries, their intimate relationship with the Spanish (later Mexicans) produced, in effect, an alliance against the Apaches, Navajos, and Comanches of the region.

The complex interaction between the Pueblos and the Spanish produced an elaborate caste system in the Southwest. At the top were the Spanish or Mexicans, who owned the largest estates and controlled the trading centers at Santa Fe and elsewhere. The Pueblos, subordinate but still largely free, were below them. Apaches, Navajos, and others—some captured in war and enslaved for a fixed time, others men and women who had voluntarily left their own tribes—were at the bottom. They were known as *genizaros*, Indians without tribes, and they had become in many ways part of Spanish society. This caste system reflected how the Spanish Empire in America was preoccupied with racial ancestry; almost every group in the Southwest—not just Spanish and Indians, but several categories of mulattoes and mestizos (people of mixed race) as well—had a clear place in an elaborate social hierarchy.

CASTE SYSTEM

The most widespread Indian presence in the West was the Plains Indians, a diverse group of tribes and language groups. Some tribes formed alliances with one another; others were in constant conflict. Some lived sedentary lives as farmers; others were highly nomadic hunters. Despite their differences, however, the tribes shared some traits. Their cultures were based on close and extended family networks and on an intimate relationship with nature. Tribes (which sometimes numbered several thousand) were generally subdivided into "bands" of up to 500 men and women. Each band had its own governing council, but the community had a decision-making process in which most members participated. Within each band, tasks were divided by gender. Women's roles were largely domestic and artistic: raising children, cooking, gathering roots and berries, preparing hides, and creating many of the impressive artworks of tribal culture. They also tended fields and gardens in those places where bands remained settled long enough to raise crops. Men worked as hunters and traders and supervised the religious and military life of the band. Most of the Plains Indians practiced a religion centered on a belief in the spiritual power of the natural world—of plants and animals and the rhythms of the days and the seasons.

PLAINS INDIANS

Many of the Plains tribes—including some of the most powerful tribes in the Sioux Nation—subsisted largely through hunting buffalo. Riding small but powerful horses, descendants of Spanish stock, the tribes moved through the grasslands following the herds. Permanent settlements were rare. When a band halted, it constructed tepees as temporary dwellings; when it departed, it left the landscape almost completely undisturbed, a reflection of the deep reverence for nature that was central to Indian culture and religion.

The buffalo, or bison, provided the economic basis for the Plains Indians' way of life. Its flesh was their principal source of food, and its skin supplied materials for clothing, shoes, tepees, blankets, robes, and utensils. "Buffalo chips"—dried manure—provided fuel; buffalo bones became knives and arrow tips; buffalo tendons formed the strings of bows.

ECONOMIC IMPORTANCE OF THE BUFFALO

The Plains Indians were proud and aggressive warriors, schooled in warfare from their frequent (and usually brief) skirmishes with rival tribes. The male members of each tribe were, in effect, a warrior class. They competed with one another to develop reputations for fierceness and bravery as both hunters and soldiers. By the early nineteenth century, the Sioux had become the most powerful tribe in the Missouri River valley and had begun expanding west and south until they dominated much of the plains.

The Plains warriors proved to be the most formidable foes white settlers encountered. But the tribes also suffered from several serious weaknesses that in the end made it impossible for them to prevail. One weakness was the inability of the various tribes (and often even of the bands within tribes) to unite against white aggression. They were seldom able to draw together a coalition large enough to counter white power. They were also frequently distracted from their battles with whites by conflicts among the tribes

BUFFALO CHASE The painter George Catlin captured this scene of Plains Indians in the 1830s hunting among the great herds of buffalo, which provided the food and materials on which many tribes relied. (© Private Collection/The Bridgeman Art Library)

themselves. At times, tribal warriors faced white forces who were being assisted by guides and even fighters from other, usually rival, tribes.

Even so, some tribes were able to overcome their divisions and unite effectively for a time. By the mid-nineteenth century, for example, the Sioux, Arapaho, and Cheyenne had

INDIAN WEAKNESSES

forged a powerful alliance that dominated the northern plains. But there remained other important ecological and economic weaknesses of the western tribes in their contest with white society. Indians were tragically vulnerable to eastern infectious diseases. Smallpox epidemics, for example, decimated the Pawnees in Nebraska in the 1840s and many of the California tribes in the early 1850s. And the tribes were, of course, at a considerable disadvantage in any long-term battle with an economically and industrially advanced people. They were, in the end, outmanned and outgunned.

HISPANIC NEW MEXICO

For centuries, much of the Far West had been part of, first, the Spanish Empire and, later, the Mexican Republic. Although the lands the United States acquired in the 1840s did not include any of Mexico's most populous regions, considerable numbers of Mexicans did live in them and suddenly became residents of American territory. Most of them stayed.

Spanish-speaking communities were scattered throughout the Southwest, from Texas to California. All of them were transformed in varying degrees by the arrival of Anglo-American migrants and, equally important, by the expansion of the American capitalist economy into the region. For some Spanish-speaking westerners, the changes created opportunities for greater wealth. But for most it meant an end to the communal societies and economies they had built over many generations.

In New Mexico, the centers of Spanish-speaking society were the farming and trading communities the Spanish had established in the seventeenth century (see p. 17). Descendants of the original Spanish settlers (and more recent migrants from Mexico) lived alongside the Pueblo Indians and some American traders and engaged primarily in cattle and sheep ranching. There was a small aristocracy of great landowners, whose estates radiated out from the major trading center at Santa Fe. And there was a large population of Spanish (later Mexican) peasants, who worked on the great estates, farmed small plots of their own, or otherwise scraped out a subsistence. There were also large groups of Indian laborers, some enslaved or indentured.

When the United States acquired title to New Mexico in the aftermath of the Mexican War, General Stephen Kearny—who had commanded the American troops in the region during the conflict—tried to establish a territorial government

that excluded the established Mexican ruling class (the landed aristocrats from around Santa Fe and the most influential priests). He drew most of the officials from among the approximately 1,000 Anglo-Americans in the region, ignoring the more than

TAOS INDIAN REBELLION

50,000 Hispanics. There were widespread fears among Hispanics and Indians alike that the new American rulers of the region would confiscate their lands and otherwise threaten their societies. In 1847, Taos Indians rebelled; they killed the new governor and other Anglo-American officials before being subdued by U.S. Army forces. New Mexico remained under military rule for three years, until the United States finally organized a territorial government there in 1850.

By the 1870s, the government of New Mexico was dominated by one of the most notorious of the many "territorial rings" that sprang up in the West in the years before statehood. These were circles of local Anglo businesspeople and ambitious politicians with access to federal money who worked together to make the territorial government mutually profitable. In Santa Fe, the ring used its influence to gain control of over 2 million acres of land, much of which had long been in the possession of the original Mexican residents of the territory. The old Hispanic elite in New Mexico had lost much of its political and economic authority.

Even without its former power and despite the expansion of Anglo-American settlement, Hispanic society in New Mexico survived and grew. The U.S. Army finally did what the Hispanic residents had been unable to accomplish for 200 years: it broke the power of the Navajo, Apache, and other tribes that had so often harassed the residents of New Mexico and had prevented them from expanding their society and commerce. The defeat of the tribes led to substantial Hispanic migration into other areas of the Southwest and as far north as Colorado. Most of the expansion involved peasants and small tradespeople who were looking for land or new opportunities for commerce.

HISPANIC WEST This color lithograph, *Tejano Ranchers, 1877,* is by James Walker (1818–1889). Walker, a painter known for depicting military subjects, here shows the lively activities on a Tejano ranch in Texas. (Private Collection/© Peter Newark Pictures/The Bridgeman Art Library)

Hispanic societies survived in the Southwest in part because they were so far from the centers of English-speaking society that Anglo-American migrants (and the railroads that carried

HISPANIC RESISTANCE

them) were slow to get there. But Mexican Americans in the region also fought at times to preserve control of their societies. In the late 1880s, for example, Mexican peasants in an area of what is now Nevada successfully fended off the encroachment of English-speaking cattle ranchers.

But by then, such successes were already the exception. The Anglo-American presence in the Southwest grew rapidly once the railroads established lines into the region in the 1880s and early 1890s. With the railroads came extensive new ranching, farming, and mining. The expansion of economic activity in the region attracted a new wave of Mexican immigrants—perhaps as many as 100,000 by 1900—who moved across the border (which was unregulated until World War I) in search of work. But the new immigrants, unlike the earlier Hispanic residents of the Southwest, were coming to a society in which they were from the beginning subordinate to Anglo-Americans. The English-speaking proprietors of the new enterprises restricted most Mexicans to the lowest-paying and least stable jobs.

HISPANIC CALIFORNIA AND TEXAS

In California, Spanish settlement began in the eighteenth century with a string of Christian missions along the Pacific coast. The missionaries and the soldiers who accompanied them gathered most of the coastal Indians into their communities, some forcibly and some by persuasion. The Indians were targets of the evangelizing efforts of the missionaries, who baptized more than 50,000 of them. But they were also a labor force for the flourishing and largely self-sufficient economies the missionaries created; the Spanish forced most of these laborers into a state of servitude little different from slavery. The missions had enormous herds of cattle, horses, sheep, and goats, most of them tended by Indian workers; they had brickmakers, blacksmiths, weavers, and farmers, most of them Indians as well. Few of the profits of the mission economy flowed to the workers.

In the 1830s, after the new Mexican government had begun reducing the power of the church, the mission society largely collapsed, despite strenuous resistance from the missionaries

DECLINE OF MISSION SOCIETY

themselves. In its place emerged a secular Mexican aristocracy, which controlled a chain of large estates (some of them former missions) in the fertile lands west of the Sierra Nevada. For them, the arrival of Anglo-Americans before and after the Civil War was disastrous. So vast were the numbers of English-speaking immigrants that the *californios* (as the Hispanic residents of the state were known) had little power to resist the onslaught. In the central and northern parts of the state, where the Anglo population growth was greatest, the *californios* experienced a series of defeats. English-speaking prospectors organized to exclude them, sometimes violently, from the mines during the gold rush. Many *californios* also lost their lands—either through corrupt business deals or through

outright seizure (sometimes with the help of the courts and often through simple occupation by squatters). Years of litigation by the displaced Hispanics had very little effect on the changing distribution of landownership.

In the southern areas of California, where there were at first fewer migrants than in other parts of the state, some Mexican landowners managed to hang on for a time. The booming Anglo communities in the north of the state created a large market for the cattle that southern *rancheros* were raising. But a combination of reckless expansion, growing indebtedness, and a severe drought in the 1860s devastated the Mexican ranching culture. By the 1880s, the Hispanic aristocracy in California had largely ceased to exist. Increasingly, Mexicans and Mexican Americans became part of the lower end of the state's working class, clustered in barrios in Los Angeles or elsewhere, or becoming migrant farmworkers. Even small landowners who managed to hang on to their farms found themselves unable to raise livestock, as the once-communal grazing lands fell under the control of powerful Anglo ranchers. The absence of herding destroyed many family economies and, by forcing farmers into migrant work, displaced much of the peasantry.

A similar pattern of dispossession occurred in Texas, where many Mexican landowners lost their land after the territory joined the United States (see pp. 342–343). This occurred as a result of fraud, coercion, and the inability of even the most substantial Mexican ranchers to compete with the enormous emerging Anglo-American ranching kingdoms. In 1859, Mexican resentments erupted in an armed challenge to American power: a raid on a jail in Brownsville, led by the rancher Juan Cortina, who freed all the Mexican prisoners

DECLINING STATUS OF HISPANICS

inside. But such resistance had little long-term effect. Cortina continued to harass Anglo communities in Texas until 1875, but the Mexican government finally captured and imprisoned him. As in California, Mexicans in southern Texas (who constituted nearly three-quarters of the population there) became an increasingly impoverished working class relegated largely to unskilled farm or industrial labor.

On the whole, the great Anglo-American migration was less catastrophic for the Hispanic population of the West than it was for the Indian tribes. Indeed, for some Hispanics, it created new opportunities for wealth and station. For the most part, however, the late nineteenth century saw the destruction of Mexican Americans' authority in a region they had long considered their own; and it saw the movement of large numbers of Hispanics—both longtime residents of the West and more recent immigrants—into an impoverished working class serving the expanding capitalist economy of the United States.

THE CHINESE MIGRATION

At the same time that ambitious or impoverished Europeans were crossing the Atlantic in search of opportunities in the New World, many Chinese crossed the Pacific in hopes of better lives than they could expect in their own poverty-stricken land. Not all came to the United States. Many Chinese moved to Hawaii, Australia, South and Central America, South Africa, and even the Caribbean–some as "coolies" (indentured servants whose condition was close to slavery).

A few Chinese had come to California even before the gold rush (see pp. 351–352), but after 1848 the flow increased dramatically. By 1880, more than 200,000 Chinese had settled in the United States, mostly in California, where they constituted nearly a tenth of the population. Almost all came as free laborers. For a time, white Americans welcomed the Chinese as a conscientious, hardworking people. In 1852, the governor of California called them "one of the most worthy classes of our newly adopted citizens" and called for more Chinese immigration to swell the territory's inadequate labor force. Very quickly, however, white opinion turned hostile–in part because the Chinese were so industrious and successful that some white Americans began considering them rivals, even threats. The experience of Chinese immigrants

RACISM

in the West became, therefore, a struggle to advance economically in the face of racism and discrimination.

In the early 1850s, large numbers of Chinese immigrants worked in the gold mines, and for a time some of them enjoyed considerable success. But opportunities for Chinese to prosper in the mines were fleeting. In 1852, the California legislature began trying to exclude the Chinese from gold mining by enacting a "foreign miners" tax (which also helped exclude Mexicans).

A series of other laws in the 1850s were designed to discourage Chinese emigration to the territory. Gradually, the effect of the discriminatory laws, the hostility of white miners, and the declining profitability of the surface mines drove most Chinese out of prospecting. Those who remained in the mountains became primarily hired workers in the mines built by corporations with financing from the East. These newer mines–which extended much deeper into the mountains than

THE TRANSCONTINENTAL RAILROAD This complicated trestle under construction by the Union Pacific was one of many large spans necessary for the completion of the transcontinental railroad. It gives some indication of the enormous engineering challenges the railroad builders had to overcome. (Universal History Archive/© UIG/The Bridgeman Art Library)

individual prospectors or small, self-financed groups had been able to go–replaced the early, smaller operations.

As mining declined as a source of wealth and jobs for the Chinese, railroad employment grew. Beginning in 1865, more

BUILDING THE TRANSCONTINENTAL RAILROAD

than 12,000 Chinese found work building the transcontinental railroad. In fact, Chinese workers formed 90 percent of the labor force of the Central Pacific and were mainly responsible for construction of the western part of the new road. The company preferred them to white workers because they had no experience of labor organization. They worked hard, made few demands, and accepted low wages. Many railroad workers were recruited in China by agents for the Central Pacific. Once employed, they were organized into work gangs under Chinese supervisors.

Work on the Central Pacific was arduous and often dangerous. As the railroad moved through the mountains, the company made few concessions to the difficult conditions and provided its workers with little protection from the elements. Work continued through the winter, and many Chinese tunneled into snowbanks at night to create warm sleeping areas for themselves. The tunnels frequently collapsed, suffocating those inside; but the company allowed nothing to disrupt construction.

Chinese laborers, however, were not always as docile as their employers imagined them to be. In the spring of 1866, 5,000 Chinese railroad workers went on strike, demanding higher wages and a shorter workday. The company isolated them, surrounded them with strikebreakers, and starved them. The strike failed, and most of the workers returned to their jobs.

In 1869 the transcontinental railroad was completed. Thousands of Chinese were now out of work. Some hired themselves out on the vast new drainage and irrigation projects in the agricultural valleys of central California. Some became common agricultural laborers, picking fruit for low wages. Some became tenant farmers, often on marginal lands that white owners saw no profit in working themselves. Some managed to acquire land of their own and establish themselves as modestly successful truck farmers.

Increasingly, however, Chinese immigrants flocked to cities. By 1900, nearly half the Chinese population of California lived

ESTABLISHMENT OF "CHINATOWNS"

in urban areas. By far the largest single Chinese community was in San Francisco. Much of community life there, and in other "Chinatowns" throughout the West, revolved around powerful organizations–usually formed by people from a single clan or community in China–that functioned as something like benevolent societies to address common social and financial issues and filled many of the roles that political machines often served in immigrant communities in eastern cities. They were often led by prominent merchants. (In San Francisco, the leading merchants–known as the "Six Companies"–often worked together to advance their interests in the city and state.) These organizations became, in effect, employment brokers, unions, arbitrators of disputes, defenders of the community against outside persecution, and dispensers of social services.

They also organized the elaborate festivals and celebrations that were such a conspicuous and important part of life in Chinatowns.

Other Chinese organizations were secret societies, known as "tongs." Some of the tongs were violent criminal organizations, involved in the opium trade and prostitution. Few people outside the Chinese communities were aware of their existence, except when rival tongs engaged in violent conflict (or "tong wars"), as occurred frequently in San Francisco in the 1880s.

Life was hard for most urban Chinese, in San Francisco and elsewhere. The Chinese usually occupied the lower rungs of the employment ladder, working as common laborers, servants, and unskilled factory hands. Some established their own small businesses, especially laundries. They moved into this business not because of experience–there were few commercial laundries in China–but because they were excluded from so many other areas of employment. Laundries could be started with very little capital and required only limited command of English. By the 1890s, Chinese constituted over two-thirds of all the laundry workers in California, many of them in shops they themselves owned and ran.

The relatively small number of Chinese women fared even worse. During the earliest Chinese migrations to California, virtually all the women who made the journey did so because they had been sold into prostitution. As late as 1880, nearly half the Chinese women in California were prostitutes. Both Anglo and Chinese reformers tried to stamp out the prostitution in Chinatowns in the 1890s, but more effective than their efforts was the growing number of Chinese women in America. Once the sex ratio became more balanced, Chinese men were more likely to seek companionship in families.

ANTI-CHINESE SENTIMENTS

As Chinese communities grew larger and more conspicuous in western cities, anti-Chinese sentiment among white residents became increasingly strong. Anti-coolie clubs emerged in the

ANTI-COOLIE CLUBS

1860s and 1870s. They sought a ban on employing Chinese and organized boycotts of products made with Chinese labor. Some of these clubs attacked Chinese workers in the streets and were suspected of setting fire to factories in which Chinese worked. Such activities reflected the resentment of many white workers toward Chinese laborers for accepting low wages and thus undercutting union members.

As the political value of attacking the Chinese grew in California, the Democratic Party took up the call. So did the Workingmen's Party of California–created in 1878 by Denis Kearney, an Irish immigrant–which gained significant political power in the state largely on the basis of its hostility to the Chinese. By the mid-1880s, anti-Chinese agitation and violence had spread up and down the Pacific coast and into other areas of the West.

But anti-Chinese sentiment did not rest on economic grounds alone. It rested on cultural and racial arguments as well. For example, the reformer Henry George, a critic of capitalism and a champion of the rights of labor (see p. 472), described the

A CHINESE FAMILY IN SAN FRANCISCO Like many other Americans, Chinese families liked to pose for photograph portraits in the late nineteenth century. And like many other immigrants, they often sent such pictures back to relatives in China. This portrait of Chun Duck Chin and his seven-year-old son, Chun Jan Yut, was taken in a studio in San Francisco in the 1870s. Both father and son appear to have dressed up for the occasion, in traditional Chinese garb, and the studio—which likely took many such portraits of Chinese families—provided a formal Chinese backdrop. The son is holding what appears to be a chicken, perhaps to impress relatives in China with the family's prosperity. (National Archives and Records Administration)

Chinese as products of a civilization that had failed to progress, that remained mired in barbarism and savagery. They were, therefore, "unassimilable" and should be excluded.

In 1882, Congress responded to the political pressure and the growing violence by passing the Chinese Exclusion Act, which banned Chinese emigration to the United States for ten years and barred Chinese already in the country from becoming naturalized citizens. Support for the act came from representatives from all regions of the country. It reflected the growing fear of unemployment and labor unrest throughout the nation and the belief that excluding "an industrial army of Asiatic laborers" would protect "American" workers and help reduce class conflict. Congress renewed the law for another ten years in 1892 and made it permanent in 1902. It had a dramatic effect on the Chinese population, which declined by more than 40 percent in the forty years after its passage.

CHINESE EXCLUSION ACT

The Chinese in America did not accept the new laws quietly. They were shocked by the anti-Chinese rhetoric that lumped them together with African Americans and Indians. They were, they insisted, descendants of a great and enlightened civilization. How could they be compared to people who knew "nothing about the relations of society"? White Americans, they said, did not protest the great waves of immigration by Italians ("the most dangerous of men," one Chinese American said) or Irish or Jews. "They are all let in, while Chinese, who are sober, are duly law abiding, clean, educated and industrious, are shut out." The Six Companies in San Francisco organized strenuous letter-writing campaigns and filed suit in federal court. Their efforts had little effect.

CHINESE RESISTANCE

MIGRATION FROM THE EAST

The great wave of new settlers in the West after the Civil War came on the heels of important earlier migrations. California and Oregon were both already states of the Union by 1860. There were large and growing Anglo-American and African American communities in Texas, which had entered the Union as a state in 1845 and had been part of the Confederacy during the war. And from Texas and elsewhere, traders, farmers, and ranchers had begun to establish Anglo-American outposts in parts of New Mexico, Arizona, and other areas of the Southwest.

But the scale of the postwar migration dwarfed everything that had preceded it. In previous decades, the settlers had come in thousands. Now they came in millions, spreading throughout the vast western territories—into empty and inhabited lands alike. Most of the new settlers were from the established Anglo-American societies of the eastern United States, but substantial numbers—more than 2 million between 1870 and 1900—were foreign-born immigrants from Europe: Scandinavians, Germans, Irish, Russians, Czechs, and others. Settlers were attracted by gold and silver deposits, by the shortgrass pastures for cattle and sheep, and ultimately by the sod of the plains and the meadowlands of the mountains, which they discovered were suitable for farming or ranching. Settlement was also encouraged by the completion of the transcontinental railroad in 1869 and the construction of the many subsidiary lines that spread out from it.

The land policies of the federal government also encouraged settlement. The Homestead Act of 1862 permitted settlers to buy plots of 160 acres for a small fee if they occupied the land they purchased for five years and improved it. The Homestead Act was intended as a progressive measure. It would give a free farm to any American who needed one. It would be a form of government relief to people who otherwise might have no prospects. And it would help create new markets and new outposts of commercial agriculture for the nation's growing economy.

HOMESTEAD ACT

But the Homestead Act rested on a number of misperceptions. The framers of the law had assumed that mere possession of land would be enough to sustain a farm family. They had not recognized the effects of the increasing mechanization of agriculture and the rising costs of running a farm. Moreover, they

SODBUSTERS As farmers moved onto the Great Plains in Nebraska and other states on the agrarian frontier, their first task was to cut through the sod that covered the land to get to soil in which they could plant crops. The sod itself was so thick and solid that some settlers (including the Summers family of West Custer County, Nebraska, pictured here in 1888) used it to build their houses. The removal of the sod made cultivation of the plains possible; it also removed the soil's protective covering and contributed to the great dust storms that plagued the region in times of drought. (© Nebraska State Historical Society)

had made many of their calculations on the basis of eastern agricultural experiences that were inappropriate for the region west of the Mississippi. A unit of 160 acres was too small for the grazing and grain farming of much of the Great Plains. Although more than 400,000 homesteaders stayed on Homestead Act claims long enough to gain title to their land, a much larger number abandoned the region before the end of the required five years, unable to cope with the bleak life on the windswept plains and the economic realities that were making it difficult for families without considerable resources to thrive.

Not for the last time, beleaguered westerners looked to the federal government for solutions to their problems. In response to their demands, Congress increased the homestead allotments. The Timber Culture Act (1873) permitted homesteaders to receive grants of 160 additional acres if they planted 40 acres of trees on them. The Desert Land **GOVERNMENT ASSISTANCE** Act (1877) provided that claimants could buy 640 acres at $1.25 an acre provided they irrigated part of their holdings within three years. The Timber and Stone Act (1878), which presumably applied to nonarable land, authorized sales at $2.50 an acre. These laws ultimately made it possible for individuals to acquire as much as 1,280 acres of land at little cost. Some enterprising settlers got much more. Fraud ran rampant in the administration of the acts. Lumber, mining, and cattle companies, by employing "dummy" registrants and using other illegal devices, seized millions of acres of the public domain.

Political organization followed on the heels of settlement. After the admission of Kansas as a state in 1861, the remaining territories of Washington, New Mexico, Utah, and Nebraska were divided into smaller units that would presumably be easier to organize. By the close of the 1860s, territorial governments were in operation in the new provinces of Nevada, Colorado, Dakota, Arizona, Idaho, Montana, and Wyoming. Statehood soon followed. Nevada became a state in 1864, Nebraska in 1867, and Colorado in 1876. In 1889, North and South Dakota, Montana, and Washington won admission; Wyoming and Idaho entered the next year. Congress denied Utah statehood until its Mormon leaders convinced the government in 1896 that polygamy (the practice of a man having more than one wife at a time) had been abandoned. At the turn of the century, only three territories remained outside the Union. Arizona and New Mexico were excluded because their scanty white populations remained minorities in the territories, because their politics were predominantly Democratic in a Republican era, and because they were unwilling to accept admission as a single state. Oklahoma (formerly Indian Territory) was opened to white settlement and granted territorial status in 1889–1890.

THE CHANGING WESTERN ECONOMY

Among the many effects of the new wave of Anglo-American settlement in the Far West was a transformation of the region's economy. The new American settlers tied the West firmly to the growing industrial economy of the East (and of much of the rest of the world). Mining, cutting and selling timber, ranching, commercial farming, and many other economic activities relied on the East for markets and for capital. Some of the most powerful economic institutions in the West were great eastern corporations that controlled mines, ranches, and farms.

LABOR IN THE WEST

As commercial activity increased, many farmers, ranchers, and miners found it necessary to recruit a paid labor force—not an easy task for those far away from major population centers and unable or unwilling to hire Indian workers. The labor shortage of the region led to higher wages for workers than were typical in most areas of the East. But working conditions were often arduous, and job security was almost nonexistent. Once a railroad was built, a crop harvested, a herd sent to market, a mine played out, hundreds and even thousands of workers could find themselves suddenly unemployed. Competition from Chinese immigrants, whom employers could usually hire for considerably lower wages than they had to pay whites, also forced some Anglo-Americans out of work. Communities of the jobless gathered in the region's few cities, in mining camps, and elsewhere; other unemployed people moved restlessly from place to place in search of work.

Those who owned no land were highly mobile, mostly male, and seldom married. Indeed, the West had the highest percentage of single adults (10 percent) of any region in the country—one reason why single women found working in dance halls and as prostitutes among the most readily available forms of employment.

Despite the enormous geographic mobility in western society, actual social mobility was limited. Many **LIMITED SOCIAL MOBILITY** Americans thought of the West as a land of limitless opportunity, but, as in the rest of the country, advancement was easiest and most rapid for those who were economically advantaged to begin with. Studies of western communities suggest that social mobility in most of them was no greater than it was in the East. And the distribution of wealth in the region was little different from that in the older states as well.

Even more than in many parts of the East, the western working class was highly multiracial. English-speaking whites worked alongside African Americans and immigrants from **RACIALLY STRATIFIED WORKING CLASS** southern and eastern Europe, as they did in the East. Even more, they worked with Chinese, Filipinos, Mexicans, and Indians. But the workforce was highly stratified along racial lines. In almost every area of the western economy, white workers (whatever their ethnicity) occupied the upper tiers of employment: management and skilled labor. The lower tiers—people who did unskilled and often arduous work in the mines, on the railroads, or in agriculture—consisted overwhelmingly of nonwhites.

Reinforcing this dual labor system was a set of racial assumptions developed and sustained largely by white employers. Chinese, Mexicans, and Filipinos, they argued, were genetically or culturally suited to manual labor. Because they were smaller than many Anglo-Americans, those who promoted these racist stereotypes argued, they could work better in deep mines than whites. Because they were accustomed to heat, they could withstand arduous work in the fields better than whites. Because they were unambitious and unconcerned about material comfort, they would accept low wages and live in conditions that white people would not tolerate. These racial myths served the interests of employers above all, but white workers tended to embrace them too. That was in part because the myths supported a system that reserved whatever mobility there was largely for whites. An Irish common laborer might hope in the course of a lifetime to move several rungs up the occupational ladder. A Chinese or Mexican worker in the same job had no realistic prospects of doing the same.

THE ARRIVAL OF THE MINERS

One of the great economic boons in the Far West after the gold rush was a result of the mineral-rich region of mountains and plateaus, where settlers hoped to make quick fortunes by finding precious metals. The life span of this mining boom was relatively brief. It began in earnest around 1860 and flourished until the 1890s. Then it abruptly declined.

News of a gold or silver strike in an area usually began with a stampede reminiscent of the California gold rush of 1849. **LIFE CYCLE OF A MINING BOOM** Individual prospectors would exploit the first shallow deposits of ore largely by hand, with pan and placer mining. After these surface deposits dwindled, corporations moved in to engage in lode or quartz mining, which dug deeper beneath the surface. Then, as those deposits dwindled, commercial mining either disappeared or continued on a restricted basis, and ranchers and farmers moved in and established a more permanent economy.

The first great mineral strikes since the California gold rush occurred just before the Civil War. In 1858, gold was discovered in the Pike's Peak district of what would soon be the territory of Colorado; the following year, 50,000 prospectors stormed in from California, the Mississippi Valley, and the East. Denver and other mining camps blossomed into "cities" overnight. Almost as rapidly as it had developed, the boom ended. After the mining frenzy died down, corporations, notably the Guggenheim interests, revived some of the profits of the gold boom, and the discovery of silver near Leadville supplied a new source of mineral wealth.

While the Colorado rush of 1859 was still in progress, news of another strike drew miners to Nevada. Gold **COMSTOCK LODE** had been found in the Washoe district, but the most valuable ore in the great Comstock Lode (first discovered in 1858 by Henry Comstock) and other veins was silver. The first prospectors to reach the Washoe fields came from California; and from the beginning, Californians dominated the settlement and development of Nevada. In a remote desert without railroad transportation, the territory produced no supplies of its own, and everything—from food and machinery to

COLORADO BOOMTOWN The Colorado silver boom began in 1879, bringing many people into the newly admitted state in search of opportunity. By the 1890s, with dwindling silver deposits, many recently wealthy communities went bust. (© Time & Life Pictures/Getty Images)

whiskey–had to be shipped from California to Virginia City, Carson City, and other gold rush settlements and towns. When the first placer (or surface) deposits ran out, California and eastern capitalists bought the claims of the pioneer prospectors and began to use the more difficult process of quartz mining, which enabled them to retrieve silver from deeper veins. For a few years these outside owners reaped tremendous profits; from 1860 to 1880, the Nevada lodes yielded bullion worth $306 million. After that, the mines quickly played out.

The next important mineral discoveries came in 1874, when gold was found in the Black Hills of southwestern Dakota Territory. Prospectors swarmed into the area until surface resources faded and corporations took over. One enormous company, the Homestake, came to dominate the fields.

In the long run, other, less glamorous natural resources proved more important to the development of the West than gold and silver. The great Anaconda copper mine launched by William Clark in 1881 marked the beginning of an industry that would remain important to Montana for many decades. In other areas, mining operations had significant success with lead, tin, quartz, and zinc.

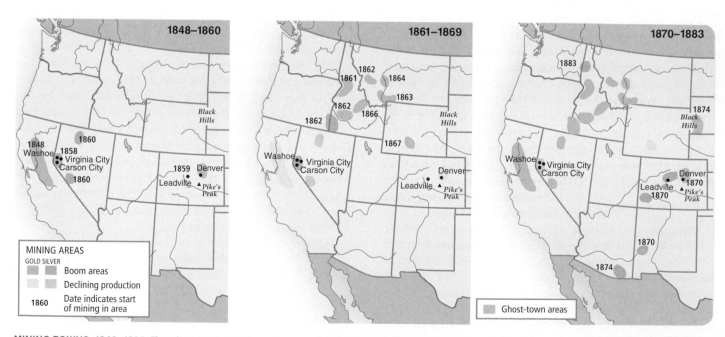

MINING TOWNS, 1848–1883 These three maps illustrate the rapid movement from boom to bust in the western mining industry in the mid-nineteenth century. Note how quickly the "boom" areas of gold and silver mining turn into places of "declining production," often in less than a decade. Note, too, how mining for both metals moved from California and Nevada in the 1860s to areas farther east and north in the 1870s and beyond. The map also shows the areas in which "ghost towns"—mining communities abandoned by their residents once production ceased—proliferated.

• *What impact did mining have on the population of the West?*

The conditions of mine life in the boom period–the presence of precious minerals, the vagueness of claim boundaries, the cargoes of gold being shipped out–attracted outlaws and "bad men," operating as individuals or gangs. When the situation became intolerable in a community, those members interested in order began enforcing their own laws through vigilante committees, an unofficial system of social control used earlier in California. Vigilantes were unconstrained by the legal system. Some vigilantes continued to operate as private "law" enforcers after the creation of regular governments.

Men greatly outnumbered women in the mining towns, and younger men in particular had difficulty finding female companions of comparable age. Those women who did gravitate to the new communities often came with their husbands, and their activities were generally (although not always) confined to the same kinds of domestic tasks that eastern women performed. Single women, or women whose **GENDER IMBALANCE** husbands were earning no money, did choose (or find it necessary) to work for wages at times, as cooks, laundresses, and tavernkeepers. And in the sexually imbalanced mining communities, there was always a ready market for prostitutes.

The thousands of people who flocked to the mining towns in search of quick wealth and who failed to find it often remained as wage laborers in corporate mines after the boom period. Working conditions were almost uniformly terrible. The corporate mines were deep and extremely hot, with temperatures often exceeding 100 degrees Fahrenheit. Some workers died of heatstroke (or of pneumonia, a result of experiencing sudden changes of temperature when emerging from the mines). Poor ventilation meant large accumulations of poisonous carbon dioxide, which caused dizziness, nausea, and headaches. Lethal dusts stayed in the stagnant air to be inhaled over and over by the miners, many of whom developed silicosis (a disabling disease of the lungs) as a result. There were frequent explosions, cave-ins, and fires, and there were many accidents with the heavy machinery the workers used to bore into the earth. In the 1870s, before technological advances eliminated some of the dangers, one worker in every thirty was disabled in the mines, and one in every eighty was killed. That rate fell later in the nineteenth century, but mining remained one of the most dangerous and arduous working environments in the United States.

THE CATTLE KINGDOM

Another important element of the changing economy of the Far West was cattle ranching. The open range–the vast grasslands of the public domain–provided a huge area on the Great Plains where cattle raisers could graze their herds free of charge and unrestricted by the boundaries of private farms.

The western cattle industry was Mexican and Texan by ancestry. Long before citizens of the United States invaded the Southwest, Mexican ranchers had devel- **MEXICAN ORIGINS** oped the techniques and equipment that the cattlemen and cowboys of the Great Plains later employed: branding (a device known in all frontier areas where stock was common), roundups, roping, and the gear of the herders–their lariats, saddles, leather chaps, and spurs. Americans in Texas adopted these methods and carried them to the northernmost ranges of the cattle kingdom. Texas also had the largest herds of cattle in the country; the animals were descended from imported Spanish stock–wiry, hardy longhorns–and allowed to run wild or semiwild. From Texas, too, came small, muscular broncos or mustangs well suited to the requirements of cattle country.

At the end of the Civil War, an estimated 5 million cattle roamed the Texas ranges. Early in 1866, some Texas cattle ranchers began driving their combined herds, as many as 260,000 cattle, north to Sedalia, Missouri, on the Missouri Pacific Railroad. Traveling over rough country and beset by outlaws, Indians, and property-conscious farmers, the caravan suffered heavy losses. Only a fraction of the animals arrived

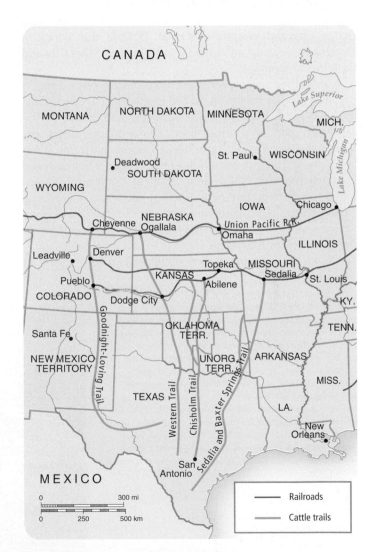

THE CATTLE KINGDOM, C. 1866–1887 Cattle ranching and cattle drives are among the most romanticized features of the nineteenth-century West. But they were also hardheaded businesses, made possible by the growing eastern market for beef and the availability of inexpensive transportation to take cattle to urban markets.

• *What brought an end to the open range?*

in Sedalia. But the drive proved that cattle could be driven to distant markets and pastured along the trail, and that they would even gain weight during the journey. This earliest of the "long drives," in other words, established the first, tentative link between the isolated cattle breeders of south and west Texas and the booming urban markets of the East. The drive laid the groundwork for the explosion of the "cattle kingdom."

Market facilities grew up at Abilene, Kansas, on the Kansas Pacific Railroad, and for years the town reigned as the railhead

CHISHOLM TRAIL

of the cattle kingdom. Between 1867 and 1871, cattlemen drove nearly 1.5 million head up the Chisholm Trail to Abilene—a town that, when filled with rampaging cowboys at the end of a drive, rivaled the mining towns in rowdiness. But by the mid-1870s, agricultural development in western Kansas was eating away at the open range land at the same time that the supply of animals was increasing. Cattlemen therefore had to develop other trails and other market outlets farther west: Dodge City and Wichita in Kansas, Ogallala and Sidney in Nebraska, Cheyenne and Laramie in Wyoming, Miles City and Glendive in Montana.

A long drive was a spectacular sight, and not surprisingly, it became the most romanticized and mythologized aspect of life in the West. It began with the spring, or calf, roundup. The cattlemen rounded up stock from the open range, herds containing the stock of many different owners, with only their brands to distinguish them from one another. The combined herds, usually numbering from 2,000 to 5,000 head, moved out. Cowboys representing each of the major ranchers accompanied them. Most of the cowboys in the early years were veterans of the Confederate army. The next-largest group consisted of African Americans—more than half a million of them. They were more numerous than white northerners or Mexicans

and other foreigners. They were usually assigned such jobs as wrangler (herdsman) or cook.

Every cattleman had to have a permanent base from which to operate, and so the ranch emerged. A ranch consisted of the employer's dwelling, quarters for employees, and a tract of grazing land. In the early years of the cattle kingdom, most ranches were small, since so much of the grazing occurred in the vast, open areas that cattlemen shared. But as farmers and sheep breeders began to compete for the open plains, ranches became larger and more clearly defined; cattlemen gradually had to learn to raise their stock on their own fenced land.

Farmers ("nesters") from the East threw fences around their claims, blocking trails and breaking up the open range. A series of "range wars"–between sheepmen and cattlemen, between ranchers and farmers–erupted out of the tensions between these competing groups, resulting in significant loss of life and extensive property damage.

Accounts of the lofty profits to be made in the cattle business–it was said that an investment of $5,000 would return $45,000 in four years–tempted eastern, English, and Scottish capital to the plains. Increasingly, the structure of the cattle economy became corporate; in one year, twenty corporations with a combined capital of $12 million were chartered in Wyoming. The inevitable result of this frenzied, speculative expansion was that the ranges, already diminished by the railroads and the farmers, became overstocked. There was not enough grass to support the crowding herds or sustain the long drives. Finally nature intervened. Two severe winters, in 1885-1886 and 1886-1887, with a searing summer between them, stung and scorched the plains. Hundreds of thousands of cattle died, streams and grass dried up, princely ranches and costly investments disappeared in a season.

The open-range industry never recovered; the long drive disappeared for good. Railroads displaced the trail as the route to

COWBOYS ON A "LONG DRIVE" The "long drive" not only provided cattle for the eastern market, it also created communities of men who spent much of their lives on the trail, working for ranchers tending cattle. These cowboys were mostly young, unmarried men, including many African Americans. Most of them later settled down with families, but many agreed with the former cowboy Charles Goodknight, who wrote years later, "All in all, my years on the trail were the happiest I ever lived. There were many hardships and dangers . . . but when all went well, there was no other life so pleasant. Most of the time we were solitary adventurers in a great land, . . . and we were free and full of the zest of darers." This photograph, dating from the 1890s, depicts cowboys herding cattle at the end of a long drive in the stockyards at Kansas City, Missouri. (© North Wind Picture Archives/Alamy)

market for livestock. But the established cattle ranches–with fenced-in grazing land and stocks of hay for winter feed–survived, grew, and prospered, eventually producing more beef than ever.

Although the cattle industry was overwhelmingly male in its early years, there were always a few women involved in ranching and driving. As ranching became more sedentary, the presence of women greatly increased. By 1890, more than 250,000 women owned ranches or farms in the western states (many of them as proxies for their husbands or fathers, but some in their own right). Indeed, the region provided women with many opportunities that were closed to them in the East–including the opportunity to participate in politics. Wyoming was the first state in the Union to guarantee woman suffrage; and throughout the West, women established themselves as an important political presence (and occasionally as significant officeholders).

Women won the vote earlier in the West than they did in the rest of the nation, although for different reasons in different places. In Utah, the Mormons granted women suffrage in an effort to stave off criticism of their practice of polygamy. In

POLITICAL GAINS FOR WOMEN

some places, women won suffrage before statehood to swell the electorate to the number required by Congress. In others, women won the vote by persuading men that they would help bring a "moral" voice into the politics of the region and strengthen the sense of community in the West. Most men (and many women) believed that women were more "generous and virtuous" than men. They might bring these special qualities to the raw societies of the region. (Many of the same arguments were ultimately used to justify suffrage in the East as well.)

THE ROMANCE OF THE WEST

The supposedly unsettled West had always occupied a special place in the Anglo-American imagination, beginning in the seventeenth century when the first white settlers along the Atlantic coast began to look to the interior. They were searching for new opportunities or for refuge from the civilized world. The vast regions of this "last frontier" had a particularly strong romantic appeal to many people.

THE WESTERN LANDSCAPE

The allure of the West was obvious. The Great Plains, the Rocky Mountains, the basin and plateau region beyond the Rockies, the Sierra Nevada, and the Cascade Range–all constituted a landscape of brilliant diversity and spectacular grandeur, different from anything white Americans had encountered before. It was little wonder that newcomers looked on the West with reverence and wonder. Painters of the "Rocky Mountain School"–of whom the best known were Albert Bierstadt and Thomas Moran–celebrated the new West in grandiose canvases, some of which were taken on

"ROCKY MOUNTAIN SCHOOL"

tours around eastern and midwestern states and attracted enormous crowds, eager for a vision of the Great West. Such paintings emphasized the ruggedness and dramatic variety of the region, and reflected the same awe toward the land that earlier regional painters had displayed toward the Hudson River valley and other areas.

The interest in paintings of the West helped inspire a growing wave of tourism. Increasingly in the 1880s and 1890s, as railroads extended farther into the region and as the Indian wars subsided, resort hotels began to spring up near some of the most spectacular landscapes in the region; and easterners began to come for visits of several weeks or more, combining residence in a comfortable hotel with hikes and excursions into the "wilderness."

THE COWBOY CULTURE

Even more appealing than the landscape was the rugged, free-spirited lifestyle that many Americans associated with the West–a lifestyle that supposedly stood in sharp contrast to the increasingly stable and ordered world of the East. Many nineteenth-century Americans came to romanticize, especially, the figure of the cowboy and transformed him remarkably quickly from the low-paid worker he actually was into a powerful and enduring figure of myth.

MYTH OF THE COWBOY

Admiring Americans seldom thought about the many dismal aspects of the cowboy's life: the tedium, the loneliness, the physical discomforts, the low pay, the few opportunities for advancement. Instead, in popular western novels such as Owen Wister's *The Virginian* (1902), they romanticized his freedom from traditional social constraints, his affinity with nature, even his supposed propensity for violence. Wister's character was a semi-educated man whose natural decency, courage, and compassion made him a powerful symbol of the supposed virtues of the frontier. But *The Virginian* was only the most famous example of a type of literature that soon swept throughout the United States: novels and stories about the West, and about the lives of cowboys in particular, that appeared in boys' magazines, pulp novels, theater, and even serious literature. The enormous popularity of traveling Wild West shows spread the cult of the cowboy still further. (See "Patterns of Popular Culture," p. 444.)

The cowboy had become perhaps the most widely admired popular hero in America, and a powerful and enduring symbol of the important American ideal of the "natural man." That symbol has survived into the twenty-first century–in popular literature, in song, in film, and on television.

THE IDEA OF THE FRONTIER

Yet it was not simply the character of the new West that made it so important to the nation's imagination. It was also that many Americans considered it the last frontier. Since the earliest moments of European settlement in America, the image of uncharted territory to the west had always comforted

THE WILD WEST SHOW

FOR many Americans, the "Old West" has always been a place of myth—a source of romantic and exciting stories. One reason the romantic depiction of the Old West persisted was the astonishing popularity of the "Wild West show" in the late nineteenth and early twentieth centuries.

PROMOTING THE WEST, C. 1895 Buffalo Bill's Wild West show was popular all over the United States and, indeed, through much of the world. He was so familiar a figure that many of his posters contained only his picture with the words "He is Coming." This more conventional poster announces a visit of the show to Brooklyn. (© Archive Photos/Getty Images)

This colorful entertainment may have had little connection with the reality of western life, but it gave its audiences an image of the West as a place of adventure and romance that has lasted for generations. The Wild West show emerged out of a number of earlier entertainment traditions. The great showman P. T. Barnum had begun popularizing the "Wild West" as early as the 1840s when he staged a "Grand Buffalo Hunt" for spectators in New York, and such shows continued into the 1870s. At about the same time, western cowboys began staging versions of the modern rodeo when their cattle drives passed near substantial towns. But the first real Wild West show opened in Omaha, Nebraska, in 1883. Its organizer was William F. Cody, better known as "Buffalo Bill."

Cody had ridden for the Pony Express, fought in the Civil War, and been a supplier of buffalo meat to workers on the transcontinental railroad (hence his celebrated nickname). But his real fame was a result of his work as a scout for the U.S. Cavalry during the Indian wars of the 1870s and as a guide for hunting parties of notable easterners.

Cody's Wild West shows included mock Indian attacks (by real Indians) on stagecoaches and wagon trains; portrayals of the Pony Express; and shooting, riding, and roping exhibitions. The grand finale—"A Grand Hunt on the Plains"—featured buffalo, elk, deer, mountain sheep, longhorn cattle, and wild horses. Cody's

ROMANTIC IMAGE OF THE WEST and inspired those who dreamed of starting life anew. Now, with the last of that unsettled land being slowly absorbed into the nation's civilization, that image exercised a stronger pull than ever.

Mark Twain, one of the great American writers of the nineteenth century, gave voice to this romantic vision of the frontier in a series of brilliant novels and memoirs. In some of his writings—notably *Roughing It* (1872)—he wrote of the Far West and of his own experience as a newspaper reporter in Nevada during the mining boom. His greatest works, however, were novels that dealt with life on an earlier frontier: the Mississippi Valley of Twain's boyhood. In *The Adventures of Tom Sawyer* (1876) and *The Adventures of Huckleberry Finn* (1885), he produced characters who repudiated the constraints of organized society and attempted to escape into a natural world. For Huck Finn, the vehicle of escape was a small raft on the Mississippi, but the yearning for freedom reflected a larger vision of the West as the last refuge from the constraints of civilization.

The painter and sculptor Frederic Remington also captured the romance of the West and its image as an alternative to the settled civilization of the East. He portrayed the cowboy as a natural aristocrat, much like Wister's Virginian, living in a natural world in which all the normal supporting structures of "civilization" were missing. The romantic quality of his work made Remington one of the most beloved and successful artists of the nineteenth century.

FREDERIC REMINGTON

Theodore Roosevelt, who was, like both Wister and Remington, a man born and raised in the East, traveled to the Dakota Badlands in the mid-1880s to help himself recover from the sudden death of his young wife. He had long romanticized the West as a place of physical regeneration—a place where a man could gain strength through rugged activity (just as Roosevelt, a sickly, asthmatic boy, had hardened himself through adherence to the idea of a strenuous life). His long sojourn into the Badlands in the 1880s cemented his love of the region, which continued to the end of his life. And like shows inspired dozens of imitators. Always, at the center of every show—whether Cody's or one of his imitators—was the effort to evoke the mythic romance of the Old West.

Buffalo Bill was always the star performer in his own productions. But the show had other celebrities, too. Annie Oakley became wildly popular for her shooting acts, during which she would throw into the air small cards with her picture on them, shoot a hole through their middle, and toss them into the audience as souvenirs.

Native Americans were important parts of the Wild West shows, and hundreds of them participated—showing off their martial skills and exotic costumes and customs. The great Sioux leader Sitting Bull toured with the show for four months in 1885, during which he discussed Indian affairs with President Cleveland, who was a member of one of Sitting Bull's audiences. The famous Chiricahua Apache warrior Geronimo, who had fought against the United States until 1886, spent a season touring with one of Buffalo Bill's competitors—having previously been paraded around the country as a prisoner by the U.S. Army.

An immediate success, Buffalo Bill's Wild West show traveled across the nation and throughout Europe. More than 41,000 people saw it on one day in Chicago in 1884. In 1886, it played for six months on Staten Island in New York, where General William T. Sherman, Mark Twain, P. T. Barnum, Thomas A. Edison, and the widow of General Custer all saw and praised it. Members of the royal family attended the show in England, and it drew large crowds as well in France, Germany, and Italy.

The Wild West shows died out not long after World War I, but many of their features survived in circuses and rodeos, and later in films, radio and television shows, and theme parks. Their popularity was evidence of the nostalgia with which late-nineteenth-century Americans looked at their own imagined past, and their eagerness to remember a "Wild West" that had never really been what they liked to believe. Buffalo Bill and his imitators confirmed the popular image of the West as a place of romance and glamour and helped keep that image alive for later generations. ●

ANNIE OAKLEY Annie Oakley had been a vaudeville and circus entertainer for years before joining Buffalo Bill's Wild West show in 1885. She was under five feet tall and weighed less than a hundred pounds, but her exploits with pistols, rifles, and horses earned her a reputation as a woman of unusual strength and skill. (© Bettmann/Corbis)

UNDERSTAND, ANALYZE, AND EVALUATE

1. How did the West portrayed in the Wild West shows contrast with the real West?
2. Why do you think Indians participated in the Wild West shows? How did their participation affect white audiences' perception of Native Americans?
3. Why has the romantic image of the Wild West remained so long-lived in American popular culture?

Wister and Remington, he made his own fascination with the West a part of the nation's popular culture. In the 1890s, he published a four-volume history, *The Winning of the West*, with a romanticized account of the spread of white civilization into the frontier. These and other books on the West enhanced his own reputation. They also contributed to the public's fascination with the "frontier."

FREDERICK JACKSON TURNER

Perhaps the clearest and most influential statements of the romantic vision of the frontier came from the historian Frederick Jackson Turner, of the University of Wisconsin. In

TURNER'S FRONTIER THESIS

1893, the thirty-three-year-old Turner delivered a memorable paper to a meeting of the American Historical Association in Chicago titled "The Significance of the Frontier in American History," in which he argued that the end of the "frontier" also marked the end of one of the most important democratizing forces in American life. (See "Debating the Past," pp. 446–447.)

In fact, Turner's assessments were both inaccurate and premature. The West had never been a "frontier" in the sense he meant the term: an empty, uncivilized land awaiting settlement. White migrants who moved into the region had joined (or displaced) already-established societies and cultures. At the same time, considerable unoccupied land remained in the West for many years to come. But Turner did express a growing and generally accurate sense that much of the best farming and grazing land was now taken, that in the future it would be more difficult for individuals to acquire valuable land for little or nothing.

THE LOSS OF UTOPIA

In accepting the idea of the "passing of the frontier," many Americans were acknowledging the end of one of their most cherished myths. As long as it had been possible for them to

THE "FRONTIER" AND THE WEST

THE American West, the Indian population, and the people of European descent who settled there have been central to the national imagination and to American historical scholarship.

FRONTIER TOWN GROWS UP This picture of present-day San Francisco conveys a very different view of a city that, at about the time just before the gold rush (about 1848), had only 1,000 people. Today, the city has left behind many overt traces of its earlier status as a frontier community. The city now has nearly a million citizens with diverse backgrounds living within the Bay Area of nearly 8.5 million people. (© Robert Harding World Imagery/Alamy)

Through most of the nineteenth century, the history of the West reflected the romantic and optimistic view of the region as a place of adventure and opportunity where brave and enterprising people endured great hardships to begin building a new civilization. The emergence of western history as an important field of scholarship can be traced to Frederick Jackson Turner's "The Significance of the Frontier in American History," a paper he delivered at a meeting of the American Historical Association in 1893.

Turner stated his thesis simply. The settlement of the West by white people—"the existence of an area of free land, its continuous recession, and the advance of American settlement westward"—was the central story of American history. The process of westward expansion transformed a desolate and savage land into a modern civilization. It also continually renewed American ideas of democracy and individualism. It shaped not just the West but the nation as a whole. The Turner thesis shaped American history for a generation, and it shaped western American history for even longer. In the first half of the twentieth century, virtually everyone who wrote about the West echoed at least part of Turner's argument. Ray Allen Billington's *Westward Expansion* (1949), a skillful revision of Turner's thesis, kept the idea of what Billington called the "westward course of empire" (the movement of

TWILIGHT ENCAMPMENT The western photographer Walter McClintock took this dramatic photograph of a Blackfoot Indian camp in the 1890s. By the time this picture was taken, the Indian tribes were already dwindling, and artists, photographers, and ethnographers were flocking to the West to record aspects of Indian civilization that they feared would soon disappear. (Courtesy Beinecke Rare Book and Manuscript Library, Yale University)

Europeans into an unsettled land) at the center of scholarship. In *The Great Plains* (1931) and *The Great Frontier* (1952), Walter Prescott Webb similarly emphasized the bravery and ingenuity of white settlers in the Southwest.

Serious efforts to displace Turner's thesis as the explanation of western American history did not begin in earnest until after World War II. In *Virgin Land* (1950), Henry Nash Smith examined many of the same heroic images of the West that Turner and his disciples. He treated those images less as descriptions of reality than as myths. Earl Pomeroy challenged Turner's notion of the West as a place of individualism, innovation, and democratic renewal, claiming that "conservatism, inheritance, and continuity bulked at least as large."

The western historians of the late 1970s launched an even more emphatic attack on the Turner thesis and the idea of the "frontier." New western historians such as Richard White, Patricia Nelson Limerick, William Cronon, Donald Worster, Peggy Pascoe, and many others challenged the Turnerians on a number of points.

Turner saw the nineteenth-century West as "free land" awaiting the expansion of Anglo-American settlement and American democracy. Pioneers settled the region by conquering the "obstacles" that stood in the way of civilization. The new western historians rejected the concept of a "frontier" and emphasized, instead, the elaborate and highly developed civilizations that already existed in the region. White, English-speaking Americans, they argued, did not so much settle the West as conquer it, though their conquest was never complete. Anglo-Americans in the West continued to share the region not only with the Indians and Hispanics who preceded them there, but also with African Americans, Asians, Latino Americans, and others who flowed into the West at the same time they did.

The Turnerian West was a place of heroism, triumph, and, above all, progress, dominated by the feats of brave white men. More-recent historians describe the West as a less triumphant (and less masculine) place in which bravery and success coexist with oppression, greed, and failure; in which decaying ghost towns, bleak Indian reservations, impoverished barrios, and ecologically devastated landscapes are as characteristic of western development as great ranches, rich farms, and prosperous cities; and in which women are as important as men in shaping the societies that emerged. This aspect of the "new western history" has attracted particular criticism from those attached to traditional accounts. The novelist Larry McMurtry, for example, has denounced the newer scholarship as "Failure Studies." He has insisted that in rejecting the romantic image westerners had of themselves, the revisionists omit an important part of the western experience.

To Turner and his disciples, the nineteenth-century West was a place where rugged individualism flourished and replenished American democracy. The newer western scholars contend that western individualism is a self-serving myth. Western "pioneers," they argue, were never self-sufficient but depended on government-subsidized railroads for access to markets, federal troops for protection from Indians, and (later) government-funded dams and canals for irrigating their fields and sustaining their towns.

While Turner defined the West as a process—a process of settlement that came to an end with the "closing of the frontier" in the late nineteenth century—more-recent historians see the West as a region whose distinctive history did not end in 1890 but continues into our own time. ●

AP HISTORICAL ARGUMENTATION AND INTERPRETATION

Questions assume cumulative content knowledge from this chapter and previous chapters.

1. Describe three major interpretations of the history of the American West. For each, identify one piece of historical evidence that could be used to support the interpretation and one piece of historical evidence that could be used to refute the interpretation.

2. Offer an explanation regarding how historians in the early 20th century might have been influenced in their perspective of American Western history.

3. With which historical interpretation of the American West do you most agree? Support your view, using historical evidence.

PSYCHOLOGICAL LOSS

consider the West an empty, open land, it was possible to believe that there were constantly revitalizing opportunities in American life. Now there was a vague and ominous sense of opportunities foreclosed, of individuals losing their ability to control their own destinies. The psychological loss was all the greater because of what historian Henry Nash Smith would later call, in *Virgin Land* (1950), the "myth of the garden": the once widely shared belief that the West had the potential to be a virtual Garden of Eden, where a person could begin life anew and where the ideals of democracy could be restored.

THE DISPERSAL OF THE TRIBES

Having imagined the West as a "virgin land" awaiting civilization by white people, many Americans tried to force the region to match their image of it. That meant, above all, ensuring that

the Indian tribes would not remain obstacles to the spread of white society.

WHITE TRIBAL POLICIES

The traditional policy of the federal government was to regard the tribes simultaneously as independent nations and as wards of the president, and to negotiate treaties with them that were solemnly ratified by the Senate. This limited concept of Indian sovereignty had been responsible for the government's attempt before 1860 to erect a permanent frontier between whites and Indians, to reserve the region west of the bend of the Missouri River as permanent Indian country. However, treaties or agreements with the tribes seldom survived the pressure of white settlers eager for access to Indian lands. The history of relations between the United States and the Native Americans was, therefore, one of nearly endless broken promises.

By the early 1850s, the idea of establishing one great enclave in which many tribes could live gave way, in the face of white demands for access to lands in Indian Territory, to a new reservations policy, known as "concentration." In 1851, each tribe was assigned its own defined reservation, confirmed by separate treaties—treaties often illegitimately negotiated with unauthorized "representatives" chosen by whites, people known sarcastically as "treaty chiefs." The new arrangement had many benefits for whites and few for the Indians. It divided the tribes from one another and made them easier to control. It allowed the government to force tribes into scattered locations and to take over the most desirable lands for white settlement. But it did not survive as the basis of Indian policy for long.

"CONCENTRATION" POLICY

In 1867, in the aftermath of a series of bloody conflicts, Congress established an Indian Peace Commission, composed of soldiers and civilians, to recommend a new and presumably permanent Indian policy. The commission recommended replacing the "concentration" policy with a plan to move all the Plains Indians into two large reservations—one in Indian Territory (Oklahoma), the other in the Dakotas. At a series of meetings with the tribes, government agents cajoled, bribed, and tricked representatives of the Arapaho, Cheyenne, Sioux, and other tribes into agreeing to treaties establishing the new reservations.

This solution worked little better than previous ones. White management of Indian matters was entrusted to the Bureau of Indian Affairs, a branch of the Department of the Interior responsible for distributing land, making payments, and supervising the shipment of supplies. Its record was appalling. The bureau's agents in the West, products of political patronage, were often men of extraordinary incompetence and dishonesty. But even the most honest and diligent agents were generally ill prepared for their jobs, had no understanding of tribal ways, and had little chance of success.

POORLY ADMINISTERED RESERVATIONS

Worsening the fate of the tribes was the white Anglos' relentless slaughtering of the buffalo herds that supported the tribes' way of life. Even in the 1850s, whites had been killing buffalo at a rapid rate to provide food and supplies for the large bands of migrants traveling to the gold rush in California. After the Civil War, the white demand for buffalo hides became a national phenomenon—partly for economic reasons and partly as a fad. (Everyone east of the Missouri seemed to want a buffalo robe from the romantic West, and there was a strong demand for buffalo leather, which was used to make machine belts in eastern factories.) Gangs of professional hunters swarmed over the plains to shoot the huge animals. Railroad companies hired riflemen (such as Buffalo Bill Cody) and arranged shooting expeditions to kill large numbers of buffalo, hoping to thin the herds, which were obstructions to railroad traffic. Some Indian tribes (notably the Blackfeet) also began killing large numbers of buffalo to sell in the booming new market.

It was not just the hunting that threatened the buffalo. The ecological changes accompanying white settlement—the reduction, and in some areas virtual disappearance, of the open plains—also decimated the buffalo population. The southern herd was virtually exterminated by 1875, and within a few years the smaller northern herd had met the same fate. In 1865, there had been at least 15 million buffalo; a decade later, fewer than a thousand of the great beasts survived. The army and the agents of the Bureau of Indian Affairs condoned and even encouraged the killing. By destroying the buffalo herds, whites were destroying the Indians' source of food and supplies and their ability to resist the white advance. They were also contributing to a climate in which Indian warriors felt the need to fight to preserve their way of life.

DECIMATION OF THE BUFFALO

CHIEF GARFIELD Edward Curtis, one of the most accomplished photographers of tribal life in the early twentieth century, made this portrait of a Jicarilla Apache chief in 1904. By then, the Jicarilla were living in a reservation in northern New Mexico, and white officials had assigned all members of the tribe Spanish or English names. The man depicted here, the head chief, had chosen the name Garfield himself. (© Stapleton Collection/Corbis)

THE INDIAN WARS

There was almost incessant fighting between whites and Indians from the 1850s to the 1880s, as Indians struggled against the growing threats to their civilizations. Indian warriors, usually traveling in raiding parties of thirty to forty men, **INDIAN RESISTANCE** attacked wagon trains, stagecoaches, and isolated ranches, often in retaliation for earlier attacks. As the U.S. Army became more deeply involved in the fighting, the tribes began to focus more of their attacks on white soldiers.

At times, this small-scale fighting escalated into something close to a war. During the Civil War, the eastern Sioux in Minnesota, cramped on an inadequate reservation and exploited by corrupt white agents, suddenly rebelled against the restrictions imposed on them by the government's policies. Led by Little Crow, they killed more than 700 whites before being subdued by a force of regulars and militiamen. Thirty-eight of the Indians were hanged, and the tribe was exiled to the Dakotas.

At the same time, fighting flared up in eastern Colorado, where the Arapaho and Cheyenne were coming into conflict with white miners settling in the region. Bands of Indians attacked stagecoach lines and settlements in an effort to regain lost territory. In response, whites called up a large territorial **SAND CREEK MASSACRE** militia. The governor urged all friendly Indians to congregate at army posts for protection before the army began its campaign. One Arapaho and Cheyenne band under Chief Black Kettle, apparently in response to the invitation, camped near Fort Lyon on Sand Creek in November 1864. Some members of the party were warriors, but Black Kettle believed he was under official protection and exhibited no hostile intention. Nevertheless, Colonel J. M. Chivington, apparently encouraged by the army commander of the district, led a volunteer militia force—largely consisting of unemployed miners, many of whom were apparently drunk—to the unsuspecting camp and massacred 133 people, 105 of them women and children. Black Kettle escaped the Sand Creek massacre. Four years later, in 1868, he and his Cheyennes, some of whom were now at war with the whites, were caught on the Washita River, near the Texas border, by Colonel George A. Custer. White troops killed the chief and slaughtered his people.

At the end of the Civil War, white troops stepped up their wars against the western Indians on several fronts. The most serious and sustained conflict was in Montana, where the army was attempting to build a road to connect Fort Laramie, Wyoming, to the new mining centers. The western Sioux resented this intrusion into the heart of their buffalo range. Led by one of their great chiefs, Red Cloud, they so harried the soldiers and the construction party—among other things, burning the forts that were supposed to guard the route—that the road could not be used.

It was not only the U.S. Army that threatened the tribes. It was also unofficial violence by white vigilantes who engaged in what became known as "Indian hunting." In California, **"INDIAN HUNTING"** in particular, tracking down and killing Indians became for some whites a kind of sport. Some who did not engage in killing offered rewards (or bounties) to those who did; these bounty hunters brought back scalps and skulls as proof of their deeds. Sometimes the killing was in response to Indian raids on white communities. But often it was in service to a more basic and terrible purpose. Considerable numbers of whites were committed to the goal of literal "elimination" of the tribes, a goal that rested on the belief in the inhumanity of Indians and the impossibility of white society's coexisting with them. In Oregon in 1853, for example, whites who had hanged a seven-year-old

HELD UP BY BUFFALO Once among the most numerous creatures in North America, the buffalo almost became extinct as a result of indiscriminate slaughter by white settlers and travelers, who often fired at herds from moving trains simply for the sport of it. (Private Collection/© Peter Newark American Pictures/The Bridgeman Art Library)

Indian boy explained themselves by saying simply "nits breed lice." In California, civilians killed close to 5,000 Indians between 1850 and 1880–one of many factors (disease and poverty being the more important) that reduced the Indian population of the state from 150,000 before the Civil War to 30,000 in 1870.

The treaties negotiated in 1867 brought a temporary lull to many of the conflicts. But new forces soon shattered the peace again. In the early 1870s, more waves of white settlers, mostly miners, began to penetrate some of the lands in Dakota Territory supposedly guaranteed to the tribes in 1867.

THE INDIAN FRONTIER As conflict erupted between Indian and white cultures in the West, the government sought increasingly to concentrate tribes on reservations. Resistance to the reservation concept helped unite the Sioux and Cheyenne, traditionally enemies, in the Dakotas during the 1870s. Along the Little Bighorn River, the impetuous Custer underestimated the strength of his Indian opponents and attacked before the supporting troops of Reno and Benteen were in a position to aid him.

• *What did the defeat of Custer's army do for the Sioux tribes?*

Indian resistance flared anew, this time with even greater strength. In the northern plains, the Sioux rose up in 1875 and left their reservation. When white officials ordered them to return, bands of warriors gathered in Montana and united under two great leaders: Crazy Horse and Sitting Bull.

Three army columns set out to round them up and force them back onto the reservation. With the expedition, as col-

LITTLE BIGHORN

onel of the famous Seventh Cavalry, was the colorful and controversial George A. Custer, a golden-haired, romantic glory seeker. At the Battle of the Little Bighorn in southern Montana in 1876–the most famous conflict between whites and Indians–the tribal warriors surprised Custer and 264 members of his regiment, surrounded them, and killed every man. Custer was accused of rashness, but he encountered something that no white man would likely have predicted. The chiefs had gathered as many as 2,500 warriors, one of the largest Indian armies ever assembled at one time in the United States.

But the Indians did not have the political organization or the supplies to keep their troops united. Soon the warriors drifted off in bands to elude pursuit or search for food, and the army eventually forced them back to the Dakota reservations. The power of the Sioux was soon broken. The proud leaders, Crazy Horse and Sitting Bull, accepted defeat and the monotony of life on reservations. Both were later killed by reservation police after being tricked or taunted into a last pathetic show of resistance.

One of the most dramatic episodes in Indian history occurred in Idaho in 1877. The Nez Percé were a small and relatively peaceful tribe, some of whose members had managed to live unmolested in Oregon into the 1870s without ever signing a treaty with the United States. But under pressure from white settlers, the government forced them to move into a reservation that another branch of the tribe had accepted by treaty in the 1850s. With no realistic prospect of resisting, the Indians began the journey to the reservation; but on the way, several younger Indians, drunk and angry, killed four white settlers.

The leader of the Nez Percé, Chief Joseph, urged his followers to flee from the American troops. They scattered in

CHIEF JOSEPH

several directions and became part of a remarkable chase. Joseph moved with 200 men and 350 women, children, and elders in an effort to reach Canada and take refuge with the Sioux there. Pursued by four columns of American soldiers, the Indians covered 1,321 miles in seventy-five days, repelling or evading the army time and again. They were finally caught just short of the Canadian boundary. Some escaped and slipped across the border; but Joseph and most of his followers, weary and discouraged, finally gave up. "Hear me, my chiefs," Joseph said after meeting with the American general Nelson Miles. "I am tired. My heart is sick and sad. From where the sun now stands, I will fight no more forever." He surrendered to Miles in exchange for a promise that his band could return to the Nez Percé reservation in Idaho. But the government refused to honor Miles's promise, and the Nez Percé were moved

THE BATTLE OF THE LITTLE BIGHORN: AN INDIAN VIEW This 1898 watercolor by one of the Indian participants portrays the aftermath of the Battle of the Little Bighorn, June 25–26, 1876, in which an army unit under the command of General George Armstrong Custer was surrounded and wiped out by Sioux and Cheyenne warriors. This grisly painting shows Indians on horseback riding over the corpses of Custer and his men. Custer can be seen lying at left center, dressed in yellow buckskin with his hat beside him. The four standing men at center are Sitting Bull, Rain-in-the-Face, Crazy Horse, and Kicking Bear (the artist). At lower right, Indian women begin preparations for a ceremony to honor the returning warriors. (© The Granger Collection, New York)

from one place to another for several years; in the process, many of them died of disease and malnutrition (although Joseph himself lived until 1908).

The last Indians to maintain organized resistance against the whites were the Chiricahua Apaches, who fought intermittently from the 1860s to the late 1880s. The two ablest chiefs of this fierce tribe were Mangas Colorados and Cochise. Mangas was murdered during the Civil War by white soldiers who tricked him into surrendering, and in 1872 Cochise agreed to peace in exchange for a reservation that included some of the tribe's traditional land. But Cochise died in 1874, and his successor, Geronimo–unwilling to bow to white pressures to assimilate–fought on for more than a decade establishing bases in the mountains of Arizona and Mexico and leading warriors in intermittent raids against white outposts. With each raid, however, the number of warring Apaches dwindled, as some warriors died and others drifted away to the reservation. By 1886, Geronimo's plight was hopeless. His band consisted of only about thirty people, including women and children, while his white pursuers numbered perhaps ten thousand. Geronimo recognized the odds and surrendered, an event that marked the end of formal warfare between Indians and whites. The Apache wars were the most violent of all the Indian conflicts, perhaps because the tribes were now the most desperate. But it was the whites who committed the most flagrant and vicious atrocities. In 1871, for example, a mob of white miners invaded an Apache camp, slaughtered more than a hundred Indians, and captured children, whom they sold as slaves to rival tribes. On other occasions, white troops murdered Indians who responded to invitations to peace conferences, once killing them with poisoned food.

Nor did the atrocities end with the conclusion of the Apache wars. Another tragic encounter occurred in 1890 as a result of a religious revival among the Sioux–a revival that itself symbolized the catastrophic effects of the white assaults on Indian civilization. The Sioux were by now aware that their culture and their glories were irrevocably fading; some were also near starvation because corrupt government agents had reduced their food rations. As other tribes had done in trying times in the past, many of these Indians turned to a prophet who led them into a religious revival.

This time the prophet was Wovoka, a Paiute who inspired a spiritual awakening that began in Nevada and spread quickly to the plains. The new revival emphasized the coming of a messiah, but its most conspicuous feature was a mass, emotional "Ghost Dance," which inspired ecstatic visions. Among these visions were images of a retreat of white people from the plains and a restoration of the great buffalo herds. White agents on the Sioux reservation watched the dances in bewilderment and fear; some believed they might be the preliminary to hostilities.

"GHOST DANCE"

On December 29, 1890, the Seventh Cavalry (which had once been Custer's regiment) tried to round up a group of about 350 cold and starving Sioux at Wounded Knee, South Dakota. Fighting broke out in which about 40 white soldiers and more than 300 of the Indians, including women and children, died. What precipitated the conflict is a matter of dispute. But the battle soon turned into a one-sided massacre, as the white soldiers turned their revolving cannons on the Indians and mowed them down in the snow.

WOUNDED KNEE

THE DAWES ACT

Even before the Ghost Dance and the Wounded Knee tragedy, the federal government had moved to destroy forever the tribal structure that had always been the cornerstone of Indian culture. Reversing its policy of nearly fifty years of creating reservations

WOUNDED KNEE This grim photograph shows Big Foot, chief of the Lakota Sioux, lying dead in the snow near Wounded Knee in South Dakota. He was one of many victims of an 1890 massacre of more than 300 members of the tribe, killed by U.S. Army soldiers after the Indians had surrendered their weapons. Whether the massacre was planned and deliberate, or whether it was a result of confusion and fear, remains in dispute. (© nsf/Alamy)

in which the tribes would be isolated from white society, Congress abolished the practice by which tribes owned reservation lands communally. Some supporters of the new policy believed they were acting for the good of the Indians, whom they considered a "vanishing race" in need of rescue by white society. But whatever the motives, the policy was designed to force Indians to become landowners and farmers, to abandon their collective society and culture and become part of white civilization.

The Dawes Severalty Act of 1887 (usually known simply as the Dawes Act) provided for the gradual elimination of tribal ownership of land and the allotment of **ASSIMILATION** tracts to individual owners: 160 acres to the head of a family, 80 acres to a single adult or orphan, 40 acres to each dependent child. Adult owners were given United States citizenship, but unlike other citizens, they could not gain full title to their property for twenty-five years (supposedly to prevent them from selling the land to speculators). The act applied to most of the western tribes. The Pueblo, who continued to occupy lands long ago guaranteed them, were excluded from its provisions. In applying the Dawes Act, the Bureau of Indian Affairs relentlessly promoted the idea of assimilation that lay behind it. Not only did they try to move Indian families onto their own plots of land; they also took some Indian children away from their families and sent them to boarding schools run by whites, where they believed the young people could be educated to abandon tribal ways. The bureau also moved to stop Indian religious rituals and encouraged the spread of Christianity and the creation of Christian churches on the reservations.

Few Indians were prepared for this wrenching change from their traditional collective society to capitalist individualism. In any case, white administration of the program was so corrupt and inept that ultimately the government simply abandoned it. Much of the reservation land, therefore, was never distributed to individual owners. Congress attempted to speed the transition with the Burke Act of 1906, but Indians continued to resist forced assimilation.

Neither then nor later did legislation provide a satisfactory solution to the plight of the Indians, largely because there was no entirely happy solution to be had. The interests of the Indians were not compatible with those of the expanding white civilization. Whites successfully settled the American West only at the expense of the region's indigenous peoples.

THE RISE AND DECLINE OF THE WESTERN FARMER

The arrival of the miners, the empire building of the cattle ranchers, the dispersal of the Indian tribes—all served as a prelude to the decisive phase of white settlement of the Far West. Even before the Civil War, farmers had begun moving into the plains region, challenging the dominance of the ranchers and the Indians and occasionally coming into conflict with both. By the 1870s, what was once a trickle had become a deluge.

Farmers poured into the plains and beyond, enclosed land that had once been hunting territory for Indians and grazing territory for cattle, and established a new agricultural region.

For a time in the late 1870s and early 1880s, the new western farmers flourished, enjoying the fruits of an agricultural economic boom comparable in many ways to the booms that eastern industry periodically enjoyed. Beginning in the mid-1880s, however, the boom turned to bust. American agriculture—not only in the new West but in the older Midwest and the South as well—was producing more than it ever had, too much for the market to absorb. For that and other reasons, prices for agricultural goods declined. Both economically and psychologically, the agricultural economy began a long, steady decline.

FARMING ON THE PLAINS

Many factors combined to produce this surge of western settlement, but the most important was the railroads. Before the Civil War, the Great Plains had been accessible only through a difficult journey by wagon. But beginning in the 1860s, a great new network of railroad lines developed, spearheaded by the transcontinental routes Congress had authorized and subsidized in 1862. They made huge new areas of settlement accessible.

The completion of the transcontinental line was a dramatic and monumental achievement. The two lines joined at Promontory Point in northern Utah in the spring of 1869.

But while this first transcontinental line captured the public imagination, the construction of subsidiary lines in the following years proved of greater importance to the West. State governments encouraged railroad development by offering financial aid, favorable loans, and more than 50 million acres of land (on top of the 130 million acres the federal government had already provided). Although operated by private corporations, the railroads were essentially public projects.

It was not only by making access to the Great Plains easier that the railroads helped spur agricultural settlement there. The railroad companies themselves actively promoted settlement, both to provide themselves with **KEY ROLE OF THE RAILROAD** customers for their services and to increase the value of their vast landholdings. In addition, the companies set rates so low for settlers that almost anyone could afford the trip west. And they sold much of their land at very low prices and provided liberal credit to prospective settlers.

Contributing further to the great surge of white agricultural expansion was a temporary change in the climate of the Great Plains. For several years in succession, beginning in the 1870s, rainfall in the plains states was well above average. White Americans now rejected the old idea that the region was the Great American Desert. Some even claimed that cultivation of the plains itself actually encouraged rainfall.

Even under the most favorable conditions, farming on the plains presented special problems. First was the challenge of fencing. Farmers had to enclose their land, if for no other reason than to protect it from the herds of the open-range cattlemen. But traditional wood or stone fences were too expensive and were

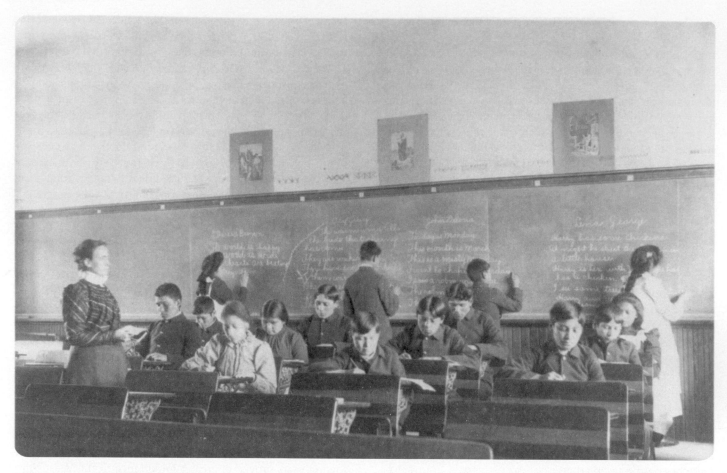

CARLISLE INDIAN SCHOOL Government authorities and private philanthropists tried in many ways to encourage Indians to assimilate into mainstream white American society after the end of the Indian wars of the late nineteenth century. The Carlisle Indian Industrial School, founded by Captain Richard Henry Pratt in 1879, was the first federally funded Native American off-reservation boarding school. Educators there believed that Native Americans were the equals of people from European backgrounds. The curriculum was designed to help Native Americans gain the skills necessary to advance in mainstream American society. (The Library of Congress (LC-USZ62-55422))

BARBED WIRE

ineffective as barriers to cattle. In 1873, however, two Illinois farmers, Joseph H. Glidden and I. L. Ellwood, solved this problem by developing and marketing barbed wire, which became standard equipment on the plains and revolutionized fencing practices all over the country.

The second problem was water. Much of the land west of the Mississippi was considerably more arid than the lands to the east. Some of it was literally desert. As a result, the growth of the West depended heavily on irrigation—providing water from sources other than rainfall. Water was diverted from rivers and streams and into farmlands throughout the West—in California and in the Southwest more than anywhere else. In other areas, farmers drilled wells or found other methods of channeling water onto their lands. The search for water—and the resulting battles over control of water (between different landowners and even between different states)—became a central and enduring characteristic of western life.

In the plains states, the problems of water created an epic disaster. After 1887, a series of dry seasons began, and lands that had been fertile now returned to semidesert. Some farm-

DROUGHT

ers dealt with the problem by using deep wells pumped by steel windmills, by turning to what was called dryland farming (a system of tillage designed to conserve moisture in the soil by covering it with a dust blanket), or by planting drought-resistant crops. In many areas of the plains, however, only large-scale irrigation could save the endangered farms. But irrigation projects of the necessary magnitude required government assistance, and neither the state nor federal governments were prepared to fund the projects.

Most of the people who moved into the region had previously been farmers in the Midwest, the East, or Europe. In the

HARD TIMES FOR FARMERS

booming years of the early 1880s, with land values rising, the new farmers had no problem obtaining extensive and easy credit and had every reason to believe they would soon be able to retire their debts. But the arid years of the late 1880s—during which crop prices were falling while production was becoming more expensive—changed that prospect. Tens of thousands of farmers could not pay their debts and were forced to abandon their farms. There was, in effect, a reverse migration: white settlers moved back east, sometimes turning once-flourishing communities into desolate ghost towns. Those who remained continued to suffer from falling prices (for example, wheat, which had sold for $1.60 a bushel at the end of the Civil War, dropped to 49 cents in the 1890s) and persistent indebtedness.

COMMERCIAL AGRICULTURE

American farming by the late nineteenth century no longer bore much relation to the comforting image many Americans continued to cherish. The sturdy, independent farmer of popular myth was being replaced by the commercial farmer–attempting to do in the agricultural economy what industrialists were doing in the manufacturing economy.

Commercial farmers were not self-sufficient and made no effort to become so. They specialized in cash crops, which they sold in national or world markets. They did not make their own household supplies or grow their own food but bought them instead at town or village stores. This kind of farming, when it was successful, raised the farmers' living standards. But it also made them dependent on bankers and interest rates, railroads and freight rates, national and European markets, world supply and demand. And unlike the capitalists of the industrial order, they could not regulate their production or influence the prices of what they sold.

Between 1865 and 1900, agriculture became an international business. Farm output increased dramatically, not only in the United States but also in Brazil, Argentina, Canada, Australia, New Zealand, Russia, and elsewhere. At the same time, modern forms of communication and transportation–the telephone, telegraph, steam navigation, railroads–were creating new markets around the world for agricultural goods. American commercial farmers, constantly opening new lands, produced much more than the domestic market could absorb; they relied on the world market to absorb their surplus, but in that market they faced major competition. Cotton farmers depended on export sales for 70 percent of their annual income, wheat farmers for 30 to 40 percent; but the volatility of the international market put them at great risk.

Beginning in the 1880s, worldwide overproduction led to a drop in prices for most agricultural goods and hence to great economic distress for many of the more than 6 million American farm families. By the 1890s, 27 percent of the farms in the country were mortgaged; by 1910, 33 percent. In 1880, 25 percent of all farms had been operated by tenants; by 1910, the proportion had grown to 37 percent. Commercial farming made some people fabulously wealthy. But the farm economy as a whole was suffering a significant decline relative to the rest of the nation.

CONSEQUENCES OF OVERPRODUCTION

THE FARMERS' GRIEVANCES

American farmers were painfully aware that something was wrong. But few yet understood the implications of national and world overproduction. Instead, they concentrated their attention and anger on immediate, comprehensible–and no less real–problems: inequitable freight rates, high interest charges, and an inadequate currency.

The farmers' first and most burning grievance was against the railroads. In many cases, the railroads charged higher freight rates for farm goods than for other goods, and higher rates in the South and West than in the Northeast. Railroads also controlled elevator and warehouse facilities in buying centers and charged arbitrary storage rates.

Farmers also resented the institutions controlling credit–banks, loan companies, insurance corporations. Since sources of credit in the West and South were few, farmers had to take loans on whatever terms they could get, often at interest rates ranging from 10 to 25 percent. Many farmers had to pay these loans back in years when prices were dropping and currency was becoming scarce. Increasing the volume of currency eventually became an important agrarian demand.

A third grievance concerned prices–both the prices farmers received for their products and the prices they paid for goods. Farmers sold their products in a competitive world market over which they had no control and of which they had no advanced knowledge. A farmer could plant a large crop at a moment when prices were high and find that by harvesttime the price had declined. Farmers' fortunes rose and fell in response to unpredictable forces. But many farmers became convinced (often with valid reason) that "middlemen"–speculators, bankers, regional and local agents–were combining to fix prices so as to benefit themselves at the growers' expense. Many farmers also came to believe (again, not entirely without reason) that manufacturers in the East were conspiring to keep the prices of farm goods low and the prices of industrial goods high. Although farmers sold their crops in a competitive world market, they bought manufactured goods in a domestic market protected by tariffs and dominated by trusts and corporations.

THE AGRARIAN MALAISE

These economic difficulties produced a series of social and cultural resentments. Farm families in some parts of the country–particularly in the prairie and plains regions, where large farms were scattered over vast areas–were virtually cut off from the outside world and human companionship. During the winter months and spells of bad weather, the loneliness and boredom could become nearly unbearable. Many farmers lacked access to adequate education for their children, to proper medical facilities, to recreational or cultural activities, to virtually anything that might give them a sense of being members of a community. Older farmers felt the sting of watching their children leave the farm for the city. They felt the humiliation of being ridiculed as "hayseeds" by the new urban culture that was coming to dominate American life.

ISOLATION

The result of this sense of isolation and obsolescence was a growing malaise among many farmers, a discontent that would help create a great national political movement in the 1890s. It found reflection, too, in the literature that emerged from rural America. Late-nineteenth-century writers often romanticized the rugged life of the cowboy and the western miner. For the farmer, however, the image was often different. Hamlin Garland, for example, reflected the growing disillusionment in a series of novels and short stories. In the past, Garland wrote in the introduction to his novel

Jason Edwards (1891), the agrarian frontier had seemed to be "the Golden West, the land of wealth and freedom and happiness. All of the associations called up by the spoken word, the West, were fabulous, mythic, hopeful." Now, however, the bright promise had faded. The trials of rural life were crushing the human spirit. "So this is the reality of the dream!" a character in *Jason Edwards* exclaims. "A shanty on a barren plain, hot and lone as a desert. My God!" Once, sturdy yeoman farmers had viewed themselves as the backbone of American life. Now they were becoming painfully aware that their position was declining in relation to the rising urban-industrial society to the east.

AP CONNECTING THEMES

Chapter 16 discussed the rising economic and political importance of the Far West. The peopling of the Far West and the consequences on the native populations were immense. Review the multiple effects of the completion of the transcontinental railroad on native populations, as well as the political, economic, and social development of the region. Also, review the chapter to assess the relative importance of the government in encouraging westward settlement. Lastly, be able to compare and contrast the economic, environmental, and political impact of the mining, cattle, and agricultural developments, both regionally and for the nation as a whole.

The following themes have heightened importance in Chapter 16. You should now be able to do the following for each listed theme:

Identity: Analyze the ways in which American concepts of identity changed as a result of westward expansion and racial prejudice.

Work, Exchange, and Technology: Explain how changes in technology and transportation affected the settlement of the Far West.
Peopling: Analyze the sources of western population growth, the ethnic makeup of the Far West, and explain the consequences of that makeup.
Politics and Power: Explain how the growth of the trans-Mississippi west influenced politics in the United States.
Environment and Geography: Analyze the impact of various aspects of western settlement on the environment of the region and the environment's impact on settlement.
Ideas, Beliefs, and Culture: Explain how the settlement of the Far West influenced cultural values and artistic expression in the United States.

AP SUGGESTED STUDY

PEOPLE/PLACES/EVENTS As you study these items, think about how they demonstrate or relate to key concepts and historical themes from this chapter and previous chapters.

AP TEST PRACTICE

Questions assume cumulative content knowledge from this chapter and previous chapters.

MULTIPLE CHOICE Use the excerpt below and your knowledge of U.S. history to answer questions 1-2.

"Since the days when the fleet of Columbus sailed into the waters of the New World, America has been another name for opportunity, and the people of the United States have taken their tone from the incessant expansion which has not only been open but has even been forced upon them. . . . Movement has been its dominant fact . . . each frontier did indeed furnish a new field of opportunity, a gate of escape from the bondage of the past; and freshness, and confidence, and scorn of older society, impatience of its restraints and its ideas, and indifference to its lessons, have accompanied the frontier."

–Frederick Jackson Turner, historian, essay titled "The Significance of the Frontier in American History," in 1893 and later collected in a book of essays by Turner titled *The Frontier in American History,* ©1920

1. Which best describes the American democratic ideal that Turner argues the American "frontier" facilitated?

    (A) The ideal of freedom of religion

    (B) The ideal of orderly settlement of society

    (C) The desirability of utopian societies

    (D) The ideal of equal opportunity

2. Which ideology best reflects Turner's perspective?

    (A) Mercantilism

    (B) Manifest Destiny

    (C) Puritan idea of predestination

    (D) Abolitionism

SHORT ANSWER Use your knowledge of U.S. history to answer questions 3-6.

3. Answer a, b, and c.

    a) Briefly explain ONE example of Native American resistance to white expansion in the American West.

    b) Briefly explain a SECOND example of ONE example of Native American resistance to white expansion in the American West.

    c) Briefly explain ONE example of government reaction to a Native American effort to resist white encroachment into the far western territories.

4. Answer a, b, and c.

    a) Briefly explain ONE example of how continued westward expansion followed developments in transportation.

    b) Briefly explain a SECOND example of how continued westward expansion affected national politics.

    c) Briefly explain ONE example of how continued westward expansion changed Americans' sense of national identity in relation to other peoples living in the North American continent.

5. Answer a, b, and c.

    a) For one of the areas below, identify ONE event or historical example and briefly explain how this event or example was affected by American westward expansion.

    • Ethnic populations

    • Environment

    • Art and popular culture

    b) Use ONE piece of historical evidence to support your explanation.

    c) Choose a second area and identify ONE event or historical example and briefly explain how this event or example was affected by American westward expansion.

6. Use the photograph on page 438 to answer a, b, and c.

    a) Briefly explain the perspective expressed by the artist concerning ONE of the following:

    • Farming

    • Family life

    • Technology

    b) Briefly explain ONE development from the period 1860 to 1890 that led to people of this ethnic background living in the Midwest at this time.

    c) Briefly explain ONE development during the period of 1860 to 1890 that would have challenged this demographic movement.

LONG ESSAY Develop a thoughtful and thorough historical argument that answers the question below. Begin your essay with a thesis statement and support it with relevant historical evidence.

7. To what extent was technology the most important factor in the development of the western United States.

17 | INDUSTRIAL SUPREMACY

1. **Historical Causation** Analyze the economic, political, and social consequences of the rise of big business during the Gilded Age.

2. **Contextualization** Analyze the reasons for the growth of big business during the Gilded Age.

3. **Historical Causation** Explain the organizational innovations that led to consolidation and centralization of big business.

4. **Historical Argumentation** To what degree and in what ways were labor unions successful in improving the lives of workers during the Gilded Age?

5. **Patterns of Continuity and Change over Time** How did consolidation and centralization of big business change the lives of workers during the Gilded Age?

6. **Contextualization** Analyze the reasons for the growth in numbers of women and children in the industrial labor force.

Key Concept Correlations

Analyze the ways the historical developments you learn about in this chapter connect to the following AP Key Concepts.

6.1 The rise of big business in the United States encouraged massive migrations and urbanization, sparked government and popular efforts to reshape the U.S. economy and environment, and renewed debates over U.S. national identity.

6.2 The emergence of an industrial culture in the United States led to both greater opportunities for, and restrictions on, immigrants, minorities, and women.

6.3 The "Gilded Age" witnessed new cultural and intellectual movements in tandem with political debates over economic and social policies.

7.1 Governmental, political, and social organizations struggled to address the effects of large-scale industrialization, economic uncertainty, and related social changes such as urbanization and mass migration.

Thematic Learning Objectives

WXT-3, 5, 6, 7; WOR-3; CUL-3, 5, 6; PEO-2, 3, 6; ID-2, 5, 6, 7; POL-3

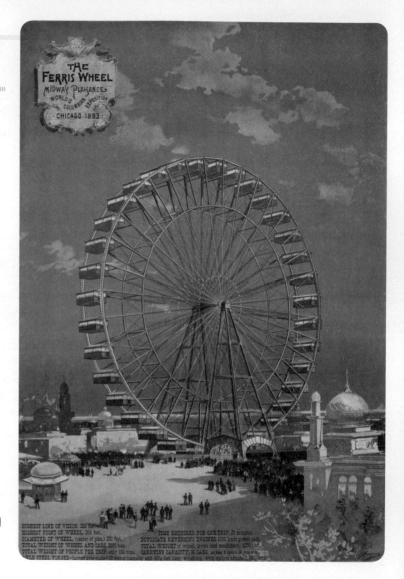

CELEBRATING A CITY AND A NATION The new industrial economy made possible many great feats that only decades before would have been unthinkable. Here is the world's first Ferris wheel, which was unveiled in 1893 at the World's Columbian Exposition in Chicago. The fair, designed in large part by Daniel Burnham and Frederick Law Olmsted, celebrated the 400th anniversary of Columbus's arrival in the New World in 1492. The grand scale and technological innovation on display at the fair not only announced a renewed city that had been severely damaged by fire, it also heralded the growing sense of American exceptionalism. (© Archive Photos/Getty Images)

CHAPTER 17 discusses the rise of big business and its political, economic, and social impact on American society. It focuses on the factors that led to increased consolidation and centralization in big business and the influence it exerted over the federal government. The chapter also discusses the development of innovative business strategies, which increased productivity and efficiency. Significant focus is also given to the reaction of disadvantaged groups to poor and unsafe working conditions, including efforts to unionize. The excesses of capitalism and unequal distribution of wealth were typically justified using the concept of Social Darwinism, but came under increasing criticism over a variety of concerns, including exploitation of the working classes, corporate and political corruption, and fears for American democracy. The American labor force experienced changes as immigration increased and more and more women and children were being employed in an industrial capacity. As you read, evaluate the following ideas:

- Large-scale production and technological innovation led to urbanization, mass migration, and significant social changes during the Gilded Age.
- The increasing efficiency of American industry made it a worldwide economic force.
- Social Darwinism was used to justify the great disparity in wealth and power during the Gilded Age, including the "conspicuous consumption" of the wealthy.
- The industrial workforce expanded through internal and international migration.
- Workers organized labor unions to fight corporate power for better working conditions and wages.
- Industrialization led to greater opportunities for immigrants, women, and minorities.
- Critics of the excesses of the capitalistic system emerged, offering alternatives to unfettered corporate power through government regulation.

SOURCES OF INDUSTRIAL GROWTH

Many factors contributed to the growth of American industry: abundant raw materials; a large and growing labor supply; a surge in technological innovation; the emergence of a talented, ambitious, and often ruthless group of entrepreneurs; a federal government eager to assist the growth of business; and a great and expanding domestic market for the products of manufacturing.

INDUSTRIAL TECHNOLOGIES

Perhaps the most important technological development in a nation whose economy rested so heavily on railroads and urban construction was the revolutionizing of iron and steel production in the late nineteenth century. Iron production had developed slowly in the United States through most of the nineteenth century; steel production had developed hardly at all by the end of the Civil War. In the 1870s and 1880s, however, iron production soared as railroads added 40,000 new miles of track, and steel production made great strides toward what would soon be its dominance in the metals industry.

The story of the rise of steel is, like so many other stories of economic development, a story of technological discovery. An Englishman, Henry Bessemer, and an American, William Kelly, had developed, almost simultaneously, a process for converting iron into the much more durable and

NEW STEEL PRODUCTION TECHNIQUES versatile steel. (The process, which took Bessemer's name, consisted of blowing air through molten iron to burn out the impurities.) The Bessemer process also relied on the discovery by the British metallurgist Robert Mushet that ingredients could be added to the iron during conversion to transform it into steel. In 1868, the New Jersey ironmaster Abram S. Hewitt introduced from Europe another method of making steel—the open-hearth process, which ultimately largely supplanted the Bessemer process. These techniques made possible the production of steel in great quantities and large dimensions, for use in the manufacture of locomotives, steel rails, and girders for the construction of tall buildings.

The steel industry emerged first in western Pennsylvania and eastern Ohio. That was partly because iron ore could be found there in abundance and because there was already a flourishing iron industry in the region. It was also because the new forms of steel production created a demand for new kinds of fuel–particularly a demand for the anthracite (or hard) coal that was plentiful in Pennsylvania. Later, new techniques made it possible to use bituminous (soft) coal (easily mined in western Pennsylvania), which could then

PITTSBURGH be converted to coke to fuel steel furnaces. As a result, Pittsburgh quickly became the center of the steel world. But the industry was growing so fast that new sources of ore were soon necessary. The upper peninsula of Michigan, the Mesabi Range in Minnesota, and the area around Birmingham, Alabama, became important ore-producing centers by the end of the century, and new centers of steel production grew up near them in Cleveland, Detroit, Chicago, and Birmingham, among others.

Until the Civil War, iron and steel furnaces were mostly made of stone and usually built against the side of a hill to reduce construction demands. In the 1870s and after, however, furnaces were redesigned as cylindrical iron shells lined with brick. These massive new furnaces were 75 feet tall and higher and could produce more than 500 tons of steel a week.

As the steel industry spread, new transportation systems emerged to serve it. The steel production in the Great Lakes region was possible only because of the availability of steam freighters that could carry ore on the lakes, which contributed to development of new and more powerful steam engines. Shippers also used new steam engines to speed the unloading of ore, a task that previously had been performed, slowly and laboriously, by men and horses.

A close relationship grew up between the emerging steel companies and the railroads. Steel manufacturers provided rails and parts for railroad cars. The Pennsylvania Railroad, for example, literally created the Pennsylvania Steel Company, provided it with substantial initial capital, and ensured it a market for its products with an immediate contract for steel rails.

The steel industry's need for lubrication for its machines helped create another important new industry in the late

RISE OF THE PETROLEUM INDUSTRY nineteenth century–oil. (Not until later did oil become important primarily for its potential as a fuel.) The existence of petroleum reserves in western Pennsylvania had been common knowledge for some time. In the 1850s,

PIONEER OIL RUN, 1865 The American oil industry emerged first in western Pennsylvania, where speculators built makeshift facilities almost overnight. An oil field on the other side of the hill depicted here had been producing 600 barrels a day, and the wells quickly spilled over the hill and down the slope shown in this photograph. (The Library of Congress)

Pennsylvania businessman George Bissell showed that the substance could be burned in lamps and that it could also yield such products as paraffin, naphtha, and lubricating oil. Bissell raised money to begin drilling; and in 1859, Edwin L. Drake, one of Bissell's employees, established the first oil well, near Titusville, Pennsylvania, which was soon producing 500 barrels of oil a month. Demand for petroleum grew quickly, and promoters soon developed other fields in Pennsylvania, Ohio, and West Virginia.

THE AIRPLANE AND THE AUTOMOBILE

Two technologies were critical to the development of the automobile. One was the creation of gasoline (or petrol). It was the result of an extraction process developed in the late nineteenth century in the United States by which lubricating oil and fuel oil were separated from crude oil. In the 1870s, designers in France, Germany, and Austria—inspired by the success of railroad engines—had begun to develop an "internal combustion engine," which used the expanding power of burning gas to drive pistons. A German, Nicolaus August Otto, created a gas-powered engine in the mid-1860s,

a precursor to automobile engines. But he did not develop a way to untether it from gas lines to be used portably in machines. One of Otto's former employees, Gottfried Daimler, later perfected an engine that could be used in automobiles (including the famous early car that took Daimler's name).

The American automobile industry developed rapidly in the aftermath of these breakthroughs. Charles and Frank Duryea built the first gasoline-driven motor vehicle in America in 1893. Three years later, Henry Ford produced the first of the famous cars that would eventually bear his name. By 1910, the industry had become a major force in the economy and the automobile was beginning to reshape American social and cultural life, as well as the nation's landscape. In 1895, there were only four automobiles on the American highways. By 1917, there were nearly 5 million.

HENRY FORD

The search for a means of human flight was as old as civilization, and had been almost entirely futile until the late nineteenth century, when engineers, scientists, and tinkerers in both the United States and Europe began to experiment with a wide range of aeronautic devices. Balloonists began to

THE FLIGHT OF THE WRIGHT BROTHERS Orville and Wilbur Wright became great celebrities after their famous flight at Kitty Hawk, North Carolina in 1903. They made few original contributions to the development of aviation technology, but their flight (with Wilbur piloting) helped publicize the "flying machine" that would soon revolutionize travel. (Historicus, Inc.)

consider ways to turn dirigibles into useful vehicles of transportation. Others experimented with kites and gliders to see if they could somehow be used to propel humans through the air.

Among those testing gliders were two brothers in Ohio, Wilbur and Orville Wright, who owned a bicycle shop in which they began to construct a glider that could be propelled through the air by an internal combustion engine (the same kind of engine that was propelling automobiles). In 1903, four years after they began their experiments, Orville made a celebrated test flight near Kitty Hawk, North Carolina, in which an airplane took off by itself and traveled 120 feet in 12 seconds under its own power before settling back to earth. By the fall of 1904, the Wright brothers had improved the plane to the point where they were able to fly over 23 miles, and in the following year they began to take a few passengers with them on their flights.

Although the first working airplane was built in the United States, aviation technology was slow to gain a foothold in America. Most of the early progress in airplane design occurred in France, where there was substantial government funding for research and development. The U.S. government created the National Advisory Committee on Aeronautics in 1915, twelve years after the Wright brothers' flight, and American airplanes became a significant presence in Europe during World War I. But the prospects for commercial flight seemed dim until the 1920s, when Charles Lindbergh's famous solo flight from New York to Paris electrified the nation and the world and helped make aviation a national obsession.

Research and Development

The rapid development of new industrial technologies encouraged business leaders to sponsor their own research to allow them to keep up with the rapid changes in industry. General Electric, fearful of technological competition, created one of the first corporate laboratories in 1900. By 1913, Bell Telephone, Du Pont, General Electric, Eastman Kodak, and

CORPORATE RESEARCH AND DEVELOPMENT about fifty other companies were budgeting hundreds of thousands of dollars each year for research by their own engineers and scientists. The emergence of corporate research and development laboratories coincided with a decline in government support for research. That helped corporations to attract skilled researchers who had once worked for government agencies. It also decentralized the sources of research funding and ensured that inquiry would move in many different directions, not just along paths determined by the government.

A rift began to emerge between scientists and engineers. Engineers—both inside and out of universities—became increasingly tied up with the research and development agendas of corporations and worked hard to be of practical use to the new economy. Many scientists scorned this "commercialization" of knowledge and preferred to stick to basic research that had no immediate practical applications. Even so, American

TRANSFORMATION OF HIGHER EDUCATION scientists were more closely connected to practical challenges than were their European counterparts, and some joined engineers in corporate research and development laboratories, which over time began to sponsor not just practical but also basic research.

American universities in the late nineteenth and early twentieth centuries developed a growing connection between university-based research and the needs of the industrial economy. University faculty and laboratories began to receive funding from corporations for research, and a partnership began to develop between the academic world and the commercial world that continued into the twenty-first century. No comparable partnership emerged in European universities in these years, and some scholars have argued that America's more rapid development in the twentieth century is in part a product of the market's success in harnessing knowledge–from the academic world and elsewhere–more effectively than the nation's competitors abroad.

The Science of Production

By the beginning of the twentieth century, many industrialists were turning to new principles of "scientific management." Those principles were often known as "Taylorism," after their leading theoretician, Frederick Winslow Taylor. Taylor's ideas were controversial during his lifetime and have remained controversial since.

Taylor urged employers to reorganize the production process by subdividing tasks. This would speed up production; it would also make workers more interchangeable and thus

"TAYLORISM" diminish a manager's dependence on any particular employee. And it would reduce

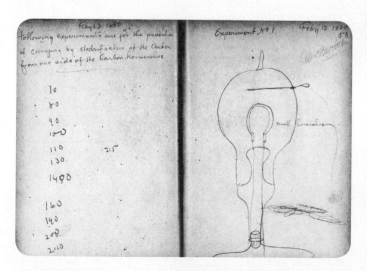

EDISON'S NOTEBOOK This page from one of Thomas Edison's notebooks shows sketches of and notes on some of his early experiments on an incandescent lamp—what we know as an electric lightbulb. Edison was not only the most celebrated inventor of his day but also, by the early twentieth century, one of the greatest popular heroes in American life in a time when scientific and technological progress was considered the defining feature of the age.
(© Archive Photos/Getty Images)

DIESEL ENGINE ASSEMBLY LINE IN "CATERPILLAR" FACTORY

INDUSTRIAL PRODUCTION This postcard conveys the assembly line at the Caterpillar manufacturing company. The factory shown here was enormous, occupying 151 acres, 53.8 of which were enclosed building areas. The men are assembling diesel engines. The company has been well known for building tractors, engines, and road machinery. (© Rykoff Collection/Corbis)

the need for highly trained skilled workers. If properly managed by trained experts, Taylor claimed, workers using modern machines could perform simple tasks at much greater speed, significantly increasing productive efficiency. Taylor and his many admirers argued that scientific management was a way to make human labor compatible with the demands of the machine age. Scientific management was also a way to increase the employer's control of the workplace and to make working people less independent.

The most important change in production technology in the industrial era was the emergence of mass production and, above all, the moving assembly line, which Henry Ford intro-

MOVING ASSEMBLY LINE

duced in his automobile plants in 1914. This revolutionary technique cut the time for assembling a chassis from 12½ hours to 1½ hours. It enabled Ford to raise the wages and reduce the hours of his workers while cutting the base price of his Model T from $950 in 1914 to $290 in 1929. Ford's assembly line became a model for many other industries.

RAILROAD EXPANSION

Despite important advances in many other forms of technology and communication, the principal agent of industrial progress in the late nineteenth century remained the railroad. Railroads were the nation's principal form of transportation. They helped determine the path by which agricultural and industrial economies developed. When railroad lines ran through sparsely populated regions, new farms and other economic activity quickly sprang up along the routes. When they reached forests, lumberers came quickly in their wake and began cutting down timber to send back to towns and cities for sale. When railroads moved through the great plains of the West, they brought buffalo hunters who nearly exterminated the great herds of bison and, later, helped transport cattle into the region and carry meat back into the cities. Because Chicago was the principal railroad hub of the central United States, it also became the place where railroads brought livestock, making the city the slaughterhouse of the nation.

Railroads even altered concepts of time. Until the 1880s, there was no standard method of keeping time from one community to another. In most places, the position of the sun determined the time, which meant that clocks were set differently even between nearby towns. This created great difficulties for railroads, which were trying to set schedules for the entire nation. On November 18, 1883, the railroad companies, working together, agreed to create four time zones across the continent, each an hour apart from its closest neighbor. Although not until 1918 did the federal government make these time zones standard for all purposes, the action by the railroads very quickly solidified the idea of "standard time" through most of the United States.

Every decade in the late nineteenth century, total railroad trackage increased dramatically: from 30,000 miles in 1860

RAPID EXPANSION OF THE RAILROAD

to 52,000 miles in 1870, to 93,000 in 1880, to 163,000 in 1890, and to 193,000 by 1900. Subsidies from federal, state, and local governments—as well as investments from abroad—were vital to these vast undertakings, which required far more capital than private entrepreneurs in America could raise by themselves. Equally important was the emergence of great railroad combinations that brought most of the nation's rails under the control of a very few men. Many railroad combinations continued to be dominated by individuals. The achievements (and excesses) of these tycoons—Cornelius Vanderbilt, James J. Hill, Collis P. Huntington, and others—became symbols to much of the nation of great economic power concentrated in individual hands. But railroad development was less significant for the individual barons it

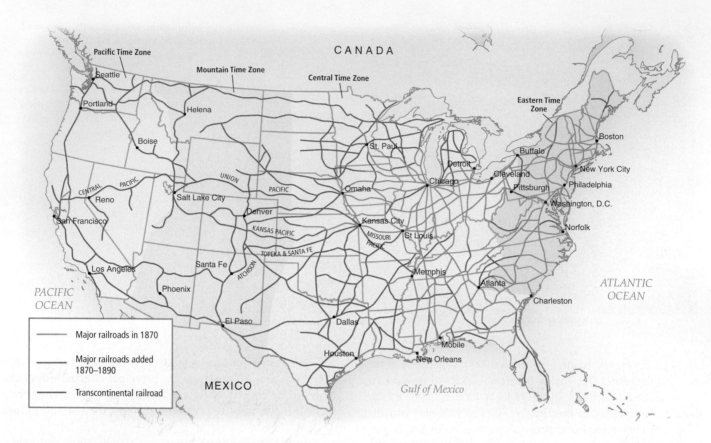

RAILROADS, 1870–1890 This map illustrates the rapid expansion of railroads in the late nineteenth century. In 1870, there was already a dense network of rail lines in the Northeast and Midwest, illustrated here by the green lines. The red lines show the further expansion of rail coverage between 1870 and 1890, much of it in the South and the areas west of the Mississippi River.

• *Why were railroads so essential to the nation's economic growth in these years?*

created than for its contribution to the growth of a new institution: the modern corporation.

The Corporation

There had been various forms of corporations in America since colonial times, but the modern corporation emerged as a major force only after the Civil War, when railroad magnates and other industrialists realized that no single person or group of limited partners, no matter how wealthy, could finance their great ventures.

Under the laws of incorporation passed in many states in the 1830s and 1840s, business organizations could raise money by **LIMITED LIABILITY** selling stock to members of the public; after the Civil War, one industry after another began doing so. At the same time, affluent Americans began to consider the purchase of stock a good investment even if they were not involved in the business whose stock they were purchasing. What made the practice appealing was that investors had only "limited liability"–that is, they risked only the amount of their investments; they were not liable for any debts the corporation might accumulate beyond that. The ability to sell stock to a broad public made it possible for entrepreneurs to gather vast sums of capital and undertake great projects.

The Pennsylvania Railroad and others were among the first to adopt the new corporate form of organization. But **ANDREW CARNEGIE** it quickly spread beyond the railroad industry. In steel, the central figure was Andrew Carnegie, a Scottish immigrant who had worked his way up from modest beginnings and in 1873 opened his own steelworks in Pittsburgh. Soon he dominated the industry. His methods were much like those of other industrial titans. He cut costs and prices by striking deals with the railroads and then bought out rivals who could not compete with him. With his associate Henry Clay Frick, he bought up coal mines and leased part of the Mesabi iron-ore range in Minnesota, operated a fleet of ore ships on the Great Lakes, and acquired railroads. Ultimately, Carnegie controlled the processing of his steel from mine to market. He financed his undertakings not only out of his own profits but out of the sale of stock as well. Then, in 1901, he sold out for $450 million to the banker J. Pierpont Morgan, who merged the Carnegie interests with others to create the giant United States Steel Corporation–a $1.4 billion enterprise that controlled almost two-thirds of the nation's steel production.

There were similar developments in other industries. Gustavus Swift developed a relatively small Chicago meatpacking

NEW
MANAGERIAL
TECHNIQUES business executive: the "middle manager," who formed a layer of command between workers and owners. Beginning in the railroad corporations, these new management techniques moved quickly into virtually every area of large-scale industry. Efficient administrative capabilities helped make possible another major feature of the modern corporation: consolidation.

CONSOLIDATING CORPORATE AMERICA

Businessmen created large, consolidated organizations primarily through two methods. One was "horizontal integration"—the

ANDREW CARNEGIE Carnegie was one of a relatively small number of great industrialists of the late nineteenth century who genuinely rose "from rags to riches." Born in Scotland, he came to the United States in 1848, at the age of thirteen, and soon found work as a messenger in a Pittsburgh telegraph office. His skill in learning to transcribe telegraphic messages (he became one of the first telegraphers in the country able to take messages by sound) brought him to the attention of a Pennsylvania Railroad official, and before he was twenty, he had begun his ascent to the highest ranks of industry. After the Civil War, he shifted his attention to the growing iron industry; in 1873 he invested all his assets in the development of the first American steel mills. Two decades later Carnegie was one of the wealthiest men in the world. In 1901 he abruptly resigned from his businesses and spent the remaining years of his life as a philanthropist. By the time of his death in 1919, he had given away more than $350 million, which by some measures would be worth well over a hundred billion dollars in 2014. (The Library of Congress (LC-DIG-ggbain-13249))

JOHN D. ROCKEFELLER Rockefeller's Standard Oil Company became perhaps the largest and most powerful monopoly in America in the late nineteenth century, and Rockefeller became one of the nation's wealthiest and most controversial men. Some historians consider Rockefeller to have been the richest person in history with a personal fortune at the time of his death of up to over a half-trillion dollars adjusted for the late 2000s. (© Hulton Archive/ Getty Images)

company into a great national corporation, in part because of profits he earned selling to the military in the Civil War. Isaac Singer patented a sewing machine in 1851 and created I. M. Singer and Company, one of the first modern manufacturing corporations.

Many of the corporate organizations developed a new approach to management. Large, national business enterprises needed more-systematic administrative structures than the limited, local ventures of the past. As a result, corporate leaders introduced a set of managerial techniques—the genesis of modern business administration—that relied on the division of responsibilities, a carefully designed hierarchy of control, modern cost-accounting procedures, and above all, a new breed of

HORIZONTAL AND VERTICAL INTEGRATION

combining of a number of firms engaged in the same enterprise into a single corporation. The consolidation of many different railroad lines into one company was an example. Another method, which became popular in the 1890s, was "vertical integration"–the taking over of all the different businesses on which a company relied for its primary function (as in the case of Carnegie Steel).

ROCKEFELLER'S STANDARD OIL

The most celebrated corporate empire of the late nineteenth century was John D. Rockefeller's Standard Oil, a great combination created through both horizontal and vertical integration. Shortly after the Civil War, Rockefeller launched a refining company in Cleveland and immediately began trying to eliminate his competition. Allying himself with other wealthy capitalists, he proceeded methodically to buy out competing refineries. In 1870, he formed the Standard Oil Company of Ohio; within a few years it had acquired twenty of the twenty-five refineries in Cleveland, as well as plants in Pittsburgh, Philadelphia, New York City, and Baltimore. So far, Rockefeller had expanded only horizontally. But soon he began expanding vertically as well. He built his own barrel factories, terminal warehouses, and pipelines. Standard Oil owned its own freight cars and developed its own marketing organization. By the 1880s, Rockefeller had established such dominance within the petroleum industry that to much of the nation he served as the leading symbol of monopoly. He controlled access to 90 percent of the refined oil in the United States.

Rockefeller and other industrialists saw consolidation as a way to cope with what they believed was the greatest curse of the modern economy: "cutthroat competition." Most businessmen claimed to believe in free enterprise and a competitive marketplace, but in fact they feared the existence of too many competing firms, convinced that substantial competition could spell instability and ruin for all. A successful enterprise, many capitalists believed (but did not say publicly), was one that could eliminate or absorb its competitors.

As the movement toward combination accelerated, new vehicles emerged to facilitate it. The railroads began making so-called pool arrangements–informal agreements among various companies to stabilize rates and divide markets (arrangements known as cartels that would later become illegal). But the pools did not work very well. If even a few firms in an industry were unwilling to cooperate (as was almost always the case), the pool arrangements collapsed.

THE TRUST AND THE HOLDING COMPANY

The failure of the pools led to new techniques of consolidation, resting less on cooperation than on centralized control. At first, the most successful such technique was the creation of the "trust"–pioneered by Standard Oil in the early 1880s and perfected by the banker J. P. Morgan. Over time, "trust"

became a term for any great economic combination. But the trust was in fact a particular kind of organization. Under a trust agreement, stockholders in individual corporations transferred their stocks to a small group of trustees in exchange for shares in the trust itself. Owners of trust certificates often had no direct control over the decisions of the trustees; they simply received a share of the profits of the combination. The trustees themselves, on the other hand, might literally own only a few companies but could exercise effective control over many.

THE TRUST AGREEMENT

In 1889, the State of New Jersey helped produce a third form of consolidation by changing its laws of incorporation to permit companies to buy up other companies. Other states soon followed. That made the trust unnecessary and permitted actual corporate mergers. Rockefeller, for example, quickly relocated Standard Oil to New Jersey and created there what became known as a "holding company"–a central corporate body that would buy up the stock of various members of the Standard Oil trust and establish direct, formal ownership of the corporations in the trust.

J. PIERPONT MORGAN This arresting portrait captures something of the intimidating power of J. Pierpont Morgan, the most powerful financier in America for decades until his death in 1913. (© The Granger Collection, New York)

RAPID CORPORATE CONSOLIDATION

By the end of the nineteenth century, as a result of corporate consolidation, 1 percent of the corporations in America were able to control more than 33 percent of the manufacturing. A system of economic organization was emerging that lodged enormous power in the hands of a very few men: the great bankers of New York such as J. P. Morgan, industrial titans such as Rockefeller (who gained control of a major bank), and others.

Whether or not this relentless concentration of economic power was the only way or the best way to promote industrial expansion became a major source of debate in America. But it is clear that, whatever else they may have done, the industrial giants of the era were responsible for substantial economic growth. They were integrating operations, cutting costs, creating a great industrial infrastructure, stimulating new markets, creating jobs for a vast new pool of unskilled workers, and opening the way to large-scale mass production. They were also creating the basis for some of the greatest public controversies of their era.

CAPITALISM AND ITS CRITICS

The rise of big business produced many critics. Farmers and workers saw in the growth of the new corporate power centers a threat to notions of a republican society in which wealth and authority were widely distributed. Middle-class critics pointed to the corruption that the new industrial titans seemed to produce in their own enterprises and in local, state, and national politics. The growing criticisms challenged the captains of industry to defend the new corporate economy, to convince the public (and themselves) that it was compatible with the ideology of individualism and equal opportunity that had long been central to the American self-image.

THE "SELF-MADE MAN"

The most common rationale for modern capitalism rested squarely on the older ideology of individualism. The new industrial economy, its defenders argued, was not reducing opportunities for individual advancement, but expanding them. It was providing every individual with a chance to succeed and attain great wealth.

There was an element of truth in such claims, but only a small one. Before the Civil War there had been few millionaires in America; by 1892 there were more than 4,000. Some were in fact what almost all millionaires claimed to be: "self-made men." Andrew Carnegie had worked as a bobbin boy in a Pittsburgh cotton mill; John D. Rockefeller had begun as a clerk in a Cleveland commission house; E. H. Harriman, a great railroad tycoon, had begun as a broker's office boy. But most of the new business tycoons had begun their careers from positions of wealth and privilege.

MYTH OF THE SELF-MADE MAN

Nor was their rise to power and prominence always a result simply of hard work and ingenuity, as they liked to claim. It was also a result of ruthlessness, arrogance, and, at times, rampant corruption. The railroad magnate Cornelius Vanderbilt expressed the attitude of many corporate tycoons with his belligerent question: "What do I care about the law? H'aint I got the power?" So did his son William, with his oft-quoted statement: "The public be damned." Industrialists made large financial contributions to politicians, political parties, and government officials in exchange for assistance and support. And more often than not, politicians responded as they hoped. Cynics said that

"MODERN COLOSSUS OF (RAIL) ROADS" Cornelius Vanderbilt, known as the "Commodore," accumulated one of America's great fortunes by consolidating several large railroad companies under his control in the 1860s. His name became a synonym not only for enormous wealth, but also (in the eyes of many Americans) for excessive corporate power—as suggested in this cartoon, showing him standing astride his empire and manipulating its parts. (The Library of Congress (LC-DIG-ds-05068))

AP CONSIDER THE SOURCE

PHILANTHROPY

THE WORD *PHILANTHROPY* ORIGINALLY meant love of humanity or goodwill toward fellow humans, but over time the term has come to mean large-scale giving by wealthy individuals. Steel magnate Andrew Carnegie accumulated a huge fortune in industry but devoted the last two decades of his life to philanthropy, establishing more than 2,500 libraries in the United States, endowing universities, and building Carnegie Hall in New York City and the Peace Palace in The Hague. In 1911, he established the Carnegie Corporation of New York "to promote the advancement and diffusion of knowledge and understanding." Carnegie articulated his philosophy of the obligation of the wealthy to use their fortunes to improve the world in the essay "Wealth," published in *North American Review* in 1889 and excerpted in the first source document below.

Investor and philanthropist Warren Buffett is the chairman and chief executive officer of Berkshire Hathaway, a conglomerate holding company whose assets include GEICO, The Pampered Chef, Fruit of the Loom, See's Candies, and Benjamin Moore & Co., among many others. Known as the "Sage of Omaha," Buffett was born in Omaha, Nebraska, in 1930 and still resides in the house he bought there in 1957 for $31,500. He made his first stock purchase at age 11 when he bought shares of Cities Service Preferred. Today Buffett is one of the world's richest men, with an estimated net worth of $45 billion in 2010. In 2006, Buffett announced that he intended to give away most of his fortune during his lifetime, rather than having the funds distributed after his death. The majority of Buffett's wealth will go to the Bill and Melinda Gates Foundation, the charitable foundation established by his close friend, bridge partner, and fellow philanthropist Bill Gates.

ANDREW CARNEGIE—1889

WEALTH

Andrew Carnegie

This, then, is held to be the duty of the man of wealth: first, to set an example of modest, unostentatious living, shunning display or extravagance; to provide moderately for the legitimate wants of those dependent upon him; and after doing so to consider all surplus revenues which come to him simply as trust funds which he is called upon to administer, and strictly bound as a matter of duty to administer in the manner which, in his judgment, is best calculated to produce the most beneficial results for the community—the man of wealth thus becoming the mere agent and trustee for his poorer brethren, bringing to their service his superior wisdom, experience, and ability to administer, doing for them better than they would or could do for themselves. . . .

In bestowing charity, the main consideration should be to help those who will help themselves; to provide part of the means by which those who desire to improve may do so; to give those who desire to rise the aids by which they may rise; to assist, but rarely or never to do all. Neither the individual nor the race is improved by almsgiving. Those worthy of assistance, except in rare cases, seldom require assistance. The really valuable men of the race never do, except in cases of accident or sudden change. Everyone has, of course, cases of individuals brought to his own knowledge where temporary assistance can do genuine good, and these he will not overlook. But the amount which can be wisely given by the individual for individuals is necessarily limited by his lack of knowledge of the circumstances connected with each. He is the only true reformer who is as careful and as anxious not to aid the unworthy as he is to aid the worthy, and, perhaps, even more so, for in almsgiving more injury is probably done by rewarding vice than by relieving virtue. . . .

Thus is the problem of rich and poor to be solved. The laws of accumulation will be left free; the laws of distribution free. Individualism will continue, but the millionaire will be but a trustee for the poor; entrusted for a season with a great part of the increased wealth of the community, but administering it for the community far better than it could or would have done for itself. The best minds will thus have reached a stage in the development of the race in which it is clearly seen that there is no mode of disposing of surplus wealth creditable to thoughtful and earnest men into whose hands it flows save by using it year by year for the general good.

This day already dawns. But a little while, and although, without incurring the pity of their fellows, men may die sharers in great business enterprises from which their capital cannot be or has not been withdrawn, and is left chiefly at death for public uses, yet the man who dies leaving behind him millions of available wealth, which was his to administer during life, will pass away "unwept, unhonored, and unsung," no matter to what uses he leaves the dross which he cannot take with him. Of such as these the public verdict will then be: "The man who dies thus rich dies disgraced."

Such, in my opinion, is the true gospel concerning wealth, obedience to which is destined some day to solve the problem of the rich and the poor, and to bring "Peace on earth, among men goodwill."

Source: *North American Review* (June 1889). Reprinted in *The Annals of America*, vol. 11, 1884-1894 (Chicago: Encyclopaedia Britannica, 1968), 222-226.

WARREN BUFFETT—2010

MY PHILANTHROPIC PLEDGE

Warren Buffett

In 2006, I made a commitment to gradually give all of my Berkshire Hathaway stock to philanthropic foundations. I couldn't be happier with that decision.

Now, Bill and Melinda Gates and I are asking hundreds of rich Americans to pledge at least 50% of their wealth to charity. So I think it is fitting that I reiterate my intentions and explain the thinking that lies behind them.

First, my pledge: More than 99% of my wealth will go to philanthropy during my lifetime or at death. Measured by dollars, this commitment is large. In a comparative sense, though, many individuals give more to others every day.

Millions of people who regularly contribute to churches, schools, and other organizations thereby relinquish the use of funds that would otherwise benefit their own families. The dollars these people drop into a collection plate or give to United Way mean forgone movies, dinners out, or other personal pleasures. In contrast, my family and I will give up nothing we need or want by fulfilling this 99% pledge.

Moreover, this pledge does not leave me contributing the most precious asset, which is time. Many people, including—I'm proud to say—my three children, give extensively of their own time and talents to help others. Gifts of this kind often prove far more valuable than money. A struggling child, befriended and nurtured by a caring mentor, receives a gift whose value far exceeds what can be bestowed by a check. My sister, Doris, extends significant person-to-person help daily. I've done little of this.

What I can do, however, is to take a pile of Berkshire Hathaway stock certificates—"claim checks" that when converted to cash can command far-ranging resources—and commit them to benefit others who, through the luck of the draw, have received the short straws in life. To date about 20% of my shares have been distributed (including shares given me by my late wife, Susan Buffett). I will continue to annually distribute about 4% of the shares I retain. At the latest, the proceeds from all of my Berkshire shares will be expended for philanthropic purposes by 10 years after my estate is settled. Nothing will go to endowments; I want the money spent on current needs.

This pledge will leave my lifestyle untouched and that of my children as well. They have already received significant sums for their personal use and will receive more in the future. They live comfortable and productive lives. And I will continue to live in a manner that gives me everything I could possibly want in life.

Some material things make my life more enjoyable; many, however, would not. I like having an expensive private plane, but owning a half-dozen homes would be a burden. Too often, a vast collection of possessions ends up possessing its owner. The asset I most value, aside from health, is interesting, diverse, and long-standing friends.

My wealth has come from a combination of living in America, some lucky genes, and compound interest. Both my children and I won what I call the ovarian lottery. (For starters, the odds against my 1930 birth taking place in the U.S. were at least 30 to 1. My being male and white also removed huge obstacles that a majority of Americans then faced.)

My luck was accentuated by my living in a market system that sometimes produces distorted results, though overall it serves our country well. I've worked in an economy that rewards someone who saves the lives of others on a battlefield with a medal, rewards a great teacher with thank-you notes from parents, but rewards those who can detect the mispricing of securities with sums reaching into the billions. In short, fate's distribution of long straws is wildly capricious.

The reaction of my family and me to our extraordinary good fortune is not guilt, but rather gratitude. Were we to use more than 1% of my claim checks on ourselves, neither our happiness nor our well-being would be enhanced. In contrast, the remaining 99% can have a huge effect on the health and welfare of others. That reality sets an obvious course for me and my family: Keep all we can conceivably need and distribute the rest to society, for its needs. My pledge starts us down that course.

Warren Buffett

("My Philanthropic Pledge," by Warren Buffet. This material is copyrighted and used with permission of the author.)

AP TEST PRACTICE

Questions assume cumulative content knowledge from this chapter and previous chapters.

1. How does Carnegie's text best reflect ideas from the times in which Carnegie lived?

   (A) Carnegie's text reflects humility, as American society at the turn of the 20th century believed that wealthy men should display modesty.

   (B) Carnegie's text reflects the influence of Social Darwinism by asserting the natural superiority of the wealthy person.

   (C) Carnegie's text reveals the wealthy industrialist's contempt for law, which was a prevalent attitude in turn-of-the-20th century America.

   (D) Carnegie's text reflects the view at the turn of the 20th century that government should play a role in shaping the economy to meet the needs of the rich and poor.

2. Which best describes Buffett's view of his own fortune versus Carnegie's view of his own fortune?

   (A) Success by way of hard work and thrift vs. success through being blessed

   (B) Achievement through help from the government vs. achievement strictly through individual ability

   (C) Luck of circumstance vs. deserved success through talent

   (D) Earnest action and devotion of time vs. pluck and wise decision-making

3. Which best describes commonalities shared by Carnegie and Buffett, as conveyed in their respective texts?

   (A) To live moderately and provide their wealth for the advancement of society

   (B) To set up large endowments for their families and use what is left for the advancement of society

   (C) Commit to living a life of poverty, so that all of their fortune can be given to address societal problems

   (D) To live modestly and save their money for distribution in the future, upon their deaths

Standard Oil did everything to the Ohio legislature except refine it. A member of the Pennsylvania legislature once reportedly said: "Mr. Speaker, I move we adjourn unless the Pennsylvania Railroad has more business for us to transact."

The average industrialist of the late nineteenth century was not, however, a Rockefeller or a Vanderbilt. For every successful millionaire, there were dozens of aspiring businessmen whose efforts failed. Some industries fell under the monopolistic control of a single firm or a small group of large firms. But most industries remained fragmented, with many small companies struggling to carve out a stable position for themselves in an uncertain, highly competitive environment. The annals of business did indeed include real stories of individuals rising from rags to riches. They also included stories of people moving from riches back to rags.

SURVIVAL OF THE FITTEST

Most tycoons liked to claim that they had attained their wealth and power through hard work, acquisitiveness, and thrift—the traditional virtues of Protestant America. Those who succeeded, they argued, deserved their success. "God gave me my money," explained John D. Rockefeller, expressing the assumption that riches were a reward for worthiness. Those who failed, they said, had earned their failure—through their own laziness, stupidity, or carelessness. "Let us remember," said a prominent Protestant minister, "that there is not a poor person in the United States who was not made poor by his own shortcomings."

Such assumptions helped strengthen a popular social theory of the late nineteenth century: Social Darwinism, the appli-

SOCIAL DARWINISM

cation of Charles Darwin's laws of evolution and natural selection among species to human society. Just as only the fittest survived in the process of evolution, Social Darwinists claimed, so in human society only the fittest individuals survived and flourished in the marketplace.

The English philosopher Herbert Spencer was the first and most important proponent of this theory. Society, he argued, benefited from the elimination of the unfit and the survival of the strong and talented. Spencer's books were popular in America in the 1870s and 1880s. And his teachings found prominent supporters among American intellectuals, most notably William Graham Sumner of Yale University who promoted similar ideas in lectures, articles, and a famous 1906 book, *Folkways*. Sumner did not agree with everything Spencer wrote, but he did share Spencer's belief that individuals must have absolute freedom to struggle, to compete, to succeed, or to fail. Many industrialists seized on the theories of Spencer and Sumner to justify their own power. "The growth of a large business is merely the survival of the fittest," Rockefeller proclaimed. "This is not an evil tendency in business. It is merely the working out of the law of nature and a law of God."

Social Darwinism appealed to businessmen because it seemed to legitimize their success and confirm their virtues. It also appealed to them because it placed their activities within

JUSTIFYING THE STATUS QUO

the context of traditional American ideas of freedom and individualism. Above all, it appealed to them because it justified their tactics. Social Darwinists insisted that all attempts by labor to raise wages by forming unions and all endeavors by government to regulate economic activities would fail, because economic life was controlled by a natural law, the law of competition. And Social Darwinism coincided with another "law" that seemed to justify business practices and business dominance: the law of supply and demand as defined by Adam Smith and the classical economists. The economic system, they argued, was like a great and delicate machine functioning by the "invisible hand" of market forces.

But Social Darwinism and the ideas of classical economics did not have much to do with the realities of the corporate economy. At the same time that businessmen were celebrating the virtues of competition and the free market, they were actively seeking to protect themselves from competition and to replace the natural workings of the marketplace with control by great combinations. Rockefeller's great Standard Oil monopoly was the clearest example of the effort to free an enterprise from competition. Many other businessmen made similar attempts on a smaller scale. Vicious competitive battle—something Spencer and Sumner celebrated and called a source of healthy progress—was in fact the very thing that American businessmen most feared and tried to eliminate.

THE GOSPEL OF WEALTH

Some businessmen attempted to temper the harsh philosophy of Social Darwinism with a more gentle, if in some ways equally self-serving, idea: the "gospel of wealth." People of great wealth, advocates of this idea argued, had not only great power but great responsibilities as well. It was their duty to use their riches to advance social progress. Andrew Carnegie elaborated on the creed in his 1901 book, *The Gospel of Wealth*, in which he wrote that the wealthy should consider all revenues in excess of their own needs as "trust funds" to be used for the good of the community; the person of wealth, he said, was "the mere trustee and agent for his poorer brethren." Carnegie was only one of many great industrialists who devoted large parts of their fortunes to philanthropic works—much of it to libraries and schools, institutions he believed would help the poor to help themselves.

The notion of private wealth as a public blessing existed alongside another popular concept: the notion of great wealth

RUSSELL CONWELL

as something available to all. Russell H. Conwell, a Baptist minister, became the most prominent spokesman for the idea by delivering one lecture, "Acres of Diamonds," reportedly more than 6,000 times between 1880 and 1900. Conwell told a series of stories, which he claimed were true, of individuals who had found opportunities for extraordinary wealth in their own backyards. (One such story involved a modest farmer who discovered a vast diamond mine in his own fields in the course

THE NOVELS OF HORATIO ALGER

A young boy, perhaps an orphan, makes his perilous way through life on the rough streets of the city by selling newspapers or peddling matches. One day, his energy and determination catch the eye of a wealthy man, who gives him a chance to improve himself. Through honesty, charm, hard work, and aggressiveness, the boy rises in the world to become a successful man.

That, in a nutshell, is the story that Horatio Alger presented to his readers in novel after novel—more than 100 of them in all—for over forty years. During Alger's lifetime, Americans bought many million copies of his novels. After his death in 1899, his books (and others written in his name) continued to sell at an astonishing rate.

Alger was born in 1832 into a middle-class New England family, attended Harvard, and spent a short time as a Unitarian minister. He never experienced the hardships he later chronicled. In the mid-1850s, he turned to writing stories and books. His most famous novel, *Ragged Dick*, was published in 1868; but there were many others almost identical to it: *Tom, the Bootblack; Sink or Swim; Jed, the Poorhouse Boy; Phil, the Fiddler; Andy Grant's Pluck.* Most of his books were aimed at young people, and almost all of them were fables of a young man's rise "from rags to riches." The purpose of his writing, he claimed, was twofold. He wanted to "exert a salutary influence upon the class of whom [I] was writing, by setting before them inspiring examples of what energy, ambition, and an honest purpose may achieve." He also wanted to show his largely middle-class readers "the life and experiences of the friendless and vagrant children to be found in all our cities."

Most Americans of the late nineteenth and early twentieth centuries were attracted to Alger because his stories helped reinforce one of the most cherished of their national myths: that with willpower and hard work, anyone could become a "self-made man." That belief was all the more important in the late nineteenth century, when the rise of large-scale corporate industrialization was making it increasingly difficult for individuals to control their own fates.

Alger placed great emphasis on the moral qualities of his heroes; their success was a reward for their virtue. But many of his readers ignored the moral message and clung simply to the image of sudden and dramatic success. After the author's death, his publishers responded to that yearning by abridging many of Alger's works to eliminate the parts of his stories where the heroes do good deeds. Instead, they focused solely on the success of Alger's heroes in rising in the world.

Alger had very mixed feelings about the new industrial order he described. His books were meant to reveal not just the opportunities for advancement it sometimes created, but also its cruelty. To Alger, the modern age

---

of working his land.) "I say to you," he told his rapt audiences, "that you have 'acres of diamonds' beneath you right here . . . that the men and women sitting here have within their reach opportunities to get largely wealthy. . . . I say that you ought to get rich, and that it is your duty to get rich." Most of the millionaires in the country, Conwell claimed (inaccurately), had begun on the lowest rung of the economic ladder and had worked their way to success. Every industrious individual had the chance to do likewise.

HORATIO ALGER Horatio Alger was the most famous promoter of the success story. (See "Patterns of Popular Culture," pp. 472–473.) Alger was originally a minister in a small town in Massachusetts but was driven from his pulpit as a result of a sexual scandal. He moved to New York, where he wrote his celebrated novels about poor boys who rise "from rags to riches"–more than 100 in all, which together sold more than 20 million copies. He became something of a folk hero in American culture. Few of his many fans were aware of his homosexuality. Like most other gay men of his era, he kept his private life carefully hidden, fearful that publicity would destroy his reputation and his career.

ALTERNATIVE VISIONS

Alongside the celebrations of competition, the justifications for great wealth, and the legitimization of the existing order stood a group of alternative philosophies, challenging the corporate ethos and at times capitalism itself.

One such philosophy emerged in the work of the sociologist Lester Frank Ward. Ward was a Darwinist, but he rejected **LESTER FRANK WARD** the application of Darwinian laws to human society. In *Dynamic Sociology* (1883) and other books, he argued that civilization was governed not by natural selection but by human intelligence, which was capable of shaping society as it wished. Unlike Sumner, who believed that state intervention to remodel the environment was futile, Ward thought that an active government engaged in positive planning was society's best hope. The people, through their government, could intervene in the economy and adjust it to serve their needs.

Other Americans skeptical of the laissez-faire ideas of the Social Darwinists adopted drastic approaches to reform. Some dissenters joined the Socialist Labor Party, founded in the 1870s and led for many years by Daniel De Leon, an immigrant from the West Indies. De Leon attracted a modest following in the industrial cities, but the party failed to become a major political force. It never polled more than 82,000 votes. A dissident faction of his party, eager to forge ties with organized labor, broke away and in 1901 formed the more enduring American Socialist Party.

Other radicals gained a wider following. One of the most influential was Henry George of California. His angrily eloquent

RISEN FROM THE RANKS Alger's novels were even more popular after his death in 1899 than they had been in his lifetime. This is a reprint of the cover of one of his many "rags-to-riches" books. *Risen from the Ranks* is about the rise of a young boy, Harry Walton, who rises from newsboy to newspaper editor. (© The Granger Collection, New York)

did not guarantee success through hard work alone; there had to be some providential assistance as well. That was one reason that in almost all his books, his heroes triumphed not just because of their own virtues or efforts, but because of some amazing stroke of luck as well. Over time Alger's admirers came to ignore his own misgivings about industrialism and to portray his books purely as celebrations of (and justifications for) laissez-faire capitalism and the accumulation of wealth.

Today, though his books are largely forgotten, the name Horatio Alger lives on, representing the idea of individual advancement through (in a phrase Alger coined) "pluck and luck." An example of the transformation of Alger into a symbol of individual achievement is the Horatio Alger Award, established in 1947 by the American Schools and Colleges Association to honor "living individuals who by their own efforts had pulled themselves up by their bootstraps in the American tradition." Among its recipients have been Presidents Dwight D. Eisenhower and Ronald Reagan, evangelist Billy Graham, and U.S. Supreme Court Justice Clarence Thomas. ●

Progress and Poverty, published in 1879, became one of the best-selling nonfiction works in American publishing history.

HENRY GEORGE George tried to explain why poverty existed amid the wealth created by modern industry. "This association of poverty with progress is the great enigma of our times," he wrote. "So long as all the increased wealth which modern progress brings goes but to build up great fortunes, to increase luxury and make sharper the contrast between the House of Have and the House of Want, progress is not real and cannot be permanent."

George blamed social problems on the ability of a few monopolists to grow wealthy as a result of rising land values. An increase in the value of land, he claimed, was a result not of any effort by the owner, but of the growth of society around the land. It was an "unearned increment," and it was rightfully the property of the community. And so George proposed a "single tax," to replace all other taxes, which would return the increment to the people. The tax, he argued, would destroy monopolies, distribute wealth more equally, and eliminate poverty. Single-tax societies sprang up in many cities. George moved east to New York; and in 1886, with the support of labor and the socialists, he narrowly missed being elected mayor.

Rivaling George in popularity was Edward Bellamy, whose utopian novel *Looking Backward*, published in 1888, sold more than 1 million copies. It described the experiences of a young Bostonian who went into a hypnotic sleep in 1887 and awoke

LOOKING BACKWARD in the year 2000 to find a new social order where want, politics, and vice were unknown. The new society had emerged from a peaceful, evolutionary process. The large trusts of the late nineteenth century had continued to grow and combine until they formed a single great trust, controlled by the government, which absorbed all the businesses of all the citizens and distributed the abundance of the industrial economy equally among all the people. Society had become a great machine, "so logical in its principles and direct and simple in its workings" that it almost ran itself. "Fraternal cooperation" had replaced competition. Class divisions had disappeared. Bellamy labeled the philosophy behind this vision "nationalism," and his work inspired the formation of more than 160 Nationalist Clubs to propagate his ideas.

THE PROBLEMS OF MONOPOLY

Relatively few Americans shared the views of those who questioned capitalism itself. But by the end of the century a growing number of people were becoming deeply concerned about a particular, glaring aspect of capitalism: the growth of monopoly (control of the market by large corporate combinations). Laborers, farmers, consumers, small manufacturers, conservative bankers and financiers, advocates of radical change—all began to assail monopoly and economic concentration.

PATTERNS OF POPULAR CULTURE

THE NOVELS OF LOUISA MAY ALCOTT

IF Horatio Alger's rags-to-riches tales captured the aspirations of many men of the late nineteenth century, Louisa May Alcott's enormously popular novels helped give voice to the often-unstated ambitions of many young women.

Alcott was born in 1832, the daughter of a prominent if generally impoverished reformer and educator, Bronson Alcott—a New England transcendentalist committed to abolishing slavery and advancing women's rights. Louisa May Alcott grew up wanting to write, one of the few serious vocations available to women. As a young adult, she wrote a series of popular adventure novels under the pen name A. M. Barnard, populated by conventional male heroes. While serving as a nurse in the Civil War, she contracted typhoid and recovered, but developed mercury poisoning through her treatment and suffered from it until her death in 1888. After the war, she chose a different path—writing realistic fiction and basing it on the lives and experiences of women. The publication of *Little Women* (1868, 1869) established Alcott as a major literary figure and as an enduring, if sometimes puzzling, inspiration for girls and, indeed, women of all ages.

Little Women—and its successors *Little Men* (1871) and *Jo's Boys* (1886)—were unlike the formulaic Horatio Alger stories, in which young men inevitably rose from humble circumstances to great success. And yet they both echoed and altered the message of those books. The fictional March family in the novels was in fact modeled on Alcott's own impoverished if intellectually lively childhood, and much of *Little Women* is a chronicle of poverty, suffering, and even death. But it is also the story of a young girl—Jo March, modeled to some degree on Alcott herself—who struggles to build a life for herself that is not defined by conventional women's roles and ambitions. Jo March, like Louisa May Alcott, becomes a writer. She spurns a conventional marriage (to her attractive and wealthy neighbor Laurie). Unlike Alcott, who never married, Jo does find a husband—an older man, a German professor who does not support Jo's literary ambitions.

Many readers have found this marriage troubling—and false to the message of the rest of the book. It seems to contradict Alcott's belief that women can have intellectual independence and achievement. But to Alcott,

CHILDREN OF WEALTH Amy Elizabeth du Pont (1880–1962), the heiress of the American industrialist du Pont family, drives her younger sister, Julia, in their own pony-driven buggy. The photograph, taken by Pierre A. Gentieu, shows the children enjoying themselves while traveling with their family in France. (© Hagley Museum & Library, Wilmington, Delaware, USA/The Bridgeman Art Library)

(© Bettmann/Corbis)

this unconventional marriage was a symbol of her own repudiation of an ordinary domestic life. "Girls write to ask who the little women marry, as if that was the only end and aim of a woman's life," Alcott wrote a friend after the publication of the first volume of the novel. "I won't marry Jo to Laurie to please any one." Jo's marriage to Professor Bhaer is in many ways a concession. "Jo should have remained a literary spinster [like Alcott herself]," she once wrote, "but so many enthusiastic ladies wrote to me clamorously demanding that she should marry Laurie, or somebody, that I didn't dare to refuse and out of perversity went and made a funny match for her."

It is tempting to see Louisa May Alcott's life—as an independent woman, a writer, and an active suffragist—as a better model to her readers than the characters in her fiction. Jo March is willful, rebellious, stubborn, ambitious, and often selfish, not the poised, romantic, submissive woman of most sentimental novels of her time. She hates housekeeping and drudgery. She yearns at times to be a boy. She resists society's expectations—through her literary aspirations, her sharp temper, and ultimately her unconventional marriage. Through those qualities, she captured the imaginations of late-nineteenth-century female readers and continues to capture the imaginations of readers today. *Little Women* has survived far longer than the Horatio Alger stories did precisely because it presents a story of growing up that, unlike Alger's, is not predictable but complicated, conflicted, and surprising. ●

UNDERSTAND, ANALYZE, AND EVALUATE

1. Do the female characters of Alcott's novels reflect the actual status of women in the late nineteenth century?

2. In what ways are Alcott's novels similar to Alger's? How do they differ?

3. *Little Women* has continued to be popular as a novel, and it has been made several times into movies and at least once into a Broadway musical. What accounts for its enduring popularity?

They blamed monopoly for creating artificially high prices and for producing a highly unstable economy. In the absence of competition, they argued, monopolistic industries could charge whatever prices they wished; railroads, in particular, charged very high rates along some routes because, in the absence of competition, they knew their customers had no choice but to pay them. Artificially high prices, moreover, contributed to the economy's instability, as production consistently outpaced demand. Beginning in 1873, the economy fluctuated erratically, with severe recessions creating havoc every five or six years, each recession worse than the previous one, until finally, in 1893, the system seemed on the verge of total collapse.

Hostility to monopoly was based on more than a concern about prices. Many Americans considered monopoly dangerous because the rise of large combinations seemed to threaten the ability of individuals to advance in the world. If a single person, or a small group, could control all economic activity in an industry, what opportunities would be left for others? To men, in particular, monopoly threatened the ideal of the wage-earning husband capable of supporting a family and prospering, because combinations seemed to reduce opportunities to succeed—to make less likely the idea of the "self-made man" memorialized in the novels of Horatio Alger. Monopoly, therefore, threatened not just competition, but certain notions of manhood as well.

Adding to the resentment of monopoly was the emergence of a new class of enormously and conspicuously wealthy people, whose lifestyles became an affront to those struggling to stay afloat. According to one estimate early in the century, 1 percent of the families in America controlled nearly 88 percent of the nation's assets. Some of the wealthy—Andrew Carnegie, for example—lived unostentatiously and donated large sums to charities. Others, however, lived in almost grotesque luxury. Like a clan of feudal barons, the Vanderbilts maintained, in addition to many country estates, seven opulent mansions on seven blocks of New York City's Fifth Avenue. Other wealthy New Yorkers lavished vast sums on parties. The most notorious, a ball on which Mrs. Bradley Martin spent $368,000, created such a furor that she and her husband fled to England to escape public abuse.

Observing their flagrant displays of wealth were the four-fifths of the American people who lived modestly and at least

INCREASING INEQUALITY

10 million people who lived below the commonly accepted poverty line. The standard of living was rising for everyone, but the gap between rich and poor was increasing. To those in difficult economic circumstances, the sense of relative deprivation could be almost as frustrating and embittering as poverty itself.

INDUSTRIAL WORKERS IN THE NEW ECONOMY

The American working class was both a beneficiary and a victim of the growth of industrial capitalism. Many workers in the late nineteenth century experienced a real rise in their standard of living. But they did so at the cost of arduous and often dangerous working conditions, diminishing control over their own work, and a growing sense of powerlessness.

THE IMMIGRANT WORKFORCE

The industrial workforce expanded dramatically in the late nineteenth century as demand for factory labor grew. There was a continuing flow of rural Americans into factory towns and cities–people disillusioned with or bankrupted by life on the farm and eager for new economic and social opportunities. And there was a great wave of immigration from Mexico, Asia, Canada, and above all Europe in the decades following the Civil War–an influx greater than that of any previous era. The 25 million immigrants who arrived in the United States between 1865 and 1915 were more than four times the number who had arrived in the fifty years before.

In the 1870s and 1880s, most of the immigrants to eastern industrial cities came from the nation's traditional sources: **NEW SOURCES OF IMMIGRATION** England, Ireland, and northern Europe. By the end of the century, however, the major sources of immigration had shifted, with large numbers of southern and eastern Europeans (Italians, Poles, Russians, Greeks, Slavs, and others) moving to America (among other nations) and into the industrial workforce. In the West, the major sources of immigration were Mexico and, until the Chinese Exclusion Act of 1882, Asia. No reliable figures are available for either group, but an estimated 1 million Mexicans entered the United States in the first three decades of the twentieth century, many of them swelling the industrial workforce of western cities.

The new immigrants were coming to America in part to escape poverty and oppression in their homelands. But they were also lured to the United States by expectations of new opportunities. Sometimes such expectations were realistic, but often they were the result of false promises. Railroads tried to lure immigrants into their western landholdings by distributing misleading advertisements overseas. Industrial employers actively recruited immigrant workers under the Contract Labor Law, which–until its repeal in 1885–permitted them to pay for the passage of workers in advance and deduct the amount later from their wages. Even after the repeal of the law, employers continued to encourage the immigration of unskilled laborers, often with the assistance of foreign-born labor brokers, such as the Greek and Italian padrones, who recruited work gangs of their fellow nationals.

The arrival of these new groups introduced heightened eth- **HEIGHTENED ETHNIC TENSIONS** nic tensions into the dynamic of the working class. Low-paid Poles, Greeks, and French Canadians began to displace higher-paid British and Irish workers in the textile factories of New England. Italians, Slavs, and Poles emerged as a major source of labor for the mining industry in the East, traditionally dominated by native workers or northern European immigrants. Chinese and Mexicans competed with Anglo-Americans and African Americans in mining, farmwork, and factory labor in California, Colorado, and Texas.

WAGES AND WORKING CONDITIONS

The average standard of living for workers rose in the years after the Civil War, but for many laborers, the return for their labor remained very small. At the turn of the century, the average income of the American worker was $400 to $500 a year–below the $600 figure widely considered the minimum for a reasonable level of comfort. Nor did workers have much job security. All workers were vulnerable to the boom-and-bust cycle of the industrial economy, and some lost their jobs because of technological advances or because of the cyclical or seasonal nature of their work. Even those who kept their jobs could find their wages suddenly and substantially cut in hard times. Few workers, in other words, were ever far from poverty.

American laborers faced other hardships as well. For first-generation workers accustomed to the patterns of agrarian life, there was a difficult

APPROACHING SHORE This image of European immigrants aboard a ship approaching the American shore captures both the excitement and the tension of these newcomers to the United States. (The Library of Congress (LC-USZ62-7307))

WOMEN ON THE ASSEMBLY LINE This image, from 1902, shows women at work on the lock and drill department assembly line at the National Cash Register Company in Dayton, Ohio. The photograph suggests the growing scale of factory enterprise at the turn of the twentieth century. (© Everett Collection Historical/Alamy)

adjustment to the nature of modern industrial labor: the performance of routine, repetitive tasks, often requiring little skill, on a strict and monotonous schedule. To skilled artisans whose once-valued tasks were now performed by machines, the new system was impersonal and demeaning. Factory laborers worked ten- to twelve-hour days, six days a week; in the steel industry they worked twelve hours a day. Many worked in appallingly unsafe or unhealthy factories. Industrial accidents were frequent and severe. Compensation to the victims, from either their employers or the government, was often limited, until many states began passing workmen's compensation laws in the early twentieth century.

For many workers, the most disturbing aspect of factory labor in the new industrial system was their loss of control over the conditions of their labor. Even semiskilled workers and common laborers had managed to maintain some control over their labor in the relatively informal working conditions of the early and mid-nineteenth century. As the corporate form of organization spread, employers set out to make the factory more efficient (often in response to the principles of scientific management). That meant, they believed, centralizing control of the workplace in the hands of managers, ensuring that workers had no authority or control that might disrupt the flow of production. This loss of control, as much as the low wages and long hours, lay behind the substantial working-class militancy in the late nineteenth century.

LOSS OF CONTROL

WOMEN AND CHILDREN AT WORK

The decreasing need for skilled work in factories induced many employers to increase the use of unskilled women and children, whom they could hire for lower wages than adult males. By 1900, women made up 17 percent of the industrial workforce, a fourfold increase since 1870; and 20 percent of all women (well over 5 million) were wage earners. Some of these working women were single and took jobs to support themselves or their parents or siblings. Many others were married and had to work to supplement the inadequate earnings of their husbands; for many working-class families, two incomes were required to support even a minimal standard of living. Many reformers, including many females, saw women as particularly vulnerable to exploitation and injury in the rough environment of the factory. They considered it inappropriate for women to work independently. The "problem" of women in the workforce became a significant public issue. In some communities the aversion to seeing married women work was so strong—among both men and women—that families struggled on inadequate wages rather than see a wife and mother take a job.

Women industrial workers were overwhelmingly white and mostly young, 75 percent of them under twenty-five. The vast majority were immigrants or the daughters of immigrants. There were some women in all areas of industry, even in some of the most arduous jobs. Most women, however, worked in a few industries where unskilled and semiskilled machine labor (as opposed to heavy manual labor) prevailed. The textile industry remained the largest single industrial employer of women. (Domestic service remained the most common female occupation overall.) Women worked for wages as low as $6 to $8 a week, well below the minimum necessary for survival (and well below the wages paid to men working the same jobs). At the turn of the century, the average annual wage for a male

POORLY PAID WOMEN

SPINDLE BOYS Young boys, some of them barefoot, clamber among the great textile machines in a Georgia cotton mill adjusting spindles. Many of them were the children of women who worked in the plants. The photograph is by Lewis Hine. (© Lewis Hine/ Corbis)

industrial worker was $597; for a woman, it was $314. Even highly skilled women workers made about half what men doing the same job earned. Advocates of a minimum-wage law for women created a sensation when several women testified at a hearing in Chicago that low wages and desperate poverty had driven them to prostitution. (The testimony was not, however, sensational enough for the Illinois legislature, which promptly defeated the bill.)

At least 1.7 million children under sixteen years of age were employed in factories and fields in 1900, more than twice the number of thirty years before. Ten percent of all girls aged ten to fifteen, and 20 percent of all boys, held jobs. This was partly because some families so desperately needed additional wages that parents and children alike were pressed into service. It was also because in some families the reluctance to permit wives to work led parents to send their children into the workforce to avoid forcing mothers to go. This did not, however, prevent reformers from seeing children

INEFFECTIVE CHILD-LABOR LAWS

working in factories as a significant social problem. Under the pressure of outraged public opinion, thirty-eight state legislatures passed child-labor laws in the late nineteenth century; but these laws were of limited impact. Sixty percent of child workers were employed in agriculture, which was typically exempt from the laws; such children often worked twelve-hour days picking or hoeing in the fields. And even for children employed in factories, the laws merely set a minimum age of twelve years and a maximum workday of ten hours, standards that employers often ignored. In the cotton mills of the South, children working at the looms all night were kept awake by having cold water thrown in their faces. In canneries, little girls cut fruits and vegetables sixteen

hours a day. Exhausted children were particularly susceptible to injury while working at dangerous machines, and they were maimed and even killed in industrial accidents at an alarming rate.

As much as the appalling conditions of women and child workers troubled the national conscience, conditions for many men were at least equally dangerous. In mills and mines, and on the railroads, the American accident rate was higher than that of any industrial nation in the world. As late as 1907, an average of twelve railroad men a week died on the job. In factories, thousands of workers faced such occupational diseases as lead or phosphorus poisoning, against which few employers took precautions.

THE STRUGGLE TO UNIONIZE

Labor leaders attempted to fight back against the poor conditions in the workplace by adopting some of the same tactics their employers had used so effectively: creating large combinations, or unions. But by the end of the century their efforts had met with little success.

There had been craft unions in America, representing small groups of skilled workers, since well before the Civil War. Alone, however, individual unions could not hope to exert

NATIONAL LABOR UNION

significant power in the new corporate economy, and in the 1860s some labor leaders began to search for ways to combine the energies of the various labor organizations. The first attempt to federate separate unions into a single national organization came in 1866, when William H. Sylvis founded the National Labor Union—a polyglot association, claiming 640,000 members, that included a variety of reform groups having little

KEHOE HANGED.

Last Scenes in the Life of the King of the Molly Maguires.

I AM NOT GUILTY.

History of Kehoe's Prominent Share in the Many Murders in the Coal Region.

EVIDENCE FROM SPIES.

Little Excitement in Pottsville on the Occasion of the Execution.

[BY TELEGRAPH TO THE HERALD.]
POTTSVILLE, Pa., Dec. 18, 1878.
The people of Pottsville have become so accustomed to executions of Molly Maguires that there is no excitement attendant upon this occasion. Jack Kehoe, the terror of the coal fields, the braggart and desperado, passed a most miserable night. The guards say that he only got a few moments' sleep. He

MOLLY McGUIRES The Molly Maguires were known for their harsh, intimidating, and at times violent tactics against the owners and managers of anthracite coal mines. This newspaper notice announces the execution of Jack Kehoe—both high constable of Mahanoy County in Pennsylvania and a member of the Molly McGuires—who was found guilty of multiple murders in this coal-producing region. He was posthumously pardoned of these crimes in 1979 suggesting that his cry "I am not guilty" was indeed true. (© American Antiquarian Society, Worcester, Massachusetts, USA/The Bridgeman Art Library)

direct relationship with labor. After the Panic of 1873, the National Labor Union disintegrated and disappeared.

The National Labor Union, like most of the individual unions that joined it, excluded women workers. Male workers argued (not entirely incorrectly) that women were used to drive down their wages; and they justified their hostility by invoking the ideal of domesticity. "Woman was created to be man's companion," a National Labor Union official said, "to be the presiding deity of the home circle." Most women

workers agreed that "man should be the breadwinner," as one female union organizer said. But many argued that as long as conditions made it impossible for men to support their families, women should have full and equal opportunities in the workplace.

Unions faced special difficulties during the recession years of the 1870s. Not only was there widespread unemployment; there was also widespread middle-class hostility toward the unions. When labor disputes with employers turned bitter

MOLLY MAGUIRES

and violent, as they occasionally did, much of the public instinctively blamed the workers (or the "radicals" and "anarchists") they believed were influencing the workers) for the trouble, rarely the employers. Particularly alarming to middle-class Americans was the emergence of the "Molly Maguires," a militant labor organization in the anthracite coal region of Pennsylvania. The Mollies operated within the Ancient Order of Hibernians, an Irish fraternal society. They attempted to intimidate the coal operators through violence and occasionally murder, and they added to the growing perception that labor activism was motivated by dangerous radicals. Much of the violence attributed to the Molly Maguires, however, was instigated or performed by informers and agents employed by the mine owners, who wanted a pretext for ruthless measures to suppress unionization.

THE GREAT RAILROAD STRIKE

Excitement over the Molly Maguires paled beside the near hysteria that gripped the country during the railroad strike of 1877, which began when the eastern railroads announced a 10 percent wage cut and which soon expanded into something approaching a class war. Strikers disrupted rail service

NATIONAL STRIKE

from Baltimore to St. Louis, destroyed equipment, and rioted in the streets of Pittsburgh and other cities. State militias were called out, and in July President Hayes ordered federal troops to suppress the disorders in West Virginia. In Baltimore, eleven demonstrators died and forty were wounded in a conflict between workers and militiamen. In Philadelphia, state militia opened fire on thousands of workers and their families who were attempting to block the railroad crossings and killed twenty people. In all, more than 100 people died before the strike finally collapsed several weeks after it had begun.

The great railroad strike was America's first major, national labor conflict, and it illustrated how disputes between workers and employers could no longer be localized in the increasingly national economy. It illustrated as well the depth of resentment among many American workers toward their employers (and toward the governments allied with them) and the lengths to which they were prepared to go to express that resentment. And finally, it was an indication of the frailty of the labor movement. The failure of the strike seriously weakened the railroad unions and damaged the reputation of labor organizations in other industries as well.

THE KNIGHTS OF LABOR

The first genuinely national labor organization was the Noble Order of the Knights of Labor, founded in 1869 under the leadership of Uriah S. Stephens. Membership was open to all who "toiled," a definition that included all workers and most business and professional people. The only excluded groups were lawyers, bankers, liquor dealers, and professional gamblers. Unlike most labor organizations of the time, the Knights welcomed women members—not just female factory workers, but domestic servants and women who worked in their own homes. Leonora Barry, an Irish immigrant who had worked in a New York hosiery factory, ran the Woman's Bureau of the Knights. Under her effective leadership, the Knights enlisted 50,000 women members (both black and white) and created over a hundred all-female locals.

The Knights were loosely organized, without much central direction. Members met in local "assemblies," which took many different forms. They were loosely affiliated with a national "general assembly." Their program was similarly vague. Although they championed an eight-hour day and the abolition of child labor, the leaders were more interested in long-range reform of the economy. Leaders of the Knights hoped to replace the "wage system" with a new "cooperative system," in which workers would themselves control a large part of the economy.

For several years, the Knights remained a secret fraternal organization. But in the late 1870s, under the leadership of Terence V. Powderly, the order moved into the open and entered a spectacular period of expansion. By 1886, it claimed a total membership of over 700,000, including some militant elements that the moderate

DISSOLUTION OF THE KNIGHTS OF LABOR

leadership could not always control. Local unions or assemblies associated with the Knights launched a series of strikes in the 1880s in defiance of Powderly's wishes. In 1885, striking railway workers forced the Missouri Pacific, a link in the Gould system, to restore wage cuts and recognize their union. But the victory was temporary. In the following year, a strike on another Gould railroad, the Texas and Pacific, was crushed, and the power of the unions in the Gould system was broken. Their failure helped discredit the organization. By 1890, the membership of the Knights had shrunk to 100,000. A few years later, the organization disappeared.

THE AFL

Even before the Knights began to decline, a rival organization based on a very different organizational concept appeared. In 1881, representatives of a number of existing craft unions formed the Federation of Organized Trade and Labor Unions of the United States and Canada. Five years later, it changed its name to the American Federation of Labor (AFL), and it soon became the most important and enduring labor group in the country. Rejecting the Knights' idea of one big union for everybody, the Federation was an association of autonomous craft unions and represented mainly skilled workers. It was generally hostile to organizing unskilled workers, who did not fit comfortably within the craft-based structure of existing organizations.

Toward women, the AFL adopted an apparently contradictory policy. On the one hand, the male leaders of the AFL were hostile to the idea of women entering the paid workforce. Because women were weak, they believed, employers could easily take advantage of them by paying them less than

OPPOSITION TO FEMALE EMPLOYMENT

KNIGHTS OF LABOR DELEGATES, 1886 The Knights of Labor was the first, and for many years the only, labor organization to welcome women unreservedly, as this portrait of delegates to the Knights 1886 convention indicates. (The Library of Congress (LC-USZ62-12485))

men. As a result, women workers drove down wages for everyone. "It is the so-called competition of the unorganized, defenseless woman worker, the girl and the wife, that often tends to reduce the wages of the father and husband," Samuel Gompers, the powerful leader of the AFL, once said. He talked often about the importance of women remaining in the home and argued (incorrectly) that "there is no necessity of the wife contributing to the support of the family by working." More than that, female labor was, the AFL newspaper wrote, "the knife of the assassin, aimed at the family circle." Gompers himself believed strongly that a test of a man's worth was his ability to support a family and that women in the workforce would undermine men's positions as heads of their families.

Although hostile to the idea of women workers, the AFL nevertheless sought equal pay for those women who did work and even hired some female organizers to encourage unionization in industries dominated by women. These positions were, in fact, less contradictory than they seem. By raising the pay of women, the AFL could make them less attractive to employers and, in effect, drive them out of the workforce.

Gompers accepted the basic premises of capitalism; his goal was simply to secure for workers a greater share of capitalism's material rewards. Gompers opposed the creation of a worker's party; he was generally hostile to any government efforts to

THE AFL'S AGENDA

protect labor or improve working conditions, convinced that what government could give it could also take away. The AFL concentrated instead on the relationship between labor and management. It supported the immediate objectives of most workers: better wages and working conditions. And while the AFL hoped to attain its goals by collective bargaining, it was ready to use strikes if necessary.

As one of its first objectives, the AFL demanded a national eight-hour day and called for a general strike if workers did not achieve the goal by May 1, 1886. On that day, strikes and demonstrations calling for a shorter workday took place all over the country, most of them staged by AFL unions but a few by radical groups.

In Chicago, a center of labor and radical strength, a strike was

HAYMARKET SQUARE

already in progress at the McCormick Harvester Company when the general strike began. City police had been harassing the strikers, and labor and radical leaders called a protest meeting at Haymarket Square. When the police ordered the crowd to disperse, someone threw a bomb that killed seven officers and injured sixty-seven other people. The police, who had killed four strikers the day before, fired into the crowd and killed four more people. Conservative, property-conscious Americans, frightened and outraged, demanded retribution, even though no one knew who had thrown the bomb. Chicago officials finally rounded up eight anarchists and charged them with murder, on the grounds that their statements had incited whoever had hurled the bomb. All eight scapegoats were found guilty after a remarkably injudicious trial. Seven were sentenced to death. One of the condemned committed suicide, four were executed, and two had their sentences commuted to life imprisonment.

To most middle-class Americans, the Haymarket bombing was an alarming symbol of social chaos and radicalism. "Anarchism" now became a code word in the public mind for terrorism and violence, even though most anarchists were relatively peaceful visionaries dreaming of a new social order. For the next thirty years, the specter of anarchism remained one of the most frightening concepts in the American middle-class imagination. It also became a constant obstacle to the goals of the AFL and other labor organizations, and it was particularly devastating to the Knights of Labor, which, as the most radical of the major labor organizations, never recovered from the post-Haymarket hysteria. However much they tried to distance themselves from radicals, unions were always vulnerable to accusations of anarchism, as the violent strikes of the 1890s occasionally illustrated.

THE HOMESTEAD STRIKE

The Amalgamated Association of Iron and Steel Workers, which was affiliated with the American Federation of Labor, was the most powerful trade union in the country. Its members were skilled workers, in great demand by employers and thus able to exercise significant power in the workplace. Employers sometimes called such workers "little shopfloor autocrats," and they resented the substantial control over working conditions these skilled laborers often had. The union had a rulebook with fifty-six pages of what workers called "legislation" limiting the power of employers. In the emerging corporate world of the late nineteenth century, such challenges to management control were beginning to seem intolerable to many employers.

By the mid-1880s, the steel industry had introduced new production methods and new patterns of organization that were streamlining the steelmaking process and, at the same time, reducing the companies' dependence on skilled labor. In the Carnegie system, the union had a foothold in only one of the corporation's three major factories—the Homestead plant

HENRY CLAY FRICK

near Pittsburgh. By 1890, Carnegie and his chief lieutenant, Henry Clay Frick, had decided that the Amalgamated "had to go," even at Homestead. Over the next two years, they repeatedly cut wages at Homestead. At first, the union acquiesced, aware that it was not strong enough to wage a successful strike.

In 1892, the company stopped even discussing its decisions with the Amalgamated, in effect denying the union's right to negotiate. Finally, when Frick announced another wage cut at Homestead and gave the union two days to accept it, the Amalgamated called for a strike. Frick abruptly shut down the plant and called in 300 guards from the Pinkerton Detective Agency to enable the company to hire nonunion workers. The hated Pinkertons were well-known strikebreakers, and their mere presence was often enough to incite workers to violence.

The Pinkertons approached the plant by river on barges on July 6, 1892. The strikers prepared for them by pouring oil on the water and setting it on fire, and they met the guards at the docks with guns and dynamite. After several hours of pitched battle, during which three guards and ten strikers were killed and many others injured, the Pinkertons surrendered and were escorted roughly out of town.

But the workers' victory was temporary. The governor of Pennsylvania, at the company's request, sent the state's entire

THE UNION DEFEATED

National Guard contingent, some 8,000 troops, to Homestead. Production resumed, with strikebreakers now protected by troops. Public opinion turned against the strikers when a radical made an attempt to assassinate Frick. Slowly, workers drifted back to their jobs; and finally–four months after the strike began–the Amalgamated surrendered. By 1900, every major steel plant in the Northeast had broken with the Amalgamated, which now had no power to resist. Its membership shrank from a high of 24,000 in 1891 (two-thirds of all eligible steelworkers) to fewer than 7,000 a decade later. Its decline was symbolic of the general erosion of union strength in the late nineteenth century, as factory labor became increasingly unskilled and workers thus became easier to replace. The AFL unions were often powerless in the face of these changes.

THE PULLMAN STRIKE

A dispute of greater magnitude and equal bitterness, if less violence, was the Pullman strike in 1894. The Pullman Palace Car Company manufactured sleeping and parlor cars for railroads, which it built and repaired at a plant near Chicago. The company built a 600-acre town, named Pullman, and rented its trim, orderly houses to the employees. George M. Pullman, owner of the company, considered the town a model solution to the industrial problem; he referred to the workers as his "children." But many residents chafed at the regimentation and the high rents.

In the winter of 1893–1894, the Pullman Company slashed wages by about 25 percent, citing the declining revenues the depression that began in 1983 was causing. At the same time, Pullman refused to reduce rents in its model town, which were 20 to 25 percent higher than rents for comparable accommodations in surrounding areas. Workers went on strike

EUGENE DEBS

and persuaded the militant American Railway Union, led by Eugene V. Debs, to support them by refusing to handle Pullman cars and equipment. Opposing the strikers was the General Managers' Association, a consortium of twenty-four Chicago railroads. It persuaded its member companies to discharge switchmen who refused to handle Pullman cars. Every time this happened, Debs's union instructed its members who worked for the offending companies to walk off their jobs. Within a few days thousands of railroad workers in twenty-seven states and territories were on strike, and transportation from Chicago to the Pacific coast was paralyzed.

Most state governors responded readily to appeals from strike-threatened businesses; but the governor of Illinois, John Peter Altgeld, was a man with demonstrated sympathies for workers and their grievances. Altgeld had criticized the trials of the Haymarket anarchists and had pardoned the convicted

THE PULLMAN STRIKE These two images portray two aspects of the great Pullman strike of 1894. The photograph above shows U.S. troops, ordered to Chicago to quell the strike, camping on the lakefront. The drawing below shows freight cars and an engine destroyed by striking workers. These images were published together in *Harper's Weekly* to illustrate the ferocity of the Pullman battle. (The Library of Congress (LC-USZ62-96506))

men who were still in prison when he took office. He refused to call out the militia to protect employers now. Bypassing Altgeld, railroad operators asked the federal government to send regular army troops to Illinois, on the pretext that the strike was preventing the movement of mail on the trains. President Grover Cleveland and Attorney General Richard Olney, a former railroad lawyer and a bitter foe of unions, complied. In July 1894, over Altgeld's objections, the president ordered 2,000 troops to the Chicago area. A federal court issued an injunction forbidding the union to continue the strike. When Debs and his associates defied it, they were arrested and imprisoned. With federal troops protecting the hiring of new workers and with the union leaders in a federal jail, the strike quickly collapsed.

SOURCES OF LABOR WEAKNESS

The last decades of the nineteenth century were years in which labor, despite its organizing efforts, made few real gains and suffered many important losses. In a rapidly expanding industrial economy, wages for workers rose hardly at all, and not nearly enough to keep up with the rising cost of living. Labor leaders won a few legislative victories: the abolition by Congress in 1885 of the Contract Labor Law; the establishment by Congress in 1868 of an eight-hour day on public works projects and in 1892 of an eight-hour day for government employees; state laws governing hours of labor and safety standards; and gradually some guaranteed compensation for workers injured on the job. But many of these laws were not enforced, and neither strikes nor protests seemed to have much effect. The end of the century found most workers with less political power and considerably less control of the workplace than they had had forty years before.

Workers failed to make greater gains for many reasons. The principal labor organizations represented only a small percentage of the industrial workforce. Four percent of all workers (fewer than 1 million) belonged to unions in 1900. The AFL, the most important, excluded unskilled workers, who were emerging as the core of the industrial workforce, and along with them most women, blacks, and recent immigrants. Women responded to this exclusion in 1903 by forming their own organization, the Women's Trade Union League (WTUL). But after several frustrating years of attempting to unionize women, the WTUL turned the bulk of its attention to securing protective legislation for women workers, not general organization and mobilization of labor. Other divisions within the workforce contributed further to union weakness. Tensions between different ethnic and racial groups kept laborers divided.

Another source of labor weakness was the shifting nature of the workforce. Many immigrant workers came to America intending to remain only briefly, to earn some money and return home. The assumption that they had no long-range future in the country (even though it was often a mistaken one) eroded their willingness to organize. Other workers—natives and immigrants alike—were in constant motion, moving from one job to another, one town to another, seldom in one place long enough to establish institutional ties or exert real power. A study of Newburyport, Massachusetts, over a thirty-year period shows that 90 percent of the workers there vanished from the town records in those years, many of them because they moved elsewhere. Even workers who stayed put often did not remain in the same job for long.

SHIFTING NATURE OF THE WORKFORCE

Some real social mobility did exist. Workers might move from unskilled to semiskilled or skilled jobs during their lifetimes; their children might become foremen or managers. The gains were small, but they were enough to inspire considerable (and often unrealistic) hopes and to persuade some workers that they were not part of a permanent working class.

Above all, workers made few gains in the late nineteenth century because of the strength of the forces arrayed against them. They faced corporate organizations of vast wealth and power, which were generally determined to crush any efforts by workers to challenge their prerogatives—not just through brute force, but also through infiltration of unions, espionage within working-class communities, and sabotage of organizational efforts. And as the Homestead and Pullman strikes suggest, the corporations usually had the support of local, state, and federal authorities, who were willing to send in troops to "preserve order" and crush labor uprisings on demand.

CORPORATE STRENGTH

Despite the creation of new labor unions, despite a wave of strikes and protests that in the 1880s and 1890s reached startling proportions, workers in the late nineteenth century failed to create successful organizations or to protect their interests in the way the large corporations managed to do. In the battle for power within the emerging industrial economy, almost all the advantages seemed to lie with capital.

AP | CONNECTING THEMES

Chapter 17 focused on the impact of industrialization and the growth of big business on all aspects of American society. As you review the chapter, pay attention to the reasons for industrial growth, the development of the corporation, and how businesses consolidated into monopolies and trusts. Review the ways in which the power of big business was increased, and how growing inequities in wealth and degenerate working conditions spurred a reaction from disadvantaged groups and other social groups. Consider the relative success various groups had in combating the power of big business. Be keenly aware of the justification of the capitalistic system and the

attacks on the excesses of the system, including calls for increased government regulation of business. How did organized labor succeed or fail in improving working conditions? How was the labor force affected by migration patterns, immigration, and the increasing employment of women and children? Lastly, consider the migration patterns that led to the growth of cities and how the urban environment affected people and society.

The following themes have heightened importance in Chapter 17. You should now be able to do the following for each listed theme:

Identity: Analyze the ways in which migration led to changes in American identity for immigrants, working class people, and first-time urban residents.

Work, Exchange, and Technology: Explain how changes in technology and the organizational structure of business affected the economic and social development of the United States.

Peopling: Analyze the sources of urban population growth by examining migration patterns during the Gilded Age.

Politics and Power: Explain the relationship between the federal government and big business during the Gilded Age.

America and the World: Describe how the second industrial revolution changed American perceptions about involvement in world affairs.

Environment and Geography: Analyze the impact of urbanization and industrialization on the American environment.

Ideas, Beliefs, and Culture: Explain how abuses in capitalism led to an outcry for social and philosophical change.

AP SUGGESTED STUDY

PEOPLE/PLACES/EVENTS As you study these items, think about how they demonstrate or relate to key concepts and historical themes from this chapter and previous chapters.

AP TEST PRACTICE

Questions assume cumulative content knowledge from this chapter and previous chapters.

MULTIPLE CHOICE Use the photograph on page 477 and your knowledge of U.S. history to answer questions 1–5.

1. The photograph reflects the increased hiring of women in factories at the turn of the 20th century, mostly due to

   (A) laws restricting the hiring of children

   (B) greater interest in education and job training for women

   (C) lack of skilled laborers for filling a boom in factory jobs

   (D) changes in factory technology and management decreasing the need for skilled labor

2. The labor system represented in the photograph had which of the following effects on workers in general at the turn of the 20th century?

   (A) Independence from the monotonous, repetitive, unskilled tasks of the farm

   (B) Loss of control over the conditions of their labor

   (C) An introduction to the idea of advancement in a career within an industry

   (D) An increase in the effectiveness of labor unions

3. Women working in factories at the turn of the 20th century such as that shown in the photograph were typically

   (A) widowed and had no other means for supporting themselves

   (B) young, white, and immigrants, or daughters of immigrants

   (C) always single, as factory work for married women was frowned upon

   (D) only immigrants from northern European nations

4. Which best describes one way in which factory employment for women in the above photo differed from factory employment for women at the beginning of industrialization in America in the early 19th century?

   (A) Lower wages, but an improvement in working conditions and personal freedom

   (B) Improved wages, but poorer working conditions

   (C) Lower wages and poorer working conditions

   (D) Lower wages, but decreased working hours

5. In which way did the system represented in the photograph most benefit the working class in America at the turn of the 20th century?

   (A) A general rise in the standard of living

   (B) A general rise in personal freedom to control their livelihoods

   (C) An increase in shared experiences

   (D) Improvement from agrarian life

SHORT ANSWER Use your knowledge of U.S. history to answer questions 6–10.

6. Answer a, b, and c.

   a) Briefly explain why ONE of the following was the primary cause of the Industrial Revolution between 1865 and 1900.

   • Immigration

   • Technological improvements

   • Increased agricultural production

   b) Provide ONE piece of historical evidence to support your conclusion.

   c) Briefly explain why ONE of the other options is not as persuasive as the one you chose in a.

7. Answer a, b, and c.

   a) Briefly explain ONE example of the causes for the rise of "big business" in America by the turn of the 20th century.

   b) Briefly explain a SECOND example of the causes for the rise of "big business" in America by the turn of the 20th century.

   c) Briefly explain ONE example of the economic consequences of "big business" in America by the turn of the 20th century.

8. Answer a, b, and c.

   a) The first Industrial Revolution prior to the Civil War and the second Industrial Revolution after the Civil War had many similar causes and effect. Briefly explain ONE important similarity in the reasons why industrialization occurred in these two time periods.

   b) Briefly explain ONE important similarity in the effects of industrialization during these two time periods.

   c) Briefly explain ONE critical response to industrialization during either period.

9. Using the political cartoon on page 467, answer a, b, and c.

   a) Briefly explain the cartoonist's perspective regarding the state of big business by the turn of the 20th century in America.

   b) Briefly explain ONE argument that supporters of the cartoonist's perspective at the turn of the 20th century would have most likely used in support.

   c) Briefly explain ONE argument that non-supporters of the cartoonist's perspective at the turn of the 20th century would have most likely used in opposition.

10. Answer a, b, and c.

   a) For ONE of the areas below, identify a historical development and briefly explain it in relation to the rise of industrial capitalism in America at the turn of the 20th century.

   • Art and literature

   • Social philosophy or values

   • Gender roles

   • Consumerism

   b) Use ONE piece of historical evidence to support your explanation.

   c) Briefly explain ONE general social reaction to the development you identified above at the turn of the 20th century.

LONG ESSAY Develop a thoughtful and thorough historical argument that answers each question below. Begin your essay with a thesis statement and support it with relevant historical evidence.

11. Some historians have argued that the rise of industrialization in America had a positive impact on the development of American society. Support, modify or refute this statement providing specific evidence in the areas of political, economic and social areas.

12. Evaluate the extent to which increasing industrialization in the United States contributed to maintaining continuity as well as fostering change in the American identity between 1865 and 1900.

18 | THE AGE OF THE CITY

AP

HISTORICAL THINKING

1. **Patterns of Continuity and Change over Time** Analyze the change in the volume and characteristics of immigrants and the American reaction to that change.

2. **Historical Causation** Analyze the reasons for the growth of urban problems and the success of municipal governments in dealing with those problems.

3. **Contextualization** Explain how the lure of the city influenced both internal and external migration patterns, leading to urbanization.

4. **Contextualization** Explain how urban planners proposed to physically alter the environment to improve the quality of life for urban residents.

5. **Historical Causation** To what degree and in what ways did improvements in urban transportation influence the settlement patterns of the rich and poor?

6. **Historical Argumentation** Analyze the impact of social criticism in art and literature on improving life for the urban poor.

7. **Contextualization** In what ways did increased leisure time influence movement toward mass consumption?

Key Concept Correlations

Analyze the ways the historical developments you learn about in this chapter connect to the following AP Key Concepts.

6.1 The rise of big business in the United States encouraged massive migrations and urbanization, sparked government and popular efforts to reshape the U.S. economy and environment, and renewed debates over U.S. national identity.

6.2 The emergence of an industrial culture in the United States led to both greater opportunities for, and restrictions on, immigrants, minorities, and women.

6.3 The "Gilded Age" witnessed new cultural and intellectual movements in tandem with political debates over economic and social policies.

7.1 Governmental, political, and social organizations struggled to address the effects of large-scale industrialization, economic uncertainty, and related social changes such as urbanization and mass migration.

SNOW IN NEW YORK, 1902 Robert Henri Cozad (1865–1929) was one of a number of painters who, in the early twentieth century, created what became known as the "Ashcan" school of painting. These artists painted scenes of the urban underworld—tenements, saloons, boxing rings. (Courtesy National Gallery of Art, Washington)

7.2 A revolution in communications and transportation technology helped to create a new mass culture and spread "modern" values and ideas, even as cultural conflicts between groups increased under the pressure of migration, world wars, and economic distress.

Thematic Learning Objectives
CUL-3, 5, 6; ID-2, 6, 7; PEO-2, 3, 6; POL-3, 6

AP CONNECTING CONCEPTS

CHAPTER 18 discusses the urbanization of America. It focuses on the reasons for migration to cities and the consequences of a rapidly expanding population, with governmental structures incapable of dealing with the problems which that growth created. Much attention is given to the sources of population growth and of rising nativist sentiment against rapidly increasing immigration. As a result of improved urban transportation, housing patterns became segregated according to class, race, and ethnicity. Cities faced growing problems of crime, fire, disease, and environmental degradation. Political machines and "boss rule" tended to take a benevolent turn toward the urban poor in return for political support. Chapter 18 also discusses the increase in leisure time and the rise of mass consumption. Finally, art and literature moved toward realistic depictions of urban life, which spurred reform efforts. As you read, evaluate the following ideas:

- Urban centers grew both in size and number during the Gilded Age.
- The increasing efficiency of American industry made it a worldwide economic force.
- Social Darwinism was used to justify both the economic inequalities of the Gilded Age and the conspicuous consumption of the upper class.
- Improvements in urban transportation led to class, racial, and ethnic segregation in urban housing patterns.
- Immigrants faced social prejudice and were conflicted between Americanizing and maintaining their cultural identity.
- Political machines provided support services for the poor in exchange for political support.
- Critics of the excesses of the capitalistic system emerged, offering alternatives to unfettered corporate power through government regulation and the Social Gospel.

THE URBANIZATION OF AMERICA

The great migration from the countryside to the city was not unique to the United States. It was occurring simultaneously throughout much of the Western world in response to industrialization and the factory system. America, a society with little experience of great cities, found urbanization both jarring and alluring.

THE LURE OF THE CITY

"We cannot all live in cities," the journalist Horace Greeley wrote shortly after the Civil War, "yet nearly all seem determined to do so." The urban population of America increased sevenfold in the half century after the Civil War. And in 1920, the census revealed that for the first time, a majority of the American people lived in "urban" areas—communities of 2,500 people or more. New York City and its environs grew from 1 million in 1860 to over 3 million in 1900. Chicago had 100,000 residents in 1860 and more than a million in 1900. Cities were experiencing similar growth in all areas of the country.

RAPID URBAN GROWTH

Natural increase accounted for only a small part of the urban growth. In fact, urban families experienced a high rate of infant mortality, a declining fertility rate, and a high death rate from disease. Without immigration, cities would have grown slowly, if at all. The city attracted people from the countryside because it offered conveniences, entertainments, and cultural experiences unavailable in rural communities. Cities gave women the opportunity to act in ways that in smaller communities would have been seen to violate "propriety." They gave gay men and lesbian women space in which to build a culture (even if still a mostly hidden one) and experiment sexually at least partly insulated from the hostile gaze of others. But most of all, cities attracted people because they offered more and better-paying jobs than were available in rural America or in the foreign economies many immigrants were fleeing.

People moved to cities, too, because new forms of transportation made it easier for them to get there. Railroads made simple, quick, and inexpensive what once was a daunting journey from parts

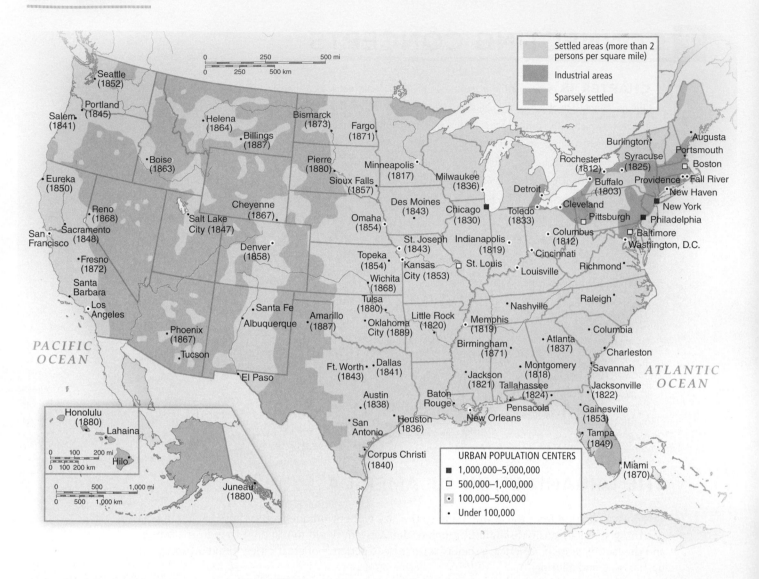

THE UNITED STATES IN 1900 This map helps illustrate the enormous increase in the nation's urban population in the nineteenth century. The map of America in 1800, on p. 194 in Chapter 7, reveals a nation with very few significant cities and with a population clustered largely along the eastern seaboard. By 1900, a much larger area of the United States had consistent areas of settlement, and many more of those areas consisted of towns and cities—including three cities (Chicago, New York, and Philadelphia) with populations of over a million and a considerable number of other cities with 100,000 or more people. Also striking, however, is the amount of land in the West with very light settlement or no settlement.

• *Do climate and geography help explain the variable patterns of settlement?*

of the American countryside to nearby cities. The development of large, steam-powered ocean liners created a highly competitive shipping industry, allowing Europeans and Asians to cross the oceans to America much more cheaply and quickly than they had in the past.

MIGRATIONS

As a result of urbanization, the late nineteenth century became an age of unprecedented geographic mobility, as Americans

GEOGRAPHIC MOBILITY left the declining agricultural regions of the East at a dramatic rate. Some who left were moving to the newly developing farmlands of the West. But many were moving to the cities of the East and the Midwest.

Among those leaving rural America for industrial cities in the late nineteenth century were young rural women, for whom opportunities in the farm economy were limited. As farms grew larger, more commercial, and more mechanized, they became increasingly male preserves; and since much of the workforce on many farms consisted of unskilled and often transient workers, there were fewer family units than before. Farm women had once been essential for making clothes and other household goods, but those goods were now available in stores or through catalogs. Hundreds of thousands of women moved to the cities, therefore, in search of work and community.

Southern blacks were also beginning what would be a nearly century-long exodus from the countryside into the cities. Their withdrawal was a testament to the poverty, debt,

Population (millions)

POPULATION GROWTH, 1860–1900 This chart illustrates the rapid increase in the nation's population in the last forty years of the nineteenth century. As you can see, the American population more than doubled in those years.

• *What were the principal factors behind this substantial population growth?*

violence, and oppression African Americans encountered in the late-nineteenth-century rural South. The opportunities they found in cities were limited. Factory jobs for blacks were rare, and professional opportunities almost nonexistent. Urban blacks tended to work as cooks, janitors, domestic servants, and in other low-paying service occupations. Because many such jobs were considered women's work, black women often outnumbered black men in the cities.

By the end of the nineteenth century, there were substantial African American communities (10,000 people or more) in over thirty cities–many of them in the South, but some (New York City, Chicago, Washington, D.C., Baltimore) in the North or in border states. Much more substantial African American migration would come during World War I and after; but the black communities established in the late nineteenth century paved the way for the great population movements of the future.

AFRICAN AMERICAN COMMUNITIES

The most important source of urban population growth in the late nineteenth century, however, was the arrival of great numbers of new immigrants from abroad: 10 million between 1860 and 1890, 18 million more in the three decades after that. Some came from Canada, Mexico, Latin America, and–particularly on the West Coast–China and Japan. But by far the greatest number came from Europe. After 1880, the flow of new arrivals began for the first time to include large numbers of people from southern and eastern Europe: Italians, Greeks, Slavs, Slovaks, Russian Jews, Armenians, and others. By the 1890s, more than half of all immigrants came from these new regions, as opposed to less than 2 percent in the 1860s.

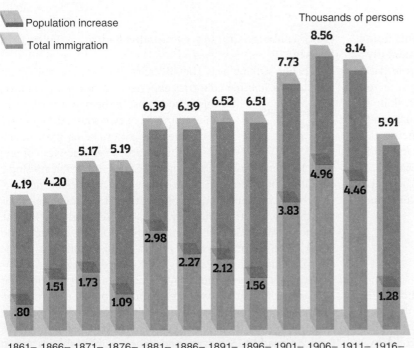

Population increase

Total immigration

Thousands of persons

IMMIGRATION'S CONTRIBUTION TO POPULATION GROWTH, 1860–1920 Immigration, mostly from Europe, was responsible for about 20 percent of the nation's population growth in the late nineteenth and early twentieth centuries.

• *What factors drew so many immigrants to the United States in these years?*

GLOBAL MIGRATIONS WOR-3

THE large waves of immigration that transformed American society in the late nineteenth and early twentieth centuries were not unique to the United States. They were part of a worldwide movement of peoples that affected every continent. These epic migrations were the product of two related forces: population growth and industrialization.

The population of Europe grew faster in the second half of the nineteenth century than it had ever grown before—almost doubling between 1850 and the beginning of World War I. The population growth was a result of growing economies able to support more people and productive agriculture that helped end debilitating famines. But the rapid growth nevertheless strained the resources of many parts of Europe and affected, in particular, rural people, who were now too numerous to live off the available land. Many decided to move to other parts of the world, where land was more plentiful or jobs were more available.

At the same time, industrialization drew millions of people from rural areas into cities—sometimes cities in their own countries, but often industrial cities in other, more economically advanced nations. From 1800 to the start of World War I, 50 million Europeans migrated to new lands overseas—people from almost all areas of Europe, but, in the later years of the century (when migration reached its peak), mostly from poor rural areas in southern and eastern Europe. Italy, Russia, and Poland were among the biggest sources of late-nineteenth-century migrants. Almost two-thirds of these immigrants came to the United States. But nearly 20 million Europeans migrated to other lands, to Canada, Australia, New Zealand, South Africa, Argentina, and other parts of South America. Many of these migrants moved to vast areas of open land in these countries and established themselves as farmers. Many others settled in the industrial cities that were growing up in all these regions.

It was not only Europeans who were transplanting themselves in these years. Vast numbers of migrants—usually poor, desperate people—left Asia, Africa, and the Pacific islands in search of better lives. Most of them could not afford the journey abroad on their own. They moved instead as indentured servants, agreeing to a term of servitude in their new land in exchange for food, shelter, and

(Private Collection/© Peter Newark American Pictures/Bridgeman Images)

In earlier stages of immigration, most new immigrants from Europe (with the exception of the Irish) were at least modestly prosperous and educated. Germans and Scandinavians in particular had headed west on their arrival, either to farm or to work as businessmen, merchants, professionals, or skilled laborers in midwestern cities such as St. Louis, Cincinnati, and Milwaukee. Most of the new immigrants of the late nineteenth century, however, lacked the capital to buy farmland and lacked the education to establish themselves in professions. So, like the poor Irish immigrants before the Civil War, they settled overwhelmingly in industrial cities, where most of them took unskilled jobs.

THE ETHNIC CITY

By 1890, the population of some major urban areas consisted of a majority of foreign-born immigrants and their children: 87 percent of the population of Chicago, 80 percent in New York City, 84 percent in Milwaukee and Detroit. (London, the largest industrial city in Europe, by contrast, had a population that was 94 percent native.) New York had more Irish than Dublin and more Germans than Hamburg. Chicago eventually had more Poles than Warsaw.

Equally striking was the diversity of the new immigrant populations. In other countries experiencing heavy immigration in this period, most of the new arrivals were coming from one or two sources: Argentina, for example, was experiencing great migrations too, but almost everyone was coming from Italy and Spain. In the United States, however, no single national group dominated. In the last four decades of the nineteenth century, substantial groups arrived from Italy, Germany, Scandinavia, Austria, Hungary, Russia, Great Britain, Ireland, Poland, Greece, Canada, Japan, China, Holland, Mexico, and many other nations. In some towns, a dozen different ethnic groups found themselves living in close proximity.

THE DIVERSE AMERICAN CITY

Most of the new immigrants were rural people, and their adjustment to city life was often painful. To help ease the transition, many national groups formed close-knit ethnic communities within the cities: Italian, Polish, Jewish, Slavic, Chinese, French-Canadian, Mexican, and other neighborhoods (often called "immigrant ghettos") that attempted to re-create in the New World many of the features of the Old.

transportation. Recruiters of indentured servants fanned out across China, Japan, areas of Africa and the Pacific islands, and, above all, India. French and British recruiters brought hundreds of thousands of Indian migrants to work in plantations in their own Asian and African colonies. Chinese laborers were recruited to work on plantations in Cuba and Hawaii; mines in Malaya, Peru, South Africa, and Australia; and railroad projects in Canada, Peru, and the United States. African indentured servants moved in large numbers to the Caribbean, and Pacific islanders tended to move to other islands or to Australia.

The migration of European peoples to new lands was largely voluntary. Most migrants moved to the United States, where indentured servitude was illegal. Non-European migration brought relatively small numbers of people to the United States, but together, these various forms of migration produced one of the greatest population movements in the history of the world and transformed not just the United States, but much of the globe as well. ●

UNDERSTAND, ANALYZE, AND EVALUATE

1. What were some of the negative factors that motivated European and non-Europeans to leave their home countries for the United States? What were some of the positive factors in the United States that attracted them?
2. Why did European empires encourage and facilitate the migration of Europeans and non-Europeans to new lands?
3. Why did more Europeans than non-Europeans migrate to the United States?

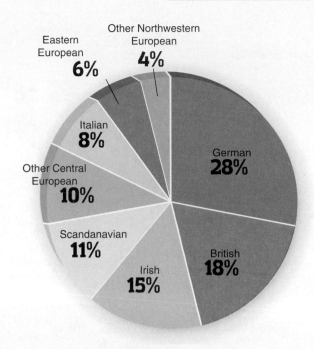

SOURCES OF IMMIGRATION FROM EUROPE, 1860–1900 This pie chart shows the sources of European immigration in the late nineteenth century. The largest number of immigrants continued to come from traditional sources (Britain, Ireland, Germany, Scandinavia), but the beginnings of what in the early twentieth century would become a major influx of immigrants from new sources—southern and eastern Europe in particular—are already visible here. Immigration from other sources—Mexico, South and Central America, and Asia—was also significant during this period.

● *Why would these newer sources of European and other kinds of immigration create controversy among older-stock Americans?*

Some ethnic neighborhoods consisted of people who had migrated to America from the same province, town, or village. Even when the population was more diverse, however, the immigrant neighborhoods offered newcomers much that was familiar. They could find newspapers and theaters in their native languages, stores selling their native foods, churches or synagogues, and fraternal organizations that provided links with their national pasts. Many immigrants also maintained close ties with their native countries. They stayed in touch with relatives who had remained behind. Some (perhaps as many as a third in the early years) returned to Europe or Asia or Mexico after a short time; others helped bring the rest of their families to America.

BENEFITS OF ETHNIC COMMUNITIES

The cultural cohesiveness of the ethnic communities clearly eased the pain of separation from the immigrants' native lands. What role it played in helping immigrants become absorbed into the economic life of America is a more difficult question to answer. It is clear that some ethnic groups (Jews and Germans in particular) advanced economically more rapidly than others (for example, the Irish). One explanation is that, by

huddling together in ethnic neighborhoods, immigrant groups tended to reinforce the cultural values of their previous societies. When those values were particularly well suited to economic advancement in an industrial society—as was, for example, the high value Jews placed on education—ethnic identification may have helped members of a group to improve their lots. When other values predominated—maintaining community solidarity, sustaining family ties, preserving order—progress could be less rapid.

ASSIMILATION

Despite the substantial differences among the various immigrant communities, virtually all groups of the foreign-born had certain things in common. Most immigrants, of course, shared the experience of living in cities (and of adapting from a rural past to an urban present). Most were young; the majority of newcomers were between fifteen and forty-five years old. And in virtually all communities of foreign-born immigrants, the strength of ethnic ties had to compete against another powerful force: the desire for assimilation.

Many of the new arrivals from abroad had come to America with romantic visions of the New World. And however disillusioning they might find their first contact with the United States, they usually

AMERICANIZATION

ETHNIC AND CLASS SEGREGATION IN MILWAUKEE, 1850–1890 This map illustrates the complex pattern of settlement in Milwaukee, a pattern that was in many ways typical of many industrial cities, in the late nineteenth century. Two related phenomena—industrialization and massive immigration from abroad—shaped the landscape of the city in these years. By 1890, first- and second-generation immigrants made up 84 percent of the city's population. Note the complicated distribution of ethnic groups in distinctive neighborhoods throughout the city, and note too the way in which middle-class people (especially "native-born" middle-class people, which included many people of German descent whose families had been in the United States for generations) isolated themselves from the areas in which the working class lived.

• *What were some of the advantages and disadvantages of this ethnic clustering to the immigrants who lived in these communities?*

retained the dream of becoming true "Americans." Even some first-generation immigrants worked hard to rid themselves of all vestiges of their old cultures, to become thoroughly Americanized. Second-generation immigrants were even more likely to attempt to break with the old ways, to try to assimilate completely into what they considered the real American culture. Some even looked with contempt on parents and grandparents who continued to preserve traditional ethnic habits and values.

The urge to assimilate put a particular strain on relations between men and women in immigrant communities. Many of the foreign-born came from cultures in which women were more subordinate to men, and more fully lodged within the family, than most women in the United States. In some immigrant cultures, parents expected to arrange their children's

CHANGING GENDER ROLES marriages and to control almost every moment of their daughters' lives until marriage. But out of either choice or economic necessity, many immigrant women (and even more of the American-born daughters of immigrants) began working outside the home and developing friendships, interests, and attachments outside the family. The result was not the collapse of the family-centered cultures of immigrant communities; those cultures proved remarkably durable. But there were adjustments to the new and more fluid life of the American city, and often considerable tension in the process.

Assimilation was not entirely a matter of choice. Native-born Americans encouraged it, both deliberately and inadvertently, in countless ways. Public schools taught children in English, and employers often insisted that workers speak English on the job. Although there were merchants in immigrant communities who sold ethnically distinctive foods and clothing, most stores by necessity sold mainly American products, forcing immigrants to adapt their diets, wardrobes, and lifestyles to American norms. Church leaders were often native-born Americans or assimilated immigrants who encouraged their parishioners to adopt American ways. Some even reformed their theology and liturgy to make it more compatible with the norms of the new country. Reform Judaism, imported from Germany to the United States in the mid-nineteenth century, was an effort by American Jewish leaders (as it had been among German leaders) to make their faith less "foreign" to the dominant culture of a largely Christian nation.

EXCLUSION

The arrival of so many new immigrants, and the way many of them clung to old ways and created culturally distinctive communities, provoked fear and resentment among some native-born Americans, just as earlier arrivals had done. Some people reacted against the immigrants out of generalized fears and prejudices, seeing in their "foreignness" the source of all the disorder and corruption of the urban world. "These people," a Chicago newspaper wrote shortly after the Haymarket bombing, referring to striking immigrant workers, "are not American, but the very scum and offal of Europe . . . Europe's human and inhuman rubbish." Native-born Americans on the West Coast had a similar cultural aversion to Mexican, Chinese, and Japanese immigrants. Other native laborers were often incensed by the willingness of the immigrants to accept lower wages and to take over the jobs of strikers.

The rising nativism provoked political responses. In 1887, Henry Bowers, a self-educated lawyer obsessed with a hatred of Catholics and foreigners, founded the American Protective Association, a group committed to stopping the immigrant tide. By 1894, membership in the organization had reportedly reached 500,000, with chapters throughout the Northeast and Midwest. That same year a more genteel organization, the Immigration Restriction League, was founded in

PUSHCART VENDOR Many immigrants to American cities aspired to be merchants. But many people with such aspirations could not afford to rent or buy a shop. So they set up business instead in pushcarts, which they parked along sidewalks and from which they sold a variety of wares. This pushcart was photographed with its owner on the Lower East Side of Manhattan around the end of the nineteenth century. (© The Granger Collection, New York)

Boston by five Harvard alumni. It was dedicated to the belief that immigrants should be screened, through literacy tests and other standards designed to separate the desirable from the undesirable. The league avoided the crude conspiracy theories and the rabid xenophobia of the American Protective Association. Its sophisticated nativism made it possible for many educated, middle-class people to support the restrictionist cause.

Even before the rise of these new organizations, politicians were struggling to find answers to the "immigration question."

In 1882 Congress had responded to strong anti-Asian sentiment in California and elsewhere and restricted Chinese immigration, even though the Chinese made up only 1.2 percent of the population of the West Coast (see pp. 434–437). In the same year, Congress denied entry to "undesirables"–convicts, paupers, the mentally incompetent–and placed a tax of 50 cents on each person admitted. Later legislation of the 1890s enlarged the list of those barred from immigrating and increased the tax.

WELCOME TO ALL!

PRO-IMMIGRATION This political cartoon from 1880, by Joseph Keppler, expresses the view that people from all over the world should be welcomed into the ever-expanding United States. While opposition to immigration from the restrictionist camp was great, immigrants were seen by many employers as a large and cheap labor supply necessary to support a rapidly growing economy. (© The Granger Collection, New York)

These laws kept out only a small number of aliens, however, and more-ambitious restriction proposals **ADVANTAGES OF CHEAP LABOR** made little progress. Congress passed a literacy requirement for immigrants in 1897, but President Grover Cleveland vetoed it. The restrictions had limited success because many native-born Americans, far from fearing immigration, welcomed it and exerted strong political pressure against the restrictionists. Immigration was providing a rapidly growing economy with a cheap and plentiful labor supply; many employers argued that America's industrial (and indeed agricultural) development would be impossible without it.

THE URBAN LANDSCAPE

The city was a place of remarkable contrasts. It had homes of almost unimaginable size and grandeur, and hovels of indescribable squalor. It had conveniences unknown to earlier generations, and problems that seemed beyond society's capacity to solve. Both the attractions and the problems were a result of the stunning pace at which cities were growing. The expansion of the urban population helped spur important new technological and industrial developments. But the rapid growth also produced misgovernment, poverty, congestion, filth, epidemics, and great fires. Planning and building simply could not match the pace of growth.

THE CREATION OF PUBLIC SPACE

In the eighteenth and early nineteenth centuries, cities had generally grown up haphazardly, with little central planning. By the mid-nineteenth century, however, reformers, planners, architects, and others began to call for a more ordered vision of the city. The result was the self-conscious creation of public spaces and public services.

Among the most important innovations of the mid-nineteenth century were great urban parks, which reflected the desire of a growing number of urban leaders to provide an antidote to the **FREDERICK LAW OLMSTED AND CALVERT VAUX** congestion of the city landscape. The most successful American promoters of this notion of the park as refuge were the landscape designers Frederick Law Olmsted and Calvert Vaux, who teamed up in the late 1850s to design New York City's Central Park. They deliberately created a public space that would look as little like the city as possible. Instead of the ordered, formal spaces common in some European cities, they created a space that seemed to be entirely natural—even though almost all of Central Park was carefully designed and constructed. Central Park was from the start one of the most popular and admired public spaces in the world, and as a result Olmsted and Vaux were recruited to design great parks and public spaces in other cities: Brooklyn, Boston, Philadelphia, Chicago, and Washington, D.C.

CENTRAL PARK BAND CONCERT By the late nineteenth century, New York City's Central Park was already considered one of the great urban landscapes of the world. To New Yorkers, it was an irresistible escape from the crowded, noisy life of the rest of the city. But the park itself sometimes became enormously crowded as well, as this well-dressed audience at a band concert makes clear. (© The Granger Collection, New York)

At the same time that cities were creating great parks, they were also creating great public buildings: libraries, art galleries, natural history museums, theaters, concert halls, and opera houses. New York City's Metropolitan Museum of Art was only the largest and best known of many great museums taking shape in the late nineteenth century; others were created in such cities as Boston, Chicago, Philadelphia, and Washington, D.C. In one city after another, new and lavish public libraries appeared as if to confirm the city's role as a center of learning and knowledge.

Wealthy residents of cities were the principal force behind the creation of the great public buildings and at times even parks. As their own material and social aspirations grew, they wanted the public life of the city to provide them with amenities to match their expectations. Becoming an important patron of a major cultural institution was an especially effective route to social distinction. But this philanthropy, whatever the motives behind it, also produced valuable assets for the city as a whole.

As the size and aspirations of the great cities increased, urban leaders launched monumental projects to remake the way their cities looked. Inspired by massive city rebuilding projects in Paris, London, Berlin, and other European cities, some American cities began to clear away older neighborhoods and streets and **"CITY BEAUTIFUL" MOVEMENT** create grand, monumental avenues lined with new, more impressive buildings. A particularly important event in inspiring this effort to remake the city was the 1893 Columbian Exposition in Chicago, a world's fair constructed to honor the 400th anniversary of Columbus's first voyage to America. At the center of the wildly popular exposition was a cluster of neoclassical buildings–the "Great White City"–constructed in the fashionable "beaux-arts" style of the time, arranged symmetrically around a formal lagoon. It became the inspiration for what became known as the "city beautiful" movement, led by the architect of the Great White City, Daniel Burnham. The movement aimed to impose a similar order and symmetry on the disordered life of cities around the country. "Make no little plans," Burnham liked to tell city planners. His influence led to the remaking of cities all across the country–from Washington, D.C., to Chicago and San Francisco. Only rarely, however, were planners able to overcome the obstacles of private landowners and complicated urban politics. They rarely achieved more than a small portion of their dreams. There were no reconstructions of American cities to match the elaborate nineteenth-century reshaping of Paris and London.

The effort to remake the city did not just focus on redesigning the existing landscape. It occasionally led to the creation of entirely new ones. In Boston in the late 1850s, a large area of marshy tidal land was gradually filled in to create the neighborhood known as "Back Bay." The landfill project took more

THE BACK BAY than forty years to complete and was one of the largest public works projects ever undertaken in America to that point. But Boston was not alone. Chicago reclaimed large areas from Lake Michigan as it expanded and at one point raised the street level for the entire city to help avoid the problems the marshy land created. In Washington, D.C., another marshy site, large areas were filled in and slated for development. In New York and other cities, the response to limited space was not so much creating new land as annexing adjacent territory. A great wave of annexations expanded the boundaries of many American cities in the 1890s and beyond.

HOUSING THE WELL-TO-DO

One of the greatest problems of this precipitous growth was finding housing for the thousands of new residents who were pouring into the cities every day. For the prosperous, however, housing was seldom a worry. The availability of cheap labor and the reduced cost of building let anyone with even a moderate income afford a house.

Many of the richest urban residents lived in palatial mansions in the heart of the city and created lavish "fashionable districts"–Fifth Avenue in New York City, Back Bay and Beacon Hill in Boston, Society Hill in Philadelphia, Lake Shore Drive in Chicago, Nob Hill in San Francisco, and many others.

The moderately well-to-do (and as time went on, increasing numbers of wealthy people as well) took advantage of the less expensive land on the edges of the city and settled in

GROWTH OF SUBURBS new suburbs, linked to the downtowns by trains or streetcars or improved roads. Chicago in the 1870s, for example, boasted nearly 100 residential suburbs connected with the city by railroad and offering the joys of "pure air, peacefulness, quietude, and natural scenery." Boston, too, saw the development of some of the earliest "streetcar suburbs"–Dorchester,

Brookline, and others–which catered to both the wealthy and the middle class. New Yorkers of moderate means settled in new suburbs on the northern fringes of Manhattan and commuted downtown by trolley or riverboat. Real estate developers worked to create and promote suburban communities that would appeal to nostalgia for the countryside that many city dwellers felt. Affluent suburbs, in particular, were notable for lawns, trees, and houses designed to look manorial. Even modest communities strove to emphasize the opportunities suburbs provided for owning land.

HOUSING WORKERS AND THE POOR

Most urban residents, however, could not afford either to own a house in the city or to move to the suburbs. Instead, they stayed in the city centers and rented. Because demand was so high and space so scarce, they had little bargaining power in the process. Landlords tried to squeeze as many rent-paying residents as possible into the smallest available space. In Manhattan, for example, the average population density in 1894 was 143 people per acre–a higher rate than that of the most crowded cities of Europe (Paris had 127 per acre, Berlin 101) and far higher than in any other American city then or since. In some neighborhoods–the Lower East Side of New York City, for example–density was more than 700 people per acre, among the highest levels in the world.

Landlords were reluctant to invest much in immigrant housing, confident they could rent dwellings for a profit regardless of their conditions. In the cities of the South–Charleston, New Orleans, Richmond–poor African Americans lived in crumbling former slave quarters. In Boston, they moved into cheap three-story wooden houses ("triple deckers"), many of them decaying fire hazards. In Baltimore and Philadelphia, they crowded into narrow brick row houses. And in New York, as in many other cities, more than a million people lived in tenements.

The word "tenement" had originally referred simply to a multiple-family rental building, but by the late nineteenth century it was being used to describe slum dwellings only. The first

TENEMENTS tenements, built in New York City in 1850, had been hailed as a great improvement in housing for the poor. "It is built with the design of supplying the laboring people with cheap lodgings," a local newspaper commented, "and will have many advantages over the cellars and other miserable abodes which too many are forced to inhabit." But tenements themselves soon became "miserable abodes," with many windowless rooms, little or no plumbing or central heating, and often a row of privies in the basement. A New York state law of 1870 required a window in every bedroom of tenements built after that date; developers complied by adding small, sunless air shafts to their buildings. Most of all, tenements were incredibly crowded, with three, four, and, sometimes many more people crammed into each small room.

Jacob Riis, a Danish immigrant and New York newspaper

JACOB RIIS reporter and photographer, shocked many middle-class Americans with his sensational (and some claimed sensationalized) descriptions and

A TENEMENT LAUNDRY Immigrant families living in tenements, in New York and in many other cities, earned their livelihoods as they could. This woman, shown here with some of her children, was typical of many working-class mothers who found income-producing activities they could pursue in the home (in this case, laundry). This room, dominated by large vats and piles of other people's laundry, is also the family's home, as the crib and religious pictures make clear. (© Bettmann/Corbis)

pictures of tenement life in his 1890 book, *How the Other Half Lives*. Slum dwellings, he said, were almost universally sunless, practically airless, and "poisoned" by "summer stenches." "The hall is dark and you might stumble over the children pitching pennies back there." But the solution many reformers (including Riis) favored, and that governments sometimes adopted, was to raze slum dwellings without building any new or better housing to replace them.

URBAN TRANSPORTATION

Urban growth posed monumental transportation challenges. Old downtown streets were often too narrow for the heavy traffic that was beginning to move over them. Most were without a hard, paved surface producing either a sea of mud or a cloud of dust. In the last decades of the nineteenth century, more and more streets were paved, usually with wooden blocks,

TRANSPORTATION PROBLEMS

bricks, or asphalt; but paving could not keep up with the number of new thoroughfares the expanding cities were creating. By 1890, Chicago had paved only about 600 of its more than 2,000 miles of streets.

But it was not simply the conditions of the streets that impeded urban transportation. It was the numbers of people who needed to move every day from one part of the city to another, numbers that mandated the development of mass transportation. Streetcars drawn on tracks by horses had been introduced into some cities even before the Civil War. But the horsecars were not fast enough, so many communities developed new forms of mass transit.

In 1870, New York opened its first elevated railway, whose noisy, filthy steam-powered trains moved rapidly above the city streets on massive iron structures. New York, Chicago, San Francisco, and other cities also experimented with cable cars, towed by continuously moving underground cables. Richmond, Virginia, introduced the

MASS TRANSIT

first electric trolley line in 1888, and by 1895 such systems were operating in 850 towns and cities. In 1897, Boston opened the first American subway when it put some of its trolley lines underground. At the same time, cities were developing new techniques of road and bridge building. One of the great technological marvels of the 1880s was the completion of the Brooklyn Bridge in New York City, a dramatic steel-cable suspension span designed by John A. Roebling.

THE "SKYSCRAPER"

Cities were growing upward as well as outward. Until the mid-nineteenth century, almost no buildings more than four or five stories high could be constructed. Construction techniques were such that it was difficult and expensive to build adequate structural supports for tall buildings. There was also a limit to the number of flights of stairs the users of buildings could be expected to climb. But by the 1850s, there had been successful experiments with machine-powered passenger elevators; and by the 1870s, new methods of construction using cast iron and steel beams made it easier to build tall buildings.

Not long after the Civil War, therefore, tall buildings began to appear in the major cities. The Equitable Building in New York City, completed in 1870 and rising seven and a half floors above the street, was one of the first in the nation to be built with an elevator. A few years later, even taller buildings of ten and twelve stories were appearing elsewhere in New York, in Chicago, and in other growing cities around the country. With each passing decade, the size and number of tall buildings increased until, by the 1890s, the term "skyscraper" became a popular description of them.

STRAINS OF URBAN LIFE

The increasing congestion of the cities and the absence of adequate public services produced many hazards. Crime, fire, disease, indigence, and pollution all placed strains on the capacities of metropolitan institutions, and both governments and private institutions were for a time poorly equipped to respond to them.

FIRE AND DISEASE

One serious problem was fires. In one major city after another, fires destroyed large downtown areas, where many buildings were still constructed of wood. Chicago and Boston suffered "great fires" in 1871. Other cities—among them Baltimore and San Francisco, where a tremendous earthquake produced a catastrophic fire in 1906—experienced similar disasters. The great fires were terrible and deadly experiences, but they also encouraged the construction of fireproof buildings and the

DEVELOPMENT OF PROFESSIONAL FIRE DEPARTMENTS

development of professional fire departments. They also forced cities to rebuild at a time when new technological and architectural innovations were available. Some of the modern, high-rise downtowns of American cities arose out of the rubble of great fires.

ENVIRONMENTAL DEGRADATION

Modern notions of environmentalism were unknown to most Americans in the late nineteenth and early twentieth centuries. But the environmental degradation of many American cities was a visible and disturbing fact of life in those years. The frequency of great fires, the dangers of disease and plague, the extraordinary crowding of working-class neighborhoods were all examples of the environmental costs of industrialization and rapid urbanization.

Improper disposal of human and industrial waste was a common feature of almost all large cities in these years. Such practices contributed to the pollution of rivers and lakes and also, in many cases, to the compromising of the city's drinking water. This was particularly true in poor neighborhoods with primitive plumbing (and sometimes no indoor plumbing), outdoor privies that leaked into the groundwater, and overcrowded tenements. The presence of domestic animals—horses, which were the principal means of transportation until the late nineteenth century, but in poor neighborhoods also cows, pigs, and other animals—contributed as well to the environmental problems.

Air quality in many cities was poor as well. Few Americans had the severe problems that London experienced in these

AIR POLLUTION

years with its perpetual "fogs" created by the debris from the burning of soft coal. But air pollution from factories and from stoves and furnaces in offices, homes, and other buildings was constant and at times severe. The incidence of respiratory infection and related diseases was much higher in cities than it was in nonurban areas, and it accelerated rapidly in the late nineteenth century.

By the early twentieth century, reformers were actively crusading to improve the environmental conditions of cities and were beginning to achieve some notable successes. By 1910, most large American cities had constructed sewage disposal systems, often at great cost, to protect the drinking water of their inhabitants and to prevent the great bacterial plagues that impure water had helped create in the past—such as the 1873 yellow fever epidemic in Memphis that killed more than 5,000 people.

Alice Hamilton, a physician who became an investigator for the U.S. Bureau of Labor, was a pioneer in the identification of

PUBLIC HEALTH SERVICE

pollution in the workplace. She documented ways in which improper disposal of such potentially dangerous substances as lead

THE GREAT FIRE IN CHICAGO This haunting photograph shows the intersection of State and Madison Streets, which Chicagoans liked to call "the world's busiest intersection," in the aftermath of the great fire of 1871. It destroyed much of the city's downtown. Horse-drawn streetcars are shown here traveling the ghostly, still smoke-filled streets. At left, posters advertise the new locations of displaced stores and offices—prompting the photographer to attach the optimistic title "Back in Business" to this image. (© Archive Photos/Getty Images)

(she was one of the first physicians to identify lead poisoning), chemical waste, and ceramic dust was creating widespread sickness. And despite considerable resistance from many factory owners, she did bring such problems to public attention and, in some states at least, inspired legislation to require manufacturers to solve them. In 1912, the federal government created the Public Health Service, which was charged with preventing such occupational diseases as tuberculosis, anemia, and carbon dioxide poisoning, which were common in the garment industry and other trades. It attempted to create common health standards for all factories; but since the agency had few powers of enforcement, it had limited impact. It did, however, establish the protection of public health as a responsibility of the federal government and also helped bring to public attention the environmental forces that endangered health. The creation of the Occupational Health and Safety Administration in 1970, which gave government the authority to require employers to create safe and healthy workplaces, was a legacy of the Public Health Service's early work.

URBAN POVERTY

Above all, perhaps, the expansion of the cities created widespread and often desperate poverty. Despite the rapid growth of urban economies, the sheer number of new residents ensured that many people would be unable to earn enough for a decent subsistence.

Public agencies and private philanthropic organizations offered very limited relief. They were generally dominated by middle-class people, who tended to believe that too much assistance would breed dependency and that poverty was the fault of the poor themselves—a result of laziness or alcoholism or other kinds of irresponsibility. Most tried to restrict aid to the "deserving poor"–those who truly could not help themselves (at least according to the standards of the organizations themselves, which conducted elaborate "investigations" to separate the "deserving" from the "undeserving").

Other charitable societies–for example, the Salvation Army, which began operating in America in 1879, one year after it

SALVATION ARMY was founded in London–concentrated more on religious revivalism than on the relief of the homeless and hungry. Tensions often arose between native Protestant philanthropists and Catholic immigrants over religious doctrine and standards of morality.

Middle-class people grew particularly alarmed over the rising number of poor children in the cities, some of them orphans or runaways, living alone or in small groups scrounging for food. These "street arabs," as they were often called, attracted more attention from reformers than any other group–although that attention produced no serious solutions to their problems.

CRIME AND VIOLENCE

Poverty and crowding naturally bred crime and violence. Much of it was relatively minor, the work of pickpockets, con

HIGH CRIME RATES artists, swindlers, and petty thieves. But some was more dangerous. The American murder rate rose rapidly in the late nineteenth century (even as such rates were declining in Europe), from 25 murders for every million people in 1880 to over 100 by the end of the century–a rate slightly higher than the relatively high rates of the 1980s and 1990s. That reflected in part a very high level of violence in some nonurban areas: the American South, where rates of lynching and homicide were particularly high; and the West, where the rootlessness and instability of new communities (cow towns, mining camps, and the like) created much violence. But the cities contributed their share to the increase in crime as well. Native-born Americans liked to believe that crime was a result of the violent proclivities of immigrant groups, and they cited the rise of gangs and criminal organizations in various ethnic communities. But native-born Americans were as likely to commit crimes as immigrants.

The rising crime rates encouraged many cities to develop larger and more professional police forces. In the early nineteenth century, police forces had often been private and informal organizations; urban governments had resisted professionalized law enforcement. By the end of the century, however, professionalized public police departments were a part of the life of virtually every city and town. They worked closely with district attorneys and other public prosecutors, who were also becoming more numerous and more important in city life. Police forces themselves could also spawn corruption and brutality, particularly since jobs on them were often filled through political patronage. And complaints about police dealing differently with white and black suspects, or with

rich and poor communities, were common in the late nineteenth century.

Some members of the middle class, fearful of urban insurrections, felt the need for even more substantial forms of protection. Urban national guard groups (many of them created and manned by middle-class elites) built imposing armories on the outskirts of affluent neighborhoods and stored large supplies of weapons and ammunition in preparation for uprisings that, in fact, never occurred.

THE MACHINE AND THE BOSS

Newly arrived immigrants, many of whom could not speak English, needed help in adjusting to American urban life: its laws, its customs, usually its language. Some ethnic communities created their own self-help organizations. But for many residents of the inner cities, the principal source of assistance was the political machine.

The urban machine was one of America's most distinctive political institutions. It owed its existence to the power vacuum

BOSS RULE that the chaotic growth of cities (and the very limited growth of city governments)

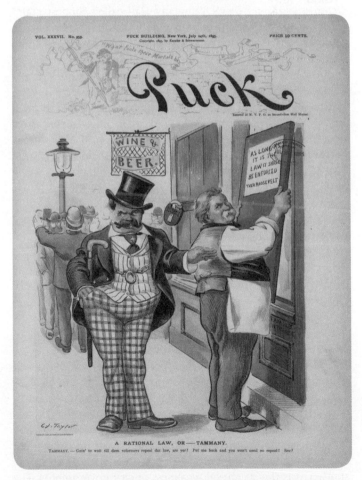

PUCK MAGAZINE *Puck* was the first successful humor magazine published in the United States. Issues were published from 1871 to 1918. It offered political cartoons, caricatures, and satire on the issues of the day. This cover takes on the graft and corruption of Tammany Hall. (The Library of Congress (LC-USZC4-7884))

had created. It was also a product of the potential voting power of large immigrant communities. Any politician who could mobilize that power stood to gain enormous influence, if not public office. And so there emerged a group of urban "bosses," themselves often of foreign birth or parentage. Many were Irish, because they spoke English and because some had acquired previous political experience from the long Irish struggle against the English at home. Almost all were men (in most states women could not yet vote). The principal function of the political boss was simple: to win votes for his organization. That meant winning the loyalty of his constituents. To do so, a boss might provide potential voters with occasional relief–baskets of groceries, bags of coal. He might step in to save those arrested for petty crimes from jail. He rewarded many of his followers with patronage: with jobs in city government or in such city agencies as the police (which the machine's elected officials often controlled); with jobs building or operating the new transit systems; and with opportunities to rise in the political organization itself.

Machines were also vehicles for making money. Politicians enriched themselves and their allies through various forms of graft and corruption. Some of it might be fairly open–what **GRAFT AND CORRUPTION** George Washington Plunkitt of New York City's Tammany Hall called "honest graft." For example, a politician might discover in advance where a new road or streetcar line was to be built, buy an interest in the land near it, and profit when the city had to buy the land from him or when property values rose as a result of the construction. But there was also covert graft: kickbacks from contractors in exchange for contracts to build streets, sewers, public buildings, and other projects; the sale of franchises for the operation of such public utilities as street railways, waterworks, and electric light and power systems. The most famously corrupt city boss was William M. Tweed, boss of New York City's Tammany Hall in the 1860s and 1870s, whose excesses finally landed him in jail in 1872.

Middle-class critics saw the corrupt machines as blights on the cities and obstacles to progress. In fact, political organizations were often responsible not just for corruption, but also for modernizing city infrastructures, for expanding the role of government, and for creating stability in a political and social climate that otherwise would have lacked a center. The motives of the bosses may have been largely venal, but their achievements were sometimes greater than those of the scrupulous reformers who challenged them.

Several factors made boss rule possible. One was the power of immigrant voters, who were less concerned with middle-class **REASONS FOR BOSS RULE** ideas of political morality than with obtaining the services that machines provided and reformers did not. Another was the link between the political organizations and wealthy, prominent citizens who profited from their dealings with bosses. Still another was the structural weakness of city governments. The boss, by virtue of his control over his machine, formed an "invisible government" that provided an alternative to what was often the inadequacy of the regular government.

The urban machine was not without competition. Reform groups frequently mobilized public outrage at the corruption of the bosses and often succeeded in driving machine politicians from office. Tammany, for example, saw its candidates for mayor and other high city offices lose almost as often as they won in the last decades of the nineteenth century. But the reform organizations typically lacked the permanence of the machine. Thus, many critics of machines began to argue for more-basic reforms: for structural changes in the nature of city government.

THE RISE OF MASS CONSUMPTION

For urban middle-class Americans, the last decades of the nineteenth century were a time of dramatic advances. Indeed, it was in those years that a distinctive middle-class culture began to exert a powerful influence over American life. Much of the **MIDDLE-CLASS CULTURE** rest of American society–the majority of the population, which was neither urban nor middle class–advanced less rapidly or not at all; but almost no one was unaffected by the rise of a new urban, consumer culture.

PATTERNS OF INCOME AND CONSUMPTION

American industry could not have grown as it did without the expansion of markets. The growth of demand occurred at almost all levels of society, a result not just of the new techniques of production and mass distribution that were making consumer goods less expensive, but also of rising incomes.

Incomes in the industrial era were rising for almost everyone, although at highly uneven rates. The most conspicuous result of the new economy was the creation of vast fortunes. But more important for society as a whole were the growth and increasing **RISING INCOME** prosperity of the middle class. The salaries of clerks, accountants, middle managers, and other "white-collar" workers rose on average by a third between 1890 and 1910–and in some parts of the middle class, salaries rose by much more. Doctors, lawyers, and other professionals, for example, experienced a particularly dramatic increase in the prestige and profitability of their professions.

Working-class incomes rose too in those years, although from a much lower base and considerably more slowly. Iron- and steelworkers, despite the setbacks their unions suffered, saw their hourly wages increase by a third between 1890 and 1910; but industries with large female, African American, or Mexican workforces–shoes, textiles, paper, laundries, many areas of commercial agriculture–saw very small increases, as did almost all industries in the South.

Also important to the new mass market were the development of affordable products and the creation of new merchandising techniques, which made many consumer goods available to a broad market for the first time. A good example

NEW MERCHANDISING TECHNIQUES

of such changes was the emergence of ready-made clothing. In the early nineteenth century, most Americans had made their own clothing–usually from cloth they bought from merchants, at times from fabrics they spun and wove themselves. Affluent people contracted with private tailors to make their clothes. But the invention of the sewing machine and the spur that the Civil War (and its demand for uniforms) gave to the manufacture of clothing created an enormous industry devoted to producing ready-made garments. By the end of the century, almost all Americans bought their clothing from stores.

Partly as a result, much larger numbers of people became concerned with personal style. Interest in women's fashion, for example, had once been a luxury reserved for the affluent. Now middle-class and even working-class women could strive to develop a distinctive style of dress. New homes, even modest ones, now included clothes closets. Even people in remote rural areas could develop stylish wardrobes by ordering from the new mail-order houses.

DEPARTMENT STORES Department stores often created "events" to help promote sales of their many wares. Here, Strawbridge and Clothier department store creates quite a stir on Market Street in Philadelphia in 1907. (© Corbis)

Another example of the rise of the mass market was the way Americans bought and prepared food. The development and mass production of tin cans in the 1880s created a large new industry devoted to packaging and selling canned food and (as a result of the techniques Gail Borden, an inventor and politician, developed in the 1850s) condensed milk. Refrigerated railroad cars made it possible for perishables–meats, vegetables, dairy products, and other foodstuffs–to travel long distances without spoiling. The development of artificially frozen ice made it possible for many more households to afford iceboxes. Among other things, the changes meant improved diets and better health; life expectancy rose six years in the first two decades of the twentieth century.

CHAIN STORES AND MAIL-ORDER HOUSES

Changes in marketing also altered the way Americans bought goods. Small local stores faced competition from new "chain stores." The Great Atlantic & Pacific Tea Company (A & P) began creating a national network of grocery stores as early as the 1850s and expanded it rapidly after the Civil War.

F. W. Woolworth opened his first "Five and Ten Cent Store" in Utica, New York, in 1879 and went on to build a national chain of dry goods stores. Chain stores were able to sell manufactured goods at lower prices than the local, independent stores because the chains had so much more volume. From the beginning, the chains faced opposition from the established merchants they threatened to displace, and from others who feared that they would jeopardize the character of their communities. (Similar controversies have continued into the twenty-first century over the spread of large chains such as Wal-Mart and Barnes & Noble.) But most customers, however loyal they might feel to a local merchant, found it difficult to resist the greater variety and lower prices the chains provided them.

Chain stores were slow to reach remote, rural areas, which remained dependent on poorly stocked and often very expensive country stores. But rural people gradually gained access to the new consumer world through the great mail-order houses. In 1872, Montgomery Ward–a Chicago-based traveling salesman–distributed a catalog of consumer goods in association with the farmers' organization, the Grange (see p. 520). By the 1880s, he was offering thousands of items at low prices to farmers throughout the Midwest and beyond. He soon faced stiff competition from Sears Roebuck, first established by Richard Sears in Chicago in 1887. Together, the bulky catalogs from Ward and Sears changed the lives of many isolated people–introducing them to (and explaining for them) new trends of fashion and home decor as well as making available new tools, machinery, and technologies for the home.

SOCIAL CONSEQUENCES OF MAIL-ORDER CATALOGS

DEPARTMENT STORES

In larger cities, the emergence of great department stores (which had appeared earlier in Europe) helped transform buying habits and turn shopping into an alluring and glamorous activity. Marshall Field in Chicago created one of the first American department stores, and others soon followed: Macy's in New York City, Abraham and Straus in Brooklyn, Jordan Marsh and Filene's in Boston, Wanamaker's in Philadelphia.

IMPACT OF THE DEPARTMENT STORE

Department stores transformed the concept of shopping in several ways. First, they brought together under one roof an enormous array of products that had previously been sold in separate shops. Second, they sought to create an atmosphere of wonder and excitement, to make shopping a glamorous activity. Department stores were elaborately decorated to suggest great luxury and elegance. They included restaurants and tearooms and comfortable lounges, to suggest that shopping could be a social event as well as a practical necessity. They hired well-dressed salesclerks, mostly women, to provide attentive service to their mostly female customers. Third, department stores—like mail-order houses—took advantage of economies of scale to sell merchandise at lower prices than many of the individual shops with which they competed.

WOMEN AS CONSUMERS

The rise of mass consumption had particularly dramatic effects on American women. Women's clothing styles changed much more rapidly and dramatically than men's, which encouraged frequent purchases. Women generally bought and prepared food for their families, so the availability of new food products changed not only the way everyone ate, but also the way women shopped and cooked.

The consumer economy produced new employment opportunities for women as salesclerks in department stores and as waitresses in the rapidly proliferating restaurants. And it spawned the creation of a new movement in which women were to play a vital role: the consumer protection movement. The National Consumers League, formed in the 1890s under the leadership of Florence Kelley, a prominent social reformer, attempted to mobilize the power of women as consumers to force retailers and manufacturers to improve wages and working conditions for women workers. By defining themselves as consumers, many middle-class women were able to find a stance from which they could become active participants in public life. Indeed, the mobilization of women behind consumer causes—and eventually many other causes—was one of the most important political developments of the late nineteenth century.

NATIONAL CONSUMERS LEAGUE

LEISURE IN THE CONSUMER SOCIETY

Closely related to the growth of consumption was an increasing interest in leisure, in part because time away from work was expanding rapidly for many people. Members of the urban middle and professional classes had increasingly large blocks of time in which they were not at work—evenings, weekends, even vacations (previously almost unknown among salaried workers). Working hours in many factories declined, from an average of nearly seventy hours a week in 1860 to under sixty in 1900. Industrial workers might still be on the job six days a week, but many of them had more time off in the evenings. Even farmers found that the mechanization of agriculture gave them more free time. The lives of many Americans were becoming compartmentalized, with clear distinctions between work and leisure.

REDEFINING LEISURE

The growth of free time produced a redefinition of the idea of "leisure." In earlier eras, relatively few Americans had considered leisure a valuable thing. On the contrary, many equated it with laziness or sloth. "Rest," as in the relative inactivity many Americans considered appropriate for the Sabbath, was valued because it offered time for spiritual reflection and prepared people for work. But leisure—time spent amusing oneself in nonproductive pursuits—was not only unavailable to most Americans, but faintly scorned as well.

NEW CONCEPTIONS OF LEISURE

But with the rapid expansion of the economy and the increasing number of hours workers had away from work, it became possible to imagine leisure time as a normal part of the lives of many people. Industrial workers, in pursuit of shorter hours, adopted the slogan "Eight hours for work, eight hours for rest, and eight hours for what we will." Others were equally adamant in claiming that leisure time was both a right and an important contribution to an individual's emotional and even spiritual health.

The economist Simon Patten was one of the first intellectuals to articulate this new view of leisure, which he tied closely to the rising interest in consumption. Patten, in *The Theory of Prosperity* (1902), *The New Basis of Civilization* (1910), and other works, challenged the centuries-old assumption that the normal condition of civilization was a scarcity of goods. "We are now in the transition stage," he wrote, "from this pain economy [the economy of scarcity] to a pleasure economy." The principal goal of such an economy, he claimed, "should be an abundance of goods and the pursuit of pleasure."

SIMON PATTEN

As Americans became more accustomed to leisure as a normal part of their lives, they began to look for new experiences with which to entertain themselves. Entertainment usually meant "going out," spending leisure time in public places where there would be not only entertainment, but also other people. Thousands of working-class New Yorkers flocked to the amusement park at Coney Island, for example, not just for the rides and shows, but for the excitement of the crowds as well. So did the thousands who spent evenings in dance halls, vaudeville houses, and concert halls. Affluent New Yorkers enjoyed afternoons in Central Park, where a principal attraction was seeing other people (and being seen by them). Moviegoers were attracted not just by the movies themselves, but also by the energy of the audiences at the lavish "movie palaces" that began to appear in cities in the early twentieth century,

PUBLIC LEISURE

just as sports fans were drawn by the crowds as well as by the games.

Mass entertainment did not always bridge differences of class, race, or gender. Saloons and most sporting events tended to be male preserves. Shopping (itself becoming a valued leisure-time activity) and going to tearooms and luncheonettes were more characteristic of female leisure. Theaters, pubs, and clubs were often specific to particular ethnic communities or particular work groups. There were, in fact, relatively few places where people of widely diverse backgrounds gathered together.

When the classes did meet in public spaces—as they did, for example, in city parks—there was often conflict over what constituted appropriate public behavior. Elites in New York City, for example, tried to prohibit anything but quiet, "genteel" activities in Central Park, while working-class people wanted to use the public spaces for sports and entertainments. But even divided by class, ethnicity, and gender, leisure and popular entertainment did help sustain a vigorous public culture.

SPECTATOR SPORTS

The search for forms of public leisure hastened the rise of organized spectator sports, especially baseball, which by the end of the century was well on its way to becoming the national pastime (see "Patterns of Popular Culture," pp. 384–385). A game much like baseball, known as "rounders" and derived from cricket, had enjoyed limited popularity in Great Britain in the early nineteenth century. Versions of the game began to appear in America in the early 1830s, well before Abner Doubleday supposedly "invented" baseball. (Doubleday, in fact, had little to do with the creation of baseball and actually cared little for sports. Alexander Cartwright, a member of a New York City baseball club in the 1840s, defined many of the rules and features of the game as we know it today.)

By the end of the Civil War, interest in baseball had grown rapidly. More than 200 amateur or semiprofessional teams or clubs existed, many of which joined a national association and agreed on standard rules. The first salaried team, the **MAJOR LEAGUE BASEBALL** Cincinnati Red Stockings, was formed in 1869. Other cities soon fielded professional teams, and in 1876, at the urging of Albert Spalding, they banded together in the National League. A rival league, the American Association, soon appeared. It eventually collapsed, but in 1901 the American League emerged to replace it. In 1903, the first modern World Series was played, in which the American League Boston Red Sox beat the National League Pittsburgh Pirates. By then, baseball had become an important business and a great national preoccupation (at least among men), attracting paying crowds in the thousands.

The second most popular game, football, appealed at first to an elite segment of the male population, in part because it originated in colleges and universities. The first intercollegiate football game in America occurred between Princeton and Rutgers in 1869, and soon the game became entrenched as part of collegiate life. Early intercollegiate football bore only an indirect relation to the modern game; it was more similar to what is now known as rugby. By the late 1870s, however, the game was becoming standardized and was taking on the outlines of its modern form.

As college football grew in popularity, it spread to other sections of the country, notably to the midwestern state **GROWTH OF COLLEGE FOOTBALL** universities, which were destined soon to replace the eastern schools as the great powers of the game. It also began to exhibit

THE AMERICAN NATIONAL GAME Long before the modern major leagues began, local baseball clubs were active throughout much of the United States, establishing the game as the "national pastime." This print of a "grand match for the championship" depicts an 1866 game at Elysian Fields, a popular park just across the river from New York City in Hoboken, New Jersey. (© National Baseball Hall of Fame and Museum, Inc.)

CONEY ISLAND

PEOPLE who lived in the crowded cities of early-twentieth-century America yearned at times for ways to escape the noise, smells, heat, and stress of the urban world. Wealthy families could travel to resorts or country houses. But most city dwellers could not afford to venture far, and for them ambitious entrepreneurs tried to provide dazzling escapes close to home. The most celebrated such escape was Coney Island in Brooklyn, New York—which became for a time the most famous and popular urban resort in America.

With its broad oceanfront beach, Coney Island, located in Brooklyn, had been an attractive destination for visitors since the early nineteenth century. In the 1870s and 1880s, investors built railroad lines from the city to the beach and began to create spectacular amusements to induce New Yorkers to visit. But the real success of Coney Island began in the 1890s, when the amusements and spectacles reached a new level. Sea Lion Park, which opened in 1895, showcased trained sea lions and exotic water rides. Steeplechase Park opened two years later, attracting visitors with a mechanical steeplechase ride in which visitors could pretend to be jockeys, and

stunt rooms with moving floors and powerful blasts of compressed air.

By then, Coney Island was a popular site for real horse racing, boxing matches, and other sports. It was

THE ELEPHANT HOTEL One of the early attractions of Coney Island as it became a popular resort was this hotel, built inside a large wooden elephant. This picture, taken in 1890, shows Coney Island at a point when development was still relatively modest. (© Photo Collection Alexander Alland, Sr./Corbis)

POSTCARD FROM LUNA PARK Visitors to Coney Island sent postcards to friends and relatives by the millions, and those cards were among the most effective promotional devices for the amusement parks. This one shows the brightly lit entrance to Luna Park, Coney Island's most popular attraction for many years. (© Bettmann/Corbis)

the taints of professionalism that have marked it ever since. Some schools used "ringers," tramp athletes who were not even registered as students. In an effort to eliminate such abuses, Amos Alonzo Stagg, athletic director and coach at the University of Chicago, led in forming the Western Conference, or Big Ten, in 1896, which established rules governing eligibility.

Football also became known for a high level of violence on the field; eighteen college students died of football-related injuries and over a hundred were seriously hurt in 1905. The carnage prompted a White House conference on organized

sports convened by President Theodore Roosevelt. As a result of its deliberations, a new intercollegiate association (which in 1910 became known as the National College Athletic Association, the NCAA) revised the rules and the required equipment of the game in an effort to make it more honest and safer.

Other popular spectator sports were emerging at about the same time. Basketball was invented in 1891 at Springfield, Massachusetts, by Dr. James A. Naismith, a Canadian working as athletic director for a local college. Boxing, which had long been a disreputable activity concentrated primarily among

STEEPLECHASE PARK Steeplechase Park opened in 1897 and immediately began attracting crowds eager to ride the mechanical steeplechase shown here. (© UIG/Getty Images)

also attracting gambling casinos, saloons, and brothels. From the beginning, among affluent middle-class people at least, Coney Island had a reputation as a rough and unsavory place. But to the working class immigrants and lower-middle-class people, it was a place of wonder, excitement, and escape.

The greatest Coney Island attraction, Luna Park, opened in 1903. It provided not just rides and stunts, but lavish reproductions of exotic places and spectacular adventures: Japanese gardens, Venetian canals with gondoliers, a Chinese theater, a simulated trip to the moon, and reenactments of such disasters as burning buildings, earthquakes, and even the volcanic eruption that destroyed Pompeii. A year later, a competing company opened Dreamland, which tried to outdo even Luna Park with a 375-foot tower, a three-ring circus, chariot races, and a Lilliputian village inspired by *Gulliver's Travels*. (A fire destroyed Dreamland in 1911.)

The popularity of Coney Island in these years was phenomenal. Thousands of people flocked to the large resort hotels that lined the beaches. Many thousands more made day trips out from the city by train and (after 1920) subway. In 1904, the average daily attendance at Luna Park alone was 90,000 people. On weekends, the Coney Island post office handled over 250,000 postcards, through which visitors helped spread the reputation of the resort across the nation.

Coney Island's popularity reflected a number of powerful impulses among urban Americans at the turn of the century. It provided visitors with an escape from the heat and crowding of the vast metropolis around it. It gave people who had few opportunities for travel a simulated glimpse of exotic places and events that they would never be able to experience in reality. For immigrants, many of whom lived in insular ethnic communities, Coney Island provided a way of experiencing American mass culture on an equal footing with people of backgrounds different from their own. Almost everyone who found Coney Island appealing did so in part because it provided an escape from the genteel standards of behavior that governed so much of American life at the time. In the amusement parks of Coney Island, people delighted in finding themselves in situations that in any other setting would have seemed embarrassing or improper: women's skirts blown above their heads with hot air; people pummeled with water and rubber paddles by clowns; hints of sexual freedom as strangers were forced to come into physical contact with one another on rides and amusements and as men and women revealed themselves to each other wearing bathing suits on the beach.

Coney Island remained popular throughout the first half of the twentieth century, and it continues to attract visitors today (although in much smaller numbers). But its heyday was in the years before World War I, when the exotic sights and thrilling adventures it offered had almost no counterparts elsewhere in American culture. When radio, movies, and eventually television began to offer their own kind of mass escapism, Coney Island gradually ceased to be the dazzling, unmatchable marvel it had seemed to earlier generations. ●

UNDERSTAND, ANALYZE, AND EVALUATE

1. How did Coney Island reflect the new culture of mass consumption?
2. What new ideas about leisure help account for the popularity of Coney Island in the early twentieth century?
3. What forms of popular culture today continue the Coney Island tradition of offering escapism, adventure, and excitement to a mass audience?

the urban working classes, had become by the 1880s a more popular and in some places more reputable sport, particularly after the adoption of the Marquis of Queensberry rules (by which fighters wore padded gloves and fought in three-minute rounds). The first modern boxing hero, John L. Sullivan, became heavyweight champion of the world in 1882. Even so, boxing remained illegal in some states until after World War I. Horse racing, popular since colonial times, became increasingly commercialized with the construction of large tracks and the establishment of large-purse races such as the Kentucky Derby.

GAMBLING AND SPORTS

Even in their infancy, spectator sports were closely associated with gambling. There was elaborate betting—some of it organized by underground gambling syndicates—on baseball and football almost from the start. One of the most famous incidents in the history of baseball was the alleged "throwing" of the 1919 World Series by the Chicago White Sox because of gambling (an incident that became known as the "Black Sox Scandal"). That event resulted in the banning of some of the game's most notable figures from the sport for life and the establishment of the office of commissioner of baseball to "clean up" the game. Boxing was troubled throughout its history by the influence of gambling and the frequent efforts of managers to "fix" fights in the interests of bettors. Horse racing as it became commercialized was openly organized around betting, with the race tracks themselves establishing odds and taking bets.

The rise of spectator sports and gambling was largely a response to the desire of men to create a distinctively male culture in cities. But not all sports were the province of men. A number of sports were emerging in which women became important participants. Golf and tennis seldom attracted crowds in the late nineteenth century, but both experienced a rapid increase in participation among relatively wealthy men and women. Bicycling and croquet also enjoyed widespread popularity in the 1890s among women as well as men. Women's colleges were beginning to introduce their students to strenuous sports as well–track, crew, swimming, and (beginning in the late 1890s) basketball–challenging the once prevalent notion that vigorous exercise was dangerous to women.

MUSIC AND THEATER

Many ethnic communities maintained their own theaters, in which immigrants listened to the music of their homelands and heard comedians making light of their experiences in the New World. Italian theaters often drew on the traditions of Italian opera to create sentimental musical events. The Yiddish theater built on the experiences of American

ETHNIC THEATER

Jews–and was the training ground for a remarkable group of musicians and playwrights who later went on to play a major role in mainstream, English-speaking theater.

Urban theaters also introduced one of the most distinctively American entertainment forms: the musical comedy, which evolved gradually from the comic operettas of European theater. George M. Cohan, an Irish vaudeville entertainer, became the first great creator of musical comedies in the early twentieth century; in the process of creating his many shows, he wrote a series of patriotic songs–"Yankee Doodle Dandy," "Over There," and "You're a Grand Old Flag"– that remained popular many decades later. Irving Berlin, a veteran of the Yiddish theater, wrote more than 1,000 songs for the musical theater during his long career, including such popular favorites as "Alexander's Ragtime Band" and "God Bless America."

Vaudeville, a form of theater adapted from French models, was the most popular urban entertainment in the first decades of the twentieth century. Even saloons and small community theaters could afford to offer their customers vaudeville, which consisted of a variety of acts (musicians, comedians, magicians, jugglers, and others) and was, at least in the beginning, inexpensive to produce. As the economic potential of vaudeville grew, some promoters– most prominently Florenz Ziegfeld of New York–staged much more elaborate spectacles. Vaudeville was also one of the few entertainment media open to black performers. They brought to it elements of the minstrel shows they had earlier developed for black audiences in the late nineteenth century. (See "Patterns of Popular Culture," pp. 420-421.)

VAUDEVILLE

THE FLORADORA SEXTET The Floradora Sextet was a popular vocal group of the late nineteenth and early twentieth centuries and became fixtures on the vaudeville and burlesque stages of many cities and resorts. They are shown here in an elaborately costumed production number at the famous Weber and Fields Music Hall in New York City, which opened in 1896. (© Bettmann/Corbis)

THE MOVIES

The most important form of mass entertainment (until the invention of radio and television) was the movies. Thomas Edison and others had created the technology of the motion picture in the 1880s. Not long after, short films became available to individual viewers through "peep shows" in pool halls, penny arcades, and amusement parks. Soon larger projectors made it possible to project the images onto big screens, which permitted substantial audiences to see films in theaters.

By 1900, Americans were becoming attracted in large numbers to these early movies—usually plotless films of trains or waterfalls or other spectacles designed mainly to show off the technology. D. W. Griffith carried the motion picture into a new era with his silent epics—*The Birth of a Nation* (1915), *Intolerance* (1916), and others—which introduced serious plots and elaborate productions to filmmaking. Some of these films—most notably *The Birth of a Nation*, with its celebration of the Ku Klux Klan and its demeaning portraits of African Americans—also contained notoriously racist messages, an indication, among other things, that the audiences for these early films were overwhelmingly white. Nevertheless, motion pictures were the first truly mass entertainment medium, reaching all areas of the country and almost all groups in the population.

THE BIRTH OF A NATION

WORKING-CLASS LEISURE

Leisure had a particular importance to working-class men and women—in part because it was a relatively new part of their lives and in part because it stood in such sharp contrast to the grueling environments in which many industrial workers labored. More than most other groups in society, workers spent their leisure time on the streets—walking alone or in groups, watching street entertainers, meeting friends, talking and joking. For people with time but little money, the life of the street was an appealing source of camaraderie and energy.

Another important setting for the leisure time of working-class men was the neighborhood saloon, which became a place where a worker could be sure of encountering a regular circle of friends. Saloons were often ethnically specific, in part because they served particular neighborhoods dominated by particular national groups. They also became political centers. Saloonkeepers were especially important figures in urban political machines, largely because they had regular contact with so many men in a neighborhood. When the Anti-Saloon League and other temperance organizations attacked the saloon, one of the reasons they cited was that eliminating saloons would weaken political machines. Opponents also noted correctly that saloons were sometimes places of crime,

IMPORTANCE OF THE SALOON

A NICKELODEON Before the rise of the great movie palaces, urban families flocked to "nickelodeons," small theaters that charged five cents for admission and showed many different films each day, including serials—dramas that drew audiences back into theaters day after day with new episodes of a running story. (© The Granger Collection, New York)

violence, and prostitution—an entryway into the dark underworld of urban life.

Boxing was a particularly popular sport among working-class men. Many workers could not afford to attend the great public boxing matches pairing such popular heroes as John L. Sullivan and "Gentleman Jim" Corbett. But there were less glittering boxing matches in small rings and even in saloons—bare-knuckled fights organized by ethnic clubs and other groups that gave men an opportunity to demonstrate their strength and courage, something that the working world did not always provide them.

THE FOURTH OF JULY

The Fourth of July played a large role in the lives of many working-class Americans. That was in part because in an age of six-day (and sometimes seven-day) workweeks and before regular vacations, it was for many decades one of the few full days of leisure—other than the Sabbath, during which activities were often restricted by law—that many workers had. Fourth of July celebrations were one of the highlights of the year in many ethnic, working-class communities. In Worcester, Massachusetts, for example, the Ancient Order of Hibernians (an Irish organization) sponsored boisterous picnics for the Irish working class of the city. Competing with them were Irish temperance organizations, which offered more sober and "respectable" entertainments to those relatively few workers who wished to avoid the heavy drinking at the Hibernian affairs. Other ethnic groups organized their own Fourth of July events—picnics, games, parades—making the day a celebration not just of the nation's independence, but of the cultures of

IMPORTANCE OF THE FOURTH OF JULY

immigrant communities. The city's affluent middle class, in the meantime, tended to stay away, remaining indoors or organizing family picnics at resort areas outside the city.

MASS COMMUNICATIONS

Urban industrial society created a vast market for new methods of transmitting news and information. Between 1870 and 1910, the circulation of daily newspapers increased nearly ninefold (from under 3 million to more than 24 million), a rate three times as great as the rate of population increase. And while standards varied widely from one paper to another, American journalism began to develop the beginnings of a professional identity. Salaries of reporters increased; many newspapers began separating the reporting of news from the expression of opinion; and newspapers themselves became important businesses.

One striking change was the emergence of national press services, which made use of the telegraph to supply news and features to papers throughout the country and which contributed as a result to the standardization of the product. By the turn of the century, important newspaper chains had emerged as well. The most powerful was William Randolph Hearst's, which by 1914 controlled nine newspapers and two magazines. Hearst and rival publisher Joseph Pulitzer helped popularize what became known as "yellow journalism"—a deliberately sensational, often lurid style of reporting presented in bold graphics, designed to reach a mass audience. (See "Patterns of Popular Culture," pp. 536–537.) Another major change occurred in the nature of American magazines. Beginning in the 1880s, new kinds of magazines appeared that were designed for a mass audience. One of the pioneers was Edward W. Bok, who took over the *Ladies' Home Journal* in 1899 and, by targeting a mass female audience, built its circulation to over 700,000.

EMERGENCE OF NEWSPAPER CHAINS

HIGH CULTURE IN THE AGE OF THE CITY

In addition to the important changes in popular culture that accompanied the rise of cities and industry, there were profound changes in the realm of "high culture"—in the ideas and activities of intellectuals and elites. Even the notion of a distinction between "highbrow" and "lowbrow" culture was relatively new to the industrial era. In the early nineteenth century, many cultural activities attracted people of widely varying backgrounds and targeted people of all classes. By the late nineteenth century, however, elites were developing a cultural and intellectual life quite separate from the popular amusements of the urban masses.

THE LITERATURE OF URBAN AMERICA

Some writers and artists—the local-color writers of the South, for example, and Mark Twain, in such novels as *Huckleberry Finn* and *Tom Sawyer*—responded to the new industrial civilization by evoking an older, more natural world. But others grappled directly with the modern order.

One of the strongest impulses in late-nineteenth- and early-twentieth-century American literature was the effort to re-create urban social reality. This trend toward realism found an early voice in Stephen Crane, who—although best known for his novel of the Civil War, *The Red Badge of Courage* (1895)—was the author of an earlier, powerful indictment of the plight of the working class. Crane created a sensation in 1893 when he published *Maggie: A Girl of the Streets*, a grim picture of urban poverty and slum life. Theodore Dreiser was even more influential in encouraging writers to abandon the genteel traditions of earlier times and turn to the social dislocations and injustices of the present. He did so both in *Sister Carrie* and in other, later novels (including *An American Tragedy*, published in 1925).

SOCIAL REALISM

Many of Dreiser's contemporaries followed him in chronicling the oppression of America's poor. In 1901 Frank Norris published *The Octopus*, an account of a struggle between oppressed wheat farmers and powerful railroad interests in California. The socialist writer Upton Sinclair published *The Jungle* in 1906, a novel designed to reveal the depravity of capitalism. It exposed abuses in the American meatpacking industry; and while it did not inspire the kind of socialist response for which Sinclair had hoped, it did help produce legislative action to deal with the problem. Kate Chopin, a southern writer who explored the oppressive features of traditional marriage, encountered widespread public abuse after publication of her shocking novel *The Awakening* in 1899. It described a young wife and mother who abandons her family in search of personal fulfillment. It was formally banned in some communities. William Dean Howells, in *The Rise of Silas Lapham* (1884) and other works, described what he considered the shallowness and corruption in the search for wealth.

Other critics of American society responded to the new civilization not by attacking it but by withdrawing from it. The historian Henry Adams published a classic autobiography in 1906, *The Education of Henry Adams*, in which he portrayed himself as a man disillusioned with and unable to relate to his society, even though he continued to live in it. The novelist Henry James lived the major part of his adult life in England and Europe and produced a series of coldly realistic novels—*The American* (1877), *Portrait of a Lady* (1881), *The Ambassadors* (1903), and others—that showed his ambivalence about the character of modern, industrial civilization.

The growing popularity of literature helped spawn a remarkable network of clubs, mostly formed and populated by women, to bring readers together to talk about books. Reading clubs proliferated rapidly in cities and even small towns, among African American as well as white women. They made literature a social experience for hundreds of thousands of women and created a tradition that has continued into the twenty-first century.

ART IN THE AGE OF THE CITY

American art through most of the nineteenth century had been overshadowed by the art of Europe. Many American artists studied and even lived in Europe. But others broke from the Old World traditions and experimented with new styles. Winslow Homer was vigorously American in his paintings of New England maritime life and other native subjects. James McNeil Whistler was one of the first Western artists to appreciate the beauty of Japanese color prints and to introduce Oriental concepts into American and European art.

By the first years of the new century, some American artists were turning decisively away from the traditional academic style, a style perhaps best exemplified in America by the brilliant portraitist John Singer Sargent. Instead, many younger painters were exploring the same grim aspects of modern life that were becoming the subject of American literature. Members of the so-called Ashcan school produced work startling in its naturalism and stark in its portrayal of the social realities of the era. John Sloan portrayed the dreariness of American urban slums; George Bellows caught the vigor and violence of his time in paintings and drawings of prize fights; Edward Hopper explored the starkness and loneliness of the modern city. The Ashcan artists were also among the first Americans to appreciate expressionism and abstraction; and they showed their interest in new forms in 1913 when they helped stage the famous and controversial Armory Show in New York City, which displayed works of the French Postimpressionists and of some American moderns.

ASHCAN SCHOOL

The work of these and other artists marked the beginning in America of an artistic movement known as modernism, a movement that had counterparts in many other areas of cultural and intellectual life as well. Rejecting the heavy reliance on established forms that characterized the "genteel tradition" of the nineteenth-century art world, modernists rejected the grip of the past and embraced new subjects and new forms. Where the genteel tradition emphasized the "dignified" and "elevated" aspects of civilization (and glorified the achievements of gifted elites), modernism gloried in the ordinary, even the coarse. Where the genteel tradition placed great importance on respect for the past and the maintenance of "standards," modernism looked to the future and gloried in the new. Eventually, modernism developed strict orthodoxies of its own. But in its early stages, it seemed to promise an escape from rigid, formal traditions and an unleashing of individual creativity.

THE IMPACT OF DARWINISM

The single most profound intellectual development in the late nineteenth century was the widespread acceptance of the theory of evolution, associated most prominently with the English naturalist Charles Darwin. Darwinism argued that the human species had evolved from earlier forms of life (and most recently from simian creatures similar to apes) through a process of "natural selection." It challenged the biblical story of the Creation and almost every other tenet of traditional American religious faith. History, Darwinism suggested, was not the working out of a divine plan, as most Americans had always believed. It was a random process dominated by the fiercest or luckiest competitors.

"NATURAL SELECTION"

The theory of evolution met widespread resistance at first from educators, theologians, and even many scientists. By the end of the century, however, the evolutionists had converted most members of the urban professional and educated classes. Even many middle-class Protestant religious leaders had accepted the doctrine, making significant alterations in theology to accommodate it. Evolution had become enshrined in schools

ON THE STEPS This painting is by George Luks (1867–1933), an American artist who belonged to the so-called Ashcan school. Luks and others revolted against what they considered the sterile formalism of academic painting and chose instead to portray realistic scenes of ordinary life. In 1913 they stirred the art world with a startling exhibition in New York, known as the Armory Show. In it they displayed not only their own work (which was relatively conventional in technique, even if sometimes daring in its choice of subjects), but also the work of innovative European artists, who were already beginning to explore wholly new artistic forms. (© David David Gallery/SuperStock)

and universities; few serious scientists any longer questioned its basic validity.

Unseen by most urban Americans at the time, however, the rise of Darwinism was contributing to a deep schism between the new, cosmopolitan culture of the city–which was receptive to new ideas such as evolution–and a traditional, provincial culture located mainly (although not wholly) in rural areas–which remained wedded to fundamentalist religious beliefs and older values. Thus the late nineteenth century saw not only the rise of a liberal Protestantism in tune with new scientific discoveries but also the beginning of an organized Protestant fundamentalism, rejecting evolution, which would make its presence felt politically in the 1920s and again in the late twentieth century and beyond.

Darwinism helped spawn other new intellectual currents. There was the Social Darwinism of William Graham Sumner **"PRAGMATISM"** and others, which industrialists used so enthusiastically to justify their favored position in American life. But there were also more sophisticated philosophies, among them a doctrine that became known as "pragmatism," which seemed peculiarly a product of America's changing material civilization. William James, a Harvard psychologist (and brother of the novelist Henry James), was the most prominent publicist of the new theory, although earlier intellectuals such as Charles S. Peirce and later ones such as John Dewey were also important to its development and dissemination. According to the pragmatists, modern society should rely for guidance not on inherited ideals and moral principles but on the test of scientific

inquiry. No idea or institution (not even religious faith) was valid, they claimed, unless it worked and unless it stood the test of experience. "The ultimate test for us of what a truth means," James wrote, "is the conduct it dictates or inspires."

A similar concern for scientific inquiry was intruding into the social sciences and challenging traditional orthodoxies. Economists such as Richard T. Ely and Simon Patten argued for a more active and pragmatic use of scientific discipline. Sociologists such as Edward A. Ross and Lester Frank Ward urged applying the scientific method to the solution of social and political problems. Historians such as Frederick Jackson Turner and Charles Beard argued that economic factors more than spiritual ideals had been the governing force in historical development. John Dewey proposed a new approach to education that placed less emphasis on the rote learning of traditional knowledge and more on a flexible, democratic approach to schooling, one that enabled students to acquire knowledge that would help them deal with the realities of their society.

The relativistic implications of Darwinism also promoted **GROWTH OF ANTHROPOLOGY** the growth of anthropology and encouraged some scholars to begin examining other cultures–most significantly, perhaps, the culture of American Indians–in new ways. A few white Americans began to look at Indian society as a coherent culture with its own norms and values that were worthy of respect and preservation, even though different from those of white society. But such ideas about Native Americans found very little support outside a few corners of the intellectual world until much later in the twentieth century.

DEMPSEY AND FIRPO The artist George Bellows began painting fight scenes in the first years of the twentieth century, when boxing appealed primarily to working-class urban communities. By 1924, when he painted this view of the Dempsey-Firpo fight, prizefighting had become one of the most popular sports in America. (© Whitney Museum of American Art, New York, USA/Bridgeman Images)

TOWARD UNIVERSAL SCHOOLING

A society that was coming to depend increasingly on specialized skills and scientific knowledge was, of course, a society with a high demand for education. The late nineteenth century, therefore, was a time of rapid expansion and reform of American schools and universities.

One example was the spread of free public primary and secondary education. In 1860, there **SPREAD OF PUBLIC EDUCATION** were only 100 public high schools in the entire United States. By 1900, the number had reached 6,000, and by 1914 over 12,000. By 1900, compulsory school attendance laws were in effect in thirty-one states and territories. But education was still far from universal. Rural areas lagged far behind urban-industrial ones in funding public education. And in the South, many blacks had no access to schools.

Educational reformers, few of whom shared the relativistic views of anthropologists, sought to provide educational opportunities for the Indian tribes as well, in an effort to "civilize" them and help were established in the last decades of the century—among them the state university systems of California, Illinois, Minnesota, and Wisconsin.

Other universities benefited from millions of dollars contributed by business and financial tycoons. Rockefeller, Carnegie, and others gave generously to such schools as the University of Chicago, Columbia, Harvard, Northwestern, Princeton, Syracuse, and Yale. Other philanthropists founded new universities or reorganized and renamed older ones to perpetuate their family names—Vanderbilt, Johns Hopkins, Cornell, Duke, Tulane, and Stanford.

EDUCATION FOR WOMEN

The post-Civil War era saw, too, an important expansion of educational opportunities for women, although such opportunities continued to lag far behind those available to men and were almost always denied to black women.

Most public high schools accepted women readily, but opportunities for higher education were few. At the end of the Civil War, only three American colleges were coeducational. In the years after the war, some of the land-grant colleges and universities in the Midwest and such private universities as Cornell and Wesleyan began to admit women along with men. But coeducation provided fewer opportunities than the creation of a network of women's colleges. Mount Holyoke, which had begun its life in 1836 as a "seminary" for women, became a full-fledged college in the 1880s. At about the same time, new female institutions were emerging: Vassar, Wellesley, Smith, Bryn Mawr, Wells, and Goucher. A few of the larger private universities created separate colleges for women on their campuses (Barnard at Columbia and Radcliffe at Harvard, for example). Proponents of women's colleges saw the institutions as places where female students would not be treated as "second-class citizens" by predominantly male student bodies and faculties.

WOMEN'S COLLEGES

The female college was part of an important phenomenon in the history of modern American women: the emergence of a distinctive women's community. Most faculty members and many administrators were women (often unmarried). And the life of the college produced a spirit of sorority and commitment among educated women that had important effects in later years, as women became the leaders of many reform activities. Most female college graduates eventually married, but many married at a later age than their non-college-educated counterparts and in some cases continued to pursue careers after marriage and motherhood. A significant minority, perhaps over 25 percent, did not marry, but devoted themselves exclusively to careers. A leader at Bryn Mawr remarked, "Our failures marry." That was surely rhetorical excess. The growth of female higher education clearly became for some women a liberating experience, persuading them that they had roles to perform in society in addition to those of wives and mothers.

WILLIAM GRAHAM SUMNER William Graham Sumner was an influential scholar who was appointed the first professor of sociology at Yale. A dynamic writer and teacher, he is best known for his promotion of "Social Darwinism"—a now-discredited theory that used the theory of evolution to explain differences among peoples. (© The Granger Collection, New York)

them adapt to white society. In the 1870s, reformers recruited small groups of Indians to attend Hampton Institute, a primarily black college. In 1879, Richard Henry Pratt, a former army officer, organized the Carlisle Indian Industrial School in Pennsylvania. Carlisle emphasized the kind of practical "industrial" education that Booker T. Washington had urged at his school at Tuskegee. Equally important, it isolated Indians from their tribes and tried to force them to assimilate to white norms. The purpose, Pratt said, was to "kill the Indian and save the man." Carlisle inspired other, similar schools in the West. Ultimately, the reform efforts failed, both because of Indian resistance and because of inadequate funding, incompetent administration, and poor teaching.

Colleges and universities were also proliferating rapidly in the late nineteenth century. They benefited particularly from the Morrill Land Grant Act of the Civil War era, by which the federal government had donated land to states for the establishment of colleges. After 1865, states in the South and West took particular advantage of the law. In all, sixty-nine "land-grant" institutions

"LAND-GRANT" INSTITUTIONS

AP CONNECTING THEMES

Chapter 18 focused on the reason for urban growth and the consequences of a rapidly increasing urban population. As you review Chapter 18, you should focus on why cities appealed to various groups of people and the factors influencing migration patterns. The increase in immigration and the changing sources of immigration provoked a nativist response, while many other Americans welcomed the new immigrants as a source of labor. The wave of immigration also affected urban growth, spurring a growth in ethnic communities and neighborhoods. Patterns of settlement and urban growth were also affected by improvements in urban transportation. Be able to discuss urban problems of poverty, crime, fire, disease, and pollution and assess the success of municipal governments in overcoming those problems. Lastly, Chapter 18 discussed the causes and effects of increased leisure time and movement toward a mass consumption society. Art and literature began to emphasize a style of "social realism," which had an effect of promoting calls to improve urban conditions, particularly for the poor.

The following themes have heightened importance in Chapter 18. You should now be able to do the following for each listed theme:

Identity: Analyze the ways in which migration led to changes in American identity for immigrants, working class people, and first-time urban residents.

Work, Exchange, and Technology: Explain the reasons for movement to a mass consumption society and the impact of increased leisure time on American society.

Peopling: Analyze the sources of urban population growth by examining migration patterns during the Gilded Age.

Politics and Power: Explain the positive and negative aspects of machine politics and boss rule on urban residents.

Environment and Geography: Analyze the impact of urbanization and industrialization on the American environment.

AP SUGGESTED STUDY

PEOPLE/PLACES/EVENTS As you study these items, think about how they demonstrate or relate to key concepts and historical themes from this chapter and previous chapters.

ALICE HAMILTON 498	HENRY JAMES 508	TAMMANY HALL 500
ARMORY SHOW 509	JACOB RIIS 495	TENEMENTS 495
ASHCAN SCHOOL 509	KATE CHOPIN 508	THEODORE DREISER 508
ASSIMILATION 491	MASS TRANSIT 496	UPTON SINCLAIR 508
BOSS RULE 499	MODERNISM 509	WILLIAM JAMES 510
"CITY BEAUTIFUL" MOVEMENT 494	MOVIES 507	WILLIAM M. TWEED 500
DARWINISM 509	NATIONAL CONSUMERS LEAGUE 502	WOMEN'S COLLEGES 511
DEPARTMENT STORES 501	NEWSPAPER CHAINS 508	YELLOW JOURNALISM 508
D.W. GRIFFITH 507	SOCIAL REALISM 508	YIDDISH THEATER 506
EDWARD HOPPER 509	STEPHEN CRANE 508	

AP TEST PRACTICE

Questions assume cumulative content knowledge from this chapter and previous chapters.

MULTIPLE CHOICE Use the graphs on page 491 and your knowledge of U.S. history to answer questions 1-3.

1. What was a direct effect of the immigration pattern shown in the graph on urban centers in America by the turn of the 20th century?

   (A) Dramatic slowing of migration of native-born Americans from rural areas to urban centers

   (B) Greater independence for immigrant women

   (C) Growth of distinct, ethnic neighborhoods

   (D) City governments subsidizing housing for the new arrivals

2. What trend developed in reaction to the events depicted in the graph, reflecting a similar trend to similar events in the earlier part of the 19th century?

   (A) Movement of African American women to urban centers in large numbers

   (B) A rise in nativist sentiment

   (C) A sharp drop in jobs available for the newly-arrived immigrants

   (D) The growth of suburbs

3. Some Americans in the late 19th century welcomed the events depicted in the graph because they allowed for

(A) a great deal of cultural diversity to experience in the cities

(B) a plentiful source for cheap labor

(C) a sharp increase in housing demands

(D) development of mass transit within urban areas, as more people needed to move about within the city

MULTIPLE CHOICE Use the map on page 488 to answer questions 4–5.

4. Which was a notable aspect of the population trend depicted by the map?

(A) Great numbers of African Americans moved from the South to the northern cities.

(B) Few immigrants in the late 19th century settled in cities, upon their arrival in America.

(C) Greater numbers of the elderly left the hardships of farm life for the cities.

(D) Greater numbers of young, rural women and of African Americans were migrating to the cities.

5. Which best describes the cause for the settlement patterns shown in the map?

(A) Availability of new lands in the West

(B) Industrialization and mechanized farming

(C) Increased diversity of immigrants to America

(D) The sharp rise in cotton and tobacco production

SHORT ANSWER Use your knowledge of U.S. history to answer questions 6–8.

6. Answer a, b, and c.

a) There were two very large surges in immigrants coming to America-one in the 1840s and 1850's and the other in the 1880s and 1890s. Briefly explain ONE major difference in these groups of people.

b) Briefly explain ONE important similar effect of these two immigration surges on American society.

c) Briefly explain ONE negative response to these surges in either period.

7. Use the photograph on page 501 to answer a, b, and c.

a) Briefly explain how the photograph demonstrates the changing nature of American society by the turn of the 20th century.

b) Briefly explain ONE development between 1860 and 1910 that led to or contributed to this change in American society.

c) Briefly explain ONE development between 1860 and 1910 that was a social consequence of this change in American society.

8. Answer a, b, and c.

a) For one of the areas below, briefly explain an intellectual development in American culture at the turn of the 20th century.

   • Art

   • Literature

   • Science

b) Provide an example of the intellectual development you explained above.

c) Briefly explain the social commentary your example is asserting relating to the modern American society of the turn of the 20th century.

LONG ESSAY Develop a thoughtful and thorough historical argument that answers the question below. Begin your essay with a thesis statement and support it with relevant historical evidence.

9. Analyze the extent to which industrialization caused social and cultural changes, leading to increased urbanization.

19 | FROM CRISIS TO EMPIRE

"A PARTY OF PATCHES," *JUDGE* MAGAZINE, JUNE 6, 1891 This political cartoon suggests the contempt and fear with which many easterners, in particular, viewed the emergence of the People's Party in 1891.
(© Kansas State Historical Society)

AP

HISTORICAL THINKING

1. **Patterns of Continuity and Change over Time** To what degree and in what ways did government policy toward big business change in the late 19th century?

2. **Historical Argumentation** Analyze the reasons for agrarian discontent in the late 19th century and evaluate the success of their efforts to resolve those issues.

3. **Historical Causation** Explain the domestic and international consequences of the Panic of 1893.

4. **Contextualization** Analyze the major problems facing the United States in the late 19th century and the response of political parties to those issues.

5. **Periodization** To what degree and in what ways did the Spanish-American War represent a turning point in American foreign policy?

Key Concept Correlations

Analyze the ways the historical developments you learn about in this chapter connect to the following AP Key Concepts.

6.1 The rise of big business in the United States encouraged massive migrations and urbanization, sparked government and popular efforts to reshape the U.S. economy and environment, and renewed debates over U.S. national identity.

6.3 The "Gilded Age" witnessed new cultural and intellectual movements in tandem with political debates over economic and social policies.

7.3 Global conflicts over resources, territories, and ideologies renewed debates over the nation's values and its role in the world while simultaneously propelling the United States into a dominant international military, political, cultural, and economic position.

Thematic Learning Objectives

WOR-3, 6, 7; WXT-3, 5, 6, 7; CUL-5; PEO-3, 6; POL-3, 6; ENV-5

CHAPTER 19 discusses politics in the Gilded Age, focusing on individual presidents who are sometimes referred to as the "forgettable presidents." The chapter describes emerging problems that the United States faced and the reaction of different political parties to those issues. In particular, it focuses on agrarian discontent and the ways farmers sought to redress those problems by organizing to combat the power of big business and government. The chapter examines the Panic of 1893 and its domestic and international impact. The chapter also looks at the psychological significance of the silver issue in the 1890s and the response of the major parties to that issue. Lastly, the chapter examines the reasons for and consequences of American emergence onto the world stage as both a military and economic power. You should pay particular attention to this development. As you read the chapter, evaluate the following ideas:

- The United States sought to expand its presence in world affairs to gain greater influence, open new markets, and gain access to new sources of raw materials.
- Popular challenges to the relationship between government and big business arose as a result of a growing disparity in the distribution of wealth.
- The Populist Party arose as farmers organized to seek redress of their grievances.
- The United States justified its new imperialism on the basis of economic, social, and political arguments.
- As a result of victory in the Spanish-American War, the United States acquired new territories and an expanded military and economic presence in the world.
- Debates between imperialists and anti-imperialists divided the country in the late 19th century.

THE POLITICS OF EQUILIBRIUM

The most striking feature of late-nineteenth-century politics was the remarkable stability of the party system. From the end of Reconstruction until the late 1890s, the electorate was divided almost precisely evenly between the Republicans and the Democrats. Sixteen states were solidly and consistently Republican, and fourteen states (most in the South) were solidly and consistently Democratic. Only five states (most importantly New York and Ohio) were usually in doubt, and their voters generally decided the results of national elections. The Republican Party captured the presidency in all but two of the elections of the era, but in the five presidential elections beginning in 1876, the average popular-vote margin separating the Democratic and Republican candidates was 1.5 percent. The congressional balance was similarly stable, with the Republicans generally controlling the Senate and the Democrats generally controlling the House.

ELECTORAL STABILITY

As striking as the balance between the parties was the intensity of public loyalty to them. In most of the country, Americans viewed their party affiliations with a passion and enthusiasm that is difficult for later generations to understand. Voter turnout in presidential elections between 1860 and 1900 averaged over 78 percent of all eligible voters (as compared with only about 50 percent in most recent elections). Even in nonpresidential years, from 60 to 80 percent of the voters turned out to cast ballots for congressional and local candidates. Large groups of potential voters were disenfranchised in these years: women in most states; almost all blacks and many poor whites in the South. But for adult white males, there were few franchise restrictions.

HIGH TURNOUT

What explains this extraordinary loyalty to the two political parties? It was not, certainly, that the parties took distinct positions on important public issues. They did so rarely. Party loyalties reflected other factors. Region was perhaps the most important. To white southerners, loyalty to the Democratic Party was a matter of unquestioned faith. It was the vehicle by which they had triumphed over Reconstruction and preserved white supremacy. To many northerners, white and black, Republican loyalties were equally intense. To them, the party of Lincoln remained a bulwark against slavery and treason.

Religious and ethnic differences also shaped party loyalties. The Democratic Party attracted most of the Catholic voters, recent immigrants, and poorer workers–groups that often overlapped. The Republican Party appealed to northern Protestants, citizens of old stock, and much of the middle class–groups that also had considerable overlap. Among the few substantive issues on which the parties took clearly different stands were matters connected with immigrants. Republicans tended to support measures restricting immigration and to favor temperance legislation, which many of them believed would help discipline immigrant communities. Catholics and immigrants viewed such proposals as assaults on them and their cultures and opposed them; the Democratic Party followed their lead.

Party identification, then, was usually more a reflection of cultural inclinations than a calculation of economic interest. Individuals might affiliate with a party because their parents had done so, or because it was the party of their region, their church, or their ethnic group.

CULTURAL BASIS OF PARTY IDENTIFICATION

THE NATIONAL GOVERNMENT

One reason the two parties managed to avoid substantive issues was that the federal government (and, to some degree, state and local governments as well) did relatively little. The government in Washington was responsible for delivering the mail, maintaining a military, conducting foreign policy, and collecting tariffs and taxes. It had few other responsibilities and few institutions with which it could have undertaken additional responsibilities even if it had chosen to do so.

There were significant exceptions. The federal government had been supporting the economic development of the nation for decades. In the late nineteenth century, that mostly meant giving tremendous subsidies to railroads, usually in the form of grants of federal land, to encourage them to extend their lines deeper into the nation. And as President Cleveland's intervention in the Pullman strike suggests, the government was also not averse to using its military and police power to protect capitalists from challenges from their workers.

In addition, the federal government administered a system of annual pensions for Union Civil War veterans who had retired from work and for their widows. At its peak, this

CIVIL WAR PENSION SYSTEM

pension system was making payments to a majority of the male citizens (black and white) of the North and to many women as well. Some reformers hoped to make the system permanent and universal. But their efforts failed, in part because the Civil War pension system was awash in party patronage and corruption. Other reformers–believers in "good government"–saw elimination of the pension system as a way to fight graft, corruption, and party rule. When the Civil War generation died out, the pension system died with it.

In most other respects, however, the United States in the late nineteenth century was a society without a modern, national government. The most powerful institutions were the two political parties (and the bosses and machines that dominated them) and the federal courts.

PRESIDENTS AND PATRONAGE

The power of party bosses had an important effect on the power of the presidency. The office had great symbolic importance, but its occupants were unable to do very much except distribute government appointments. A new president and his tiny staff had to make almost 100,000 appointments (most of them in the post office, the only really large government agency); and even in that function, presidents had limited latitude, since they had to avoid offending the various factions within their own parties.

Sometimes that proved impossible, as the presidency of Rutherford B. Hayes (1877-1881) demonstrated. By the end of his term, two groups–the Stalwarts, led by Roscoe Conkling of New

STALWARTS AND HALF-BREEDS

York, and the Half-Breeds, captained by James G. Blaine of Maine–were competing for control of the Republican Party. Rhetorically, the

PRESIDENT CHESTER A. ARTHUR Although originally a Stalwart and a follower of Roscoe Conkling, upon becoming president on the assassination of James A. Garfield, Chester A. Arthur attempted to reform the spoils system. The Pendleton Act, passed by Congress in 1883, required that some civil service jobs be filled by competitive examinations rather than patronage. (The Library of Congress (LC-DIG-ppmsca-28490))

Stalwarts favored traditional, professional machine politics, while the Half-Breeds favored reform. In fact, both groups were mainly interested in a larger share of the patronage pie. Hayes tried to satisfy both and ended up satisfying neither.

The battle over patronage overshadowed all else during Hayes's unhappy presidency. His one important substantive initiative—an effort to create a civil service system—attracted no support from either party. And his early announcement that he would not seek reelection only weakened him further. (His popularity in Washington was not enhanced by the decision of his wife, a temperance advocate widely known as "Lemonade Lucy," to ban alcoholic beverages from the White House.) Hayes's presidency was a study in frustration.

The Republicans managed to retain the presidency in 1880 in part because they agreed on a ticket that included a Stalwart and a Half-Breed. They nominated James A. Garfield, a veteran congressman from Ohio and a Half-Breed, for president and Chester A. Arthur of New York, a Stalwart, for vice president. The Democrats nominated General Winfield Scott Hancock, a minor Civil War commander with no national following. Benefiting from the end of the recession of 1879, Garfield won a decisive electoral victory, although his popular-vote margin was very thin. The Republicans also captured both houses of Congress.

Garfield began his presidency by trying to defy the Stalwarts in his appointments and by showing support for civil service

GARFIELD ASSASSINATED

reform. He soon found himself embroiled in an ugly public quarrel with Conkling and the Stalwarts. It was never resolved. On July 2, 1881, only four months after his inauguration, Garfield was shot twice while standing in the Washington railroad station by an apparently deranged gunman (and unsuccessful office seeker) who shouted, "I am a Stalwart and Arthur is president now!" Garfield lingered for nearly three months but finally died, a victim as much of inept medical treatment as of the wounds themselves.

Chester A. Arthur, who succeeded Garfield, had spent a political lifetime as a devoted, skilled, and open spoilsman and a close ally of Roscoe Conkling. But on becoming president, he tried—

PENDLETON ACT

like Hayes and Garfield before him—to follow an independent course and even to promote reform, aware that the Garfield assassination had discredited the traditional spoils system. To the dismay of the Stalwarts, Arthur kept most of Garfield's appointees in office and supported civil service reform. In 1883, Congress passed the first national civil service measure, the Pendleton Act, which required that some federal jobs be filled by competitive written examinations rather than by patronage. Relatively few offices fell under civil service at first, but its reach extended steadily.

CLEVELAND, HARRISON, AND THE TARIFF

In the unsavory election of 1884, the Republican candidate for president was Senator James G. Blaine of Maine—known to his admirers as the "Plumed Knight" but to many others as a symbol of seamy party politics. A group of disgruntled "liberal Republicans," known by their critics as the "mugwumps," announced they

would bolt the party and support an honest Democrat. Rising to the bait, the Democrats nominated Grover Cleveland, the reform governor of New York. He differed from Blaine on no substantive issues but had acquired a reputation as an enemy of corruption.

In a campaign filled with personal invective, what may have decided the election was the last-minute introduction of a religious controversy. Shortly before the election, a delegation

ELECTION OF 1884

of Protestant ministers called on Blaine in New York City; their spokesman, Dr. Samuel Burchard, referred to the Democrats as the party of "rum, Romanism, and rebellion." Blaine was slow to repudiate Burchard's indiscretion, and Democrats quickly spread the news that Blaine had tolerated a slander on the Catholic Church. Cleveland's narrow victory was probably a result of an unusually heavy Catholic vote for the Democrats in New York. Cleveland won 219 electoral votes to Blaine's 182; his popular margin was only 23,000.

Grover Cleveland was respected, if not often liked, for his stern and righteous opposition to politicians, grafters, pressure groups, and Tammany Hall. He had become famous as the "veto governor," as an official who was not afraid to say no. He was the embodiment of an era in which few Americans believed the federal government could, or should, do very much. Cleveland had always doubted the wisdom of protective tariffs. The existing high rates, he believed, were responsible for the annual surplus in federal revenues, which was tempting Congress to pass "reckless" and "extravagant" legislation, which he frequently vetoed. In December 1887, therefore, he asked Congress to reduce the tariff rates. Democrats in the House approved a tariff reduction, but Senate Republicans defiantly passed a bill of their own actually raising the rates. The resulting deadlock made the tariff an issue in the election of 1888.

The Democrats renominated Cleveland and supported tariff reductions. The Republicans settled on former senator Benjamin Harrison of Indiana, who was obscure but respectable (the grandson of President William Henry Harrison); he endorsed high tariffs. The campaign was the first since the Civil War to involve a clear question of economic difference between the parties. It was also one of the most corrupt (and closest) elections in American history. Harrison won an electoral majority of 233 to 168, but Cleveland's popular vote exceeded Harrison's by 100,000.

NEW PUBLIC ISSUES

Benjamin Harrison's record as president was little more substantial than that of his grandfather, who had died a month after taking office. Harrison had few visible convictions, and he made no effort to influence Congress. And yet during Harrison's passive administration, public opinion was beginning to force the government to confront some of the pressing social and economic issues of the day. Most notably, sentiment was rising in favor of legislation to curb the power of trusts.

By the mid-1880s, fifteen western and southern states had adopted laws prohibiting combinations that restrained competition. But corporations found it easy to escape limitations by incorporating in states, such as New Jersey and Delaware, that

LABOR AND MONOPOLY This 1883 cartoon appeared in *Puck*, a magazine popular for its satirical treatment of American politics. It expresses a common sentiment of the Populists and many others: that ordinary men and women (portrayed here by the pathetic figure of "labor" and by the grim members of the audience) were almost hopelessly overmatched by the power of corporate monopolies. The knight's shield, labeled "corruption of the legislature," and his spear, labeled "subsidized press," make clear that—in the view of the cartoonist at least—corporations had many allies in their effort to oppress workers. (The Library of Congress (LC-DIG-ppmsca-2412))

SHERMAN ANTITRUST ACT

offered them special privileges. If antitrust legislation was to be effective, its supporters believed, it would have to come from the national government. Responding to growing popular demands, both houses of Congress passed the Sherman Antitrust Act in July 1890, almost without dissent. Most members of Congress saw the act as a symbolic measure, one that would help deflect public criticism but was not likely to have any real effect on corporate power. For over a decade after its passage, the Sherman Act—indifferently enforced and steadily weakened by the courts—had almost no impact. As of 1901, the Justice Department had instituted many antitrust suits against labor unions, but only fourteen against business combinations; there had been few convictions.

The Republicans were more interested, however, in the issue they believed had won them the 1888 election: the tariff. Representative William McKinley of Ohio and Senator Nelson

McKINLEY TARIFF

W. Aldrich of Rhode Island drafted the highest protective measure ever proposed to Congress. Known as the McKinley Tariff, it became law in October 1890. But Republican leaders apparently misinterpreted public sentiment. The party suffered a stunning reversal in the 1890 congressional election. The

Republicans' substantial Senate majority was slashed to 8; in the House, the party retained only 88 of the 323 seats. McKinley himself was among those who went down in defeat. Nor were the Republicans able to recover in the course of the next two years. In the presidential election of 1892, Benjamin Harrison once again supported protection; Grover Cleveland, renominated by the Democrats, once again opposed it. A new third party, the People's Party, with James B. Weaver as its candidate, advocated substantial economic reform. Cleveland won 277 electoral votes to Harrison's 145 and had a popular margin of 380,000. Weaver ran far behind. For the first time since 1878, the Democrats won a majority of both houses of Congress.

The policies of Cleveland's second term were much like those of his first—devoted to minimal government and hostile to active efforts to deal with social or economic problems. Again, he supported a tariff reduction, which the House approved but the Senate weakened. Cleveland denounced the result but allowed it to become law as the Wilson-Gorman Tariff. It included only very modest reductions.

But public pressure was growing in the 1880s for other reforms, among them regulation of the railroads. Farm organizations in the Midwest (most notably the Grangers) had persuaded several state legislatures to pass regulatory legislation in the early

SHACKLED BY THE TARIFF This 1894 cartoon by the political satirist Louis Dalrymple portrays an unhappy Uncle Sam bound hand and foot by the McKinley Tariff and by what tariff opponents considered a closely related evil—monopoly. Members of the Senate are portrayed as tools of the various industries and special interests protected by the tariff. The caption, "A Senate for Revenue Only," is a parody of the antitariff rallying cry, "A tariff for revenue only," meaning that duties should be designed only to raise money for the government, not to stop imports of particular goods to protect domestic industries. A particularly provocative element of the cartoon is the image of two African American legislators promoting another controversial issue: "free silver" (see pp. 525–527). (© The Granger Collection, New York)

1870s. But in 1886, the Supreme Court—in *Wabash, St. Louis, and Pacific Railway Co. v. Illinois,* known as the *Wabash* case—ruled one of the Granger Laws in Illinois unconstitutional. According to the Court, the law was an attempt to control interstate commerce and thus infringed on the exclusive power of Congress. Later, the federal courts limited the powers of the states to regulate commerce even within their own boundaries.

Effective railroad regulation, it was now clear, could come only from the federal government. Congress responded to public pressure in 1887

INTERSTATE COMMERCE ACT

with the Interstate Commerce Act, which banned discrimination in rates between long and short hauls, required that railroads publish their rate schedules and file them with the government, and declared that all interstate rail rates must be "reasonable and just"—although the act did not define what that meant. A five-person agency, the Interstate Commerce Commission (ICC), was to administer the act. But it had to rely on the courts to enforce its rulings. For

THE STATE, WAR, AND NAVY BUILDING This sprawling Victorian office building was one of the largest in Washington, D.C., when it was constructed shortly after the Civil War. It housed the State, War, and Navy Departments until not long before World War II. It suggests both the degree to which the federal government was growing in the late nineteenth century and, more importantly, the degree to which it remained a tiny entity compared to what it would later become. This building, which stands directly next door to the White House, today houses a part (but only a part) of the president's staff. (The Library of Congress)

almost twenty years after its passage, the Interstate Commerce Act—which was, like the Sherman Act, haphazardly enforced and narrowly interpreted by the courts—had little practical effect.

THE AGRARIAN REVOLT

No group watched the performance of the federal government in the 1880s with more dismay than American farmers. Suffering from a long economic decline, afflicted with a painful sense of obsolescence, rural Americans were keenly aware of the problems of the modern economy and particularly eager for government assistance in dealing with them. The result of their frustrations was the emergence of one of the most powerful movements of political protest in American history: what became known as Populism.

The Grangers

According to popular myth, American farmers were the most individualistic of citizens. In reality, however, farmers had been making efforts to organize for many decades. The first major farm organization appeared in the 1860s: the Grange.

The Grange had its origins shortly after the Civil War in a tour through the South by a minor Agriculture Department

ORIGINS

official, Oliver H. Kelley. Kelley was appalled by what he considered the isolation and drabness of rural life. In 1867 he left the government and, with other department employees, founded the National Grange of

"THE GRANGE AWAKENING THE SLEEPERS" This 1873 cartoon illustrates the way the Grange embraced many of the same concerns that the Farmers' Alliances and their People's Party later expressed. A farmer is attempting to arouse passive citizens (lying in place of the "sleepers," or cross ties on railroad tracks), who are about to be crushed by a train. The cars bear the names of the costs of the railroads' domination of the agrarian economy. (© The Granger Collection, New York)

A POPULIST GATHERING Populism was a response to real economic and political grievances. But like most political movements of its time, it was also important as a cultural experience. For farmers in sparsely settled regions in particular, it provided an antidote to isolation and loneliness. This gathering of Populist farmers in Dickinson County, Kansas, shows how the political purposes of the movement were tightly bound up with its social purposes. (© Kansas State Historical Society)

the Patrons of Husbandry, to which he devoted years of labor as secretary and from which emerged a network of local organizations. At first, the Grangers defined their purposes modestly. They attempted to bring farmers together to learn new scientific agricultural techniques—to keep farming "in step with the music of the age." The Grangers also hoped to create a feeling of community, to relieve the loneliness of rural life.

The Grangers grew slowly for a time. But when the depression of 1873 caused a major decline in farm prices, membership rapidly increased. By 1875, the Grange claimed more than 800,000 members and 20,000 local lodges; it had chapters in almost every state but was strongest in the great staple-producing regions of the South and the Midwest.

As membership grew, the lodges in the Midwest began to focus less on the social benefits of organization and more on the economic possibilities. They attempted to organize marketing cooperatives to allow farmers to circumvent the hated "middlemen" (people who managed the sale of farmers' crops, taking a large cut of the profits for themselves). And they urged cooperative political action to curb monopolistic practices by railroads and warehouses.

ECONOMIC GRIEVANCES

The Grangers set up cooperative stores, creameries, elevators, warehouses, insurance companies, and factories that produced machines, stoves, and other items. More than 400 enterprises were in operation at the height of the movement, and some of them forged lucrative relationships with existing businesses. One corporation emerged specifically to meet the needs of the Grangers: the first mail-order business, Montgomery Ward and Company, founded in 1872, which helped farmers escape from overpriced local stores. Eventually, however, most of the Grange enterprises failed, both because of the inexperience of their operators and because of the opposition of the middlemen they were challenging.

The Grangers also worked to elect state legislators pledged to their program. Usually they operated through the existing parties, although occasionally they ran candidates under such independent party labels as "Antimonopoly" and "Reform." At their peak, they managed to gain control of the legislatures in most of the midwestern states. Their purpose was to subject the railroads to government controls. The Granger laws of the early 1870s imposed strict regulations on railroad rates and practices.

POLITICAL PROGRAM

But the new regulations were soon destroyed by the courts. That defeat, combined with the political inexperience of many Grange leaders and, above all, the temporary return of agricultural prosperity in the late 1870s, produced a dramatic decline in the power of the association. Some of the Granger cooperatives survived as effective economic vehicles for many years, but the movement as a whole dwindled rapidly. By 1880, its membership had shrunk to 100,000.

THE FARMERS' ALLIANCES

The successor to the Grange as the leading vehicle of agrarian protest began to emerge even before the Granger movement had faded. As early as 1875, farmers in parts of the South (most notably in Texas) were banding together in so-called Farmers' Alliances. By 1880, the Southern Alliance had more than 4 million members; and a comparable Northwestern Alliance was taking root in the plains states and the Midwest and developing ties with its southern counterpart.

Like the Granges, the Alliances were principally concerned with local problems. They formed cooperatives and other marketing mechanisms. They established stores, banks, processing plants, and other facilities for their members—to free them from the hated "furnishing merchants" who kept so many farmers in debt. Some Alliance leaders, however, also saw the movement as an effort to build a society in which economic competition might give way to cooperation. They argued for a sense of mutual, neighborly responsibility that would enable farmers to resist oppressive outside forces. Alliance lecturers traveled throughout rural areas attacking the concentration of power in great corporations and financial institutions and promoting cooperation as an alternative economic system.

From the beginning, women were full voting members in most local Alliances. Many held offices and served as lecturers. A few, most notably Mary E. Lease, went on to become fiery Populist orators. (Lease was

MARY LEASE

MARY E. LEASE The fiery Populist orator Mary E. Lease was a fixture on the Alliance lecture circuit in the 1890s. She made some 160 speeches in 1890 alone. Her critics called her the "Kansas Pythoness," but she was popular among populist farmers with her denunciations of banks, railroads, and "middlemen," and her famous advice to "raise less corn and more hell." (© Corbis)

BEARING THE CROSS OF GOLD The cartoonist Grant Hamilton created this image of William Jennings Bryan shortly after he made his famous "Cross of Gold" speech at the Democratic National Convention, which led to his nomination for president. The cartoon highlights two of the most powerful images in Bryan's speech—a "crown of thorns" and a "cross of gold," both biblical references and both designed to represent the oppression that the gold standard imposed on working people. (© The Granger Collection, New York)

famous for urging farmers to "raise less corn and more hell.") Others emphasized issues of particular concern to women, especially temperance. Like their urban counterparts, agrarian women argued that sobriety was a key to stability in rural society. Alliances (and the Populist Party they eventually created) advocated extending the vote to women in many areas of the country.

Although the Alliances quickly became far more widespread than the Granges had ever been, they suffered from similar problems. Their cooperatives did not always work well, partly because the market forces operating against them were sometimes too strong to be overcome, partly because the cooperatives themselves were often mismanaged. These economic frustrations helped push the movement into a new phase at the end of the 1880s: the creation of a national political organization.

In 1889, the Southern and Northwestern Alliances, despite continuing differences between them, agreed to a loose merger. The next year the Alliances held a national convention at Ocala, Florida, and issued the so-called Ocala Demands, which

were, in effect, a party platform. In the 1890 off-year elections, candidates supported by the Alliances won partial or complete control of the legislatures in twelve states. They also won six governorships, three seats in the U.S. Senate, and approximately fifty in the U.S. House of Representatives. Many of the successful Alliance candidates were Democrats who had benefited–often passively–from Alliance endorsements. But dissident farmers drew enough encouragement from the results to contemplate further political action, including forming a party of their own.

Sentiment for a third party was strongest among the members of the Northwestern Alliance. But several southern lead-

BIRTH OF THE PEOPLE'S PARTY

ers supported the idea as well–among them Tom Watson of Georgia, the only southern congressman elected in 1890 openly to identify with the Alliance, and Leonidas L. Polk of North Carolina, perhaps the ablest mind in the movement. Alliance leaders discussed plans for a third party at meetings in

Cincinnati in May 1891 and St. Louis in February 1892. Then, in July 1892, 1,300 exultant delegates poured into Omaha, Nebraska, to proclaim the creation of the new party, approve an official set of principles, and nominate candidates for the presidency and vice presidency. The new organization's official name was the People's Party, but its members were more commonly known as Populists.

The election of 1892 (which restored Grover Cleveland to the presidency) demonstrated the potential power of the new movement. The Populist presidential candidate was James B. Weaver of Iowa, a former Greenbacker who received the nomination after the death of Leonidas Polk, the early favorite. Weaver polled more than 1 million votes, 8.5 percent of the total, and carried six mountain and plains states for 22 electoral votes. Nearly 1,500 Populist candidates won election to seats in state legislatures. The party elected three governors, five senators, and ten congressmen. It could also claim the support of many Republicans and Democrats in Congress who had been elected by appealing to populist sentiment.

THE POPULIST CONSTITUENCY

The Populists dreamed of creating a broad political coalition. But populism always appealed principally to farmers, particularly to small farmers with little long-range economic security—people whose operations were minimally mechanized, if at all, who relied on one crop, and who had access only to limited credit. In the Midwest, the Populists were usually family farmers struggling to hold on to their land (or to get it back). In the South, there were many modest landowners too, but in addition there were significant numbers of sharecroppers and tenant farmers. Whatever their differences, however, most Populists had at least one thing in common: they were engaged in a type of farming that was becoming less viable in the face of new, mechanized, diversified, and consolidated commercial agriculture.

Populists tended to be not only economically but also culturally marginal. The movement appealed above all to geographically isolated farmers who felt cut off from the mainstream of national life and resented their isolation. Populism gave such people an outlet for their grievances; it also provided them with a social experience, a sense of belonging to a community that they had previously lacked.

The Populists were also notable for the groups they failed to attract. There were energetic efforts to include labor within the coalition. Representatives of the Knights of Labor attended early organizational meetings; the new party added a labor plank to its platform—calling for shorter hours for workers and restrictions on immigration, and denouncing the use of private detective agencies as strikebreakers in labor disputes. On the whole, however, Populism never attracted significant labor support, in part because the economic interests of labor and the interests of farmers were often at odds.

One exception was the Rocky Mountain states, where the Populists did have some significant success in attracting miners to their cause. They did so partly because local Populist

"FREE SILVER" leaders endorsed a demand for "free silver," the idea of permitting silver to become, along with gold, the basis of the currency so as to expand the money supply. In Colorado, Idaho, Nevada, and other areas of the Far West, silver mining was an important activity, and the People's Party enjoyed substantial, if temporary, success there.

In the South, white Populists struggled with the question of whether to accept African Americans into the party. Their numbers and poverty made black farmers possibly valuable allies. There was an important black component to the movement—a network of "Colored Alliances" that by 1890 had more than one and a quarter million members. But most white Populists were willing to accept the assistance of African Americans only as long as it was clear that whites would remain indisputably in control. When southern conservatives began to attack the Populists for undermining white supremacy, the interracial character of the movement quickly faded.

"COLORED ALLIANCES"

Most of the Populist leaders were members of the rural middle class: professional people, editors and lawyers, or long-time politicians and agitators. Many active Populists were women. Some Populist leaders were somber, serious theoreticians; others were semihysterical rabble-rousers. In the South, in particular, Populism produced the first generation of what was to become a distinctive and enduring political breed—the "southern demagogue." Tom Watson in Georgia, Jeff Davis in Arkansas, and others attracted widespread popular support by arousing the resentment of poor southerners against the entrenched planter aristocracy.

POPULIST IDEAS

The reform program of the Populists was spelled out first in the Ocala Demands of 1890 and then, even more clearly, in the Omaha platform of 1892. It proposed a system of "subtreasuries," which would replace and strengthen the cooperatives of Grangers and Alliances that had been experimenting for years. The government would establish a network of warehouses, where farmers could deposit their crops. Using those crops as collateral, growers could then borrow money from the government at low rates of interest and wait for the price of their goods to go up before selling them. In addition, the Populists called for the abolition of national banks, the end of absentee ownership of land, the direct election of U.S. senators (which would weaken the power of conservative state legislatures), and other devices to improve the ability of the people to influence the political process. They called as well for regulation and (after 1892) government ownership of railroads, telephones, and telegraphs. And they demanded a system of government-operated postal savings banks, a graduated income tax, and the inflation of the currency. Eventually, the party as a whole embraced the demand of its western members for the remonetization of silver.

POPULIST PLATFORM

Some Populists were openly anti-Semitic, pointing to the Jews as leaders of the obscure financial forces attempting to enslave

THE CHAUTAUQUAS

EDUCATION and oratory were part of American life in the nineteenth century. Starting in 1826, lyceums were among the first public organizations to provide adults with both. Participants met in libraries, vacant schools, and elsewhere. Organizers estimated that 13,000 people attended public lectures. An even-larger movement to provide instructional lectures and speeches arose during the 1880s and 1890s from the Populist movement. Men and women flocked by the hundreds or even thousands to hear speeches and discussions provided by itinerant speakers.

The most famous of these lectures were the Chautauquas, founded in the summer of 1874 by two enterprising men from the Chautauqua Lakes area in western New York State. Within a few years, the Chautauqua Assembly had expanded to include lectures on literary, scientific, theological, and practical subjects and was attracting ever-larger audiences for one- or two-week "schools." In 1883, the New York State legislature granted the Assemblies a charter and gave them the name "The Chautauqua University."

So successful (and profitable) were the Chautauqua Assemblies that scores of towns and villages began establishing lecture series of their own—"Little Chautauquas"—throughout the Midwest. At the peak of this movement, a Chicago promoter organized traveling programs to tour rural areas across the United States—visiting more than 8,000 different communities within a single year.

From 1904 through the mid-1920s, these "traveling Chautauquas" attracted enormous crowds and generated great excitement almost everywhere they went. On the day of a Chautauqua lecture, roads

CHAUTAUQUA ASSEMBLY This Chautauqua meeting occurred in Clarinda, Iowa. It was one of hundreds of such meetings during the 1880s and 1890s that met the need of thousands of people across the country for knowledge and learning. (The Library of Congress (LC-USZ62-24372A))

were sometimes clogged for miles in every direction with buggies and, later, automobiles transporting farm families

them. Others were anti-intellectual, anti-eastern, and anti-urban. A few of the leading Populists gave an impression of personal failure, brilliant instability, and brooding communion with mystic forces. Ignatius Donnelly, for example, wrote one book locating the lost isle of Atlantis, another claiming that Bacon had written Shakespeare's plays, and still another–*Caesar's Column* (1891)–presenting a deranged vision of bloody revolution and the creation of a populist utopia. Tom Watson, once a champion of interracial harmony, ended his career baiting blacks and Jews.

Yet the occasional bigotry of some Populists should not dominate the image of Populism as a whole, which was a serious effort to find solutions to real problems. Populists emphat-

POPULISM'S IDEOLOGICAL CHALLENGE

ically rejected the laissez-faire orthodoxies of their time, including the idea that the rights of ownership are absolute. They raised one of the most overt and powerful challenges of the era to the direction in which American industrial capitalism was moving.

THE CRISIS OF THE 1890s

The agrarian protest was only one of many indications of the national political crisis emerging in the 1890s. There was a severe depression, widespread labor unrest and violence, and the continuing failure of either major party to respond to the growing distress. The rigid conservatism of Grover Cleveland, who

took office for the second time just at the moment the economy collapsed, meant that the federal government did little to alleviate the crisis. Out of this growing sense of urgency came some of the most heated political battles in American history, culminating in the dramatic campaign of 1896, on which, many Americans came to believe, the future of the nation was hanging.

THE PANIC OF 1893

The Panic of 1893 precipitated the most severe depression the nation had yet experienced. It began in March 1893, when the Philadelphia and Reading Railroad, unable to meet payments on loans, declared bankruptcy. Two months later, the National Cordage Company failed as well. Together, the two corporate failures triggered a collapse of the stock market. And since many of the major New York banks were heavy investors in the stock market, a wave of bank failures soon began. That caused a contraction of credit, which meant that many of the new, aggressive, and loan-dependent businesses soon went bankrupt.

There were other, longer-range causes of the financial col-

OVEREXPANSION AND WEAK DEMAND

lapse. Depressed prices in agriculture since 1887 had weakened the purchasing power of farmers, the largest group in the population. Depression conditions in Europe caused a loss of American markets abroad and a withdrawal by foreign investors of gold invested in the United States. Railroads and other major industries had expanded too rapidly, well

BRYAN AT CHAUTAUQUA William Jennings Bryan, the most famous orator of the early twentieth century, was a fixture at Chautauqua meetings, not only at the original Chautauqua in New York but also at the traveling and tented Chautauquas that spread across the country. Here he is shown speaking in Madison, Wisconsin. (The Library of Congress (LC-USZC4-4646))

dressed in their best clothes, carrying picnic baskets, straining excitedly to see the tents, posters, and crowds.

Chautauqua speakers were drawn from many walks of life, but they included some of the greatest figures of the age: William Jennings Bryan, William McKinley, Theodore Roosevelt, Booker T. Washington, Eugene V. Debs, and many others. The Chautauquas themselves also made some speakers rich and famous. The Philadelphia minister Russell Conwell, for example, made a great name (and a great fortune) with his famous "Acres of Diamonds" lectures, which he delivered thousands of times over the course of several decades, preaching a simple and attractive message: "Get rich . . . for money is power and power ought to be in the hands of good people." Conwell's sermon was characteristic of one kind of popular Chautauqua event – lectures that stressed self-improvement. Other such lectures stressed religion and health.

overexpansion of ambitious organizers. But the original Chautauqua Assembly in upstate New York survived, although in much-diminished form. It exists today as a resort that continues to offer lectures and other educational events to a large and dedicated clientele. ●

UNDERSTAND, ANALYZE, AND EVALUATE

1. During a time when they faced so many economic problems, why would farmers have found the Chautauquas so appealing?
2. Why would so many prominent public figures have participated in the Chautauquas?
3. Can you think of any parallels today to the Chautauqua movement of the early twentieth century?

The Chautauqua circuit was one of the best ways for a speaker to reach large numbers of people, which is one reason why so many progressive leaders and feminist reformers eagerly joined in. It was, for a time, one of the most powerful forms of communication in the nation.

The traveling Chautauquas declined during the 1920s and almost vanished in the 1930s—victims of radio, movies, and the automobile; the spread of public education to rural areas; and the reckless

beyond market demand. The depression reflected the degree to which the American economy was now interconnected, the degree to which failures in one area affected all other areas. And the depression showed how dependent the economy was on the health of the railroads, which remained the nation's most powerful corporate and financial institutions. When the railroads suffered, as they did beginning in 1893, everything suffered.

Once the panic began, its effects spread with startling speed. Within six months, more than 8,000 businesses, 156 railroads, and 400 banks failed. Already low agricultural prices tumbled further. Up to 1 million workers, 20 percent of the labor force, lost their jobs—the highest level of unemployment in American history to that point. The depression was unprecedented not only in its severity but also in its persistence. Although there was some improvement beginning in 1895, prosperity did not fully return until 1901.

The suffering the depression caused naturally produced social unrest, especially among the enormous numbers of unemployed workers. In 1894, Jacob S. Coxey, an Ohio businessman **"COXEY'S ARMY"** and Populist, began advocating a massive public works program to create jobs for the unemployed and an inflation of the currency. When it became clear that his proposals were making no progress in Congress, Coxey announced that he would "send a petition to Washington with boots on"—a march of the unemployed to the capital to present their demands to the government. "Coxey's Army," as it was known, numbered only about

500 when it reached Washington, D.C., after having marched on foot from Masillon, Ohio. Armed police barred them from the Capitol and arrested Coxey. He and his followers were herded into camps because their presence supposedly endangered public health. Congress took no action on their demands.

To many middle-class Americans, the labor turmoil of the time–the Homestead and Pullman strikes, for example (see pp. 481-483)–was a sign of a dangerous instability, even perhaps a revolution. Labor radicalism–some of it real, more of it imagined by the frightened middle class–heightened the general sense of crisis among the public.

THE SILVER QUESTION

The financial panic weakened the government's monetary system. President Cleveland believed that the instability of the currency was the primary cause of the depression. The "money question," therefore, became the basis for some of the most dramatic political conflicts of the era.

At the heart of the complicated debate was the question of what would form the basis of the dollar. Today, the value of the dollar rests on little more than public confidence in the government. But in the nineteenth century, many people believed that currency was worthless if there was not something concrete behind it—precious metal (specie), which holders of paper money could collect if they presented their currency to a bank or to the Treasury.

During most of its existence as a nation, the United States had recognized two metals—gold and silver—as a basis for the dollar, a situation known as "bimetallism." In the 1870s, however, that had changed. The official ratio of the value of silver to the value of gold for purposes of creating currency (the "mint ratio") was 16 to 1: sixteen ounces of silver equaled one ounce of gold. But the actual commercial value of silver (the "market ratio") was much higher than that. Owners of silver could get more by selling it for manufacture into jewelry and other objects than they could by taking it to the mint for conversion to coins. So they stopped taking it to the mint, and the mint stopped coining silver.

In 1873, Congress passed a law that seemed simply to recognize the existing situation by officially discontinuing silver coinage. Few people objected at the time. But in the course of the 1870s, the market value of silver fell well below the official mint ratio of 16 to 1. (Sixteen ounces of silver, in other words, were now worth less, not more, than one ounce of gold.) Silver became attractive for coinage again. In discontinuing silver coinage, Congress had eliminated a potential method of expanding the currency (and had eliminated a potential market for silver miners). Before long, many Americans concluded that a conspiracy of big bankers had been responsible for the "demonetization" of silver and referred to the law as the "Crime of '73."

Two groups of Americans were especially determined to undo the "Crime of '73." One consisted of the silver-mine owners,

"CRIME OF '73" now understandably eager to have the government take their surplus silver and pay them much more than the market price. The other group consisted of discontented farmers, who wanted an increase in the quantity of money—an inflation of the currency—as a means of raising the prices of farm products and easing payment of the farmers' debts. The inflationists demanded that the government return at once to "free silver"—that is, to the "free and unlimited coinage of silver" at the old ratio of 16 to 1. But by the time the depression began in 1893, Congress had made no more than a token response to their demands.

At the same time, the nation's gold reserves were steadily dropping. President Cleveland believed that the chief cause of the weakening gold reserves was the Sherman Silver Purchase Act of 1890 (a sop to silver miners), which had required the government to purchase (but not to coin) silver and to pay for it in gold. Early in his second administration, therefore, a special session responded to Cleveland's request and repealed the Sherman Act—although only after a bitter and divisive battle that helped create a permanent split in the Democratic Party. The president's gold policy had aligned the southern and western Democrats in a solid alliance against him and his eastern followers.

By now, both sides had invested the currency question **SYMBOLIC IMPORTANCE OF THE CURRENCY QUESTION** with great symbolic and emotional importance. Indeed, the issue aroused passions rarely seen in American politics, culminating in the tumultuous presidential election

TAKING ARMS AGAINST THE POPULISTS Kansas was a Populist stronghold in the 1890s, but the new party faced powerful challenges. In 1893, state Republicans disputed an election that the Populists believed had given them control of the legislature. When the Populists occupied the statehouse, Republicans armed themselves, drove out the Populists, and seized control of the state government. Republican members of the legislature pose here with their weapons in a photograph perhaps intended as a warning to any Populists inclined to challenge them. (© Kansas State Historical Society)

COXEY'S ARMY Jacob S. Coxey leads his "army" of unemployed men through the town of Allegheny, Pennsylvania, in 1894, en route to Washington, D.C., where he hoped to pressure Congress to approve his plans for a massive public works program to put people back to work. (© Archive Photos/Getty Images)

of 1896. Supporters of the gold standard considered its survival essential to the honor and stability of the nation. Supporters of free silver considered the gold standard an instrument of tyranny. "Free silver" became to them a symbol of liberation. Silver would be a "people's money," as opposed to gold, the money of oppression and exploitation. It would eliminate the indebtedness of farmers and of whole regions of the country. A graphic illustration of the popularity of the silver issue was the enormous success of William H. Harvey's *Coin's Financial School,* published in 1894, which became one of the great best-sellers of its age. The fictional Professor Coin ran an imaginary school specializing in finance, and the book consisted of his lectures and his dialogues with his students. The professor's brilliant discourses left even his most vehement opponents dazzled as he persuaded his listeners, with simple logic, of the almost miraculous restorative qualities of free silver: "It means the reopening of closed factories, the relighting of fires in darkened furnaces; it means hope instead of despair; comfort in place of suffering; life instead of death."

"A CROSS OF GOLD"

Most Populists did not pay much attention to the silver issue at first. But as the party developed strength, the money question became more important to its leaders. The Populists desperately needed funds to finance their campaigns. Silver-mine owners were willing to provide assistance but insisted on an elevation of the currency plank. The Populists also needed to form alliances with other political groups. The "money question" seemed a way to win the support of many people not engaged in farming but nevertheless starved for currency.

POPULISM

THE scholarly debates over Populism have tended to reflect a larger debate among historians on populist politics. Some historians viewed the Populists with suspicion and hostility.

(The Library of Congress (LC-USZC4-1473))

Others have viewed Populism approvingly. To them, the Populists have appeared as essentially admirable, democratic activists.

This latter view shaped the first, and for many years the only, general history of Populism: John D. Hicks's *The Populist Revolt* (1931). Hicks described Populists as people reacting rationally and progressively to economic misfortune. They were proposing reforms that would limit the power of the new financial titans and restore a measure of control to the farmers. Populism was, he wrote, "the last phase of a long and perhaps a losing struggle—the struggle to save agricultural America from the devouring jaws of industrial America." A losing struggle, perhaps, but not a vain one; for many of the reforms the Populists advocated, Hicks implied, became the basis of later progressive legislation.

An alternative to this generally approving view of Populism appeared in the early 1950s when some scholars, recalling the European fascism of World War II and wary about contemporary communism, took a more hostile view of mass popular politics. A leading proponent of this harsh new view was Richard Hofstadter. In *The Age of Reform* (1955), Hofstadter conceded that Populism embraced some progressive

THE EMERGENCE OF BRYAN

As the election of 1896 approached, Republicans, watching the failure of the Democrats to deal effectively with the depression, were confident of success. Party leaders, led by the

WILLIAM McKINLEY Ohio boss Marcus A. Hanna, settled on Governor William McKinley of Ohio, who had as a member of Congress authored the 1890 tariff act, as the party's presidential candidate. The Republican platform opposed the free coinage of silver except by agreement with the leading commercial nations (which everyone realized was unlikely). Thirty-four delegates from the mountain and plains states walked out of the convention in protest and joined the Democratic Party.

The Democratic National Convention of 1896 was the scene of unusual drama. Southern and western delegates, eager to neutralize the challenge of the People's Party, were determined to seize control of the party from conservative easterners and incorporate some Populist demands–among them free silver–into the Democratic platform. They wanted as well to nominate a pro-silver presidential candidate.

Defenders of the gold standard seemed to dominate the debate, until the final speech. Then William Jennings Bryan, a handsome, thirty-six-year-old congressman from Nebraska

"CROSS OF GOLD" SPEECH already well known as an effective orator, mounted the podium to address the convention. His great voice echoed through the hall as he defended "free silver" in what became one of the most famous political speeches in American history. The closing passage sent his audience into something close to a frenzy: "Having behind us the producing masses of this nation and the world, supported by the commercial interests, the laboring interests and the toilers everywhere, we will answer their demand for a gold standard by saying to them: 'You shall not press down upon the brow of labor this crown of thorns; you shall not crucify mankind upon a cross of gold.'" It became known as the "Cross of Gold" speech.

In the aftermath of Bryan's powerful speech, the convention voted to adopt a pro-silver platform. And the following day, Bryan (as he had eagerly and not entirely secretly hoped) was nominated for president on the fifth ballot. He was, and remains, the youngest person ever nominated for president by ideas and advocated some sensible reforms, but he concentrated primarily on exposing both the "soft" and the "dark" sides of the movement. Populism was "soft," Hofstadter claimed, because it rested on a nostalgic and unrealistic myth, because it romanticized the nation's agrarian past and refused to confront the realities of modern life. It was "dark," he argued, because it was permeated with bigotry and ignorance. Populists, he claimed, revealed anti-Semitic tendencies, and they displayed animosity toward intellectuals, easterners, and urbanites as well.

Challenges to Hofstadter's thesis arose almost immediately. Norman Pollack argued in a 1962 study, *The Populist Response to Industrial America,* that the agrarian revolt had rested not on nostalgic, romantic concepts but, rather, on a sophisticated, farsighted, and even radical vision of reform—one that recognized the realities of an industrial economy, but that sought to make that economy more equitable and democratic by challenging many of the premises of capitalism. Walter T. K. Nugent, in *Tolerant Populists* (1963), argued that the Populists in Kansas were far from bigoted, that they not only tolerated but welcomed Jews and other minorities into their party, and that they offered a practical, sensible program. Lawrence Goodwyn, in *Democratic Promise* (1976), argued similarly that the Populists advocated an intelligent, and above all a democratic, alternative to the inequities of modern capitalism.

Historians were debating not only the question of what Populism meant. They were also arguing over who the Populists were. Hicks, Hofstadter, and Goodwyn disagreed on many things, but they shared a general view of the Populists as victims of economic distress—usually one-crop farmers in marginal agricultural regions victimized by drought and debt. Other scholars, however, suggested that the problem of identifying the Populists is more complex. Sheldon Hackney, in *Populism to Progressivism in Alabama* (1969), argued that the Populists were not only economically troubled but also socially rootless, "only tenuously connected to society by economic function, by personal relationships, by stable community membership, by political participation, or by psychological identification with the South's distinctive myths." Peter Argersinger, Stanley Parsons, James Turner, and others have similarly suggested that Populists were characterized by a form of social and even geographic isolation. Steven Hahn's 1983 study, *The Roots of Southern Populism,* identified poor white farmers in the "upcountry" as the core of Populist activity in Georgia; and Hahn argued that Populists were reacting not simply to the psychic distress of being "left behind," but also to a real economic threat to their way of life—to the encroachments of a new commercial order of which they had never been a part.

Another debate concerns the legacy of Populism. In *Roots of Reform* (1999), Elizabeth Sanders contends that Populism did not die as a movement after the 1896 election. On the contrary, she argues, the Populists succeeded in dominating much of the Democratic Party in the following decades and turning it into a vehicle for advancing the interests of farmers and the broader reform causes for which Populists had fought. Michael Kazin, in *The Populist Persuasion* (1994), argues that a Populist tradition has survived throughout much of American history, influencing movements as disparate as those led by Huey Long in the 1930s, the New Left and George Wallace in the 1960s, Ross Perot in the 1990s, and the Tea Party movement in the aftermath of the 2008 economic collapse. Other historians, however, maintain that the term *populism* has been used (and misused) so widely as to have become virtually meaningless, that it really applies only to the agrarian insurgents of the 1890s. ●

AP HISTORICAL ARGUMENTATION AND INTERPRETATION

Questions assume cumulative content knowledge from this chapter and previous chapters.

1. Identify the respective arguments of four of the historians discussed, regarding Populism. For each, provide one piece of historical evidence that supports the argument.

2. Describe an example that was discussed, in which the times in which the historian lived most likely influenced his or her view.

3. With which historian's interpretation do you most agree? Explain why, supporting your argument with historical evidence.

---

a major party. Republican and conservative Democrats attacked Bryan as a dangerous demagogue. But his many admirers hailed him as the Great Commoner. He was a potent symbol of rural, Protestant, middle-class America.

The choice of Bryan and the nature of the Democratic platform created a quandary for the Populists. They had **"FUSION"** expected both major parties to adopt conservative programs and nominate conservative candidates, leaving the Populists to represent the growing forces of protest. But now the Democrats had stolen much of their thunder. The Populists faced the choice of naming their own candidate and splitting the protest vote or endorsing Bryan and losing their identity as a party. By now, the Populists had embraced the free-silver cause, but most Populists still believed that other issues were more important. Many argued that "fusion" with the Democrats—who had endorsed free silver but ignored most of the other Populist demands—would destroy their party. But the majority concluded that there was no viable alternative. Amid considerable acrimony, the convention voted to support Bryan.

THE CONSERVATIVE VICTORY

The campaign of 1896 produced desperation among conservatives. The business and financial community, frightened beyond reason at the prospect of a Bryan victory, contributed lavishly to the Republican campaign, which may have spent as much as $7 million, as compared to the Democrats' $300,000. From his home at Canton, Ohio, McKinley hewed to the tradition by which candidates for president did not actively campaign for the office. He conducted a dignified "front-porch" campaign by receiving pilgrimages of the Republican faithful, organized and paid for by Hanna.

Bryan showed no such restraint. He became the first presidential candidate in American history to stump every section of the country systematically, to appear in villages and hamlets, **BIRTH OF MODERN CAMPAIGNING** indeed the first to say frankly to the voters that he wanted to be president. He traveled 18,000 miles and addressed an estimated 5 million people. But Bryan may have done himself more harm than good. By violating a long-standing tradition of presidential candidates' remaining aloof from their own campaigns (the tradition by which they "stood" for office rather than "running" for it), Bryan helped establish the modern form of presidential politics. But he also antagonized many voters, who considered his campaign undignified.

On election day, McKinley polled 271 electoral votes to Bryan's 176 and received 51.1 percent of the popular vote to Bryan's 47.7. Bryan carried the areas of the South and West where miners or struggling staple farmers predominated. The Democratic program, like that of the Populists, had been too narrow to win a national election.

For the Populists and their allies, the election results were a disaster. They had gambled everything on their "fusion" with the

END OF THE PEOPLE'S PARTY

Democratic Party and lost. Within months of the election, the People's Party began to dissolve. Never again would American farmers unite so militantly to demand economic reform.

BRYAN WHISTLE-STOPPING By long-established tradition, candidates for the presidency did not actively campaign after receiving their party's nomination. Nineteenth-century Americans considered public "stumping" to be undignified and inappropriate for a future president. But in 1896, William Jennings Bryan—a young candidate little known outside his own region, a man without broad support even among the leaders of his own party—decided that he had no choice but to go directly to the public for support. He traveled widely and incessantly in the months before the election, appearing before hundreds of crowds and hundreds of thousands of people. (The Library of Congress (LC-USZC2-6259))

McKinley and Recovery

The administration of William McKinley, which began in the aftermath of turmoil, saw a return to relative calm. One reason was the exhaustion of dissent. By 1897, when McKinley took office, the labor unrest that had so frightened many middle-class Americans and so excited working-class people had subsided. With the simultaneous decline of agrarian protest, the greatest destabilizing forces in the nation's politics were—temporarily at least—in retreat. Another reason was the shrewd character of the McKinley administration itself, committed as it was to reassuring stability. Most important, however, was the gradual easing of the economic crisis, a development that undercut many of those who were agitating for change.

McKinley and his allies committed themselves fully to only one issue, one on which they knew virtually all Republicans agreed: the need for higher tariff rates. Within weeks of his inauguration, the administration won approval of the Dingley Tariff, raising duties to the highest point in American history. The administration dealt more gingerly with the explosive silver question (an issue that McKinley himself had never considered very important in any case). McKinley sent a commission to Europe to explore the possibility of a silver agreement with Great Britain and France. As he and everyone else anticipated, the effort produced no agreement. The Republicans then enacted the Currency,

CURRENCY ACT

or Gold Standard, Act of 1900, which confirmed the nation's commitment to the gold standard by assigning a specific gold value to the dollar and requiring all currency issued by the United States to hew to that value.

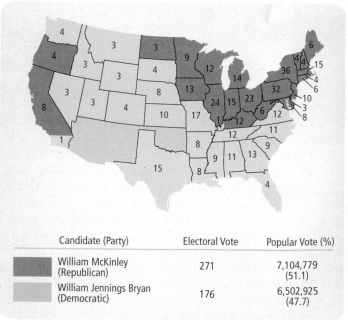

Candidate (Party)	Electoral Vote	Popular Vote (%)
William McKinley (Republican)	271	7,104,779 (51.1)
William Jennings Bryan (Democratic)	176	6,502,925 (47.7)

ELECTION OF 1896 The results of the presidential election of 1896 are, as this map shows, striking for the regional differentiation they reveal. William McKinley won the election by a comfortable but not enormous margin, but his victory was not broad-based. He carried all the states of the Northeast and the industrial Midwest, along with California and Oregon, but virtually nothing else. Bryan carried the entire South and almost all of the agrarian West.

• *What campaign issues in 1896 help account for the regional character of the results?*

And so the "battle of the standards" ended in victory for the forces of conservatism. Economic developments at the time seemed to vindicate the Republicans. Prosperity began to return in 1898. Foreign crop failures sent farm prices surging upward, and American business entered another cycle of expansion. Prosperity and the gold standard, it seemed, were closely allied.

But while the free-silver movement had failed, it had raised an important question for the American economy. In the quarter-century before 1900, the countries of the Western world had experienced a spectacular growth in productive facilities and population. Yet the supply of money had not kept pace with economic progress, because the supply was tied to gold and the amount of gold had remained practically constant. Had it not been for a dramatic increase in the gold supply in the late 1890s (a result of new techniques for extracting gold from low-content ores and the discovery of huge new gold deposits in Alaska, South Africa, and Australia), Populist predictions of

financial disaster might in fact have proved correct. In 1898, two and a half times as much gold was produced as in 1890, and the currency supply was soon inflated far beyond anything Bryan and the free-silver forces had anticipated.

By then, however, Bryan–like many other Americans–was becoming engaged with another major issue: a growing United States presence in world affairs and the possibility of America becoming an imperialist nation.

STIRRINGS OF IMPERIALISM

For over two decades after the Civil War, the United States expanded hardly at all. By the 1890s, however, some Americans were ready–indeed, eager–to resume the course of Manifest Destiny that had inspired their ancestors to wrest an empire from Mexico in the expansionist 1840s.

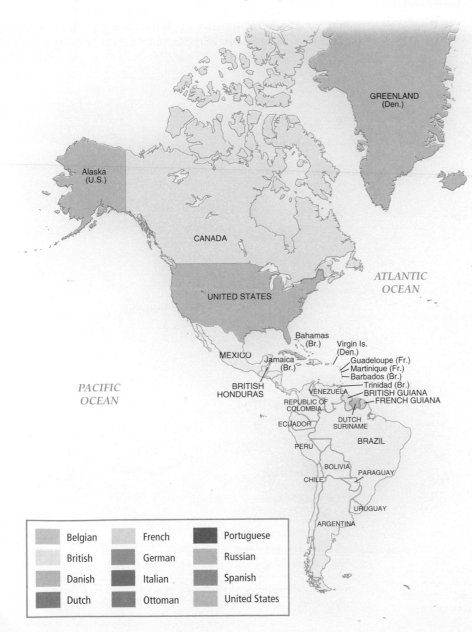

IMPERIALISM AT HIGH TIDE: 1900 The United States became a formal imperial power in 1898, when it acquired colonies in the aftermath of the Spanish American War. But the U.S. was a decided latecomer to imperialism. During the nineteenth century, European nations dramatically expanded the reach of their empires, moving in particular into Africa and Asia. Although the British remained the world's largest imperial power by a significant margin, vast areas of the globe came under the control of other European colonizers, as this map shows.

• *How did the United States and the European imperial nations justify their acquisition of empire?*

THE NEW MANIFEST DESTINY

Several developments helped shift American attention to lands across the seas. The experience of subjugating the Indian tribes had established a precedent for exerting colonial control over dependent peoples. The concept of the "closing of the frontier," widely heralded by Frederick Jackson Turner and many others in the 1890s, produced fears that natural resources would soon dwindle and that alternative sources must be found abroad. The depression of the 1890s encouraged some businessmen to look overseas for new markets. The bitter social protests of the time–the Populist movement, the free-silver crusade, the bloody labor disputes–led some politicians to urge a more aggressive foreign policy as an outlet for frustrations that would otherwise destabilize domestic life.

INCREASING IMPORTANCE OF TRADE — Foreign trade became increasingly important to the American economy in the late nineteenth century. The nation's exports had totaled about $392 million in 1870; by 1890, the figure was $857 million; and by 1900, $1.4 billion.

Many Americans began to consider the possibility of acquiring colonies that might expand such markets further.

Americans were well aware of the imperialist fever that was raging through Europe and leading the major powers to partition most of Africa among themselves and to turn eager eyes on the Far East and the feeble Chinese Empire. Some Americans feared that their nation would soon be left out, that no territory would remain to be acquired. Senator Henry Cabot Lodge of Massachusetts, a leading imperialist, warned that the United States "must not fall out of the line of march." The same distortion of Darwinism that industrialists and others had long been applying to domestic economic affairs in the form of Social Darwinism was now applied to world affairs. Many writers and public figures contended that nations or "races," like biological species, struggled constantly for existence and that only the fittest could survive. For strong nations to dominate weak ones was, therefore, in accordance with the laws of nature.

The popular writer John Fiske predicted in an 1885 article in *Harper's Magazine* that the English-speaking peoples would eventually control every land that was not already the seat of an "established civilization." The experience of white Americans in subjugating the native population of their own continent, Fiske argued, was "destined to go on" in other parts of the world.

John W. Burgess, founder of Columbia University's School of Political Science, gave a stamp of scholarly approval to imperial-

INTELLECTUAL JUSTIFICATIONS FOR IMPERIALISM

ism. In his 1890 study: *Political Science and Comparative Law*, he flatly stated that the Anglo-Saxon and Teutonic nations possessed the highest political talents. It was their duty, therefore, to uplift less fortunate peoples, even to force superior institutions on them if necessary. "There is," he wrote, "no human right to the status of barbarism."

The ablest and most effective apostle of imperialism was Alfred Thayer Mahan, a captain and later admiral in the U.S. Navy. Mahan's thesis, presented in *The Influence of Sea Power upon History* (1890) and other works, was

ALFRED THAYER MAHAN

simple: countries with sea power were the great nations of history; the greatness of the United States, bounded by two oceans,

would rest on its naval strength. The prerequisites for sea power were a productive domestic economy, foreign commerce, a strong merchant marine, a navy to defend trade routes—and colonies, which would provide raw materials and markets and could serve as naval bases. Mahan advocated that the United States construct a canal across the isthmus of Central America to join the oceans, acquire defensive bases on both sides of the canal in the Caribbean and the Pacific, and take possession of Hawaii and other Pacific islands.

Mahan feared the United States did not have a large enough navy to play the great role he envisioned. But during the 1870s and 1880s, the government launched a shipbuilding program that by 1898 had moved the United States to fifth place among the world's naval powers, and by 1900 to third.

HEMISPHERIC HEGEMONY

James G. Blaine, who served as secretary of state in two Republican administrations in the 1880s, led early efforts to

HAWAIIAN SUGARCANE PLANTATION The sugarcane plantations of nineteenth-century Hawaii (like the sugar plantations of Barbados in the seventeenth and eighteenth centuries) required a vast labor force that the island's native population could not provide. The mostly American owners of the plantations imported more than 300,000 Asian workers from China, Japan, and Korea to work in the fields between 1850 and 1920. The work was arduous, as the words of a song by Japanese sugar workers suggests: "Hawaii, Hawaii, But when I came what I saw was Hell. The boss was Satan, The lunas [overseers] his helpers." (© Corbis)

IMPERIALISM WOR-6

EMPIRES were not, of course, new to the nineteenth century, when the United States acquired its first overseas colonies. They have existed since the early moments of recorded history—in ancient Greece, Rome, China, and many other parts of the world. But in the mid- and late nineteenth century, the construction of empires took on a new and different form from those of earlier eras, and the word "imperialism" emerged for the first time to describe it. European powers now created colonies not by sending large numbers of migrants to settle and populate new lands but, instead, by creating military, political, and business structures that allowed them to dominate and profit from the existing populations. This new imperialism changed the character of the imperial nations themselves, enriching them greatly and producing new classes of people whose lives were shaped by the demands of imperial business and administration. It changed the character of colonized societies even more, by drawing them into the vast nexus of global industrial capitalism and by introducing European customs, institutions, and technologies to the subject peoples.

Champions of the new imperialism argued that the acquisition of colonies was essential for the health, even the survival, of their own industrializing nations. Colonies were sources of raw materials vital to industrial production, they were markets for manufactured goods, and they could be suppliers of cheap labor. Defenders of the idea of empire argued as well that imperialism was good for the colonized people too. Many saw colonization as an opportunity to export Christianity to "heathen" lands, while secular apologists argued that imperialism helped bring colonized people into the modern world. The British poet Rudyard Kipling was perhaps the most famous spokesman for empire. In his celebrated poem "The White Man's Burden," he spoke of the duty of the colonizers to lift up primitive peoples, to "fill full the mouth of famine and bid the sickness cease."

The greatest imperial power of the nineteenth century, indeed one of the greatest imperial powers in all of human history, was Great Britain. By 1800, despite its recent loss of the colonies that became the United States, it already possessed vast territory in North America, the Caribbean, and the Pacific—most notably Canada and Australia. But in the second half of the nineteenth century, Britain greatly expanded its empire. Its most important acquisition was India. In 1857, when native Indians revolted against British authority, British forces brutally crushed the rebellion and established formal colonial control over the land. British officials, backed by substantial military power, now governed India through a large civil service staffed mostly by

THE BRITISH RAJ The Drum Corps of the Royal Fusiliers in India poses here for a formal portrait, taken in 1877. Although the drummers are British, an Indian associate is included at top left. This blending of the dominant British with subordinate Indians was characteristic of the administration of the British Empire in India—a government known as the "raj," from the Indian word for "rule." (Time & Life Pictures/Getty Images)

expand American influence into Latin America, where, he believed, the United States must look for markets for its surplus goods. In October 1889, Blaine helped organize the first Pan-American Congress, which attracted delegates from nineteen nations. The delegates agreed to create the Pan-American Union, a weak international organization located in Washington, D.C., that served as a clearinghouse of information to the member nations. But they rejected Blaine's more substantive proposals: for an inter-American customs union and arbitration procedures for hemispheric disputes.

The Cleveland administration took a similarly active interest in Latin America. In 1895, it supported Venezuela in a dispute with Great Britain. When the British ignored American demands

VENEZUELAN DISPUTE

that the matter be submitted to arbitration, Secretary of State Richard Olney charged that Britain was violating the Monroe Doctrine. Cleveland then created a special commission to settle the dispute: if Britain resisted the commission's decision, he insisted, the United States should be willing to go to war to enforce it. As war talk raged throughout the country, the British government prudently agreed to arbitration.

HAWAII AND SAMOA

The islands of Hawaii in the mid-Pacific had been an important way station for American ships in the China trade since the people from England and Scotland, but with some Indians serving in minor or symbolic positions. The British invested heavily in railroads, telegraphs, canals, harbors, and agricultural improvements to enhance the economic opportunities available to them. They created schools for Indian children in an effort to draw them into British culture and make them supporters of the imperial system.

Britain also extended its empire into Africa and other parts of Asia. Cecil Rhodes expanded a small existing British colony at Cape Town into a substantial colony that included what is now South Africa. In 1895, he added new territories to the north, which he named Rhodesia (today, Zimbabwe and Zambia). Other imperialists spread British authority into Kenya, Uganda, Nigeria, and much of Egypt. With the acquisition of Singapore, Hong Kong, Burma, and Malaya, Britain extended its empire into east Asia.

Other European states, watching the vast expansion of the British Empire, quickly jumped into the race for colonies. France created colonies in Indochina (Vietnam and Laos), Algeria, west Africa, and Madagascar. Belgium moved into the Congo in west Africa. Germany established colonies in the Cameroons, Tanganyika, and other parts of Africa, and in the Pacific islands north of Australia. Dutch, Italian, Portuguese, Spanish, Russian, and Japanese imperialists created colonies in Africa, Asia, and the Pacific—driven both by their own commercial interests and by the frenzied competition that had developed among rival imperial powers. In 1898, the United States was drawn into the imperial race as an unanticipated result of the Spanish-American War. But Americans also sought colonies, although only a few, as a result of the efforts of pro-imperialists (among them Theodore Roosevelt), who believed that in the modern industrial-imperial world a nation without colonies would have difficulty remaining, or becoming, a true great power. ●

UNDERSTAND, ANALYZE, AND EVALUATE

1. What motivated the European nations' drive for empire in the late nineteenth century?
2. Why was Great Britain so successful in acquiring its vast empire?
3. How do the imperial efforts and ambitions of the United States at the end of the nineteenth century compare with those of the European powers that were also acquiring empires at this time?

early nineteenth century. By the 1880s, officers of the expanding American navy were looking covetously at Pearl Harbor on the island of Oahu as a possible permanent base for U.S. ships. Pressure for an increased American presence in Hawaii was emerging from another source as well: the growing number of Americans who had settled on the islands and who had gradually come to dominate their economic and political life.

In doing so, the Americans had been wresting authority away from the leaders of an ancient civilization. Settled by Polynesian people beginning in about 1500 BCE, Hawaii had **SELF-SUFFICIENT SOCIETIES** developed an agricultural and fishing society in which different islands (and different communities on the same islands), each with its own chieftain, lived more or less self-sufficiently. When the first Americans arrived in Hawaii in the 1790s on merchant ships from New England, there were perhaps a half-million people living there. Battles among rival communities were frequent, as ambitious chieftains tried to consolidate power over their neighbors. In 1810, after a series of such battles, King Kamehameha I established his dominance, welcomed American traders, and helped them develop a thriving trade between Hawaii and China, from which the natives profited along with the merchants. But Americans soon wanted more than trade. Missionaries began settling there in the early nineteenth century; and in the 1830s, William Hooper, a Boston trader, became the first of many Americans to buy land and establish a sugar plantation on the islands.

The arrival of these merchants, missionaries, and planters was devastating to traditional Hawaiian society. The newcomers inadvertently brought infectious diseases to which the Hawaiians, like the American Indians before them, were tragically vulnerable. By the mid-nineteenth century, more than half the native population had died. By 1900, disease had more than halved the population again. But the Americans brought other incursions as well. Missionaries worked to undermine native religion. Other white settlers introduced liquor, firearms, and a commercial economy, all of which eroded the traditional character of Hawaiian society. By the 1840s, American planters had spread throughout the islands; and an American settler, G. P. Judd, had become prime minister of Hawaii under King Kamehameha III, who had agreed to establish a constitutional monarchy. Judd governed Hawaii for over a decade.

In 1887, the United States negotiated a treaty with Hawaii that permitted it to open a naval base at Pearl Harbor. By then, growing sugar for export to America had become the basis of the Hawaiian economy—as a result of an 1875 agreement allowing Hawaiian sugar to enter the United States duty-free. The American-dominated sugar plantation system not only displaced native Hawaiians from their lands but also sought to build a workforce with Asian immigrants, whom the Americans considered more reliable and more docile than the natives. Indeed, finding adequate labor and keeping it under control were the principal concerns of many planters. Some planters deliberately sought to create a mixed-race workforce (Chinese, Japanese, native Hawaiians, Filipinos, Portuguese, and others) as a way to keep the workers divided and unlikely to challenge them.

Native Hawaiians did not accept their subordination without protest. In 1891, they elevated a powerful nationalist to **QUEEN LILIUOKALANI** the throne: Queen Liliuokalani, who set out to challenge the growing American control of the islands. But she remained in power only two years. By 1890, the United States had eliminated the privileged position of Hawaiian sugar in international trade. The result was devastating to the economy of the islands, and American planters concluded that the only way for them to recover was to become part of the United States (and hence exempt from its tariffs). In 1893, they staged a revolution and called on the United States for protection. After the American minister ordered marines from a warship in

YELLOW JOURNALISM

JOSEPH Pulitzer was a successful newspaper publisher in St. Louis, Missouri, when he traveled to New York City in 1883 to buy a struggling paper, the *New York World*. "There is room in this great and growing city," he wrote in one of his first editorials, "for

THE YELLOW PRESS AND THE WRECK OF THE *MAINE* No evidence was ever found tying the Spanish to the explosion in Havana harbor that destroyed the American battleship *Maine* in February 1898. Indeed, most evidence indicated that the blast came from inside the ship, a fact that suggests an accident rather than sabotage. Nevertheless, the newspapers of Joseph Pulitzer and William Randolph Hearst ran sensational stories about the incident that were designed to arouse public sentiment in support of a war against the Spanish. This front page from Pulitzer's *New York World* is an example of the lurid coverage the event received. Circulation figures at the top right of the page indicate, too, how successful the coverage was in selling newspapers. (© The Granger Collection, New York)

a journal that is not only cheap, but bright, not only bright but large, not only large but truly democratic . . . that will serve and battle for the people with earnest sincerity." Within a year, the *World*'s daily circulation had soared from 10,000 to over 60,000. By 1886, it had reached 250,000 and was making enormous profits.

The success of Pulitzer's *World* marked the birth of what came to be known as "yellow journalism," a phrase that reportedly derived from a character in one of the *World*'s comic strips: "the Yellow Kid." Color printing in newspapers was relatively new, and yellow was the most difficult color to print; so in the beginning, the term "yellow journalism" was a comment on the new technological possibilities that Pulitzer was so eagerly embracing. Eventually, however, it came to refer to a sensationalist style of reporting and writing that spread quickly through urban America and changed the character of newspapers forever.

Sensationalism was not new to journalism in the late nineteenth century, of course. Political scandal sheets had been publishing lurid stories since before the American Revolution. But the yellow journalism of the 1880s and 1890s took the search for a mass audience to new levels. The *World* created one of the first Sunday editions, with lavishly colored special sections, comics, and illustrated features. It expanded coverage of sports, fashion, literature, and theater. It pioneered large, glaring, overheated headlines that captured the eyes of people who were passing newsstands. It published exposés of political corruption. It made considerable efforts to bring drama and energy to its coverage of crime. It tried to involve readers directly in its stories (as when a *World* campaign helped raise $300,000 to build a base for the Statue of Liberty, with much of the money coming in donations of five or ten cents from working-class readers). And it introduced a self-consciously populist style of writing that appealed to working-class readers. "The American people want something terse, forcible, picturesque, striking," Pulitzer said. His reporters wrote short, forceful sentences. They did not shy away from expressing sympathy or outrage. And they were not always constrained by the truth.

Honolulu harbor to go ashore to aid the rebels, the queen yielded her authority.

A provisional government, dominated by Americans (who constituted less than 5 percent of the population of the islands), immediately sent a delegation to Washington to negotiate a treaty of annexation. But debate continued until 1898, when the Republicans returned to power and approved the agreement.

Three thousand miles south of Hawaii, the Samoan islands had also long served as a way station for American ships in the Pacific trade. As American commerce with Asia increased,

Pulitzer very quickly produced imitators, the most important of them the California publisher William Randolph Hearst, who in 1895 bought the *New York Journal*, cut its price to one cent (Pulitzer quickly followed suit), copied many of the *World*'s techniques, and within a year raised its circulation to 400,000. Hearst soon made the *Journal* the largest-circulation paper in the country—selling more than a million copies a day. Pulitzer, whose own circulation was not far behind, accused him of "pandering to the worst tastes of the prurient and the horror-loving" and "dealing in bogus news." But the *World* wasted no time before imitating the *Journal*. The competition between these two great "yellow" journals soon drove both to new levels of sensationalism. Their success drove newspapers in other cities around the nation to copy their techniques.

The civil war in Cuba in the 1890s gave both papers their best opportunities yet for combining sensational reporting with shameless appeals to patriotism and moral outrage. They avidly published exaggerated reports of Spanish atrocities toward the Cuban rebels, fanning popular anger toward Spain. When the American battleship *Maine* mysteriously exploded in Havana harbor in 1898, both papers (without any evidence) immediately blamed Spanish authorities. The *Journal* offered a $50,000 reward for information leading to the conviction of those responsible for the explosion, and it crowded all other stories off its front page ("There is no other news," Hearst told his editors) to make room for such screaming headlines as THE WHOLE COUNTRY THRILLS WITH WAR FEVER and HAVANA POPULACE INSULTS THE MEMORY OF THE *MAINE* VICTIMS. In the three days following the *Maine* explosion, the *Journal* sold more than 3 million copies, a new world's record for newspaper circulation.

In the aftermath of the *Maine* episode, the more conservative press launched a spirited attack on yellow journalism. That was partly in response to Hearst's boast that the conflict in Cuba was "the *Journal*'s war." He sent a cable to one of his reporters in Cuba saying: "You furnish the pictures, and I'll furnish the war." Growing numbers of critics tried to discourage yellow journalism, which

"respectable" editors both deplored and feared. Some schools, libraries, and clubs began to banish the papers from their premises. But the techniques the "yellow" press pioneered in the 1890s helped map the way for a tradition of colorful, popular journalism—later embodied in "tabloids," some elements of which eventually found their way into television news—that has endured into the present day. ●

UNDERSTAND, ANALYZE, AND EVALUATE

1. Did Pulitzer's *World*, Hearst's *Journal*, and their imitators report the news or manufacture it?
2. How did the "yellow" press influence the public's perception of the Spanish-American War?
3. How does television news continue the tradition of "yellow" journalism? In what other mass media do you see the style and techniques pioneered by the "yellow" press?

"THE YELLOW DUGAN KID" *Hogan's Alley*, one of the most popular cartoons of the late nineteenth and early twentieth centuries, debuted in the *New York World* in 1895. Perhaps its best-known character was Mickey Dugan, the goofy-looking creation of cartoonist Richard Outcault, known as "the Yellow Kid," whose nickname very likely was the source of the term "yellow journalism." *Hogan's Alley* was the forerunner of modern serial cartoons—not least because it was one of the first newspaper features to make elaborate use of color. (The drawing above accompanied Outcault's letter requesting copyright registration for the character of what he called "the yellow Dugan kid.") (The Library of Congress)

business groups in the United States and the American navy began urging the government to annex the Samoan harbor at Pago Pago. In 1878, the Hayes administration extracted a treaty from Samoan leaders for an American naval station there.

ACQUISITION OF SAMOA

But Great Britain and Germany were also interested in the islands, and they too secured treaty rights from the native princes. For the next ten years the three powers jockeyed for dominance in Samoa, occasionally coming dangerously close to war. Finally, the three nations agreed to share power over Samoa. The three-way arrangement failed to halt the rivalries of its members; and in 1899, the United States and Germany divided the islands between them, compensating Britain with territories elsewhere in the Pacific. The United States retained the harbor at Pago Pago.

WAR WITH SPAIN

Imperial ambitions had thus begun to stir within the United States well before the late 1890s. But a war with Spain in 1898 turned those stirrings into overt expansionism. The war transformed America's relationship to the rest of the world and left the nation with a far-flung overseas empire.

CONTROVERSY OVER CUBA

The Spanish-American War was a result of events in Cuba, which along with Puerto Rico now represented all that remained of Spain's once extensive American empire. Cubans had been resisting Spanish rule since at least 1868. Many Americans had sympathized with the Cubans during that long struggle, but the United States had not intervened.

In 1895, the Cubans rebelled again. This revolution produced a ferocity on both sides that horrified many Americans. **CUBAN REVOLT** The Cubans deliberately devastated the island to force the Spaniards to leave. The Spanish, commanded by General Valeriano Weyler, confined civilians in some areas to hastily prepared concentration camps, where they died by the thousands, victims of disease and malnutrition. The American press took to calling the general "Butcher Weyler." The Spanish had used some of these same savage methods during earlier struggles in Cuba without shocking American sensibilities. But the revolt of 1895 was reported more fully and sensationally by the American press, which helped create the impression that the Spaniards were committing all the atrocities, when in fact there was considerable brutality on both sides.

The conflict in Cuba came at a particularly opportune moment for the publishers of some American newspapers, Joseph Pulitzer with his *New York World* and William Randolph Hearst with his *New York Journal*. (See "Patterns of Popular Culture," pp. 536–537.) In the 1890s, Hearst and Pulitzer were engaged in a ruthless circulation war, and they both sent batteries of reporters and illustrators to the island with orders to provide accounts of Spanish atrocities. A growing population of Cuban émigrés in the United

THE DUTY OF THE HOUR:—TO SAVE HER NOT ONLY FROM SPAIN BUT FROM A WORSE FATE.

"THE DUTY OF THE HOUR" This 1892 lithograph was no doubt inspired by the saying "Out of the frying pan and into the fire." A despairing Cuba, struggling to escape from the frying pan of Spanish misrule, contemplates an even more dangerous alternative: "anarchy" (or home rule). Cartoonist Louis Dalrymple here suggests that the only real solution to Cuba's problems is control by the United States, whose "duty" to Cuba is "To Save Her Not Only from Spain but from a Worse Fate." (© The Granger Collection, New York)

States–centered in Florida, New York City, Philadelphia, and Trenton, New Jersey–gave extensive support to the Cuban Revolutionary Party (whose headquarters were in New York City) and helped publicize the Cuban cause as effectively as those of the yellow journalists in generating American support for the revolution.

The mounting storm of indignation against Spain did not persuade President Cleveland to support intervention. But when McKinley became president in 1897, he formally protested Spain's "uncivilized and inhuman" conduct, causing the Spanish government (fearful of American intervention) to recall Weyler, modify the concentration policy, and grant the island a qualified autonomy.

But whatever chances there were for a peaceful settlement vanished as a result of two dramatic incidents in February 1898. The first occurred when a Cuban agent stole a private letter written by Dupuy de Lôme, the Spanish minister in Washington, and turned it over to the American press. The letter described McKinley as a weak man and "a bidder for the admiration of the crowd." This was no more than many Americans, including some Republicans, were saying about their president. (Theodore Roosevelt described McKinley as having "no more backbone than a chocolate eclair.") But coming from a foreigner, it created intense popular anger. Dupuy de Lôme promptly resigned.

While excitement over the de Lôme letter was still high, the American battleship *Maine* blew up in Havana harbor

THE MAINE with a loss of more than 260 people. The ship had been ordered to Cuba in January to protect American lives and property. Many Americans assumed that the Spanish had sunk the ship, particularly when a naval court of inquiry hastily and inaccurately reported that an external explosion by a submarine mine had caused the disaster. (Later evidence suggested that the disaster was actually the result of an accidental explosion inside one of the engine rooms.) War hysteria swept the country, and Congress unanimously appropriated $50 million for military preparations. "Remember the *Maine*!" became a national chant for revenge.

McKinley still hoped to avoid a conflict. But others in his administration (including Assistant Secretary of the Navy Theodore Roosevelt) were clamoring for war. In March 1898, the president asked Spain to agree to an armistice, negotiations for a permanent peace, and an end to the concentration camps. Spain agreed to stop the fighting and eliminate the concentration camps but refused to negotiate with the rebels and reserved the right to resume hostilities at its discretion. That satisfied neither public opinion nor the Congress; and a few days later the United States declared war on Spain.

"A SPLENDID LITTLE WAR"

Secretary of State John Hay called the Spanish-American conflict "a splendid little war," an opinion that most Americans–except many of the enlisted men who fought in it–seemed to

share. Declared in April, it was over in August, in part because Cuban rebels had already greatly weakened the Spanish resistance, which made the American intervention in many respects little more than a "mopping-up" exercise. Only 460 Americans were killed in battle or died of wounds, although

SUPPLY AND MOBILIZATION PROBLEMS some 5,200 others perished of disease: malaria, dysentery, and typhoid, among others. Casualties among Cuban insurgents, who continued to bear the brunt of the fighting, were much higher.

And yet the American war effort was not without difficulties. United States soldiers faced serious supply problems: a shortage of modern rifles and ammunition, uniforms too heavy for the warm Caribbean weather, inadequate medical services, and skimpy, almost indigestible food. The regular army numbered only 28,000 troops and officers, most of whom had experience in quelling Indian outbreaks but none in larger-scale warfare. As in the Civil War, the United States had to rely heavily on National Guard units, organized by local communities and commanded for the most part by local leaders without military experience.

There were racial conflicts. A significant proportion of the American invasion force consisted of black soldiers. Some were volunteer troops put together by African American communities (although some governors refused to allow the formation of such units). Others were members of the four black regiments in the regular army, who had been stationed on the frontier to defend white settlements against Indians and were now transferred east to fight in Cuba. As the black soldiers traveled through the South toward the training camps, they chafed at the rigid segregation to which they were subjected and occasionally resisted the restrictions openly. African American soldiers in Georgia deliberately made use of a "whites only" park; in Florida, they beat a soda-fountain operator for refusing to serve them; in Tampa, white provocations and black retaliation led to a nightlong riot that left thirty people wounded.

Racial tensions continued in Cuba, where African Americans played crucial roles in some of the important battles of the war (including the famous charge at San Juan Hill) and won many medals. Nearly half the Cuban insurgents fighting with the Americans were of African descent, and unlike their American counterparts they were fully integrated into the rebel army. (Indeed, one of the leading insurgent generals, Antonio Maceo, was a black man.) The sight of black Cuban soldiers fighting alongside whites as equals gave African Americans a stronger sense of the injustice of their own position.

SEIZING THE PHILIPPINES

By an accident of history, the assistant secretary of the navy during the Cuban revolution was Theodore Roosevelt, an ardent Anglophile eager to see the United States join the British and other nations as imperial powers. Roosevelt was, in fact, a relatively minor figure in the Navy Department, but

MEMORIALIZING NATIONAL HISTORY

PUBLIC MONUMENTS ARE CONSTRUCTED FOR A VARIETY OF REASONS: to remember tragedy, to commemorate sacrifice, to celebrate specific persons or groups, and to honor acts of courage, heroism, and endurance. The structures differ in purpose, theme, and meaning, but all serve to satisfy our need to reflect upon the meaning of events, groups, or people memorialized.

The explosion of the battleship *Maine* in Havana Harbor in February 1898 resulted in the deaths of 266 men and served to propel the United States into war with Spain. Twelve years after the conclusion of the short-lived war, work began on a monument to memorialize the *Maine* and commemorate the men who died in the explosion. Dedicated on February 15, 1915, the monument, located in Arlington National Cemetery and pictured in the first two images below, includes the main mast from the *Maine*. The names of those killed in the disaster are inscribed around the base of the monument, which represents the turret of a battleship.

A memorial commemorating those killed in the terrorist attacks of September 11, 2001, in New York City, Pennsylvania, and at the Pentagon, as well as those killed in the February 1993 bombing of the World Trade Center in New York, opened at the site of the attack on September 12, 2011. A museum dedicated to the events around the destruction of the World Trade Towers opened in May of 2014. The memorial

THE MAINE—1898/1915

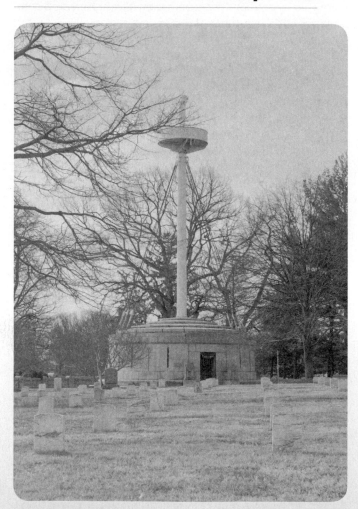

(The Library of Congress (381569pu))

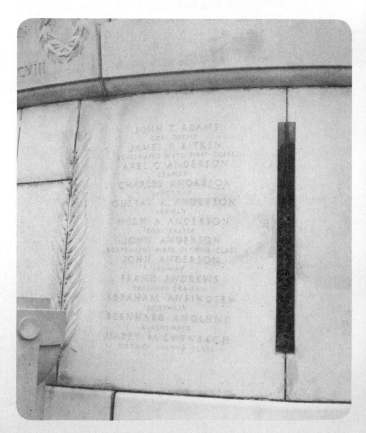

(The Library of Congress (381579pu))

consists of two pools, each approximately one acre in size, set within the footprints of the Twin Towers of the World Trade Center. The names of every person killed have been inscribed around the edges of the pools. Four hundred oak trees have been planted to add to the site a sense of quiet solemnity and reminder of enduring life.

THE VICTIMS OF TERRORISM—2014

(© Aristide Economopoulos/Star Ledger/Corbis)

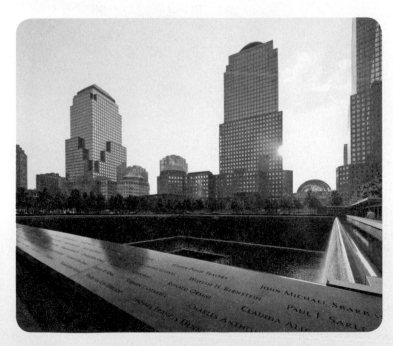

(© Atlantide Phototravel/Corbis)

AP | TEST PRACTICE

Questions assume cumulative content knowledge from this chapter and previous chapters.

1 Based on the images and the information provided, what is a common feature shared by both memorials?

(A) Each is highly representational, or realistic, in artistic style.

(B) Each is located at the place in which the event happened.

(C) Each references the main structural object(s) that suffered destruction in the respective event.

(D) Each displays as a very prominent feature an actual, physical part of the main structural object(s) that suffered destruction in the respective event.

2. Each memorial includes inscriptions of the names of those killed in the event. What do the respective decisions for the locale of the memorial most suggest about differences between each event?

(A) The location of the *Maine* memorial suggests that military lives were lost, while the locale of the September 11 memorial suggests that civilian lives were lost.

(B) The location of the *Maine* memorial suggests that the event was a national matter, while the location of the September 11 memorial suggests that the event was not.

(C) The differences in the kind of locale selected for each respective memorial suggest that the September 11 memorial was more controversial.

(D) The differences in the kind of locale selected for each respective memorial suggest that the *Maine* event was more controversial.

3. Consider what you have learned about the national response to and the consequences of the destruction of the *Maine*. What does the fact of the construction of these particular memorials discussed most suggest about why a nation might choose to memorialize certain events over other events?

(A) A nation will memorialize events that only celebrate its victories overseas.

(B) A nation will only memorialize events that celebrate heroes.

(C) A nation most typically will memorialize events that individual citizens petition for.

(D) A nation is more likely to memorialize events that unite a nation and propel it to major national political action.

he was determined to expand his power. British friends had persuaded him that the war in Cuba gave the United States a rare opportunity to expand the American empire. Roosevelt responded by sending the navy's Pacific fleet to the Philippines, with orders to attack as soon as American declared war. On May 1, 1898, Commodore George Dewey led the fleet into Manila Harbor, quickly destroyed the aging Spanish fleet, and forced the Spanish government to surrender with hardly a shot fired. He became the first American hero of the war.

In the rejoicing over Dewey's victory, few Americans paused to note that the character of the war was changing. What had begun as a war to free Cuba was becoming a war to strip Spain of its colonies. The United States was now confronted with the question of what to do with the Spanish possessions it was suddenly acquiring.

THE BATTLE FOR CUBA

The war in Cuba continued after the capture of the Philippines. At first, the American commanders planned a long period of training before actually sending troops into combat. But when a Spanish fleet under Admiral Pascual Cervera slipped past the American navy into Santiago harbor on the southern coast of Cuba, plans changed quickly. The American Atlantic fleet quickly bottled Cervera up in the harbor. And the U.S. Army's commanding general, Nelson A. Miles, hastily altered his strategy and left Tampa in June with a force of 17,000 to attack Santiago. Both the departure from Florida and the landing in Cuba were scenes of fantastic incompetence. It took five days for this relatively small army to go ashore, even with the enemy offering no opposition.

General William R. Shafter, the American commander, moved toward Santiago, which he planned to

THE ROUGH RIDERS

surround and capture. On the way he met and defeated Spanish forces at Las Guasimos and, a week later, in two simultaneous battles, El Caney and San Juan Hill. At the center of the fighting (and on the front pages of the newspapers) during many of these engagements was a cavalry unit known as the Rough Riders. Nominally commanded by General Leonard Wood, its real leader was Colonel Theodore Roosevelt, who had resigned from the Navy Department to get into the war and who had struggled to ensure that his regiment made it to the front before the fighting ended. His passion to join the war undoubtedly reflected the decision of his beloved father, Theodore Roosevelt Sr., not to fight in the Civil War, a source of private shame within his family that his son sought to erase.

Roosevelt rapidly emerged as a hero of the conflict. His fame rested in large part on his role in leading a bold, if perhaps

THE SPANISH-AMERICAN WAR IN CUBA, 1898 The military conflict between the United States and Spain in Cuba was a brief affair. The Cuban rebels and an American naval blockade had already brought the Spanish to the brink of defeat. The arrival of American troops was simply the final blow. In the space of about a week, U.S. troops won four decisive battles in the area around Santiago in southeast Cuba—one of them (the Battle of Kettle Hill) the scene of Theodore Roosevelt's famous charge up the adjacent San Juan Hill. This map shows the extent of the American naval blockade, the path of American troops from Florida to Cuba, and the location of the actual fighting.

• *What were the implications of the war in Cuba for Puerto Rico?*

reckless, charge up Kettle Hill (a charge that was a minor part of the larger battle for the adjacent San Juan Hill) directly into the face of Spanish guns. Roosevelt himself emerged unscathed, but nearly a hundred of his soldiers were killed or wounded. He remembered the battle as "the great day of my life."

AFRICAN AMERICAN CAVALRY Substantial numbers of African Americans fought in the U.S. Army during the Spanish-American War. Although confined to all-black units, they engaged in combat alongside white units and fought bravely and effectively. This photograph shows a troop of African American cavalry in formation in Cuba. (© Corbis)

Although Shafter was now in position to assault Santiago, his army was so weakened by sickness that he feared he might have to abandon his position, particularly once the commander of the American naval force blockading Santiago refused to enter the harbor because of mines. But unknown to the Americans, the Spanish government had by now decided that Santiago was lost and had ordered Cervera to evacuate. On July 3, Cervera tried to escape from the harbor. The waiting American squadron destroyed his entire fleet. On July 16, the commander of Spanish ground forces in Santiago surrendered. At about the same time, an American army landed in Puerto Rico and occupied it against virtually no opposition. On August 12, an armistice ended the war.

Under the terms of the armistice, Spain recognized the independence of Cuba. It ceded Puerto Rico (now occupied by American troops) and the Pacific island of Guam to the United States. And it accepted continued American occupation of Manila pending the final disposition of the Philippines.

PUERTO RICO AND THE UNITED STATES

The annexation of Puerto Rico produced relatively little con-

ANNEXATION OF PUERTO RICO

troversy in the United States. The island of Puerto Rico had been a part of the Spanish Empire since Ponce de León arrived there in 1508, and it had contained

Spanish settlements since the founding of San Juan in 1521. The native people of the island, the Arawaks, had mostly disappeared as a result of infectious diseases, Spanish brutality, and poverty. Puerto Rican society developed, therefore, with a Spanish ruling class and a large African workforce for the coffee and sugar plantations that came to dominate its economy.

As Puerto Rican society became increasingly distinctive, resistance to Spanish rule began to emerge, just as it had in Cuba. Uprisings occurred intermittently beginning in the 1820s; the most important of them–the so-called Lares Rebellion–was, like the others, effectively crushed by the Spanish in 1868. But the growing resistance did prompt some reforms: the abolition of slavery in 1873, representation in the Spanish parliament, and other changes. Demands for independence continued to grow, and in 1898, in response to political pressure organized by the popular politician Luis Muñoz Rivera, Spain granted the island a degree of independence. But before the changes had any chance to take effect, control of Puerto Rico shifted to the United States. American military forces occupied the island during the war. They remained in control until 1900, when the Foraker Act ended military rule and established a formal colonial government: an American governor and a two-chamber legislature (the members of the upper chamber appointed by the United States, the members of the lower elected by the Puerto Rican people). The United States could amend or veto any legislation the Puerto Ricans passed. Agitation for independence continued, and in 1917, under pressure to clarify the relationship between Puerto Rico and America, Congress passed the Jones Act, which declared Puerto Rico to be United States territory and made all Puerto Ricans American citizens.

The Puerto Rican sugar industry flourished as it took advantage of the American market that was now open to it without tariffs. As in Hawaii, Americans

SUGAR ECONOMY

began establishing large sugar plantations on the island and hired natives to work them; many of the planters did not even live in Puerto Rico. The growing emphasis on sugar as a cash crop, and the transformation of many Puerto Rican farmers into paid laborers, led to a reduction in the growing of food for the island. Puerto Ricans became increasingly dependent on imported food and hence increasingly a part of the international commercial economy. When international sugar prices were high, Puerto Rico did well. When they dropped, the island's economy sagged, pushing the many plantation workers–already poor–into destitution. Unhappy with the instability, the poverty among natives, and the American threat to Hispanic culture, many Puerto Ricans continued to agitate for independence. Others, however, began to envision closer relations with the United States, even statehood.

THE DEBATE OVER THE PHILIPPINES

Although the annexation of Puerto Rico produced relatively little controversy, the annexation of the Philippines created a

THE ROUGH RIDERS Theodore Roosevelt resigned as assistant secretary of the navy to lead a volunteer regiment in the Spanish-American War. They were known as the Rough Riders, and their bold charge during the battle of San Juan Hill made Roosevelt a national hero. Roosevelt is shown here (at center with glasses) posing with the other members of the regiment. (© Bettmann/Corbis)

long and impassioned debate. Controlling a nearby Caribbean island fit reasonably comfortably into the United States's sense of itself as the dominant power in the Western Hemisphere. Controlling a large and densely populated territory thousands of miles away seemed different and, to many Americans, more ominous.

McKinley claimed to be reluctant to support annexation. But, according to his own accounts, he came to believe there

THE PHILIPPINES QUESTION

were no acceptable alternatives. Emerging from what he described as an "agonizing night of prayer," he claimed divine guidance for his decision to annex the islands. Returning them to Spain would be "cowardly and dishonorable," he claimed. Turning them over to another imperialist power (France, Germany, or Britain) would be "bad business and discreditable." Granting the islands independence would be irresponsible; the Filipinos were "unfit for self government." The only solution was "to take them all and to educate the Filipinos, and uplift and Christianize them, and by God's grace do the very best we could by them."

The Treaty of Paris, signed in December 1898, brought a formal end to the war. It confirmed the terms of the armistice concerning Cuba, Puerto Rico, and Guam. American negotiators startled the Spanish by demanding that they cede the Philippines to the United States, something the original armistice had not included. The Spanish objected briefly, but an American offer of $20 million for the islands softened their resistance. They accepted all the American terms.

In the U.S. Senate, however, resistance was fierce. During debate over ratification of the treaty, a powerful anti-imperialist movement

ANTI-IMPERIALIST LEAGUE

arose around the country to oppose acquisition of the Philippines. The anti-imperialists included some of the nation's wealthiest and most powerful figures: Andrew Carnegie, Mark Twain, Samuel Gompers, Senator John Sherman, and others. Their motives were various. Some believed simply that imperialism was immoral, a repudiation of America's commitment to human freedom. Some feared "polluting" the American population by introducing "inferior" Asian races into it. Industrial workers feared being undercut by a flood of cheap laborers from the new colonies. Conservatives worried about the large standing army and entangling foreign alliances that they believed imperialism would require and that they feared would threaten American liberties. Sugar growers and others feared unwelcome competition from the new territories. The Anti-Imperialist League, established late in 1898 by upper-class Bostonians, New Yorkers, and others to fight against annexation, attracted a widespread following in the Northeast and waged a vigorous campaign against ratification of the Paris treaty.

Favoring ratification was an equally varied group. There were the exuberant imperialists such as Theodore Roosevelt, who saw the acquisition of empire as a way to reinvigorate the nation and keep alive what they considered the healthy, restorative influence of the war. Some businessmen saw opportunities to dominate the Asian trade. And most Republicans saw partisan advantages in acquiring valuable new territories through a war fought and won by a Republican administration. Perhaps the strongest argument in favor of annexation, however, was that the United States already possessed the islands.

When anti-imperialists warned of the danger of acquiring territories with large populations who might have to become citizens, the imperialists had a ready answer: the nation's long-standing policies toward Indians—treating them as dependents rather than as citizens—had created a precedent for annexing land without absorbing people. Supporters of annexation argued that the "uncivilized" Filipinos "would occupy the same status precisely as our Indians. . . . They are, in fact, 'Indians'—and the Fourteenth Amendment does not make citizens of Indians."

The fate of the treaty remained in doubt for weeks, until it received the unexpected support of William Jennings Bryan, a fervent anti-imperialist. He backed ratification not because he approved of annexation but because he hoped to move the issue out of the Senate and make it the subject of a national referendum in 1900, when he expected to be the

Democratic presidential candidate again. Bryan persuaded a number of anti-imperialist Democrats to support the treaty so as to set up the 1900 debate. The Senate ratified it finally on February 6, 1899.

But Bryan miscalculated. If the election of 1900 was in fact a referendum on the Philippines, as Bryan expected, it proved beyond doubt that the nation had decided in favor of imperialism. Once again Bryan ran against McKinley; and once again McKinley won–even more decisively than in 1896. It was not only the issue of the colonies, however, that ensured McKinley's victory. The Republicans were the beneficiaries of growing prosperity– and also of the colorful personality of their vice presidential candidate, Theodore Roosevelt, the hero of San Juan Hill.

ELECTION OF 1900

THE REPUBLIC AS EMPIRE

The new American empire was small by the standards of the great imperial powers of Europe. But it embroiled the United States in the politics of both Europe and the Far East in ways the nation had always tried to avoid in the past. It also drew Americans into a brutal war in the Philippines.

GOVERNING THE COLONIES

Three of the American dependencies–Hawaii, Alaska (acquired from Russia in 1867), and Puerto Rico–presented relatively few problems. They received territorial status (and their residents American citizenship) relatively quickly: Hawaii in 1900, Alaska in 1912, and Puerto Rico in 1917. The U.S. Navy took control of the Pacific islands of Guam and Tutuila. Some of the smallest, least populated Pacific islands now under American control the United States simply left alone. Cuba was a thornier problem. American military forces, commanded by General Leonard Wood, remained there until 1902 to prepare the island for independence. They built roads, schools, and hospitals, reorganized the legal, financial, and administrative systems, and introduced medical and sanitation reforms. But the United States also laid the basis for years of American economic domination of the island.

When Cuba drew up a constitution that made no reference to the United States, Congress responded by passing the Platt Amendment in 1901 and pressured Cuba into incorporating its terms into its constitution. The Platt Amendment barred Cuba from making treaties with other nations (thus, in effect, giving the United States control of Cuban foreign policy); it gave the United States the right to intervene in Cuba to preserve independence, life, and property; and it required Cuba to permit American naval stations on its territory. The amendment left Cuba with only nominal political independence.

PLATT AMENDMENT

American investments, which quickly took over the island's economy, made the new nation an American economic

"MEASURING UNCLE SAM FOR A NEW SUIT," BY J. S. PUGHE, IN *PUCK* **MAGAZINE, 1900** President William McKinley is favorably depicted here as a tailor, measuring his client for a suit large enough to accommodate the new possessions the United States obtained in the aftermath of the Spanish-American War. This detail from a larger cartoon tries to link this expansion with earlier, less controversial ones such as the Louisiana Purchase. (The Library of Congress (LC-DIG-ppmsca-25453))

appendage as well. Americans poured into Cuba, buying up plantations, factories, railroads, and refineries. Absentee American ownership of many of the island's most important resources was the source of resentment and agitation for decades. Resistance to "Yankee imperialism" produced intermittent revolts against the Cuban government–revolts that at times prompted U.S. military intervention. American troops occupied the island from 1906 to 1909 after one such rebellion; they returned again in 1912, to suppress a revolt by black plantation workers. As in Puerto Rico and Hawaii, sugar production–spurred by access to the American market–increasingly dominated the island's economy and subjected it to the same cycle of booms and busts that so plagued other sugar-producing appendages of the United States economy.

AMERICAN ECONOMIC DOMINANCE

THE PHILIPPINE WAR

Americans did not like to think of themselves as imperial rulers in the European mold. Yet, like other imperial powers, the United States soon discovered–as it had discovered at home in its relations with the Indians–that subjugating another people required more than ideals; it also required strength and brutality. That, at least, was the lesson of the American experience in the Philippines, where American forces soon became engaged in a long and bloody war with insurgent forces fighting for independence.

The conflict in the Philippines is the least remembered of all American wars. It was also one of the longest, lasting from 1898 to 1902, and one of the most vicious. It involved 200,000 American troops and resulted in 4,300 American deaths, nearly ten times the number who had died in combat in the Spanish-American War. The number of Filipinos killed in the conflict has long been a matter of dispute, but it seems likely that at least 50,000 natives (and perhaps many more) died. The American occupiers faced brutal guerrilla tactics in the Philippines, very similar to those the Spanish occupiers had faced prior to 1898 in Cuba. And they soon found themselves drawn into the same pattern of brutality that had outraged so many Americans when Weyler had used them in the Caribbean.

The Filipinos had been rebelling against Spanish rule even before 1898. And as soon as they realized the Americans had come to stay, they rebelled against them as well. Ably led by Emilio Aguinaldo, who claimed to head the legitimate government of the nation, Filipinos harried the American army of occupation from island to island for more than three years. At first, American commanders believed the rebels had only a small popular following. But by early 1900, General Arthur MacArthur, an American commander in the islands (and father of General Douglas MacArthur), was writing: "I have been reluctantly compelled to believe that the Filipino masses are loyal to Aguinaldo and the government which he heads."

EMILIO AGUINALDO

To MacArthur and others, that realization was not a reason to moderate American tactics or conciliate the rebels. It was a reason to adopt much more severe measures. Gradually, the American military effort became more systematically vicious and brutal. Captured Filipino guerrillas were treated not as prisoners of war, but as murderers. Many were summarily executed. On some islands, entire communities were evacuated—the residents forced into concentration camps while American troops destroyed their villages, farms, crops, and livestock. A spirit of savagery grew among some American soldiers, who came to view the Filipinos as almost subhuman and at times seemed to take pleasure in killing arbitrarily. One American commander ordered his troops "to kill and burn, the more you kill and burn the better it will please me. . . . Shoot everyone over the age of 10." Over fifteen Filipinos were killed for every one wounded; in the American Civil War—the bloodiest conflict in U.S. history to that point—one person had died for every five wounded.

By 1902, reports of the brutality and of the American casualties had soured the American public on the war. But by then, the rebellion had largely exhausted itself and the occupiers had established control over most of the islands. The key to their victory was the March 1901 capture of Aguinaldo, who later signed a document urging his followers to stop fighting and declaring his own allegiance to the United States. (Aguinaldo then retired from public life and lived quietly until 1964.) Fighting continued in some places for another

GROWING ECONOMIC DEPENDENCE

FILIPINO PRISONERS American troops guard captured Filipino guerrillas in Manila. The suppression of the Filipino insurrection was a much longer and costlier military undertaking than the Spanish-American War, by which the United States first gained possession of the islands. By mid-1900 there were 70,000 American troops in the Philippines, under the command of General Arthur MacArthur (whose son Douglas won fame in the Philippines during World War II). (The Library of Congress)

THE AMERICAN SOUTH PACIFIC EMPIRE, 1900 Except for Puerto Rico, all of the colonial acquisitions of the United States in the wake of the Spanish-American War occurred in the Pacific. The new attraction of imperialism persuaded the United States to annex Hawaii in 1898. The war itself gave America control of the Philippines, Guam, and other, smaller Spanish possessions in the Pacific. When added to the small, scattered islands that the United States had acquired as naval bases earlier in the nineteenth century, these new possessions gave the nation a far-flung Pacific empire, even if one whose total territory and population remained small by the standards of the other great empires of the age.

• *What was the reaction in the United States to the acquisition of this new empire?*

year, and the war revived intermittently until as late as 1906; but American possession of the Philippines was now secure. In the summer of 1901, the military transferred authority over the islands to William Howard Taft, who became their first civilian governor. Taft announced that the American mission in the Philippines was to prepare the islands for independence, and he gave the Filipinos broad local autonomy. The Americans also built roads, schools, bridges, and sewers; instituted major administrative and financial reforms; and established a public health system. The Philippine economy–dominated by fishing, agriculture, timber, and mining–also became increasingly linked to the economy of the United States. Americans did not make many investments in the Philippines, and few Americans moved there. But trade with the United States grew to the point that the islands were almost completely dependent on American markets.

In the meantime, a succession of American governors gradually increased Filipino political autonomy. On July 4, 1946, the islands gained their independence.

THE OPEN DOOR

The acquisition of the Philippines greatly increased the already strong American interest in Asia. Americans were particularly concerned about the future of China, with which the United States had an important trade and which was now so enfeebled that it provided a tempting target for exploitation by stronger countries. By 1900, England, France, Germany, Russia, and Japan were beginning to carve up China among themselves. They pressured the Chinese government for "concessions," which gave them effective control over various regions, most along the coast of China. In some cases, they simply seized Chinese territory and claimed it as their own. Many Americans feared that the process would soon cut them out of the China trade altogether.

Eager for a way to advance American interests in China without risking war, McKinley issued a statement in September 1898 saying the United States wanted access to China, but no special advantages there. "Asking only the open door for ourselves, we are ready to accord the open door to others." The next year, Secretary of State John Hay translated those words into policy when he addressed identical messages–which **HAY'S "OPEN DOOR NOTES"** became known as the "Open Door notes"– to England, Germany, Russia, France, Japan, and Italy. He asked them to approve three principles: each nation with a sphere of influence in China was to respect the rights and privileges of other nations in its sphere; Chinese officials were to continue to collect tariff duties in all spheres (the existing tariff favored the United States); and nations were not to discriminate against other nations in levying port dues and railroad rates within their own spheres. Together, these principles would allow the United States to trade freely with the Chinese without fear of interference and without having to become militarily involved in the region. They would also retain the illusion of Chinese sovereignty and thus prevent formal colonial dismemberment of China, which might also create obstacles to American trade.

Europe and Japan received the Open Door proposals coolly. Russia openly rejected them; the other powers claimed to accept them in principle but to be unable to act unless all the other powers agreed. But Hay refused to consider this a rebuff. He boldly announced that all the powers had accepted the principles of the Open Door in "final and definitive" form and that the United States expected them to observe those principles.

No sooner had the diplomatic maneuvering over the Open Door ended than the Boxers, a secret Chinese martial-arts society with highly nationalist convictions and a somewhat mystical vision of their invulnerability to bullets, launched a revolt against foreigners in China. The Boxer Rebellion spread widely across eastern China, attacking Westerners wherever they could find them–including many Christian missionaries. But the climax of the revolt was a siege of the entire Western foreign diplomatic corps, which took refuge in the British embassy in Beijing. The imperial powers (including the United States) sent an international expeditionary force into China to rescue the diplomats. In August 1900, it fought its way into Peking and broke the siege.

The Boxer Rebellion became an important event for the role of the United States in China. McKinley and Hay had agreed to American participation in quelling the Boxer Rebellion so as to secure a voice in the settlement of the uprising and to prevent the partition of China by the European **BOXER REBELLION** powers. Hay now won support for his Open Door approach from England and Germany and induced the other participating powers to accept compensation from the Chinese for the damages the Boxer Rebellion had caused. Chinese territorial integrity survived at least in name, and the United States retained access to its lucrative trade.

A MODERN MILITARY SYSTEM

The war with Spain had revealed glaring deficiencies in the American military system. The army had exhibited the greatest weaknesses, but the entire military organization had demonstrated problems of supply, training, and coordination. Had the United States been fighting a more powerful foe,

THE BOXER REBELLION, 1900 This photograph shows imprisoned Boxers in Beijing. Days earlier, they had been involved in the siege of the compound in which Western diplomats lived. An expeditionary force of numerous European powers in China, and of the United States, had broken the siege and captured the Boxers. (© Bettmann/Corbis)

disaster might have resulted. After the war, McKinley appointed Elihu Root, an able corporate lawyer in New York, as secretary of war to supervise a major overhaul of the armed forces. (Root was one of the first of several generations of attorney-statesmen who moved easily between public and private roles and constituted much of what has often been called the American "foreign policy establishment.")

Between 1900 and 1903, the Root reforms enlarged the regular army from 25,000 to a maximum of 100,000. They established federal army standards for the National Guard, ensuring that never again would the nation fight a war with volunteer regiments trained and equipped differently than those in the regular army. They sparked the creation of a system of officer training schools, including the Army Staff College (later the **ROOT'S MILITARY REFORMS** Command and General Staff School) at Fort Leavenworth, Kansas, and the Army War College in Washington. And in 1903, a general staff (named the Joint Chiefs of Staff) was established to act as military advisers to the secretary of war. It was this last reform that Root considered most important: the creation of a central planning agency modeled on the example of European general staffs. The Joint Chiefs were charged with many functions. They were to "supervise" and "coordinate" the entire army establishment and to establish an office that would plan for possible wars. An Army and Navy Board was to foster interservice cooperation. As a result of the new reforms, the United States entered the twentieth century with something resembling a modern military system.

AP CONNECTING THEMES

Chapter 19 focused on the politics of the Gilded Age, the discontent among farmers, and the rise of the United States as a world military and economic power. As you review the chapter, focus on the similarities and differences in the platforms of various political parties, including third parties, in addressing these developments. Be aware of the reasons for agrarian discontent and the means by which farmers attempted to remedy those problems. Particularly important is the rise of the Populist Party and its platform's challenge to the status quo. The emergence of William Jennings Bryan as a key political figure is important, as is the adoption of significant portions of the Populist platform by the Democratic Party. Next, this chapter also discussed how U.S. involvement in world affairs increased, highlighted by the Spanish-American War and the acquisition of new territories. Reasons why the United States moved to a more imperialistic stance and the results of that involvement were discussed.

The following themes have heightened importance in Chapter 19. You should now be able to do the following for each listed theme:

Identity: Analyze the ways in which the acquisition of overseas territories challenged the concept of American identity.
Work, Exchange, and Technology: Explain the consequences of economic hardship on both the domestic and international scene.
Peopling: Describe how the acquisition of new overseas territories affected migration patterns.
America in the World: Explain the motives for and consequences of the new imperialism economically, politically, and socially.
Politics and Power: Explain the challenges to the relationship between government and big business and the response of government to those challenges.
Environment and Geography: Explain several ways in which the new imperialism of the late 19th century changed America's status in the world.
Ideas, Beliefs, and Culture: Compare and contrast the debate over imperialism, demonstrating an understanding of the justifications used by each side.

AP SUGGESTED STUDY

PEOPLE/PLACES/EVENTS As you study these items, think about how they demonstrate or relate to key concepts and historical themes from this chapter and previous chapters.

ALFRED THAYER MAHAN 533
ANTI-IMPERIALIST LEAGUE 544
BOXER REBELLION 548
CUBAN REVOLT 538
EMILIO AGUINALDO 546
FARMERS' ALLIANCES 521
FORAKER ACT 543
FOREIGN TRADE 532
"FREE SILVER" 523
HAWAII 534

IMPERIALISM 531
HALF-BREEDS 516
INTERSTATE COMMERCE ACT 519
JACOB COXEY 525
MARY E. LEASE 521
THE *MAINE* 539
"OPEN DOOR" POLICY 547
PLATT AMENDMENT 545
PANIC OF 1893 524
PENDLETON ACT 517

POPULISM 520
POPULIST PARTY (PEOPLE'S) 522
PUERTO RICO 543
SHERMAN ANTITRUST ACT 518
SPANISH-AMERICAN WAR 539
THE GRANGE 520
THE PHILIPPINES 539
WILLIAM JENNINGS BRYAN 528
WILLIAM MCKINLEY 528
YELLOW JOURNALISM 536

AP TEST PRACTICE

Questions assume cumulative content knowledge from this chapter and previous chapters.

MULTIPLE CHOICE Use the political cartoon on page 538 and your knowledge of U.S. history to answer questions 1–3.

1. What argument used by some at the time to justify American imperialism is most being implied in the cartoon?
   (A) The need to expand American markets
   (B) The superiority of the white races and their duty to civilize the more "barbaric" races
   (C) The need to compete with the European imperial powers
   (D) The duty of America to control the Western Hemisphere

2. Which of the following was most directly a reason for American imperialism in the late 19th century?
   (A) Increasing importance of foreign trade to the national economy
   (B) Increasing public awareness of Latin and Pacific Asian countries
   (C) The lack of natural resources in the western United States
   (D) The declining influence of Spain in the Western Hemisphere

3. Which was a result of the events being referenced in the cartoon?

   (A) Sharply increased competition with Great Britain as an imperial power

   (B) Annexation of the Hawaiian Islands

   (C) Spanish-American War

   (D) American annexation of Cuba

SHORT ANSWER Use your knowledge of U.S. history to answer questions 4–7.

4. Answer a, b, and c.

   a) Briefly explain ONE example of how government policy towards big business changed near the turn of the 20th century.

   b) Briefly explain ONE example of how government policy towards big business remained constant from the mid-19th century to the turn of the 20th century.

   c) Briefly explain ONE example demonstrating the nature of big business's relationship with government in the late 19th century through the turn of the 20th century.

5. Answer a, b, and c.

   a) Briefly explain why the Spanish-American War is considered the point at which America was considered a world power.

   b) Provide ONE piece of historical evidence to support this assertion.

   c) Briefly explain why ONE other point in American history might be a better choice to mark this turning point.

6. Answer a, b, and c.

   a) For one of the areas below, identify ONE challenge that American farmers as a group found themselves confronting at the turn of the 20th century.

   • Economic

   • Political

   • Cultural

   b) Briefly explain the event you identified above.

   c) Choose a SECOND area and explain why agrarian issues in that area were not as challenging at turn of the 20th century.

7. Use the political cartoon on page 545 to answer a, b, and c.

   a) Briefly explain the perspective regarding America's new imperialism of the late 19th century that the cartoon is expressing.

   b) Briefly explain ONE argument which those in agreement with the perspective of the cartoon would have given in the political debate over American imperialism in the late 19th century.

   c) Briefly explain ONE argument which those in disagreement with the perspective of the cartoon would have given in the political debate over American imperialism in the late 19th century.

LONG ESSAY Develop a thoughtful and thorough historical argument that answers the question below. Begin your essay with a thesis statement and support it with relevant historical evidence.

8. To what extent were the political and economic causes for American imperialism in the 1890s a continuation as well as a departure from the political and economic causes for America's Manifest Destiny during the 1840s and 1850s?

20 | THE PROGRESSIVES

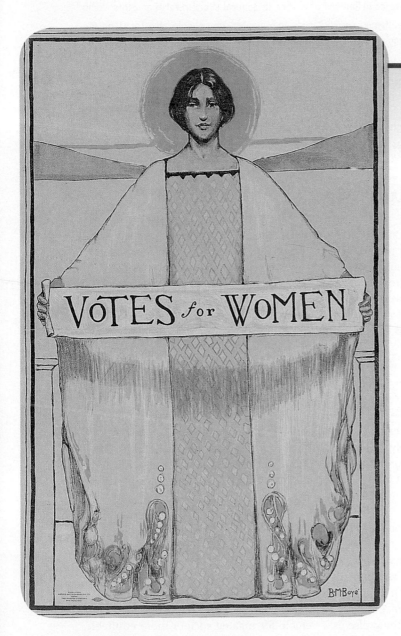

"VOTES FOR WOMEN," BY B. M. BOYE This striking poster was the prize-winning entry in a 1911 contest sponsored by the College Equal Suffrage League of Northern California. (The Schlesinger Library, Radcliffe Institute, Harvard University)

AP

HISTORICAL THINKING

1. **Historical Argumentation** To what degree and in what ways were Progressives able to make the American political system more democratic at the national, state, and local levels?

2. **Historical Argumentation** To what degree and in what ways did the Progressive movement improve life for average Americans through the regulation of big business?

3. **Historical Causation** To what degree and in what ways were Progressives able to enact social welfare legislation?

4. **Contextualization** Analyze the sources of support for Progressive reform and the reasons for that support.

5. **Contextualization** Analyze the role of women in the Progressive movement, reforms they sought to attain, and their relative success in realizing those goals.

6. **Comparison** Compare and contrast the views of big business and conservationists on the use of natural resources.

7. **Comparison** Compare and contrast New Nationalism with New Freedom.

8. **Historical Argumentation** Evaluate the positions of Booker T. Washington and W.E.B. Du Bois on how to best attain equal rights for African Americans.

Key Concept Correlations

Analyze the ways the historical developments you learn about in this chapter connect to the following AP Key Concepts.

6.2 The emergence of an industrial culture in the United States led to both greater opportunities for, and restrictions on, immigrants, minorities, and women.

6.3 The "Gilded Age" witnessed new cultural and intellectual movements in tandem with political debates over economic and social policies.

7.1 Governmental, political, and social organizations struggled to address the effects of large-scale industrialization, economic uncertainty, and related social changes such as urbanization and mass migration.

Thematic Learning Objectives
WOR-3; ID-7; WXT-3, 5, 6, 7, 8; POL-2, 3; ENV-5; CUL-5

CHAPTER 20 discusses the progressive reform movement and the beliefs and philosophies that drove the impulse. It discusses the strategies of reformers for realizing their agenda, as well as their relative success. The chapter deals extensively with the positive contributions of women to general social reform and to specific issues of interest, such as prohibition and suffrage. As you study the chapter, you should also focus on the political agendas of Theodore Roosevelt, William Taft, and Woodrow Wilson, particularly on comparing and contrasting the ideas of Roosevelt's New Nationalism and Wilson's New Freedom. Pay close attention also to the discussion of diverse views concerning environmental protection. As you read, evaluate the following ideas:

- Progressives pressured government to take a more active role in democratizing the political system, reining in the power of big business, and enacting social welfare legislation.
- The middle class, women, and journalists played prominent roles in initiating progressive reforms.

THE PROGRESSIVE IMPULSE

BELIEF IN PROGRESS Progressivism was, first, an optimistic vision. Progressives believed, as their name implies, in the idea of progress. They believed that society was capable of improvement and that continued growth and advancement were the nation's destiny.

But progressives believed, too, that growth and progress could not continue to occur recklessly, as they had in the late nineteenth century. The "natural laws" of the marketplace, and the doctrines of laissez faire and Social Darwinism that celebrated those laws, were not sufficient. Direct, purposeful human intervention in social and economic affairs was, they argued, essential to ordering and bettering society.

VARIETIES OF PROGRESSIVISM

Progressives did not always agree on the form their intervention should take, and the result was a variety of reform impulses that sometimes seemed to have little in common. One powerful impulse was the spirit of "antimonopoly," the fear of concentrated power and the urge to limit **"ANTIMONOPOLY"** and disperse authority and wealth. This vaguely populist impulse appealed not only to many workers and farmers but to some middle-class Americans as well. And it encouraged government to regulate or break up trusts at both the state and national level.

Another progressive impulse was a belief in the importance of social cohesion: the belief that individuals are part of a great web of social relationships, that each person's welfare is dependent on the welfare of society as a whole. That assumption produced a concern about the "victims" of industrialization and other people who had difficult lives.

Still another impulse was a deep faith in knowledge–in the possibilities of applying to society the principles of natural and social sciences. Many reformers believed that knowledge was more **FAITH IN KNOWLEDGE** important than anything else as a vehicle for making society more equitable and humane. Most progressives believed, too, that a modernized government could–and must–play an important role in the process of improving and stabilizing society. Modern life was too complex to be left in the hands of party bosses, untrained amateurs, and antiquated institutions.

THE MUCKRAKERS

Among the first people to articulate the new spirit of reform were crusading journalists who began to direct public attention toward social, economic, and political injustices. They became known as the "muckrakers," after Theodore Roosevelt accused one of them of raking up muck through his writings. They were committed to exposing scandal, corruption, and injustice to public view.

At first, their major targets were the trusts and particularly the railroads, which the muckrakers considered powerful and deeply corrupt. Exposés of the great corporate organizations began to appear as early as the 1860s, when Charles Francis Adams Jr. and others uncovered corruption among the railroad barons. One of the most notable muckrakers was the journalist Ida Tarbell's enormous study of the Standard Oil trust (published first in magazines and then as a two-volume book in 1904). By the turn of the century, many muckrakers were turning their attention to government, particularly to the urban political machines. The most influential, perhaps, was Lincoln Steffens, a reporter for *McClure's* magazine and the author of a famous book based on his articles, *The Shame of the Cities* (1904). His portraits of "machine government" and "boss rule"; his exposure of "boodlers" in cities as diverse as St. Louis, Minneapolis, Cleveland, Cincinnati, Chicago, Philadelphia, and New York; his tone of studied moral outrage—all helped arouse sentiment for urban political reform. The alternative to leaving government in the hands of corrupt party leaders, the muckrakers argued, was for the people themselves to take a greater interest in public life.

IDA TARBELL AND LINCOLN STEFFENS

The muckrakers reached the peak of their influence in the first decade of the twentieth century. By presenting social problems to the public with indignation and moral fervor, they helped inspire other Americans to take action.

THE SOCIAL GOSPEL

The growing outrage at social and economic injustice helped produce many reformers committed to the pursuit of what came to be known as "social justice." (Social justice is a term widely used around the world to describe a kind of justice that goes beyond the individual, seeking justice for society as a whole. Advocates of social justice are likely to believe in an egalitarian society and support for poor and oppressed people.) That impulse helped create the rise of what became known as the "Social Gospel." By the early twentieth century, it had become a powerful movement within American Protestantism (and, to a lesser extent, within American Catholicism and Judaism). It was chiefly concerned with redeeming the nation's cities.

The Salvation Army, which began in England but soon spread to the United States, was one example of the fusion of religion with reform. A Christian social welfare organization with a vaguely military structure, by 1900 it had recruited 3,000 "officers" and 20,000 "privates" and was offering both material aid and spiritual service to the urban poor. In addition, many ministers, priests, and rabbis left traditional parish work to serve in the troubled cities. Charles Sheldon's *In His Steps* (1898), the story of a young minister who abandoned a comfortable post to work among the needy, sold more than 15 million copies. It was one of the most successful novels of the era.

Walter Rauschenbusch, a Protestant theologian from Rochester, New York, published a series of influential discourses on the possibilities for human salvation through Christian reform. To him, the message of Darwinism was not the survival of the fittest. He believed, rather, that all individuals should work to ensure a humanitarian evolution of the social fabric. Some American Catholics seized on the 1893 publication of Pope Leo XIII's encyclical *Rerum Novarum* (New Things) as justification for their own crusade for social justice. Catholic liberals such as Father John A. Ryan took to heart the pope's warning that "a small number of very rich men have been able to lay upon the masses of the poor a yoke little better than slavery itself." For decades, he worked to expand the scope of Catholic social welfare organizations.

FATHER JOHN RYAN

THE SETTLEMENT HOUSE MOVEMENT

An element of much progressive thought was the belief in the influence of the environment on individual development. Social Darwinists such as William Graham Sumner had argued that people's fortunes reflected their inherent "fitness" for survival. Progressive theorists disagreed. Ignorance, poverty, even criminality, they argued, were not the result of inherent genetic failings or of the workings of providence; they were, rather, the effects of an unhealthy environment. To elevate the distressed, therefore, required an improvement of the conditions in which they lived.

Nothing produced more distress, many urban reformers believed, than crowded immigrant neighborhoods, which publicists such as Jacob Riis were exposing through vivid photographs and lurid descriptions. One response to the problems of such communities, borrowed from England, was the settlement house. The most famous, and one of the first, was Hull House, which opened in 1889 in Chicago as a result of the efforts of the social worker Jane Addams. It became a model for more than 400 similar institutions throughout the nation. Staffed by members of the educated middle class, settlement houses sought to help immigrant families adapt to the language and customs of their new country. Settlement houses avoided the condescension and moral disapproval of earlier philanthropic efforts. But they generally embraced a belief that middle-class Americans had a responsibility to impart their own values to immigrants and to teach them how to create middle-class lifestyles.

JANE ADDAMS AND HULL HOUSE

Young college women (mostly unmarried) were important participants in the settlement house movement. Working in a settlement house, which was a protected site that served mostly women, was consistent with the widespread assumption that women needed to be sheltered from difficult environments. The clean and well-tended buildings that settlement houses created were not only a model for immigrant women, but an appropriate site for elite women as well.

"THE BOSSES OF THE SENATE" (1889), BY JOSEPH KEPPLER Keppler was a popular political cartoonist of the late nineteenth century who shared the growing concern about the power of the trusts—portrayed here as bloated, almost reptilian figures standing menacingly over the members of the U.S. Senate, to whose chamber the "people's entrance" is "closed." (© The Granger Collection, New York)

The settlement houses helped create another important element of progressive reform: the profession of social work. Workers at Hull House, for example, maintained a close relationship with the University of Chicago's pioneering work in the field of sociology. A growing number of programs for the professional training of social workers began to appear in the nation's leading universities, partly in response to the activities of the settlements.

THE ALLURE OF EXPERTISE

As the emergence of the social work profession suggests, progressives involved in humanitarian efforts placed a high value on knowledge and expertise. Even nonscientific problems, they believed, could be analyzed and solved scientifically. Many reformers came to believe that only enlightened experts and well-designed bureaucracies could create the stability and order America needed.

Some reformers even spoke of the creation of a new civilization, in which the expertise of scientists and engineers could be brought to bear on the problems of the economy and

society. The social scientist Thorstein Veblen, for example, proposed a new economic system in which power would reside in the hands of highly trained engineers. Only they, he argued, could fully understand the "machine process" by which modern society must be governed.

THE PROFESSIONS

The late nineteenth century saw a dramatic expansion in the number of Americans engaged in administrative and professional tasks. Industries needed managers, technicians, and accountants as well as workers. Cities required commercial, medical, legal, and educational services. New technology required scientists and engineers, who, in turn, required institutions and instructors to train them. By the turn of the century, those performing these services had come to constitute a distinct social group–what some historians have called a new middle class.

The new middle class placed a high value on education and individual accomplishment. By the early twentieth century, its millions of members were building organizations and establishing standards to secure their position in society. The idea of professionalism had been a frail one in America even as late as 1880. When every patent-medicine salesman could claim to be a doctor, when every frustrated politician could set up shop as a lawyer, when anyone who could read and write could pose as a teacher, a professional label by itself carried little weight. There were, of course, skilled and responsible doctors, lawyers, teachers, and others; but they had no way of controlling or distinguishing themselves clearly from the amateurs, charlatans, and incompetents who presumed to practice their trades. As the demand for professional services increased, so did the pressures for reform.

Among the first to respond was the medical profession. In 1901, doctors who considered themselves trained profes-

AMERICAN MEDICAL ASSOCIATION

sionals reorganized the American Medical Association into a national professional society. By 1920, nearly two-thirds of all American doctors were members. The AMA quickly called for strict, scientific standards for admission to the practice of medicine, with doctors themselves serving as protectors of the standards. State governments responded by passing new laws requiring the licensing of all physicians. By 1900, medical education at a few medical schools—notably Johns Hopkins in Baltimore (founded in 1893)—compared favorably with that in the leading institutions of Europe. Doctors such as William H. Welch at Hopkins revolutionized the teaching of medicine by moving students out of the classrooms and into laboratories and clinics.

There was similar movement in other professions. By 1916, lawyers in all forty-eight states had established professional bar associations. The nation's law schools accordingly expanded greatly. Businessmen supported the creation of schools of business administration and created their own national organizations: the National Association of Manufacturers in 1895 and the United States Chamber of Commerce in 1912. Even farmers, long

NATIONAL ASSOCIATION OF MANUFACTURERS

the symbol of the romantic spirit of individualism, responded to the new order by forming, through the National Farm Bureau Federation, a network of agricultural organizations designed to spread scientific farming methods.

While removing the untrained and incompetent, the admission requirements also protected those already in the professions from excessive competition and lent prestige and status to their trades. Some professionals used their entrance requirements to exclude blacks, women, immigrants, and other "undesirables" from their ranks. Others used them simply

THE INFANT WELFARE SOCIETY, CHICAGO The Infant Welfare Society was one of many "helping" organizations in Chicago and other large cities—many of them closely tied to the settlement houses—that strove to help immigrants adapt to American life and create safe and healthy living conditions. Here, a volunteer helps an immigrant mother learn to bathe her baby. (The Library of Congress (LC-DIG-npcc-33267))

to keep the numbers down, to ensure that demand would remain high.

WOMEN AND THE PROFESSIONS

Both by custom and by active barriers of law and prejudice, American women found themselves excluded from most of the emerging professions. But a substantial number of middle-class women—particularly those emerging from the new women's colleges and coeducational state universities—entered professional careers nevertheless.

A few women managed to establish themselves as physicians, lawyers, engineers, scientists, and corporate managers in

FEMALE-DOMINATED PROFESSIONS

the early 1900s. Several leading medical schools admitted women, and in 1900 about 5 percent of all American physicians were female (a proportion that remained unchanged until the 1960s). Most, however, turned by necessity to those "helping" professions that society considered vaguely domestic and thus suitable for women: settlement houses, social work, and most important, teaching. Indeed, in the late nineteenth century, more than two-thirds of all grammar school teachers were women, and perhaps 90 percent of all professional women were teachers. For educated black women, in particular, the existence of segregated schools in the South created a substantial market for African American teachers.

Women also dominated other professional activities. Nursing had become primarily a women's field during and after the Civil War. By the early twentieth century, it was

PROGRESSIVISM

UNTIL the early 1950s, most historians generally agreed on the central characteristics of progressivism. It was just what progressives themselves said it was: a movement by the "people" to curb the power of the "special interests."

George Mowry challenged this traditional view in *The California Progressives* (1951). He described the reform movement in California not as a people's protest, but, rather, as an effort by a small and privileged group of business and professional men to limit the power of large new corporations and labor unions. Richard Hofstadter expanded on this idea in *The Age of Reform* (1955), describing progressives throughout the country as people suffering from "status anxiety"—old, formerly influential, upper-middle-class families seeking to restore their fading prestige by challenging the powerful new institutions that had begun to displace them.

The Mowry-Hofstadter thesis provoked new challenges and new interpretations of the meaning of progressivism. Gabriel Kolko, in *The Triumph of Conservatism* (1963), rejected the Mowry-Hofstadter idea that progressivism represented the efforts of a displaced elite. Progressivism, he argued, was an effort to regulate business undertaken, not by the "people" or "displaced elites," but by corporate leaders, who saw in government supervision a way to protect themselves from competition. Martin Sklar's *The Corporate Reconstruction of American Capitalism* (1988) is a more sophisticated version of a similar argument.

A more moderate challenge to the "psychological" interpretation of progressivism came from historians embracing a new "organizational" view of history. In *The Search for Order, 1877–1920* (1967), Robert Wiebe presented progressivism as a response to dislocations in American life brought on by rapid changes in the economy. Economic power had moved to large, national organizations, while social and political life remained centered primarily in local communities. The result was widespread disorder and unrest. Progressivism, Wiebe argued, was the effort of a "new middle class"—a class tied to the emerging national economy—to stabilize and enhance their position in society by creating national institutions suitable for the new national economy.

Some historians continued to argue that progressivism was a movement of the people against the special interests. J. Joseph Huthmacher argued in 1962 that much of the force behind progressivism came from members of the working class, especially immigrants, who pressed for such reforms as workmen's compensation and wage and hour laws. John Buenker, in *Urban Liberalism and Progressive Reform* (1973), claimed that political machines and urban "bosses" were important sources of reform energy and helped create twentieth-century liberalism.

Other historians writing in the 1970s and 1980s attempted to link reform to some of the broad processes of political change that had created the public battles of the era. Richard L. McCormick's *From Realignment to Reform* (1981), a study of political change in New York State, argued that the crucial change in this era was the decline of the political parties and the rise of interest groups working for particular social and economic goals.

Many historians see progressivism as rooted in gender and have focused on the role of women (and the vast network of voluntary associations they created) in shaping and promoting progressive reform. Historians Kathryn Sklar, Linda Gordon, Ruth Rosen, and Elaine Tyler May, among others, argued that some progressive battles were part of an effort by women to protect their interests within the domestic sphere in the face of jarring challenges from the new industrial world. This protective urge drew women reformers to such issues as temperance, divorce, prostitution, and the regulation of female and child labor. Other women worked to expand their own roles in the public world. Progressivism cannot be understood, historians of women contend, adopting professional standards. And many women entered academia–often receiving advanced degrees at such predominantly male institutions as the University of Chicago, MIT, or Columbia, and finding professional opportunities in the new and expanding women's colleges.

WOMEN AND REFORM

KEY ROLE OF WOMEN IN REFORM CAUSES

The prominence of women in reform movements is one of the most striking features of progressivism. In most states in the early twentieth century, women could not vote. They almost never held public office. They had footholds in only a few (and usually primarily female) professions and lived in a culture in which most people, male and female, believed that women were not suited for the public world. What, then, explains the prominent role so many women played in the reform activities of the period?

THE "NEW WOMAN"

SOCIOECONOMIC ORIGINS OF THE NEW WOMAN

The phenomenon of the "new woman," widely remarked upon at the time, was a product of social and economic changes that affected the private world as much as the public one, even if such changes affected mostly middle-class people. By the end of the nineteenth century, almost all income-producing activity had moved out of the home and into the factory or the office. At the same time, children were beginning school at earlier ages and spending more time there. For many wives and mothers who did not work for wages, the home

WOMANS HOLY WAR.
Grand Charge on the Enemy's Works.

(© Private Collection/The Bridgeman Art Library)

McGerr, in *A Fierce Discontent* (2003), and Alan Dawley, in *Changing the World* (2003), have characterized progressivism as a fundamentally moral undertaking. McGerr viewed it as an effort by the middle class to create order and stability, whereas Dawley saw it as an effort by groups on the left to attack social injustice.

Given the range of disagreement over the nature of the progressive movement, it is hardly surprising that some historians have despaired of finding any coherent definition for the term. Peter Filene, for one, suggested in 1970 that the concept of progressivism as a "movement" had outlived its usefulness. But Daniel Rodgers, in an important 1982 article, "In Search of Progressivism," disagreed. The very diversity of progressivism, he argued, accounted both for its enormous impact on its time and for its capacity to reveal to us today the "noise and tumult" of an age of rapid social change. ●

AP HISTORICAL ARGUMENTATION AND INTERPRETATION

Questions assume cumulative content knowledge from this chapter and previous chapters.

1. Identify five interpretations concerning the progressive era made by historians. For each, provide one piece of historical evidence that supports the argument.
2. Identify the interpretations that view Progressivism through a psychological lens. Identify the arguments that view Progressivism through a gender lens. Identify the arguments that view Progressivism through an organizational lens.
3. With which historian's interpretation do you most agree? Explain why, supporting your argument with historical evidence.

without understanding the role of women and the importance of issues involving the family and the private world within it.

Other historians have sought to place progressivism in a broader context. Daniel Rodgers's *Atlantic Crossings* (1998) is a study of how European reforms influenced American progressives. Both Michael

was no longer an all-consuming place. Technological innovations such as running water, electricity, and eventually household appliances made housework less onerous (even if higher standards of cleanliness counterbalanced many of these gains).

Declining family size also changed the lives of many women. Middle-class white women in the late nineteenth century had fewer children than their mothers and grandmothers had borne. They also lived longer. Many women thus now spent fewer years with young children in the home and lived more years after their children were grown.

Some educated women shunned marriage, believing that only by remaining single could they play the roles they envisioned in the public world. Single women were among the most prominent female reformers of the time: Jane Addams and Lillian Wald in the settlement house movement, Frances Willard in the temperance movement, Anna Howard Shaw in

the suffrage movement, and many others. Some of these women lived alone. Others lived with other women, often in

"BOSTON MARRIAGES"

long-term relationships—some of them quietly romantic—that were known at the time as "Boston marriages." The divorce rate also rose rapidly in the late nineteenth century, from one divorce for every twenty-one marriages in 1880 to one in nine by 1916; women initiated the majority of them.

THE CLUBWOMEN

Among the most visible signs of the increasing public roles of women in the late nineteenth and early twentieth centuries were the women's clubs, which proliferated rapidly beginning in the 1880s and 1890s and became the vanguard of many important reforms.

The women's clubs began largely as cultural organizations to provide middle- and upper-class women with an outlet for their intellectual energies. In 1892, when women formed the

GFWC General Federation of Women's Clubs to coordinate the activities of local organizations, there were more than 100,000 members in nearly 500 clubs. By 1917, there were over 1 million.

By the early twentieth century, the clubs were becoming less concerned with cultural activities and more concerned with contributing to social betterment. Because many club members were from wealthy families, some organizations had substantial funds at their disposal to make their influence felt. And ironically, because women could not vote, the clubs had a nonpartisan image that made them difficult for politicians to dismiss.

Black women occasionally joined clubs dominated by whites. But most such clubs excluded blacks, and so African Americans formed clubs of their own. Some of them affiliated with the General Federation, but most became part of the independent National Association of Colored Women. Some black clubs also took positions on issues of particular concern to African Americans, such as lynching and aspects of segregation.

The women's club movement seldom raised overt challenges to prevailing assumptions about the proper role of women in society. Few clubwomen were willing to accept the arguments

A PUBLIC SPACE FOR WOMEN of such committed feminists as Charlotte Perkins Gilman, who in her 1898 book, *Women and Economics*, argued that the traditional definition of gender roles was exploitive and obsolete. Instead, the club movement allowed women to define a space for themselves in the public world without openly challenging the existing, male-dominated order.

Much of what the clubs did was uncontroversial: planting trees; supporting schools, libraries, and settlement houses; building hospitals and parks. But clubwomen were also an important force in winning passage of state (and ultimately federal) laws that regulated the conditions of woman and child labor, established government inspection

THE COLORED WOMEN'S LEAGUE OF WASHINGTON, D.C. The women's club movement spread widely through American life and produced a number of organizations through which African American women gathered to improve social and political conditions. The Colored Women's League of Washington, D.C., members of which appear in this 1894 photograph, was founded in 1892 by Sara Fleetwood, a registered nurse who was the wife of Christian Fleetwood, one of the first African American soldiers to receive the Congressional Medal of Honor for his heroism in the Civil War. The league she founded was committed to "racial uplift," and it consisted mostly of teachers, who created nurseries for the infants of women who worked and evening schools for adults. Members of the League are shown here gathered on the steps of Frederick Douglass's home on Capitol Hill. Sara Fleetwood is in the second row on the far right. (The Library of Congress)

of workplaces, regulated the food and drug industries, reformed policies toward the Indian tribes, applied new standards to urban housing, and, perhaps most notably, outlawed the manufacture and sale of alcohol. They were instrumental in pressuring state legislatures in most states to provide "mother's pensions" to widowed or abandoned mothers with small children—a system that ultimately became absorbed into the Social Security system. In 1912, they pressured Congress into establishing the Children's Bureau in the Labor Department, an agency directed to develop policies to protect children.

In many of these efforts, the clubwomen formed alliances with other women's groups, such as the Women's Trade Union **WOMEN'S TRADE UNION LEAGUE** League (WTUL), founded in 1903 by female union members and upper-class reformers. It was committed to persuading women to join unions. In addition to working on behalf of protective legislation for women, WTUL members held public meetings on behalf of female workers, raised money to support strikes, marched on picket lines, and bailed striking women out of jail.

WOMAN SUFFRAGE

Perhaps the largest single reform movement of the progressive era, indeed one of the largest in American history, was the fight for woman suffrage.

It is sometimes difficult for today's Americans to understand **RADICAL CHALLENGE OF WOMEN'S SUFFRAGE** why the suffrage issue could have become the source of such enormous controversy. But at the time, suffrage seemed to many of its critics a very radical demand, in part because of the rationale some of its early

supporters used to advance it. Throughout the late nineteenth century, many suffrage advocates presented their views in terms of "natural rights," arguing that women deserved the same rights as men—including, first and foremost, the right to vote. Elizabeth Cady Stanton, for example, wrote in 1892 of woman as "the arbiter of her own destiny . . . if we are to consider her as a citizen, as a member of a great nation, she must have the same rights as all other members." This was an argument that boldly challenged the views of the many men and women who believed that society required a distinctive female "sphere" in which women would serve first and foremost as wives and mothers. And so a powerful antisuffrage movement emerged, dominated by men but with the active support of many women. Opponents railed against the threat suffrage posed to the "natural order" of civilization. Antisuffragists, many of them women, associated suffrage with divorce (not without some reason, since many suffrage advocates also supported making it easier for women to obtain a divorce). They linked suffrage with promiscuity, immorality, and neglect of children.

In the first years of the twentieth century, the suffrage movement began to overcome this opposition and win some substantial victories, in part because suffragists were becoming better organized and more politically sophisticated than their opponents. Under the leadership of Anna Howard Shaw, a Boston social worker, and Carrie Chapman Catt, a journalist **NAWSA** from Iowa, membership in the National American Woman Suffrage Association (NAWSA) grew from about 13,000 in 1893 to over 2 million in 1917. The movement gained strength because many of its most prominent leaders began to justify suffrage in "safer," less threatening ways. Suffrage, some supporters began to argue, would not challenge the "separate sphere" in which women resided. It was, they claimed, precisely because women occupied

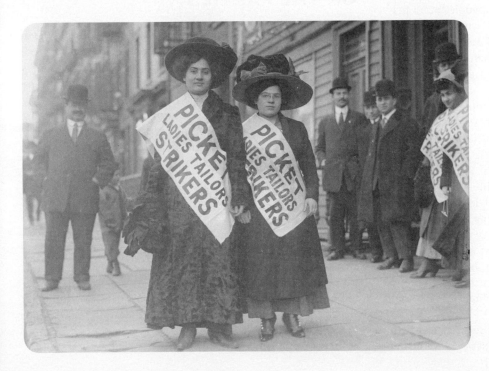

SHIRTWAIST WORKERS ON STRIKE The Women's Trade Union League was notable for bringing educated, middle-class women together with workers in efforts to improve factory and labor conditions. These picketing women are workers in the "Ladies Tailors" garment factory in New York. (The Library of Congress (LC-DIG-ggbain-04507))

SUFFRAGE PAGEANT, 1913 On March 3, 1913—the day before Woodrow Wilson's inauguration as president—more than 5,000 supporters of woman suffrage staged a parade in Washington, D.C., that overshadowed Wilson's own arrival there. Crowds estimated at over half a million watched the parade, not all of them admirers of the woman suffrage movement, and some of the onlookers attacked the marchers. The police did nothing to stop the attacks. This photograph depicts a suffragist, Florence Noyes, costumed as Liberty, posing in front of the U.S. Treasury Building, part of a pageant accompanying the parade. Woman suffrage was one of the most important and impassioned reform movements of the progressive era. (The Library of Congress)

a distinct sphere–because as mothers and wives and home-makers they had special experiences and special sensitivities to bring to public life–that woman suffrage could make such an important contribution to politics.

In particular, many suffragists argued that enfranchising women would help the temperance movement, by giving its largest group of supporters a political voice. Some suffrage advocates claimed that once women had the vote, war would become a thing of the past, since women would–by their calming, maternal influence–help curb the belligerence of men. That was one reason why World War I gave a final, decisive push to the movement for suffrage.

Suffrage also attracted support for other, less optimistic rea-

CONSERVATIVE ARGUMENTS FOR SUFFRAGE

sons. Many middle-class people found persuasive the argument that if blacks, immigrants, and other "base" groups had access to the franchise, then it was a matter not only of justice but of common sense to allow educated, "well-born" women to vote.

The principal triumphs of the suffrage movement began in 1910, when Washington became the first state in four-

NINETEENTH AMENDMENT

teen years to extend suffrage to women. California followed a year later, and four other western states in 1912. In 1913, Illinois became the first state east of the Mississippi to embrace woman suffrage. And in 1917 and 1918, New York and Michigan–two of the most populous states in the Union–gave women the vote. By 1919, thirty-nine states had granted women the right to vote in at least some elections; fifteen had allowed them full participation. In 1920, finally, suffragists won ratification of the Nineteenth Amendment, which guaranteed political rights to women throughout the nation.

To some feminists, however, the victory seemed less than complete. Alice Paul, head of the militant National Woman's

Party (founded in 1916), never accepted the relatively conservative "separate sphere" justification for suffrage. She argued that the Nineteenth Amendment alone would not be sufficient to protect women's rights. Women needed more: a constitutional amendment that would provide clear, legal protection for their rights and would prohibit all discrimination on the basis of sex. But Alice Paul's argument found limited favor even among many of the most important leaders of the recently triumphant suffrage crusade.

THE ASSAULT ON THE PARTIES

Sooner or later, most progressive goals required the involvement of government. Only government, reformers agreed, could effectively counter the many powerful private interests that threatened the nation. But American government at the dawn of the new century was, progressives believed, poorly

REFORMING GOVERNMENT

adapted to perform their ambitious tasks. At every level, political institutions were outmoded, inefficient, and corrupt. Before progressives could reform society effectively, they would have to reform government itself. Many reformers believed the first step must be an assault on the dominant role the political parties played in the life of the state.

EARLY ATTACKS

Attacks on party dominance had been frequent in the late nineteenth century. Greenbackism and Populism, for example, had been efforts to break the hammerlock with which the Republicans and Democrats controlled public life. The Independent Republicans (or mugwumps) had also attempted to challenge the grip of partisanship.

These early assaults enjoyed some success. In the 1880s and 1890s, for example, most states adopted the secret ballot. Prior to that, the political parties themselves had printed ballots (or "tickets"), with the names of the party's candidates, and no others. They distributed the tickets to their supporters, who then simply went to the polls to deposit them in the ballot box. The old system had made it possible for bosses to monitor the voting behavior of their constituents; it had also made it difficult for voters to "split" their tickets–to vote for candidates of different parties for different offices. The new secret ballot–printed by the government and distributed at the polls to be filled out and deposited in secret–helped chip away at the power of the parties over voters.

MUNICIPAL REFORM

Many progressives, such as Lincoln Steffens, believed the impact of party rule was most damaging in the cities. Municipal government therefore became one of the first targets of those working for political reform.

The muckrakers struck a responsive chord among a powerful group of urban, middle-class progressives. For several decades after the Civil War, "respectable" citizens of the nation's large cities had avoided participation in municipal government. Viewing politics as a debased and demeaning activity, they shrank from contact with the "vulgar" elements **MIDDLE-CLASS PROGRESSIVES** who were coming to dominate public life. By the end of the century, however, a new generation of activists–some of them members of old aristocratic families, others a part of the new middle class–were taking a growing interest in government.

These activists faced a formidable array of opponents. In addition to challenging the powerful city bosses and their entrenched political organizations, they were attacking a large group of special interests: saloon owners, brothel keepers, and, perhaps most significantly, those businessmen who had established lucrative relationships with the urban political machines and who viewed reform as a threat to their profits. Finally, there was the great constituency of urban working people, many of them recent immigrants, to whom the machines were a source of needed jobs and services. Gradually, however, the reformers gained in political strength.

NEW FORMS OF GOVERNANCE

One of the first major successes came in Galveston, Texas, where the old city government proved unable **COMMISSION PLAN** to deal with the effects of a destructive tidal wave in 1900. Capitalizing on public dismay, reformers, many of them local businessmen, won approval of a new city charter. The mayor and council were replaced by an elected, nonpartisan commission. In 1907, Des Moines, Iowa, adopted its own version of the commission plan, and other cities followed.

Another approach to municipal reform was the city-manager plan, by which elected officials hired an outside expert–often a professionally trained business manager or engineer–to take **CITY-MANAGER PLAN** charge of the city government. The city manager would presumably remain untainted by the corrupting influence of politics. By the end of the progressive era in the early 1920s, almost 400 cities were operating under commissions, and another 45 employed city managers.

In most urban areas, the enemies of partnership had to settle for less absolute victories. Some cities made the election of mayors nonpartisan (so that the parties could not choose the candidates) or moved them to years when no presidential or congressional races were in progress (to reduce the influence of the large turnouts that party organizations produced). Reformers tried to make city councilors run at large, to limit the influence of ward leaders and district bosses. They tried to strengthen the power of the mayor at the expense of the city council, on the assumption that reformers were more likely to succeed in getting a sympathetic mayor elected than they were to win control of the entire council.

Some of the most successful reformers emerged from conventional political structures that progressives came to control.

TOM JOHNSON As sentiment for municipal reform grew in intensity in the late nineteenth century, it became possible for progressive mayors committed to ending "boss rule" to win election over machine candidates in some of America's largest cities. One of the most prominent was Tom Johnson, the reform mayor of Cleveland. Johnson made a fortune in the steel and streetcar business and then entered politics, partly as a result of reading Henry George's *Poverty and Progress*. He became mayor in 1901 and in his four terms waged strenuous battles against party bosses and corporate interests. He won many fights, but he lost what he considered his most important one: the struggle for municipal ownership of public utilities. (© Western Reserve Historical Society)

SOCIAL DEMOCRACY WOR-3

ENORMOUS energy, enthusiasm, and organization drove the reform efforts in America in the late nineteenth and early twentieth centuries, much of it a result of social crises and political movements in the United States. But the "age of reform," as some scholars have called it, was not just an American phenomenon. It was part of a wave of social experimentation that was occurring through much of the industrial world.

Several industrializing nations—the United States, Britain, Germany, and France—adopted the term "progressivism" for their efforts, but the term that most broadly defined the new reform energies was "social democracy." Social democrats in many countries shared a belief in the betterment of society, not through religion or inherited ideology, but through the accumulation of knowledge. They favored improving the social condition of all people through economic reforms and government programs of social protection. And they believed that these changes could come through peaceful political change, rather than through radicalism or revolution. Political parties committed to these goals emerged in several countries: the Labour Party in Britain, Social Democratic parties in various European nations, and the short-lived Progressive Party in the United States. Intellectuals, academics, and government officials across the world shared the knowledge they were accumulating and observed social programs. An important moment in the growth of social democracy were the many Paris expositions of 1889 and 1900. Their symbol was the famous Eiffel Tower, and their meaning for many progressives was the possibilities of progress through industrial innovation. Not only tourists, but progressive experts as well, visited the Paris expositions; and they held meetings while they were there to share their visions of the future.

At the turn of the century, American reformers visited Germany, France, Britain, Belgium, and the Netherlands, observing the reforms in progress there, while European reformers visited the United States. Reformers from both the United States and Europe were also fascinated by the advanced social experiments in Australia and, especially, New Zealand—which the American reformer Henry Demarest Lloyd once called "the political brain of the modern world." New Zealand's dramatic experiments in factory regulation, woman suffrage, old-age pensions, progressive taxation, and labor arbitration gradually found counterparts in many other nations. William Allen White, a progressive journalist from Kansas, said of this time: "We were parts of one another, in the United States and Europe. Something was welding us into one social and economic whole with local political variations . . . [all] fighting a common cause."

FIGARO ILLUSTRÉ

(© Archives Charmet/The Bridgeman Art Library)

Social democracy—or, as it was sometimes called in the United States and elsewhere, social justice or the Social Gospel—was responsible for many public programs. Germany began a system of social insurance for its citizens in the 1880s while undertaking a massive

---

Tom Johnson, the celebrated reform mayor of Cleveland, waged a long war against the powerful streetcar interests in his city, fighting to lower streetcar fares to 3 cents, and ultimately to impose municipal ownership on certain basic utilities. After Johnson's defeat and death, his talented aide Newton D. Baker won election as mayor and helped maintain Cleveland's reputation as the best-governed city in America. Hazen Pingree of Detroit, Samuel "Golden Rule" Jones of Toledo, and other mayors effectively challenged local party bosses to bring the spirit of reform into city government.

TOM JOHNSON

STATEHOUSE PROGRESSIVISM

The assault on boss rule in the cities did not, however, always produce results. Consequently, many progressives turned to state government as an agent for reform. They looked with particular scorn on state legislatures, whose ill-paid, undistinguished members, they believed, were generally incompetent, often corrupt, and totally controlled by party bosses. Reformers

began looking for ways to circumvent the boss-controlled legislatures by increasing the power of the electorate.

Two of the most important changes were innovations first proposed by Populists in the 1890s: the initiative and the referendum. The initiative allowed reformers to circumvent state legislatures by submitting new legislation directly to the voters in general elections. The referendum provided a method by which actions of the legislature could be returned to the electorate for approval. By 1918, more than twenty states had enacted one or both of these reforms.

INITIATIVE AND REFERENDUM

Similarly, the direct primary and the recall were efforts to limit the power of party and improve the quality of elected officials. The primary election was an attempt to take the selection of candidates away from the bosses and give it to the people. (In the South, it was also an effort to limit black voting–since primary voting, many white southerners believed, would be easier to control than general elections.) The

DIRECT PRIMARY AND RECALL

study of society that produced more than 140 volumes of "social investigation" of almost every aspect of the nation's life. French reformers pressed in the 1890s for factory regulation, assistance to the elderly, and progressive taxation. Britain pioneered the settlement houses in working-class areas of London—a movement that soon spread to the United States as well—and, like the United States, witnessed growing challenges to the power of monopolies at both the local and national level.

In many countries, social democrats felt pressure from the rising worldwide labor movement and from the rise of socialist parties in many industrial countries. Strikes, sometimes violent, were common in France, Germany, Britain, and the United States in the late nineteenth century. The more militant workers became, the more unions grew. Social democrats did not always welcome the rise of militant labor movements, but they took them seriously and tried to use them to support their own reform efforts.

The politics of social democracy represented a great shift in the character of public life all over the industrial world. Instead of battles over the privileges of aristocrats or the power of monarchs, reformers now focused on the social problems of ordinary people and attempted to improve their lot. "The politics of the future are social politics," the British reformer Joseph Chamberlain said in the 1880s, referring to efforts to deal with the problems of ordinary citizens. That belief was fueling progressive efforts across the world in the years that Americans have come to call the "progressive era." ●

UNDERSTAND, ANALYZE, AND EVALUATE

1. What is social democracy? How does it differ from socialism?
2. What progressive era reforms in American social and political life can be seen in other nations as well?
3. Social democratic political parties continue to exist in many countries throughout the world. Why was the Progressive Party in the United States so short-lived?

recall gave voters the right to remove a public official from office at a special election, which could be called after a sufficient number of citizens had signed a petition. By 1915, every state in the nation had instituted primary elections for at least some offices. The recall encountered more strenuous opposition, but a few states (such as California) adopted it as well.

Other reform measures attempted to clean up the legislatures themselves. Between 1903 and 1908, twelve states passed laws restricting lobbying by business interests in state legislatures. In those same years, twenty-two states banned campaign contributions by corporations, and twenty-four states forbade public officials to accept free passes from railroads. Many states also struggled successfully to create systems of workmen's compensation for workers injured on the job. And starting in 1911, reformers successfully created pensions for widows with dependent children.

Reform efforts proved most effective in states that elevated vigorous and committed politicians to positions of leadership. In New York, Governor Charles Evans Hughes exploited progressive sentiment to create a commission to regulate public utilities. In California, Governor Hiram Johnson limited the political power of the Southern Pacific Railroad. In New Jersey, Woodrow Wilson, the Princeton University president elected governor in 1910, used executive leadership to win reforms designed to end New Jersey's widely denounced position as the "mother of trusts."

The most celebrated state-level reformer was Robert M. La Follette of Wisconsin. Elected governor in 1900, he helped

ROBERT LA FOLLETTE

turn his state into what reformers across the nation described as a "laboratory of progressivism." Under his leadership the Wisconsin progressives won approval of direct primaries, initiatives, and referendums. They regulated railroads and utilities. They passed laws to regulate the workplace and provide compensation for laborers injured on the job. They instituted graduated taxes on inherited fortunes, and they nearly doubled state levies on railroads and other corporate interests. La Follette used his personal magnetism to widen public awareness of progressive goals. Reform was the responsibility not simply of politicians, he argued, but of newspapers, citizens' groups, educational institutions, and business and professional organizations as well.

PARTIES AND INTEREST GROUPS

The reformers did not, of course, eliminate parties from American political life. But they did contribute to a decline in

DECLINE OF PARTY INFLUENCE

party influence. Evidence of their impact came from, among other things, the decline in voter turnout. In the late nineteenth century, up to 81 percent of eligible voters routinely turned out for national elections because of the

ROBERT LA FOLLETTE CAMPAIGNING IN WISCONSIN After three terms as governor of Wisconsin, La Follette began a long career in the U.S. Senate in 1906, during which he worked uncompromisingly for advanced progressive reforms—so uncompromisingly, in fact, that he was often almost completely isolated. He titled a chapter of his autobiography "Alone in the Senate." La Follette had a greater impact on his own state, whose politics he and his sons dominated for nearly forty years and where he was able to win passage of many reforms that the federal government resisted. (The Library of Congress (LC-DIG-ggbain-06406))

strength of party loyalty. In the early twentieth century, while turnout remained high by today's standards, the figure declined markedly as parties grew weaker. In the presidential election of 1900, 73 percent of the electorate voted. By 1912, that figure had declined to about 59 percent. Never again did voter turnout reach as high as 70 percent.

Why did voter turnout decline in these years? The secret ballot was one reason. Party bosses had less ability to get voters to the polls. Illiterate voters had trouble reading the new ballots. Party bosses lost much of their authority and were unable to mobilize voters as successfully as they had in the past. But perhaps the most important reason for the decline of party rule (and voter turnout) was that other power centers were beginning to replace them. They have become known as "interest groups." Beginning late in the nineteenth century and accelerating rapidly in the twentieth, new organizations emerged outside the party system: professional organizations, trade associations representing businesses and industries, labor organizations, farm lobbies, and many others. Social workers, the settlement house movement, women's clubs, and others learned to operate as interest groups to advance their demands.

SOURCES OF PROGRESSIVE REFORM

Middle-class reformers, most of them from the East, dominated the public image and much of the substance of progressivism in the late nineteenth and early twentieth centuries. But they were not alone in seeking to improve social conditions. Working-class Americans, African Americans, westerners, and even party bosses also played crucial roles in advancing some of the important reforms of the era.

LABOR, THE MACHINE, AND REFORM

Although the American Federation of Labor, and its leader Samuel Gompers, remained largely aloof from many of the reform efforts of the time (reflecting Gompers's firm belief that workers should not rely on government to improve their lot), some unions played important roles in reform battles. Between 1911 and 1913, thanks to political pressure from labor groups such as the newly formed Union Labor Party, California passed a child-labor law, a workmen's compensation law, and a limitation on working hours for women. Union pressures contributed to the passage of similar laws in many other states as well.

One result of the assault on the parties was a change in the party organizations themselves, which attempted to adapt to the new realities so as to preserve their influence. They sometimes allowed their machines to become vehicles of social reform. One example was New York City's Tammany Hall, the

nation's oldest and most notorious city machine. Its astute leader, Charles Francis Murphy, began in the early years of the century to fuse the techniques of boss rule with some of the concerns of social reformers. Tammany began to use its political power on behalf of legislation to improve working conditions, protect child laborers, and eliminate the worst abuses of the industrial economy.

In 1911, a terrible fire swept through the factory of the Triangle Shirtwaist Company in New York City; 146 workers, most of them women, died. Many of them had been trapped inside the burning building because management had locked the emergency exits to prevent malingering. For the next three years, a state commission studied not only the background of the fire but also the general condition of the industrial workplace. It was responding to intense public pressure from women's groups and New York City labor unions—and to quiet pressure from Tammany Hall. By 1914, the commission had issued a series of reports calling for major reforms in the conditions of modern labor. The report itself was a classic progressive document, based on the testimony of experts, filled with statistics and technical data.

TRIANGLE SHIRTWAIST FIRE

Yet, when its recommendations reached the New York legislature, its most effective supporters were not middle-class progressives but two Tammany Democrats from working-class backgrounds: Senator Robert F. Wagner and Assemblyman Alfred E. Smith. With the support of Murphy and the backing

VOTER PARTICIPATION IN PRESIDENTIAL ELECTIONS, 1876–1920 One of the striking developments of early-twentieth-century politics was the significant decline in popular participation in politics. This chart shows the steady downward progression of voter turnout in presidential elections from 1876 to 1920. Turnout remained high by modern standards (except for the aberrant election of 1920, in which turnout dropped sharply because women had recently received the vote but had not yet begun to participate in elections in large numbers). But from an average rate of participation of about 79 percent in the last quarter of the nineteenth century, turnout dropped to an average of about 65 percent between 1900 and 1916.

• What were some of the reasons for this decline?

of other Tammany legislators, they steered through a series of pioneering labor laws that imposed strict regulations on factory owners and established effective mechanisms for enforcement.

WESTERN PROGRESSIVES

The American West produced some of the most notable progressive leaders of the time: Hiram Johnson of California, George Norris of Nebraska, William Borah of Idaho, and others—almost all of whom spent at least some of their political careers in the U.S. Senate. For western states, the most important target of reform energies was not state or local governments, which had relatively little power, but the federal government, which exercised a kind of authority in the West that it had never possessed in the East. That was in part because some of the most important issues to the future of the West required action above the state level. Disputes over water, for example, almost always involved rivers and streams that crossed state lines. The question of which states had the rights to the waters of the Colorado River created a political battle that no state government could resolve; the federal government had to arbitrate.

More significant, perhaps, the federal government exercised enormous power over the lands and resources of the western states and provided substantial subsidies to the region in the form of land grants and support for railroad and water projects. Huge areas of the West remained (and still remain) public lands, controlled by Washington—a far greater proportion than in any states east of the Mississippi. Much of the growth of the West was (and continues to be) a result of federally funded dams and water projects.

AFRICAN AMERICANS AND REFORM

One social question that received little attention from white progressives was race. But among African Americans themselves, the progressive era produced some significant challenges to existing racial norms.

VICTIMS OF THE TRIANGLE FIRE, 1911 In this bleak photograph, victims of the fire in the factory of the Triangle Shirtwaist Company are laid out on the sidewalk near the building, as police and passersby look up at the scene of the blaze. The tragedy of the Triangle Fire galvanized New York legislators into passing laws to protect women workers. (© The Granger Collection, New York)

African Americans faced greater obstacles than any other group in challenging their own oppressed status and seeking reform. Thus it was not surprising, perhaps, that so many embraced the message of Booker T. Washington in the late nineteenth century, to "put down your bucket where you are," to work for immediate self-improvement rather than long-range social change. Not all African Americans, however, were content with this approach. And by the turn of the century a powerful challenge was emerging–a challenge to the philosophy of Washington but, more important, to the entire structure of race relations. The chief spokesman for this new approach was W. E. B. Du Bois.

Du Bois, unlike Washington, had never known slavery. Born in Massachusetts, educated at Fisk University in Nashville and at

W. E. B. Du Bois

Harvard, he grew to maturity with a more expansive view than Washington of the goals of his race and the responsibilities of white society to eliminate prejudice and injustice. In *The Souls of Black Folk* (1903), he launched an open attack on the philosophy of Washington, accusing him of encouraging white efforts to impose segregation and of limiting the aspirations of his race. "Is it possible and probable," he asked, "that nine millions of men can make effective progress in economic lines if they are deprived of political rights, made a servile caste, and allowed only the most meager chance for developing their exceptional men? If history and reason give any distinct answer to these questions, it is an emphatic No."

Rather than content themselves with education at the trade and agricultural schools, Du Bois advocated, talented blacks should accept nothing less than a full university education. They should aspire to the professions. They should, above all, fight for their civil rights, not simply wait for them to be granted as a reward for patient striving. In 1905, Du Bois and a group of his supporters met at Niagara Falls–on the Canadian side of the border because no hotel on the American side of the Falls would

NAACP Founded

have them–and launched what became known as the Niagara Movement. Four years later, after a race riot in Springfield, Illinois, they joined with white progressives sympathetic to their cause to form the National Association for the Advancement of Colored People (NAACP). Whites held most of the offices at first, but Du Bois, its director of publicity and research, was the guiding spirit. In the ensuing years, the new organization led the drive for equal rights, using as its principal weapon lawsuits in the federal courts.

Within less than a decade, the NAACP had begun to win some important victories. In *Guinn v. United States* (1915), the Supreme Court supported its position that the grandfather clause in an Oklahoma law was unconstitutional. (The statute denied the vote to any citizen whose ancestors had not been enfranchised in 1860.) In *Buchanan v. Worley* (1917), the Court struck down a Louisville, Kentucky, law requiring residential segregation. The NAACP established itself, particularly after Booker T. Washington's death in 1915, as one of the nation's leading black organizations, a position it would maintain for many years.

Among the many issues that engaged the NAACP and other African American organizations was the phenomenon of lynching in the South. Du Bois was an outspoken critic of lynching and an advocate of a federal law making it illegal (since state courts

THE YOUNG W. E. B. DU BOIS This formal photograph of W. E. B. Du Bois was taken in 1899, when he was thirty-one years old and a professor at Atlanta University. He had just published *The Philadelphia Negro*, a classic sociological study of an urban community, which startled many readers with its description of the complex class system among African Americans in the city. (© Hulton Archive/Getty Images)

in the South routinely refused to prosecute lynchers). But the most determined opponents of lynching were southern women. They included white women such as Jessie Daniel Ames. The most effective crusader was a black woman, Ida Wells Barnett, who worked both on her own (at great personal risk) and with such organizations as the National Association of Colored Women and the Women's Convention of the National Baptist Church to try to discredit lynching and challenge segregation.

CRUSADE FOR SOCIAL ORDER AND REFORM

Reformers directed many of their energies at the political process. But they also crusaded on behalf of what they considered moral issues. There were campaigns to eliminate alcohol from national life, to curb prostitution, to limit divorce, and to restrict immigration. Proponents of each of those reforms believed that success would help regenerate society as a whole.

THE TEMPERANCE CRUSADE

Many progressives considered the elimination of alcohol from American life a necessary step in restoring order to society. Scarce wages vanished as workers spent hours in the saloons. Drunkenness spawned violence, and occasionally murder, within urban families. Working-class wives and mothers hoped through temperance to reform male behavior and thus improve women's lives. Employers, too, regarded alcohol as an impediment to industrial efficiency; workers often missed time on the job because of drunkenness or came to the factory intoxicated. Critics of economic privilege denounced the liquor industry as one of the nation's most sinister trusts. And political reformers, who (correctly) looked on the saloon as one of the central institutions of the urban machine, saw an attack on drinking as part of an attack on the bosses. Out of such sentiments emerged the temperance movement.

Temperance had been a major reform movement before the Civil War, mobilizing large numbers of people in a **WCTU** crusade with strong evangelical overtones. In 1873, the movement developed new strength. Temperance advocates formed the Women's Christian Temperance Union (WCTU), led after 1879 by Frances Willard. By 1911, it had 245,000 members and had become the single largest women's organization in American history to that point. In 1893, the Anti-Saloon League joined the temperance movement and, along with the WCTU, began to press for a specific legislative solution: the legal abolition of saloons. Gradually, that demand grew to include the complete prohibition of the sale and manufacture of alcoholic beverages.

Despite substantial opposition from immigrant and working-class voters, pressure for prohibition grew steadily through the first decades of the new century. By 1916, nineteen states had passed prohibition laws. **EIGHTEENTH AMENDMENT** But since the consumption of alcohol was actually increasing in many unregulated areas, temperance advocates were beginning to advocate a national prohibition law. America's entry into World War I, and the moral fervor it unleashed, provided the last push to the advocates of prohibition. In 1917, with the support of rural fundamentalists who opposed alcohol on moral and religious grounds, progressive advocates of prohibition steered through Congress a constitutional amendment embodying their demands. Two years later, after ratification by every state in the nation except Connecticut and Rhode Island (bastions of Catholic immigrants), the Eighteenth Amendment became law, to take effect in January 1920.

Total immigration during five-year periods (in millions)

4.96 · 4.46 · 3.83 · 1.28

| 1901–1905 | 1906–1910 | 1911–1915 | 1916–1920 |

Year

TOTAL IMMIGRATION, 1900–1920 Emigration to the United States reached the highest level in the nation's history to that point in the first fifteen years of the twentieth century. In the nineteenth century, there was no five-year period when as many as 3 million immigrants arrived in America. In the first fifteen years of the twentieth century, more than 3 million newcomers arrived in every five-year period—and in one of them, as this chart reveals, the number reached almost 5 million. (The Library of Congress (3a38144u))

• *Why did the flow of immigrants drop so sharply in the period 1916–1920?*

IMMIGRATION RESTRICTION

Virtually all reformers agreed that the growing immigrant population had created social problems, but there was wide disagreement on how best to respond. Some progressives believed that the proper approach was to help the new residents adapt to American society. Others argued that efforts at assimilation had failed and that the only solution was to limit the flow of new arrivals.

In the first decades of the century, pressure grew to close the nation's gates. New scholarly theories, appealing to the progressive respect for expertise, argued that the introduction of immigrants into American society was polluting the nation's racial stock. Among the theories created to support this argument was eugenics, the science of altering the reproductive processes of plants and animals to produce new hybrids or breeds. In the early twentieth century, there was an effort, funded by the Carnegie Foundation, to turn eugenics into a method of altering human reproduction as well. But the eugenics movement when applied to humans was not an effort to "breed" new people, an effort for which no scientific tools existed. It was, rather, an effort to grade races and ethnic groups according to their genetic qualities. Eugenicists advocated the forced sterilization of the mentally retarded, criminals, and others. But they also spread the belief that

EUGENICS AND NATIVISM

human inequalities were hereditary and that immigration was contributing to the multiplication of the unfit. Skillful publicists such as Madison Grant, whose *The Passing of the Great Race* (1916) established him as the nation's most effective nativist, warned of the dangers of racial "mongrelization" and of the importance of protecting the purity of Anglo-Saxon and other Nordic stock from pollution by eastern Europeans, Latin Americans, and Asians.

A special federal commission of "experts," chaired by Senator William P. Dillingham of Vermont, issued a study filled with statistics and scholarly testimony. It argued that the newer immigrant groups—largely southern and eastern Europeans—had proven themselves less assimilable than earlier immigrants. Immigration, the report implied, should be restricted by nationality. Many people who rejected these racial arguments nevertheless supported limiting immigration as a way to solve such urban problems as overcrowding, unemployment, strained social services, and social unrest.

The combination of these concerns gradually won for the nativists the support of some of the nation's leading progressives, among them former president Theodore Roosevelt. Powerful opponents—employers who saw immigration as a source of cheap labor, immigrants themselves, and their political representatives—managed to block the restriction movement for a time. But by the beginning of World War I (which effectively blocked immigration temporarily), the nativist tide was gaining strength.

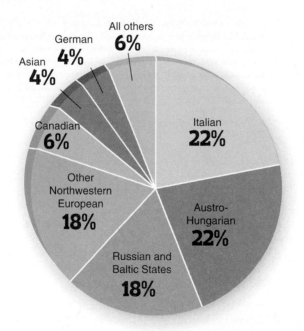

SOURCES OF IMMIGRATION, 1900–1920 At least as striking as the increase in immigration in the early twentieth century was the change in its sources. In the nineteenth century, the vast majority of immigrants to the United States had come from northern and western Europe (especially Britain, Ireland, Germany, and Scandinavia). Now, as this chart shows, the major sources were southern and eastern Europe, with over 60 percent coming from Italy, Russia, and the eastern European regions of the Austro-Hungarian Empire.

• *What impact did these changing sources have on attitudes toward immigration in the United States?*

CHALLENGING THE CAPITALIST ORDER

If there was one issue that overshadowed, and helped to shape, all others in the minds of reformers, it was the character of the dramatically growing modern industrial economy. Most of the problems that concerned progressives could be traced back, directly or indirectly, to the growing power and influence—and also, reformers believed, corruption—of corporate America. So it is not surprising that prominent among progressive concerns was reshaping or reforming the behavior of the capitalist world.

THE DREAM OF SOCIALISM

At no time in the history of the United States to that point, and seldom after, did radical critiques of the capitalist system attract more support than in the period 1900-1914. Although never a force to rival or even seriously threaten the two major parties, the Socialist Party of America grew during these years into a force of considerable strength. In the election of 1900, it had attracted the support of fewer than 100,000 voters; in 1912, its durable leader and perennial presidential candidate, Eugene V. Debs, received nearly 1 million ballots. Strongest in urban immigrant

EUGENE DEBS

MAY DAY, 1908 The American Socialist Party staged this vast rally in New York City's Union Square to celebrate May Day in 1908. The Second Socialist International had designated May Day as the official holiday for radical labor in 1899. (© Corbis)

communities, particularly among Germans and Jews, it also attracted the loyalties of a substantial number of Protestant farmers in the South and Midwest. Socialists won election to over 1,000 state and local offices. And they had the support at times of such intellectuals as Lincoln Steffens, the crusader against municipal corruption, and Walter Lippmann, the brilliant young journalist and social critic. Florence Kelley, Frances Willard, and other women reformers were attracted to socialism, too, in part because of its support for pacifism and labor organizing.

Virtually all socialists agreed on the need for basic structural changes in the economy, but they differed widely on the extent of those changes and the tactics necessary to achieve them. Some socialists endorsed the radical goals of European Marxists; others envisioned a moderate reform that would allow small-scale private enterprise to survive but would nationalize major industries. Some believed in working for reform through electoral politics; others favored militant direct action. Among the militants was the radical labor union the Industrial Workers of the World (IWW), known to opponents as the "Wobblies"

"WOBBLIES"

(a nickname of unknown origin). Under the leadership of William ("Big Bill") Haywood, the IWW advocated a single union for all workers and abolition of the "wage slave" system; it rejected political action in favor of strikes–especially the general strike. The Wobblies were widely believed to have been responsible for the dynamiting of railroad lines and power stations and other acts of terror in the first years of the twentieth century.

The IWW was one of the few labor organizations of the time to champion the cause of unskilled workers and had particular strength in the West–where a large group of migratory laborers (miners, timbermen, and others) found it very difficult to organize or sustain conventional unions. In 1917, a strike by IWW timber workers in Washington and Idaho shut down production in the industry. That brought down upon the union the wrath of the federal government, which had just begun mobilizing for war and needed timber for war production. Federal authorities imprisoned the leaders of the union, and state governments between 1917 and 1919 passed a series of laws that outlawed the IWW. The organization survived for a time but never fully recovered.

LOUIS BRANDEIS Brandeis graduated from Harvard Law School in 1877 with the best academic record of any student in the school's previous or subsequent history. His success in his Boston law practice was such that by the early twentieth century he was able to spend much of his time in unpaid work for public causes. His investigations of monopoly power soon made him a major figure in the emerging progressive movement. Woodrow Wilson nominated him for the U.S. Supreme Court in January 1916. He was one of the few nominees in the Court's history never to have held prior public office, and he was the first Jew ever to have been nominated. The appointment aroused five months of bitter controversy in the Senate before Brandeis was finally confirmed. For the next twenty years, he was one of the Court's most powerful members—all the while lobbying behind the scenes on behalf of the many political causes (preeminent among them Zionism, the founding of a Jewish state) to which he remained committed. (© Bettmann/Corbis)

Moderate socialists who advocated peaceful change through political struggle dominated the Socialist Party. They empha-

SOCIALISM'S DEMISE

sized a gradual education of the public to the need for change and patient efforts within the system to enact it. But World War I dramatically weakened the socialists. They had refused to support the war effort, and a growing wave of antiradicalism subjected them to enormous harassment and persecution.

DECENTRALIZATION AND REGULATION

Most progressives retained a faith in the possibilities of reform within a capitalist system. Rather than nationalize basic industries, many reformers hoped to restore the economy to a "more human" scale. Few envisioned a return to a society of small, local enterprises; some consolidation, they recognized, was inevitable. They did, however, argue that the federal government should work to break up the largest combinations and enforce a balance between the need for bigness and the need for competition.

This viewpoint came to be identified particularly closely with Louis D. Brandeis, a brilliant lawyer and later justice of the Supreme Court, who wrote widely (most notably in his 1913 book, *Other People's Money*) about the "curse of bigness."

Brandeis and his supporters opposed bigness in part because they considered it inefficient. But their opposition had a moral

THE PROBLEM OF CORPORATE CENTRALIZATION

basis as well. Bigness was a threat not just to efficiency but to freedom as well. It limited the ability of individuals to control their own destinies. It encouraged abuses of power. Government must, Brandeis insisted, regulate competition in such a way as to ensure that large combinations did not emerge.

Other progressives were less enthusiastic about the virtues of competition. More important to them was efficiency, which they believed economic concentration encouraged. What government should do, they argued, was not to fight "bigness,"

"GOOD TRUSTS" AND "BAD TRUSTS"

but to guard against abuses of power by large institutions. It should distinguish between "good trusts" and "bad trusts," encouraging the good while disciplining the bad. Since economic consolidation was destined to remain a permanent feature of American society, continuing oversight by a strong, modernized government was essential. One of the most influential spokesmen for this emerging "nationalist" position was Herbert Croly, whose 1909 book, *The Promise of American Life*, became an influential progressive document.

Increasingly, the attention of nationalists such as Croly focused on some form of coordination of the industrial economy. Society must act, Walter Lippmann wrote in a notable 1914 book, *Drift and Mastery*, "to introduce plan where there has been clash, and purpose into the jungles of disordered growth." To some nationalists, that meant businesses themselves learning new ways of cooperation and self-regulation. To others, the solution was for government to play a more active role in regulating and planning economic life. One of those who came to endorse that position (although not fully until after 1910) was Theodore Roosevelt, who once said: "We should enter upon a course of supervision, control, and regulation of those great corporations." Roosevelt became for a time the most powerful symbol of the reform impulse at the national level.

THEODORE ROOSEVELT AND THE MODERN PRESIDENCY

"Presidents in general are not lovable," the famous writer and columnist Walter Lippmann, who had known many, said near the end of his life. "They've had to do too much to get where they are. But there was one President who was lovable–Teddy Roosevelt–and I loved him."

Lippmann was not alone. To a generation of progressive reformers, Theodore Roosevelt was more than an admired public figure; he was an idol. No president before, and few since, had attracted such attention and devotion. Yet, for all his popularity among reformers, Roosevelt was in many respects decidedly conservative. He earned his extraordinary popularity less because of the extent of the reforms he championed than because he brought to his office a broad conception of its powers and invested the presidency with something of its modern status as the center of national political life.

THE ACCIDENTAL PRESIDENT

When President William McKinley suddenly died in September 1901, the victim of an assassination, Roosevelt (who had been elected vice president less than a year before) was only forty-two years old, the youngest man ever to assume the presidency. "I told William McKinley that it was a mistake to nominate that wild man at Philadelphia," party boss Mark Hanna was reported to have exclaimed. "Now look, that damned cowboy is President of the United States!"

Roosevelt's reputation as a wild man was a result less of the substance of his early political career than of its style. As a **ROOSEVELT'S BACKGROUND** young member of the New York legislature, he had displayed an energy seldom seen in that lethargic body. As a rancher in the Dakota Badlands (where he retired briefly after the sudden death of his first wife), he had helped capture outlaws. As New York City police commissioner, he had been a flamboyant battler against crime and vice. As assistant secretary of the navy, he had been a bold proponent of American expansion. As commander of the Rough Riders, he had led a heroic, if militarily useless, charge in the battle of San Juan Hill in Cuba during the Spanish-American War.

But Roosevelt as president rarely rebelled against the leaders of his party. He became, rather, a champion of cautious, moderate change. Reform, he believed, was a vehicle less for remaking American society than for protecting it against radical challenges.

GOVERNMENT, CAPITAL, AND LABOR

Roosevelt allied himself with those progressives who urged regulation (but not destruction) of the trusts. At the heart of **ROOSEVELT'S VISION OF FEDERAL POWER** Roosevelt's policy was his desire to win for government the power to investigate the activities of corporations and publicize the results. The new Department of Commerce and Labor, established in 1903 (later to be divided into two separate departments), was to assist in this task through its investigatory arm, the Bureau of Corporations.

Although Roosevelt was not a trustbuster at heart, he made a few highly publicized efforts to break up combinations. In 1902, he ordered the Justice Department to invoke the Sherman Antitrust Act against a great new railroad monopoly in the Northwest, the Northern Securities Company, a $400 million

PRESIDENT THEODORE ROOSEVELT To a generation of progressive reformers, Theodore Roosevelt was an idol. No president before, and few since, had attracted such attention and devotion from the American people. (The Library of Congress (LC-DIG_ppmsca-37602))

enterprise pieced together by J. P. Morgan and others. To **NORTHERN SECURITIES COMPANY** Morgan, accustomed to a warm, supportive relationship with Republican administrations, the action was baffling. He told the president, "If we have done anything wrong, send your man to my man and they can fix it up." Roosevelt proceeded with the case nonetheless, and in 1904 the Supreme Court ruled that the Northern Securities Company must be dissolved. Although he filed more than forty additional antitrust suits during the remainder of his presidency, Roosevelt had no serious commitment to reverse the prevailing trend toward economic concentration.

A similar commitment to establishing the government as an impartial regulatory mechanism shaped Roosevelt's policy toward labor. In the past, federal intervention in industrial disputes had almost always meant action on behalf of employers. Roosevelt was willing to consider labor's position as well. When a bitter 1902 strike by the United Mine Workers endangered coal supplies for the coming winter, Roosevelt asked both the operators and the miners to accept impartial federal arbitration. When the mine owners balked, Roosevelt threatened to send federal troops to seize the mines. The operators finally relented. Arbitrators awarded the strikers a 10 percent wage increase and a nine-hour day, although no recognition of their union—less than they had wanted but more than they would likely have

DEDICATED TO CONSERVING AMERICA

A LEADER IN AMERICA'S CONSERVATION MOVEMENT, naturalist John Muir (1838–1914) was born in Scotland and grew up in Wisconsin. He went to California in 1868 and spent several years in the American West exploring the land and studying the trees, forests, and glaciers of the area before settling permanently in California in 1880. He campaigned for the establishment of Yosemite National Park, a goal achieved in 1890. Through his friendship with President Theodore Roosevelt, he persuaded the president to greatly increase the amount of protected public land. As a dedicated conservationist, Muir wrote articles attempting to rouse the public to the need to protect public lands. In addition to the public lands he helped protect and preserve, Muir created another lasting legacy—the Sierra Club, an organization that he co-founded and that is still thriving today.

The two source documents below are thus both connected to John Muir. The first is an excerpt from his book *Our National Parks*. The second is a reprinting of the Sierra Club's current stated purposes and goals.

OUR NATIONAL PARKS—1901

FROM CHAPTER 1, "THE WILD PARKS AND FOREST RESERVATIONS OF THE WEST," BY JOHN MUIR

The tendency nowadays to wander in wildernesses is delightful to see. Thousands of tired, nerve-shaken, over-civilized people are beginning to find out that going to the mountains is going home; that wildness is a necessity; and that mountain parks and reservations are useful not only as fountains of timber and irrigating rivers, but as fountains of life. Awakening from the stupefying effects of the vice of over-industry and the deadly apathy of luxury, they are trying as best they can to mix and enrich their own little ongoings with those of Nature, and to get rid of rust and disease. Briskly venturing and roaming, some are washing off sins and cobweb cares of the devil's spinning in all-day storms on mountains; sauntering in rosiny pine-woods or in gentian meadows, brushing through chaparral, bending down and parting sweet, flowery sprays; tracing rivers to their sources, getting in touch with the nerves of Mother Earth; jumping from rock to rock, feeling the life of them, learning the songs of them, panting in whole-souled exercise, and rejoicing in deep, long-drawn breaths of pure wildness. This is fine and natural and full of promise. So also is the growing interest in the care and preservation of forests and wild places in general, and in the half wild parks and gardens of towns. . . .

When, like a merchant taking a list of his goods, we take stock of our wildness, we are glad to see how much of even the most destructible kind is still unspoiled. Looking at our continent as scenery when it was all wild, lying between beautiful seas, the starry sky above it, the starry rocks beneath it, to compare its sides, the East and the West, would be like comparing the sides of a rainbow. But it is no longer equally beautiful. . . . [T]he continent's outer beauty is fast passing away, especially the plant part of it, the most destructible and most universally charming of all.

Only thirty years ago, the great Central Valley of California, five hundred miles long and fifty miles wide, was one bed of golden and purple flowers. Now it is ploughed and pastured out of existence, gone forever,–scarce a memory of it left in fence corners and along the bluffs of the streams. . . . The same fate, sooner or later, is awaiting them all, unless awakening public opinion comes forward to stop it. . . .

The Grand Cañon Reserve of Arizona, of nearly two million acres, or the most interesting part of it, as well as the Rainier region, should be made into a national park, on account of their supreme grandeur and beauty. . . . No matter how far you have wandered hitherto, or how many famous gorges and valleys you have seen, this one, the Grand Cañon of the Colorado, will seem as novel to you, as unearthly in the color and grandeur and quantity of its architecture, as if you had found it after death, on some other star; so incomparably lovely and grand and supreme is it above all the other cañons in our fire-moulded, earthquake-shaken, rain-washed, wave-washed, river and glacier sculptured world. . . .

SIERRA CLUB—2006

SIERRA CLUB PURPOSES AND GOALS

The purposes of the Sierra Club are to explore, enjoy, and protect the wild places of the earth; to practice and promote the responsible use of the earth's ecosystems and resources; to educate and enlist humanity to protect and restore the quality of the natural and human environment; and to use all lawful means to carry out these objectives.

Ideal Goals—for Environment and Society

- To sustain natural life-support systems, avoid impairing them, and avoid irreversible damage to them.
- To facilitate species survival; to maintain genetic diversity; to avoid hastened extinction of species; to protect prime natural habitat.
- To establish and protect natural reserves, including representative natural areas, wilderness areas in each biome, displays of natural phenomena, and habitats for rare and endangered species.
- To control human population growth and impacts; to limit human population numbers and habitat needs within Earth's carrying capacity; to avoid needless human consumption of resources; to plan and control land use, with environmental impact assessment and safeguards, and rehabilitation of damaged sites.
- To learn more about the facts, interrelationships, and principles of the Earth's ecosystems, and the place and impact of humans in them; to understand the consequences of human activities within the biosphere.
- To develop responsible and appropriate technology matched to end-uses; to introduce sophisticated technology gradually after careful assessment and with precautionary monitoring.
- To control pollution of the biosphere; to minimize waste residuals with special care of hazardous materials; to use the best available control technology at sources; and to recycle wastes.
- To manage resources soundly; to avoid waste with long-term plans; to sustain the yield of living resources and maintain their productivity and breeding stocks; to prolong availability of nonliving resources such as fossil fuels, minerals, and water.
- To impart a sense of social responsibility among consumers, developers, and public authorities concerning environmental protection; to regulate threats to public health; to avoid private degradation of public resources; to minimize impacts on innocent parties and future generations.

As the Sierra Club prepares for its second century, we offer to America and the world our vision of humanity living in harmony with nature. We dedicate ourselves to achieving this vision as we reaffirm our passionate commitment to explore, enjoy, and protect the Earth.

....

(*From the Current Articles of Incorporation & Bylaws,* June 20, 1981, updated July 13, 2006. Excerpted from, Sierra Club Goals Pamphlet, 1985-1989. Reproduced from sierraclub.org with permission of the Sierra Club. ©2006 Sierra Club. All Rights Reserved.)

AP TEST PRACTICE

Questions assume cumulative content knowledge from this chapter and previous chapters.

1. Which of the following groups would most agree with the excerpt from *Our National Parks?*

(A) Southern romantic aristocrats

(B) Western settlers in the 19th century

(C) Those who championed ideas of self-reliance and self-realization in the mid-19th century

(D) Protestant evangelists

2. Which best describes how Muir's argument in *Our National Parks* reflects the economic and social history of the time?

(A) Muir is responding to a sense of societal disorder due to developments of his time, such as rapid industrialization.

(B) Muir is responding to a sense of political injustice, due to the relationship between government and big business at the time.

(C) Muir is responding to the social critiques of the power of monopolies to do as they please.

(D) Muir is responding to the demands of farmers to increase arable lands through irrigation projects.

3. Which progressive value does the Sierra Club's statement of purposes and goals best reflect?

(A) A strong belief in the ideal of spiritual self-improvement

(B) A strong belief in the role of government in regulating use of environmental resources

(C) A strong belief in the role of purposeful human action in bettering a society

(D) A strong belief in social justice

BOYS IN THE MINES These young boys, covered in grime and no more than twelve years old, pose for the noted photographer Lewis Hine outside the coal mine in Pennsylvania where they separated coal from slate in coal breakers. The rugged conditions endured by mine workers were one cause of the great strike of 1902, in which Theodore Roosevelt intervened. (The Library of Congress)

won without Roosevelt's intervention. Roosevelt viewed himself as no more the champion of labor than as a champion of management. On several occasions, he ordered federal troops to intervene in strikes on behalf of employers.

THE "SQUARE DEAL"

During Roosevelt's first years as president, he was principally concerned with winning reelection, which required that he not antagonize the conservative Republican Old Guard. By skillfully dispensing patronage to conservatives and progressives alike, and by winning the support of northern businessmen while making adroit gestures to reformers, Roosevelt had neutralized his opposition within the party by early 1904. He won its presidential nomination with ease. And in the general election, where he faced a dull conservative Democrat, Alton B. Parker, he captured over 57 percent of the popular vote and lost no states outside the South.

During the 1904 campaign, Roosevelt boasted that he had worked in the anthracite coal strike to provide everyone with a "square deal." One of his first targets after the election **HEPBURN ACT** was the powerful railroad industry. The Interstate Commerce Act of 1887, establishing the Interstate Commerce Commission (ICC), had been an early effort to regulate the industry; but over the years, the courts had sharply limited its influence. Roosevelt asked Congress for legislation to increase the government's power to oversee railroad rates. The Hepburn Railroad Regulation Act of 1906 sought to restore some regulatory authority to the government, although the bill was so cautious that it satisfied few progressives.

Roosevelt also pressured Congress to enact the Pure Food and Drug Act, which restricted the sale of dangerous or ineffective

medicines. When Upton Sinclair's powerful novel *The Jungle* appeared in 1906, featuring appalling **PURE FOOD AND DRUG ACT** descriptions of conditions in the meatpacking industry, Roosevelt pushed for passage of the Meat Inspection Act, which helped eliminate many diseases once transmitted in impure meat. Starting in 1907, he proposed, but mostly failed to achieve, even more stringent reforms: an eight-hour workday, broader compensation for victims of industrial accidents, inheritance and income taxes, regulation of the stock market, and others. He also started openly to criticize conservatives in Congress and the judiciary who were obstructing these programs. The result was a widening gulf between the president and the conservative wing of his party.

ROOSEVELT AND CONSERVATION

Roosevelt's aggressive policies on behalf of conservation contributed to that gulf. Using executive powers, he restricted private development on millions of acres of undeveloped government land—most of it in the West—by adding them to the previously modest national forest system. When conservatives in Congress restricted his authority over public lands in 1907, Roosevelt and his chief forester, Gifford Pinchot, seized all the forests and many of the water power sites still in the public domain before the bill became law.

Roosevelt was the first president to take an active interest in the new and struggling American conservation movement. In the early twentieth century, the idea of preserving the natural world for ecological reasons was not well established. Instead, many people who considered themselves "conservationists"–such as Pinchot, the first director of the National Forest Service (which he helped to create)–promoted policies to protect land for carefully managed development.

The Old Guard eagerly supported another important aspect of Roosevelt's natural resource policy: public reclamation and irriga-

FEDERAL AID TO THE WEST

tion projects. In 1902, the president backed the National Reclamation Act, better known as the Newlands Act (named for its sponsor, Nevada senator Francis Newlands). The Newlands Act provided federal funds for the construction of dams, reservoirs, and canals in the West–projects that would open new lands for cultivation and (years later) provide cheap electric power.

ROOSEVELT AND PRESERVATION

Despite his sympathy with Pinchot's vision of conservation, Roosevelt also shared some of the concerns of the naturalists–those within the conservation movement committed to protecting the natural beauty of the land and the health of its wildlife from human intrusion. Early in his presidency, Roosevelt even spent four days camping in the Sierras with

John Muir, the nation's leading preservationist and the founder of the Sierra Club.

Roosevelt added significantly to the still-young National Park System, whose purpose was to protect public land from any exploitation or development. Congress had created the first national park–Yellowstone, in Wyoming, in 1872–and had authorized others in the 1890s: Yosemite and Sequoia in California, and Mount Rainier in Washington State. Roosevelt added land to several existing parks and also created new ones: Crater Lake in Oregon, Mesa Verde in Utah, Platt in Oklahoma, and Wind Cave in South Dakota.

THE HETCH HETCHY CONTROVERSY

The contending views of the early conservation movement came to a head beginning in 1906 in a sensational controversy over the Hetch Hetchy Valley in Yosemite National Park. Hetch Hetchy (a name derived from a local Indian term

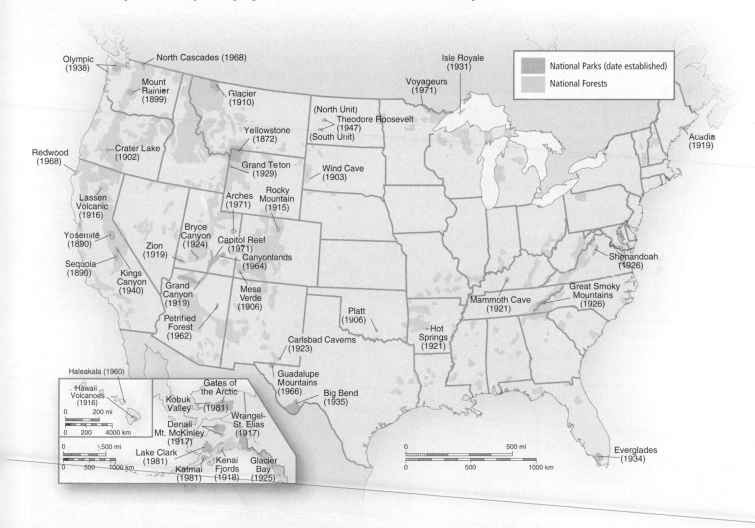

ESTABLISHMENT OF NATIONAL PARKS AND FORESTS This map illustrates the steady growth throughout the late nineteenth and early twentieth centuries of the systems of national parks and national forests in the United States. Although Theodore Roosevelt is widely and correctly remembered as a great champion of national parks and forests, the greatest expansions of these systems occurred after his presidency. Note, for example, how many new areas were added in the 1920s.

• What is the difference between national parks and national forests?

meaning "grassy meadows") was a spectacular, high-walled valley popular with naturalists. But many residents of San Francisco, worried about finding enough water to serve their growing population, saw Hetch Hetchy as an ideal place for a dam, which would create a large reservoir for the city—a plan that Muir and other naturalists furiously opposed.

In 1906, San Francisco suffered a devastating earthquake and fire. Widespread sympathy for the city strengthened the case for the dam; and Theodore Roosevelt—who had initially expressed some sympathy for Muir's position—turned the decision over to Gifford Pinchot. Pinchot had no interest in Muir's aesthetic and spiritual arguments. He approved construction of the dam.

For over a decade, a battle raged between naturalists and the advocates of the dam, a battle that consumed the energies of John Muir for the rest of his life and that eventually, many people believed, led to his death. "Dam Hetch Hetchy!" Muir once said. "As well dam for water-tanks the people's cathedrals and churches, for no holier temple has ever been consecrated by the heart of man." To Pinchot, there was no question that the needs of the city were more important than the claims of preservation. Muir helped place a referendum question on the ballot in 1908, certain that the residents of the city would oppose the project "as soon as light is cast upon it." Instead, San Franciscans approved the dam by a huge margin. Although there were many more delays in succeeding years, construction of the dam finally began after World War I.

COMPETING CONSERVATIONIST VISIONS

This setback for the naturalists was not, however, a total defeat. The fight against Hetch Hetchy helped mobilize a new coalition of people committed to preservation, not "rational use," of wilderness.

THE PANIC OF 1907

Despite the flurry of reforms Roosevelt was able to enact, the government still had relatively little control over the industrial economy. That became clear in 1907, when a serious panic and recession began.

Conservatives blamed Roosevelt's "mad" economic policies for the disaster. And while the president naturally (and correctly) disagreed, he nevertheless acted quickly to reassure business leaders that he would not interfere with their recovery efforts. J. P. Morgan, in a spectacular display of his financial power, helped construct a pool of the assets of several important New York banks to prop up shaky financial institutions. The key to the arrangement, Morgan told the president, was the purchase by U.S. Steel of the shares of the Tennessee Coal and Iron Company, currently held by a threatened New York bank. He would, he insisted, need assurances that the purchase would not prompt antitrust action. Roosevelt tacitly agreed, and the Morgan plan proceeded. Whether or not as a result, the panic soon subsided.

TENNESSEE COAL AND IRON COMPANY

Roosevelt loved being president. As his years in office produced increasing political successes, as his public popularity continued to rise, more and more observers began to assume that he would run for reelection in 1908, despite the long-standing tradition of presidents serving no more than two terms. But the Panic of 1907, combined with Roosevelt's growing

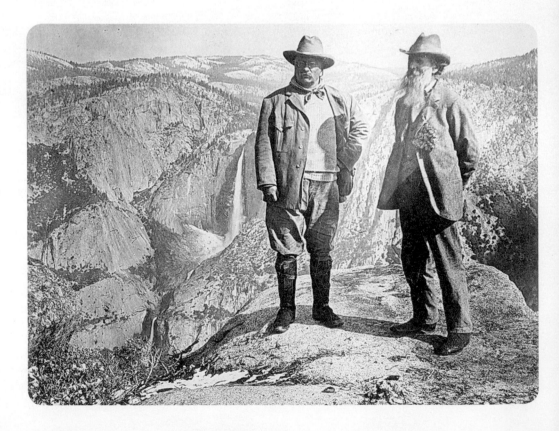

ROOSEVELT AND MUIR IN YOSEMITE John Muir, founder and leader of the Sierra Club, considered Theodore Roosevelt a friend and ally—a relationship cemented by a four-day camping trip the two men took together in Yosemite National Park in 1903. Roosevelt was indeed a friend to the national park and national forest systems and added considerable acreage to both. Among other things, he expanded Yosemite (at Muir's request). But unlike Muir, Roosevelt was also committed to economic development. As a result, he was not always a reliable ally of the most committed preservationists. (© Bettmann/Corbis)

"radicalism" during his second term, so alienated conservatives in his own party that he might have had difficulty winning the Republican nomination. In 1904, moreover, he had made a public promise to step down four years later. And so in 1909, Roosevelt, fifty years old, retired from public life–briefly.

THE TROUBLED SUCCESSION

William Howard Taft, who assumed the presidency in 1909, had been Theodore Roosevelt's most trusted lieutenant and his handpicked successor; progressive reformers believed him to be one of their own. But Taft had also been a restrained and

WILLIAM HOWARD TAFT moderate jurist, a man with a punctilious regard for legal process; conservatives expected him to abandon Roosevelt's aggressive use of presidential powers. By seeming acceptable to almost everyone, Taft easily won election to the White House in 1908. He received his party's nomination virtually uncontested. His victory in the general election in November– over William Jennings Bryan, running for the Democrats for the third time–was a foregone conclusion.

Four years later, however, Taft would leave office the most decisively defeated president of the twentieth century, his party deeply divided and the government in the hands of a Democratic administration for the first time in twenty years.

TAFT AND THE PROGRESSIVES

Taft's first problem arose in the opening months of the new administration, when he called Congress into special session to

PAYNE-ALDRICH TARIFF lower protective tariff rates, an old progressive demand. But the president made no effort to overcome the opposition of the congressional Old Guard, arguing that to do so would violate the constitutional doctrine of separation of powers. The result was the feeble Payne-Aldrich Tariff, which reduced tariff rates scarcely at all and in some areas raised them. Progressives resented the president's passivity.

Taft may not have been a champion of reform, but neither was he a consistent opponent of change. In 1912, he supported and signed legislation to create a federal Children's Bureau to investigate "all matters pertaining to the welfare of children and child life." Julia Lathrop, the first chief of the bureau, was a veteran of Hull House and a close associate of Jane Addams. She helped make the Children's Bureau a force for progressive change not just in federal policy, but also in state and local governments.

But a sensational controversy broke out late in 1909 that helped put an end to Taft's popularity with reformers. Many progressives had been unhappy when Taft replaced Roosevelt's secretary of the interior, James R. Garfield, an aggressive conservationist, with Richard A. Ballinger, a conservative corporate lawyer. Suspicion of Ballinger grew when he attempted to invalidate Roosevelt's removal of nearly 1 million acres of forests and mineral reserves from private development.

WILLIAM HOWARD TAFT Taft could be a jovial companion in small groups, but his public image was of a dull, stolid man who stood in sharp and unfortunate contrast to his dynamic predecessor, Theodore Roosevelt. Taft also suffered public ridicule for his enormous size. He weighed as much as 350 pounds at times, and wide publicity accompanied his installation of an oversized bathtub in the White House. (© Bettmann/Corbis)

In the midst of this mounting concern, Louis Glavis, an Interior Department investigator, charged Ballinger with having

BALLINGER-PINCHOT DISPUTE once connived to turn over valuable public coal lands in Alaska to a private syndicate for personal profit. Glavis took the evidence to Gifford Pinchot, still head of the Forest Service and a critic of Ballinger's policies. Pinchot took the charges to the president. Taft investigated them and decided they were groundless. But Pinchot was not satisfied, particularly after Taft fired Glavis for his part in the episode. He leaked the story to the press and asked Congress to investigate the scandal. The president discharged him for insubordination. The congressional committee appointed to study the controversy, dominated by Old Guard Republicans, exonerated Ballinger. But progressives throughout the country supported Pinchot. The controversy aroused as much public passion as any dispute of its time; and when it was over, Taft had alienated the supporters of Roosevelt completely and, it seemed, irrevocably.

THE RETURN OF ROOSEVELT

During most of these controversies, Theodore Roosevelt was far away: on a long hunting safari in Africa and an extended tour of Europe. To the American public, however, Roosevelt remained a formidable presence thanks to intensive newspaper coverage of his every move abroad. His return to New York in the spring of 1910 was a major public event. Roosevelt insisted that he had no plans to reenter politics, but within a month he announced that he would embark on a national speaking tour before the end of the summer. Furious with Taft, he was becoming convinced that he alone was capable of reuniting the Republican Party.

The real signal of Roosevelt's decision to assume leadership of Republican reformers came in a speech he gave on September 1, 1910, in Osawatomie, Kansas. In it he outlined a set of principles, which he labeled the "New Nationalism," that made clear he had moved a considerable way from the cautious conservatism of the first years of his presidency. He argued that social justice was possible only through the vigorous efforts of a strong federal government whose executive acted as the "steward of the public welfare." Those who thought primarily of property rights and personal profit "must now give way to the advocate of human welfare." He supported graduated income and inheritance taxes, workers' compensation for industrial accidents, regulation of the labor of women and children, tariff revision, and firmer regulation of corporations.

"NEW NATIONALISM"

SPREADING INSURGENCY

The congressional elections of 1910 provided further evidence of how far the progressive revolt had spread. In primary elections, conservative Republicans suffered defeat after defeat while almost all the progressive incumbents were reelected. In the general election, the Democrats, who were now offering progressive candidates of their own, won control of the House of Representatives for the first time in sixteen years and gained strength in the Senate. But Roosevelt still denied any presidential ambitions and claimed that his real purpose was to pressure Taft to return to progressive policies. Two events, however, changed his mind. The first, on October 27, 1911, was the announcement by the administration of a suit against U.S. Steel, which charged, among other things, that the 1907 acquisition of the Tennessee Coal and Iron Company had been illegal. Roosevelt had approved that acquisition in the midst of the 1907 panic, and he was enraged by the implication that he had acted improperly.

Roosevelt was still reluctant to become a candidate for president because Senator Robert La Follette, the great Wisconsin progressive, had been working since 1911 to secure the presidential nomination for himself. But La Follette's candidacy stumbled in February 1912 when, exhausted, and distraught over the illness of a daughter, he appeared to suffer a nervous breakdown during a speech in Philadelphia. Roosevelt announced his candidacy on February 22.

ROOSEVELT VERSUS TAFT

La Follette retained some diehard support. But for all practical purposes, the campaign for the Republican nomination had now become a battle between Roosevelt and Taft. Roosevelt scored overwhelming victories in all thirteen presidential primaries. Taft, however, remained the choice of most party leaders, who controlled the nominating process.

The battle for the nomination at the Chicago convention revolved around an unusually large number of contested delegates: 254 in all. Roosevelt needed fewer than half the disputed seats to clinch the nomination. But the Republican National Committee, controlled by the Old Guard, awarded all

ROOSEVELT AT OSAWATOMIE
Roosevelt's famous speech at Osawatomie, Kansas, in 1910 was the most radical of his career and openly marked his break with the Taft administration and the Republican leadership. "The essence of any struggle for liberty," he told his largely conservative audience, "has always been, and must always be to take from some one man or class of men the right to enjoy power, or wealth, or position or immunity, which has not been earned by service to his or their fellows." (© The Granger Collection, New York)

but 19 of them to Taft. At a rally the night before the convention opened, Roosevelt addressed 5,000 cheering supporters. "We stand at Armageddon," he told the roaring crowd, "and we battle for the Lord." The next day, he led his supporters out of the convention, and out of the party. The convention then quietly nominated Taft on the first ballot.

Roosevelt summoned his supporters back to Chicago in August for another convention, this one to launch the new

THE PROGRESSIVE PARTY

Progressive Party and nominate himself as its presidential candidate. Roosevelt approached the battle feeling, as he put it, "fit as a bull moose" (thus giving his new party an enduring nickname).

The "Bull Moose" party was notable for its strong commitment to a wide range of progressive causes that had grown in popularity over the previous two decades. The party advocated additional regulation of industry and trusts, sweeping reforms of many areas of government, compensation by the government for workers injured on the job, pensions for the elderly and for widows with children, and (alone among the major parties) woman suffrage. The delegates left the party's convention filled with hope and excitement.

Roosevelt himself, however, entered the fall campaign aware that his cause was almost hopeless, partly because many of the insurgents who had supported him during the primaries refused to follow him out of the Republican Party. His pessimism was also a result of the man the Democrats had nominated for president.

WOODROW WILSON AND THE NEW FREEDOM

The 1912 presidential contest was not simply one between conservatives and reformers. It was also one between two brands of progressivism. And it matched the two most important national leaders of the early twentieth century in unequal contest.

WOODROW WILSON

Reform sentiment had been gaining strength within the Democratic as well as the Republican Party in the first years of the century. At the 1912 Democratic National Convention in Baltimore in June, Champ Clark, the conservative Speaker of the House, was unable to assemble the two-thirds majority necessary for nomination because of progressive opposition. Finally, on the forty-sixth ballot, Woodrow Wilson, the governor of New Jersey and the only genuinely progressive candidate in the race, emerged as the party's nominee.

Wilson had risen to political prominence by an unusual path. He had been a professor of political science at Princeton until 1902, when he was named president of the university. Elected governor of New Jersey in 1910, he demonstrated a commitment to reform. During his two years in the statehouse, he earned a national reputation for winning passage of progressive

WILSON'S "NEW FREEDOM"

legislation. As a presidential candidate in 1912, Wilson presented a progressive program that came to be called the "New Freedom." Roosevelt's New Nationalism advocated accepting economic concentration and using government to regulate and control it. But Wilson seemed to side with those who (like Louis Brandeis) believed that bigness was both unjust and inefficient, that the proper response to monopoly was not to regulate it but to destroy it.

The 1912 presidential campaign was an anticlimax. William Howard Taft, resigned to defeat, barely campaigned. Roosevelt campaigned energetically (until a gunshot wound from a would-be assassin forced him to the sidelines during the last weeks before the election), but he failed to draw any significant numbers of Democratic progressives away from Wilson. In November, Roosevelt and Taft split the Republican vote; Wilson held on to most Democrats and won. He polled only 42 percent of the vote, compared with 27 percent for Roosevelt, 23 percent for Taft, and 6 percent for the socialist Eugene V. Debs. But in the electoral college, Wilson won 435 of the 531 votes. Roosevelt had carried only six states, Taft two, Debs none.

THE SCHOLAR AS PRESIDENT

Wilson was a bold and forceful president. He exerted firm control over his cabinet, and he delegated real authority only to those whose loyalty to him was beyond question. His most powerful adviser, Colonel Edward M. House, was an intelligent and ambitious Texan who held no office and whose only claim to authority was his personal intimacy with the president.

In legislative matters, Wilson skillfully welded together a coalition that would support his program. Democratic majorities in both houses of Congress made his task easier.

LOWERING THE TARIFF

Wilson's first triumph as president was the fulfillment of an old Democratic (and progressive) goal: a substantial lowering of the protective tariff. The Underwood-Simmons Tariff provided cuts substantial enough, progressives believed, to introduce real competition into American markets and thus to help break the power of trusts. To make up for the loss of revenue under the new tariff, Congress approved a graduated income tax, which the recently adopted Sixteenth Amendment to the Constitution now permitted. This first modern income tax imposed a 1 percent tax on individuals and corporations earning more than $4,000 a year, with rates ranging up to 6 percent on annual incomes over $500,000.

Wilson held Congress in session through the summer to work on a major reform of the American banking system: the Federal Reserve Act, which Congress passed and the president signed on December 23, 1913. It created twelve regional

FEDERAL RESERVE ACT

banks, each to be owned and controlled by the individual banks of its district. The regional Federal Reserve banks would hold a certain percentage of the assets of their member banks in reserve; they would use those reserves to support loans to private banks at an interest (or "discount") rate that the Federal Reserve system would set; they would issue a new type of paper currency—Federal Reserve notes—that would become

WOODROW WILSON Woodrow Wilson, the 28th president of the United States, was a Virginian (the first southerner to be elected president since before the Civil War), a professor of political science and later president of Princeton University, governor of New Jersey, and known as a brilliant progressive. His election to the presidency brought the first Democrat to the White House since 1896. (The Library of Congress (3a21763v))

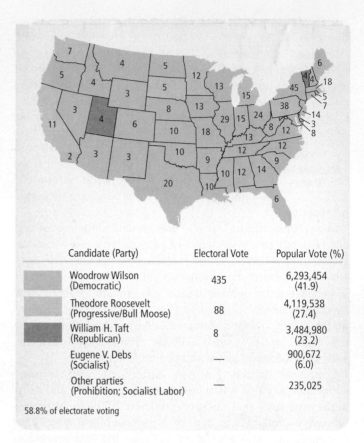

Candidate (Party)	Electoral Vote	Popular Vote (%)
Woodrow Wilson (Democratic)	435	6,293,454 (41.9)
Theodore Roosevelt (Progressive/Bull Moose)	88	4,119,538 (27.4)
William H. Taft (Republican)	8	3,484,980 (23.2)
Eugene V. Debs (Socialist)	—	900,672 (6.0)
Other parties (Prohibition; Socialist Labor)	—	235,025

58.8% of electorate voting

ELECTION OF 1912 The election of 1912 was one of the most unusual in American history because of the dramatic schism within the Republican Party. Two Republican presidents—William Howard Taft, the incumbent, and Theodore Roosevelt, his predecessor—ran against each other in 1912, opening the way for a victory by the Democratic candidate, Woodrow Wilson, who won with only about 42 percent of the popular vote. A fourth candidate, the socialist Eugene V. Debs, received a significant 6 percent of the vote.

• *What events caused the schism between Taft and Roosevelt?*

the nation's basic medium of trade and would be backed by the government. Most important, they would be able to shift funds quickly to troubled areas–to meet increased demands for credit or to protect imperiled banks. Supervising and regulating the entire system was a national Federal Reserve Board, whose members were appointed by the president. Nearly half the nation's banking resources were represented in the system within a year, and 80 percent by the late 1920s.

In 1914, turning to the central issue of his 1912 campaign, Wilson proposed two measures to deal with the problem of monopoly. In the process he revealed how his own approach to the issue was beginning to change. There was a proposal to create a federal agency through which the government would help business police itself–a regulatory commission of the type Roosevelt had advocated in 1912. There were also proposals to strengthen the government's ability to break up trusts–a decentralizing approach characteristic of Wilson's 1912 campaign. The two measures took shape as the Federal Trade Commission Act and the Clayton Antitrust Act. The Federal Trade Commission Act created a regulatory agency that would help businesses determine in advance whether their actions would be acceptable to the government. The agency would also have authority to launch prosecutions against "unfair trade practices," and it would have wide power to investigate corporate behavior. Wilson signed the Federal Trade Commission Bill happily. But he seemed to lose

interest in the Clayton Antitrust Bill and did little to protect it from conservative assaults, which greatly weakened it. The future, he had apparently decided, lay with government supervision.

RETREAT AND ADVANCE

By the fall of 1914, Wilson believed that the program of the New Freedom was essentially complete and that agitation for reform would now subside. He refused to support the movement for national woman suffrage. Deferring to southern Democrats, and reflecting his own southern background, he condoned the reimposition of segregation in the agencies of the federal government (in contrast to Roosevelt, who had ordered the elimination of many such barriers). When congressional progressives attempted to enlist his support for new reform legislation, Wilson dismissed their proposals as unconstitutional or unnecessary.

The congressional elections of 1914, however, shattered the president's complacency. Democrats suffered major losses in Congress, and voters who in 1912 had supported the Progressive Party began returning to the Republicans. Wilson would not be able to rely on a divided opposition when he ran for reelection in 1916. By the end of 1915, therefore, Wilson had begun to support a second flurry of reforms. In January 1916, he appointed Louis Brandeis to the Supreme Court, making him not only the first Jew but also the most progressive justice to serve there. Later, he supported a measure to make it easier for farmers to receive credit and one creating a system of workers' compensation for federal employees.

Wilson was sponsoring measures that expanded the powers of the national government in important ways. In 1916, for example, he supported the Keating-Owen Act, the first federal

CHILD-LABOR LAWS
law regulating child labor. The measure prohibited the shipment of goods produced by underage children across state lines, thus giving an expanded importance to the constitutional clause assigning Congress the task of regulating interstate commerce. The president similarly supported measures that used federal taxing authority as a vehicle for legislating social change. After the Court struck down Keating-Owen, a new law attempted to achieve the same goal by imposing a heavy tax on the products of child labor. (The Court later struck it down too.) And the Smith-Lever Act of 1914 demonstrated another way in which the federal government could influence local behavior; it offered matching federal grants to support agricultural extension education. Over time, these innovative uses of government overcame most of the constitutional objections and became the foundation of a long-term growth in federal power over the economy.

AP CONNECTING THEMES

Chapter 20 emphasized the goals, successes, and limitations of the progressive movement. Review the role of women in instituting social reforms and consider how their participation in progressive reform efforts broadened opportunities and to what degree ideas concerning the "cult of domesticity" were affected. Also, you should now be familiar with the role of muckrakers in promoting reform, as well as knowing about geographical divisions and the bases for support or emphasis on various types of reform. Chapter 20 discussed Theodore Roosevelt's actions regarding corporate trusts and environmental conservation. Also discussed was the unusual election of 1912 and the factors that led Woodrow Wilson to be elected president. Compare Wilson's New Freedom program to Roosevelt's New Nationalism program. Lastly, the chapter compared the respective views of Booker T. Washington and W.E.B. Du Bois on achieving racial equality. Think about how the progressive movement played a role in assisting certain minorities in their struggles for equal rights.

The following themes have heightened importance in Chapter 20. You should now be able to do the following for each listed theme:

Identity: Explain the ways in which class consciousness was accentuated during the progressive era and explain changes in the perception of gender roles.

Work, Exchange, and Technology: Explain the consequences of economic hardship on both the domestic and international scenes. Also, be able to explain the changing view toward big business on the part of the federal government.

Politics and Power: Discuss the degree to which the progressive movement was successful in making the government more responsible to the people at the national, state, and local levels.

Environment and Geography: Describe the debate over conservation of resources versus preservation of resources.

Ideas, Beliefs, and Culture: Explain how concepts about the legitimate role of the federal government in looking out for the welfare of its citizens changed during the progressive era.

**Additional note: You should be able to contrast the reform movements of the progressive era with those of the Jacksonian era. Additionally, in looking ahead, you should ultimately be able to compare and contrast the progressive era with other eras of reform such as the New Deal and the Great Society.

AP SUGGESTED STUDY

PEOPLE/PLACES/EVENTS As you study these items, think about how they demonstrate or relate to key concepts and historical themes from this chapter and previous chapters.

ALICE PAUL 560	IDA TARBELL 553	NEW FREEDOM 579
"BAD TRUSTS" 570	INTERSTATE COMMERCE ACT 574	NEWLANDS ACT 575
"BULL MOOSE" PARTY 579	IWW ("WOBBLIES") 569	NEW NATIONALISM 578
ELIZABETH CADY STANTON 559	JANE ADDAMS 553	PANIC OF 1907 576
EUGENE DEBS 568	LINCOLN STEFFENS 553	PROFESSIONAL ASSOCIATIONS 555
EUGENICS 568	LOUIS BRANDEIS 570	PROHIBITION 567
FATHER JOHN RYAN 553	MUCKRAKERS 552	PURE FOOD AND DRUG ACT 574
FEDERAL RESERVE ACT 579	MUNICIPAL REFORMS 561	REFERENDUM 562
GIFFORD PINCHOT 574	NAACP 566	ROBERT LA FOLLETTE 563
"GOOD TRUSTS" 570	NATIONAL AMERICAN WOMAN	SETTLEMENT HOUSES 553
HETCH HETCHY 575	SUFFRAGE ASSOCIATION	SIERRA CLUB 575
HULL HOUSE 553	(NAWSA) 559	SOCIAL GOSPEL 553

AP TEST PRACTICE

Questions assume cumulative content knowledge from this chapter and previous chapters.

MULTIPLE CHOICE Use the photograph on page 555 and your knowledge of U.S. history to answer questions 1–2.

1. The subject matter of the photograph most reflects which progressive belief?

   (A) The progressive belief in participation in municipal government

   (B) The progressive belief in the "natural laws" of the marketplace

   (C) The progressive belief in individual accomplishment and professionalism

   (D) The progressive belief in the influence of the environment on human individual development

2. During which earlier period in American history was there a similar concern for social welfare for the underprivileged of different ethnic backgrounds?

   (A) 17th century Puritan New England

   (B) 18th century Enlightenment period

   (C) Post Second Great Awakening secular movements

   (D) Post-Civil War western towns

SHORT ANSWER Use your knowledge of U.S. history to answer questions 3–6.

3. Answer a, b, and c.

   a) Briefly explain ONE example of a variety of progressive reform.

   b) Briefly explain a SECOND example of a variety of progressive reform.

   c) Briefly explain ONE example of a commonality in philosophy, motives, or goals between the varieties of movement you identified above.

4. Answer a, b, and c.

   a) For ONE of the groups below, identify a political, social, or economic issue it tackled in the progressive era.

   • Labor

   • Political Parties

   • African Americans

   b) Briefly explain ONE example of a success or advancement the group achieved regarding the issue.

   c) Briefly explain ONE development that would support an argument that the success or advancement was limited.

5. Answer a, b, and c.

   a) For ONE of the areas below, briefly explain its influence on progressive ideals.

   • Enlightenment

   • Second Great Awakening

   • Early 19th-century Romanticism

   b) Provide ONE example of an event or development to support your explanation.

   c) Briefly explain why ONE of the other options is not as useful to explaining influences leading to the development of progressivism at the turn of the 20th century.

6. Use the political cartoon on page 554 to answer a, b, and c.

   a) Briefly explain the opinion expressed by the artist about ONE of the following:

   • Monopolies

   • Senators

   • Public opinion

   b) Briefly explain ONE development from 1889 to 1910 that might give some validity to its claim.

   c) Briefly explain ONE way in which this political issue was reformed between 1889 and 1910.

LONG ESSAY For each question below, develop a thoughtful and thorough historical argument that answers the question. Begin your essay with a thesis statement and support it with relevant historical evidence.

7. Evaluate the extent to which the reform movements of the progressive era of the early 20th century were a continuation as well as a departure from the reform movements of the 1820s and 1830s in regard to their philosophies, goals, and motivations.

8. Some historians have argued that the progressive era was a turning point in the women's rights movement. Support, modify, or refute this interpretation, providing specific evidence to justify your answer.

21 | AMERICA AND THE GREAT WAR

THE WAR TO END ALL WARS The horror of World War I was unprecedented in human history. More than 9 million people died between July 28, 1914, when the war started and November 11, 1918, when it came to an end. The astronomical number of casualties was due to advanced technologies of combat. Here, an American soldier is succumbing to poison gas, one of the most feared weapons of the war. (Private Collection/© Peter Newark Pictures/Bridgeman Images)

AP
HISTORICAL THINKING

1. **Contextualization** Analyze the reasons for increased U.S. involvement in world affairs.

2. **Historical Argumentation** To what degree and in what ways were the wartime goals of the United States realized in the post-war era?

3. **Comparison** Compare and contrast the foreign policy goals of Theodore Roosevelt, William Howard Taft, and Woodrow Wilson and the results.

4. **Patterns of Continuity and Change over Time** Analyze the impact of World War I on African Americans and the reactions to the changes it brought.

5. **Interpretation** Analyze the economic impact of World War I and its impact on progressive reform.

6. **Contextualization** To what degree and in what way were civil liberties suppressed and repressed during World War I?

7. **Interpretation** Analyze the degree to which and the ways in which organized labor lost favor with the American public during and after the war.

8. **Historical Argumentation** Analyze the reasons for the Red Scare following World War I and its effects.

Key Concept Correlations

Analyze the ways the historical developments you learn about in this chapter connect to the following AP Key Concepts.

7.1 Governmental, political, and social organizations struggled to address the effects of large-scale industrialization, economic uncertainty, and related social changes such as urbanization and mass migration.

7.2 A revolution in communications and transportation technology helped to create a new mass culture and spread "modern" values and ideas, even as cultural conflicts between groups increased under the pressure of migration, world wars, and economic distress.

7.3 Global conflicts over resources, territories, and ideologies renewed debates over the nation's values and its role in the world while simultaneously propelling the United States into a dominant international military, political, cultural, and economic position.

Thematic Learning Objectives

WOR-3, 4, 7; ID-3, 6, 8; PEO-2, 3, 6, 7; POL-6, 7; WXT-6

AP CONNECTING CONCEPTS

CHAPTER 21 discusses increasing U.S. involvement in world affairs in the early 20th century. Pay particular attention to the foreign policy of the presidents and their views and roles regarding internationalism during the time period. Consider how foreign policy might have become more jingoistic. The chapter also discusses the debate over neutrality and preparedness and the reasons the U.S. eventually enter World War I. Important to the chapter discussion is the impact of the war on the American economy, civil liberties, and migration patterns. Discussion also focuses on the decline of organized labor, increasing racial and ethnic tensions, and the impact of the war on African Americans. As you read, evaluate the following ideas:

- Changing demography led to cultural and racial conflict.
- World War I increased xenophobic tendencies among portions of the American people.
- World War I created a climate in which civil liberties were significantly restricted.
- Labor strikes and racial tension disrupted American society during World War I partially enabling the Red Scare.
- World War I significantly altered migration patterns both internally and externally.
- While debate continued over U.S involvement in world affairs, the United States clearly shed its isolationistic background and became a major player on the world stage.
- The United States justified expansion on the basis of economic, political, and social motives.
- The United States entered World War I for humanitarian and democratic goals.
- The United States refused to join the League of Nations and returned to a somewhat isolationist position after the war.

THE "BIG STICK": AMERICA AND THE WORLD, 1901–1917

To the general public, foreign affairs remained largely remote. Walter Lippmann once wrote: "I cannot remember taking any interest whatsoever in foreign affairs until after the outbreak of the First World War." But to Theodore Roosevelt and later presidents, that made foreign affairs even more appealing. There the president could act with less regard for the Congress or the courts. There he could free himself from concerns about public opinion. Overseas, the president could exercise power unfettered and alone.

Roosevelt and "Civilization"

Theodore Roosevelt believed in the value and importance of using American power in the world (a conviction he once described by citing the proverb "Speak softly, but carry a big stick"). But he had two different standards for using that power.

Roosevelt believed that an important distinction existed between the "civilized" and "uncivilized" nations of the world. "Civilized" nations, as he defined them, were predominantly white and Anglo-Saxon or Teutonic; "uncivilized" nations were generally nonwhite, Latin, or Slavic. But racism was only partly the basis of the distinction. Equally important was economic development. He believed, therefore, that Japan, a rapidly industrializing society, had earned admission to the ranks of the civilized. A civilized society, he argued, had the right and duty to intervene in the affairs of a "backward" nation to preserve order and stability. That belief was one important reason for Roosevelt's early support of the development of American sea power. By 1906, the American navy had attained a size and strength surpassed only by that of Great Britain (although Germany was fast gaining ground).

RACIAL AND ECONOMIC BASIS OF ROOSEVELT'S DIPLOMACY

Protecting the "Open Door" in Asia

In 1904, the Japanese staged a surprise attack on the Russian fleet at Port Arthur in southern Manchuria, a province of China that both Russia and Japan hoped to control. Roosevelt, hoping to

THE WORLD'S CONSTABLE.

"**THE NEW DIPLOMACY**" This 1904 drawing by the famous Puck cartoonist Louis Dalrymple conveys the new image of America as a great power that Theodore Roosevelt was attempting to project to the world. Roosevelt the world policeman deals effectively with "less civilized" peoples (Asians and Latin Americans, seen clamoring at left) by using the "big stick" and deals equally effectively with the "civilized" nations (at right) by offering arbitration. (© The Granger Collection, New York)

prevent either nation from becoming dominant there, agreed to a Japanese request to mediate an end to the conflict. Russia, faring badly in the war, had no choice but to agree. At a peace conference in Portsmouth, New Hampshire, in 1905, Roosevelt extracted from the embattled Russians a recognition of Japan's territorial gains and from the Japanese an agreement to cease the fighting and expand no further. At the same time, he negotiated a secret agreement with the Japanese to ensure that the United States could continue to trade freely in the region.

Roosevelt won the Nobel Peace Prize in 1906 for his work in ending the Russo-Japanese War. But in the years that followed, relations between the United States and Japan steadily deteriorated. Japan now emerged as the preeminent naval

"GREAT WHITE FLEET"

power in the Pacific and soon began to exclude American trade from many of the territories it controlled. To be sure the Japanese government recognized the power of the United States, he sent sixteen battleships of the new American navy (known as the "Great White Fleet" because the ships were temporarily painted white for the voyage) on an unprecedented journey around the world that included a call on Japan.

THE IRON-FISTED NEIGHBOR

Roosevelt took a particular interest in events in what he (and most other Americans) considered the nation's special sphere of interest: Latin America. He established a pattern of U.S. intervention in the region that would long survive his presidency.

Early in 1902, the financially troubled government of Venezuela began to renege on debts to European bankers. Naval forces of Britain, Italy, and Germany blockaded the Venezuelan coast in response. Then German ships began to bombard a Venezuelan port amid rumors that Germany planned to establish a permanent base in the region. Roosevelt used the threat of American naval power to pressure the German navy to withdraw.

The incident helped persuade Roosevelt that European intrusions into Latin America could result not only from

"ROOSEVELT COROLLARY"

aggression but also from instability or irresponsibility (such as defaulting on debts) within the Latin American nations themselves. As a result, in 1904 he announced what came to be known as the "Roosevelt Corollary" to the Monroe Doctrine.

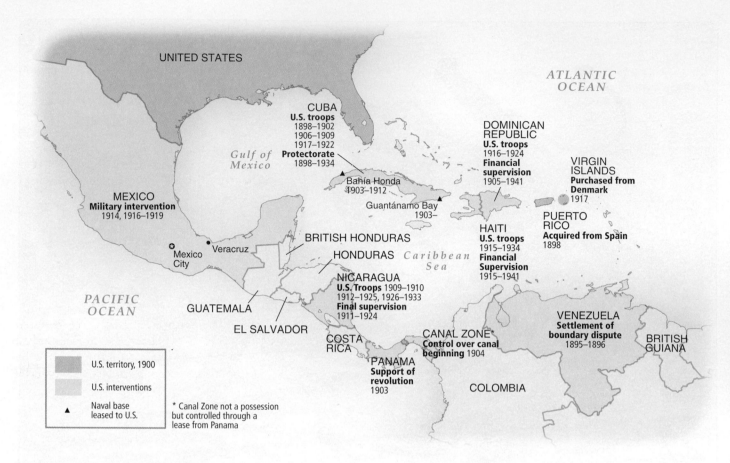

THE UNITED STATES AND LATIN AMERICA, 1895–1941 Except for Puerto Rico, the Virgin Islands, and the Canal Zone, the United States had no formal possessions in Latin America and the Caribbean in the late nineteenth century and the first half of the twentieth. But as this map reveals, the U.S. exercised considerable influence in these regions throughout this period—political and economic influence, augmented at times by military intervention. Note the particularly intrusive presence of the United States in the affairs of Cuba, Haiti, and the Dominican Republic—as well as the canal-related interventions in Colombia and Panama.

• *What were some of the most frequent reasons for U.S. intervention in Latin America?*

The United States, he claimed, had the right not only to oppose European intervention in the Western Hemisphere but also to intervene in the domestic affairs of its neighbors if those neighbors proved unable to maintain order and national sovereignty on their own.

The immediate motivation for the Roosevelt Corollary, and the first opportunity for using it, was a crisis in the Dominican Republic. A revolution had toppled its corrupt and bankrupt government in 1903, but the new regime proved no better able to make good on the country's $22 million in debts to European nations. Roosevelt established, in effect, an American receivership, assuming control of Dominican customs and distributing 45 percent of the revenues to the Dominicans and the rest to foreign creditors. This arrangement lasted, in one form or another, for more than three decades.

In 1902, the United States granted political independence to Cuba, but only after the new government had agreed to the Platt Amendment to its constitution (see p. 545). The amendment gave the United States the right to prevent any other foreign power from intruding into the new nation. In 1906, when domestic uprisings seemed to threaten the internal stability of the island,

PLATT AMENDMENT

American troops landed in Cuba, quelled the fighting, and remained there for three years.

THE PANAMA CANAL

The most celebrated accomplishment of Roosevelt's presidency was the construction of the Panama Canal, which linked the Atlantic and the Pacific. At first, Roosevelt and many advocates of a canal favored a route across Nicaragua, which would permit a sea-level canal requiring no locks. But they soon turned instead to the narrow Isthmus of Panama in Colombia, the site of an earlier, failed effort by a French company to construct a channel. Although the Panama route was not at sea level (and would thus require locks), it was shorter than the one in Nicaragua. And construction was already about 40 percent complete. When the French company lowered the price for its holdings, the United States chose Panama.

Roosevelt dispatched John Hay, his secretary of state, to negotiate an agreement with Colombian diplomats in Washington that would allow construction to begin without delay. Under heavy American pressure, the Colombian chargé d'affaires, Tomas Herrén, unwisely signed an agreement giving the United States perpetual rights to a six-mile-wide "canal zone" across Colombia. The outraged Colombian senate refused to ratify it. Colombia then sent a new representative to Washington with instructions to demand a higher payment from the Americans plus a share of the payment to the French.

Roosevelt was furious and began to look for ways to circumvent the Colombian government. Philippe Bunau-Varilla, chief engineer of the French canal project, was a ready ally. In November 1903, he helped organize and finance a revolution in Panama.

PANAMANIAN REVOLT There had been many previous revolts, all of them failures, but this one had the support of the United States. Roosevelt landed troops from the USS *Nashville* in Panama to "maintain order." Their presence prevented Colombian forces from suppressing the rebellion, and three days later Roosevelt recognized Panama as an independent nation. The new Panamanian government quickly agreed to the terms the Colombian senate had rejected. Work on the canal proceeded rapidly, and it opened in 1914.

TAFT AND "DOLLAR DIPLOMACY"

Like his predecessor, William Howard Taft worked to advance the nation's economic interests overseas. But he showed little interest in Roosevelt's larger vision of world stability. Taft's secretary of state, the corporate attorney Philander C. Knox, worked aggressively to extend American investments into less developed regions. Critics called his policies "Dollar Diplomacy."

It was particularly visible in the Caribbean. When a revolution broke out in Nicaragua in 1909, the administration quickly

INTERVENTION IN NICARAGUA sided with the insurgents (who had been inspired to revolt by an American mining company) and sent troops into the country to seize the customs houses. As soon as peace was restored, Knox encouraged American bankers to offer substantial loans to the new government, thus increasing Washington's financial leverage over the country. When the new pro-American government faced an insurrection less than two years later, Taft again landed troops in Nicaragua, this time to protect the existing regime. The troops remained there for more than a decade.

DIPLOMACY AND MORALITY

Woodrow Wilson entered the presidency with relatively little interest or experience in international affairs. Yet he faced international challenges of a scope and gravity unmatched by those of any president before him. In many respects, he continued—and even strengthened—the Roosevelt-Taft approach to foreign policy.

OPENING THE PANAMA CANAL The great Miraflores locks of the Panama Canal open in October 1914 to admit the first ship to pass through the channel. The construction of the canal was one of the great engineering feats of the early twentieth century. But the heavy-handed political efforts of Theodore Roosevelt were at least equally important to its completion. (© Bettmann/Corbis)

Having already seized control of the finances of the Dominican Republic in 1905, the United States established a military government there in 1916. The military occupation lasted eight years. In neighboring Haiti, Wilson landed marines in 1915 to quell a revolution, in the course of which a mob had murdered an unpopular president. American military forces remained in the country until 1934, and American officers drafted the new Haitian constitution adopted in 1918. When Wilson began to fear that the Danish West Indies might be about to fall into the hands of Germany, he bought the colony from Denmark and renamed it the Virgin Islands. Concerned about the possibility of European influence in Nicaragua, he signed a treaty with that country's government ensuring that no other nation would build a canal there and winning for the United States the right to intervene in Nicaragua to protect American interests.

But Wilson's view of America's role in the world was not entirely similar to the views of his predecessors, as became

WILSON'S MORAL DIPLOMACY

clear in his dealings with Mexico. For many years, under the friendly auspices of the corrupt dictator Porfirio Díaz, American businessmen had been establishing an enormous economic presence in Mexico. In 1910, however, Díaz had been overthrown by the popular leader Francisco Madero, who seemed hostile to American businesses in Mexico. The United States quietly encouraged a reactionary general, Victoriano Huerta, to depose Madero early in 1913, and the Taft administration, in its last weeks in office, prepared to recognize the new Huerta regime and welcome back a receptive environment for American investments in Mexico. Before it could do so, however, the new government murdered Madero, shortly before Woodrow

Wilson took office in Washington. The new president instantly announced that he would never recognize Huerta's "government of butchers."

At first, Wilson hoped that simply by refusing to recognize Huerta he could help topple the regime and bring to power the opposing Constitutionalists, led by Venustiano Carranza. But when Huerta, with the support of American business interests, established a full military dictatorship in October 1913, the president became more assertive. In April 1914, an officer in Huerta's army briefly arrested several American sailors from the USS *Dolphin* who had gone ashore in Tampico, on Mexico's east coast. The men were immediately released, but the American admiral–unsatisfied with the apology he received–demanded that the Huerta forces fire a twenty-one-gun salute to the American flag as a public display of penance. The Mexicans refused. Wilson used the trivial incident as a pretext for seizing the Mexican port of Veracruz.

Wilson had envisioned a bloodless action, but in a clash with Mexican troops in Veracruz, the Americans killed 126

VERACRUZ

Mexican soldiers and suffered 19 casualties of their own. Now at the brink of war, Wilson began to look for a way out. His show of force, however, had helped strengthen the position of the Carranza faction, which captured Mexico City in August and forced Huerta to flee the country. At last, it seemed, the crisis might be over.

But Wilson was not yet satisfied. He reacted angrily when Carranza refused to accept American guidelines for the creation of a new government, and he briefly considered throwing his support to still another aspirant to leadership: Carranza's erstwhile lieutenant Pancho Villa, who was now leading

PANCHO VILLA AND HIS TROOPS Pancho Villa (fourth from left in the front row) poses with some of the leaders of his army, whose members Americans came to consider bandits once they began staging raids across the U.S. border. He was a national hero in Mexico. (The Library of Congress (LC-DIG-ggbain-29882))

a rebel army of his own. When Villa's military position deteriorated, however, Wilson abandoned him and finally, in October 1915, granted preliminary recognition to the Carranza government. By now, however, he had created yet another crisis. Villa, angry at what he considered an American betrayal, retaliated in January 1916 by shooting sixteen American mining engineers in northern Mexico. Two months later, he led his soldiers (or "bandits," as the United States called them) across the border into Columbus, New Mexico, where they killed seventeen more Americans.

With the permission of the Carranza government, Wilson ordered General John J. Pershing to lead an American expedi-

INTERVENTION IN MEXICO

tionary force across the Mexican border in pursuit of Villa. The American troops never found Villa, but they did engage in two ugly skirmishes with Carranza's army, in which forty Mexicans and twelve Americans died. Again, the United States and Mexico stood at the brink of war. But at the last minute, Wilson drew back. He quietly withdrew American troops from Mexico, and in March 1917, he at last granted formal recognition to the Carranza regime. By now, however, Wilson's attention was turning elsewhere—to the far greater international crisis engulfing the European continent and ultimately much of the world.

THE ROAD TO WAR

The causes of the war in Europe—indeed the question of whether there were any significant causes at all, or whether the entire conflict was the result of a tragic series of blunders—have been the subject of continued debate for nearly a century. What is clear is that the European nations had by 1914 created an unusually precarious international system that careened into war very quickly on the basis of what most historians agree was a relatively minor series of provocations.

THE COLLAPSE OF THE EUROPEAN PEACE

The major powers of Europe were organized by 1914 in two great, competing alliances. The "Triple Entente" linked Britain, France, and Russia. The "Triple Alliance" united Germany, the Austro-Hungarian Empire, and Italy. The chief rivalry, however, was not between the two alliances, but between the

COMPETING ALLIANCES

great powers that dominated them: Great Britain and Germany—the former long established as the world's most powerful colonial and commercial nation, the latter ambitious to expand its own empire and become at least Britain's equal. The Anglo-German rivalry may have been the most important underlying source of the tensions that led to World War I, but it was not the immediate cause of its outbreak. The conflict emerged most directly out of a controversy involving nationalist movements within the Austro-Hungarian Empire. On June 28, 1914, Archduke Franz Ferdinand, heir to the throne of the tottering

empire, was assassinated while paying a state visit to Sarajevo. Sarajevo was the capital of Bosnia, a province of Austria-Hungary that Slavic nationalists wished to annex to neighboring Serbia; the archduke's assassin was a Serbian nationalist.

This local controversy quickly escalated through the workings of the system of alliances that the great powers had constructed. With support from Germany, Austria-Hungary launched a punitive assault on Serbia. The Serbians called on Russia to help with their defense. The Russians began mobilizing their army on July 30. Things quickly careened out of control. By August 3, Germany had declared war on both Russia and France and had invaded Belgium in preparation for a thrust across the French border. On August 4, Great Britain—ostensibly to honor its alliance with France but, more importantly, to blunt the advance of its principal rival—declared war on Germany. Russia and the Austro-Hungarian Empire formally began hostilities on August 6. Italy, although an ally of Germany in 1914, remained neutral at first and later entered the war on the side of the British and French. The Ottoman Empire (centered in Turkey) and other, smaller nations all joined the fighting later in 1914 or in 1915. Within less than a year, virtually the entire European continent and part of Asia were embroiled in a catastrophic war.

WILSON'S NEUTRALITY

Wilson called on his fellow citizens in 1914 to remain "impartial in thought as well as deed." But that was an impossible task, for several reasons. Some Americans sympathized with the German cause (German Americans because of affection for Germany, Irish Americans because of hatred of Britain). Many more (including Wilson himself) sympathized with Britain. Wilson was only one of many Americans who fervently admired England—its traditions, its culture, its political system; almost instinctively, these Americans attributed to the cause of the Allies (Britain, France, Italy, Russia) a moral quality that they denied to the Central Powers (Germany, the Austro-Hungarian Empire, and the Ottoman Empire). Lurid reports of German atrocities in Belgium and France, skillfully exaggerated by British propagandists, strengthened the hostility of many Americans toward Germany.

Economic realities also made it impossible for the United States to deal with the belligerents on equal terms. The British had imposed a naval blockade on Germany to prevent munitions and supplies from reaching the enemy.

ECONOMIC TIES TO BRITAIN

As a neutral, the United States had the right, in theory, to trade with both Britain and Germany; but for Americans to trade with Germany, they would have to defy the British blockade. A truly neutral response to the blockade would have been to stop trading with Britain as well. But while the United States could survive an interruption of its relatively modest trade with the Central Powers, it could not easily weather an embargo on its much more extensive trade with the Allies, particularly when war orders from Britain and France soared after 1914, helping to produce one of the greatest economic booms in the nation's history. So America

IT IS FAR BETTER TO FACE THE BULLETS THAN TO BE KILLED AT HOME BY A BOMB

JOIN THE ARMY AT ONCE & HELP TO STOP AN AIR RAID

GOD SAVE THE KING

BULLETS BETTER THAN BOMBS? At the beginning of World War I, Britain largely relied on a volunteer army. To attract recruits, the government used propaganda posters such as the one shown here. While this was very successful in attracting recruits, the need for soldiers was enormous, compelling Parliament to enact in January 1916 a Military Service Bill that introduced conscription. By the end of the war, more than 5 million men had joined up. (© Archive Photos/Alamy)

tacitly ignored the blockade of Germany and continued trading with Britain. By 1915, the United States had gradually transformed itself from a neutral power into the arsenal of the Allies.

The Germans, in the meantime, were resorting to a new and, in American eyes, barbaric tactic: submarine warfare. Unable to challenge British domination on the ocean's surface, Germany began early in 1915 to use the newly improved submarine to try to stem the flow of supplies to England. Enemy vessels, the Germans announced, would be sunk on sight. Months later, on

LUSITANIA May 7, 1915, a German submarine sank the British passenger liner *Lusitania* without warning, causing the deaths of 1,198 people, 128 of them Americans. The ship was, it later became clear, carrying both passengers and munitions; but most Americans considered the attack what Theodore Roosevelt called it: "an act of piracy."

Wilson angrily demanded that Germany promise not to repeat such outrages and that the Central Powers affirm their

commitment to neutral rights. The Germans finally agreed to Wilson's demands, but tensions between the nations continued to grow. Early in 1916, in response to an announcement that the Allies were now arming merchant ships to sink submarines, Germany proclaimed that it would fire on such vessels without warning. A few weeks later Germany attacked the unarmed French steamer *Sussex*, injuring several American passengers. Again Wilson demanded that Germany abandon its "unlawful" tactics; again the German government relented, still hoping to keep America out of the war.

PREPAREDNESS VERSUS PACIFISM

Despite the president's increasing bellicosity in 1916, he was still far from ready to commit the United States to war. One obstacle was American domestic politics. Facing a difficult battle for reelection, Wilson could not ignore the powerful factions that continued to oppose intervention.

The question of whether America should make military and economic preparations for war provided the first issue over which pacifists and interventionists could openly debate. Wilson at first sided with the antipreparedness forces, denouncing the idea of an American military buildup as needless and provocative. As tensions between the United States and Germany grew, however, he changed his mind. In the fall of 1915, he endorsed an ambitious proposal for a large and rapid increase in the nation's armed forces. Amid expressions of outrage from pacifists in Congress and elsewhere, he worked hard to win approval of it, even embarking on a national speaking tour early in 1916 to arouse support for the proposal.

Still, the peace faction wielded considerable political strength, as became clear at the Democratic Convention in the summer

1916 ELECTION of 1916. The convention became especially enthusiastic when the keynote speaker punctuated his list of Wilson's diplomatic achievements with the chant "What did we do? What did we do? . . . We didn't go to war! We didn't go to war!" That speech helped produce one of the most prominent slogans of Wilson's reelection campaign: "He kept us out of war." During the campaign, Wilson did nothing to discourage those who argued that the Republican candidate, the progressive New York governor Charles Evans Hughes (supported by the bellicose Theodore Roosevelt), was more likely than he to lead the nation into war. And when pro-war rhetoric became particularly heated, Wilson spoke defiantly of the nation being "too proud to fight." He ultimately won reelection by a small margin: fewer than 600,000 popular votes and only 23 electoral votes. The Democrats retained a precarious control over Congress.

A WAR FOR DEMOCRACY

The election was behind him, and tensions between the United States and Germany remained high. But Wilson still required a justification for American intervention that would unite public opinion and satisfy his own sense of morality. In the end, he created that rationale himself. The United States,

Wilson insisted, had no material aims in the conflict. Rather, the nation was committed to using the war as a vehicle for constructing a new world order, one based on some of the same progressive ideals that had motivated reform in America. In a speech before Congress in January 1917, he presented a plan for a postwar order in which the United States would help maintain peace through a permanent league of nations—a peace that would ensure self-determination for all nations, a "peace without victory." These were, Wilson believed, goals worth fighting for if there was sufficient provocation. Provocation came quickly.

In January, after months of inconclusive warfare in the trenches of France, the military leaders of Germany decided on one last dramatic gamble to achieve victory. They launched a series of major assaults on the enemy's lines in France. At the same time, they began unrestricted submarine warfare (against American as well as Allied ships) to cut Britain off from vital supplies. The Allied defenses would collapse, they hoped, before the United States could intervene. The new German policy made American entry into the war virtually inevitable. Two additional events helped clear the way. On February 25,

ZIMMERMANN TELEGRAM

the British gave Wilson a telegram intercepted from the German foreign minister, Arthur Zimmermann, to the government of Mexico. It proposed that in the event of war between Germany and the United States, the Mexicans should join with Germany against the Americans to regain their "lost provinces" (Texas and much of the rest of the American Southwest) when the war was over. Widely publicized by British propagandists and in the American press, the Zimmermann telegram inflamed public opinion and helped build popular sentiment for war. A few weeks later, in March 1917, a revolution in Russia toppled the reactionary czarist regime and replaced it with a new, republican government. The United States would now be spared the embarrassment of allying itself with what most Americans considered a despotic monarchy.

On the rainy evening of April 2, two weeks after German submarines had torpedoed three American ships, Wilson appeared before a joint session of Congress and asked for a declaration of war:

> It is a fearful thing to lead this great peaceful people into war, into the most terrible and disastrous of all wars, civilization itself seeming to be in the balance. But the right is more precious than peace, and we shall fight for the things which we have always carried nearest our hearts—for democracy, for the right of those who submit to authority to have a voice in their own Governments, for the rights and liberties of small nations, for a universal dominion of right by such a concert of free peoples as shall bring peace and safety to all nations and make the world itself at last free.

Even then, opposition remained. For four days, pacifists in Congress carried on a futile struggle. When the declaration of war finally passed on April 6, fifty representatives and six senators voted against it.

"WAR WITHOUT STINT"

Armies on both sides in Europe were decimated and exhausted by the time of Woodrow Wilson's declaration of war. The German offensives of early 1917 had failed to produce an end to the struggle, and French and British counteroffensives had accomplished little beyond adding to the casualties. The Allies looked to the United States for help. Wilson, who had called on the nation to wage war "without stint or limit," was ready to oblige.

STALEMATE

ENTERING THE WAR

By the spring of 1917, Great Britain was suffering such vast losses from attacks by German submarines—one of every four ships setting sail from British ports never returned—that its ability to continue receiving vital supplies from across the Atlantic was in question. Within weeks of joining the war, a fleet of American destroyers began aiding the British navy in its assault on German submarines. Other American warships

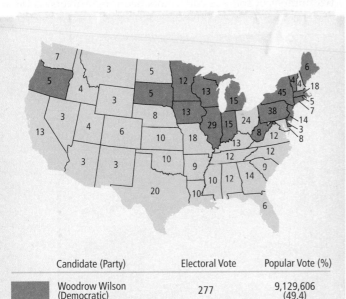

Candidate (Party)	Electoral Vote	Popular Vote (%)
Woodrow Wilson (Democratic)	277	9,129,606 (49.4)
Charles E. Hughes (Republican)	254	8,538,221 (46.2)
A. L. Benson (Socialist)	—	585,113 (3.2)
Other parties (Prohibition; Socialist Labor)	—	233,909

61.6% of electorate voting

ELECTION OF 1916 Woodrow Wilson had good reason to be concerned about his reelection prospects in 1916. He had won only about 42 percent of the vote in 1912, and the Republican Party—which had been divided four years earlier—was now reunited around the popular Charles Evans Hughes. In the end, Wilson won a narrow victory over Hughes with just under 50 percent of the vote and an even narrower margin in the electoral college. Note the striking regional character of his victory.

• *How did Wilson use the war in Europe to bolster his election prospects?*

escorted merchant vessels across the Atlantic. Americans also helped sow antisubmarine mines in the North Sea. The results were dramatic. Sinkings of Allied ships had totaled nearly 900,000 tons in April 1917; by December, the figure had dropped to 350,000, and by October 1918 to 112,000. The convoys also helped the United States protect its own soldiers en route to Europe. No American troop ship was lost at sea in World War I.

Many Americans had hoped that providing naval assistance alone would be enough to turn the tide in the war, but it quickly became clear that American ground forces would also be neces-

RUSSIAN REVOLUTION

sary to shore up the tottering Allies. Britain and France had few remaining reserves. By early 1918, Russia had withdrawn from the war. After the Bolshevik Revolution in November 1917, the new government, led by V.I. Lenin, negotiated a hasty and costly peace with the Central Powers, thus freeing additional German troops to fight on the western front.

THE AMERICAN EXPEDITIONARY FORCE

There were only about 120,000 soldiers in the army in 1917 and perhaps 80,000 more in the National Guard. Neither group had any combat experience; and except for the small number of officers who had participated in the Spanish-American War two decades before and the Mexican intervention of 1916, few commanders had any experience in battle either.

Some politicians urged a voluntary recruitment process to raise the needed additional forces. Among the advocates of this approach was Theodore Roosevelt, now old and ill, who swallowed his hatred of Wilson and called on him at the White House with an offer to raise a regiment to fight in Europe. Wilson rejected his offer. In the new age of warfare, he sensed, the old tradition of civilians becoming officers and recruiting troops (a common practice in the Civil War), seemed obsolete. The president and his secretary of war, Newton D. Baker, decided that only a national draft could provide the needed men; and despite the protests of those who agreed with

SELECTIVE SERVICE ACT

House Speaker Champ Clark that "there is precious little difference between a conscript and a convict," he won passage of the Selective Service Act in mid-May. The draft brought nearly 3 million men into the army; another 2 million joined various branches of the armed services voluntarily. Together, they formed what became known as the American Expeditionary Force (AEF).

It was the first time in American history that any substantial number of soldiers and sailors had fought overseas for an

THE WARTIME DRAFT The World War I draft was the first centrally organized effort by the federal government to require military service from its citizens. Although some Americans evaded the draft in 1917 and 1918 (and were reviled by others as "shirkers"), most of those drafted complied with the law. (The Library of Congress (LC-DIG-npcc-00293))

extended period. The military did its best to keep up morale among men who spent most of their time living in the trenches, but it was a difficult task. The trenches were frequently shelled and even when calm were muddy, polluted, and infested with rats. But when soldiers had time away from the front, they were usually less interested in the facilities the Red Cross tried to make available for them than in exploring the bars and brothels of local towns. More than one in every ten American soldiers in Europe contracted venereal disease during World War I, which inspired elaborate official efforts to prevent infection and to treat it when it occurred.

In some respects, the AEF was the most diverse fighting force the United States had ever assembled. For the first time, women were permitted to enlist in the military—more than ten thousand in the navy and a few hundred in the marines. They were not allowed to participate in combat, but they served auxiliary roles in hospitals and offices.

Nearly 400,000 African Americans enlisted in or were drafted into the army and navy as well. (The marines would not accept them.) And while most of them performed menial tasks on military bases in the United States, more than 50,000 **AFRICAN AMERICAN SOLDIERS** went to France. African American soldiers served in segregated, all-black units under white commanders; and even in Europe, most of them were assigned to noncombat duty. But some black units fought valiantly in the great offensives of 1918. Most African American soldiers learned to live with the racism they encountered—in part because they hoped their military service would ultimately improve their status. But a few responded to provocations violently. In August 1917, a group of black soldiers in Houston, Texas, subjected to continuing abuse by people in the community, used military

weapons to kill seventeen whites. Thirteen African American soldiers were hanged, and another forty were sentenced to life terms in military jails.

Having assembled this first genuinely national army, the War Department permitted the American Psychological Association to study it. The psychologists gave thousands of soldiers new tests designed to measure intelligence: the "Intelligence Quotient," or "IQ," test and other newly designed aptitude tests. In fact, the tests were less effective in measuring intelligence than in measuring education; and they reflected the educational expectations of the white middle-class people who had devised them. Half the whites and the vast majority of the African Americans taking the test scored at levels that classified them as "morons." In reality, most of them were simply people who had not had much access to education.

THE MILITARY STRUGGLE

The engagement of these forces in combat was intense but brief. Not until the spring of 1918 were significant numbers of American ground troops available for battle. Eight months later, the war was over. Under the command of General John J. Pershing, who had only recently led the unsuccessful American pursuit of Pancho Villa, the American Expeditionary Force—although it retained a command structure independent of the other Allies—joined the existing Allied forces. **GENERAL JOHN PERSHING**

The experience of American troops during World War I was very different from those of other nations, which had already been fighting for nearly four years by the time the U.S. forces arrived in significant numbers. British, French, German, and other troops had by then spent years living in the vast

LIFE IN THE TRENCHES For most British, French, German, and ultimately American troops in France, the most debilitating part of World War I was the seeming endlessness of life in the trenches. Some young men lived in these cold, wet, muddy dugouts for months, even years, surrounded by filth, sharing their space with vermin, eating mostly rotten food. Occasional attacks to try to dislodge the enemy from its trenches usually ended in failure and became the scenes of terrible slaughters. (National Archives and Records Administration (NWDNS-111-SC-12151))

network of trenches that had been dug into the French countryside. Modern weapons made conventional, frontal battles a recipe for mass suicide. Instead, the two sides relied on heavy shelling of each other's trenches and occasional, usually inconclusive, and always murderous assaults across the "no-man's land" dividing them. Life in the trenches was almost indescribably terrible. The trenches were places of extraordinary physical stress and discomfort. They were also places of intense boredom, laced with fear. By the time the Americans arrived, morale on both sides was declining, and many soldiers had come to believe that the war would be virtually endless.

Although the American forces had trench experiences of their own, they were very brief compared to those of the European armies. Instead, the United States tipped the balance of power in the battle and made it possible for the Allies at last to break out of their entrenched positions and advance against the Germans. In early June 1918, American forces at Château-Thierry assisted the French in repelling a German offensive that had brought German forces within fifty miles of Paris. Six weeks later, after over a million American troops had flooded into France, the Americans helped turn away another assault, at Rheims, farther south. By July 18, the Allies had halted the German advance and were beginning a successful offensive of their own.

CHÂTEAU-THIERRY

On September 26, the American fighting force joined a large assault against the Germans in the Argonne Forest that lasted nearly seven weeks. By the end of October, despite terrible weather, they had helped push the Germans back toward their own border and had cut the enemy's major supply lines to the front.

MEUSE-ARGONNE OFFENSIVE

Faced with an invasion of their own country, German military leaders now began to seek an armistice–an immediate cease-fire that would, they hoped, serve as a prelude to negotiations among the belligerents. Pershing wanted to drive on into Germany itself; but other Allied leaders, after first insisting on terms that made the agreement little different from a surrender, accepted the German proposal. On November 11, 1918, the Great War shuddered to a close.

THE NEW TECHNOLOGY OF WARFARE

World War I was a proving ground for a range of military and other technologies. The trench warfare that characterized the conflict was necessary because of the enormous destructive power of newly improved machine guns and higher-powered artillery. It was no longer feasible to send troops out into an open field, or even to allow them to camp in the open. The new weaponry would slaughter them in an instant. Trenches sheltered troops while allowing limited, and usually inconclusive, fighting. But technology overtook the trenches, too, as mobile weapons–tanks and flamethrowers–proved capable of piercing entrenched positions. Most terrible of all, new chemical weapons–poisonous mustard gas, which required troops to carry gas masks at all times–made it possible to attack entrenched soldiers without direct combat.

The new forms of technological warfare required elaborate maintenance. Faster machine guns needed more ammunition. Motorized vehicles required fuel and spare parts and mechanics capable of servicing them. The logistical difficulties of supply became a major factor in planning tactics and strategy. Late in the war, when advancing toward Germany, Allied armies frequently had to stop for days at a time to wait for their equipment to catch up with them.

AMERICA IN WORLD WAR I: THE WESTERN FRONT, 1918 These maps show the principal battles in which the United States participated in the last year of World War I. The small map on the upper right helps locate the area of conflict within the larger European landscape. The larger map at left shows the long, snaking red line of the western front in France—stretching from the border between France and southwest Germany all the way to the northeast border between Belgium and France. Along that vast line, the two sides had been engaged in murderous, inconclusive warfare for over three years by the time the Americans arrived. Beginning in the spring and summer of 1918, bolstered by reinforcements from the United States, the Allies began to win a series of important victories that finally enabled them to begin pushing the Germans back. American troops, as this map makes clear, were decisive along the southern part of the front.

• At what point did the Germans begin to consider putting an end to the war?

World War I was the first conflict in which airplanes played a significant role. The planes themselves were relatively simple and not very maneuverable; but anti-aircraft technology was not yet highly developed either, so their effectiveness was still considerable. Planes began to be constructed to serve various functions: bombers, fighters (planes that would engage in "dogfights" with other planes), and reconaissance aircraft.

The most "modern" part of the military during World War I was the navy. New battleships emerged—of which the British *Dreadnought* was perhaps the most visible example—that made use of new technologies such as turbine propulsion, hydraulic gun controls, electric light and power, wireless telegraphy, and advanced navigational aids. Submarines, which had made a brief appearance in the American Civil War, now became significant weapons (as the German U-boat campaign in 1915 and 1916 made clear). The new submarines were driven by diesel engines, which had the advantage of being more compact than a steam engine and whose fuel was less explosive than that of a gasoline engine. The diesel engine also had a much greater range than ships powered by other fuels.

The new technologies were to a large degree responsible for the most stunning and horrible characteristic of World War I—its appalling level of casualties. A million men representing the British Empire (Britain, Canada, Australia, India, and others) died. France lost 1.7 million men; Germany, 2 million; the former Austro-Hungarian Empire, 1.5 million; Italy, 460,000; and Russia, 1.7 million. The number of Turkish dead, which was surely large, was never known. In Britain, one-third of the men born between 1892 and 1895 died in the war. Similarly terrible percentages could be calculated for other warring nations. Even greater numbers of men returned

HIGH CASUALTY RATES

home with injuries, some of them permanently crippling. The United States, which entered the war near its end and became engaged only in the last successful offensives, suffered very light casualties in comparison–112,000 dead, half of them victims of influenza, not battle. But the American casualties were very high in the battles in which U.S. troops were centrally involved.

THE WAR AND AMERICAN SOCIETY

The American experience in World War I was relatively brief, but it had profound effects on the government, the economy, and society. Mobilizing an industrial economy for total war required an unprecedented degree of government involvement in industry, agriculture, and other areas. It also required, many Americans believed, a strenuous effort to ensure the loyalty and commitment of the people.

ORGANIZING THE ECONOMY FOR WAR

By the time the war ended, the U.S. government had spent $32 billion for expenses directly related to the conflict. This

FINANCING THE WAR

was a staggering sum by the standards of the time. The entire federal budget had seldom exceeded $1 billion before 1915, and as recently as 1910 the nation's entire gross national product had been only $35 billion. To finance the war, the government relied on two devices. First, it launched a major drive to solicit loans from the American people by selling "Liberty Bonds" to the public. By 1920, the sale of bonds, to both individuals and institutions, accompanied by elaborate patriotic appeals, had produced $23 billion. At the same time, new taxes were bringing in an additional sum of nearly $10 billion–some from levies on the "excess profits" of corporations, much from new, steeply graduated income and inheritance taxes that ultimately rose as high as 70 percent in some brackets.

An even greater challenge was organizing the economy to meet war needs. In 1916, Wilson established a Council of National Defense, composed of members of his cabinet, and a Civilian Advisory Commission, which set up local defense councils in every state and locality. Economic mobilization, according to this first plan, was to rest on a dispersal of power to local communities.

But this early administrative structure soon proved unworkable. Some members of the Council of National Defense, many of them disciples of the social engineering gospel of Thorstein Veblen and the "scientific management" principles of Frederick Winslow Taylor, urged a centralized approach. Instead of dividing the economy geographically, they proposed dividing it functionally by organizing a series of planning bodies, each to supervise a specific sector of the economy. The administrative structure that slowly emerged

from such proposals was dominated by a series of "war boards," one to oversee the railroads, one to supervise fuel supplies (largely coal), another to handle food (a board that helped elevate to prominence the brilliant young engineer and business executive Herbert Hoover). The boards generally succeeded in meeting essential war needs without paralyzing the domestic economy.

At the center of the effort to rationalize the economy was the War Industries Board (WIB), an agency created in July

WAR INDUSTRIES BOARD

1917 to coordinate government purchases of military supplies. Casually organized at first, it stumbled badly until March 1918, when Wilson restructured it and placed it under the control of the Wall Street financier Bernard Baruch. From then on, the board wielded powers greater (in theory at least) than any other government agency had ever possessed. Baruch decided which factories would convert to the production of which war materials and set prices for the goods they produced. When materials were scarce, Baruch decided to whom they should go. When corporations were competing for government contracts, he chose among them. He was, it seemed, providing the centralized regulation of the economy that some progressives had long urged.

In reality, the celebrated efficiency of the WIB was something of a myth. The agency was, in fact, plagued by mismanagement and inefficiency. Its apparent success rested in large part on the sheer extent of American resources and productive capacities. Nor was the WIB in any real sense an example of state control of the economy. Baruch viewed himself as the partner of business; and within the WIB, businessmen themselves–the so-called dollar-a-year men, who took paid leave from their corporate jobs and worked for the government for a token salary–supervised the affairs of the private economy. Baruch ensured that manufacturers who coordinated their efforts with his goals would be exempt from antitrust laws. He helped major industries earn enormous profits from their efforts.

The effort to organize the economy for war produced some spectacular accomplishments: Hoover's efficient organization of domestic food supplies, William McAdoo's success in untangling the railroads, and others. In some areas, however, progress was so slow that the war was over before many of the supplies ordered

LESSONS OF THE MANAGED ECONOMY

for it were ready. Even so, many leaders of both government and industry emerged from the experience convinced of the advantages of a close, cooperative relationship between the public and private sectors. Some hoped to continue the wartime experiments in peacetime.

LABOR AND THE WAR

The growing link between the public and private sectors extended, although in greatly different form, to labor. The National War Labor Board, established in April 1918 to resolve labor disputes, pressured industry to grant important concessions to workers: an eight-hour day, the maintenance of minimal living standards, equal pay for women doing equal work, recognition of the right of unions to organize and bargain collectively. In return, it insisted that workers forgo all strikes and that employers not engage in lockouts. Membership in labor unions increased by more than 1.5 million between 1917 and 1919.

The war provided workers with important, if usually temporary, gains. But it did not stop labor militancy. That was particularly clear in the West, where the Western Federation of Miners staged a series of strikes to improve the terrible conditions in the underground mines. The bloodiest of them occurred just before the war. In Ludlow, Colorado, in 1914, workers (mostly Italians, Greeks, and Slavs) walked out of coal mines owned by John D. Rockefeller. Joined by their wives and daughters, they continued the strike even after they had been evicted from company housing and had moved into hastily erected tents. The state militia was called into the town to protect the mines, but in fact (as was often the case), it actually worked to help employers defeat the strikers.

Joined by strikebreakers and others, the militia attacked the workers' tent colony; and in the battle that followed, thirty-nine people died, among them eleven children. But these events, which became known as the Ludlow Massacre, were only precursors to continued conflict in the mines that the war itself did little to discourage.

LUDLOW MASSACRE

ECONOMIC AND SOCIAL RESULTS OF THE WAR

Whatever its other effects, the war helped produce a remarkable period of economic growth in the United States—a boom that began in 1914 (when European demands for American products began to increase) and accelerated after

ON THE TOWN IN HARLEM Harlem, once a suburb of Manhattan where middle-class commuters lived, became in the early twentieth century the center of African American life in New York. The Lafayette Theatre was the first New York theater to desegregate, in as early as 1912. African American theatergoers could sit in the orchestra section rather than just in the balcony as was the practice in other New York theaters. (© John Springer Collection/Corbis)

WOMEN INDUSTRIAL WORKERS In World War II, such women were often called "Rosie the Riveter." Their presence in these previously all-male work environments was no less startling to Americans during World War I. These women are shown working with acetylene torches to bevel armor plate for tanks. *(Photo by Margaret Bourke-White/© Time & Life Pictures/Getty Images)*

1917 (in response to demand from the United States war effort). Industrial production soared, and manufacturing activity expanded in regions that had previously had relatively little of it. The shipbuilding industry, for example, grew rapidly on the West Coast (enabled by the Panama Canal). Employment increased dramatically; and because so many white men were away at war, new opportunities for female, African American, Mexican, and Asian workers appeared. Some workers experienced a significant growth in income, but inflation cut into the wage increases and often produced a net loss in purchasing power. The agricultural economy profited from the war as well. Farm prices rose to their highest levels in decades, and agricultural production increased dramatically as a result.

One of the most important social changes of the war years was the migration of hundreds of thousands of African Americans from the rural South into northern industrial cities. It became known as the "Great Migration." Like most

"GREAT MIGRATION" migrations, it was a result of both a "push" and a "pull." The push was the poverty, indebtedness, racism, and violence many black men and women experienced in the South. The pull was the prospect of factory jobs in the urban North and the opportunity to live in communities where blacks could enjoy more freedom and autonomy. In the labor-scarce economy of the war years, northern factory owners dispatched agents to the South to recruit African American workers. Black newspapers advertised the prospects for employment in the North. And perhaps most important, those who migrated sent word back to friends and families of the opportunities they encountered—which explains the heavy concentration of migrants from a single area of the South in certain cities in the North. In Chicago, for example, the more than 70,000 new black residents came disproportionately from a few areas of Alabama and Mississippi.

The result was a dramatic growth in black communities in northern industrial cities such as New York, Chicago, Cleveland, and Detroit. Some older, more established African American residents of these cities were unsettled by these new arrivals, with their country ways and their revivalistic religion; many people in the existing African American communities considered the newcomers coarse and feared that their presence would increase their own vulnerability to white racism. But the movement could not be stopped. New churches sprang up in black neighborhoods (many of them simple storefronts, from which self-proclaimed preachers searched for congregations). Low-paid black workers crowded into inadequate housing. As

RACE RIOTS the black communities expanded, they inevitably began to rub up against white neighborhoods, with occasionally violent results. In East St. Louis, Illinois, a white mob attacked a black neighborhood on July 2, 1917, burned down many houses, and shot the residents of some of them as they fled. As many as forty African Americans died.

For American women, black and white, the war meant new opportunities for employment. A million or more women worked in a wide range of industrial jobs that, in peacetime, were considered male preserves: steel, munitions, trucking, public transportation. Most of them had been working in other, lower-paying jobs. But whatever changes the war brought were temporary ones. As soon as the war was over, almost all of the women working in previously male industrial jobs quit or were fired; in fact, the percentage of women working for wages actually declined between 1910 and 1920. The government had created the Women in Industry Board to oversee the movement of these women into the jobs left behind by men. After the war, the board became the Women's Bureau, a permanent agency dedicated to protecting the interests of women in the workforce.

THE FUTILE SEARCH FOR SOCIAL UNITY

The idea of unity–not only in the direction of the economy but in the nation's social purpose as well–had been the dream of many progressives for decades. To them, the war seemed to offer an unmatched opportunity for America to close ranks behind a great common cause. In the process, they hoped, society could achieve a lasting sense of collective purpose. The dream of social unity helped drive many efforts–the peace movement, the labor movement, and even the government. But it also drove a period of political and social oppression and an egregious violation of civil liberties

THE PEACE MOVEMENT

Government leaders, and many others, realized that public sentiment about American involvement in the war had been deeply divided before April 1917 and remained so even after the declaration of war.

The peace movement in the United States before 1917 had many constituencies: German Americans, Irish Americans, religious pacifists (Quakers, Mennonites, and others), intellectuals and groups on the left such as the Socialist Party and the Industrial Workers of the World, all of whom considered the war a meaningless battle among capitalist nations for commercial supremacy–an opinion many others, in America and Europe, later came to share.

WOMAN'S PEACE PARTY

But the most active and widespread peace activism came from the women's movement. In 1915, Carrie Chapman Catt, a leader of the fight for woman suffrage, helped create the Woman's Peace Party, with a small but active membership. As the war in Europe intensified, the party's efforts to keep the United States from intervening grew.

Women peace activists were sharply divided once America entered the war in 1917. The National American Woman Suffrage Association, the largest women's organization, supported the war and, more than that, presented itself as a patriotic organization dedicated to advancing the war effort. Its membership grew dramatically as a result. Catt, who was among those who abandoned the peace cause, now began calling for woman suffrage as a "war measure," to ensure that women (whose work was essential to the war effort) would feel fully a part of the nation. But many other women refused to support the war even after April 1917. Among them were Jane Addams, who was widely reviled as a result, and Charlotte Perkins Gilman, a leading feminist activist.

MATERNAL OPPOSITION TO WAR

Women peace activists shared many of the same objections to the war as did the members of the Socialist Party (to which some of them belonged). But some criticized the war on other grounds as well, arguing that as "the mother half of humanity," they had a special moral and maternal basis for their pacifism.

SELLING THE WAR AND SUPPRESSING DISSENT

World War I was not as popular among the American people as World War II would be, but most of the country supported the intervention once it began. In communities across the nation, there were outbursts of fervent patriotism, floods of voluntary enlistments in the military, and greatly increased displays of patriotism. Women joined their local Red Cross in an effort to contribute to the war effort. Children raised money for war bonds in their schools. Churches included prayers for the president and the troops in their services. And the war also gave a large boost to the wave of religious revivalism that had been growing for a decade before 1917; revivalism, in turn, became a source of support for the war. Billy Sunday, the leading revivalist of his time, dropped his early opposition to intervention in 1917 and became a fervent champion of the American military effort.

Nevertheless, government leaders (and many others) remained deeply concerned about the significant minorities who continued to oppose the war even after the United States entered the conflict. Many believed that a crucial prerequisite for victory

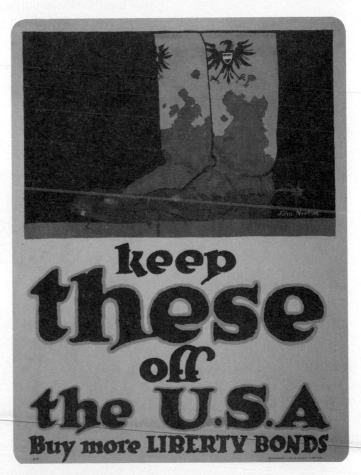

WARTIME PROPAGANDA This poster—one of many lurid images of imperial Germany used by the U.S. government to generate enthusiasm for American involvement in World War I—shows bloodstained German boots with the German eagle clearly visible. The demonization of Germany was at the heart of government efforts to portray the war to Americans. (The Library of Congress (LC-USZC4-9853))

RACE, GENDER, AND MILITARY SERVICE

MUCH CAN BE LEARNED ABOUT A SOCIETY'S VALUES from how it handles the raising of an army. In wartime, nations typically clarify the terms of citizenship and service—asking some people to fight, others to stay home, and appealing to the public for participation and support. The government sets the terms of service, but they must align with popular values to be successful.

During World War I, as part of the broad national effort to explain, justify, and fight the war, the government disseminated the two posters below (the "1917-1918" documents). The first poster was part of a recruiting drive for the U.S. Navy; the second was part of a campaign to sell "liberty loans," interest-bearing bonds that funded roughly two-thirds of the war's $32 billion price tag. Both images suggest that women not only served in the military and industrial sectors—they also served as *symbols*.

By the time of the war on terrorism of the early twenty-first century, the landscape of military recruitment had changed dramatically. The new war was more limited in scale than World War I, and the draft had been suspended in 1973, converting the military to an all-volunteer force. This put a high premium on recruiting and marketing—and the materials used for those purposes remained just as illuminating as ever (see the "2006-2014" documents). In 2006, the U.S. Army launched its "Army Strong" campaign to communicate

WORLD WAR I—1917–1918

WARTIME POSTERS

(The Library of Congress (LC-USZC4-1124))

(The Library of Congress (LC-USZC4-9884))

the message that the army builds not only physical but also mental and emotional strengths in its recruits. The second images shows the welcoming attitude of today's army.

WAR ON TERRORISM—2006–2014

ARMY RECRUITMENT AND MARKETING

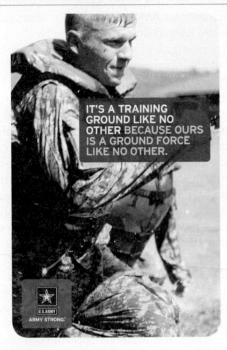

IT'S A TRAINING GROUND LIKE NO OTHER BECAUSE OURS IS A GROUND FORCE LIKE NO OTHER.

U.S. ARMY
ARMY STRONG.

(The U.S. Army)

(The U.S. Army)

AP TEST PRACTICE

Questions assume cumulative content knowledge from this chapter and previous chapters.

1. The World War I recruiting posters, in comparison to the present-day posters, depict only white people, despite the fact that many African Americans and ethnic minorities served in World War I. What does that difference say about mainstream attitudes toward race and ethnicity during World War I?

   (A) African Americans were integrated with white society

   (B) Whites were viewed as superior and the legitimate citizens of the nation

   (C) For purposes of the war, the various races were all considered part of the "white" population

   (D) Whites were viewed as equally desirable as recruits from minority groups

2. In comparing the way the genders are portrayed between the posters from the different time periods, which best describes the general societal understanding of gender roles in the early 20th century?

   (A) There was a general expectation that women would enlist in addition to men.

   (B) Women were viewed as equal to men.

   (C) Men played subordinate roles to women.

   (D) Women were generally expected to embody virtue.

3. What do the different styles of persuasion between the posters of the two time periods suggest about changing popular attitudes towards military enlistment from the early 20th century to the early 21st century?

   (A) A continuation of the idea of military enlistment as one of patriotic duty

   (B) A change from a romantic idea of duty to one of practical personal benefit and opportunity

   (C) A change from the idea of military enlistment as protecting the nation to one of adventure

   (D) A continuation of the ideal of practical benefit for the individual was an energetic, even coercive, effort to unite public opinion behind the military effort.

The most conspicuous government effort to rally public support was a vast propaganda campaign orchestrated by the new Committee on Public Information (CPI). It was directed by the Denver journalist George Creel, who spoke openly of the importance of achieving social unity. The CPI supervised the distribution of tons of pro-war literature (75 million pieces of printed material). War posters plastered the walls of offices, shops, theaters, schools, churches, and homes. Newspapers dutifully printed official government accounts of the reasons for the war and the prospects for quick victory. Creel encouraged reporters to exercise "self-censorship" when reporting news about the conflict.

CPI

As the war continued, the CPI's tactics became increasingly crude. Government-promoted posters and films became lurid portrayals of the savagery of the Germans, bearing such titles as *The Prussian Cur* and *The Kaiser: Beast of Berlin,* encouraging Americans to think of the German people as something close to savages.

The government soon began more coercive efforts to suppress dissent. The CPI ran full-page advertisements in popular magazines like the *Saturday Evening Post* urging citizens to notify the Justice Department when they encountered "the man who spreads the pessimistic stories . . . , cries for peace, or belittles our efforts to win the war." The Espionage Act of 1917 gave the government new tools with which to respond to such reports. It created stiff penalties for spying, sabotage, or obstruction of the war effort (crimes that were often broadly defined); and it empowered the Post Office Department to ban "seditious" material from the mails. Sedition, Postmaster General Albert Sidney Burleson said, included statements that might "impugn the motives of the government and thus encourage insubordination," anything that suggested "that the government is controlled by Wall Street or munitions manufacturers, or any other special interests." He included in that category all publications of the Socialist Party.

ESPIONAGE ACT

More repressive were two measures of 1918: the Sabotage Act of April 20 and the Sedition Act of May 16. These bills expanded the meaning of the Espionage Act to make illegal any public expression of opposition to the war; in practice, it allowed officials to prosecute anyone who criticized the president or the government.

SEDITION ACT

The most frequent targets of the new legislation (and one of the reasons for its enactment in the first place) were such anticapitalist groups (and antiwar) groups as the Socialist Party and the Industrial Workers of the World (IWW). Many Americans had favored the repression of socialists and radicals even before the war; the wartime policies now made it possible to move against them legally. Eugene V. Debs, the humane leader of the Socialist Party and an opponent of the war, was sentenced to ten years in prison in 1918. Only a pardon by President Warren G. Harding ultimately won his release in 1921. Big Bill Haywood and members of the IWW were especially energetically prosecuted. Only by fleeing to the Soviet Union did Haywood avoid long imprisonment. More than 1,500 people were arrested in 1918 for the crime of criticizing the government.

State and local governments, corporations, universities, and private citizens contributed as well to the climate of repression. Vigilante mobs sprang up to "discipline" those who dared challenge the war. A dissident Protestant clergyman in Cincinnati was pulled from his bed one night by a mob, dragged to a nearby hillside, and whipped "in the name of the women and children of Belgium." An IWW organizer in Montana was seized by a mob and hanged from a railroad bridge.

REPRESSING DISSENT

A cluster of citizens' groups emerged to mobilize "respectable" members of their communities to root out disloyalty. The American Protective League, probably the largest of such groups, enlisted the services of 250,000 people, who served as "agents"–prying into the activities and thoughts of their neighbors, opening mail, tapping telephones, and in general attempting to impose unity of opinion on their communities. It received government funds to support its work. Attorney General Thomas W. Gregory, a particularly avid supporter of repressing dissent, described the league and similar organizations approvingly as "patriotic organizations." Other vigilante organizations–the National Security League, the Boy Spies of America, the American Defense Society–performed much the same function.

There were many victims of such activities: socialists, labor activists, female pacifists. But the most frequent targets of repression were immigrants: Irish Americans because of their historic animosity toward the British, Jews because many had expressed opposition to the anti-Semitic policies of the Russian government, and others. "Loyalist" citizens' groups policed immigrant neighborhoods. They monitored meetings and even conversations for signs of disloyalty. Even some settlement house workers, many of whom had once championed ethnic diversity, contributed to such efforts. The director of the National Security League described the origins of the anti-immigrant sentiment, which was producing growing support for what many citizens were now calling "100 percent Americanism":

"100 PERCENT AMERICANISM"

> The melting pot has not melted. . . . There are vast communities in the nation thinking today not in terms of America, but in terms of Old World prejudices, theories, and animosities.

The greatest target of abuse was the German American community. Most German Americans supported the American war effort once it began. Still, public opinion turned bitterly hostile. A campaign to purge society of all things German quickly gathered speed, at times assuming ludicrous forms. Sauerkraut was renamed "liberty cabbage." Frankfurters became "liberty sausage." Performances of German music were frequently banned. German books were removed from the shelves of libraries. Courses in the German language were removed from school curricula; the California Board of Education called it "a language that disseminates the ideals of autocracy, brutality, and hatred." Germans were routinely fired from jobs in war industries, lest they "sabotage" important tasks. Some were fired from positions entirely unrelated to the war—for example, Karl Muck, the German-born conductor of the Boston Symphony Orchestra. Vigilante groups routinely subjected Germans to harassment and beatings, including a lynching in southern Illinois in 1918. Relatively few Americans favored such extremes, but many came to agree with the belief of the eminent psychologist G. Stanley Hall that "there is something fundamentally wrong with the Teutonic soul."

THE SEARCH FOR A NEW WORLD ORDER

Woodrow Wilson had led the nation into war promising a more just and stable peace at its conclusion. Well before the armistice, he was preparing to lead the fight for what he considered a democratic postwar settlement.

THE FOURTEEN POINTS

On January 8, 1918, Wilson appeared before Congress to present the principles for which he claimed the nation was fighting. The war aims had fourteen distinct provisions, widely known as the Fourteen Points; but they fell into three broad categories. First, Wilson's proposals contained eight specific

WILSON'S IDEALISTIC VISION

recommendations for adjusting postwar boundaries and for establishing new nations to replace the defunct Austro-Hungarian and Ottoman Empires. Those recommendations reflected his belief in the right of all peoples to self-determination. Second, there were five general principles to govern international conduct in the future: freedom of the seas, open covenants instead of secret treaties, reductions in armaments, free trade, and impartial mediation of colonial claims. Finally, there was a proposal for a league of nations that would help implement these new principles and territorial adjustments and resolve future controversies.

There were serious flaws in Wilson's proposals. He provided no formula for deciding how to implement the "national self-determination" he promised for subjugated peoples. He said little about economic rivalries and their effect on international relations, even though such economic tensions had been in large part responsible for the war. Nevertheless, Wilson's international vision quickly came to enchant not only much of his own generation (in both America and Europe), but also members of generations to come. It reflected his belief, strongly rooted in the ideas of progressivism, that the world was as capable of just and efficient government as were individual nations; that once the international community accepted certain basic principles of conduct, and once it constructed modern institutions to implement them, the human race could live in peace.

The Fourteen Points were also an answer to the new Bolshevik government in Russia. In December 1917, Lenin had issued his own statement of war aims, strikingly similar to

Wilson's. Wilson's announcement, which came just three weeks later, was, among other things, a last-minute (and unsuccessful) effort to persuade the Bolshevik regime to keep Russia in the war. But Wilson also realized that Lenin was now a competitor in the effort to lead the postwar order. And he announced the Fourteen Points in part to ensure that the world looked to the United States, not Russia, for guidance.

LENIN'S CHALLENGE

EARLY OBSTACLES

Wilson was confident, as the war neared its end, that popular support would enable him to win Allied approval of his peace plan. But there were ominous signs both at home and abroad that his path might be more difficult than he expected. In Europe, leaders of the Allied forces, many resenting what they considered Wilson's tone of moral superiority, were preparing to resist him even before the armistice was signed. They had reacted unhappily when Wilson refused to make the United States their "ally" but had kept his distance as an "associate" of his European partners, keeping American military forces separate from the Allied armies they were joining.

Most of all, however, Britain and France, having suffered incalculable losses in their long years of war, and having stored

ALLIED INTRANSIGENCE

up an enormous reserve of bitterness toward Germany as a result, were in no mood for a benign and generous peace. The British prime minister, David Lloyd George, insisted for a time that the German kaiser be captured and executed. He and Georges Clemenceau, president of France, remained determined to the end to gain something from the struggle to compensate them for the catastrophe they had suffered.

At the same time, Wilson was encountering problems at home. In 1918, with the war almost over, he unwisely appealed to the American voters to support his peace plans by electing Democrats to Congress in the November elections. A Republican victory, he declared, would be "interpreted on the other side of the water as a repudiation of my leadership." Days later, the Republicans captured majorities in both houses. Domestic economic troubles, more than international issues, had been the most important factor in the voting; but because of the president's ill-timed appeal, the results damaged his ability to claim broad popular support for his peace plans.

The leaders of the Republican Party, in the meantime, were developing their own reasons for opposing Wilson. Some were angry that he had tried to make the 1918 balloting a referendum on his war aims, especially since many Republicans had been supporting the Fourteen Points. Wilson further antagonized them when he refused to appoint any important Republicans to the negotiating team that would represent the United States at the peace conference in Paris. But the president considered such matters unimportant. Only one member of the American negotiating party would have any real authority: Wilson himself. And once he had produced a just and moral treaty, he believed, the weight of world and American opinion would compel his enemies to support him.

THE PARIS PEACE CONFERENCE

Wilson arrived in Europe to a welcome such as few men in history have experienced. To the war-weary people of the Continent, he was nothing less than a savior, the man who would create a new and better world. When he entered Paris on December 13, 1918, he was greeted, some observers claimed, by the largest crowd in the history of France. The negotiations themselves, however, proved less satisfying.

THE BIG FOUR

The principal figures in the negotiations were the leaders of the victorious Allied nations: David Lloyd George representing Great Britain; Georges Clemenceau representing France; Vittorio Orlando, the prime minister of Italy; and Wilson, who hoped to dominate them all. From the beginning, the atmosphere of idealism Wilson had sought to create was competing with a spirit of national aggrandizement. There was, moreover, a strong sense of unease about the unstable situation in eastern Europe and the threat of communism. Russia, whose new Bolshevik government was still fighting "White" counterrevolutionaries, was unrepresented in Paris; but the radical threat it seemed to pose to Western governments was never far from the minds of any of the delegates, least of all Wilson himself.

Indeed, not long before he came to Paris, Wilson ordered the landing of American troops in the Soviet Union. They were there, he claimed, to help a group of 60,000 Czech soldiers trapped in Russia to escape. But the Americans soon became involved, at least indirectly, in assisting the White Russians (the anti-Bolsheviks) in their fight against the new regime. Some American troops remained in Russia as late as April 1920. Lenin's regime survived these challenges. Wilson refused to recognize the new government. Diplomatic relations between the United States and the Soviet Union were not restored until 1933.

WILSON'S RETREAT

In the tense and often vindictive atmosphere of the negotiations in Paris, Wilson was unable to win approval of many of the broad principles he had espoused: freedom of the seas, which the British refused even to discuss; free trade; "open covenants openly arrived at" (the Paris negotiations themselves were often conducted in secret). Despite his support for "impartial mediation" of colonial claims, he was forced to accept a transfer of German colonies in the Pacific to Japan; the British had promised them in exchange for Japanese assistance in the war. Wilson's pledge of "national self-determination" for all peoples suffered numerous assaults. Economic and strategic demands were constantly coming into conflict with the principle of cultural nationalism.

REPARATIONS

The treaty departed most conspicuously from Wilson's ideals on the question of reparations. As the conference began, the president opposed demanding compensation from the defeated Central Powers. The other Allied leaders, however, were insistent, and slowly Wilson gave way and accepted the principle of reparations, the specific sum to be set later by a commission. That figure, established in 1921, was $56 billion, supposedly to pay for damages to civilians and for military pensions. Continued negotiations over the next decade scaled the sum back considerably. In the end, Germany paid only $9 billion, which was still more than its crippled economy could afford. The reparations, combined with other territorial and economic penalties,

THE BIG FOUR IN PARIS Surface cordiality during the Paris Peace Conference disguised serious tensions among the so-called Big Four, the leaders of the victorious nations in World War I. As the conference progressed, the European leaders developed increasing resentment of Woodrow Wilson's high (and some of them thought sanctimonious) moral posture in the negotiations. Shown here are, from left to right, David Lloyd George of Great Britain, Vittorio Orlando of Italy, Georges Clemenceau of France, and Wilson. (The Library of Congress (LC-DIG-ggbain-29038))

constituted an effort to keep Germany weak for the indefinite future. Never again, the Allied leaders believed, should the Germans be allowed to become powerful enough to threaten the peace of Europe.

Wilson did manage to win some important victories in Paris in setting boundaries and dealing with former colonies. He secured approval of a plan to place many former colonies and imperial possessions (among them Palestine) in "trusteeship" under the League of Nations–the so-called mandate system. He blocked a French proposal to break up western Germany into a group of smaller states. He helped design the creation of two new nations: Yugoslavia and Czechoslovakia, which were welded together out of, among other territories, pieces of the former Austro-Hungarian Empire. Each nation contained an uneasy collection of ethnic groups that had frequently battled one another in the past.

But Wilson's most visible triumph, and the one most important to him, was the creation of a permanent international organization to oversee world affairs and prevent future

LEAGUE OF NATIONS

wars. On January 25, 1919, the Allies voted to accept the "covenant" of the League of Nations; and with that, Wilson believed, the peace treaty was transformed from a disappointment into a success. Whatever mistakes and inequities had emerged from the peace conference, he was convinced, could be corrected later by the League.

The covenant provided for an assembly of nations that would meet regularly to debate means of resolving disputes and protecting the peace. Authority to implement League decisions would rest with a nine-member executive council; the United States would be one of five permanent members of the council, along with Britain, France, Italy, and Japan. The covenant left many questions unanswered, most notably how the League would enforce its decisions. Wilson, however, was confident that once established, the new organization would find suitable answers.

THE RATIFICATION BATTLE

Wilson was well aware of the political obstacles awaiting him at home. Many Americans, accustomed to their nation's isolation from Europe, questioned the wisdom of this major new commitment to internationalism. Others had serious reservations about the specific features of the treaty and the covenant. After a brief trip to Washington in February 1919, during which he listened to harsh objections to the treaty from members of the Senate and others, he returned to Europe and insisted on several modifications in the covenant to satisfy his critics. The revisions ensured that the United States would not be obliged to accept a League mandate to oversee a territory and that the League would not challenge the Monroe Doctrine. But the changes were not enough to mollify his opponents, and Wilson refused to go further.

Wilson presented the Treaty of Versailles (which took its name from the palace outside Paris where the final negotiating sessions had taken place) to the Senate on July 10, 1919, asking, "Dare we reject it and break the heart of the world?" In the

WILSON'S INTRANSIGENCE

weeks that followed, he refused to consider even the most innocuous compromise. His deteriorating physical condition–he was suffering from hardening of the arteries and had apparently experienced something like a mild stroke (undiagnosed) in Paris–may have contributed to his intransigence.

The Senate, in the meantime, was raising many objections. Some senators–the fourteen so-called irreconcilables, many of them western isolationists–opposed the agreement on principle. But other opponents, with less fervent convictions, were principally concerned with constructing a winning issue for the Republicans in 1920 and with weakening a president whom some members of the Senate had come to despise. Most notable of these was Senator Henry Cabot Lodge of Massachusetts, the

HENRY CABOT LODGE

powerful chairman of the Foreign Relations Committee. A man of stunning arrogance and a close friend of Theodore Roosevelt (who had died early in 1919, spouting hatred of Wilson to the end), Lodge loathed the president with genuine passion. "I never thought I could hate a man as I hate Wilson," he once admitted. He used every possible tactic to obstruct, delay, and amend the treaty. Wilson, for his part, despised Lodge as much as Lodge despised him.

Public sentiment clearly favored ratification, so at first Lodge could do little more than play for time. When the document reached his committee, he spent two weeks slowly reading aloud each word of its 300 pages; then he held six weeks of public hearings to air the complaints of every disgruntled minority (Irish Americans, for example, angry that the settlement made no provision for an independent Ireland). Gradually, Lodge's general opposition to the treaty crystallized into a series of "reservations"–amendments to the League covenant limiting American obligations to the organization.

At this point, Wilson might still have won approval if he had agreed to some relatively minor changes in the language of the treaty. But the president refused to yield. When he realized the Senate would not budge, he decided to appeal to the public.

WILSON'S ORDEAL

What followed was a political disaster and a personal tragedy. Wilson embarked on a grueling, cross-country speaking tour to arouse public support for the treaty. In a little more than three weeks, he traveled over 8,000 miles by train, speaking as often as four times a day, resting hardly at all. Finally, he reached the end of his strength. After speaking at Pueblo, Colorado, on September 25, he collapsed with severe headaches. Canceling the rest of his itinerary, he rushed back to Washington, D.C., where, a few days later, he suffered a major stroke. For two weeks he was close to death; for six weeks more, he was so seriously ill that he could conduct virtually no public business. His wife and his doctor formed an almost impenetrable barrier around him, shielding him from any official pressures that might impede his recovery, preventing the public from receiving any accurate information about the gravity of his condition.

Wilson ultimately recovered enough to resume a limited official schedule, but he was essentially an invalid for the remaining eighteen months of his presidency. His left side was partially paralyzed; more important, like many stroke victims, he had only

LEAGUE MEMBERSHIP REJECTED

partial control of his mental and emotional state. His condition only intensified what had already been his strong tendency to view public issues in moral terms and to resist any attempts at compromise. When the Senate Foreign Relations Committee finally sent the treaty to the full Senate for ratification, recommending nearly fifty amendments and reservations, Wilson refused to consider any of them. When the full Senate voted in November to accept fourteen of the reservations, Wilson gave stern directions to his Democratic allies: they must vote only for a treaty with no changes whatsoever; any other version must be defeated. On November 19, 1919, forty-two Democrats, following the president's instructions, joined with the thirteen Republican "irreconcilables" to reject the amended treaty. When the Senate voted on the original version without any reservations, thirty-eight senators, all but one Democrats, voted to approve it; fifty-five senators (some Democrats among them) voted no.

There were sporadic efforts to revive the treaty over the next few months. But Wilson's opposition to anything but the precise settlement he had negotiated in Paris remained too formidable an obstacle. He was, moreover, becoming convinced that the 1920 national election would serve as a "solemn referendum" on the League. By now, however, public interest in the peace process had begun to fade—partly as a reaction against the tragic bitterness of the ratification fight, but more in response to a series of other crises.

A SOCIETY IN TURMOIL

Even during the Paris Peace Conference, many Americans were less concerned about international matters than about turbulent

NEW SOCIAL ENVIRONMENT

events at home. The American economy experienced a severe postwar recession. And much of middle-class America responded to demands for change with a fearful, conservative hostility. The aftermath of war brought not the age of liberal reform that progressives had predicted, but a period of repression and reaction.

INDUSTRY AND LABOR

Citizens of Washington, D.C., on the day after the armistice, found it impossible to place long-distance telephone calls: the lines were jammed with officials of the war agencies canceling government contracts. The fighting had ended sooner than anyone had anticipated, and without warning, without planning, the nation was launched into the difficult task of economic reconversion.

At first, the wartime boom continued. But the postwar prosperity rested largely on the lingering effects of the war (government deficit spending continued for some months after the armistice) and on sudden, temporary demands

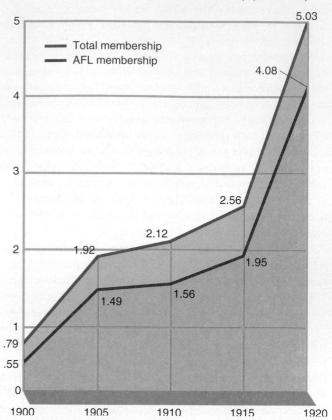

Total membership (in millions)

UNION MEMBERSHIP, 1900–1920 This chart illustrates the steady increase in union membership in the first part of the twentieth century—a membership dominated by unions associated with the AFL. Note the particularly sharp increase between 1915 and 1920, the years of World War I.

• Why did the war years see such an expansion of union labor?

(a booming market for scarce consumer goods at home and a strong market for American products in the war-ravaged nations of Europe). This brief postwar boom was accompanied, however, by raging inflation, a result in part of the rapid abandonment of wartime price controls. Through most of 1919 and 1920, prices rose at an average of more than 15 percent a year.

Finally, late in 1920, the economic bubble burst, as many of the temporary forces that had created it disappeared and as inflation began killing the market for consumer goods. Between

POSTWAR RECESSION

1920 and 1921, the gross national product (GNP) declined nearly 10 percent; 100,000 businesses went bankrupt; 453,000 farmers lost their land; nearly 5 million Americans lost their jobs. In this unpromising economic environment, leaders of organized labor set out to consolidate the advances they had made in the war, which now seemed in danger of being lost. The raging inflation of 1919 wiped out the modest wage gains workers had achieved during the war; many laborers worried about job security as hundreds of thousands of veterans returned to the workforce; arduous working conditions—such as the twelve-hour workday in the steel industry—continued to be a source of discontent. Employers aggravated the resentment by using the end of the war (and the end of government controls) to rescind benefits they had been forced to give workers in 1917 and 1918–most notably recognition of unions.

The year 1919, therefore, saw an unprecedented wave of strikes–more than 3,600 in all, involving over 4 million workers. In January, a walkout by shipyard workers in Seattle, Washington, evolved into a general strike that brought the entire city almost to a standstill. The mayor requested and received the assistance of U.S. Marines to keep the city running, and eventually the strike failed. But the brief success of a general strike, something Americans associated with European radicals, made the Seattle incident reverberate loudly throughout the country.

In September, there was a strike by the Boston police force, which was responding to layoffs and wage cuts by demanding recognition of its union. Seattle had

BOSTON POLICE STRIKE

remained generally calm during its strike, but with its police off the job, Boston erupted in violence and looting. Efforts by local businessmen, veterans, and college students to patrol the streets proved ineffective; and finally Governor Calvin Coolidge called in the National Guard to restore order. (His public statement that "there is no right to strike against the public safety by anybody, anywhere, any time" attracted national acclaim.) Eventually, Boston officials dismissed the entire police force and hired a new one.

In September 1919, the greatest strike in American history began, when 350,000 steelworkers in several eastern and mid-western cities walked off the job, demanding an eight-hour

STEELWORKERS' STRIKE DEFEATED

workday and recognition of their union. The steel strike was long, bitter, and violent–most of the violence coming from employers, who hired armed guards to disperse picket lines and escort strikebreakers into factories. It climaxed in a riot in Gary, Indiana, in which eighteen strikers were killed. Steel executives managed to keep most plants running with nonunion labor, and public opinion was so hostile to the strikers that the AFL–having at first endorsed the strike–soon timidly repudiated it. By January, the strike had collapsed. It was a setback from which organized labor would not recover for more than a decade.

THE DEMANDS OF AFRICAN AMERICANS

The nearly 400,000 black men who had served in the armed forces during the war came home in 1919 and marched

THE BOSTON POLICE STRIKE National Guardsmen stand guard in front of a store where broken windows suggest looting has already occurred, during the Boston Police Strike of 1919. (© Bettmann/Corbis)

down the main streets of the industrial cities with other returning troops. And then (in New York and other cities), they marched again through the streets of black neighborhoods such as Harlem, led by jazz bands, cheered by thousands of African Americans, worshiped as heroes. The black soldiers were an inspiration to thousands of urban African Americans, a sign, they thought, that a new age had come, that the glory of black heroism in the war would make it impossible for white society ever again to treat African Americans as less than equal citizens. W. E. B. Du Bois, watching the African American soldiers returning home, conveyed his hopes for a new life for them. "We are returning from war!" he wrote, "The Crisis and tens of thousands of black men were drafted into the great struggle . . . we fought gladly and to the last drop of blood; for America and her highest ideals, we fought in far-off hope." But recalling the past he added, "This country of ours, despite all its better souls have done and dreamed, is yet a shameful land."

In fact, that black soldiers had fought in the war had almost no impact on white attitudes. But it did have a profound effect on black attitudes: it accentuated African American bitterness—and increased black determination to fight for their rights. For soldiers, there was an expectation of some social reward for their service. For many other African Americans, the war had raised economic expectations, as they moved into industrial and other jobs vacated by white workers, jobs to which they had previously had no access. Just as black soldiers expected their military service to enhance their social status, so black factory workers regarded their move north as an escape from racial prejudice and an opportunity for economic gain.

NEW BLACK ATTITUDES

By 1919, however, the racial climate had become savage and murderous. In the South, there was a sudden increase in lynchings: more than seventy blacks, some of them war veterans, died at the hands of white mobs in 1919 alone. In the North, black factory workers faced widespread layoffs as returning white veterans displaced them from their jobs. African American veterans found no significant new opportunities for advancement. Rural black migrants to northern cities encountered white communities unfamiliar with and generally hostile to them; and as whites became convinced that black workers with lower wage demands were hurting them economically, animosity grew rapidly.

The wartime riots in East St. Louis and elsewhere were a prelude to a summer of much worse racial violence in 1919. In Chicago, a black teenager swimming in Lake Michigan on a hot July day happened to drift toward a white beach. Whites on shore allegedly stoned him unconscious; he sank and drowned. Angry blacks gathered in crowds and marched into white neighborhoods to retaliate; whites formed even larger crowds and roamed into black neighborhoods shooting, stabbing, and beating passersby, destroying homes and properties. For more than a week, Chicago was virtually at war. In the end, 38 people died—15 whites and 23 blacks—and 537 were injured; over 1,000 people were left homeless. The Chicago riot was the worst but not the only racial violence during the so-called red summer of 1919; in all, 120 people died in such racial outbreaks in little more than three months.

CHICAGO RACE RIOTS

Racial violence, and even racially motivated urban riots, was not new. The deadliest race riot in American history had

THE FIFTEENTH REGIMENT ON FIFTH AVENUE The all-black Fifteenth Army Regiment marches up Fifth Avenue in New York City in 1917, shortly after the United States entered World War I. They are en route to an army training camp in New York State before traveling to the front in Europe. Less than two years later, many of these same men marched through Harlem on their return from the war, and again down Fifth Avenue, before cheering crowds—convinced, wrongly, that their service in the war would win them important new freedoms at home. (© Bettmann/Corbis)

occurred in New York during the Civil War. But the 1919 riots were different in one respect: they did not just involve white people attacking blacks; they also involved blacks fighting back. The NAACP signaled this change by urging African Americans not just to demand government protection, but also to retaliate, to defend themselves. The poet Claude McKay, one of the major figures of what would shortly be known as the Harlem Renaissance, wrote a poem after the Chicago riot called "If We Must Die":

Like men we'll face the murderous cowardly pack.
Pressed to the wall, dying, but fighting back.

At the same time, a Jamaican, Marcus Garvey, began to attract a wide American following—mostly among poor urban blacks—with an ideology of black nationalism. Garvey encouraged African Americans to take pride in their own achievements and to develop an awareness of their African heritage—to **MARCUS GARVEY'S BLACK NATIONALISM** reject assimilation into white society and develop pride in what Garvey argued was their own superior race and culture. His United Negro Improvement Association (UNIA) launched a chain of black-owned grocery stores and pressed for the creation of other black businesses. Eventually, Garvey began urging his supporters to leave America and "return" to Africa, where they could create a new society of their own. In the 1920s, the Garvey movement experienced explosive growth for a time; and the UNIA became notable for its mass rallies and parades, for the opulent uniforms of its members, and for the growth of its enterprises. It began to decline, however, after Garvey was indicted in 1923 on charges of business fraud. He was deported to Jamaica two years later.

But the allure of black nationalism, which he helped make visible to millions of African Americans, survived in black culture long after Garvey himself was gone.

THE RED SCARE

To much of the white middle class at the time, the industrial warfare, the racial violence, and other forms of dissent all appeared to be frightening omens of instability and radicalism. This was in part because the Russian Revolution of November 1917 made it clear that communism was no longer simply a theory, but now an important regime.

Concerns about the communist threat grew in 1919 when the Soviet government announced the formation of the Communist International (or Comintern), whose purpose was to export revolution around the world. And in America itself, there were, in addition to the great number of imagined radicals, a modest number of real ones. The American Communist Party was formed in 1919, and there were other radical groups (many of them dominated by immigrants from Europe who had been involved in radical politics before coming to America). Some of these radicals were presumably responsible for a series of bombings in the spring of 1919 that produced great national alarm. In April, the Post Office Department, intercepted several dozen parcels addressed to leading businessmen and politicians that were triggered to explode when opened. Several of them reached their destinations, and one of them exploded, severely injuring a domestic servant of a public official in Georgia. Two months later, eight bombs exploded in eight cities within minutes of one another, suggesting a nationwide conspiracy. One of them damaged the

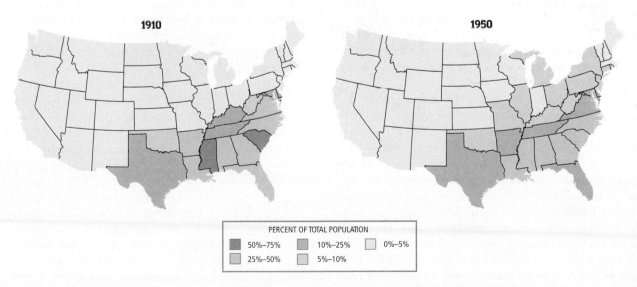

AFRICAN AMERICAN MIGRATION, 1910–1950 Two great waves of migration produced a dramatic redistribution of the African American population in the first half of the twentieth century—one around the time of World War I, the other during and after World War II. The map on the left shows the almost exclusive concentration of African Americans in the South as late as 1910. The map on the right shows both the tremendous increase of black populations in northern states by 1950 and the relative decline of black populations in parts of the South. Note in particular the changes in Mississippi and South Carolina.

• Why did the wars produce such significant migration out of the South?

MARCUS GARVEY Marcus Garvey rejected the idea of African Americans assimilating into white society. Instead, he encouraged his supporters to leave America and "return" to Africa to create their own society. (Private Collection/© Peter Newark American Pictures/ Bridgeman Images)

façade of Attorney General A. Mitchell Palmer's home in Washington. In 1920, there was a terrible explosion in front of the Morgan bank on Wall Street, which killed thirty people (only one of them—a clerk—in the bank itself).

The bombings crystallized what was already a growing determination among many middle-class Americans (and some government officials) to fight back against radicalism—a determination steeled by the repressive atmosphere of the war years. This antiradicalism accompanied, and reinforced, the already strong commitment among old-stock Protestants to the idea of "100 percent Americanism." And it produced what became known as the Red Scare.

POPULAR ANTIRADICALISM

Antiradical newspapers and politicians now began to portray almost every form of instability or protest as a sign of a radical threat. Race riots, one newspaper claimed, were the work of "armed revolutionaries running rampant through our cities." The steel strike, the *Philadelphia Inquirer* claimed, was "penetrated with the Bolshevik idea . . . steeped in the doctrines of the class struggle and social overthrow." Nearly thirty states enacted new peacetime sedition laws imposing harsh penalties on those who promoted revolution; some 300 people went to jail as a result—many of them people whose "crime" had been nothing more than opposition to the war. There were spontaneous acts of violence against supposed radicals in some communities. A mob of off-duty soldiers in New York City ransacked the offices of a socialist newspaper and beat up its staff. Another mob, in Centralia, Washington, dragged an IWW agitator from jail and castrated him before hanging him from a bridge. Citizens in many communities removed "subversive" books from the shelves of libraries; administrators in some universities dismissed "radical" members from their faculties. Women's groups such as the National Consumers League came under attack by antiradicals because so many feminists had opposed American intervention in the fighting in Europe.

Perhaps the greatest contribution to the Red Scare came from the federal government. On New Year's Day, 1920, Attorney General A. Mitchell Palmer and his ambitious assistant, J. Edgar Hoover, orchestrated a series of raids on alleged radical centers throughout the country and arrested more than 6,000 people.

PALMER RAIDS

The Palmer Raids had been intended to uncover large caches of weapons and explosives; they discovered only three pistols. Most of those arrested were ultimately released, but about 500 who were not American citizens were summarily deported.

The ferocity of the Red Scare soon abated, but its effects lingered well into the 1920s, most notably in the celebrated case of Sacco and Vanzetti. In May 1920, two Italian immigrants, Nicola Sacco and Bartolomeo Vanzetti, were charged with the murder of a paymaster in Braintree, Massachusetts. The evidence against them was questionable; but because both men were confessed anarchists, they faced a widespread public presumption of guilt. They were convicted in a trial of extraordinary injudiciousness, before an openly prejudiced judge, Webster Thayer, and were sentenced to death. Over the next several years, public support for Sacco and

SACCO AND VANZETTI

Vanzetti grew to formidable proportions. But all requests for a new trial or a pardon were denied. On August 23, 1927, amid widespread protests around the world, Sacco and Vanzetti, still proclaiming their innocence, died in the electric chair. Theirs was a cause that a generation of Americans never forgot.

REFUTING THE RED SCARE

An unexpected result of postwar turmoil was the emergence of a vigorous defense of civil liberties that not only discredited the Red Scare, but helped give new force of the Bill of Rights as well. The heavy-handed actions of the federal government after the war created a powerful backlash. It destroyed the career of A. Mitchell Palmer. It almost nipped in the bud the ascent of J. Edgar Hoover. It damaged the Democratic Party. And it led to an organization committed to protecting civil liberties: the National Civil Liberties Bureau, launched in 1917, which in 1920 was renamed the American Civil Liberties Union (ACLU), which remains a prominent institution today. At the same time, members of the Supreme

Court—most notably Justices Oliver Wendell Holmes and Louis Brandeis—gradually moved toward a strong position of defense of unpopular speech. The clash of "fighting faiths," Holmes wrote in a dissent in 1920, was best resolved "by free trade in ideas—that the best test of truth is . . . the competition of the market." This and other dissents eventually became law as other justices committed themselves to a robust defense of speech, however unpopular.

THE RETREAT FROM IDEALISM

On August 26, 1920, the Nineteenth Amendment, guaranteeing women the right to vote, became part of the Constitution. To the woman suffrage movement, this was the culmination of nearly a century of struggle. To many progressives, who had seen the inclusion of women in the electorate as a way of bolstering their political strength, it seemed to promise new support for reform. In some respects, the amendment helped fulfill that promise. Because of woman suffrage, members of Congress—concerned that women would vote as a bloc on the basis of women's issues—passed the Sheppard-Towner Maternity and Infancy Act in 1921, one of the first pieces of federal welfare legislation that provided funds for supporting the health of women and infants. Concern about the women's vote also appeared to create support for the 1922 Cable Act, which granted women the rights of U.S. citizenship independent of their husbands' status, and for the proposed (but never ratified) 1924 constitutional amendment to outlaw child labor.

In other ways, however, the Nineteenth Amendment marked less the beginning of an era of reform than an ending. Economic problems, feminist demands, labor unrest, racial tensions, and the intensity of the antiradicalism they helped create—all combined in the years immediately following the war to produce a general sense of disillusionment.

That became particularly apparent in the election of 1920. Woodrow Wilson wanted the campaign to be a referendum on the League of Nations, and the Democratic candidates, Ohio governor James M. Cox and Assistant Secretary of the Navy Franklin D. Roosevelt, tried to keep Wilson's ideals alive. The Republican presidential nominee, however, offered a different vision. He was Warren Gamaliel Harding, an obscure Ohio senator whom party leaders had chosen as their nominee confident that he would do their bidding once in office. Harding offered few ideals, only a vague promise of a return, as he later phrased it, to "normalcy." He won in a landslide. The Republican ticket received 61 percent of the popular vote and carried every state outside the South. The party made major gains in Congress as well. Woodrow Wilson, who had tried and failed to create a postwar order based on democratic ideals, stood repudiated. Early in 1921, he retired to a house on S Street in Washington, where he lived quietly until his death in 1924. In the meantime, for most Americans, a new era had begun.

RETURN TO "NORMALCY"

THE PALMER RAIDS In the years following World War I, many Americans feared political radicalism, especially from the left. The United States Department of Justice, led by Attorney General A. Mitchell Palmer, conducted raids and arrested and deported more than 500 foreign citizens, including several prominent leftist leaders. (© Everett Collection Inc./Alamy)

AP CONNECTING THEMES

Chapter 21 emphasized the movement of the United States from a posture of isolationism to involvement in world affairs and the reasons for and outcomes of that movement. As you review, evaluate the presidential role in orchestrating that change. You should now also be aware of the factors that led to U.S. involvement in World War I, the perceived goals of the war effort, and the degree of success in attaining those goals. You should also have a good understanding of the impact of the war on the economy, the home-front, and on African Americans, women, and other minority groups. Further, you should now understand the impact of the war on civil liberties and the restrictions on personal freedoms. Important to recognize is the significant change in the way Americans viewed non-conformity, particularly with regard to ethnic and racial minorities. Be able to compare and contrast post-war views on U.S. involvement in world affairs and the role that personalities played in the ultimate decision. Be able to assess the degree to which the Red Scare reflected real or perceived threats.

The following themes have heightened importance in Chapter 21. You should now be able to do the following for each listed theme:

Identity: Explain the ways in which World War I changed perceptions of American identity.

Work, Exchange, and Technology: Examine the ways in which World War I affected the American economy and the role it played in increasing opportunities for women and minorities.

Politics and Power: Explain conflict over U.S. involvement in World War I between political parties, both before and after the war.

America and the World: Explain the reasons and consequences of increased U.S. involvement in world affairs.

Environment and Geography: Explain the debate over conservation of resources versus preservation of resources.

Ideas, Beliefs, and Culture: Explain the increase in racial tensions and beliefs about what constituted loyalty during and after the war.

AP SUGGESTED STUDY

PEOPLE/PLACES/EVENTS As you study these items, think about how they demonstrate or relate to key concepts and historical themes from this chapter and previous chapters.

ALLIES **589**
AMERICAN EXPEDITIONARY FORCE **592**
CENTRAL POWERS **589**
DOLLAR DIPLOMACY **587**
GENERAL JOHN J. PERSHING **589**
"GREAT MIGRATION" **598**
LEAGUE OF NATIONS **605**
LUDLOW MASSACRE **597**
LUSITANIA **590**

MARCUS GARVEY **609**
NICOLA SACCO AND BARTOLOMEO VANZETTI **610**
NINETEENTH AMENDMENT **611**
PALMER RAIDS **610**
PANCHO VILLA **589**
RED SCARE **609**
ROOSEVELT COROLLARY **585**
SENATOR HENRY CABOT LODGE **605**

THE FOURTEEN POINTS **603**
TREATY OF VERSAILLES **605**
TRENCH WARFARE **594**
TRIPLE ALLIANCE **589**
TRIPLE ENTENTE **589**
UNITED NEGRO IMPROVEMENT ASSOCIATION **609**
ZIMMERMANN TELEGRAM **591**

AP TEST PRACTICE

Questions assume cumulative content knowledge from this chapter and previous chapters.

MULTIPLE CHOICE Use the photograph on page 597 and your knowledge of U.S. history to answer questions 1–4.

1. Which significant social change in America in the early 20th century is most directly evidenced by the photograph?

   (A) A sharp rise in ethnic tensions among communities of the urban North

   (B) A dramatic surge in a uniquely American popular culture

   (C) The beginnings of desegregation policies in the South

   (D) The "Great Migration" of African Americans from the rural South to the industrial North

2. Which of the following best explains the rise of communities such as that represented in the photograph?

   (A) Public fervor in embracing a vision of self-determination and peace for world communities

   (B) Increased opportunities for jobs due to WWI and prospects for greater personal autonomy

   (C) Prospects for greater personal freedom, due to WWI

   (D) Poor national economic conditions, due to strains placed on the economy by WWI

3. The growth of the community represented by the photograph most created conditions for

(A) an integration of various ethnic communities

(B) expanded tenement settlements

(C) a wave of public recognition of women's rights

(D) a flowering of urban, African American cultural arts

4. The development represented by the photograph best suggests which regarding the nature of American life by the early 20th century?

(A) A continuing growth in urbanization and industrialization

(B) A boom in the agricultural economies of both the Midwest and South

(C) A notable slowing in the transition from a rural society to an urban society

(D) Continuing large increases in population

SHORT ANSWER Use your knowledge of U.S. history to answer questions 5–8.

5. Answer a, b, and c.

a) Briefly explain ONE example of government repression of civil liberties in America, stemming from American involvement in World War I.

b) Briefly explain ONE example of private citizen efforts to repress civil liberties in America, stemming from American involvement in World War I.

c) Briefly explain ONE example of targets of repression in American society, stemming from American involvement in World War I.

6. Answer a, b, and c.

a) For one of the groups below, briefly explain how it was affected by the participation of America in World War I.

• Immigrants

• Women

• Pacifists or non-interventionists

b) Briefly explain ONE example that could be used to support your explanation.

c) Briefly explain a SECOND example that could be used to support your explanation.

7. Answer a, b, and c.

a) Choose ONE area in which America's participation in World War I had the most dramatic effect?

• Economic

• Political

• Social

b) Provide ONE piece of historical evidence that supports your choice in part a.

c) Contrast your choice against ONE of the others and explain why that effect was not as profound as the effect on your choice.

8. Answer a, b, and c.

a) Racism was very evident against African Americans both in the 1910's and 1920's. Briefly explain ONE important similarity in the reasons why this racism emerged in these time periods.

b) Use ONE piece of historical evidence to support your explanation in part a.

c) Briefly explain ONE critical response by African-Americans to this racism in either time period.

LONG ESSAY For each question below, develop a thoughtful and thorough historical argument that answers the question. Begin your essay with a thesis statement and support it with relevant historical evidence.

9. To what extent was the Red Scare and xenophobia of the 1920's a continuation as well as a change in past cultural practices in America?

10. Evaluate the extent to which increasing migration of African Americans to the North contributed to maintaining continuity as well as fostering change in the North between 1910 and 1925.

22 | THE "NEW ERA"

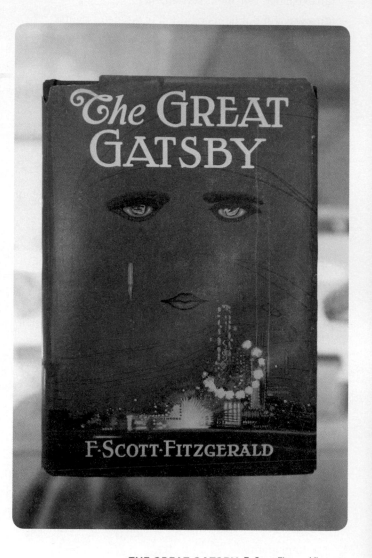

THE GREAT GATSBY F. Scott Fitzgerald's great novel, one of the most famous of the "Lost Generation," critiques the excesses of capitalism and explores the personal sense of alienation experienced by many in the years following World War I. (© Getty Images News/Getty Images)

CONNECTING CONCEPTS

CHAPTER 22 discusses the social, political, and economic climate of the 1920s. Economically, the United States returned to the normalcy of the Gilded Age, fostering a close relationship between government and business, while organized labor had declining influence. Politically, the country moved away from the liberal reforms of the Progressive era to a significantly more conservative posture. Socially, the 1920s witnessed a search for new cultural norms, often rejecting traditional values. Advances in technology and communications led to the creation of a society largely based on mass consumerism. As you read, evaluate the following ideas:

- The United States continued its move from a rural, agrarian society to an urban industrial society.
- Revolutionary changes in communications and technology created a new "mass culture," which challenged the traditional values of American society.
- The rise of an urban industrial society created new challenges and opportunities for women and African Americans.
- World War I resulted in intensified nativist sentiment and led to increasingly restrictive immigration laws.
- The United States turned to a more isolationistic and conservative stance during the 1920s.

THE NEW ECONOMY

After the recession of 1921–1922, the United States began a period of almost uninterrupted prosperity and economic expansion. Less visible at the time, but equally significant, was the survival (and even the growth) of inequalities and imbalances.

TECHNOLOGY AND ECONOMIC GROWTH

No one could deny the remarkable, some believed miraculous, feats of the American economy in the 1920s. The nation's manufacturing output rose by more than 60 percent during the decade. Per capita income grew by a third. Inflation was negligible. A mild recession in 1923 interrupted the pattern of growth, but when it subsided early in 1924, the economy expanded with greater vigor than before.

The economic boom was a result of many factors. An immediate cause was the debilitation of European industry in the aftermath of World War I, which left the United States for the next ten years or so the only truly healthy industrial power in the world. More important in the long run

SOURCES OF THE BOOM was technology and the great industrial expansion it made possible. The automobile industry, as a result of the development of the assembly line and other innovations, now became one of the most important industries in the nation. It stimulated growth in many related industries as well. Auto manufacturers purchased the products of steel, rubber, glass, and tool companies. Auto owners bought gasoline from the oil corporations. Road construction in response to the proliferation of motor vehicles became an important industry. The increased mobility the automobile made possible increased the demand for suburban housing, fueling a boom in the construction industry.

Other new industries benefiting from technological innovations contributed as well to the economic growth. Radio began to become a popular technology even before commercial

RADIO broadcasting began in 1920. Early radio had been able to broadcast little besides pulses, which meant that radio communication could occur only through the Morse code. But with the discovery of the theory of modulation, pioneered by the Canadian scientist Reginald Fessenden, it became possible to transmit speech and music. (Modulation also eventually made possible the transmission of video signals that later helped create radar and television.) Once commercial broadcasting began, families flocked to buy conventional radio sets, which, unlike the cheaper "shortwave" or "ham" radios, could receive high-quality signals over short and medium distances. They were powered by vacuum tubes that were much more reliable than earlier models. By 1925, there were 2 million sets in

COMMUNICATIONS TECHNOLOGY

SCOTTISH-BORN INVENTOR AND SCIENTIST Alexander Graham Bell received a patent for his invention of the telephone on March 7, 1876. The Bell Telephone Company was formed in July of the following year; in the first month of the company's existence, it sold only six phones. By the end of the year, however, more than 3,000 telephones were in service in the United States. The nation's first telephone system (or exchange) was installed in Hartford, Connecticut, that same year. The first exchange linking two major cities was established in 1883 between New York City and Boston. By the turn of the century there were more than 5 million phones in the United States. As the map below shows, in 1914 telephone exchanges linked more than 70,000 places and 8 million subscribers in the United States. The telephone served as the basic communication link in the United States for over 100 years.

One of the next big revolutions in communications technology occurred in the 1970s, with the development of the Internet. The Soviet Union's launch of the satellite *Sputnik* in 1957 spurred the United States to develop computers and computer communications technology largely for defense-related purposes. The Department of Defense's Advanced Research Projects Agency (ARPA) formed the first computer network (ARPANET) in 1969, linking the computers of four universities–Stanford, UCLA, the University of California at Santa Barbara, and the University of Utah. By 1971, the ARPANET had expanded to twenty-three hosts at universities and government research centers throughout the United States. The Department of Defense withdrew from ARPANET in the early 1980s for security reasons. Now free to develop independently, the network–renamed the Internet–expanded rapidly, not only throughout the United States but across the globe as well.

THE TELEPHONE—1914

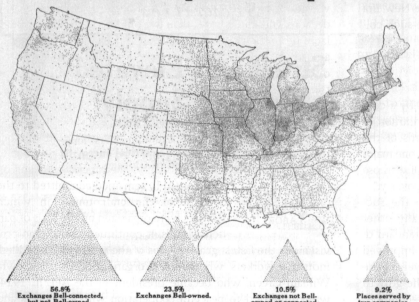

What the Telephone Map Shows

56.8%	23.5%	10.5%	9.2%
Exchanges Bell-connected, but not Bell-owned.	Exchanges Bell-owned.	Exchanges not Bell-owned or connected.	Places served by two companies.

EVERY dot on the map marks a town where there is a telephone exchange, the same sized dot being used for a large city as for a small village. Some of these exchanges are owned by the Associated Bell companies and some by independent companies. Where joined together in one system they meet the needs of each community and, with their suburban lines, reach 70,000 places and over 8,000,000 subscribers.

The pyramids show that only a minority of the exchanges are Bell-owned, and that the greater majority of the exchanges are owned by independent companies and connected with the Bell System.

At comparatively few points are there two telephone companies, and there are comparatively few exchanges, chiefly rural, which do not have outside connections.

The recent agreement between the Attorney General of the United States and the Bell System will facilitate connections between all telephone subscribers regardless of who owns the exchanges.

Over 8,000 different telephone companies have already connected their exchanges to provide universal service for the whole country.

AMERICAN TELEPHONE AND TELEGRAPH COMPANY
AND ASSOCIATED COMPANIES

One Policy   **One System**   **Universal Service**

For our Mutual Advantage mention Popular Electricity and Modern Mechanics when writing to Advertisers.

(Popular Electricity and Modern Mechanics, September, 19, 1914)

GLOBAL COMMUNICATION NETWORKS (© iStock Vectors/Getty Images)

AP TEST PRACTICE

Questions assume cumulative content knowledge from this chapter and previous chapters.

1. What similar effect did both the telephone and Internet have on American society?

 (A) Each was controlled by a dominant communications company

 (B) Each greatly expanded Americans' communications ability

 (C) Each was initially developed for national defense purposes

 (D) Each greatly reduced the need for the American people to travel

2. Which pattern is most supported by the illustrations?

 (A) The coastal regions have or had the most access to the new respective technologies, when compared to the other regions of the U.S.

 (B) The northern Midwest region and the Northeast have or had greater access to the new technology of the time, in comparison to other regions of the U.S.

 (C) The Northwest has or had the most access to the new technology of the time, in both eras.

 (D) The Great Basin and Great Plains had the most access to both technologies.

3. Based on what you have learned about the southern region of the U.S, which best explains the pattern of telephone exchanges in the South in 1914?

 (A) Due to the romantic cultural legacy of the South, fewer individuals in the South sought to purchase the new technology.

 (B) The South was more rural and, therefore, less densely populated between cities and villages.

 (C) The Northern cities took up most of the available capacity, leaving little for the South.

 (D) The technology was not available in the South.

PREPARING WOMEN FOR WORK This school was established during World War I by the Northern Pacific Telegraph Company to train new women employees to be telephone operators. Both during and after the war, telephone companies were among the largest employers of women. (© Bettmann/Corbis)

in menial jobs in California, despite the continuing hostility of the white population. They worked on railroads, construction sites, and farms, and in many other low-paying workplaces. Some Japanese managed to escape the ranks of the unskilled by forming their own small businesses or setting themselves up as truck farmers (farmers who grow small food crops for local sale). Many of the *Issei* (Japanese immigrants) and *Nisei* (their American-born children) enjoyed significant economic success—so much so that California passed laws in 1913 and 1920 to make it more difficult for them to buy land. Other Asians—most notably Filipinos—also swelled the unskilled workforce and generated considerable hostility. Anti-Filipino riots in California beginning in 1929 helped produce legislation in 1934 virtually eliminating immigration from the Philippines.

Mexican immigrants formed a major part of the unskilled workforce throughout the Southwest and California. Nearly half a million Mexicans entered the United States in the 1920s, more than any other national group, increasing the total Mexican population to over a million. Most lived in California, Texas, Arizona, and New Mexico; and by 1930, most lived in

Migration after 1914 had few opportunities for union representation. The skilled crafts represented in the AFL often

A. PHILIP RANDOLPH

worked actively to exclude blacks from their trades and organizations. Most blacks worked in jobs in which the AFL took no interest—as janitors, dishwashers, garbage collectors, commercial laundry attendants, and domestics, and in other types of service jobs. This general reluctance to organize service-sector workers was in part because AFL leaders did not want women and minorities to become union members. The Brotherhood of Sleeping Car Porters, founded in 1925 and led for years by A. Philip Randolph, was a notable exception: a vigorous union, led by an African American and representing a virtually all-black workforce. Over time, Randolph won some significant gains for his members—increased wages, shorter working hours, and other benefits. He also enlisted the union in battles for civil rights for African Americans.

In the West and the Southwest, the ranks of unskilled workers included considerable numbers of Asians and Hispanics, few of them organized, most of them actively excluded from white-dominated unions. In the wake of the Chinese Exclusion Acts of the late nineteenth century, Japanese immigrants increasingly took the place of the Chinese

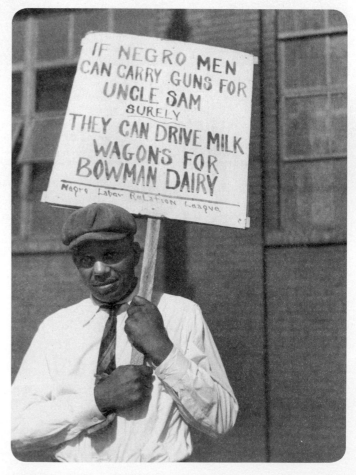

AFRICAN AMERICAN WORKER PROTESTING The frail union movement among African Americans in the 1920s, led by A. Philip Randolph and others against imposing obstacles, slowly built up a constituency within the black working class. Here, an aspiring black dairy worker draws attention to the contrast between African American patriotism in war and the discriminatory treatment African Americans faced at home. (© John Vachon/Getty Images)

cities. Large Mexican barrios—usually raw urban communities, often without even such basic services as plumbing and sewage—grew up in Los Angeles, El Paso, San Antonio, Denver, and many other cities and towns. Some of the residents found work locally in factories and shops; others traveled to mines or did migratory labor on farms, but returned to the cities between jobs. Mexican workers, too, faced hostility and discrimination from the Anglo population of the region; but there were few efforts actually to exclude them. Employers in the relatively underpopulated West needed this ready pool of low-paid, unskilled, and unorganized workers.

THE "AMERICAN PLAN"

Whatever the weaknesses of the unions and of unorganized, unskilled workers, the strength of the corporations was the

PROTECTING THE OPEN SHOP

principal reason for the absence of effective labor organization. After the turmoil of 1919, corporate leaders worked hard to spread the doctrine that unionism was somehow subversive, that a crucial element of democratic capitalism was the protection of the open shop (a shop in which

no worker could be required to join a union). The crusade for the open shop, euphemistically titled the "American Plan," received the endorsement of the National Association of Manufacturers in 1920 and became a pretext for a harsh campaign of union busting across the country.

When such tactics proved insufficient to counter union power, government assistance often made the difference. In 1921, the Supreme Court upheld a lower-court ruling that declared picketing illegal and supported the right of courts to issue injunctions against strikers. In 1922, the Justice Department intervened to quell a strike by 400,000 railroad workers. In 1924, the courts refused protection to members of the United Mine Workers Union when mine owners launched a violent campaign in western Pennsylvania to drive the union from the coal fields. As a result of these developments, union membership fell from more than 5 million in 1920 to under 3 million in 1929.

AGRICULTURAL TECHNOLOGY AND THE PLIGHT OF THE FARMER

Like industry, American agriculture in the 1920s was embracing new technologies for increasing production. The number

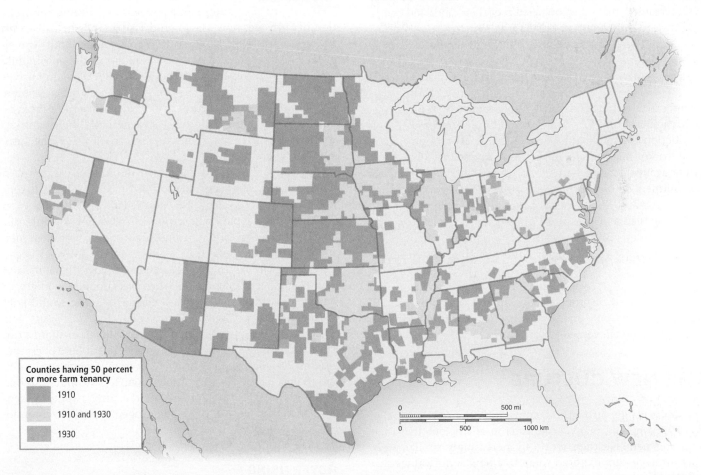

Counties having 50 percent or more farm tenancy

- 1910
- 1910 and 1930
- 1930

FARM TENANCY, 1910–1930 This map illustrates the significant increase in farm tenancy—that is, the number of farmers who did not own their land but worked as tenants for others—between 1910 and 1930. The dark green areas of the map show how extensive tenancy was even in 1910; over 50 percent of the land in those areas was farmed by tenants. The gold and purple parts of the map show the significant expansion of tenancy between 1910 and 1930—creating many new areas in which more than half the farmers were tenants.

• *How did the increasing efficiency and technological progress of agriculture in these years contribute to the growth of tenancy?*

MECHANIZED FARMING of tractors on American farms, for example, quadrupled during the 1920s, especially after they began to be powered by internal combustion engines (like automobiles) rather than by the cumbersome steam engines of the past. They helped to open 35 million new acres to cultivation. Increasingly sophisticated combines and harvesters were proliferating, helping make it possible to produce more crops with fewer workers.

Agricultural researchers were already at work on other advances that would later transform food production in America and around the world: the invention of hybrid corn (made possible by advances in genetic research), which became available to farmers in 1921 but was not grown in great quantities until the 1930s; and the creation of chemical fertilizers and pesticides, which also began to have limited use in the 1920s but proliferated quickly in the 1930s and 1940s.

The new technologies greatly increased agricultural productivity, both in the United States and in other parts of the world. But the demand for agricultural goods was not rising as fast as production. The results were substantial surpluses, a disastrous decline in food prices, and a severe drop in farmers' income beginning early in the 1920s. More than 3 million people left agriculture in the course of the decade. Of those who remained, many lost ownership of their lands and had to rent instead from banks or other landlords.

In response, some farmers began to demand relief in the form of government price supports. One price-raising scheme **"PARITY"** in particular came to dominate agrarian demands: the idea of "parity." Parity was a complicated formula for setting an adequate price for farm goods and ensuring that farmers would earn back at least their production costs no matter how the national or world agricultural market might fluctuate. Champions of parity urged high tariffs against foreign agricultural goods and a government commitment to buy surplus domestic crops at parity and sell them abroad at whatever the market would bring.

The legislative expression of the demand for parity was the McNary-Haugen Bill, named after its two principal sponsors in **MCNARY-HAUGEN BILL** Congress and introduced repeatedly between 1924 and 1928. In 1926 and again in 1928, Congress (where farm interests enjoyed disproportionate influence) approved a bill requiring parity for grain, cotton, tobacco, and rice, but President Coolidge vetoed it both times.

THE NEW CULTURE

The increasingly urban and consumer-oriented culture of the 1920s helped many Americans in all regions live their lives and perceive their world in increasingly similar ways. That same culture exposed them to a new set of values that reflected the prosperity and complexity of the modern economy. But the new culture could not, of course, erase the continuing, and indeed increasing, diversity of the United States.

CONSUMERISM

Among the many changes industrialization produced in the United States was the creation of a mass consumer culture. By **GROWING MASS CONSUMPTION** the 1920s, America was a society in which many men and women could afford not merely the means of subsistence, but a considerable measure of additional, discretionary goods and services; a society in which people could buy items not just because of need but for pleasure as well. Middle-class families purchased such new appliances as electric refrigerators, washing machines, electric irons, and vacuum cleaners, which revolutionized housework and had a particularly dramatic impact on the lives of women. Men and women wore wristwatches and smoked cigarettes. Women purchased cosmetics and mass-produced fashions. Above all, Americans bought automobiles. By the end of the decade, there were more than 30 million cars on American roads.

The automobile affected American life in countless ways. It greatly expanded the geographic horizons of millions of **SOCIAL IMPACT OF THE AUTOMOBILE** people who in the past had seldom ventured far from their homes. Rural men and women, in particular, found in the automobile a means of escaping the isolation of farm life; now they could visit friends or drive into town quickly and at will, rather than spending hours traveling by horse or foot. City dwellers found in the automobile an escape from the congestion of urban life. Weekend drives through the countryside became a staple of urban leisure. Many families escaped the city in a permanent sense: by moving to the new suburbs that were rapidly growing up around large cities in response to the ease of access the automobile had created.

The automobile also transformed the idea of vacations. In the past, the idea of traveling for pleasure had been a luxury reserved for the wealthy. Now many middle-class and even working-class people could aspire to travel considerable distances for vacations, which were a new concept for most men and women in this era. Many businesses and industries began to include paid vacations among their employee benefits; and many employers encouraged their vacationing workers to travel, on the assumption that a change of scene would help restore their energy and vigor at work.

For young people in families affluent enough to afford a car, the automobile was often a means of a different kind of escape. It allowed them to move easily away from parents and family and to develop social lives of their own. It contributed to one of the distinctive developments of the early twentieth century: the emergence of a well-developed and relatively independent youth culture.

ADVERTISING

No group was more aware of the emergence of consumerism (or more responsible for creating it) than the advertising industry. The first advertising and public relations firms (N. W. Ayer and

BREAKING DOWN RURAL ISOLATION: THE EXPANSION OF TRAVEL HORIZONS IN OREGON, ILLINOIS This map uses the small town of Oregon, Illinois—west of Chicago—to illustrate the way in which railroads and then automobiles reduced the isolation of rural areas in the first decades of the twentieth century. The gold and purple areas of the two maps show the territory that residents of Oregon could reach within two hours. Note how small that area was in 1900 and how much larger it was in 1930, by which time an area of over a hundred square miles had become easily accessible to the town. Note, too, the significant network of paved roads in the region by 1930, few of which had existed in 1900.

• *Why did automobile travel do so much more than railroads to expand the travel horizons of small towns?*

J. Walter Thompson) had appeared well before World War I; but in the 1920s, partly as a result of techniques pioneered by wartime propaganda, advertising came of age. Publicists no longer simply conveyed information; they sought to identify products with a particular lifestyle, to invest them with glamour and prestige, and to persuade potential consumers that purchasing a commodity could be a personally fulfilling and enriching experience.

Advertisers also encouraged the public to absorb the values of promotion and salesmanship and to admire those who were effective "boosters" and publicists. One of the most

THE MAN NOBODY KNOWS successful books of the 1920s was *The Man Nobody Knows,* by advertising executive Bruce Barton. It portrayed Jesus Christ as not only a religious prophet but also a "super salesman," who "picked up twelve men from the bottom ranks of business and forged them into an organization that conquered the world." The parables, Barton claimed, were "the most powerful advertisements of all time." Barton's message was fully in tune with the new spirit of the consumer culture. Jesus had been a man concerned with living a full and rewarding life in this world; twentieth-century men and women should do the same. ("Life is meant to live and enjoy as you go along," Barton once wrote.) Jesus had succeeded because he knew how to make friends, to become popular, to please others; that talent was a prescription for success in the modern era as well.

The advertising industry could never have had the impact it did without the emergence of new vehicles of communication that made it possible to reach large audiences quickly and easily. Newspapers were being absorbed into national chains, and wire services were making it possible even for independent newspapers to carry nationally syndicated material.

New or expanded mass-circulation magazines also attracted broad, national audiences. *The Saturday Evening Post,* which began publication as a magazine in 1871, appealed to rural and small-town families with its homey stories and its conspicuous traditionalism; its popularity was, in some respects, evidence of a yearning for an earlier time. But other magazines responded directly to the realities of modern, urban life. The *Reader's Digest,* founded in 1921 by DeWitt and Lila Wallace, condensed stories and even books originally published in other places in an effort to make the expanding world of knowledge and information available in a brief, efficient form for people who would otherwise have no access to it. *Time* magazine, founded in 1923 by Henry Luce and Briton Hadden, set out to condense the news of the week into a brief, accessible, lively format for busy people who did not have the time or desire to read newspapers.

THE MOVIES AND BROADCASTING

At the same time, movies were becoming an ever more popular and powerful form of mass communication. More than 100 million people saw films in 1930, as compared to 40 million in 1922. The addition of sound to motion pictures—beginning in **HOLLYWOOD** 1927 with the first feature-length "talkie," *The Jazz Singer* with Al Jolson—created nationwide excitement. An embarrassing scandal in 1921 involving the popular comedian Fatty Arbuckle produced public outrage and political pressure to "clean up" Hollywood. In response, the film industry introduced "standards" to its films. Studio owners created the Motion Picture Association, a new trade association, and hired former postmaster general Will Hays to head it. More important, they gave Hays broad powers to review films and to ban anything likely to offend viewers (or politicians). Hays exercised his powers broadly and imposed on the film industry a safe, sanctimonious conformity for many years.

The most important communications vehicle was the only one truly new to the 1920s: radio. The first commercial radio station in America, KDKA in Pittsburgh, began broadcasting in 1920; and the first national radio network, the National Broadcasting Company, was formed in 1927. By 1923, there were more than 500 radio stations, covering every area of the country. The radio industry, too, feared government regulation and control, and thus monitored program content carefully and excluded controversial or provocative material. But radio was much less centralized than filmmaking. Individual stations had considerable autonomy, and even carefully monitored stations and networks could not control the countless hours of programming as effectively as the Hays office could control films. Radio programming, therefore, was more diverse—and at times more controversial and even subversive—than film.

MODERNIST RELIGION

The influence of the consumer culture, and its increasing emphasis on immediate, personal fulfillment, was visible even in religion. Theological modernists taught their followers to abandon some of the traditional tenets of evangelical Christianity (literal interpretation of the Bible, belief in the

RADIO NEWS In the early 1920s, when radio was still new, many people considered it a "hobby," appropriate to people interested in technology. By the end of the decade, radio was a normal part of the everyday lives of almost everyone. *Radio News* started off in 1919 as a magazine for amateur radio enthusiasts. By the time of its last issue, in 1971, the magazine had expanded to cover all technical aspects of radio and electronics. (© Buyenlarge/SuperStock)

Trinity, attribution of human traits to the deity) and to accept a faith that would help individuals to live more fulfilling lives in the present world.

The most influential spokesman for liberal Protestantism in the 1920s was Harry Emerson Fosdick, the pastor of Riverside Church in New York City. The basis of Christian religion, he claimed, was not unexamined faith, but a fully developed personality. In his 1926 book, *Abundant Religion*, he argued that Christianity would "furnish an inward spiritual dynamic for radiant and triumphant living."

HARRY EMERSON FOSDICK

Most Americans, even most middle-class Americans, stopped well short of this view of religion as a vehicle for advancing "man's abundant life" and remained faithful to traditional religious messages. But many other middle-class Americans were gradually devaluing religion, assigning it a secondary role (or at times no role) in their lives. When the sociologists Robert and Helen Merrell Lynd studied the society of Muncie, Indiana, in the mid-1920s, they were struck by how many people there claimed that they paid less attention to religion than their parents had. They no longer devoted much time to teaching their children the tenets of their faith; they seldom prayed at home or attended church on any day but Sunday. Even the Sabbath was becoming not a day of rest and religious reflection but, rather, a holiday filled with activities and entertainments.

PROFESSIONAL WOMEN

In the 1920s, college-educated women were no longer pioneers. There were now two and even three generations of graduates of women's or coeducational colleges and universities; many such women were making their presence felt in professional areas that in the past they had rarely penetrated.

Still, professional opportunities for women remained limited by prevailing assumptions (prevalent among many women as well as men) about what were suitable female occupations. Although there were notable success stories about female business executives, journalists, doctors, and lawyers, most professional women remained confined to such traditionally "feminine" fields as fashion, education, social work, and nursing, or to the lower levels of business management. Some middle-class women now combined marriage and careers, but most still had to choose between work and family. The majority of the 25 percent of married women who worked outside the home in the 1920s were working class. The "new professional woman" was a vivid and widely publicized image in the 1920s. In reality, however, most middle-class married women did not work outside the home.

LIMITED OPPORTUNITIES FOR WOMEN

CHANGING IDEAS OF MOTHERHOOD

Yet the 1920s constituted a new era for middle-class women nonetheless. In particular, the decade saw a redefinition of the idea of motherhood. Shortly after World War I, an influential group of psychologists—the "behaviorists," led by John B. Watson—began to challenge the long-held assumption that women had an instinctive capacity for motherhood. Maternal affection was not, they claimed, sufficient preparation for child rearing. Instead, mothers should rely on the advice and assistance of experts and professionals: doctors, nurses, and trained educators in nursery schools and kindergartens.

For many middle-class women, these changes helped redefine what had been an all-consuming activity. Motherhood was no less important in behaviorist theory than it had been before; if anything, it was more so. But for many women it was **"COMPANIONATE MARRIAGES"** less emotionally fulfilling, less connected to their instinctive lives, more dependent on (and tied to) people and institutions outside the family. Many attempted to compensate by devoting new attention to their roles as wives and companions, to developing what became known as "companionate marriage." The middle-class wife shared increasingly in her husband's social life; she devoted more attention to cosmetics and clothing; she was less willing to allow children to interfere with their marriage. Most of all, many more women considered their sexual relationships with their husbands not simply as a means of procreation, as earlier generations had been taught to do, but as an important and pleasurable experience in its own right, as the culmination of romantic love.

Progress in the development of birth control was both a cause and a result of this change. The pioneer of the American birth-control movement was Margaret Sanger, who had become committed to the cause in part because of the influence of

Emma Goldman—a Russian immigrant and political radical who had agitated for birth control before World War I. Sanger began **BIRTH CONTROL** her career promoting the diaphragm and other birth-control devices out of a concern for working-class women, believing that large families were among the major causes of poverty and distress in poor communities. By the 1920s, partly because she had limited success in persuading working-class women to accept her teachings, she was becoming more concerned with persuading middle-class women of the benefits of birth control. Women, she argued, should be free to enjoy the pleasures of sexual activity without any connection to procreation. Birth-control devices began to find a large market among middle-class women, even though some techniques remained illegal in many states (and abortion remained illegal nearly everywhere).

THE "FLAPPER": IMAGE AND REALITY

The new, more secular view of womanhood had effects on women beyond the middle class as well. Some women concluded that in the "New Era" it was no longer necessary to maintain a rigid, Victorian female "respectability." Women could smoke, drink, dance, wear seductive clothes and makeup, and attend lively parties. They could strive for physical and emotional fulfillment, for release from repression and inhibition. (The wide popularity of Freudian ideas in the 1920s—often simplified and distorted for mass consumption—contributed to the growth of these attitudes.)

THE FLAPPER By the mid-1920s, the flapper—the young woman who challenged traditional expectations—had become not only a social type but a movement in fashion as well. Here, Catherine Dear is shown posing in the latest "beach costume," a fashion a long way from the rigid "respectability" of Victorian age women. (© Bettmann/Corbis)

THE CINEMA WOR-4, 7

THERE is probably no cultural or commercial product more closely identified with the United States than motion pictures—or, as they are known in much of the world, the cinema. Although the technology of cinema emerged from the work of inventors in England and France as well as the United States, the production and distribution of films has been dominated by Americans almost from the start. The United States was the first nation to create a film "industry," and it did so at a scale vaster than that of any other country. The 700 feature films a year that Hollywood produced in the 1920s was more than ten times the number created by any other nation, and its films were dominating not only the vast American market, but much of the world's market as well. Seventy percent of the films seen in France, 80 percent of those seen in Latin America, and 95 percent of the movies viewed in Canada and Great Britain were produced in the United States in the 1920s.

As early as the 1930s, the penetration of other nations by American movies was already troubling many governments. The Soviet Union responded to the popularity of Walt Disney's Mickey Mouse cartoons by inventing a cartoon hero of its own—a porcupine, designed to entertain in a way consistent with socialist values and not the capitalist ones that the Soviets believed Hollywood conveyed. During World War II, American films were banned in occupied France (prompting some antifascist dissidents to screen such American films as Frank Capra's *Mr. Smith Goes to Washington* in protest).

American dominance was a result in part of World War I and its aftermath, which debilitated European filmmaking just as movies were vigorously growing in the United States. By the end of World War I, half the theaters of the world were in America. Two decades later, despite an extraordinary expansion of theaters in other nations, the United States continued to have over 40 percent of the world's cinemas. And while the spread of theaters through other areas of the world helped launch film industries in many other countries, it also increased the market (and the appetite) for American films and strengthened American supremacy in their production. "The sun, it now appears," *The Saturday Evening Post* commented in the mid-1920s, "never sets on the British empire and the American motion picture." Movies were then, and perhaps remain still, America's most influential cultural export. Even American popular music, which has enormous global reach, faces more significant local competition than American movies do in most parts of the world.

Despite this American dominance, however, filmmaking has flourished—and continues to flourish—in many countries around the world. India's fabled "Bollywood," for example, produces an enormous number of movies for its domestic market—almost as many as the American industry creates, even

VALENTINO The popularity of the film star Rudolph Valentino among American women was one of the most striking cultural phenomena of the 1920s. Valentino was slight and delicate, not at all like the conventional image of "manliness." But he developed an enormous following among women, in part—as this poster is obviously intended to suggest—by baring his body on screen. Valentino was Italian, which made him seem somehow strange and foreign to many older-stock Americans, and he was almost always cast in exotic roles, never as an American. His sudden death in 1926 (at the age of 31) created enormous outpourings of grief among many American women. (© UA/Photofest)

Such assumptions became the basis of the "flapper"–the modern woman whose liberated lifestyle found expression in dress, hairstyle, speech, and behavior. The flapper lifestyle had a particular impact on lower-middle-class and working-class single women, who were flocking to new jobs in industry and the service sector. (The young, affluent, upper-class "Bohemian" women most often associated with the flapper image were, in fact, imitating a style that emerged first among this larger working-class group.) At night, such women flocked, often alone, to clubs and dance halls in search of excitement and companionship.

Despite the image of liberation the flapper evoked in popular culture, most women remained highly dependent on men–both in the workplace, where they were usually poorly paid, and in the home–and relatively powerless when men exploited that dependence.

PRESSING FOR WOMEN'S RIGHTS

The realization that the "new woman" was as much myth as reality inspired some American feminists to continue their crusade for reform. The National Woman's Party, under the leadership of Alice Paul, pressed on with its campaign to make the Equal Rights Amendment, first proposed in 1923, a part of the Constitution, although it found little

EQUAL RIGHTS AMENDMENT support in Congress (and met continued resistance from other feminist groups). Nevertheless, women's organizations and female political activities grew in many ways in the 1920s. Responding to the suffrage victory, women organized the League of Women Voters and the women's auxiliaries of both the Democratic and Republican Parties. Female-dominated though few of them are widely exported. The global cinema has had a significant impact on American filmmaking, just as American films have influenced filmmakers abroad. The small British film industry had a strong early influence on American movies partly because of the quality and originality of British films, and partly because of the emigration of talented actors, directors, and screenwriters to the United States. The great Alfred Hitchcock, for example, made his first films in London before moving to Hollywood, where he spent the rest of his long career. After World War II, French "new wave" cinema helped spawn a new generation of highly individualistic directors in the United States. Asian cinema—especially the thriving film industry in Hong Kong, with its gritty realism—helped lead to some of the powerfully violent American films of the 1980s and beyond, as well as the genre of martial-arts films that has become popular around the world. German, Italian, Swedish, Dutch, Japanese, Australian, and Indian filmmakers also had influence on Hollywood—and over time perhaps even greater influence on the large and growing "independent film" movement in the United States.

In recent decades, as new technologies and new styles have transformed films around the world, the American movie industry has continued to dominate global cinema. But national boundaries no longer adequately describe moviemaking in the twenty-first century. It is becoming a truly globalized enterprise in the same way that so many other commercial ventures are becoming international. "American" films today are often produced abroad, often have non-American directors and actors, and are often paid for with international financing. Hollywood still dominates worldwide filmmaking, but Hollywood itself is now an increasingly global community. ●

UNDERSTAND, ANALYZE, AND EVALUATE

1. Did American movies, as the Soviet Union claimed in the 1930s, promote capitalism?
2. Why has the American movie industry continued to dominate global cinema?
3. With the increasing globalism of the movie industry, is there still an identifiable American cinema?

consumer groups grew rapidly and increased the range and energy of their efforts.

Women activists won a significant triumph in 1921, when they helped secure passage in Congress of a measure in keeping with the traditional feminist goal of securing "protective" legislation for women: the Sheppard-Towner Act. It provided federal funds to states to establish prenatal and child health-care programs. From the start, however, the bill produced controversy. Alice Paul and her supporters opposed the measure, arguing that it classified all women as mothers. Margaret Sanger's objection was that the new programs would discourage birth-control efforts. More important, the American Medical Association fought Sheppard-Towner, warning that it would introduce untrained outsiders into the health-care field. In 1929, Congress terminated the program.

EDUCATION AND YOUTH

The growing secularism of American culture and its expanding emphasis on training and expertise found reflection in the increasingly important role of education in the lives of American youth. First, more people were going to school in the 1920s than ever before. High-school attendance more than doubled during the decade, from 2.2 million to more than 5 million. Enrollment in colleges and universities increased threefold between 1900 and 1930, with much of that increase occurring after World War I. In 1918, there had been 600,000 college students; in 1930, there were 1.2 million, nearly 20 percent of the college-age population. Attendance was increasing as well at trade and vocational schools and in other institutions providing the specialized training that the modern economy demanded. Schools were beginning to offer instruction not only in the traditional disciplines, but also in modern technical skills: engineering, management, economics.

The growing importance of education contributed to the emergence of a separate youth culture. The idea of adolescence as a distinct period in the life of an individual was for the most part new to the twentieth century. In some measure it was a result of the influence of Freudian psychology. But it was a result, too, of society's recognition that a more extended period of training and preparation was necessary before a young person was ready to move into the workplace. Schools and colleges provided adolescents with a setting in which they could develop their own social patterns, their own hobbies, their own interests and activities. An increasing number of students saw school as a place not just for academic training, but also for organized athletics, extracurricular activities, clubs, and fraternities and sororities—that is, as an institution that allowed them to define themselves less in terms of their families and more in terms of their peer group.

THE DISENCHANTED

The generation that lived through (and in many cases fought in) the Great War quickly came to see the conflict as a useless waste of lives lost for no purpose. For many young people in the 1920s, disenchantment with the war contributed to a growing disenchantment with the United States. The newly prosperous and consumer-driven era they encountered seemed meaningless and vulgar to many artists and intellectuals in particular. As a result, they came to view their own culture with contempt. Rather than trying to influence and reform their society, they isolated themselves from it and embarked on a restless search for personal fulfillment. The American writer Gertrude Stein once referred to the young Americans emerging from World War I as a "Lost Generation." For some writers and intellectuals, at least, it was an apt description.

DANCE HALLS

IN the booming, boisterous, consumer-oriented world of the 1920s, many Americans—especially those living in urban areas—challenged the inhibitions of traditional public culture. They looked instead for freedom, excitement, and release. Nowhere did they do so more vigorously and visibly than in the great dance halls that were proliferating in cities across the nation in these years.

The dance craze that swept urban America in the 1920s and 1930s was a result of many things. The great African American migration during World War I had helped bring new forms of jazz out of the South and into the urban North—where the phonograph and the radio popularized it. The growth of a distinctive youth culture—and the increasing tendency of men and women to socialize together in public—created an audience for uninhibited, sexually titillating entertainment. The relative prosperity of the 1920s enabled many young working-class people to afford to spend evenings out. And prohibition, by closing down most saloons and taverns, limited their other options.

Night after night, in big cities and small, young people flocked to dance halls to hear the powerful, pulsing new music; to revel in dazzling lights and ornate surroundings; to show off new clothes and hairstyles; and, of course, most of all, to dance. Like the new movie palaces that were being built at the same time, many of the dance halls provided a sense of grandiosity and glamour. Some of the larger dance halls in the big cities—Roseland and the Savoy in New York, the Trianon and the Aragon in Chicago, the Raymor in Boston, the Greystone in Detroit, the Hollywood Paladium, and many others—were truly cavernous, capable of accommodating thousands of couples at once. Over 10 percent of the men and women between the ages of 17 and 40 in New York went dancing at least once a week, and the numbers were comparable in other large cities.

JITTERBUGGERS As dance halls became more popular, dancing became more exuberant—perhaps never more so than when the "jitterbug" became popular in the 1930s. This photograph shows an acrobatic pair of dancers during a huge dance event in Los Angeles designed to raise money for the Salvation Army. More than 10,000 people attended the event, and the police on hand to keep order had to call for reinforcements as the crowd became more and more frenzied and enthusiastic. (© Bettmann/Corbis)

What drew so many people to the dance halls? In large part, it was the music, which both its defenders and critics recognized as something very new in mainstream American culture. Dancing was "moral ruin," the *Ladies' Home Journal* primly warned in 1921, prompting "carelessness, recklessness, and laxity of moral responsibility" with its "direct appeal to the body's sensory centers." Many young dancers might have agreed with the description, if not with the moral judgment. Jazz encouraged a kind of uninhibited, even frenetic dancing—expressive, athletic, sensual—that young couples, in particular, found extraordinarily exciting, a welcome release from the often staid worlds of family, school, or work. Performances by some of the most famous bands and musicians of the day, Paul Whiteman, Ben Pollack, Fletcher Henderson, Bix Beiderbecke, Louis Armstrong, and Duke Ellington—already familiar to everyone through radio performances and recordings—drew enormous crowds.

Some of the less savory halls also attracted dancers for illicit reasons—as sources of bootleg liquor or as places to buy drugs. "Taxi-dance" ballrooms, which allowed men without their own partners to buy tickets to dance with "hostesses" and "instructresses," were sometimes closed by municipal authorities for "lewd" dancing and prostitution. Managers of the larger ballrooms tried to distance themselves from the unsavory image of the taxi-dance halls by imposing dress codes and making at least some efforts, usually futile, to require "decorum" among their patrons.

Dance halls were particularly popular with young men and women from working-class, immigrant communities. For them, going dancing was part of becoming American, a way to escape—even if momentarily—the insular world of the immigrant neighborhood. (Their parents saw it that way too, and often tried to stop their children from going because they

THE SAVOY The Savoy ballroom in New City's Harlem was one of the largest and most popular dance halls in America, and a regular home to many of the most noted dance bands in the 1920s and 1930s. (© Archive Photos/Getty)

At the heart of the Lost Generation's critique of modern society was a sense of personal alienation. The repudiation of Wilsonian idealism, the restoration of "business as usual," the growing emphasis on materialism and consumerism suggested that the war had been a fraud; that the suffering and the dying

LOST GENERATION'S CRITIQUE

had been in vain. Ernest Hemingway, one of the most celebrated (and most commercially successful) of the new breed of writers, expressed the generation's contempt for the war in his novel *A Farewell to Arms* (1929). Its

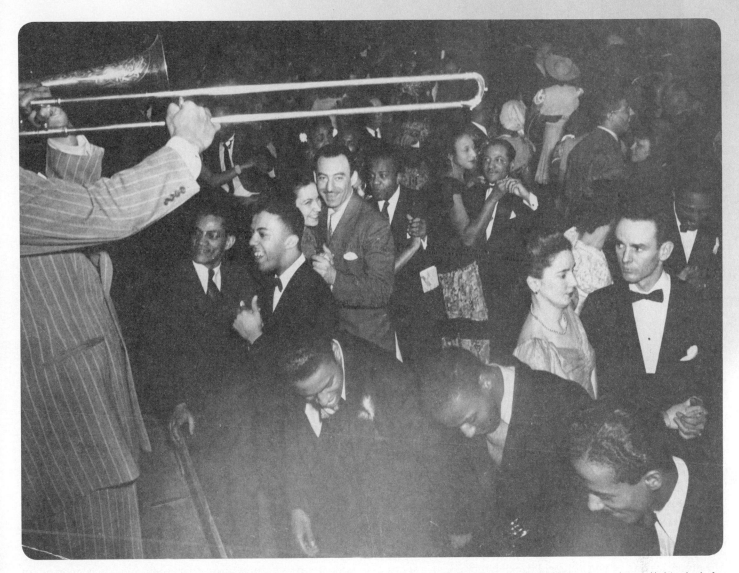

DANCING AT THE SAVOY This photograph of the interior of the famous Savoy ballroom shows the crowds of men and women who typically flocked there to dance to the great black jazz bands of the 1920s and 1930s. (© International Center of Photography/Getty Images)

feared the dance halls would pull them out of the family and the community.) Going dancing was a chance to mingle with hundreds, sometimes thousands, of strangers of diverse backgrounds, and to participate in a cultural ritual that had no counterpart in ethnic cultures.

But dance halls were not melting pots. African Americans—who flocked to ballrooms at least as eagerly as whites—usually gathered at clubs in black neighborhoods, where there were only occasional white patrons. White working-class people might encounter a large number of different ethnic groups in a great hall at once, but the groups did not mix very much. In Chicago's Dreamland, for example, Italians congregated near the door, Poles near the band, and Jews in the middle of the floor. Still, the experience of the dance hall—like the experience of the movie palace or the amusement park—drew people into the growing mass culture that was competing with and beginning to overwhelm the close-knit ethnic cultures into which many young Americans had been born. ●

UNDERSTAND, ANALYZE, AND EVALUATE

1. Besides the music, what was the appeal of the dance hall?
2. Although thousands of young people attended dance halls, why were the halls unable to break down the ethnic or racial barriers of those who flocked to them?
3. Is there an equivalent today of the dance hall of the 1920s and 1930s? If so, what is its appeal? Who are its customers? How is it different from the dance halls of the earlier era?

protagonist, an American officer fighting in Europe, decides that there is no justification for his participation in the conflict and deserts the army with a nurse with whom he has fallen in love. Hemingway suggested that the officer was to be admired for doing so.

One result of this alienation was a series of savage critiques of modern society by a wide range of writers, some of whom **H. L. MENCKEN** were known as the "debunkers." Among them was the Baltimore journalist H. L. Mencken. His magazines—first the *Smart Set* and later the

American Mercury–ridiculed everything most middle-class Americans held dear: religion, politics, the arts, even democracy itself. Mencken could not believe, he claimed, that "civilized life was possible under a democracy," because it was a form of government that placed power in the hands of the common people, whom he ridiculed as the "booboisie." Echoing Mencken's contempt was the novelist Sinclair Lewis, the first American to win a Nobel Prize in Literature. In a series of savage novels–*Main Street* (1920), *Babbitt* (1922), *Arrowsmith* (1925), and others–he lashed out at one aspect of modern society after another: the small town, the modern city, the medical profession, popular religion. The novelist F. Scott Fitzgerald

REJECTING SUCCESS

ridiculed the American obsession with material success in *The Great Gatsby* (1925). The novel's title character, Jay Gatsby, spends his life accumulating wealth and social prestige in order to win the woman he loves. The world to which he has aspired, however, turns out to be one of pretension, fraud, and cruelty, and it ultimately destroys him.

THE HARLEM RENAISSANCE

In postwar Harlem in New York City, a new generation of black artists and intellectuals created a flourishing African American culture widely described as the "Harlem Renaissance." There were nightclubs (among them the famous Cotton Club) featuring many of the great jazz musicians who would later become staples of national popular culture: Duke Ellington, Jelly Roll Morton, Fletcher Henderson, and others. There were

theaters featuring ribald musical comedies and vaudeville acts. Many white New Yorkers traveled up to Harlem for the music and theater, but the audiences were largely black.

Harlem in the 1920s was above all a center of literature, poetry, and art that drew heavily from both American and African roots. Black artists were trying in part to demonstrate the richness of their own racial heritage (and, not incidentally, to prove to whites that their race was worthy of respect). The poet Langston Hughes captured much of the

THE ART OF THE HARLEM RENAISSANCE Aaron Douglas (1899–1979), one of the most significant African American artists of the 1920s, combined an interest in African and African American themes with an attraction to the modernist trends in American art during this period. (© Archive Photos/Getty Images)

AFRICAN
AMERICAN
PRIDE

spirit of the movement in a single sentence: "I am a Negro—and beautiful." One of the leaders of the Harlem Renaissance was Alain Locke, who assembled a notable collection of black writings published in 1925 as *The New Negro*. Gradually, white publishers began to notice and take an interest in the writers Locke helped launch. Hughes, Zora Neale Hurston, Countee Cullen, Claude McKay, James Weldon Johnson, and others gradually found readerships well beyond the black community. The painter Aaron Douglas, talented chronicler of the African American experience, eventually found himself commissioned to create important murals in universities and public buildings.

HARLEM, 1925 Well-dressed schoolchildren gather on a street in Harlem, illustrating the growing affluence of the African American elite in New York. (© Bettmann/Corbis)

A CONFLICT OF CULTURES

The modern, secular culture of the 1920s was not unchallenged. It grew up alongside older, more traditional cultures, with which it continually and often bitterly competed.

PROHIBITION

When the prohibition of the sale and manufacture of alcohol went into effect in January 1920, it had the support of most

FAILURE OF
PROHIBITION

members of the middle class and most of those who considered themselves progressives. Within a year, however, it had become clear that the "noble experiment," as its defenders called it, was not working well. Prohibition did substantially reduce drinking, at least in some regions of the country. But it also produced conspicuous and growing violations that made the law an almost immediate source of disillusionment and controversy. The federal government hired only 1,500 agents to enforce the prohibition laws, and in many places they

ALCOHOL AND
ORGANIZED
CRIME

received little help from local police. Before long, it was almost as easy to acquire illegal alcohol in much of the country as it had once been to acquire legal alcohol. And since an enormous, lucrative industry was now barred to legitimate businessmen, organized crime figures took it over. In Chicago, Al Capone built a criminal empire based largely on illegal alcohol. He guarded it against interlopers with an army of as many as 1,000 gunmen, whose zealousness contributed to the violent deaths of more than 250 people in the city between 1920 and 1927. Other regions produced gangsters and gang wars of their own.

Many middle-class progressives who had originally supported prohibition soon soured on the experiment. But an enormous constituency of provincial, largely rural, Protestant Americans continued vehemently to defend it.

Opponents of prohibition (or "wets," as they came to be known) gained steadily in influence. Not until 1933, however, when the Great Depression added weight to their appeals, were they finally able effectively to challenge the "drys" and win repeal of the Eighteenth Amendment.

NATIVISM AND THE KLAN

Agitation for a curb on foreign emigration to the United States had begun in the nineteenth century; and like the prohibition movement, it had gathered strength in the years before the war largely because of the support of middle-class progressives. Such concerns had not been sufficient in the first years of the century to win passage of curbs on immigration; too many employers fought to keep low-paid immigrant workers flooding into the country. But in the troubled and repressive years immediately following the war, many old-stock Americans began to associate immigration with radicalism.

Sentiment on behalf of restriction grew rapidly as a result. In 1921, Congress passed an emergency immigration act, establishing a quota system by which annual immigration from any country could not exceed 3 percent of the number of persons of that nationality who had been in the United States in 1910. The new law cut immigration from 800,000 to 300,000 in any single year, but nativists remained unsatisfied and pushed for a harsher law. The National Origins Act of 1924

NATIONAL
ORIGINS ACT
OF 1924

strengthened the exclusionist provision of the 1921 law. It banned immigration from east Asia entirely. That provision deeply angered the Japanese, who understood that they were the principal target; Chinese immigration had been illegal since 1882. The law also reduced the quota for Europeans from 3 percent to 2 percent. The quota would be based, moreover, not on the 1910 census, but on the census of 1890, a year in which there had been many fewer southern

PROHIBITION, 1921 A New York City police commissioner oversees agents pouring illegal liquor into the street. This raid occurred in the early months of prohibition, when the battle against alcohol was still popular—hence the eagerness of the commissioner to appear in the photograph. (The Library of Congress (LC-USZ62-123257))

and eastern Europeans in the country. What immigration there was, in other words, would heavily favor northwestern Europeans—people of "Nordic" or "Teutonic" stock. Five years later, a further restriction set a rigid limit of 150,000 immigrants a year. In the years that followed, immigration officials seldom permitted even half that number actually to enter the country.

But the nativism of the 1920s extended well beyond restricting immigration. Among other things, this nativism helped instigate the rebirth of the Ku Klux Klan as a major force in American society.

The first Klan, founded during Reconstruction, had died in the 1870s. But in 1915, another

THE NEW KLAN group of white southerners met on Stone Mountain near Atlanta and established a new version of the society. Nativist passions had swelled in Georgia and elsewhere in response to the case of Leo Frank, a Jewish factory manager in Atlanta convicted in 1914 (on very flimsy evidence) of murdering a female employee; a mob stormed Frank's jail and lynched him. The premiere (also in

TOTAL IMMIGRATION, 1920–1960 After many years of extremely high rates of immigration from Europe and elsewhere, the United States experienced several decades of much lower immigration beginning in the 1920s. Immigration-restriction legislation passed in 1921 and 1924 was one important reason for the decline.

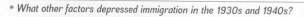

• *What other factors depressed immigration in the 1930s and 1940s?*

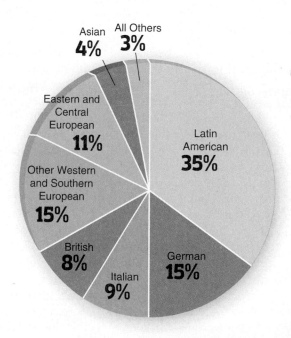

SOURCES OF IMMIGRATION, 1920–1960 This chart shows a significant change in the sources of immigration between 1920 and 1960, a direct result of the National Origins Act of 1924, which established national quotas for immigrants to the United States based on the number of such immigrants who had been in the country in 1890. Note the shift back toward northern and western Europe and away from Italy and other southern and eastern European nations (which had not been heavily represented in the immigration of the 1890s). But the most dramatic change was the huge increase in the proportion of immigrants from Latin America, a region explicitly exempted from the quota system established in 1924.

• *Why were Latin Americans treated differently than Europeans in immigration law in these years?*

Atlanta) of D. W. Griffith's film *The Birth of a Nation*, which glorified the early Klan, also helped inspire white southerners to form a new one. At first the new Klan, like the old, was largely concerned with intimidating African Americans, who, according to Klan leader William J. Simmons, were becoming insubordinate. And at first it remained small, obscure, and almost entirely southern. After World War I, however, concern about African Americans became secondary to concern about Catholics, Jews, and foreigners. At that point, membership in the Klan expanded rapidly and dramatically, not just in the small towns and rural areas of the South, but also in industrial cities in the North and Midwest. Indiana had the largest Klan membership of any state, and there were substantial Klans in Chicago, Detroit, and other northern industrial cities. The Klan was also strong in the West, with particularly large and active chapters in Oregon and Colorado. By 1924, there were reportedly 4 million members.

In some communities, where Klan leaders came from the most "respectable" segments of society, the organization operated much like a fraternal society, engaging in nothing more dangerous than occasional political pronouncements. Many Klan units (or "klaverns") tried to present themselves as patriots and community leaders. Some established women's and even children's auxiliaries to demonstrate their commitment to the family. Often, however, the Klan also operated as a brutal, even violent, opponent of "alien" groups and as a defender of traditional, fundamentalist morality. Some Klansmen systematically terrorized blacks, Jews, Catholics, and foreigners and boycotted their businesses, threatened their families, and attempted to drive them out of their communities. Occasionally, they resorted to violence: public whipping, tarring and feathering, arson, and lynching.

What the Klan feared, it soon became clear, was not simply "foreign" or "racially impure" groups; it was anyone who posed a challenge to "traditional values," as the Klan defined them. Klansmen persecuted not only immigrants and African Americans, but also those white Protestants they considered guilty of irreligion, sexual promiscuity, or drunkenness. The Klan worked to enforce prohibition; it attempted to institute compulsory Bible reading in schools; it worked to punish divorce. It also provided its members, many of them people of modest means with little real power in society, with a sense of community and seeming authority. Its bizarre costumes, its elaborate rituals, its "secret" language, its burning crosses—all helped produce a sense of excitement and cohesion.

DEFENDING "TRADITIONAL VALUES"

The Klan declined quickly after 1925, when a series of internal power struggles and several sordid scandals discredited some of its most important leaders. The most damaging episode involved David Stephenson, head of the Indiana Klan, who raped a young secretary, kidnapped her, and watched her die rather than call a doctor after she swallowed poison. The Klan staggered on in some areas into the 1930s, but by World

DAVID STEPHENSON

KLAN INITIATION A Ku Klux Klan chapter in Jackson, Mississippi, holds an initiation ceremony for new members in August 1923. (The Library of Congress (LC-USZ62-28024))

War II it was effectively dead. (The postwar Ku Klux Klan, which still survives, is modeled on but has no direct connection to the Klan of the 1920s and 1930s.)

RELIGIOUS FUNDAMENTALISM

Another bitter cultural controversy of the 1920s challenged the place of religion in contemporary society. By 1921, American Protestantism was divided into two warring camps. On one side stood the modernists: mostly urban, middle-class people who had attempted to adapt religion to the teachings of science and to the realities of their modern, secular society. On the other side stood the defenders of traditional faith: provincial, largely rural men and women, fighting to maintain the centrality of traditional religion in American life. They became known as "fundamentalists," a term derived from an influential set of pamphlets, *The Fundamentals*, published before World War I. The fundamentalists were outraged at the abandonment of traditional beliefs in the face of scientific discoveries. They insisted the Bible was to be interpreted literally. Above all, they opposed the teachings of Charles Darwin, who had openly challenged the biblical story of the Creation. Human beings had not evolved from lower orders of animals, the fundamentalists insisted; they had been created by God, as described in Genesis.

Fundamentalism was a highly evangelical movement, interested in spreading the doctrine to new groups. Fundamentalist evangelists, among them the celebrated Billy Sunday, traveled from state to state (particularly in the South and parts of the West) attracting huge crowds to their revival meetings. Protestant modernists looked on much of this activity with condescension and amusement. But by the mid-1920s, to their great alarm, evangelical fundamentalism was gaining political strength in some states with its demands for legislation to forbid the teaching of evolution in the public schools. In Tennessee in March 1925, the legislature adopted a measure making it illegal for any public school teacher "to teach any theory that denies the story of the divine creation of man as taught in the Bible."

The Tennessee law attracted the attention of the fledgling American Civil Liberties Union, which had been founded in 1920 by men and women alarmed by the repressive legal and social climate of World War I and its aftermath. The ACLU offered free counsel to any Tennessee educator willing to defy the law and become the defendant in a test case. A twenty-four-year-old biology teacher in the town of Dayton, John T. Scopes, agreed to have himself arrested. And when the ACLU decided to send the famous attorney Clarence Darrow to

SCOPES "MONKEY TRIAL" defend Scopes, the aging William Jennings Bryan (now an important fundamentalist spokesman) announced that he would travel to Dayton to assist the prosecution. Journalists from across the country flocked to Tennessee to cover what became known as the "Monkey Trial," which opened in an almost circuslike atmosphere. Scopes had, of course, clearly violated the law; and a verdict of guilty was a foregone conclusion, especially when the judge refused to permit "expert" testimony by evolution scholars. Scopes was fined $100, and the case was ultimately dismissed in a higher court because of a technicality. Nevertheless, Darrow scored an important victory for the modernists by calling Bryan to the stand to testify as an "expert on the Bible." In the course of the cross-examination, which was broadcast by radio to

BRYAN AND DARROW IN DAYTON
Clarence Darrow (left), a famous lawyer who defended Scopes, and William Jennings Bryan, an even more famous politician who supported the prosecution, pose for photographers during the 1925 Scopes trial. Both men had removed their jackets because of the intense heat, and Bryan had shocked many of his admirers by revealing that he was not wearing suspenders (as most country people did), but a belt—which in rural Tennessee was a symbol of urban culture. (© Archive Photos/Getty Images)

much of the nation, Darrow made Bryan's stubborn defense of biblical truths appear foolish and finally tricked him into admitting the possibility that not all religious dogma was subject to only one interpretation.

The Scopes trial was a traumatic experience for many fundamentalists. It isolated and ultimately excluded them from many mainstream Protestant denominations. It helped put an end to much of their political activism. But it did not change their religious convictions. Even without connection to traditional denominations, fundamentalists continued to congregate in independent churches or new denominations of their own.

THE DEMOCRATS' ORDEAL

The anguish of provincial Americans attempting to defend an embattled way of life proved particularly troubling to the Democratic Party, which suffered during the 1920s as a result of tensions between its urban and rural factions. More than the Republicans, the Democrats were a diverse coalition of interest groups, linked to the party by local traditions. Among those interest groups were prohibitionists, Klansmen, and fundamentalists on one side and Catholics, urban workers, and immigrants on the other.

In 1924, the tensions between them proved devastating. At the Democratic National Convention in New York City that summer, bitter conflict broke out over the platform when the party's urban wing attempted to win approval of planks calling for the repeal of prohibition and a denunciation of the Klan. Both planks narrowly failed. More damaging to the party was a deadlock in the balloting for a presidential candidate. Urban Democrats supported Alfred E. Smith, the Irish Catholic Tammanyite who had risen to become a progressive governor of New York. Rural Democrats backed William McAdoo, Woodrow Wilson's Treasury secretary (and son-in-law), later to become a senator from California; he had skillfully positioned himself to win the support of southern and western delegates suspicious of Tammany Hall and modern urban life. The convention dragged on for 103 ballots, until finally, after both Smith and McAdoo withdrew, the party settled on a compromise: the bland corporate lawyer John W. Davis, who had served as solicitor general and ambassador to Britain under Wilson. He was easily defeated by President Calvin Coolidge.

A similar schism plagued the Democrats again in 1928, when Al Smith finally secured his party's nomination for president after a much shorter battle. Smith was not, however, able to unite his divided party—largely because of widespread anti-Catholic sentiment, especially **AL SMITH** in the South. He was the first Democrat since the Civil War not to carry the entire South. Elsewhere, although he did well in the large cities, he carried only Massachusetts and Rhode Island. Smith's opponent, and the victor in the presidential election, was a man who perhaps more than any other contemporary politician seemed to personify the modern, prosperous, middle-class society of the New Era: Herbert Hoover.

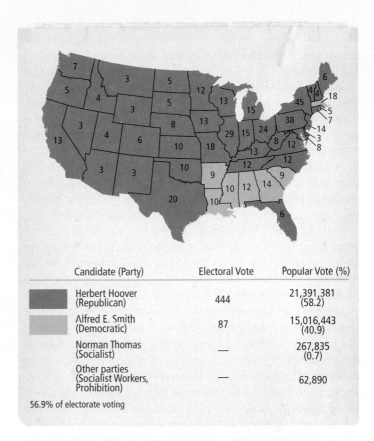

Candidate (Party)	Electoral Vote	Popular Vote (%)
Herbert Hoover (Republican)	444	21,391,381 (58.2)
Alfred E. Smith (Democratic)	87	15,016,443 (40.9)
Norman Thomas (Socialist)	—	267,835 (0.7)
Other parties (Socialist Workers, Prohibition)	—	62,890

56.9% of electorate voting

ELECTION OF 1928 The election of 1928 was, by almost any measure, highly one-sided. Herbert Hoover won over 58 percent of the vote to Alfred Smith's 41. Smith carried only Massachusetts, Rhode Island, and some traditionally Democratic states in the South.

• *Why did Smith do so poorly even in some of the South?*

REPUBLICAN GOVERNMENT

For twelve years, beginning in 1921, both the presidency and the Congress were in the hands of the Republican Party—a party in which the power of reformers had greatly dwindled since the heyday of progressivism before the war. For most of those years, the federal government enjoyed a warm and supportive relationship with the American business community. Yet the government of the New Era was more than the passive, pliant instrument that critics often described. It also attempted to serve as an active agent of economic change.

HARDING AND COOLIDGE

Nothing seemed more clearly to illustrate the unadventurous character of 1920s politics than the characters of the two men who served as president during most of the decade: Warren G. Harding and Calvin Coolidge.

Harding was elected to the presidency in 1920, having spent many years in public life doing little of note. An undistinguished senator from Ohio, he had received the Republican presidential nomination as a result of an agreement among leaders of his party, who considered him, as one noted, a "good second-rater." Harding appointed capable men to the most important cabinet offices, and he attempted to stabilize the nation's troubled foreign policy. But even as he attempted to rise to his office, he seemed baffled by his responsibilities, as if he recognized his own unfitness. "I am a man of limited talents from a small town," he reportedly told friends on one occasion. "I don't seem to grasp that I am President." Harding's intellectual limits were compounded by personal weaknesses: his penchant for gambling, illegal alcohol, and attractive women.

Harding lacked the strength to abandon the party hacks who had helped create his political success. One of them, Harry Daugherty, the Ohio party boss principally responsible **TEAPOT DOME** for his meteoric political ascent, he appointed attorney general. Another, New Mexico senator Albert B. Fall, he made secretary of the Interior. Members of the so-called Ohio Gang filled important offices throughout the administration. Unknown to the public (and perhaps also to Harding), Daugherty, Fall, and others were engaged in fraud and corruption. The most spectacular scandal involved the rich naval oil reserves at Teapot Dome, Wyoming, and Elk Hills, California. At the urging of Fall, Harding transferred control of those reserves from the Navy Department to the Interior Department. Fall then secretly leased them to two wealthy businessmen and received in return nearly half a million dollars in "loans" to ease his private financial troubles. Fall was ultimately convicted of bribery and sentenced to a year in prison; Daugherty barely avoided a similar fate for his part in another scandal.

In the summer of 1923, only months before Senate investigations and press revelations brought the scandals to light, a tired and depressed Harding left Washington for a speaking tour in the West. In Seattle late in July, he suffered severe pain, which his doctors wrongly diagnosed as food poisoning. A few days later, in San Francisco, he suffered two major heart attacks and died.

In many ways, Calvin Coolidge, who succeeded Harding in the presidency, was utterly different from his predecessor. **CALVIN COOLIDGE** Where Harding was genial, garrulous, and debauched, Coolidge was dour, silent, even puritanical. And while Harding was, if not perhaps personally corrupt, then at least tolerant of corruption in others, Coolidge seemed honest beyond reproach. In other ways, however, Harding and Coolidge were similar figures. Both took an essentially passive approach to their office.

Like Harding, Coolidge had risen to the presidency on the basis of few substantive accomplishments. Elected governor of Massachusetts in 1919, he had won national attention with his laconic response to the Boston police strike that year. That was enough to make him his party's vice presidential nominee in 1920. Three years later, after Harding's death, he took the oath of office from his father, a justice of the peace, by the light of a kerosene lamp.

If anything, Coolidge was even less active as president than Harding, partly as a result of his conviction that government should interfere as little as possible in the life of the nation. In 1924, he received his party's presidential nomination virtually unopposed. Running against John W. Davis, he won a comfortable victory: 54 percent of the popular vote and 382 of the 531 electoral votes. Robert La Follette, the candidate of the reincarnated Progressive Party, received 16 percent of the popular vote but carried only his home state of Wisconsin. Coolidge probably could have won renomination and reelection in 1928. Instead, in characteristically laconic fashion, he walked into a press room one day and handed each reporter a slip of paper containing a single sentence: "I do not choose to run for president in 1928."

HARDING AND FRIENDS President Warren G. Harding (center left, holding a rod) poses with companions during a fishing trip to Miami in 1921. He enjoyed these social and sporting events with wealthy friends and political cronies. Two of his companions here, Attorney General Harry Daugherty (to the left of Harding) and Interior Secretary Albert Fall (at far right) were later principal figures in the scandals that rocked the administration before and after Harding's death. (© Bettmann/Corbis)

CALVIN COOLIDGE AT LEISURE Coolidge was a silent man of simple tastes. But he was not really an outdoorsman, despite his efforts to appear so. He is shown here fishing in Simsbury, Connecticut, carefully attired in suit, tie, hat, and rubber boots. (© Bettmann/Corbis)

GOVERNMENT AND BUSINESS

The story of Harding and Coolidge themselves, however, is only a part—and by no means the most important part—of the story of their administrations. However passive the New Era presidents may have been, much of the federal government was working effectively and efficiently during the 1920s to **ANDREW MELLON** adapt public policy to the widely accepted goal of the time: helping business and industry operate with maximum efficiency and productivity. The close relationship between the private

sector and the federal government that had been forged during World War I continued. Secretary of the Treasury Andrew Mellon, a wealthy steel and aluminum tycoon, devoted himself to working for substantial reductions in taxes on corporate profits, personal incomes, and inheritances. Largely because of his efforts, Congress cut them all by more than half. Mellon also worked closely with President Coolidge after 1924 on a series of measures to trim dramatically the already modest federal budget. The administration even managed to retire half the nation's World War I debt.

The most energetic member of the cabinet was Commerce Secretary Herbert Hoover, who considered himself, and was considered by others, a notable progressive. During his eight years in the Commerce Department, Hoover encouraged voluntary cooperation in the private sector as the best avenue to stability. But the idea of voluntarism, he believed, did not require that the government remain passive; on the contrary, public institutions, Hoover insisted, should **HOOVER'S "ASSOCIATIONALISM"** play an active role in creating the new, cooperative order. Above all, Hoover became the champion of the concept of business "associationalism"—a concept that envisioned the creation of national organizations of businessmen in particular industries. Through these trade associations, private entrepreneurs could, Hoover believed, stabilize their industries and promote efficiency in production and marketing.

Many progressives derived encouragement from the election of Herbert Hoover to the presidency in 1928. Hoover easily defeated Al Smith, the Democratic candidate. And he entered office promising bold new efforts to solve the nation's remaining economic problems. But Hoover had few opportunities to prove himself. Less than a year after his inauguration, the nation plunged into the severest and most prolonged economic crisis in its history—a crisis that brought many of the optimistic assumptions of the New Era crashing down and launched the nation into a period of unprecedented social innovation and reform

AP CONNECTING THEMES

Chapter 22 discussed the 1920s, with particular focus on social change. Review the chapter to study the impact of technological change, particularly in communications, and the role that change played in creating a mass culture. Be certain to understand the concepts of mass society and consumerism. Chapter 22 also focused on political changes, which led the United States to a more conservative, pro-business stance, as well as to reduce its role in world affairs. Further, chapter 22 discussed the conflict of cultural values in such areas as religion, women's roles in society, prohibition, and rising nativism. Attention was given to the elements of society that were

doing well economically and those doing poorly. Finally, think back to World War I. Chapter 22 discussed the disillusionment brought on by the failure to realize the very idealistic goals the country had pursued. Consider how that disillusionment influenced the mindset of society in the 1920s.

The following themes have heightened importance in Chapter 22. You should now be able to do the following for each listed theme:

Identity: Explain the ways in which World War I changed perceptions of American identity during the 1920s.

Work, Exchange, and Technology: Examine the ways in which new technology and communications contributed to the growth of a mass consumer society.

Politics and Power: Explain the reasons for and the consequences of movement toward a more conservative political posture.

America and the World: Explain the reasons for the reduction of the role of the United States in world affairs.

Ideas, Beliefs, and Culture: Explain the reasons for and consequences of the challenge to traditional values during the 1920s.

AP SUGGESTED STUDY

PEOPLE/PLACES/EVENTS As you study these items, think about how they demonstrate or relate to key concepts and historical themes from this chapter and previous chapters.

AP TEST PRACTICE

Questions assume cumulative content knowledge from this chapter and previous chapters.

MULTIPLE CHOICE Use the maps on page 623 and your knowledge of U.S. history to answer questions 1-2.

1. Which significant social change in America in the first half of the early 20th century was most directly the result of the trends shown in the maps?

   (A) Railroads greatly expanded their number of short lines, linking many major lines together.

   (B) Americans experienced greater consumerism.

   (C) Americans experienced greater personal mobility.

   (D) Rural Americans traveled to towns less often.

2. The development depicted by the maps most suggests that

   (A) Fewer Americans were able to purchase consumer goods.

   (B) Railroads remained the most important means of personal travel.

   (C) Regional distinctions were still prevalent.

   (D) Consumer goods became more affordable for the average American.

SHORT ANSWER Use your knowledge of U.S. history to answer questions 3-4.

3. Using the photographs on page 620, answer parts a, b, and c.

   a) Briefly explain ONE major difference between the photographs depicting the telegraph trainees and the African American protestor.

   b) Briefly explain how someone supporting female worker training could use ONE piece of evidence from the period between 1900 and 1930 that shows progress for this group in other areas of American life.

   c) Briefly explain how someone supporting the protestor could use ONE piece of evidence from the period between 1900 and 1930 not mentioned in the caption to show lack of progress for this group in other areas of American life.

4. Answer a, b, and c.

   a) For one of the areas below, identify a new technology or development, which had a significant social or cultural impact.
   • Communications
   • Transportation
   • Agriculture

   b) Briefly explain ONE example of how that technology or development affected American society by the early 20th century.

   c) Briefly explain ONE example of how American society remained the same, despite the changes brought by the new technology or development.

LONG ESSAY For the question below, develop a thoughtful and thorough historical argument that answers the question. Begin your essay with a thesis statement and support it with relevant historical evidence.

5. Evaluate the extent to which technological advancements and mass consumerism contributed to maintaining continuity as well as fostering change in American Identity during the first three decades of the 20th century.

23 | THE GREAT DEPRESSION

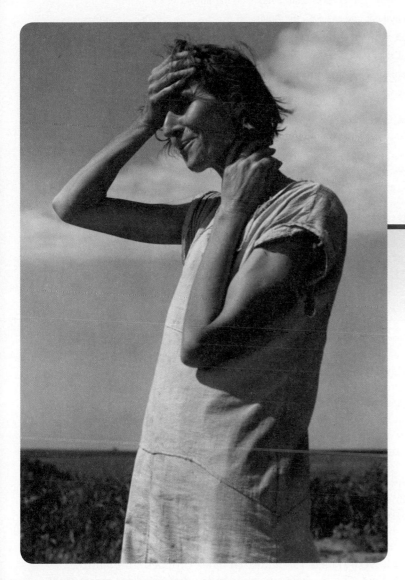

***WOMAN OF THE HIGH PLAINS "IF YOU DIE,
YOU'RE DEAD—THAT'S ALL"*** This poignant
photograph, taken by Dorothea Lange (1895–1965) in
1938, shows a plains woman, Nettie Featherston, enduring
one of the great natural disasters in U.S. history: the Dust
Bowl of the 1930s. Featherston, a migrant laborer's wife
and mother of three, lived in the draught-ridden Texas
Panhandle. Her despair could not be more evident.
(© New York Public Library, USA/Bridgeman Images)

AP
HISTORICAL THINKING

1. **Historical Causation** Analyze the causes of the Great
   Depression.

2. **Patterns of Continuity and Change over Time** To what
   degree and in what ways did the Great Depression change
   the lives of farmers, minorities, and women?

3. **Historical Causation** Analyze the causes and the impact of
   the collapse of the banking system on the Great Depression.

4. **Comparison** Analyze the degree to which Hoover broke
   with traditional views of government response to economic
   depression and the degree to which he maintained a
   traditional approach.

5. **Contextualization** Analyze the impact of the Great
   Depression on artistic expression.

Key Concept Correlations

Analyze the ways the historical developments you learn about in this chapter
connect to the following AP Key Concepts.

7.1 Governmental, political, and social organizations struggled to
address the effects of large-scale industrialization, economic uncertainty,
and related social changes such as urbanization and mass migration.

7.2 A revolution in communications and transportation technology
helped to create a new mass culture and spread "modern" values and
ideas, even as cultural conflicts between groups increased under the
pressure of migration, world wars, and economic distress.

Thematic Learning Objectives
PEO-3, 6; ID-7: WXT-3, 5, 6, 7, 8; POL-3; WOR-4, 7

AP CONNECTING CONCEPTS

CHAPTER 23 discusses the causes and effects of the Great Depression. Particularly, it focuses on the impact of economic depression on farmers, minorities, and women. The chapter examines in depth the domestic and international causes of the Great Depression. The chapter also focuses on the impact of the failure of the banking system and on the impact of unemployment and relief on the American psyche. The chapter also notes the growth of more radical politics as a result of poverty and depression. Some time is spent on an examination of cultural and literary reactions to the Great Depression. Finally, the chapter discusses the attempts by President Hoover to end the Great Depression and the unprecedented actions he took, many of which hurt his popularity. As you read, evaluate the following ideas:

- The Great Depression transformed the United States into a limited welfare state.
- New technology led to increased cultural and political conflict.
- Economic necessity drove many Americans to migrate during the Great Depression.

THE COMING OF THE GREAT DEPRESSION

The sudden economic decline that began in 1929 came as an especially severe shock because it followed so closely a period in which the New Era seemed to be performing another series of economic miracles.

THE GREAT CRASH

In February 1928, stock prices began a steady rise that continued, with only a few temporary lapses, for a year and a half. Between May 1928 and September 1929, the average price of stocks

STOCK MARKET BOOM

increased over 40 percent. The stocks of the major industrials–the stocks that are used to determine the Dow Jones Industrial Average–doubled in value in that same period. Trading mushroomed from 2 or 3 million shares a day to over 5 million and, at times, to as many as 10 or 12 million. A widespread speculative fever grew steadily more intense, particularly once brokerage firms began encouraging the mania by recklessly offering easy credit.

In the autumn of 1929, the great bull market began to fall apart. On October 21 and again on October 23, there were alarming declines in stock prices, in both cases followed by temporary recoveries (the second of them engineered by J. P. Morgan and Company and other big bankers,

"BLACK TUESDAY"

who conspicuously bought up stocks to restore public confidence). But on October 29, "Black Tuesday," all efforts to save the market failed. Sixteen million shares of stock were traded; the industrial index dropped 43 points; stocks in many companies became worthless. The market remained deeply depressed for more than four years.

Many people believed that the stock market crash was the beginning, and even the cause, of the Great Depression. But although October 1929 might have been the first visible sign of the crisis, the Depression had earlier beginnings and more important causes.

CAUSES OF THE DEPRESSION

Economists, historians, and others have argued for decades about the causes of the Great Depression without reaching any consensus. (See "Debating the Past," pp. 642-643.) But most agree on several things. They agree, first, that what is remarkable about the crisis is not that it occurred; periodic recessions are a normal feature of capitalist economies. What is remarkable is that it was so severe and that it lasted so long. The important question, therefore, is not so much why there was a depression, but why it was such a bad one. Most observers agree, too, that a number of different

AFTERMATH OF THE CRASH Walter Thornton, shown here in October 1929 next to an expensive roadster he had bought not long before, was one of the affluent Americans who suffered substantial losses in the crash of the stock market in the fall of 1929. In popular mythology, many such people committed suicide in despair. In reality, very few people did. Much more common were efforts such as this to sell off assets to make up for the losses. Thornton was more fortunate than many victims of the Depression. Most had few assets to sell. (© Bettmann/Corbis)

LACK OF DIVERSIFICATION

factors account for the severity of the crisis, even if there is considerable disagreement about which was the most important.

One of those factors was a lack of diversification in the American economy in the 1920s. Prosperity had depended excessively on a few basic industries, notably construction and automobiles. In the late 1920s, those industries began to decline. Expenditures on construction fell from $11 billion to less than $9 billion between 1926 and 1929. Automobile sales fell by more than a third in the first nine months of 1929. Newer industries were emerging to take up the slack—among them petroleum, chemicals, plastics, and others oriented toward the expanding market for consumer goods—but had not yet developed enough strength to compensate for the decline in other sectors.

A second factor was the maldistribution of purchasing power and, as a result, a weakness in consumer demand, which was too small to create an adequate market for the goods the economy was producing. Even in 1929, after nearly a decade of economic growth, more than half the families in America lived on the edge of or below the minimum subsistence level—too poor to buy the goods the industrial economy was producing.

MALDISTRIBUTION OF WEALTH

Another major problem was the credit structure of the economy. Farmers were deeply in debt—their land mortgaged, crop prices too low to allow them to pay off what they owed. Small banks, especially those tied to the agricultural economy, were in constant trouble in the 1920s as their customers defaulted on loans; many of these small banks failed. Large banks were in trouble, too. Although most

THE UNEMPLOYED, 1930 Thousands of unemployed men wait to be fed outside the Municipal Lodgers House in New York City. (The Library of Congress)

CAUSES OF THE GREAT DEPRESSION

WHAT were the causes of the Great Depression? Economists and historians have debated this question since the economic collapse began and still have not reached anything close to agreement on an answer to it. In the process, however, they have produced several very different theories about how a modern economy works.

During the Depression itself, different groups offered interpretations of the crisis that fit comfortably with their own self-interests. Some corporate leaders claimed that the Depression was the result of a lack of "business confidence," that businessmen were reluctant to invest because they feared government regulation and high taxes. The Hoover administration, unable to solve the crisis with the tools it considered acceptable, blamed international economic forces and sought, therefore, to stabilize world currencies and debt structures. New Dealers, determined to find a domestic solution to the crisis and ideologically inclined to place limits on corporate power, argued that the Depression was a crisis of "underconsumption"—that low wages and high prices had made it too difficult to buy the products of the industrial economy—and that a lack of demand had led to the economic collapse.

Scholars in the years since the Great Depression have also created interpretations that fit their views of how the economy works. One of the first important postwar interpretations came from the economists Milton Friedman and Anna Schwartz, in their *Monetary History of the United States* (1963). In a chapter titled "The Great Contraction," they argued for what has become known as the "monetary" interpretation. The Depression, they claimed, was a result of a drastic contraction of the currency (a result largely of mistaken decisions by the Federal Reserve Board, which raised interest rates when it should have lowered them). These deflationary measures, Friedman and Schwartz argue, turned an ordinary recession into the Great Depression. Friedman, in particular, advocated for many years that sound monetary policy is the best way to solve economic problems—as opposed to fiscal policies, such as taxation and spending.

A second, very different argument, known as the "spending" interpretation, is identified with, among others, the economist Peter Temin and his book *Did Monetary Forces Cause the Great Depression?* (1976). Temin's answer to his own question is "no." The cause of the crisis was not monetary contraction (although the contraction made it worse), but a drop in investment and consumer spending, which preceded the decline in the money supply and helped to cause it. Here again, there are obvious political implications. If a decline in spending was the cause of the Depression, then the proper response was an effort to stimulate demand—raising government spending, increasing purchasing power, redistributing wealth. According to this theory, the New Deal never ended the Depression because it did not spend enough. World War II did end it because it pumped so much public money into the economy. This is a liberal, Keynesian explanation, just as the "monetary hypothesis" is a conservative explanation.

In *The Great Depression* (1987), the economic historian Michael Bernstein avoids trying to explain why the economic downturn occurred and asks, instead, why it lasted so long. The reason the recession of 1929

American bankers were very conservative, some of the nation's biggest banks were investing recklessly in the stock market or making unwise loans. When the stock market crashed, many of these banks suffered losses greater than they could absorb.

A fourth factor contributing to the coming of the Depression was America's position in international trade. Late in the

DECLINING EXPORTS 1920s, European demand for American goods began to decline. That was partly because of high American tariffs, partly because European industry and agriculture were becoming more productive, and partly because some European nations (most notably Germany, under the Weimar Republic) were having financial difficulties and could not afford to buy goods from overseas. But it was also because the European economy was being destabilized by, a fifth factor contributing to the Depression, the international debt structure that had emerged in the aftermath of World War I.

When the war ended in 1918, all the European nations that had been allied with the United States owed large sums of money to American banks, sums much too large to be repaid out of their shattered economies. That was one reason the

UNSTABLE INTERNATIONAL DEBT STRUCTURE Allies had insisted (over Woodrow Wilson's objections) on reparation payments from Germany and Austria. Reparations, they believed, would provide them with a way to pay off their own debts. But Germany and Austria were themselves in economic trouble after the war; they were no more able to pay the reparations than the Allies were able to pay their debts.

The U.S. government refused to forgive or reduce the debts. Instead, American banks began making large loans to European governments, with which they paid off their earlier loans. Thus debts (and reparations) were being paid only by piling up new and greater debts. In the late 1920s, particularly after the American economy began to weaken in 1929, the European nations found it much more difficult to borrow money from the United States. At the same time, high American protective tariffs were making it difficult for them to sell their goods in American markets. Without any source of foreign exchange with which to repay their loans, they began to default. The collapse of the international credit structure was one of the reasons the Depression spread to Europe (and grew much worse in America) after 1931. (See "America in the World," pp. 644–645.)

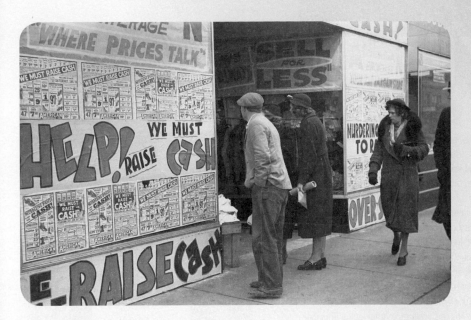

SHOP WINDOW Arthur Rothstein, one of the most significant photographers of the Great Depression, photographed this shop window in West Frankfort, Illinois, in 1939. The windows are plastered with signs pleading for customers to help them by purchasing their goods. (© The Granger Collection, New York)

after the war. This is, in other words, an explanation of the Depression that seems to support some of the economic ideas that became popular in the 1970s and 1980s calling for a more direct government role in stimulating the growth of new industries. Other explanations include the rise of protectionism (increased by the ill-advised Smoot-Hawley Tariff of 1931, which stifled international trade); the weakness of the banking system; the reckless credit policies of the 1920s; and many others.

In the end, however, no single explanation of the Great Depression has ever seemed adequate to most scholars. The event, the economist Robert Lucas once argued, is simply "inexplicable" by any rational calculation. ●

HISTORICAL ARGUMENTATION AND INTERPRETATION

Questions assume cumulative content knowledge from this chapter and previous chapters.

1. Explain the respective arguments made by three different groups during the Great Depression for the causes of the depression. How were these groups affected by their self-interests or values?
2. Explain two historians' views on how the economy works and how this influenced their interpretations of the causes of the Great Depression.
3. With which historical argument do you most agree? Explain why, supporting your argument with historical evidence.

became the Depression of the 1930s, he argues, was the timing of the collapse. The recession began as an ordinary cyclical downturn. Had it begun a few years earlier, the basic strength of the automobile and construction industries in the 1920s would have led to a reasonably speedy recovery. Had it begun a few years later, a group of newer, emerging industries would have helped produce a recovery in a reasonably short time. But the recession began in 1929, too late for the automobile and construction industries to help and too soon for emerging new industries to help, since they were still in their infancies. One of the reasons World War II was so important to the long-term recovery of the U.S. economy, Bernstein's argument suggests, was not just that it pumped money into the economy, but that much of that money contributed to developing new industries that would help sustain prosperity

PROGRESS OF THE DEPRESSION

The stock market crash of 1929 did not so much cause the Depression, then, as help trigger a chain of events that exposed long-standing weaknesses in the American economy. During the next three years, the crisis steadily worsened.

A collapse of much of the banking system followed the stock market crash. More than 9,000 American banks either went bankrupt or closed their doors to avoid bankruptcy between 1930 and 1933. Depositors lost over $2.5 billion in deposits. Partly as a result of these banking closures, the total money supply of the nation fell by more than a third between 1930 and 1933. The declining money supply meant a decline in purchasing power, and thus deflation. Manufacturers and merchants began reducing prices, cutting back on production, and laying off workers. Some economists argue that a severe depression could have been avoided if the Federal Reserve system had acted more responsibly. But the members of the Federal Reserve Board, concerned about protecting its own solvency in a dangerous economic environment, raised interest rates in 1931, which contracted the money supply even further.

BANKING COLLAPSE

The American gross national product plummeted from more than $104 billion in 1929 to $76.4 billion in 1932—a 25 percent decline in three years. In 1929, Americans had spent $16.2 billion in capital investment; in 1933, they invested only a third of a billion. The consumer price index declined 25 percent between 1929 and 1933, the wholesale price index 32 percent. Gross farm income dropped from $12 billion to $5 billion in four years.

SEVERE CONTRACTION

THE AMERICAN PEOPLE IN HARD TIMES

Someone asked the British economist John Maynard Keynes in the 1930s whether he was aware of any historical era comparable to the Great Depression. "Yes," Keynes replied. "It was called the Dark Ages, and it lasted 400 years." The Depression did not, of course, last 400 years, but it did bring unprecedented despair to the economies of the United States and much of the Western world. And it had far-reaching effects on American society and culture.

THE GLOBAL DEPRESSION WOR-3

THE Great Depression began in the United States, but it did not end there. The collapse of the American economy—the largest in the world—sent shock waves around the globe. By 1931, the American depression had become a world depression.

The origins of the worldwide depression lay in the pattern of debts that had emerged during and after World War I, when the United States loaned billions of dollars to European nations. In 1931, large banks in New York began calling in their loans from Germany and Austria. That precipitated the failure of one of Austria's largest banks, which in turn created panic through much of central Europe. The economic collapse in Germany and Austria meant that those nations could not continue paying reparations to Britain and France (required by the Treaty of Versailles of 1919), which meant in turn that Britain and France could not continue paying off their loans to the United States.

This spreading financial crisis was accompanied by a dramatic contraction of international trade, precipitated in part by the Smoot-Hawley Tariff in the United States, which established the highest import duties in history and stifled much global commerce. Depressed agricultural prices—a result of worldwide overproduction—also contributed to the downturn. By 1932, worldwide industrial production had declined by more than a third, and world trade had plummeted by nearly two-thirds. By 1933, thirty million people in industrial nations were unemployed, five times the number four years before.

But the Depression was not confined to industrial nations. Imperialism and industrialization drew almost all regions of the world into the international industrial economy. Colonies and nations in Africa, Asia, and South America—critically dependent on exporting raw materials and agricultural goods to industrial countries—experienced a decline in demand for their products, which led to rising levels of poverty and unemployment. Some nations—among them the Soviet Union and China—remained unconnected to the global economy and suffered relatively little from the Great Depression. But in most parts of the world, the Depression caused tremendous social and economic hardship.

It also created political turmoil. Among the countries hardest hit by the Depression was Germany, where industrial production had declined by 50 percent and unemployment reached 35 percent in the early 1930s. The desperate economic conditions there contributed greatly to the rise of the Nazi Party and its leader, Adolf Hitler, who became chancellor in 1932. Japan suffered greatly as well, and as in Germany, Japan's economic troubles produced political turmoil and aided the rise of a new militaristic regime. In Italy, the fascist government of Benito Mussolini, which had first taken power in

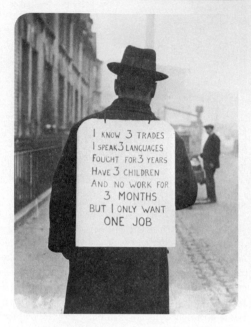

LOOKING FOR WORK IN LONDON, 1935 An unemployed London man wears a sign that seems designed to convince passersby that he is an educated, respectable person despite his present circumstances. (© Hulton Archive/Getty Images)

the 1920s, also saw militarization and territorial expansion as a way out of economic difficulties.

In other nations, governments sought solutions to the Depression through reform of their domestic economies. Among the most common responses to the

UNEMPLOYMENT AND RELIEF

In the industrial Northeast and Midwest, cities were becoming paralyzed by unemployment. Cleveland, Ohio, in 1932 had an unemployment rate of roughly 50 percent; Akron, 60 percent; Toledo, 80 percent. Many industrial workers were accustomed to periods of unemployment, but no one was prepared for the scale and duration of the joblessness of the 1930s.

Most Americans had been taught to believe that every individual was responsible for his or her own fate, that unemployment and poverty were signs of personal failure. Many adult men, in particular, felt deeply ashamed of their joblessness; the helplessness of unemployment was a challenge to traditional notions of masculinity. Unemployed workers walked through the streets day after day looking for jobs that did not exist.

BELIEF IN PERSONAL RESPONSIBILITY

An increasing number of families were turning to state and local public relief systems, just to be able to eat. But those systems, which in the 1920s had served only a small number of indigent persons, were unequipped to handle the new demands. In many places, relief simply collapsed. Private charities attempted to supplement the public relief efforts, but the problem was far beyond their capabilities as well. State governments felt pressure to expand their own assistance to the unemployed; but tax revenues were declining along with everything else, and state leaders balked at placing additional strains on already tight budgets. Moreover, many public officials believed that an extensive welfare system would undermine the moral fiber of its clients.

Breadlines stretched for blocks outside Red Cross and Salvation Army kitchens. Thousands of people sifted through garbage cans for scraps of food or waited outside restaurant kitchens in hopes of receiving plate scrapings. Nearly 2 million

Depression around the world was substantial government investment in public works. The United States, Britain, France, Germany, Italy, the Soviet Union, and other countries made substantial investments in roads, bridges, dams, public buildings, and other large projects. All the industrial countries of the world also experimented with some form of government-funded relief for the unemployed, often borrowing ideas from one another in the process.

Furthermore, because classical models of economic behavior seemed unable to explain, or provide solutions to, the crisis, the Depression helped create new approaches to economics. The great British economist John Maynard Keynes revolutionized economic thought in much of the world. His 1936 book, *The General Theory of Employment, Interest, and Money*, despite its bland title, created a sensation by arguing that the Depression was a result not of declining production but, rather, of inadequate consumer demand. Governments, he said, could stimulate their economies by increasing the money supply and creating investment—through a combination of lowering interest rates and public spending. Keynesianism, as Keynes's theories became known, began to have an impact in the United States in 1938, and in much of the rest of the world in subsequent years.

The Great Depression was an important turning point not only in American history, but in the history of the twentieth-century world as well. It transformed ideas of public policy and economics in many nations. It toppled old regimes and created new ones. Above all, it was a major factor—maybe the single most important factor—in the coming of World War II. ●

UNDERSTAND, ANALYZE, AND EVALUATE

1. How did the 1919 Treaty of Versailles and the Hawley-Smoot Tariff contribute to the global depression of the 1930s?
2. How did the governments of European nations respond to the depression?
3. What effect did the global depression have on economic theory? Why was Keynes's economic theory so revolutionary?

men, most of them young (and a much smaller number of women), took to the roads, riding freight trains from city to city, living as nomads.

Farm income declined by 60 percent between 1929 and 1932. A third of all American farmers lost their land. In addition, a large area of agricultural settlement in the Great Plains of the South and West was suffering from a catastrophic **"DUST BOWL"** natural disaster: one of the worst droughts in the history of the nation. Beginning in 1930, a large area of the nation, stretching north from Texas into the Dakotas, came to be known as the "Dust Bowl." It began to experience a steady decline in rainfall and an accompanying increase in heat. The drought continued for a decade, turning what had once been fertile farm regions into deserts. In Kansas, the soil in some places was without moisture as far as three feet below the surface. In Nebraska, Iowa, and other affected states, summer temperatures were averaging over

100 degrees. Swarms of grasshoppers were moving from region to region, devouring what meager crops farmers were able to raise, often even devouring fenceposts or clothes hanging out to dry. Great dust storms–called "black blizzards"–swept across the plains, blotting out the sun and suffocating livestock as well as people unfortunate or foolish enough to stay outside.

Even with these disastrous conditions, the farm economy continued through the 1930s to produce far more food than American consumers could afford to buy. Farm prices fell so low that few growers made any profit on their crops. As a result, many farmers, like many urban unemployed, left their homes in search of work. In the South, in particular, many dispossessed farmers–black and white–wandered from town to town, hoping to find jobs or handouts. Hundreds of thou-**"OKIES"** sands of families from the Dust Bowl (often known as "Okies," since many came from Oklahoma) traveled to California and other states, where they found conditions little better than those they had left. Many worked as agricultural migrants, traveling from farm to farm picking fruit and other crops at starvation wages.

Throughout the nation, problems resulting from malnutrition and homelessness grew at an alarming rate. Hospitals pointed to a striking increase in deaths from starvation. On the outskirts of cities, families lived in makeshift shacks constructed of flattened tin cans, scraps of wood, abandoned crates, and other debris. Many homeless Americans simply kept moving–sleeping in freight cars, city parks, subways, or unused sewer ducts.

AFRICAN AMERICANS AND THE DEPRESSION

As the Depression began, over half of all black Americans still lived in the South. Most were farmers. The collapse of prices for cotton and other staple crops left some with no income. Many **AFRICAN AMERICAN SUFFERING** left the land altogether–either by choice or forced by landlords who no longer found the sharecropping system profitable. Some migrated to southern cities. But unemployed whites in the urban South believed they had first claim to all work and began to take positions as janitors, street cleaners, and domestic servants, displacing the African Americans who formerly had occupied such jobs.

As the Depression deepened, whites in many southern cities began to demand that all blacks be dismissed from their jobs. In Atlanta in 1930, an organization calling itself the Black Shirts organized a campaign with the slogan "No Jobs for Niggers Until Every White Man Has a Job!" In other areas, whites used intimidation and violence to drive blacks from jobs. By 1932, over half the African Americans in the South were without employment. And what limited relief there was went almost invariably to whites first.

Unsurprisingly, therefore, many black southerners–perhaps 400,000–left the South in the 1930s and journeyed to the cities of the North. There they generally found less blatant discrimination. But conditions were little better than in the South. In New York, and in many other cities, black unemployment

MIGRANT FAMILY Dorothea Lange, one of the great photographers of the Depression era, worked in the 1930s for the photographic division of the Farm Security Administration (FSA). The FSA photographers sought to record the conditions of life in America's troubled agrarian world during the Great Depression in the hopes of stimulating reform. Lange's photograph here represents a family in transit as they, like thousands of others, moved from the Great Plains to California. (Photo by Dorothea Lange/© Time & Life Pictures/Getty Images)

associated with the Communist Party, came to the aid of the accused youths and began to publicize the case. Later, the National Association for the Advancement of Colored People (NAACP) provided assistance as well. The trials continued throughout the 1930s. Although the white southern juries who sat on the case never acquitted any of the defendants, all of them eventually gained their freedom–four because the charges were dropped, four because of early paroles, and one because he escaped. But the last of the Scottsboro defendants did not leave prison until 1950.

The Depression was a time of important changes in the role and behavior of leading black organizations. The NAACP, for example, began to work diligently to win a position for blacks within
the emerging labor movement, supporting the formation of the Congress of Industrial Organizations and helping to break down racial barriers within labor unions. Walter White, secretary of the NAACP, once made a personal appearance at an auto plant to implore African Americans not to work as strikebreakers. Partly as a result of such efforts, more than half a million blacks were able to join the labor movement. In the Steelworkers Union, for example, African Americans constituted about 20 percent of the membership.

NAACP's CHANGING ROLE

MEXICAN AMERICANS IN DEPRESSION AMERICA

Similar patterns of discrimination confronted the large and growing population of Mexicans and Mexican Americans, which numbered approximately 2 million in the 1930s.

Mexican Americans filled many of the same menial jobs in the West and elsewhere that African Americans filled in other regions. Some farmed small, marginal tracts. Some became agricultural migrants, traveling from region to region harvesting fruit, lettuce, and other crops. But most lived in urban areas–in California, New Mexico, and Arizona, but also in Detroit, Chicago, New York, and other eastern industrial cities–and occupied the lower ranks of the unskilled labor force in such industries as steel, automobiles, and meatpacking.

As in the South, unemployed white Anglos in the Southwest demanded jobs held by Hispanics. Thus Mexican unemployment rose quickly to levels far higher than those for Anglos. Some Mexicans were, in effect, forced to leave the country by officials who arbitrarily removed them from relief rolls or simply rounded them up and transported them across the border. Perhaps half a million Chicanos left the United States for Mexico in the first years of the Depression. Most relief programs excluded Mexicans from their rolls or

DISCRIMINATION AGAINST HISPANICS

was 50 percent or more. In other cities, it was higher. Two million African Americans were on some form of relief by 1932.

Traditional patterns of segregation and disenfranchisement in the South survived the Depression largely unchallenged. But a few particularly notorious examples of racism did attract national attention. The most celebrated was the Scottsboro case. In March 1931, nine black teenagers were taken off a freight train in Alabama (in a small town near Scottsboro) and arrested for vagrancy and disorder. Later, two white women who had also been riding the train accused them of rape. In fact, there was overwhelming evidence, medical and otherwise, that the women had not been raped– that they may have made their accusations out of fear of being arrested themselves. Nevertheless, an all-white jury in Alabama quickly convicted all nine of the "Scottsboro boys" (as they were known to both friends and foes) and sentenced eight of them to death.

The Supreme Court overturned the convictions in 1932, and a series of new trials began that attracted increasing national attention. The International Labor Defense, an organization

SCOTTSBORO CASE

DUST STORM, SOUTHWEST PLAINS, 1937 The dust storms of the 1930s were a terrifying experience for all who lived through them. Resembling a black wall sweeping in from the western horizon, such a storm engulfed farms and towns alike, blotting out the light of the sun and covering everything with fine dirt. (© Bettmann/Corbis)

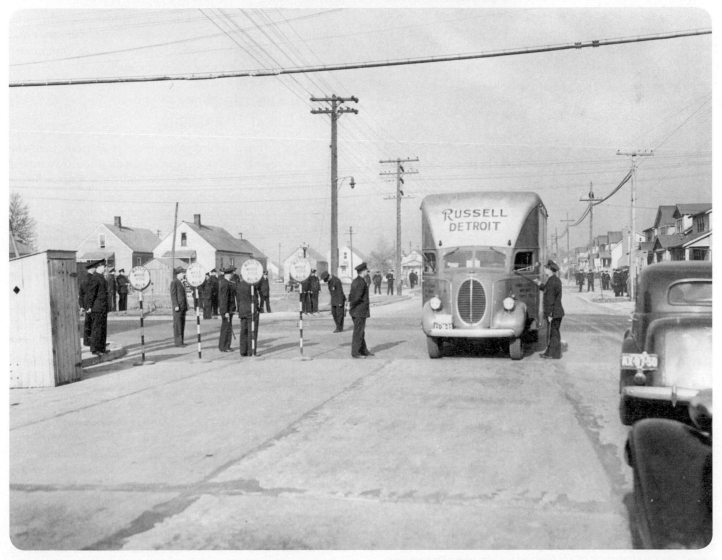

BLACK MIGRANTS The Great Migration of African Americans from the rural South into the cities had begun before World War I. But in the 1930s and 1940s the movement accelerated. Northerners were not always so welcoming. Here, vans move African Americans to the federal Sojourner Truth Housing Project in Detroit under the guard of Michigan state troopers and police. (© The Granger Collection, New York)

offered them benefits far below those available to whites. Latinos generally had no access to American schools. Many hospitals refused them admission.

Occasionally, there were signs of organized resistance by Mexican Americans themselves, most notably in California, where some formed a union of migrant farmworkers. But harsh repression by local growers and the public authorities allied with them prevented such organizations from having much impact. Like African American farmworkers, many Mexicans began as a result to migrate to cities such as Los Angeles, where they lived in a poverty comparable to that of urban blacks in the South and Northeast.

ASIAN AMERICANS IN HARD TIMES

For Asian Americans, too, the Depression reinforced long-standing patterns of discrimination and economic marginalization. In California, where the largest Japanese American and Chinese American populations resided, even educated Asians had always found it difficult, if not impossible, to move into mainstream professions. Japanese American college graduates often found themselves working at family fruit stands; 20 percent of

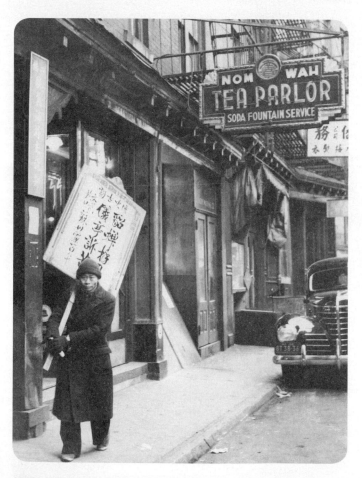

CHINATOWN, NEW YORK A Chinese man carries a "sandwich board" through the streets of New York's Chinatown bearing the latest news of the war between China and Japan, which in 1938 was already well under way. Chinese Americans had the dual challenge in the 1930s of dealing both with large-scale unemployment and with continuing news of catastrophe from China, where most still had many family members. (© Hulton Archive/Getty Images)

all Japanese Americans in Los Angeles worked at such stands at the end of the 1930s. For those who found jobs (usually poorly paid) in the industrial or service economy, employment was precarious; like blacks and Hispanics, they often lost jobs to white Americans desperate for work that a few years earlier they would not have considered. Japanese farmworkers, like Chicano farmworkers, suffered from the increasing competition for even these low-paying jobs from white migrants from the Great Plains.

In California, younger men and women organized Japanese American Democratic Clubs in several cities, which worked for,

JAPANESE AMERICAN CITIZENS LEAGUE among other things, laws protecting racial and ethnic minorities from discrimination. At the same time, some Japanese American businessmen and professionals tried to overcome obstacles by encouraging other Japanese to become more assimilated, more "American." They formed the Japanese American Citizens League in 1930 to promote their goals. By 1940, it had nearly 6,000 members.

Chinese Americans fared no better. The overwhelming majority continued to work in Chinese-owned laundries and restaurants. Those who moved outside the Asian community could rarely find jobs above the entry level.

WOMEN AND THE WORKPLACE IN THE GREAT DEPRESSION

The economic crisis served in many ways to strengthen the widespread belief that a woman's proper place was in the

POPULAR DISAPPROVAL OF WOMEN'S EMPLOYMENT home. Most men and many women believed that what work there was should go to men. Many people believed that no woman whose husband was employed should accept a job.

But the widespread assumption that married women, at least, should not work outside the home did not stop them from doing so. Both single and married

INCREASED FEMALE EMPLOYMENT women worked in the 1930s, despite public condemnation of the practice, because they or their families needed the money. In fact, the largest new group of female workers consisted of wives and mothers. By the end of the Depression, 20 percent more women were working than had been doing so at the beginning.

The increase occurred despite considerable obstacles. Professional opportunities for women declined because unemployed men began moving into professions, such as teaching and social work, that had previously been considered women's fields. Female industrial workers were more likely to be laid off or to experience wage reductions than their male counterparts. But white women also had certain advantages in the workplace. The nonprofessional jobs that women traditionally held—as salesclerks and stenographers, and in other service positions—were less likely to disappear than the predominantly male jobs in heavy industry. Nor were many men, even unemployed men, likely to ask for such jobs.

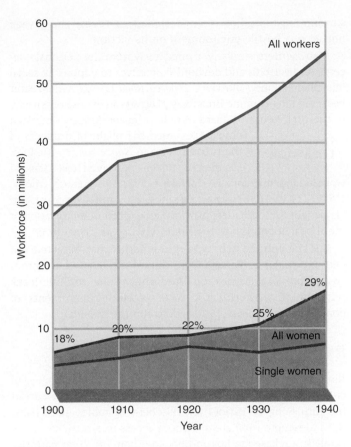

WOMEN IN THE PAID WORKFORCE, 1900–1940 The participation of women in the paid workforce increased slowly but steadily in the first forty years of the twentieth century. Note, however, the general leveling off of the participation of single women—who traditionally accounted for the vast majority of women workers—after 1920, at the same time that the total number of women in the paid workforce was rising. Many more married women began entering the paid workforce in these years, particularly in the 1930s.

• *Why did so many married women begin doing paid work during the Great Depression?*

Black women suffered massive unemployment because of a great reduction of domestic service jobs. As many as half of all black working women lost their jobs in the 1930s. Even so, at the end of the 1930s, 38 percent of black women were employed, as compared to 24 percent of white women. That was because black women—both married and unmarried—had always been more likely to work than white women, less out of preference than out of economic necessity.

For American feminists, the Depression years were, on the whole, a time of frustration. Although economic pressures pushed more women into the workforce, those same pressures helped to erode the frail support that feminists had won in the 1920s for the idea of women becoming economically and professionally independent.

DEPRESSION FAMILIES

The economic hardships of the Depression years placed great strains on American families, many of whom had become accustomed in the 1920s to a steadily rising standard of living but now found themselves plunged suddenly into uncertainty.

Such circumstances forced many families to retreat from the consumer patterns they had developed in the 1920s. Women often returned to sewing clothes for themselves and

RETREAT FROM CONSUMERISM their families and to preserving their own food rather than buying such products in stores. Others engaged in home businesses—taking in laundry, selling baked goods, accepting boarders. Many households expanded to include distant relatives. Parents often moved in with their children and grandparents with their grandchildren, or vice versa.

But the Depression also eroded the strength of many family units. There was a decline in the divorce rate, but largely because divorce was now too expensive for some. More common was the informal breakup of families, particularly the desertion of families by unemployed men bent on escaping the humiliation of being unable to earn a living. The marriage and birth rates declined simultaneously for the first time since the early nineteenth century.

THE DEPRESSION AND AMERICAN CULTURE

The Great Depression was a traumatic experience for millions of Americans, and it shook the confidence of many people in themselves or in their nation or both. Out of the crisis emerged some of the most probing criticisms of American society and the American economic system of the industrial age. At the same time, the Depression produced powerful confirmations of traditional values and reinforced many traditional goals. There was not one Depression culture, but many.

DEPRESSION VALUES

American social values seemed to change relatively little in response to the Depression. Instead, many people responded to hard times by redoubling their commitment to familiar ideas and goals. The sociologists Robert Lynd and Helen Merrell Lynd, who had published a celebrated study of Muncie, Indiana, *Middletown*, in 1929, returned there in the mid-1930s to see how the city had changed. They concluded in their 1937 book, *Middletown in Transition*, that in most respects "the texture of Middletown's culture has not changed. . . . Middletown is overwhelmingly living by the values by which it lived in 1925." Above all, the men and women of "Middletown"—and by implication many other Americans—remained committed to the traditional American emphasis on the individual.

In some respects, the economic crisis worked to undermine the traditional "success ethic" in America.

PERSISTENCE OF THE "SUCCESS ETHIC" Many people began to look to government for assistance; many blamed corporate moguls, international bankers, "economic royalists," and others for their distress. Yet the Depression did not, in the end, seriously erode the success ethic.

Some victims of the Depression expressed anger and struck out at the economic system. Many, however, seemed to blame themselves. Nothing so surprised foreign observers of America in the 1930s as the apparent passivity of **SELF-BLAME** the unemployed, many of whom were so ashamed of their joblessness that they refused to leave their homes.

At the same time, millions of people responded eagerly to reassurances that they could, through their own efforts, restore themselves to prosperity and success. The writer and lecturer Dale Carnegie's self-help manual *How to Win Friends and Influence People* (1936) was one of the best-selling books of the decade. Carnegie's message was not only that personal initiative was the route to success; it was also that the best way for people to get ahead was to fit in and make other people feel important.

ARTISTS AND INTELLECTUALS IN THE GREAT DEPRESSION

Just as many progressives had become alarmed when, early in the twentieth century, they "discovered" the existence of **"DISCOVERY" OF RURAL POVERTY** widespread poverty in the cities, so many Americans were shocked during the 1930s at their discovery of debilitating rural poverty. Among those who were most effective in conveying the dimensions of this poverty was a group of documentary photographers, many of them employed by the federal Farm Security Administration in the late 1930s, who traveled through the South recording the nature of agricultural life. Roy Stryker, Walker Evans, Arthur Rothstein, Ben Shahn, Margaret Bourke-White, Dorothea Lange, and others produced memorable studies of farm families and their surroundings, studies often designed to reveal the savage impact of a hostile environment on its victims.

Many writers, similarly, turned away from the personal concerns of the 1920s and devoted themselves to exposés of social injustice. Erskine Caldwell's *Tobacco Road* (1932), which later became a long-running Broadway play, was an exposé of poverty in the rural South. Richard Wright, a major African American **DEPRESSION LITERATURE** novelist, exposed the plight of residents of the urban ghetto in *Native Son* (1940). John Steinbeck's novels portrayed the trials of workers and migrants in California. John Dos Passos's trilogy, *U.S.A.* (1930–1936), attacked modern capitalism outright. Playwright Clifford Odets provided an explicit demonstration of the appeal of political radicalism in *Waiting for Lefty* (1935).

But the cultural products of the 1930s that attracted the widest popular audiences were those that diverted attention away from the Depression. And they came to Americans primarily through the two most powerful instruments of popular culture in the 1930s–radio and the movies.

RADIO

Almost every American family had a radio in the 1930s. In cities and towns, radio consoles were now as familiar a part of the furnishing of parlors and kitchens as tables and chairs. Even in remote rural areas without access to electricity, many families purchased radios and hooked them up to car batteries when they wished to listen.

Unlike in later times, radio in the 1930s was often a community experience. Young people would place radios on their front porches and invite friends over to sit, talk, or dance. In poor urban neighborhoods, many people who could not afford

A RADIO PLAY Among the most popular entertainments of the 1930s were live readings of plays over the radio—many of them mysteries or romances written specifically for the new medium. Here, a group of actors performs a radio comedy over WNBC in New York City in the early 1930s. The actors (from left to right) are Jack Benny, George Murphy, Jean Cranford, and Reginald Gardiner. (© Hulton Archive/Getty Images)

A NIGHT AT THE OPERA The antic comedy of the Marx Brothers provided a popular and welcome escape from the rigors of the Great Depression. The Marx Brothers, shown here in a poster for one of their most famous films, effectively lampooned dilemmas that many Americans faced in their ceaseless, and usually unsuccessful, efforts to find an easy route to wealth and comfort. (© Everett Collection)

other kinds of social activities would gather on a street or in a backyard to listen to sporting events or concerts. Within families, the radio often drew parents and children together in the evening to listen to favorite programs.

What did Americans hear on the radio? Although radio stations occasionally carried socially and politically provocative

ESCAPIST PROGRAMMING

programs, the staple of broadcasting was escapism: comedies such as *Amos 'n Andy* (with its humorous, if demeaning, picture of urban blacks); adventures such as *Superman, Dick Tracy*, and *The Lone Ranger;* and other entertainment programs. Radio brought a new kind of comedy—previously limited to vaudeville or to ethnic theaters—to a wide audience. Jack Benny, George Burns and Gracie Allen, and other masters of elaborately timed jokes and repartee began to develop broad followings (that they would later take with them to television).

Soap operas, also later to become staples of television programming, were enormously popular on radio in the 1930s, especially with women who were alone in the house during the day. (That was one reason they became known as soap operas; soap companies—whose advertising was targeted at women—generally sponsored them.)

Almost invariably, radio programs were broadcast live; and as a result, radio spawned an enormous number of public performances. Radio comedies and dramas were often performed before audiences in theaters or studios. Band concerts were broadcast from dance halls, helping jazz and swing bands to achieve broad popularity. Classical music, too, was broadcast live from studios.

Radio provided Americans with their first direct access to important public events, and radio news and sports divisions grew rapidly to meet the demand. Some of the most dramatic

moments of the 1930s were a result of radio coverage of celebrated events: the World Series, major college football games, the Academy Awards, political

RADIO'S IMPACT

conventions, presidential inaugurations. When the German dirigible the *Hindenburg* crashed in flames in Lakehurst, New Jersey, in 1937 after a transatlantic voyage, it produced an enormous national reaction largely because of the live radio account by a broadcaster overcome with emotion who cried out, as he watched the terrible crash, "Oh the humanity! Oh the humanity!" The actor/director Orson Welles created another memorable event in 1938 when he broadcast "War of the Worlds," which created panic among millions of people who believed for a while that the fictional events it described were real. (See "Patterns of Popular Culture," pp. 696–697.)

Radio was important for the way it drew the nation together by creating the possibility of shared experiences and common access to culture and information. It was also significant for the way it helped reshape the social life of the nation, for the way it encouraged many families and individuals to center their lives more around the home than they had in the past.

MOVIES IN THE NEW ERA

Moviegoing would seem particularly vulnerable to hard times. Families struggling to pay the rent or buy food could easily decide to forgo an evening at the movies. In the first years of

CONTINUING POPULARITY OF MOVIES

the Depression, movie attendance did drop significantly. By the mid-1930s, however, most Americans had resumed their moviegoing habits—in part because movies were a less expensive entertainment option than many other possibilities, and in part because the movies themselves (all of them now with sound, and by the end of the decade many of them in color) were becoming more appealing.

In many ways, movies were as safely conventional in the 1930s as they had been in the late 1920s. Hollywood continued to exercise tight control over its products in the 1930s through its resilient censor Will Hays, who ensured that most movies carried no sensational or controversial messages. The studio system—through which a few large movie companies exercised iron control over actors, writers, and directors, and through which a few great moguls, such as Louis B. Mayer or Jack Warner, could single-handedly decide the fate of most projects—also worked to ensure that Hollywood films avoided controversy.

But neither the censor nor the studio system could (or wished to) prevent films from exploring social questions altogether. A few films, such as King Vidor's *Our Daily Bread* (1932) and John Ford's adaptation of John Steinbeck's novel *The Grapes of Wrath* (1940), did explore political themes. The director Frank Capra provided a muted social message in several of his comedies—*Mr. Deeds Goes to Town* (1936), *Mr. Smith Goes to Washington* (1939), and *Meet John Doe* (1941)—which

THE FILMS OF FRANK CAPRA

FRANK Capra is probably best remembered today for his last successful film, *It's a Wonderful Life* (1946), widely replayed every year at Christmas. In it, George Bailey, a kind and compassionate small-town savings-and-loan operator (played by Jimmy Stewart), is almost destroyed by a wealthy, greedy, and malicious banker. In despair and contemplating suicide, Bailey receives a visit from an angel who shows him what life in his community, Bedford Falls, would have been like had George never been born. After a few hours of wandering through a coarse, corrupt, degraded version of the town he knew, Bailey comes to understand the value of his own life. He returns to the real Bedford Falls to find that his family, friends, and neighbors have rallied together to rescue him from his financial difficulties and affirm his value to them, and theirs to him.

By the time *It's a Wonderful Life* appeared, Frank Capra had been the most famous and successful director in Hollywood for more than a decade. His films during those years had almost all been great commercial and critical successes. Capra's popularity was a result in part of his tremendous talent as a director. But it was also a result of his ideas. Most of his films expressed a vision of society, and of politics, that resonated clearly with the concerns of millions of Americans as they struggled through the years of the Great Depression.

Capra was born in 1897 in a small village in Sicily and moved with his family to America six years later. After working his way through college, he found a job in the still-young movie industry in California and eventually became a director of feature films. His great

MR. DEEDS GOES TO TOWN Gary Cooper, playing the newly wealthy Longfellow Deeds, leaves the friendly, virtuous small town of Mandrake Falls en route to New York to receive the fortune he has inherited. Capra's evocation of the warmth and generosity of Mandrake Falls was part of his effort to contrast the decent America of ordinary people with the grasping and corrupt America of the wealthy and the city. (© Columbia Pictures/Photofest)

PROMOTING CAPRA Capra was unusual among directors of the 1930s in having a distinct following of his own. Most films attempted to attract audiences by highlighting their stars. Capra films highlighted Capra himself. (© Columbia Pictures/Photofest)

celebrated the virtues of the small town and the decency of the common people in contrast to the selfish, corrupt values of the city and the urban rich. (See "Patterns of Popular Culture," pp. 652-653.) Gangster movies such as *Little Caesar* (1930) and *The Public Enemy* (1931) portrayed a dark, gritty, violent world with which few Americans were familiar, but their desperate stories were popular nevertheless with those engaged in their own difficult struggles.

More often, however, the commercial films of the 1930s were deliberately and explicitly escapist: lavish musicals such as *Gold Diggers of 1933* (whose theme song was "We're in the Money"), "screwball" comedies such as Capra's *It Happened One Night,* or the many films of the Marx Brothers–films designed to divert audiences from their troubles and, often, indulge their fantasies about quick and easy wealth.

The 1930s saw the beginning of Walt Disney's long reign as the champion of animation and children's entertainment. After producing cartoon shorts for theaters in the late 1920s–many of them starring the newly created character of Mickey Mouse, who made his debut

WALT DISNEY

ordinary man—played again by Gary Cooper—is manipulated by a fascist cartel to dupe the public on their behalf. He comes to his senses just in time and, by threatening suicide, rallies ordinary people to turn against the malign plans of the fascists. He then disappears into the night.

Capra was entirely conscious of the romantic populism that he brought to his films. He was intensely patriotic, and he believed fervently that America stood for individual opportunity and was defined by the decency of ordinary people. He did not like the term "masses" and found it "insulting, degrading." He saw the people, rather, as a "collection of free individuals . . . each an island of human dignity."

When America entered World War II, Capra collaborated with the government (and the Walt Disney studios) to make a series of films designed to explain to new soldiers what the war was about—a series known as *Why We Fight*. They contrasted the individualistic democracy of the American small town with the dark collectivism of the Nazis and Fascists. Capra poured into them all his skills as a filmmaker and all his romantic, patriotic images. *It's a Wonderful Life*, released a year after the war ended, continued his evocation of the decency of ordinary people.

In the decades that followed, Capra ceased to be an important force in American cinema. The sentimental populism and comic optimism that had been so appealing to audiences during the hard years of the Depression and the war gave way to a harder, more realistic style of filmmaking in the 1950s and 1960s; and Capra—a romantic to the end—was never fully able to adjust. But in a time of crisis, Capra had helped his audiences find solace in his romantic vision of the American past, and in the warmth and goodness of small towns and the decency of ordinary people. ●

FRANK CAPRA Frank Capra was one of the most famous and successful Hollywood movie directors of the 1930s and 1940s. His films evoked a romantic populism and patriotism during a time of great stress and deprivation. (© Moviepix/Getty Images)

breakthrough came in 1934 with *It Happened One Night*, a now-classic comedy that won five major Academy Awards, including best picture and best director. Over the next seven years, he built on that success by making a series of more-pointed films through which he established himself as a powerful voice of a comfortably populist vision of democracy and American life.

Capra made no secret of his romantic image of the small town and the common man, his distaste for cities, his contempt for opportunistic politicians, and his condemnation of what he considered the amoral (and often immoral) capitalist marketplace. In *Mr. Deeds Goes to Town* (1936), a simple man from a small town inherits a large fortune, moves to the city, and—not liking the greed and dishonesty he finds there—gives the money away and moves back home. In *Mr. Smith Goes to Washington* (1939), a decent man from a western state is elected to the U.S. Senate, refuses to join in the self-interested politics of Washington, and dramatically exposes the corruption and selfishness of his colleagues. (The rugged western actor Gary Cooper portrayed Mr. Deeds, and Jimmy Stewart played Mr. Smith.) In *Meet John Doe* (1941), released on the brink of American entry into World War II, an

UNDERSTAND, ANALYZE, AND EVALUATE

1. Why were Capra's films so popular with people suffering through the economic crisis of the Great Depression?
2. What social messages do Capra's films convey?
3. If Capra's style was considered dated after World War II, why has his film *It's a Wonderful Life* continued to be so popular?

in the 1928 cartoon *Steamboat Willie*–Disney began to produce feature-length animated films, starting in 1937 with *Snow White*. Other enormously popular films of the 1930s were adaptations of popular novels: *The Wizard of Oz* and *Gone with the Wind*, both released in 1939.

POPULAR LITERATURE AND JOURNALISM

The social and political strains of the Great Depression found voice much more successfully in print than they did on the

airwaves or the screen. Much literature and journalism in the 1930s dealt directly or indirectly with the tremendous disillusionment, and the increasing radicalism, of the era.

Not all literature, of course, was challenging or controversial. The most popular books and magazines of the time were as escapist and romantic as the most popular radio shows and movies. Two of the best-selling novels of the decade were romantic sagas set in earlier eras: Margaret Mitchell's *Gone with the Wind* (1936) and Hervey Allen's *Anthony Adverse* (1933). Leading magazines

LIFE MAGAZINE

focused more on fashions, stunts, scenery, and the arts than on the social conditions of the nation. The enormously popular new photographic journal *Life*, which began publication in 1936 and quickly became one of the most successful magazines in American history, had one of the largest readerships of any publication in the United States. It devoted some attention to politics and to the economic conditions of the Depression, more, in fact, than did many of its competitors. But it was best known for stunning photographs of sporting and theater events, natural landscapes, and impressive public projects. Its first cover was a striking photograph by Margaret Bourke-White of a New Deal hydroelectric project. One of its most popular features was "*Life* Goes to a Party," which took the chatty social columns of daily newspapers and turned them into glossy photographic glimpses of Americans having fun.

Other Depression writing, however, was frankly and openly challenging to the dominant values of American popular culture. In the first years of the Depression, some of the most significant literature offered corrosive portraits of the harshness and emptiness of American life: Nathanael West's *Miss Lonelyhearts* (1933), the story of an advice columnist overwhelmed by the sadness he encounters in the lives of those who consult him; Jack Conroy's *The Disinherited* (1933), a harsh portrait of the lives of coal miners; and James T. Farrell's *Studs Lonigan* (1932), a portrait of a lost, hardened working-class youth.

THE POPULAR FRONT AND THE LEFT

In the later 1930s, much of the political literature was a result of the rise of the Popular Front, a broad coalition of "antifascist" groups on the left, of which the most important was the American Communist Party. The party had long been a harsh and unrelenting critic of American capitalism and the government it claimed was controlled by it. But in 1935, under instructions from the Soviet Union, the party softened its attitude toward Franklin Roosevelt (whom Stalin considered a potential ally in the coming battle against Hitler) and formed loose alliances with many other "progressive" groups. The party began to praise the New Deal. It even supported John L. Lewis, a powerful (and strongly anticommunist) labor leader. The party adopted the slogan "Communism is twentieth-century Americanism." In its heyday, the Popular Front did much to enhance the reputation and influence of the Communist Party, whose formal membership grew to perhaps 100,000 in the mid-1930s, the highest it had ever been or would be again. But it also helped mobilize writers, artists, and intellectuals—many of them unconnected with (and many of them uninterested in) the Communist Party—behind a pattern of social criticism.

For some intellectuals, the Popular Front offered an escape from the lonely and difficult stance of detachment and alienation they had embraced in the 1920s. The Spanish Civil War was important to many American intellectuals, especially those on the left. It helped give meaning and purpose to individual lives. The war in Spain pitted the fascists of Francisco Franco

SPANISH CIVIL WAR

(who was receiving support from Hitler and Mussolini) against the existing republican government. It attracted a substantial group of young Americans—more than 3,000—who formed the Abraham Lincoln Brigade (directed and in part created by the American Communist Party) and traveled to Spain to join the fight against the fascists. About a third of its members died in combat. Ernest Hemingway, who spent time as a correspondent in Spain during the conflict, wrote in his novel *For Whom the Bell Tolls* (1940) of how the war provided those Americans who fought in it with "a part in something which you could believe in wholly and completely and in which you felt an absolute brotherhood with others who were engaged in it."

The Communist Party was active as well in organizing the unemployed in the early 1930s and staged a hunger march in Washington, D.C., in 1931. Party members were among the most effective union organizers in some industries. And the party was among the few political organizations that took a firm stand in favor of racial justice; its active defense of the Scottsboro defendants was but one example of its efforts to ally itself with the aspirations of African Americans.

The American Communist Party was not, however, the open, patriotic organization it tried to appear. It was always under the close and rigid supervision of the Soviet Union. Its leaders took their orders from the Comintern in Moscow. Most members obediently followed the "party line" (although there were many areas in which Communists were active for which there was no party line, areas in which members acted independently). The subordination of the party leadership to the Soviet Union was most clearly demonstrated in 1939, when Stalin signed a nonaggression pact with Nazi Germany. Moscow then sent orders to the American Communist Party to abandon the Popular Front and return to its old stance of harsh criticism of American liberals; and Communist Party leaders in the United States immediately obeyed—although thousands of disillusioned members left the party as a result.

The Socialist Party of America, under the leadership of Norman Thomas, also cited the economic crisis as evidence of the failure of capitalism and sought vigorously to win public support for its own political program. Among other things, it attempted to mobilize support among the rural poor. The Southern Tenant Farmers' Union (STFU), supported by the party and organized by a young socialist, H. L. Mitchell, attempted to create a biracial coalition of sharecroppers, tenant farmers, and others to demand economic reform. Neither the STFU nor the party itself, however, made any real progress toward establishing socialism as a major force in American politics. By 1936, membership in the Socialist Party had fallen below 20,000.

SOUTHERN TENANT FARMERS' UNION

Antiradicalism was a powerful force in the 1930s, just as it had been during and after World War I and would be again in the 1940s and 1950s. Hostility toward the Communist Party, in particular, was intense at many levels of government. Congressional committees chaired by Hamilton Fish of New York and Martin Dies of Texas investigated communist influence wherever they

MIGRANT FAMILY This photograph by the great Depression photographer Dorothea Lange portrays a family of migrants leaving Texas in search of work in California. It suggests the plight of hundreds of thousands of families who fled the regions affected by drought in the 1930s—a devastation that became known as the Dust Bowl. (© The Granger Collection, New York)

could find it (or imagine it). State and local governments harried and sometimes imprisoned communist organizers. White southerners tried to drive communist organizers out of the countryside, just as growers in California and elsewhere tried (unsuccessfully) to keep communists from organizing Mexican American and other workers.

Even so, only a few times before in American history (and in few since) did being part of the left seem so respectable and even conventional among workers, intellectuals, and others. Thus the 1930s witnessed a significant, if temporary, widening of the ideological range of mainstream art and politics. The New Deal sponsored artistic work through the Works Projects Administration that was frankly challenging to the capitalist norms of the 1920s. The filmmaker Pare Lorentz, with funding from New Deal agencies, made a series of powerful and polemical documentaries–*The Plow That Broke the Plains* (1936), *The River* (1937)–that combined a celebration of New Deal programs with a harsh critique of the exploitation of people and the environment that industrial capitalism had produced.

THE LEFT'S NEWFOUND RESPECTABILITY

Perhaps the most successful chronicler of social conditions in the 1930s was the novelist John Steinbeck, particularly in his celebrated novel *The Grapes of Wrath,* published in 1939. In telling the story of the Joad family, migrants from the Dust Bowl to California who encounter an unending string of calamities and failures, he offered not only a harsh portrait of the exploitive features of agrarian life in the West, but also a tribute to the endurance of his main characters–and to the spirit of community they represent.

THE GRAPES OF WRATH

THE UNHAPPY PRESIDENCY OF HERBERT HOOVER

Herbert Hoover began his presidency in March 1929 believing, like most Americans, that the nation faced a bright and prosperous future. For the first six months of his Republican administration, he attempted to expand the policies he had advocated during his eight years as secretary of commerce, policies that would, he believed, complete a stable system of cooperative individualism and sustain a successful economy. The economic crisis that began before the year was out forced the president to deal with a new set of problems, but for most of the rest of his term, he continued to rely on the principles that had always governed his public life.

THE HOOVER PROGRAM

Hoover's first response to the Depression was to attempt to restore public confidence in the economy. "The fundamental business of this country, that is, production and distribution of commodities," Hoover said in 1930, "is on a sound and prosper-

FAILURE OF VOLUNTARISM

ous basis." He then summoned leaders of business, labor, and agriculture to the White House and urged them to adopt a program of voluntary cooperation for recovery. He implored businessmen not to cut production or lay off workers; he talked labor leaders into forgoing demands for higher wages or better hours. But by mid-1931, economic conditions had deteriorated so much that the modest structure of voluntary cooperation he had erected collapsed.

Hoover also attempted to use government spending as a tool for fighting the Depression. The president proposed to Congress an increase of $423 million–a significant sum by the standards of the time–in federal public works programs, and he exhorted state and local governments to fund public construction. But the spending was not nearly enough in the face of such devastating problems. And when economic conditions worsened, he became less willing to increase spending, worrying instead about creating large government deficits. In 1932, at the depth of the Depression, he proposed a tax increase to help the government avoid a deficit.

Even before the stock market crash, Hoover had begun to construct a program to assist the already troubled agricultural economy. In April 1929, he proposed the Agricultural Marketing Act, which established the first major government program to

AGRICULTURAL MARKETING ACT

help farmers maintain prices. A federally sponsored Farm Board would make loans to national marketing cooperatives or establish corporations to buy surpluses and thus raise prices. At the same time, Hoover attempted to protect American farmers from international competition by raising agricultural tariffs. The Tariff Act of 1930 (also known as the Smoot-Hawley Tariff and the Hawley-Smoot Tariff) increased protection on seventy-five farm products. But neither the Agricultural Marketing Act nor the Hawley-Smoot Tariff ultimately helped American farmers significantly. The tariff, on the contrary, harmed the agricultural economy by stifling exports of food.

By the spring of 1931, Herbert Hoover's political position had deteriorated considerably. In the 1930 congressional elections, Democrats won control of the House and made substantial inroads in the Senate by promising increased government

HOOVER'S DECLINING POPULARITY

assistance to the economy. Many Americans held the president personally to blame for the crisis and began calling the shantytowns that unemployed people established on the outskirts of cities "Hoovervilles." Democrats urged the

HOOVER THE PATRICIAN Although Herbert Hoover grew up in a family of modest means in a small town in Iowa, his critics in the 1930s delighted in portraying him as an aloof aristocrat, fond of fancy dinners and elegant surroundings. As this formal portrait shows, Hoover gave his critics many opportunities to strengthen that image. (© Corbis)

president to support more-vigorous programs of relief and public spending. Hoover continued to believe his policies were working.

The international financial panic of the spring of 1931 destroyed the illusion that the economic crisis was coming to an end. Throughout the 1920s, European nations had depended on loans from American banks to allow them to make payments on their debts. After 1929, when they could no longer get such loans, the financial fabric of several European nations began to unravel. In May 1931, one of the largest banks in Austria collapsed. Over the next several months, panic gripped the financial institutions of neighboring countries. The American economy rapidly declined to new lows.

By the time Congress convened in December 1931, conditions had grown so desperate that Hoover supported a series of measures designed to keep endangered banks afloat and protect homeowners from foreclosure on their mortgages. More important was a bill passed in January 1932 establishing the

RECONSTRUCTION FINANCE CORPORATION

Reconstruction Finance Corporation (RFC), a government agency whose purpose was to provide federal loans to troubled banks, railroads, and other businesses. It even

HOOVERVILLES Herbert Hoover remained a symbol of despair for many Americans enduring the stresses of the Great Depression. This shanty town in Seattle and many others throughout the country were called by critics of the president "Hoovervilles." (© World History Archive/Alamy)

made funds available to local governments to support public works projects and assist relief efforts. Unlike some earlier Hoover programs, it operated on a large scale. In 1932, the RFC had a budget of $1.5 billion for public works alone.

Nevertheless, the new agency failed to deal directly or forcefully enough with the real problems of the economy to produce any significant recovery. The RFC lent funds only to financial institutions with sufficient collateral; much of its money went to large banks and corporations. At Hoover's insistence, it helped finance only those public works projects that promised ultimately to pay for themselves (toll bridges, public housing, and others). Above all, the RFC did not have enough money to make any real impact on the Depression, and it did not even spend all the money it had. Of the $300 million available to support local relief efforts, the RFC lent out only $30 million in 1932. Of the $1.5 billion public works budget, it released only about 20 percent.

POPULAR PROTEST

For the first several years of the Depression, most Americans were either too stunned or too confused to raise any effective protest. By the middle of 1932, however, dissident voices began to be heard.

In the summer of 1932, a group of unhappy farm owners gathered in Des Moines, Iowa, to establish a new organization:

**FARMERS'
HOLIDAY
ASSOCIATION** the Farmers' Holiday Association, which endorsed the withholding of farm products from the market—in effect a farmers' strike. The strike began in August in western Iowa, spread briefly to a few neighboring areas, and succeeded in blockading several markets, but in the end it dissolved in failure.

A more celebrated protest movement emerged from American veterans. In 1924, Congress had approved the payment of a $1,000 bonus to all those who had served in World War I, the money to be paid beginning in 1945. By 1932, however, many veterans were demanding that the bonus be paid immediately. Hoover, concerned about balancing the budget, rejected their appeal. In June, more than 20,000 veterans, members of the self-proclaimed Bonus Expeditionary Force, or "Bonus Army," marched into Washington, built crude camps around the city, and promised to stay until Congress approved legislation to pay the bonus. Some of the veterans departed in July, after Congress voted down their proposal. Many, however, remained where they were.

Their continued presence in Washington disturbed President Hoover. Finally, in mid-July, he ordered police to clear the marchers out of several abandoned federal buildings in which they had been staying. A few marchers threw rocks at the police, and someone opened fire; two veterans fell dead. Hoover considered the incident evidence of growing violence and radicalism, and he ordered the U.S. Army to assist the police in clearing out the buildings.

General Douglas MacArthur, the army chief of staff, carried out the mission himself (with the assistance of his aide, Dwight D. Eisenhower) and greatly exceeded the president's orders.

**DEMISE OF THE
BONUS ARMY** He led the Third Cavalry (under the command of George S. Patton), two infantry regiments, a machine-gun detachment, and six tanks down Pennsylvania Avenue in pursuit of the Bonus Army. The veterans fled in terror. MacArthur followed them across the Anacostia River, where he ordered the soldiers to burn their tent city to the ground. More than 100 marchers were injured.

CLEARING OUT THE BONUS MARCHERS In July 1932, President Hoover ordered the Washington, D.C., police to evict the Bonus marchers from some of the public buildings and land they had been occupying. The result was a series of pitched battles (one of them visible here), in which both veterans and police sustained injuries. Such skirmishes persuaded Hoover to call out the U.S. Army to finish the eviction. (© Bettmann/Corbis)

Roosevelt had been a well-known figure in the for many years already. A Hudson Valley aristoc distant cousin of Theodore Roosevelt (a conne strengthened by his marriage in 1904 to the preside niece, Eleanor), and a handsome, charming young m he progressed rapidly: from a seat in the New York Sta legislature to a position as assistant secretary of th navy during World War I to his party's vice presidentia nomination in 1920 on the ill-fated ticket with James M. Cox. Less than a year later, he was stricken with polio. Although he never regained use of his legs (and eventually could appear to walk only by using crutches and braces), he built up sufficient physical strength to return to politics in 1928. When Al Smith received the Democratic nomination for president that year, Roosevelt was elected to succeed him as governor of New York. In 1930, he easily won reelection.

Roosevelt worked no miracles in New York, but he did initiate enough positive programs of government assistance to be able to present himself as a more energetic and imaginative leader than Hoover. In national politics, he avoided such divisive cultural issues as religion and prohibition and emphasized the economic grievances that most Democrats shared. He was able as a result to assemble a broad coalition within the party and win his party's nomination. In a dramatic break with tradition, he flew to Chicago to address the convention in person and accept the nomination. In the course of his acceptance speech, Roosevelt aroused the delegates with his ringing promise: "I pledge you, I pledge myself, to a new deal for the American people," giving his future program a name that would long endure. Neither then nor in the subsequent campaign did Roosevelt give much indication of what that program would be. But Herbert Hoover's unpopularity virtually ensured Roosevelt's election.

In November, to the surprise of no one, Roosevelt won by a landslide. He received 57.4 percent of the popular vote to

1932 ELECTION Hoover's 39.7. In the electoral college, the result was even more overwhelming. Hoover carried Delaware, Pennsylvania, Connecticut, Vermont, New Hampshire, and Maine. Roosevelt won everything else. Democrats won majorities in both houses of Congress. It was a broad and convincing mandate.

The incident served as perhaps the final blow to Hoover's already-battered political standing. Hoover's own reserved personality reinforced the public image of him as aloof and unsympathetic to distressed people. The Great Engineer, the personification of the optimistic days of the 1920s, had become a symbol of the nation's failure to deal effectively with its startling reversal of fortune.

THE ELECTION OF 1932

As the 1932 presidential election approached, few people doubted the outcome. The Republican Party dutifully renominated Herbert Hoover for a second term of office, but the

FDR NOMINATED gloomy atmosphere of the convention made it clear that few delegates believed he could win. The Democrats, in the meantime, gathered jubilantly in Chicago to nominate the governor of New York, Franklin Delano Roosevelt.

THE "INTERREGNUM"

The period between the election and the inauguration (which in the early 1930s lasted more than four months) was a season of growing economic crisis. Presidents-elect traditionally do not involve themselves directly in government. But in a series of brittle exchanges with Roosevelt in the months following the election, Hoover tried to exact from the president-elect a pledge to maintain policies of economic orthodoxy. Roosevelt genially refused.

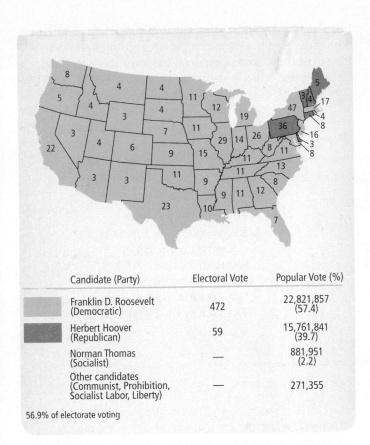

Candidate (Party)	Electoral Vote	Popular Vote (%)
Franklin D. Roosevelt (Democratic)	472	22,821,857 (57.4)
Herbert Hoover (Republican)	59	15,761,841 (39.7)
Norman Thomas (Socialist)	—	881,951 (2.2)
Other candidates (Communist, Prohibition, Socialist Labor, Liberty)	—	271,355

56.9% of electorate voting

ELECTION OF 1932 Like the election of 1928, the election of 1932 was exceptionally one-sided. But this time, the landslide favored the Democratic candidate, Franklin Roosevelt, who overwhelmed Herbert Hoover in all regions of the country except New England. Roosevelt obviously benefited primarily from popular disillusionment with Hoover's response to the Great Depression.

• *But what characteristics of Roosevelt himself contributed to his victory?*

THE CHANGING OF THE GUARD Herbert Hoover and Franklin D. Roosevelt travel together to the Capitol for Roosevelt's inauguration. The ride appeared uncomfortable for the outgoing president. Hoover seems glum and uncommunicative whereas Roosevelt seems ready to take on his new responsibilities. (© Bettmann/Corbis)

In February, only a month before the inauguration, a new crisis developed when the collapse of the American banking system suddenly and rapidly accelerated. Public confidence in

BANKING CRISIS

the banks was ebbing; depositors were withdrawing their money in panic; and one bank after another was closing its doors and declaring bankruptcy. Hoover again asked Roosevelt to give prompt public assurances that there would be no tinkering with the currency, no heavy borrowing, no unbalancing of the budget. Roosevelt again refused.

March 4, 1933, was, therefore, a day of both economic crisis and considerable personal bitterness. On that morning, Herbert Hoover, convinced that the United States was headed for disaster, rode glumly down Pennsylvania Avenue with a beaming, buoyant Franklin Roosevelt, who would shortly be sworn in as the thirty-second president of the United States.

AP CONNECTING THEMES

Chapter 23 discussed the causes and results of the Great Depression. Review the chapter, focusing on both the long- and short-term causes of the Great Depression. You should pay close attention to the impact of the Great Depression on Americans' sense of identity–Americans' perceptions of others and of themselves. Also, the chapter emphasized the impact of the economic depression on disadvantaged groups. The chapter explained the impact of unemployment on patterns of migration within and into the United States. The chapter also gave significant discussion of the impact of the Great Depression on the culture and literature of the 1930s. Lastly, as you review, you should also focus on the campaign strategies of both parties in the election of 1932.

The following themes have heightened importance in Chapter 23. You should now be able to do the following for each listed theme:

Identity: Explain how the Great Depression changed the way disadvantaged people looked at themselves and the way in which others viewed the disadvantaged.

Work, Exchange, and Technology: Examine the ways in which technological advances and foreign trade policies helped lead to the Great Depression.

Politics and Power: Explain the degree to which the election of 1932 represents a significant turning point in American history.

Peopling: Explain how the Great Depression caused significant changes in the migration patterns of American society.

Ideas, Beliefs, and Culture: Examine the impact of the Great Depression on literature and culture in the United States during the 1930s.

AP SUGGESTED STUDY

PEOPLE/PLACES/EVENTS As you study these items, think about how they demonstrate or relate to key concepts and historical themes from this chapter and previous chapters.

AGRICULTURAL MARKETING ACT 656
"BLACK TUESDAY" 640
BONUS ARMY 657
CLIFFORD ODETS 650
DUST BOWL 645
ERSKINE CALDWELL 650
FRANK CAPRA 651

HINDENBURG 651
HOOVERVILLES 656
JOHN DOS PASSOS 650
JOHN STEINBECK 650
LIFE magazine 653
"OKIES" 645
ORSON WELLES 651

POPULAR FRONT 654
RECONSTRUCTION FINANCE
    CORPORATION 657
RICHARD WRIGHT 650
SCOTTSBORO CASE 646
SOAP OPERAS 651
TARIFF ACT OF 1930 656

AP TEST PRACTICE

Questions assume cumulative content knowledge from this chapter and previous chapters.

MULTIPLE CHOICE Use the photograph on page 639 and your knowledge of U.S. history to answer questions 1-2.

1. How did many Americans respond to the event to which the woman in the photograph is responding?

    (A) Migrating overseas in search of work

    (B) Advocating for high American protective tariffs

    (C) Staying on their farms and continuing to produce more food than Americans could afford to purchase

    (D) Migrating westward to California and other states, often working as migrant laborers

2. Photographs of the era such as this one were generally taken by the photographer to

    (A) directly help the subjects of the photographs find jobs

    (B) show the harsh rural poverty of the time, hoping to generate reform

    (C) generate work for themselves

    (D) document the era for posterity

SHORT ANSWER Use your knowledge of U.S. history to answer question 3.

"The Depression, they claimed, was a result of a drastic contraction of the currency (a result largely of mistaken decisions by the Federal Reserve Board, which raised interest rates when it should have lowered them). These deflationary measures, . . . , turned an ordinary recession into the Great Depression."

–Brinkley's interpretation of Milton Friedman and Anna Schwartz's thesis in *Monetary History of the United States* (1963)

"The Cause of the crisis was not monetary contraction (although the contraction made it worse), but a drop in investment and consumer spending, which preceded the decline in money supply and helped to cause it."

–Brinkley's interpretation of Peter Temin's thesis in *Did Monetary Forces Case the Great Depression?* (1976)

3. Using the excerpts above concerning the causes of the Great Depression, answer parts a, b, and c.

    a) Briefly explain ONE major difference between Friedman/Schwartz's and Temin's interpretations of the causes of the Great Depression.

    b) Briefly explain ONE action taken during the New Deal between 1933 and 1940 that attempted to overcome the issue identified by Friedman/Schwartz between 1933 and 1941.

    c) Briefly explain ONE action taken during the New Deal between 1933 and 1940 that attempted to overcome the issue presented by Temin's thesis.

LONG ESSAY For the question below, develop a thoughtful and thorough historical argument that answers the question. Begin your essay with a thesis statement and support it with relevant historical evidence.

4. Some historians have maintained that the Great Depression greatly affected America's sense of identity and that this effect was reflected in the mass media, art, and literature of the 1930s. Support, modify, or refute this interpretation providing specific evidence to justify your answer.

24 | THE NEW DEAL

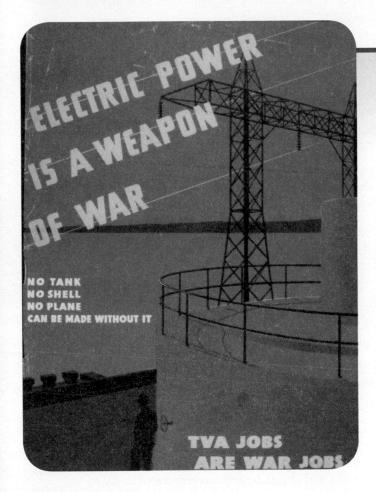

ELECTRIC POWER IS A WEAPON OF WAR

NO TANK
NO SHELL
NO PLANE
CAN BE MADE WITHOUT IT

TVA JOBS
ARE WAR JOBS

TVA JOBS ARE WAR JOBS The Tennessee Valley Authority, a federally owned corporation, sought to revitalize a region devastated by depression and other catastrophes. By the time of World War II, much of the work of the TVA centered on producing hydroelectric power with which to build war matériel. (© war posters/Alamy)

HISTORICAL THINKING

1. **Historical Argumentation** Analyze the means by which Roosevelt sought to restore confidence and the degree of success he had in realizing his goal.

2. **Contextualization** How did Roosevelt attempt to restore confidence in the banking system?

3. **Historical Causation** Analyze the specific measures taken to restore economic viability in both agriculture and industry?

4. **Contextualization** Analyze the arguments of critics of the New Deal on both "the left" and "the right."

5. **Comparison** Compare and contrast the relative successes of the First and Second New Deals.

6. **Patterns of Continuity and Change over Time** Analyze the fundamental changes the New Deal brought to the United States, relative to the role of the federal government in the economy.

7. **Comparison** Compare the attitude of the federal government toward organized labor during the Gilded Age with that of the government's attitude toward labor during the New Deal.

8. **Contextualization** Analyze the degree to which the New Deal led to political realignment of the parties.

9. **Interpretation** To what degree and in what ways was the New Deal a failure and to what degree and in what ways was it a success?

10. **Patterns of Continuity and Change over Time** Analyze the impact of the New Deal in changing the lives of African Americans and American Indians.

11. **Interpretation** Analyze the impact of Eleanor Roosevelt in changing perceptions of the role of women in politics.

Key Concept Correlations

Analyze the ways the historical developments you learn about in this chapter connect to the following AP Key Concepts.

7.1 Governmental, political, and social organizations struggled to address the effects of large-scale industrialization, economic uncertainty, and related social changes such as urbanization and mass migration.

7.2 A revolution in communications and transportation technology helped to create a new mass culture and spread "modern" values and ideas, even as cultural conflicts between groups increased under the pressure of migration, world wars, and economic distress.

Thematic Learning Objectives

WXT-8, POL-2, 3, 4; ID-3; CUL-5

AP CONNECTING CONCEPTS

CHAPTER 24 discusses the New Deal policies of relief, recovery, and reform, meant to alleviate suffering, to put America on the road to economic prosperity, and to reform the economic system to prevent catastrophic depressions in the future. The chapter focuses on specific attempts by the Roosevelt administration to promote industrial and agricultural recovery. The chapter also deals with critics of the New Deal—on both "the left" and "the right"—concerning too much or too little government involvement in the economy. The chapter also notes a positive change in the attitude of the federal government toward organized labor. Another major focus of this chapter is the major accomplishment of the Second New Deal and of perceived threats to those programs from the Supreme Court. Important, also, is the political realignment of ethnic groups, including African Americans, and labor brought about by the New Deal. Significant change is also made regarding the federal government's treatment of American Indians, undoing much of the policies of the Dawes Act. Lastly, the chapter examines the contributions of Eleanor Roosevelt, who worked tirelessly to improve the lives of disadvantaged groups. As you read, evaluate the following ideas:

- Economic depression led for calls to increase the regulatory powers of the federal government.
- National reformers responded to the Great Depression by transforming the United States into a limited welfare state.
- The New Deal sought to promote relief for those in need, recovery of the American economy, and reform of the economic system to prevent future depressions.
- Conservatives and the Supreme Court worked to limit the New Deal.
- While the New Deal failed to end the Great Depression, it did lead to political realignment that strengthened the Democratic Party.
- Economic necessity drove many Americans to migrate during the Great Depression.

LAUNCHING THE NEW DEAL

Roosevelt's first task upon taking office was to alleviate the panic that was threatening the financial system. He did so in part by force of personality and in part by constructing very rapidly an ambitious and diverse program of legislation.

RESTORING CONFIDENCE

Much of Roosevelt's success was a result of his ebullient personality. In his inaugural address, he assured the American people that "the only thing we have to fear is fear itself," and promised to

ROOSEVELT'S PERSONALITY
take drastic, even warlike, action against the emergency. He projected an infectious optimism that helped alleviate the growing despair. He was the first president to make regular use of the radio, and his friendly "fireside chats,"
during which he explained his programs and plans to the people, helped build public confidence in the administration. Roosevelt held frequent informal press conferences and won the respect and friendship of most reporters. Their regard for him was such that by unwritten agreement, no journalist ever photographed the president getting into or out of his car or sitting in his wheelchair. Much of the American public remained unaware throughout the Roosevelt years that the president's legs were completely paralyzed.

But Roosevelt could not rely on image alone. On March 6, 1933, two days after taking office, he issued a proclamation closing all American banks for four days until Congress could meet in special session to consider banking-reform legislation. So great was the panic about bank failures that the "bank holiday," as the president euphemistically described it, created a general sense of

"BANK HOLIDAY"
relief. Three days later, Roosevelt sent to Congress the Emergency Banking Act, a generally conservative bill (much of it drafted by Hoover administration holdovers) designed primarily to protect the larger banks from being dragged down

Agricultural Adjustment

These initial actions were largely stopgaps, to buy time for comprehensive programs. The first of them was the Agricultural Adjustment Act, which Congress passed in May 1933. Its most important feature was its provision for reducing crop production to end agricultural surpluses and halt the downward spiral of farm prices.

Under the provisions of the act, producers of seven basic commodities (wheat, cotton, corn, hogs, rice, tobacco, and dairy products) would decide on production limits for their crops.

AAA The government, through the Agricultural Adjustment Administration (AAA), would then tell individual farmers how much they should produce and would pay them subsidies for leaving some of their land idle. A tax on food processing (for example, the milling of wheat) would provide the funds for the new payments. Farm prices would be subsidized up to the point of parity.

The AAA helped bring about a rise in prices for farm commodities in the years after 1933. Gross farm income increased by half in the first three years of the New Deal, and the agricultural economy emerged from the 1930s much more stable and prosperous than it had been in many years. The AAA did, however, favor larger farmers over smaller ones, particularly since local administration of its programs often fell into the hands of the most powerful producers in a community. By distributing payments to landowners, not those who worked the land, the government did little to discourage planters who were reducing their acreage from evicting tenants and sharecroppers and firing field hands.

In January 1936, the Supreme Court struck down the crucial provisions of the Agricultural Adjustment Act, arguing that the government had no constitutional authority to require farmers to limit production. But within a few weeks the administration had secured passage of new legislation (the Soil Conservation and Domestic Allotment Act), which permitted the government to pay farmers to reduce production so as to "conserve soil," prevent erosion, and accomplish other secondary goals. The Court did not interfere with the new laws.

The administration launched several efforts to assist poor farmers as well. The Resettlement Administration, established in 1935, and its successor, the Farm Security Administration, created in 1937, provided loans to help farmers cultivating submarginal soil to relocate to better lands. But the programs

"Rural Electrification" never moved more than a few thousand farmers. More effective was the Rural Electrification Administration, created in 1935, which worked to make electric power available for the first time to thousands of farmers through utility cooperatives.

Industrial Recovery

Ever since 1931, leaders of the U.S. Chamber of Commerce and many others had been urging the government to adopt an antideflation scheme that would permit trade associations to cooperate in stabilizing prices within their industries. Existing

THE "RADIO PRESIDENT" Franklin D. Roosevelt was the first American president to master the use of radio. Beginning in his first days in office, he regularly bypassed the newspapers and communicated directly with the people through his famous "fireside chats." He is shown here speaking in 1938, urging communities to continue to provide work relief for the unemployed. (© Bettmann/Corbis)

by the weakness of smaller ones. The bill provided for Treasury Department inspection of all banks before they would be allowed to reopen, for federal assistance to some troubled institutions, and for a thorough reorganization of those in the greatest difficulty. A confused and frightened Congress passed the bill within four hours of its introduction. "I can assure you," Roosevelt told the public on March 12, in his first fireside chat, "that it is safer to keep your money in a reopened bank than under the mattress." Whatever else the new law accomplished, it helped dispel the panic. Three-quarters of the banks in the Federal Reserve system reopened within the next three days, and $1 billion in hoarded currency and gold flowed back into them within a month. The immediate banking crisis was over.

On the morning after passage of the Emergency Banking Act, Roosevelt sent to Congress another measure—the Economy Act—designed to convince fiscally conservative Americans (especially the business community) that the federal government was in safe, responsible hands. The act proposed to balance the federal budget by cutting the salaries of government employees and reducing pensions to veterans by as much as 15 percent. Otherwise, the president warned, the nation faced a $1 billion budget deficit. Like the banking bill, this one passed Congress almost instantly—despite heated protests from some congressional progressives.

Roosevelt also moved in his first days in office to put to rest one of the divisive issues of the 1920s. He supported and then signed a bill to legalize the manufacture and sale of beer with

Prohibition Repealed a 3.2 percent alcohol content—an interim measure pending the repeal of prohibition, for which a constitutional amendment (the Twenty-First) was already in process. The amendment was ratified later in 1933.

BANKING CRISES

WHEN FRANKLIN DELANO ROOSEVELT TOOK OFFICE AS PRESIDENT IN 1933, the U.S. banking system was close to collapse. As depositors, panicked by the worsening Depression, withdrew their savings from the banks, bank after bank was forced to close. To prevent a complete collapse of the banking system, FDR first declared a "bank holiday," calling for the closing of all banks, and then called Congress into special session to pass banking-reform legislation, the Emergency Banking Act. In his first fireside chat on March 12, 1933–excerpted in the first source document below–the president sought to explain to the public the actions he and Congress had undertaken and to reassure his listeners that their money would be safe in banks.

Some seventy-five years after the Great Depression of the 1930s, the nation once again experienced a serious financial crisis in the Great Recession of 2007–2010. Once again, Congress passed banking-reform legislation calling for closer regulation of banks and providing greater protections for consumers. In his address of July 21, 2010, President Barack Obama outlined the provisions of the new legislation and sought to reassure the public. Excerpts from this address comprise the second source in this feature.

THE GREAT DEPRESSION—1933

FRANKLIN DELANO ROOSEVELT: "THE BANKING CRISIS (FIRST FIRESIDE CHAT)"

First of all, let me state the simple fact that when you deposit money in a bank, the bank does not put the money into a safe deposit vault. It invests your money in many different forms of credit in bonds, in commercial paper, in mortgages and in many other kinds of loans. In other words, the bank puts your money to work to keep the wheels of industry and of agriculture turning around. . . .

What, then, happened during the last few days of February and the first few days of March? Because of undermined confidence on the part of the public, there was a general rush by a large portion of our population to turn bank deposits into currency or gold, a rush so great that the soundest banks couldn't get enough currency to meet the demand. . . . By the afternoon of March third, a week ago last Friday, scarcely a bank in the country was open to do business. Proclamations closing them, in whole or in part, had been issued by the Governors in almost all the states. It was then that I issued the proclamation providing for the national bank holiday, and this was the first step in the Government's reconstruction of our financial and economic fabric.

The second step, last Thursday, was the legislation promptly and patriotically passed by the Congress confirming my proclamation and broadening my powers so that it became possible in view of the requirement of time to extend the holiday and lift the ban of that holiday gradually in the days to come. This law also gave authority to develop a program of rehabilitation of our banking facilities. . . .

The new law allows the twelve Federal Reserve Banks to issue additional currency on good assets and thus the banks that reopen will be able to meet every legitimate call. . . . It is necessary that the reopening of banks be extended over a period [of several days] in order to permit the banks to make applications for the necessary loans, to obtain currency needed to meet their requirements, and to enable the Government to make common sense checkups. . . .

We have had a bad banking situation. Some of our bankers had shown themselves either incompetent or dishonest in their handling of the people's funds. They had used the money entrusted to them in speculations and unwise loans. This was, of course, not true in the vast majority of our banks, but it was true in enough of them to shock the people of the United States, for a time, into a sense of insecurity and to put them into a frame of mind where they did not differentiate, but seemed to assume that the acts of a comparative few had tainted them all. And so it became the Government's job to straighten out this situation and do it as quickly as possible. And that job is being performed. . . .

[T]here is an element in the readjustment of our financial system more important than currency, more important than gold, and that is the confidence of the people themselves. Confidence and courage are the essentials of success in carrying out our plan. You people must have faith; you must not be stampeded by rumors or guesses. Let us unite in banishing fear. We have provided the machinery to restore our financial system, and it is up to you to support and make it work.

Source: whitehouse.c-span.org

THE GREAT RECESSION OF 2007–2010

BARACK OBAMA: SIGNING OF DODD-FRANK WALL STREET REFORM AND CONSUMER PROTECTION ACT

Over the past two years, we have faced the worst recession since the Great Depression. Eight million people lost their jobs. Tens of millions saw the value of their homes and retirement savings plummet. Countless businesses have been unable to get the loans they need and many have been forced to shut their doors. And although the economy is growing again, too many people are still feeling the pain of the downturn.

Now, while a number of factors led to such a severe recession, the primary cause was a breakdown in our financial system. It was a crisis born of a failure of responsibility from certain corners of Wall Street to the halls of power in Washington. For years, our financial sector was governed by antiquated and poorly enforced rules that allowed some to game the system and take risks that endangered the entire economy.

Unscrupulous lenders locked consumers into complex loans with hidden costs. Firms like AIG placed massive, risky bets with borrowed money. And while the rules left abuse and excess unchecked, they also left taxpayers on the hook if a big bank or financial institution ever failed.

Now, let's put this in perspective. The fact is, the financial industry is central to our nation's ability to grow, to prosper, to compete and to innovate. There are a lot of banks that understand and fulfill this vital role, and there are a whole lot of bankers who want to do right–and do right–by their customers. This reform will help foster innovation, not hamper it. It is designed to make sure that everybody follows the same set of rules, so that firms compete on price and quality, not on tricks and not on traps. . . .

[R]eform will also rein in the abuse and excess that nearly brought down our financial system. It will finally bring transparency to the kinds of complex and risky transactions that helped trigger the financial crisis. Shareholders will also have a greater say on the pay of CEOs and other executives, so they can reward success instead of failure.

And finally, because of this law, the American people will never again be asked to foot the bill for Wall Street's mistakes. There will be no more tax-funded bailouts–period. If a large financial institution should ever fail, this reform gives us the ability to wind it down without end   angering the broader economy. And there will be new rules to make clear that no firm is somehow protected because it is "too big to fail." . . .

The fact is every American–from Main Street to Wall Street–has a stake in our financial system. Wall Street banks and firms invest the capital that makes it possible for start-ups to sell new products. They provide loans to businesses to expand and to hire. They back mortgages for families purchasing a new home. That's why we'll all stand to gain from these reforms. We all win when investors around the world have confidence in our markets. We all win when shareholders have more power and more information. We all win when consumers are protected against abuse. And we all win when folks are rewarded based on how well they perform, not how well they evade accountability.

Source: www.whitehouse.gov

AP TEST PRACTICE

Questions assume cumulative content knowledge from this chapter and previous chapters.

1. Based on the excerpts, which major cause did both crises share?

(A) Banks refused to lend money to individuals

(B) A rush by the public to withdraw their savings from banks

(C) Irresponsible speculation by banks

(D) The general public not understanding how the financial system worked

2. A comparison of the documents provides the most evidence of which difference in the lead-up to the Great Recession versus the Great Depression?

(A) No panic on the part of the public vs. great panic on the part of the public

(B) Failure of the government to enforce banking regulations vs. very little to no government regulation of banks

(C) Too strict of government enforcement of banking and finance regulations vs. no government enforcement

(D) Too many government regulations to keep track of vs. none

3. What governmental banking policies changed as a result of the Great Depression which led to President Obama stating, "(lender policies) left taxpayers on the hook if a big bank or financial institution ever failed?"

(A) More regulations placed on bank loaning policies

(B) More disclosures required by government regulators to ensure truth in bank assets

(C) A government program insured bank savings accounts

(D) A government regulation required all bank loans be backed by government funds

SALUTING THE BLUE EAGLE Several thousand San Francisco schoolchildren assembled on a baseball field in 1933 to form the symbol of the National Recovery Administration: an eagle clutching a cogwheel (to symbolize industry) and a thunderbolt (to symbolize energy). This display is evidence of the widespread (if brief) popular enthusiasm the NRA produced. NRA administrators drew from their memories of World War I Liberty Loan drives and tried to establish the Blue Eagle as a symbol of patriotic commitment to recovery. (© Bettmann/Corbis)

antitrust laws clearly forbade such practices, and Herbert Hoover had refused to endorse suspension of the laws. The Roosevelt administration was more receptive. In exchange for relaxing antitrust provisions, however, New Dealers insisted on other provisions. Business leaders would have to make important concessions to labor—recognize the workers' right to bargain collectively through unions—to ensure that the incomes of workers would rise along with prices. And to help create jobs and increase consumer buying power, the administration added a major program of public works spending. The result of these and many other impulses was the National Industrial Recovery Act, which Congress passed in June 1933.

At first, the new industrial recovery program appeared to work well. At its center was a new federal agency, the National Recovery Administration (NRA), under the direction of the flamboyant and energetic Hugh S. Johnson. Johnson called on every business establishment in the nation to accept a temporary "blanket code": a minimum wage of between 30 and 40 cents an hour, a maximum workweek of thirty-five to forty hours, and the abolition of child labor. Adherence to the code, he claimed, would raise consumer purchasing power and increase employment. At the same time, Johnson negotiated another, more specific set of codes with leaders of the nation's major industries. These industrial codes set floors below which no company would lower prices or wages in its search for a competitive advantage. He quickly won agreements from almost every major industry in the country.

NRA

From the beginning, however, the NRA encountered serious difficulties. The codes themselves were hastily and often poorly written. Administering them was beyond the capacities of federal officials with no prior experience in running so vast a program. Large producers consistently dominated the code-writing process and ensured that the new regulations would work to their advantage and to the disadvantage of smaller firms. And the codes at times did more than simply set

floors under prices; they actively and artificially raised them—sometimes to levels higher than the market could sustain.

Other NRA goals did not progress as quickly as the efforts to raise prices. Section 7(a) of the National Industrial Recovery Act promised workers the right to form unions and engage in collective bargaining and encouraged many workers to join unions for the first time. But Section 7(a) contained no enforcement mechanisms. Hence recognition of unions by employers (and thus the significant wage increases the unions were committed to winning) did not follow. The Public Works Administration (PWA), established in 1933 to administer the National Industrial Recovery Act's spending programs, only gradually allowed the $3.3 billion in public works funds to trickle out. Not until 1938 was the PWA budget pumping an appreciable amount of money into the economy.

SECTION 7(A)

Perhaps the clearest evidence of the NRA's failure was that industrial production actually declined in the months after the agency's establishment—from an index of 101 in July 1933 to 71 in November—despite the rise in prices that the codes had helped to create. By the spring of 1934, the NRA was besieged by criticism, and businessmen were ignoring many of its provisions. That fall, Roosevelt pressured Johnson to resign and established a new board of directors to oversee the NRA. Then, the Supreme Court intervened.

In 1935, a case came before the Court involving alleged NRA code violations by the Schechter brothers, who operated a wholesale poultry business confined to Brooklyn, New York. The Court ruled unanimously that the Schechters were not engaged in interstate commerce (and thus not subject to federal regulation) and, further, that Congress had unconstitutionally delegated legislative power to the president to draft the NRA codes. The justices struck down the legislation establishing the agency. Roosevelt denounced the justices for their "horse-and-buggy" interpretation of the interstate commerce

THE TENNESSEE VALLEY AUTHORITY The Tennessee Valley Authority was one of the largest experiments in government-funded public works and regional planning in American history to that point. The federal government had helped fund many projects in its history—canals, turnpikes, railroads, bridges, dams, and others. But never before had it undertaken a project of such great scope, and never before had it maintained such close control and ownership over the public works it helped create. This map illustrates the broad reach of the TVA within the Tennessee Valley region, which spanned seven states. TVA dams throughout the region helped control floods and also provided a source for hydroelectric power, which the government sold to consumers. Note the dam near Muscle Shoals, Alabama, in the bottom left of the map. It was begun during World War I, and efforts to revive it in the 1920s helped create the momentum that produced the TVA.

• *Why were progressives so eager to see the government enter the business of hydroelectric power in the 1920s?*

clause. He was rightly concerned, for the reasoning in the Schechter case threatened many other New Deal programs as well. But the Court's destruction of the NRA itself gave the New Deal a convenient excuse for ending a failed experiment.

REGIONAL PLANNING

The AAA and the NRA largely reflected the beliefs of New Dealers who favored economic planning but wanted private interests (farmers or business leaders) to dominate the planning process. Other reformers believed that the government itself should be the chief planning agent in the economy. Their most conspicuous success, and one of the most celebrated accomplishments of the New Deal, was an unprecedented experiment in regional planning: the Tennessee Valley Authority (TVA).

The TVA had its roots in a political controversy of the 1920s. Progressive reformers had agitated for years for public development of the nation's water resources as a source of cheap electric power. In particular, they had urged completion of a great dam at Muscle Shoals on the Tennessee River in Alabama—a dam begun during World War I and left unfinished when the war ended. But opposition from the utility companies had been too powerful to overcome.

TVA

In 1932, however, one of the great utility empires–that of the electricity magnate Samuel Insull–collapsed spectacularly, amid widely publicized exposés of corruption. Hostility to the utilities soon grew so intense that the companies were no longer able to block the public power movement. The result in May 1933 was the Tennessee Valley Authority. The TVA was authorized to complete the dam at Muscle Shoals and build others in the region, and to generate and sell electricity from them to the public at reasonable rates. It was also intended to be an agent for a comprehensive redevelopment of the entire region: for stopping the disastrous flooding that had plagued the Tennessee Valley for centuries, for encouraging the development of local industries, for supervising a substantial program of reforestation, and for helping farmers improve productivity.

The TVA revitalized the region in numerous ways. It improved water transportation, virtually eliminated flooding in the region, and provided electricity to thousands who had never before had it. Throughout much of the country, largely because of the "yard-stick" provided by the TVA's cheap production of electricity, private power rates declined. Even so, the Tennessee Valley remained a generally impoverished region despite the TVA's efforts. And like many other New Deal programs, the TVA made no serious effort to challenge local customs and racial prejudices.

CURRENCY, BANKS, AND THE STOCK MARKET

Roosevelt soon came to consider the gold standard a major obstacle to the restoration of adequate prices. On April 18, 1933, he made the shift off the gold standard official with an executive order. By itself, the repudiation of the gold standard meant relatively little. But both before and after the April decision, the administration experimented in various ways with manipulating the value of the dollar–by making substantial purchases of gold and silver and later by establishing a new, fixed standard for the dollar (reducing its gold content substantially from the 1932 amount). The resort to government-managed currency–that is, to a dollar whose value could be raised or lowered by government policy according to economic circumstances–created an important precedent for future federal policies and permanently altered the relationship between the public and private sectors. It did not, however, have any immediate impact on the depressed American economy.

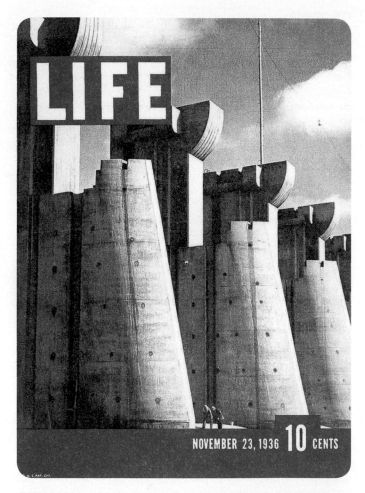

PUBLIC WORKS Among the most visible products of the New Deal was a vast network of public works in almost all areas of the country, but concentrated particularly in the South and the West. The great dams that the government built in the Tennessee Valley and elsewhere were particularly effective at capturing the public imagination. This dramatic photograph by Margaret Bourke-White appeared on the cover of the first issue of Life in 1936, which very quickly became the most popular and successful magazine in America. It shows the Fort Peck Dam on the Missouri River. (Margaret Bourke White/© Time & Life Pictures/Getty Images)

Through other legislation, the early New Deal increased federal authority over previously unregulated or weakly regulated areas of the economy. The Glass-Steagall Act of June 1933 gave the government authority to curb irresponsible speculation by banks. It also established a wall between commercial banking and investment banking. Equally important, it established the Federal Deposit Insurance Corporation, which guaranteed all bank deposits up to $2,500. Finally, in 1935, Congress passed a major banking act that transferred much of the authority once wielded by the regional Federal Reserve banks to the Federal Reserve Board in Washington.

GLASS-STEAGALL ACT

To protect investors in the stock market, Congress passed the so-called Truth in Securities Act of 1933, requiring corporations issuing new securities to provide full and accurate information about them to the public. Another act of June 1934 established the Securities and Exchange Commission (SEC) to police the stock market. Among other things, the establishment of the SEC was an indication of how far the financial establishment had fallen in public estimation. The criminal trials of a number of once-respected Wall Street figures for grand larceny and fraud eroded the public stature of the financial community still further.

SEC

THE GROWTH OF FEDERAL RELIEF

Among Roosevelt's first acts in office was the establishment of the Federal Emergency Relief Administration (FERA), which provided cash grants to states to prop up bankrupt relief agencies. To administer the program, he chose the director of the New York State relief agency, Harry Hopkins, who disbursed the FERA grants widely and rapidly. But both Hopkins and Roosevelt had misgivings about establishing a government "dole."

They felt more comfortable with another form of government assistance: work relief. Thus, when it became clear that the FERA grants were not enough, the administration established a second program: the Civil Works Administration (CWA). Between November 1933 and April 1934, it put more than 4 million people to work on temporary projects. Some of the projects were of lasting value, such as the construction of roads, schools, and parks; others were little more than make-work. To Hopkins, however, the important thing was pumping money into an economy badly in need of it and providing assistance to people with nowhere else to turn.

CWA

Roosevelt's favorite relief project was the Civilian Conservation Corps (CCC). Established in the first weeks of the new administration, the CCC was designed to provide employment to the millions of young men who could find no jobs in the cities. The CCC created camps in national parks and forests and in other rural and wilderness settings. There young men (women were largely excluded from the program) worked in a semimilitary environment on such projects as planting trees, building reservoirs, developing parks, and improving agricultural irrigation. CCC camps were segregated by race. The vast majority of

CCC

them were restricted to white men, but a few were available to African Americans, Mexicans, and Indians.

Mortgage relief was a pressing need for millions of farm owners and homeowners. The Farm Credit Administration, which within two years refinanced one-fifth of all farm mortgages in the United States, was one response to that problem. The Frazier-Lemke Farm Bankruptcy Act of 1933 was another. It enabled some farmers to regain their land even after foreclosure on their mortgages. Despite such efforts, however, 25 percent of all American farm owners had lost their land by 1934. Homeowners were similarly troubled, and in June 1933 the administration established the Home Owners Loan Corporation, which by 1936 had refinanced the mortgages of more than 1 million householders. A year later, Congress established the Federal Housing Administration to insure mortgages for new construction and home repairs.

THE NEW DEAL IN TRANSITION

Seldom has an American president enjoyed such remarkable popularity as Franklin Roosevelt did during his first two years in office. But with no end to the Depression yet in sight, the New Deal gradually found itself the target of fierce public criticism. In the spring of 1935, partly in response to these growing attacks, Roosevelt launched an ambitious new program of legislation that has often been called the "Second New Deal."

CRITICS OF THE NEW DEAL

Some of the most strident attacks on the New Deal came from critics on the right. Roosevelt had tried for a time to conciliate conservatives and business leaders. By the end of 1934, however, it was clear that the American right in general, and much of the corporate world in particular, had become irreconcilably hostile to the New Deal. In August 1934, a group of the most fervent (and wealthiest) Roosevelt opponents, led by members of the Du Pont family, reshaped the American Liberty League (formed initially to oppose prohibition of liquor), to arouse public opposition to the New Deal's "dictatorial" policies and its supposed attacks on free enterprise. But the new organization was never able to expand its constituency much beyond the northern industrialists who had founded it.

AMERICAN LIBERTY LEAGUE

Roosevelt's critics on the far left also managed to produce alarm among some supporters of the administration, but like the conservatives, they proved to have only limited strength. The Communist Party, the Socialist Party, and other radical and semiradical organizations were at times harshly critical of the New Deal. But they, too, failed to attract genuine mass support.

More menacing to the New Deal than either the far right or the far left was a group of dissident political movements that defied easy ideological classification. Some gained substantial public support within particular states and regions. And three men succeeded in mobilizing genuinely national followings. Dr. Francis E. Townsend, an elderly California physician, rose from obscurity to lead a movement of more than 5 million members with his plan for federal pensions for the elderly. According to the Townsend Plan, all Americans over the age of sixty would receive monthly government pensions of $200, provided they retired (thus freeing jobs for younger, unemployed Americans) and spent the money in full each month (which would pump needed funds into the economy). By 1935, the Townsend Plan had attracted the support of many older men and women. And while the plan itself was defeated in Congress in 1935, the public sentiment behind it helped build support for the Social Security system, which Congress did approve in 1935.

TOWNSEND PLAN

Father Charles E. Coughlin, a Catholic priest in the Detroit suburb of Royal Oak, Michigan, achieved even greater renown through his weekly sermons, launched in 1926 and broadcast nationally over the radio. In later years, Coughlin became notorious for his sympathy for fascism and his outspoken anti-Semitism. But until at least 1937, he was known primarily as an advocate for changing the banking and currency systems. He proposed a series of monetary reforms—remonetization of silver, issuing of greenbacks, and nationalization of the banking system—that he insisted would restore prosperity and ensure economic justice. At first a warm supporter of Franklin Roosevelt, by late 1934 Coughlin had become disheartened by

THE NEW DEAL Of the many resources at Roosevelt's disposal was the impression of his sunny personality during dark times. It conveyed to many a sense of hope and optimism. In this political cartoon from about 1934, Roosevelt is seen steering the ship of state towards economic recovery. His detractors are shown grumbling under the cloud of depression. (© The Granger Collection, New York)

what he claimed was the president's failure to deal harshly enough with the "money powers." In the spring of 1935, he established his own political organization, the National Union for Social Justice. He was widely believed to have one of the largest regular radio audiences of anyone in America.

More alarming to the administration was the growing national popularity of Senator Huey P. Long of Louisiana. Long had risen to power in his home state through his strident attacks on the banks, oil companies, and utilities and on the conservative political oligarchy allied with them. Elected

HUEY LONG governor in 1928, he launched an assault on his opponents so thorough and forceful that they were soon left with virtually no political power. Many critics in Louisiana claimed that Long had, in effect, become a dictator. But he also maintained the overwhelming support of the Louisiana electorate, in part because of his flamboyant personality and in part because of his solid record of conventional progressive accomplishments: building roads, schools, and hospitals; revising the tax codes; distributing free textbooks; lowering utility rates. Barred by law from succeeding himself as governor, he ran in 1930 for a seat in the U.S. Senate and won easily.

Long, like Coughlin, supported Franklin Roosevelt in 1932. But within six months of Roosevelt's inauguration, he had broken with the president. As an alternative to the New Deal, he advocated a drastic program of wealth redistribution, a program he ultimately named the Share-Our-Wealth Plan. The government, he claimed, could end the Depression easily by using the tax system to confiscate the surplus riches of the wealthiest men and women in America and distribute these surpluses to the rest of the population. That would, he claimed, allow the government to guarantee every family a minimum "homestead" of $5,000 and an annual wage of $2,500. In 1934, Long established his own national organization: the Share-Our-Wealth Society, which soon

SHARE-OUR-WEALTH SOCIETY attracted a large following through much of the nation. A poll by the Democratic National Committee in the spring of 1935 disclosed that Long might attract more than 10 percent of the vote if he ran as a third-party candidate, possibly enough to tip a close election to the Republicans.

THE "SECOND NEW DEAL"

Roosevelt launched the so-called Second New Deal in the spring of 1935 in response both to the growing political pressures and to the continuing economic crisis. The new proposals represented, if not a new direction, at least a shift in the emphasis of New Deal policy. Perhaps the most conspicuous change was in the administration's attitude toward big business. Symbolically at least, the president was now willing to attack corporate interests openly. In March, for example, he proposed to Congress an act designed to break up the great utility holding companies, and he spoke harshly of monopolistic control of their industry. The Holding Company Act of 1935 was the result, although furious lobbying by the utilities led to amendments that sharply limited its effects.

HUEY LONG Few public speakers could arouse a crowd more effectively than Huey Long of Louisiana, known to many as "the Kingfish" (a nickname borrowed from the popular radio show *Amos 'n Andy*). It was Long's effective use of radio, however, that contributed most directly to his spreading national popularity in the early 1930s. (© Archive Photos/Getty Images)

Equally alarming to affluent Americans was a series of tax reforms proposed by the president in 1935, a program conservatives quickly labeled a "soak-the-rich" scheme. Apparently designed to undercut the appeal of Huey Long's Share-Our-Wealth Plan, the Roosevelt proposals called for establishing the highest and most progressive peacetime tax rates in history–although the actual impact of these rates was limited.

The Supreme Court decision in 1935 to strike down the National Industrial Recovery Act also invalidated Section 7(a) of the act, which had guaranteed workers the right to orga-

NATIONAL LABOR RELATIONS BOARD nize and bargain collectively. A group of progressives in Congress led by Senator Robert F. Wagner of New York introduced what became the National Labor Relations Act of 1935. The new law, popularly known as the Wagner Act, provided workers with a crucial enforcement mechanism missing from the 1933 law: the National Labor Relations Board (NLRB), which would have power to compel employers to recognize and bargain with legitimate unions. The president was not entirely happy with the bill, but he signed it anyway. That was in large part because American workers themselves had by 1935 become so important and vigorous a force that Roosevelt realized his own political future would depend in part on responding to their demands.

LABOR MILITANCY

The emergence of a powerful trade union movement in the 1930s was one of the most important social and political developments of the decade. It occurred partly in response to government efforts to enhance the power of unions, but it was also a result of the increased pressure from American workers and their leaders.

The growing labor militancy first became obvious in 1934, when recently organized workers (many of them inspired by the collective bargaining provisions of the National Industrial Recovery Act) demonstrated a new assertiveness. It was soon clear, however, that without stronger legal protection, most organizing drives would end in frustration. Once the Wagner Act became law, the search for more-effective forms of organization rapidly gained strength in labor ranks.

The American Federation of Labor (AFL) remained committed to the idea of the craft union: organizing workers on the basis of their skills. But that concept had little to offer unskilled laborers, who now constituted the bulk of the industrial workforce. During the 1930s, therefore, a newer **INDUSTRIAL UNIONISM** concept of labor organization challenged the craft union ideal: industrial unionism. Advocates of this approach argued that all workers in a particular industry should be organized in a single union, regardless of what functions the workers performed: all autoworkers should be in a single automobile union; all steelworkers should be in a single steel union. United in this way, workers would greatly increase their power.

Leaders of the AFL craft unions for the most part opposed the new concept. But industrial unionism found a number of important advocates, most prominent among them John L. Lewis, the talented, flamboyant, and eloquent leader of the United Mine Workers. At first, Lewis and his allies attempted to work within the AFL, but friction between the new industrial organizations Lewis was promoting and the older craft unions grew rapidly. At the 1935 AFL convention, Lewis became embroiled in a series of angry confrontations (and one celebrated fistfight) with craft union leaders before finally walking out. A few weeks later, he created the Committee on Industrial Organization. When the AFL expelled the new committee and all the industrial unions it represented, Lewis **CIO** renamed the committee the Congress of Industrial Organizations (CIO), established it in 1936 as an organization directly rivaling the AFL, and became its first president.

The CIO expanded the constituency of the labor movement. It was more receptive to women and to blacks than the AFL had been, in part because women and blacks were more likely to be relegated to unskilled jobs and in part because CIO organizing drives targeted previously unorganized industries (textiles, laundries, tobacco factories, and others) where women and minorities constituted much of the workforce. The CIO was also a more militant organization than the AFL. By the time of the 1936 schism, it was already engaged in major organizing battles in the automobile and steel industries.

ORGANIZING BATTLES

Out of several competing auto unions, the United Auto Workers (UAW) was gradually emerging preeminent in the early and mid-1930s. But although it was gaining recruits, it was making little **SIT-DOWN STRIKE** progress in winning recognition from the automobile corporations. In December 1936, however, autoworkers employed a controversial and effective new technique for challenging corporate opposition: the sit-down strike. Employees in several General Motors plants in Detroit simply sat down inside the plants, refusing either to work or to leave, thus preventing the company from using strikebreakers. The tactic spread to other locations, and by February 1937 strikers had occupied seventeen GM plants. While male workers remained in the factories, female supporters—relatives, friends, and coworkers of the strikers—demonstrated on behalf of the strikers, lobbied on their behalf with state and local officials, and provided food, clothing, and other necessities to the men inside. The strikers ignored court orders and local police efforts to force them to vacate the buildings. When Michigan's governor, Frank Murphy, a liberal Democrat, refused to call up the National Guard to clear out the strikers, and when the federal government also refused to intervene on behalf of employers, General Motors relented. In February 1937, GM became the first major manufacturer to recognize the UAW; other automobile companies soon did the same. The sit-down strike proved effective for rubber workers and others as well, but it survived only briefly as a labor technique. Its apparent illegality aroused so much public opposition that labor leaders soon abandoned it.

In the steel industry, the battle for unionization was less easily won. In 1936, the Steel Workers' Organizing Committee (SWOC; later the United Steelworkers of America) began a major organizing drive involving thousands of workers and frequent, at times bitter, strikes. In March 1937, U.S. Steel, the giant of the industry, recognized the union rather than risk a costly strike at a time when it sensed itself on the verge of recovery from the Depression. But the smaller companies (known collectively as "Little Steel") were less accommodating. On Memorial Day 1937, a group of striking workers from Republic Steel gathered with their families for a picnic and demonstration in South Chicago. When they attempted to march peacefully (and legally) toward the steel plant, police opened fire on them. Ten demonstrators were killed; another ninety were wounded. Despite a public outcry against the "Memorial Day Massacre," the harsh tactics of Little Steel companies succeeded. The 1937 strike failed.

But the victory of Little Steel was one of the last gasps of the kind of brutal strikebreaking that had proved so effective in the past. In 1937 alone, there were 4,720 strikes—over 80 percent of them settled in favor of the unions. By the end of the year, more **ORGANIZED LABOR'S RAPID GROWTH** than 8 million workers were members of unions recognized as official bargaining units by employers (compared with 3 million in 1932). By 1941, that number had expanded to 10 million and included the workers of Little Steel, whose employers had finally recognized the SWOC.

THE "MEMORIAL DAY MASSACRE" The bitterness of the labor struggles of the 1930s was nowhere more evident than in Chicago in 1937, when striking workers attempting to march on a Republic Steel plant were brutally attacked by Chicago police, who used clubs, tear gas, and guns to turn the marchers away. Ten strikers were killed and many others were injured. (© Carl Linde/AP Images)

SOCIAL SECURITY

In 1935, Roosevelt gave public support to what became the Social Security Act, which Congress passed the same year. It established several distinct programs. For the elderly, there were two types of assistance. Those who were presently destitute could receive up to $15 a month in federal assistance. More important for the future, many Americans presently working were incorporated into a pension system, to which they and their employers would contribute by paying a payroll tax; it would provide them with an income on retirement. Pension payments would not begin until 1942 and even then would provide only $10 to $85 a month to recipients. And broad categories of workers (including domestic servants and agricultural laborers, occupations with disproportionate numbers of blacks and women) were excluded from the program. But the act was a crucial first

step in building the nation's most important social program for the elderly.

In addition, the Social Security Act created a system of unemployment insurance, which employers alone would finance and

UNEMPLOYMENT INSURANCE

which made it possible for workers laid off from their jobs to receive temporary government assistance. It also established a limited system (later expanded) of federal aid to people with disabilities and a program of aid to dependent children.

The framers of the Social Security Act wanted to create a system of "insurance," not "welfare." And the largest programs (old-age pensions and unemployment insurance) were in many ways similar to private insurance programs, with contributions from participants and benefits available to all. But the act also provided considerable direct assistance based on need—to the elderly poor, to those with disabilities, to dependent children and their mothers. These groups were widely perceived to be small and genuinely unable to support themselves. But in later generations the programs for these groups would expand considerably.

NEW DIRECTIONS IN RELIEF

Social Security was designed primarily to fulfill long-range goals. But millions of unemployed Americans had immediate needs. To help them, the Roosevelt administration established the

WPA

Works Progress Administration (WPA) in 1935. Like the Civil Works Administration and earlier efforts, the WPA established a system of work relief for the unemployed. But it was much bigger than the earlier agencies, both in the size of its budget ($5 billion in its first two years) and in the energy and imagination of its operations.

Under the direction of Harry Hopkins, the WPA was responsible for building or renovating 110,000 public buildings (schools, post offices, government office buildings) and for

SOCIAL SECURITY POSTER, 1935 Within months of the passage of the Social Security Act of 1935, the new Social Security Board began publicizing the benefits the new system offered to working Americans—the most dramatic of which was a monthly pension to retired Americans who had paid into the system. (The Library of Congress)

constructing almost 600 airports, more than 500,000 miles of roads, and over 100,000 bridges. In the process, the WPA kept an average of 2.1 million workers employed and pumped needed money into the economy.

The WPA displayed flexibility and imagination in offering assistance to those whose occupations did not fit into any traditional category of relief. The Federal Writers' Project of the WPA, for example, gave unemployed writers a chance to do their work and receive a government salary. The Federal Arts Project, similarly, helped painters, sculptors, and others to continue their careers. The Federal Music Project and the Federal Theater Project oversaw the production of concerts and plays, creating work for unemployed musicians, actors, and directors. Other relief agencies emerged alongside the WPA. The National Youth Administration (NYA) provided work and scholarship assistance to high-school and college-age men and women. The Emergency Housing Division of the Public Works Administration began federal sponsorship of public housing.

Men and women alike were in distress in the 1930s (as in all difficult times). But the new welfare system dealt with members of the two sexes in very different ways. For men, the government concentrated mainly on work relief—on such programs as the CCC, the CWA, and the WPA, all of which were overwhelmingly male, and—through the Social Security Act—pensions and unemployment insurance, both structured initially to assist mostly men. The principal government aid to women was not work relief but cash assistance—most notably through the Aid to Dependent Children program of Social Security, which was designed largely to assist single mothers. This disparity in treatment reflected a widespread assumption that men constituted the bulk of the paid workforce and that women needed to be treated within the context of the family. In fact, millions of women were already employed by the 1930s.

THE 1936 "REFERENDUM"

For a time in 1935 there had seemed reason to question the president's prospects for reelection. But by the middle of 1936—with the economy visibly reviving—there could be

ALF LANDON

little doubt that he would win a second term. The Republican Party nominated the moderate governor of Kansas, Alf M. Landon, who waged a weak campaign. Roosevelt's dissident challengers now appeared powerless. One reason was the violent death of their most effective leader, Huey Long, who was assassinated in Louisiana in September 1935. Another reason was the ill-fated alliance among Father Coughlin, Dr. Townsend, and Gerald L. K. Smith (an intemperate henchman of Huey Long), who joined forces that summer to establish a new political movement—the Union Party, which nominated an undistinguished North Dakota congressman, William Lemke, for president.

The result was the greatest landslide in American history to that point. Roosevelt polled just under 61 percent of the

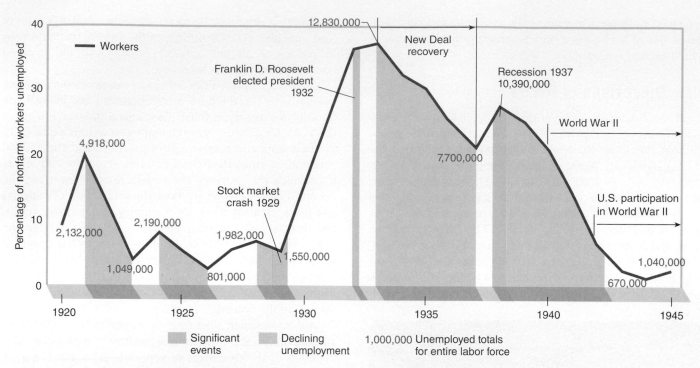

40

— Workers

12,830,000

New Deal recovery

30

Franklin D. Roosevelt elected president 1932

Recession 1937 10,390,000

World War II

4,918,000

20

Percentage of nonfarm workers unemployed

Stock market crash 1929

7,700,000

2,190,000

U.S. participation in World War II

10

2,132,000

1,982,000

1,049,000

1,550,000

1,040,000

801,000

670,000

0

1920   1925   1930   1935   1940   1945

| ▨ | Significant events | ▨ | Declining unemployment | 1,000,000 | Unemployed totals for entire labor force |

UNEMPLOYMENT, 1920–1945 This chart shows the shifting patterns of unemployment from 1920 to the end of World War II. As it reveals, nonfarm unemployment was very high in the early 1920s, in the last year of the postwar recession, but remained relatively low from 1923 to 1929. The beginning of the Great Depression sent unemployment soaring—to a peak of nearly 13 million people in early 1933—an unemployment rate of 25 percent. The New Deal helped create a partial recovery from the Depression over the next four years, but unemployment remained very high throughout the 1930s, and spiked sharply higher again during the recession of 1937–1938, before falling rapidly after war began in Europe.

• *Why was the war so much more successful than the New Deal in ending unemployment?*

WPA WORKERS ON THE JOB The Works Progress Administration funded an enormous variety of work projects to provide jobs for the unemployed. But most WPA employees worked on construction sites of one kind or another. (© Jospeh Schwartz/ Corbis)

WPA MURAL ART The Federal Arts Project of the Works Progress Administration commissioned an impressive series of public murals from the artists it employed. Many of these murals adorned post offices, libraries, and other public buildings constructed by the WPA. Shown here is a portion of a mural of shipbuilders at the Rincon Center, San Francisco. This mural is unusual in showing an African American worker. Most WPA iconography portrayed workers as white men only. (© Architec Tour/Alamy)

vote to Landon's 36 percent and carried every state except Maine and Vermont. The Democrats increased their already large majorities in both houses of Congress. The Union Party received fewer than 900,000 votes.

ELECTORAL REALIGNMENT The election results demonstrated the party realignment that the New Deal had produced. The Democrats now controlled a broad coalition of western and southern farmers, the urban working classes, the poor and unemployed, and the black communities of northern cities, as well as traditional progressives and committed new liberals—a coalition that constituted a substantial majority of the electorate. It would be decades before the Republican Party could again create a lasting majority coalition of its own.

THE NEW DEAL IN DISARRAY

Roosevelt emerged from the 1936 election at the zenith of his popularity. Within months, however, the New Deal was mired in serious new difficulties—a result of continuing opposition, the president's own political errors, and major economic setbacks.

THE COURT FIGHT

The 1936 mandate, Franklin Roosevelt believed, made it possible for him to do something about the problem of the Supreme Court. No program of reform, he had become convinced, could long survive the conservative justices, who had already struck down the NRA and the AAA and threatened to invalidate even more legislation.

In February 1937, Roosevelt sent a surprise message to Capitol Hill proposing a general overhaul of the federal court system; included among the many provisions was one to add up to six new justices to the Supreme Court, with a new justice added for every sitting justice over the age of seventy. The courts were "overworked," he claimed, and needed additional manpower and fresh ideas to enable them to cope with their increasing burdens. But Roosevelt's real purpose was to give himself the opportunity to appoint new, liberal justices and change the ideological balance of the Court.

COURT PACKING

Conservatives were outraged at the "Court-packing plan," and even many Roosevelt supporters were disturbed by what they considered evidence of the president's hunger for power. Still, Roosevelt might well have persuaded Congress to approve at least a compromise measure had not the Supreme Court itself intervened. Of the nine justices, three reliably supported the New Deal, and four reliably opposed it. Of the remaining two, Chief Justice Charles Evans Hughes often sided with the progressives and Associate Justice Owen J. Roberts usually voted with the conservatives. On March 29, 1937, Roberts, Hughes, and the three progressive justices voted together to uphold a state minimum-wage law—in the case of *West Coast Hotel v. Parrish*—thus appearing to reverse a 5-to-4 decision of the previous year invalidating a similar law. Two weeks later, again by a 5-to-4 margin, the Court upheld the Wagner Act, and in May it validated the Social Security Act. Whether or not for that reason, the Court's newly moderate position made the Court-packing bill seem unnecessary. Congress ultimately defeated it.

On one level, the affair was a significant victory for Franklin Roosevelt. The Court was no longer an obstacle to New Deal reforms, particularly after the older justices began to retire, to be replaced by Roosevelt appointees. But the Court-packing episode did lasting political damage to the administration. From 1937 on, southern Democrats and other conservatives voted against Roosevelt's measures much more often than they had in the past.

THE GOLDEN AGE OF COMIC BOOKS

IN the troubled years of the Great Depression and World War II, many Americans sought release from their anxieties in fantasy. Movies, plays, books, radio shows, and other diversions drew people out of their own lives and into a safer or more glamorous or more exciting world. Beginning in 1938, one of the most popular forms of escape for many young Americans became the comic book.

SUPERMAN The most popular action figure in the history of comic books was Superman, whose superhuman powers were particularly appealing fantasies to Americans suffering through the Depression and, later, World War II. (© Hulton Archive/Getty Images)

In February 1935, Malcolm Wheeler-Nicholson founded the first comics magazine—what we now know as the "comic book"—titled *New Fun*. *New Fun* was not successful, but Wheeler founded a new company, Detective Comics, and began in 1937 to design a new magazine called *Action Comics*. Wheeler ran out of money before he could publish anything, but the company continued without him. In 1938, the first issue of *Action Comics* appeared with a startling and controversial cover—a powerful man in a skintight suit lifting a car over his head. His name was Superman, and he became the most popular cartoon character of all time.

Within a year, Superman had a comic book named after him, which was selling over 1.2 million copies each issue. By 1940, there was a popular Superman radio show introduced by a breathless announcer crying, "It's a bird! It's a plane! It's . . . Superman!" Soon other publishers began developing new "superheroes" (a term invented by the creators of Superman) to capitalize on this growing new popular appetite. In 1939, a second great comic book publisher appeared—Marvel Comics. By the early 1940s, Superman had been joined by other superheroes: the Human Torch, the Sub-Mariner, Batman, the Flash, and Wonder Woman, a character created in part to signal the importance of women to the war effort.

It is not hard to imagine why superheroes would be so appealing to Americans—particularly to the teenage boys who were the largest single purchasers of comic books—in the 1930s and 1940s. Superman and other superheroes were idealized versions of the ideal boy—smart, good, "the perfect Boy Scout," as one fan put it. But they were also all-powerful, capable of righting wrong and preventing catastrophe. At a time when catastrophe was an ever-present possibility in the world, superheroes were a comforting escape from fear.

Many of the early comic book writers were young Jewish men, conscious of their outsider status in an American culture not yet wholly open to them. Almost all the characters they created had alter egos, identities they used while living within the normal world. Superman was Clark Kent, a "mild-mannered reporter." Batman was Bruce Wayne, a wealthy heir. The superhero characters were outsiders themselves—but outsiders endowed with special powers and abilities unavailable to ordinary people.

Even before America entered World War II, the comic superheroes were battling the Axis powers. Marvel's the Human Torch and the Sub-Mariner joined forces against the German navy. Superman fought spies and saboteurs at home. Captain America, a new character created in March 1941, was a frail young man rejected by the army who, after being given a secret serum by a military doctor, became extraordinarily powerful. The cover of the first issue of *Captain America* showed the title character punching Hitler in his headquarters in Germany.

The end of the war was also the end of this first "golden age" of American comic books. Many superhero magazines ceased publication as peacetime reduced the popular appetite for fantasy. In their place emerged new comic books, which emphasized romance and even mild sexuality.

In the late 1940s and early 1950s, comic books began to come under attack from educators, psychiatrists, journalists, and even the federal government. Congress took no legal action against comic book publishers or writers, but the comic book industry itself created a trade association, which produced a "Comics Code" to prevent indecency in the industry.

Comic books experienced an unexpected revival in the late 1950s and 1960s. Old superheroes—Captain America, the Human Torch, and others—reappeared. New ones—Spiderman, Iron Man, the Silver Surfer—joined them. Superman, who had never disappeared, enjoyed newfound popularity and became the hero for a time of a popular television show. But these new or

RETRENCHMENT AND RECESSION

By the summer of 1937, the gross national product, which had dropped from $82 billion in 1929 to $40 billion in 1932, had risen back to nearly $72 billion. Other economic indices showed similar advances. Roosevelt seized on these improvements as an excuse to try to balance the federal budget, convinced by Treasury Secretary Henry Morgenthau and many economists that the real danger now was no longer depression but inflation. Between January and August 1937,

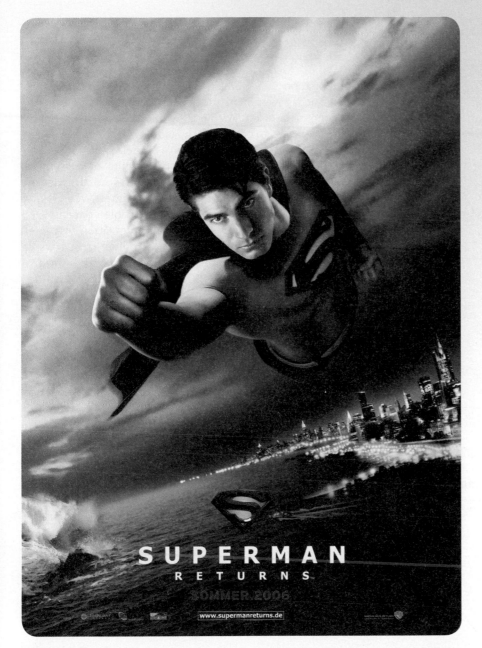

SUPERMAN TODAY Superman continues to appeal to the fantasies of Americans, as shown by this poster of the movie *Superman Returns* from 2006. Another film, *Man of Steel*, was released in 2013. And yet another is in the works for 2015 or 2016. (© Warner Bros./Photofest)

revised heroes were not entirely like those of the 1930s and 1940s. They reflected the realities of an increasingly complex and complicated world, which their characters—like their mostly young readers—were struggling to understand. ●

UNDERSTAND, ANALYZE, AND EVALUATE

1. What could comic books offer readers suffering through the crisis of the Great Depression?
2. How and why have comic book superheroes changed over time?
3. What might account for the upsurge in comic books' popularity in the late 1950s and 1960s?

he cut the WPA in half, laying off 1.5 million relief workers. A few weeks later, the fragile boom collapsed. Other cuts in spending followed. The index of industrial production dropped from 117 in August 1937 to 76 in May 1938. Four million additional workers lost their jobs. Economic conditions were soon almost as bad as they had been in the bleak days of 1932–1933.

The recession of 1937, known to the president's critics as the "Roosevelt recession," was a result of many factors. But to many observers at the time (including, apparently, the

Federal Budget and Surplus/Deficit, 1920–1940

Gross National Product, 1920–1940

Budget and Surplus/Deficit as Percentage of GNP, 1920–1940

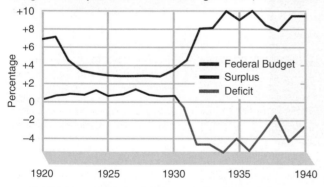

FEDERAL BUDGET SURPLUS/DEFICIT AND GNP, 1920–1940 Among its many other effects, the Great Depression produced dramatic changes in the fiscal condition of the federal government. In the first of these three charts, note the sharp decline in federal spending in the early 1920s (as the nation demobilized from World War I) and the appearance of significant budget surpluses. Note, too, the dramatic increase in government spending (and the appearance of significant deficits) once the Depression began and, particularly, once Franklin Roosevelt became president. The second chart illustrates the varying fortunes of the nation's economy by showing the rise and fall of gross national product—the total of goods and services produced by the economy. The GNP fell sharply in the first years of the Depression, but by the end of the 1930s was nearing its 1929 levels again. The final chart gives some perspective on these figures by illustrating the relationship between federal spending (and federal surpluses and deficits) and the total size of the economy. At its peak in these years, federal spending was never more than about 9 percent of the GNP and the deficit never more than about 5 percent. In recent decades, the federal budget has often exceeded 20 percent of the GNP. Deficits—much higher in absolute numbers than those of the 1930s—were rarely higher as a percentage of the GNP than those of the 1930s until the first decade of the twenty-first century.

• *Why did government deficits increase so sharply during the Great Depression?*

president himself), it seemed to be a direct result of the administration's unwise decision to reduce

ROOSEVELT RECESSION

spending. And so in April 1938, the president asked Congress for an emergency appropriation of $5 billion for public works and relief programs, and government funds soon began pouring into the economy once again. Within a few months, another tentative recovery seemed to be under way, and the advocates of spending pointed to it as proof of the validity of their approach.

At about the same time, at the urging of a group of younger, antimonopolist liberals in the administration, Roosevelt sent a stinging message to Congress, vehemently denouncing what he called an "unjustifiable concentration of economic power" and asking for the creation of a commission to consider major reforms in the antitrust laws. In response, Congress established the Temporary National Economic Committee (TNEC), whose members included representatives of both houses of Congress and officials from several executive agencies. Also that spring, Roosevelt appointed a new head of the antitrust division of the Justice Department: Thurman Arnold, a Yale Law School professor who soon proved to be the most vigorous director ever to serve in that office.

Later in 1938, the administration successfully supported one of its most ambitious pieces of labor legislation, the Fair Labor Standards Act, which for the first time established a national minimum wage and a forty-hour workweek, and which also placed strict limits on child labor. Like Social Security, the act at first excluded from its provisions the great majority of women and minority workers.

Despite these achievements, however, by the end of 1938 the New Deal had essentially come to an end. Congressional opposition now made it difficult for the president to enact any major new programs. But more important, perhaps, the threat

END OF THE NEW DEAL

of world crisis hung heavy in the political atmosphere, and Roosevelt was gradually growing more concerned with persuading a reluctant nation to prepare for war than with pursuing new avenues of reform.

LIMITS AND LEGACIES OF THE NEW DEAL

In the 1930s, Roosevelt's principal critics were conservatives, who accused him of abandoning the Constitution and establishing a menacing, even tyrannical, state. In later years, the New Deal's most visible critics attacked it from the left, pointing to the major problems it left unsolved and the important groups it failed to represent. And beginning in the early twenty-first century, conservative attacks on the New Deal would emerge again. A full understanding of the New Deal requires coming to terms with the sources of both critiques, by examining both its achievements and its limits.

THE IDEA OF THE "BROKER STATE"

In 1933, many New Dealers dreamed of using their new popularity and authority to remake American capitalism—to produce new forms of cooperation and control that would create a genuinely harmonious, ordered economic world. By 1939, it was clear that what they had created was in fact something quite different. But rather than bemoan the gap between their original intentions and their ultimate achievements, New Deal liberals, both in 1939 and in later years, chose to accept what they had produced and to celebrate it—to use it as a model for future reform efforts.

What they had created was something that in later years would become known as the "broker state." Instead of forging all elements of society into a single, harmonious unit, as some reformers had once hoped to do, the real achievement of the New Deal was to elevate and strengthen new interest groups so as to allow them to compete more effectively in the national marketplace. The New Deal made the federal government a mediator in that continuous competition—a force that could intervene when necessary to help some groups and limit the power of others. In 1933, there had been only one great interest group (albeit a varied and divided one) with genuine power in the national economy: the corporate world. By the end of the 1930s, American business found itself competing for influence with an increasingly powerful labor movement, an organized agricultural economy, and aroused consumers. In later years, the "broker state" idea would expand to embrace other groups as well: racial, ethnic, and religious minorities;

ESTABLISHMENT OF THE "BROKER STATE"

women; and many others. Thus, one of the enduring legacies of the New Deal was to make the federal government a protector of interest groups and a supervisor of the competition among them, rather than an instrument attempting to create a universal harmony of interests.

What determines which interest groups receive government assistance in a "broker state"? The experience of the New Deal suggests that such assistance goes largely to those groups able to exercise enough political or economic power to demand it. Thus in the 1930s, farmers—after decades of organization and agitation—and workers—as the result of militant action and mass mobilization—won from the government new and important protections. Other groups, less well organized, perhaps, but politically important because so numerous and visible, won limited assistance as well: imperiled homeowners, the unemployed, the elderly.

By the same token, the interest-group democracy that the New Deal came to represent offered much less to those groups either too weak to demand assistance or not visible enough to arouse widespread public support. And yet those same groups were often the ones most in need of help from their government. One of the important limits of the New Deal, therefore, was its very modest record on behalf of several important social groups.

AFRICAN AMERICANS AND THE NEW DEAL

One group the New Deal did relatively little to assist was African Americans. The administration was not hostile to black aspirations. On the contrary, the New Deal was probably more sympathetic to them than any previous government of the

ELEANOR ROOSEVELT First Lady Eleanor Roosevelt was among the first women to play an important role in politics and government. She oversaw Franklin Roosevelt's political campaigns before he became president as well as developed an important career of her own working on social programs in New York. When she moved to the White House, she served her husband by traveling widely (something that Franklin Roosevelt, whose legs were paralyzed by polio, could not often do), and she took on issues that her husband chose not to embrace. An example is this photograph of Eleanor Roosevelt riding in a car to a Washington, D.C., jail to inspect the facility, which had a reputation for being overcrowded and obsolete. (© Underwood & Underwood/Corbis)

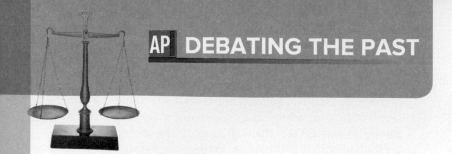

THE NEW DEAL

FOR many years, debate among historians over the nature of the New Deal mirrored the debate among Americans in the 1930s over the achievements of the Roosevelt administration. Historians struggled, just as contemporaries had done, to decide whether the New Deal was a good thing or a bad thing.

By far the dominant view of the New Deal among scholars has been an approving, liberal interpretation, and the first important voice of that view was Arthur M. Schlesinger Jr., who argued in the three volumes of *The Age of Roosevelt* (1957–1960) that the New Deal marked a continuation of the long struggle between public power and private interests. Roosevelt had moved that struggle to a new level, challenging the unrestrained power of the business community and offering far more protection for workers, farmers, consumers, and others than they had enjoyed in the past.

The first systematic "revisionist" interpretation of the New Deal came in 1963, in William Leuchtenburg's *Franklin D. Roosevelt and the New Deal.* Leuchtenburg was a sympathetic critic, arguing that most of the limitations of the New Deal were a result of the restrictions imposed on Roosevelt by the political and ideological realities of his time—that the New Deal probably could not have done much more than it did. Nevertheless, Leuchtenburg could not agree with others who called the New Deal a revolution in social policy. He was able to muster only enough enthusiasm to call it a "halfway revolution," one that enhanced the positions of some previously disadvantaged groups (notably farmers and factory workers) but did little or nothing for many others (including blacks, sharecroppers, and the urban poor). Ellis Hawley augmented these moderate criticisms of the Roosevelt record in *The New Deal and the Problem of Monopoly* (1966). In examining 1930s economic policies, Hawley argued that New Deal efforts were in many cases designed to enhance the position of private entrepreneurs—even, at times, at the expense of some of the liberal reform goals that administration officials espoused.

Much harsher criticisms of the New Deal emerged in the 1960s and later. Barton Bernstein in a 1968 essay concluded that the Roosevelt administration may have saved capitalism, but it failed to help—and in many ways actually harmed—groups most in need of assistance. Ronald Radosh, Thomas Ferguson, and, more recently, Colin Gordon took such arguments further. They cited the close ties between the New Deal and internationalist financiers and industrialists; the liberalism of the 1930s was a product of their shared interest in protecting capitalists and stabilizing capitalism.

Most scholars in the 1980s and 1990s, however, seemed largely to have accepted the revised liberal view: that the New Deal was a significant (and, most agreed, valuable) chapter in the history of reform, but one that worked within rigid, occasionally crippling limits. Much of the recent work on the New Deal has focused on the constraints within which it was operating. The sociologist Theda Skocpol (along with other scholars) has emphasized the issue of "state capacity" as an important New Deal constraint; ambitious reform ideas often foundered, she argued, because no government bureaucracy had sufficient strength and expertise to shape or administer them. James T. Patterson, Barry Karl, Mark Leff, and others have emphasized the political constraints the New Deal encountered. Both in Congress and among the public, conservative inhibitions about government remained strong.

Frank Freidel, Ellis Hawley, Herbert Stein, and many others point as well to the ideological constraints affecting Franklin Roosevelt and his supporters. Alan Brinkley, in *The End of Reform* (1995), described an ideological shift in New Deal liberalism that shifted from the initial regulatory view of government to one that envisioned relatively little direct governmental interference in the corporate world and centered instead on Keynesian welfare state programs. David Kennedy, in *Freedom from Fear* (1999), argued by contrast that the aggressive anticapitalism of early New Deal liberalism actually hampered the search for recovery. Only when Roosevelt

twentieth century. Eleanor Roosevelt spoke throughout the 1930s on behalf of racial justice and put continuing pressure on her husband and others in the federal government to ease discrimination against blacks. She was also partially responsible for what was, symbolically at least, one of the most important events of the decade for African Americans. When the renowned African American concert singer Marian Anderson was refused permission in the spring of 1939 to give a concert in the auditorium of the Daughters of the American Revolution (Washington's only major concert hall), Eleanor Roosevelt resigned from the organization and then (along with Interior Secretary Harold Ickes, another champion of racial equality) helped secure government permission for her to sing on the steps of the Lincoln Memorial. Anderson's Easter Sunday concert attracted 75,000 people and became, in effect, one of the first modern civil rights demonstrations.

The president himself appointed a number of black officials to significant second-level positions in his administration. Roosevelt appointees such as Robert Weaver, William Hastie, and Mary McLeod Bethune created an informal network of officeholders who consulted frequently with one another and who became known as the "Black Cabinet." Eleanor Roosevelt, Harold Ickes, and Harry Hopkins all made efforts to ensure that New Deal relief programs did not exclude blacks; and by 1935, perhaps a quarter of all African Americans were receiving some form of government assistance. One result was a historic change in black electoral behavior. As late as 1932, most African Americans were voting Republican, as they had since the Civil War. By 1936, more than 90 percent of them were voting Democratic—the beginnings of a political alliance that would endure for decades.

"BLACK CABINET"

embraced measures that unleashed the power of the market did prosperity begin to return.

The phrase "New Deal liberalism" has come in the postwar era to seem synonymous with modern ideas of aggressive federal management of the economy, elaborate welfare systems, a powerful bureaucracy, and large-scale government spending. Many historians of the New Deal, however, would argue that the modern idea of "New Deal liberalism" bears only a limited relationship to the ideas that New Dealers themselves embraced. The liberal accomplishments of the 1930s can be understood only in the context of their own time; later liberal efforts drew from that legacy but also altered it to fit the needs and assumptions of very different eras. ●

AP HISTORICAL ARGUMENTATION AND INTERPRETATION

Questions assume cumulative content knowledge from this chapter and previous chapters.

1. Describe the development of historical interpretations discussed of the nature of the New Deal and its achievements.
2. How might a historian who was a Progressive in the early 20th century have evaluated the achievements or degree of success of the New Deal?
3. With which historical argument do you most agree? Explain why, supporting your argument with historical evidence.

FDR IN ALBANY Before he became president, Franklin Roosevelt served as governor of New York, where he developed a reputation of being an activist working to confront the Great Depression. In this 1930 photograph, he is sitting at his desk in the state capitol. Two years later, he would be elected president. (© AFP/Getty Images)

African Americans supported Franklin Roosevelt because they knew he was not their enemy. But they had few illusions that the New Deal represented a major turning point in American race relations. For example, the president was never willing to risk losing the backing of southern Democrats by supporting legislation to make lynching a federal crime. Nor would he endorse efforts in Congress to ban the poll tax, one of the most potent tools by which white southerners kept blacks from voting.

New Deal relief agencies did not challenge, and indeed reinforced, existing patterns of discrimination. The Civilian Conservation Corps established separate black camps. The NRA codes tolerated paying blacks less than whites doing the same jobs. African Americans were largely excluded from employment in the TVA. The Federal Housing Administration refused to provide mortgages to African

EXISTING DISCRIMINATION REINFORCED

Americans moving into white neighborhoods, and the first public housing projects financed by the federal government were racially segregated. The WPA routinely relegated black, Hispanic, and Asian workers to the least-skilled and lowest-paying jobs, or excluded them altogether; when funding ebbed, nonwhites, like women, were among the first to be dismissed.

The New Deal was not hostile to African Americans, and it did much to help them advance. But it refused to make the issue of race a significant part of its agenda.

THE NEW DEAL AND THE "INDIAN PROBLEM"

In many respects, government policies toward the Indian tribes in the 1930s were simply a continuation of the long-established effort to encourage Native Americans to assimilate into the larger society and culture.

But the principal elements of federal policy in the New Deal years worked to advance a very different goal, largely because of the efforts of the extraordinary commissioner of Indian affairs in those years, John Collier. Collier was a former social worker who had become committed to the cause of the Indians after exposure to tribal cultures in New Mexico in the 1920s. More important, he was greatly influenced by the work of twentieth-century anthropologists who promoted the idea of cultural relativism, which challenged the three-centuries-old assumption among white Americans that Indians were "savages" and that white society was inherently superior and more "civilized."

JOHN COLLIER

Collier promoted legislation that would, he hoped, reverse the pressures on Native Americans to assimilate and would allow them the right to live in traditional Indian ways. Not all tribal leaders agreed with Collier; indeed, his belief in the importance of preserving Indian culture would not find its broadest support among the tribes until the 1960s. Nevertheless, Collier effectively promoted legislation–which became the Indian Reorganization Act of 1934–that restored to the tribes the right to own land collectively. (It reversed the allotment policy adopted in 1887, which encouraged the breaking up of tribal lands into individually owned plots–a policy that had led to the loss of over 90 million acres of tribal land to white speculators and others.) In the thirteen years after passage of the 1934 bill, tribal land increased by nearly 4 million acres, and Indian agricultural income increased from under $2 million in 1934 to over $49 million in 1947.

INDIAN REORGANIZATION ACT

Even with the redistribution of lands under the 1934 act, however, Indians continued to possess, for the most part, only territory whites did not want–much of it arid, some of it desert. And as a group, they continued to constitute the poorest segment of the population. The efforts of the 1930s did not solve what some white people called the "Indian problem." They did, however, provide Indians with some tools for rebuilding the viability of the tribes.

WOMEN AND THE NEW DEAL

As with African Americans, the New Deal was not hostile to feminist aspirations, but neither did it do a great deal to advance them. That was largely because such aspirations did not have sufficiently widespread support (even among women) to make it politically advantageous for the administration to back them.

There were, to be sure, important symbolic gestures on behalf of women. Roosevelt appointed the first female cabinet member in the nation's history, Secretary of Labor Frances Perkins. He also named more than 100 other women to positions at lower levels of the federal bureaucracy. They created an active female network within the government and cooperated

HARLEM, THE "NEGRO CAPITAL OF AMERICA" Photographer Jack Manning took this picture, *Street Portrait 5 Young Boys*, as part of Aaron Siskind's project called the "Harlem Document," which portrayed life in what *Look* magazine called "the Negro capital of America." This photo was taken in 1938 or 1939. (Jack Manning/© The New York Times/Redux)

with one another in advancing causes of interest to women. Such appointments were in part a response to pressure from Eleanor Roosevelt, who was a committed advocate of women's rights and a champion of humanitarian causes. Molly Dewson, head of the Women's Division of the Democratic National Committee, was also influential in securing federal appointments for women as well as in increasing their role within the Democratic Party. Several women received appointments to the federal judiciary. And one, Hattie Caraway of Arkansas, became in 1934 the first woman elected to a full term in the U.S. Senate. (She was running to succeed her husband, who had died in office.)

SYMBOLIC GAINS FOR WOMEN

But New Deal support for women operated within limits, partly because New Deal women themselves had limited views of what their aims should be. Frances Perkins and many others in the administration emerged out of the feminist tradition of the progressive era, which emphasized not so much gender equality as special protections for women. Perkins and other women reformers were instrumental in creating support for, and shaping the character of, the Social Security Act of 1935. But they built into that bill their own notion of women's special place in a male-dominated economy. The principal provision of the bill specifically designed for women–the Aid to Dependent Children program–was modeled on the state-level mothers' pensions that generations of progressive women had worked to pass earlier in the century.

The New Deal generally supported the prevailing belief that in hard times women should withdraw from the workplace to open up more jobs for men. New Deal relief agencies offered relatively little employment for women. The NRA sanctioned wage practices that discriminated against women. The Social Security program at first excluded domestic servants, waitresses, and other predominantly female occupations.

PREVAILING GENDER NORMS BUTTRESSED

THE NEW DEAL IN THE WEST AND THE SOUTH

Two regions of the United States that did receive special attention from the New Deal were the West and the South, both of which benefited disproportionately from New Deal relief and public works programs. The West received more federal funds per capita through New Deal relief programs than any other region, and parts of the South were not far behind.

Most westerners were eager for the assistance New Deal agencies provided, but their political leaders were not always as supportive. In Colorado, for example, the state legislature refused to provide the required matching funds for FERA relief in 1933. When, in response, Harry Hopkins cut Colorado off from the program, unemployed people rioted in Denver and looted food stores. Only then did the legislature reverse course and provide funding.

In the South, locally administered New Deal relief programs did not challenge prevailing racial norms. In the West, too, New Deal programs accepted existing racial and ethnic prejudices. In several states, relief agencies paid different groups at different rates: white Anglos received the most generous aid; blacks, Indians, and Mexican Americans received lower levels of support.

FAILURE TO CHALLENGE JIM CROW

In the CCC camps in New Mexico, Hispanics and Anglos sometimes worked in the same camps, but there were frequent tensions and occasional conflicts between them. But the main reason for the New Deal's impact on the West was that conditions in the region made the government's programs especially important. Federal agricultural programs had an enormous impact on the West because farming remained so much more central to the economy of the region than it did in much of the East. The largest New Deal public works programs–the great dams and power stations–were mainly in the West, both because the best locations for such facilities were there and because the West had the most need for new sources of water and power. The Grand Coulee Dam on the Columbia River was the largest public works project in American history to that point. It provided cheap electric power for much of the Northwest and, along with the construction of smaller dams and water projects nearby, created a basis for economic development in the region.

Without this enormous public investment by the federal government, much of the economic development that transformed the West after World War II would have been much more difficult, if not impossible, to achieve. But the region paid a price for the government's beneficence: for generations after the Great Depression, the federal government maintained a much greater and more visible bureaucratic presence in the West than in any other region.

NEW DEAL'S LEGACY IN THE WEST

The New Deal located fewer great infrastructure projects in the South than it did in the West–although the largest of them, the TVA, was an entirely southern venture. But many of the economic development efforts the Roosevelt administration undertook were of disproportionate benefit to the South, largely because the South was the least economically developed region of the nation in the 1930s. One example was rural electrification, which had a large impact on many agrarian areas of the nation but a particular impact on the South, where vast parts of the countryside remained without access to power lines until the Rural Electrification Administration provided them.

The New Deal also directed national attention toward the economic condition of the South in a way that no previous administration had done. Many Americans outside the South had long believed the South to be "backward," but they tended to attribute that backwardness to racism, segregation, and prejudice. In a 1938 economic report sponsored by the federal government, a group of social scientists and others called the South "the nation's number one economic problem." Although the report made some reference to the South's racial customs, it spoke mostly about its lack of sufficiently developed economic institutions and facilities.

THE NEW DEAL AND THE NATIONAL ECONOMY

The most frequent criticisms of the New Deal involve its failure genuinely to revive or reform the American economy. New Dealers never fully embraced government spending as a vehicle for recovery, and their efforts along other lines never succeeded in ending the Depression. The economic boom sparked by World War II, not the New Deal, finally ended the crisis. Nor did the New Deal substantially alter the distribution of power within American capitalism; and it had only a small impact on the distribution of wealth among the American people.

FAILURE TO ACHIEVE RECOVERY

Nevertheless, the New Deal did have important and lasting effects on both the behavior and the structure of the American economy. It helped elevate new groups–workers, farmers, and others–to positions from which they could at times effectively challenge the power of the corporations. It contributed to the economic development of the West and, to a lesser degree, the South. It increased the regulatory functions of the federal government in ways that helped stabilize previously troubled areas of the economy: the stock market, the banking system, and others. (Many of these regulations were weakened or repealed beginning in the 1970s and beyond.) And the administration helped establish the basis for new forms of federal fiscal policy, which in the postwar years would give the government tools for promoting and regulating economic growth.

The New Deal also created the basis of the federal welfare state, through its many relief programs and above all through the Social Security system. The conservative inhibitions New

MAJOR LEGISLATION OF THE NEW DEAL

1933	Emergency Banking Act
	Economy Act
	Civilian Conservation Corps
	Agricultural Adjustment Act
	Tennessee Valley Authority
	National Industrial Recovery Act
	Banking Act
	Federal Emergency Relief Act
	Home Owners Refinancing Act
	Civil Works Administration
	Federal Securities Act
1934	National Housing Act
	Securities and Exchange Act
	Home Owners Loan Act

1935	Works Progress Administration
	National Youth Administration
	Social Security Act
	National Labor Relations Act
	Public Utilities Holding Company Act
	Resettlement Administration
	Rural Electrification Administration
	Revenue Act ("wealth tax")
1936	Soil Conservation and Domestic Allotment Act
1937	Farm Security Administration
	National Housing Act
1938	Second Agricultural Adjustment Act
	Fair Labor Standards Act
1939	Executive Reorganization Act

FEDERAL WELFARE STATE ESTABLISHED Dealers brought to this task ensured that the welfare system would be limited in its impact (at least in comparison with those of other industrial nations), would reinforce some traditional patterns of gender and racial discrimination, and would be expensive and cumbersome to administer. But for all its limits, the new system marked a historic break with the federal government's traditional reluctance to offer public assistance to its neediest citizens.

THE NEW DEAL AND AMERICAN POLITICS

Perhaps the most dramatic effect of the New Deal was on the structure and behavior of American government and on the character of American politics. Franklin Roosevelt helped enhance the power of the federal government. By the end of the 1930s, state and local governments were clearly of second-ary importance to the government in Washington. Roosevelt also established the presidency as the preeminent center of authority within the federal government.

Finally, the New Deal had a profound impact on how the American people defined themselves politically. It took a weak, divided Democratic Party, which had been a minority **NEW EXPECTATIONS OF GOVERNMENT** force in American politics for many decades, and turned it into a mighty coalition that would dominate national party competition for more than thirty years. It turned the attention of many voters away from some of the cultural issues that had preoccupied them in the 1920s and awakened in them an interest in economic matters of direct importance to their lives. And it created among the American people greatly increased expectations of government—expectations that the New Deal did not always fulfill but that survived to become the basis of new liberal crusades in the postwar era.

AP CONNECTING THEMES

Chapter 24 focused on the specific acts and consequences of New Deal attempts to end the Great Depression. As you review the chapter, focus on how Roosevelt used personality and technology to attempt to restore confidence in the economy. Also, pay attention to the major pieces of legislation during the First and Second New Deals and their relative successes or failures (but don't get bogged down in memorizing every agency). Understand the arguments of critics from both "the left" and "the right" and Roosevelt's responses to those threats. Focus on the changing attitude of government toward organized labor, African Americans, and American Indians. Extremely important is to understand the causes and results of political realignment during the 1930s. Finally, focus on the impact of the Great Depression on women and of Eleanor Roosevelt's efforts to improve the lives of disadvantaged people.

The following themes have heightened importance in Chapter 24. You should now be able to do the following for each listed theme:

Work, Exchange, and Technology: Examine the impact of "make-work" projects on the American economy and on the self-image of unemployed workers.

Politics and Power: Explain the reasons for and results of political realignment of many disadvantaged groups to the Democratic Party.

Environment and Geography: Examine the impact of climatic changes on the economy and the impact of New Deal programs on environmental reclamation.

Ideas, Beliefs, and Culture: Examine how the New Deal changed the philosophical mindset of the American people toward the role of the federal government in the economy.

AP SUGGESTED STUDY

PEOPLE/PLACES/EVENTS As you study these items, think about how they demonstrate or relate to key concepts and historical themes from this chapter and previous chapters.

AGRICULTURAL ADJUSTMENT ACT
  (AAA) 663
"BANK HOLIDAY" 662
BROKER STATE 679
CHARLES E. COUGHLIN 669
CONGRESS OF INDUSTRIAL
  ORGANIZATIONS (CIO) 671
COURT-PACKING PLAN 675
ELEANOR ROOSEVELT 680
FEDERAL WRITERS' PROJECT 673

FRANCES PERKINS 682
FRANCIS E. TOWNSEND 669
GLASS-STEAGALL ACT 668
HARRY HOPKINS 673
HUEY LONG 670
JOHN COLLIER 682
JOHN L. LEWIS 671
MARIAN ANDERSON 680
NATIONAL RECOVERY ADMINISTRATION
  (NRA) 666

SCHECHTER BROTHERS CASE 666
SECOND NEW DEAL 670
SECURITIES AND EXCHANGE
  COMMISSION (SEC) 668
SIT-DOWN STRIKE 671
SOCIAL SECURITY ACT 672
TENNESSEE VALLEY AUTHORITY
  (TVA) 667

AP TEST PRACTICE

Questions assume cumulative content knowledge from this chapter and previous chapters.

MULTIPLE CHOICE Use the graph on page 674 and your knowledge of U.S. history to answer questions 1-2.

1. In which way might the New Deal have most directly contributed to the trend between 1932 and 1936?

    (A) Establishment of pensions for future retirees

    (B) Establishment of work relief programs

    (C) Providing direct cash assistance to women

    (D) Creating a system of unemployment insurance

2. Based on your studies of World War I, which is the more reasonable explanation for the trend shown on the graph from the start of World War II?

    (A) An increase in government funded jobs programs

    (B) A rise in demand for American products as competitor countries were at war

    (C) Effective redistribution of power within the American capitalist system, achieved by the New Deal by the time of the war

    (D) The increased strength of the power of unions by the start of the war

SHORT ANSWER Use your knowledge of U.S. history to answer questions 3-4.

3. Answer a, b, and c.

    a) For ONE of the areas below, briefly explain how effective the New Deal was in achieving its goals.

    • Providing relief to the poverty-stricken

    • Stimulating the economy

    • Instituting economic reforms

    b) Provide ONE piece of historical evidence to prove its effectiveness.

    c) Choose ONE other area and explain why New Deal programs were not as effective in achieving its goals as it was for the area you chose.

4. Using the pictures on page 672 and 674, answer a, b, and c.

    a) For ONE of the groups below, briefly explain how the New Deal addressed issues the group faced.

    • Women

    • African Americans

    • Union members

    b) Provide at least ONE example of how the New Deal assisted this group.

    c) Provide ONE example that demonstrates how the New Deal failed to help the group that you chose.

LONG ESSAY For each question below, develop a thoughtful and thorough historical argument that answers the question. Begin your essay with a thesis statement and support it with relevant historical evidence.

5. Some critics of the New Deal have maintained that it did not bring lasting stability for the American society, minority groups, or the economy. Support, modify or refute this interpretation, providing specific evidence to justify your answer.

6. Analyze to what extent the New Deal helped to reshape the Democratic Party and increase support for the party among ethnic minorities and the working class.

25 THE GLOBAL CRISIS, 1921–1941

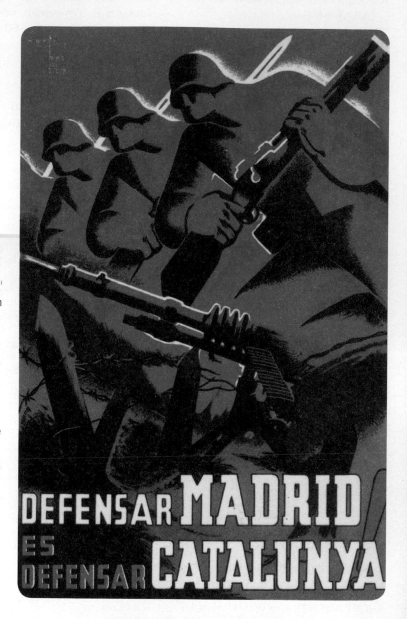

AP
HISTORICAL THINKING

1. **Historical Argumentation** Analyze the degree to which disillusionment with World War I influenced U.S. foreign policy in the 1920s and early 1930s.

2. **Historical Causation** To what degree and in what ways did Franklin Roosevelt attempt to change the mind-set of the American people toward involvement in European affairs prior to the attack on Pearl Harbor?

3. **Comparison** To what degree and in what ways was the foreign policy of the United States isolationist and to what degree and in what ways was it internationalist?

4. **Historical Causation** What factors led the American public to move from an isolationist stance to one which favored U.S. involvement in international conflict between 1930 and 1941?

5. **Patterns of Continuity and Changes over Time** Analyze both the continuity and changes in American foreign policy toward Latin America and the Soviet Union between 1918 and 1940.

Key Concept Correlations

Analyze the ways the historical developments you learn about in this chapter connect to the following AP Key Concepts.

7.3 Global conflicts over resources, territories, and ideologies renewed debates over the nation's values and its role in the world while simultaneously propelling the United States into a dominant international military, political, cultural, and economic position.

Thematic Learning Objectives
WOR-4, 6, 7; ENV-5; POL-6; ID-3

"DEFENDING MADRID" The Spanish Civil War, in which the forces led by Francisco Franco overturned the existing republican government, was an early signal to many Americans of the dangers of fascism and the threat to democracy. Although the United States government remained aloof from the conflict, several thousand Americans volunteered to fight on behalf of the republican forces. This 1938 Spanish war poster contains the words "Defending Madrid Is Defending Catalonia," an effort by the government in Madrid to enlist the support of the surrounding regions to defend the capital against Franco forces. (© Archive Photos/Getty Images)

CHAPTER 25 deals with changes in U.S. foreign affairs from the 1920s through the attack on Pearl Harbor. It focuses on the reasons for the debate between isolationists and internationalists. The chapter also focuses on the impact of the Great Depression and the attitudes of the American people regarding foreign policy. Significant attention is paid to the factors that gradually led Americans to favor involvement in World War II. That discussion includes specific international developments, as well as domestic changes leading to turning American public opinion. In spite of this development, some Americans made great efforts to limit U.S. involvement in world affairs. Finally, the chapter deals with the causes that led to the attack on Pearl Harbor in 1941. As you read, evaluate the following ideas:

- Disillusionment with the perceived failure of the United States to achieve idealistic goals in World War I led the American people to favor an isolationistic stance.
- The unstable international situation between 1920 and 1941 led to significant debate over the role of the United States in global affairs.
- The United States pursued a policy of independent internationalism during the 1920s, choosing when and where to become involved.
- During the 1930s the American people generally opposed U.S. involvement in global disputes until the attack on Pearl Harbor in 1941.

THE DIPLOMACY OF THE NEW ERA

Critics of American foreign policy in the 1920s often used a single word to describe the cause of their disenchantment: isolationism. Having rejected the Wilsonian vision of a new world order,

MYTH OF ISOLATIONISM

they claimed, the nation had turned its back on the rest of the globe and repudiated its international responsibilities. In fact, the United States played a more active role in world affairs in the 1920s than it had at almost any previous time in its history—even if not the role the Wilsonians had prescribed.

REPLACING THE LEAGUE

It was clear when the Harding administration took office in 1921 that American membership in the League of Nations was no longer a realistic possibility. As if finally to bury the issue, Secretary of State Charles Evans Hughes secured legislation from Congress in 1921 declaring the war with Germany at an end, and then proceeded to negotiate separate peace treaties with the former Central Powers. Through these treaties, American policymakers believed, the United States would receive all the advantages of the Versailles Treaty with none of the burdensome responsibilities. But Hughes was also committed to finding something to replace the League as a guarantor of world peace and stability. He embarked, therefore, on a series of efforts to build safeguards against future wars—but safeguards that would not hamper American freedom of action in the world.

The most important such effort was the Washington Conference of 1921–an attempt to prevent what was threatening to become a costly and destabilizing naval armaments race between the United States, Britain, and Japan. In his opening speech, Hughes startled the delegates by proposing

WASHINGTON CONFERENCE OF 1921

a plan for dramatic reductions in the fleets of all three nations and a ten-year moratorium on the construction of large warships. He called for the scrapping of nearly 2 million tons of existing shipping. Far more surprising than the proposal was the fact that the conference ultimately agreed to accept most of its terms, something that Hughes apparently had not anticipated. The Five-Power Pact of February 1922 established both limits for total naval tonnage and a ratio of armaments among the signatories. For every 5 tons of American and British warships, Japan would maintain 3 and France and Italy 1.75 each. (Although the treaty seemed to confirm the military inferiority of Japan, in fact it sanctioned Japanese dominance in East Asia. The United States and Britain had to spread their fleets across the globe; Japan was concerned only with the Pacific.) The Washington Conference also produced two other, related treaties: the Nine-Power Pact, pledging a continuation of the Open Door policy in China, and the Four-Power Pact, by which the United States, Britain, France, and Japan promised to respect one another's Pacific territories and cooperate to prevent aggression.

The Washington Conference began the New Era effort to protect the peace (and the international economic interests of

KELLOGG-BRIAND PACT

the United States) without accepting active international duties. The Kellogg-Briand Pact of 1928 concluded it. When the French foreign minister, Aristide Briand, asked the United States in 1927 to join an alliance against Germany, Secretary of State Frank Kellogg (who had replaced Hughes in 1925) instead proposed a multilateral treaty outlawing war as an instrument of national policy. Fourteen nations signed the agreement in Paris on August 27, 1928, amid great solemnity and wide international acclaim. Forty-eight other nations later joined the pact. It contained no instruments of enforcement but rested, as Kellogg put it, on the "moral force" of world opinion.

DEBTS AND DIPLOMACY

The first responsibility of diplomacy, Hughes, Kellogg, and others agreed, was to ensure that American overseas trade faced no obstacles to expansion and would remain free of interference. Preventing a dangerous armaments race and reducing the possibility of war were steps to that end. So were new financial arrangements that emerged at the same time.

The United States was most concerned about Europe, on whose economic health American prosperity in large part depended. Not only were the major European industrial powers suffering from the devastation World War I had produced; they were also staggering under a heavy burden of debt. The Allied forces were struggling to repay $11 billion in loans they had contracted with the United States during and shortly after the war, loans that the Republican administrations were unwilling to reduce or forgive. "They hired the money, didn't they?" Calvin Coolidge once replied when asked if he favored offering Europe relief from their debts. At the same time, an even more debilitated Germany was attempting to pay the reparations levied against it by the Allies. With the financial structure of Europe on the brink of collapse, the United States stepped in with a solution.

In 1924 Charles G. Dawes, an American banker and diplomat, negotiated an agreement under which American banks would provide enormous loans to the Germans, enabling them

CIRCULAR LOANS

to meet their reparations payments; in return, Britain and France would agree to reduce the amount of those payments. Dawes won the Nobel Peace Prize for his efforts, but in fact the Dawes Plan did little to solve the problems it addressed. It led to a troubling circular pattern in international finance. America would lend money to Germany, which would use that money

U.S. PRODUCTION METHODS IN THE SOVIET UNION This photograph, from about 1930, shows American turbines used in a Soviet power station built by Americans as part of the first Five Year Plan of Soviet economic growth. Soviet planners were so impressed with American methods of mass production, they called the system of large-scale factory production "Fordism," after American automobile manufacturer Henry Ford. (© The Granger Collection, New York)

to pay reparations to France and England, which would in turn use those funds (as well as large loans they themselves were receiving from American banks) to repay war debts to the United States. The flow was able to continue only by virtue of the enormous debts Germany and the other European nations were accumulating to American banks and corporations.

Those banks and corporations were doing more than providing loans. They were becoming a daily presence in the economic life of Europe. American automobile manufacturers were opening European factories, capturing a large share of the overseas market. Other American industries in the 1920s were establishing subsidiaries worth more than $10 billion throughout the Continent, taking advantage of the devastation of European industry and the inability of domestic corporations to recover. Some groups within the U.S. government warned that the reckless expansion of overseas loans and investments, many in enterprises of dubious value, threatened disaster; that the United States was becoming too dependent on unstable European economies.

The high tariff barriers that the Republican Congress had erected (through the Fordney-McCumber Act of 1922) were creating additional problems, such skeptics warned. European nations, unable to export their goods to the United States, were finding it difficult to earn the money necessary to repay their loans. Such warnings fell for the most part on deaf ears.

The U.S. government felt even fewer reservations about assisting American economic expansion in Latin America.

ECONOMIC EXPANSION IN LATIN AMERICA

During the 1920s, American military forces maintained a presence in numerous countries in the region. United States investments in Latin America more than doubled between 1924 and 1929; American corporations built roads and other facilities in many areas—partly, they argued, to weaken the appeal of revolutionary forces in the region, but at least equally to increase their own access to Latin America's rich natural resources. United States banks were offering large loans to Latin American governments, just as they were in Europe; and just as in Europe, the Latin Americans were having great difficulty earning the money to repay them in the face of the formidable U.S. tariff barrier. By the end of the 1920s, resentment of "Yankee imperialism" was growing rapidly. The economic troubles after 1929 would only accentuate such problems.

HOOVER AND THE WORLD CRISIS

After the relatively placid international climate of the 1920s, the diplomatic challenges facing the Hoover administration must have seemed ominous and bewildering. The world financial crisis that began in 1929 and greatly intensified after 1931 was not only creating economic distress; it was also producing a dangerous nationalism that threatened the weak international agreements established during the previous decade. Above all, the Depression was toppling some existing political leaders and replacing them with powerful, belligerent governments bent on expansion as a solution to their economic problems. Hoover was confronted, therefore, with the beginning of a process that would ultimately lead to war.

In Latin America, Hoover worked studiously to repair some of the damage created by earlier American policies. He made a ten-week goodwill tour through the region before his inauguration. Once in office, he tried to abstain from intervening in the internal affairs of neighboring nations and moved to withdraw American troops from Haiti. When economic distress led to the collapse of one Latin American regime after another, Hoover announced a new policy: the United States would grant diplomatic recognition to any sitting government in the region without questioning the means it had used to obtain

power. He even repudiated the Roosevelt corollary to the Monroe Doctrine by refusing to permit U.S. intervention when several Latin American countries defaulted on debt obligations to the United States in October 1931.

In Europe, the administration enjoyed few successes in its efforts to promote economic stability. When Hoover's proposed moratorium on debts in 1931 failed to attract broad support or produce financial stability (see pp. 641–643), many economists and political leaders appealed to the president to cancel all war debts to the United States. Like his predecessors, Hoover refused; and several European nations promptly went into default, severely damaging an already tense international climate.

The ineffectiveness of diplomacy in Europe was particularly troubling in view of some of the new governments coming to power on the Continent. Benito Mussolini's Fascist Party had been in control of Italy since the early 1920s; by the 1930s, the regime was growing increasingly nationalistic and militaristic, and Fascist leaders were loudly threatening an active campaign of imperial expansion. More ominous was the growing power of the National Socialist (or Nazi) Party in Germany. By the late 1920s, the Weimar Republic, the nation's government since the end of World War I, had lost virtually all popular support, discredited by, among other things, a ruinous inflation. Adolf Hitler, the stridently nationalistic leader of the Nazis, was rapidly growing in popular favor. Although he lost a 1932 election for chancellor, Hitler would sweep into power less than a year later. His belief in the racial superiority of the Aryan (German) people, his commitment to providing *Lebensraum* (living space) for his "master race," his pathological anti-Semitism, and his passionate militarism—all posed a great threat to European, and world, peace.

More immediately alarming to the Hoover administration was a major crisis in Asia—another early step toward World War II.

HITLER AND MUSSOLINI The German and Italian dictators (shown here reviewing Nazi troops in the mid-1930s) acted publicly as if they were equals. Privately, Hitler treated Mussolini with contempt, and Mussolini complained constantly of being a junior partner in the relationship.
(© Popperfoto/Getty Images)

The Japanese, reeling from an economic depression of their own, were concerned about the increasing strength of the Soviet Union and of Premier Chiang Kai-shek's national-ist China. In particular, they were alarmed at Chiang's insistence on expanding his government's power in Manchuria, which remained officially a part of China but over which the Japanese had maintained effective economic control since 1905. When the moderate government of Japan failed to take forceful steps to counter Chiang's ambitions, Japan's military leaders staged what was, in effect, a coup in the autumn of 1931–seizing control of foreign policy from the weakened liber-als. Weeks later, they launched a major invasion of northern Manchuria. (See "America in the World," pp. 692–693.)

MANCHURIA

The American government had few options. For a while, Secretary of State Henry Stimson (who had served as secretary of war under Taft) continued to hope that Japanese moderates would regain control of the Tokyo government and halt the invasion. The militarists, however, remained in command; and by the beginning of 1932, the conquest of Manchuria was complete. Stimson issued stern (but ineffectual) warnings to Japan and tried to use moral suasion to end the crisis. But Hoover forbade him to cooperate with the League of Nations in imposing economic sanctions against the Japanese. Stimson's only real tool in dealing with the Manchurian invasion was a refusal to grant diplomatic recognition to the new Japanese territories. Japan was unconcerned and early in 1932 expanded its aggression farther into China, attacking the city of Shanghai and killing thousands of civilians.

By the time Hoover left office early in 1933, it was clear that the international system the United States had attempted to create in the 1920s–a system based on voluntary cooperation among nations and on an American refusal to commit to the interests of other countries–had collapsed. The United States faced a choice. It could adopt a more energetic form of internationalism and enter into firmer and more meaningful associations with other nations. Or it could resort to nationalism and rely on its own devices for dealing with its own (and the world's) problems. For the next six years, it experimented with elements of both approaches.

FAILURE OF AMERICA'S INTERWAR DIPLOMACY

ISOLATIONISM AND INTERNATIONALISM

The administration of Franklin Roosevelt faced a dual chal-lenge as it entered office in 1933: it had to deal with the worst economic crisis in the nation's history, and it had to deal with

THE BOMBING OF CHUNGKING, 1940 Chungking (now Chongqing) was the capital of China under the nationalist government of Chiang Kai-shek during World War II. It was also the site of some of the most savage fighting of the Sino-Japanese War. This photograph shows buildings in Chungking burning after Japanese bombing in 1940. (© Hulton Archive/Getty Images)

the effects of a decaying international structure. The two problems were not unrelated. It was the worldwide Depression itself that was producing much of the political chaos throughout the globe.

Through most of the 1930s, however, the United States was unwilling to make more than faint gestures toward restoring stability to the world. Like many other peoples suffering economic hardship, most Americans were turning inward. Yet the realities of world affairs were not to allow the nation to remain isolated for very long—as Franklin Roosevelt soon realized.

DEPRESSION DIPLOMACY

Perhaps Roosevelt's sharpest break with the policies of his predecessor was on the question of American economic relations with Europe. Hoover had argued that only by resolving the question of war debts and reinforcing the gold standard could the American economy hope to recover. He had therefore agreed that the United States would participate in the World Economic Conference, to be held in London in June 1933, to

FDR's "BOMBSHELL"

try to resolve these issues. By the time the conference assembled, however, Roosevelt was president. He had already decided to allow the gold value of the dollar to fall to enable American goods to compete in world markets. Shortly after the conference convened, Roosevelt released a famous "bombshell" message repudiating the orthodox views of most of the delegates and rejecting any agreement on currency stabilization. The conference quickly dissolved without reaching agreement, and not until 1936 did the administration finally agree to new negotiations to stabilize Western currencies.

At the same time, Roosevelt abandoned the commitments of the Hoover administration to settle the issue of war debts through international agreement. In effect, he simply let the issue die. In April 1934, he signed a bill to forbid American banks to make loans to any nation in default on its debts. The result was to stop the old, circular system; within months, war-debt payments from every nation except Finland stopped for good.

Although the new administration had no interest in international currency stabilization or settlement of war debts, it did have an active interest in improving America's position in world trade. Roosevelt approved the Reciprocal Trade Agreement Act of 1934, authorizing the administration to negotiate treaties lowering tariffs by as much as 50 percent in return for reciprocal reductions by other nations. By 1939, Secretary of State Cordell Hull, a devoted free trader, had negotiated new treaties with twenty-one coun-

RECIPROCAL TRADE AGREEMENT ACT

tries. The result was an increase in American exports of nearly 40 percent. But most of the agreements admitted only products not competitive with American industry and agriculture, so imports into the United States continued to lag. Thus other nations were not obtaining the American currency needed to buy American products or pay off debts to American banks.

AMERICA AND THE SOVIET UNION

America's hopes of expanding its foreign trade helped produce efforts by the Roosevelt administration to improve relations with the Soviet Union. The United States and Russia had viewed each other with mistrust and even hostility since the Bolshevik Revolution of 1917, and the American government still had not officially recognized the Soviet regime by 1933. But powerful voices within the United States were urging a change in policy because the Soviet Union appeared to be a possible source of trade. The Russians, too, were eager for a new relationship. They were hoping in particular for American cooperation in containing the power of Japan, which Soviet leaders feared as a threat to Russia from the southeast. In November 1933, therefore, Soviet foreign minister Maxim Litvinov reached an agreement with President Roosevelt in Washington: the Soviets would cease their propaganda efforts in the United States and protect American citizens in Russia; in return, the United States would recognize the Soviet regime.

Despite this promising beginning, however, relations with the Soviet Union soon soured once again. American trade failed to establish much of a foothold in Russia; and the Soviets received no reassurance from the United States that it was interested in stopping Japanese expansion in Asia. By the end of 1934, as a result of these disappointed hopes on both sides, the Soviet Union and the United States were once again viewing each other with considerable mistrust.

THE GOOD NEIGHBOR POLICY

Somewhat more successful were American efforts to enhance both diplomatic and economic relations with Latin America through what became known as the "Good Neighbor Policy." Latin America was one of the most important targets of the new policy of trade reciprocity. During the 1930s, the United States succeeded in increasing both exports to and imports from the other nations of the Western Hemisphere by over 100 percent. Closely tied to these new economic relationships was a new U.S. attitude toward intervention in Latin America. The Hoover administration had unofficially abandoned the earlier U.S. practice of using military force to compel Latin American governments to repay debts, respect foreign investments, or otherwise behave "responsibly." The Roosevelt administration went further. At the Inter-American Conference in Montevideo in December 1933, Secretary of State Hull

INTER-AMERICAN CONFERENCE

signed a formal convention declaring: "No state has the right to intervene in the internal or external affairs of another." Roosevelt respected that pledge throughout his years in office. The Good Neighbor Policy did not mean, however, that the United States had abandoned its influence in Latin America. Instead of military force, Americans now tried to use economic influence. The new reliance on economic pressures eased tensions between the United States and its neighbors considerably. It did nothing to stem the growing U.S. domination of the Latin American economies.

THE SINO-JAPANESE WAR, 1931–1941 WOR-3, 7

LONG before Pearl Harbor, well before war broke out in Europe in 1939, the first shots of what would become World War II had been fired in the Pacific in a conflict between Japan and China.

Japan emerged from World War I as a great world power, with a proud and powerful military and growing global trade. But the Great Depression created severe economic problems for the Japanese (in part because of stiff new American tariffs on silk imports). As in other parts of the world,

ENTERING MANCHURIA, 1931 Japanese troops pour into Mukden (now Shenyang), the capital of the Chinese province of Manchuria, in 1931—following a staged incident that allowed Japan to claim that its troops had been attacked. The so-called Mukden Incident marked the beginning of the long Sino-Japanese War. (© Hulton Archive/Getty Images)

the crisis strengthened the political influence of highly nationalistic and militaristic leaders. Japanese militarists dreamed of a new empire in the Pacific that would give Japan access to fuel, raw materials, and markets for its industries, as well as land for its agricultural needs and its rapidly increasing population. Such an empire, they argued, would free Asia from exploitation by Europe and America and would create a "new world order based on moral principles."

During World War I, Japan had seized territory and economic concessions in China and had created a particularly strong presence in the northern Chinese region of Manchuria. There, in September 1931, a group of militant young army officers seized on a railway explosion to justify a military campaign through which they conquered the entire province. Both the United States government and the League of Nations demanded that Japan evacuate Manchuria. The Japanese ignored them and, for the next six years, consolidated their control over their new territory.

On July 7, 1937, Japan began a wider war when it attacked Chinese troops at the Marco Polo Bridge outside Beijing. Over the next few weeks, Japanese forces overran a large part of southern China, including most of the port cities, killing many Chinese soldiers and civilians in the process. Particularly notorious was the Japanese annihilation of many thousands of civilians in the city of Nanjing (the number has long been in dispute, but estimates range from 80,000 to more than 300,000) in an event that became known in China and the West as the Nanjing Massacre. The Chinese government fled to the mountains. As in 1931, the United States and the League of Nations protested in vain.

The China that the Japanese had invaded was a nation in turmoil. It was engaged in a civil war between the so-called Kuomintang, a nationalist party led by Chiang Kai-shek, and the Chinese Communist Party, led by Mao Zedong; and this internal struggle weakened

THE RISE OF ISOLATIONISM

The first years of the Roosevelt administration marked not only the death of Hoover's hopes for international economic agreements, but the end of any hopes for world peace through treaties and disarmament as well.

The arms control conference in Geneva had been meeting, without result, since 1932; and in May 1933, Roosevelt attempted to spur it to action by submitting a new American proposal for arms reductions. Negotiations stalled and then broke down; and only a few months later, first Hitler and then

Mussolini withdrew from the talks. Two years later, Japan withdrew from the London Naval Conference, which was attempting to draw up an agreement to continue the limitations on naval armaments negotiated at the Washington Conference of 1921.

Faced with a choice between more-active efforts to stabilize the world and more-energetic attempts to isolate the nation from it, most Americans unhesitatingly chose the latter. Support for isolationism emerged

SOURCES OF ISOLATIONISM

from many quarters. Old Wilsonian internationalists had grown disillusioned with

China's capacity to resist invasion. But beginning in 1937, the two Chinese rivals agreed to an uneasy truce and began fighting the Japanese together, with some success—bogging the Japanese military down in a seemingly endless war and imposing hardships on the Japanese people at home. The Japanese government and the military, however, remained determined to continue the war against China, whatever the sacrifices.

One result of the costs of the war for Japan was its growing dependence on the United States for steel and oil to meet civilian and military needs. In July 1941, in an effort to pressure the Japanese to stop their expansion, the Roosevelt administration made it impossible for the Japanese to continue buying American oil. Japan now faced a choice between ending its war in China and finding other sources of fuel to keep its war effort (and its civilian economy) going. It chose to extend the war beyond China in a search for oil. The best available sources were in the Dutch East Indies; but the only way to secure that European colony, the Japanese believed, would be to neutralize the United States in Asia. Visionary military planners in Japan began advocating a daring move to immobilize the Americans in the Pacific before expanding the war elsewhere—with an attack on the U.S. naval base at Pearl Harbor. The first blow of World War II in America, therefore, was the culmination of more than a decade of Japanese efforts to conquer China. ●

UNDERSTAND, ANALYZE, AND EVALUATE

1. What were the goals of the Japanese militarists in the 1930s that led to the attacks on China?
2. Why was China unable to stop Japanese aggression in the 1930s?
3. What role did the United States play in the Sino-Japanese War?

the League of Nations and its inability to stop Japanese aggression in Asia. Other Americans were listening to the argument (popular among populist-minded politicians in the Midwest and West) that powerful business interests–Wall Street, munitions makers, and others–had tricked the United States into participating in World War I. An investigation by a Senate committee chaired by Senator Gerald Nye of North Dakota revealed exorbitant profiteering and blatant tax evasion by many corporations during the war, and it suggested (on the basis of little evidence) that bankers had pressured Wilson to intervene in the war so as to protect their loans abroad. Roosevelt himself shared some of the suspicions voiced by the isolationists and claimed to be impressed by the findings of the Nye investigation. Nevertheless, he continued to hope for at least a modest American role in maintaining world peace. In 1935, he asked the Senate to ratify a treaty to make the United States a member of the World Court–a treaty that would have expanded America's symbolic commitment to internationalism without increasing its actual responsibilities in any important way. Nevertheless, isolationist opposition (spurred by unrelenting hostility from the Hearst newspapers and a passionate broadcast by Father Charles Coughlin on the eve of the Senate vote) resulted in the defeat of the treaty. It was a devastating political blow to the president, and he did not soon again attempt to challenge the isolationist tide.

That tide seemed to grow stronger in the following months. Through the summer of 1935, it became clear that Mussolini's Italy was preparing to invade Ethiopia in an effort to expand its colonial holdings in Africa. Fearing that a general European war would result, American legislators began to design legal safeguards to prevent the United States from being dragged into the conflict. The result was the Neutrality Act of 1935.

The 1935 act, and the Neutrality Acts of 1936 and 1937 that followed, was designed to prevent a recurrence of the events that many Americans now believed had pressured the United States into World War I. The 1935 law established a

NEUTRALITY ACTS

mandatory arms embargo against both victim and aggressor in any military conflict and empowered the president to warn American citizens that they might travel on the ships of warring nations only at their own risk. Thus, isolationists believed, the "protection of neutral rights" could not again become an excuse for American intervention in war. The 1936 Neutrality Act renewed these provisions. And in 1937, with world conditions growing even more precarious, Congress passed a new Neutrality Act that established the so-called cash-and-carry policy, by which belligerents could purchase only nonmilitary goods from the United States and had to pay cash and carry the goods away on their own vessels.

The American stance of militant neutrality gained support in October 1935 when Mussolini finally launched his

ETHIOPIA

long-anticipated attack on Ethiopia. When the League of Nations protested, Italy simply resigned from the organization, completed its conquest of Ethiopia, and formed an alliance (the "Axis") with Nazi Germany. Most Americans responded to the news with renewed determination to isolate themselves from European instability. Two-thirds of those responding to public opinion polls at the time opposed any American action to deter aggression. Isolationist sentiment showed its strength once again in 1936-1937 in response to the civil war in Spain. The Falangists, a group much like the Italian fascists, revolted in July 1936 against the existing republican government. Hitler and Mussolini supported General Francisco Franco, who became the leader of the Falangists in 1937,

THE SPANISH CIVIL WAR Many Americans took up arms to help the republican forces fight against Franco and his army. The novelist Ernest Hemingway joined them in Spain as a reporter (and supporter of the republicans), and he spent much of his time talking with both American and Spanish troops. His novel *For Whom the Bell Tolls* was inspired by his experience in the civil war. (Robert Capa/© International Center of Photography/Magnum Photos)

both vocally and with weapons and supplies. Some individual Americans traveled to Spain to assist the republican cause; but the U.S. government joined with Britain and France in an agreement to offer no assistance to either side—although all three governments were sympathetic to the republicans.

Particularly disturbing was the deteriorating situation in Asia. Japan's aggressive designs against China had been clear

"QUARANTINE" SPEECH since the invasion of Manchuria in 1931. In the summer of 1937, Tokyo launched an even broader assault, attacking China's five northern provinces. (See "America in the World," pp. 692-693.) The United States, Roosevelt believed, could not allow the Japanese aggression to go unremarked or unpunished. In a speech in Chicago in October 1937, therefore, the president warned forcefully of the dangers that Japanese aggression posed to world peace. Aggressors, he proclaimed, should be "quarantined" by the international community to prevent the contagion of war from spreading. The president was deliberately vague about what such a "quarantine" would mean. Nevertheless, public response to the speech was disturbingly hostile. As a result, Roosevelt drew back.

Only months later, another episode provided renewed evidence of how formidable the obstacles to Roosevelt's efforts remained. On December 12, 1937, Japanese aviators bombed and sank the U.S. gunboat *Panay* as it sailed the Yangtze River in China. The attack was almost undoubtedly deliberate. It occurred in broad daylight, with clear visibility. A large American flag had been painted conspicuously on the *Panay's*

deck. Even so, isolationists seized eagerly on Japanese protestations that the bombing had been an accident and pressured the administration to accept Japan's apologies.

THE FAILURE OF MUNICH

Hitler's determination to expand German power became fully visible in 1936, when he moved the revived German army into the Rhineland, violating the Versailles treaty and rearming an area that France had, in effect, controlled since World War I. In March 1938, German forces marched into Austria, and Hitler proclaimed a union (or *Anschluss*) between Austria, his native land, and Germany, his adopted one—thus fulfilling his longtime dream of uniting the German-speaking peoples in one great nation. Neither in America nor in most of Europe was there much more than a murmur of opposition. The Austrian invasion, however, soon created another crisis, because Hitler had by now occupied territory surrounding three sides of western Czechoslovakia, a region he dreamed of annexing to provide Germany with the *Lebensraum* (living space) he believed it needed. In September 1938, he demanded that Czechoslovakia cede to him part of that region, the Sudetenland, an area on the Austro-German border in which many ethnic Germans lived. Czechoslovakia, which possessed substantial military power of its own, was prepared to fight rather than submit. But it realized it could not hope for success without help from other European nations. It received none. Most Western nations were appalled at the prospect of another war and were willing to pay almost any price to settle the crisis peacefully. Anxiety ran almost as high in the United States as it did in Europe during and after the crisis, and helped produce such strange expressions of fear as the hysterical response to the famous "War of the Worlds" radio broadcast in October. (See "Patterns of Popular Culture," pp. 696-697).

On September 29, Hitler met with the leaders of France and Great Britain at Munich in an effort to resolve the crisis. The **MUNICH CONFERENCE** French and British agreed to accept the German demands for Czechoslovakia in return for Hitler's promise to expand no farther. "This is the last territorial claim I have to make in Europe," the führer solemnly declared. And Prime Minister Neville Chamberlain returned to England to a hero's welcome, assuring his people that the agreement ensured "peace in our time." Among those who had cabled him with encouragement at Munich was Franklin Roosevelt.

The Munich accords were the most prominent element of a policy that came to be known as "appeasement" and that **FAILURE OF "APPEASEMENT"** came to be identified (not altogether fairly) almost exclusively with Chamberlain. Whoever was to blame, however, it became clear almost immediately that the policy was a failure. In March 1939, Hitler occupied the remaining areas of Czechoslovakia, violating the Munich agreement unashamedly. And in April, he began issuing threats against Poland. At that point, both Britain and France gave assurances to the Polish government that they would come to its assistance in case of an invasion; they even flirted, too late, with the Stalinist regime in Russia, attempting to draw it into a mutual defense agreement. Stalin, however, had already decided that he could expect no protection from the West; after all, he had not even been invited to attend the Munich Conference. Accordingly, he signed a nonaggression pact with Hitler in August 1939, freeing the Germans for the moment from the danger of a two-front war. For a few months, Hitler had been trying to frighten the Poles into submitting to German demands. When that failed, he staged an incident on the Polish border to allow him to claim that Germany had been attacked; and on September 1, 1939, he launched a full-scale invasion of Poland. Britain and France, true to their pledges, declared war on Germany two days later. World War II in Europe had begun.

FROM NEUTRALITY TO INTERVENTION

"This nation will remain a neutral nation," the president declared shortly after the hostilities began in Europe, "but I cannot ask that every American remain neutral in thought as well." It was a statement that stood in stark and deliberate contrast to Woodrow Wilson's 1914 plea that the nation remain neutral in both deed and thought; and it was clear from the start that among those whose opinions were decidedly unneutral in 1939 was the president himself.

NEUTRALITY TESTED

There was never any question that both the president and the majority of the American people favored Britain, France, and the other Allied nations in the conflict. The question was how much the United States was prepared to do to assist them. At the very least, Roosevelt believed, the United States should **CASH-AND-CARRY** make armaments available to the Allied armies to help them counter the highly productive German munitions industry. In September 1939, he asked Congress for a revision of the Neutrality Acts. The original measures had forbidden the sale of American weapons to any nation engaged in war; Roosevelt wanted the arms embargo lifted. Powerful isolationist opposition forced him to accept a weaker revision than he would have liked; as passed by Congress, the 1939 measure maintained

THE OCCUPATION OF POLAND, 1939 A German motorized detachment enters a Polish town that has already been battered by heavy bombing from the German air force (the *Luftwaffe*). The German invasion of Poland, which began on September 1, 1939, sparked the formal beginning of World War II. (© Bettmann/Corbis)

ORSON WELLES AND THE "WAR OF THE WORLDS"

ON the evening of October 30, 1938, about 6 million Americans were listening to the weekly radio program *The Mercury Theatre on the Air,* produced by the actor/filmmaker Orson Welles and broadcast over the CBS network. A few minutes into the show, an announcer interrupted some dance music with a terrifying report:

> At least forty people, including six state troopers, lie dead in a field east of Grover's Mill [New Jersey], their bodies burned and distorted beyond recognition. . . . Good heavens, something's wriggling out of the shadow like a gray snake! Now it's another one and another. . . . It's large as a bear and it glistens like black leather. But that face . . . it's indescribable! I can hardly force myself to keep looking at it.

The panicky announcer was describing the beginning of an alien invasion of earth and the appearance of Martians armed with "death rays," determined to destroy the planet. Later in the evening, an announcer claiming to be broadcasting from Times Square reported the destruction of New York City before falling dead at the microphone.

THE MERCURY THEATRE ON THE AIR Orson Welles, the founder and director of *The Mercury Theatre on the Air,* directs a corps of actors during a rehearsal for one of the show's radio plays. (© Popperfoto/Getty Images)

WELLES ON THE AIR Welles is shown here during the broadcast of the "War of the Worlds" in 1938. Although announcers told listeners throughout the broadcast that it was fiction, Welles came under intense criticism in following days for the panic it caused among many listeners. (© Bettmann/Corbis)

The dramatic "news bulletins" were part of a radio play by Howard Koch, loosely adapted from H. G. Wells's 1898 novel, *The War of the Worlds.* Announcers reminded the audience repeatedly throughout the broadcast that they were listening to a play, but many people either did not hear or did not notice the disclaimers. By the end of the hour, according to some estimates, as many as a million Americans were flying into panics, convinced that the end of the world was imminent.

Thousands of listeners in New York and New Jersey fled their homes and tried to drive along clogged highways into the hills or the countryside. In Newark, people ran from their buildings with wet towels wrapped around their faces or wearing gas masks—as if defending themselves against the chemical warfare that many remembered from the trenches in World War I. In cities across the country, people flocked into churches to pray; called police and hospitals for help;

the prohibition on American ships entering war zones. It did, however, permit belligerents to purchase arms on the same cash-and-carry basis that the earlier Neutrality Acts had established for the sale of nonmilitary materials.

After the German armies had quickly subdued Poland, the war in Europe settled into a long, quiet lull that lasted through the winter and spring—a "phony war," many people called it. The only real fighting during this period occurred not between the Allies and the Axis, but between Russia and its neighbors.

Taking advantage of the situation in the West, the Soviet Union overran and annexed the small Baltic republics of Latvia, Estonia, and Lithuania and then, in late November, invaded Finland. Most Americans were outraged, but neither Congress nor the president was willing to do more than impose an ineffective "moral embargo" on the shipment of armaments to Russia. By March 1940, the Soviet advance was complete.

Whatever illusions anyone may have had about the reality of the war in western Europe were shattered in the spring of flooded the switchboards of newspapers, magazines, and radio stations desperate for information. "I never hugged my radio so closely as I did last night," one woman later explained. "I held a crucifix in my hand and prayed while looking out of my open window for falling meteors." The *New York Times* described it the next day as "a wave of mass hysteria." For weeks thereafter, Orson Welles and other producers of the show were the focus of a barrage of criticism for what many Americans believed had been a deliberate effort to create public fear. For years, sociologists and other scholars studied the episode for clues about mass behavior.

Welles and his colleagues claimed to be surprised by the reaction their show created. The broadcast proved more effective than they had expected because it touched on anxieties that ran deep in American life at the time. The show aired only a few weeks after the war fever that had preceded the Munich pact among Germany, Britain, and France; Americans already jittery about the possibility of war proved easy prey to fears of another kind of invasion. The show also tapped longer-standing anxieties about the fragility of life that afflicted many Americans during the long depression of the 1930s, and it seemed to frighten working-class people—those most vulnerable to unexpected catastrophes—in particular.

Most of all, however, the "War of the Worlds" unintentionally exploited the enormous power that radio had come to exercise in American life, and the great trust many people had developed in what they heard over the air. For many people, the broadcasts they received over the radio had become their principal, even their only, source of information about the outside world. When the actors from *The Mercury Theatre* began to use the familiar phrases and cadences of radio news announcers, it was easy for members of their audience to assume that they were hearing the truth.

Welles concluded the broadcast by describing the play as "the Mercury Theater's own radio version of dressing up in a sheet and jumping out of a bush and saying Boo! . . . So good-bye everybody, and remember, please, for the next day or so, the terrible lesson you learned tonight. The grinning, glowing, globular invader of your living room is an inhabitant of the pumpkin patch, and if your doorbell rings and there's no one there, that was no Martian . . . it's Halloween." But the real lesson of the "War of the Worlds" was the lesson of the enormous, and at times frightening, power of the medium of broadcasting. ●

From *War of the Worlds* by Howard Koch. Copyright © 1938 Howard Koch.

MASS HYSTERIA A *New York Daily News* headline the morning after the famous "War of the Worlds" broadcast of *The Mercury Theatre on the Air* reports on the panic the radio show caused the night before. Thousands of listeners throughout the nation panicked as they listened to a broadcast based on H. G. Wells's fantasy *The War of the Worlds*. Many believed that an interplanetary conflict had started with invading Martians spreading wide death and destruction in New Jersey and New York. (© New York Daily News/Getty Images)

UNDERSTAND, ANALYZE, AND EVALUATE

1. Why did Welles's "War of the Worlds" broadcast create so much panic and hysteria?
2. What responsibility did Welles and his producers bear for the hysteria that followed the program? Could they have done more to prevent that hysteria and reassure their audience? If so, should they have done more?
3. Do the media today hold as much power and influence as radio did in the 1930s? Would an audience today be as likely to react with panic and hysteria to a broadcast similar to that of the "War of the Worlds"?

FALL OF FRANCE 1940 when Germany launched an invasion to the west—first attacking Denmark and Norway, sweeping next across the Netherlands and Belgium, and driving finally deep into the heart of France. Allied efforts proved futile against the Nazi blitzkrieg. One western European stronghold after another fell into German hands. On June 10, Mussolini brought Italy into the war, invading France from the south as Hitler was attacking from the north. On June 22, finally, France fell to the German onslaught. Nazi troops marched into Paris; a new collaborationist regime assembled in Vichy; and in all Europe, only the shattered remnants of the British army, rescued from the beaches of Dunkirk by a flotilla of military and civilian vessels assembled miraculously quickly, remained to oppose the Axis forces.

Roosevelt had already begun to increase American aid to the Allies. He also began preparations to resist a possible Nazi invasion of the United States. On May 16, he asked Congress for an additional $1 billion for defense (much of it for the

THE BLITZ, LONDON The German *Luftwaffe* terrorized London and other British cities in 1940–1941 and again late in the war by bombing civilian areas indiscriminately in an effort to break the spirit of the English people. The effort failed, and the fortitude of the British in the face of the attack did much to arouse support for their cause in the United States. St. Paul's Cathedral, largely undamaged throughout the raids, looms in the background of this photograph, as other buildings crumble under the force of German bombs. (© Daily Mail/Rex/Alamy)

construction of an enormous new fleet of warplanes) and received it quickly. With France weakening a few weeks later, he proclaimed that the United States would "extend to the opponents of force the material resources of this nation." And on May 15, Winston Churchill, the new British prime minister, sent Roosevelt the first of many long lists of requests for ships, armaments, and other assistance without which, he insisted, England could not long survive. Many Americans (including the U.S. ambassador to London, Joseph P. Kennedy) argued that the British plight was already hopeless, that any aid to the English was a wasted effort. The president, however, made the politically dangerous decision to make war materials available to Churchill. He even circumvented the cash-and-carry provisions of the Neutrality Act by trading fifty American destroyers (most of them left over from World War I) to England in return for the right to build American bases on British territory in the Western Hemisphere; and he returned to the factories a number of new airplanes purchased by the American government so that the British could buy them instead.

Roosevelt was able to take such steps in part because of a major shift in American public opinion. Before the invasion of France, most Americans had believed that a German victory in the war would not be a threat to the United **SHIFTING PUBLIC OPINION** States. By July, with France defeated and Britain threatened, more than 66 percent of the American Public (according to opinion polls) believed that Germany posed a direct threat to the United States. Congress was aware of the change and was becoming more willing to permit expanded American

assistance to the Allies. It was also becoming more concerned about the need for internal preparations for war, and in September it approved the Burke-Wadsworth Act, inaugurating the first peacetime military draft in American history.

But while the forces of isolation may have weakened, they were far from dead. A spirited and at times vicious debate began in the spring of 1940 between those activists who advocated expanded American involvement in the war (who were termed, often inaccurately, "interventionists") and those who continued to insist on neutrality. The celebrated journalist William Allen White served as chairman of a new Committee to Defend America by Aiding the Allies whose members lobbied actively for increased American assistance to the Allies but opposed actual intervention. Other activists went so far as to urge an immediate declaration of war (a position that as yet had little public support) and in April 1941 created an organization of their own, the Fight for Freedom Committee.

Opposing them was a powerful new lobby called the America First Committee, which attracted some of America's most prominent leaders. Its chairman was General Robert E. Wood, until recently the president of Sears Roebuck; and its membership included **AMERICA FIRST COMMITTEE** Charles Lindbergh, General Hugh Johnson, Senator Gerald Nye, and Senator Burton Wheeler. It won the editorial support of the Hearst chain and other influential newspapers, and it had at least the indirect support of a large proportion of the Republican Party. (It also, inevitably, attracted a fringe of Nazi sympathizers and anti-Semites.) The debate between the two sides was loud and bitter. Through the summer and fall of 1940, moreover, it was complicated by a presidential campaign.

THE THIRD-TERM CAMPAIGN

For many months, the politics of 1940 revolved around the question of Franklin Roosevelt's intentions. Would he break with tradition and run for an unprecedented third term? The president never publicly revealed his own wishes. But by refusing to withdraw from the contest, he made it impossible for any rival Democrat to establish a foothold within the party. Just before the Democratic National Convention in July, he let it be known that he would accept a "draft" from his party. The Democrats quickly renominated him and even reluctantly swallowed his choice for vice president: Agriculture Secretary Henry A. Wallace, a man too liberal for the taste of many party leaders.

With Roosevelt effectively straddling the center of the defense debate, favoring neither the extreme isolationists nor the extreme interventionists, the Republicans had few

WENDELL
WILLKIE
obvious alternatives. Succumbing to a remarkable popular movement (carefully orchestrated by, among others, *Time* and *Life* magazines), they nominated a dynamic and attractive but politically inexperienced businessman, Wendell Willkie.

Willkie took positions little different from Roosevelt's: he would keep the country out of war but would extend generous assistance to the Allies. An appealing figure and a vigorous campaigner, he managed to evoke more public enthusiasm than any Republican candidate in decades. In the end, however, he was no match for Franklin Roosevelt. The election was closer than it had been in either 1932 or 1936, but Roosevelt nevertheless won decisively. He received 55 percent of the popular vote to Willkie's 45 percent, and won 449 electoral votes to Willkie's 82.

NEUTRALITY ABANDONED

In the last weeks of 1940, with the election behind him, Roosevelt began to make subtle but profound changes in the American role in the war. More than aiding Britain, he was moving the United States closer to entering the war.

In December 1940, Great Britain was virtually bankrupt. No longer could the British meet the cash-and-carry requirements imposed by the Neutrality Acts; yet England's needs, Churchill insisted, were greater than ever. The president, therefore, suggested a method that would "eliminate the dol-
LEND-LEASE
lar sign" from all arms transactions. The new system was labeled "lend-lease." It would allow the government not only to sell but also to lend or lease armaments to any nation deemed "vital to the defense of the United States." In other words, America could funnel weapons to England on the basis of no more than Britain's promise to return or pay for them when the war was over. Isolationists attacked the measure bitterly, arguing (correctly) that it was simply a device to tie the United States more closely to the Allies; but Congress enacted the bill by wide margins.

With lend-lease established, Roosevelt soon faced another serious problem: ensuring that the American supplies would actually reach Great Britain. Shipping lanes in the Atlantic had become extremely dangerous; German submarines destroyed as much as a half-million tons of shipping each month. The British navy was losing ships more rapidly than it could replace them and was finding it difficult to transport materials across the Atlantic from America. Secretary of War Henry Stimson (who had been Hoover's secretary of state and who returned to the cabinet at Roosevelt's request in 1940) argued that the United States should itself convoy vessels to England; but Roosevelt decided to rely instead on the concept of "hemispheric defense," by which the United States navy would defend transport ships only in the western Atlantic—which he argued was a neutral zone and the responsibility of the American nations. By July 1941, American ships were patrolling the ocean as far east as Iceland, escorting convoys of merchant ships, and radioing information to British vessels about the location of Nazi submarines.

At first, Germany did little to challenge these obviously hostile American actions. By the fall of 1941, however, events
GERMANY
INVADES THE
USSR
in Europe changed its position. German forces had invaded the Soviet Union in June of that year, shattering the 1939 Nazi-Soviet pact. The Germans drove quickly and forcefully deep into Russian territory. When the Soviets did not surrender, as many military observers had predicted they would, Roosevelt persuaded Congress to extend lend-lease privileges to them—the first step toward creating a new relationship with Stalin that would ultimately lead to a formal Soviet-American alliance. Now American industry was providing crucial assistance to Hitler's foes on two fronts, and the navy was playing a more active role than ever in protecting the flow of goods to Europe.

In September, Nazi submarines began a concerted campaign against American vessels. Early that month, a German U-boat fired on the American destroyer *Greer* (which was radioing the U-boat's position to the British at the time). Roosevelt responded by ordering American ships to fire on German submarines "on sight." In October, Nazi submarines hit two American destroyers and sank one of them, the *Reuben James*, killing many American sailors. Enraged members of Congress now voted approval of a measure allowing the United States to arm its merchant vessels and to sail all the way into belligerent ports. The United States had, in effect, launched a naval war against Germany.

At the same time, a series of meetings, some private and one public, were tying the United States and Great Britain more closely together. In April 1941, senior military officers of the two nations met in secret and agreed on the joint strategy they would follow if the United States entered the war. In
ATLANTIC
CHARTER
August, Roosevelt met with Churchill aboard a British vessel anchored off the coast of Newfoundland. The president made no military commitments, but he did join the prime minister in releasing a document that became known as the Atlantic Charter, in which the two nations set out "certain common principles" on which to base "a better future for the world." It was, in only vaguely disguised form, a statement of war aims that called openly for, among other things, "the final destruction of the Nazi tyranny."

By the fall of 1941, it seemed only a matter of time before the United States became an official belligerent. Roosevelt remained convinced that public opinion would support a declaration of war only in the event of an actual enemy attack. But an attack seemed certain to come, if not in the Atlantic, then in the Pacific.

THE ROAD TO PEARL HARBOR

Japan took advantage of the crisis that had preoccupied the Soviet Union and the two most powerful colonial powers in

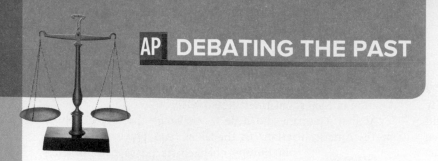

THE QUESTION OF PEARL HARBOR

THE phrase "Remember Pearl Harbor!" became a rallying cry during World War II—reminding Americans of the surprise Japanese attack on the American naval base in Hawaii and arousing the nation to exact revenge. But within a few years of the end of hostilities, some Americans began to challenge the official version of the attack on December 7, 1941, and their charges sparked a debate that has never fully subsided. Was the Japanese attack on Pearl Harbor unprovoked, and did it come without warning? Or was it part of a deliberate plan by the Roosevelt administration to make the Japanese attack to force a reluctant United States into the war? Most controversial of all, did the administration know of the attack in advance? Did Roosevelt deliberately refrain from warning the commanders in Hawaii so that the air raid's effect on the American public would be more profound?

Among the first to challenge the official version of Pearl Harbor was the historian Charles A. Beard, who maintained in *President Roosevelt and the Coming of the War* (1948) that the United States had deliberately forced the Japanese into a position whereby they had no choice but to attack. By cutting off Japan's access to the raw materials it needed for its military adventure in China, by stubbornly refusing to compromise, the United States ensured that the Japanese would strike out into the southwest Pacific to take the needed supplies by force—even at the risk of war with the United States. The administration, which had some time before cracked the Japanese code, must have known weeks in advance of Japan's plan to attack—although Beard did not claim that officials knew the attack would come at Pearl Harbor. Beard supported his argument by citing Secretary of War Henry Stimson's comment in his diary: "The question was how we should maneuver them into the position of firing the first shot." This view has reappeared more recently in Thomas Fleming, *The New Dealers' War* (2001), which also argues that Roosevelt deliberately (and duplicitously) maneuvered the United States into war with Japan.

Basil Rauch, in *Roosevelt from Munich to Pearl Harbor* (1950), challenged Beard's thesis. Rauch argued that the administration did not know in advance of the planned attack on Pearl Harbor. It did, however, expect an attack somewhere; and it made subtle efforts to "maneuver" Japan into firing the first shot in the conflict.

Richard N. Current, in *Secretary Stimson: A Study in Statecraft* (1954), offered an even stronger challenge to Beard. Stimson did indeed anticipate an attack, Current argued, but not an attack on American territory; rather, he anticipated an assault on British or Dutch possessions in the Pacific. The problem confronting the administration was how to find a way to make a Japanese attack on British or Dutch territory appear to be an attack on America. Only thus, Stimson believed, could Congress be persuaded to approve a declaration of war.

Roberta Wohlstetter, in *Pearl Harbor: Warning and Decision* (1962), the most thorough scholarly study to appear to that point, undertook to answer the question of whether the Roosevelt administration knew of the attack in advance. She concluded that the United States had ample warning of Japanese intentions and should have realized that the Pearl Harbor raid was imminent. But government officials failed to interpret the evidence correctly, largely because their preconceptions about Japanese intentions were at odds with the evidence they confronted. Admiral Edwin T. Layton, who had been a staff officer at Pearl Harbor in 1941, also blamed political and bureaucratic failures for the absence of advance warning of the attack. In a 1985 memoir, *And I Was There,* he argued that the Japanese attack was a result not only of "audacious planning and skillful execution" by

TRIPARTITE PACT Asia, Britain and France, to extend its empire in the Pacific. In September 1940, Japan signed the Tripartite Pact, a loose defensive alliance with Germany and Italy that seemed to extend the Axis into Asia. (In reality, the European Axis powers never developed a strong relationship with Japan, and the wars in Europe and the Pacific were largely separate conflicts.)

Roosevelt had already displayed his animosity toward Japanese policies by harshly denouncing their assault on China and by terminating a long-standing American commercial treaty with the Tokyo government. Still the Japanese drive continued. In July 1941, imperial troops moved into Indochina and seized the capital of Vietnam, a colony of France. The United States, having broken the Japanese codes, knew that Japan's next target would be the Dutch East Indies; and when Tokyo failed to respond to Roosevelt's stern warnings, the president froze all Japanese assets in the United States and

established a complete trade embargo, severely limiting Japan's ability to purchase essential supplies (including oil). American public opinion, shaped by strong anti-Japanese prejudices developed over several decades, generally supported these hostile actions.

Tokyo now faced a choice. Either it would have to repair relations with the United States to restore the flow of supplies, or it would have to find those supplies elsewhere, most notably by seizing British and Dutch possessions in the Pacific. At first the Japanese prime minister, Prince Konoye, seemed willing to compromise. In October, however, militants in Tokyo forced Konoye out of office and replaced him with the leader of the war party, General Hideki Tojo. With Japan's need for new sources of fuel becoming desperate, there now seemed little alternative to war.

For several weeks, the Tojo government kept up a pretense of wanting to continue negotiations. On November 20, 1941,

PEARL HARBOR, DECEMBER 7, 1941 At least seven 18-inch aerial torpedoes and two bombs struck the battleship USS *West Virginia* on that fateful morning. Repair workers discovered 66 bodies of *West Virginia* crewmembers. After it was restored to fighting condition, the ship reentered the war and participated in the Battles of Iwo Jima and Okinawa. (© GL Archive/Alamy)

"revisionists" (Beard and his successors) that the president had deliberately maneuvered the nation into the war by permitting the Japanese to attack. Instead, he emphasized the enormous daring and great skill with which the Japanese orchestrated an ambitious operation that few Americans believed possible.

The revisionist claims have not been laid to rest. John Toland revived the charges of a Roosevelt betrayal in 1982, in *Infamy: Pearl Harbor and Its Aftermath,* claiming to have discovered new evidence (the testimony of an unidentified seaman) that proves the navy knew at least five days in advance that Japanese aircraft carriers were heading toward Hawaii. From that, Toland concluded that Roosevelt must have known that an attack was forthcoming and that he allowed it to occur in the belief that a surprise attack would arouse popular support for entering the war. But like the many other writers who have made the same argument, Toland was unable to produce any direct evidence of Roosevelt's knowledge of the planned attack. ●

HISTORICAL ARGUMENTATION AND INTERPRETATION

Questions assume cumulative content knowledge from this chapter and previous chapters.

1. Identify the arguments of four historians from the discussion regarding the Japanese attack on Pearl Harbor.
2. Review the arguments and the evidence given by the revisionists and those who challenge them. Why might the argument regarding the attack continue to persist.
3. With which argument do you most tend to agree? Explain why, supporting your argument with historical evidence.

the Japanese, but also of "a dramatic breakdown in our intelligence process . . . related directly to feuding among high-level naval officers in Washington."

The most thorough study of Pearl Harbor to date is Gordon W. Prange's *At Dawn We Slept* (1981). Like Wohlstetter, Prange concluded that the Roosevelt administration was guilty of a series of disastrous blunders in interpreting Japanese strategy; the American government had possession of enough information to predict the attack, but failed to do so. But Prange dismissed the arguments of the

Tokyo proposed a modus vivendi highly favorable to itself and sent its diplomats in Washington to the State Department to discuss it. But Tokyo had already decided that it would not

TOKYO'S DECISION FOR WAR

yield on the question of China, and Washington had made clear that it would accept nothing less than a reversal of that policy. Secretary of State Cordell Hull rejected the Japanese overtures out of hand; on November 27, he told Secretary of War Henry Stimson, "I have washed my hands of the Japanese situation, and it is now in the hands of you and [Secretary of the Navy Frank] Knox, the Army and Navy." He was not merely speculating. American intelligence had already decoded Japanese messages, which made clear that war was imminent, that after November 29 an attack would be only a matter of days.

But Washington did not know where the attack would take place. Most officials were convinced that the Japanese would

move first not against American territory but against British or Dutch possessions to the south. American intelligence took note of a Japanese naval task force that began sailing east from the Kuril Islands in the general direction of Hawaii on November 25, and radioed a routine warning to the U.S. naval facility at Pearl Harbor, near Honolulu. But officials were paying more attention to a large Japanese convoy moving southward through the China Sea. A combination of confusion and miscalculation led the government to overlook indications that Japan intended a direct attack on American forces–partly because Hawaii was so far from Japan that few officials believed such an attack possible.

At 7:55 A.M. on Sunday, December 7, 1941, a wave of Japanese bombers–taking off from aircraft carriers hundreds of

PEARL HARBOR

miles away–attacked the United States naval base at Pearl Harbor. A second wave came an hour later. Military commanders in Hawaii had taken

HIDEKI TOJO Tojo was a general of the Imperial Japanese Army and, for most of World War II, the prime minister of Japan. He was directly responsible for the attack on Pearl Harbor, although planning for it had begun before he took office. After the war, Tojo was arrested, convicted of war crimes, and hanged. (© LAPI/Roger-Viollet/The Image Works)

no precautions against such an attack and had allowed ships to remain bunched up defenselessly in the harbor and airplanes to remain parked in rows on airstrips. The consequences of the raid were disastrous for America. Within two hours, the United States lost 8 battleships, 3 cruisers, 4 other vessels, 188 airplanes, and several vital shore installations. More than 2,000 soldiers and sailors died, and another 1,000 were injured. The Japanese suffered only light losses.

American forces were now greatly diminished in the Pacific (although by a fortunate accident, none of the American aircraft carriers–the heart of the Pacific fleet–had been at Pearl Harbor on December 7). Nevertheless, the raid on Pearl Harbor did virtually overnight what more than two years of effort by Roosevelt and others had been unable to do: it unified the American people in a fervent commitment to war. On December 8, the president traveled to Capitol Hill, where he grimly addressed a joint session of Congress: "Yesterday, December 7, 1941–a date which will live in infamy–the United States of America was suddenly and deliberately attacked by the naval and air forces of the Empire of Japan." Within four hours, the Senate unanimously and the House 388 to 1 (the lone dissenter being Jeannette Rankin of Montana, who had voted against war in 1917 as well) approved a declaration of war against Japan. Three days later, Germany and Italy, Japan's European allies, declared war on the United States; and on the same day, December 11, Congress reciprocated without a dissenting vote. For the second time in twenty-five years, the United States was engaged in a world war.

AP CONNECTING THEMES

The primary focus of Chapter 25 was on involvement by the United States in world affairs in the inter-war period. As you review, pay close attention to the reasons for, the debates about, and the chronological sequence of events that led the United States to move from an isolationistic foreign policy to one of internationalism. Think about how foreign policy in this period compares with foreign policy in previous periods of American history. You should also focus on the nature of changing relations between the United States and the Soviet Union and Latin America, and the reasons those changes occurred. Think about the impact of the Great Depression on U.S. involvement in foreign affairs and its impact on the coming of World War II. Understand the reasons for and the progression of changing attitudes of the American people toward involvement in World War II during the 1930s. Finally, be able to explain the factors that led the United States to enter the war on the side of the Allies.

The following themes have heightened importance in Chapter 25. You should now be able to do the following for each listed theme:

Identity: Explain the impact of U.S. failure to achieve its idealistic goals in World War I on some Americans' view of foreigners during the 1920s.

Peopling: Explain the causes that led to significant immigration restrictions during the 1920s.

Politics and Power: Explain the degree to which American public opinion influenced U.S. involvement in world affairs and the degree to which actions of the federal government altered public opinion.

America and the World: Explain and support with specific factual evidence the movement of the United States from a policy of isolationism to a policy of internationalism.

Ideas, Beliefs, and Culture: Analyze the degree to which and the ways in which the debate over isolationism versus internationalism gradually changed between 1920 and 1941.

AP SUGGESTED STUDY

PEOPLE/PLACES/EVENTS As you study these items, think about how they demonstrate or relate to key concepts and historical themes from this chapter and previous chapters.

ADOLF HITLER 689
APPEASEMENT 695
ATLANTIC CHARTER 699
BENITO MUSSOLINI 689
CORDELL HULL 691

DAWES PLAN 688
GOOD NEIGHBOR POLICY 691
HENRY STIMSON 699
HIDEKI TOJO 700
KELLOGG-BRIAND PACT 688

LEND-LEASE 699
NEUTRALITY ACTS 693
PEARL HARBOR 701
WASHINGTON CONFERENCE
OF 1921 687

AP TEST PRACTICE

Questions assume cumulative content knowledge from this chapter and previous chapters.

MULTIPLE CHOICE Use the photograph on page 698 and your knowledge of U.S. history to answer questions 1-2.

1. As with World War I, what American foreign policy debate recurred, but which German actions like that in the photograph started pulling American public opinion into a more unified direction?

   (A) Issue of increasing import tariffs, regarding foreign trade
   (B) Continued implementation of Manifest Destiny
   (C) Isolationism vs. intervention
   (D) Imperialism vs. anti-imperialism

2. Which best describes a characteristic of America's eventual effort in World War II, which partly resulted from average Americans' reaction to events like that in the photograph between 1940 and 1941?

   (A) Being reminded of the destitution of the Great Depression and not wanting a return to such conditions
   (B) A determination to remain neutral in judgment about the causes of the war
   (C) A steadfastness on the part of Americans to advancing democratic ideals
   (D) Conviction that arms supply to Great Britain early in the war had been wasted

SHORT ANSWER Use your knowledge of U.S. history to answer questions 3-4.

3. Answer a, b, and c.

   a) For one of the areas below, identify ONE event contributing to the Japanese decision to attack Pearl Harbor.
   • Events in Europe
   • American government actions
   • Events in Japan or Asia

   b) Briefly explain how that event affected or played a role in Japan's decision.
   c) Choose a SECOND area and briefly explain why events in that area are not as relevant to Japan's decision to attack Pearl Harbor.

4. Answer a, b, and c.

   a) Briefly explain ONE example of American efforts in the 1920s and 1930s to deal with increasing global political crises, while still remaining in a relatively isolationist position.
   b) Briefly explain a SECOND example of American efforts in the 1920s and 1930s to deal with increasing global political crises, while still remaining in a relatively isolationist position.
   c) Briefly explain ONE example of American efforts in the 1920s and 1930s to deal with economic issues in its foreign policy.

LONG ESSAY For the question below, develop a thoughtful and thorough historical argument that answers the question. Begin your essay with a thesis statement and support it with relevant historical evidence.

5. Some historians have argued that despite seeming isolationist policies, the United States played a more active role in international affairs in the 1920s than at almost any previous time. Support, modify, or refute this interpretation, providing specific evidence to support your answer.

26 | AMERICA IN A WORLD AT WAR

"SOMEONE TALKED" This World War II poster, created by the graphic artist Henry Koerner, was one of many stern reminders to Americans from the government of the dangers of disclosing military secrets. In particular, wartime leaders were worried about soldiers and their families talking loosely about troop and ship locations (hence the title of another such poster: "Loose Lips Sink Ships"). (© K. J. Historical/Corbis)

WINNER R. HOE & CO., INC. AWARD – NATIONAL WAR POSTER COMPETITION
HELD UNDER AUSPICES OF ARTISTS FOR VICTORY, INC.–COUNCIL FOR DEMOCRACY–MUSEUM OF MODERN ART

AP HISTORICAL THINKING

1. **Contextualization** Analyze the general strategies of the Allies in their effort to win the war on both the European and Pacific fronts.

2. **Patterns of Continuity and Change over Time** To what degree and in what ways did World War II change employment patterns in the United States?

3. **Historical Causation** Analyze the impact of the war on both internal and external migration patterns.

4. **Historical Causation** Analyze the reasons for the emergence of the United States from World War II as the dominant world power.

5. **Comparison** Compare and contrast the restriction on civil liberties during World War II with the restrictions on civil liberties during World War I.

Key Concept Correlations

Analyze the ways the historical developments you learn about in this chapter connect to the following AP Key Concepts.

7.2 A revolution in communications and transportation technology helped to create a new mass culture and spread "modern" values and ideas, even as cultural conflicts between groups increased under the pressure of migration, world wars, and economic distress.

7.3 Global conflicts over resources, territories, and ideologies renewed debates over the nation's values and its role in the world while simultaneously propelling the United States into a dominant international military, political, cultural, and economic position.

Thematic Learning Objectives

ID-3, 6, 8; PEO-3; WOR-4, 7; POL-5

AP CONNECTING CONCEPTS

CHAPTER 26 examines the impact of World War II on American society. The chapter contains a general overview of the progress of the war, with particular emphasis on turning points, and the impact of technological development on the outcome of the war. The chapter also focuses on the impact of the war on the U.S. economy and the increase in opportunities for traditionally underemployed minorities and women and their challenges to overcoming discrimination. It examines the war's impact on specific minority groups and the impact of the war on civil liberties, particularly, regarding Japanese American citizens. As you read, evaluate the following ideas:

- World War II led to greater internal migration in the United States.
- World War II transformed the role of the United States in world affairs to that of a dominant world power.
- Economic growth spurred by World War II ended the Great Depression.
- Economic expansion during World War II led to increased opportunities for those who were traditionally underemployed.
- The development of new technology helped the United States win the war and become a dominant world power.

WAR ON TWO FRONTS

Whatever political disagreements and social tensions may have existed among the American people during World War II, there was striking unity of opinion about the conflict itself—"a unity," as one member of Congress proclaimed shortly after Pearl Harbor, "never before witnessed in this

AMERICA UNITED

country." America's unity and confidence were severely tested in the first, troubled months of 1942. Despite the impressive display of patriotism and the dramatic flurry of activity, the war was going very badly. Britain appeared ready to collapse. The Soviet Union was staggering. One after another, Allied strongholds in the Pacific were falling to the forces of Japan. The first task facing the United States, therefore, was less to achieve victory than to stave off defeat.

CONTAINING THE JAPANESE

Ten hours after the strike at Pearl Harbor, Japanese airplanes attacked the American airfields at Manila in the Philippines, destroying much of America's remaining air power in the Pacific. Three days later Guam, an American possession, fell to Japan; then Wake Island and the British colony Hong Kong. The great British fortress of Singapore surrendered in February 1942, the Dutch East Indies in March, Burma in April. In the Philippines, exhausted Filipino and American troops gave up their defense of the islands on May 6.

American strategists planned two broad offensives to turn the tide against the Japanese. One, under the command of General Douglas MacArthur, would move north from Australia, through New Guinea, and eventually back to the Philippines. The other, under Admiral Chester Nimitz, would move west from Hawaii toward major Japanese island outposts in the central Pacific. Ultimately, the two offensives would come together to invade Japan itself.

The Allies achieved their first important victory in the Battle of Coral Sea, just northwest of Australia, on May 7–8, 1942, when American forces turned back the previously unstoppable

MIDWAY

Japanese fleet. A month later, there was an even more important turning point northwest of Hawaii. An enormous battle raged for four days, June 3–6, 1942, near the small American outpost at Midway Island, at the end of which the United States, despite great losses, was clearly victorious. The American navy destroyed four Japanese aircraft carriers while losing only one, and regained control of the central Pacific for the United States.

The Americans took the offensive for the first time several months later in the southern Solomon Islands, to the east of New Guinea. In August 1942, American forces assaulted three of

GUADALCANAL

the islands: Gavutu, Tulagi, and Guadalcanal. A ferocious struggle (with, before it was over, terrible savagery) developed at Guadalcanal and continued for six months, inflicting heavy losses on both sides. In the end, however, the Japanese were forced to abandon the island–and with it their last chance of launching an effective offensive to the south.

Thus, in both the southern and central Pacific, the initiative had shifted to the United States by mid-1943. The Japanese advance had come to a stop. With aid from Australians and New Zealanders, the Americans now began the slow, arduous process of moving toward the Philippines and toward Japan itself.

HOLDING OFF THE GERMANS

In the European war, the United States had less control over military operations. It was fighting in cooperation with Britain and with the exiled "Free French" forces in the west; and it was trying also to conciliate its new ally, the Soviet Union, which was fighting Hitler in the east. The army chief of staff, General George C. Marshall, supported a plan for a major Allied invasion of France across the English Channel in the spring of 1943. But the American plan faced challenges from the Allies. The Soviet Union, which was absorbing (as it would throughout the war) the brunt of the German effort, wanted the Allied invasion to proceed at the earliest possible moment. The British, on the other hand, wanted first to launch a series of Allied offensives around the edges of the Nazi empire–in northern Africa and southern Europe–before undertaking the major invasion of France.

WORLD WAR II IN THE PACIFIC This map illustrates the changing fortunes of the two combatants in the Pacific phase of World War II. The long red line stretching from Burma to Manchuria represents the eastern boundary of the vast areas of the Pacific that had fallen under Japanese control by the summer of 1942. The blue lines illustrate the advance of American forces back into the Pacific beginning in May 1942 and accelerating in 1943 and after, which drove the Japanese forces back. The American advance was a result of two separate offensives—one in the central Pacific, under the command of Chester Nimitz, which moved west from Hawaii; the other, under the command of Douglas MacArthur, which moved north from Australia. By the summer of 1945, American forces were approaching the Japanese mainland and were bombing Tokyo. The dropping of two American atomic bombs, on Hiroshima and Nagasaki, finally brought the war to an end.

• Why did the Soviet Union enter the Pacific war in August 1945, as shown in the upper left corner of the map?

Roosevelt realized that to support the British plan would antagonize the Soviets and might delay the important cross-channel invasion. But he also knew that the invasion of Europe would take a long time to prepare, and he was reluctant to wait so long before getting American forces into combat. And so, over the objections of some of his most important advisers, he decided to support the British plan. At the end of October 1942, the British opened a counteroffensive against Nazi forces in North Africa under General Erwin Rommel, who was threatening the Suez Canal at El Alamein, and forced the Germans to retreat from Egypt. On November 8, Anglo-American forces landed at Oran and Algiers in Algeria and at Casablanca in Morocco—areas under the Nazi-controlled French government at Vichy—and began moving east toward Rommel.

The Germans threw the full weight of their forces in Africa against the inexperienced Americans and inflicted a serious defeat on them at the Kasserine Pass in Tunisia. General George S. Patton, however, regrouped the American troops and began an effective counteroffensive. With the help of Allied air and naval power and of British forces attacking from the east under General Bernard Montgomery (the hero of El Alamein), the American offensive finally drove the last Germans from Africa in May 1943. The North Africa campaign had tied up a large proportion of the Allied resources and contributed to the postponement of the planned May 1943 cross-channel invasion of France. That produced angry complaints from the Soviet Union. By now, however, the threat of a Soviet collapse seemed much diminished, for during the winter of 1942–1943

STALINGRAD the Red Army had successfully held off a major German assault at Stalingrad in southern Russia. Hitler had committed such enormous forces to the battle, and had suffered such appalling losses, that he could not continue his eastern offensive.

The Soviet victory had come at a horrible cost. The German siege of Stalingrad had decimated the civilian population of the city and devastated the surrounding countryside. Indeed, throughout the war, the Soviet Union absorbed losses far greater than any other warring nation (up to 20 million casualties)—a fact that continued to haunt the Russian memory and affect Soviet policy generations later. But the Soviet success in beating back the German offensive persuaded Roosevelt to agree, in a January 1943 meeting with Churchill in Casablanca, to an Allied invasion of Sicily. General Marshall opposed the plan, arguing that it would further delay the vital invasion of France. But Churchill prevailed with the argument that the operation in Sicily might knock Italy out of the war and tie up German divisions

that might otherwise be stationed in France. On the night of July 9, 1943, American and British armies landed in southeast Sicily; thirty-eight days later they had conquered the island and were moving onto the Italian mainland. In the face of these setbacks, Mussolini's government collapsed and the deposed dictator fled north to Germany. Mussolini's successor, Pietro Badoglio, quickly committed Italy to the Allies, but Germany moved eight divisions into the country and established a powerful defensive line south of Rome. The Allied offensive on the Italian peninsula, which began on September 3, 1943, soon bogged down, especially after a serious setback at Monte Cassino that winter. Not until May 1944 did the Allies resume their northward advance. On June 4, 1944, they captured Rome.

AUSCHWITZ, DECEMBER 1944 This photograph, taken near the end of World War II, shows a group of imprisoned children behind a barbed wire fence in one of the most notorious Nazi concentration camps. By the time this picture was taken, the Nazis had been driven out of Auschwitz and were under the control of Allied soldiers. (© Keystone/Getty Images)

The invasion of Italy contributed to the Allied war effort in several important ways. But it postponed the invasion of France by as much as a year, deeply embittering the Soviet Union, many of whose leaders believed that the United States and Britain were deliberately delaying the cross-channel invasion in order to allow the Russians to absorb the brunt of the fighting. The postponement also gave the Soviets time to begin moving toward the countries of eastern Europe.

DISPUTE OVER THE SECOND FRONT

AMERICA AND THE HOLOCAUST

In dealing with the global crisis, the leaders of the American government were confronted with one of history's great horrors: the Nazi campaign to exterminate the Jews of Europe–the Holocaust. As early as 1942, high officials in Washington had incontrovertible evidence that Hitler's forces were rounding up Jews and others (including non-Jewish Poles, gypsies, homosexuals, and communists) from all over Europe, transporting them to concentration camps in eastern Germany and Poland,

and systematically murdering them, often in factory-like gas chambers. (The death toll would ultimately reach 6 million Jews and approximately 4 million others.) News of the atrocities was reaching the public as well, and public pressure began to build for an Allied effort to end the killing or at least to rescue some of the surviving Jews.

The American government consistently resisted almost all such entreaties. Although Allied bombers were flying missions within a few miles of the most notorious death camp at Auschwitz in Poland, pleas that the planes try to destroy the crematoria at the camp were rejected as militarily unfeasible. So were similar requests that the Allies try to destroy railroad lines leading to the camps.

The United States also resisted entreaties that it admit large numbers of the Jewish refugees attempting to escape Europe–a pattern established well before Pearl Harbor. One ship, the German passenger liner *St. Louis,* had arrived off Miami in 1939 (after having already been turned away from Havana, Cuba) carrying nearly 1,000 escaped German Jews, only to be refused entry and forced to return to Europe. Both before and during

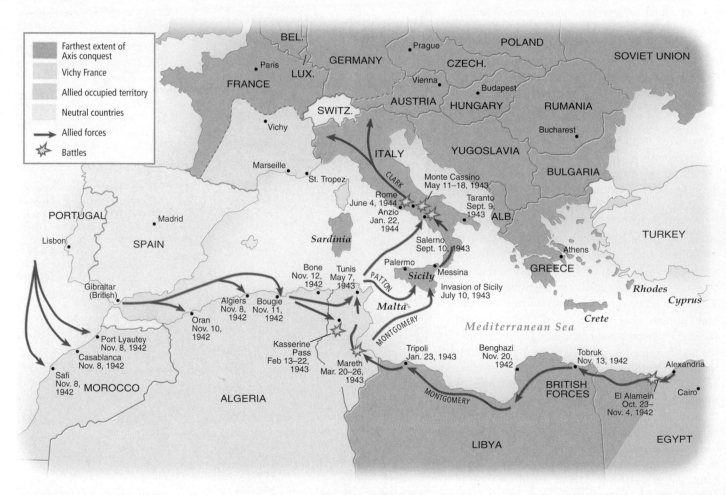

WORLD WAR II IN NORTH AFRICA AND ITALY: THE ALLIED COUNTEROFFENSIVE, 1942–1943 The United States and Great Britain understood from the beginning that an invasion of France across the English Channel would eventually be necessary for a victory in the European war. In the meantime, however, they began a campaign against Axis forces in North Africa, and in the spring of 1943 they began an invasion across the Mediterranean into Italy. This map shows the points along the coast of North Africa where Allied forces landed in 1942—with American forces moving east from Morocco and Algeria, and British forces moving west from Egypt. The two armies met in Tunisia and moved into Italy from there.

• *Why were America and Britain reluctant to launch the cross-channel invasion in 1942 or 1943?*

the war, the State Department did not even use up the number of visas permitted by law; almost 90 percent of the quota remained untouched. This disgraceful record was not a result of inadvertence. There was a deliberate effort by officials in the State Department—spearheaded by Assistant Secretary Breckinridge Long, a genteel anti-Semite—to prevent Jews from entering the United States in large numbers. One opportunity after another to assist imperiled Jews was either ignored or rejected.

OFFICIAL ANTI-SEMITISM

After 1941, there was probably little American leaders could have done, other than defeat Germany, to save most of Hitler's victims. But more forceful action by the United States (and Britain, which was even less amenable than America to Jewish requests for assistance) might well have saved some lives. Policymakers at the time justified their inaction by arguing that most of the proposed actions—bombing the railroads and the death camps, for example—would have had little effect. They insisted that the most effective thing they could do for the victims of the Holocaust was to concentrate their attention solely on the larger goal of winning the war.

THE AMERICAN PEOPLE IN WARTIME

"War is no longer simply a battle between armed forces in the field," an American government report of 1939 concluded. "It is a struggle in which each side strives to bring to bear against the enemy the coordinated power of every individual and of every material resource at its command. The conflict extends from the soldier in the front line to the citizen in the remotest hamlet in the rear." The United States had experienced wars before. But not since the Civil War had the nation undergone so consuming a military experience as World War II. American armed forces engaged in combat around the globe for nearly four years. American society, in the meantime, underwent changes that reached into virtually every corner of the nation.

PROSPERITY

World War II had its most profound impact on American domestic life by at last ending the Great Depression. By the middle of 1941, the economic problems of the 1930s—unemployment, deflation, industrial sluggishness—had virtually vanished before the great wave of wartime industrial expansion.

WAR-INDUCED ECONOMIC RECOVERY

The most important agent of the new prosperity was federal spending, which after 1939 was pumping more money into the economy each year than all the New Deal relief agencies combined had done. In 1939, the federal budget had been $9 billion, the highest level it had ever reached in peacetime; by 1945, it had risen to $100 billion. Largely as a result, the gross national product soared: from $91 billion in 1939 to $166 billion in 1945. Personal incomes in some areas grew by as much as 100 percent or more. The demands of wartime production created a shortage of consumer goods, so many wage earners diverted much of their new affluence into savings, which would help keep the economic boom alive in the postwar years.

THE ST. LOUIS The fate of the German liner *St. Louis* has become a powerful symbol of the indifference of the United States and other nations to the fate of European Jews during the Holocaust, even though its forlorn journey preceded both the beginning of World War II and the beginning of systematic extermination of Jews by the Nazi regime. The *St. Louis* carried a group of over 900 Jews fleeing from Germany in 1939, carrying exit visas of dubious legality cynically sold to them by members of Hitler's Gestapo. It became a ship without a port as it sailed from country to country—Mexico, Paraguay, Argentina, Costa Rica, and Cuba—where its passengers were refused entry time and again. Most of the passengers were hoping for a haven in the United States, but the U.S. State Department refused to allow the ship even to dock as it sailed up the American eastern seaboard. Eventually, the *St. Louis* returned to Europe and distributed its passengers among Britain, France, Holland, and Belgium (where this photograph was taken showing refugees smiling and waving as they prepare to disembark in Antwerp in June 1939). Less than a year later, all those nations except Britain fell under Nazi control. (© Bettmann/Corbis)

AP CONSIDER THE SOURCE

THE FACE OF THE ENEMY

POLITICAL CARTOONISTS USE A VARIETY OF TECHNIQUES TO PRESENT THEIR MESSAGE, including caricature, symbolism, exaggeration, irony, and juxtaposition. Their work both reflects and draws public attention to contemporary issues, and often captures the emotional response to an issue better than the written word. Theodore Geisel, better known as Dr. Seuss, drew some 400 cartoons for *PM*, a left-wing daily newspaper, during World War II in which he lambasted the wartime enemies of the United States. One of these cartoons ("What have YOU done today to help save your country from them?") is reproduced below. The second image from World War II, depicting Japanese prime minister Hideki Tojo, was drawn by Arthur Szyk and appeared on the cover of *Collier's* magazine in December 1942.

Political cartoons were also used during earlier conflicts. The image on page 711 was drawn during the War of 1812 to celebrate American naval victories and portrays American President James Madison giving Britain's King George III a bloody nose.

WORLD WAR II—1942

"WHAT HAVE *YOU* DONE TODAY TO HELP SAVE YOUR COUNTRY FROM THEM?" (*PM*, March 5, 1942. http://orpheus.ucsd.edu/speccoll/dspolitic/Frame.htm. Courtesy Mandeville Special Collections Library, University of California, San Diego.)

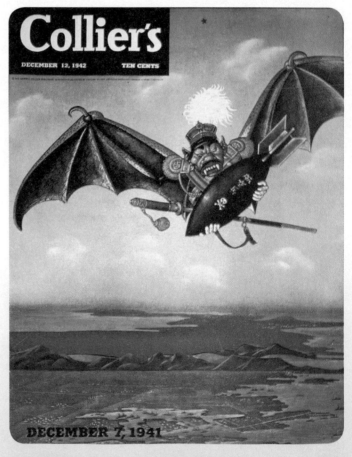

ARTHUR SZYK, *COLLIER'S* COVER, DECEMBER 12, 1942 (Private Collection/ Peter Newark Military Pictures/Bridgeman Art Library International/© Estate of Arthur Szyk)

WAR OF 1812—1812

A BOXING MATCH, OR ANOTHER BLOODY NOSE FOR JOHN BULL, WILLIAM CHARLES,
1813 (© Library of Congress Prints & Photographs Division [LC-DIG-ppmsca-10754])

AP TEST PRACTICE

Questions assume cumulative content knowledge from this chapter and previous chapters.

1. The first World War II cartoon's perspective most suggests which attitude towards the two individuals and their respective countries in 1942?

    (A) One was viewed as self-important and the other, inferior

    (B) One was viewed as humble, and the other, silly

    (C) One was viewed as superior, and the other, imperial

    (D) Both were viewed as imperious

2. What can most likely be deduced from the fact that the Szyk cartoon was the cover page for a popular magazine almost exactly one year after the event?

    (A) That the Japanese were determined to achieve their goals

    (B) That the event was a turning point in American history

    (C) That the event did not have a great impact on America

    (D) That the event was more about Japanese aggression than about America's response

3. What do the Seuss and the Charles cartoons share in their suggestion about American identity in the face of the two different crises at different time periods?

    (A) Americans react recklessly to such crises.

    (B) Americans are inexperienced against such crises.

    (C) Americans are steadfast against aggression.

    (D) Americans are singularly united and do not experience differences of opinion within their society during such crises.

THE WAR AND THE WEST

The impact of government spending was perhaps most dramatic in the West, which had long relied on federal largesse more than other regions. The West Coast, naturally, became the launching point for most of the naval war against Japan; and the government created large manufacturing facilities in California and elsewhere to serve the needs of its military. Altogether, the government made almost $40 billion worth of capital investments (factories, military and transportation facilities, highways, power plants) in the West during the war, more than in any other region. Ten percent of all the money the federal government spent between 1940 and 1945 went to California. Other western states also shared disproportionately in war contracts and government-funded capital investments.

By the end of the war, the economy of the Pacific Coast and, to a lesser extent, other areas of the West had been transformed. The Pacific Coast had become the center of the growing American aircraft industry. New yards in southern California, Washington State, and elsewhere made the West a center of the shipbuilding industry. Los Angeles, formerly a medium-sized city notable chiefly for its film industry, now became a major industrial center as well.

Once a lightly industrialized region, parts of the West were now among the most important manufacturing areas in the country. Once a region without adequate facilities to support substantial economic growth, the West now stood poised to become the fastest-growing region in the nation after the war.

LABOR AND THE WAR

Instead of the prolonged and debilitating unemployment that had been the most troubling feature of the Depression economy, the war created a serious labor shortage. The armed forces took more than 15 million men and women out of the civilian workforce at the same time that the demand for labor was rising rapidly. Nevertheless, the civilian workforce increased by almost 20 percent during the war. The 7 million people who had previously been unemployed accounted for some of the increase; the employment of many people previously considered inappropriate for the workforce–the very young, the elderly, and, most important, several million women–accounted for the rest.

The war gave an enormous boost to union membership, which rose from about 10.5 million members in 1941 to more than 13 million in 1945. But it also created

UNION GAINS important new restrictions on the ability of unions to fight for their members' demands. The government was principally interested in preventing inflation and in keeping production moving without disruption. It managed to win important concessions from union leaders on both scores. One was the so-called Little Steel formula, which set a 15 percent limit on wartime wage increases. Another was the "no-strike" pledge, by which unions agreed not to stop production in wartime. In return, the government provided labor with a

"maintenance-of-membership" agreement, which insisted that the thousands of new workers pouring into unionized defense plants would be automatically enrolled in the unions. The agreement ensured the continued health of the union organizations, but in return workers had to give up the right to demand major economic gains during the war.

Many rank-and-file union members, and some local union leaders, resented the restrictions imposed on them by the government and the labor movement hierarchy. Despite the no-strike pledge, there were nearly 15,000 work stoppages during the war, mostly wildcat strikes (strikes unauthorized by the union leadership). When the United Mine Workers defied the government by striking in May 1943, Congress reacted by passing, over Roosevelt's veto, the Smith-Connally Act (or the War Labor Disputes Act), which required unions to wait thirty days before striking and empowered the president to seize a struck war plant. In the meantime, public animosity toward labor rose rapidly, and many states passed laws to limit union power.

STABILIZING THE BOOM

The fear of deflation, the central concern of the 1930s, gave way during the war to a fear of inflation, particularly after

OFFICE OF PRICE ADMINISTRATION prices rose 25 percent in the two years before the attack on Pearl Harbor. In October 1942, Congress grudgingly responded to the president's request and passed the Anti-Inflation Act, which gave the administration authority to freeze agricultural prices, wages, salaries, and rents throughout the country. Enforcement of these provisions was the task of the Office of Price Administration (OPA), led first by Leon Henderson and then by Chester Bowles. In part because of its success, inflation was a much less serious problem during World War II than it had been during World War I.

Even so, the OPA was never popular. There was widespread resentment of its controls over wages and prices. And there was only grudging acquiescence in its complicated system of rationing scarce consumer goods: coffee, sugar, meat, butter, canned goods, shoes, tires, gasoline, and fuel oil. Black-marketing and overcharging grew to proportions far beyond OPA policing capacity.

From 1941 to 1945, the federal government spent a total of $321 billion–twice as much as it had spent in the entire 150 years of its existence to that point, and ten times as much as the cost of World War I. The national debt rose from $49 billion in 1941 to $259 billion in 1945. The government borrowed about half the revenues it needed by selling $100 billion worth of bonds–some sold to ordinary citizens, but most to financial institutions. Much of the rest it raised by radically increasing income taxes through the Revenue Act of 1942, which established a 94 percent rate for the highest brackets and, for the first time, imposed taxes on the lowest-income families as well. To simplify collection, Congress enacted a withholding system of payroll deductions in 1943.

MOBILIZING PRODUCTION

The search for an effective mechanism to mobilize the economy for war began as early as 1939 and continued for nearly four years. One failed agency after another attempted to bring order to the mobilization effort. Finally, in January 1942, the president responded to widespread criticism by creating the War Production Board (WPB), under the direction of former Sears Roebuck executive Donald Nelson. In theory, the WPB was to be a "superagency," with broad powers over the economy. In fact, it never had as much authority as its World War I equivalent, the War Industries Board. And the genial Donald Nelson never displayed the administrative or political strength of his 1918 counterpart, Bernard Baruch.

WAR PRODUCTION BOARD

The WPB was never able to win control over military purchases; the army and navy often circumvented the board entirely in negotiating contracts with producers. It was never able to satisfy the complaints of small business, which charged (correctly) that most contracts were going to large corporations. Gradually, the president transferred much of the WPB's authority to a new office located within the White House: the Office of War Mobilization, directed by former Supreme Court justice and South Carolina senator James F. Byrnes. But the OWM was only slightly more successful than the WPB.

Despite the administrative problems, the war economy managed to meet almost all the nation's critical war needs. Enormous new factory complexes sprang up in the space of a few months, many of them funded by the federal government's Defense Plants Corporation. An entire new industry producing synthetic rubber emerged, to make up for the loss of access to natural rubber in the Pacific. By the beginning of 1944, American factories were, in fact, producing more of most goods than the government needed. Their output was twice that of all the Axis countries combined. There were even complaints late in the war from some officials that military production was becoming excessive, that a limited resumption of civilian production should begin before the fighting ended. The military staunchly and successfully opposed almost all such demands.

WARTIME SCIENCE AND TECHNOLOGY

More than any previous American war, World War II was a watershed for technological and scientific innovation. That was partly because the American government poured substantial funds into research and development beginning in 1940. In that year the government created the National Defense Research Committee, headed by the MIT scientist Vannevar Bush, who had been a pioneer in the early development of the computer. By the end of the war, the new agency had spent more than $100 million on research, more than four times the amount spent by the government on military research and development in the previous forty years.

NATIONAL DEFENSE RESEARCH COMMITTEE

In the first years of the war, all the technological advantages seemed to lie with the Germans and Japanese. Germany had made great advances in tanks and other mechanized armor in the 1930s, particularly during the Spanish Civil War, when it had helped arm Franco's fascist forces. It used its armor effectively during its blitzkrieg in Europe in 1940 and again in North Africa in 1942. German submarine technology was significantly advanced compared to British and American capabilities in 1940, and German U-boats were, for a time, devastatingly effective in disrupting Allied shipping. Japan had developed extraordinary capacity in its naval-air technology. Its highly sophisticated fighter planes, launched from distant aircraft carriers, conducted the successful raid on Pearl Harbor in December 1941.

But Britain and America had advantages of their own, which quickly helped redress these imbalances. American techniques of mass production—the great automotive assembly lines in particular—were converted efficiently to military production in 1941 and 1942 and soon began producing airplanes, ships, tanks, and other armaments in much greater numbers than the Germans and Japanese could produce. Allied scientists and engineers moved quickly as well to improve Anglo-American aviation and naval technology, particularly to improve the performance of submarines and tanks. By late 1942, Allied weaponry was at least as advanced as that of the enemy.

In addition, each technological innovation by the enemy produced a corresponding innovation to limit the damage of the new techniques. American and British physicists made rapid advances in improving radar and sonar technology—taking advantage of advances in radio technology in the 1920s and beyond—which helped Allied naval forces decimate German U-boats in 1943 and effectively end their effectiveness in the naval war. Particularly important was the creation in 1940 of "centimetric radar," which used narrow beams of short wavelength that made radar more efficient and effective than ever before—as the British navy discovered in April 1941 when the instruments on one of its ships detected a surfaced submarine ten miles away at night and, on another occasion, spotted a periscope at three-quarters of a mile range. With earlier technologies, the sub and periscope would have been undetectable. This new radar could also be effectively miniaturized, which was critical to its use on airplanes and submarines in particular. It required only a small rotating aerial, and it used newly advanced cavity magnetron valves of great power. These innovations put the Allies far in advance of Germany and Japan in radar and sonar technology. The Allies also learned early how to detect and disable German naval mines; and when the Germans tried to counter this progress by introducing an "acoustic" mine, which detonated when a ship came near it, not necessarily just on contact, the Allies developed acoustical countermeasures of their own, which transmitted sounds through the water to detonate mines before ships came near them.

RADAR AND SONAR

Anglo-American antiaircraft technology—both on land and on sea—also improved, although never to the point where it

RADAR SCOPE, 1944 Navy technicians are shown here demonstrating the new radar scopes that revolutionized the tracking of ships and planes during World War II. (National Archives and Records Administration)

could stop bombing raids. Germany made substantial advances in the development of rocket technology in the early years of the war, and it managed to launch some rocket-propelled bombs (the V1s and V2s) across the English Channel, aimed at London. The psychological effects of the rockets on the British people were considerable. But the Germans were never able to create a production technology capable of building enough such rockets to make a real difference in the balance of military power.

Beginning in 1942, British and American forces seized the advantage in the air war by producing new and powerful four-engine bombers in great numbers—among them the British Lancaster B1 and the American Boeing B17F, capable of flying a bomb load of 6,000 pounds for 1,300 miles, and capable of reaching 37,500 feet. Because they were able to fly higher and longer than the German equivalents, they were able to conduct extensive bombing missions over Germany (and later Japan) with much less danger of being shot down.

But the success of the bombers rested heavily as well on new electronic devices capable of guiding their bombs to their targets. The Gee navigation system, which was also valuable to the navy, used electronic pulses to help pilots plot their exact location–something that in the past only a highly skilled navigator could do, and then only in good weather. In March 1942, eighty Allied bombers fitted with Gee systems staged a devastatingly effective bombing raid on German industrial and military installations in the Ruhr Valley. Studies showed that the Gee system doubled the accuracy rate of night bombing raids. Also effective was the Oboe system, a radio device that sent a sonic message to airplanes to tell them when they were within twenty yards of their targets, first introduced in December 1942.

The area in which the Allies had perhaps the greatest advantages in technology and knowledge was the gathering of intelligence, much of it through Britain's top-secret Ultra project. Some of

ULTRA

the advantages the Allies enjoyed came from successful efforts to capture or steal German and Japanese intelligence devices. More important, however, were the efforts of cryptologists to puzzle out the enemy's systems, and advances in computer technology that helped the Allies decipher coded messages sent by the Japanese and the Germans. Much of Germany's coded communication made use of the so-called Enigma machine, which was effective because it constantly changed the coding systems it used.

In the first months of the war, Polish intelligence had developed an electro-mechanical computer, which it called the "Bombe," that could decipher some Enigma messages. After the fall of Poland, British scientists, led by the brilliant computer pioneer Alan Turing, took the Bombe, which was too slow to keep up with the increasingly frequent changes of coding the Germans were using, and greatly improved it. On April 15, 1940, the new, improved, high-speed Bombe broke the coding of a series of German messages within hours (not days, as had previously been the case). A few weeks later, it began decrypting German messages at the rate of 1,000 a day, providing the British (and later the Americans) with a constant flow of information about enemy operations that continued—unknown to the Germans—until the end of the war.

Later in the war, British scientists working for the intelligence services built the first real programmable, digital computer—the Colossus II, which became operational less than a week before the beginning of the Normandy invasion. It was able to decipher an enormous number of intercepted German messages almost instantly.

The United States also had some important intelligence breakthroughs, including, in 1941, a dramatic success by the **MAGIC** American Magic operation (the counterpart to the British Ultra) in breaking a Japanese coding system not unlike the German Enigma, a mechanical device known to the Allies as Purple. The result was that Americans had access to intercepted information that, if properly interpreted, could have alerted them to the Japanese raid on Pearl Harbor in December 1941. But because such a raid had seemed entirely inconceivable to most American officials prior to its occurrence, those who received the information failed to understand or disseminate it in time.

AFRICAN AMERICANS AND THE WAR

During World War I, many African Americans had eagerly seized the chance to serve in the armed forces, believing that their patriotic efforts would win them an enhanced position in postwar society. They had been cruelly disappointed. As World War II approached, blacks were again determined to use the conflict to improve their position in society—this time, however, not by currying favor but by making demands.

In the summer of 1941, A. Philip Randolph, president of the predominantly black Brotherhood of Sleeping Car Porters, began to insist that the government require companies receiving defense contracts to integrate their workforces. To mobilize support for the demand, Randolph planned a massive march on Washington, which would, he promised, bring more than 100,000 demonstrators to the capital. Roosevelt was afraid of both the possibility of violence and the certainty of political embarrassment. He finally persuaded Randolph to cancel the march in return for a promise to **FEPC** establish a Fair Employment Practices Commission (FEPC) to investigate discrimination in war industries. The FEPC's enforcement powers, and thus its effectiveness, were limited, but its creation was a rare symbolic victory for African Americans making demands of the government.

The demand for labor in war plants greatly increased the migration of blacks from the rural areas of the South into industrial cities—a migration that continued for more than a decade after the war and brought many more African Americans into northern cities than the Great Migration of 1914–1919 had done. The migration bettered the economic condition of many African Americans, but it also created urban tensions. On a hot June day in Detroit in 1943, a series of altercations between blacks and whites at a city park led to two days of racial violence in which thirty-four people died, twenty-five of them African Americans.

Despite such tensions, the leading black organizations redoubled their efforts during the war to challenge the system **CORE** of segregation. The Congress of Racial Equality (CORE), organized in 1942, mobilized mass popular resistance to discrimination in a way that the older, more conservative organizations had never done. Randolph, Bayard Rustin, James Farmer, and other, younger black leaders helped organize sit-ins and demonstrations in segregated theaters and restaurants. In 1944, CORE won a much-publicized victory by forcing a Washington, D.C., restaurant to agree to serve African Americans. CORE's defiant spirit would survive into the 1950s and help produce the civil rights movement.

Pressure for change was also growing within the military. At first, the armed forces maintained their traditional practice of limiting blacks to the most menial assignments, keeping them in segregated training camps and units, and barring them entirely from the Marine Corps and the Army Air Forces. Gradually, however, military leaders were forced to make adjustments—in part because of public and political pressures, but also because they recognized that these forms of segregation were wasting manpower. By the end of the war, the number of black servicemen had increased sevenfold, to 700,000; some training camps were being at least partially integrated; African Americans were beginning to serve on ships with white sailors; and more black units were being sent into combat than at the beginning of the war. But tensions remained. In some of the partially integrated army bases—Fort Dix, New Jersey, for example—riots occasionally broke out when African Americans protested having to serve in segregated divisions. Substantial discrimination survived in all the services until well after the war. But within the military, as within the society at large, the traditional pattern of race relations was slowly eroding.

NATIVE AMERICANS AND THE WAR

Approximately 25,000 Native Americans performed military service during World War II. Many of them served in combat (among them Ira Hayes, one of the men who memorably raised the American flag at Iwo Jima). Others worked as "code-talkers," working in military communications and speaking their own languages (which enemy forces would be unlikely to understand) over the radio and the telephones.

"CODE-TALKERS"

The war had important effects, too, on those Native Americans who remained civilians. Little war work reached the tribes, and government subsidies dwindled. Many talented young people left the reservations, some to serve in the military, others (more than 70,000) to work in war plants. This brought many Indians into close contact with white society for the first time and awakened in some of them a taste for the material benefits of life in capitalist America that they would retain after the war. Some never returned to the reservations, but chose to remain in the non-Indian world and assimilate to its ways. Others found that after the war, employment opportunities that had been available to them during the fighting became unavailable once again, drawing them back to the reservations.

The wartime emphasis on national unity undermined support for the revitalization of tribal autonomy that the Indian Reorganization Act of 1934 had launched. New pressures emerged to eliminate the reservation system and require the tribes to assimilate into white society—pressures so severe that John Collier, the director of the Bureau of Indian Affairs who had done so much to promote the reinvigoration of the reservations, resigned in 1945.

MEXICAN AMERICAN WAR WORKERS

Large numbers of Mexican workers entered the United States during the war in response to labor shortages on the Pacific Coast, in the Southwest, and eventually in almost all areas of the nation. The American and Mexican governments agreed in 1942 to a program by which *braceros* (contract laborers) would be admitted to the United States for a limited time to work at specific jobs, and American employers in some parts of the Southwest began actively recruiting Mexican American workers.

During the Depression, many Mexican American farmworkers had been deported to make room for unemployed white workers. The wartime labor shortage caused farm owners to begin hiring Mexican Americans again. More important, however, Mexican Americans were able for the first time to find significant numbers of factory jobs. They formed the second-largest group of migrants (after African Americans) to American cities in the 1940s. Over 300,000 of them served in the United States military.

EMPLOYMENT GAINS FOR MEXICAN AMERICANS

The sudden expansion of Mexican American neighborhoods created tensions and occasionally conflict in some

VICTORY GARDENS During both World War I and II, private and public lands were cultivated by non-combattant civilians, often children, to reduce the pressure on the public food supply. In addition to help solving practical needs of food production, these gardens served to boost the morale of citizens across the country as they supported the war effort. Here, gardeners work a plot of of land in Saint Gabriel's Park, in New York City, with the Chrysler Building looming in the background. (© Bettmann/Corbis)

American cities. Some white residents of Los Angeles became alarmed at the activities of Mexican American teenagers, many of whom were joining street gangs (*pachucos*). The *pachucos* were particularly distinctive because of their members' style of dress, which whites considered outrageous. They wore "zoot suits"—long, loose jackets with padded shoulders, baggy pants tied at the ankles—long watch chains, broad-brimmed hats, and greased, ducktail hairstyles. (It was a style borrowed in part from fashions in Harlem.)

In June 1943, animosity toward the zoot-suiters produced a four-day riot in Los Angeles, during which white sailors stationed at a base in Long Beach invaded Mexican American communities and attacked zoot-suiters (in response to alleged attacks). The city police did little to restrain the sailors, who grabbed Mexican American teenagers, tore off and burned their clothes, cut off their ducktails, and beat them. But when Mexican Americans tried to fight back, the police moved in and arrested them. In the aftermath of the "zoot-suit riots," Los Angeles passed a law prohibiting the wearing of zoot suits.

ZOOT-SUIT RIOTS

WOMEN AND CHILDREN AT WAR

The war drew increasing numbers of women into roles from which, by either custom or law, they had been largely barred.

The number of women in the workforce increased by nearly 60 percent, and women accounted for a third of paid workers in 1945 (as opposed to a quarter in 1940). These wage-earning women were more

DRAMATIC INCREASE IN FEMALE EMPLOYMENT

likely to be married and older than most women who had entered the workforce in the past.

Many women entered the industrial workforce to replace male workers serving in the military. But while economic and military necessity eroded some of the popular objections to women in the workplace, obstacles remained. Many factory owners continued to categorize jobs by gender. (Female work, like male work, was also categorized by race: black women were usually assigned more menial tasks, and paid at a lower rate, than their white counterparts.) Employers also made substantial investments in automated assembly lines to reduce the need for heavy labor.

Special recruiting materials for women made domestic analogies. Cutting airplane wings was compared to making a dress pattern, mixing chemicals to making a cake. Still, women did make important inroads in industrial employment during the war. Women had been working in industry for over a century, but some began now to take on heavy industrial jobs that had long been considered "men's work."

"ROSIE THE RIVETER" The famous wartime image of "Rosie the Riveter" symbolized the new importance of the female industrial workforce. Women workers joined unions in substantial numbers, and they helped erode at least some of the prejudice, including the prejudice against working mothers, that had previously kept many of them from paid employment.

Most women workers during the war were employed not in factories but in service-sector jobs. Above all, they worked for the government, whose bureaucratic needs expanded dramatically alongside its military and industrial needs. Washington, D.C., in particular, was flooded with young female clerks, secretaries, and typists–known as "government girls"–most of whom lived in cramped quarters in boardinghouses, private homes, and government dormitories and worked long hours in the war agencies. Public and private clerical employment for women expanded in other urban areas as well, creating high concentrations of young women in places largely depleted of young men. Even within the military, which enlisted substantial numbers of women as WACs (army) and WAVEs (navy), most female work was clerical.

The new opportunities produced new problems. Many mothers whose husbands were in the military **LIMITED CHILD CARE** had to combine working with caring for their children. The scarcity of child-care facilities or other community services meant that some women had no choice but to leave young children–often known as "latchkey children" or "eight-hour orphans"–at home alone (or sometimes locked in cars in factory parking lots) while they worked.

Perhaps in part because of the family dislocations the war produced, juvenile crime rose markedly in the war years. Young boys were arrested at rapidly increasing rates for car theft and burglary, vandalism, and vagrancy. The arrest rate for prostitutes, many of whom were teenage girls, rose too, as did the incidence of sexually transmitted disease. For many children, however, the distinctive experience of the war years was not crime but work. More than a third of all teenagers between the ages of fourteen and eighteen were employed late in the war, causing some reduction in high-school enrollments.

The return of prosperity during the war helped increase the rate and lower the age of marriage after the Depression decline, **BEGINNING OF THE "BABY BOOM"** but many of these young marriages were unable to survive the pressures of wartime separation. The divorce rate rose rapidly. The rise in the birth rate that accompanied the increase in marriages was the first sign of what would become the great postwar "baby boom."

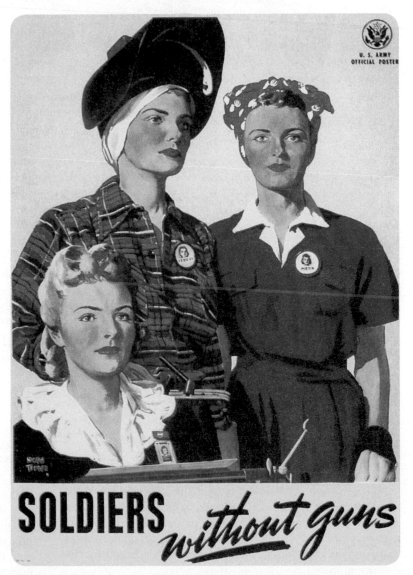

SOLDIERS *without guns*

WOMEN AT WAR Many American women enlisted in the army and navy women's corps during World War II, but an equally important contribution of women to the war effort was their work in factories and offices—often in jobs that would have been considered inappropriate for them in peacetime but that they were now encouraged to assume because of the absence of so many men. (The Library of Congress)

LIFE: THE GREAT MAGAZINE

THE birth of a great era of photographs in the twentieth century created many new magazines. One of the finest was *Life*, first published in 1936 by Henry Luce. It soon became the most popular magazine in America. Luce himself wrote a minor classic of journalism for his new magazine:

HENRY LUCE (© Time & Life Pictures/Getty Images)

To see life; to see the world; to eyewitness great events; to watch the faces of the poor and the gestures of the proud; to see strange things—machines, armies, multitudes, shadows in the jungle and on the moon; to see man's work. . . . Thus to see, and to be shown, is now the will and new expectancy of half of mankind.

Luce and his partner, Briton Hadden, began a remarkable empire when they started *Time* magazine in 1923. But Hadden died suddenly in 1929, and Luce took charge. He began a successful business magazine—*Fortune*. But it was *Life* that made Luce famous and wealthy. The Cowles family of Iowa followed Luce with *Look*, which was also successful. But for most Americans, *Life* was the most important magazine.

Life, which began just three years before World War II presented many stories on the coming conflict. Building for the war was growing fast by 1942. Detroit and other cities turned their automobile production into the manufacture of planes, armored vehicles, jeeps, and other war matériel. *Life* reporters warned that "the morale situation is perhaps worst in the U.S. . . . For Detroit can either blow up Hitler or it can blow up the U.S."

Life sent a large pool of photographers and graphic artists across the Atlantic to cover the war. The magazine turned the conflict into a great visual story and became renowned for its striking imagery.

Life's remarkable popularity continued throughout the war. It's first issue after the Japanese attack on Pearl Harbor featured the word "WAR" set in large black type on its first page. Photographers were not allowed to use many of the pictures they took of the tremendous damage until 1943, because editors feared that people at home would be shocked if they saw

WARTIME LIFE AND CULTURE

The war created considerable anxiety in American life. Families worried about loved ones at the front and struggled to adjust to the absence of husbands, fathers, brothers, sons—and to the new mobility of women, which also drew family members away from home. Businesses and communities struggled to compensate for shortages of goods and the absence of men.

But the abundance of the war years also created a striking buoyancy in American life that the conflict itself only partially subdued. Suddenly, people had money to spend again

ECONOMIC GOOD TIMES

and—despite the many shortages of consumer goods—at least some things to spend it on. Audiences equal to about half the population attended movies each week, often to watch heroic war films. Magazines, particularly pictorial ones such as *Life*, reached the peak of their popularity, satisfying the seemingly insatiable hunger of readers for pictures of and stories about the war. (See "Patterns of Popular Culture," pp. 718-719.) Radio ownership and listening also increased, for the same reason.

Resort hotels, casinos, and race tracks were jammed with customers. Dance halls were packed with young people drawn to the seductive music of swing bands; soldiers and sailors

THE STORY OF WAR *Life* reporters and photographers told the story of the war to everyone, including these soldiers, shown reading the magazine that they will in turn appear in. (Photo by US Army/© Time & Life Pictures/Getty Images)

UNDERSTAND, ANALYZE, AND EVALUATE

1. In what ways did *Life* magazine influence the way news stories are reported and presented today?
2. Analyze the cover of *Life* magazine shown above. What were the messages the magazine wanted to convey about the war to its readers?
3. How does the motive of making a profit influence how the news is reported?

military personnel who were injured or killed. But, eventually, Americans saw what the war really was through images that included flag-draped coffins. At the end of the war, on VJ Day, the great photographer Alfred Eisenstadt captured a moment of peace and joy when he took the famous picture of a sailor embracing a young woman in Times Square.

After the war, although there were still serious essays on politics and foreign affairs, *Life* began another effort—to show America as a prosperous and happy nation. The magazine began to show "Modern Living," along with "football games, automobile trips, family trips, and all the pleasant trivia of the American way of life." *Life* was eager to show the great bounty of American life. "How can one feel thankful for too much," one reporter wrote.

Through most of the 1950s, *Life* remained an enormously prosperous venture. But toward the end of that decade, *Life* started to decline, as many magazines began to lose their impact with the growing popularity of television. Advertisers who would have bought ad space in magazines began buying television advertisements. Magazines, including *Life,* lost a vital source of their revenue. In December 1972, *Life* published its last issue. But the great *Life* photographs remain a remarkable archive of events around the world during a large part of the twentieth century. ●

home on leave, or awaiting shipment overseas, were especially attracted to the dances and the big band.

Advertisers, and at times even the government, exhorted Americans to support the war effort to ensure a future of material comfort and consumer choice for themselves and their children. "Your people are giving their lives in useless sacrifice," *The Saturday Evening Post* wrote in a mock letter to the leaders of wartime Japan. "Ours are fighting for a glorious future of mass employment, mass production and mass distribution and ownership." Even troops at the front seemed at times to justify their efforts with reference to the comforts of home more than to the character of the enemy or the ideals

FIGHTING FOR FUTURE PROSPERITY

America claimed to be defending. "They are fighting for home," the writer John Hersey once wrote from Guadalcanal (with at least a trace of dismay), because "Home is where the good things are–the generosity, the good pay, the comforts, the democracy, the pie."

For men at the front, the image of home was a powerful antidote to the rigors of wartime. They dreamed of music, food, movies, material comforts. Many also dreamed of women–wives and girlfriends, but also movie stars and others who became the source of one of the most popular icons of the front: the pinup.

For the servicemen who remained in America during the war, and for soldiers and sailors in cities far from home in particular, the company of friendly, "wholesome" women was, the
USO
military believed, critical to maintaining morale. USOs recruited thousands of young women to serve as hostesses in their clubs—women who were expected to dress nicely, dance well, and chat happily with lonely men. Other women joined "dance brigades" and traveled by bus to military bases for social evenings with servicemen. They, too, were expected to be pretty, to dress attractively (and conservatively), and to interact comfortably with men they had never met before and would likely never see again. The USO forbade women to have dates with soldiers after parties in the clubs, and the members of the "dance brigades" were expected to have no contact with servicemen except during the dances. Clearly, such regulations were sometimes violated. But while the military took elaborate measures to root out homosexual men and women from their ranks (unceremoniously dismissing many of them with undesirable discharges), it quietly tolerated "healthy heterosexuality."

THE INTERNMENT OF JAPANESE AMERICANS

World War I had produced widespread hatred, vindictiveness, and hysteria in America, as well as widespread and flagrant violations of civil liberties. World War II did not produce a comparable era of repression. The government barred from the mails a few papers it considered seditious, among them Father Coughlin's anti-Semitic and pro-fascist *Social Justice,* but there was no general censorship of dissident publications. The most ambitious effort to punish domestic fascists, a sedition trial of twenty-eight people, ended in a mistrial, and the defendants went free. Unlike during World War I, the government generally left socialists and communists (most of whom strongly supported the war effort) alone—although the Roosevelt administration summarily and secretly executed a number of German spies who had entered the country.

Nor was there much of the ethnic or cultural animosity that had shaped the social climate of the United States during World War I. The "zoot-suit" riots in Los Angeles and occasional racial conflicts in American cities and on military bases made clear that traditional racial and ethnic hostilities had not
ETHNIC DISTINCTIONS BLURRED
disappeared. So did wartime restrictions imposed on some Italians—including provisions forbidding many of them to travel and imprisoning several hundred. The great opera singer Ezio Pinza was classified as an "enemy alien." But on the whole, the war worked more to blur ethnic distinctions than to heighten them. Americans continued to eat sauerkraut without calling it by the World War I name "liberty cabbage." They displayed relatively little hostility toward German or Italian Americans. Instead, they seemed to share the view of their government's propaganda: that the enemy was less the German and Italian people than the vicious political systems to which they had succumbed. In popular culture, and in everyday interactions, ethnicity seemed less a source of menacing

difference—as it often had in the past—and more evidence of healthy diversity. The participation and frequent heroism of American soldiers of many ethnic backgrounds encouraged this change.

But there was a glaring exception to the general rule of tolerance: the treatment of the small, politically powerless group of Japanese Americans. From the beginning, Americans adopted a different attitude toward their Asian enemy than they did toward their European foes. The Japanese, both government and private propaganda encouraged Americans to believe, were a devious, malign, and cruel people. The infamous attack on Pearl Harbor seemed to many Americans to confirm that assessment.

This racial animosity soon extended to Americans of Japanese descent. There were not many Japanese Americans in the continental United States—only about 127,000, most of them concentrated in a few areas in California. About a third of them were unnaturalized, first-generation immigrants (Issei); two-thirds were naturalized or native-born citizens of the United States (Nisei). The Japanese in America, like the Chinese, had long been the target of ethnic and racial animosity; and unlike members of European ethnic groups, who had encountered similar resentment, Asians seemed unable to dispel prejudice against them no matter how assimilated they became. Many white Americans
ANTI-JAPANESE PREJUDICE
continued to consider Asians (even native-born citizens) so "foreign" that they could never become "real" Americans. Partly as a result, much of the Japanese American population in the West continued to live in close-knit, to some degree even insular, communities, which reinforced the belief that they were alien and potentially menacing.

The attack on Pearl Harbor inflamed these long-standing suspicions and turned them into active animosity. Wild stories circulated about how the Japanese in Hawaii had helped sabotage Pearl Harbor and how Japanese Americans in California were conspiring to aid an enemy landing on the Pacific coast. There was no evidence to support any of these charges; but according to Earl Warren, then attorney general of California, the apparent passivity of the Japanese Americans was itself evidence of the danger they posed. Because they did nothing to allow officials to gauge their intentions, Warren claimed, it was all the more important to take precautions against conspiracies.

Although there was some public pressure in California to remove the Japanese "threat," popular sentiment was generally more tolerant of the Nisei and Issei (and more willing to make distinctions between them and the Japanese in Japan) than was official sentiment. The real impetus for taking action came from the government. Secretary of the Navy Frank Knox, for example, said shortly after Pearl Harbor that "the most effective fifth column [a term for internal sabotage] work of the entire war was done in Hawaii." That statement—clearly referring to the large Japanese population there—later proved to be entirely false. General John L. DeWitt, the senior military commander on the West Coast, claimed to have "no confidence in [Japanese American] loyalty whatsoever." When asked about the distinction between unnaturalized Japanese immigrants and American citizens, he said, "A Jap is a Jap. It makes no difference whether he is an American citizen or not."

In February 1942, in response to such pressure (and over the objections of the attorney general and J. Edgar Hoover, the director of the FBI), President Roosevelt authorized the army to "intern" the Japanese Americans. He created the War Relocation Authority (WRA) to oversee the project. More than 100,000 people (Issei and Nisei alike) were rounded up, told to dispose of their property however they could (which often meant simply abandoning it), and taken to what the government euphemistically termed "relocation centers" in the "interior." In fact, they were facilities little different from prisons, many of them located in the western mountains and the desert. Conditions in the internment camps were not brutal, but they were harsh and uncomfortable. Government officials talked of them as places where the Japanese could be socialized and "Americanized." But the internment camps were more a target of white economic aspirations than of missionary work. The governor of Utah, where many of the internees were located, wanted the federal government to turn over thousands of Japanese Americans to serve as forced laborers. Washington did not comply, but the WRA did hire out many inmates as agricultural laborers.

"RELOCATION CENTERS"

The internment never produced significant popular opposition. For the most part, once the Japanese were in the camps, other Americans (including their former neighbors on the West Coast) largely forgot about them—except to make strenuous efforts to acquire the property they had abandoned. Even so, beginning in 1943 conditions slowly improved. Some young Japanese Americans left the camps to attend colleges and universities (mostly in the East—the WRA continued to be wary of letting Japanese return to the Pacific Coast). Others were permitted to move to cities to take factory and service jobs (although, again, not on the West Coast). Some young

men joined and others were drafted into the American military; a Nisei army unit fought with distinction in Europe.

In 1944, the Supreme Court ruled in *Korematsu v. U.S.* that the relocation was constitutionally permissible. In another case the same year, it barred the internment of "loyal" citizens, but left the interpretation of "loyal" to the discretion of the government. Nevertheless, by the end of 1944, most of the internees had been released; and in early 1945, they were finally permitted to return to the West Coast—where they faced continuing harassment and persecution, and where many found their property and businesses irretrievably lost. In 1988, they won some compensation for their losses, when, after years of agitation by survivors of the camps and their descendants, Congress voted to award them reparations. But by then, many of the former internees had died.

KOREMATSU V. U.S.

CHINESE AMERICANS AND THE WAR

Just as America's conflict with Japan undermined the position of Japanese Americans, the American alliance with China during World War II significantly enhanced both the legal and social status of Chinese Americans. In 1943, partly to improve relations with the government of China, Congress finally repealed the Chinese Exclusion Act, which had barred almost all Chinese immigration since 1882. The new quota for Chinese immigrants was minuscule (105 a year), but a substantial number of Chinese women managed to gain entry into the country through other provisions covering war brides and fiancées. Over 4,000 Chinese women entered the United States in the first three years after the war. Permanent residents of the United States who were of Chinese descent were finally permitted to become citizens.

CHINESE EXCLUSION ACTS REPEALED

Racial animosity toward the Chinese did not disappear, but it did decline—in part because government propaganda and popular culture began presenting positive images of the Chinese (partly to contrast them with the Japanese); in part because Chinese Americans (like African Americans and other previously marginal groups) began taking jobs in war plants and other booming areas suffering from labor shortages and hence moving out of the isolated world of the Chinatowns. A higher proportion of Chinese Americans (22 percent of all adult males) were drafted than of any other national group, and the entire Chinese community in most cities worked hard and conspicuously for the war effort.

THE RETREAT FROM REFORM

Late in 1943, Franklin Roosevelt publicly suggested that "Dr. New Deal," as he called it, had served its purpose and should now give way to "Dr. Win-the-War." The statement reflected the president's own genuine shift in concern: that victory was now more important

MANZANAR RELOCATION CENTER During World War II, more than 100,000 Japanese Americans were interned by the government in "relocation centers" such as the one shown here. Many of these U.S. citizens were forced to give up their property and to work for little or no money. Here, sequestered citizens wait for lunch. (The Library of Congress (LC-A35-6-M-22))

than reform. But it also reflected the political reality that had emerged during the first two years of war. Liberals in government were finding themselves unable to enact new programs. They were even finding it difficult to protect existing ones from conservative assault.

Within the administration itself, many liberals found themselves displaced by the new managers of the wartime agencies, who came overwhelmingly from large corporations and conservative Wall Street law firms. But the greatest assault on

DISMANTLING THE NEW DEAL

New Deal reforms came from conservatives in Congress, who seized on the war as an excuse to do what many of them had wanted to do in peacetime: dismantle many of the achievements of the New Deal. They were assisted by the end of mass unemployment, which decreased the need for such relief programs as the Civilian Conservation Corps and the Works Progress Administration (both of which were abolished by Congress). They were assisted, too, by their own increasing numbers. In the congressional elections of 1942, Republicans gained 47 seats in the House and 10 in the Senate. Roosevelt continued to talk at times about his commitment to social progress and liberal reform, in part to bolster the flagging spirits of his traditional supporters. But increasingly, the president quietly accepted the defeat or erosion of New Deal measures in order to win support for his war policies and peace plans. He also accepted the changes because he realized that his chances for reelection in 1944 depended on his ability to identify himself less with domestic issues than with world peace.

Republicans approached the 1944 election determined to exploit what they believed was resentment of wartime regimentation and privation and unhappiness with Democratic reform. They nominated as their candidate the young and vigorous governor of New York, Thomas E. Dewey. Roosevelt was unopposed within his party, but Democratic leaders pressured him to abandon the controversial Vice President Henry Wallace, an outspoken liberal and hero of the CIO. Roosevelt, tired and frail, seemed to take little interest in the matter and passively acquiesced in the selection of Senator Harry S. Truman of Missouri, a man he barely knew. Truman was not a prominent figure in the party, but he had won acclaim as chairman of the Senate War Investigating Committee (known as the Truman Committee), which had compiled an impressive record of uncovering waste and corruption in wartime production.

The conduct of the war was not an issue in the campaign. Instead, the election revolved around domestic economic

1944 ELECTION

issues and, indirectly, the president's health. The president was in fact gravely ill, suffering from, among other things, arteriosclerosis. But the campaign seemed momentarily to revive him. He made several strenuous public appearances late in October, which dispelled popular doubts about his health and ensured his reelection. Roosevelt captured 53.5 percent of the popular vote to Dewey's 46 percent, and won 432 electoral votes to Dewey's 99. Democrats lost 1 seat in the Senate, gained 20 in the House, and maintained control of both.

THE DEFEAT OF THE AXIS

By the middle of 1943, America and its allies had succeeded in stopping the Axis advance in both Europe and the Pacific. In the next two years, the Allies themselves seized the offensive and launched a series of powerful drives that rapidly led the way to victory.

THE LIBERATION OF FRANCE

By early 1944, American and British bombers were attacking German industrial installations and other targets almost around the clock, drastically cutting production and impeding transportation. Especially devastating was the massive bombing of

STRATEGIC BOMBING

such German cities as Leipzig, Dresden, and Berlin—attacks that often made few distinctions between industrial sites and residential ones. A February 1945 incendiary raid on Dresden created a great firestorm that destroyed three-fourths of the previously undamaged city and killed approximately 135,000 people, almost all civilians.

Military leaders claimed that the bombing destroyed industrial facilities, demoralized the population, and cleared the way for the great Allied invasion of France planned for the late spring. The air battles over Germany considerably weakened the *Luftwaffe* (the German air force) and made it a less formidable obstacle to the Allied invasion. Preparations for the invasion were also assisted by the breaking of the Enigma code.

An enormous invasion force had been gathering in England for two years: almost 3 million troops, and perhaps the greatest array of naval vessels and armaments ever assembled in one

D-DAY

place. On the morning of June 6, 1944, D-Day, General Dwight D. Eisenhower, the Supreme Commander of the Allied forces, sent this vast armada into action. The landing came not at the narrowest part of the English Channel, where the Germans had expected and prepared for it, but along sixty miles of the Cotentin Peninsula on the coast of Normandy. While airplanes and battleships offshore bombarded the Nazi defenses, 4,000 vessels landed troops and supplies on the beaches. (Three divisions of paratroopers had been dropped behind the German lines the night before, amid scenes of great confusion, to seize critical roads and bridges for the push inland.) Fighting was intense along the beach, but the superior manpower and equipment of the Allied forces gradually prevailed. Within a week, the German forces had been dislodged from virtually the entire Normandy coast.

For the next month, further progress remained slow. But in late July in the Battle of Saint-Lô, General Omar Bradley's First Army smashed through the German lines. General George S. Patton's Third Army, spearheaded by heavy tank attacks, then moved through the hole Bradley had created and began a drive into the heart of France. On August 25, Free French forces arrived in Paris and liberated the city from four years of German occupation. And by mid-September, the Allied armies had driven the Germans almost entirely out of France and Belgium.

WORLD WAR II IN EUROPE: THE ALLIED COUNTEROFFENSIVE, 1943–1945 This map illustrates the climactic movements in the war in Europe—the two great offensives against Germany that began in 1943 and culminated in 1945. From the east, the armies of the Soviet Union, having halted the Germans at Stalingrad and Moscow, swept across eastern Europe toward Germany. From the west and the south, American, British, and other Allied forces moved toward Germany through Italy and—after the Normandy invasion in June 1944—through France. The two offensives met in Berlin in May 1945.

• *What problems did the position of the Allied forces at the end of the war help to produce?*

The great Allied drive came to a halt, however, at the Rhine River in the face of a firm line of German defenses and a period of cold weather, rain, and floods. In mid-December, German forces struck in desperation along fifty miles of front in the

BATTLE OF THE BULGE

Ardennes Forest. In the Battle of the Bulge (named for a large bulge that appeared in the American lines as the Germans pressed forward), they drove fifty-five miles toward Antwerp before they were finally stopped at Bastogne. The battle ended serious German resistance in the west.

While the Allies were fighting their way through France, Soviet forces were sweeping westward into central Europe and the Balkans. In late January 1945, the Russians launched a great offensive toward the Oder River inside Germany. In early spring, they were ready to launch a final assault against Berlin. By then, Omar Bradley's First Army was pushing into Germany from the west. Early in March, his forces captured the city of Cologne, on the west bank of the Rhine. The next day, in a remarkable stroke of good fortune, he discovered and seized an undamaged bridge over the river at Remagen;

THE NORMANDY INVASION This photograph, taken from a landing craft, shows American troops wading ashore and onto the Normandy beaches, where one of the decisive battles of World War II was taking shape. The invasion was launched despite threatening weather and rough seas. (© Popperfoto/Getty Images)

Allied troops were soon pouring across the Rhine. In the following weeks the British field marshal Bernard Montgomery, commander of Allied ground operations on D-Day and after, pushed into northern Germany with a million troops, while Bradley's army, sweeping through central Germany, completed the encirclement of 300,000 German soldiers in the Ruhr.

The German resistance was now broken on both fronts. American forces were moving eastward faster than they had anticipated and could have beaten the Russians to Berlin and Prague. Instead, the American and British high commands decided to halt the advance along the Elbe River in central Germany to await the Russians. That decision enabled the Soviets to occupy eastern Germany and Czechoslovakia.

On April 30, with Soviet forces on the outskirts of Berlin, Adolf Hitler killed himself in his bunker in the capital. And **GERMANY DEFEATED** on May 8, 1945, the remaining German forces surrendered unconditionally. V-E (Victory in Europe) Day prompted great celebrations in western Europe and in the United States, tempered by the knowledge of the continuing war against Japan.

THE PACIFIC OFFENSIVE

In February 1944, American naval forces under Admiral Chester Nimitz won a series of victories in the Marshall Islands and cracked the outer perimeter of the Japanese Empire. Within a month, the navy had destroyed other vital Japanese bastions. American submarines, in the meantime, were decimating Japanese shipping and crippling the nation's domestic economy. By the summer of 1944, the already skimpy food rations for the Japanese people had been reduced by nearly a quarter; there was also a critical gasoline shortage.

America's principal ally in Asia was China, and the United States hoped that the Chinese forces would help defeat the Japanese. To assist them, the army sent General Joseph W. Stilwell to help provide critical supplies to China by a land route through India and across the Himalayas. It was a brutal task. The Japanese blocked them at several points, and Stilwell had to rely for a time on airlifts of supplies over the mountains. But finally in the fall of 1944, Stilwell's forces succeeded in constructing a road and pipelines across the mountains into China—a route that came to be known by several names: the Burma Road, the Ledo Road, and at times the Stilwell Road.

COMING HOME Euphoric American soldiers arrive in New York Harbor back aboard the *Queen Elizabeth* after the end of the war in Europe in 1945. (© AP Images)

Japanese forces consistently threatened the Burma Road. More dangerously, the Japanese were also threatening the wartime capital of China in Chungking. Chiang Kai-shek, the Chinese premier, was reluctant to use his troops against the Japanese and seemed more concerned with attacking Chinese communists, who were also fighting the Japanese. This helped create a famous feud between Stilwell and Chiang. Stilwell began to call Chiang—not entirely privately—the "peanut." The dispute continued for many months until Stilwell finally left China. Stilwell's successors had little more success in prodding Chiang to confront the Japanese.

The decisive battles of the Pacific war occurred not in China but at sea. In mid-June 1944, an enormous American armada struck the heavily fortified Mariana Islands and, after some of the bloodiest operations of the war, captured Tinian, Guam, and Saipan, 1,350 miles from Tokyo. In September, American forces landed on the western Carolines. And on October 20, General MacArthur's troops landed on Leyte Island in the Philippines. As the American forces pushed closer to Japan itself, the Japanese used their entire fleet against the

BATTLE OF LEYTE GULF

Allied invaders in three major encounters—which together constituted the decisive Battle of Leyte Gulf, the largest naval

engagement in history. American forces held off the Japanese onslaught and sank four Japanese carriers, all but destroying Japan's capacity to continue a serious naval war.

Nevertheless, the Japanese forces seemed only to increase their resistance. In February 1945, American marines seized the tiny volcanic island of Iwo Jima, only 750 miles from Tokyo, but only after the costliest single battle in the history of the Marine Corps. The marines suffered over 25,000 casualties, and the Japanese forces suffered even greater losses.

The battle for Okinawa, an island only 370 miles south of Japan, was further evidence of the strength of the Japanese

OKINAWA

resistance in those last desperate months. Week after week, the Japanese sent kamikaze (suicide) planes against American and British ships, sacrificing 3,500 of them while inflicting great damage. Japanese troops on shore launched desperate nighttime attacks on the American lines. The United States and its allies suffered nearly 50,000 casualties before finally capturing Okinawa in late June 1945. More than 100,000 Japanese died in the siege.

The same kind of bitter fighting seemed to await the Americans in Japan itself. But there were also signs early in 1945 that such an invasion might not be necessary. The

OKINAWA The invasion of Okinawa, an island near Japan, was one of the last major battles of World War II. In this photograph, taken June 18, 1945, a bullet-scarred monument provides shelter to members of the 7th Infantry of the U.S. Tenth Army as they look ahead at Japanese action. Over 11,000 Americans (and more than 80,000 Japanese) died in the rugged battle for the island, which consumed nearly three months. It ended three days after this photograph was taken. Two months later—after the bombing of Hiroshima and Nagasaki—Japan surrendered. (© Bettmann/Corbis)

Japanese had almost no ships or planes left with which to fight. In July 1945, for example, American warships stood off the shore of Japan and shelled industrial targets (many already in ruins from aerial bombings) with impunity. A brutal firebombing of Tokyo in March, in which American bombers dropped napalm on the city, created a massive firestorm in which at least 83,000 and perhaps as many as 100,000, mostly civilians, died. It further weakened the Japanese will to resist. Moderate Japanese leaders, who had long since decided that the war was lost, were struggling for power within the government and were looking for ways to bring the war to an end. After the invasion of Okinawa, Emperor Hirohito appointed a new premier and gave him instructions to sue for peace; but the new leader could not persuade military leaders to give up the fight. The premier did try, along with the emperor, to obtain mediation through the Soviet Union. The Russians, however, showed little interest in playing the role of arbitrator.

Whether the moderates could ultimately have prevailed is a question about which historians and others continue to disagree. In any case, the question eventually became moot. In mid-July, American scientists conducted a successful test of a new atomic bomb, which led to a major event in world history, significant only in part because it ended World War II.

THE MANHATTAN PROJECT

Reports had reached the United States in 1939 that Nazi scientists had taken the first step toward the creation of an atomic bomb. The United States and Britain immediately began a race to develop the weapon before the Germans did.

The search for the new weapon emerged from theories developed by atomic physicists, beginning early in the century, and particularly from some of the founding ideas of modern science developed by Albert Einstein. Einstein's famous theory of relativity had revealed the relationships between mass and energy. More precisely, he had argued that, in theory at least, matter could be converted into a tremendous force of energy. It was Einstein, by then living in the United States, who warned Franklin Roosevelt that the Germans were developing atomic weapons and that the United States must begin trying to do the same. The effort to build atomic weapons centered on the use of uranium, whose atomic structure made possible the creation of a nuclear chain reaction. A nuclear chain reaction occurs when the atomic nuclei in radioactive matter are split (a process known as nuclear fission) by neutrons. Each fission creates new neutrons that produce fissions in additional atoms at an ever-increasing and self-sustaining pace.

The construction of atomic weapons had become feasible by the 1940s because of the discovery of the radioactivity of uranium in the 1930s by Enrico Fermi in Italy. In 1939, the **ENRICO FERMI** great Danish physicist Niels Bohr sent news of German experiments in radioactivity to the United States. In 1940, scientists at Columbia University began chain-reaction experiments with uranium and produced persuasive evidence of the feasibility of using uranium as fuel for a weapon. The Columbia experiments stalled in 1941, and the work moved to UC Berkeley and the University of Chicago, where Enrico Fermi (who had emigrated to the United States in 1938) achieved the first controlled fission chain reaction in December 1942.

By then, the army had taken control of the research and appointed General Leslie Groves to reorganize the project—which soon became known as the Manhattan Project (because it was devised in the Manhattan Engineer District Office of the Army Corps of Engineers). Over the next three years, the U.S. government secretly poured nearly $2 billion into the Manhattan Project—a massive scientific and technological effort conducted at hidden laboratories in Oak Ridge, Tennessee; Los Alamos, New Mexico; Hanford, Washington; and other sites. Scientists in Oak Ridge, who were charged with finding a way to create a nuclear chain reaction that could be feasibly replicated within the confined space of a bomb, began experimenting with plutonium—a derivative of uranium first discovered by scientists at UC Berkeley. Plutonium proved capable of providing a practical fuel for the weapon. Scientists in Los Alamos, under the direction of J. Robert Oppenheimer, were charged with the construction of the actual atomic bomb.

Despite many unforeseen problems, the scientists pushed ahead much faster than anyone had predicted. Even so, the war in Europe ended before they were ready to test the first weapon. Just before dawn on July 16, 1945, in the desert near Alamogordo, New Mexico, the scientists gathered to witness the first atomic explosion in history: the detonation of a plutonium-fueled bomb that its creators had named Trinity.

THE TRINITY BOMB

The explosion—a blinding flash of light, probably brighter than any ever seen on earth, followed by a huge, billowing mushroom cloud—created a vast crater in the barren desert.

ATOMIC WARFARE

News of the explosion reached President Harry S. Truman (who had taken office in April on the death of Roosevelt) in Potsdam, Germany, where he was attending a conference of Allied leaders. He issued an ultimatum to the Japanese (signed jointly by the British) demanding that they surrender by August 3 or face complete devastation. The Japanese premier wanted to accept the Allied demand, but he still could not persuade the military leaders to agree. There was a hint from Tokyo that the government might agree to surrender, in return for a promise that the Japanese could retain their emperor. The American government, firmly committed to the idea of "unconditional surrender," dismissed those proposals. They were convinced (perhaps correctly) that the moderates who were making the peace overtures did not have the power to deliver them. When the deadline passed with no surrender, Truman ordered the air force to use the new atomic weapons against Japan.

Controversy has raged for decades over whether Truman's decision to use the bomb was justified and what his motives were. (See "Debating the Past," pp. 728–729.) Some people have argued that the atomic attack was unnecessary, that had the United States agreed to the retention of the emperor (which it ultimately did agree to, in any case), or waited only a few more weeks, the Japanese would have surrendered. Others

DEBATING THE BOMB'S USE

THE EMPEROR SURVEYS THE RUINS In the aftermath of the American firebombing of Tokyo, which caused as much damage and death as the atomic bomb attacks on Hiroshima and Nagasaki, and just before the formal Japanese surrender in September 1945, Emperor Hirohito—previously visible to most Japanese only in formal portraits—walked through the ruins of the city and allowed himself to be photographed. This photograph is widely considered the first picture of the emperor to reveal any expression on his face. It was taken by Carl Mydans, a photographer for *Life* magazine. (Photo by Carl Mydans/© Time & Life Pictures/Getty Images)

THE DECISION TO DROP THE ATOMIC BOMB

IN the fall of 1994, the Air and Space Museum of the Smithsonian Institution in Washington, D.C., installed in its main hall the fuselage of the *Enola Gay*, the airplane that dropped the first atomic bomb ever used in warfare. It was used in 1945 on the Japanese city of Hiroshima. Originally, the airplane was to have been accompanied by an exhibit that would include discussions of the many popular and academic controversies over whether the United States should have used the bomb. But a powerful group of critics demanded that the exhibit should reflect only the "official" explanation of the decision. In the end, the museum decided to mount no exhibit at all. The *Enola Gay* hangs in the Smithsonian today without any explanation for the millions of tourists who see it each year.

The furor that surrounded the *Enola Gay* exhibit reflects the passions that the bombing of Hiroshima and Nagasaki continue to arouse among people around the world. It also reflects the continuing debate since 1945 among historians about how to explain and evaluate President Truman's decision to use the atomic bomb in the war against Japan.

Truman himself, both at the time and in his 1955 memoir, insisted that the decision was a simple and straightforward one. The alternative to using atomic weapons, he claimed, was an invasion of mainland Japan that might have cost as many as a million American lives. Given that choice, he said, the decision was easy. "I regarded the bomb as a military weapon and never had any doubt that it should be used." Truman's explanation of his decision has been supported by the accounts of many of his contemporaries: Secretary of War Henry Stimson, Winston Churchill, and several of Truman's senior military advisers. It has also received considerable support from historians. Herbert Feis argued in *The Atomic Bomb and the End of World War II* (1966) that Truman had made his decision on purely military grounds—to ensure a speedy American victory. David McCullough, author of the popular biography *Truman*, published in 1992, also accepted Truman's own account of his actions largely uncritically, as did Alonzo L. Hamby in *Man of the People* (1995), an important scholarly study of Truman. "One consideration weighed most heavily on Truman," Hamby concluded. "The longer the war lasted, the more Americans killed." Robert J. Donovan, author of an extensive history of the Truman presidency, *Conflict and Crisis* (1977), reached the same conclusion: "The simple reason Truman made the decision to drop the bomb was to end the war quickly and save lives."

Other scholars have strongly disagreed. As early as 1948, a British physicist, P. M. S. Blackett, wrote in *Fear, War, and the Bomb* that the destruction of Hiroshima and Nagasaki was "not so much the last military act of the second World War as the first major operation of the cold diplomatic war with Russia."

An important critic of Truman's decision is the historian Gar Alperovitz, the author of two influential books on the subject: *Atomic Diplomacy: Hiroshima and Potsdam* (1965) and *The Decision to Use the Atomic Bomb and the Architecture of an American Myth* (1995). Alperovitz dismissed the argument that the bomb was used to shorten the war and save lives. Japan was likely to have surrendered soon even if the bomb had not been used, he claimed. Instead, he argued, the United States used the bomb less to influence Japan than to intimidate the Soviet Union. Truman made his decision to bomb Hiroshima following a discouraging meeting with Stalin at Potsdam. He was heavily influenced, therefore, by his belief that America needed a new way to force Stalin to change his behavior, "to make Russia more manageable in Europe."

Martin J. Sherwin, in *A World Destroyed* (1975), argued similarly that the danger Stalin posed to the peace made American policymakers aware that the effective use of atomic weapons could help strengthen the American hand in the nation's critical relationship with the Soviet Union.

John W. Dower's *War Without Mercy* (1986) contributed, by implication at least, to another controversial explanation of the American decision: racism. Throughout World War II, many Americans looked upon the Japanese as members of an almost bestial race, almost a subhuman species. And while Dower himself stops short of saying so, other historians have suggested that this racialized image of the Japanese contributed to American willingness to drop atomic bombs on Japanese cities. Even many of Truman's harshest critics, however, note that it is, as Alperovitz

argue that nothing less than the atomic bombs could have persuaded the hard-line military leaders of Japan to surrender without a costly American invasion. Some critics of the decision, including some of the scientists involved in the Manhattan Project, have argued that whatever the Japanese intentions, the United States, as a matter of morality, should not have used the terrible new weapon. One horrified physicist wrote the president shortly before the attack: "This thing must not be permitted to exist on this earth. We must not be the most hated and feared people in the world."

The nation's military and political leaders, however, showed little concern about such matters. Truman, who had not even known of the existence of the Manhattan Project

until he became president, was apparently making what he believed to be a simple military decision. A weapon was available that would end the war quickly; he could see no reason not to use it.

Still more controversy has existed over whether there were other motives at work behind Truman's decision. With the Soviet Union poised to enter the war in the Pacific, did the United States want to end the conflict quickly to forestall an expanded communist presence in Asia? Did Truman use the bomb to intimidate Stalin, with whom he was engaged in difficult negotiations, so that the Soviet leader would accept American demands? Little direct evidence is available to support (or definitively refute) either of these accusations.

has written, "all but impossible to find specific evidence that racism was an important factor in the decision to attack Hiroshima and Nagasaki."

The debate over the decision to drop the atomic bomb is an unusually emotional one, and it has inspired bitter professional and personal attacks on advocates of almost every position. It illustrates clearly how history has often been, and remains, a powerful force in the way societies define their politics, their values, and their character. ●

AP HISTORICAL ARGUMENTATION AND INTERPRETATION

Questions assume cumulative content knowledge from this chapter and previous chapters.

1. Identify four historians' arguments presented in the discussion regarding the decision to drop the atomic bomb on Hiroshima and Nagasaki.
2. Why might the debate or interpretations of the dropping of the atomic bomb provoke such passions, that the *Enola Gay* exhibit at the Smithsonian Institution in Washington, D.C. offers no explanation of the event?
3. With which historical argument discussed do you most agree? Explain why, supporting your argument with historical evidence.

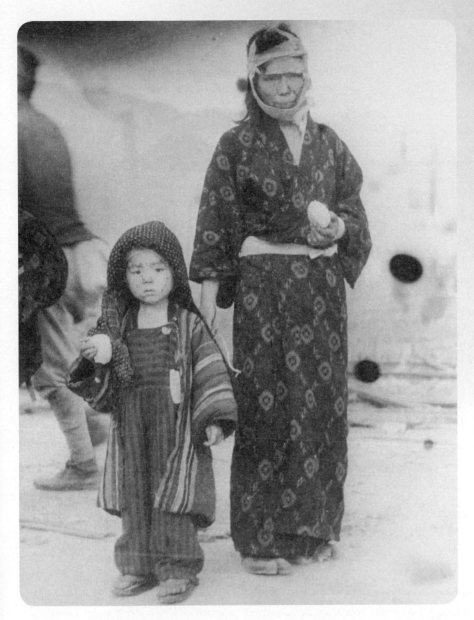

NAGASAKI SURVIVORS A Japanese woman and child look grimly at a photographer as they hold pieces of bread in the aftermath of the dropping of the second American atomic bomb—this one on Nagasaki.
(© Bettmann/Corbis)

On August 6, 1945, an American B-29, the *Enola Gay*, dropped an atomic weapon on the Japanese industrial center at Hiroshima. With a single bomb, the United States completely incinerated a four-square-mile area at the center of the previously undamaged city. More than 80,000 civilians died, according to later American estimates. Many more survived to suffer the crippling effects of radioactive fallout or to pass those effects on to their children in the form of birth defects.

HIROSHIMA

The Japanese government, stunned by the attack, was at first unable to agree on a response. Two days later, on August 8, the Soviet Union declared war on Japan. And the following day, the United States sent

NAGASAKI

another American plane to drop another atomic weapon—this time on the city of Nagasaki—causing more than 100,000 deaths in another unfortunate community. Finally, the emperor intervened to break the stalemate in the cabinet, and on August 14 the government announced that it was ready to give up. On September 2, 1945, on board the American battleship *Missouri*, anchored in Tokyo Bay, Japanese officials signed the articles of surrender.

The most catastrophic war in the history of mankind had come to an end, and the United States had emerged not only victorious but in a position of unprecedented power, influence, and prestige as well. It was a victory, however, that few could greet with unambiguous joy. Fourteen million combatants had died in the struggle. As many as 40 million civilians may have died–mostly from bombings, from disease and starvation, from genocidal campaigns of extermination. The United States had suffered only light casualties in comparison with many other nations, but the cost had still been high: 322,000 dead, another 800,000 injured. And despite the sacrifices, the world continued to face an uncertain future, menaced by the threat of nuclear warfare and by the emerging antagonism between the world's two strongest nations–the United States and the Soviet Union–that would darken the peace for many decades to come.

AP CONNECTING THEMES

Chapter 26 focused on World War II. In terms of the war, itself, as you review, focus on understanding the general overview of the conduct of the war in both the European and Pacific theaters, with particular emphasis on the turning points of the war in both areas. Be certain to concentrate on understanding how the war affected the U.S. economy and, specifically, how it affected opportunities for traditionally underemployed groups. Also, think about the impact of traditional patterns of discrimination and how they manifested themselves during the war. Be able to explain how the war changed internal and external migration patterns. Finally, be able to explain how the war, itself, and technological development led the United States to emerge from the war as the dominant world power.

The following themes have heightened importance in Chapter 26. You should now be able to do the following for each listed theme:

Identity: Explain the impact of World War II on American identity, both generally and for specific minority groups.

Work, Exchange, and Technology: Explain the impact of World War II on employment opportunities for traditionally underemployed groups as well as the war's impact on organized labor.

Work, Exchange, and Technology: Explain the impact of technology in helping the United States win the war and emerge as a dominant world power.

Work, Exchange, and Technology: Explain how the industrial power of the United States helped the Allies win the war.

Peopling: Trace the changes in both internal and external migration patterns caused by World War II.

Politics and Power: Explain the degree to which the war was used as a political tool to undermine Democratic political dominance.

America and the World: Understand the reasons that World War II led to the United States becoming a dominant world power.

Environment and Geography: Describe the potential impact of the development of atomic power on both physical and human geography.

Ideas, Beliefs, and Culture: Explain the degree to which World War II led to debate over traditional American values.

AP SUGGESTED STUDY

PEOPLE/PLACES/EVENTS As you study these items, think about how they demonstrate or relate to key concepts and historical themes from this chapter and previous chapters.

ATOMIC BOMB 726
A. PHILIP RANDOLPH 715
BATTLE OF THE BULGE 723
BRACEROS 716
COLOSSUS II 715
CONGRESS OF RACIAL EQUALITY (CORE) 715
D-DAY 722
DWIGHT D. EISENHOWER 722
ENOLA GAY 729

ENRICO FERMI 726
GUADALCANAL 705
HARRY S. TRUMAN 722
HIROSHIMA 729
HOLOCAUST 708
KOREMATSU v. U.S. 721
LUFTWAFFE 722
MANHATTAN PROJECT 726
MIDWAY 705
NISEI UNIT 721

OFFICE OF PRICE ADMINISTRATION (OPA) 712
OKINAWA 725
"RELOCATION CENTERS" 721
"ROSIE THE RIVETER" 717
SONAR 713
VICHY 707
ZOOT SUITS 720

AP TEST PRACTICE

Questions assume cumulative content knowledge from this chapter and previous chapters.

MULTIPLE CHOICE Use the poster on page 717 and your knowledge of U.S. history to answer questions 1-2.

1. What does the poster best provide evidence of regarding how World War II ended the Great Depression?

   (A) Finally allowing more women to work expanded the economy.

   (B) The Great Depression was still weighing down the economy.

   (C) The government greatly increased taxes to help fund the war.

   (D) An abundance of jobs was created.

2. What does the poster best suggest about the changing identity of American women?

   (A) That women were equal to men

   (B) That women regardless of race were equal

   (C) That women were equal to men in terms of military service

   (D) That women could do jobs traditionally held by men

SHORT ANSWER Use your knowledge of U.S. history to answer questions 3-5.

3. Answer a, b, and c.

   a) Briefly explain ONE example of how ethnic minorities were affected by America entering World War II.

   b) Briefly explain ONE example of how women were affected by America entering World War II.

   c) Briefly explain ONE example of how Native Americans were affected by America entering World War II.

4. Answer a, b, and c.

   a) For one of the areas below, briefly explain its role in the American war effort during World War II.

   • Popular patriotism

   • Technology

   • Industrial production

   b) Provide one example that supports your argument.

   c) Choose a second area, and briefly explain why it might have played a more important or a less important role in contributing to the Allied victory in World War II.

5. Use the historical argument below to answer a, b, and c.

It has been said that World War II was one of the major catalysts for the modern Civil Rights movement.

   a) Briefly explain why this assertion might be considered true.

   b) Briefly explain ONE piece of historical evidence from the period between 1941 and 1945, which could be used to support this assertion.

   c) Briefly explain ONE piece of evidence, which could be used to refute this assertion.

LONG ESSAY For each question below, develop a thoughtful and thorough historical argument that answers the question. Begin your essay with a thesis statement and support it with relevant historical evidence.

6. Evaluate the extent to which World War I and World War II governmental policies maintained continuity as well as fostered change in the civil liberties Americans enjoyed at home.

7. Analyze Allied strategy in World War II, identifying key events which you believe were turning points in the history of World War II.

27 | THE COLD WAR

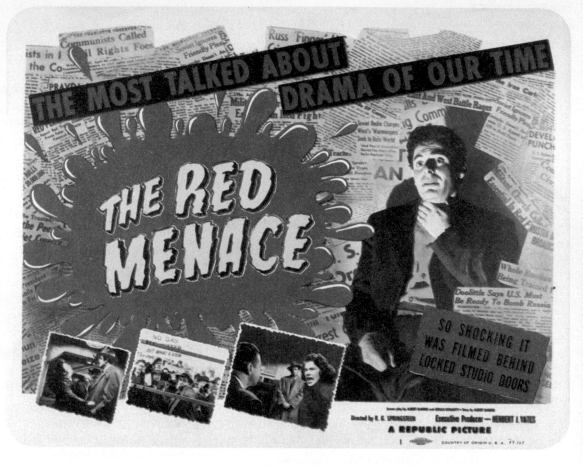

THE RED MENACE This 1949 movie poster suggests how much attention was directed to the threat of communism. The film, produced by Republic Pictures and directed by R. G. Springsteen, told the story of a man and a woman who joined the Communist Party, only to become disillusioned when they watched the murder of a party member who begins to doubt the party's principles. This movie—and most others like it—got poor reviews and did not attract large audiences.
(© Republic Pictures/Photofest)

AP

HISTORICAL THINKING

1. **Historical Interpretation** Analyze the reasons for the development of tensions between the Soviet Union and the United States.

2. **Historical Argumentation** Analyze the degree of success the policy of containment achieved between 1945 and 1953.

3. **Historical Causation** Analyze the reasons for the growth of anti-labor sentiment following World War II.

4. **Historical Causation** Analyze the reasons for and results of the second Red Scare.

5. **Contextualization** Analyze the ways in which the United States prepared to avoid a serious economic recession following World War II.

6. **Comparison** Compare and contrast the response of the American people to the end of World War II to the American people's response to the end of World War I.

7. **Contextualization** Analyze the political debates over the uses of atomic technology in the post–World War II era.

8. **Patterns of Continuity and Change over Time** To what degree and in what ways did post–World War II foreign policy represent a fundamental change from previous foreign policy?

Key Concept Correlations

Analyze the ways the historical developments you learn about in this chapter connect to the following AP Key Concepts.

7.3 Global conflicts over resources, territories, and ideologies renewed debates over the nation's values and its role in the world while simultaneously propelling the United States into a dominant international military, political, cultural, and economic position.

8.1 The United States responded to an uncertain and unstable postwar world by asserting and attempting to defend a position of global leadership, with far-reaching domestic and international consequences.

Thematic Learning Objectives

WOR-3, 4, 7; ID-3, 7; POL-6; CUL-5

CHAPTER 27 focuses on the development and consequences of the Cold War on both international relations and domestic affairs. It begins with a discussion of the reasons for rising tension between the Soviet Union and the United States both during and after World War II. The chapter focuses on the development of the policy of containment and examples of both military and economic measures designed to implement the policy, as well as a discussion concerning the relative success of the policy. It also deals with attempts to prevent a post-war recession similar to the one experienced after World War I. The chapter examines the reasons for the movement of the American public to a more conservative posture and the effects of that shift on organized labor and politics, culminating with the election of Eisenhower in 1952. Significant time is spent on the impact of the second Red Scare on the American domestic scene and its threats to civil liberties. Attention is also given to U.S. involvement in Korea and debates over the uses of nuclear power. As you read, evaluate the following ideas:

- Following World War II, the United States attempted to limit the extension of the Soviet Union's military and ideological expansion through a policy of military and economic containment.
- The United States developed a policy of international involvement that challenged traditional American values concerning involvement in international affairs.
- During the Cold War era, international tensions resulted in periodic thaws in Cold War tensions followed by renewed confrontations toward the opposition.
- Decolonization of European colonies forced the Unites States to support their European allies in their attempts to suppress colonial insurrections, leading to deteriorating relations between the United States and rising third world nations.
- The second Red Scare led to renewed debate over the limiting of personal liberty versus the federal government's attempts to ensure national security.

ORIGINS OF THE COLD WAR

Few issues in twentieth-century American history have aroused more debate than the question of the origins of the Cold War. Some historians have claimed that Soviet duplicity and expansionism created the international tensions, while others have proposed that American provocations and imperial ambitions were at least equally to blame. Most historians agree, however, that wherever the preponderance of blame may lie, both the United States and the Soviet Union contributed to the atmosphere of hostility and suspicion that quickly clouded the peace. (See "Debating the Past," pp. 736-737.)

SOURCES OF SOVIET-AMERICAN TENSION

At the heart of the rivalry between the United States and the Soviet Union in the 1940s was a fundamental difference in the ways the great powers envisioned the postwar world. One vision, first openly outlined in the Atlantic Charter in 1941, was of a world in which nations abandoned

AMERICA'S POSTWAR VISION

their traditional beliefs in military alliances and spheres of influence and governed their relations with one another through democratic processes, with an international organization serving as the arbiter of disputes and the protector of every nation's right of self-determination. That vision–inspired in part by Woodrow Wilson–appealed to many Americans, including Franklin Roosevelt.

The other vision was that of the Soviet Union and to some extent, it gradually became clear, of Great Britain. Both Stalin and Churchill had signed the Atlantic Charter. But Britain had always

SPHERES OF INFLUENCE

been uneasy about the implications of the self-determination ideal for its own enormous empire. And the Soviet Union was determined to create a secure sphere for itself in Central and Eastern Europe as protection against possible future aggression from the West. Both Churchill and Stalin, therefore, tended to envision a postwar structure in which the great powers would control areas of strategic interest to them, in which something vaguely similar to the traditional European balance of power would reemerge. Gradually, the differences between these two positions would turn the peacemaking process into a form of warfare.

WARTIME DIPLOMACY

Serious strains had already begun to develop in the alliance with the Soviet Union in January 1943, when Roosevelt and Churchill met in Casablanca, Morocco, to discuss Allied strategy. (Stalin had declined Roosevelt's invitation to attend.) The two leaders could not accept Stalin's most important demand–the immediate opening of a second front in western Europe. But they tried to reassure Stalin by announcing that they would accept nothing less than the unconditional surrender of the Axis powers, thus indicating that they would not negotiate a separate peace with Hitler and leave the Soviets to fight on alone.

In November 1943, Roosevelt and Churchill traveled to Teheran, Iran, for their first meeting with Stalin. By now, however, Roosevelt's most effective bargaining tool–Stalin's need for American assistance in his struggle against Germany–had been largely removed. The German advance against Russia had been halted; Soviet forces were now launching their own westward offensive. Nevertheless, the Teheran Conference seemed in most respects a success. Roosevelt and Stalin established a cordial personal relationship. Stalin agreed to an American request that the Soviet Union enter the war in the Pacific soon after the end of hostilities in Europe. Roosevelt, in turn, promised that an Anglo-American second front would be established within six months.

On other matters, however, the origins of future disagreements were already visible. Most important was the question of the future of Poland. Roosevelt and Churchill were willing to agree to a movement of the Soviet border westward, allowing Stalin to annex some historically Polish territory. But on the nature of the **DISPUTE OVER POLAND** postwar government in the rest of Poland, there were sharp differences. Roosevelt and Churchill supported the claims of the Polish government-in-exile that had been functioning in London since 1940; Stalin wished to install another pro-communist exiled government that had spent the war in Lublin, in the Soviet Union. The three leaders avoided a bitter conclusion to the Teheran Conference only by leaving the issue unresolved.

YALTA

More than a year later, in February 1945, Roosevelt joined Churchill and Stalin for a peace conference in the Soviet city of Yalta–a resort on the Black Sea that was once a summer palace for the tsars. On a number of issues, the "Big Three," as Roosevelt, Churchill, and Stalin were known, reached agreements. In return for Stalin's renewed promise to enter the Pacific war, Roosevelt agreed that the Soviet Union should receive some of the territory in the Pacific that Russia had lost in the 1904 Russo-Japanese War.

The negotiators also agreed to a plan for a new international organization, a plan that had been hammered out the previous

YALTA Churchill, Roosevelt, and Stalin (known during the war as the "Big Three") meet at Yalta in the Crimea in February 1945 to try to agree on the outlines of the peace that they knew was soon to come. Instead, they settled on a series of vague compromises that ultimately left all parties feeling betrayed. (© Bettmann/Corbis)

UNITED NATIONS summer at a conference in Washington, D.C., at the Dumbarton Oaks estate. The new United Nations would contain a General Assembly, in which every member would be represented, and a Security Council, with permanent representatives of the five major powers (the United States, Britain, France, the Soviet Union, and China), each of which would have veto power. The Security Council would also have temporary delegates from several other nations. These agreements became the basis of the United Nations charter, drafted at a conference of fifty nations beginning April 25, 1945, in San Francisco. The U.S. Senate ratified the charter in July by a vote of 80 to 2 (in striking contrast to the slow and painful defeat it had administered to the charter of the League of Nations twenty-five years before).

On other issues, however, the Yalta Conference produced no real accord. Basic disagreement remained about the postwar Polish government. Stalin, whose armies now occupied Poland, had already installed a government composed of the pro-communist "Lublin" Poles. Roosevelt and Churchill insisted that the pro-Western "London" Poles must be allowed a place in the Warsaw regime. Roosevelt envisioned a government based on free, democratic elections–which both he and Stalin recognized the pro-Western forces would win. Stalin agreed only to a vague compromise by which an unspecified number of pro-Western Poles would be granted a place in the government. He reluctantly consented to hold "free and unfettered elections" in Poland on an unspecified future date. They did not take place for almost fifty years.

Nor was there agreement about the future of Germany. Roosevelt seemed to want a reconstructed and reunited Germany. Stalin wanted to impose heavy reparations on Germany and to ensure a permanent dismemberment of the nation. The final agreement was, like the Polish accord, vague and unstable. The **DISAGREEMENTS OVER GERMANY** decision on reparations would be referred to a future commission. The United States, Great Britain, France, and the Soviet Union would each control its own "zone of occupation" in Germany–the zones to be determined by the position of troops at the end of the war. Berlin, the German capital, was already well inside the Soviet zone, but because of its symbolic importance it would be divided into four sectors, one for each nation to occupy. At an unspecified date, Germany would be reunited; but there was no agreement on how the reunification would occur. As for the rest of Europe, the conference produced a murky accord on the establishment of governments "broadly representative of all democratic elements" and "responsible to the will of the people."

The Yalta accords, in other words, were less a settlement of postwar issues than a set of loose principles that sidestepped the most difficult questions. Roosevelt, Churchill, and Stalin returned home from the conference each apparently convinced that he had signed an important agreement. But the Soviet interpretation of the accords differed so sharply from the Anglo-American interpretation that the illusion endured only briefly. In the weeks following the Yalta Conference, Roosevelt watched with growing alarm as the Soviet Union moved systematically to establish pro-communist governments in one Central or Eastern European nation after another and as Stalin refused to make the changes in Poland that the president believed he had promised.

But Roosevelt did not abandon hope. Still believing the differences could be settled, he left Washington early in the spring for a vacation at his retreat in Warm Springs, Georgia. There, on April 12, 1945, he suffered a sudden, massive stroke and died.

THE COLLAPSE OF THE PEACE

Harry S. Truman, who succeeded Roosevelt in the presidency, had little familiarity with international issues. And he did not share Roosevelt's apparent faith in the flexibility of the Soviet Union. Roosevelt had hoped that Stalin was a reasonable man with whom an ultimate accord might be reached. Truman, in contrast, sided with those in the government (and there were many) who considered the Soviet Union fundamentally untrustworthy and who viewed Stalin with suspicion and even loathing.

THE FAILURE OF POTSDAM

Truman had been in office only a few days before he decided to, as he put it, "get tough" with the Soviet Union. Truman met on April 23 with Soviet foreign minister Molotov and sharply chastised him for violations of the Yalta accords. **TRUMAN'S "GET TOUGH" POLICY** In fact, Truman had only limited leverage by which to compel the Soviet Union to carry out its agreements. Truman insisted that the United States should be able to get "85 percent" of what it wanted, but he was ultimately forced to settle for much less.

Truman conceded first on Poland. When Stalin made a few minor concessions to the pro-Western exiles, Truman recognized the Warsaw government, hoping that noncommunist forces might gradually expand their influence there. Until the 1980s, they did not. Other questions remained, above all the question of Germany. To settle them, Truman met in July at Potsdam, in Russian-occupied Germany, with Churchill (who, after elections in Britain in the midst of the talks, was replaced as prime minister by Clement Attlee) and Stalin. Truman reluctantly accepted the adjustments of the Polish-German border that Stalin had long demanded; he refused, however, to permit the Russians to claim any reparations from the American, French, and British zones of Germany. This stance effectively confirmed that Germany would remain divided, with the western zones united into one nation, friendly to the United States, and the Russian zone surviving as another nation, with a Soviet-dominated, communist government.

THE CHINA PROBLEM

Central to American hopes for an open, peaceful world "policed" by the great powers was a strong, independent China. But even **CHIANG KAI-SHEK** before the war ended, the American government was aware that those hopes faced a major, perhaps insurmountable, obstacle:

ORIGINS OF THE COLD WAR

THE Cold War may be over, but the debate over its origins is not. For more than a decade after the end of World War II, few historians in the United States challenged the official American interpretation of the beginnings of the Cold War. Most students of the conflict agreed that relations with the Soviet Union broke down because Stalin violated the Yalta accords and because he was spreading communism throughout the world.

Not long after the war, as communism was spreading in Europe, George F. Kennan wrote an important telegraph arguing that the Soviet Union needed to be "contained," that while the United States should not invade communist nations it should work to stop their growing influence. Over time, he suggested, containment would weaken the Soviet Union.

In debates from the 1950s on, scholars began to offer different, more critical views about the Cold War. William Appleman Williams, writing in *The Tragedy of American Diplomacy* (1959), disagreed with the containment theory. The Cold War, he said, was simply the most recent version of a consistent American effort in the twentieth century to maintain an "open door" for American trade in world markets. According to Williams, the confrontation with the Soviet Union was less a response to Russian aggressive designs than an expression of the American belief in the necessity of capitalist expansion.

Later revisionists modified Williams's claims, but most accepted his basic outlook. The United States had been primarily to blame for the Cold War, many scholars asserted. Claims were made that the Soviet Union was too weak and exhausted at the end of World War II to pose a serious threat to America; that the United States used its nuclear monopoly to threaten and intimidate Stalin; that Harry Truman recklessly abandoned the conciliatory tone taken by Franklin Roosevelt (who died in 1945), taking instead a provocative hard line against the Russians. The Soviet response, these scholars

(National Archives and Records Administration)

the Chinese government of Chiang Kai-shek. Chiang was generally friendly to the United States, but his government was corrupt and incompetent with feeble popular support, and Chiang was unable or unwilling to face the problems that were threatening to engulf him. Since 1927, the nationalist government he headed had been engaged in a prolonged and bitter rivalry with the communist armies of Mao Zedong. So successful had the communist challenge grown that Mao was in control of one-fourth of the population by 1945.

Some Americans urged the government to find a "third force" to support as an alternative to either Chiang or Mao. A few argued that the United States should try to reach some accommodation with Mao. Truman, however, decided reluctantly that he had no choice but to continue supporting Chiang. For the next several years, as the long struggle between the nationalists and the communists erupted into a full-scale civil war, the United States continued to send money and weapons to Chiang. Eventually, Truman sent General George Marshall, former army chief of staff and future secretary of state, to study the Chinese problem and recommend a policy for the United States. Many American friends in China—known generally as the China Lobby—pressured Marshall to expand the American military presence as a way to combat the continuing expansion of

communist control. Marshall came to believe that nothing short of an all-out war with China would be necessary to defeat the communists, and he was unwilling to recommend that the president should accept such a war. That decision was the source of many embittered attacks on Marshall, Truman, and many others for decades to come.

Instead, the American government was beginning to consider an alternative to China as the strong, pro-Western force in Asia:

RESTORING JAPAN a revived Japan. Abandoning the strict occupation policies of the first years after the war (when General Douglas MacArthur had governed the nation), the United States lifted restrictions on industrial development and encouraged rapid economic growth in Japan. The vision of an open, united world was giving way in Asia, as it was in Europe, to an acceptance of a divided world with a strong, pro-American sphere of influence.

THE CONTAINMENT DOCTRINE

By the end of 1945, any realistic hope of a postwar world constructed according to the Atlantic Charter ideals that Roosevelt and Churchill had agreed upon was in shambles. Instead, a new American policy, known as containment, was asserted, reflected a legitimate fear of capitalist encirclement. Walter LaFeber, in *America, Russia, and the Cold War, 1945–1966* (1967 and later editions), maintained that America's supposedly idealistic internationalism at the close of the war was in reality an effort to ensure a world shaped in the American image that would guarantee its influence, especially regarding trade.

Ultimately, the revisionist interpretation began to produce a reaction of its own, a "postrevisionist" view of the conflict. Some manifestations of this reaction consisted of little more than a reaffirmation of the traditional view of the Cold War, but the dominant works of postrevisionist scholarship attempted to strike a balance between the two camps, to identify areas of blame and misperception on both sides of the conflict. Thomas G. Paterson, in *Soviet-American Confrontation* (1973), viewed Russian hostility and American efforts to dominate the postwar world as equally responsible for the Cold War. John Lewis Gaddis, in *The United States and the Origins of the Cold War, 1941–1947* (1972) and other works, similarly maintained that "neither side can bear sole responsibility for the onset of the Cold War." American policymakers, he argued, had only limited options because of the pressures of domestic politics. And Stalin was immobilized by his obsessive concern with maintaining his own power and ensuring absolute security for the Soviet Union. But if neither side was entirely to blame, Gaddis concluded, the Soviets must be held more accountable for the problems, for Stalin was in a much better position to compromise, given his broader power within his own government, than the politically hamstrung Truman. Melvyn Leffler's *Preponderance of Power* (1991) argued similarly that American policymakers genuinely believed in the existence of a Soviet threat and were determined to remain consistently stronger than the Soviets in response.

A more complex view of the Cold War has emerged out of the postrevisionist literature. The Cold War, historians now suggest, was not so much the fault of one side or the other as it was the natural, perhaps inevitable, result of tensions between the world's two most powerful nations—nations that had been suspicious of, if not hostile toward, one another for nearly a century. "The United States and the Soviet Union were doomed to be antagonists," Ernest May wrote in 1984. "There probably was never any real possibility that the post-1945 relationship could be anything but hostility verging on conflict."

Since the fall of the Soviet Union in 1991, scholars have had access to Russian archives that have enriched—though not fundamentally changed—the way historians view the Cold War. John Lewis Gaddis, in *We Now Know: Rethinking Cold War History* (1998) and *The Cold War: A History* (2005), argues that the strong anticommunist positions of Margaret Thatcher, Ronald Reagan, and Pope John Paul II had a larger impact on the weakening of the Soviet Union than was previously understood. In *The Global Cold War* (2005), Arne Westad, also making use of the released archives,

roots the origins of the dangerous instability in the so-called Third World in the frequent interventions of both the Soviet Union and the United States in the Cold War era. And John Lewis Gaddis, in *The Cold War: A History*, looks back on the Cold War that he chronicled for several decades in the midst of the Cold War. He argues that, despite all the anxieties it raised and all the violence it helped to create, the containment policy that shaped American foreign policy beginning in the mid-1940s was ultimately a significant success. ●

AP HISTORICAL ARGUMENTATION AND INTERPRETATION

Questions assume cumulative content knowledge from this chapter and previous chapters.

1. For each view regarding the origins of the Cold War, identify a representative historical argument: traditional, revisionist, postrevisionist.
2. Why might the historical debate or interpretations regarding the origins of the Cold War have become more complex with the passage of time?
3. With which historical argument discussed regarding the origins of the Cold War do you most agree? Explain why, supporting your argument with historical evidence.

---

slowly emerging. Rather than attempting to create a unified, "open" world, the United States and its allies would work to "contain" the threat of further Soviet expansion.

The new doctrine emerged in part as a response to events in Europe in 1946. In Turkey, Stalin was trying to win control over the vital sea lanes to the Mediterranean. In Greece,

TRUMAN DOCTRINE

communist forces were threatening the pro-Western government. The British had announced they could no longer provide assistance. Faced with these challenges, Truman decided to enunciate a firm new policy. In doing so, he drew from the ideas of the influential American diplomat George F. Kennan, who had warned not long after the war that the only appropriate diplomatic approach to dealing with the Soviet Union was "a long-term, patient but firm and vigilant containment of Russian expansive tendencies." On March 12, 1947, Truman appeared before Congress and used Kennan's warnings as the basis of what became known as the Truman Doctrine. "I believe," he argued, "that it must be the policy of the United States to support free peoples who are resisting attempted subjugation by armed minorities or by outside pressures." In the same speech he requested $400 million—part of it to bolster the armed forces of Greece and Turkey, another part

to provide economic assistance to Greece. Congress quickly approved the measure.

The American commitment ultimately helped ease Soviet pressure on Turkey and helped the Greek government defeat the communist insurgents. More important, it established a basis for American foreign policy that would survive for more than forty years.

THE MARSHALL PLAN

An integral part of the containment policy was a proposal to aid in the economic reconstruction of Western Europe. There were many motives: humanitarian concern for the European people; a

REBUILDING EUROPE

fear that Europe would remain an economic drain on the United States if it could not quickly rebuild and begin to feed itself; a desire for a strong European market for American goods. But above all, American policymakers believed that unless something could be done to strengthen the shaky pro-American governments in Western Europe, those governments might fall under the control of rapidly growing domestic communist parties.

In June 1947, therefore, Secretary of State George C. Marshall announced a plan to provide economic assistance to all

PEACE-MONGERING

SALUTING THE MARSHALL PLAN In another age, a chimney spouting smoke would evoke environmental damage. But in the aftermath of World War II, the rebuilding of Europe's industrial capacity was a great achievement—helped by (and celebrated by) the United States and the Marshall Plan. (© The Granger Collection, New York)

MOBILIZATION AT HOME

That the United States had accepted a continuing commitment to the containment policy became clear in 1947 and 1948 through a series of measures designed to maintain American military power at near wartime levels. In 1948, at President Truman's request, Congress approved a new military draft and revived the Selective Service System. In the meantime, the United States, having failed to reach agreement with the Soviet Union on international control of nuclear weapons, redoubled its own efforts in atomic research, elevating nuclear weaponry to a central place in its military arsenal. The Atomic Energy Commission, established in 1946, became the supervisory body charged with overseeing all nuclear research, both civilian and military. And in 1950, the Truman administration approved the development of the new hydrogen bomb, a nuclear weapon far more powerful than the bombs the United States had used in 1945.

The National Security Act of 1947 reshaped the nation's major military and diplomatic institutions. It created a new

NATIONAL SECURITY ACT OF 1947

Department of Defense to oversee all branches of the armed services, combining functions previously performed separately by the War and Navy Departments. A National Security Council (NSC), operating out of the White House, would oversee foreign and military policy. A Central Intelligence Agency (CIA) would replace the wartime Office of

European nations (including the Soviet Union) that would join in drafting a program for recovery. Although Russia and its Eastern satellites quickly and predictably rejected the plan, sixteen Western European nations eagerly participated. Whatever domestic opposition to the plan there was in the United States largely vanished after a sudden coup in Czechoslovakia in February 1948 that established a Soviet-dominated communist government there. In April, Congress approved the creation of the Economic Cooperation Administration, the agency that would administer the Marshall Plan, as it became known. Over the next three years, the Marshall Plan channeled over $12 billion of American aid into Europe, helping to spark a substantial economic revival. By the end of 1950, European industrial production had risen 64 percent, communist strength in the member nations had declined, and opportunities for American trade had revived.

SURVIVING NUCLEAR WAR Preoccupation with the possibility of a nuclear war reached a fever pitch in the first years of the atomic era. The Federal Civil Defense Agency, which in 1950 issued these simple rules for civilians to follow in dealing with an atomic attack, was one of many organizations attempting to convince the American public that a nuclear war was survivable. (Federal Civil Defense Agency)

Survival Secrets for Atomic Attacks

ALWAYS PUT FIRST THINGS FIRST

Try to Get Shielded

If you have time, get down in a basement or subway. Should you unexpectedly be caught out-of-doors, seek shelter alongside a building, or jump in any handy ditch or gutter.

Drop Flat on Ground or Floor

To keep from being tossed about and to lessen the chances of being struck by falling and flying objects, flatten out at the base of a wall, or at the bottom of a bank.

Bury Your Face in Your Arms

When you drop flat, hide your eyes in the crook of your elbow. That will protect your face from flash burns, prevent temporary blindness and keep flying objects out of your eyes.

NEVER LOSE YOUR HEAD

Strategic Services and would be responsible for collecting information through both open and covert methods; as the Cold War continued, the CIA would also engage secretly in political and military operations. The National Security Act, in other words, gave the president expanded powers with which to pursue the nation's international goals.

THE ROAD TO NATO

At about the same time, the United States was moving to strengthen the military capabilities of Western Europe.

Convinced that a reconstructed Germany was essential to the hopes of the West, Truman reached an agreement with England and France to merge the three western zones of occupation into a new West German republic (which would include the former American, British, and French sectors of Berlin, even though that city lay well within the East German zone). Stalin responded quickly. On June 24, 1948, he imposed a tight blockade around the western sectors of Berlin. If Germany was to be officially divided, he was implying, then the country's western government would have to abandon its outpost in the heart of the Soviet-controlled eastern zone. Truman refused to do so.

DIVIDED EUROPE AFTER WORLD WAR II This map shows the sharp division that emerged in Europe after World War II between the area under the control of the Soviet Union and the area allied with the United States. In the east, Soviet control or influence extended into all the nations shaded brown—including the eastern half of Germany. In the west and south, the green-shaded nations were allied with the United States as members of the North Atlantic Treaty Organization (NATO). The countries shaded gold were aligned with neither of the two superpowers. The small map in the upper right shows the division of Berlin among the various occupying powers at the end of the war. Eventually, the American, British, and French sectors were combined to create West Berlin, a city governed by West Germany but entirely surrounded by communist East Germany.

• *How did the West prevent East Germany from absorbing West Berlin?*

Unwilling to risk war through a military challenge to the blockade, he ordered a massive airlift to supply the city with food, fuel, and other needed goods. The airlift continued for more than ten months, transporting nearly 2.5 million tons of material, keeping a city of 2 million people alive, and transforming West Berlin into a symbol of the West's resolve to resist communist expansion. In the spring of 1949, Stalin lifted the now-ineffective blockade. And in October, the division of Germany into two nations–the Federal Republic in the west and the Democratic Republic in the east–became official.

The crisis in Berlin accelerated the consolidation of what was already in effect an alliance among the United States and the countries of Western Europe. On
NATO
April 4, 1949, twelve nations signed an agreement establishing the North Atlantic Treaty Organization (NATO) and declaring that an armed attack against one member would be considered an attack against all. The NATO countries would, moreover, maintain a standing military force in Europe to defend against what many policymakers believed was the threat of a Soviet invasion. The formation of NATO eventually spurred the Soviet Union to create an alliance of its own with the communist governments in Eastern Europe–an alliance formalized in 1955 by the Warsaw Pact.

REEVALUATING COLD WAR POLICY

A series of events in 1949 propelled the Cold War in new directions. An announcement in September that the Soviet Union had successfully exploded its first atomic weapon, years earlier than predicted, shocked and frightened many Americans. So did the collapse of Chiang Kai-shek's nationalist government in China, which occurred with startling speed in the last months of 1949. Chiang fled with his political allies and the remnants of his army to the offshore island of Formosa (Taiwan), and the entire Chinese mainland came under the control of a communist government that many Americans believed to be an extension of the Soviet Union. The United States refused to recognize the new communist regime and, instead, devoted increased attention to the revitalization of Japan as a buffer against Asian communism, ending the American occupation in 1952.

In this atmosphere of escalating crisis, Truman called for a thorough review of American foreign policy. The result was a
NSC-68
National Security Council report, issued in 1950 and commonly known as NSC-68, which outlined a shift in the American position. The first statements of the containment doctrine–the writings of George Kennan, the Truman Doctrine speech–had made at least some distinctions between areas of vital interest to the United States and areas of less importance to the nation's foreign policy and called on America to share the burden of containment with its allies. But the April 1950 document argued that the United States could no longer rely on other nations to take the initiative in resisting communism. It must itself establish firm and active leadership of the noncommunist world. And it must move to stop communist expansion virtually anywhere it occurred,

PROCLAIMING THE VICTORY OF THE REVOLUTION Chairman Mao Zedong, standing on the rostrum of the Tiananmen Square Gate in Beijing, speaks by radio to the Chinese people on October 1, 1949, to proclaim the founding of the People's Republic of China. This was shortly after the communist victory in the nation's civil war and the departure of Chiang Kai-shek and his followers to the island of Taiwan. (© AP Images)

regardless of the intrinsic strategic or economic value of the lands in question. Among other things, the report called for a major expansion of American military power, with a defense budget almost four times the previously projected figure.

THE CONSERVATIVE OPPOSITION TO CONTAINMENT

The containment doctrine for dealing with the Cold War attracted broad bipartisan support. But not everyone believed that containment was the right approach to take. Some Americans on the left believed that containment was unnecessarily belligerent and that the United States could have made peace with the Russians. But greater opposition to containment came from conservative Americans who believed that it was too weak a response to communism and saw containment as a kind of appeasement.

Among the conservatives who disdained containment was an anticommunist organization known as the John Birch

Society. Its leader was Robert Welch, a man so fearful of communism that he believed some of the most important leaders of American government were trying to undermine the United States by collaborating with the Soviets. Welch presented his opposition in *The Blue Book of the John Birch Society*, in which he argued that much of the American government was riddled with treason. "For years," he wrote, "we have been taken steadily down the road to Communism by steps supposedly designed . . . as ways of *fighting* communism." But instead, he argued, it was communist Americans themselves who were undermining the nation. "Both the U.S. and Soviet governments are controlled by the same furtive conspiratorial cabal of internationalists, greedy bankers, and corrupt politicians," Welch wrote. "If left unexposed, the traitors inside the U.S. government would betray the country's sovereignty to the United Nations for a collectivist New World Order, managed by a 'one-world government.'" Among the sources of treason, Welch claimed, were the United Nations and other international institutions. Many Americans considered the John Birch Society an extremist organization, but the belief that communism was the greatest danger facing the United States was widely supported by many people.

The opposition to containment reached some of the highest levels of the government. John Foster Dulles, who would become secretary of state in the Eisenhower administration, wrote the foreign policy plank of the Republican platform in 1952. "We charge that the leaders of the Administration in power lost the peace so dearly earned by World War II," Dulles stated. "They abandoned friendly nations such as Latvia, Lithuania, Estonia, Poland, and Czechoslovakia." Containment, opponents such as Dulles argued, was a policy of weakness that had allowed the communists to take over much of the world. Many of those who argued against containment called for what was known as "rollback": instead of containing communism, the United States should be pushing back the borders of communism, despite the possibility of another war. President Eisenhower, however, did not share Dulles's belief in rollback, and the government abided by the containment strategy throughout the 1950s and beyond.

AMERICAN SOCIETY AND POLITICS AFTER THE WAR

The crises overseas were not the only frustrations the American people encountered after the war. The nation also faced serious economic difficulties in adapting to peacetime. The resulting instability contributed to an increasingly heated political climate.

THE PROBLEMS OF RECONVERSION

The bombs that destroyed Hiroshima and Nagasaki ended the war months earlier than almost anyone had predicted and propelled the nation precipitously into a process of reconversion.

There had been many predictions that peace would bring a return of Depression unemployment, as war production ceased and returning soldiers flooded the labor market. But there was no general economic collapse in 1946–for several reasons. Government spending dropped sharply and abruptly, to be sure; $35 billion of war contracts were canceled within weeks of the Japanese surrender. But increased consumer demand soon compensated. Consumer goods had been generally unavailable during the war, so many workers had saved a substantial portion of their wages and were now ready to spend. A $6 billion tax cut pumped additional money into general circulation. The Servicemen's Readjustment Act of 1944, better known as the GI Bill of Rights, provided economic and educational assistance to veterans, increasing spending even further.

GI BILL

This flood of consumer demand ensured that there would be no new depression, but it contributed to more than two years of serious inflation, during which prices rose at rates of 14 to 15 percent annually. In the summer of 1946, President Truman vetoed an extension of the authority of the wartime Office of Price Administration, thus eliminating price controls. (He was opposed not to the controls, but to congressional amendments that had weakened the OPA.) Inflation soared to 25 percent before he relented a month later and signed a bill little different from the one he had rejected.

Compounding the economic difficulties was a sharp rise in labor unrest, driven in part by the impact of inflation. By the end of 1945, there had already been major strikes in the automobile, electrical, and steel industries. In April 1946, John L. Lewis led the United Mine Workers on strike, shutting down the coal fields for forty days. Fears grew rapidly that without vital coal supplies, the entire economy might grind to a halt. Truman finally forced the miners to return to work by ordering

POSTWAR LABOR UNREST

THE GI BILL The Servicemen's Readjustment Act of 1944, better known as the GI Bill provided a wide range of benefits to all honorably discharged service personnel who served during the war. Benefits included low-cost mortgages, low-interest loans to start a business, cash payments of tuition and living expenses to attend university, high school or vocational education, as well as one year of unemployment compensation. By 1956, roughly 2.2 million veterans had used the G.I. Bill education benefits to attend colleges or universities. An additional 5.6 million veterans used these benefits for some kind of training program. (© Bettmann/Corbis)

government seizure of the mines. But in the process, he pressured mine owners to grant the union most of its demands, which he had earlier denounced as inflationary. Almost simultaneously, the nation's railroads suffered a total shutdown—the first in the nation's history—as two major unions walked out on strike. By threatening to use the army to run the trains, Truman pressured the workers back to work after only a few days.

Reconversion was particularly difficult for the millions of women and minorities who had entered the workforce during the war. With veterans returning home and looking for jobs in the industrial economy, employers tended to push women, blacks, Hispanics, Chinese, and others out of the plants to make room for white males. Some of the war workers, particularly women, left the workforce voluntarily, out of a desire to return to their former domestic lives. But as many as 80 percent of women workers, and virtually all black, Hispanic, and Asian males, wanted to continue working. The postwar inflation, the pressure to meet the rising expectations of a high-consumption society, the growing divorce rate, which left many women responsible for their own economic well-being—all combined to create among women a high demand for paid employment. As they found themselves excluded from industrial jobs, therefore, women workers moved increasingly into other areas of the economy (above all, the service sector).

THE FAIR DEAL REJECTED

Days after the Japanese surrender, Truman submitted to Congress a twenty-one-point domestic program outlining what

TRUMAN'S "FAIR DEAL" he later termed the "Fair Deal." It called for expansion of Social Security benefits, the raising of the legal minimum wage from 40 to 65 cents an hour, a program to ensure full employment through aggressive use of federal spending and investment, a permanent Fair Employment Practices Act, public housing and slum clearance, long-range environmental and public works planning, and government promotion of scientific research. Weeks later he added other proposals: federal aid to funding for the St. Lawrence Seaway, nationalization of atomic energy, and, perhaps most important, national health insurance—a dream of welfare-state liberals for decades, but one deferred in 1935 when the Social Security Act was written. The president was declaring an end to the wartime moratorium on liberal reform. He was also symbolizing, as he later wrote, "my assumption of the office of President in my own right."

But many of the Fair Deal programs fell victim to the same public and congressional conservatism that had crippled the last years of the New Deal. Indeed, that conservatism seemed to be intensifying, as the November 1946 congressional elections suggested. Using the simple but devastating slogan "Had Enough?," the Republican Party won control of both houses of Congress.

The new Republican Congress quickly moved to reduce government spending and chip away at New Deal reforms. The president bowed to what he claimed was the popular mandate

to lift most remaining wage and price controls, and Congress moved further to deregulate the economy. Inflation rapidly increased. When a public outcry arose over the soaring prices for meat, Senator Robert Taft, perhaps the most influential Republican conservative in Congress, advised consumers to "eat less," and added, "We have got to break with the corrupting idea that we can legislate prosperity, legislate equality, legislate opportunity." True to the spirit of Taft's words, the Republican Congress refused to appropriate funds to aid education, increase Social Security, or support reclamation and power projects in the West. It defeated a proposal to raise the minimum wage. It passed tax measures that cut rates dramatically for high-income families and moderately for those with lower incomes. Only vetoes by the president finally forced a more progressive bill.

The most notable action of the new Congress was its assault on the Wagner Act of 1935. Conservatives had always

TAFT-HARTLEY ACT resented the new powers the legislation had granted unions; and in light of the labor difficulties during and after the war, such resentments intensified sharply. The result was the Labor-Management Relations Act of 1947, better known as the Taft-Hartley Act. It made illegal the so-called closed shop (a workplace in which no one can be hired without first being a member of a union). And although it continued to permit the creation of so-called union shops (in which workers must join a union after being hired), it permitted states to pass "right-to-work" laws prohibiting even that. Repealing this provision, the controversial Section 14(b), would remain a goal of the labor movement for decades. Outraged workers and union leaders denounced the measure as a "slave labor bill." Truman vetoed it, but both the House and the Senate easily overruled him the same day.

The Taft-Hartley Act did not destroy the labor movement, as many union leaders had predicted. But it did damage weaker unions in relatively lightly organized industries such as chemicals and textiles; and it made more difficult the organizing of workers who had never been union members, especially women, minorities, and most workers in the South.

THE ELECTION OF 1948

Truman and his advisers believed the American public was not ready to abandon the achievements of the New Deal, despite the 1946 election results. As they planned strategy for the 1948 campaign, therefore, they placed their hopes in an appeal to enduring Democratic loyalties. Throughout 1948, Truman proposed one reform measure after another. Although Congress ignored or defeated them all, the president was building campaign issues for the fall.

There remained, however, the problems of Truman's personal unpopularity—the belief among much of the electorate

DEMOCRATIC DEFECTIONS that he and his administration were weak and inept—and the deep divisions within the Democratic Party. At the Democratic National Convention that summer, two factions abandoned

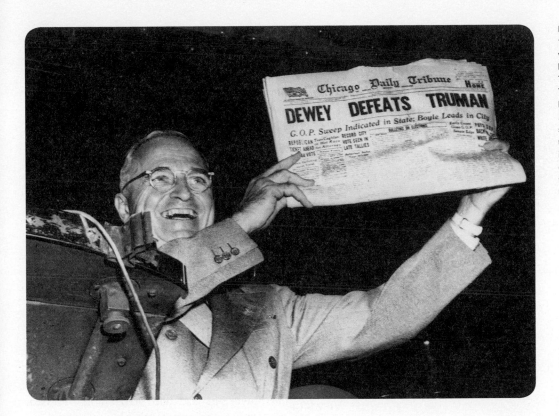

the party: southern conservatives reacted angrily to Truman's proposed civil rights bill (the first major one of the century) and to the approval at the convention of a civil rights plank in the platform (engineered by Hubert Humphrey, the mayor of Minneapolis). These two factions formed the States' Rights (or "Dixiecrat") Party, with Governor Strom Thurmond of South Carolina as its presidential nominee. At the same time, the Democratic Party's left wing formed a new Progressive Party, with Henry A. Wallace as its candidate. Wallace supporters objected to what they considered the slow and ineffective domestic policies of the Truman administration, but they resented even more the president's confrontational stance toward the Soviet Union.

In addition, many Democratic liberals unwilling to leave the party attempted to dump the president in 1948. The Americans for Democratic Action (ADA), a coalition of liberals, tried to entice Dwight D. Eisenhower, the popular war hero, to contest the nomination. Only after Eisenhower had refused did liberals bow to the inevitable and concede the nomination to Truman. The Republicans, in the meantime, had once again nominated Governor Thomas E. Dewey of New York, whose substantial reelection victory in 1946 had made him one of the nation's leading political figures. Austere, dignified, and competent, he seemed to offer an unbeatable alternative to the president. Polls showed Dewey with an apparently insurmountable lead in September, so much so that some opinion analysts stopped taking surveys. Dewey conducted a subdued, statesmanlike campaign and tried to avoid antagonizing anyone. But Truman, seemingly alone, believed he could win. As the campaign gathered momentum, Truman became more and more aggressive, turning the fire away from himself and toward Dewey and the "do-nothing, good-for-nothing" Republican Congress, which was, he told the voters, responsible for fueling inflation and abandoning workers and the middle class. To dramatize his point, he called Congress into a special session in July to give it a chance, he said, to enact the liberal measures the Republicans had recently written into their platform. Congress met for two weeks and, predictably, did almost nothing.

The president traveled nearly 32,000 miles and made 356 speeches, delivering blunt, extemporaneous attacks. He had told Senator Alben Barkley of Kentucky, his running mate, "I'm going to fight hard. I'm going to give them hell." He called for repeal of the Taft-Hartley Act, increased price supports for farmers, and strong civil rights protection for blacks. (He was the first president to campaign in Harlem.) He sought, in short, to re-create much of Franklin Roosevelt's New Deal coalition. To the surprise of virtually everyone, he succeeded. On election night, Truman won a narrow but decisive victory: 49.5 percent of the popular vote to Dewey's 45.1 percent (with the two splinter parties dividing the small remainder between them), and an electoral vote margin of 303 to 189. Democrats, in the meantime, regained both houses of Congress by substantial margins.

TRUMAN'S SURPRISING VICTORY

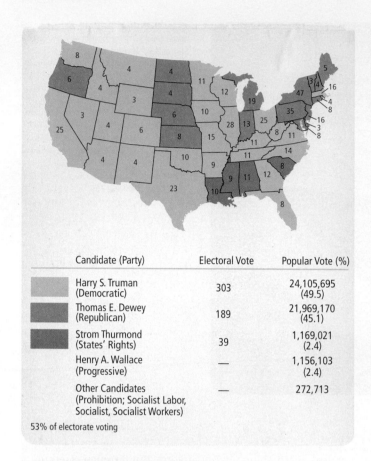

Candidate (Party)	Electoral Vote	Popular Vote (%)
Harry S. Truman (Democratic)	303	24,105,695 (49.5)
Thomas E. Dewey (Republican)	189	21,969,170 (45.1)
Strom Thurmond (States' Rights)	39	1,169,021 (2.4)
Henry A. Wallace (Progressive)	—	1,156,103 (2.4)
Other Candidates (Prohibition; Socialist Labor, Socialist, Socialist Workers)	—	272,713

53% of electorate voting

ELECTION OF 1948 Despite the widespread expectation that the Republican candidate, Thomas Dewey, would easily defeat Truman in 1948, the president in fact won a substantial reelection victory that year. This map shows the broad geographic reach of Truman's victory. Dewey swept most of the Northeast, but Truman dominated almost everywhere else. Strom Thurmond, the States' Rights candidate, carried four states in the South.

• *What had prompted Thurmond to desert the Democratic Party and run for president on his own?*

THE FAIR DEAL REVIVED

Despite the Democratic victories, the Eighty-First Congress was little more hospitable to Truman's Fair Deal reform than its Republican predecessor. Truman did win some important victories. Congress raised the legal minimum wage from 40 cents to 75 cents an hour. It approved an important expansion of the Social Security system, increasing benefits by 75 percent and extending them to 10 million additional people. And it passed the National Housing Act of 1949, which provided for the construction of 810,000 units of low-income housing, accompanied by long-term rent subsidies. (Inadequate funding plagued the program for years, and it reached its initial goal only in 1972.)

But on other issues—among them national health insurance and aid to education—Truman made no progress. Nor was he able to persuade Congress to accept the civil rights legislation he proposed in 1949, which would have made lynching a federal crime,

TRUMAN STYMIED

provided federal protection of black voting rights, abolished the poll tax, and established a new Fair Employment Practices Commission to curb discrimination in hiring (to replace the wartime commission Roosevelt had established in 1941). Southern Democrats filibustered to kill the bill.

Truman did proceed on his own to battle several forms of racial discrimination. He ordered an end to discrimination in the hiring of government employees. He began to dismantle segregation within the armed forces. And he allowed the Justice Department to become actively involved in court battles against discriminatory statutes. In the meantime, the Supreme Court signaled its own growing awareness of the issue by ruling, in *Shelley v. Kraemer* (1948), that the courts could not be used to enforce private "covenants" meant to bar African Americans from residential neighborhoods.

THE NUCLEAR AGE

Looming over the political, economic, and diplomatic struggles of the postwar years was the image of the great and terrible mushroom clouds that had risen over Alamogordo, Hiroshima, and Nagasaki. Americans greeted these terrible new instruments of destruction with fear and awe, but also with expectation. Postwar culture, therefore, was torn in many ways. There was the dark image of the nuclear war that many Americans feared would be a result of the rivalry with the Soviet Union. But there was also the bright image of a dazzling technological future that atomic power might help to produce.

CONFLICTING VIEWS OF NUCLEAR POWER

The fear of nuclear weapons was not hard to find in popular culture, even if it was often disguised in other ways. The late 1940s and early 1950s were the heyday of the *film noir*, a kind of filmmaking that had originated in France and had been named for the dark lighting characteristic of the genre. American *film noir* movies portrayed the loneliness of individuals in an impersonal world—a staple of American culture for many decades—but also suggested the menacing character of the age, the looming possibility of vast destruction. Sometimes, films and television programs addressed nuclear fear explicitly—for example, the celebrated television show of the 1950s and early 1960s *The Twilight Zone*, which frequently featured dramatic portrayals of the aftermath of nuclear war; or postwar comic books, which depicted powerful superheroes saving the world from destruction.

Such images resonated with the public because awareness of nuclear weapons was increasingly built into their daily lives. Schools and office buildings had regular air raid drills, to prepare people for the possibility of nuclear attack. Radio stations regularly tested the emergency broadcast systems. Fallout shelters sprang up in public buildings and private homes, stocked with water and canned goods. America was a nation filled with anxiety.

And yet at the same time, the United States was also an exuberant nation, dazzled by its own prosperity and excited by the technological innovations that were transforming the world. Among those innovations was nuclear power—which

PROMISE OF CHEAP NUCLEAR POWER

offered the possibility that the same scientific knowledge that could destroy the world might also lead it into a dazzling future. A Gallup poll late in 1948 revealed that approximately two-thirds of those who had an opinion on the subject believed that, "in the long run," atomic energy would "do more good than harm." Nuclear power plants began to spring up in many areas of the country, welcomed as the source of cheap and unlimited electricity, their potential dangers scarcely even discussed by those who celebrated the creation of atomic power.

THE KOREAN WAR

On June 24, 1950, the armies of communist North Korea swept across their southern border and invaded the pro-Western half of the Korean peninsula to the south. Within days, they had occupied much of South Korea, including Seoul, its capital. Almost immediately, the United States committed itself to defeating the North Korean offensive. It was the nation's first military engagement of the Cold War.

THE DIVIDED PENINSULA

Before the end of World War II, both the United States and the Soviet Union had sent troops into Korea in an effort to weaken Japanese occupation. Once the war was over and the Japanese expelled, the United States and the Soviet Union each supported different governments—the Soviets supporting a communist regime in the North and the United States supporting a pro-Western government in the

SYNGMAN RHEE

South. Instead, they had divided the nation, supposedly temporarily, along the 38th parallel. The Russians departed in 1949, leaving behind a communist government in the north with a strong, Soviet-equipped army. The Americans left a few months later, handing control to the pro-Western government of Syngman Rhee, who was anticommunist but only nominally democratic. He had a relatively small military, which he used primarily to suppress internal opposition.

The relative weakness of the south offered a strong incentive to nationalists in the North Korean government who wanted to reunite the country. The temptation to invade grew stronger when the American government implied that it did not consider South Korea within its own "defense perimeter." The role of the Soviet Union in North Korea's calculations prior to the 1950 invasion remains unclear; there is reason to believe that the North Koreans acted without Stalin's prior approval. But the Soviets supported the offensive once it began.

The Truman administration responded quickly to the invasion. On June 27, 1950, the president appealed to the United Nations to intervene. The Soviet Union was boycotting the Security Council at the time (to protest the council's refusal to recognize the new communist government of China) and thus was unable to exercise its veto power. As a result, American delegates were able to win UN agreement to a resolution calling for international assistance to the Rhee government. On June 30, the United States ordered its own ground forces into Korea, and Truman appointed General Douglas MacArthur to command the overwhelmingly American UN operations there.

The intervention in Korea was the first expression of the newly expansive American foreign policy outlined in NSC-68. But the administration quickly went beyond NSC-68 and decided that the war would be an effort not simply at containment but also at "liberation." After a surprise American invasion at Inchon in September had routed the North Korean

"LIBERATION"

forces from the south and sent them fleeing back across the 38th parallel, Truman gave MacArthur permission to pursue the communists into their own territory. His aim, as an American-sponsored UN resolution proclaimed in October, was to create "a unified, independent and democratic Korea."

FROM INVASION TO STALEMATE

For several weeks, MacArthur's invasion of North Korea proceeded smoothly. On October 19, the capital, Pyongyang, fell to the UN forces. Victory seemed near—until the new communist government of China, alarmed by the movement of American forces toward its border, intervened. By November 4, eight divisions of the Chinese army had entered the war. The UN offensive stalled and then collapsed. Through December 1950, outnumbered American forces fought a bitter, losing battle against the Chinese divisions, retreating at almost every juncture. Within weeks, communist forces had pushed the Americans back below the 38th parallel once again and had captured the South Korean capital of Seoul a second time. By mid-January 1951 the rout had ceased; and by March the UN armies had managed to regain much of the territory they had recently lost, taking back Seoul and pushing the communists north of the 38th parallel once more. But with that, the war degenerated into a protracted stalemate.

From the start, Truman was determined to avoid a direct conflict with China, which he feared might lead to a new world war. Once China entered the war, he began seeking a negotiated solution to the struggle, and for the next two years he insisted that there be no wider war. But he faced a formidable opponent in General MacArthur, who resisted any limits on his military discretion. The United States was fighting the Chinese, he argued. It should therefore attack China itself, if not through an actual invasion, then at least by bombing communist forces massing north of the Chinese border. In March 1951, MacArthur indicated his unhappiness in a public letter to House Republican leader Joseph W.

DISARRAY IN KOREA This disturbing picture by the noted *Life* magazine photographer Carl Mydans conveys something of the air of catastrophe that surrounded the rout of Americans from North Korea by the Chinese in 1951. Having approached the Chinese border, the Americans confronted a massive invasion of Korea by Chinese troops, who soon pushed them back below the border between the North and the South and well beyond. Shown here are U.S. Marines following a vehicle carrying corpses after a battle with Chinese and North Korean troops. They had been trapped by the enemy in North Korea and had fought their way forty miles south before being rescued. (Photo by Carl Mydans/© Time & Life Pictures/Getty Images)

Martin that concluded: "There is no substitute for victory." His position had wide popular support.

The Martin letter came after nine months during which MacArthur had opposed Truman's decisions. More than once,

TRUMAN-MACARTHUR CONTROVERSY

the president had warned the general to keep his objections to himself. The release of the Martin letter, therefore, struck the president as intolerable insubordination. On April 11, 1951, he relieved MacArthur of his command.

There was a storm of public outrage. Sixty-nine percent of the American people supported MacArthur, a Gallup poll reported. When the general returned to the United States later in 1951, he was greeted with wild enthusiasm. His televised farewell appearance before a joint session of Congress—which he concluded by saying, "Old soldiers never die, they just fade away"—attracted an audience of millions. Public criticism of Truman abated somewhat when a number of prominent military figures, including General Omar Bradley, publicly sup-

ported the president's decision. But substantial hostility toward Truman remained. In the meantime, the Korean stalemate continued. Negotiations between the opposing forces began at Panmunjom in July 1951, but the talks—and the war—dragged on until 1953.

LIMITED MOBILIZATION

Just as the war in Korea produced only a limited American military commitment abroad, so it created only a limited economic mobilization at home. Still, the government did try to control the wartime economy in several important ways.

First, Truman set up the Office of Defense Mobilization to fight inflation by holding down prices and discouraging high union wage demands. When these cautious regulatory efforts failed, the president took more-drastic action. When railroad workers walked off the job in 1951, Truman ordered the government to seize control of the railroads. That helped keep the

THE KOREAN WAR, 1950–1953 These two maps illustrate the changing fortunes of UN forces (which were mostly American) during the 1950–1953 Korean War. The map at the left shows the extent of the North Korean invasion of the South in 1950; communist forces for a time controlled all of Korea except a small area around Pusan in the southeast. On September 15, 1950, UN troops under Douglas MacArthur landed in force at Inchon and soon drove the North Koreans back across the border. MacArthur then pursued the North Koreans well into their own territory. The map at right shows the very different circumstances once the Chinese entered the war in November 1950. Chinese forces drove the UN army back below the 38th parallel and, briefly, deep into South Korea, below Seoul. The UN troops fought back to the prewar border between North and South Korea late in 1951, but the war then bogged down into a stalemate that continued for a year and a half.

• *What impact did the Korean War have on American politics in the early 1950s?*

WARTIME ECONOMIC REGULATION trains running, but it had no effect on union demands. Workers ultimately got most of what they had demanded. In 1952, during a nationwide steel strike, Truman seized the steel mills, citing his powers as commander in chief. But in a 6-to-3 decision, the Supreme Court ruled that the president had exceeded his authority, and Truman was forced to relent.

The Korean War gave a significant boost to economic growth by pumping new government funds into the economy at a point when many people believed a recession was about to begin. But as the long stalemate continued, leaving 140,000 Americans dead or wounded, frustration turned to anger. Many began to believe that something must be deeply wrong—not only in Korea but within the United States as well. Such fears contributed to the rise of the second major campaign of the century against domestic communism.

THE CRUSADE AGAINST SUBVERSION

Why did the American people develop a growing fear of internal communist subversion that by the early 1950s had reached the point of near hysteria? There are many possible answers, but no single definitive explanation.

One factor was obvious. Communism was not an imagined enemy in the 1950s. It had tangible shape, in Joseph Stalin and the Soviet Union. In addition, America had encountered setbacks in its battle against communism: the Korean stalemate, the "loss" of China, the Soviet development of an atomic bomb. Searching for someone to blame, many people were attracted to the idea of a communist conspiracy within American borders. But there were other factors as well, rooted in American domestic politics.

SOURCES OF THE RED SCARE

HUAC AND ALGER HISS

Much of the anticommunist furor emerged out of the Republican Party's search for an issue with which to attack the Democrats, and out of the Democrats' efforts to stifle that issue. Beginning in 1947 (with Republicans temporarily in control of Congress), the House Un-American Activities Committee (HUAC) held widely publicized investigations to prove that, under Democratic rule, the government had tolerated (if not actually encouraged) communist subversion. The committee turned first to the movie industry, arguing that communists had infiltrated Hollywood. Writers and producers, some of them former communists, were called to testify; and when several of them ("the Hollywood Ten") refused to answer questions about their own political beliefs and those of their colleagues, they were jailed for contempt. Some writers were barred from employment in the movie industry when Hollywood, attempting to protect its public image, adopted a blacklist of those of "suspicious loyalty."

More alarming to much of the public was HUAC's investigation into charges of disloyalty leveled against a former high-ranking member of the State Department: Alger Hiss. In 1948, Whittaker Chambers, a self-avowed former communist agent who had turned vehemently against the party and become an editor at *Time* magazine, told the committee that Hiss had passed classified State Department documents through him to the Soviet Union in 1937 and 1938. When Hiss sued him for slander, Chambers produced microfilms of the documents (called the "pumpkin papers," because Chambers had kept them hidden in a pumpkin in his garden). Hiss could not be tried for espionage because of the statute of limitations (a law that protects individuals from prosecution for most crimes after seven years have passed). But largely because of the relentless efforts of Richard M. Nixon, a freshman Republican congressman from California and a member of HUAC, Hiss was convicted of perjury and served several years in prison. The Hiss case not only discredited a prominent young diplomat; it also cast suspicion on a generation of liberal Democrats and made it possible for many Americans to believe that communists had actually infiltrated the government.

ALGER HISS

THE FEDERAL LOYALTY PROGRAM AND THE ROSENBERG CASE

Partly to protect itself against Republican attacks, partly to encourage support for the president's foreign policy initiatives, the Truman administration in 1947 initiated a widely publicized program to review the loyalty of federal employees. In August 1950, the president authorized sensitive agencies to fire people deemed "bad security risks." By 1951, more than 2,000 government employees had resigned under pressure and 212 had been dismissed.

The employee loyalty program established a widely cited list of supposedly subversive organizations. The director of

THE McCARRAN INTERNAL SECURITY ACT

the Federal Bureau of Investigation (FBI), J. Edgar Hoover, investigated and harassed alleged radicals. In 1950, Congress passed the McCarran Internal Security Act, requiring all communist organizations to register with the government. Truman vetoed the bill. Congress easily overrode his veto.

The successful Soviet detonation of a nuclear weapon in 1949 convinced many people that there had been a conspiracy to pass American atomic secrets to the Russians. In 1950, Klaus Fuchs, a young British scientist, seemed to confirm those fears when he testified that he had delivered to the Russians details of the manufacture of the bomb. The case ultimately settled on an obscure New York couple, Julius and Ethel Rosenberg, members of the Communist Party, whom the federal government claimed had been the masterminds of the conspiracy. The case against them rested in large part on testimony by Ethel's brother, David Greenglass, a machinist who had worked on the Manhattan Project. Greenglass admitted to channeling secret information to the Soviet Union through other agents (including Fuchs). His sister and brother-in-law had, he claimed, planned and orchestrated the espionage. The Rosenbergs were convicted and, on April 5, 1951, sentenced to death. After two years of appeals and protests by sympathizers, they died in the electric chair on June 19, 1953.

All these factors–the HUAC investigations, the Hiss trial, the loyalty investigations, the McCarran Act, the Rosenberg case–helped to intensify public fear of communist subversion. By the early 1950s, the fear seemed to have gripped much of the country. State and local governments, the judiciary, schools and universities, labor unions–all sought to purge themselves

ANTICOMMUNIST HYSTERIA

of real or imagined subversives. A pervasive fear settled on the country–not only the fear of communist infiltration but also the fear of being suspected of communist subversion. It was a climate that made possible the rise of an extraordinary public figure, whose behavior at any other time might have been dismissed as preposterous.

McCARTHYISM

Joseph McCarthy was a relatively undistinguished first-term Republican senator from Wisconsin when, in February 1950, he suddenly burst into national prominence. In the midst of a speech in Wheeling, West Virginia, he raised a sheet of paper and claimed to "hold in my hand" a list of 205 known communists currently working in the U.S. State Department. No person of comparable stature had ever made so bold a charge against the federal government; and in the weeks to come, as McCarthy repeated and expanded his accusations, he emerged as the nation's most prominent leader of the crusade against domestic subversion.

Within weeks of his charges against the State Department, McCarthy was leveling accusations at other agencies. After 1952, with the Republicans in control of the Senate and McCarthy the chairman of a special subcommittee, he conducted highly publicized investigations of subversion in many areas of the government. His ambitious assistants, Roy Cohn

McCARTHYISM'S APPEAL

and David Schine, sauntered arrogantly through federal offices and American embassies overseas looking for evidence of communist influence. One hapless government official after another appeared before McCarthy's subcommittee, where the senator belligerently and often cruelly badgered witnesses and destroyed public careers. McCarthy never produced solid evidence of actual communist subversion. But a growing constituency adored him nevertheless for his coarse, "fearless" assaults on a government establishment that many Americans considered arrogant, elitist, even traitorous. Republicans, in particular, rallied to his claims that the Democrats had been responsible for "twenty years of treason," that only a change of parties could rid the country of subversion. McCarthy, in short, provided his followers with an issue into which they could channel a wide range of resentments: fear of communism, animosity toward the country's "eastern establishment," and frustrated partisan ambitions.

For a time, McCarthy intimidated all but a few people from opposing him. Even the highly popular Dwight D. Eisenhower, running for president in 1952, did not speak out against him, although he disliked McCarthy's tactics and was outraged at McCarthy's attacks on General George Marshall.

THE REPUBLICAN REVIVAL

Public frustration over the stalemate in Korea and popular fears of internal subversion combined to make 1952 a bad year for the Democratic Party. Truman, whose popularity had greatly diminished, wisely decided not to run again. The party united instead behind Governor Adlai E. Stevenson of Illinois, whose dignity, wit, and eloquence made him a beloved figure to many liberals and intellectuals. But Republicans charged that Stevenson lacked the strength or the will to combat communism sufficiently. McCarthy described him as "soft" and took delight in deliberately confusing him with Alger Hiss.

Stevenson's greatest problem, however, was the Republican candidate opposing him. Rejecting the efforts of conservatives to nominate Robert Taft or Douglas MacArthur, the Republicans turned to a man who had no previous identifi-

DWIGHT EISENHOWER

cation with the party: General Dwight D. Eisenhower, military hero, commander of NATO, president of Columbia University in New York. Eisenhower won nomination on the first ballot. He chose as his running mate the young California senator who had gained national prominence through his crusade against Alger Hiss: Richard M. Nixon. Eisenhower and Nixon were a powerful combination in the autumn campaign. While

"McCarthyism"

WHEN the American Civil Liberties Union warned in the early 1950s, at the peak of the anticommunist fervor that is now known as "McCarthyism," that "the threat to civil liberties today is the most serious in the history of our country," it was expressing a view with which many Americans wholeheartedly agreed. But while many Americans accept that there were unusually powerful challenges to freedom of speech and association in the late 1940s and early 1950s, there is wide disagreement about the causes and meaning of those challenges.

The simplest argument—and one that continues to attract scholarly support—is that the postwar Red Scare expressed real and legitimate concerns about communist subversion in the United States. William O'Neill, in *A Better World* (1982), and Richard Gid Powers, in *Not Without Honor* (1995), have both argued that anticommunism was a serious, intelligent, and patriotic movement, despite its excesses. The American Communist Party, according to this view, was an agent of Stalin and the Soviet Union within the United States, actively engaged in espionage and subversion. The effort to root communists out of public life was both understandable and justifiable—and the hysteria it sometimes produced was an unhappy but predictable by-product of an essentially rational and justifiable effort. "Anticommunism," Powers wrote, "expressed the essential American determination to stand against attacks on human freedom and foster the growth of democracy throughout the world. . . . To superimpose on this rich history the cartoon features of Joe McCarthy is to reject history for the easy comforts of moralism."

Most interpretations, however, have been much less charitable. In the 1950s, in the midst of the Red Scare, an influential group of historians and social scientists began to portray the anticommunist fervor of their time as an expression of social maladjustment—an argument perhaps

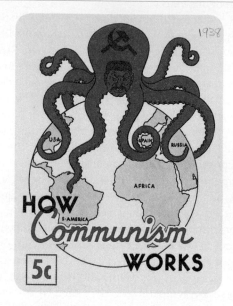

(Rare Book and Special Collections Division, The Library of Congress)

Eisenhower attracted support through his geniality and his statesmanlike pledges to settle the Korean conflict (at one point dramatically promising to "go to Korea" himself), Nixon effectively exploited the issue of communist subversion. After surviving early accusations of financial improprieties (which he effectively neutralized in a famous television address, the "Checkers speech"), Nixon went on to launch harsh attacks on Democratic "cowardice," "appeasement," and "treason."

Eisenhower won by both a popular and electoral landslide: 55 percent of the popular vote to Stevenson's 44 percent, 442 electoral votes to Stevenson's 89. Republicans gained control of both houses of Congress for only the second time in two decades. The election of 1952 ended twenty years of Democratic government. And while it might not have seemed so at the time, it also signaled the end of some of the worst turbulence of the postwar era.

AP CONNECTING THEMES

Chapter 27 discussed the development of the Cold War and its political and social effects. As part of the discussion, the chapter examined the impact of the second Red Scare on perceptions of what it meant to be an American and the impulse to create conformity of thought. Review the chapter for specific examples of the U.S. policy of containment and assess the degree to which the policy was a success. Also, as you review the chapter you should focus on the similarities and differences between post-World War I society and post-World War II society. Be able to compare postwar foreign policies, American public opinion about the respective war efforts, and the political movements following each of

the wars. You should also focus on how the Cold War changed America's perceptions about involvement in world affairs. Consider how wars have affected civil liberties and be able to relate the impact to both previous and subsequent time periods.

The following themes have a heightened importance in Chapter 27. You should now be able to do the following for each listed theme:

American Identity: Explain the impact of the Cold War on perceptions of American identity, particularly, relating to the second Red Scare.

most closely associated with Richard Hofstadter's essay "The Paranoid Style in American Politics." There was, they argued, no logical connection between the modest power of actual communists in the United States and the anticommunist hysteria. The fear of communism, they maintained, was rooted in social and cultural anxieties that had only an indirect connection with the political world. Extreme anticommunism, they claimed, was something close to a pathology; it expressed fear of and alienation from the modern world. A person afflicted with the "paranoid style," Hofstadter wrote:

> believes himself to be living in a world in which he is spied upon, plotted against, betrayed, and very likely destined for total ruin. He feels that his liberties have been arbitrarily and outrageously invaded. He is opposed to almost everything that has happened in American politics in the past twenty years.

Other scholars, writing not long after the decline of McCarthyism, rejected the sociocultural argument but shared the belief that the crusade against subversion was a distortion of normal public life. They saw the anticommunist crusade as an example of party politics run amok. Richard Freeland, in *The Truman Doctrine and the Origins of McCarthyism* (1971), argued that the Democrats began the effort to purge the government of radicals to protect themselves from attacks by the Republicans. Nelson Polsby, Robert Griffith, and others have noted how Republicans seized on the issue of communism in government in the late 1940s to reverse their nearly twenty-year exclusion from power. With each party trying to outdo the other in its effort to demonstrate its anticommunist credentials, it was hardly surprising that the crusade reached extraordinarily intense proportions.

Still other historians have emphasized the role of powerful government officials and agencies with a strong commitment to anticommunism—most notably J. Edgar Hoover and the FBI. Athan Theoharis and Kenneth O'Reilly introduced the idea of an anticommunist bureaucracy in work published in the 1970s and 1980s. Ellen Schrecker, in *Many Are the Crimes* (1998), argues that the Red Scare was, at its heart, directed largely against the left and that it was orchestrated by an interlocking cluster of official agencies with a deep commitment to the project.

Several scholars, finally, have presented an argument that does not so much challenge other interpretations as complement them. Anticommunist zealots were not alone to blame for the excesses of McCarthyism, they argue. It was also the fault of liberals—in politics, in academia, and perhaps above all in the media—who were so intimidated by the political climate, or so imprisoned within the conventions of their professions, that they found themselves unable to respond effectively to the distortions and excesses they recognized around them. ●

AP HISTORICAL ARGUMENTATION AND INTERPRETATION

Questions assume cumulative content knowledge from this chapter and previous chapters.

1. Identify five different historical arguments discussed regarding "McCarthyism."
2. How might a sociocultural approach to an analysis of the subject differ from a purely political approach?
3. With which historical argument discussed regarding the origins of the Cold War do you most agree? Explain why, supporting your argument with historical evidence.

Work, Exchange, and Technology: Explain the Cold War's impact on the American economy both in regard to foreign trade and domestic production.

Politics and Power: Explain the movement of American public opinion to a more conservative posture as reflected by the election of 1952.

America and the World: Explain how the Cold War altered the relationship of the United States within American-bloc, Soviet-bloc, and non-aligned nations.

Ideas, Beliefs, and Culture: Explain the ways in which the Cold War altered American perceptions about foreign affairs and challenges to the establishment.

AP SUGGESTED STUDY

PEOPLE/PLACES/EVENTS As you study these items, think about how they demonstrate or relate to key concepts and historical themes from this chapter and previous chapters.

AP TEST PRACTICE

Questions assume cumulative content knowledge from this chapter and previous chapters.

MULTIPLE CHOICE Use the map on page 739 and your knowledge of U.S. history to answer questions 1-3.

1. The political division of countries as shown on the map was most directly a result of

   (A) The Soviet Union's economic goals for free trade

   (B) America's policy of containment against the Soviet Union

   (C) America's commitment to maintaining military power at wartime levels

   (D) America's and the Soviet Union's desire to have an international, peaceful order

2. Which best explains the reasoning for America's economic policy in the years immediately following World War II towards the countries allied with it?

   (A) The U.S. wanted to prevent Asia's growth into an economic power.

   (B) The U.S. wanted to prevent disputes between the nations that were a part of its alliance.

   (C) The U.S. wanted to pursue the vision of an international organization that would enforce the right of every nation to self-determination.

   (D) Strong economies would help the pro-American governments of these nations solidify their power against domestic Communist forces.

3. Which best describes how American foreign policy toward the Cold War shifted in 1950?

   (A) U.S. policy became less aggressive, asserting that other nations needed to take active responsibility for stopping communist expansion within their own nations.

   (B) The U.S. policy took a more aggressive stance, in which it asserted it should take active leadership in stopping communist expansion anywhere in the world.

   (C) The U.S. added many Asian countries into the alliance, to stem any chance of the spread of communism.

   (D) The U.S. asserted that it would only protect countries from communist expansion only in instances in which the country was of vital interest to America.

SHORT ANSWER Use your knowledge of U.S. history to answer questions 4-5.

4. Use the political cartoon on page 738 to answer a, b, and c.

   a) Briefly explain the opinion expressed by the artist about ONE of the following:

   • The economic state of Western Europe

   • The efficacy of the Marshall Plan

   • Soviet Union's foreign policy

   b) Briefly explain ONE development, not specifically referenced, from the period 1948-1956 that supports the cartoonist's opinion.

   c) Briefly explain ONE way in which developments during the period 1948-1956 challenged the view shown by the cartoon.

5. Answer a, b, and c.

   a) Briefly explain why ONE of the following issues most contributed to domestic political divisions and acrimony in the U.S. in the years immediately following World War II.

   • New Deal

   • Civil Rights

   • Labor

   b) Provide one example that supports your argument.

   c) Choose a second area, and briefly explain why it played a lesser role in contributing to domestic political divisions and acrimony in the U.S. in the years immediately following World War II.

LONG ESSAY For each question below, develop a thoughtful and thorough historical argument that answers the question. Begin your essay with a thesis statement and support it with relevant historical evidence.

6. Some historians have maintained that the second Red Scare following WWII was deeper and more severe than the first Red Scare that followed WWI. Support, modify or refute this analysis by providing specific political, social and economic evidence to back your argument.

7. Evaluate the extent to which the development of the atomic bomb affected American culture in the 1950s.

28 | THE AFFLUENT SOCIETY

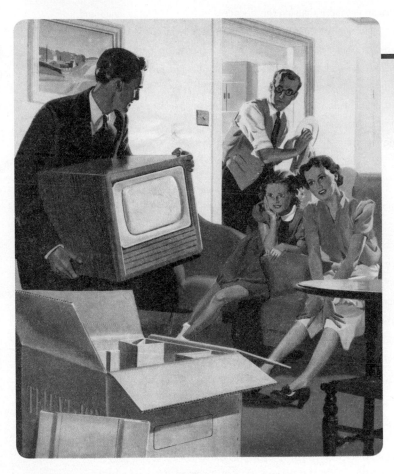

AMERICAN TV The arrival of television into American homes signaled a rapid, pervasive, and profound change in American life. TV viewing affected how Americans experienced entertainment and received their news. Television advertising helped create an enormous market for American products. With television, newspapers, radios, and the movies all lost some of their impact on American culture.
(© Doug Steley C/Alamy (RF))

AP
HISTORICAL THINKING

1. **Historical Causation** Analyze the reasons for the development of a prolonged and robust economy during the 1950s.

2. **Historical Interpretation** Analyze the factors that led to the homogenization of American society during the 1950s.

3. **Historical Argumentation** Analyze the reasons for the growth of the civil rights movement during the 1950s and the degree of success it achieved.

4. **Patterns of Continuity and Change over Time** Analyze the continuity and change in migration patterns in the United States during the 1950s.

5. **Comparison** Analyze the positive and negative effects of increased scientific and technological development during the 1950s.

6. **Historical Argumentation** Evaluate the reasons for and the success of American foreign policy during the 1950s.

7. **Contextualization** Analyze how mass media influenced traditional perceptions of gender roles during the 1950s.

8. **Patterns of Continuity and Change over Time** To what degree and in what ways did post-World War II American society mirror post-World War I society politically, economically, and socially.

Key Concept Correlations

Analyze the ways the historical developments you learn about in this chapter connect to the following AP Key Concepts.

8.1 The United States responded to an uncertain and unstable post-war world by asserting and attempting to defend a position of global leadership, with far-reaching domestic and international consequences.

8.2 Liberalism, based on anticommunism abroad and a firm belief in the efficacy of governmental and especially federal power to achieve social goals at home, reached its apex in the mid-1960s and generated a variety of political and cultural responses.

8.3 Postwar economic, demographic, and technological changes had a far-reaching impact on American society, politics, and the environment.

Thematic Learning Objectives

WOR-3, 4, 7; ENV-5; ID-3, 6, 7, 8; POL-3, 5, 7; CUL-5, 6, 7; WXT-3, 5; PEO-3, 6

CHAPTER 28 focuses on the economic and social fabric of American society during the 1950s. The chapter examines the factors that led to American prosperity during the decade and the role that science and technology played in that development. It also examines the emergence of a significantly stronger civil rights movement and the impact of the movement on American society and on the demands by minorities beyond African Americans. The chapter spends considerable time examining population migration patterns, with special emphasis on suburban and urban migration. Another key focus is the development of a mass consumer society and the responses to the conformity it created. The chapter also focuses on the problems in foreign affairs the U.S. faced in various regions of the world in its attempt to contain communism in light of foreign nationalistic revolutions. As you read, evaluate the following ideas:

- The United States reacted to conflicts in Asia, Europe, Latin America, and the Middle East.
- Decolonization of European colonies forced the Unites States to support their European allies in their attempts to suppress colonial insurrections, leading to deteriorating relations between the United States and rising third world nations.
- The civil rights movement gained momentum following *Brown v. Board of Education* but found progress slow as opponents adopted a policy of massive resistance.
- Despite the emergence of an "affluent society," pockets of poverty continued to persist in the "other America."
- Post-war America experienced an economic boom as a result of government spending, the consolidation of industry, and a dramatically increased birth rate.
- Migration patterns within the United States underwent significant change due to suburbanization, movement from the "Rust Belt" to the "Sun Belt," and white flight from inner-cities.

"THE ECONOMIC MIRACLE"

Among the most striking features of American society in the 1950s and early 1960s was a booming economic growth that made even the heady 1920s seem pale by comparison. It was a better-balanced and more widely distributed prosperity than that of thirty years earlier, but it was not as universal as some Americans liked to believe.

SOURCES OF ECONOMIC GROWTH

Between 1945 and 1960, the gross national product grew by 250 percent, from $200 billion to over $500 billion. Unemployment, which during the Depression had averaged between 15 and 25 percent, remained throughout the 1950s and early 1960s at about 5 percent or lower. Inflation, in the meantime, hovered around 3 percent a year or less.

The causes of this growth and stability were varied. Government spending, which had ended the Depression in the 1940s, continued to stimulate growth through public funding of schools,

GOVERNMENT SPENDING housing, veterans' benefits, welfare, the $100 billion interstate highway program, which began in 1956, and above all, military spending. Economic growth was at its peak (averaging 4.7 percent a year) during the first half of the 1950s, when military spending was highest because of the Korean War. In the late 1950s, with spending on armaments in decline, the annual rate of growth declined by more than half, to 2.25 percent.

The national birth rate reversed a long pattern of decline with the so-called baby boom, which had begun during the war and peaked in 1957. The nation's population rose almost 20 percent in the decade, from 150 million in 1950 to 179 million in 1960. The baby boom contributed to increased consumer demand and expanding economic growth.

The rapid expansion of suburbs–the suburban population grew 47 percent in the 1950s, more than twice as fast as the population as a whole–helped stimulate growth in several important sectors

Births per thousand women 15–44 years old

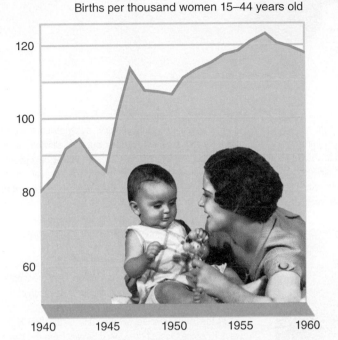

THE AMERICAN BIRTH RATE, 1940–1960 This chart shows how the American birth rate grew rapidly during and after World War II (after a long period of decline in the 1930s) to produce what became known as the "baby boom." At the peak of the baby boom, during the 1950s, the nation's population grew by 20 percent. (© Archive Photos/Getty Images)

• *What impact did the baby boom have on the nation's economy?*

SUBURBAN GROWTH of the economy. The number of privately owned cars (essential for most suburban living) more than doubled in a decade, sparking a great boom in the automobile industry. Demand for new homes helped sustain a vigorous housing industry. The construction of roads and highways stimulated the economy as well.

Because of this unprecedented growth, the economy grew nearly ten times as fast as the population in the thirty years after the war. And while that growth was far from equally distributed, it affected most of society. The average American in 1960 had over 20 percent more purchasing power than in 1945, and more than twice as much as during the prosperous 1920s. By 1960, per capita income was over $1,800, $500 more than it had been in 1945. The American people had achieved the highest standard of living of any society in the history of the world.

THE RISE OF THE MODERN WEST

No region of the country profited more from economic growth than the American West. Its population expanded dramatically; its cities boomed; its industrial economy flourished. Before World War II, most of the West had been, economically at least, an appendage of the great industrial economy of the East. The West provided the East with raw materials and agricultural goods. By the 1960s, however, some parts of the West had become among the most important (and populous) industrial and cultural centers of the nation in their own right. As during World War II, much of the growth of the West was a result of federal spending and investment—on the dams, power

stations, highways, and other infrastructure projects that made economic development possible; and on the military contracts that continued to flow disproportionately to factories in California and Texas, many of them built with government funds during the war. But other factors played a role as well. The enormous increase in automobile use after World War II—a result, among other things, of suburbanization and improved highway systems—gave a large stimulus to the petroleum industry and contributed to the rapid growth of oil fields in Texas and Colorado, and also to the metropolitan centers serving them: Houston, Dallas, and Denver. State governments in the West invested heavily in their universities. The University of Texas and University of California systems, in particular, became among the nation's largest and best; as centers of research, they helped attract technology-intensive industries to the region.

Climate also contributed to economic growth. California, Nevada, and Arizona, in particular, attracted many migrants from the East because of their warm, dry climates. The growth

FAVORABLE CLIMATE of Los Angeles after World War II was a particularly remarkable phenomenon. More than 10 percent of all new businesses in the United States between 1945 and 1950 began in Los Angeles. Its population rose by over 50 percent between 1940 and 1960.

THE NEW ECONOMICS

The discovery of the power of the American economic system was a major cause of the confident tone of much American political life in the 1950s. During the Depression, politicians, intellectuals, and others had often questioned the viability of capitalism. In the 1950s, such doubt vanished. Two features in particular made the postwar economy a source of national confidence.

First was the belief that Keynesian economics made it possible for government to regulate and stabilize the economy without

KEYNESIAN ECONOMICS intruding directly into the private sector. The British economist John Maynard Keynes had argued as early as the 1920s that by varying the flow of government spending and taxation (fiscal policy) and managing the supply of currency (monetary policy), the government could stimulate the economy to cure recession and dampen growth to prevent inflation. The experience of the last years of the Depression and the first years of the war had seemed to confirm this argument. By the mid-1950s, Keynesian theory was rapidly becoming a fundamental article of faith—not only among professional economists but also among much of the public.

The "new economics," as its supporters came to call it, finally won official acceptance in 1963, when John Kennedy proposed a tax cut to stimulate economic growth. Although it took Kennedy's death and the political skills of Lyndon Johnson to win passage of the measure in 1964, the result seemed to confirm all that the Keynesians had predicted: an increase in private demand, which stimulated economic growth and reduced unemployment.

As the economy continued to expand far beyond what anyone had predicted only a few years before, many Americans assumed that such growth was now without bounds. By the mid-1950s, reformers concerned about poverty were arguing

PATTERNS OF POPULAR CULTURE

ON THE ROAD

PEOPLE have traveled across the Americas for thousands of years, often with considerable difficulty. Indians had to make paths over rough terrain. Immigrants from England, Scotland, Mexico, and many other places began to move from town to town often on log roads. Later, they used stones and pebbles to create new byways. Wagons and carriages often rode on bumpy or muddy surfaces. Of course, many years later more-efficient, comfortable roads were built across the American continent, a development that changed American life dramatically.

JACK KEROUAC Beat author Jack Kerouac's *On the Road* captured in literature the energy of a country on the move. The book's emphasis on jazz, beat poetry, and drugs, however, made it a notorious expression of the prevailing counterculture. (© Hulton Archive/Getty Images)

In the mid-twentieth century, automobiles traveled more slowly than they do today. But cars allowed travelers to discover interesting places and meet new people as they moved from town to town. Jack Kerouac, in his famous book *On the Road* (1957), was one of the first to capture in writing the new spirit of automobile travel. "It was drizzling and mysterious at the beginning of our journey," Kerouac wrote as he got his battered car ready. "I could see that it was all going to be one big saga of the mist. . . . We were all delighted, when we all realized we were leaving confusion and nonsense behind and performing our one and noble function of the time, *move*. And we moved!"

In the 1950s, Route 66 was one of the first highways to cross most of the United States, from the West Coast to Chicago. But Route 66 became more than a road; it became a popular symbol of a country on the move. Travelers could drive along the famous highway while listening to the hit song "(Get Your Kicks On) Route 66" on the radio. A television series called *Route 66* depicted characters becoming involved in all sorts of drama as they traveled the storied route.

People traveling long distances, perhaps even across the continent, needed restaurants, motels, and shops, a development that encouraged the creation of fast-food chains, many of which began with drive-in restaurants where customers could be served and eat in their cars. The first drive-in restaurant, Royce Hailey's Pig Stand, opened in Dallas in 1921, followed later in the decade by the White Tower. Ray Kroc's McDonald's opened its first outlets in Des Plaines,

ENDING POVERTY THROUGH ECONOMIC GROWTH that the solution lay not in redistribution but in economic growth. The affluent would not have to sacrifice in order to eliminate poverty; the nation would simply have to produce more abundance, thus raising the quality of life of even the poorest citizens to a level of comfort and decency.

CAPITAL AND LABOR

Over 4,000 corporate mergers took place in the 1950s; and more than ever before, a relatively small number of large-scale organizations controlled an enormous proportion of the nation's economic activity. This was particularly true in industries benefiting

CORPORATE CONSOLIDATION from government defense spending. As during World War II, the federal government tended to award military contracts to a few large corporations. In 1959, for example, half of all defense contracts went to only twenty firms. By the end of the decade, half the net corporate income in the nation was going to only slightly more than 500 firms, or one-tenth of 1 percent of the total number of corporations.

A similar consolidation was occurring in the agricultural economy. As increasing mechanization reduced the need for farm labor, the agricultural workforce declined by more than half in the two decades after the war. Mechanization also endangered one of the most cherished American institutions: the family farm. By the 1960s, relatively few individuals could

756

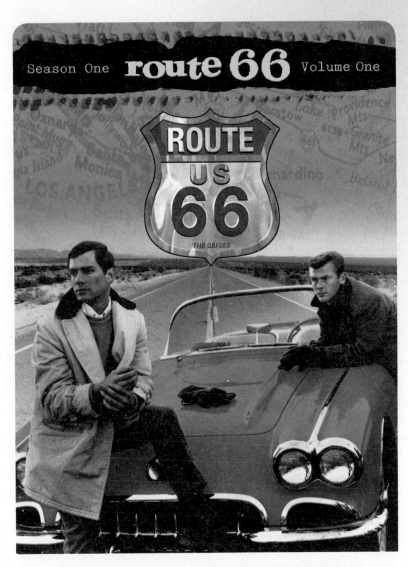

Season One **route 66** Volume One

ROUTE
US
66
THE SERIES

ROUTE 66 The television show *Route 66,* starring George Maharis and Martin Milner, conveyed in popular culture the optimistic energy of a driving nation. (© CBS/Photofest)

Illinois, and southern California in 1955. Five years later, there were 228 outlets. In time, with thousands of restaurants, McDonald's became the most recognizable symbol of food in the world. Large supermarket chains—catering to customers with automobiles—replaced smaller, family-owned markets in town centers. Large centers and shopping malls moved the center of retailing out of cities and into separate, sprawling complexes surrounded by large parking lots.

Eventually, with President Eisenhower's encouragement, the Federal Aid Highway Act of 1956 provided money to build the interstate highway system. This network of highways made it possible for people to travel long distances quickly and efficiently. ●

UNDERSTAND, ANALYZE, AND EVALUATE

1. How did television programs like *Route 66* of the mid-1950s reflect much older American myths about the American West?
2. In what other ways than those described in this feature did the interstate highway system help the American economy?
3. What military advantages did the highway system provide?

any longer afford to buy and equip a modern farm, and much of the nation's most productive land had been purchased by financial institutions and corporations.

Corporations enjoying booming growth were reluctant to allow strikes to interfere with their operations. As a result, business leaders made important concessions to unions. As early as 1948, Walter Reuther, president of the United Automobile Workers, obtained a contract from General Motors that included a built-in "escalator clause"–an automatic cost-of-living increase pegged to the consumer price index. In 1955, Reuther received a guarantee from Ford Motor Company of continuing wages to auto workers even during layoffs. By the mid-1950s, factory wages in all industries had risen substantially.

By the early 1950s, large labor unions had developed a new kind of relationship with employers, a relationship sometimes

THE "POSTWAR CONTRACT" known as the "postwar contract." Workers in steel, automobiles, and other large unionized industries were receiving generous increases in wages and benefits; in return, the unions tacitly agreed to refrain from raising other issues–issues involving control of the workplace and a voice for workers in the planning of production. Strikes became far less frequent.

The economic successes of the 1950s helped pave the way for a reunification of the labor movement. In December 1955,

AFL-CIO the American Federation of Labor and the Congress of Industrial Organizations ended their twenty-year rivalry and merged to create the AFL-CIO, under the leadership of George Meany. Relations between the leaders of the former AFL and the former CIO were not always comfortable. CIO leaders believed (correctly) that the AFL hierarchy was dominating the relationship. AFL leaders were suspicious of what they considered the radical past of the CIO leadership. Even so, the union of the two great labor movements of the 1930s survived; and gradually tensions subsided.

Success bred corruption in some union bureaucracies. In 1957, the powerful Teamsters Union became the subject of a congressional investigation, and its president, David Beck, was charged with misappropriation of union funds. Beck ultimately stepped down to be replaced by Jimmy Hoffa, whom government investigators pursued for nearly a decade before finally winning a conviction against him (for tax evasion) in 1967. The United Mine Workers, the union that had spearheaded the industrial movement in the 1930s, similarly became tainted by suspicions of corruption and by violence. John L. Lewis's last years as head of the union were plagued with scandals and dissent within the organization. His successor, Tony Boyle, was ultimately convicted of complicity in the 1969 murder of the leader of a dissident faction within the union.

While the labor movement enjoyed significant success in winning better wages and benefits for workers already organized in strong unions, the majority of laborers who were as

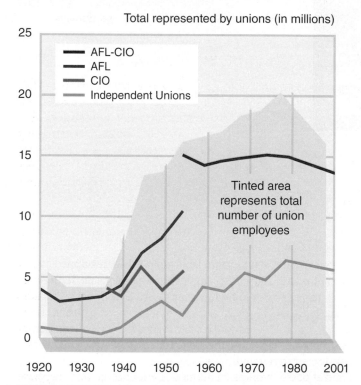

Total represented by unions (in millions)

AFL-CIO
AFL
CIO
Independent Unions

Tinted area represents total number of union employees

WORKERS REPRESENTED BY UNIONS, 1920–2001 This chart shows the number of workers represented by unions over an eighty-year period. Note the dramatic rise in the unionized workforce during the 1930s and 1940s, the slower but still-significant rise in the 1960s and 1970s, and the steady decline that began in the 1980s. The chart, in fact, understates the decline of unionized labor in the postwar era, since it shows union membership in absolute numbers and not as a percentage of the rapidly growing workforce.

• Why did unions cease recruiting new members successfully in the 1970s, and why did they begin losing members in the 1980s?

LIMITED GAINS FOR UNORGANIZED WORKERS

yet unorganized made fewer advances. Total union membership remained relatively stable throughout the 1950s, at about 16 million; and while this was in part a result of a shift in the workforce from blue-collar to white-collar jobs, it was also a result of new obstacles to organization. The 1947 Taft-Hartley Act and the state "right-to-work" laws that it created made it more difficult to form (or even sustain) many unions. The CIO launched a major organizing drive in the South shortly after World War II, targeting the poorly paid workers in textile mills in particular. But "Operation Dixie," as it was called, was a failure—as were most other organizing drives for at least thirty years after World War II.

THE EXPLOSION OF SCIENCE AND TECHNOLOGY

In 1961, *Time* magazine selected as its "man of the year" not a specific person but "the American Scientist." The choice was an indication of the widespread fascination with which Americans viewed science and technology. But it was also a sign of the remarkable, and remarkably rapid, scientific and technological advances in many areas during the postwar years.

MEDICAL BREAKTHROUGHS

A particularly important advance in medical science was the development of new antibacterial drugs capable of fighting infections that in the past had been all but untreatable.

The development of antibiotics had its origins in the discoveries of Louis Pasteur and Jules-François Joubert. Working **ANTIBIOTICS** in France in the 1870s, they produced the first conclusive evidence that virulent bacterial infections could be defeated by other, more ordinary bacteria. Using their discoveries, the English physician Joseph Lister revealed the value of antiseptic solutions in preventing infection during surgery.

But the practical use of antibacterial agents to combat disease did not begin until many decades later. In the 1930s, scientists in Germany, France, and England demonstrated the power of so-called sulfa drugs—drugs derived from an antibacterial agent known as sulfanilamide—which could be used effectively to treat streptococcal blood infections. New sulfa drugs were soon being developed at an astonishing rate, and were steadily improved, with dramatic results in treating what had once been a major cause of death.

In 1928, in the meantime, Alexander Fleming, an English medical researcher, accidentally discovered the antibacterial properties of an organism that he named penicillin. There was little progress in using penicillin to treat human illness, however, until a group of researchers at Oxford **PENICILLIN** University, directed by Howard Florey and Ernest Chain, learned how to produce stable, potent penicillin in sizable enough quantities to make it a practical weapon against bacterial disease. The first human trials of the new drug, in 1941, were dramatically successful, but progress toward the mass availability of penicillin was stalled in England because of World War II. American laboratories took the next crucial steps in developing methods for the mass production and commercial distribution of penicillin, which became widely available to doctors and hospitals around the world by 1948. Since then, a wide range of new antibiotics of highly specific character have been developed so that bacterial infections are now among the most successfully treated of all human illnesses.

There was also dramatic progress in immunization. The first great triumph was the development of the smallpox vaccine by the English researcher Edward Jenner in the late eighteenth century. A vaccine effective against typhoid was developed by an English bacteriologist, Almorth Wright, in 1897, and was in wide use by World War I. Vaccination against tetanus became widespread in many countries just before and during World War II. Medical scientists also developed a vaccine, BCG, against another major killer, tuberculosis, in the 1920s; but controversy over its safety stalled its adoption, especially in the United States, for many years. It was not widely used in the United States until after World War II, when it largely eliminated tuberculosis.

Viruses are much more difficult to prevent and treat than bacterial infections, and progress toward vaccines against viral infections—except for smallpox—was relatively slow. Not until the 1930s, when scientists discovered how to grow viruses in laboratories in tissue cultures, could researchers study them with any real effectiveness. Gradually, they discovered how to produce forms of a virus incapable of causing a disease but capable of triggering antibodies in vaccinated people that would protect them from contracting the disease. An effective vaccine against yellow fever was developed in the late 1930s, and one against some forms of influenza—one of the great killers of the first half of the twentieth century—appeared in 1945.

A particularly dramatic postwar triumph was the development of a vaccine against polio. In 1954, the American scientist **SALK VACCINE** Jonas Salk introduced an effective vaccine against the virus that had killed and crippled thousands of children and adults (among them Franklin Roosevelt). It was provided free to the public by the federal government beginning in 1955. After 1960, an oral vaccine developed by Albert Sabin—usually administered in a sugar cube—made widespread vaccination even easier. By the early 1960s, these vaccines had virtually eliminated polio from American life and much of the rest of the world.

As a result of these and many other medical advances, both infant mortality and the death rate among young children declined significantly in the first twenty-five years after the war (although not by as much as in Western Europe). Average life expectancy in that same period rose by five years, to seventy-one.

PESTICIDES

At the same time that medical researchers were finding cures and vaccines against infectious diseases, other scientists were developing new kinds of chemical pesticides, which they hoped would protect crops from destruction by insects and protect humans from such insect-carried diseases as typhus and malaria. The most famous of the new pesticides was dichlorodiphenyltrichloroethane, generally known as DDT, a compound discovered in 1939 by a Swiss chemist named Paul **DDT** Muller. He had found that although DDT seemed harmless to human beings and other mammals, it was extremely toxic to insects. American scientists learned of Muller's discovery in 1942, just as the army was grappling with the insect-borne tropical diseases—especially malaria and typhus—that threatened American soldiers overseas during World War II.

Under these circumstances, DDT seemed a godsend. It was first used on a large scale in Italy in 1943-1944 during a typhus outbreak, which it quickly helped end. Soon it was being sprayed in mosquito-infested areas of Pacific islands where American troops were fighting the Japanese. No soldiers suffered any apparent ill effects from the sprayings, and the incidence of malaria dropped precipitously. DDT quickly gained a reputation as a miraculous tool for controlling insects, and it undoubtedly saved thousands of lives. Only later did scientists recognize that DDT had long-term toxic effects on animals and humans.

POSTWAR ELECTRONIC RESEARCH

The 1940s and 1950s saw dramatic new developments in electronic technology. Researchers in the 1940s produced the first commercially viable televisions and created a technology that **INVENTION OF TELEVISION** made it possible to broadcast programming over large areas. Later, in the late 1950s, scientists at RCA's David Sarnoff Laboratories in New Jersey developed the technology for color television, which first became widely available in the early 1960s.

In 1948 Bell Labs, the research arm of AT&T, produced the first transistor, a small solid-state device capable of amplifying electrical signals, which was much smaller and more efficient than the cumbersome vacuum tubes that had powered most electronic equipment in the past. Transistors made possible the miniaturization of many devices (radios, televisions, audio equipment, hearing aids) and were also important in aviation, weaponry, and satellites. They contributed as well to another major breakthrough in electronics: the development of integrated circuitry in the late 1950s.

Integrated circuits combined a number of once-separate electronic elements (transistors, resistors, diodes, and others) and embedded them into a single, microscopically small device. They made it possible to create increasingly complex electronic devices requiring complicated circuitry that would have been impractical to produce through other means. Most of all, integrated circuits helped advance the development of the computer.

THE SALK VACCINE Dr. Jonas Salk, a medical researcher at the University of Pittsburgh, developed in the mid-1950s the first vaccine that proved effective in preventing polio. In its aftermath, scenes similar to this one—a mass inoculation of families in a municipal stadium in Evansville, Indiana—repeated themselves all over the country. A few years later, Dr. Albert Sabin of the University of Cincinnati created a vaccine that could be administered more easily, through sugar cubes. (© AP Images)

POSTWAR COMPUTER TECHNOLOGY

Prior to the 1950s, computers had been constructed mainly to perform complicated mathematical tasks, such as those required to break military codes. In the 1950s, they began to perform commercial functions for the first time, as data-processing devices used by businesses and other organizations.

The first significant computer of the 1950s was the Universal Automatic Computer (or **UNIVAC**), which was developed initially for the U.S. Bureau of the Census by the Remington Rand Company. It was the first computer able to handle both alphabetical and numerical information easily. It used tape storage and could perform calculations and other functions much faster than its predecessor, the ENIAC, developed in 1946 by the same researchers at the University of Pennsylvania who were responsible for the UNIVAC. Searching for a larger market than the census for their very expensive new device, Remington Rand arranged to use a UNIVAC to predict the results of the 1952 election for CBS television news. It would, they believed, produce valuable publicity for the machine. Analyzing early voting results, the UNIVAC accurately predicted an enormous landslide victory for Eisenhower over Stevenson. Few Americans had ever heard of a computer before that night, and the UNIVAC's television debut became, therefore, a critical breakthrough in public awareness of computer technology.

Remington Rand had limited success in marketing the UNIVAC, but in the mid-1950s the International Business Machines Company (IBM) introduced its first major data-processing computers and began to find a wide market for them among businesses in the United States and abroad.

These early successes, combined with the enormous amount of money IBM invested in research and development, made the company the worldwide leader in computers for many years.

BOMBS, ROCKETS, AND MISSILES

In 1952, the United States successfully detonated the first hydrogen bomb. (The Soviet Union tested its first H-bomb a year later.) Unlike the plutonium and uranium bombs developed during World War II, the hydrogen bomb derives its power not from fission (the splitting of atoms) but from fusion (the joining of lighter atomic elements with heavier ones). It is capable of producing explosions of vastly greater power than the earlier, fission bombs.

THE HYDROGEN BOMB

The development of the hydrogen bomb gave considerable impetus to a stalled scientific project in both the United States and the Soviet Union—the effort to develop unmanned rockets and missiles capable of carrying the

THE DAWN OF THE COMPUTER AGE This massive computer, powered by tubes, was part of the first generation of mainframes developed after World War II. They served mostly government agencies and large corporations. By the 1990s, a small desktop computer could perform all the functions of this huge computer at much greater speed. (© Time & Life Pictures/Getty Images) new weapons, which were not suitable for delivery by airplanes, to their targets. Both nations began to put tremendous resources into their development. The United States, in particular, benefited from the emigration to America of some of the German scientists who had helped develop rocketry for Germany during World War II.

In the United States, early missile research was conducted almost entirely by the Air Force. There were significant early successes in developing rockets capable of traveling several hundred miles. But American and Soviet leaders were both struggling to build longer-range missiles that could cross oceans and continents—intercontinental ballistic missiles, or ICBMs, capable of traveling through space to distant targets. American scientists experimented in the 1950s with first the Atlas and then the Titan ICBM. There were some early successes, but there were also many setbacks, particularly because of the difficulty of massing sufficient, stable fuel to provide the tremendous power needed to launch missiles beyond

the atmosphere. By 1958, scientists had created a solid fuel to replace the volatile liquid fuels of the early missiles; and they had also produced miniaturized guidance systems capable of ensuring that missiles could travel to reasonably precise destinations. Within a few years, a new generation of missile, known as the Minuteman, with a range of several thousand miles, became the basis of the American atomic weapons arsenal. American scientists also developed a nuclear missile capable of being carried and fired by submarines—the Polaris, which could launch from below the surface of the ocean by compressed air. A Polaris was first successfully fired from underwater in 1960.

THE SPACE PROGRAM

The origins of the American space program can be traced most directly to a dramatic event in 1957, when the Soviet Union

THE SHOCK OF *SPUTNIK*

announced that it had launched an earth-orbiting satellite—*Sputnik*—into outer space. The United States had yet to perform any similar feats, and the American government (and much of American society) reacted to the announcement with alarm, as if the Soviet achievement was also a massive American failure. Federal policy began encouraging (and funding) strenuous efforts to improve scientific education in the schools, to create more research laboratories, and, above all, to speed the development of America's own exploration of outer space. The United States launched its first satellite, *Explorer I*, in January 1958.

The centerpiece of space exploration, however, soon became the manned space program, established in 1958 through the creation of a new agency, the National Aeronautics and Space Administration (NASA), and through the selection of the first American space pilots, or "astronauts." They quickly became among the nation's most revered heroes. NASA's initial effort, the Mercury Project, was designed to launch manned vehicles into space to orbit the earth. On May 5, 1961, Alan Shepard became the first American launched into space. But his short, suborbital flight came several months after a Soviet "cosmonaut," Yuri Gagarin, had made a flight in which he had orbited the earth. On February 2, 1962, John Glenn (later a U.S. senator) became the first American to orbit the globe. NASA later introduced the Gemini program, whose spacecraft could carry two astronauts at once.

Mercury and Gemini were followed by the Apollo program, whose purpose was to land men on the moon. It had some catastrophic setbacks, most notably a fire

THE APOLLO PROGRAM

in January 1967 that killed three astronauts. But on July 20, 1969, Neil Armstrong, Edwin Aldrin, and Michael Collins successfully traveled in a space capsule into orbit around the moon. Armstrong and Aldrin then detached a smaller craft from the capsule, landed

LAUNCHING A SATELLITE, 1961 Four years after the successful Russian launching of the satellite *Sputnik* in 1957 threw Americans into something close to a panic, a Thor-Able Star rocket takes off from Cape Canaveral, Florida, carrying an American satellite. The satellite contained a nuclear generator capable of providing it with extended continuous power for its radio transmitters. (National Archives and Records Administration)

APOLLO 11 Edwin ("Buzz") Aldrin is photographed by his fellow astronaut Neil Armstrong in August 1969, when they became the first humans to set foot on the surface of the moon. They traveled into orbit around the moon in the spaceship *Apollo 11* and then traveled from the spaceship to the moon in a "lunar module," which they then used to return to the ship for the journey home. (NASA)

on the surface of the moon, and became the first humans to walk on a body other than earth. Six more lunar missions followed, the last in 1972. Not long after that, however, the government began to cut the funding for missions, and popular enthusiasm for the program began to wane.

The future of the manned space program did not lie primarily in efforts to reach distant planets, as originally envisioned. Instead, the program became a more modest effort to make travel in near space easier and more practical through the development of the "space shuttle," an airplane-like device launched by a missile but capable of both navigating in space and landing on earth much like a conventional aircraft. The first space shuttle was successfully launched in 1982. The explosion of one shuttle, *Challenger*, in January 1986 shortly after takeoff, killing all seven astronauts, stalled the program for two years. Missions resumed in the late 1980s, driven in part by commercial purposes. The space shuttle launched and repaired communications satellites, and inserted the Hubble Space Telescope into orbit in 1990

(and later repaired its flawed lens). But problems continued to plague the program into the early twenty-first century.

The space program, like the military development of missiles, gave a tremendous boost to the American aeronautics industry and was responsible for the development of many technologies that proved valuable in other areas.

PEOPLE OF PLENTY

Among the most striking social developments of the postwar era was the rapid expansion of a middle-class lifestyle and outlook. The new prosperity of social groups that had previously lived on the margins; the growing availability of consumer products at affordable prices and the rising public fascination with such products; and the massive population movement from the cities to the suburbs—all helped make the American middle class a larger, more powerful, more homogeneous, and more dominant force than ever before.

THE CONSUMER CULTURE

At the center of middle-class culture in the 1950s, as it had been for many decades before, was a growing absorption with consumer goods. That was a result of increased prosperity, of the increasing variety and availability of products, and of advertisers' adeptness in creating a demand for those products. It was also a result of the growth of consumer credit, which increased by 800 percent between 1945 and 1957 through the development of credit cards, revolving charge accounts, and easy-payment plans. Prosperity fueled the automobile industry, and Detroit responded to the boom with ever-flashier styling and accessories. Consumers also responded eagerly to the development of such new products as dishwashers, garbage disposals, televisions, hi-fis, and stereos. To a large degree, the prosperity of the 1950s and 1960s was consumer driven (as opposed to investment driven).

Because consumer goods were so often marketed (and advertised) nationally, the 1950s were notable for the rapid spread of great national consumer crazes. For example, children, adolescents, and even some adults became entranced in the late 1950s with the hula hoop—a large plastic ring kept spinning around the waist. The popularity of the Walt Disney–produced children's television show *The Mickey Mouse Club* created a national demand for related products such as Mickey Mouse watches and hats. It also helped produce the stunning success of Disneyland, an amusement park near Los Angeles that re-created many of the characters and events of Disney entertainment programs.

CONSUMER CRAZES

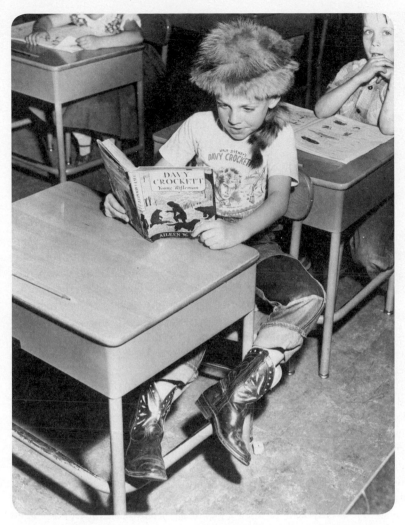

THE DAVY CROCKETT CRAZE In the 1950s Walt Disney introduced a television show about American folk hero Davy Crockett. This boy wears to school his hero's famous "coon-skin" (that is, raccoon skin) cap and Davy Crockett T-shirt as he reads about Crockett. In addition to merchandising products associated with Crockett, Disney believed that it was time for Americans "to get acquainted, or renew acquaintance with, the robust, cheerful, energetic and representative folk heroes" from the American past. (© Bettmann/Corbis)

THE LANDSCAPE AND THE AUTOMOBILE

The success of Disneyland depended largely on the ease of highway access from the dense urban areas around it, as well as the vast parking lots that surrounded the park. It was, in short, a symbol of the overwhelming influence of automobiles on American life and on the American landscape in the postwar era. Between 1950 and 1980, the nation's population increased by 50 percent, but the numbers of automobiles owned by Americans increased by 400 percent.

The Federal Highway Act of 1956, which appropriated $25 billion for highway construction, was one of the most important alterations of the national landscape in modern history.

INTERSTATE HIGHWAYS Great ribbons of concrete—40,000 miles of them—spread across the nation, spanning rivers and valleys, traversing every state, and providing links to every major city (and between cities and their suburbs). These highways dramatically reduced the time necessary to travel from one place to another. They also made trucking a more economical way than railroads to transport goods to markets. They made travel by automobile, truck, and bus as fast as or faster than travel by trains, resulting in the long, steady decline of railroads.

Highways also encouraged the movement of economic activities—manufacturing in particular—out of cities and into surburban and rural areas where land was cheaper. The decline of many traditional downtowns soon followed, as many workers moved outside the urban core. There was rapid growth of what eventually became known as "edge cities" and other new centers of industry and commerce outside traditional city centers.

The proliferation of automobiles and the spread of highways also made it easier for families to move into homes that were far away from where they worked. This enabled many people to live in larger houses with larger lots than they could have afforded previously. Garages began to be built onto houses in great numbers after World War II, and such suburban amenities as swing sets, barbecues, and private swimming pools became more common as backyards became more the focus of family life. The shift of travel from train to automobile helped launch a tremendous proliferation of motels—26,000 by 1948, 60,000 by 1960, well over 100,000 by 1970. The first Holiday Inn (starting what would soon become the largest motel chain in America) opened along a highway connecting Memphis and Nashville, Tennessee, in 1952. Drive-in theaters—a distinctively American phenomenon that had begun to appear in the 1930s—spread rapidly after the war. There were 4,000 drive-ins by 1958.

THE SUBURBAN NATION

By 1960, a third of the nation's population was living in suburbs. Suburbanization was partly a result of important innovations in home-building, which made single-family houses affordable to millions of people. The most famous

"LEVITTOWN" of the postwar suburban developers, William Levitt, used new mass-production techniques to construct a large housing development on Long Island, near New York City. This first "Levittown" (there would later be others in New Jersey and Pennsylvania) consisted of several thousand two-bedroom Cape Cod–style houses, with identical interiors and only slightly varied façades, each perched on its own concrete slab (to eliminate excavation costs), facing curving, treeless streets. Levittown houses, and other, similarly low-priced homes, sold for under $10,000, and they helped meet an enormous and growing demand for housing. Young couples—often newly married and the husband a war veteran, eager to start a family, assisted by low-cost, government-subsidized mortgages provided by the GI Bill (see p. 741)—rushed to purchase the inexpensive homes.

Why did so many Americans want to move to the suburbs? One reason was the enormous importance postwar Americans placed on family life after five years of disruptive war. Suburbs

INTERSTATES The interstate highway system changed the physical landscape of the United States. Its great, sprawling ribbons of concrete—such as this photograph that shows the Hollywood Freeway, Harbor Freeway, and Arroyo Seco Freeway intersecting on multiple levels—sliced through cities, towns, and rural areas. But its biggest impact was in facilitating the movement of urban populations out of cities and into increasingly distant suburbs. (Photo by J. R. Eyerman/© Time & Life Pictures/Getty Images)

provided families with larger homes than they could find (or afford) in the cities. Many people were attracted by the idea of living in a community populated largely by people of similar age and background and found it easier to form friendships and social circles there than in the city. Women in particular often valued the presence of other nonworking mothers living nearby to share the tasks of child raising. Another factor motivating white Americans to move to the suburbs was race. There were some African American suburbs, but most suburbs were restricted to whites—both because relatively few blacks could afford to live in them and because formal and informal barriers kept out even prosperous African Americans. In an era when the black population of most cities was rapidly growing, many white families moved to the suburbs to escape the integration of urban neighborhoods and schools.

Suburban neighborhoods had many things in common with one another. But they were not uniform. Levittowns and inexpensive developments like them ultimately became the homes of mainly lower-middle-class people one step removed from the inner city. Other, more affluent suburbs became enclaves of wealthy families. In virtually every city, a clear hierarchy emerged of upper-class suburban neighborhoods and more modest ones, just as such gradations had emerged years earlier among urban neighborhoods.

THE SUBURBAN FAMILY

For professional men (many of whom worked in cities, at some distance from their homes), suburban life generally meant a rigid division between their working and personal worlds. For many middle-class, married women, it meant increased isolation

from the workplace. The enormous cultural emphasis on family life in the 1950s strengthened popular prejudices against women entering the professions, or occupying any paid job at all. Many middle-class husbands considered it demeaning for their wives to be employed. And many women shied away from the workplace when they could afford to stay at home full-time with their children.

One of the most influential books in postwar American life was a famous guide to child rearing:

DR. BENJAMIN SPOCK

Dr. Benjamin Spock's *Baby and Child Care*, first published in 1946 and reissued (and revised) repeatedly for decades thereafter. Dr. Spock's approach to raising babies was child-centered, as opposed to parent-centered. The purpose of motherhood, he taught, was to help children learn and grow and realize their potential. All other considerations, including the mother's own physical and emotional requirements, should be subordinated to the needs of the child. Dr. Spock at first envisioned only a very modest role for fathers in the process of child rearing, although he changed his views on this (and on many other issues) over time.

Women who could afford not to work faced pressures to remain in the home and concentrate on raising their children. But as expectations of material comfort rose, many middle-class families needed a second income to maintain the standard of living they desired. As a result, the number of married women working outside the home actually increased in the postwar years—even as the social pressure for them to stay out of the workplace grew. By 1960, nearly a third of all married women were part of the paid workforce.

THE BIRTH OF TELEVISION

Television, the most powerful medium of mass communication in the second half of the twentieth century, was central to the culture of the postwar era. Experiments in broadcasting pictures (along with sound) had begun as early as the 1920s, but commercial television began only shortly after World War II. Its growth was phenomenally rapid. In 1946, there were only 17,000 sets in the country; by 1957, there were 40 million television sets in use—almost as many sets as there were families. More people had television sets, according to one report, than had refrigerators.

The television industry emerged directly out of the radio industry, and all three major networks—the National Broadcasting Company, the Columbia Broadcasting System, and the American Broadcasting Company—had started as radio companies. Like radio, the television business was driven by advertising. The need to attract advertisers determined most programming decisions; and in the early days of television, sponsors often played a direct, powerful, and continuing role in determining the content of the programs they chose to

OZZIE AND HARRIET In addition to depicting American life as predominantly white, middle class, and suburban, television in the 1950s and 1960s often portrayed Americans as optimistic and upwardly mobile. Here the Nelson family, characters from the show *The Adventures of Ozzie and Harriet*, enjoys time together in their backyard pool. (© ABC/Photofest)

sponsor. Many early television shows bore the names of the corporations that were paying for them: the GE Television Theater, the Chrysler Playhouse, the Camel News Caravan, and others. Some daytime serials were actually written and produced by Procter & Gamble and other companies.

The impact of television on American life was rapid, pervasive, and profound. By the late 1950s, television news had replaced newspapers, magazines, and radios as the nation's most important vehicle of information. Television advertising

SOCIAL CONSEQUENCES OF TELEVISION

helped create a vast market for new fashions and products. Televised athletic events gradually made professional and college sports one of the most important sources of entertainment (and one of the biggest businesses) in America. Television entertainment programming–almost all of it controlled by the three national networks and their corporate sponsors–replaced movies and radio as the principal source of diversion for American families.

Much of the programming of the 1950s and early 1960s created a common image of American life–an image that was predominantly white, middle-class, and suburban, and that was epitomized by such popular situation comedies as *Ozzie*

TELEVISION'S HOMOGENIZING MESSAGE

and Harriet and *Leave It to Beaver*. Programming also reinforced the concept of gender roles that most men (and many women) unthinkingly embraced. Most situation comedies, in particular, showed families in which, as the title of one of the most popular put it, *Father Knows Best*, and in which most women were mothers and housewives striving to serve their children and please their husbands.

But television also conveyed other images: gritty, urban, working-class families in Jackie Gleason's *The Honeymooners;* the childless show-business family of the early *I Love Lucy;* unmarried professional women in *Our Miss Brooks* and *My Little Margie;* hapless African Americans in *Amos 'n Andy*. Television not only sought to create an idealized image of a homogeneous suburban America. It also sought to convey experiences at odds with that image–but to convey them in warm, unthreatening terms.

Yet television also, inadvertently, created conditions that could accentuate social conflict. Even those unable to share in the affluence of the era could, through television news and other venues, acquire a vivid picture of how the rest of their society lived. And at the same time that television was reinforcing the homogeneity of the white middle class, it was also contributing to the sense of alienation and powerlessness among groups excluded from the world it portrayed.

TRAVEL, OUTDOOR RECREATION, AND ENVIRONMENTALISM

The idea of a paid vacation for American workers, and the association of that idea with travel, entered American culture beginning in the 1920s. But it was not until the postwar years that vacation travel became truly widespread among middle-income Americans. The construction of the interstate highway system contributed dramatically to the growth of travel. So did the increasing affluence of workers, which made it possible for them to buy cars.

Nowhere was this surge in travel and recreation more visible than in America's national parks, which experienced the

CITY ANNEXATIONS

■ Original city (1837)

■ 1837–1889

■ 1890–1939

■ 1940–1990

ORIGINAL SUBURBAN
MUNICIPAL
INCORPORATIONS

■ 1837–1889

■ 1890–1939

■ 1940–1990

CHICAGO'S ANNEXATIONS AND THE SUBURBAN NOOSE This map uses Chicago as an example of two important processes in the growth of American cities—municipal consolidation and suburbanization. In 1837, Chicago consisted of a small area on the shore of Lake Michigan (represented by the small dark orange area on the right center of the map. Over the next fifty years, Chicago annexed an enormous amount of additional land around its original borders, followed by a few smaller annexations in the twentieth century. At the same time, however, many of the areas around Chicago were separating themselves from the city by incorporating as independent communities—suburbs—with a particular wave of such incorporations in the first decades of the twentieth century, continuing into the 1990s. A map of New York, and of many other cities, would reveal a similar pattern.

• *What were the consequences for the city of its legal and financial separation from so many suburban communities?*

beginnings of what became a permanent surge in attendance in the 1950s. People who traveled to national parks did so for many

ECHO PARK reasons—some to hike and camp; some to fish and hunt (activities that themselves grew dramatically in the 1950s and helped create a large number of clubs); some simply to look in awe at the landscape. Many visitors to national parks came in search less of conventional recreation than of wilderness. The importance of that search became clear in the early 1950s in the first of many battles over development of wilderness areas: the fight to preserve Echo Park.

Echo Park is a spectacular valley in the Dinosaur National Monument, on the border between Utah and Colorado, near the southern border of Wyoming. In the early 1950s, the federal government's Bureau of Reclamation—created early in the century to encourage irrigation, develop electric power, and increase water supplies—proposed building a dam across the Green River, which runs through Echo Valley, so as to create a lake for recreation and a source of hydroelectric power. The American environmental movement had been relatively quiet since its searing defeat early in the century in its effort to stop a similar dam in the Hetch Hetchy Valley at Yosemite National Park (see p. 575). But the Echo Park proposal helped rouse it from its slumber.

In 1950, Bernard DeVoto—a well-known writer and a great champion of the American West—published an essay in *The Saturday Evening Post* titled "Shall We Let Them Ruin Our National Parks?" It had a sensational impact, arousing opposition to the Echo Valley dam from many areas of the

SIERRA CLUB REBORN country. The Sierra Club, relatively quiet in previous decades, moved into action; the controversy helped elevate a new and aggressive leader, David Brower, who eventually transformed the club into the nation's leading environmental organization. By the mid-1950s, a large coalition of environmentalists, naturalists, and wilderness vacationers had been mobilized in opposition to the dam, and in 1956 Congress—bowing to the public pressure—blocked the project and preserved Echo Park in its natural state. The controversy was a major victory for those who wished to preserve the sanctity of the national parks, and it was an important impetus to the dawning environmental consciousness that would become so important in later decades.

ORGANIZED SOCIETY AND ITS DETRACTORS

White-collar workers came to outnumber blue-collar laborers for the first time in the 1950s, and an increasing proportion of them worked in corporate settings with rigid hierarchical structures. Industrial workers also confronted large bureaucracies, both in the workplace and in their own unions. Consumers discovered the frustrations of bureaucracy in dealing with the large national companies from whom they bought goods and services. More and more Americans were becoming convinced that the key to a successful future lay in acquiring the specialized training and skills necessary for work in large organizations.

The American educational system responded to the demands of this increasingly organized society by experimenting with changes in curriculum and philosophy. Elementary and secondary schools gave increased attention to the teaching of science, mathematics, and foreign languages (particu-

GROWTH OF SPECIALIZED EDUCATION larly after the launching of the Soviet Union's *Sputnik*)—all of which educators considered important for the development of skilled, specialized professionals. Universities in the meantime were expanding their curricula to provide more opportunities for students to develop specialized skills. The idea of the "multiversity"–a phrase first coined by the chancellor of the University of California at Berkeley to describe his institution's diversity–represented a commitment to making higher education a training ground for specialists in a wide variety of fields.

The debilitating impact of bureaucratic life on the individual slowly became a central theme of popular and scholarly debate. William H. Whyte Jr. produced one of the most widely discussed books of the decade: *The Organization Man* (1956), which attempted to describe the special mentality of the worker in a large, bureaucratic setting. Self-reliance, Whyte claimed, was losing place to the ability to "get along" and "work as a team" as the most valued trait in the modern character. Sociologist David Riesman had made similar observations in *The Lonely Crowd* (1950), in which he argued that the traditional "inner-directed" man, who judged himself on the basis of his own values and the esteem of his family, was giving way to a new "other-directed" man, more concerned with winning the approval of the larger organization or community.

Novelists, too, expressed misgivings in their work about the impersonality of modern society. Saul Bellow produced a series of novels–*The Adventures of Augie March* (1953), *Seize the Day* (1956), *Herzog* (1964), and many others–that chronicled the difficulties American Jewish men had in finding fulfillment in modern urban America. J. D. Salinger wrote in *The Catcher in the Rye* (1951) of a prep-school student, Holden Caulfield, who was unable to find any area of society–school, family, friends, city–in which he could feel secure or committed.

THE BEATS AND THE RESTLESS CULTURE OF YOUTH

The most caustic critics of bureaucracy, and of middle-class society in general, were a group

THE BEAT GENERATION'S CRITIQUES

of young poets, writers, and artists generally known as the "beats" (or, derisively, as "beatniks"). They wrote harsh critiques of what they considered the sterility and conformity of American life, the meaninglessness of American politics, and the banality of popular culture. Allen Ginsberg's dark, bitter poem "Howl" (1955) decried the "Robot apartments! invincible suburbs! skeleton treasuries! blind capitals! demonic industries!" of modern life. Jack Kerouac produced the bible of much of the Beat Generation in his novel *On the Road* (1957)–an account of a cross-country automobile trip that depicted the rootless, iconoclastic lifestyle of Kerouac and his friends.

The beats were the most visible evidence of a widespread restlessness among young

Americans in the 1950s. In part, that restlessness was a result of prosperity itself–of a growing sense among young people of limitless possibilities, and of the declining power of such traditional values as thrift, discipline, and self-restraint. Young middle-class Americans were growing up in a culture that encouraged them to expect rich and fulfilling lives; but they were living in a world in which almost all of them experienced obstacles to that fulfillment.

Tremendous public attention was directed at the phenomenon of "juvenile delinquency," and in both politics and popular culture there were dire warnings about the growing criminality of American youth. The 1955 film *Blackboard Jungle*, for example, was a frightening depiction of crime and violence in city schools. Scholarly studies, presidential commissions, and journalistic exposés all contributed to the sense of alarm about the spread of delinquency–although in fact youth crime did not dramatically increase in the 1950s.

The culture of alienation that the beats so vividly represented had counterparts even in ordinary middle-class behavior: teenage rebelliousness toward parents, youthful fascination with fast cars and motorcycles, and the increasing visibility of teenage sex, assisted by the greater availability of birth-control devices. The popularity of James Dean, in such movies as *Rebel Without a Cause* (1955), *East of Eden* (1955), and *Giant* (1956), conveyed a powerful image of youth culture in the 1950s. Both in the roles he played (moody, alienated teenagers and young men with a streak of self-destructive violence) and in the way he lived his own life (he died in 1955, at the age of 24,

ELVIS Elvis Presley is almost certainly the most famous and influential rock musician of the twentieth century. Born in Mississippi and influenced by the African American of the South, he became a singer in the mid-1950s and continued to be extraordinarily popular until his death in 1977. This photograph shows him very early in his career. (© AP Images)

LUCY AND DESI

THE most popular show in the history of television began as an effort by a young comedian to strengthen her troubled marriage. In 1950, Lucille Ball was performing in a popular weekly CBS radio comedy, *My Favorite Husband,* in which she portrayed a slightly zany housewife who tangled frequently with her banker husband, played by Richard Denning. The network proposed to transfer the show from radio to television. Lucy said she would do so only if she could replace Denning with her real-life husband of ten years, Desi Arnaz—a Cuban-born bandleader whose almost constant traveling was putting a strain on their marriage. Network officials tried in vain to talk her out of the idea. Arnaz had no acting experience, they told her. Lucy herself recognized another reason for their reluctance: the radicalism of portraying an ethnically mixed marriage on the air. But she held her ground.

On Monday, October 15, 1951, the first episode of *I Love Lucy* was broadcast over CBS. Desi Arnaz played Ricky Ricardo, a Cuban bandleader and singer who spoke, at times, with a comically exaggerated Latin accent. Lucille Ball was Lucy Ricardo, his stage-struck and slightly dizzy wife. Performing with them were William Frawley and Vivian Vance, who played their neighbors and close friends, Fred and Ethel Mertz. In the premiere episode, "The Girls Want to Go to a Nightclub," Ricky and Fred want to go to a boxing match on the night of Fred and Ethel's anniversary, while the wives are arranging an evening at a nightclub.

The opening episode contained many of the elements that characterized the show throughout its long run and ensured its extraordinary success: the remarkable chemistry among the four principal actors, the unexpected comedic talent of Desi Arnaz, and most of all the brilliance of Lucille Ball. She was a master of physical comedy, and many of her funniest moments involved scenes of absurdly incongruous situations (Lucy working an assembly line, Lucy stomping grapes in Italy). Her characteristic yowl of frustration became one of the most familiar sounds in American culture. She was a beautiful woman, but she never hesitated to make herself look ridiculous. "She was everywoman," her longtime writer Jess Oppenheim once wrote; "her little expressions and inflections stimulated the shock of recognition in the audience."

But it was not just the great talents of its cast that made *I Love Lucy* such a phenomenon. It was the skill of its writers in evoking some of the most common experiences and desires of television viewers in the 1950s. Lucy, in particular, mined the frustrations of domestic life for all they were worth, constantly engaging in zany and hilarious schemes to break into show business or somehow expand her world. The husbands wanted calm and conventional domestic lives—and time to themselves for conspicuously male activities: boxing, fishing, baseball. In the first seasons, the fictional

LUCY AT HOME Although Lucy and Desi at first portrayed a childless, ethnically mixed couple living in a Manhattan apartment, many of the comic situations in the early years of the show were purely domestic. Here, Lucy, wearing an apron, deals with one of her many household predicaments with the extraordinary physical comedy that was part of her great success. Desi, watching skeptically, was a talented straight man to Lucy's zaniness. (© CBS/Photofest)

couples lived as neighbors, without children, in a Manhattan apartment building. Later, Lucy had a child and they all moved to the suburbs. (The show used Lucy's real-life pregnancy on the air; and on January 19, 1953—only hours after Lucille Ball gave birth to her real

---

in a car accident), Dean became an icon of the unfocused rebelliousness of American youth in his time.

ROCK 'N' ROLL

One of the most powerful cultural forces for American youth was the enormous popularity of rock 'n' roll—and of the greatest early rock star, Elvis Presley. Presley became a symbol of a

ELVIS PRESLEY youthful determination to push at the borders of the conventional and acceptable. His sultry good looks; his self-conscious effort to dress in the vaguely rebellious style of urban gangs (motorcycle jackets and slicked-back hair); and most of all, the open sexuality of his music and his public performances made him wildly popular among young Americans in the 1950s. His first great hit,

"Heartbreak Hotel," established him as a national phenomenon in 1956, and he remained a powerful figure in American popular culture until—and indeed beyond—his death in 1977.

Presley's music, like that of most early white rock musicians, drew heavily from black rhythm and blues traditions,

ROCK 'N' ROLL'S BLACK ROOTS which appealed to some white youths in the early 1950s because of their pulsing, sensual rhythms and their hard-edged lyrics. Sam Phillips, a local record promoter who had recorded some of the important black rhythm and blues musicians of his time (among them B. B. King), reportedly said in the early 1950s: "If I could find a white man with a Negro sound, I could make a billion dollars." Soon after that, he found Presley. But there were others as well. Among them were Buddy Holly and Bill Haley (whose 1955 song

VITAMEATAVEGAMIN One of the most popular episodes of *I Love Lucy* portrays Lucy at a trade show promoting a new health product called "Vitameatavegamin." In the course of the show, she herself drinks a great deal of the concoction, which has a high alcohol content and leaves her hilariously drunk. (© CBS/Photofest)

PROMOTING THE SHOW The marriage of Lucille Ball and Desi Arnaz, which paralleled the television marriage of Lucy and Ricky Ricardo, was one of the most effective promotional devices for *I Love Lucy*. Here, Lucy and Desi pose for a promotional still—one of many they made for advertisements, magazine covers, and posters until their marriage (and the show) dissolved in 1960. (© Photofest)

son and second child—CBS aired a previously filmed episode of the fictional Lucy giving birth to a fictional son, "Little Ricky" Ricardo.)

Lucille Ball remained a major television star for nearly twenty years after *I Love Lucy* (and its successor, *The Lucille Ball–Desi Arnaz Comedy Hour*) left the air in 1960. Desi Arnaz, whom Lucy divorced in 1960, remained for a time one of Hollywood's most powerful and successful studio executives as the head of Desilu Productions. And nearly sixty-five years after the first episode of *I Love Lucy* aired, the series remains extraordinarily popular all over the world—shown so frequently in reruns that in some American cities it is sometimes possible to see six Lucy episodes in a single evening. "People identified with the Ricardos," Lucille Ball once said, "because we had the same problems they had. We just took ordinary situations and exaggerated them." ●

UNDERSTAND, ANALYZE, AND EVALUATE

1. In what ways did *I Love Lucy* reflect American society and family life of the 1950s?
2. How have television situation comedies since *I Love Lucy* copied the formula for success established by that program? Do you see elements of the *I Love Lucy* pattern in today's situation comedies?
3. Why do you think *I Love Lucy* has continued to be so popular, both in the United States and throughout the world?

"Rock Around the Clock"–used in the film *Blackboard Jungle*–served to announce the arrival of rock 'n' roll to millions of young people), who were closely connected to African American musical traditions. Rock drew from other sources too: from country western music (another strong influence on Presley), from gospel music, even from jazz. But its most important influence was its roots in rhythm and blues.

The rise of such white rock musicians as Presley was a result in part of the limited willingness of white audiences to accept black musicians. But the 1950s did see a growth in the popularity of African American bands and singers among both black and white audiences. Chuck Berry, Little Richard, B. B. King, Chubby Checker, the Temptations, and others–many of them recorded by the African American producer Berry Gordy, the founder and president of Motown Records in

Detroit–never rivaled Presley in their popularity among white youths. But they did develop a significant multiracial audience of their own.

The rapid rise and enormous popularity of rock owed a great deal to innovations in radio and television programming. By the 1950s, radio stations no longer felt obliged to present mostly live programming. Instead, many radio stations devoted themselves to playing recorded music. Early in the 1950s, a new breed of radio announcers, known now as "disc jockeys," began to create programming aimed specifically at young fans of rock music; and when those programs became wildly successful, other stations followed suit. *American Bandstand*, a televised showcase for rock 'n' roll hits that began in 1957, featured a live audience dancing to mostly recorded music. The show helped spread the popularity of rock–and made its host, Dick Clark, one of the best-known figures in America among young Americans.

Radio and television were important to the recording industry, of course, because they encouraged the sale of records. Also important were jukeboxes, which played individual songs on 45s (records with one song on each side) and

"PAYOLA" SCANDALS

proliferated in soda fountains, diners, bars, and other places where young people were likely to congregate. Sales of records increased threefold—from $182 million to $521 million—between 1954 and 1960. So eager were record promoters to get their songs on the air that some routinely made secret payments to station owners and disc jockeys to encourage them to showcase their artists. These payments, which became known as "payola," produced a briefly sensational series of scandals when they were exposed in the late 1950s and early 1960s.

THE "OTHER AMERICA"

It was relatively easy for white, middle-class Americans in the 1950s to believe that the world they knew—a world of economic growth, personal affluence, and cultural homogeneity—was the world all Americans experienced; that the values and assumptions they shared were ones that most other Americans shared too. But such assumptions were false. Even within the middle class, there was considerable restiveness—among women, intellectuals, young people, and others who found the middle-class consumer culture somehow unsatisfying, even stultifying. More importantly, large groups of Americans remained outside the circle of abundance and shared in neither the affluence of the middle class nor its values.

ON THE MARGINS OF THE AFFLUENT SOCIETY

In 1962, the socialist writer Michael Harrington created a sensation by publishing a book called *The Other America*, in which

THE OTHER AMERICA

he chronicled the continuing existence of poverty in America. The conditions he described were not new. Only the attention he was bringing to them was.

The great economic expansion of the postwar years reduced poverty significantly but did not eliminate it. In 1960, at any given moment, more than a fifth of all American families (over 30 million people) continued to live below what the government defined as the poverty line (down from a third of all families fifteen years before). Many millions more lived just above the official poverty line, but with incomes that gave them little comfort and no security.

Most of the poor experienced poverty intermittently and temporarily. Eighty percent of those classified as poor at any particular moment were likely to have moved into poverty recently and might move out of it again as soon as they found a job—an indication of how unstable employment could be at the lower levels of the job market. But approximately 20 percent of the poor were people for whom poverty was a continuous, debilitating reality, from which there

PERSISTENT POVERTY

was no easy escape. That included approximately half the nation's elderly and a large proportion of African Americans and Hispanics. Native Americans constituted the single poorest group in the country, a result of government policies that undermined the economies of the reservations and drove many Indians into cities, where some lived in a poverty worse than that they had left. These were the people Harrington had written about in *The Other America*, people who suffered from what he called "a system designed to be impervious to hope."

This "hard-core" poverty rebuked the assumptions of those who argued that economic growth would eventually lead everyone into prosperity; that, as many claimed, "a rising tide lifts all boats." It was a poverty that the growing prosperity of the postwar era seemed to affect hardly at all.

RURAL POVERTY

Among those on the margins of the affluent society were many rural Americans. In 1948, farmers had received 8.9 percent of the national income; in 1956, they received only 4.1 percent. In part, this decline reflected the steadily shrinking farm population; in 1956 alone, nearly 10 percent of the rural population

DECLINING AGRICULTURAL PRICES

moved into or was absorbed by cities. But it also reflected declining farm prices. Because of enormous surpluses in basic staples, prices fell 33 percent in those years, even though national income as a whole rose 50 percent at the same time. Even most farmers who managed to survive experienced substantial losses of income at the same time that the prices of many consumer goods rose.

Not all farmers were poor. Some substantial landowners weathered, and even managed to profit from, the changes in American agriculture. Others moved from considerable to only modest affluence. But the agrarian economy did produce substantial numbers of genuinely impoverished people. Black sharecroppers and tenant farmers continued to live at or below subsistence level throughout the rural South—in part because of the mechanization of cotton picking beginning in 1944, in part because of the development of synthetic fibers that reduced demand for cotton. (Two-thirds of the cotton acreage of the South went out of production between 1930 and 1960.) Migrant farmworkers, a group concentrated especially in the West and Southwest and containing many Mexican American and Asian American workers, lived in similarly dire circumstances. In rural areas without much commercial agriculture—such as the Appalachian region in the East, where the decline of the coal economy reduced the one significant source of support for the region—whole communities lived in desperate poverty, increasingly cut off from the market economy. All these groups were vulnerable to malnutrition and even starvation.

The Inner Cities

As white families moved from cities to suburbs in vast numbers, many inner-city neighborhoods became vast repositories for the poor, "ghettos" from which there was no easy escape. The growth of these neighborhoods owed much to a vast

BLACK URBAN MIGRATION

migration of African Americans out of the countryside and into industrial cities. More than 3 million black men and women moved from the South to northern cities between 1940 and 1960. Chicago, Detroit, Cleveland, New York, and other eastern and midwestern industrial cities experienced a great expansion of their black populations—both in absolute numbers and, even more, as a percentage of the whole, since so many whites were leaving these cities at the same time.

Similar migrations from Mexico and Puerto Rico expanded poor Hispanic neighborhoods at the same time. Between 1940 and 1960, nearly a million Puerto Ricans moved into American cities (the largest group to New York). Mexican workers crossed the border in Texas and California and swelled the already substantial Latino communities of such cities as San Antonio, Houston, San Diego, and Los Angeles (which by 1960 had the largest Mexican American population of any city, approximately 500,000 people).

Why so many inner-city communities, populated largely by racial and ethnic minorities, remained so poor in the midst of growing affluence has been the subject of considerable debate. Some critics have argued that the new migrants were victims, in part, of their own pasts, that the work habits, values, and family structures they brought with them from their rural homes were poorly adapted to the needs of the modern industrial city. Others have argued that the inner city itself—its crippling poverty, its crime, its violence, its apparent hopelessness—created a "culture of poverty" that made it difficult for individuals to advance.

Many others argue that a combination of declining blue-collar jobs, inadequate support for minority-dominated public schools, and barriers to advancement rooted in racism—not the culture and values of the poor themselves—was the source of inner-city poverty. It is indisputable that inner cities were filling up with poor minority residents at the same time that the unskilled industrial jobs they were seeking were diminishing. Employers were relocating factories and mills from old industrial cities to new locations in suburbs, smaller cities, and even abroad—places where the cost of labor was lower. Even in the factories that remained, automation was reducing the number of unskilled jobs. The economic opportunities that had helped earlier immigrant groups to rise up from poverty were unavailable to most of the postwar migrants. Nor can there be any doubt that historic patterns of racial discrimination in hiring, education, and housing doomed many members of these communities to continuing, and in some cases increasing, poverty.

For many years, the principal policy response to the poverty of inner cities was "urban renewal": the effort to tear down buildings in the poorest and most degraded areas. In the

"URBAN RENEWAL"

twenty years after World War II, urban renewal projects destroyed over 400,000 buildings, among them the homes of nearly 1.5 million people. In some cases, urban renewal provided new public housing for poor city residents. Some of it was considerably better than the housing they left; some of it was poorly designed and constructed, and deteriorated rapidly into dismal and dangerous slums.

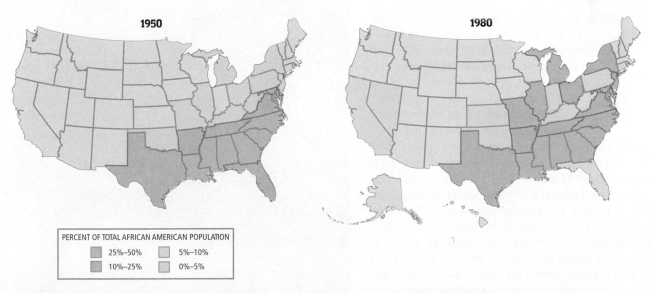

AFRICAN AMERICAN MIGRATION, 1950–1980 Although there had been a substantial migration of African Americans out of the South and into northern industrial cities around the time of World War I and again during World War II, that process accelerated in the thirty years after 1950. By 1980, fewer southern states had black populations that accounted for 25 percent or more of their total population than in 1950. In the rest of the country, the number of states whose black populations exceeded 5 and 10 percent (the states shaded orange and purple) greatly increased.

• *What were some of the factors that produced the African American migration in this period?*

THE RISE OF THE CIVIL RIGHTS MOVEMENT

After decades of skirmishes, an open battle began in the 1950s against racial segregation and discrimination. Although white Americans played an important role in the civil rights movement, pressure from African Americans themselves was the crucial element in raising the issue of race to prominence.

THE *BROWN* DECISION AND "MASSIVE RESISTANCE"

On May 17, 1954, the Supreme Court announced its decision in the case of *Brown v. Board of Education of Topeka.* In consid-

BROWN V. BOARD OF EDUCATION

ering the legal segregation of a Kansas public school system, the Court rejected its own 1896 *Plessy v. Ferguson* decision, which had ruled that communities could provide blacks with separate facilities as long as the facilities were equal to those of whites.

The *Brown* decision was the culmination of many decades of effort by black opponents of segregation, and particularly by a group of talented NAACP lawyers, many of them trained at Howard University in Washington, D.C., by the great legal educator Charles Houston. Thurgood Marshall, William Hastie, James Nabrit, and others spent years filing legal challenges to segregation in one state after another, nibbling at the edges of the system, and accumulating precedents to support their assault on the "separate but equal" doctrine itself. The same lawyers filed the suits against the school boards of Topeka, Kansas, and several other cities that became the basis for the *Brown* decision.

The Topeka suit involved the case of an African American girl who had to travel several miles to a segregated public school every day even though she lived

"SEPARATE BUT EQUAL" DOCTRINE OVERTURNED

virtually next door to a white elementary school. When the case arrived before the Supreme Court, the justices examined it not simply in terms of legal precedent but in terms of history, sociology, and psychology. They concluded that school segregation inflicted unacceptable damage on those it affected, regardless of the relative quality of the separate schools. Chief Justice Earl Warren explained the unanimous opinion of his colleagues: "We conclude that in the field of public education the doctrine of 'separate but equal' has no place. Separate educational facilities are inherently unequal." The following year, the Court issued another decision (known as "*Brown* II") to provide rules for implementing the 1954 order. It ruled that communities must work to desegregate their schools "with all deliberate speed," but it set no timetable and left specific decisions up to lower courts.

In some communities—for example, Washington, D.C.—compliance came relatively quickly and quietly. More often,

"MASSIVE RESISTANCE"

however, strong local opposition (what came to be known in the South as "massive resistance") produced long delays and bitter conflicts. Some school districts ignored the ruling altogether. Others attempted to circumvent it with purely token efforts to integrate. More than 100 southern members of Congress signed a "manifesto" in 1956 denouncing the *Brown* decision and urging their constituents to defy it. Southern governors, mayors, local school boards, and nongovernmental pressure groups (including hundreds of "White Citizens' Councils") all worked to obstruct desegregation. Many school districts enacted "pupil placement laws" allowing school officials to place students in schools according to their scholastic abilities and social behavior. Such laws were transparent devices for maintaining segregation; but in 1958, the Supreme

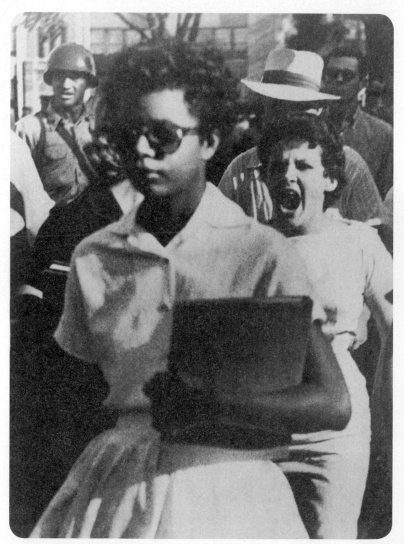

LITTLE ROCK, ARKANSAS African American student Elizabeth Eckford passes by jeering whites on her way to Little Rock Central High School, newly integrated by federal court order. The black students later admitted that they had been terrified during the first difficult weeks of integration. But in public, most of them acted with calm and dignity. (© Everett Collection/SuperStock)

Court (in *Shuttlesworth v. Birmingham Board of Education*) refused to declare them unconstitutional.

By the fall of 1957, only 684 of 3,000 affected school districts in the South had even begun to desegregate their schools. Many white parents simply withdrew their children from the public schools and enrolled them in all-white "segregation academies"; some state and local governments diverted money from newly integrated public schools and used it to fund the new, all-white academies. The *Brown* decision, far from ending segregation, had launched a prolonged battle between federal authority and state and local governments, and between those who believed in racial equality and those who did not.

The Eisenhower administration was not eager to commit itself to that battle. The president himself had greeted the *Brown* decision with skepticism (and once said it had set back progress on race relations "at least fifteen years"). But in September 1957, he faced a case of direct state defiance of federal authority and felt compelled to act. Federal courts had ordered the desegregation of Central High School in Little Rock, Arkansas. An angry white mob tried to prevent implementation of the order by blockading the entrances to the school, and Governor Orval Faubus refused to do anything to stop the obstruction. President Eisenhower responded by federalizing the Arkansas National Guard and sending troops to Little Rock to restore order and ensure that the court orders would be obeyed. Only then did Central High School admit its first black students.

LITTLE ROCK

THE EXPANDING MOVEMENT

The *Brown* decision helped spark a growing number of popular challenges to segregation in the South. On December 1, 1955, Rosa Parks, an African American woman, was arrested in Montgomery, Alabama, when she refused to give up her seat on a Montgomery bus to a white passenger. Parks, an active civil rights leader in the community, had apparently decided spontaneously to resist the order to move. Her feet were tired, she later explained. But black leaders in Montgomery had been waiting for such an incident, which they wanted to use to challenge the segregation of the buses. The arrest of this admired woman produced outrage in the city's African American community and helped local leaders organize a successful boycott of the bus system to demand an end to segregated seating.

The bus boycott owed much of its success to the prior existence of well-organized black citizens' groups. A black women's political caucus had, in fact, been developing plans for a boycott of the segregated buses for some time. They seized on Rosa Parks as a symbol of the movement. Once launched, the boycott was almost completely effective. Black workers who needed to commute to their jobs (of whom the largest group consisted of female domestic servants) formed car pools to ride back and forth to work, or simply walked, at times over long distances. The boycott put economic pressure not only on the bus company (a private concern) but on many Montgomery

MONTGOMERY BUS BOYCOTT

merchants as well. The bus boycotters found it difficult to get to downtown stores and tended to shop instead in their own neighborhoods. Still, the boycott might well have failed had it not been for a Supreme Court decision late in 1956, inspired in part by the protest, that declared segregation in public transportation to be illegal. The buses in Montgomery abandoned their discriminatory seating policies, and the boycott came to a close.

An important result of the Montgomery boycott was the rise to prominence of a new figure in the movement for civil rights. The man chosen to head the boycott movement was a local Baptist pastor, Martin Luther King Jr., the son of a prominent Atlanta minister, a powerful orator, and a gifted leader. At first King was reluctant to lead the movement. But once he accepted the role, he became consumed by it.

King's approach to black protest was based on the doctrine of nonviolence—that is, of passive resistance even in the face of direct attack. He drew from the teachings of Mahatma Gandhi, the Indian nationalist leader; from Henry David Thoreau and his doctrine of civil disobedience; and from Christian doctrine. And he produced an approach to racial struggle that captured the moral high ground for his supporters. He urged African Americans to engage in peaceful demonstrations; to allow themselves to be arrested, even beaten, if necessary; and to respond to hate with love. For the next thirteen years—as leader of the Southern Christian Leadership Conference, an interracial group he founded shortly after the bus boycott—he was the most influential and most widely admired black leader in the country. The popular movement he came to represent soon spread throughout the South and throughout the country.

MARTIN LUTHER KING'S STRATEGY

Pressure from the courts, from northern liberals, and from African Americans themselves also speeded the pace of racial change in other areas. One important color line had been breached as early as 1947, when the Brooklyn Dodgers signed Jackie Robinson as the first African American to play Major League baseball. By the mid-1950s, blacks had established themselves as a powerful force in almost all professional sports. Within the government, President Eisenhower completed the integration of the armed forces, attempted to desegregate the federal workforce, and in 1957 signed a civil rights act (passed, without active support from the White House, by a Democratic Congress) providing federal protection for African Americans who wished to register to vote. It was a weak bill, with few mechanisms for enforcement, but it was the first civil rights bill of any kind to win passage since the end of Reconstruction, and it served as a signal that the executive and legislative branches were beginning to join the judiciary in the federal commitment to the "Second Reconstruction."

CAUSES OF THE CIVIL RIGHTS MOVEMENT

Why did a civil rights movement begin to emerge at this particular moment? The injustices it challenged and the goals it promoted were hardly new; in theory, African Americans could have launched the same movement fifty or a hundred years earlier, or decades later. Why did they do so in the 1950s and 1960s?

Several factors contributed to the rise of African American protest in these years. The legacy of World War II was one of

LEGACY OF WORLD WAR II

the most important. Millions of black men and women had served in the military or worked in war plants during the war and had derived from the experience a broader view of the world, and of their place in it.

Another factor was the growth of an urban black middle class, which had been developing for decades but which began

URBAN BLACK MIDDLE CLASS

to flourish after the war. Much of the impetus for the civil rights movement came from the leaders of urban black communities–ministers, educators, professionals–and much of it came as well from students at black colleges and universities, which had expanded significantly in the previous decades. Men and women with education and a stake in society were often more aware of the obstacles to their advancement than poorer and more oppressed people, to whom the possibility of advancement may have seemed too remote even to consider. And urban blacks had considerably more freedom to associate with one another and to develop independent institutions than did rural blacks, who were often under the very direct supervision of white landowners.

Television and other forms of popular culture were another factor in the rising consciousness of racism among blacks. More than any previous generation, postwar African Americans had constant, vivid reminders of how the white majority lived–of the world from which they were effectively excluded. Television also conveyed the activities of demonstrators to a national audience, ensuring that activism in one community would inspire similar protests in others. In addition to the forces that were inspiring African Americans to mobilize, other forces were at work mobilizing many white Americans to support the movement once it began. One was the Cold War, which made racial injustice an embarrassment to Americans trying to present their nation as a model to the world. Another was the political mobilization of northern blacks, who were now a substantial voting bloc within the Democratic Party; politicians from northern industrial states could not ignore their views. Labor unions with substantial black memberships also played an important part in supporting (and funding) the civil rights movement.

EISENHOWER REPUBLICANISM

Dwight D. Eisenhower was one of the least experienced politicians to serve in the White House in the twentieth century. He was also among the most popular and politically successful presidents of the postwar era. At home, he pursued essentially moderate policies, avoiding most new initiatives but accepting the work of earlier reformers. Abroad, he continued and even intensified American commitments to oppose communism

but brought to some of those commitments a measure of restraint that his successors did not always match.

"WHAT WAS GOOD FOR . . . GENERAL MOTORS"

The first Republican administration in twenty years staffed itself with men drawn from the same quarter as those who

BUSINESS LEADERS' NEW OUTLOOK

had staffed Republican administrations in the 1920s: the business community. But by the 1950s, many business leaders had acquired a social and political outlook very different from that of their predecessors. Above all, many had reconciled themselves to at least the broad outlines of the Keynesian welfare state the New Deal had launched. Indeed, some corporate leaders had come to see it as something that actually benefited them–by helping maintain social order, by increasing mass purchasing power, and by stabilizing labor relations.

To his cabinet, Eisenhower appointed wealthy corporate lawyers and business executives who were not apologetic about their backgrounds. Charles Wilson, president of General Motors, assured senators considering his nomination for secretary of defense that he foresaw no conflict of interest because he was certain that "what was good for our country was good for General Motors, and vice versa."

Eisenhower's consistent inclination was to limit federal activities and encourage private enterprise. He supported the private rather than public development of natural resources. To the chagrin of farmers, he lowered federal support for farm prices. He also removed the last limited wage and price controls maintained by the Truman administration. He opposed the creation of new social service programs such as national health insurance. He strove constantly to reduce federal expenditures (even during the recession of 1958) and balance the budget. He ended 1960, his last full year in office, with a $1 billion budget surplus.

THE SURVIVAL OF THE WELFARE STATE

The president took few new initiatives in domestic policy, but he resisted pressure from the right wing of his party to disman-

FEDERAL HIGHWAY ACT OF 1956

tle those welfare policies of the New Deal that had survived the conservative assaults of the war years and after. He agreed to extend the Social Security system to an additional 10 million people and unemployment compensation to an additional 4 million, and he agreed to increase the legal minimum hourly wage from 75 cents to $1. Perhaps the most significant legislative accomplishment of the Eisenhower administration was the Federal Highway Act of 1956, which authorized $25 billion for a ten-year project that built over 40,000 miles of interstate highways–the largest public works project in American history. The program was to be funded through a highway "trust fund," whose revenues would come from new taxes on the purchase of fuel, automobiles, trucks, and tires.

In 1956, Eisenhower ran for a second term, even though he had suffered a serious heart attack the previous year. With Adlai Stevenson opposing him once again, he won by another, even greater landslide, receiving nearly 57 percent of the popular vote and 457 electoral votes to Stevenson's 73. Democrats retained control of both houses of Congress, which they had won back in 1954. And in 1958–during a serious recession–they increased that control by substantial margins.

THE DECLINE OF MCCARTHYISM

The Eisenhower administration did little in its first years in office to discourage the anticommunist furor that had gripped the nation. By 1954, however, the crusade against subversion was beginning to produce significant popular opposition–an indication that the anticommunist passion of several years earlier was beginning to abate. The clearest signal of that change was the political demise of Senator Joseph McCarthy.

During the first year of the Eisenhower administration, McCarthy continued to operate with impunity. But in January 1954 he overreached when he attacked Secretary of the Army Robert Stevens and the armed services in general. At that point, the administration and influential members of Congress organized a special investigation of the charges, which became known as the Army-McCarthy hearings. They were among the first congressional hearings to be nationally televised. The result was devastating to McCarthy. Watching McCarthy in action–bullying witnesses, hurling groundless (and often cruel) accusations, evading issues–much of the public began to see him as a villain, and even a buffoon. In December 1954, the Senate voted 67 to 22 to condemn him

ARMY-MCCARTHY HEARINGS

for "conduct unbecoming a senator." Three years later, with little public support left, he died–a victim, apparently, of complications arising from alcoholism.

EISENHOWER, DULLES, AND THE COLD WAR

The threat of nuclear war with the Soviet Union created a sense of high anxiety in international relations in the 1950s. But the nuclear threat had another effect as well. With the potential devastation of an atomic war so enormous, both superpowers began to edge away from direct confrontations. The attention of both the United States and the Soviet Union began to turn to the rapidly escalating instability in the poor and developing nations of the Third World.

DULLES AND "MASSIVE RETALIATION"

Eisenhower's secretary of state, and (except for the president himself) the dominant figure in the nation's foreign policy in the 1950s, was John Foster Dulles, an aristocratic corporate lawyer with a stern moral revulsion to communism. He entered office denouncing the containment policies of the Truman years as excessively passive, arguing that the United States should pursue an active program of "liberation," which would lead to a "rollback" of communist expansion. Once in power, however, he had to defer to the more moderate views of the president himself.

The most prominent of Dulles's innovations was the policy of "massive retaliation," which Dulles announced early in 1954.

The United States would, he explained, respond to communist threats to its allies not by using conventional forces in local conflicts (a policy that had led to so much frustration in Korea) but by relying on "the deterrent of massive retaliatory power" (by which he meant nuclear weapons). In part, the new doctrines reflected Dulles's inclination for tense confrontations, an approach he once defined as "brinksmanship"–pushing the Soviet Union to the brink of war in order to exact concessions. But the real force behind the massive-retaliation policy was economics. With pressure growing both in and out of government for a reduction in American military expenditures, an increasing reliance on atomic weapons seemed to promise, as some advocates put it, "more bang for the buck."

ECONOMIC BENEFITS OF "MASSIVE RETALIATION"

FRANCE, AMERICA, AND VIETNAM

What had been the most troubling foreign policy concern of the Truman years–the war in Korea–plagued the Eisenhower administration only briefly. On July 27, 1953, negotiators at Panmunjom finally signed an agreement ending the hostilities. Each antagonist was to withdraw its troops a mile and a half from the existing battle line, which ran roughly along the 38th parallel, the prewar border between North and South Korea. A conference in Geneva was to consider means by which to reunite the nation peacefully–although in fact the 1954 meeting produced no agreement and left the cease-fire line as the apparently permanent border between the two countries.

Almost simultaneously, however, the United States was being drawn into a long, bitter struggle in Southeast Asia. Vietnam, a colony of France, was facing strong opposition from nationalists, led by Ho Chi Minh, a communist.

When French troops became surrounded in a disastrous siege in North Vietnam, only American intervention, it was clear, could prevent the total collapse of the French military effort. Yet despite the urgings of Secretary of State Dulles, Vice President Nixon, and others, Eisenhower refused to permit direct American military intervention in Vietnam, claiming that neither Congress nor America's other allies would support such action.

DIEN BIEN PHU

COLD WAR CRISES

American foreign policy in the 1950s rested on a reasonably consistent foundation: the containment policy, as revised by the Truman and Eisenhower administrations. But the nation's leaders spent much of their time reacting to both real and imagined crises in far-flung areas of the world. Among the Cold War challenges the Eisenhower administration

EISENHOWER AND DULLES Although President Eisenhower was a somewhat colorless television personality, his was the first administration to make extensive use of the new medium to promote its policies and dramatize its actions. The president's press conferences were frequently televised, and on several occasions Secretary of State John Foster Dulles reported to the president in front of the cameras. Dulles is shown here in the Oval Office on May 17, 1955, reporting after his return from Europe, where he had signed the treaty restoring sovereignty to Austria. (© AP Images)

confronted were a series of crises in the Middle East, a region in which the United States had been little involved until after World War II.

On May 14, 1948, after years of Zionist efforts and a dramatic decision by the new United Nations, Israel proclaimed its independence. President Truman recog-

RECOGNIZING ISRAEL nized the new Jewish homeland the next day. But the creation of Israel, while it resolved some conflicts, created others. Palestinian Arabs, unwilling to accept being displaced from what they considered their own country, joined with Israel's Arab neighbors and fought determinedly against the new state in 1948—the first of several Arab-Israeli wars.

Committed as the American government was to Israel, it was also concerned about the stability and friendliness of the Arab regimes in the oil-rich Middle East, in which American petroleum companies had major investments. Thus the United States reacted with alarm as it watched Mohammad Mossadegh, the nationalist prime minister of Iran, begin to resist the presence of Western corporations in his nation in the early 1950s. In 1953, the American CIA joined forces with conservative Iranian military leaders to engineer a coup that drove Mossadegh from office. To replace him, the CIA helped elevate the young shah of Iran, Mohammad Reza Pahlevi, from his position as token constitutional monarch to that of virtually absolute ruler. The shah remained closely tied to the United States for the next twenty-five years.

American policy was less effective in dealing with the nationalist government of Egypt, under the leadership of General Gamal Abdel Nasser, which began to develop a trade relationship with the Soviet Union in the

SUEZ CRISIS early 1950s. In 1956, to punish Nasser for his friendliness toward the communists, Dulles withdrew American offers to assist in building the great Aswan Dam across the Nile. A week later, Nasser retaliated by seizing control of the Suez Canal from the British, saying that he would use the income from it to build the dam himself.

On October 29, 1956, Israeli forces attacked Egypt. The next day the British and French landed troops in the Suez to drive the Egyptians from the canal. Dulles and Eisenhower feared that the Suez crisis would drive the Arab states toward the Soviet Union and precipitate a new world war. By refusing to support the invasion, and by joining in a United Nations denunciation of it, the United States helped pressure the French and British to withdraw and helped persuade Israel to agree to a truce with Egypt.

Cold War concerns affected American relations in Latin America as well. In 1954, the Eisenhower administration ordered the CIA to help topple the new, leftist government of Jacobo Arbenz Guzmán in Guatemala, a regime that Dulles (responding to the entreaties of the United Fruit Company, a major investor in Guatemala fearful of Arbenz) argued was potentially communist.

No nation in the region had been more closely tied to America than Cuba. Its leader, Fulgencio Batista, had ruled as a military dictator since 1952, when with American assistance

FIDEL CASTRO he had toppled a more moderate government. Cuba's relatively prosperous economy had become a virtual fiefdom of American corporations, which controlled almost all the island's natural resources and had cornered over half the vital sugar crop. American organized-crime syndicates controlled much of Havana's lucrative hotel and nightlife business. In 1957, a popular movement of resistance to the Batista regime began to gather strength under the leadership of Fidel Castro. On January 1, 1959, with Batista having fled to exile in Spain, Castro marched into Havana and established a new government.

Castro soon began implementing radical policies of land reform and expropriating foreign-owned businesses and resources. Cuban-American relations deteriorated rapidly as a result. When Castro began accepting assistance from the Soviet Union in 1960, the United States cut back the "quota" by which Cuba could export sugar to America at a favored price. Early in 1961, as one of its last acts, the Eisenhower administration severed diplomatic relations with Castro. Isolated by the United States, Castro soon cemented an alliance with the Soviet Union.

EUROPE AND THE SOVIET UNION

Although the problems of the Third World were moving slowly toward the center of American foreign policy, the direct relationship with the Soviet Union and the effort to resist communist expansion in Europe remained the principal concerns of the Eisenhower administration. In 1955,

HUNGARIAN REVOLUTION OF 1956

Eisenhower and other NATO leaders met with the Soviet premier, Nikolai Bulganin, at a cordial summit conference in Geneva. But when a subsequent conference of foreign ministers met to try to resolve specific issues, they could find no basis for agreement. Relations between the Soviet Union and the West soured further in 1956 in response to the Hungarian Revolution. Hungarian dissidents had launched a popular uprising in November to demand democratic reforms. Before the month was out, Soviet tanks and troops entered Budapest to crush the uprising and restore an orthodox, pro-Soviet regime. The Eisenhower administration refused to intervene.

THE U-2 CRISIS

In November 1958, Nikita Khrushchev, who had succeeded Bulganin as Soviet premier and Communist Party chief earlier that year, renewed the demands of his predecessors that the NATO powers abandon West Berlin. When the United States and its allies predictably refused, Khrushchev suggested

THE CUBAN REVOLUTION Fidel Castro is shown here in the Cuban jungle in 1957 with a small group of his staff and their revolutionary forces. Kneeling in the foreground is Castro's brother Raoul. Two years later, Castro's forces toppled the existing government and elevated Fidel to the nation's leadership, where he remained for almost fifty years. (© Bettmann/Corbis)

that he and Eisenhower discuss the issue personally, both in visits to each other's countries and at a summit meeting in Paris in 1960. The United States agreed. Khrushchev's 1959 visit to America produced a cool but mostly polite public response. Plans proceeded for the summit conference and for Eisenhower's visit to Moscow shortly thereafter. Only days before the scheduled beginning of the Paris meeting, however, the Soviet Union announced that it had shot down an American U-2, a high-altitude spy plane, over Russian territory. Its pilot, Francis Gary Powers, was in captivity. Khrushchev lashed out angrily at the American incursion into Soviet air space, breaking up the Paris summit almost before it could begin and withdrawing his invitation to Eisenhower to visit the Soviet Union.

After eight years in office, Eisenhower had failed to eliminate, and in some respects had actually increased, the tensions between the United States and the Soviet Union. Yet

EISENHOWER'S RESTRAINT

Eisenhower had brought to the Cold War his own sense of the limits of American power. He had resisted military intervention in Vietnam. And he had placed a measure of restraint on those who urged the creation of an enormous American military establishment. In his Farewell Address in January 1961, he warned of the "unwarranted influence" of a vast "military-industrial complex." His caution, in both domestic and international affairs, stood in marked contrast to the attitudes of his successors, who argued that the United States must act more boldly and aggressively on behalf of its goals at home and abroad.

AP CONNECTING THEMES

Chapter 28 discussed the social and economic fabric of American society in the 1950s. As you review the chapter, you should focus on the reasons behind and results of economic growth in the post-World War II era. You should be able to compare and contrast the 1950s with other periods of U.S. history, particularly, the Gilded Age, the 1920s, and, eventually, the 1980s. Focus on the factors which encouraged conformity of thought in the 1950s and particularly how mass media reinforced traditional stereotypes. Understand the background, strategies, and results of the civil rights movement and resistance to it. You should think about the role of the baby boom and youth culture in challenging the traditional values of established society. Important as well is the consideration of the degree to which the 1950s attempted to dislodge New Deal programs and the degree to which it accepted them. Be able to analyze the problems U.S. foreign policy makers faced as former colonies of U.S. allies staged nationalistic rebellions.

The following themes have a heightened importance in Chapter 28. You should now be able to do the following for each listed theme:

Identity: Explain the impact of the conformity and the civil rights movement on perceptions of American identity by minorities and women.

Work, Exchange, and Technology: Explain the changes that increased automation and technology brought to the American worker.

Peopling: Explain the changes in migration patterns brought on by increased affluence, white flight, and the baby boom.

Politics and Power: Explain the movement of American public opinion to a more conservative posture as reflected by the election of 1952.

America and the World: Explain the difficulties that foreign nationalistic revolutions posed for the United States and the degree to which those problems were resolved.

Environment and Geography: Explain the growing concern over the impact of new chemical fertilizers and pesticides on the environment.

Ideas, Beliefs, and Culture: Explain the ways in which and degree to which the mass society of the 1950s was similar to and different from the mass society of the 1920s.

AP SUGGESTED STUDY

PEOPLE/PLACES/EVENTS As you study these items, think about how they demonstrate or relate to key concepts and historical themes from this chapter and previous chapters.

ALLEN GINSBERG 767

"BEATS" 767

BRINKSMANSHIP 776

BROWN V. BOARD OF EDUCATION OF TOPEKA 772

DIEN BIEN PHU 776

ECHO PARK 766

ELVIS PRESLEY 768

FIDEL CASTRO 777

J. D. SALINGER 767

JACKIE ROBINSON 773

JACK KEROUAC 767

JOHN FOSTER DULLES 775

JONAS SALK 759

LEVITTOWN 763

MARTIN LUTHER KING JR. 773

MASSIVE RETALIATION 775

MICHAEL HARRINGTON 770

ROSA PARKS 773

SAUL BELLOW 767

SPUTNIK 761

UNIVAC 760

WILLIAM H. WHYTE JR. 767

WILLIAM LEVITT 763

AP TEST PRACTICE

Questions assume cumulative content knowledge from this chapter and previous chapters.

MULTIPLE CHOICE Use the photograph on page 765 and your knowledge of U.S. history to answer questions 1–3.

1. Which of the following economic developments in the 1950s most directly led to the family lifestyle being depicted in the photograph?

    (A) The advent of television

    (B) Proliferation of automobiles and the building of highways

    (C) The growth of large shopping centers away from the urban centers

    (D) Advances in advertising techniques creating a demand for consumer products

2. Which notable feature of American society of the 1950s is most reinforced in the photograph?

    (A) Desire of Americans to live in neighborhoods with families of similar backgrounds and ages

    (B) The increase in the number of homes owning televisions

    (C) Increasing number of women working outside the home in order to maintain a certain standard of living

    (D) Idealized gender roles

3. Which of the following depictions of American society in the 1950's is best illustrated by the photograph?

    (A) Development of a rebellious youth culture

    (B) Increased homogeneity in mass culture

    (C) Cultural anxiety stemming from the Cold War

    (D) Fear of challenges to the traditional family

SHORT ANSWER Use your knowledge of U.S. history to answer questions 4–8.

4. Answer a, b, and c.

    a) Briefly explain ONE example of a significant development in the field of medicine in the 1950s.

    b) Briefly explain a SECOND example of a significant development in the field of chemistry in the 1950s.

    c) Briefly explain ONE example of a significant development in the field of electronics in the 1950s.

5. Answer a, b, and c.

    a) For one of the areas below, identify one event which had negative consequences for the U.S. in the Cold War.

    • Military

    • Ideological

    • Economic

    b) Briefly explain how that event affected the U.S. negatively.

    c) Provide an example or argument that could be used to challenge your view that the event had negative consequences for the U.S.

6. Answer a, b, and c.

    a) For one of the groups below, offer a statement that describes cultural changes it experienced in the 1950s.

    • Military

    • Youth

    • Women

    • Workers

    b) Provide one example that supports your statement.

    c) Provide one example that could be used to support the view that not much changed for the group in the 1950s.

7. Use the photograph on page 772 to answer a, b, and c.

    a) Explain an example of judicial action, which helped lead to the event depicted in the photograph.

    b) Explain an example of African American activism, which helped lead to the event depicted in the photograph.

    c) Explain an example of white American resistance to events like that depicted in the photograph.

8. Answer a, b and c.

    a) Mass consumerism was striking in its social development in the 1920s and 1950s. Briefly explain ONE similarity in the reasons why this development occurred during these two decades.

    b) Briefly explain ONE important similarity in the effects of mass consumerism on American society in both periods.

    c) Briefly explain ONE way in which some responded critically to this consumerism in either period.

LONG ESSAY For each question below, develop a thoughtful and thorough historical argument that answers the question. Begin your essay with a thesis statement and support it with relevant historical evidence.

9. Evaluate the extent to which World War II and the Cold War both positively and negatively affected the development of American society during the 1950's.

10. Evaluate the extent to which governmental actions and decisions in the 1950's contributed to maintaining continuity as well as fostering change in the economic, legal and social lives of African-Americans during that decade of the 1950's.

29 | CIVIL RIGHTS, VIETNAM, AND THE ORDEAL OF LIBERALISM

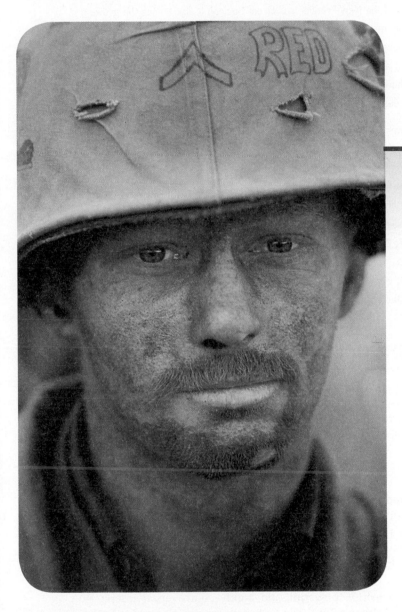

KHE SANH, VIETNAM, 1968 A beleaguered American soldier shows his exhaustion during the 76-day siege of the American marine base at Khe Sanh, which began shortly before the 1968 Tet offensive in Vietnam. American forces sustained record casualties in the fierce fighting at Khe Sanh; the Vietnamese communist forces suffered far more. (© Robert Ellison/Black Star)

AP HISTORICAL THINKING

1. **Contextualization** Analyze the reasons for the realignment of political parties during the 1960s.

2. **Patterns of Continuity and Change over Time** Analyze the impact of growing militancy in the civil rights movement.

3. **Historical Interpretation** Analyze the political, social, and economic impact of the war in Vietnam on American society.

4. **Patterns of Continuity and Change over Time** Analyze the degree to which the civil rights movement of the 1960s resolved issues left unsettled by Reconstruction.

5. **Contextualization** Analyze the factors that led some moderate Americans to abandon the liberal agenda by the late 1960s.

6. **Historical Argumentation** Analyze the degree to which the Great Society was successful in accomplishing its goals and the degree to which it failed to achieve lasting change.

7. **Periodization** To what degree and in what ways could the year 1968 be considered a turning point in U.S. History?

Key Concept Correlations

Analyze the ways the historical developments you learn about in this chapter connect to the following AP Key Concepts.

8.1 The United States responded to an uncertain and unstable post-war world by asserting and attempting to defend a position of global leadership, with far-reaching domestic and international consequences.

8.2 Liberalism, based on anticommunism abroad and a firm belief in the efficacy of governmental and especially federal power to achieve social goals at home, reached its apex in the mid-1960s and generated a variety of political and cultural responses.

Thematic Learning Objectives

WOR-3, 4, 7, 8; ID-3, 7, 8, POL-3, 4, 7; CUL-5, 6, 7; WXT-3; PEO-7

Chapter 29 focuses on the political and social fabric of American society during the 1960s. The chapter examines the factors that led to an initial wave of liberalism in the Kennedy and Johnson administrations and both the realized and unrealized accomplishments of the New Frontier and Great Society. It also traces the growing militancy of the civil rights movement and the impact on eroding support from white Americans and challenges to the established civil rights leaders. Extensive coverage is given to the war in Vietnam and growing concern about how it impacted the economic system and ruptured the social fabric of American society. Finally, the chapter deals with the election of 1968 and how it served to realign political parties and further divide American society. As you read, evaluate the following ideas:

- The United States sought to contain communism in Southeast Asia.
- Protests against the war in Vietnam continued to grow as escalation of the war expanded.
- The war in Vietnam caused significant polarization in American society.
- Civil rights leaders attempted to fulfill post-Civil War promises for African Americans.
- Successes in the civil rights movement encouraged other minorities to protest for equal rights.
- Many civil rights leaders began to pursue a more militant strategy during the mid-1960s.
- Liberalism reached its high point during the Lyndon Johnson administration while at the same time creating a conservative backlash.
- The 1960s witnessed growing concern over the human impact on the environment which led to legislation designed to mitigate and undo some of the damage.

EXPANDING THE LIBERAL STATE

Those who yearned for a more active government in the late 1950s, and who accused the Eisenhower administration of allowing the nation to "drift," looked above all to the presidency for leadership. The two men who served in the White House through most of the 1960s—John Kennedy and Lyndon Johnson—seemed for a time to be the embodiment of these liberal hopes.

JOHN KENNEDY

The presidential campaign of 1960 produced two young candidates who claimed to offer the nation active leadership. The Republican nomination went almost uncontested to Vice President Richard Nixon, who promised moderate reform. The Democrats, in the meantime, emerged from a spirited primary campaign united, somewhat uneasily, behind John Fitzgerald Kennedy, an attractive and articulate senator from Massachusetts who had narrowly missed being the party's vice presidential candidate in 1956.

John Kennedy was the son of the wealthy, powerful, and highly controversial Joseph P. Kennedy, former American ambassador to Britain. But while he had grown up in a world of ease

ELECTION OF 1960

and privilege, he became a spokesman for personal sacrifice and energetic progress. His appealing public image was at least as important as his political positions in attracting popular support. He overcame doubts about his youth (he turned forty-three in 1960) and religion (he was Catholic) to win with a tiny plurality of the popular vote (49.7 percent to Nixon's 49.6 percent) and only a slightly more comfortable electoral majority (303 to 219).

Kennedy had campaigned promising a set of domestic reforms more ambitious than any since the New Deal, a program he described as the "New Frontier." But his thin popular mandate and a Congress dominated by a coalition of Republicans and conservative Democrats frustrated many of his hopes. Kennedy did manage to win approval of tariff reductions his administration had negotiated, and he began to build an ambitious legislative agenda that he hoped he might eventually see enacted—including a call for a significant tax cut to promote economic growth.

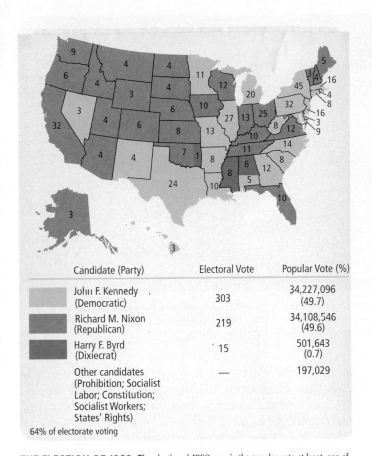

Candidate (Party)	Electoral Vote	Popular Vote (%)
John F. Kennedy (Democratic)	303	34,227,096 (49.7)
Richard M. Nixon (Republican)	219	34,108,546 (49.6)
Harry F. Byrd (Dixiecrat)	15	501,643 (0.7)
Other candidates (Prohibition; Socialist Labor; Constitution; Socialist Workers; States' Rights)	—	197,029

64% of electorate voting

THE ELECTION OF 1960 The election of 1960 was, in the popular vote at least, one of the closest in American history. John Kennedy's margin over Richard Nixon was less than one-third of 1 percent of the total national vote, but greater in the electoral college. Note the distribution of electoral strength of the two candidates. Kennedy was strong in the industrial Northeast and the largest industrial states of the Midwest, and he retained at least a portion of his party's traditional strength in the South and Southwest. But Nixon made significant inroads into the upper South, carried Florida, and swept most of the Plains and Mountain states.

• *What was the significance of this distribution of strength to the future of the two parties?*

More than any other president of the century (except perhaps the two Roosevelts and, later, Ronald Reagan), Kennedy made his own personality an integral part of his presidency

KENNEDY ASSASSINATED

and a central focus of national attention. Nothing illustrated that more clearly than the popular reaction to the tragedy of November 22, 1963. Kennedy had traveled to Texas with his wife and Vice President Lyndon Johnson for a series of political appearances. While the presidential motorcade rode slowly through the streets of Dallas, shots rang out. Two bullets struck the president—one in the throat, the other in the head. He was sped to a nearby hospital, where minutes after arriving he was pronounced dead. Lee Harvey Oswald, who appeared to be a confused and embittered Marxist, was arrested for the crime later that day, and then mysteriously murdered by a Dallas nightclub owner, Jack Ruby, two days later. Most Americans at the time accepted the conclusions of a federal commission, appointed by President Johnson and chaired by Chief Justice Earl Warren, which found that both Oswald and Ruby had acted alone, that there was no conspiracy. In later years, however,

many Americans came to believe that the Warren Commission report had ignored evidence of a broad conspiracy behind the murders. Even after fifty years, some people still believe in the conspiracies associated with the president's assassination. And fifty years after his death, Kennedy's popularity remains high.

LYNDON JOHNSON

The Kennedy assassination was a national trauma—a defining event for almost everyone old enough to be aware of it. At the time, however, much of the nation took comfort in the personality and performance of Kennedy's successor in the White House, Lyndon Baines Johnson. Johnson was a native of the poor "hill country" of west Texas and had risen to become majority leader of the U.S. Senate by dint of extraordinary, even obsessive, effort and ambition. Having failed to win the Democratic nomination for president in 1960, he surprised many who knew him by agreeing to accept the second position on the ticket with Kennedy. The events in Dallas thrust him into the White House.

JOHN KENNEDY The new president and his wife, Jacqueline, attend one of the five balls in Washington marking Kennedy's inauguration in 1961. (Photo by Paul Schutzer/© Time & Life Pictures/Getty Images)

Johnson's rough-edged, even crude personality could hardly have been more different from Kennedy's. But like Kennedy, Johnson was a man who believed in the active use of power. Between 1963 and 1966, he compiled the most impressive legislative record of any president since Franklin Roosevelt. He was aided by the tidal wave of emotion that followed the death of President Kennedy, which helped win

THE "GREAT SOCIETY"

support for many New Frontier proposals. But Johnson also constructed a remarkable reform program of his own, one that he ultimately labeled the "Great Society." And he won approval of much of it through the same sort of skillful lobbying in Congress that had made him an effective majority leader.

Johnson envisioned himself as a great "coalition builder." He wanted the support of everyone, and for a time he nearly got it. His first year in office was, by necessity, dominated by the campaign for reelection. There was little doubt that he would win–particularly after the Republican Party fell under the sway of its right wing and nominated the conservative Senator Barry Goldwater of Arizona. In the November 1964 election, the president received a larger plurality of the popular vote, over 61 percent, than any candidate before or since. Goldwater managed to carry only his home state of Arizona and five states in the Deep South. Record Democratic majorities in both houses of Congress, many of whose members had been swept into office only because of the margin of Johnson's victory, ensured that the president would be able to fulfill many of his goals.

THE ASSAULT ON POVERTY

For the first time since the 1930s, the federal government took steps in the 1960s to create important new social welfare pro-

MEDICARE AND MEDICAID

grams. The most important of these, perhaps, was Medicare: a program to provide federal aid to the elderly for medical expenses. Its enactment in 1965 came at the end of a bitter, twenty-year debate between those who believed in the concept of national health assistance and those who denounced it as "socialized medicine." But the program as it went into effect pacified many critics. For one thing, it avoided the stigma of "welfare" by making Medicare benefits available to all elderly Americans, regardless of need (just as Social Security had done with pensions). That created a large middle-class constituency for the program. The program also defused the opposition of the medical community by allowing doctors serving Medicare patients to practice privately and to charge their normal fees; Medicare simply shifted responsibility for paying those fees from the patient to the government. In 1966, Johnson steered to passage the Medicaid program, which extended federal medical assistance to welfare recipients and other indigent people of all ages.

Medicare and Medicaid were early steps in a much larger assault on poverty–one that Kennedy had been planning in

ETERNAL FLAME The John F. Kennedy Eternal Flame memorializes the slain president. It is located at Kennedy's grave site in Arlington National Cemetery. The site was designed by architect John Carl Warnecke, a long-time friend of the president. (© Getty Images News/Getty Images)

the last months of his life and that Johnson launched only weeks after taking office. The centerpiece of this "war on poverty," as Johnson called it, was the Office of Economic Opportunity (OEO), which created an array of new educational, employment, housing, and health-care programs. But the OEO was controversial from the start, in part because of its commitment to the idea of "Community Action."

Community Action was an effort to involve members of poor communities themselves in the planning and administration of the programs designed to help them. The Community Action programs provided jobs for many poor people and gave them valuable experience in administrative and political work. Many men and women who went on to significant careers in

COMMUNITY ACTION PROGRAM

politics or community organizing, including many black and Hispanic politicians, as well as many Indians, got their start in Community Action programs. But despite its achievements, the Community Action approach proved impossible to sustain, both because of administrative failures and because the apparent excesses of a few agencies damaged the popular image of the Community Action programs and, indeed, the war on poverty as a whole.

The OEO spent nearly $3 billion during its first two years of existence, and it helped reduce poverty in some areas. But it fell far short of eliminating poverty. That was in part because of the weaknesses of the programs themselves and in part because funding for them, inadequate from the beginning, dwindled as the years passed and a costly war in Southeast Asia became the nation's first priority.

CITIES, SCHOOLS, AND IMMIGRATION

Closely tied to the antipoverty program were federal efforts to promote the revitalization of decaying cities and to strengthen the nation's schools. The Housing Act of 1961 offered $4.9 billion in federal grants to cities for the preservation of open spaces, the

HOUSING AND URBAN DEVELOPMENT

development of mass-transit systems, and the subsidization of middle-income housing. In 1966, Johnson established a new cabinet agency, the Department of Housing and Urban Development (whose first secretary, Robert Weaver, was the first African American ever to serve in the cabinet). Johnson also inaugurated the Model Cities program, which offered federal subsidies for urban redevelopment pilot programs.

Kennedy had long fought for federal aid to public education, but he had failed to overcome two important obstacles: many Americans feared that aid to education was the first step toward federal control of the schools, and Catholics insisted that federal assistance must extend to parochial as well as public schools. Johnson managed to circumvent both objections with the Elementary and Secondary Education Act of 1965 and a series of subsequent measures. The bills extended aid to both private and parochial schools and based the aid on the economic conditions of the students, not on the needs of the schools themselves. Total annual federal expenditures for education and technical training rose from $5 billion to $12 billion between 1964 and 1967.

The Johnson administration also supported the Immigration Act of 1965, one of the most important pieces of legislation of

IMMIGRATION ACT OF 1965

the 1960s. The law maintained a strict limit on the number of newcomers admitted to the country each year (170,000), but it eliminated the "national origins" system established in the 1920s, which gave preference to immigrants from northern Europe over those from other parts of the world. It continued to restrict immigration from some parts of Latin America, but it allowed people from all parts of Europe, Asia, and Africa to enter the United States on an equal basis. By the early 1970s, the character of American immigration had changed, with members of new national groups—and particularly large groups of Asians—entering the United States and changing the character of the American population.

LEGACIES OF THE GREAT SOCIETY

Taken together, the Great Society reforms meant a significant increase in federal spending. For a time, rising tax revenues from the growing economy nearly compensated for the new expenditures. In 1964, Johnson managed to win passage of the $11.5 billion tax cut that Kennedy had first proposed in 1962. The cut increased the federal deficit, but substantial economic growth over the next several years made up for much of the revenue initially lost. As Great Society programs began to multiply, however, and particularly as they began to compete with the escalating costs of America's military ventures, federal spending rapidly outpaced increases in revenues. In 1961, the federal government had spent $94.4 billion. By 1970, that sum had risen to $196.6 billion.

The high costs of the Great Society programs, the deficiencies and failures of many of them, and the inability of the government to find the revenues to pay for them contributed to a growing disillusionment in later years with the idea of

FAILURES AND ACHIEVEMENTS OF THE GREAT SOCIETY

federal efforts to solve social problems. By the 1980s, many Americans had become convinced that the Great Society experiments had not worked and that, indeed, government programs to solve social problems could not work. But the Great Society, despite many failures, was also responsible for some significant achievements. It substantially reduced hunger in America. It made medical care available to millions of elderly and poor people who would otherwise have had great difficulty affording it. It contributed to the greatest reduction in poverty in American history. In 1959, according to the most widely accepted estimates, 21 percent of the American people lived below

THE JOHNSON TREATMENT Lyndon Johnson was legendary for his powers of persuasion—for a combination of charm and intimidation that often worked on even the most experienced politicians. He is shown here in the Oval Office meeting with his old friend Senator Richard Russell of Georgia and demonstrating one of his most powerful and unsettling techniques of persuasion: moving so close to the person with whom he was talking as to be almost touching him. (LBJ Library Photo by Yoichi Okamoto)

the official poverty line. By 1969, only 12 percent remained below that line. The improvements affected blacks and whites in about the same proportion: 56 percent of the black population had lived in poverty in 1959, while only 32 percent did so ten years later–a 42 percent reduction; 18 percent of all whites had been poor in 1959, but only 10 percent were poor a decade later–a 44 percent reduction. Much of that progress was a result of economic growth, but some of it was a result of Great Society programs.

THE BATTLE FOR RACIAL EQUALITY

The nation's most important domestic initiative in the 1960s was the effort to provide justice and equality to African Americans. It was the most difficult commitment, the one that produced the severest strains on American society. It was also the most urgent. Black Americans were themselves ensuring that the nation would have to deal with the problem of race.

EXPANDING PROTESTS

John Kennedy had long been sympathetic to the cause of racial justice, but he was hardly a committed crusader. His intervention during the 1960 campaign to help win the release of Martin Luther King Jr. from a Georgia prison won him a large plurality of the black vote. But like many presidents before him, he feared alienating southern Democratic voters and members of Congress.

His administration set out to contain the racial problem by expanding enforcement of existing laws and supporting litigation to overturn existing segregation statutes, hoping to make modest progress without creating politically damaging divisions.

But the pressure for more fundamental change could not be contained. In February 1960, black college students in Greensboro, North Carolina, staged a sit-in at a segregated

SNCC

Woolworth's lunch counter; and in the following weeks, similar demonstrations spread throughout much of the South, forcing many merchants to integrate their facilities. In the fall of 1960, some of those who had participated in the sit-ins formed the Student Nonviolent Coordinating Committee (SNCC), which worked to keep the spirit of resistance alive.

In 1961, an interracial group of students, working with the Congress of Racial Equality (CORE), began what they called

"FREEDOM RIDES"

"freedom rides" (reviving a tactic CORE had tried, without much success, in the 1940s). Traveling by bus throughout the South, the freedom riders tried to force the desegregation of bus stations. In some places, they met with such savage violence at the hands of enraged whites that the president finally dispatched federal marshals to help keep the peace. Kennedy also ordered the integration of all bus and train stations. In the meantime, SNCC workers began fanning out through black communities and even into remote rural areas to encourage African Americans to challenge the obstacles to voting that the Jim Crow laws had created. The Southern Christian Leadership Conference (SCLC) also created citizen-education and other programs–many of them organized by Ella Baker, one of the most successful grassroots leaders of the movement–to mobilize black workers, farmers, housewives, and others to challenge segregation, disenfranchisement, and discrimination.

Continuing judicial efforts to enforce the integration of public education increased the pressure on national leaders to respond to the civil rights movement. In October 1962, a federal court ordered the University of Mississippi to enroll its first black student, James Meredith; Governor Ross Barnett, a strident segregationist, refused to enforce the order. When angry whites in Oxford, Mississippi, began rioting to protest the court decree, President Kennedy sent federal troops to the city to restore order and protect Meredith's right to attend the university.

Events in Alabama in 1963 helped bring the growing movement to something of a climax. In April, Martin Luther King Jr. helped launch a series of nonviolent demonstrations in Birmingham, Alabama, a city perhaps unsurpassed in its commitment to segregation. Police Commissioner Eugene "Bull" Connor supervised a brutal effort to break up the peaceful marches, arresting hundreds of

BIRMINGHAM, 1963 In one of the scenes that horrified many Americans watching on television, police in Birmingham, Alabama, turn fire hoses full force on civil rights demonstrators, knocking many of them to the ground. (© AP Images)

demonstrators and using attack dogs, tear gas, electric cattle prods, and fire hoses—at times even against small children—as

BIRMINGHAM much of the nation watched televised reports in horror. Two months later, Governor George Wallace—who had won election in 1962 pledging staunch resistance to integration—pledged to stand in the doorway of a building at the University of Alabama to prevent the court-ordered enrollment of several black students. Only after the arrival of federal marshals and a visit from Attorney General Robert Kennedy did Wallace give way. His stand won him wide popularity among whites throughout the nation who were growing uncomfortable with the pace of integration. That same night, NAACP official Medgar Evers was murdered in Mississippi.

A NATIONAL COMMITMENT

The events in Alabama and Mississippi were a warning to the president that he could no longer contain or avoid the issue of race. In an important television address the night of the University of Alabama confrontation and the murder of Evers, President Kennedy spoke eloquently of the "moral issue" facing the nation. "If an American," he asked, "because his skin is dark, . . . cannot enjoy the full and free life which all of us want, then who among us would be content to have the color of his skin changed and stand in his place? Who among us would then be content with the counsels of patience and delay?" Days later, he introduced a series of new legislative proposals prohibiting segregation in "public accommodations" (stores, restaurants, theaters, hotels), barring discrimination in employment, and increasing the power of the government to file suits on behalf of school integration.

To generate support for the legislation, and to dramatize the power of the growing movement, more than

MARCH ON WASHINGTON 200,000 demonstrators marched down the Mall in Washington, D.C., in August 1963 and gathered before the Lincoln Memorial for the greatest civil rights demonstration in the nation's history. President Kennedy, who had at first opposed the idea of the march, in the end gave it his open support after receiving pledges from organizers that speakers would not criticize the administration. Martin Luther King Jr., in one of the greatest speeches of his distinguished oratorical career, roused the crowd with a litany of images prefaced again and again by the phrase "I have a dream." The march was the high-water mark of the peaceful, interracial civil rights movement.

The assassination of President Kennedy three months later gave new impetus to the battle for civil rights legislation. The ambitious measure that Kennedy had proposed in June 1963 had stalled in the Senate after having passed through the House of Representatives with relative ease. Early in 1964, after Johnson applied both

public and private pressure, supporters of the measure finally mustered the two-thirds majority necessary to close debate and end a filibuster by southern senators; and the Senate passed the most comprehensive civil rights bill in the nation's history.

THE BATTLE FOR VOTING RIGHTS

Having won a significant victory in one area, the civil rights movement shifted its focus to another: voting rights. During the summer of 1964, thousands of civil rights workers, black

"FREEDOM SUMMER" and white, northern and southern, spread out through the South, but primarily in Mississippi, to work on behalf of black voter registration and participation. The campaign was known as "freedom summer," and it produced a violent response from some southern whites. Three of the first freedom workers to

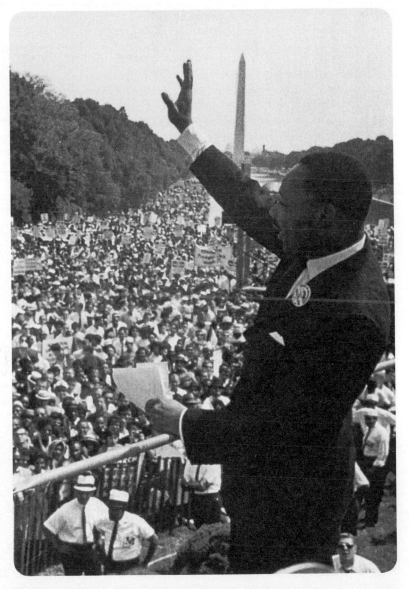

MARTIN LUTHER KING JR. IN WASHINGTON, D.C. Moments after completing his memorable speech during the August 1963 March on Washington, King waves to the vast and enthusiastic crowd that has gathered in front of the Lincoln Memorial to demand "equality and jobs." (© AP Images)

THE CIVIL RIGHTS MOVEMENT

THE early histories of the civil rights movement rest on a heroic narrative of moral purpose and personal courage by which great men and women inspired ordinary people to rise up and struggle for their rights. This narrative generally begins with the *Brown* decision of 1954 and the Montgomery bus boycott of 1955, continues through the civil rights campaigns of the early 1960s, and culminates in the Civil Rights Acts of 1964 and 1965. Central events in this narrative are the 1963 March on Washington, with Martin Luther King Jr.'s famous "I Have a Dream" speech, and King's assassination in 1968, which has often symbolized the end of the movement and the beginning of a different, more complicated period of the black freedom struggle. The key element of these narratives is the central importance to the movement of a few great leaders, most notably King himself. Among the best examples of this kind of narrative are Taylor Branch's powerful studies of the life and struggles of King, *Parting the Waters* (1988), *Pillar of Fire* (1998), and *At Canaan's Edge* (2006), as well as David Garrow's important study, *Bearing the Cross* (1986).

Few historians would deny the importance of King and other leaders to the successes of the civil rights movement. But a number of scholars have argued that the leader-centered narrative obscures the vital contributions of ordinary people in communities throughout the South, and the nation, to the struggle. John Dittmer's *Local People: The Struggle for Civil Rights in Mississippi* (1994) and Charles Payne's *I've Got the Light of Freedom* (1995) both examine the day-to-day work of the movement's rank and file in the early 1960s and argue that their collective efforts were at least as important as those of King and other leaders. Only by understanding the local origins of the movement, these and other scholars argue, can we understand its true character.

Scholars also disagree about the time frame of the movement. Rather than beginning the story in 1954 or 1955 (as in Robert Weisbrot's excellent 1991 synthesis *Freedom Bound* or William Chafe's important 1981 local study *Civilities and Civil Rights,* which examined the Greensboro sit-ins of 1961), a number of scholars have tried to move the story into both earlier periods and later ones. Robin Kelley's *Race Rebels* (1994) emphasizes the important contributions of working-class African Americans, who organized some of the earliest civil rights demonstrations—sit-ins, marches, and other efforts to challenge segregation—long before the conventional dates for the beginning of the movement. Gail O'Brien's *The Color of the Law* (1999) examines a 1946 "race riot" in Columbia, Tennessee, citing it as a signal of the early growth of African American militancy.

Other scholars have looked beyond the 1960s and beyond the South to incorporate events outside the orbit of the formal "movement" in the history of the civil rights struggle. A growing literature on northern, urban, and relatively radical activists emphasizes the challenges facing northern African Americans and the very different tactics and strategies that they often chose to pursue their goals. The enormous attention historians have given to the life and legacy of Malcolm X—among them Alex Haley's influential *Autobiography of Malcolm X* (1965) and Michael Eric Dyson's *Making Malcolm* (1996)—is one example of this, as is the increasing attention scholars have given to black radicalism in the late 1960s and beyond and to such militant groups as the Black Panthers.

arrive in the South—two whites, Andrew Goodman and Michael Schwerner, and one African American, James Chaney—were brutally murdered by Ku Klux Klan members with the support of local police in Neshoba County, Mississippi.

The "freedom summer" also produced the Mississippi Freedom Democratic Party (MFDP), an integrated alternative to the regular state party organization. Under the leadership of Fannie Lou Hamer and others, the MFDP challenged the regular party's right to its seats at the Democratic National Convention that summer. President Johnson, eager to avoid antagonizing anyone (even southern white Democrats who seemed likely to support his Republican opponent), enlisted King's help to broker a compromise. It permitted the MFDP to be seated as observers, with promises of party reforms later on, while the regular state party retained its official standing. Both sides grudgingly accepted the agreement. Both were embittered by it.

A year later, in March 1965, King helped organize a major demonstration in Selma, Alabama, to press the demand for the right of blacks to register to vote. Selma sheriff Jim Clark led local police in a brutal attack on the demonstrators—which, as in Birmingham, received graphic television coverage past

horrified many viewers across the nation. Two northern whites participating in the Selma march were murdered in the course of the effort there—one, a minister, beaten to death in the streets of the town; the other, a Detroit housewife, shot as she drove along a highway at night with a black passenger in her car. The national outrage that followed the events in Alabama helped push Lyndon Johnson to propose and win passage of the Civil Rights Act of 1965, better known as the Voting Rights Act, which provided federal protection to blacks attempting to exercise their right to vote. But important as such gains were, they failed to satisfy the rapidly rising expectations of African Americans as the focus of the movement began to move from political to economic issues.

VOTING RIGHTS ACT

THE CHANGING MOVEMENT

For decades, the nation's African American population had been undergoing a major demographic shift; and by the 1960s, the problem of racial injustice was no longer primarily southern and rural, as it had been earlier in the century. By 1966, 69 percent

BROWN V. BOARD OF EDUCATION This photograph, taken for an Atlanta newspaper, illustrated the long and dangerous walk that Linda Brown, one of the plaintiffs in the famous desegregation case that ultimately reached the Supreme Court, had to travel each day on her way to a segregated school in Topeka, Kansas. An all-white school was located close to her home, but to reach the black school she had to attend required a long walk and a long bus ride each day. Not only does the picture illustrate the difficulties segregation created for Linda Brown, it was also a part of a broad publicity campaign launched by the supporters of the case. (Photo by Carl Iwasaki/© Time & Life Pictures/Getty Images)

Even *Brown v. Board of Education* (1954), the great landmark of the legal challenge to segregation, has been subject to reexamination. Richard Kluger's narrative history of the *Brown* decision, *Simple Justice* (1975), is a classic statement of the traditional view of *Brown* as a triumph over injustice. But critics have been less certain of the dramatic success of the ruling. James T. Patterson's *Brown v. Board of Education: A Civil Rights Milestone and Its Troubled Legacy* (2001) argues that the *Brown* decision long preceded any national consensus on the need to end segregation and that its impact was far less decisive than earlier scholars have suggested. Michael Klarman's *From Jim Crow to Civil Rights* (2004) examines the role of the Supreme Court in advancing civil rights and suggests, among other things, that the *Brown* decision may actually have retarded racial progress in the South for a time because of the enormous backlash it created. Charles Ogletree's *All Deliberate Speed* (2004) and Derrick Bell's *Silent Covenants* (2004) both argue that the Court's decision did not provide an effective enforcement mechanism for desegregation and in many other ways failed to support measures that would have made school desegregation a reality. They note as evidence for this view that American public schools are now more segregated—even if not forcibly by law—than they were at the time of the *Brown* decision.

As the literature on the African American freedom struggles of the twentieth century has grown, historians have begun to speak of civil rights *movements*, rather than a single, cohesive movement. In this way, scholars recognize that struggles of this kind take many more forms, and endure through many more periods of history, than the traditional accounts suggest. ●

AP HISTORICAL ARGUMENTATION AND INTERPRETATION

Questions assume cumulative content knowledge from this chapter and previous chapters.

1. Describe three major strands of historical interpretations of the Civil Rights movement presented in the discussion.
2. Why might historical narratives that focus on the moral purpose and courage of a few great leaders remain the most widely accepted view of the movement?
3. With which historical interpretation presented in the discussion do you most agree? Explain why, supporting your argument with historical evidence.

of American blacks were living in metropolitan areas and 45 percent outside the South. Although the economic condition of much of American society was improving, in the poor urban communities in which the black population was concentrated, things were getting significantly worse. Well over half of all American nonwhites lived in poverty at the beginning of the 1960s; black unemployment was twice that of whites.

By the mid-1960s, therefore, the issue of race was moving out of the South and into the rest of the nation. The battle against school desegregation had moved beyond the initial assault on de jure segregation (segregation by law) to an attack on de facto segregation (segregation in practice, as through residential patterns), thus carrying the fight into northern cities. Many African American leaders (and their white supporters) were demanding, similarly, that the battle against job discrimination move to a new level: employers not only should abandon negative measures to deny jobs to blacks; they also should adopt positive measures to recruit minorities, thus compensating for past injustices. Lyndon Johnson gave his tentative support to the concept of "affirmative action" in 1965. Over the

DE JURE AND DE FACTO SEGREGATION

next decade, affirmative action guidelines gradually extended to all institutions doing business with or receiving funds from the federal government (including schools and universities)–and to many others as well.

A symbol of the movement's new direction, and of the problems it would cause, was a major campaign in the summer of 1966 in Chicago, in which King played a prominent role. Organizers of the Chicago campaign hoped to direct national attention to housing and employment discrimination in northern industrial cities in much the same way similar campaigns had exposed legal racism in the South. But the Chicago campaign not only evoked vicious and at times violent opposition from white residents of that city; it also failed to arouse the national conscience in the way events in the South had.

URBAN VIOLENCE

Well before the Chicago campaign, the problem of urban poverty was thrust into national attention when violence broke out in black neighborhoods in major cities. There were a few scattered disturbances in the summer of 1964, most notably in

Harlem. The first large race riot since the end of World War II occurred the following summer in the Watts section of Los Angeles. In the midst of a seemingly routine traffic arrest, a

WATTS RIOT white police officer struck a protesting black bystander with his club. The incident triggered a storm of anger and a week of violence (and revealed how deeply African Americans in Los Angeles, and in other cities, resented their treatment at the hands of local police). As many as 10,000 people were estimated to have participated in the violence in Watts—attacking white motorists, burning buildings, looting stores, and sniping at policemen. Thirty-four people died during the Watts uprising, which was eventually quelled by the National Guard; twenty-eight of the dead were black. In the summer of 1966, there were forty-three additional outbreaks, the most serious of them in Chicago and Cleveland. And in the summer of 1967, there were eight major outbreaks, including the largest of them all—a racial clash in Detroit in which forty-three people (thirty-three of them black) died.

Televised reports of the violence alarmed millions of Americans and created both a new sense of urgency and a growing sense of doubt among many of those whites who had embraced the cause of racial justice only a few years

before. A special Commission on Civil Disorders, created by the president in response to the disturbances, issued a celebrated report in the spring of 1968 recommending massive spending to eliminate the abysmal conditions of the ghettos. "Only a commitment to national action on an unprecedented scale," the commission concluded, "can shape a future compatible with the historic ideals of American society." To many white Americans, however, the lesson of the riots was the need for stern measures to stop violence and lawlessness.

BLACK POWER

Disillusioned with the ideal of peaceful change in cooperation with whites, an increasing number of African Americans were

SHIFT FROM INTEGRATION TO RACIAL DISTINCTION turning to a new approach to the racial issue: the philosophy of "black power." Black power could mean many different things. But in all its forms, it suggested a move away from interracial cooperation and toward increased awareness of racial distinctiveness. It was part of a long nationalist tradition among African Americans that extended back into slavery and that had its most visible

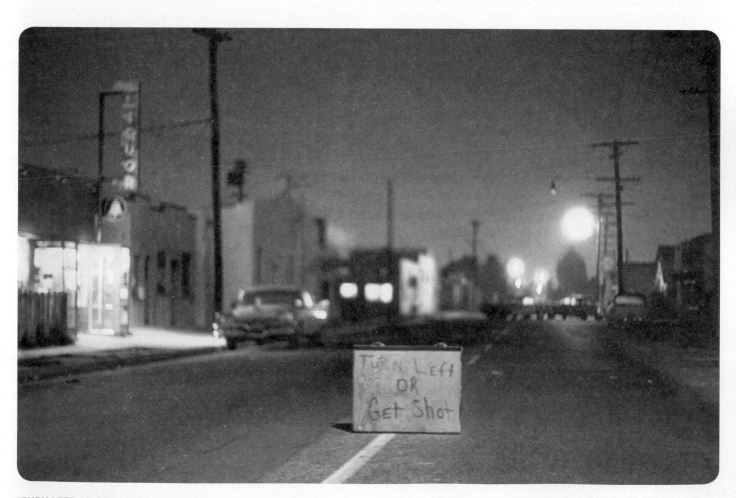

"TURN LEFT OR GET SHOT" This chilling sign, erected at an intersection in the Watts neighborhood in Los Angeles during the 1965 riot there, illustrates the escalating racial tensions that were beginning to explode in American cities in the mid-1960s. (© Bettmann/Corbis)

twentieth-century expression in the Garvey movement of the 1920s.

Perhaps the most enduring impact of the black-power ideology was a social and psychological one: instilling racial pride in African Americans, who lived in a society whose dominant culture generally portrayed African Americans as inferior to whites. It encouraged the growth of black studies in schools and universities. It helped stimulate important black literary and artistic movements. It produced a new interest among many African Americans in their African roots. It led to a rejection by some blacks of certain cultural practices borrowed from white society: "Afro" hairstyles began to replace artificially straightened hair; some blacks began to adopt African styles of dress and new, African names.

But black power had political manifestations as well, most notably in creating a deep schism within the civil rights movement. Traditional black organizations that had emphasized cooperation with sympathetic whites–groups such as the NAACP, the Urban League, and King's Southern Christian

AN INCREASINGLY DIVIDED CIVIL RIGHTS MOVEMENT

Leadership Conference–now faced competition from radical groups. The Student Nonviolent Coordinating Committee and the Congress of Racial Equality had both begun as relatively moderate, interracial organizations; SNCC was originally a student branch of the SCLC. By the mid-1960s, however, these and other groups were calling for radical and occasionally even violent action against the racism of white society and were openly rejecting the approaches of older, more established black leaders.

Particularly alarming to many whites (and to some African Americans as well) were organizations that existed outside the mainstream civil rights movement. In Oakland, California, the Black Panther Party (founded by Huey Newton and Bobby Seale) promised to defend black rights even if that required violence. Black Panthers organized along semimilitary lines and wore weapons openly and proudly. They were, in fact, more the victims of violence from the police than they were practitioners of violence themselves. But they created an image, quite deliberately, of militant radicals willing to fight for justice, in Newton's words, "through the barrel of a gun."

MALCOLM X

In Detroit, a once-obscure black nationalist group, the Nation of Islam, gained new prominence. Founded in 1931 by Elijah Poole

NATION OF ISLAM

(who converted to Islam and renamed himself Elijah Muhammad), the movement taught African Americans to take responsibility for their own lives, to live by strict codes of behavior, and to reject any dependence on whites. The most celebrated of the Black Muslims, as whites often termed them, was Malcolm Little, a former drug addict and pimp who had spent time in prison and had rebuilt his life after joining the movement. He adopted the name Malcolm X ("X" to denote his lost African surname).

Malcolm became one of the movement's most influential spokesmen, particularly among younger blacks, as a result of his intelligence, his oratorical skills, and his harsh, uncompromising opposition to all forms of racism and oppression. He did not advocate violence, as his critics often claimed; but he insisted that black people had the right to defend themselves, violently if necessary, from those who assaulted them. Malcolm died in 1965 when black gunmen, presumably under orders from rivals within the Nation of Islam, assassinated him in New York.

But Malcolm's influence did not die with him. A book he had been working on before his death with the writer Alex Haley (*The Autobiography of Malcolm X*) attracted wide attention after its publication in 1965 and spread his reputation broadly through the nation. Years after his death, he was to many African Americans as important and revered a symbol as Martin Luther King Jr.

MALCOLM X Malcolm X, a leader of the militant Nation of Islam, arrives in Washington, D.C., in May 1963 to set up a headquarters for the organization there. Malcolm was hated and feared by many whites during his lifetime. After he was assassinated in 1965, he became a widely revered hero among African Americans. (© Bettmann/Corbis)

"FLEXIBLE RESPONSE" AND THE COLD WAR

In international affairs as much as in domestic reform, the optimistic liberalism of the Kennedy and Johnson administrations dictated a more positive, more active approach to dealing with the nation's problems than in the past. And just as the new activism in domestic reform proved more difficult and divisive than liberals had imagined, so too it created frustrations and failures in foreign policy.

DIVERSIFYING FOREIGN POLICY

The Kennedy administration entered office convinced that the United States needed to be able to counter communist aggression in more-flexible ways than the atomic-weapons-oriented

"FLEXIBLE RESPONSE" defense strategy of the Eisenhower years had permitted. In particular, Kennedy was unsatisfied with the nation's ability to meet communist threats in "emerging areas" of the Third World–the areas in which, Kennedy believed, the real struggle

against communism would be waged in the future. He gave enthusiastic support to the expansion of the Special Forces (or "Green Berets," as they were soon known)–soldiers trained specifically to fight guerrilla conflicts and other limited wars.

Kennedy also favored expanding American influence through peaceful means. To repair the badly deteriorating relationship with Latin America, he proposed an "Alliance for Progress": a series of projects for peaceful development and stabilization of the nations of that region. Kennedy also inaugurated the Agency for International Development (AID) to coordinate foreign aid. And he established what became one of his most popular innovations: the Peace Corps, which sent young American volunteers abroad to work in developing areas.

Among the first foreign policy ventures of the Kennedy administration was a disastrous assault on the Castro government in Cuba. The Eisenhower administration had begun the project; and by the time Kennedy took office, the CIA had been working

BAY OF PIGS for months to train a small army of anti-Castro Cuban exiles in Central America. On April 17, 1961, with the approval of the new president, 2,000 of the armed exiles landed at the Bay of Pigs in Cuba, expecting first American air support and then a spontaneous uprising

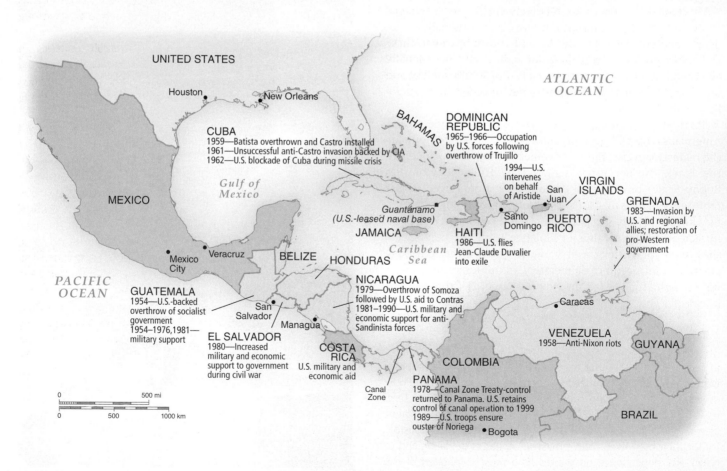

THE UNITED STATES IN LATIN AMERICA, 1954–1996 The Cold War greatly increased the readiness of the United States to intervene in the affairs of its Latin American neighbors. This map presents the many times and ways in which Washington ordered interventions in Central America, the Caribbean, and the northern nations of South America. During much of this period, the interventions were driven by Cold War concerns—by fears that communists might take over nations near the United States as they had taken over Cuba in the early 1960s.

• *What other interests motivated the United States to exert influence in Latin America, even after the end of the Cold War?*

by the Cuban people on their behalf. They received neither. At the last minute, as it became clear that things were going badly, Kennedy withdrew the air support, fearful of involving the United States too directly in the invasion. The expected uprising did not occur. Instead, well-armed Castro forces easily crushed the invaders, and within two days the entire mission had collapsed.

CONFRONTATIONS WITH THE SOVIET UNION

In the grim aftermath of the Bay of Pigs, Kennedy traveled to Vienna in June 1961 for his first meeting with Soviet premier Nikita Khrushchev. Their frosty exchange of views did little to reduce tensions between the two nations—nor did Khrushchev's veiled threat of war if the United States continued to support a noncommunist West Berlin in the heart of East Germany.

Khrushchev was particularly unhappy about the mass exodus of residents of East Germany to the West through the easily traversed border in the center of Berlin. But he ultimately found a method short of war to stop it. Before dawn on August 13, 1961, the East German government, complying with directives from Moscow, began constructing a wall between East and West Berlin. Guards fired on those who continued to try to escape from East to West. For nearly thirty years, the Berlin Wall served as the most potent physical symbol of the conflict between the communist and noncommunist worlds.

The rising tensions culminated the following October in the most dangerous and dramatic crisis of the Cold War. On October 14, aerial reconnaissance photos produced clear evidence that the Soviets were constructing sites in Cuba for offensive nuclear weapons. To the Soviets, placing missiles in Cuba probably seemed a reasonable—and relatively inexpensive—way to counter the presence of American missiles in Turkey (and a way to deter any future American invasion of Cuba). But to Kennedy and most other Americans, the missile sites represented an act of aggression by the Soviets toward the United States. Almost immediately, the president decided that the weapons could not be allowed to remain. On October 22, he ordered a naval and air blockade around Cuba, a "quarantine" against all offensive weapons. Preparations were under way for an American air attack on the missile sites when, late in the evening of October 26, Kennedy received a message from Khrushchev implying that the Soviet Union would remove the missile bases in exchange for an American pledge not to invade Cuba. Ignoring other, tougher Soviet messages, the president agreed. The crisis was over.

CUBAN MISSILE CRISIS

JOHNSON AND THE WORLD

Lyndon Johnson entered the presidency lacking John Kennedy's prior, albeit limited, experience with international affairs. He was eager, therefore, not only to continue the policies of his predecessor but also to prove quickly that he too was a strong and forceful leader.

An internal rebellion in the Dominican Republic gave him an early opportunity to do so. A 1961 assassination had toppled the repressive dictatorship of General Rafael Trujillo, and for the next four years various factions in the country had struggled for dominance. In the spring of 1965, a conservative military regime began to collapse in the face of a revolt by a broad range of groups on behalf of the left-wing nationalist Juan Bosch. Arguing (without any evidence) that Bosch planned to establish a pro-Castro, communist regime, Johnson dispatched 30,000 American troops to quell the disorder. Only after a conservative candidate defeated Bosch in a 1966 election were the forces withdrawn.

INTERVENTION IN THE DOMINICAN REPUBLIC

From Johnson's first moments in office, however, his foreign policy was almost totally dominated by the bitter civil war in Vietnam and by the expanding involvement of the United States there.

THE AGONY OF VIETNAM

George Kennan, who helped devise the containment doctrine that drew America into war in Vietnam, once called the conflict "the most disastrous of all America's undertakings over

KENNEDY IN BERLIN, 1963 President John F. Kennedy looks across the Berlin Wall from a platform built to allow him to see into East Berlin. Shortly afterward he gave a powerful speech to a vast crowd of West Berliners. The speech was well received in Europe and America. But it followed another important speech in which Kennedy spoke of easing the tensions between the West and the communist world. (© Rue des Archives/The Granger Collection, New York)

AP DEBATING THE PAST

THE VIETNAM COMMITMENT

IN 1965, the Department of Defense released a film intended for American soldiers about to embark for service in Vietnam and designed to explain why the United States had found it necessary to commit so many lives and resources to the defense of a small and distant land. The film was titled *Why Vietnam?*—a question many Americans have pondered and debated in the decades

(© AFP/Getty Images)

since. The debate has centered on two questions. One is an effort to assess the broad objectives Americans believed they were pursuing in Vietnam. The other is an effort to explain how and why policymakers made the specific decisions that led to the American commitment.

The Defense Department film offered one answer to the question of America's broad objectives: the United States was fighting in Vietnam to defend freedom and stop aggression and to prevent the spread of communism. This explanation continued to attract support well after the war ended. Political scientist Guenter Lewy contended, in *America in Vietnam* (1978), that the United States entered Vietnam to help an ally combat "foreign aggression." Historian Ernest R. May stated: "The paradox is that the Vietnam War, so often condemned by its opponents as hideously immoral, may well have been the most moral or at least the most selfless war in all of American history. For the impulse guiding it was not to defeat an enemy or to serve a national interest; it was simply not to abandon friends."

Other scholars have taken a starkly different view. They see America's intervention in Vietnam as a form of imperialism—part of a larger effort by the United States after World War II to impose a particular political and economic order on the world. "The Vietnam War," historian Gabriel Kolko wrote in *Anatomy of a War* (1985), "was for the United States the culmination of its frustrating postwar effort to merge its arms and politics to halt and reverse the emergence of states and

the whole 200 years of its history." Yet at first, the Vietnam War seemed simply one more Third World struggle on the periphery of the Cold War, a struggle in which the United States would try to tip the balance against communism without becoming too deeply or directly engaged. No single president really "decided" to go to war in Vietnam. Rather, the American involvement there emerged from years of gradually increasing commitments that slowly and almost imperceptibly expanded.

THE FIRST INDOCHINA WAR

Vietnam had a long history both as an independent kingdom and a major power in its region, and as a subjugated province of China. In the mid-nineteenth century, Vietnam became a colony of France. And like other European possessions in Asia, it fell under the control of Japan during World War II. After the defeat of Japan, the question arose of what was to happen to Vietnam in the postwar world. There were two opposing forces attempting

to answer that question, both of them appealing to the United States for help. The French wanted to reassert their colonial control over Vietnam. Challenging them was a powerful nationalist **THE VIETMINH** movement within Vietnam committed to creating an independent country. The nationalists were organized into a political party, the Vietminh, which had been created in 1941 and led ever since by Ho Chi Minh, a communist educated in Paris and Moscow, and a fervent Vietnamese nationalist. In the fall of 1945, after the collapse of Japan and before the Western powers had time to return, the Vietminh declared Vietnam an independent nation and set up a nationalist government under Ho Chi Minh in Hanoi.

President Truman was under heavy pressure from both the British and the French to support France in its effort to reassert its control over Vietnam. The French argued that without Vietnam, their domestic economy would collapse. And since the economic revival of Western Europe was quickly becoming one of the Truman administration's top priorities, the social systems opposed to the international order Washington sought to establish." Marilyn Young, in *The Vietnam Wars, 1945–1990* (1991), argued that the United States intervened in Vietnam as part of a broad and continuing effort to organize the post–World War II world along lines compatible with American interests and ideals.

Those who looked less at the nation's broad objectives than at the internal workings of the policy-making process likewise produced competing explanations. Journalist David Halberstam's *The Best and the Brightest* (1972) argued that policymakers deluded themselves into thinking they could achieve their goals in Vietnam by ignoring, suppressing, or dismissing the information that might have suggested otherwise. The foreign policy leaders of the Kennedy and Johnson administrations were so committed to the idea of American activism and success that they refused to consider the possibility of failure; the Vietnam disaster was thus, at least in part, a result of the arrogance of the nation's leaders.

Larry Berman offered a somewhat different view in *Planning a Tragedy* (1982) and *Lyndon Johnson's War* (1989). Berman argued that Johnson committed American troops to the war in Vietnam in 1965 not because he expected to win (in fact, he never believed that a real victory was within sight), but because he feared that allowing Vietnam to fall would ruin him politically. To do otherwise, Johnson feared, would destroy his hopes for winning approval of his Great Society legislation at home.

Leslie H. Gelb and Richard K. Betts saw the roots of the involvement in the larger imperatives of the American foreign policy system. In *The Irony of Vietnam: The System Worked* (1979), they argued that intervention in Vietnam was the logical, perhaps even inevitable, result of a political and bureaucratic order shaped by the doctrine of containment. American foreign policy operated in response to a single, overriding imperative: the need to prevent the expansion of communism. Only when the national and international political situation had shifted to the point where it was possible for American policymakers to reassess the costs of the commitment (a shift that began to occur in the early 1970s) was it possible for the United States to begin disengaging.

More-recent studies have questioned the idea that intervention was inevitable or that there were no viable alternatives. David Kaiser, in *American Tragedy* (2000), argues that John Kennedy was not a hawkish supporter of escalation. Rather, his skepticism about the judgment of his military advisers had led him to believe that the United States should find a negotiated settlement to the war. His successor, Lyndon Johnson, harbored no such skepticism and sided with those who favored a military solution. The death of John Kennedy, therefore, becomes a vital event in the history of America in Vietnam. Fredrik Logevall, in *Choosing War: The Lost Chance for Peace and the Escalation of the War in Vietnam* (1999), argues that there were significant opportunities for a negotiated settlement of the war in the early 1960s, but that American leaders (including both Kennedy and Johnson) chose a military response instead—in part to protect themselves politically from charges of weakness.

That the debate over the Vietnam War has been so continuous over the past few decades is a reflection of the enormous role the U.S. failure there has played in shaping the way Americans have thought about politics and policy ever since. Because the "lessons of Vietnam" remain a subject of intense popular concern, the debate over the history of Vietnam is likely to continue. ●

(© Leif Skoogfors/Corbis)

AP HISTORICAL ARGUMENTATION AND INTERPRETATION

Questions assume cumulative content knowledge from this chapter and previous chapters.

1. Identify five historical interpretations presented in the discussion of why America committed to the Vietnam War.
2. What does the continued, intense concern over the "lessons of Vietnam" suggest about the significance of the Vietnam War on the American psyche and how historical objectivity might be affected?
3. With which historical interpretation presented in the discussion do you most agree? Explain why, supporting your argument with historical evidence.

United States did nothing to stop the French as they moved back into Vietnam in 1946 and began a struggle with the Vietminh to reestablish control over the country.

For the next four years, during what has become known as the First Indochina War, Truman and then Eisenhower supported the French military campaign against the Vietminh; by 1954, by some calculations, the United States was paying 80 percent of France's war costs. But the war went badly for the French in spite of the American support. Finally, late in 1953, Vietminh forces engaged the French in a major battle in the far northwest corner of the country, at Dien Bien Phu, an isolated and almost indefensible site. The French were surrounded, and the battle turned into a prolonged and horrible siege, with the French position steadily deteriorating. It was at this point that the Eisenhower administration decided not to intervene to save the French (see p. 776). The defense of Dien Bien Phu collapsed and the French government decided the time had come to get out. The First Indochina War had come to an end.

GENEVA AND THE TWO VIETNAMS

An international conference at Geneva, planned many months before to settle the Korean dispute and other controversies, now took up the fate of Vietnam as well. The Geneva Conference produced an agreement to end the Vietnam conflict without American participation. There would be an immediate cease-fire in the war; Vietnam would be temporarily partitioned along the 17th parallel, with the Vietminh in control of North Vietnam and a pro-Western regime in control of the South. In 1956, elections would be held to reunite the country under a single government.

GENEVA CONFERENCE

AMERICA AND DIEM

As soon as the Geneva accords established the partition, the French finally left Vietnam. The United States almost immediately stepped into the vacuum and became the principal benefactor of the new government in the South, led by Ngo Dinh Diem. Diem was an aristocratic Catholic from central

NGO DINH DIEM

Vietnam, an outsider in the South. But he was also a nationalist, uncontaminated by collaboration with the French. And he was, for a time, successful. With the help of the American CIA, Diem waged an effective campaign against some of the powerful religious sects and the South Vietnamese mafia, which had challenged the authority of the central government. As a result, the United States came to regard Diem as a powerful and impressive alternative to Ho Chi Minh. Lyndon Johnson once called him the "Churchill of Southeast Asia."

The U.S. government supported South Vietnamese President Diem's refusal in 1956 to permit the elections called for by the Geneva accords (see above), reasoning, correctly, that Ho Chi Minh would easily win any such election. Ho could count on almost 100 percent of the vote in the north, with its much larger population, and at least some support in the south. In the meantime, the United States poured military and economic aid into South Vietnam. By 1956, it was the second largest recipient of American military aid in the world, after Korea.

Diem's early successes in suppressing the sects in Vietnam led him in 1959 to begin a similar campaign to eliminate the Vietminh supporters who had stayed behind in the south after the partition. He was quite successful for a time, so successful,

THE NLF

in fact, that the North Vietnamese found it necessary to respond. Ho Chi Minh resumed his armed struggle for national unification. In 1959, the Vietminh cadres in the south created the National Liberation Front (NLF), known to many Americans as the Viet Cong—an organization closely allied with the North Vietnamese government. It was committed to overthrowing the "puppet regime" of Diem and reuniting the nation. In 1960, under orders from Hanoi, and with both material and manpower support from North Vietnam, the NLF began military operations in the South.

By 1961, NLF forces were very successfully destabilizing the Diem regime. They were killing more than 4,000 government officials a year (mostly village leaders) and establishing effective control over many areas of the countryside. Diem was also by now losing the support of many other groups in South Vietnam, and he was even losing support within his own military. In 1963, the Diem regime precipitated a major crisis by trying to discipline and repress the South Vietnamese Buddhists in an effort to make Catholicism the dominant religion of the country. The Buddhists began to stage enormous antigovernment demonstrations. Several Buddhist monks doused themselves with gasoline, sat cross-legged in the streets of downtown Saigon, and set themselves on fire—in view of photographers and television cameras.

The Buddhist crisis caused the U.S. government to reconsider its commitment to Diem—although not to the survival of

DIEM OVERTHROWN

South Vietnam. American officials pressured Diem to reform his government, but Diem made no significant concessions. In the fall of 1963, Kennedy gave his tacit approval to a plot by a group of South Vietnamese generals to topple Diem. In early November 1963, the generals staged the coup, assassinated Diem and his

brother and principal adviser, Ngo Dinh Nhu (murders the United States had not wanted or expected), and established the first of a series of new governments, which were, for over three years, even less stable than the one they had overthrown. A few weeks after the coup, John Kennedy too was dead.

FROM AID TO INTERVENTION

Lyndon Johnson thus inherited what was already a substantial American commitment to the survival of an anticommunist South Vietnam. During his first two years in office, he expanded that commitment into a full-scale American war. Why he did so has long been a subject of debate (see "Debating the Past," pp. 794–795).

Many factors played a role in Johnson's decision. But the most obvious explanation is that the new president faced many pressures to expand the American involvement and very few to limit it. As the untested successor to a revered and martyred president, he felt obliged to prove his worthiness for the office

PRESSURE FOR AMERICAN INTERVENTION

by continuing the policies of his predecessor. Johnson also felt it necessary to retain in his administration many of the important figures of the Kennedy years. In doing so, he surrounded himself with a group of foreign policy advisers—Secretary of State Dean Rusk, Secretary of Defense Robert McNamara, National Security Adviser McGeorge Bundy, and others—who firmly believed that the United States had an obligation to resist communism in Vietnam. Congress raised little protest to, and indeed at one point openly endorsed, Johnson's use of executive powers to lead the nation into war.

Above all, intervention in South Vietnam was fully consistent with nearly twenty years of American foreign policy. An anticommunist ally was appealing to the United States for assistance; all the assumptions of the containment doctrine, as it had come to be defined by the 1960s, seemed to require the nation to intervene. Vietnam, Johnson believed, was a test of American willingness to fight communist aggression, a test he was determined not to fail.

During his first months in office, Johnson expanded the American involvement in Vietnam only slightly, sending an additional 5,000 military advisers there and preparing to send 5,000 more. Then, early in August 1964, the president announced that American destroyers on patrol in international waters in the Gulf

GULF OF TONKIN RESOLUTION

of Tonkin had been attacked by North Vietnamese torpedo boats. Later information raised doubts as to whether the administration reported the attacks accurately. At the time, however, virtually no one questioned Johnson's portrayal of the incident as a serious act of aggression, or his insistence that the United States must respond. By a vote of 416 to 0 in the House and 88 to 2 in the Senate, Congress hurriedly passed the Gulf of Tonkin Resolution, which authorized the president to "take all necessary measures" to protect American forces and "prevent further aggression" in Southeast Asia. The resolution became, in Johnson's view at least, an open-ended legal authorization for escalation of the conflict.

THE WAR IN VIETNAM AND INDOCHINA, 1964–1975 Much of the Vietnam War was fought in small engagements in widely scattered areas and did not conform to traditional notions of combat. But as this map shows, there were traditional battles and invasions and supply routes as well. The red arrows in the middle of the map show the general path of the Ho Chi Minh Trail, the main supply route by which North Vietnam supplied its troops and allies in the South. The blue arrow in southern South Vietnam indicates the point at which American troops invaded Cambodia in 1970.

• *What is there in the geography of Indochina, as presented on this map, that helps to explain the great difficulty the American military had in securing South Vietnam against communist attacks?*

Map labels: CHINA · NORTH VIETNAM · Lao Cai · Dien Bien Phu · Thai Nguyen · Hanoi · Haiphong · BURMA · Luang Prabang · *PLAIN OF JARS* · Thanh Hoa · *Gulf of Tonkin* · *Hainan* · LAOS · Vinh · Vientiane · Udon Thani · Phanom · THAILAND · FRIENDSHIP HIGHWAY · Sepone · Khe Sanh · Hue · Phu Bai · Da Nang · Hoi An · *South China Sea* · Partition Line 1954 · DMZ (Demilitarized Zone) · Takhli · Don Muang · Ratchasima · Udon Rarchathani · Chulai · My Lai · Quang Ngai · Dak To · Kon Tum · Ankhe · Bangkok · CAMBODIA · Barrambang · *Tonle Sap* · Ploiku · Qui Nhon · *CENTRAL HIGHLANDS* · SOUTH VIETNAM · Pursat · Kompong Cham · Nha Trang · Phnom Penh · Bo Duc · Da Lat · Camranh Bay · Phanrang · 1970—U.S. and South Vietnam troops entered Viet Cong strongholds inside Cambodia · Tay Ninh · Song Be · *Gulf of Thailand* · *PLAIN OF REEDS* · Saigon · Sihanoukville · Can Tho · Cantho · *Mekong River Delta*

Legend:
- ■ U.S. bases
- → U.S. and South Vietnam invasion of Cambodia
- → Ho Chi Minh Trail (communist supply route)

Scale: 0 — 200 mi · 0 — 200 — 400 km

With the South Vietnamese leadership still in disarray, more and more of the burden of opposition to the Viet Cong fell on the United States. In February 1965, seven marines died when communist forces attacked an American military base at Pleiku. Johnson retaliated by ordering the first American bombings of the north since the 1964 Tonkin crisis in an attempt to destroy the depots and transportation lines responsible for the flow of North Vietnamese soldiers and supplies into South Vietnam. The bombing continued intermittently until 1972. A month later, in March 1965, two battalions of American marines landed at Da Nang in South Vietnam. There were now more than 100,000 American troops in Vietnam.

Four months later, the president finally admitted that the character of the war had changed. American soldiers would now, he announced, begin playing an active combat role in the conflict. By the end of the year, there were more than 180,000 American combat troops in Vietnam; in 1966, that number doubled; and by the end of 1967, over 500,000 American soldiers were there—along with a considerable number of civilian personnel working in various capacities. In the meantime, the air war intensified; ultimately the tonnage of bombs dropped on North Vietnam would exceed that in all theaters during World War II. And American casualties were mounting. In 1961,

MOUNTING CASUALTIES

THE FOLK-MUSIC REVIVAL

TWO impulses of the 1960s—the renewed interest among young people in the politics of the left, and the search for an "authentic" alternative to what many considered the artificial, consumerist culture of modern America—helped produce the revived popularity of folk music in that turbulent era. Although the harder, harsher, and more sensual music of rock 'n' roll was more visible and more popular in the 1960s, folk music more clearly expressed many of the political ideas and aspirations that were welling up in the youth culture of the time.

The folk-music tradition, like most American musical traditions, had many roots. It drew from some of the black musical traditions of the South, and from the white country music of Appalachia. And it drew most immediately from a style of music developed by musicians associated with the Communist Party's Popular Front in the 1930s. Woody Guthrie, Pete Seeger, the Weavers, and others whose music would become popular again in the 1960s began their careers singing in Popular Front and union rallies during the Great Depression. Their music, like the Popular Front itself, set out to seem entirely American, rooted in the nation's folk traditions.

Folk music remained alive in the 1940s and 1950s, but it had only a modest popular following. Pete Seeger and the Weavers continued to perform and to attract attention on college campuses. Harry Belafonte and the Kingston Trio recorded slick, pop versions of folk songs in an effort to bring them to mass audiences. In 1952, Folkway Records released the *Anthology of American Folk Music*, a collection of eighty-four performances recorded in the 1920s and 1930s that became an inspiration and an important source of material to many younger folk musicians. Folk-music festivals—at Berkeley, Newport, and Chicago—began to proliferate beginning in 1959. And an important community of folk musicians lived and performed together in the 1950s and early 1960s in New York City's Greenwich Village.

As the politics of the 1960s became more heated, and as young people in particular became politically aroused, it was folk music that most directly reflected their new values and concerns. Peter, Paul, and Mary—although only intermittently political—became icons to much of the New Left, beginning with their 1962 recording of "If I Had a Hammer," a song first performed at Communist Party rallies in the 1940s by Pete Seeger and the Weavers. Bob Dylan, whose own politics were never wholly clear to the public, had a large impact on the 1960s left, even inadvertently providing a name to the most radical offshoot of Students for a Democratic Society (SDS), the Weathermen, who named themselves after a line from one of his songs: "You don't need a weatherman to know which way the wind blows."* Joan Baez, whose politics were no secret to anyone, was actively engaged in the antiwar movement and was arrested several times for participating in militant protests.

RALLYING AGAIN The music of Woody Guthrie and other musicians of the 1930s, 1940s and 1950s inspired a revival of popular music sympathetic to the protesting generation of the 1960s. (© Everett Collection Inc./Alamy)

But it was not just the overt political messages of folk musicians that made them so important to young Americans in the 1960s. In addition, folk was a kind of music that seemed to reflect the "authenticity" the youth culture was attempting to find. In truth, neither the musicians themselves nor the young Americans attracted to them had much real connection with the traditions they were trying to evoke. The audiences for folk music—a

---

14 Americans had died in Vietnam. By the spring of 1966, more than 4,000 Americans had been killed.

The United States finally succeeded in 1965 in creating a reasonably stable government in the south under General Nguyen Van Thieu. But the new regime was hardly less corrupt or brutal than its predecessors, and no more able than they to establish its authority in its own countryside. The Viet Cong, not the Thieu regime, controlled the majority of South Vietnam's villages and hamlets.

THE QUAGMIRE

Central to the American war effort was a commitment to what the military called "attrition," a strategy premised on the

STRATEGY OF "ATTRITION" belief that the United States could inflict so many casualties and so much damage on the enemy that eventually they would be

unable and unwilling to continue the struggle. But the attrition strategy failed because the North Vietnamese proved willing to commit many more soldiers to the conflict than the United States had expected. The United States relied heavily on its bombing of the north to eliminate the communists' war-making capacity. By the end of 1967, most of the identifiable targets of any strategic importance in North Vietnam had been destroyed. But the bombing had produced none of the effects that the United States had expected. North Vietnam was not a modern, industrial society; it had few of the sorts of targets against which bombing is effective. The North Vietnamese responded to the air raids with ingenuity: They created a great network of underground tunnels, shops, and factories. They also secured increased aid from the Soviet Union and China. Infiltration of the south was unaffected; the North Vietnamese kept moving the Ho Chi Minh Trail, the routes by which North Vietnam soldiers infiltrated the South.

COFFEEHOUSE MUSIC The Feejon Coffee House in Manhattan was popular among young writers, poets, and others in the late 1950s, in part because it was a gathering place for folk musicians, two of whom are shown here performing at right. (© John Orris/Getty images)

PETE SEEGER Pete Seeger was one of several folk musicians who provided a link between the Popular Front—labor movement folk music of the 1930s and the folk revival of the 1960s. He is shown here in concert in 1966. (© Archive Photos/Getty Images)

product of rural and working-class traditions—were overwhelmingly urban, middle-class people. But the message of folk music—that there is a "real" America rooted in values of sharing and community, hidden beneath the crass commercialism of modern culture—resonated with the yearnings of many people in the 1960s (and beyond) for an alternative to their own troubled world. When young audiences responded to Woody Guthrie's famous ballad "This Land Is Your Land," they were expressing a hope for a different America—more democratic, more honest, and more natural than the land they knew. ●

*Bob Dylan, "Subterranean Homesick Blues." Copyright © 1965 by Warner Bros. Music. Copyright renewed 1993 by Special Rider Music. All rights reserved. International copyright secured. Reprinted by permission.

UNDERSTAND, ANALYZE, AND EVALUATE

1. What did folk music, with roots in the musical traditions of blacks, rural folk, and working-class people, offer that made it so appealing to and popular with urban, middle-class audiences?
2. What similarities between the 1930s and the 1960s might help explain the popularity of folk music during both those decades?
3. What musical style or form today continues the folk music tradition of expressing a political message and reflecting the search for "authenticity"?

Another crucial part of the American strategy was the "pacification" program, which was intended to push the Viet Cong from areas chosen by the United States and then "pacify" those regions by winning the "hearts and minds" of the people. But American forces were not adept at establishing the kind of rapport with provincial Vietnamese that the Viet Cong had created.

"HEARTS AND MINDS"

Gradually, the pacification program gave way to a heavy-handed relocation strategy, through which American troops uprooted villagers from their homes, sent them fleeing to refugee camps or into the cities (producing by 1967 more than 3 million refugees), and then destroyed the vacated villages and surrounding countryside. But the Viet Cong responded by moving to new sanctuaries elsewhere. The futility of the United States's effort was suggested by the statement of an American officer after flattening one such hamlet that it had been "necessary to destroy [the village] in order to save it."

As the war dragged on and victory remained elusive, some American officers and officials began to urge the president to expand the military efforts. The Johnson administration, however, resisted. Unwilling to abandon its commitment to South Vietnam for fear of destroying American "credibility" in the world, the government was also unwilling to expand the war too far, for fear of provoking direct intervention by the Chinese, the Soviets, or both. In the meantime, the president began to encounter additional obstacles and frustrations at home.

THE WAR AT HOME

As late as the end of 1965, few Americans, and even fewer influential ones, had protested the American involvement in Vietnam. But as the war dragged on, political support for it began to erode. A series of "teach-ins" on university campuses, beginning at the University of Michigan in 1965, sparked a national debate over

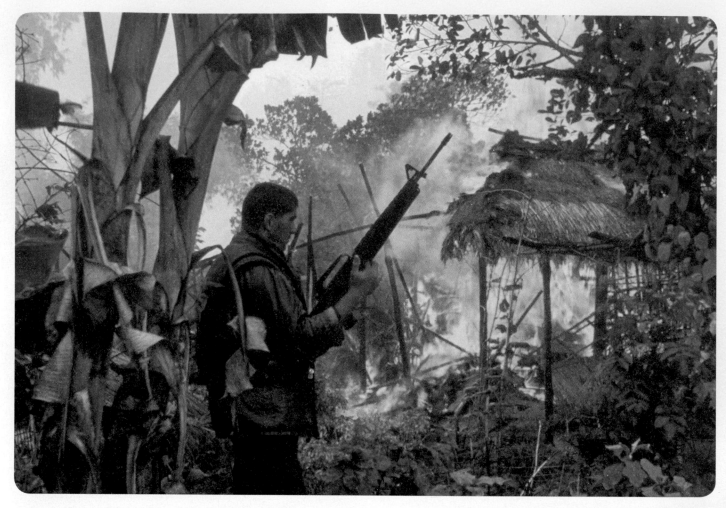

SEARCH AND DESTROY U.S. troops in Vietnam, often unable to distinguish enemy forces from the civilian population, increasingly sought to destroy places they considered possible enemy sanctuaries. Here an American soldier watches the burning of a village, one of many that U.S. troops destroyed. (© Topham/The Image Works)

the war. By the end of 1967, American students opposed to the war had become a significant political force. Enormous peace marches in New York, Washington, D.C., and other cities drew broad public attention to the antiwar movement. Opposition to the war became a central issue in left-wing politics and in the culture of colleges and universities. It had penetrated popular cultures as well—most visibly in the rising popularity of folk musicians, many of whom used their songs to express opposition to the war. In the meantime, a growing number of journalists, particularly reporters who had spent time in Vietnam, helped sustain the antiwar movement with their frank revelations about the brutality and apparent futility of the war. The growing chorus of popular protest soon began to stimulate opposition to the war from within the government.

GROWING OPPOSITION TO THE WAR

Senator J. William Fulbright of Arkansas, chairman of the powerful Senate Foreign Relations Committee, turned against the war and in January 1966 began to stage highly publicized congressional hearings to air criticisms of it. Distinguished figures such as George F. Kennan and retired general James Gavin testified against the conflict, giving opposition to the war greater respectability. Other members of Congress joined Fulbright in opposing Johnson's policies—including, in 1967, Robert F. Kennedy, brother of the slain president and now a senator from New York. Even within the administration, the consensus seemed to be crumbling. Robert McNamara, who had done much to help extend the American involvement in Vietnam, quietly left the government, disillusioned, in 1968. His successor as secretary of defense, Clark Clifford, became a quiet but powerful voice within the administration on behalf of a cautious scaling down of the commitment in troops and funding.

In the meantime, the American economy was beginning to suffer. Johnson's commitment to fighting the war while continuing his Great Society reforms—his promise of "guns and butter"—proved impossible to maintain. The inflation rate, which had remained at 2 percent through most of the early 1960s, rose to 3 percent in 1967, 4 percent in 1968, and 6 percent in 1969. In August 1967, Johnson asked Congress for a tax increase—a 10 percent surcharge that was widely labeled a "war tax"—which he knew was necessary if the nation was to avoid even more ruinous inflation. In return, congressional conservatives demanded and received a $6 billion reduction in the funding for Great Society programs.

WAR-INDUCED INFLATION

THE TRAUMAS OF 1968

By the end of 1967, the twin crises of the war in Vietnam and the deteriorating racial situation at home–crises that fed upon and inflamed each other–had produced profound social and political tensions. In the course of 1968, those tensions seemed suddenly to burst to the surface and to threaten the nation with genuine chaos.

THE TET OFFENSIVE

On January 31, 1968, the first day of the Vietnamese New Year (Tet), communist forces launched an enormous, concerted attack on American strongholds throughout South Vietnam. A few cities fell to the communists. During their occupation of the provincial capital, Hue, the communist forces rounded up supporters of the Saigon regime and massacred them. Other cities suffered major disruptions.

Americans saw vivid reports on television of communist forces in the heart of Saigon, setting off bombs, shooting South Vietnamese officials and troops, and holding down fortified areas (including, briefly, the grounds of the American embassy). Such images shocked many Americans and proved devastating to popular support for the war. The Tet offensive also suggested to the American public something of the brutality of the struggle in Vietnam. In the midst of the fighting, television cameras recorded the sight of a captured Viet Cong soldier being led up to a South Vietnamese officer in the streets of Saigon. Without a word, the officer pulled out his pistol and shot the young man in the head, leaving him lying dead in the street. Few single events did more to galvanize support for the war in the United States.

American forces soon dislodged the Viet Cong from most of the positions they had seized, and the Tet offensive in the end cost the communists such appalling casualties that they were significantly weakened for months to come. The Tet defeats permanently depleted the ranks of the NLF and forced North Vietnamese troops to take on a much larger share of the subsequent fighting. Tet may have been a military victory for the United States, but it was a political defeat for the administration.

POLITICAL AND PSYCHOLOGICAL DEFEAT

MY LAI MASSACRE On March 16, 1968 U.S. Army soldiers killed between 347 and 504 unarmed men, women, and children in South Vietnam. Twenty-six soldiers were charged with criminal offenses. Only Lieutenant William Calley, Jr., a platoon leader, was convicted. The incident increased domestic opposition to the war when its horrific scope and the initial attempt by the army to cover it up were exposed. (© Image Asset Management Ltd./Alamy)

1968 WOR-4, 7

THE year 1968 was one of the most turbulent in the postwar history of the United States. Much of what caused these upheavals was specifically American events—the growing controversy over the war in Vietnam, the assassinations of Martin Luther King Jr. and Robert Kennedy, racial unrest in the nation's cities, student protests on campuses throughout America. But the turmoil of 1968 was not confined to the United States. There were tremendous upheavals in many parts of the world that year.

PRAGUE SPRING Czech demonstrators march through Wenceslas Square in Prague following a radio address by their reform president, Alexander Dubcek, in August 1968. By this time, the great hopes awakened by Dubcek's reforms during the "Prague Spring" of several months ago had been crushed by Soviet pressure, including the arrival of Soviet tanks in the streets of Prague. These demonstrators are demanding the "brutal truth" from their leaders about the price Czechoslovakia paid to keep Dubcek in power. (© Bettmann/Corbis)

The most common form of turbulence around the world in 1968 was student unrest. A student uprising in France in May 1968 far exceeded in size and ferocity anything that occurred in the United States. It attracted the support of French workers, briefly paralyzed Paris and other cities, and contributed to the downfall of the government of Charles de Gaulle a year later. In England, Ireland, Germany, Italy, the Netherlands, Mexico, Canada, Japan, and South Korea, students and other young people also demonstrated in great numbers, sometimes violently, against governments and universities and other structures of authority. In Czechoslovakia, hundreds of thousands of citizens took to the streets in support of what became known as "Prague Spring"—a demand for greater democracy and a repudiation of many of the oppressive rules and structures imposed on the nation by its Soviet-dominated communist regimes—until Russian tanks rolled into the city to crush the uprising.

One factor that contributed to the worldwide turbulence of 1968 was simple numbers. The postwar baby boom, which occurred in many nations, had created a very large age cohort that by the late 1960s was reaching adulthood. The sheer size of the new generation produced a tripling of the number of people attending colleges and universities, and a heightened sense of the power of youth. The long period of postwar prosperity and relative peace in which this generation had grown up contributed to heightened expectations of what the world should offer them—and a greater level of impatience than previous generations had demonstrated with the obstacles that stood in the way of their hopes. A new global youth culture emerged that was in many ways at odds with the dominant culture of older generations. It valued nonconformity, personal freedom, and even rebellion.

A second force contributing to the widespread turbulence of 1968 was the power of global media. Satellite technology introduced in the early 1960s made it

In the following weeks, opposition to the war grew substantially. Leading newspapers and magazines, television commentators, and mainstream politicians began taking public stands in favor of de-escalation of the conflict. Within weeks of the Tet offensive, public opposition to the war had almost doubled. And Johnson's personal popularity rating had slid to 35 percent, the lowest of any president since Harry Truman.

THE POLITICAL CHALLENGE

Beginning in the summer of 1967, dissident Democrats (led by the activist Allard Lowenstein) tried to mobilize support behind an antiwar candidate who would challenge Lyndon Johnson in the 1968 primaries. When Robert Kennedy declined their invitation, they turned to Senator Eugene McCarthy of Minnesota. A brilliantly orchestrated campaign by Lowenstein and thousands of young volunteers in the New Hampshire primary produced a startling showing by McCarthy in March; he nearly defeated the president.

A few days later, Robert Kennedy entered the campaign, embittering many McCarthy supporters, but bringing his own substantial strength among African Americans, the poor, and workers to the antiwar cause. Polls showed the president trailing badly in the next scheduled primary, in Wisconsin. Indeed, possible to transmit live news instantly across the world. Videotape technology and the creation of lightweight portable television cameras enabled media organizations to respond to events much more quickly and flexibly than in the past. And the audience for these televised images was by now global and enormous, particularly in industrial nations but even in the poorest areas of the world. Protests in one country were suddenly capable of inspiring protests in others. Demonstrators in Paris, for example, spoke openly of how campus protests in the United States in 1968—for example, the student uprising at Columbia University in New York City—had helped motivate French students to rise up as well. Just as American students were protesting against what they considered the antiquated paternalistic features of their universities, French students demanded an end to the rigid, autocratic character of their own academic world.

In most parts of the world, the 1968 uprisings came and went without fundamentally altering the institutions and systems they were attacking. But many changes came in the wake of these protests. Universities around the globe undertook significant reforms. Religious observance in mainstream churches and synagogues in the West declined dramatically after 1968. New concepts of personal freedom gained legitimacy, helping to inspire new social movements in the years that followed—among them the dramatic growth of feminism in many parts of the world. The events of 1968 did not produce a revolution, in the United States or in most of the rest of the world, but they did help launch a period of dramatic social, cultural, and political change that affected the peoples of many nations. ●

UNDERSTAND, ANALYZE, AND EVALUATE

1. What factors combined to produce the turbulence that resulted in the uprisings of 1968?
2. Did the demonstrators of 1968 succeed or fail to achieve their objectives? What were the long-term effects of the 1968 uprisings?
3. Has there been a year or period since 1968 in which similar worldwide protests and uprisings have occurred? If so, what events triggered these later demonstrations?

public animosity toward the president was now so intense that Johnson did not even dare leave the White House to campaign. On March 31, Johnson went on television to announce a limited halt in the bombing of North Vietnam—his first major concession to the antiwar forces—and, more surprising, his withdrawal from the presidential contest.

ROBERT KENNEDY

Robert Kennedy quickly established himself as the champion of the Democratic primaries. In the meantime, however, Vice President Hubert Humphrey, with the support of President Johnson, entered the contest and began to attract the support of party leaders and of the many delegations that were selected not by popular primaries but by state party organizations. He soon appeared to be the front-runner in the race.

THE KING AND KENNEDY ASSASSINATIONS

In the midst of this bitter political battle, in which the war had been the dominant issue, attention suddenly turned back to the nation's bitter racial conflicts. On April 4, Martin Luther King Jr., who had traveled to Memphis, Tennessee, to lend his support to striking black sanitation workers in the city, was shot and killed while standing on the balcony of his motel. The presumed assassin, James Earl Ray, who was captured days later in London and eventually convicted, had no apparent motive. Later evidence suggested that he had been hired by others to do the killing, but he never revealed the identity of his employers.

King's tragic death produced an outpouring of grief matched in recent memory only by the reaction to the death of John Kennedy. Among African Americans, it also produced anger. In the days after the assassination, major riots broke out in more than sixty American cities. Forty-three people died; more than 3,000 suffered injuries; as many as 27,000 people were arrested.

RIOTS

For two months following the death of King, Robert Kennedy continued his campaign for the presidential nomination. Late on the night of June 6, he appeared in the ballroom of a Los Angeles hotel to acknowledge his victory in that day's California primary. As he left the ballroom after his victory statement, Sirhan Sirhan, a young Palestinian apparently enraged by pro-Israeli remarks Kennedy had recently made, emerged from a crowd and shot him in the head. Early the next morning, Kennedy died.

THE "KENNEDY LEGACY"

By the time of his death, Robert Kennedy–who earlier in his career had been widely considered a cold, ruthless agent of his more appealing brother–had emerged as a figure of enormous popular appeal. More than John Kennedy, Robert identified his hopes with the American "underclass"–with blacks, Hispanics, Native Americans, the poor. Indeed, Robert Kennedy, much more than John, shaped what some would later call the "Kennedy legacy," a set of ideas that would for a time become central to American liberalism: the fervent commitment to using government to help the powerless. The passions Kennedy aroused made his violent death a particularly shattering experience for many Americans.

The presidential campaign continued gloomily during the last weeks before the convention. Hubert Humphrey, who had seemed likely to win the nomination even before Robert Kennedy's death, now faced only minor opposition. The approaching Democratic National Convention, therefore, began to take on the appearance of an exercise in futility; and antiwar activists, despairing of winning any victories within the convention, began to plan major demonstrations outside it.

When the Democrats finally gathered in Chicago in August, even the most optimistic observers were predicting a turbulent convention. Inside the hall, delegates bitterly debated

DEMOCRATIC
NATIONAL
CONVENTION

an antiwar plank in the party platform that both Kennedy and McCarthy supporters favored. Miles away, in a downtown park, thousands of antiwar protesters were staging demonstrations. On the third night of the convention, as the delegates were beginning their balloting on the now inevitable nomination of Hubert Humphrey, demonstrators and police clashed in a bloody riot in the streets of Chicago. Hundreds of protesters were injured as police attempted to disperse them with tear gas and billy clubs. Aware that the violence was being televised, the demonstrators taunted the authorities with the chant, "The whole world is watching!" And Hubert Humphrey, who had spent years dreaming of becoming his party's candidate for president, received a nomination that appeared at the time to be almost worthless.

THE CONSERVATIVE RESPONSE

The turbulent events of 1968 persuaded many observers that American society was in the throes of revolutionary change. In

CHICAGO, 1968 Demonstrators climb on a statue in a Chicago park during the 1968 Democratic National Convention, protesting both the Vietnam War and the harsh treatment they had received from Mayor Richard Daley's Chicago police. (© Dennis Brack/Black Star)

fact, however, the response of most Americans to the turmoil was a conservative one.

The most visible sign of the conservative backlash was the surprising success of the campaign of the segregationist Alabama governor George Wallace for the presidency. In 1964, he had run in a few Democratic presidential primaries and had done surprisingly well, even in several states outside the South. In 1968, he became a third-party candidate for president, basing his campaign on a host of conservative grievances, not all of them connected to race. He denounced the forced busing of students, the proliferation of government regulations and social programs, and the permissiveness of authorities toward race riots and antiwar demonstrations. There was never any serious chance that Wallace would win the election; but his standing in the polls at times rose to over 20 percent.

GEORGE
WALLACE

A more effective effort to mobilize the "silent majority" in favor of order and stability was under way within the Republican Party. Richard Nixon, whose political career had seemed at an end after his losses in the presidential race of 1960 and a California gubernatorial campaign two years later,

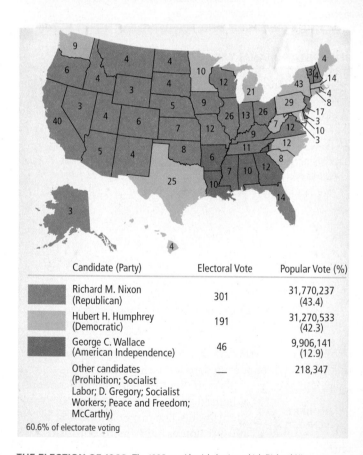

Candidate (Party)	Electoral Vote	Popular Vote (%)
Richard M. Nixon (Republican)	301	31,770,237 (43.4)
Hubert H. Humphrey (Democratic)	191	31,270,533 (42.3)
George C. Wallace (American Independence)	46	9,906,141 (12.9)
Other candidates (Prohibition; Socialist Labor; D. Gregory; Socialist Workers; Peace and Freedom; McCarthy)	—	218,347

60.6% of electorate voting

THE ELECTION OF 1968 The 1968 presidential election, which Richard Nixon won, was almost as close as the election of 1960, which he had lost. Nixon might have won a more substantial victory had it not been for the independent candidacy of Governor George C. Wallace, who attracted many of the same conservative voters to whom Nixon appealed.

• How does the distribution of Democratic and Republican strength in this election compare to that in 1960?

reemerged as the preeminent spokesman for what he called "Middle America." Nixon recognized that many Americans were tired of hearing about their obligations to the poor, tired of hearing about the sacrifices necessary to achieve racial justice, tired of judicial reforms that seemed designed to help criminals. By offering a vision of stability, law and order, government retrenchment, and "peace with honor" in Vietnam, he easily captured the Republican presidential nomination. And after the spectacle of the Democratic National Convention, he enjoyed a commanding lead in the polls as the November election approached.

That lead diminished greatly in the last weeks before the voting. Old doubts about Nixon's character continued to haunt the Republican candidate. A skillful last-minute surge by Hubert Humphrey, who managed to restore a tenuous unity to the Democratic Party, narrowed the gap further. And the Wallace campaign appeared to be hurting the Republicans more than the Democrats. In the end, however, Nixon eked out a victory almost as narrow as his defeat in 1960. He received 43.4 percent of the popular vote to Humphrey's 42.3 percent (a margin of only about 800,000 votes), and 301 electoral votes to Humphrey's 191. George Wallace, who like most third-party

NIXON VICTORIOUS candidates faded in the last weeks of the campaign, still managed to poll 12.9 percent of the popular vote and to carry five southern states with a total of 46 electoral ballots–the best showing by a third-party candidate since the 1920s. Nixon had not won a decisive personal mandate. But the election made clear that a majority of the American electorate was more interested in restoring stability than in promoting social change.

AP CONNECTING THEMES

Chapter 29 discussed the social and political fabric of American society in the 1960s. As you review, you should focus on the reasons behind and results of the movement toward liberalism in the early years of the decade and judge the relative success or failure of various programs. It is also important that you keep in mind the notion that the surge of liberalism is largely spent by the later part of the decade, and you need to understand the factors that led to its demise. You need to have a good grasp of the methods, accomplishments, and support of various civil rights groups and how the methods, accomplishments, and support changed over time. Pay particular attention to the role that the war in Vietnam played in dividing society. Finally, pay close attention to the election of 1968 and the ways in which the year 1968 might represent a turning point in American history.

The following themes have a heightened importance in Chapter 29. You should now be able to do the following for each listed theme:

Identity: Explain how the rising tide of protest by minority groups changed both their perceptions of themselves and the perceptions of others toward them.

Work, Exchange, and Technology: Explain the growing polarization of blue collar workers from their traditional attachment to liberal ideals.

Politics and Power: Explain the movement of American public opinion to a more conservative posture as reflected by the election of 1968.

America and the World: Explain the impact of the war in Vietnam on U.S. foreign relations during the 1960s.

Environment and Geography: Explain how the growing concern over the environment led to specific pieces of legislation designed to remedy those concerns.

Ideas, Beliefs, and Culture: Explain the ways in which domestic and foreign affairs led society to splinter along ideological lines.

AP SUGGESTED STUDY

PEOPLE/PLACES/EVENTS As you study these items, think about how they demonstrate or relate to key concepts and historical themes from this chapter and previous chapters.

BAY OF PIGS 792	GREAT SOCIETY 784	NEW FRONTIER 782
BLACK POWER 790	GULF OF TONKIN RESOLUTION 796	NGO DINH DIEM 796
COMMUNITY ACTION PROGRAM 784	HO CHI MINH 794	RICHARD NIXON 804
CONGRESS OF RACIAL EQUALITY (CORE) 786	HO CHI MINH TRAIL 798	ROBERT KENNEDY 802
CUBAN MISSILE CRISIS 793	IMMIGRATION ACT OF 1965 785	STUDENT NONVIOLENT COORDINATING COMMITTEE (SNCC) 786
DIEN BIEN PHU 795	JOHN KENNEDY 782	TET OFFENSIVE 801
FREEDOM RIDES 786	MALCOLM X 791	VIET CONG 796
FREEDOM SUMMER 787	MARCH ON WASHINGTON 787	
GEORGE WALLACE 787	MEDICAID 784	
	MEDICARE 784	

AP TEST PRACTICE

Questions assume cumulative content knowledge from this chapter and previous chapters.

MULTIPLE CHOICE Use the photograph on page 787 and your knowledge of U.S. history to answer questions 1–2.

1. Which best describes how the focus of the African American civil rights movement changed in the decade following the event depicted in the photograph?

   (A) Movement to obtain citizenship for African Americans

   (B) Movement to completely end the economic system of sharecropping in the South

   (C) Movement from challenging segregation laws to challenging discrimination in social and economic "practices"

   (D) Movement to remain committed to nonviolent protest tactics

2. Which would become a competing vision in the approach to achieving African American civil rights to the approach exemplified by the main individual in the photograph?

   (A) A movement for self-improvement over advocating for long-range social change

   (B) A black nationalistic movement

   (C) A movement advocating for voting rights for African Americans

   (D) A view that African Americans should patiently strive for equal rights

SHORT ANSWER Use your knowledge of U.S. history to answer questions 3–6.

3. Answer a, b, and c.

   a) Briefly explain ONE example of continuing efforts by African Americans to gain civil rights in the early 1960s.

   b) Briefly explain ONE example of federal government actions in support of civil rights for African Americans in the early 1960s.

   c) Briefly explain ONE example of a political or social crisis arising from events in the civil rights movement of African Americans in the early 1960s.

4. Answer a, b, and c.

   a) For one of the time periods below, identify one event which pushed the United States into greater involvement in Vietnam.

   • 1945–1953

   • 1954–1960

   • 1964–1967

   b) Briefly explain how that event influenced or led to U.S. involvement in Vietnam.

   c) Choose a second time period, and explain why events from this time period were not as important a factor in pushing the U.S. into greater involvement in Vietnam.

5. Use the map on page 792 to answer a, b, and c.

   a) Briefly explain the change in Cold War policy in the 1960s, as represented by the map.

   b) Provide one example of that change.

   c) Provide a second example of that change.

6. Answer a, b, and c.

   a) Both the election of 1968 and 1860 occurred during extremely critical time periods in American history. Explain any similar economic or political context that existed during both election years.

   b) Briefly explain ONE important difference in the economic or political events occurring during both election years.

   c) Briefly explain ONE way in which elements of society critically responded to the election outcome.

LONG ESSAY For each question below, develop a thoughtful and thorough historical argument that answers the question. Begin your essay with a thesis statement and support it with relevant historical evidence.

7. Some historians have maintained that U.S. foreign policy in Vietnam between 1954 and 1973 was misguided. Support, modify or refute this interpretation, providing specific diplomatic, social, and political evidence to justify your answer.

8. Evaluate the extent to which the Great Society contributed to maintaining continuity with previous domestic policies as well as fostered change in American society between 1964 and 1975.

30 | THE CRISIS OF AUTHORITY

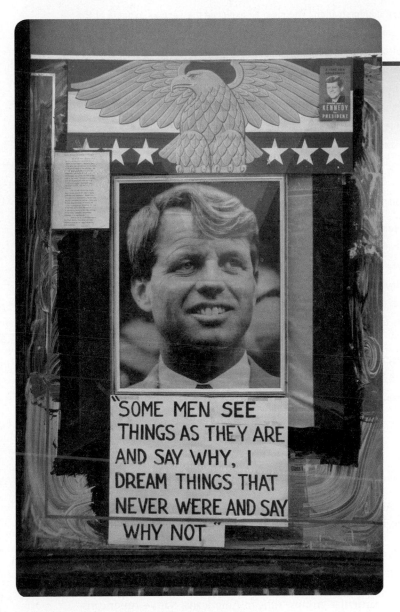

ROBERT KENNEDY THE ICON This photo and statement from Robert Kennedy date from 1968, the year of his presidential campaign and assassination. Almost immediately after his death, Kennedy became a symbol of a lost era—and he remains a powerful image into our own time. In 2008, the Triborough Bridge in New York City was renamed the RFK Bridge. (© Henry Diltz/Corbis).

AP HISTORICAL THINKING

1. **Historical Argumentation** Analyze the success of the youth movement in challenging traditional American values.

2. **Patterns of Continuity and Change over Time** To what degree and in what ways were attempts by minorities (including women, Latinos, American Indians, and gay rights advocates) successful in realizing their goals?

3. **Historical Causation** Analyze the political, social, and economic causes that led the United States to withdraw from Vietnam.

4. **Patterns of Continuity and Change over Time** To what degree and in what ways was American foreign policy during the 1960s and early 1970s a continuation of past U.S. foreign policy and to what degree and in what ways was it a departure from previous U.S. foreign policy?

5. **Contextualization** Analyze the degree to which the new conservative movement challenged the policies of the Great Society.

6. **Comparison** Compare and contrast the elections of 1964, 1968, and 1972.

7. **Historical Interpretation** Analyze the impact and ramifications of the Watergate scandal on Americans' perception of government.

Key Concept Correlations

Analyze the ways the historical developments you learn about in this chapter connect to the following AP Key Concepts.

8.1 The United States responded to an uncertain and unstable postwar world by asserting and attempting to defend a position of global leadership, with far-reaching domestic and international consequences.

8.2 Liberalism, based on anticommunism abroad and a firm belief in the efficacy of governmental and especially federal power to achieve social goals at home, reached its apex in the mid-1960s and generated a variety of political and cultural responses.

8.3 Postwar economic, demographic, and technological changes had a far-reaching impact on American society, politics, and the environment.

Thematic Learning Objectives

WOR-3, 4, 7, 8; ENV-5; ID-3, 6, 7, 8; POL-3, 5, 7; CUL-5, 6, 7; WXT-3, 8; PEO-3, 7

CHAPTER 30 focuses on the political, economic, and social changes during the 1960s and early 1970s, with particular emphasis on the Nixon administration. The chapter explores the various aspects of the youth culture of the time period as baby boomers reached maturity and examines the impact of young people on American beliefs and culture. There is also discussion of the rising tide of protest among minority groups, particularly Latinos, American Indians, and gay rights activists. The chapter examines the reasons for the growth of and the degree of success of the new feminist movement. Significant attention is paid to the reasons for and success of the rising sense of urgency concerning the environment. In terms of foreign policy, the chapter examines the escalation and end of the war in Vietnam, the window of diplomatic opportunity to improve relations with the Soviet Union and China, and problems associated with the Arab oil embargo. The chapter also examines the economic problems of stagflation and deindustrialization as the United States moved from a manufacturing economy to a service-based economy. Finally, there is discussion of the Watergate scandal and its impact on the American psyche regarding government. As you read, evaluate the following ideas:

- The United States sought to contain communism in Southeast Asia.
- Protests against the war in Vietnam continued to grow as escalation of the war expanded.
- The United States moved toward a more conciliatory stance with the Soviet Union and China.
- U.S. involvement in the Middle East took on added importance because of dependence on oil.
- Latinos and American Indians organized protests to gain equal rights and fair treatment.
- New feminists and gay rights activists attempted to change popular assumptions concerning their legitimate place in society.
- There was significant backlash against the liberal policies of the Great Society.
- The youth culture of the 1960s and 1970s challenged traditional American values.
- Presidential actions led many Americans to question the power of the federal government.

THE YOUTH CULTURE

Perhaps most alarming to conservative Americans in the 1960s and 1970s was a pattern of social and cultural protest that was emerging from younger Americans, who were giving vent to two related impulses. One was the impulse, originating with the political left, to create a great new community of "the people," which would rise up to break the power of elites and force the nation to end the war, pursue racial and economic justice, and transform its political life. The other, equally powerful, impulse was the vision of "liberation." It found expression through the efforts of particular groups–African Americans, Native Americans, Hispanics, women, gays and lesbians, and others–to define and assert themselves and make demands on the larger society. It also found expression through the efforts of individuals to create a new culture that would allow them to escape from what they considered the dehumanizing pressures of what some called the modern "technocracy."

"LIBERATION"

"THE NEW LEFT"

In retrospect, it seems unsurprising that young Americans became so assertive and powerful in American culture and politics in the 1960s. The postwar baby-boom generation–the unprecedented number of people born in a few years just after World War II–was growing up. By 1970, more than half the American population was under thirty years old; more than 8 million Americans– eight times the number in 1950–were attending college. This was the largest generation of youth in American history, and it was coming to maturity in a time of unprecedented affluence, opportunity, and–for many–frustration.

CHE ERNESTO "Che" Guevara was an Argentine Marxist revolutionary who played a significant role in the Cuban Revolution. His stylized portrait remains a major symbol of countercultural rebellion the world over. (Axiom Photographic/© Design Pics/SuperStock)

One of the most visible results of the increasingly assertive youth movement was a radicalization of many American college and university students, who in the 1960s formed what

SOURCES OF THE NEW LEFT

became known as the New Left—a large, diverse group of men and women energized by the polarizing developments of their time. The New Left embraced the cause of African Americans and other minorities, but its own ranks consisted overwhelmingly of white people. Blacks and minorities formed political movements of their own. Some members of the New Left were the children of radical parents (members of the so-called Old Left of the 1930s and 1940s).

The New Left drew from the writings of some of the important social critics of the 1950s—among them C. Wright Mills, a sociologist at Columbia University who wrote a series of scathing and brilliant critiques of modern bureaucracies. Relatively few members of the New Left were communists, but many were drawn to the writings of Karl Marx and of contemporary Marxist theorists. Some came to revere Third World Marxists

such as Che Guevara, the South American revolutionary and guerrilla leader; Mao Zedong; and Ho Chi Minh. But the New Left drew its inspiration above all from the civil rights movement, in which many idealistic young white Americans had become involved in the early 1960s.

In 1962, a group of students, most of them from prestigious universities, gathered in Michigan to form an organization to

SDS

give voice to their demands: Students for a Democratic Society (SDS). Their declaration of beliefs, the Port Huron Statement, expressed their disillusionment with the society they had inherited and their determination to build a new politics.

Some members of SDS moved into inner-city neighborhoods and tried for a time, without great success, to mobilize poor, working-class people politically. But most members of the New Left were students, and their radicalism centered in part on issues related to the modern university. A 1964 dispute at the University of California at Berkeley over the rights of students to engage in political activities on campus gained national atten-

FREE SPEECH MOVEMENT

tion. The Free Speech Movement, as it called itself, created turmoil at Berkeley as students challenged campus police, occupied administrative offices, and produced a strike in which nearly three-quarters of the Berkeley students participated. The immediate issue was the right of students to pass out literature and recruit volunteers for political causes on campus. But the protest quickly became as well an expression of a basic critique of the university and the society it seemed to represent.

The revolt at Berkeley was the first outburst of what was to be nearly a decade of campus turmoil. Students at Berkeley and elsewhere protested the impersonal character of the modern university, and they denounced the role of educational institutions in sustaining what they considered corrupt or immoral public policies. The antiwar movement greatly inflamed the challenge and expanded it to the universities; and beginning in 1968, campus demonstrations, riots, and building seizures became almost commonplace. At Columbia University in New York City, students seized several buildings, including the offices of the president, and occupied them for days until local police forcibly and violently ejected them. Harvard University had a similar, and even more violent, experience a year later.

Also in 1969, Berkeley became the scene of perhaps the most prolonged and traumatic conflict of any American college campus in the 1960s: a battle over the efforts of a few students to build a "People's Park" on a vacant lot the university planned to use to build a parking garage. This seemingly minor event precipitated weeks of impassioned and often violent conflicts between the university administration, which sought to evict the intruders from the land, and the students, many of whom supported the advocates of the park and who saw the university's efforts to close it as a symbol of the struggle between liberation and oppression.

By the end of the People's Park battle, which lasted for over a week, the Berkeley campus was completely polarized; even students who had not initially supported or even noticed the

PEOPLE'S PARK

People's Park (the great majority) were, by the end, committed to its defense;

ROCK MUSIC IN THE SIXTIES

THE rock music of the late 1960s and 1970s, even more than the rock 'n' roll of the 1950s and early 1960s, emphasized release. It gave vent to impulse and instinct, to physical and emotional urges. That was one reason it was so enormously popular among young people in an age of cultural and sexual revolution. It was also why it seemed so menacing and dangerous to many conservative Americans seeking to defend traditional values and behavior.

Rock in the late 1960s seemed simultaneously subversive and liberating. That was partly because of the behavior and lifestyles of rock musicians, whose appearance and behavior were often deliberately outrageous. Rock musicians were connected at times to the drug culture of the 1960s (especially through the so-called psychedelic-rock groups inspired by experiences with the hallucinogen LSD). They had links to mystical Eastern religions (most notably the Beatles, who had spent time in India studying Transcendental Meditation and who, beginning in 1967 with their album *Sergeant Pepper's Lonely Hearts Club Band*, incorporated those themes into their music). And they often reveled in flouting social conventions, beginning with the Rolling Stones and culminating, perhaps, in the extreme and self-destructive behavior of Jimi Hendrix, Jim Morrison, and Janis Joplin, all of whom died very young of drug-related causes.

Late-sixties rock was among many expressions of the impulses that came to be known as the counterculture; and like the counterculture, it inspired widely varying reactions. To its

WOODSTOCK MUSIC & ART FAIR
presents
AN AQUARIAN EXPOSITION
in
WHITE LAKE, N.Y.

3 DAYS of PEACE & MUSIC

WITH

Joan Baez	Keef Hartley	The Band
Arlo Guthrie	Canned Heat	Jeff Beck Group
Tim Hardin	Creedence Clearwater	Blood, Sweat and Tears
Richie Havens	Grateful Dead	Joe Cocker
Incredible String Band	Janis Joplin	Crosby, Stills and Nash
Ravi Shankar	Jefferson Airplane	Jimi Hendrix
Sly And The Family Stone	Mountain	Iron Butterfly
Bert Sommer	Quill	Ten Years After
Sweetwater	Santana	Johnny Winter
	The Who	

FRI. AUG. 15   **SAT. AUG. 16**   **SUN. AUG. 17**

All programs subject to change without notice
*White Lake, Town of Bethel, Sullivan County, N.Y.

ADVERTISING WOODSTOCK Even before the thousands of spectators gathered for the famous rock concert at Woodstock in 1969, organizers envisioned it as something more than a performance. It would, this poster claims, be a search for peace as well as for music. (© Hulton Archive/Getty Images)

★★★★
FINAL

SUNDAY NEWS
NEW YORK'S PICTURE NEWSPAPER ®
20¢
Vol. 49. No. 16   New York, N.Y. 10017, Sunday, August 17, 1969*

HIPPIES MIRED IN SEA OF MUD

They Don't Melt . . . Rockstars, undaunted by rain, mud and food shortages, trek to Woodstock folk-rock festival at White Lake, N.Y. Several thousand fled the desolated area and headed for Manhattan by a fleet of buses last night and this morning. The exodus made little dent in the crowd, numbering more than 400,000. —Stories p. 3; other pics centerfold

REPORTING WOODSTOCK The *New York Daily News*, whose largely working-class readership was not notably sympathetic toward the young people at Woodstock, ran this slightly derisive front-page story on the concert as heavy rains turned the concert site into a sea of mud. ["They Don't Melt," the caption said.] (© New York Daily News/Getty Images)

defenders, the new rock, with its emphasis on emotional release, was a healthy rebuke to the repressive norms of mainstream culture. To them, its virtues were symbolized by the great rock festival at Woodstock, New York, in August 1969, where over 400,000 young people gathered on a remote piece of farmland for several days to hear performances by such artists as the Who, Jimi Hendrix, the Grateful Dead, Janis Joplin, Joe Cocker, the Jefferson Airplane, and many others. The festival was

85 percent of the 15,000 students voted in a referendum to leave the park alone. Student radicals were, for the first time, winning large audiences for their extravagant rhetoric linking university administrators, the police, and the larger political and economic system, describing them all as part of one united, oppressive force.

Most campus radicals were rarely if ever violent (except at times in their rhetoric). But the popular image of student radicalism in mainstream culture was one of chaos and disorder, based in part on the disruptive actions of small groups of militants, among them the "Weathermen," a violent offshoot of SDS. The Weathermen were responsible for several cases of arson and bombing that destroyed campus buildings and claimed several

lives. Not many people, not even many students, ever accepted the most radical political views that lay at the heart of the New Left. But many supported the position of SDS and other groups on particular issues and, above all, on the Vietnam War. Student activists tried to drive out training programs for military officers (ROTC) and bar military recruiters from college campuses. They attacked the laboratories and corporations that were producing weapons for the war. And between 1967 and 1969, they organized some of the largest political demonstrations in American history. The October 1967 march on the Pentagon, where demonstrators were met by a solid line of armed troops; the "spring mobilization" of April 1968, which attracted hundreds of

ALTAMONT Hell's Angels "security guards" club a spectator near the stage during the rock concert at Altamont as other concertgoers—some curious, some aghast—watch. One spectator died as a result of the beatings. (© Photofest)

end the cold war he has borne / against his own kind of flesh." The festival and its music, many claimed, had shown the path to an age of love and peace and justice. Altamont, however, suggested a dark underside of the rock culture, its potential for destruction and violence. "As far as I was concerned," one participant said, "Altamont was the death knell of all those things that we thought would last forever. I personally felt like the sixties had been an extravagant stage show and I had been a spectator in the audience. Altamont had rung down the curtain to no applause."* ●

*Allen Ginsberg's estate is affiliated with the Naropa Institute, Boulder, CO.

UNDERSTAND, ANALYZE, AND EVALUATE

1. How does rock music of the 1960s differ from rock 'n' roll of the 1950s? What accounts for these differences?
2. What two characteristics of the counterculture are represented by Woodstock and Altamont? Was there an "Altamont" nation, just as there was a "Woodstock" nation?
3. Does popular music today challenge the prevailing culture, as rock music of the 1960s challenged the culture of that era? What lasting effects, if any, did 1960s rock have on U.S. society and culture?

marred by heavy rains that produced a sea of mud and by supplies and facilities completely inadequate for the unexpectedly large crowd. Drugs were everywhere in evidence, as was a kind of open sexual freedom that a decade earlier would have seemed unthinkable to all but a few Americans. But Woodstock remained peaceful, friendly, and harmonious. There was rhapsodic talk at the time of how Woodstock represented the birth of a new youth culture, the "Woodstock nation."

Critics of the new rock, and the counterculture, were not impressed with the idea of the "Woodstock nation." To them, the essence of the counterculture was a kind of numbing hopelessness and despair, with a menacing and violent underside. To them, the appropriate symbol was not Woodstock, but another great rock concert, which more than 300,000 people attended only four months after Woodstock, at the Altamont Speedway east of San Francisco. The concert featured many of the groups that had been at Woodstock, but the Rolling Stones, who had organized the event, were the main attraction. As at Woodstock, drugs were plentiful and sexual exhibitionism was frequent. But unlike Woodstock, Altamont was far from peaceful. Instead, it became ugly, brutal, and violent, and resulted in the deaths of four people. Several of them died accidentally, one, for example, from a bad drug trip, during which he fell into a stream and drowned. But numerous people were brutally beaten by members of the Hell's Angels motorcycle gang, who had been hired by the Rolling Stones as security guards. One man was beaten and stabbed to death in front of the stage while the Stones were playing "Sympathy for the Devil."

Woodstock and Altamont, then, became symbols of two aspects of the counterculture of the late 1960s and early 1970s, and of the rock music that created its anthems. The beat poet Allen Ginsberg wrote an ecstatic poem proclaiming that at Woodstock "a new kind of man has come to his bliss / to

thousands of demonstrators in cities around the country; the Vietnam "moratorium" of the fall of 1969, during which millions of opponents of the war gathered in major rallies across the nation; and countless other demonstrations, large and small—all helped thrust the issue of the war into the center of American politics.

Closely related to opposition to the war was opposition to the military draft. The gradual abolition of many traditional deferments—for graduate students, teachers, husbands, fathers, and others—swelled the ranks of those faced with conscription (and thus of those likely to oppose it). Some draft-age Americans simply refused induction, accepting what occasionally were long terms in jail as a result. Others fled to Canada, Sweden,

and elsewhere (where they were joined by deserters from the armed forces) to escape conscription. Not until 1977, when President Jimmy Carter issued a general pardon to draft resisters and a limited amnesty for deserters, did the Vietnam exiles begin to return to the country in substantial numbers.

THE COUNTERCULTURE

Closely related to the New Left was a new youth culture openly scornful of the values and conventions of middle-class society.

"HIPPIES"

As if to display their contempt for conventional standards, young Americans flaunted

BERKELEY, 1969 The People's Park controversy at the University of California at Berkeley turned the campus and the town into something close to a war zone. In this photograph, National Guardsmen with fixed bayonets stand in the way of a planned march to protest the closing of People's Park on May 30, 1969, more than two weeks after they first arrived to keep peace in Berkeley. (© AP Images)

long hair, shabby or flamboyant clothing, and a rebellious disdain for traditional speech and decorum. Also central to the counterculture, as it became known, were drugs: marijuana–which after 1966 became almost as common a youthful diversion as beer–and the less widespread but still substantial use of other, more potent hallucinogens, such as LSD.

There was also a new, more permissive view of sexual behavior–the beginnings of what came to be known as a "sexual revolution." To some degree, the emergence of relaxed approaches to sexuality was a result less of the counterculture than of the new accessibility of effective contraceptives, most notably the birth-control pill and, after 1973, legalized abortion. But the new sexuality also reflected the counterculture's belief that individuals should strive for release from inhibitions and give vent to their instincts and desires.

The counterculture challenged the structure of modern American society, attacking its banality, hollowness, artificiality, materialism, and isolation from nature. The most committed adherents of the counterculture–the hippies, who came to dominate the Haight-Ashbury neighborhood of San Francisco and other places, and the social dropouts, some of whom retreated to rural communes–rejected modern society and attempted to find refuge in a simpler, more "natural" existence.

HAIGHT-ASHBURY

The effects of the counterculture reached out to the larger society and helped create a new set of social norms that many young people (and some adults) chose to imitate. Long hair and freakish clothing became the badge not only of hippies and radicals but of an entire generation as well. The use of marijuana, the freer attitudes toward sex, the iconoclastic (and sometimes obscene) language–all spread far beyond the realm of the true devotees of the counterculture.

Perhaps the most pervasive element of the new youth society was one that even the least radical members of the generation embraced: rock music. Rock 'n' roll, drawn in part from African American music, first achieved wide popularity in the 1950s, on the strength of such early performers as Buddy Holly and, above all, Elvis Presley. Early in the 1960s, its influence spread, largely as a result of the phenomenal popularity of the Beatles, the English group whose first visit to the United States in 1964 created a remarkable sensation, "Beatlemania." For a time, most rock musicians–like most popular musicians before them–concentrated largely on uncontroversial, romantic themes. By the late 1960s, however, rock had begun to reflect many of the new iconoclastic values of its time. The Beatles, for example, abandoned their once simple and seemingly innocent style for a new, experimental, even mystical approach that reflected the growing popular fascination with drugs and Eastern religions. Other groups, such as the Rolling Stones, turned even more openly to themes of anger, frustration, and rebelliousness. Rock's driving rhythms, its sensuality, its often harsh and angry tone–all

GROWING INFLUENCE OF ROCK 'N' ROLL

WOODSTOCK In the summer of 1969, more than 400,000 people gathered for a rock concert on a farm near Woodstock, New York. Despite mostly terrible weather, the gathering was remarkably peaceful—sparking talk among some enthusiasts of the new youth culture about the "Woodstock nation." (© Shelly Rustin/Black Star)

made it an appropriate vehicle for expressing the themes of the social and political unrest of the late 1960s. A powerful symbol of the fusion of rock music and the counterculture was the great music festival at Woodstock, New York, in the summer of 1969. (See "Patterns of Popular Culture," pp. 810–811.)

THE MOBILIZATION OF MINORITIES

The growth of African American protest, the New Left, and the counterculture encouraged other minorities to assert themselves and demand redress of their grievances. For Native Americans, Hispanic Americans, gay men and women, and minorities, the late 1960s and the 1970s were a time of growing self-expression and political activism.

SEEDS OF INDIAN MILITANCY

Few minorities had deeper or more justifiable grievances against the prevailing culture than American Indians—or Native Americans, as some began to call themselves in the 1960s.

Indians were the least prosperous, least healthy, and least stable group in the nation. They were also one of the smallest,

NATIVE AMERICAN GRIEVANCES

constituting less than 1 percent of the population. Average annual family income for Indians was $1,000 less than that for blacks. The Native American unemployment rate was ten times the national rate. Joblessness was particularly high on the reservations, where nearly half the Indians lived. But even most Indians living in cities suffered from their limited education and training and could find only menial jobs. Life expectancy among Indians was some twenty years less than the national average. Suicides among Indian youths were a hundred times more frequent than among white youths. And while black Americans attracted the attention (for good or for ill) of many whites, Indians for many years remained largely ignored.

For much of the postwar era, particularly after the resignation of John Collier as commissioner of Indian Affairs in 1946, federal policy toward the tribes moved toward incorporating Indians into mainstream American society. (This policy was similar to failed "assimilation" efforts in the late nineteenth century.) Two laws passed in 1953 established what became known as "termination." Through termination,

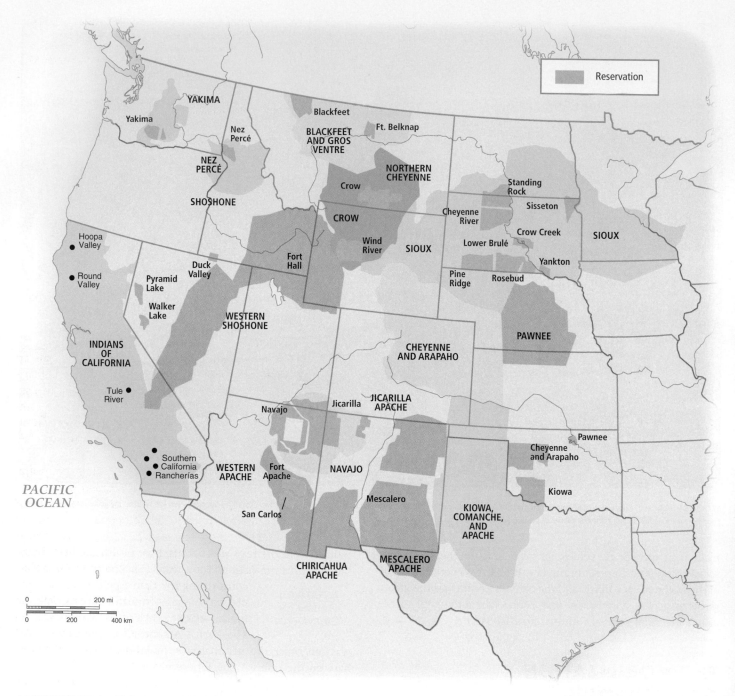

ABORIGINAL TERRITORIES AND MODERN RESERVATIONS OF WESTERN INDIAN TRIBES This map shows the rough distribution of the Native American population in the western United States before the establishment of reservations by the federal government in the nineteenth century. The large shaded regions in colors other than purple represent the areas in which the various tribes were dominant a century and more ago. The purple shaded areas show the much smaller areas set aside for them as reservations after the Indian wars of the late nineteenth century.

• *What impact did life on the reservations have on the rise of Indian activism in the 1960s and 1970s?*

the federal government withdrew all official recognition of the tribes as legal entities, administratively separate from state governments, and made them subject to the same local jurisdictions as white residents. At the same time, the government encouraged Indians to assimilate into the larger society and worked to funnel Native Americans into cities, where, presumably, they would adapt to the white world and lose their cultural distinctiveness.

To some degree, the termination and assimilation policies achieved their objectives. The tribes grew weaker, and many Native Americans adapted to life in the cities became less able to fend off white influence. On the whole, however, the new policies were a disaster for the tribes and a failure for the reformers who had promoted them. Termination led to widespread corruption and abuse. And Indians fought so bitterly against it

FAILURE OF "TERMINATION"

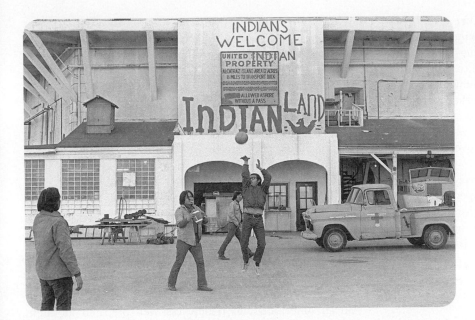

that in 1958 the Eisenhower administration barred further "terminations" without the consent of the affected tribes. In the meantime, the struggle against termination had mobilized a new generation of Indian militants and had breathed life into the principal Native American organization, the National Congress of American Indians (NCAI), created in 1944. The new militancy also benefited from the rapid increase in the Indian population, which was growing much faster than that of the rest of the nation (nearly doubling between 1950 and 1970, to a total of about 800,000).

THE INDIAN CIVIL RIGHTS MOVEMENT

In 1961, more than 400 members of 67 tribes gathered in Chicago to discuss ways of bringing all Indians together in an effort to redress common wrongs. The manifesto they issued, the Declaration of Indian Purpose, stressed the "right to choose our own way of life." One result of the movement was a gradual change in the way popular culture depicted Indians. By the 1970s, almost no films or television westerns any longer portrayed Indians as brutal savages attacking peaceful white people. And Indian activists even persuaded some white institutions to abandon what they considered demeaning references to them; Dartmouth College, for example, ceased referring to its athletic teams as the "Indians." In 1968, a group

AIM of young militant Indians established the American Indian Movement (AIM), which drew its greatest support from those Indians who lived in urban areas but soon established a significant presence on the reservations as well.

The new activism had some immediate political results. In 1968, Congress passed the Indian Civil Rights Act, which recognized the legitimacy of tribal laws within the reservations. But leaders of AIM and other insurgent groups were not satisfied and turned increasingly to direct action. In 1968,

Indian fishermen clashed with Washington State officials on the Columbia River and in Puget Sound, where Indians claimed that treaties gave them the exclusive right to fish. The following year, members of several tribes made a symbolic protest by occupying the abandoned federal prison on Alcatraz Island in San Francisco Bay and claiming the site "by right of discovery."

In response to the growing pressure, the Nixon administration appointed a Mohawk-Sioux to the position of commissioner of Indian Affairs in 1969; and in 1970, the president promised both increased tribal self-determination and an increase in federal aid. But the protests continued. In November 1972, nearly a thousand demonstrators, most of them Sioux, forcibly occupied the building of the Bureau of Indian Affairs in Washington, D.C., for six days.

A more celebrated protest occurred in February 1973 at Wounded Knee, South Dakota, the site of the 1890 massacre of

OCCUPATION OF WOUNDED KNEE Sioux by federal troops. Members of AIM seized and occupied the town of Wounded Knee for two months, demanding radical changes in the administration of the reservation and insisting that the government honor its long-forgotten treaty obligations. A brief clash between the occupiers and federal forces left one Indian dead and another wounded.

More immediately effective than these militant protests were the victories that various tribes were achieving in the federal courts. In *United States v. Wheeler* (1978), the Supreme Court confirmed that tribes had independent legal standing and could not be "terminated" by Congress. Other decisions ratified the authority of tribes to impose taxes on businesses within their reservations and to perform other sovereign functions. In 1985, the U.S. Supreme Court, in *County of Oneida v. Oneida Indian Nation*, supported Indian claims to 100,000 acres in upstate New York that the Oneida tribe claimed by virtue of treaty rights long forgotten by whites.

The Indian civil rights movement, like other civil rights movements of the same time, fell far short of winning full justice and equality for its constituents. To some Indians, the principal goal was to defend tribal autonomy, to protect the right of Indians (and, more to the point, individual tribal groups) to remain separate and distinct. To others, the goal was equality–to win for Indians a place in society equal to that of other groups of Americans. Because there was no single Indian culture or tradition in America, the movement never united all Indians.

IMPORTANT LEGAL VICTORIES For all its limits, however, the Indian civil rights movement helped the tribes win a series of new legal rights and protections that gave them a stronger position than they had enjoyed at any previous time in the twentieth century.

LATINO ACTIVISM

Far more numerous than Indians were Latinos (or Hispanic Americans), the fastest-growing minority group in the United States. They were no more a single, cohesive group than the Indians were. Some–including the descendants of early Spanish settlers in New Mexico–had roots as deep in American history as those of any other group. Others were men and women who had immigrated since World War II.

Large numbers of Puerto Ricans had migrated to eastern cities, particularly New York City. South Florida's substantial Cuban population began with a wave of middle-class refugees fleeing the Castro regime in the early 1960s, followed by a second, much poorer wave of Cuban immigrants in 1980–the so-called Marielitos, named for the port from which they left Cuba. Later in the 1980s, large numbers of immigrants (both legal and illegal) began to arrive from the troubled nations of Central and South America–from Guatemala, Nicaragua, El Salvador, Peru, and others. But the most numerous and important Latino group in the United States was Mexican Americans.

During World War II, large numbers of Mexican Americans had entered the country in response to the labor shortage, and many had remained in the cities of the Southwest and the Pacific Coast. After the war, when the legal agreements that had allowed Mexican contract workers to enter the country expired, large numbers of immigrants continued to move to the United States illegally. In 1953, the government launched what it called Operation Wetback to deport the illegals, but the effort failed to stem the flow of new arrivals. By 1960, there were substantial Mexican American neighborhoods (barrios) in American cities from El Paso to Detroit. The largest (with more than 500,000 people, according to census figures) was in Los Angeles, which had a bigger Mexican population than any other place except Mexico City.

SURGING LATINO IMMIGRATION But the greatest expansion in the Mexican American population was yet to come. In 1960, the census reported slightly more than 3 million Latinos living in the United States (the great majority of them Mexican Americans). By 1970, that number had grown to 9 million, and by 2009 to 48 million. Since there was also an uncounted but very large number of illegal immigrants in those years, the real number was undoubtedly larger.

By the late 1960s, Mexican Americans were one of the largest population groups in the West–outnumbering African Americans–and had established communities in most other parts of the nation as well. They were also among the most urbanized groups in the population; almost 90 percent lived and worked in cities. Many of them (particularly members of the older and more assimilated families of Mexican descent) were affluent and successful. Wealthy Cubans in Miami filled influential positions in the professions and local government; in the Southwest, Mexican Americans elected their own leaders to seats in Congress and to governorships.

But most newly arrived Mexican Americans and other Hispanics were less well educated than either "Anglo" or African Americans and hence less well prepared for high-paying jobs. Some of them found good industrial jobs in unionized industries, and some Mexican Americans became important labor organizers in the AFL-CIO. But many more (including most illegal immigrants) worked in low-paying service jobs, with few if any benefits and no job security.

"CHICANO" ACTIVISM Partly because of language barriers, partly because the family-centered culture of many Latino communities discouraged effective organization, and partly because of discrimination, Mexican Americans and other Hispanics were slower to develop political influence than other minorities. But some did respond to the highly charged climate of the 1960s by strengthening their ethnic identification and organizing for political and economic power. Young Mexican American activists began to call themselves "Chicanos" (once a term of derision used by whites) as a way of emphasizing the shared culture of Spanish-speaking Americans. Some Chicanos advocated a form of nationalism not unlike the ideas of black power advocates. The Texas leaders of La Raza Unida, a Chicano political party in the Southwest, called for the creation of an autonomous Mexican American state within a state; it demonstrated significant strength at the polls in the 1970s.

CÉSAR CHÁVEZ One of the most visible efforts to organize Mexican Americans occurred in California, where an Arizona-born Latino farmworker, César Chávez, created an effective union of itinerant farmworkers. In 1965, his United Farm Workers (UFW), a largely Mexican American organization, launched a prolonged strike against growers to demand recognition of their union and increased wages and benefits. When employers resisted, Chávez enlisted the cooperation of college students, churches, and civil rights groups (including CORE and SNCC) and organized a nationwide boycott, first of table grapes and then of lettuce. In 1968, Chávez campaigned openly for Robert Kennedy. Two years later, he won a substantial victory when the growers of half of California's table grapes signed contracts with his union.

KENNEDY AND CHÁVEZ César Chávez, the magnetic leader of the largely Mexican American United Farm Workers, a union that represented mostly migrant workers, staged a hunger strike in 1968 to demand that its members receive better treatment by growers. Robert F. Kennedy, just beginning his campaign for the presidency, paid him a visit in Delano, California, to show his support. Chávez, who had by then been fasting for many weeks, looks visibly weak here. Kennedy's visit helped persuade him to end the fast. (Photo by Michael Rougier/© Time & Life Pictures/Getty Images)

Latino Americans were at the center of another controversy of the 1970s and beyond: the issue of bilingualism. It was a question that aroused the opposition not only of many whites but of some Hispanics as well. Supporters of bilingualism in education argued that non-English-speaking Americans were entitled to schooling in their own language, that otherwise they would be at a grave disadvantage in comparison with native English speakers. The U.S. Supreme Court confirmed the right of non-English-speaking students to schooling in their native language in 1974. Opponents cited not only the cost and difficulty of bilingualism but also the dangers it posed to students' ability to assimilate into the mainstream of American culture.

GAY LIBERATION

Another important liberation movement that made gains in the 1960s was the effort by homosexuals to win political and economic rights and, equally important, social acceptance. Homosexuality and lesbianism had been unacknowledged realities throughout American history; not until

many years after their deaths did many Americans know, for example, that revered cultural figures such as Walt Whitman and Horatio Alger were homosexuals. But by the late 1960s, the liberating impulses that had affected other groups helped mobilize gay men and lesbians to fight for their own rights.

On June 27, 1969, police officers raided the Stonewall Inn, a gay bar in New York City's Greenwich Village, and began arresting patrons simply for frequenting the place. The raid was not unusual; police had been harassing gay bars (and homosexual men and women) for years. The accumulated resentment of this long history of assaults and humiliations caused the extraordinary response that summer night. Gay onlookers taunted the police, then attacked them. Someone started a blaze in the Stonewall Inn, almost trapping the policemen inside. Rioting continued throughout Greenwich Village (a center of New York's gay community) through much of the night.

The "Stonewall Riot" helped make the gay liberation movement—a movement that had been gaining strength since

"STONEWALL RIOT"

could be as significant and worthy of respect as heterosexual ones. Even the ravages of the AIDS epidemic, which affected the gay community more disastrously than it affected any other group, failed to halt the growth of gay liberation. In many ways, it strengthened it.

By the early 1990s, gay men and lesbians were achieving some of the same milestones that other oppressed minorities had attained in earlier decades. Some openly gay politicians won election to public office. Universities were establishing gay and lesbian studies programs. And laws prohibiting discrimination on the basis of sexual preference were making slow, halting progress at the local level.

But gay liberation also produced a powerful backlash. This became especially evident in 1993, when President Bill Clinton's effort to lift the ban on gays and lesbians serving in the military met a storm of criticism from members of Congress and from within the military itself. The backlash proved so strong that the administration retreated from its position and settled for a weak compromise ("Don't ask, don't tell") by which the military would not ask recruits about their sexual preferences, while those who enlisted in the military were expected not to reveal them.

A decade later, issues involving gays and lesbians reached a high level of intensity again, sparked in part by the efforts of several cities and states to legalize same-sex marriage. President George W. Bush proposed a constitutional amendment to ban same-sex marriage, and the issue became a major element of Republican election campaigns. Many states put referenda on their ballots banning gay marriage, and most such referenda were decisively approved by the voters.

By 2014, the federal government, 17 states, and the District of Columbia authorized same-sex marriage. In 2013, the Supreme Court bolstered the rights of same-sex couples when it ruled, in *United States v. Windsor*, that restricting the definition of marriage to include only heterosexual couples was unconstitutional. The ruling extended on the federal level the same rights enjoyed by married heterosexuals to same-sex couples. The ruling left intact any state laws prohibiting same-sex marriage. Also in 2013, Congress passed the Don't Ask, Don't Tell Repeal Act, making it possible for gay people to serve openly in the military.

THE QUILT In the early years of gay liberation, the movement focused mostly on ending discrimination and harassment. By the 1990s, however, with the AIDS epidemic affecting large numbers of gay men, activists shifted much of their attention to pressing for a cure and to remembering those who had died. One of the most remarkable results of that effort was the AIDS Quilt. Friends and relatives of victims of the disease made individual patches in memory of those they had lost. Then, in many different cities, thousands of quilters would join their pieces to create a vast testament to bereavement and memory. The enormity of the project was most visible in October 1996, when hundreds of thousands of pieces of the quilt were laid out on the Mall in Washington, stretching from the Washington Monument to the Capitol. (© Ron Edmunds/AP Images)

at least the 1950s–a significant and highly public force. New organizations sprang up around the country. Public discussion and media coverage of homosexuality, long subject to an unofficial taboo, quickly and dramatically increased. Gay and lesbian activists had some success in challenging the longstanding assumption that homosexuality was "aberrant" behavior. They argued that no sexual preference was any more "normal" than another.

Most of all, however, the gay liberation movement transformed the outlook of gay men and lesbians themselves. It

IMPACT OF THE
GAY LIBERATION
MOVEMENT

helped them to "come out," to express their preferences openly and unapologetically, and to demand from society a recognition that gay relationships

THE NEW FEMINISM

American women constitute a slight majority of the population. But during the 1960s and 1970s, many women began to identify with minority groups and to demand a liberation of their own. As a result, the role of women in American life changed more dramatically than that of any other group in the nation.

THE REBIRTH

Feminism had been a weak and often-embattled force in American life for more than forty years after the adoption of the woman suffrage amendment in 1920. Yet in the 1960s and 1970s, it evolved very quickly from relative obscurity to one of the most powerful social movements in American history.

The 1963 publication of Betty Friedan's *The Feminine Mystique* is often cited as an important early event of con-

THE FEMININE MYSTIQUE

temporary women's liberation. Friedan, a magazine journalist, had traveled around the country interviewing the women

who had graduated with her from Smith College in 1942. Most of these women were living out the dream that postwar American society had created for them: they were affluent wives and mothers living in comfortable suburbs. And yet many of them were deeply frustrated and unhappy. The suburbs, Friedan claimed, had become a "comfortable concentration camp," providing the women who inhabited them with no outlets for their intelligence, talent, and education. The "feminine mystique," she wrote, was responsible for "burying millions of women alive." By chronicling their unhappiness and frustration, Friedan did not so much cause

the revival of feminism as help give voice to a movement that was already stirring.

By the time *The Feminine Mystique* appeared, John Kennedy had established the President's Commission on the Status of Women; it brought national attention to sexual discrimination and helped create important networks of feminist activists who would lobby for legislative redress. Also in 1963, the Kennedy administration helped win passage of the Equal Pay Act, which barred the pervasive practice of paying women less than men for equal work. A year later, Congress incorporated into the Civil Rights Act of 1964 an amendment–Title VII– that extended to women many of the same legal protections against discrimination that were being extended to African Americans.

The events of the early 1960s helped expose a contradiction that had been developing for decades between the image of happy domesticity, what Friedan had called the "feminine mystique," and the reality of women's roles in America. The reality was that increasing numbers of women (including, by 1963, over a third of all married women) had already entered the workplace and were encountering widespread discrimination there; and that many other women were finding their domestic lives suffocating and frustrating.

In 1966, Friedan joined with other feminists to create the

NOW FOUNDED

National Organization for Women (NOW), which soon became the nation's largest and most influential feminist organization.

Like other movements for liberation, feminism drew much of its inspiration from the black struggle for freedom.

The new organization responded to the complaints of the women Friedan's book had examined–affluent suburbanites with no outlet for their interests–by demanding greater educational opportunities for women and denouncing the domestic ideal and the traditional concept of marriage. But the heart of the movement, at least in the beginning, was directed toward the needs of women already in the workplace. NOW denounced the exclusion of women from professions, from politics, and from countless other areas of American life. It decried legal and economic discrimination, including the practice of paying women less than men for equal work (a practice the Equal Pay Act had not effectively eliminated). The organization called for "a fully equal partnership of the sexes, as part of the worldwide revolution of human rights."

WOMEN'S LIBERATION

By the late 1960s, new and more radical feminist demands were also attracting a large following. The new feminists were mostly younger, the vanguard of the baby-boom gen-

NEW DIRECTIONS IN THE WOMEN'S MOVEMENT

eration. Many of them drew inspiration from the New Left and the counterculture. Some were involved in the civil rights movement, others in the antiwar crusade. Many had found that even

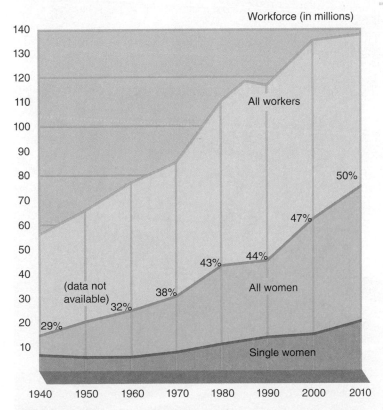

WOMEN IN THE PAID WORKFORCE, 1940–2010 The number of women working for wages steadily expanded from 1940 on, to the point that in 2010, they constituted half the total workforce.

• *What role did this growing participation in the paid workforce have on the rise of feminism in the 1960s and beyond?*

within those movements, they faced discrimination and exclusion or subordination to male leaders.

By the early 1970s, a significant change was visible in the tone and direction of the women's movement. New books by younger feminists expressed a harsher critique of American society than Friedan had offered. Kate Millett's *Sexual Politics,* (1969) signaled the new direction by arguing that "every avenue of power within the society is entirely within male hands." The answer to women's problems, in other words, was not, as Friedan had suggested, for individual women to search for greater personal fulfillment; it was for women to band together to assault the male power structure. Shulamith Firestone's *The Dialectic of Sex* (1970) was subtitled "The Case for Feminist Revolution." By the early 1970s, large numbers of women were coming to see themselves as an exploited group organizing against oppression and developing a culture and communities of their own.

EXPANDING ACHIEVEMENTS

By the early 1970s, the public and private achievements of the women's movement were already substantial. In 1971, the government extended its affirmative action guidelines to include women—linking sexism with racism as an officially acknowledged social problem. In the meantime, women were making rapid progress in their efforts to move into the economic and political mainstream. The nation's major all-male educational institutions began to open their doors to women. (Princeton and Yale did so in 1969, and most other all-male colleges and universities soon followed.) Some women's colleges, in the meantime, began accepting male students.

Women were also becoming an important force in business and the professions. Nearly half of all married women held jobs by the mid-1970s, and almost 90 percent of all women with college degrees worked. (By 2010, women constituted half the total workforce.) The two-career family, in which both husband and wife maintained active professional lives, was becoming a widely accepted norm; many women were postponing marriage or motherhood for the sake of their careers. There were also important symbolic changes, such as the refusal of many women to adopt their husbands' names when they married and the use of the term "Ms." in place of

POLITICAL AND ECONOMIC SUCCESS

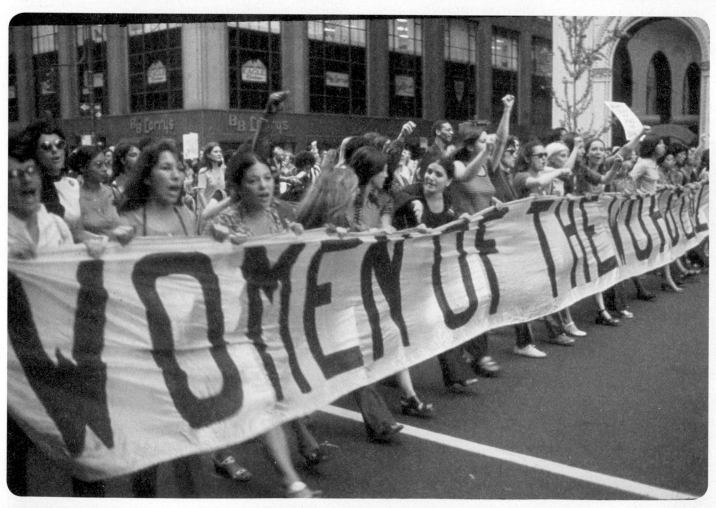

MARCHING FOR WOMEN'S RIGHTS By the end of the 1960s, the struggle for individual rights—which the African American civil rights movement had helped push to the center of national consciousness—had inspired a broad range of movements. Perhaps the most important in the long run was the drive for women's rights, which was already formidable in the summer of 1970, when thousands of women joined this march through New York City. (© Werner Wolff/Black Star)

"Mrs." or "Miss" to denote the irrelevance of a woman's marital status in the public world. In politics, women were beginning to compete effectively with men for both elected and appointive positions. By 2010, considerable numbers of women were serving in both houses of Congress (including a Speaker of the House, Nancy Pelosi), in numerous federal cabinet positions (including three secretaries of state), as governors, and in many other positions. Ronald Reagan appointed the first female Supreme Court justice, Sandra Day O'Connor, in 1981; in 1993, Bill Clinton appointed the second, Ruth Bader Ginsburg; and Barack Obama appointed two women justices, Sonia Sotomayor and Elena Kagan in 2009 and 2010, respectively. In 1984, the Democratic Party chose Representative Geraldine Ferraro of New York as its vice presidential candidate, and in 2008, Hillary Clinton became a formidable candidate in the race for the Democratic presidential nomination. In academia, women were expanding their presence in traditional scholarly fields; they were also creating a field of their own—women's studies, which in the 1980s and early 1990s was among the fastest-growing areas of American scholarship.

In professional athletics, women were beginning to compete with men both for attention and for an equal share of prize money. By the late 1970s, the federal government was pressuring colleges and universities to provide women with athletic programs equal to those available to men.

In 1972, Congress approved the Equal Rights Amendment to the Constitution, which some feminists had been promoting **FAILURE OF ERA** since the 1920s, and sent it to the states. For a while, ratification seemed almost certain. By the late 1970s, however, the momentum behind the amendment had died. The ERA was in trouble not because of indifference but because of a rising chorus of objections to it from people (including many antifeminist women) who feared it would disrupt traditional social patterns. In 1982, the amendment died when the time allotted for its ratification expired.

THE ABORTION CONTROVERSY

A vital element of American feminism since the 1920s has been women's effort to win greater control of their own sexual and reproductive lives. In its least controversial form, this impulse helped produce an increasing awareness in the 1960s and 1970s of the problems of rape, sexual abuse, and wife beating. There continued to be some controversy over the dissemination of contraceptives and birth-control information; but that issue, at least, seemed to have lost much of the explosive character it had had in the 1920s. A related issue, however, stimulated as much popular passion as any question of its time: abortion.

Abortion had once been legal in much of the United States, but by the beginning of the twentieth century it was banned by statute in most of the country and remained so into the **ROE v. WADE** 1960s (although many abortions continued to be performed quietly, and often dangerously, out of sight of the law). But the women's movement created strong new pressures on behalf of legalizing abortion.

Several states had abandoned restrictions on abortion by the end of the 1960s. And in 1973, the Supreme Court's decision in *Roe v. Wade*, based on a relatively new theory of a constitutional "right to privacy," first recognized by the Court only a few years earlier in *Griswold v. Connecticut* (1965), invalidated all laws prohibiting abortion during the "first trimester"—the first three months of pregnancy. The decision would become the most controversial ruling of the century.

ENVIRONMENTALISM IN A TURBULENT SOCIETY

Like feminism, environmentalism entered the 1960s with a long history and little public support. Also like feminism, environmentalism both profited from and transcended the turbulence of the era and emerged by the 1970s as a powerful and enduring force in American and global life.

The rise of this new movement was in part a result of the environmental degradation that had become increasingly evident in the advanced industrial society of the late twentieth century. It was a result, too, of the growth of the science of ecology, which provided environmentalists with new and powerful arguments. And it was a product of some of the countercultural movements of the time: movements that rejected aspects of the modern, industrial, consumer society and called for a return to a more "natural" existence.

THE NEW SCIENCE OF ECOLOGY

Until the mid-twentieth century, most people who considered themselves environmentalists (or, to use the traditional term, conservationists) based their commitment on aesthetic or moral grounds: they wanted to preserve nature because it was too beautiful to despoil, or because it was a mark of divinity on the world. In the course of the twentieth century, however, scientists in the United States and other nations—drawing from earlier, relatively obscure scientific writings—began to create a new rationale for environmentalism. They called it "ecology."

Ecology is the science of the interrelatedness of the natural world. It rests on an assumption—as the American zoologist **IDEA OF AN INTERRELATED WORLD** Stephen A. Forbes wrote as early as 1880—that "primeval nature . . . presents a settled harmony of interaction among organic groups," and that this harmony "is in strong contrast with the many serious maladjustments of plants and animals found in countries occupied by man." Such problems as air and water pollution, the destruction of forests, the extinction of species, and toxic wastes are not, ecology teaches, separate, isolated problems. All elements of the earth's environment are intimately and delicately linked. Damaging any one of those elements, therefore, risks damaging all the others.

A number of American scientists built on Forbes's ideas in the early twentieth century, but perhaps the greatest early

RACHEL CARSON Rachel Carson, who began her career as a marine biologist, wrote the world's best-selling book about the ocean environment in the 1950s. Carson's abiding love for the creatures of shore and surf led to her concern about the harm pesticides might do them. (© Bettmann/Corbis)

contribution to popular knowledge of ecology came not from a scientist, but from the writer and naturalist Aldo Leopold. During a career in forest management, Leopold sought to apply the new scientific findings on ecology to his interactions with the natural world. And in 1949, he published a classic of environmental literature, *The Sand County Almanac*, in which he argued that humans have a responsibility to understand and maintain the balance of nature, that they should behave in the natural world according to a code that he called the "land ethic." By then, the science of ecology was spreading widely in the scientific community. Among the findings of ecologists were such now-common ideas as the "food chain," the "ecosystem," "biodiversity," and "endangered species."

The influence of these emerging ideas of ecology could be seen especially clearly in the sensational 1962 book by Rachel Carson, *Silent Spring*. Carson was a marine biologist who had become a successful science writer. In 1957, she received a letter from a friend reporting the deaths of songbirds in her yard after the area had been sprayed with the insecticide DDT—the chemical developed in the 1930s to kill mosquitoes. Carson began investigating the impact of DDT and discovered growing signs of danger. DDT was slowly being absorbed into the food chain through water and plants, and the animals who ate and drank them. It was killing some animals (especially birds and fish) and inhibiting the ability of others to reproduce. Carson wrote eloquently about the growing danger of a "silent spring," in which birds would no longer sing and in which sickness and death would soon threaten large numbers of animals and, perhaps, people.

Silent Spring was an enormously influential book and had a direct, if delayed, influence on the decision to ban DDT in the United States in 1972. It was evidence of the growing power of environmentalism, and of the science of ecology, on public policy and national culture. But *Silent Spring* was also a very controversial book that enraged the chemical industry. Critics of Carson attempted to suppress the book and, when that effort failed, to discredit its findings.

ECOLOGY'S POSTWAR GROWTH

Between 1945 and 1960, the number of ecologists in the United States grew rapidly, and that number doubled again between 1960 and 1970. Funded by government agencies, by universities, by foundations, and eventually even by some corporations, ecological science gradually established itself as a significant field of its own. By the early twenty-first century, there were programs in and departments of ecological science in major universities throughout the United States and in many other nations.

Much more than other scientists, however, ecologists tend to fuse their commitment to research with a commitment to publicizing their work and promoting responsible public action to deal with environmental crises.

ENVIRONMENTAL ADVOCACY

Among the most important environmental organizations of the late twentieth and early twenty-first centuries were the Wilderness Society, the Sierra Club, the National Audubon Society, the Nature Conservancy, the National Wildlife Federation, and the National Parks and Conservation Association. All of these organizations predated the rise of modern ecological science, but all of them entered the twenty-first century reenergized and committed to the new concepts of environmentalism. They found allies among other not-for-profit organizations that had no previous experience with environmentalism but now chose to join the battle—among them such groups as the American Civil Liberties Union, the League of Women Voters, the National Council of Churches, and even the AFL-CIO.

NEW PROFESSIONAL ENVIRONMENTAL ACTIVISTS

Out of these organizations emerged a new generation of professional environmental activists able to contribute to the legal and political battles of the movement. Scientists provided the necessary data. Lawyers fought battles with government agencies and in the courts. Lobbyists used traditional techniques of political persuasion with legislators and other officials—knowing that many corporations and other opponents of environmental efforts would be doing the same in opposition to their goals. Perhaps most of all, these organizations learned how to mobilize public opinion on their behalf.

ENVIRONMENTAL DEGRADATION

Perhaps the greatest force behind environmentalism was the condition of the environment itself. By the 1960s, the damage to the natural world from the dramatic economic growth of the postwar era was becoming impossible to ignore. Water pollution—which had been a problem in some areas of the country for many decades—was becoming so widespread that almost every major city was dealing with the unpleasant sight and odor, as well as the very real health risks, of polluted rivers and lakes. In Cleveland, Ohio, for example, the Cuyahoga River burst into flame from time to time beginning in the 1950s from the petroleum waste being dumped into it.

WATER AND AIR POLLUTION

Perhaps more alarming was the growing awareness that the air itself was becoming unhealthy, that toxic fumes from factories and power plants and, most of all, automobiles were poisoning the atmosphere. Weather forecasts and official atmospheric information began to refer to "smog" levels—using a new word formed from a combination of "smoke" and "fog." In some large cities—Los Angeles and Denver among them—smog became a perpetual fact of life, rising steadily through the day, blotting out the sun, and creating respiratory difficulties for many citizens.

Environmentalists also brought to public attention some longer-term dangers of unchecked industrial development: the rapid depletion of oil and other irreplaceable fossil fuels; the destruction of lakes and forests as a result of "acid rain" (rainfall polluted by chemical contaminants); the rapid destruction of vast rain forests, in Brazil and elsewhere, which limited the earth's capacity to replenish its oxygen supply; the depletion of the ozone layer as a result of the release of chlorofluorocarbons into the atmosphere, which threatened to limit the earth's protection from dangerous ultraviolet rays from the sun; and most alarming, global warming, which if unchecked would create dramatic changes in the earth's climate and would threaten existing cities and settlements in coastal areas all over the world by causing a rise in ocean levels. Many of these claims became controversial, with skeptics arguing that environmentalists had not conclusively proven their cases. But most environmentalists—and many scientists—came to believe that the problems were real and deserving of immediate, urgent attention.

EARTH DAY AND BEYOND

On April 22, 1970, people all over the United States gathered in schools and universities, in churches and clubs, in parks and auditoriums, for the first "Earth Day." Originally proposed by Wisconsin senator Gaylord Nelson as a series of teach-ins on college campuses, Earth Day gradually took on a much larger life. Carefully managed by people who wanted to avoid associations with the radical left, it had an unthreatening quality that appealed to many people for whom antiwar demonstrations and civil rights rallies seemed threatening. According to some estimates, over 20 million Americans participated in some part of the Earth Day observances, which may have made it the largest single demonstration in the nation's history.

THE FIRST "EARTH DAY"

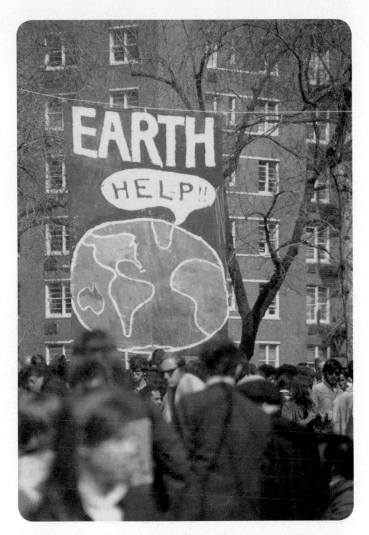

EARTH DAY, 1970 The first "Earth Day," April 22, 1970, was an important event in the development of the environmental movement. Conceived by Wisconsin senator Gaylord Nelson, Earth Day quickly gathered support in many areas of the United States and produced large demonstrations such as this one in New York City, where crowds surround a large banner portraying the earth crying out for help. (© Hulton Archive/Getty Images)

The cautious, centrist character of Earth Day and related efforts to popularize environmentalism helped create a movement that had little of the divisiveness of other, more controversial causes. Gradually, environmentalism became more than simply a series of demonstrations and protests. It became part of the consciousness of the vast majority of Americans—absorbed into popular culture, built into primary and secondary education, endorsed by almost all politicians (even if many of them opposed some environmental goals).

It also became part of the fabric of public policy. In 1970, Congress passed and President Nixon signed the National Environmental Protection Act, which created a new agency—the Environmental Protection Agency—to enforce antipollution standards on businesses and consumers. The Clean Air Act, also passed in 1970, and the Clean Water Act, passed in 1972, added tools to the government's arsenal of weapons against environmental degradation.

EPA ESTABLISHED

THE END OF COLONIALISM WOR-7, 8

ON July 4, 1946, less than a year after the close of World War II, the United States voluntarily ended its five-decade-old colonial control of the Philippines, which it had acquired as part of the spoils from the 1898 Spanish-American War. Philippine independence was only a small part of a dramatic change in the political structure of the world. The close of World War II marked not only the defeat of fascism in Germany, Italy, and Japan, but also the beginning of the end of the formal system of imperialism that European powers had maintained for centuries. Like most fundamental geopolitical changes, the drive for colonial independence was turbulent and often violent.

Although its divestiture of the Philippines was relatively peaceful, the United States was not quite as ready to cede its military and economic presence in the region as it was to give up political responsibility over the islands. Philippine independence came with important caveats: the United States maintained control of its military bases there, forbade the Philippines to engage in any direct economic competition with the United States, and required the new Philippine government to revise its constitution to allow American interests free access to the nation's natural resources. In fact, many Filipinos argue that their nation only achieved full independence in 1991, after the Philippine Senate refused to ratify a treaty that would have extended the American lease on the Subic Bay Naval Base. A year later, the United States closed the base and left, marking the first time in 400 years that the Philippines (once a Spanish possession) were not home to a foreign military power.

Britain, whose imperial holdings were the vastest in the world, withdrew from most of its colonies after World War II—beginning in 1947 with India, its largest and most important colony. As often happened when colonial rule ended, suppressed conflicts in the native population quickly emerged—in the case of India, between Hindus and Muslims. The price of Indian independence was the partition of the country into India and Pakistan (and, several decades later, Bangladesh). A year later, Britain gave up its World War I mandate of Palestine, ceding the territory to the United Nations (and allowing for the creation of Israel), as well as many of its holdings in Southeast Asia. In 1982, Britain passed the Canada Act, effectively severing Canada from the United Kingdom and culminating a move toward full Canadian self-government. Finally, in 1997, Britain returned Hong Kong to the control of China, effectively bringing an end to the era of the British Empire.

The dissolution of the British Empire did not always proceed smoothly. The Suez Crisis of 1956 dealt a decisive blow to Britain's status as a major power in the Middle East. The efforts of Britain, France, and Israel to prevent Egypt from seizing the British-controlled Suez Canal, which ran through Egyptian territory, ended in a humiliating defeat. In 1982, a dispute over the tiny Falkland Islands (just off the coast of Argentina) soon erupted into war between Britain and Argentina, which claimed the islands as its own. After the deaths of 258 British and 649 Argentine soldiers, Britain maintained its control of the Falklands, although Argentina continues to assert its right to the islands.

Despite these controversies, the dissolution of the British Empire proceeded relatively smoothly compared to the experience of the French. In late 1946, Vietnamese nationalists rose up against the French colonial government that controlled the region. The French effort to return to Vietnam culminated ultimately in the French defeat at Dien Bien Phu in 1954 and their subsequent withdrawal from Indochina. France also became embroiled in—and tried to suppress by force—other violent colonial uprisings, in Madagascar, Cameroon, and most notably Algeria. The Algerian War (1954–1962) was a particularly bloody and costly conflict, involving guerrilla warfare, torture, acts of terrorism, and, eventually, the collapse of the French Fourth Republic in 1958. Algeria ultimately won its independence, but the scars created by the long and ugly war were slow to heal.

The end of the colonial system had its greatest impact on Africa. European powers had carved up almost all of sub-Saharan Africa in the nineteenth century. But in the decades after World War II, almost all the African colonies won their independence even if not always easily. African nationalism, however, was troubled for decades by political instability and, in some countries, extreme poverty. Africa is currently home to 34 of the 48 poorest and 24 of the 32 least developed

NIXON, KISSINGER, AND THE WAR

Richard Nixon assumed office in 1969 committed not only to restoring stability at home but also to creating a new and more stable order in the world. Central to his hopes was a resolution of the stalemate in Vietnam. Yet the new president felt no freer than his predecessor to abandon the American commitment there. He realized that the war was threatening both the nation's domestic stability and its position in the world. But he feared that a precipitous retreat would destroy American honor and "credibility." American involvement in Indochina continued for four more years, during which the war expanded in its geographic scope and its bloodiness.

VIETNAMIZATION

Despite Nixon's own passionate interest in international affairs, he brought with him into government a man who ultimately seemed to overshadow him in the conduct of diplomacy: Henry Kissinger, a Harvard professor whom the president appointed as his national security adviser. Kissinger quickly established dominance over the secretary of state, William Rogers, and the secretary of defense, Melvin Laird, who were both more experienced in public life than Kissinger was. That was in part a result of Nixon's passion for concentrating decision making in the White House. But Kissinger's keen intelligence, bureaucratic skills, and success in handling the press were at least equally important. Together, Nixon and Kissinger set out to find an acceptable solution to the stalemate in Vietnam.

HENRY KISSINGER

countries in the world, in no small part a result of the lingering shadow cast by centuries of colonial exploitation of the continent.

The most recent epicenter of independence movements has been in the lands that used to comprise the former Soviet Union. A long and costly war in Afghanistan began in the 1970s as the Soviet Union struggled to retain control of the nation in the face of powerful local insurgencies. The war was one of the principal factors in the unraveling of the Soviet Empire that began in 1991. Many of the former Soviet republics—which considered themselves colonies of Russia—soon separated from Russia and became independent nations in their own right. Even after the dissolution of the Soviet Union, Russia continues to deal with the problems of empire. A vicious conflict with Chechnya, an Islamic area of Russia insisting on independence, has created terror and instability for years. In 2014, Russia reclaimed Crimea, which since the collapse of the Soviet Union had been a part of Ukraine. This action threatened to heighten tensions between Russia and the West to levels not seen since the Cold War.

The end of colonialism marked the end to an imperial system that was based on the assumption of European (and American) superiority over non-Western peoples. But if formal colonialism came to an end in the post–World War II era, other aspects of imperialism did not. Many former colonies still struggle with the indirect exercise of power, especially economic power, that wealthy Western nations continue to exert over much of the nonindustrialized world.   ●

UNDERSTAND, ANALYZE, AND EVALUATE

1. How did the experience of World War II contribute to the end of colonialism?
2. Why was the end of colonialism so often accompanied by violence?
3. What have been the effects of colonialism—and the end of colonialism—on Africa? Why have the effects been so pronounced on that continent, more so than in other areas of the world?

The new Vietnam policy moved along several fronts. One was an effort to limit domestic opposition to the war. Aware that the military draft was one of the most visible targets of dissent, the administration devised a new "lottery" system, through which only a limited group–those nineteen-year-olds with low lottery numbers–would be subject to conscription. Later, the president urged the creation of an all-volunteer army. By 1973, the Selective Service System was on its way to at least temporary extinction.

More important in stifling dissent, however, was the new policy of "Vietnamization" of the war–the training and equip-

CONSEQUENCES OF "VIETNAMIZATION" ping of the South Vietnamese military to take over the burden of combat from American forces. In the fall of 1969, Nixon announced reduction of American ground troops from Vietnam by 60,000, the first reduction in U.S. troop strength

since the beginning of the war. The reductions continued steadily for more than three years. From a peak of more than 540,000 American troops in 1969, the number had dwindled to about 60,000 by 1972.

Vietnamization helped quiet domestic opposition to the war. But it did nothing to break the stalemate in the negotiations with the North Vietnamese in Paris. The new administration quickly decided that new military pressures would be necessary to do that.

ESCALATION

By the end of their first year in office, Nixon and Kissinger had concluded that the most effective way to tip the military balance in America's favor was to destroy the bases in Cambodia from which, the American military believed, the North Vietnamese were launching many of their attacks. Very early in his presidency, Nixon ordered the air force to begin bombing Cambodian territory to destroy the enemy sanctuaries. He kept the raids secret from Congress and the public. In the spring of 1970, possibly with U.S. encouragement and support, conservative military leaders overthrew the neutral government of Cambodia and established a new, pro-American regime under General Lon Nol. Lon Nol quickly gave his approval to American incursions into his territory; and on April 30, Nixon went on television to announce that he was ordering American troops across the border into Cambodia to "clean out" the bases that the enemy had been using for its "increased military aggression."

Almost overnight, the Cambodian invasion restored the dwindling antiwar movement to vigorous life. The first days of May saw the most widespread and vocal antiwar demonstrations since the beginning of the war. Hundreds of thousands of protesters gathered in Washington, D.C., to denounce the president's policies. Millions, perhaps, participated in other demonstrations on campuses nationwide. The mood of crisis intensified greatly on May 4, when four college students were killed and nine others injured when members of

KENT STATE the National Guard opened fire on antiwar demonstrators at Kent State University in Ohio. Ten days later, police killed two black students at Jackson State University in Mississippi during a demonstration there.

The clamor against the war quickly spread into the government and the press. Congress angrily repealed the Gulf of Tonkin Resolution in December, stripping the president of what had long served as the legal basis for the war. Nixon ignored the action. Then, in June 1971, first the *New York Times* and later other newspapers began publishing excerpts from a secret study of the war prepared by the Defense Department during the Johnson administration. What came to be known as the Pentagon Papers, leaked to the press by former Defense Department official Daniel Ellsberg, provided evidence of what many critics of the war had long believed: that the government had been dishonest, both in reporting the military progress of the war and in explaining its own motives for American involvement. The administration went to court to suppress the documents, but the Supreme Court finally ruled that the press had the right to publish them.

Morale and discipline were rapidly deteriorating among U.S. troops in Vietnam, who had been fighting a savage and inconclusive war for more than five years. The trial and conviction in 1971 of Lieutenant William Calley, **MY LAI MASSACRE** who was charged with overseeing a massacre of more than 300 unarmed South Vietnamese civilians, attracted wide public attention. Many Americans believed that the My Lai tragedy was not an isolated incident. Less publicized were other, more widespread problems among American troops in Vietnam: desertion, drug addiction, racial hostilities, refusal to obey orders, even the occasional killing of unpopular officers by enlisted men.

By 1971, nearly two-thirds of those interviewed in public opinion polls were urging American withdrawal from Vietnam, including many conservatives, who considered Nixon's policies as too timid. If the war was not designed for victory, they believed, it should not be fought.

In March 1972, the North Vietnamese mounted the biggest offensive since 1968 (the so-called Easter offensive). American and South Vietnamese forces managed to halt the North Vietnam advance, but it was clear that without **EASTER OFFENSIVE** American support the offensive would have succeeded. At the same time, Nixon ordered American planes to bomb targets near Hanoi, the capital of North Vietnam, and Haiphong, its principal port, and called for the mining of seven North Vietnamese harbors to stop the flow of supplies from China and the Soviet Union.

"PEACE WITH HONOR"

As the 1972 presidential election approached, the administration stepped up its efforts to produce a breakthrough in negotiations with the North Vietnamese. In April 1972, the president dropped his longtime insistence on a removal of North Vietnamese troops from the south before any American withdrawal. Meanwhile, Henry Kissinger was meeting privately in Paris with the North Vietnamese foreign secretary, Le Duc Tho, to work out terms for a cease-fire. On October 26, only days before the presidential election, Kissinger announced that "peace is at hand." But several weeks later (after the election), negotiations broke down once again. The American and the North Vietnamese governments appeared ready to accept the Kissinger-Tho plan for a cease-fire, but the regime of General Nguyen Van Thieu balked, still insisting on a full withdrawal of North Vietnamese forces from the south. Kissinger tried to win additional concessions from the communists to meet Thieu's objections, but on December 16 talks broke off.

The next day, December 17, American B-52s began the heaviest and most destructive air raids of the entire war on Hanoi, Haiphong, and other North Vietnamese targets. Civilian casualties were high, and fifteen American B-52s were shot down by the North Vietnamese; in the entire war to that point, the United States had lost only one of the giant bombers. On December 30, Nixon terminated **"CHRISTMAS BOMBING"** the "Christmas bombing." The United States and the North Vietnamese soon returned to the conference table. And on January 27, 1973, they signed an "agreement on ending the war and restoring peace in Vietnam." Nixon claimed that the Christmas bombing had forced the North Vietnamese to relent. At least equally important, however, was the enormous American pressure on Thieu to accept the cease-fire.

The terms of the Paris accords were little different from those Kissinger and Tho had accepted in principle a few months before. There would be an immediate cease-fire. The North Vietnamese would release several hundred American prisoners of war. The Thieu regime would survive for the moment–the principal North Vietnamese concession to the United States–but North Vietnamese forces already in the south would remain there. An undefined committee would work out a permanent settlement.

DEFEAT IN INDOCHINA

American forces were hardly out of Indochina before the Paris accords collapsed. During the first year after the cease-fire, the contending Vietnamese armies suffered greater battle losses than the Americans had absorbed during ten years of fighting. Finally, in March 1975, the North Vietnamese launched a full-scale offensive against the now greatly weakened forces of the south. Thieu appealed to **FALL OF SAIGON** Washington for assistance; the president (now Gerald Ford; Nixon had resigned in 1974) appealed to Congress for additional funding; Congress refused. Late in April 1975, communist forces marched into Saigon, shortly after officials of the Thieu regime and the staff of the American embassy had fled the country in humiliating disarray. Communist forces quickly occupied the capital, renamed it Ho Chi Minh City, and began the process of reuniting Vietnam under the Hanoi government. At about the same time, the Lon Nol regime in Cambodia fell to the murderous communists of Pol Pot and the Khmer Rouge–whose genocidal policies led to the deaths of more than a third of the country's people over the next several years. That was the grim end of over a decade of direct American military involvement in Vietnam. More than 1.2 million Vietnamese soldiers had died in combat, along with countless civilians throughout the region. The United States paid a heavy price as well. The war had cost the nation almost $150 billion in direct costs and much more indirectly. It had resulted in the deaths of over 55,000 young Americans and the injury of 300,000 more. And the nation had suffered a heavy blow to its confidence and self-esteem.

NIXON, KISSINGER, AND THE WORLD

The continuing war in Vietnam provided a dismal backdrop to what Nixon considered his larger mission in world affairs: the construction of a new international order. The president had become convinced that old assumptions of a "bipolar" world—in which the United States and the Soviet Union were the only truly great powers—were now obsolete. Instead, America must adapt to the new "multipolar" international structure, in which China, Japan, and Western Europe would become major, independent forces. "It will be a safer world and a

TOWARD A "MULTIPOLAR" WORLD

better world," he said in 1971, "if we have a strong, healthy United States, Europe, Soviet Union, China, Japan—each balancing the other, not playing one against the other, an even balance."

CHINA AND THE SOVIET UNION

For more than twenty years, ever since the fall of Chiang Kai-shek in 1949, the United States had treated China, the second-largest nation on earth, as if it did not exist. Instead, America recognized the regime-in-exile on the island of Taiwan as the legitimate government of mainland China. Nixon and Kissinger wanted to forge a new relationship with the Chinese communists—in part to strengthen them as a counterbalance to the Soviet Union. The Chinese, for their part, were eager to forestall what they feared was the possibility of a Soviet-American alliance against China and to end China's own isolation from the international arena.

In July 1971, Nixon sent Henry Kissinger on a secret mission to Beijing. When Kissinger returned, the president made the startling announcement that he would

NIXON'S CHINA VISIT

visit China within the next few months. That fall, with American approval, the United Nations admitted the communist government of China and expelled the representatives of the Taiwan regime. Finally, in February 1972, Nixon paid a formal visit to China, which erased much of the deep American animosity toward the Chinese communists.

The initiatives in China coincided with (and probably assisted) an effort by the Nixon administration to improve relations with the Soviet Union. In 1969, American and Soviet diplomats met in Helsinki, Finland, to begin talks on limiting nuclear weapons. In 1972,

SALT I

they produced the first Strategic Arms Limitation Treaty (SALT I), which froze the nuclear missiles (ICBMs) of both sides at present levels.

THE PROBLEMS OF MULTIPOLARITY

Nixon and Kissinger believed that great-power relationships could not alone ensure international stability, for the "Third World" remained the most volatile and dangerous source of international tension.

Central to the Nixon-Kissinger policy toward the Third World was the effort to maintain a stable status quo

NIXON DOCTRINE

without involving the United States too deeply in local disputes. In 1969 and 1970, the president described what became known as the Nixon Doctrine, by which the United States would "participate in the defense and development of allies and friends" but would leave the "basic

THE EVACUATION OF SAIGON A harried U.S. official struggles to keep panicking Vietnamese from boarding an already-overburdened helicopter on the roof of the American embassy in Saigon. The hurried evacuation of Americans took place only hours before the arrival of North Vietnamese troops, signaling the final defeat of South Vietnam. (© AP Images)

NIXON IN CHINA President Richard Nixon's 1972 visit to China was an important step in normalizing relations between the US and the People's Republic of China. Here Nixon toasts the developing relationship with Prime Minister Zhou Enlai. (© Universal Images Group/Getty Images)

responsibility" for the future of those "friends" to the nations themselves.

In the Middle East, conditions grew more volatile in the aftermath of the 1967 "Six-Day War," in which Israel routed Egyptian, Syrian, and Jordanian forces, gained control of the **"SIX-DAY WAR"** whole of the long-divided city of Jerusalem, and occupied substantial new territories: on the west bank of the Jordan River, the Gaza Strip, the Golan Heights, and elsewhere. The war also increased the number of refugee Palestinians—Arabs who claimed the lands now controlled by Israel and who, dislodged from their homes, became a source of considerable instability in Jordan, Lebanon, and the other surrounding countries into which they now moved.

In October 1973, on the Jewish High Holy Day of Yom Kippur, Egyptian and Syrian forces again attacked Israel. For ten days, the Israelis struggled to recover from the surprise attack; finally, they launched an effective counteroffensive against Egyptian forces in the Sinai. At that point, the United States intervened, placing heavy pressure on Israel to accept a cease-fire rather than press its advantage.

The imposed settlement of the Yom Kippur War demonstrated the growing dependence of the United States and its allies on Arab oil. Permitting Israel to continue its drive into Egypt **ARAB OIL EMBARGO** might have jeopardized the ability of the United States to purchase needed petroleum from the Arab states. A brief but painful embargo by the Arab governments on the sale of oil to supporters of Israel (including America) in 1973 provided an ominous warning of the costs of losing access to the region's resources.

POLITICS AND ECONOMICS UNDER NIXON

The Nixon administration described its policies as an attempt to restore balance: between the needs of the poor and the desires of the middle class, between the power of the federal government and the interests of states and local communities. In the end, however, economic and political crises—some beyond the administration's control, some of its own making—sharply limited Nixon's ability to fulfill his domestic goals.

DOMESTIC INITIATIVES

Many of Nixon's domestic policies were a response to what he believed to be the demands of his own constituency—conservative, middle-class people whom he liked to call the **DISMANTLING THE GREAT SOCIETY** "silent majority" and who wanted to reduce federal "interference" in local affairs. Nixon tried, unsuccessfully, to persuade Congress to pass legislation prohibiting the use of forced busing to achieve school desegregation. He blocked the Department of Health, Education, and Welfare from cutting off federal funds from school districts that had failed to comply with court orders to integrate. At the same time, he began to reduce or dismantle many of the social programs of the Great Society and the New Frontier. In 1973, for example, he abolished the Office of Economic Opportunity, the centerpiece of the antipoverty program of the Johnson years.

Yet Nixon's domestic efforts were not entirely conservative. One of the administration's boldest efforts was an attempt to overhaul the nation's enormous welfare system. Nixon proposed replacing the existing system, which almost everyone agreed was cumbersome, expensive, and inefficient, with what he called the Family Assistance Plan (FAP). It would in effect have created a guaranteed annual income for all Americans: $1,600 in federal grants, which could be supplemented by outside earnings up to $4,000. Even many liberals applauded the proposal as an important step toward expanding federal responsibility for the poor. Nixon, however, presented the plan in conservative terms: as something that would reduce the role of government and transfer to welfare recipients themselves daily responsibility for their own lives. Although the FAP won approval in the House in 1970, concerted attacks by welfare recipients (who considered the benefits inadequate), members of the welfare bureaucracy (whose own influence stood to be sharply diminished by the bill), and conservatives (who opposed a guaranteed income on principle) helped kill it in the Senate.

FROM THE WARREN COURT TO THE NIXON COURT

Of all the liberal institutions that had aroused the enmity of the "silent majority" in the 1950s and 1960s, none had evoked more anger and bitterness than the Supreme Court. Not only had its rulings on racial matters disrupted traditional social patterns, but its staunch defense of civil liberties had, in the opinions of many Americans, contributed to the increase in crime, disorder, and moral decay. In *Engel v. Vitale* (1962), the Court ruled that prayers in public schools violated the constitutional separation of church and state, sparking outrage among religious fundamentalists and others. In *Roth v. United States* (1957), the Court had sharply limited the authority of local governments to curb pornography. In *Gideon v. Wainwright* (1963), the Court ruled that every felony defendant was entitled to a lawyer regardless of his or her ability to pay. In *Escobedo v. Illinois* (1964), it ruled that a defendant must be allowed access to a lawyer before questioning by police. In *Miranda v. Arizona* (1966), the Court confirmed the obligation of authorities to inform a criminal suspect of his or her rights. By 1968, the Warren Court had become the target of Americans of all kinds who felt the balance of power in the United States had shifted too far toward the poor and dispossessed at the expense of the middle class, and toward criminals at the expense of law-abiding citizens.

One of the most important decisions of the Warren Court in the 1960s was *Baker v. Carr* (1962), which required state

BAKER V. CARR

legislatures to apportion electoral districts so that all citizens' votes would have equal weight. In dozens of states, systems of legislative districting had given disproportionate representation to sparsely populated rural areas, hence diminishing the voting power of urban residents. The reapportionment that the decision required greatly strengthened the voting power of African Americans, Hispanics, and other groups concentrated in cities.

Nixon was determined to use his judicial appointments to give the Court a more conservative cast. His first opportunity came almost as soon as he entered office. When Chief Justice Earl Warren resigned early in 1969, Nixon replaced him with a federal appeals court judge of conservative leanings, Warren Burger. A few months later, Associate Justice Abe Fortas resigned after allegations of financial improprieties. To replace him, Nixon named Clement F. Haynsworth, a respected federal circuit court judge from South Carolina. But Haynsworth came under fire from Senate liberals, black organizations, and labor unions for his conservative record on civil rights and for what some critics claimed was a conflict of interest in several of the cases on which he had sat. The Senate rejected him. Nixon's next choice was G. Harrold Carswell, a judge of the Florida federal appeals court of little distinction and widely considered unfit for the Supreme Court. The Senate rejected his nomination too.

Nixon was careful thereafter to choose justices of standing within the legal community to fill vacancies on the Supreme Court: Harry Blackmun, a moderate jurist from Minnesota; Lewis F. Powell Jr., a respected judge from Virginia; and William Rehnquist, a member of the Nixon Justice Department.

The new Court, however, fell short of what many conservatives had expected. Rather than retreating from its commitment to social reform, the Court in many areas became more committed. In *Swann v. Charlotte-Mecklenburg Board of Education* (1971), it ruled in favor of the use of forced busing to achieve racial balance in schools. In *Furman v. Georgia* (1972), the Court overturned existing capital punishment

statutes and established strict new guidelines for such laws in the future. In *Roe v. Wade* (1973), it struck down laws forbidding abortions. In other decisions, however, the Burger

BAKKE V. BOARD OF REGENTS OF CALIFORNIA

Court was more moderate. Although the justices approved busing as a tool for achieving integration, they rejected, in *Milliken v. Bradley* (1974), a plan to transfer students across district lines (in this case, between Detroit and its suburbs) to achieve racial balance. While the Court upheld the principle of affirmative action in its celebrated 1978 decision *Bakke v. Board of Regents of California*, it established restrictive new guidelines for such programs in the future.

THE ELECTION OF 1972

Nixon entered the presidential race in 1972 with a substantial reserve of strength. He had made significant achievements in foreign policy and in the de-escalation of the Vietnam War. His energetic reelection committee collected enormous sums of money to support the campaign. The president himself used the powers of incumbency with great effect, refraining from campaigning and concentrating on highly publicized international decisions and state visits. Agencies of the federal government dispensed funds and favors to strengthen Nixon's political standing in critical areas.

Nixon was most fortunate in 1972, however, in his opposition. The return of George Wallace to the presidential fray caused some early concern. Nixon was delighted to see Wallace run in the Democratic primaries and quietly encouraged him to do so. But he feared that Wallace would again launch a third-party campaign. The possibility of such a campaign vanished in May, when a would-be assassin shot the Alabama governor during a campaign rally in Maryland. Paralyzed from the waist down, Wallace was unable to continue campaigning.

The Democrats, in the meantime, were making their own

GEORGE MCGOVERN

contributions to the Nixon cause by nominating for president a representative of their most liberal wing: Senator George S. McGovern of South Dakota. An outspoken critic of the war, a forceful advocate of advanced liberal positions on most social and economic issues, McGovern seemed to embody many aspects of the turbulent 1960s that middle-class Americans were most eager to reject. McGovern profited greatly from party reforms (which he had helped to draft) that reduced the power of party leaders and gave increased influence to inexperienced delegates in the selection of the Democratic ticket. But those same reforms helped make the Democratic Convention of 1972 an unappealing spectacle to much of the public.

NIXON'S LANDSLIDE

On election day, Nixon won reelection by one of the largest margins in history: 60.7 percent of the popular vote compared with 37.5 percent for the forlorn McGovern, and an electoral margin of 520 to 17.

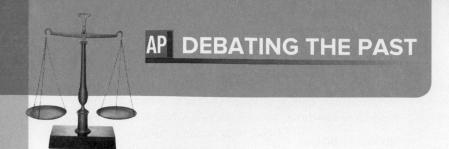
WATERGATE

DECADES after Watergate—one of the most famous political scandals in American history—historians and others continue to argue about its causes and significance. Their interpretations fall into several broad categories.

One argument emphasizes the evolution of the institution of the presidency over time and sees Watergate as the result of a much larger pattern of presidential usurpations of power that stretched back at least several decades. Arthur Schlesinger Jr. helped develop this argument in his 1973 book, *The Imperial Presidency,* which argues that ever since World War II, Americans have believed that the nation was in a state of permanent crisis, threatened from abroad by the menace of communism, threatened from within by the danger of insufficient will. The belief of a succession of presidents in the urgency of this crisis, and in their duty to take whatever measures might be necessary to combat it, led them gradually to usurp more and more power from Congress, the courts, and the public. Initially, this expansion of presidential power came in the realm of international affairs: covert and at times illegal activities overseas.

But in the postwar world, domestic politics began to seem inseparable from international politics. Gradually, presidents began to look for ways to circumvent constraints in domestic matters as well. Nixon's actions in the Watergate crisis were, in other words, a culmination of this long and steady expansion of covert presidential power. Jonathan Schell, in *The Time of Illusion* (1975), offers a variation of this argument, tying the crisis of the presidency to the pressure that nuclear weapons place on presidents to protect the nation's—and their own—"credibility." Other commentators (but few serious historical studies) go even further and argue that what happened to produce the Watergate

scandals was not substantively different from the normal patterns of presidential behavior, that Nixon simply got caught where other presidents had not, and that a long-standing liberal hostility toward Nixon ensured that he would pay a higher price for his behavior than other presidents would.

A second explanation of Watergate emphasizes the difficult social and political environment of the late 1960s and early 1970s. Nixon entered office, according to this view, facing an unprecedentedly radical opposition that would stop at nothing to discredit the war and destroy his authority. He found himself, therefore, drawn into taking similarly desperate measures of his own to defend himself from these extraordinary challenges. Nixon made this argument in his own 1975 memoirs:

It was this epidemic of unprecedented domestic terrorism that prompted our efforts to discover the best means by which to deal with this new phenomenon of highly organized and highly skilled revolutionaries

THE TROUBLED ECONOMY

For three decades, the American economy had been the envy of the world. It had produced as much as a third of the world's industrial goods and had dominated international trade. The American dollar had been the strongest currency in the world, and the American standard of living had risen steadily from its already substantial heights. Many Americans assumed that this remarkable prosperity was the normal condition of their society. In fact, however, it rested in part on several advantages that were rapidly disappearing by the late 1960s: above all, the absence of significant foreign competition and easy access to raw materials in the Third World.

Inflation, which had been creeping upward for several years when Richard Nixon took office, soon began to soar; it would be the most disturbing economic problem of the 1970s. Its most visible cause was a significant increase in federal deficit spending that began in the 1960s, when the

INFLATION Johnson administration tried to fund the war in Vietnam and its ambitious social programs without raising taxes. But there were other, equally important causes. No longer did the United States have exclusive access to cheap raw materials around the globe; not only were other industrial nations now competing for increasingly

scarce raw materials, but Third World suppliers of those materials were beginning to realize their value and to demand higher prices for them.

Annual percentage change in Consumer Price Index

INFLATION, 1960–2010 Inflation was the biggest economic worry of most Americans in the 1970s and early 1980s, and this chart shows why. Having remained very low through the early 1960s, inflation rose slowly in the second half of the decade and then dramatically in the mid- and late 1970s, before beginning a long and steady decline in the early 1980s.

• *What caused the great spike in inflation in the 1970s?*

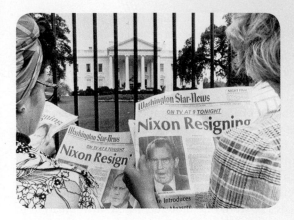

NIXON QUITS Tourists outside the White House learn that Nixon will likely resign the presidency the next day: August 9, 1974. (© Bettmann/Corbis)

dedicated to the violent destruction of our democratic system.*

The historian Herbert Parmet echoes parts of this argument in *Richard Nixon and His America* (1990). Stephen Ambrose offers a more muted version of the same view in *Richard Nixon* (1989).

Most of those who have written about Watergate, however, search for the explanation not in institutional or social forces, but in the personalities of the people involved and, most notably, in the personality of Richard Nixon. Even many of those who have developed structural explanations (Schlesinger, Schell, and Ambrose, for example) return eventually to Nixon himself as the most important explanation for Watergate. Others begin there, perhaps most notably Stanley I. Kutler, in *The Wars of Watergate* (1990) and, later, *Abuse of Power* (1997), in which he presents extensive excerpts from conversations about Watergate taped in the Nixon White House. Kutler emphasizes Nixon's lifelong resort to vicious political tactics and his long-standing belief that he was a special target of unscrupulous enemies and had to "get" them before they got him. Watergate was rooted, Kutler argues, "in the personality and history of Nixon himself." A "corrosive hatred," he claims, "decisively shaped Nixon's own behavior, his career, and eventually his historical standing." ●

*From *RN: The Memoirs of Richard Nixon* (New York: Grosset & Dunlap, 1978). Copyright © 1978 by Richard Nixon.

AP HISTORICAL ARGUMENTATION AND INTERPRETATION

Questions assume cumulative content knowledge from this chapter and previous chapters.

1. Identify three broad categories of historical interpretations about the Watergate scandal. For each category identify a historian's argument, which falls in that category.
2. If you were writing a historical interpretation of Watergate—the causes and its significance—from the perspective of one of the categories above, offer two questions you might ask for research purposes? Offer two questions you might ask for one of the other categories.
3. With which historical interpretation presented in the discussion do you most agree? Explain why, supporting your argument with historical evidence.

The greatest immediate blow to the American economy was the increasing cost of energy. More than any nation on earth, the United States based its economy on the easy availability of cheap and plentiful fossil fuels. Domestic petroleum reserves were no longer sufficient to meet this demand, and the nation was heavily dependent on imports from the Middle East and Africa.

For many years, the Organization of Petroleum Exporting Countries (OPEC) had operated as an informal bargaining unit

OPEC

for the sale of oil by Third World nations, but had seldom managed to exercise any real strength. But in the early 1970s, OPEC began to use its oil as both an economic tool and a political weapon. In 1973, in the midst of the Yom Kippur War, Arab members of OPEC announced that they would no longer ship petroleum to nations supporting Israel—which meant the United States and its allies in Western Europe. At about the same time, the OPEC nations agreed to raise their prices by 400 percent. These twin shocks produced momentary economic chaos in the West. The United States suffered its first fuel shortage since World War II. And although the boycott ended a few months later, the price of energy continued to skyrocket both because of OPEC's new militant policies and because of the weakening competitive position of the dollar in world markets.

But inflation was only one of the new problems facing the U.S. economy. Another was the decline of the nation's manufacturing sector. American industry had flourished in the aftermath of World War II. By the 1970s, however, the climate for American manufacturing had changed significantly. Many of the great industrial plants were now many decades old, much less efficient than the newer plants that Japan and European industrial nations had constructed after the war. In some industries (notably steel and automobiles), management had become complacent and bureaucratic. Most important, American manufacturing now faced major competition from abroad—not only in world trade (which still constituted only a small part of the U.S. economy) but also at home. Automobiles, steel, and many other manufactured goods from Japan and Europe established major footholds in the U.S. markets. Some of America's new competitors benefited from lower labor costs than their U.S. counterparts.

Thus the 1970s marked the beginning of a long, painful process of deindustrialization, during which thousands of

DEINDUSTRIALIZATION

factories across the country closed their gates and millions of workers lost their jobs. New employment opportunities were becoming available in other, growing areas of the economy: technology, information systems, and many other "knowledge-based" industries that would ultimately drive an extraordinary (if unbalanced) economic revival in the 1980s and 1990s. But many industrial workers were poorly equipped to move into those jobs. The result was a growing pool of unemployed and underemployed workers; the virtual disappearance of industrial jobs from many inner cities, where large numbers of minorities lived; and the impoverishment of communities dependent on particular industries. Some of the nation's manufacturing sectors ultimately revived, but few regained the size and dominance they had enjoyed in the 1950s and 1960s.

Inequality

Inequality in income and wealth is a characteristic of every nation; but in the last four decades, that inequality has become dramatically more unequal in the United States. From the end of World War II to the middle of the 1970s, increases in incomes (and, to a lesser extent, increases in total wealth) grew at about the same rate across the range of incomes. People in the bottom 20 percent of the income scale saw their incomes increase at about the same rate that people in the top 20 percent of the income scale did. But beginning in about 1973, that pattern began to change dramatically. The top 20 percent of earners saw their incomes rise at a much higher rate than did the earners below them. The top 5 percent did even better. And the top 1 percent did far better still–earning 24 percent of total income. At the same time, people in the bottom 20 percent saw their incomes slowly decrease, while the middle-class earners saw their earnings remain relatively stagnant, with incomes rising at about the same rate as inflation.

There are many explanations for this growing inequality. The decline of industry in the United States has pushed many once-well-paid workers into much-lower-paid nonunion jobs. Income tax reductions have increased the incomes of the wealthiest Americans much more rapidly than they have increased the incomes of lower-income people. The growth of the financial sector, and the extraordinary wealth that many financiers have accumulated in recent decades, has helped concentrate income and wealth at the top in unprecedented ways. Whether this inequality is a danger to American democracy, as many people believe, or a product of economic success that has improved, or will improve, the lot of everyone, as many others believe, it is nevertheless the case that the incomes in the United States are far more unequal today than they were a generation or more ago.

The Nixon Response

The Nixon administration responded to these mounting economic problems by focusing on the one thing it thought it could control: inflation. Placing conservative economists at the head of the Federal Reserve Board, he ensured sharply higher interest rates and a contraction of the money supply. But the tight money policy did little to curb inflation: the cost of living rose a cumulative 15 percent during Nixon's first two and a half years in office. Economic growth, in the meantime, declined. The United States was encountering a new and puzzling dilemma: "stagflation," a combination of rising prices and general economic stagnation.

"Stagflation"

In the summer of 1971, Nixon imposed a ninety-day freeze on all wages and prices at their existing levels. Then, in November, he launched what he called Phase II of his economic plan: mandatory guidelines for wage and price increases, to be administered by a federal agency. Inflation subsided temporarily, but the recession continued. Fearful that the recession would be more damaging than inflation in an election year, the administration reversed itself late in 1971: interest rates were allowed to drop sharply, and government spending grew. The new tactics helped revive the economy in the short term, but inflation rose substantially–particularly after the administration abandoned the strict Phase II controls.

In 1973, prices rose 9 percent; in 1974, after the Arab oil embargo and the OPEC price increases, they rose 12 percent–the highest rate since the relaxation of price controls shortly after World War II. The value of the dollar continued to slide, and the nation's international trade continued to decline.

THE WATERGATE CRISIS

Although economic problems greatly concerned the American people in the 1970s, another stunning development almost entirely preoccupied the nation beginning early in 1973: the fall of Richard Nixon.

The Scandals

Nixon's crisis was in part a result of long-term changes in the presidency. Public expectations of the president had increased dramatically in the years since World War II; yet the constraints placed on the authority of the office had grown as well. In response, a succession of presidents had sought new methods for the exercise of power, often stretching the law, occasionally breaking it. Nixon greatly accelerated these trends. Facing a Democratic Congress hostile to his goals, he attempted to find ways to circumvent the legislature whenever possible. Saddled with a federal bureaucracy unresponsive to his wishes, he constructed a hierarchy in which virtually all executive power became concentrated in the White House. Operating within a rigid, even autocratic staff structure, the president became a solitary, at times brooding figure. Unknown to all but a few intimates, he also became mired in a pattern of illegalities and abuses of power that in late 1972 began to break through to the surface.

The Changing Presidency

Early on the morning of June 17, 1972, police arrested five men who had broken into the offices of the Democratic National Committee in the Watergate office building in

**THE
WATERGATE
BREAK-IN**
Washington, D.C. Two others were seized a short time later and charged with supervising the break-in. When reporters for the *Washington Post* began researching the backgrounds of the culprits, they discovered that among those involved in the burglary were former employees of the Committee for the Re-election of the President. One of them had worked in the White House. Moreover, they had been paid to execute the break-in from a secret fund of the reelection committee, a fund controlled by members of the White House staff.

Public interest in the disclosures grew slowly in the last months of 1972. Early in 1973, however, the Watergate burglars went on trial; and under relentless prodding from federal judge John J. Sirica, one of the defendants, James W. McCord, agreed to cooperate both with the grand jury and with a special Senate investigating committee. McCord's testimony opened a floodgate of confessions, and for months a parade of White House and campaign officials exposed one illegality after another. Foremost among them was a member of the inner circle of the White House, counsel to the president John Dean, who leveled allegations against Nixon himself.

Two different sets of scandals emerged from the investigations. One was a general pattern of abuses of power involving both the White House and the Nixon campaign committee,
"COVER-UP" which included, but was not limited to, the Watergate break-in. The other scandal, and the one that became the major focus of public attention for nearly two years, was the way in which the administration tried to manage the investigations of the Watergate break-in and other abuses—a pattern of behavior that became known as the "cover-up." There was never any conclusive evidence that the president had planned or approved the Watergate burglary in advance. But there was evidence that he had been involved in illegal efforts to obstruct investigations and withhold information. Testimony before the Senate provided evidence of the complicity of Dean, Attorney General John Mitchell, top White House assistants H. R. Haldeman and John Ehrlichman, and others. As interest in the case grew to something approaching a national obsession, the investigation focused increasingly on a single question: in the words of Senator Howard Baker of Tennessee, "What did the President know and when did he know it?"

Nixon accepted the departure of those members of his administration implicated in the scandals. But he continued to insist that he himself was innocent. There the matter might have rested, had it not been for the disclosure during the Senate hearings of a White House taping system that had recorded virtually every conversation in the president's office during the period in question. All the groups investigating the scandals sought access to the tapes; Nixon, pleading "executive privilege," refused to release them. A special prosecutor appointed by the president to handle the Watergate cases, Harvard law professor Archibald Cox, took Nixon to court in October 1973 in an effort to force him to relinquish the recordings. Nixon fired Cox and suffered the humiliation of watching both Attorney General Elliot Richardson and his deputy resign in protest. This "Saturday night massacre" made the president's predicament infinitely worse. Not only did public pressure
**"SATURDAY
NIGHT
MASSACRE"** force him to appoint a new special prosecutor, Texas attorney Leon Jaworski, who proved just as determined as Cox to subpoena the tapes; but the episode also precipitated an investigation by the House of Representatives into the possibility of impeachment.

THE FALL OF RICHARD NIXON

Nixon's situation deteriorated further in the following months. Late in 1973, Vice President Spiro Agnew became embroiled in a scandal of his own when evidence surfaced that he had accepted bribes and kickbacks while serving as governor of Maryland and even as vice president. In return for a Justice Department agreement not to press the case, Agnew pleaded no contest to a lesser charge of income-tax evasion and resigned from the government. With the controversial Agnew no longer in line to succeed to the presidency, the prospect of removing Nixon from the White House became less worrisome to his opponents. The new vice president (the first appointed under the terms of the Twenty-Fifth Amendment, which had been adopted in 1967) was House Minority Leader Gerald Ford, an amiable and popular Michigan congressman.

In April 1974, in an effort to head off further subpoenas of the tapes, the president released transcripts of a number of relevant conversations, claiming that they proved his innocence. But even these edited tapes seemed to suggest Nixon's
**U.S. V.
RICHARD M.
NIXON** complicity in the cover-up. In July, the crisis reached a climax. First the Supreme Court ruled unanimously, in *United States v. Richard M. Nixon*, that the president must relinquish the tapes to Special Prosecutor Jaworski. Days later, the House Judiciary Committee voted to recommend three articles of impeachment, charging that Nixon had, first, obstructed justice in the Watergate cover-up; second, misused federal agencies to violate the rights of citizens; and third, defied the authority of Congress by refusing to deliver tapes and other materials subpoenaed by the committee.

Even without additional evidence, Nixon might well have been impeached by the full House and convicted by the Senate. Early in August, however, he provided at last what many wavering members of Congress had begun to call the "smoking gun." Among the tapes that the Supreme Court compelled Nixon to relinquish were several that offered apparently incontrovertible evidence of his involvement in the Watergate cover-up. Only days after the burglary, the recordings disclosed, the president had ordered the FBI to stop investigating the break-in. Impeachment and conviction now seemed inevitable.

For several days, Nixon brooded in the White House. Finally, on August 8, 1974, he announced his resignation—the
NIXON RESIGNS first president in American history ever to do so. At noon the next day, while Nixon

NIXON'S FAREWELL Only moments before, Nixon had been in tears saying good-bye to his staff in the East Room of the White House. But as he boarded a helicopter to begin his trip home to California shortly after resigning as president, he flashed his trademark "victory" sign to the crowd on the White House lawn. (© Bettmann/Corbis)

and his family were flying west to their home in California, Gerald Ford took the oath of office as president.

Many Americans expressed relief and exhilaration that, as the new president put it, "Our long national nightmare is over." But the wave of good feeling could not obscure the deeper and more lasting damage of the Watergate crisis. In a society in which distrust of leaders and institutions of authority was already widespread, the fall of Richard Nixon seemed to confirm the most cynical assumptions about the character of American public life.

AP CONNECTING THEMES

Chapter 30 examined the United States' economic, political, and social development during the late 1960s and early 1970s. As you review, you should focus on the impact of youth culture in challenging traditional American values. Concentrate on understanding the reasons for the emergence of growing protests by minorities for fair treatment and their relative success in achieving those goals. Examine the reasons for and consequences of the growing environmental movement. In terms of foreign policy, you need to be able to assess the degree to which U.S. foreign policy changed during the period and the degree to which it remained consistent with the foreign policy of previous years. You should also focus on the rise of a new conservatism and the degree to which it attempted to roll back liberal initiatives from earlier in the decade. Pay attention to economic problems of the time period, their causes, and attempts to overcome them. Finally, understand the issue surrounding the Watergate scandal and its consequences for the American people.

The following themes have a heightened importance in Chapter 30. You should now be able to do the following for each listed theme:

Identity: Explain how the rising tide of protest by minority groups changed both their perception of themselves and the perception of others toward them.

Work, Exchange, and Technology: Explain economic problems associated with stagflation, the Arab oil embargo, and deindustrialization of the American economy.

Politics and Power: Explain the impact of the war in Vietnam and the Watergate scandal on the American people's perception of government. Explain why the elections of 1964, 1968, and 1972 showed such varied results.

America and the World: Explain the degree to which American foreign policy reduced Cold War tensions and the degree to which it intensified them.

Ideas, Beliefs, and Culture: Explain the ways in which the youth culture of the 1960s challenged traditional American value systems.

AP SUGGESTED STUDY

PEOPLE/PLACES/EVENTS As you study these items, think about how they demonstrate or relate to key concepts and historical themes from this chapter and previous chapters.

AMERICAN INDIAN MOVEMENT (AIM) 815
BETTY FRIEDAN 819
CÉSAR CHÁVEZ 816
COUNTERCULTURE 811
"DON'T ASK, DON'T TELL" 818
FREE SPEECH MOVEMENT 809
GEORGE MCGOVERN 829
GERALD FORD 833

HENRY KISSINGER 824
NATIONAL ORGANIZATION FOR WOMEN (NOW) 819
NEW LEFT 808
NIXON DOCTRINE 827
OPEC 831
RACHEL CARSON 822
ROE V. WADE 821
"SILENT MAJORITY" 828

SPIRO AGNEW 833
"STAGFLATION" 832
STONEWALL RIOT 817
STUDENTS FOR A DEMOCRATIC SOCIETY (SDS) 809
VIETNAMIZATION 824
WATERGATE 832
WEATHERMEN 810
WOUNDED KNEE 815

AP TEST PRACTICE

Questions assume cumulative content knowledge from this chapter and previous chapters.

MULTIPLE CHOICE Use the photograph on page 820 and your knowledge of U.S. history to answer questions 1–2.

1. Which of the following was most likely an issue of particular concern at the time for the women in the photograph?

   (A) Free speech

   (B) Voting rights

   (C) An eight-hour workday

   (D) Equal pay

2. A major impetus for and source of frustration for many educated, middle-class women who mobilized the movement in the photograph most directly paralleled which of the following from the early 19th century?

   (A) The slow pace of reform for African American civil rights

   (B) The ideal of the female domestic "sphere"

   (C) A widening gap between rich and poor

   (D) The absence of educational opportunities for females

SHORT ANSWER Use your knowledge of U.S. history to answer questions 3–6.

3. Answer part a, b and c.

   a) A women's movement emerged during the first half of the 19th century and in the latter half of the 20th

century. Briefly explain ONE important similarity in the reasons why a women's movement emerged in these two time periods.

   b) Briefly explain ONE important similarity in the effects of the women's movement in these two time periods.

   c) Briefly explain ONE critical response to the women's movement in either period.

4. Use the map on page 814 to answer a, b, and c.

   a) Briefly explain ONE major reason why the modern reservations as they exist are not parallel in size to their original land holdings in the early 19th century.

   b) Briefly explain ONE piece of evidence regarding why this development occurred.

   c) Briefly explain ONE historical event that illustrates a reaction by western Indian tribes to this development.

5. Answer a, b, and c.

   a) For one of the groups below briefly [...] or social issue for which the group [...]

   • Native Americans

   • Latinos

   • Gay and lesbian Americans

b) Briefly explain a civic action it took in fighting for its cause.

c) Briefly explain a success achieved by the group in their struggle for social and economic equality.

6. Answer a, b, and c.

a) A conservative movement emerged during the early 20th century and in the late 20th century, both to defend traditional values. Briefly explain ONE important similar historical context present during both periods that gave rise to these conservative movements.

b) Briefly explain ONE important similarity in the effects of the conservative movements from these two time periods.

c) Briefly explain ONE critical response to the conservative movement from one of the periods.

LONG ESSAY For each question below, develop a thoughtful and thorough historical argument that answers the question. Begin your essay with a thesis statement and support it with relevant historical evidence.

7. Evaluate the extent to which the new conservatism of the 1960's and 70's contributed to maintaining continuity as well as fostering change in governmental policies in terms of economic, political and social issues between 1964 and the late 1970's.

31 | FROM THE "AGE OF LIMITS" TO THE AGE OF REAGAN

RONALD AND NANCY REAGAN
The president and the first lady greet guests at a White House social event. Nancy Reagan was most visible in her efforts to make the White House, and her husband's presidency, seem more glamorous than those of most recent administrations. But she also played an important, if quiet, policy role in the administration. (© Dirck Halstead/Time & Life Pictures/ Getty Images)

AP

HISTORICAL THINKING

1. **Historical Argumentation** Analyze the relative success of the Ford and Carter administrations in both domestic and foreign policy.

2. **Comparison** To what degree and in what ways were the economic policies of the Reagan administration similar to the economic policies of the Gilded Age and the 1920s?

3. **Contextualization** Analyze the reasons for the rise of the new conservatism and party realignment between 1968 and 1992.

4. **Historical Argumentation** To what degree and in what ways did American foreign policy in the 1970s and 1980s intensify Cold War conflict and to what degree and in what ways did it reduce Cold War tensions?

5. **Historical Interpretation** To what degree and in what ways did the election of Ronald Reagan constitute a "revolution?"

6. **Historical Argumentation** Analyze the positive and negative aspects of deregulation on the economy and the environment.

7. **Historical Interpretation** Analyze the impact and ramifications of U.S. entry into the Gulf War.

Key Concept Correlations

Analyze the ways the historical developments you learn about in this chapter connect to the following AP Key Concepts.

8.2 Liberalism, based on anticommunism abroad and a firm belief in the efficacy of governmental and especially federal power to achieve social goals at home, reached its apex in the mid-1960s and generated a variety of political and cultural responses.

8.3 Postwar economic, demographic, and technological changes had a far-reaching impact on American society, politics, and the environment.

9.1 A new conservatism grew to prominence in U.S. culture and politics, defending traditional social values and rejecting liberal views about the role of government.

9.2 The end of the Cold War and new challenges to U.S. leadership in the world forced the nation to redefine its foreign policy and global role.

9.3 Moving into the 21st century, the nation continued to experience challenges stemming from social, economic, and demographic changes.

Thematic Learning Objectives

POL-2, 3, 4; WXT-3, 7, 8; CUL-5, 6, 7; WOR-3, 7, 8; ENV 5; ID-6, 7

AP CONNECTING CONCEPTS

CHAPTER 31 focuses mostly on changes brought about by the election of Ronald Reagan in 1980. It does discuss, to a limited degree, the presidencies of Gerald Ford and Jimmy Carter and their domestic and foreign policy challenges. The election of 1980 represented the enshrinement of conservative values into American politics that would last throughout the decade. Emphasis is placed on the emergence of organized religion as a force in the political arena and the consequence of that development in moving social and moral agendas into the political spotlight. There is significant discussion of the impact of "Reaganomics" (or "supply-side" economics), deregulation of industry, and the relaxation of environmental controls on the economy as well as on various socio-economic classes. The chapter also discusses changing relations with the Soviet Union and an emerging role of the United States in international peacekeeping missions. As you read, evaluate the following ideas:

- The new conservatism changed American politics and society.
- Conservative Christian religious movements organized their constituents and became a major player on the political scene.
- While new conservatives were successful in changing the role of the government in the economy, they were less successful in politicizing their moral and social agenda.
- While the Reagan administration initially rejected the notion of accommodation with the Soviet Union, by the end of the decade the Cold War had faded.
- Economic inequality increased as a result of the economic policies of the 1980s.
- Internal and external migration resulted in population growth in the South and West which, in turn, increased the regions' political influence.

POLITICS AND DIPLOMACY AFTER WATERGATE

In the aftermath of Richard Nixon's departure from office, many Americans wondered whether trust in the presidency, and in the government as a whole, could easily be restored. The administrations of the two presidents who succeeded Nixon tried to answer those questions.

THE FORD CUSTODIANSHIP

Gerald Ford inherited the presidency under unenviable circumstances. He had to try to rebuild confidence in government after the Watergate scandals and to restore economic prosperity in the midst of difficult domestic and international conditions.

NIXON PARDONED
The new president's effort to establish himself as a symbol of political integrity suffered a setback only a month after he took office, when he granted Richard Nixon "a full, free, and absolute pardon" for any crimes he may have committed during his presidency. Much of the public suspected a secret deal with the former president. The pardon caused a decline in Ford's popularity from which he never fully recovered.

The Ford administration enjoyed less success in its effort to solve the problems of the American economy. In his efforts to curb inflation, the president rejected the idea of wage and price controls and called instead for largely ineffective voluntary efforts. Ford had to deal with a serious recession in 1974 and 1975–a task made more difficult by the continuing energy crisis. In the aftermath of the Arab oil embargo of 1973, the OPEC cartel began to raise the price of oil–by 400 percent in 1974 alone, one of the principal reasons why inflation reached 11 percent in 1976.

FORD'S DIPLOMATIC SUCCESSES
Ford retained Henry Kissinger as secretary of state and continued the policies of the Nixon years. Late in 1974, Ford met with Soviet premier Leonid Brezhnev at Vladivostok in Siberia and signed an arms control accord that was to serve as the basis for SALT II, thus achieving a goal the Nixon administration had long sought. Meanwhile, in the Middle East, Henry Kissinger helped produce a new accord, by which Israel agreed to return large portions of the occupied Sinai to Egypt.

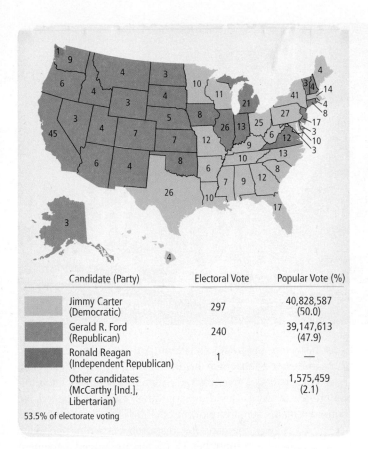

Candidate (Party)	Electoral Vote	Popular Vote (%)
Jimmy Carter (Democratic)	297	40,828,587 (50.0)
Gerald R. Ford (Republican)	240	39,147,613 (47.9)
Ronald Reagan (Independent Republican)	1	—
Other candidates (McCarthy [Ind.], Libertarian)	—	1,575,459 (2.1)

53.5% of electorate voting

THE ELECTION OF 1976 Jimmy Carter, a former governor of Georgia, swept the South in the 1976 election and carried enough of the industrial states of the Northeast and Midwest to win a narrow victory over President Gerald R. Ford. His showing indicated the importance to the Democratic Party of having a candidate capable of attracting support in the South, which was becoming increasingly Republican by the 1970s.

• *What drove so many southerners into the Republican Party?*

Ford's policies came under attack from both the right and the left. In the 1976 Republican primary campaign, Ford faced a powerful challenge from former California governor Ronald Reagan, leader of the party's conservative wing. He spoke for many on the right who were unhappy with any conciliation of communists. The president only barely survived the assault to win his party's nomination. The Democrats, in the meantime, were gradually uniting behind a new and, before 1976, little-known candidate: Jimmy Carter, a former governor of Georgia who organized a brilliant primary campaign by offering honesty, piety, and an outsider's skepticism of the federal government. And while Carter's mammoth lead in opinion polls dwindled by election day, unhappiness with the economy and a general disenchantment with Ford enabled the Democrat to hold on for a narrow victory. Carter emerged with 50 percent of the popular vote to Ford's 47.9 percent and 297 electoral votes to Ford's 240.

THE TRIALS OF JIMMY CARTER

Like Ford, Jimmy Carter assumed the presidency at a moment when the nation faced problems of staggering complexity and difficulty.

Carter had campaigned for the presidency as an "outsider," representing Americans suspicious of entrenched bureaucracies and complacent public officials. He surrounded himself in the White House with a group of close-knit associates from Georgia. Carter was exceptionally intelligent, but his critics charged that he provided no overall vision or direction to his government. His ambitious legislative agenda included major reforms of the tax and welfare systems; Congress passed virtually none of it.

CARTER'S LACK OF DIRECTION

Carter devoted much of his time to the problems of energy and the economy. Entering office in the midst of a recession, he moved first to reduce unemployment by raising public spending and cutting federal taxes. Unemployment declined, but inflation soared–largely because of the continuing increases in energy prices imposed on the West by OPEC. During Carter's last two years in office, oil prices rose at well over a 10 percent annual rate. Like

HIGH INTEREST RATES

CARTER IN THE WHITE HOUSE Jimmy Carter made a strenuous effort to bring a sense of informality to the presidency, in contrast to the "imperial" style many people had complained about during the Nixon years. He began on his inauguration day, when he and his family walked down Pennsylvania Avenue from the Capitol to the White House instead of riding in the traditional limousines. Here, Carter sits in a room in the White House preparing for a television address. He is sitting in front of a fire wearing a cardigan sweater, with his notes in his lap rather than on a desk. (© Bettmann/Corbis)

SIGNING THE CAMP DAVID ACCORDS Jimmy Carter experienced many frustrations during his presidency, but his successful efforts in 1978 to negotiate a peace treaty between Israel and Egypt was his finest hour. Egyptian president Anwar Sadat and Israeli prime minister Menachem Begin join Carter here in the East Room of the White House in March 1979 to sign the accords. (© D.B. Owen/Black Star)

Nixon and Ford before him, Carter responded with a combination of tight money and calls for voluntary restraint. By 1980, interest rates had risen to the highest levels in American history; at times, they exceeded 20 percent.

In the summer of 1979, instability in the Middle East produced a second major fuel shortage in the United States. OPEC announced another major price increase. Faced with increasing pressure to act (and with a dismal approval rating of 26 percent), Carter retreated to Camp David, the presidential retreat in the Maryland mountains. Ten days later, he emerged to deliver a remarkable television address. It included a series of proposals for resolving the energy crisis. But it was most notable for Carter's bleak assessment of the national condition. Speaking with unusual fervor, he complained of a "crisis of confidence" that had struck "at the very heart and soul of our national will." The address became known as the "malaise" speech (although Carter himself had never used that word), and it helped fuel charges that the president was trying to blame his inability to deal with the nation's problems on the American people.

HUMAN RIGHTS AND NATIONAL INTERESTS

Among Carter's most frequent campaign promises was a pledge to build a new basis for American foreign policy, one in which the defense of "human rights" would replace the pursuit of "selfish interests." Carter spoke out sharply and often about violations of human rights in many countries (including, most prominently, the Soviet Union). Beyond that general commitment, the Carter administration focused on several more traditional concerns. Carter completed negotiations begun several years earlier on a pair of treaties to turn over control of the Panama Canal to the government of Panama. After an acrimonious debate, the Senate ratified the treaties by 68 to 32, only one vote more than the necessary two-thirds majority.

Carter's greatest achievement was his success in arranging a peace treaty between Egypt and Israel. Middle East negotia-

tions between Egyptian president Anwar Sadat and Israeli prime minister Menachem Begin had begun in 1977. When those talks stalled, Carter invited Sadat and Begin to a summit conference at Camp David in September 1978, and persuaded them to remain there for two weeks while he and others helped

CAMP DAVID ACCORDS

mediate the disputes between them. On September 17, Carter announced agreement on a framework for an Egyptian-Israeli peace treaty. On March 26, 1979, Begin and Sadat returned together to the White House to sign a formal peace treaty—known as the Camp David accords—between their two nations.

In the meantime, Carter tried to improve relations with China and the Soviet Union and to complete a new arms agreement. He responded eagerly to the overtures of Deng Xiaoping, the new Chinese leader who was attempting to open his nation to the outside world. On December 15, 1978, Washington and Beijing announced the resumption of formal diplomatic relations. A few months later, Carter traveled to Vienna to meet with the aging Brezhnev to finish drafting the new SALT II arms control agreement. The treaty set limits on the number of long-range missiles, bombers, and nuclear warheads for both the United States and the USSR. Almost immediately, however, SALT II met with fierce conservative opposition in the United States.

THE YEAR OF THE HOSTAGES

Ever since the early 1950s, the United States had provided political support and military assistance to the government of the shah of Iran, hoping to make his nation a bulwark against Soviet expansion in the Middle East. By 1979, however, many Iranians

IRANIAN REVOLUTION

had come to resent his autocratic rule. At the same time, Islamic clergies (and much of the fiercely religious populace) opposed his efforts to modernize and Westernize a fundamentalist society. That produced a powerful revolutionary movement. In January 1979, the shah fled the country.

WAITING FOR KHOMEINI Iranian women, dressed in traditional Islamic garb, stand in a crowd in Teheran waiting for a glimpse of the Ayatollah Khomeini, the spiritual and eventually also political leader of the Iranian Revolution. (© Alain Dejean/Sygma/Corbis)

The United States made cautious efforts in the first months after the shah's abdication to establish cordial relations with the militant regimes that followed. By late 1979, however, revolutionary chaos in Iran was making any normal relations impossible. What power there was resided with a zealous religious leader, the Ayatollah Ruhollah Khomeini. In late October 1979, the deposed shah arrived in New York to be treated for cancer. Days later, on November 4, an armed group of militants invaded the American embassy in Teheran, seized the diplomats and military personnel inside, and demanded the return of the shah to Iran in exchange for their freedom. Fifty-three Americans remained hostages in the embassy for over a year.

Only weeks after the hostage seizure, on December 27, 1979, Soviet troops invaded Afghanistan, the mountainous Islamic nation lying between the USSR and Iran. The Soviet Union had in fact been a power in Afghanistan for years, and the dominant force since April 1978, when a coup had established a Marxist government there with close ties to the Kremlin. Carter called it the "gravest threat to world peace since World War II" and angrily imposed a series of economic sanctions on the Russians, canceled American participation in the 1980 summer Olympic Games in Moscow, and announced the withdrawal of SALT II from Senate consideration. The Soviet invasion of Afghanistan became a military quagmire and seriously weakened the Soviet regime.

CARTER'S FALLING POPULARITY The combination of domestic economic troubles and international crises created widespread anxiety, frustration, and anger in the United States—damaging President Carter's already low standing with the public and giving added strength to an alternative political force that had already made great strides.

THE RISE OF THE NEW AMERICAN RIGHT

Much of the anxiety in the 1970s was a result of public events that left many men and women shaken and uncertain about their leaders and their government. But much of it was also a result of significant changes in America's economy, society, and culture. Together these changes provided the right with its most important opportunity in generations to seize a position of authority in American life.

PATTERNS OF POPULAR CULTURE

THE MALL

THE modern mall is the direct descendant of an earlier retail innovation, the automobile-oriented shopping center, which strove to combine a number of different shops in a single structure, with parking for customers. The first modern shopping center, the Country Club Plaza, opened in Kansas City in 1924. By the mid-1950s, shopping centers—ranging from small "strips" to large integrated complexes—had proliferated throughout the country and were challenging traditional downtown shopping districts, which suffered from lack of parking and from the movement of middle-class residents to the suburbs.

In 1956, the first enclosed, climate-controlled shopping mall—the Southdale Shopping Center—opened in Minneapolis, followed quickly by similar ventures in New York, New Jersey, Illinois, North Carolina, and Tennessee. As the malls spread, they grew larger and more elaborate. By the 1970s, vast "regional malls" were emerging—Tyson's Corner in Fairfax, Virginia; Roosevelt Field on Long Island; the Galleria in Houston, and many others—that drew customers from great distances and dazzled them not only with acres of varied retail space, but also with restaurants, movie theaters, skating rinks, bowling alleys, hotels, video arcades, and large public spaces with fountains, benches, trees, gardens, and concert spaces. "The more needs you fulfill, the longer people stay," one developer observed.

Malls had become self-contained imitations of cities—but in a setting from which many of the troubling and abrasive features of downtowns had been eliminated. Malls were insulated from the elements. They were policed by private security forces, who (unlike real police) could and usually did keep "undesirable" customers off the premises. They were purged of bars, pornography shops, and unsavory businesses. They were off limits to beggars, vagrants, the homeless, and anyone else the managers considered unattractive to their customers. Malls set out to "perfect" urban space, recasting the city as a protected, controlled, and socially homogeneous site attractive to, and in many cases dominated by, white middle-class people.

Some malls also sought to become community centers in sprawling suburban areas that had few real community spaces of their own. A few malls built explicitly civic spaces—meeting halls and conference

SHOPPING CENTER, NORTHERN VIRGINIA This small shopping center near Washington, D.C., was characteristic of the new "strip malls" that were emerging in the 1950s to serve suburban customers who traveled almost entirely by automobile. (Photo by Charles Fenno Jacobs/© Time & Life Pictures/Getty Images)

centers, where community groups could gather. Some published their own newspapers. Many staged concerts, plays, and dances. But civic activities had a difficult time competing with the principal attraction of the malls: consumption.

Malls were designed with women, the principal consumers in most families, mainly in mind. "I wouldn't know how to design a center for a man," one architect said of the

THE SUNBELT AND ITS POLITICS

The most widely discussed demographic phenomenon of the 1970s was the rise of what became known as the "Sunbelt"—

RISE OF THE "SUNBELT" a term coined by the political analyst Kevin Phillips. The Sunbelt included the Southeast (including Florida), the Southwest (particularly Texas), and above all, California, which became the nation's most populous state, surpassing New York, in 1964. By 1980, the population of the Sunbelt had risen to exceed that of the older industrial regions of the North and the East.

The rise of the Sunbelt helped produce a change in the political climate. The strong populist traditions in the South and the West were capable of producing progressive politics. But more often in the late twentieth century, they produced a strong opposition to the growth of government and a resentment of the proliferating regulations and restrictions that the liberal state was producing. Many of those regulations and restrictions—environmental laws, land-use restrictions, even the 55-mile-per-hour speed limit created during the energy crisis to force motorists to conserve fuel—affected the West more than any other region.

The so-called Sagebrush Rebellion, which emerged in parts of the West in the late 1970s, mobilized conservative opposition to environmental laws and restrictions on development. It sought to portray the West (which had probably benefited more than

SAGEBRUSH REBELLION any other region from federal investment) as a victim of government control. Its members complained about the large amounts of land the federal government owned in many western states and demanded that the land be opened for development.

Some of the most conservative communities in America—among them Orange County in southern California—were in

SUBURBAN CONSERVATISM suburbs. Many suburbs insulated their residents from contact with diverse groups—through the relative homogeneity of the population, through the transferring of retail and even work space into suburban office parks and shopping malls.

THE POLITICS OF RELIGION

In the 1960s, many social critics had predicted the extinction of religious influence in American life. *Time* magazine had reported such assumptions in 1966 with a celebrated and controversial cover emblazoned with the question "Is God Dead?"

842

EARLY MALLS In the 1960s most malls, such as Bullock's Fashion Square in Sherman Oaks, CA, were outdoor collections of stores focused largely on shopping. (© AP Images)

TODAY'S MALLS Contemporary malls, such as the Grove shopping mall, in Los Angeles, CA, combine shopping with entertainment. By 2014 business in many malls began to decrease owing to online purchasing. (© SUNNYphotography.com/Alamy)

UNDERSTAND, ANALYZE, AND EVALUATE

1. How did the shopping mall change suburban life?
2. Are malls a unifying influence on social life? In what ways are malls divisive?
3. Originally, malls were designed to cater largely to women, especially mothers. Has the target audience for malls changed? If so, to whom do malls principally cater today?

complexes he built. They catered to the concerns of mothers about their own and their children's safety, and they offered products of particular interest to them. (Male-oriented stores—men's clothing, sporting goods, hardware stores—were much less visible in most malls than shops marketing women's and children's clothing, jewelry, lingerie, and household goods.)

Malls also became important to teenagers, who flocked to them in the way that earlier generations had flocked to street corners and squares in traditional downtowns. The malls were places for teenagers to meet friends, go to movies, avoid parents, hang out. They were places to buy records, clothes, or personal items. And they were places to work. Low-paying retail jobs, plentiful in malls, were typical first working experiences for many teens.

The proliferation of malls has dismayed many people, who see in them a threat to the sense of community in America. By insulating people from the diversity and conflict of urban life, critics argue, malls divide groups from one another and erode the bonds that make it possible for those groups to understand one another. But malls, like the suburbs they usually serve, also create a kind of community. They are homogeneous and protected, to be sure, but they are also social gathering places in many areas where the alternative is not the rich, diverse life of the downtown but the even more isolated experience of shopping in distant strips—or through catalogs, telephone, and the Internet. ●

But religion in America was far from dead. Indeed, in the 1970s the United States experienced the beginning of a major religious revival, perhaps the most powerful since the Second Great Awakening of the early nineteenth century. It continued in various forms into the early twenty-first century.

Some of the new religious enthusiasm found expression in the rise of various cults and pseudo-faiths: the Church of Scientology; the Unification Church of the Reverend Sun Myung Moon; even the tragic People's Temple, whose members committed mass suicide in their jungle retreat in Guyana in 1978.

But the most important impulse of the religious revival was the growth of evangelical Christianity. Evangelicalism is the basis of many forms of Christian faith, but evangelicals have in **EVANGELICAL CHRISTIANITY** common a belief in personal conversion (being "born again") through direct communication with God. Evangelical religion had been the dominant form of Christianity in America through much of its history, and a substantial subculture since the late nineteenth century. In its modern form, it became increasingly visible during the early 1950s, when evangelicals such as Billy Graham and Pentecostals such as Oral Roberts began to attract huge national (and international) followings for their energetic revivalism.

By the 1970s, more than 70 million Americans described themselves as "born-again" Christians—men and women who had established a "direct personal relationship with Jesus." Christian evangelicals owned their own newspapers, magazines, radio stations, television networks, and later Internet-based forms of communication. They operated their own schools and universities.

For some evangelicals, Christianity formed the basis for a commitment to racial and economic justice and to world peace. For many other evangelicals, the message of the new religion was very different—but no less political. They were alarmed by what they considered the spread of immorality and disorder in American life. They feared the growth of feminism and the threat they believed it posed to the traditional family. Particularly alarming to them were Supreme Court decisions eliminating religious observance from schools and, later, the decision guaranteeing women the right to an abortion.

Despite the historic antagonism between many evangelical Protestants and the Catholic Church, the growing politicization of religion in the 1970s and beyond brought some former rivals together. Catholics were the first major opponents of the Supreme Court's decision legalizing abortion in *Roe v. Wade,*

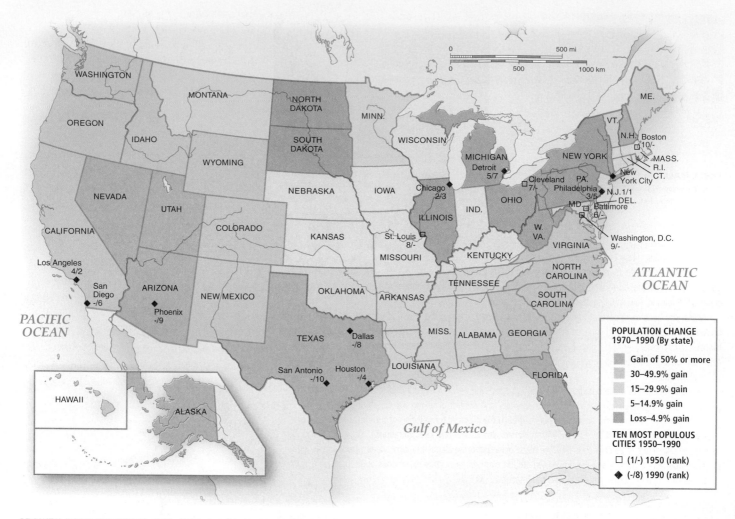

GROWTH OF THE SUNBELT, 1970–1990 One of the most important demographic changes of the last decades of the twentieth century was the shift of population out of traditional population centers in the Northeast and Midwest and toward the states of the so-called Sunbelt—most notably the Southwest and the Pacific Coast. This map gives a dramatic illustration of the changing concentration of population between 1970 and 1990. The orange/brown states are those that lost population, while the purple and blue states are those that made very significant gains (30 percent or more).

• *What was the impact of this population shift on the politics of the 1980s?*

but evangelical Protestants soon joined them in the battle. The rapidly growing Mormon Church, long isolated from both Catholics and traditional Protestants, also became increasingly engaged with the political struggles of other faiths. Mormons were instrumental in the 1982 defeat of the Equal Rights Amendment to the Constitution, which would have guaranteed women the same rights as men. And they too supported the evangelical agenda of opposition to abortion and homosexuality.

THE "NEW RIGHT"

Conservative Christians were an important part, but only a part, of what became known as the "New Right"–a diverse but powerful coalition that enjoyed rapid growth in the 1970s and early 1980s. Its origins lay in part in the 1964 presidential election. After Republican senator Barry Goldwater's shattering defeat, Richard Viguerie, a conservative activist and organizer, took a list of 12,000 contributors to the Goldwater campaign

and used it to begin a formidable conservative communications and fund-raising organization. Beginning in the 1970s, largely because of these and other organizational advances, conservatives usually found themselves better funded and organized than their opponents. By the late 1970s, there were right-wing think tanks, consulting firms, lobbyists, foundations, and schools.

Another factor in the revival of the right was the emergence of a credible right-wing leadership to replace the defeated conservative hero, Barry Goldwater. Ronald Reagan, a well-known film actor turned political activist, became the hope of the right. As a young man, he had been a liberal and a fervent admirer of Franklin Roosevelt. But he moved decisively to the right after his second marriage, to Nancy Davis, a woman of strong conservative convictions, and after he became embroiled, as president of the Screen Actors Guild, in battles with communists in the union. In the early 1950s, Reagan became a corporate spokesman for General Electric and won a wide following on the right

RONALD REAGAN

with powerful speeches in defense of individual freedom and private enterprise.

In 1964, Reagan delivered a memorable television speech on behalf of Goldwater. After Goldwater's defeat, he worked quickly to seize the leadership of the conservative wing of the Republican Party. In 1966, with the support of a group of wealthy conservatives, Reagan won the first of two terms as governor of California.

The presidency of Gerald Ford also played an important role in the rise of the right, by destroying the fragile equilibrium that had enabled the right wing and the moderate wing of the Republican Party to coexist. Ford touched on some of the right's rawest nerves. He appointed as vice president Nelson Rockefeller, the liberal Republican governor of New York and an heir to one of America's great fortunes. This appointment was offensive to many conservatives. Ford proposed an amnesty program for draft resisters, embraced and even extended the Nixon-Kissinger policies of détente, presided over the fall of Vietnam, and agreed to cede the Panama Canal to Panama. When Reagan challenged Ford in the 1976 Republican primaries, the president survived, barely, only by dropping Nelson Rockefeller from the ticket and agreeing to a platform largely written by one of Reagan's allies.

THE TAX REVOLT

Equally important to the success of the New Right was a new and potent conservative issue: the tax revolt. It had its public beginnings in 1978, when Howard Jarvis, a conservative activist in California, launched the first successful major citizens' tax revolt in California with Proposition 13, a referendum question on the state ballot rolling back property tax rates. Similar anti-tax movements soon began in other states and eventually spread to national politics.

PROPOSITION 13

The tax revolt helped the right solve one of its biggest problems. For more than thirty years after the New Deal, Republican conservatives had struggled to halt and even reverse the growth of the federal government. But attacking government programs directly, as right-wing politicians from Robert Taft to Barry Goldwater discovered, was not often the way to attract majority support. Every federal program had a political constituency. The biggest and most expensive programs—Social Security, Medicare, Medicaid, and others—had the broadest support.

In Proposition 13 and similar initiatives, members of the right separated the issue of taxes from the issue of what taxes supported. That helped them achieve some of the most controversial elements of the conservative agenda (eroding the government's ability to expand and launch new programs) without openly antagonizing the millions of voters who supported specific programs. Virtually no one liked to pay taxes, and as the economy weakened, that resentment naturally rose. The right exploited that resentment and, in the process, greatly expanded its constituency.

ATTACKING TAXES

THE CAMPAIGN OF 1980

By the time of the crises in Iran and Afghanistan, Jimmy Carter was in political trouble—his standing in popularity polls lower than that of any president in history. Senator Edward Kennedy, younger brother of John and Robert Kennedy, challenged him in the primaries. And while Carter managed to withstand the confrontation with Kennedy and win his party's nomination, he entered the fall campaign badly weakened.

The Republican Party, in the meantime, rallied enthusiastically behind Ronald Reagan. He linked his campaign to the spreading tax revolt by promising substantial tax cuts. Equally important, he called for restoration of American "strength" and "pride." Reagan clearly benefited from the frustration at Carter's inability to resolve the Iranian hostage crisis. He benefited even more from the accumulated frustrations of more than a decade of domestic and international disappointments.

On election day 1980, the one-year anniversary of the seizure of the hostages in Iran, Reagan swept to victory, winning 51 percent of the vote to 41 percent for Jimmy Carter, and 7 percent for John Anderson—a moderate Republican congressman from Illinois who had mounted an independent campaign. Carter carried only

1980 ELECTION

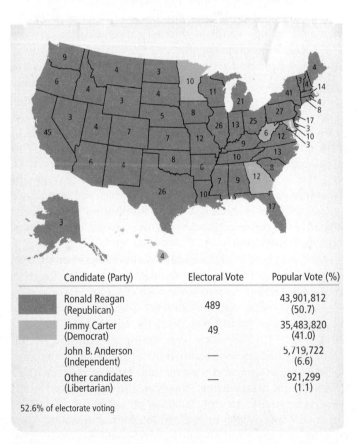

Candidate (Party)	Electoral Vote	Popular Vote (%)
Ronald Reagan (Republican)	489	43,901,812 (50.7)
Jimmy Carter (Democrat)	49	35,483,820 (41.0)
John B. Anderson (Independent)	—	5,719,722 (6.6)
Other candidates (Libertarian)	—	921,299 (1.1)

52.6% of electorate voting

THE ELECTION OF 1980 Although Ronald Reagan won only slightly more than half of the popular vote in the 1980 presidential election, his electoral majority was overwhelming—a reflection to a large degree of the deep unpopularity of President Jimmy Carter in 1980.

• *What had made Carter so unpopular?*

five states and the District of Columbia, for a total of 49 electoral votes to Reagan's 489. The Republican Party won control of the Senate for the first time since 1952 (53 Republicans versus 46 Democrats), and the Democrats retained a majority in the House by 277 to 158.

On the day of Reagan's inauguration, the American hostages in Iran were released after their 444-day ordeal. The government of Iran, desperate for funds to support its floundering war against neighboring Iraq, had ordered the hostages freed in return for a release of billions in Iranian assets that the Carter administration had frozen in American banks.

THE "REAGAN REVOLUTION"

Ronald Reagan assumed the presidency in January 1981, promising a change in government more fundamental than any since the New Deal of fifty years before. He had only moderate success in redefining public policy. But he succeeded brilliantly in making his own engaging personality the face of American politics in the 1980s.

THE REAGAN COALITION

Reagan owed his election to the widespread disillusionment with Carter and to the crises and disappointments that many voters associated with him. But he owed it as well to the emergence of a powerful coalition of conservative groups.

The Reagan coalition included an influential group of wealthy Americans associated with the corporate and financial world. What united this group was their firm commitment to capitalism and unfettered economic growth; a belief that the market offers the best solutions to most problems; a deep hostility to most government interference in markets. Central to this group's agenda in the 1980s was opposition to what it considered the "redistributive" politics of the federal government (especially its highly progressive tax structure) and hostility to the rise of what it believed were "antibusiness" government regulations. Reagan courted these free-market conservatives carefully and effectively.

CORPORATE ELITES

A second element of the Reagan coalition was even smaller, but also disproportionately influential: a group of intellectuals commonly known as "neo-conservatives," a firm base among "opinion leaders." Some of these people had once been liberals and, before that, socialists. But during the turmoil of the 1960s, they had become alarmed by what they considered to be the dangerous and destructive radicalism that they believed was destabilizing American life. Neo-conservatives were sympathetic to the demands of capitalists, but their principal concern was to reaffirm Western democratic, anti-communist values and commitments. Some neo-conservative intellectuals went on to become important figures in the battle against multiculturalism and "political correctness" within academia.

"NEO-CONSERVATIVES"

These two groups joined in an uneasy alliance in 1980 with the populist New Right. But several things differentiated the New Right from the corporate conservatives and the neo-conservatives. Perhaps the most important was the New Right's fundamental distrust of the "eastern establishment": a suspicion of its motives and goals; a sense that it exercised a dangerous, secret power in American life; a fear of the hidden influence of such establishment institutions and people as the Council on Foreign Relations, the Trilateral Commission, Henry Kissinger, and the Rockefellers.

POPULIST CONSERVATIVES

These populist conservatives expressed the kinds of concerns that outsiders, non-elites, have traditionally voiced in American society: an opposition to centralized power and influence, a fear of living in a world where distant, hostile forces are controlling society and threatening individual freedom and community autonomy. It was a testament to Ronald Reagan's political skills and personal charm that he was able to generate enthusiastic support from these populist conservatives while appealing to elite conservative groups whose concerns were in some ways antithetical to those of the New Right.

REAGAN IN THE WHITE HOUSE

Even many people who disagreed with Reagan's policies found themselves drawn to his attractive and carefully honed public image. Reagan was a master of television, a gifted public speaker, and–in public at least–rugged, fearless, and seemingly impervious to danger or misfortune. He turned seventy weeks after taking office and was the oldest man ever to serve as U.S. president. But through most of his presidency, he appeared to be vigorous, resilient, even youthful. He spent his many vacations on a California ranch, where he chopped wood and rode horses. When he was wounded in an assassination attempt in 1981, he joked with doctors on his way into surgery and appeared to bounce back from the ordeal with remarkable speed.

Reagan was not much involved in the day-to-day affairs of running the government; he surrounded himself with tough, energetic administrators who insulated him from many of the pressures of the office. At times, the president revealed a startling ignorance about the nature of his own policies. Instead, he used the actions of his subordinates. But Reagan made active use of his office to support his administration's programs by fusing his proposals with a highly nationalistic rhetoric.

"SUPPLY-SIDE" ECONOMICS

Reagan's 1980 campaign for the presidency had promised to restore the economy to health by a bold experiment that became known as "supply-side" economics or, to some, "Reaganomics." Supply-side economics operated from the assumption that the woes of the American economy were in large part a result of excessive taxation, which left inadequate capital available to investors to stimulate growth. The solution, therefore, was to reduce taxes, with particularly generous benefits to corporations and wealthy individuals, in order to encourage new investments. Because a

"REAGANOMICS"

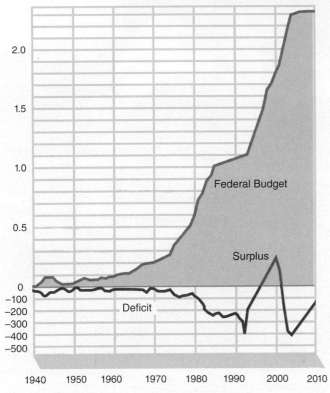

Federal Budget and Surplus/Deficit, 1940–2010
(in trillions of current dollars)

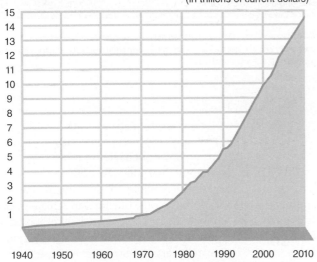

Gross National Product, 1940–2010
(in trillions of current dollars)

Budget and Surplus/Deficit as Percent of GNP, 1940–2010

tax cut would reduce government revenues (at least at first), it would also be necessary to reduce government expenses. A goal of the Reagan economic program was a significant reduction of the federal budget.

Men and women whom Reagan appointed fanned out through the executive branch of government, reducing the role

DEREGULATION

of government. Secretary of the Interior James Watt, previously a major figure in the Sagebrush Rebellion, opened up public lands and water to development. The Environmental Protection Agency (before its directors were indicted for corruption) relaxed or entirely eliminated enforcement of many environmental laws and regulations. The Civil Rights Division of the Justice Department eased enforcement of civil rights laws. The Department of Transportation slowed implementation of new rules limiting automobile emissions and imposing new safety standards on cars and trucks. By getting government "out of the way," Reagan officials promised, they were ensuring economic revival.

By early 1982, the nation had sunk into a severe recession. Unemployment reached 11 percent, its highest level in over forty years. But the economy recovered relatively rapidly. By late 1983, unemployment had fallen to 8.2 percent, and it declined steadily for several years after that. The gross national product had grown 3.6 percent in a year, the largest one-year increase since the mid-1970s. Inflation had fallen below 5 percent. The economy continued to grow, and both inflation and unemployment remained low through most of the decade.

THE FISCAL CRISIS

The economic revival did little at first to reduce federal budget deficits or to slow the growth in the national debt (the debt the nation accumulates over time as a result of its annual

SOARING NATIONAL DEBT

deficits). By the mid-1980s, the sense of a growing fiscal crisis had become one of the central issues in American politics. Having entered office promising a balanced budget within four years, Reagan had record budget deficits and accumulated more debt in his eight years in office than the American government had accumulated in its entire previous history.

The enormous deficits had many causes, some of them stretching back over decades of American

WELFARE BENEFITS CUT

public policy decisions. In particular, the budget suffered from enormous increases

FEDERAL BUDGET SURPLUS/DEFICIT, 1940–2010 These charts help illustrate why the pattern of federal deficits seemed so alarming to Americans in the 1980s, and also why those deficits proved much less damaging to the economy than many economists had predicted. The upper chart shows a dramatic increase in the federal budget from the mid-1960s on. It shows as well a corresponding, and also dramatic, increase in the size of federal deficits. Gross national product (GNP) also increased dramatically, especially in the 1980s and 1990s, as the middle chart shows. When the federal budgets and deficits of these years, shown in the bottom chart, are calculated not in absolute numbers, but as a percentage of GNP, they seem much more stable and much less alarming. After 2000, these deficits rose significantly and became a much larger percentage of GNP.

• *What factors contributed to the increasing deficits of the 1980s? How were those deficits eliminated in the 1990s?*

POVERTY IN AMERICA The American poverty rate declined sharply beginning in the 1950s and reached a historic low in the late 1970s. But the dramatic increase in income and wealth inequality that began in the mid-1970s gradually pushed the poverty rate upward again. By the mid-1980s, the poverty rate was approaching 15 percent, the highest in twenty years. In the image above, a group of children huddle against a barrier at an emergency center for homeless families in New York City in 1987. (© Richard Falco/BlackStar)

in the costs of "entitlement" programs (especially Social Security, Medicare, and Medicaid), a result of the aging of the population and dramatic increases in the cost of health care. But some of the causes of the deficit lay in the policies of the Reagan administration. The 1981 tax cuts, the largest in American history to that point, contributed to the deficit. The massive increase in military spending by the Reagan administration added much more to the federal budget than its cuts in domestic spending removed.

Reagan and the World

Reagan encountered a similar combination of triumphs and difficulties in international affairs. Determined to restore American pride and prestige in the world, he argued that the United States should once again become active and assertive in opposing communism and in supporting friendly governments whatever their internal policies.

Relations with the Soviet Union, which had been steadily deteriorating in the last years of the Carter administration, grew still more chilly in the first years of the Reagan presidency. The

president spoke harshly of the Soviet regime (which he once called the "evil empire"), accusing it of sponsoring world terrorism and declaring that any armaments negotiations must be linked to negotiations on Soviet behavior in other areas.

Although the president had long denounced the SALT II arms control treaty as unfavorable to the United States, he continued to honor its provisions. But Reagan remained skeptical about arms control. In fact, the president proposed the

SDI

most ambitious new military program in many years: the Strategic Defense Initiative (SDI), known to some as "Star Wars." Reagan claimed that SDI, through lasers and satellites, could provide an effective shield against incoming missiles and thus make nuclear war obsolete. The Soviet Union claimed that the new program would elevate the arms race to new and more dangerous levels and insisted that any arms control agreement begin with an American abandonment of SDI.

The escalation of Cold War tensions and the slowing of arms control initiatives helped produce an important popular movement in Europe and the United States in the 1980s calling for an end to nuclear weapons buildups. In America, the principal goal

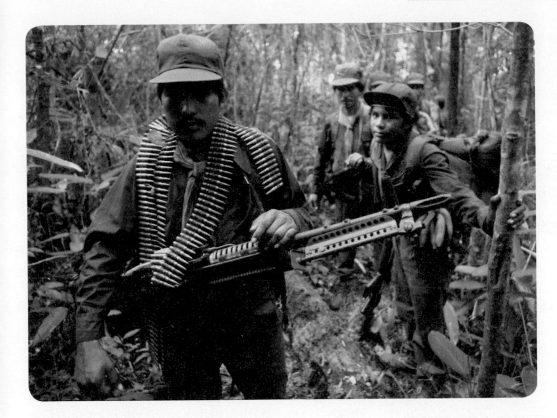

CONTRAS ON PATROL The Reagan administration's support for the Nicaraguan "contras," who opposed the leftist Sandinista regime, was the source of some of its greatest problems. Here, a small band of contras pause in the Nicaraguan jungle to catch their breath. The machine gunner carries an M-60 American weapon. (© Steven Clevenger/Corbis)

of the movement was a "nuclear freeze," an agreement between the two superpowers not to expand their atomic arsenals.

The Reagan administration supported opponents of communism anywhere in the world, whether or not they had any direct connection to the Soviet Union. This new policy became known as the Reagan Doctrine, and it meant a new American activism in the Third World. In October 1982, the administration sent American soldiers and marines into the tiny Caribbean island of Grenada to oust an anti-American Marxist regime that showed signs of a relationship with Moscow. In Nicaragua, a pro-American dictatorship had fallen to the revolutionary "Sandinistas" in 1979; the new government had grown increasingly anti-American (and increasingly Marxist) throughout the early 1980s. The Reagan administration supported the so-called contras, a guerrilla movement drawn from several antigovernment groups and trying to topple the Sandinista regime.

REAGAN DOCTRINE

In June 1982, the Israeli army launched an invasion of Lebanon in an effort to drive guerrillas of the Palestinian Liberation Organization from the country. An American peacekeeping force entered Beirut to supervise the evacuation of PLO forces from Lebanon. American marines then remained in the city to protect the fragile Lebanese government. As a result, Americans became the targets in 1983 of a terrorist bombing of a U.S. military barracks in Beirut that left 241 marines dead. Rather than become more deeply involved in the Lebanese struggle, Reagan withdrew American forces.

The tragedy in Lebanon was an example of the changing character of Third World struggles: an increasing reliance on terrorism by otherwise powerless groups to advance their political aims. A series of terrorist acts in the 1980s–attacks on airplanes, cruise ships, commercial and diplomatic posts; the seizing of American and other Western hostages alarmed and frightened much of the Western world.

TERRORISM

THE ELECTION OF 1984

Reagan approached the campaign of 1984 at the head of a united Republican Party firmly committed to his candidacy. The Democrats followed a more fractious course. Former vice president Walter Mondale, the early front-runner, fought off challenges from Senator Gary Hart of Colorado and the magnetic Jesse Jackson, who had established himself as the nation's most prominent spokesman for minorities and the poor. Mondale brought excitement to the Democratic campaign by selecting a woman, Representative Geraldine Ferraro of New York, to be his running mate and the first female candidate to appear on a national ticket.

In the campaign that fall, Reagan spoke of what he claimed was the remarkable revival of American fortunes and spirits under his leadership. His campaign emphasized such phrases as "It's Morning in America" and "America Is Back." Reagan's victory in 1984 was decisive. He won approximately 59 percent of the vote and carried every state but Mondale's native Minnesota and the District of Columbia. But Reagan was stronger than his party. Democrats gained a seat in the Senate and maintained only slightly reduced control of the House of Representatives.

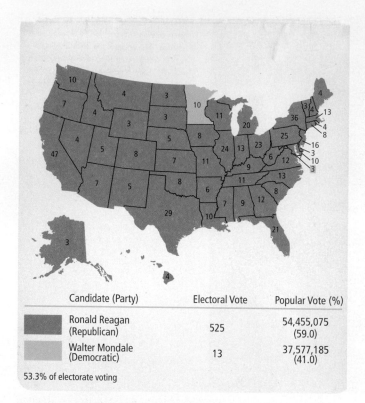

Candidate (Party)	Electoral Vote	Popular Vote (%)
Ronald Reagan (Republican)	525	54,455,075 (59.0)
Walter Mondale (Democratic)	13	37,577,185 (41.0)

53.3% of electorate voting

THE ELECTION OF 1984 In 1984, Ronald Reagan repeated (and slightly expanded) his electoral landslide of 1980 and added to it the popular landslide that had eluded him four years earlier. As this map shows, Mondale succeeded in carrying only his home state of Minnesota and the staunchly Democratic District of Columbia.

• *What were some of the factors that made Reagan so popular in 1984?*

AMERICA AND THE WANING OF THE COLD WAR

Many factors contributed to the collapse of the Soviet empire. The long, stalemated war in Afghanistan proved at least as disastrous to the Soviet Union as the Vietnam War had been to America. The government in Moscow had failed to address a long-term economic decline in the Soviet republics and the Eastern-bloc nations. Restiveness with the heavy-handed policies of communist police states was growing throughout much of the Soviet empire. But the most visible factor at the time was the emergence of Mikhail Gorbachev, who succeeded to the leadership of the Soviet Union in 1985 and, to the surprise of almost everyone, very quickly became the most revolutionary figure in world politics in several decades.

THE FALL OF THE SOVIET UNION

Gorbachev transformed Soviet politics with two dramatic new initiatives. The first he called *glasnost* (openness): the dismantling

MIKHAIL GORBACHEV of many of the repressive mechanisms that had been conspicuous features of Soviet life for over half a century. The other policy Gorbachev called *perestroika* (reform): an effort to restructure the

rigid and unproductive Soviet economy by introducing such elements of capitalism as private ownership and the profit motive.

The severe economic problems at home evidently convinced Gorbachev that the Soviet Union could no longer sustain its extended commitments around the world. As early as 1987, he began reducing Soviet influence in Eastern Europe. And in 1989, in the space of a few months, every communist state in Europe–Poland, Hungary, Czechoslovakia, Bulgaria, Romania, East Germany, Yugoslavia, and Albania–either overthrew its government or forced it to transform itself into a noncommunist (and, in some cases, actively anticommunist) regime.

The challenges to communism were not successful everywhere. In May 1989, students in China launched a mass movement calling for greater democratization. But in June, hard-line leaders seized control of the government and sent military forces

TIANANMEN SQUARE to crush the uprising. The result was a bloody assault on June 3, 1989, in Tiananmen Square in Beijing, in which a still-unknown number of demonstrators died. The assault crushed the democracy movement and restored the hard-liners to power. It did not, however, stop China's efforts to modernize and even Westernize its economy.

Early in 1990, the government of South Africa, long an international pariah for its rigid enforcement of "apartheid" (a system designed to protect white supremacy), began a cautious retreat from its traditional policies. It legalized the chief black party in the nation, the African National Congress (ANC), which had been banned for decades. On February 11, 1990, it released from prison the leader of the ANC, and a revered hero to black South Africans, Nelson Mandela. He had been in jail for twenty-seven years. Over the next several years, the South African government repealed its apartheid laws. And in 1994, after national elections in which all South Africans could participate, Nelson Mandela became the first black president of South Africa.

In 1991, communism began to collapse at the site of its birth: the Soviet Union. An unsuccessful coup by hard-line Soviet leaders on August 19 precipitated a dramatic unraveling of

DISSOLUTION OF THE USSR communist power. Within days, the coup itself collapsed in the face of resistance from the public and, more important, crucial elements within the military. Mikhail Gorbachev returned to power, but it soon became evident that the legitimacy of both the Communist Party and the central Soviet government had been fatally injured. By the end of August, many of the republics of the Soviet Union had declared independence; the Soviet government was clearly powerless to stop the fragmentation. Gorbachev resigned as leader of the now virtually powerless Communist Party and Soviet government, and the Soviet Union ceased to exist.

REAGAN AND GORBACHEV

Reagan was skeptical when Gorbachev took power in 1985, but he gradually became convinced that the Soviet leader was sincere in his desire for reform. At a summit meeting with Reagan in Reykjavik, Iceland, in 1986, Gorbachev proposed

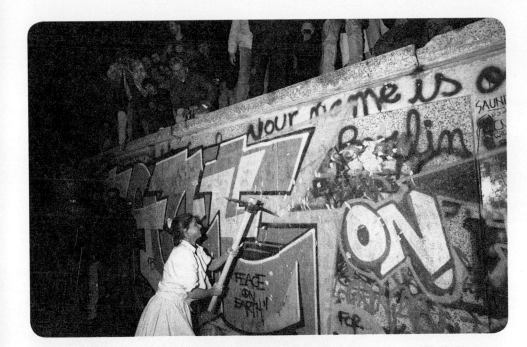

THE FALL OF THE BERLIN WALL The Berlin Wall is widely considered to have "fallen" on November 9, 1989. Starting on that date and in the days and weeks that followed, people used sledgehammers and picks to tear the wall down, often keeping the broken pieces as souvenirs of this symbolic conclusion of the Cold War. (© DIZ München GmbH/Alamy)

reducing the nuclear arsenals of both sides by 50 percent or more, although continuing disputes over Reagan's commitment to the SDI program prevented agreements. But in 1988, after Reagan and Gorbachev exchanged cordial visits to each other's capitals, the two superpowers signed a treaty eliminating American and Soviet intermediate-range nuclear forces (INF) from Europe—the most significant arms control agreement of the nuclear age. At about the same time, Gorbachev ended the Soviet Union's long and frustrating military involvement in Afghanistan.

THE FADING OF THE REAGAN REVOLUTION

For a time, the dramatic changes around the world and Reagan's personal popularity deflected attention from a series of political scandals. There were revelations of illegality, corruption, and ethical lapses in the Environmental Protection Agency, the CIA, the Department of Defense, the Department of Labor, the Department of Justice, and the Department of Housing and Urban Development. A more serious scandal emerged within the savings and loan industry, which the Reagan administration had helped deregulate in the early 1980s.

SAVINGS AND LOAN CRISIS

But the most politically damaging scandal of the Reagan years came to light in November 1986, when the White House conceded that it had sold weapons to the revolutionary government of Iran as part of a largely unsuccessful effort to secure the release of several Americans being held hostage by radical Islamic groups in the Middle East. Even more damaging was the revelation that some of the money from the arms deal with Iran had been covertly and illegally funneled into a fund to aid the contras in Nicaragua.

In the months that followed, aggressive reporting and congressional hearings exposed a widespread pattern of illegal covert activities orchestrated by the White House and dedicated to advancing the administration's foreign policy aims. The Iran-contra scandal, as it became known, did serious damage to the Reagan presidency.

IRAN-CONTRA SCANDAL

THE ELECTION OF 1988

The fraying of the Reagan administration helped the Democrats regain control of the U.S. Senate in 1986 and fueled hopes for a presidential victory in 1988. Even so, several of the most popular figures in the Democratic Party refused to run, and the nomination finally went to a previously little-known figure: Michael Dukakis, a three-term democratic governor of Massachusetts. Dukakis was a flat and somewhat dull campaigner. But Democrats were optimistic about their prospects in 1988, largely because their opponent, Vice President George H. W. Bush, had failed to spark public enthusiasm.

Beginning at the Republican Convention, however, Bush staged a remarkable turnaround by making his campaign a long, relentless attack on Dukakis, tying him to all the unpopular social and cultural stances Americans had come to identify with "liberals." The campaign revealed the new political aggressiveness of the Republican right. Bush won a substantial victory in November: 54 percent of the popular vote to Dukakis's 46 percent, and 426 electoral votes to Dukakis's 112. But the Democrats retained secure majorities in both houses of Congress.

THE FIRST BUSH PRESIDENCY

The broad popularity George H. W. Bush enjoyed during his first three years in office was partly a result of his subdued, unthreatening public image. But it was primarily because of the wonder and excitement with which Americans viewed

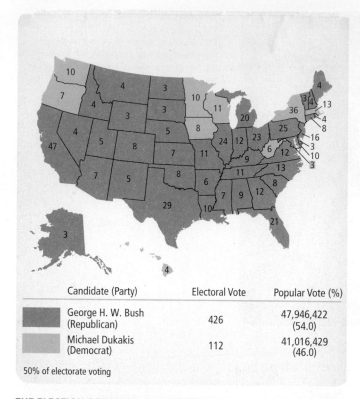

Candidate (Party)	Electoral Vote	Popular Vote (%)
George H. W. Bush (Republican)	426	47,946,422 (54.0)
Michael Dukakis (Democrat)	112	41,016,429 (46.0)

50% of electorate voting

THE ELECTION OF 1988 Democrats had high hopes going into the election of 1988, but Vice President George Bush won a decisive victory over Michael Dukakis, who did only slightly better than Walter Mondale had done four years earlier.

• *What made it so difficult for a Democrat to challenge the Republicans in 1988 after eight years of a Republican administration?*

the dramatic events in the rest of the world. Bush moved cautiously at first in dealing with the changes in the Soviet Union. But like Reagan, he eventually cooperated with Gorbachev and reached a series of significant agreements with the Soviet Union in its waning years. The United States and the Soviet Union moved rapidly toward even more far-reaching arms reduction agreements.

On domestic issues, the Bush administration was less successful. His administration inherited a heavy burden of debt **POLITICAL GRIDLOCK** and a federal deficit that had been growing for nearly a decade. The president's pledges to reduce the deficit and simultaneously to promise "no new taxes" were in conflict with one another. Bush faced a Democratic Congress with an agenda very different from his own.

The Congress and the White House managed on occasion to agree on significant measures. They cooperated in producing the plan to salvage the floundering savings and loan industry. In 1990, the president bowed to congressional pressure and agreed to a significant tax increase as part of a multiyear "budget package" designed to reduce the deficit—thus violating his own 1988 campaign pledge.

But the most serious domestic problem facing the Bush administration was one for which neither the president nor Congress had any answer: a recession that began late in 1990 and slowly increased its grip on the national economy in 1991

THE BUSH CAMPAIGN, 1988 Vice President George Bush had never been an effective campaigner, but in 1988 he revived his candidacy with an unabashed attack on his opponent's values and patriotism. Bush missed no chance to surround himself with patriotic symbols, including this red, white, and blue hot-air balloon in Kentucky. (Photo by Cynthia Johnson/© Time & Life Pictures/Getty Images)

1990 RECESSION and 1992. Because of the enormous level of debt that corporations (and individuals) had accumulated in the 1980s, the recession caused an unusual number of bankruptcies. It also increased fear and frustration among middle- and working-class Americans and put pressure on the government to address such problems as the rising cost of health care.

THE FIRST GULF WAR

The collapse of the Soviet Union in 1989-1991 had left the United States in the unanticipated position of being the only real superpower in the world. One result was that the United States would reduce its military strength and concentrate its energies and resources on pressing domestic problems. Another was that America would continue to use its power actively, not to fight communism but to defend its regional and economic interests. In 1989, that led the administration to

BURNING OIL FIELDS With the advance of Coalition forces into Kuwait, the retreating Iraqi military set fire to hundreds of oil wells and other oil-related resources to punish Kuwaiti overproduction and to create smoke screens to block "smart weapons" (guided bombs) and satellites. (© Peter Turnley/Corbis)

order an invasion of Panama, which overthrew the unpopular military leader Manuel Noriega (under indictment in the United States for drug trafficking) and replaced him with an elected, pro-American regime.

On August 2, 1990, the armed forces of Iraq invaded and **INVASION OF KUWAIT** quickly overwhelmed their small, oil-rich neighbor, the emirate of Kuwait. Saddam Hussein, the militaristic leader of Iraq, soon announced that he was annexing Kuwait and set out to entrench his forces there. After some initial indecision, the Bush administration agreed to lead other nations in a campaign to force Iraq out of Kuwait—through the pressure of economic sanctions if possible, through military force if necessary. Within a few weeks, Bush had persuaded virtually every important government in the world, including the Soviet Union and almost all the Arab and Islamic states, to join in a United Nations-sanctioned trade embargo of Iraq.

At the same time, the United States and its allies (including the British, French, Egyptians, and Saudis) began deploying a large military force along the border between Kuwait and Saudi Arabia, a force that ultimately reached 690,000 troops (425,000 of them American). On November 29, the United Nations, at the request of the United States, voted to authorize military action to expel Iraq from Kuwait if Iraq did not leave by January 15, 1991. On January 12, both houses of Congress voted to authorize the use of force against Iraq. And on January 16, American and allied air forces began a massive bombardment of Iraqi forces in Kuwait and of military and industrial installations in Iraq itself.

The allied bombing continued for six weeks. On February 23, allied (primarily American) forces under the command of General Norman Schwarzkopf began a major ground offensive—not primarily against the heavily entrenched Iraqi forces along the Kuwait border, as expected, but to the north of them into Iraq itself. The allied armies encountered almost no resistance and suffered relatively few casualties (141 fatalities). Estimates of Iraqi deaths in the war were 100,000 or more. On February 28, Iraq announced its acceptance of allied terms for a cease-fire, and the brief Persian Gulf War came to an end.

The quick and (for America) relatively painless victory over Iraq was highly popular in the United States. But the tyrannical regime of Saddam Hussein survived, weakened but still ruthless.

The Gulf War preserved an independent nation and kept an important source of oil from falling into the hands of Iraq. But many Muslims, watching Americans attacking their fellow religionists, became incensed by the U.S. presence in the region. The most conservative and militant Muslims were insulted by the presence of women in the United Nations forces. But even more-moderate Middle East Muslims began to believe that America was a threat to their world. Even before the Gulf War, Middle Eastern terrorists had been targeting Americans in the region. Their determination to threaten America grew significantly in its aftermath.

THE ELECTION OF 1992

President Bush's popularity reached a record high in the immediate aftermath of the Gulf War. But the glow of that victory faded quickly as the recession worsened in late 1991, and as the administration declined to propose any policies for combating it.

Because the early maneuvering for the 1992 presidential election occurred when President Bush's popularity remained **BILL CLINTON** high, many leading Democrats declined to run. That gave Bill Clinton, the young five-term governor of Arkansas, an opportunity to emerge early as the front-runner. He went on to run a skillful campaign.

Complicating the campaign was the emergence of Ross Perot, a blunt, forthright Texas billionaire who became an independent candidate by tapping popular resentment of the federal

THE ELECTION OF 1992 In the 1992 election, for the first time since 1976, a Democrat captured the White House. And although the third-party candidacy of Ross Perot deprived Bill Clinton of an absolute majority, he nevertheless defeated George Bush by a decisive margin in both the popular and electoral vote.

• *What factors had eroded President Bush's once-broad popularity by 1992? What explained the strong showing of Ross Perot?*

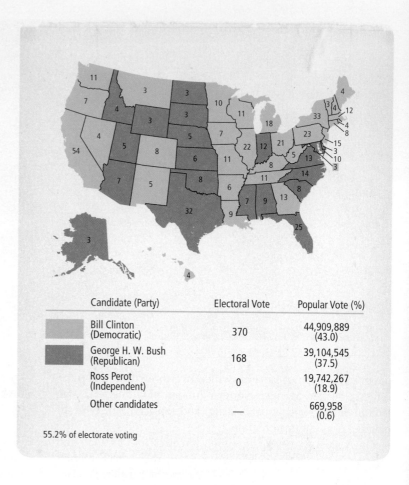

Candidate (Party)	Electoral Vote	Popular Vote (%)
Bill Clinton (Democratic)	370	44,909,889 (43.0)
George H. W. Bush (Republican)	168	39,104,545 (37.5)
Ross Perot (Independent)	0	19,742,267 (18.9)
Other candidates	—	669,958 (0.6)

55.2% of electorate voting

ROSS PEROT bureaucracy and by promising tough, uncompromising leadership to deal with the fiscal crisis. At several moments in the spring, Perot led both Bush and Clinton in public opinion polls. In July, as Perot began to face hostile scrutiny from the media, he abruptly withdrew from the race. But early in October, he reentered and soon regained much (although never all) of his early support.

Clinton won a clear, but hardly overwhelming, victory over Bush and Perot. He received 43 percent of the vote in the three-way race, to the president's 38 percent and Perot's 19 percent (the best showing for a third-party or independent candidate since Theodore Roosevelt in 1912). Clinton won 370 electoral votes to Bush's 168; Perot won none. Democrats retained control of both houses of Congress.

AP CONNECTING THEMES

Chapter 31 discussed the political, diplomatic, economic, and social climate of the United States during the 1980s. As you review, focus first on the administrations of Gerald Ford and Jimmy Carter and their relative success in both domestic and foreign policy. Be familiar with the concept of new conservatism, the reasons for its emergence as a dominant force in politics, and the impact it had on both policy decisions and the attitudes of the American people. Understand the change in relations with the Soviet Union between the beginning and end of the Reagan administration. Be aware that there is intense dispute as to whether the Reagan administration prolonged or ended the Cold War. Finally, be able to see characteristic similarities and differences between the 1980s and other periods of American history, particularly the Gilded Age and the 1920s.

The following themes have a heightened importance in Chapter 31. You should now be able to do the following for each listed theme:

Identity: Explain how the rising tide of conservatism altered perceptions of what it was to be an American.

Work, Exchange, and Technology: Explain the principles of "Reaganomics" and compare and contrast it to economic policy during the Gilded Age and the 1920s. Explain the impact of economic policies of the 1980s on various socioeconomic groups.

Peopling: Explain why migration to the South and West occurred and explain how that migration affected the regions' political clout.

Politics and Power: Explain the reasons for geographic and class realignment in the political arena in the 1980s and the degree to which religion played a role in that realignment.
America and the World: Explain the degree to which foreign policy changed under the Reagan administration.

Environment and Geography: Explain the impact of the political policies of the 1980s on environmental issues.
Ideas, Beliefs, and Culture: Discuss the ways in which and the degree to which political and religious movements in the 1980s affected Americans' beliefs and values.

AP SUGGESTED STUDY

PEOPLE/PLACES/EVENTS As you study these items, think about how they demonstrate or relate to key concepts and historical themes from this chapter and previous chapters.

AYATOLLAH RUHOLLAH KHOMEINI 841
BILL CLINTON 854
CAMP DAVID ACCORDS 840
GEORGE H. W. BUSH 851
GERALD FORD 838
GLASNOST 850
IRAN-CONTRA SCANDAL 851
JIMMY CARTER 839

MIKHAIL GORBACHEV 850
NEO-CONSERVATIVES 846
NEW RIGHT 844
PERESTROIKA 850
REAGAN DOCTRINE 849
REAGANOMICS 846
RONALD REAGAN 838
ROSS PEROT 854

SADDAM HUSSEIN 853
SAGEBRUSH REBELLION 842
SUNBELT 842
STRATEGIC DEFENSE INITIATIVE
(SDI) 848
TIANANMEN SQUARE 850

AP TEST PRACTICE

Questions assume cumulative content knowledge from this chapter and previous chapters.

MULTIPLE CHOICE Use the map on page 792 of Chapter 29 and your knowledge of U.S. history to answer questions 1-2.

1. By the late 1980s which was a major criticism by those who did not support the policy represented in the map?
   (A) That the U.S. did not intervene in enough of the countries
   (B) That the U.S. found itself backing repressive regimes
   (C) That the U.S. needed to be more adept at fighting communism
   (D) That the U.S. interventions caused destabilization of the entire Western Hemisphere

2. The reason for the evolution of American foreign policy in the Western Hemisphere by the 1980s as shown by the map was
   (A) to establish a series of military bases in Latin America to pre-empt Soviet influence
   (B) to remain neutral in the politics of countries in Latin America
   (C) to actively oppose communism of any origin anywhere in the world
   (D) to reduce U.S. intervention in countries in which communist movement was arising from within the country

SHORT ANSWER Use your knowledge of U.S. history to answer questions 3-4.

3. Answer a, b and c.
   a) Briefly explain ONE example of how the American electorate became more conservative during the 1970s and 1980s.
   b) Briefly explain a SECOND example of how the American electorate became more conservative during the 1970s and 1980s.
   c) Briefly explain ONE issue that was of concern for the conservative electorate.

4. Use the graph on page 847 to answer a, b, and c.
   a) Briefly explain one example of government action in the 1980s to reduce the trend represented in the top graph.
   b) Briefly explain an effect of that action.
   c) Briefly explain an action of the government in the 1980s which contributed to the trend on the map.

LONG ESSAY For each question below, develop a thoughtful and thorough historical argument that answers the question. Begin your essay with a thesis statement and support it with relevant historical evidence.

5. Some historians have argued that the religious conservative movement that arose in the 1980s is very similar to the Second Great Awakening at the turn of the 19th century. Support, modify, or refute this interpretation, providing specific evidence to justify your answer.

6. To what extent were the Cold War policies of the 1980s a continuation as well as a departure from the policies of the late 1940s and early 1950s?

32 | THE AGE OF GLOBALIZATION

DRONES Unmanned combat air vehicles (UCAV), also known as drones, have become weapons of choice during many recent US military engagements throughout the world. Pilots operate these vehicles from remote sites. For example, drones used for combat in Afghanistan may be operated from bases in the western United States thus raising many ethical questions about the contemporary nature of war in the global environment. (© Kirsty Wigglesworth/AP Images)

AP
HISTORICAL THINKING

1. **Contextualization** Analyze the conflict over liberalism and conservatism in the 1990s and cite specific examples of conflict and accommodation.

2. **Historical Argumentation** Analyze the reasons for and the results of the highly contested elections of 2000 and 2004.

3. **Historical Causation** Analyze the impact of an increasingly aging demographic on the political, economic, and social aspects of American society.

4. **Contextualization** To what degree and in what ways did American foreign policy respond to direct and indirect threats to American security from terrorist organizations?

5. **Contextualization** Analyze the controversy over global warming and environmental issues in defining party alignment.

6. **Historical Argumentation** Analyze the reasons for and the results of the extreme polarization of political parties after 2008.

7. **Historical Argumentation** Assess the impact of U.S. involvement in Iraq and Afghanistan on American public opinion.

Key Concept Correlations

Analyze the ways the historical developments you learn about in this chapter connect to the following AP Key Concepts.

9.1 A new conservatism grew to prominence in U.S. culture and politics, defending traditional social values and rejecting liberal views about the role of government.

9.2 The end of the Cold War and new challenges to U.S. leadership in the world forced the nation to redefine its foreign policy and global role.

9.3 Moving into the 21st century, the nation continued to experience challenges stemming from social, economic, and demographic changes.

Thematic Learning Objectives

POL-3, 7; WXT-3, 7, 8; WOR-3, 7, 8; ENV-5; CUL-7; ID-6, 7; PEO-7

CHAPTER 32 focuses on the 1990s through the present. The chapter assesses the successes and failures of the Clinton administration. In doing so, it emphasizes political fluctuation and the seeming inability of the American people to force a consistent ideological stance. It also looks at the hotly contested presidential races in 2000, 2004, and 2008. The chapter focuses on increasing income disparity between classes and the impact of the financial crisis beginning in 2008 and attempts by the federal government to mitigate its impact. The chapter also discusses the impact of the aging of American society, particularly, of the baby boomers. Significant focus is placed on the role of computer technology in altering social relationships and connecting America more definitively within a global context. Consideration is also given to the debate over the environment and global warming as well as perceived threats to the environment by increased exploration for sources of energy. The war on terror and its consequences are dealt with in significant detail. Finally, there is a discussion of the extreme polarization of political parties and the impact on perceptions of the ability of Congress and the presidency to effectively govern. As you read, evaluate the following ideas:

- Following the end of the Cold War, the United States increased its role as international peacekeeper.
- The war on terror initially saw overwhelming support, which faded as concerns over government infringement on personal liberties and questions about the success of the strategy began to surface.
- An increasingly inequitable distribution of wealth called into question the equity of the capitalistic system.
- Continued debate raged over the dependence on foreign oil.
- Computer technology dramatically changed the ways of social interaction and led to increased globalization.
- The influx of migrants from Latin America led to increased nativist sentiment.
- The extreme polarization of political parties led to gridlock and declining confidence of the American people in the ability of government to successfully resolve problems facing the country.

A RESURGENCE OF PARTISANSHIP

Bill Clinton took the oath of office in January 1993 with a domestic agenda more ambitious than that of any other president in nearly thirty years. But having won the votes of well under half the electorate, he had no powerful mandate. The Republican leadership in Congress was highly adversarial and opposed the president with unusual unanimity on many issues. A tendency toward reckless personal behavior, both before and during his presidency, caused Clinton continuing problems and gave his many enemies repeated opportunities to discredit him.

WILLIAM JEFFERSON CLINTON

LAUNCHING THE CLINTON PRESIDENCY

The Clinton administration encountered many missteps and misfortunes in its first months. Several of his early appointments became so controversial, he had to withdraw them.

Despite its many problems, the Clinton administration could boast of some major achievements in its first year. The president narrowly won approval of a budget that marked a significant turn away from the policies of the Reagan-Bush years. It included a substantial tax increase on the wealthiest Americans, a large reduction in many areas of government spending, and a major expansion of tax credits to low-income working people.

Clinton was a committed advocate of free trade and a proponent of many aspects of what came to be known as globalism. He made that clear through his strong support of a series of new and controversial free-trade agreements. After a long and difficult battle, he won approval of the North American Free Trade Agreement (or NAFTA), which eliminated most trade barriers among the United States, Canada, and Mexico. Later he won approval of other far-reaching trade agreements negotiated in the General Agreement on Trade and Tariffs (or GATT).

NAFTA

FAILURE OF HEALTH-CARE REFORM

The president's most ambitious initiative was a major reform of the nation's health-care system. Early in 1993, he appointed a task force chaired by his wife, Hillary Rodham Clinton. He proposed a sweeping reform designed to guarantee coverage to every American and hold down the costs of medical care. Substantial opposition from the right doomed the plan in 1994.

The foreign policy of the Clinton administration was not without some successes. The small Balkan nation Bosnia was embroiled in a bloody civil war between its two major ethnic groups: one Muslim, the other Serbian and Christian. The American negotiator Richard Holbrooke finally brought the warring parties together in 1995 and crafted an agreement to partition Bosnia.

THE REPUBLICAN RESURGENCE

In 1994, for the first time in forty years, Republicans gained control of both houses of Congress. Throughout 1995, the Republican Congress worked at a sometimes feverish pace to construct an ambitious and even radical legislative program. The Republicans proposed a series of measures to transfer important powers from the federal government to the states. They proposed dramatic reductions in federal spending, including a major restructuring of the Medicare program. In all these efforts, they could count on a disciplined Republican majority in the House and an only slightly less united Republican majority in the Senate.

President Clinton responded to the 1994 election results by proclaiming that "the era of big government is over" and shifting his own agenda conspicuously to the center. He announced his own plan to cut taxes and balance the budget. But compromise between the president and the Republicans in Congress became difficult. In November 1995 and again in January 1996, the federal government shut down for several days because the president and Congress could not agree on a budget. That proved to be an epic political blunder. Public opinion turned quickly and powerfully against the Republican leadership and much of its agenda. House Speaker Newt Gingrich quickly became discredited, while President Clinton slowly improved his standing in the polls.

CLINTON VERSUS DOLE

THE ELECTION OF 1996

By 1996, President Clinton was in a commanding position to win reelection. Unopposed for the Democratic nomination, he faced a Republican opponent–Senator Robert Dole of Kansas–who inspired little enthusiasm even within his own party. Clinton's revival was a result of his adroitness in taking centrist positions that undermined the Republicans and in championing traditional Democratic issues that were broadly popular. But his greatest strength came from the remarkable success of the American economy. Like Reagan in 1984, he could campaign as the champion of peace, prosperity, and national well-being.

As the election approached, Congress passed several important bills. It raised the legal minimum wage for the first time in more than a decade. And it passed a welfare reform bill, which President Clinton somewhat reluctantly signed, that marked the most important change in aid to the poor since the Social Security Act of 1935. The bill ended the fifty-year federal guarantee of assistance to families with dependent children and turned most of the responsibility for allocating federal welfare funds (now greatly reduced) to the states. Most important, it shifted the bulk of welfare benefits away from those without jobs and toward support for low-wage workers.

Clinton's buoyant campaign flagged slightly in the last weeks, but the president nevertheless received just over 49 percent of the popular vote. Clinton won 379 electoral votes to Dole's 159 (Ross Perot received 0 electoral votes). But other

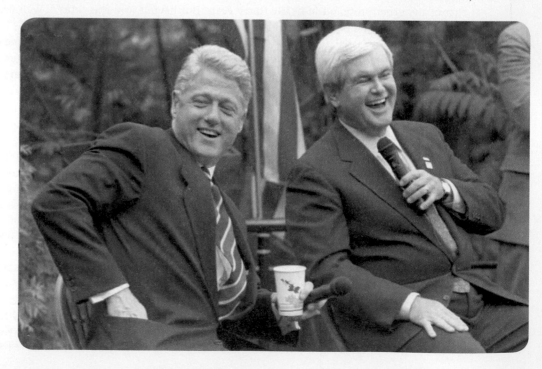

CLINTON AND GINGRICH For a time after Republicans won control of both houses of Congress in 1994, some observers suggested that Newt Gingrich was now the most powerful figure in government, and that President Clinton was (as some journalists suggested) irrelevant. But Clinton surprised everyone by working cordially with Gingrich and, in the process, rebuilding his own popularity. They are seen here together in public at a senior center in Claremont, New Hampshire. (John Mottern/© AFP/Getty Images)

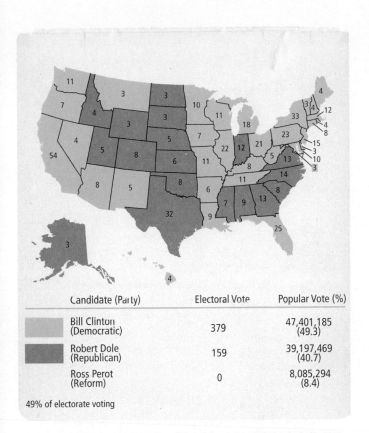

Candidate (Party)	Electoral Vote	Popular Vote (%)
Bill Clinton (Democratic)	379	47,401,185 (49.3)
Robert Dole (Republican)	159	39,197,469 (40.7)
Ross Perot (Reform)	0	8,085,294 (8.4)

49% of electorate voting

THE ELECTION OF 1996 Ross Perot did much less well in 1996 than he had in 1992, and President Clinton came much closer than he had four years earlier to winning a majority of the popular vote. Once again, Clinton defeated his Republican opponent, this time Robert Dole, by a decisive margin in both the popular and electoral vote. After the 1994 Republican landslide in the congressional elections, Bill Clinton had seemed permanently weakened.

• *What explains Clinton's political revival?*

Democrats made only modest gains and failed to regain either house of Congress.

CLINTON TRIUMPHANT AND EMBATTLED

Bill Clinton was the first Democratic president to win two terms as president since Franklin Roosevelt. He still faced a hostile Republican Congress. He proposed a modest domestic agenda, consisting of tax cuts and tax credits targeted at middle-class Americans to help them educate their children. He also negotiated effectively with the Republican leadership on a plan for a balanced budget, which passed late in 1997. By the end of 1998, the federal budget was generating its first surplus in thirty years.

BUDGET SURPLUSES

Clinton needed the popularity he had gained from the budget surplus when the most serious crisis of his presidency emerged. Clinton had been bedeviled by scandals from his first weeks in office. In early 1998, the president was charged with having had a sexual relationship with a young White House intern, Monica Lewinsky, and lying about it in a deposition. Those revelations produced a new investigation by the independent counsel in the Whitewater case, Kenneth Starr, a former judge and official in the Reagan Justice Department.

MONICA LEWINSKY

Clinton forcefully denied the charges, and the public strongly backed him. His popularity soared to record levels and remained high throughout the year that followed.

The Lewinsky scandal revived again in August 1998, when Lewinsky struck a deal with the independent counsel and testified about her relationship with Clinton. Starr then subpoenaed Clinton himself, who finally admitted that he and Lewinsky had what he called an "improper relationship." A few weeks later, Starr recommended that Congress impeach the president.

The House Judiciary Committee and then, on December 19, 1998, the full House, approved two counts of impeachment: lying to the grand jury and obstructing justice. The matter then moved to the Senate, where a trial of the president—the first since the trial of Andrew Johnson in 1868—began in early January. The trial ended with a decisive acquittal of the president.

IMPEACHMENT

In 1999, the president faced the most serious foreign policy crisis of his presidency, once again in the Balkans. A long-simmering conflict between the Serbian government of Yugoslavia and Kosovo separatists erupted into a savage civil war in 1998. In May 1999, NATO forces—dominated and led by the United States—began a bombing campaign against the Serbians, which after little more than a week led the leader of Yugoslavia, Slobodan Milosevic, to agree to a cease-fire. Serbian troops withdrew from Kosovo. They were replaced by NATO peacekeeping forces. A precarious peace returned to the region.

KOSOVO

Clinton finished his eight years in office with his popularity higher than it had been when he had taken office. Indeed, public approval of Clinton's presidency—a presidency marked by astonishing prosperity and general world stability—was consistently among the highest of any postwar president, despite the many scandals and setbacks he suffered in the White House.

THE ELECTION OF 2000

The 2000 presidential election was one of the most extraordinary in American history—not because of the campaign that preceded it, but because of the sensational controversy over its results.

George W. Bush—a Republican, a son of the former president, and a second-term governor of Texas—and Vice President Al Gore, a Democrat, easily won the nominations of their parties.

GEORGE W. BUSH VERSUS AL GORE

Both men ran cautious, centrist campaigns. Polls showed an exceptionally tight race right up to the end. In the congressional races, Republicans maintained control of the House of Representatives by five seats, while the Senate split evenly between Democrats and Republicans. In the presidential race, Gore won the national popular vote by about 540,000 votes out of about 100 million cast (or. 05%). But on election night, both candidates remained short of the 270 electoral votes needed for victory because no one could determine who had won the electoral votes of Florida. After a mandatory recount over the next two days, Bush led Gore in the state by fewer than 300 votes.

FLORIDA

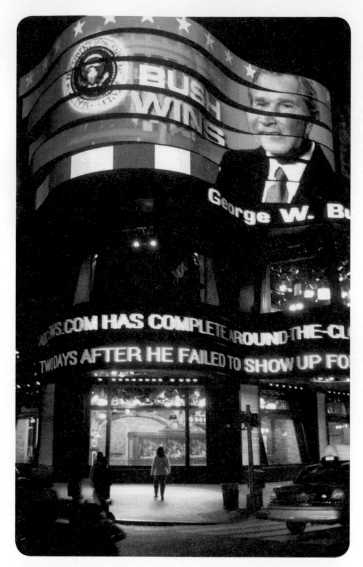

ELECTION NIGHT, 2000 The electronic billboard in New York City's Times Square, showing network coverage of the presidential contest, reports George Bush the winner of the 2000 presidential race late on election night. A few hours later, the networks retracted their projections because of continuing uncertainty over the results in Florida. Five weeks later, and then only because of the controversial intervention of the Supreme Court, Bush finally emerged the victor. (© Chris Hondros/Getty Images)

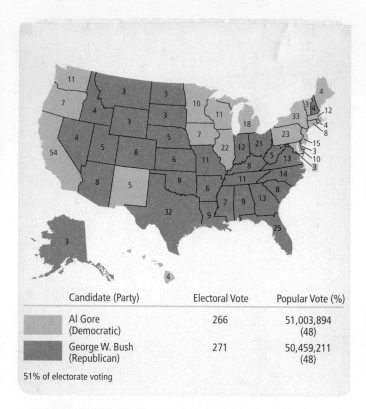

Candidate (Party)	Electoral Vote	Popular Vote (%)
Al Gore (Democratic)	266	51,003,894 (48)
George W. Bush (Republican)	271	50,459,211 (48)

51% of electorate voting

THE ELECTION OF 2000 The 2000 presidential election was one of the closest and most controversial in American history. It also starkly revealed a new pattern of party strength, which had been developing over the previous decade. Democrats swept the Northeast and most of the industrial Midwest and carried all the states of the Pacific Coast. Republicans swept the South, the plains states, and the mountain states (with the exception of New Mexico) and held on to a few traditional Republican strongholds in the Midwest.

• *Compare this map to those of earlier elections, in particular the election of 1896, and ask how the pattern of party support changed over the course of the twentieth century.*

When a court-ordered deadline arrived, the recount was not yet complete. The Florida secretary of state, a Republican, then certified Bush the winner in Florida by a little more than 500 votes. The Gore campaign contested the results. Late on December 12, the U.S. Supreme Court issued a controversial 5-4 decision for Bush and the long election ended.

THE SUPREME COURT'S DECISION

THE SECOND BUSH PRESIDENCY

George W. Bush assumed the presidency in January 2001 burdened by both the controversies surrounding his election and the perception that he was ill prepared for the office.

Bush's principal campaign promise had been that he would use the predicted budget surplus to finance a massive tax

BUSH TAX CUTS reduction. He narrowly won passage of the largest tax cut in American history—$1.35 trillion over several years.

Having campaigned as a moderate adept at building coalitions across party lines, Bush governed as a staunch conservative, relying on one of the most orthodox members of his own party for support. The president's political adviser, Karl Rove, encouraged the administration to take increasingly conservative positions. Bush appealed to the gun lobby by refusing to support a renewal of the assault weapons ban that Clinton had enacted. He proposed a constitutional amendment to ban gay marriage. The Bush administration was part of a broad and successful effort to mobilize evangelical Christians as an active part of the Republican coalition. But almost from the beginning, the aftermath of the September 11 attacks dominated both Bush's presidency and the nation's politics.

THE ELECTION OF 2004

The 2004 election pitted President Bush, who was unopposed within his party, against John Kerry, a Democratic senator from Massachusetts. Throughout the months before the election, voters were almost evenly divided again. The election itself,

FLIP-FLOPPING The tradition of accusing opponents of changing their public positions for political gain, called flip-flopping, has been a long-time feature of American politics. Here, a supporter of George W. Bush uses her footwear to ridicule his opponent, Senator John Kerry as a flip-flopper on the issue of the war with Iraq. (© Wilfredo Lee/AP Images)

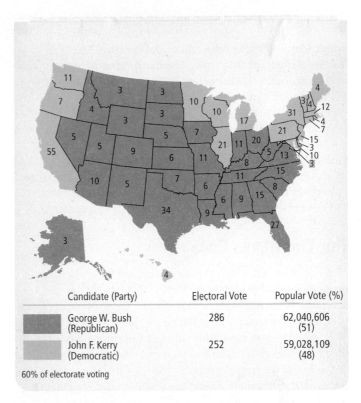

Candidate (Party)	Electoral Vote	Popular Vote (%)
George W. Bush (Republican)	286	62,040,606 (51)
John F. Kerry (Democratic)	252	59,028,109 (48)

60% of electorate voting

THE ELECTION OF 2004 The 2004 election repeated the pattern established in 2000. The Democrats, led this time by Massachusetts senator John F. Kerry, swept the Northeast, most of the industrial Midwest, and the Pacific Coast. The Republicans, led by President Bush, carried almost everything else. Although Bush's popular and electoral margins were both larger than they had been in 2000, the election remained extremely close.

although very close, was more decisive than the election of 2000. Bush won 51 percent of the popular vote to Kerry's 48.

THE ECONOMIC BOOM

The last three decades have seen remarkable changes in American life—some a result of the end of the Cold War, some the changing character of the American population, and some a product of a rapidly evolving culture. But most of these changes were at least in part a product of the dramatic transformation of the American economy.

FROM "STAGFLATION" TO GROWTH

The roots of the economic growth of the 1980s, 1990s, and 2000s lay in part in the troubled years of the 1970s, when the United States seemed for a time to be losing its ability to produce long-term prosperity. In the face of the sluggish growth and persistent inflation of those years, however, many American corporations began making important changes in the way they ran their businesses—changes that contributed to both the prosperity of the last decades of the twentieth century and the growing inequality that accompanied it. Businesses invested heavily in new technology, to make themselves more efficient and productive. Corporations began to consider mergers to provide themselves with a more diversified basis for growth. Many enterprises created more-energy-efficient plants and offices. Perhaps most important of all, American businesses sought to

NEW BUSINESS PRACTICES

reduce their labor costs, which were among the highest in the world and which many economists and business leaders believed had made the United States uncompetitive against the many emerging economies that relied on low-wage workers.

Businesses cut labor costs in many ways. They took a much harder line against unions. Nonunion companies became more successful in staving off unionization drives. Some companies moved their operations to areas of the country where unions were weak and wages low—the American South and Midwest in particular. And many companies moved much of their production out of the United States, to such nations as Mexico and China, where there were large available pools of cheaper labor.

Digital technology made possible an enormous range of new products: computers, the Internet, cellular phones, digital music, video, and cameras, personal digital assistants, and many other products. The technology industries created many new jobs and produced new consumer needs and appetites. But they did not create as many jobs as older industrial sectors had.

TECHNOLOGY INDUSTRIES

The American economy experienced rapid growth in the last decades of the twentieth century and into the twenty-first. The gross national product (the total of goods and services produced by the United States) almost quadrupled in twenty years—from $2.7 trillion in 1980, to over $9.8 trillion in 2000, to $15.7 trillion by 2013. Inflation was low throughout these decades, never rising above 3 percent in any year. Stock prices soared to unprecedented levels, and with few interruptions, from the mid-1980s to the end of the century. The Dow Jones Industrial Average, the most common index of stock performance, stood at 1,000 in late 1980. Late in 1999, it passed 11,000, and in November 2013 it peaked at 16,000 for the first time ever. Economic growth was particularly robust in the last years of the 1990s. In 1997 and 1998, annual growth rates reached 5 percent for the first time since the 1960s. Most impressive of all was the longevity of the boom. From 1994 to 2000, the economy recorded growth—at times very substantial growth—in every year, indeed in every quarter, something that had never before happened so continuously in peacetime.

THE TWO-TIERED ECONOMY

Although the American economy revived from the sluggishness of the 1970s and early 1980s, the benefits of the new economy were less widely shared than those of earlier boom times. The increasing abundance of the late twentieth and early twenty-first centuries created enormous new wealth that enriched those talented or lucky enough to profit from the areas of booming growth. The rewards for education—particularly in such areas as science and engineering—increased substantially.

The gross domestic product was more than $15 trillion at the end of 2013. Even so, incomes remained flat for most Americans. Poverty in the country had steadily declined, sometimes dramatically, in the years after World War II, so that by the end of the 1970s the percentage of people living in poverty had fallen to 12 percent (from 20 percent in preceding decades). But the decline in poverty did not continue, and in 2013 it reached 15 percent of the population, which means that 46 million Americans were living in poverty.

GLOBALIZATION

Perhaps the most important economic change was what became known as the "globalization" of the economy. The great prosperity of the 1950s and 1960s had rested on the relative insulation of the United States from the pressures of international competition. As late as 1970, international trade still played a relatively small role in the American economy, which thrived on the basis of the huge domestic market in North America.

By the end of the 1970s, however, the world had intruded on the American economy in profound ways, and that intrusion increased unabated into the twenty-first century. Exports rose from just under $43 billion in 1970 to over $1 trillion in 2006. But imports rose even more dramatically: from just over $40 billion in 1970 to over $1.8 trillion in 2006. Most American products, in other words, now faced foreign competition inside the United States. The first American trade imbalance in the postwar era occurred in 1971; only twice since then, in 1973 and 1975, has the balance been favorable.

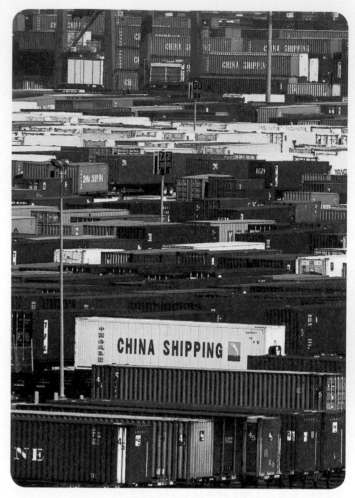

THE GLOBAL ECONOMY Hundreds of shipping containers, virtually all of them from China, stand waiting for delivery at the Yang Ming container terminal in Los Angeles in February 2001—an illustration of the increasing penetration of the American market by overseas manufacturers and of the growing interconnections between the U.S. economy and that of the rest of the world. (© Reed Saxon/AP Images)

SCIENCE AND TECHNOLOGY IN THE NEW ECONOMY

The "new economy" that emerged in the late twentieth and early twenty-first centuries was driven by dramatic new scientific and technological discoveries that had profound effects on the way Americans—and peoples throughout the world—lived.

THE DIGITAL REVOLUTION

The most visible element of the technological revolution to most Americans was the dramatic growth in the use of computers and other digital electronic devices in almost every area of life.

Among the most significant innovations that contributed to the digital revolution was the development of the microprocessor, first introduced in 1971 by Intel, which represented a notable advance in the technology of integrated circuitry. A microprocessor miniaturized the central processing unit of a computer, making it possible for a small machine to perform calculations that in the past only very large machines could do. Considerable technological innovation was needed before the microprocessor could actually become the basis of what was at first known as a "minicomputer" and then a "personal computer." But in 1977, Apple launched its Apple II personal computer, the first such machine to be widely available to the public. Several years later,

DEVELOPMENT OF THE PC IBM entered the personal computer market with the first "PC." IBM had engaged a small software development company, Microsoft, to design an operating system for its new computer. Microsoft produced a program known as MS-DOS (DOS for "disk operating system"). No PC could operate without it. The PC, and its software, made its debut in August 1981 and immediately became enormously successful.

The computer revolution created thousands of new, lucrative businesses: computer manufacturers (new companies quickly began to rival IBM in the PC market); makers of the tiny silicon chips that ran the computers and allowed smaller and smaller machines to become more and more powerful; and manufacturers of accessories and software.

THE INTERNET

Out of the computer revolution emerged another dramatic source of information and communication: the Internet. It had

ARPA its beginning in 1963, in the U.S. government's Advanced Research Projects Agency (ARPA), which funneled federal funds into scientific research projects, many of them defense related.

By 1971, twenty-three computers were linked together in ARPA's network, which served mostly research labs and universities. Gradually, interest in the system began to spread, and with it the number of computers connected to it. The network, soon renamed the Internet, was then free to develop independently. It did so rapidly, especially after the invention of technologies that made possible digital mail (e-mail) and the emergence of the personal computer, which vastly increased the

TWENTY-FOUR HOUR NEWS CYCLE With the vast popularity of digital communication news events are reported every hour of every day rather than during scheduled television programs or from reading the newspaper. With a portable tablets or smart phones, a person can keep up with what is new at any time or any place. Politicians now have much less control over how their messages are transmitted and received. (© Ian Dagnall/Alamy)

number of potential users of the Internet. As late as 1984, there remained fewer than a thousand host computers connected to the Internet. A decade later, there were over 6 million. And by 2013, over two billion computers were in use around the world.

As the amount of information on the Internet proliferated, without any central direction, new forms of software emerged to make it possible for individual users to navigate through the vast

WORLD WIDE WEB number of Internet sites. In 1989, Tim Berners-Lee, a British scientist working at a laboratory in Geneva, introduced the World Wide Web, through which individual users could publish information for the Internet. It helped establish an orderly system for both the distribution and retrieval of electronic information.

BREAKTHROUGHS IN GENETICS

Computer technology helped fuel explosive growth in all areas of scientific research, particularly genetics. Early discoveries in genetics by Gregor Mendel, Thomas Hunt Morgan, and others had laid the groundwork for more-dramatic breakthroughs—the discovery of DNA by the British scientists Oswald Avery, Colin MacLeod, and Maclyn McCarty in 1944; and in 1953, the discovery by the American biochemist James Watson and the British biophysicist Francis Crick of its double-helix structure, and thus of the key to identifying genetic codes. From these discoveries emerged the new science—and ultimately the new industry—of genetic engineering, through which new medical treatments and new techniques for hybridization of plants and animals became possible.

Little by little, scientists began to identify specific genes in humans and other living things that determine particular traits, and to learn how to alter or reproduce them. But the

HUMAN GENOME PROJECT identification of genes was painfully slow. In 1989, the federal government appropriated $3 billion to fund the National Center for the Human Genome, to accelerate the mapping of human genes. The Human Genome Project identified 3 billion genes by 2013.

In the meantime, DNA research had already attracted considerable public attention. The DNA structure of an individual, scientists have discovered, is as unique and as identifiable as a fingerprint. DNA testing, therefore, makes it possible to identify individuals through their blood, semen, skin, or even hair. It plays a major role in criminal investigations, among other things.

A CHANGING SOCIETY

The American population changed dramatically in the late twentieth and early twenty-first centuries. It grew larger, older, and more racially and ethnically diverse.

A SHIFTING POPULATION

Decreasing birth rates and growing life spans contributed to one of the most important characteristics of the American

THE HUMAN GENOME This computerized image is a digital representation of part of the human genome, the constellation of genetic material that makes up the human body. The Human Genome Project, one of the most ambitious in the history of science, set out in the late 1990s to chart the human genetic structure. Each color in this image represents one of the four chemical components of DNA, the principal material of genes. (© Mario Tama/Getty Images)

population in the twenty-first century: its increasing agedness. The enormous "baby boom" generation–people born in the first ten years after World War II–drove the median age steadily upward (from 34 in 1996 to 37 in 2010 to a projected 39 by 2035). This growing population of aging Americans contributed to stresses on the Social Security and Medicare systems, including the provisions of the Affordable Care Act introduced by President Obama. It also had important implications for the workforce. In the last twenty years of the twentieth century, the number of people aged 25-54 (known statistically as the prime workforce) grew by over 26 million. In the first ten years of the twenty-first century, the number of workers in that age group did not grow at all.

The slowing growth of the native-born population, and the workforce shortages it has helped to create, is one reason for the rapid growth of immigration. In 2010, the number of foreign-born residents of the United States was the highest in American history–more than 36 million people, over 12 percent of the total population. These immigrants came from a wider variety of backgrounds than ever before, as a result of the 1965 Immigration Reform Act, which eliminated national origins as a criterion for admission. The growing presence of the foreign-born contributed to a significant

drop in the percentage of white residents in the United States–from 90 percent in 1965 (the year of the Immigration Reform Act) to 74 in 2014. Latinos and Asians were by far

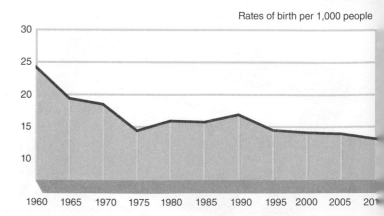

Rates of birth per 1,000 people

THE AMERICAN BIRTH RATE, 1960–2010 This chart shows the striking change in the pattern of the nation's birth rate from the twenty years after 1940, which produced the great "baby boom." From 1960 onward, the nation's birth rate steadily, and in the 1960s and 1970s dramatically, declined.

*What effect did this declining birth rate have on the age structure of the population?

the largest groups of immigrants in these years. But others came in significant numbers from Africa, the Middle East, Russia, and eastern Europe.

AFRICAN AMERICANS IN THE POST–CIVIL RIGHTS ERA

The civil rights movement and the other liberal efforts of the 1960s had two very different effects on African Americans. On the one hand, there were increased opportunities for advancement available to those in a position to take advantage of them. On the other hand, as the industrial economy declined and government services dwindled, there was a growing sense of helplessness and despair among large groups of nonwhites who continued to find themselves barred from upward mobility.

For the black middle class, which in the first decade of the twenty-first century constituted over half of the African American population of America, progress was

ECONOMIC PROGRESS FOR AFRICAN AMERICANS

remarkable in the decades after the high point of the civil rights movement. African American families moved into more-affluent urban and suburban communities. The percentage of black high-school graduates going on to college was virtually the same as that of white high-school graduates by the early twenty-first century (although a smaller proportion of blacks than whites completed high school). Just over 20 percent of African Americans over the age of twenty-four held bachelor's degrees or higher in 2010, compared to 30 percent of whites, a significant advance from twenty years earlier. And African Americans were making rapid strides in many professions in which only a generation earlier they had been barred or segregated. Over half of all employed blacks in the United States had skilled white-collar jobs in 2010. There were few areas of American life from which blacks were any longer entirely excluded.

But there were still many other African Americans whom the economic growth and the liberal programs of the 1960s and beyond had never reached. These impoverished people–sometimes described as the "underclass"–made up as

THE "UNDERCLASS"

much as a third of the nation's black population. Many of them lived in isolated, decaying, and desperately poor inner-city neighborhoods. As more successful blacks moved out of the inner cities, the poor were left behind in their decaying neighborhoods. Less than half of young inner-city African Americans finished high school in 2006; more than 60 percent were unemployed. The black family structure suffered as well from the dislocations of urban poverty. There was a radical increase in the number of single-parent, female-headed black households. In 1970, only 59 percent of all black children under 18 lived with both their parents (already down from 70 percent a decade earlier). In 2010, only 35 percent of black children lived in such households, while 74 percent of white children did.

Total immigration during five-year periods (in millions)

TOTAL IMMIGRATION, 1960–2010 This chart shows the tremendous increase in immigration to the United States in the decades since the Immigration Reform Act of 1965. The immigration of the 1980s and 1990s was the highest since the late nineteenth century. (© Comstock)

• *What role did the 1965 act have in increasing immigration levels?*

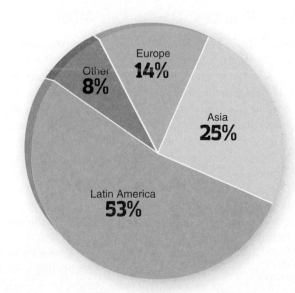

SOURCES OF IMMIGRATION, 1995–2010 The Immigration Reform Act of 1965 lifted the national quotas imposed on immigration policy in 1924 and opened immigration to large areas of the world that had previously been restricted. In 1965, 90 percent of the immigrants to the United States came from Europe. As this chart shows, by 2010 almost the reverse was true. Well over 80 percent of all immigrants came from non-European sources. The most important countries of origin in this period were (in order) Mexico, China, the Philippines, India, Vietnam, and Cuba.

• *What impact did this new immigration have on American politics?*

Whites

1%

15%

22%

62%

Blacks

.3%

24%

23%

53%

Occupational Sector

Manufacturing
White-collar
Service
Agriculture

COMPARISON OF BLACK AND WHITE OCCUPATIONAL DISTRIBUTION, 2005 By the early twenty-first century, as this chart makes clear, the African-American middle class had grown dramatically. Over half of all employed black workers in the United States worked in "white-collar" jobs. Perhaps even more striking, given the distribution of the black population a half century earlier, is that almost no African Americans (about one-third of 1 percent) were working in agriculture by the early 2000s. But the gap between black and white workers remained wide in several areas, particularly in the percentage of each group employed in low-wage service jobs.

• What factors contributed to the increase of the black middle class in the years after 1960?

MODERN PLAGUES: DRUGS AND AIDS

Two new and deadly epidemics ravaged many American communities beginning in the 1980s. One was a dramatic increase in drug use, which penetrated nearly every community in the nation. The enormous demand for drugs, particularly for "crack" cocaine in the late 1980s and early 1990s, spawned what was in effect a multibillion-dollar industry. Drug use declined significantly among middle-class people beginning in the late 1980s, but the epidemic declined much more slowly in the poor urban neighborhoods where it was doing the most severe damage.

The drug epidemic was related to another scourge of the late twentieth century: the epidemic spread of a new and often lethal disease first documented in 1981 and soon named AIDS (acquired immune deficiency syndrome). AIDS is the
AIDS EPIDEMIC product of the HIV virus, which is transmitted by the exchange of bodily fluids (blood or semen). The first American victims of AIDS (and for many years the group among whom cases remained the most numerous) were gay men. But by the late 1980s, as the gay community began to take preventive measures, the most rapid increase in the spread of the disease occurred among heterosexuals, many of them intravenous drug users, who spread the virus by sharing contaminated hypodermic needles.

In the mid-1990s, AIDS researchers, after years of frustration, began discovering effective treatments for the disease. By taking a combination of powerful drugs on a rigorous schedule, even people with advanced cases of AIDS experienced dramatic improvement—so much so that in many cases there were no measurable quantities of the virus left in their bloodstreams. The new drugs gave promise for the first time of dramatically extending the lives of people with AIDS, perhaps to normal life spans. But the drugs were very expensive and difficult to administer; poor AIDS patients often could not obtain access to them. And the drugs remained scarce in Africa and other less-affluent parts of the world where the epidemic was rampant. The United Nations, many philanthropic organizations, and a number of governments, including the United States, committed significant funds to fight the AIDS crisis in Africa in the 2000s, but progress remained slow.

A CONTESTED CULTURE

American culture changed dramatically in the years after World War II. By the 1960s, the roles of women began to change profoundly. The sexual revolution changed traditional American values. American culture also became more diverse, open, and contentious than it had been in the past. As a result, new controversies and issues emerged.

BATTLES OVER FEMINISM AND ABORTION

Among the goals of what was known as the "New Right" were challenges to feminism and its achievements. Conservatives had campaigned successfully against the proposed Equal Rights Amendment to the Constitution. They also played a central role in the most divisive issue of the last thirty years: the controversy over abortion rights.

For those who favored allowing women to choose to terminate unwanted pregnancies, the Supreme Court's decision in *Roe v. Wade* (1973) had seemed to settle the question. By the 1980s, abortion was the most commonly performed surgical procedure in the country. But at the
"RIGHT-TO-LIFE" MOVEMENT same time, opposition to abortion was creating a powerful grassroots movement. The right-to-life movement, as it called itself, found its most fervent supporters among Catholics; and indeed, the Catholic Church itself lent its institutional authority to the battle against legalized abortion. Religious doctrine also motivated the anti-abortion stance of many Mormons, evangelical Christians, and other groups. The opposition of some other anti-abortion activists had less to do with religion than with their commitment to traditional notions of family and gender relations. To them, abortion was part of a much larger assault by feminists on the role of women as wives and mothers. It was also, many foes contended, a form of murder. Fetuses, they claimed, were human beings who had a "right to life" from the moment of conception.

Although the right-to-life movement was persistent in its demand for a reversal of *Roe v. Wade* or, barring that, a constitutional amendment banning abortion, it also attacked abortion in more-limited ways, at its most vulnerable points. Starting in the late 1970s, Congress and many state legislatures began barring the use of public funds to pay for abortions, thus making them almost inaccessible for many poor women in some states. The Reagan and the two Bush administrations imposed further restrictions on federal funding and even on the right of doctors in federally funded clinics to give patients any information on abortion. Extremists in the right-to-life movement began picketing, occupying, and at times bombing abortion clinics. Several anti-abortion activists murdered doctors who performed abortions; other physicians were subject to campaigns of terrorism and harassment. The changing composition of the Supreme Court between 1981 and 2010 (during which time new conservative justices were appointed to the Court) renewed the right-to-life movement's hopes for a reversal of *Roe v. Wade*.

The changing judicial climate of the late twentieth and early twenty-first centuries mobilized defenders of abortion as never before. They called themselves the "pro-choice" movement, because they were defending not so much abortion itself as every woman's right to choose whether and when to bear a child. The pro-choice movement was in many parts of the country at least as strong as, and in some areas much stronger than, the right-to-life movement. With the election of President Clinton in 1992, a supporter of "choice," the immediate threat to *Roe v. Wade* seemed to fade. Clinton's reelection in 1996 was evidence that the pro-choice movement maintained considerable political strength. But abortion rights remained highly vulnerable. Clinton's successor, George W. Bush, openly opposed abortion. Barack Obama supported the right to abortion when he became president.

"PRO-CHOICE" MOVEMENT

THE GROWTH OF ENVIRONMENTALISM

The environmental movement grew dramatically in the early 1970s and continues to develop in the present. An early milestone was Earth Day, held on April 22, 1970, a day that generated wide-scale interest in the environment. The federal government displayed only light interest in the subject, but many people became invested in studying the effects of "global warming"–a steady rise in the earth's temperature resulting from emissions from burned fossil fuels, most notably coal and oil. Many other people either ignored or disavowed the impact of such industrial waste on the environment. In 1997, representatives of the major industrial nations met in Kyoto, Japan, and agreed to a broad treaty to reduce carbon emissions to slow or reverse global warming. Republicans in Congress prevented the ratification of this treaty in the United States. The United States again refused to participate in this global initiative during the presidency of George W. Bush, who argued that doing so would place too great of an economic burden on the country. Barack Obama, too, has done little about global warming. Without the participation of the United States and China, another country that has not signed the Kyoto Protocol, most environmentalists consider the treaty to be dead.

THE PERILS OF GLOBALIZATION

The celebration of the beginning of a new millennium on January 1, 2000, was a notable moment not just because of the change in the calendar. It was notable above all as a global event–a shared and for the most part joyous experience that united the world in its exuberance. But if the millennium celebrations suggested the bright promise of globalization, other events at the dawn of the new century suggested its dark perils.

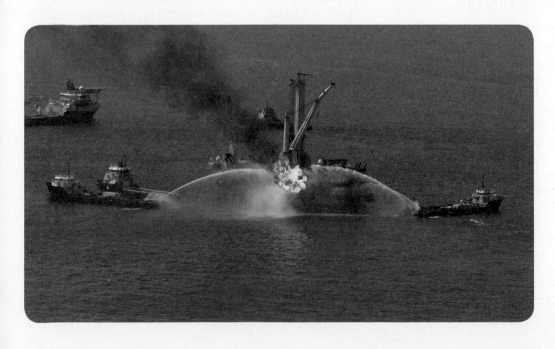

BP OIL SPILL This photograph shows the efforts of BP attempting to cap the oil spill that was a result of an explosion on an offshore drilling platform. The oil leaked for months, and it continues to damage the ecology of the Gulf of Mexico even a year later. (© Julie Dermansky/Corbis)

RAP

THE long musical lineage of rap includes elements of the disco and street funk of the 1970s; of the fast-talking jive of black radio DJs in the 1950s; of the onstage patter of Cab Calloway and other African American stars of the first half of the twentieth century. It contains reminders of tap and break dancing—even of the boxing-ring poetry of Muhammad Ali.

Rap's most important element is its words. Rap is as much a form of language as a form of music. It bears a distant resemblance to some traditions of African American pulpit oratory, which also included forms of spoken song. It draws from some of the verbal traditions of urban black street life, including the "dozens"—a ritualized trading of insults particularly popular among young black men.

But rap is also the product of a distinctive place and time: the South Bronx in the 1970s and 1980s and the hip hop culture that was born there and that soon dominated the appearance and public behavior of many young black males. "Hip hop is how you walk, talk, live, see, act, feel," said one Bronx hip hopper. Some elements of hip hop culture faded, and by the 1990s the most popular element of hip hop culture was rap, which had by then been developing for nearly twenty years.

Beginning in the early 1970s, Bronx DJs began setting up their equipment on neighborhood streets and staging block parties, where they not only played records but also put on shows of their own—performances that featured spoken rhymes, jazzy phrases, and pointed comments about the audience, the neighborhood, and themselves. Gradually, the DJs began to bring "rappers" into shows—young men who developed the DJ style into a much more elaborate form of performance, usually accompanied by dancing. As rap grew more popular in the inner city, record promoters began signing some of its new stars. In 1979, the Sugarhill Gang's "Rapper's Delight" became the first rap single to be played on mainstream commercial radio and the first to become a major hit. In the early 1980s, Run-DMC became the first national rap superstars. From there, rap moved quickly to become one of the most popular and commercially successful forms of popular music. In the 1990s and early 2000s, rap recordings routinely sold millions of copies.

Rap has taken many forms. There have been white rappers (Eminem, House of Pain), female rappers (Missy Elliot, Queen Latifah), even religious rappers and children's rappers. But it has always been primarily a product of the young male culture of the inner city, and some of the most successful rap has conveyed the frustration and anger that these men have felt about their lives—"a voice for the oppressed people," one rap artist said, "that in many other ways don't have a voice." In 1982, the rap group Grandmaster Flash and the Furious Five released a rap called "The Message,"* a searing description of ghetto culture:

> Got a bum education, double-digit inflation
> Can't take the train to the job, there's a strike at the station
> Don't push me, 'cause I'm close to the edge
> I'm tryin' not to lose me head
> It's like a jungle sometime it makes me wonder
> How I keep from going under.

In the late 1980s, the Compton and Watts neighborhoods of Los Angeles—two of the most distressed minority communities in the city—produced their own style, known as West Coast rap, with such groups as Ice Cube, Ice T, Tupac Shakur, and Snoop Doggy Dog. West Coast rap often had a harsh, angry character, and at its extremes (the so-called gangsta' rap), it could be strikingly violent and highly provocative. Scandals erupted over controversial lyrics—Ice T's "Cop Killer," which some critics believed advocated murdering

OPPOSING THE "NEW WORLD ORDER"

In the United States and other industrial nations, opposition to globalization–or to what President George H. W. Bush once called "the new world order"–took several forms. Many

CRITICS OF INTERVENTION
Americans on both the left and the right opposed the nation's increasingly interventionist foreign policy. Critics on the left charged that the United States was using military action to advance its economic interests, in the 1991 Gulf War and, above all, in the Iraq War that began in 2003. Critics on the right claimed that the nation was allowing itself to be swayed by the interests of other nations–as in the humanitarian interventions in Somalia in 1993 and the Balkans in the late 1990s– and was ceding its sovereignty to international organizations.

But the most impassioned opposition to globalization in the West came from an array of groups that saw it as an economic threat. Labor unions insisted that the rapid expansion of free-trade agreements led to the export of jobs from advanced nations to less developed ones. Other groups attacked working conditions in new manufacturing countries on humanitarian grounds, arguing that the global economy was creating new classes of "slave laborers" working in conditions that few Western nations would tolerate. Environmentalists argued that globalization, in exporting industry to low-wage countries, also exported industrial pollution and toxic waste to nations that had no effective laws to control them, and contributed significantly to global warming. And still others opposed global economic arrangements on the grounds that they enriched and empowered large multinational corporations and threatened the freedom and autonomy of individuals and communities.

The opponents of globalization were mostly agreed on the targets of their discontent: not just free-trade agreements, but also the multinational institutions that policed and advanced

GLOBALIZATION PROTESTED
the global economy. Among them were the World Trade Organization, which monitored the enforcement of the GATT treaties of the 1990s; the International Monetary Fund, which controlled international credit and exchange rates; and the World Bank, which made money available for development projects in many countries. In November 1999, when the leaders of the

KANYE WEST Testifying to the continued popularity of rap, as of 2014 rapper Kanye West remains one of the best selling artists of all time, having sold over 21 million albums and 66 million digital downloads. Time magazine has named West one of the 100 most influential people in the world. He is a rapper, songwriter, record producer, film director, entrepreneur and fashion designer. (© Getty Images Entertainment/Getty Images)

police; and the sexually explicit lyrics of 2 Live Crew and other groups, which critics accused of advocating violence against women.

But it was not just the lyrics that caused the furor. Rap artists were almost all products of tough inner-city neighborhoods, and the rough-edged styles many took with them into the public eye made many people uncomfortable. Some rappers got caught up in highly publicized trouble with the law. Several—including two of rap's biggest stars, Tupac Shakur and Notorious B.I.G.—were murdered. The business of rap, particularly the confrontational business style of Death Row Records (founded by Dr. Dre, a veteran of the first major West Coast rap group NWA), was a source of public controversy as well.

These controversies at times unfairly dominated the image of rap as a whole. Some rap is angry and cruel, as are many of the realities of the world from which it comes. But much of it is

explicitly positive, some of it deliberately gentle. Chuck D and other successful rappers use their music to exhort young black men to avoid drugs and crime, to take responsibility for their children, to get an education. And the form, if not the content, of the original rappers has spread widely through American culture. Rap came to dominate the music charts in America, and its styles made their way onto *Sesame Street* and other children's shows, into television commercials, Hollywood films, and the everyday language of millions of people, young and old, black and white. It became another of the arresting, innovative African American musical traditions that have shaped American culture for more than a century. ●

*Edward Fletcher, M. Glover, and S. Robinson, "The Message," recorded 1982 by Grand Master Flash & The Furious Five. Reprinted by permission of Sugar Hill Music Publishing Ltd.

UNDERSTAND, ANALYZE, AND EVALUATE

1. What other African American musical forms have helped shape American popular culture?

2. If rap is so closely associated with the inner-city culture where it originated, what accounts for its widespread popularity and commercial success? What other forms or styles of popular music enjoy a popularity that extends far beyond its cultural origins?

3. Do you think rap's popularity will endure? Why or why not?

PROTESTS IN SEATTLE, 1999 When the World Trade Organization held its annual meeting in Seattle, Washington, in late 1999, thousands of demonstrators crowded into the city to protest the WTO's role in the globalization of the economy and, they believed, the exploitation of working people in the United States and around the world. Their rowdy and at times violent demonstrations postponed the opening of the conference. In this photograph, a protester faces Seattle police in a cloud of tear gas, waiting to be arrested. Similar demonstrations disrupted other meetings of global economic organizations over the next several years, including protests in Washington and Genoa, Italy. (© Andy Clark/Reuters/Corbis)

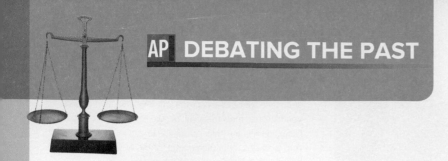

WOMEN'S HISTORY

HISTORIANS have long considered the influence of ideas, economic interests, class, and race and ethnicity on the course of history. Women's history challenged them to consider as well the role of gender. Throughout history, many scholars now argue, societies have created distinctive roles for men and women. How those roles have been defined, and the ways in which the roles affect how people and cultures behave, should be central to our understanding of both the past and the present.

In the nineteenth century, women's history generally stressed the unrecognized contributions of women to history—for example, Sarah Hale's 1853 *Record of All Distinguished Women from "the Beginning" till A.D. 1850.* Work of the same sort continued into the twentieth century and, indeed, continues today.

But after 1900, people committed to progressive reform movements began to produce a different kind of women's scholarship, focusing primarily on the ways in which women were victimized by industrialism. Feminist scholars such as Edith Abbott, Margaret Byington, and Katherine Anthony examined the impact of economic change on working-class families, with a special focus on women; and they looked at the often deplorable conditions in which women worked in factories, mills, and other people's homes. Their goal was less to celebrate women's contributions than to direct attention to the oppression of women by harsh working conditions and arouse sentiment for reform.

After the victory of the suffrage movement in 1920, women's history entered a half century of relative inactivity. Women continued to write important histories in many fields, and some—for example, Eleanor Flexner, whose *Century of Struggle* (1959) became a classic history of the suffrage crusade—wrote explicitly about women. Mary Beard, best known for her sweeping historical narratives written in collaboration with her husband, Charles Beard, published *Women as a Force in History* (1964), in which she argued for the historical importance of ordinary women as shapers of society. But such work at first had little impact on the writing of history as a whole.

---

seven leading industrial nations (and the leader of Russia) gathered for their annual meeting in Seattle, Washington, they were confronted with tens of thousands of protesters. Most of the protesters were peaceful, but some were violent, clashing with police, smashing store windows, and all but paralyzing the city. A few months later, a smaller but still substantial demonstration disrupted meetings of the IMF and the World Bank in Washington, D.C. And in July 2001, at a meeting of the same leaders in Genoa, Italy, an estimated 50,000 demonstrators clashed violently with police in a melee that left one protester dead and several hundred injured. The participants in the meeting responded to the demonstrations by pledging $1.2 billion to fight the AIDS epidemic in developing countries, and also by deciding to hold future meetings in remote locations far from major cities.

DEFENDING ORTHODOXY

Outside the industrialized West, the impact of globalization created other concerns. Many citizens of nonindustrialized nations resented the way the world economy had left them in poverty and, in their view, exploited and oppressed. In some parts of the nonindustrialized world–particularly in some of the Islamic nations of the Middle East–the increasing reach of globalization created additional grievances, rooted not just in economics but also in religion and culture.

The Iranian Revolution of 1979, in which orthodox Muslims ousted a despotic government whose leaders had embraced many aspects of modern Western culture, was one of the first large and visible manifestations of a phenomenon that would

RISE OF ISLAMIC FUNDAMENTALISM eventually reach across much of the Islamic world and threaten the stability of the globe. In one Islamic nation after another, waves of fundamentalist orthodoxy emerged to defend traditional culture against incursions from the West.

One product of these resentments was a growing resort to violence as a way to fight the influence of the West. Militants in various parts of the world used isolated incidents of violence and mayhem, designed to disrupt Western societies and governments and to create fear among their peoples. Such tactics are known to the world as terrorism.

THE RISE OF TERRORISM

The term "terrorism" was used first during the French Revolution in the 1790s to describe the actions of the radical Jacobins against the French government. The word continued to be used intermittently throughout the nineteenth and early

ORIGINS OF TERRORISM twentieth centuries to describe the use of violence as a form of intimidation against peoples and governments. But the widespread understanding of terrorism as an important fact of modern life is largely a product of the end of the twentieth century and the beginning of the twenty-first.

Acts of what we have come to call terrorism have occurred in many parts of the world. Irish revolutionaries engaged in terrorism regularly against the English through much of the twentieth century. Jews used it in Palestine against the British before the creation of Israel, and Palestinians used it frequently against Jews in Israel–over several decades. Revolutionary

Along with the rise in modern feminism in the 1960s and 1970s, interest in women's history revived as well. Gerda Lerner, one of the pioneers of the new women's history, once wrote of the impact of feminism on historical studies: "The recognition that we had been denied our history came to many of us as a staggering insight, which altered our consciousness irretrievably." Much of the early work was in the "contributionist" tradition, stressing the way in which women had played more notable roles in major historical events than historians had usually acknowledged. Other work stressed ways in which women had been victimized by their subordination to men and by their powerlessness within the industrial economy.

Increasingly, however, women's history began to question the nature of gender itself. Some scholars began to emphasize the artificiality of gender distinctions, arguing that the difference between women and men was socially constructed, superficial, and (in the public world, at least) unimportant. The history of women was, therefore, the history of how men (with the unwitting help of many women) had created and maintained a set of fictions about women's capacities that modern women were now attempting to shatter.

By the early 1980s, some feminists had begun to make a very different argument: that there were basic differences between women and men—not just biological differences, but differences in values, sensibilities, and culture. The feminists of the 1970s and 1980s did not see these differences as evidence of women's incapacities. They saw them, rather, as evidence of an alternative female culture capable of challenging (and improving) the male-dominated world. By the twenty-first century, some historians of women, therefore, began exploring areas of female experience that revealed the special character of women's culture and values: family, housework, motherhood, women's clubs and organizations, female literature, the social lives of working-class women, women's sexuality, and many other subjects that suggested "difference" more than "contributions" or "victimization." Partly in response, some historians began to make the same argument about men—that understanding "masculinity" and its role in shaping men's lives was as important as understanding notions of "femininity" in explaining the history of women.

The notion of gender as a source of social and cultural difference raised a powerful challenge to the way in which scholars view the past. Many historians continue to believe that other categories (race and class in particular) have in fact been more important than gender in shaping the lives of men and women. But, as Joan Scott, a theorist of gender studies, contends, it is not enough simply to expand the existing story to make room for women. Rather, recognizing gender as a central force in the lives of societies calls for a reconceptualization of the past. ●

AP | HISTORICAL ARGUMENTATION AND INTERPRETATION

Questions assume cumulative content knowledge from this chapter and previous chapters.

1. Identify three major threads of interpretation of women's history. For each, identify a representative interpretation made by a historian discussed.
2. What was the impact of the feminist movement of the 1960s and 1970s on the writing of women's history?
3. With which historical interpretation do you most agree? Explain why, supporting your argument with historical evidence.

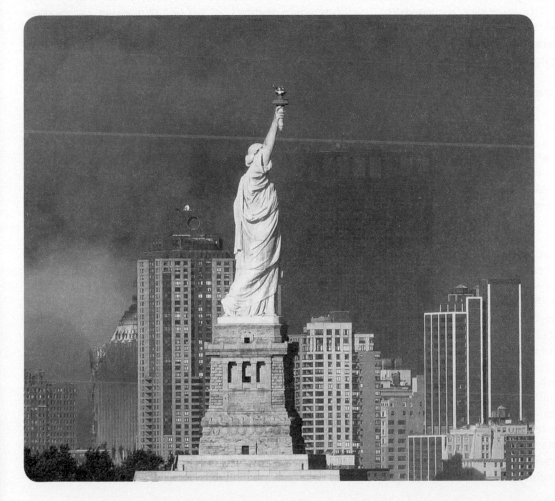

SEPTEMBER 11, 2001 One great American symbol, the Statue of Liberty, stands against a sky filled with the thick smoke from the destruction of another American symbol, New York City's World Trade Center towers, a few hours after terrorists crashed two planes into them. (© Daniel Hulshizer/AP Images)

groups in Italy, Germany, Japan, and France have engaged in terrorist acts intermittently over the past several decades.

The United States, too, has experienced terrorism for many years, much of it against American targets abroad. These included the bombing of the Marine barracks in Beirut in 1983, the explosion that brought down an American airliner over Lockerbie, Scotland, in 1988, the bombing of American embassies in 1998, the assault on the U.S. naval vessel *Cole* in 2000, and other events around the world. Terrorist incidents were relatively rare, but not unknown, within the United States itself prior to September 11, 2001. Militants on the American left performed various acts of terror in the 1960s and early 1970s. In February 1993, a bomb exploded in the parking garage of the World Trade Center in New York City killing six people and causing serious, but not irreparable, structural damage to the towers. Several men connected with militant Islamic organizations were convicted of the crime. In April 1995, a van containing explosives blew up in front of a federal building in Oklahoma City, killing 168 people. Timothy McVeigh, a former Marine who had become part of a militant antigovernment movement of the American right, was convicted of the crime in 1997 and executed in 2001.

Most Americans, however, considered terrorism a problem that mainly plagued other nations. One of the many results of the terrible events of September 11, 2001, was to jolt the American people out of complacency and alert them to the presence of continuing danger. That awareness increased in the years following September 11. New security measures changed the way in which Americans traveled. New government regulations altered immigration policies and affected the character of international banking. Warnings of possible new terrorist attacks created widespread tension and uneasiness.

THE WAR ON TERRORISM

In the aftermath of September 2001, the United States government launched what President Bush called a "war against terrorism." The attacks on the World Trade Center and the Pentagon, government intelligence indicated, had been planned and orchestrated by Middle Eastern agents of a powerful terrorist network known as al-Qaeda. Its

AL-QAEDA

leader, Osama bin Laden—until 2001 little known outside the Arab world—quickly became one of the most notorious figures in the world. Convinced that the militant "Taliban" government of Afghanistan had sheltered and supported bin Laden and his organization, the United States began a sustained campaign of bombing against the regime and sent in ground troops to help a resistance organization overthrow the Afghan government. Afghanistan's Taliban regime quickly collapsed, and its leaders—along with the al-Qaeda fighters allied with them—fled the capital, Kabul. American and anti-Taliban Afghan troops pursued them into the mountains, but failed to capture bin Laden and the other leaders of his organization.

American forces in Afghanistan rounded up several hundred people suspected of connections to the Taliban and al-Qaeda in the aftermath of the fighting and eventually moved these prisoners to a facility at the American base in Guantánamo, Cuba. They were among the first suspected terrorists to be handled under the new laws created by the federal government to deal with terrorism after September 11, 2001. The Patriot Act of 2001 was the most important of these new laws. The post-September 11 laws and policies made it possible for suspected terrorists to be held for months, and in many cases years, without access to lawyers, without facing formal charges, subjected to intensive interrogation and torture. They became examples to many critics of the dangers to basic civil liberties they believed the war on terrorism had created.

Several Supreme Court rulings, including one in 2008, dismissed the Bush administration's argument that detainees in Guantánamo were outside the reach of American law. But the administration was slow to comply. Before his election in 2008, Barack Obama promised to close the Guantánamo prison, which had become a symbol to many people of unfair treatment. But once in office, Obama found it difficult to keep this promise because of popular opposition to moving prisoners into facilities in the United States.

THE IRAQ WAR

In his State of the Union address to Congress in January 2002, President Bush spoke of an "axis of evil," which included the nations of Iraq, Iran, and North Korea—all nations with anti-American regimes, all nations that either possessed or were thought to be trying to acquire nuclear weapons. Although President Bush did not say so at the time, many people around the world interpreted these words to mean that the United States would soon try to topple the government of Saddam Hussein in Iraq.

SADDAM HUSSEIN On December 14, 2003, American forces captured Hussein at a farmhouse near Tikrit, Iraq. He was tried and found guilty of crimes against humanity for the death of 148 Iraqi Shi'ites. Hussein was hanged on December 30, 2006.
(© Getty Images News/Getty Images)

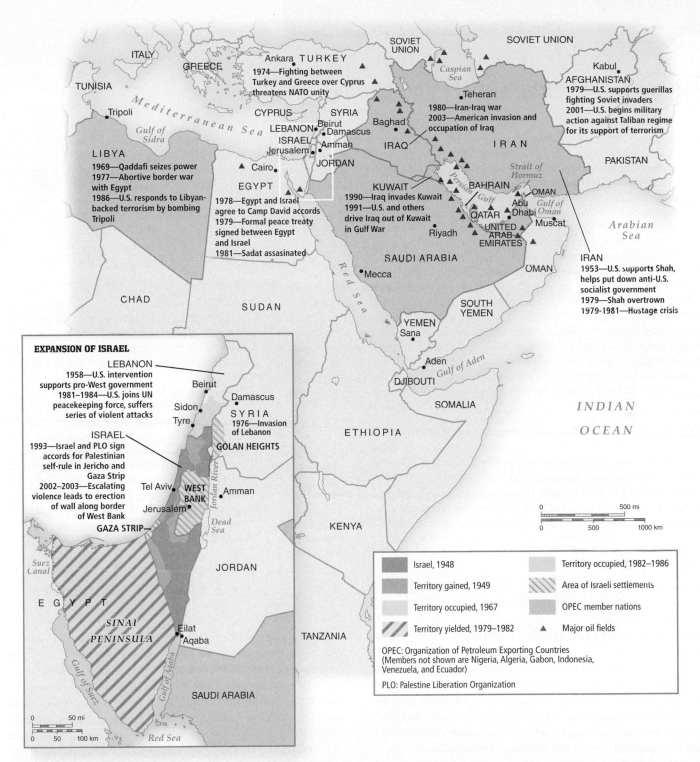

CRISES IN THE MIDDLE EAST In the 1970s and beyond, the Middle East became one of the most turbulent regions of the world and one of the regions most vital to, and difficult for, the United States. The United States intervened in the Middle East frequently during the Cold War and beyond, in ways both large and small, as this map reveals. After the events of September 2001, those interventions increased.

• Why did the United States have so much at stake in the Middle East?

For over a year after that, the Bush administration slowly built a public case for invading Iraq. Much of that case rested on two claims. One was that Iraq was supporting terrorist groups that were hostile to the United States. The other, and eventually the more important, was that Iraq either had or was developing what came to be known as "weapons of mass destruction," which included nuclear weapons and agents of chemical and biological warfare. Less central to these arguments, at least in the United States, was the charge that the Hussein government was responsible for major violations of

THE GLOBAL ENVIRONMENTAL MOVEMENT WOR-8

AN international movement for well over a century, environmentalism has grown rapidly throughout the world in the late twentieth and early twenty-first centuries. What began as a series of efforts to preserve wilderness sites and to clean up air and water in particular nations has evolved into a broad effort to deal with problems that affect, and threaten, the entire globe.

Organizations both in the United States and elsewhere have sought to create an international environmental movement. The World Wildlife Fund (WWF) was created in Switzerland in 1961. It eventually attracted more than 5 million supporters in over 90 countries and now claims to be the world's largest independent conservation organization. Greenpeace was founded in Canada in 1971 in opposition to U.S. nuclear testing in Alaska. It too has grown into an international organization, with 2.9 million financial supporters worldwide and a presence in 42 nations. Leading American environmental associations include the Wilderness Society, the Sierra Club, and the National Audubon Society.

Nongovernmental organizations (NGOs) such as Greenpeace and WWF were not the only institutions to recognize environmental concerns. In June 1972, the United Nations held its first Conference on the Human Environment. Representatives of 113 countries attended the conference to discuss issues of global environmental importance—including the role of chlorofluorocarbons (CFCs), a chemical compound used in refrigerants and aerosol sprays, in depleting the ozone layer. After the conference, the UN created the United Nations Environment Programme (UNEP) to help coordinate international efforts for environmentalism and encourage sustainable development in poorer nations around the world.

The world's first "Green" parties—political parties explicitly devoted to environmental concerns (and often also to other issues of social justice)—appeared in 1972, beginning in New Zealand (the Values Party) and Tasmania (the United Tasmania Group). Since then, Green parties have proliferated throughout the world, including in the United States. The most powerful Green party to date has been *Die Grüne* in Germany, founded in 1980.

Large-scale ecological catastrophes have often helped galvanize the global environmental movement. Among the more significant of these events was the Bhopal disaster of 1984, in which a gas leak at a Union Carbide pesticide plant in Bhopal, India, resulted in the deaths of an estimated 3,000 to 15,000 people. Two years later, a nuclear reactor accident in the Soviet city of Chernobyl in Ukraine caused 56 direct deaths, with predictions of many thousands more deaths to follow as a result of exposure. The area around Chernobyl is expected to be partially contaminated for 24,000 years, the radioactive half-life of plutonium-239. A less catastrophic nuclear accident at Three Mile Island, Pennsylvania, in 1979 heightened antinuclear sentiment in the United States. In 1989, the oil tanker *Exxon Valdez* ran aground on Bligh Reef in Prince William Sound, Alaska, and spilled approximately 10.9 million gallons of crude oil. Eventually covering thousands of square miles of ocean water (and 1,300 miles of Alaska shoreline) in oil, the spill killed hundreds of thousands of animals instantly and devastated the fragile ecosystem of the Sound. An even greater oil spill occurred in the Gulf of Mexico in 2010 from an explosion in a deep well established by BP. Eleven people died in the explosion, and almost 5 million barrels of petroleum were released into the water.

In developed, industrialized nations, environmental advocacy has largely focused on energy policy, conservation, clean technologies, and changing individual and social attitudes about consumption (as in the recycling movement). In the developing world, however, the growth of environmentalism is often linked to issues of human and democratic rights and freedom from First World exploitation. For example, the Green Belt Movement in Kenya, begun in 1977 by Wangari Maathai, encouraged Kenyan women to plant over 30 million trees across the nation to address the challenges of deforestation, soil erosion, and lack of water. The Green Belt Movement

---

human rights. Except for the last, none of these claims turned out to be accurate.

In March 2003, American and British troops, with scant support from other countries and partial authorization from the United Nations, invaded Iraq and quickly toppled the Hussein regime. Hussein went into hiding but was eventually captured in December 2003 and executed in 2006. In May 2003, shortly after the American capture of Baghdad, President Bush made a dramatic appearance on an aircraft carrier off the coast of California, where, standing in front of a large sign reading "Mission Accomplished," he declared victory in the Iraq War.

In fact, the war in Iraq continued for six more years, during which 3,600 soldiers were killed (out of just over 4,200 in total). Support for the war in the United States steadily declined in the first months of the war, especially when it became clear that the "weapons of mass destruction" in Iraq turned out not to exist. Reports of torture of Iraqi prisoners by American soldiers increased the unpopularity of the war.

The invasion of Iraq was the most visible evidence of a basic change in the structure of American foreign policy under the presidency of George W. Bush. Ever since the late 1940s, when the containment policy became the cornerstone of America's role in the world, the United States had worked to maintain stability in the world by containing, but not often directly threatening or attacking, its adversaries. Even after the Cold War ended, the United States continued to demonstrate a reasonable level of constraint, despite its unchallenged military preeminence. In the administrations of George H. W. Bush and Bill Clinton, for example, American leaders worked closely with the United Nations and NATO to achieve U.S. international goals and usually resisted taking unilateral military action. ·

There had always been those who criticized these constraints. They believed that America should do more than maintain stability, and should move actively to topple undemocratic regimes and destroy potential enemies of the United States. In the administration of George W. Bush, became an important human rights and women's rights organization, focused on reducing poverty and promoting peaceful democratic change through environmental conservation and protection. Maathai, winner of the 2004 Nobel Peace Prize, has since served as Kenya's assistant minister for Environment and Natural Resources.

In the past two decades the environmental movement has grown even more global in scope, with multilateral environmental treaties and worldwide summits becoming principal strategies of advocates. In 1997, an international effort to reduce global warming by mandating the lowering of greenhouse gas emissions culminated in the Kyoto protocols, which as of late 2010 had been ratified by 183 nations (with the United States a conspicuous exception). A leading figure in bringing the issue of global warming to wide attention both in the United States and around the world has been former vice president Al Gore, whose 2006 film, *An Inconvenient Truth,* may have done more to raise awareness of the threat of global warming than any other recent event. The film won an Academy Award as Best Documentary Feature, and Gore won the 2007 Nobel Peace Prize for his efforts on behalf of the movement he has championed. His co-winner was the International Panel on Climate Change, launched in Switzerland in 1988 and affiliated with the United Nations. ●

UNDERSTAND, ANALYZE, AND EVALUATE

1. Why are environmental movements in developing nations often linked to issues of human rights and protection from exploitation by developed nations? How do developed nations threaten the environment of developing nations?
2. How did the 2010 BP explosion and oil spill in the Gulf of Mexico affect the environment? What was the effect on the environmental movement?
3. Environmental organizations include grassroots associations, worldwide NGOs, and national political parties. How do these groups focus attention on environmental issues? Which type of organization do you think would be most successful at reaching its goals? Why?

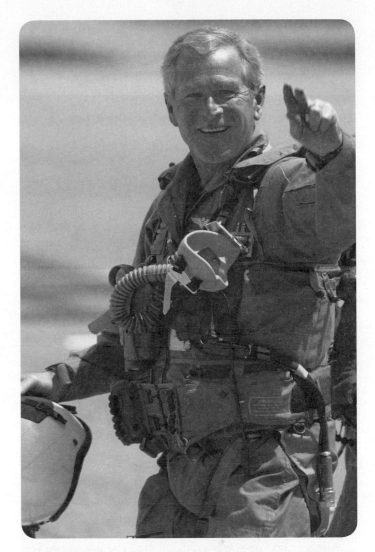

"MISSION ACCOMPLISHED," 2003 President George W. Bush chose the USS *Abraham Lincoln,* an aircraft carrier moored just off the coast of San Diego, for his first major address after the end of formal hostilities in the Iraq War on May 1, 2003. To strengthen his own identification with the military, he flew in on an S-3 Viking that landed on the carrier's deck and appeared before cameras wearing a flight suit and carrying a helmet. Later, dressed in a conventional business suit, he addressed a crowd of service men and women on the deck, standing beneath a large banner reading "Mission Accomplished." Later, as fighting in Iraq continued with no clear end in sight, and as the war became increasingly unpopular, Bush received much criticism and ridicule for what many Americans considered a premature celebration of victory. (© Reuters/Corbis)

these critics took control of American foreign policy and began to reshape it. The legacy of containment was repudiated. Instead, the public stance of the American government was Bush Foreign Policy that the United States had the right and the responsibility to spread freedom throughout the world—not just by exhortation and example, but also, when necessary, by military force. In Latvia in May 2005, President Bush spoke of the decision at the end of World War II not to challenge Soviet domination of Eastern Europe, a decision that had rested on the belief that such a challenge would lead the United States into another war. The controversial agreement negotiated at Yalta in 1945 by Roosevelt, Churchill, and Stalin, which failed to end the Soviet occupation of Poland and other Eastern European nations, was, the president said, part of an "unjust tradition" by which powerful governments sacrificed the interests of small nations. "This attempt to sacrifice freedom for the sake of stability," the president continued, "left a continent divided and unstable."

The lesson, Bush suggested, was that the United States and other great powers should value stability less and freedom more, and should be willing to take greater risks in the world to end tyranny and oppression.

TURBULENT POLITICS

The last years of the George W. Bush administration and those of Barack Obama's presidency were difficult for each man. Bush suffered from the growing unpopularity of the Iraq War, the weak federal response to Hurricane Katrina that devastated New Orleans and the Gulf coast, and the loss of

Republican majorities in both houses of Congress. President Obama struggled to maintain support in light of the flagging support for the war in Afghanistan, a hostile Congress, and difficulties in rolling out his Affordable Care Act, the Administration's comprehensive health care plan.

THE UNRAVELING OF THE BUSH PRESIDENCY

For most of the first three years of his presidency, George W. Bush enjoyed broad popularity because of his resolute stance against terrorism. Indeed, his firm position even buoyed his approval ratings during the controversial Iraq War, at least for a while. Bush's domestic policies did little to strengthen him politically, however. The president's tax cuts of 2001 disproportionately benefitted wealthy Americans, reflecting the view of White House economists that the best way to ensure growth was to put money into the hands of people most likely to invest. The tax cuts also contributed to the nearly $10 trillion increase in the national debt during the Bush presidency. Also controversial was one of Bush's most significant domestic accomplishments, an education bill known as "No Child Left Behind," which tied federal funding in schools to the success of students in taking standardized tests. Some educators and parents favored No Child Left Behind, but many others felt that students spent too many hours in the classroom learning how to take tests rather than think for themselves. By 2004, when the president faced reelection, it seemed by no means certain that he would be returned to office. Senator John Kerry of Massachusetts, a Vietnam veteran who opposed the war in Iraq, mounted a strong attack against the president by criticizing the his policies. But harsh assaults on Kerry in return, combined with the mobilization of large numbers of conservatives, helped Bush win a narrow victory.

Bush's second term was a difficult one. The war in Iraq was going badly, and its growing unpopularity added to the rapidly declining approval ratings of the president himself–ratings that by mid-2008 had reached the lowest level of presidential approval in the history of polling.

Perhaps even more damaging to President Bush was the government's response to a disastrous hurricane, Katrina, that devastated a massive swath of the coastline of the Gulf of Mexico in August 2005 and gravely damaged the city of New Orleans. The federal government's slow response aroused anger throughout the nation, contributing to the loss of the Republican majorities in both houses and leaving Bush with little support. At the same time, there were scandals in the Justice Department, revelations of illegal violations of civil liberties, and declining economic prospects that would culminate in the financial crisis of 2008.

HURRICANE KATRINA

THE ELECTION OF 2008 AND THE FINANCIAL CRISIS

Both parties began the 2008 campaign with large fields of candidates, but by spring the contest had narrowed considerably. Senator John McCain of Arizona emerged from the early primaries with the Republican nomination assured. Senator Hillary Rodham Clinton of New York (the former First Lady) and Senator Barack Obama of Illinois campaigned aggressively against each other for months. Clinton might have been the first female U.S. president. But Obama's organizational power among young voters and his inspirational messages of hope and change helped him secure primary votes and win the Democratic nomination. He entered the general election with a chance to become the nation's first African American president.

McCain and Obama entered the campaign with very different programs. McCain supported the Iraq War and Obama did not. Obama wanted national health insurance and McCain did not. McCain wanted additional tax cuts to spur investment, while Obama urged tax increases on the wealthiest Americans. Obama went with experience and name recognition in picking

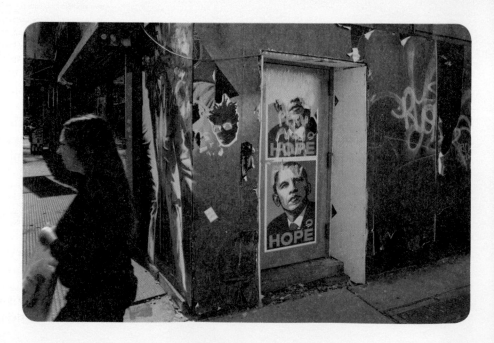

OBAMANIA Posters of and about Barack Obama were widely visible during the 2008 presidential campaign. In this photograph, a New Yorker walks past one example of the Obama street art that spread through many American cities—and, indeed, through cities around the world. Among the depictions of Obama during the campaign were the work of leading artists, who saw in him a figure of possibly historic significance. (© Chris McGrath/Getty Images)

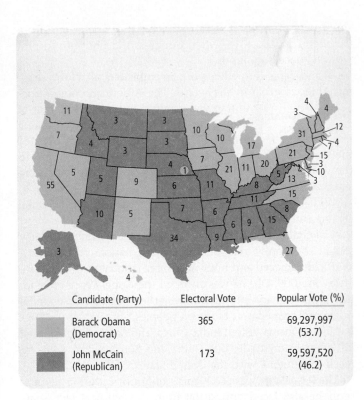

Candidate (Party)	Electoral Vote	Popular Vote (%)
Barack Obama (Democrat)	365	69,297,997 (53.7)
John McCain (Republican)	173	59,597,520 (46.2)

THE ELECTION OF 2008 The election of 2008 broke the pattern of very close divisions between the two parties and instead produced a decisive victory for Barack Obama. For the first time since 1996, Democrats won states in the South and carried most of the "swing states." The election also carried large majorities for the Democrats in both the House and the Senate, only to see the Republicans carry a majority of the House in 2010.

his vice presidential running mate, Senator Joe Biden of Delaware. McCain chose an almost unknown figure to share his ticket—Governor Sarah Palin of Alaska. Palin soon became the hero of many conservatives in the Republican convention. But her inexperience seemed to damage the Republican campaign. Before the conventions, Obama was already leading strongly in the polls.

As the nomination campaigns were heating up, a series of financial problems had arisen in mid-2007. By 2008, the nation was facing its worst financial crisis since the Great Depression. For years, financial institutions had been developing new credit instruments intended to make borrowing easier and cheaper, which lured millions of people into taking on large and risky mortgages. One such instrument, called an adjustable rate mortgage (ARM), offered homebuyers mortgages with initially low interest rates that would increase in later years. Other loans, called "jumbo loans," extended credit to people who lacked the financial means needed to pay them back. For a while, the sale of houses, many of which were based on these risky mortgages, increased, causing a "housing bubble"—a rapid rise in housing prices fueled by high demand. These business practices were made possible with the repeal of the Glass-Steagall Act in 1999. Glass-Steagall had been passed in 1933 to prevent irresponsible banking practices by mandating layers of government oversight designed to catch fraud or risky investment strategies. With more and more purchases, the price of homes fell. In time,

however, many people with the reset higher mortgage rates or jumbo loans could not sell the homes that they could no longer afford. In many cases, the market value of the home sank below the value of the mortgages held, causing some homeowners to walk away from their property and default on their loans. Foreclosures were numerous across the country. Many of the nation's largest banks had invested heavily in the securities that backed these risky loans; now, with the collapse of the housing market, they lost vast sums of money.

The so-called Great Recession of 2008, influenced by the loan crisis, also pushed down wages and triggered widespread job layoffs making it impossible for the additional owners of ARMS and jumbo loans to make payments thus increasing the number of home foreclosures. Many Americans could not meet their other financial obligations such as the repayment of school loans or credit card debt. There was also less money available for investing, or economic growth. The increased unemployment rate further accelerated the downward economic spiral.

2008 FINANCIAL CRISIS

By mid-September 2008, the financial crisis suggested an economy falling out of control. Secretary of the Treasury Henry Paulson, supported by other economic leaders, proposed the massive use of federal funds to help the government bail out banks that were failing. Both the Bush administration and eventually the Obama administration won congressional support for $750 billion in the form of the Troubled Asset Relief Program (TARP) to shore up the tottering financial institutions. The bailout kept the economy from collapsing, but it remained very weak for several years, with exceptionally high unemployment rates.

During this crisis, McCain and Obama fought out the last two months of their campaign. Obama benefited from George W. Bush's unpopularity. With the incoming president facing another powerful downturn in the economy, McCain's response seemed to associate him with Bush's policies, increasingly viewed by many Americans as causing the financial meltdown, whereas Obama conveyed a message that seemed to signal new and more hopeful possibilities. What had been at times a close race ended in a strong showing for Obama, and on November 4, 2008, he won the popular vote 53 percent to 46 percent and the electoral vote by an even larger margin.

THE OBAMA PRESIDENCY

Few modern presidents have entered the White House with higher expectations from the nation and even the world, so it was inevitable that many of Obama's supporters would eventually be disappointed. The enormity of the tasks Obama faced—managing the worst economy since the 1930s, one war in Iraq and another in Afghanistan, and a polarized political climate—made his presidency extraordinarily difficult.

At the time of Obama's inauguration, millions of Americans were unemployed. Major companies, especially in the automobile industry, faced bankruptcy. The home mortgage and other financial industries were still on the verge of collapse despite Bush's intervention. Obama's initial aspirations had to be put aside to confront the very dangerous reality that the country was on the verge of an economic depression possibly greater in scope and impact than the one of the 1930s.

To shore up the faltering economy, Obama engineered the largest economic stimulus in history. The Obama stimulus package, announced in 2009, included tax cuts, expanded

STIMULUS PACKAGE

unemployment benefits, and increased spending on education, infrastructure, police, health care, and job creation. The total funding for all of these programs reached $787 billion. Though controversial and passed by only a slight margin in Congress, in 2014 most economists agree that the stimulus measures saved the economy from catastrophe. Still, a large number of critics believe that Obama's stimulus package was a significant waste of money that added considerably to the national debt.

Even in such a precarious economic environment, Obama pressed for the passage of his Patient Protection and Affordable Care Act to realize the dream of many liberals since the 1930s: universal health care. The act urged all Americans to purchase health insurance, making provisions to help those of limited financial means to acquire it. Though the bill finally passed Congress in March 2010 despite threats of filibustering, the Republicans condemned this reform as "socialized medicine" and vowed to repeal it or defeat it through judicial action. Most of the benefits of the Affordable Care Act, as it is more commonly known, did not go into effect until 2014, that is, until Obama's second term. To the embarrassment of the administration and delight of critics, the rollout of the plan in October 2013 experienced significant technical problems when the federal website designed to process new insurance applications failed to work properly.

There were many opponents of "Obamacare"—as many derisively called the Affordable Care Act. Some of Obama's political adversaries were a group of evangelical, conserva-

TEA PARTY

tive, and libertarian Republicans who came to be known as the "Tea Party." An early leader of the Tea Party was Senator Ted Cruz of Texas. Although the Tea Party could not stop passage of the Affordable Care Act, they used their opposition to it to spearhead their overall conservative agenda: deficit reduction, tax reduction, and smaller government. The Tea Party's appeal to wealthy conservatives brought large financial contributions that gave this group a disproportionate political influence that belied its relatively small numbers. With the help of the conservative media, the Tea Party exerted increasing pressure on the Republican Party as a whole. In the 2010 midterm elections, 130 Tea Party–endorsed candidates were sworn in as members of Congress. The Tea Party contributed to the strong polarization of the federal government that resulted in a great deal of legislative gridlock, including a shutdown of many federal services and operations from October 1 to 16, 2013, when Congress did not vote to provide the necessary funds.

Obama came into office with an ambitious plan for reshaping America's role in the world. The American combat role

INTERNATIONAL RELATIONS

in Iraq was diminishing in the last year of the Bush administration, but Obama brought it to an end in August 2010. At the same time, he committed significant additional troops to the war in Afghanistan, where Americans had been fighting since 2001.

With former rival Hillary Clinton as his secretary of state, Obama sought peace between Israel and Palestine—an effort that, like all previous ones, was extraordinarily difficult. They sought to improve relations with many nations that the Iraq War had damaged and built new international trade opportunities. In 2009, Obama was awarded the Nobel Peace Prize for his "extraordinary efforts to strengthen international diplomacy and cooperation between peoples." In the fall of 2010, President Obama visited India, China, and South Korea hoping for progress on trade, but China and South Korea failed to reach agreements with the United States.

The Tea Party wasn't Obama's only critic during his first term—he also faced opposition from the political left. Some Democrats felt that he had moved too far to the right and had unnecessarily compromised core Democratic goals. Many people believed that Obama had failed to do many of the things he had promised to do in the campaign, such as closing the Guantánamo prison. Disgruntled critics protested that the president did not punish those financiers whom they held responsible for the global economic crisis. The so-called Occupy Wall Street movement arose as a populist response to the perception of increasing economic inequality. Protesters gathering in New York's Zuccotti Park near Wall

OCCUPY WALL STREET

Street and in other cities across the country used the title of an article by economist Joseph Stiglitz, "Of the 1%, by the 1%, for the 1%," to animate their position. In his article, Stiglitz argued that the wealthiest 1 percent of Americans owned over 40 percent of the nation's wealth. The crowd roared back "We are the 99 percent" to heighten the disparity between the fabulously wealthy and everyone else. Economic inequality became an important theme in the presidential election of 2012.

The impact of money on politics became mainstream news in 2010 with the Supreme Court decision in *Citizens United v. Federal Election Commission*. In this case, the conservative-leaning court ruled that government couldn't limit campaign-related expenditures from corporations or unions. Critics of the decision, including people sympathetic to the "Occupy" movement, felt that it favored the Republicans because wealthy donors tended to donate to that party. The ability of corporations to donate freely to individual campaigns would change the financing associated with the coming 2012 presidential election; indeed, more money was spent on that election than on any other in history.

While Barack Obama and Joe Biden once again occupied the Democratic ticket, the Republican primaries were tough contests involving a large field of candidates. Businessman and former Massachusetts governor Mitt Romney finally prevailed to win the Republican nomination with his vice presidential running mate, Representative Paul Ryan of Wisconsin. Originally a moderate Republican, Romney changed his position on a range of issues, including abortion and health care, apparently to appeal to the increasingly conservative nature of his party. Democrats would make his changed positions a focus of their campaign.

The key issues of the 2012 election included health-care reform, immigration reform, the federal budget deficit, and taxation and spending. The strained economy kept the focus more on domestic than international concerns. Perhaps the most pressing issue, though, was the high rate of unemployment–a problem that President Obama had struggled to remedy throughout most of his first term. Despite this lingering problem, Obama outlined his successes and pointed to them as the justification for a second term. He had withdrawn most of the troops from Iraq, as promised. Most dramatically, he had succeeded in overseeing the tracking down and, on May 2, 2011, the killing of al-Qaeda leader Osama bin Laden, the mastermind of the 9/11 attacks. One of Obama's greatest legislative achievements–the Affordable Care Act–also survived a challenge to its constitutionality in the Supreme Court's 2012 decision in *National Federation of Independent Business v. Sebelius*.

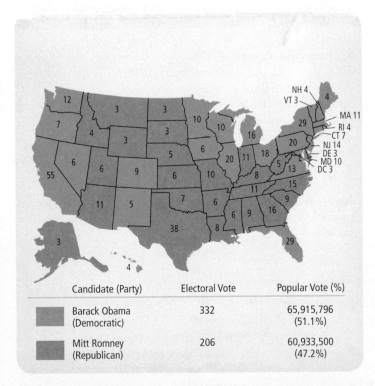

Candidate (Party)	Electoral Vote	Popular Vote (%)
Barack Obama (Democratic)	332	65,915,796 (51.1%)
Mitt Romney (Republican)	206	60,933,500 (47.2%)

THE ELECTION OF 2012 President Obama and Vice President Biden won a decisive victory over Mitt Romney and Paul Ryan. Republicans retained control of the House while Democrats kept control of the Senate.

The head-to-head contest between Romney and Obama at times seemed close, but a generally improving economy, the death of bin Laden, and several political missteps by Romney helped Obama. When voters finally cast their ballots, Obama won 51 percent of the popular vote to Romney's 47 percent, translating into 332 electoral votes for the president and 206 for his rival.

President Obama's second term posed many challenges on both the domestic and international fronts. One event that extended to both realms was the disclosure of a large number of classified documents by computer specialist Edward Snowden. On June 5, 2013, Snowden, a former contractor for the National Security Agency (NSA), released a vast number of classified documents to several media outlets. This action was viewed by many observers as the most serious leak since Daniel Ellsworth released the Pentagon Papers in 1971. The released documents showed extensive governmental surveillance of private Internet and telephone data, including the monitoring of the personal phone lines of such foreign leaders as Germany's Chancellor Angela Merkel. Snowden fled the United States, first to China and then to Russia, to avoid criminal charges. Some called Showden a traitor, others, a heroic champion of civil liberties.

NSA CONTROVERSY

One of the most serious international events during President Obama's second term took place in Syria, a country locked in violent civil war since 2011. Opponents of the Ba'ath government sought the ouster of President Bashar al-Assad and his repressive regime. Assad unleashed the army in response, killing an estimated 120,000 of his own people by September 2013. The displacement of hundreds of thousands of Syrians into neighboring countries threatened to further destabilize the region. Assad's use of chemical weapons triggered a strong condemnation by the United States and its European allies. Working with Russia, a traditional ally of the Assad regime, the United States and Europe brokered a deal to remove the stockpile of chemical weapons from the country. Obama, aware of the national unwillingness for the United States to become involved in another ground war, resisted calls for sending troops to dislodge Assad. The violent struggle continued through 2014 with no solution in sight.

The political gridlock of Obama's presidency continued into his second term. Many of his initiatives either encountered serious obstacles or did not come to pass. After his second inaugural, Obama and his strategists hoped to cement their gains among the Latino population revealed in the general election. Many Republicans, as well, believed that their party should reach out to this growing sector of the population by pushing through an immigration reform bill. On June 27, 2013, the Senate passed the Border Security, Economic Opportunity, and Immigration Modernization Act of 2013 as a comprehensive package of provisions, including a path to US citizenship for illegal immigrants already in the country. As of spring 2014, the House had not passed the bill owing to powerful conservative Republican opposition.

POLITICAL GRIDLOCK

OBAMA GRIEVES WITH A NATION President Barak Obama speaks at a memorial service for the 26 people killed on December 16, 2012 by a gunman at the Sandy Hook Elemetary School. His subsequent attempts at gun control reform were blocked by the House of Representative whose majority argued for the right of Americans to keep and bear arms without interference from the government. (© AFP/Getty Images)

Another disappointment for President Obama and his supporters involved the failure to enact meaningful gun control measures despite a series of horrific shootings occurring during his terms in office, including the shooting of twenty children and six adults at the Sandy Hook Elementary School in Newtown, Connecticut, on December 14, 2012. Despite the president's promise to exert "whatever power this office holds" to generate such gun control reform, the Congress resisted enacting any such legislation. The National Rifle Association and the conservative wing of the Republican Party successfully warded off any change on the federal level of the right of Americans to buy and use guns.

The gridlock of the House also dashed any hopes President Obama had of gaining a grand budget deal. The Congress remained sharply divided on questions of taxation, budget deficits, and government spending. In early 2014, the federal government did avert another shutdown in a move that some in the media interpreted as a sign of restored power to the mainstream Republican leadership and a lessening of the influence of the Tea Party.

AP CONNECTING THEMES

Chapter 32 discussed the political, diplomatic, economic, and social climate of the United States from 1990 to the present. In reviewing the chapter, focus on the political disarray demonstrated by the American people as they flip-flop between liberal and conservative ideologies. That trend continues into the 2000s, as evidenced by extremely close elections in 2000, 2004, and 2008. Also focus on the reasons and repercussions of growing inequities in the distribution of wealth. Pay close attention to the polarization of the two major political parties and the impact of the polarization on the ability to resolve pressing issues of the time. Think about the consequences of the aging of the American populace and the ramifications of an older populace on the economic and social structure of the nation. Consider the war on terror and the continuing issue of national security versus personal liberty. Also pay close attention to the proliferation of computer technology and the consequences of this technology on all aspects of American society.

The following themes have heightened importance in Chapter 32. You should now be able to do the following for each listed theme:

Identity: Explain how the new wave of immigration has led to conflict over American identity.

Work, Exchange, and Technology: Explain the impact of globalization on the American workforce and the character of available jobs.

Peopling: Explain the reasons for and consequences of accelerated immigration from Latin American countries into the United States.

Politics and Power: Explain consequences of the extreme polarization of the American party system on the ability of government to resolve critical issues.

America and the World: Explain the degree to which communications have "shrunk" the world and increased the interconnection of nations.

Environment and Geography: Explain the reasons for increased concerns over global warming and the role the United States has played in international environmental protection.

Ideas, Beliefs, and Culture: Explain the growing concern over the inability of the federal government to resolve critical problems.

AP SUGGESTED STUDY

PEOPLE/PLACES/EVENTS As you study these items, think about how they demonstrate or relate to key concepts and historical themes from this chapter and previous chapters.

AP TEST PRACTICE

Questions assume cumulative content knowledge from this chapter and previous chapters.

MULTIPLE CHOICE Use the excerpt below and your knowledge of U.S. history to answer questions 1–2.

"There is a real danger that the new regime established by the [Patriot] act could produce a massive database on Americans, freely available to all units of government.

The Patriot Act makes the same mistake the F.B.I. and C.I.A. have long made: favoring information quantity over quality. The universe of data that is shared should be narrowed, to focus on information closely related to suspected terrorism, and rather than being indiscriminately dumped, it should be given only to officials, at whatever agency, engaged in investigating terrorism."

–*The New York Times* editorial entitled "Revising the Patriot Act," April 10, 2005

1. Which phenomenon from earlier in the 20th century might the editorial writer have most likely condemned with similar logic?
   (A) The civil rights movement against segregation in the South
   (B) The Progressive movement's reliance on knowledge and gathering data
   (C) The moral tone of the temperance crusade in the early 20th century
   (D) The anti-communist hysteria of "rooting" out communists during the mid-century

2. Which recurring American debate would this editorial most be a part of?
   (A) Civil liberties vs. social order
   (B) Imperialistic foreign policy vs. non-imperialistic foreign policy
   (C) The role of the federal government
   (D) States' rights vs. federal power

SHORT ANSWER Use your knowledge of U.S. history to answer questions 3–4.

3. Answer a, b, and c.
   a) Briefly explain ONE example of political polarization in the late 20th and early 21st centuries regarding an environmental issue.
   b) Briefly explain ONE example of political polarization in the late 20th and early 21st centuries regarding an economic issue.
   c) Briefly explain ONE example of political polarization in the late 20th and early 21st centuries regarding a social issue.

4. Answer a, b and c.
   a) America became a unilateral superpower by the early 21st century. Explain one similarity between the Cold War foreign policy and that of the first decade of the 21st century.
   a) Explain ONE way America's foreign policy is different in the two periods.
   a) Explain ONE critical response to American foreign policy in the first decade of the 21st century.

LONG ESSAY For each question below, develop a thoughtful and thorough historical argument that answers the question. Begin your essay with a thesis statement and support it with relevant historical evidence.

5. Consider the following statement: The United States has been experiencing globalization since its colonial beginnings. Support, modify, or refute this interpretation, choosing from an economic, political, or social lens.

APPENDIXES

TOPOGRAPHICAL MAP OF THE UNITED STATES

Vancouver
Island

Puget Sound

COAST RANGE

CASCADE RANGE

Columbia R.

COLUMBIA
PLATEAU

ROCKY MOUNTAINS

Marias R.

Milk R.

Missouri R.

Yellowstone R.

Tongue R.

Powder R.

Little Missouri R.

Missouri R.

James R.

Lake
Winnipegosis

Assiniboine R.

Bighorn R.

Belle Fourche R.

BLACK
HILLS

Cheyenne R.

Snake R.

Great
Salt
Lake

SIERRA NEVADA

Humboldt R.

Sacramento R.

Central Valley

San Joaquin R.

DEATH
VALLEY

COAST RANGES

MOHAVE
DESERT

Colorado R.

Gila R.

Gila R.

Sevier R.

Virgin R.

White R.

Green R.

Colorado R.

Gunnison R.

N. Platte R.

Lodgepole R.

Niobrara R.

Platte R.

Republican R.

Smoky Hill R.

Arkansas R.

ROCKY MOUNTAINS

COLORADO
PLATEAU

Verde R.

Rio Grande

Pecos R.

Canadian R.

Colo

PACIFIC
OCEAN

RUSSIA

ARCTIC OCEAN

Bering Strait

BROOKS RANGE

ALASKA

Yukon R.

CANADA

Mt. McKinley

ALASKA RANGE

Bering
Sea

ALEUTIAN ISLANDS

Gulf of Alaska

0   250   500 miles

0   250   500 kilometers

Kauai

Niihau   Oahu

Molokai

Lanai

Kahoolawe

PACIFIC
OCEAN

Maui

HAWAII

Hawaii

0   50   100 miles

0   50   100 kilometers

Nueces R.

Rio Grande

MEXICO

C A N A D A

Lake Nipigon

Lake Superior

Lake Huron

Lake Michigan

Lake Ontario

Lake Erie

St. Lawrence R.

Kennebec R.

Lake Champlain

Connecticut R.

ADIRONDACK MTS.

Mohawk R.

Hudson R.

Allegheny R.

Delaware R.

Susquehanna R.

Potomac R.

Rock R.

Fox R.

Kankakee R.

Illinois R.

Scioto R.

ALLEGHENY MTS.

APPALACHIAN MOUNTAINS

SHENANDOAH VALLEY

Kanawha R.

James R.

Chesapeake Bay

PLAINS

Wabash R.

Ohio R.

Roanoke R.

Missouri R.

Cumberland R.

BLUE RIDGE MTS.

ATLANTIC OCEAN

Mississippi R.

White R.

Tennessee R.

ATLANTIC COASTAL PLAIN

Saluda R.

Arkansas R.

Ouachita R.

Yazoo R.

Tombigbee R.

Alabama R.

Chattahoochee R.

Savannah R.

Altamaha R.

Pearl R.

Gulf of Mexico

Lake Okeechobee

B A H A M A S

ATLANTIC OCEAN

PUERTO RICO

Caribbean Sea

CUBA

| 0 | 150 | 300 miles |
| 0 | 150 | 300 kilometers |

Land Elevation

Feet	Meters
Over 13,000	Over 3,000
6,560–13,000	2,000–3,000
3,280–6,560	1,000–2,000
660–3,280	2001–1,000
0–660	0–200
Below sea level	Below sea level

| 0 | 50 | 100 miles |
| 0 | 50 | 100 kilometers |

UNITED STATES TERRITORIAL EXPANSION, 1783–1898

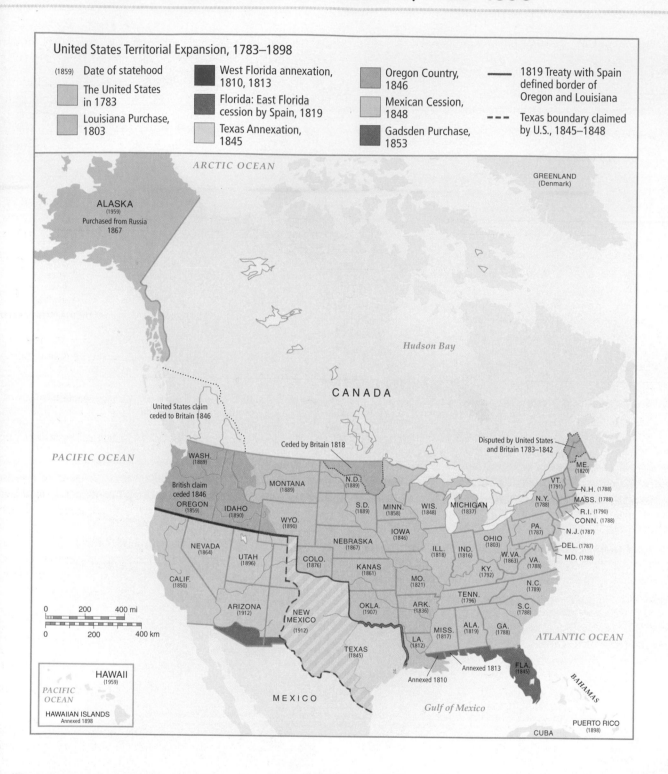

United States Territorial Expansion, 1783–1898

- (1859) Date of statehood
- The United States in 1783
- Louisiana Purchase, 1803
- West Florida annexation, 1810, 1813
- Florida: East Florida cession by Spain, 1819
- Texas Annexation, 1845
- Oregon Country, 1846
- Mexican Cession, 1848
- Gadsden Purchase, 1853
- —— 1819 Treaty with Spain defined border of Oregon and Louisiana
- --- Texas boundary claimed by U.S., 1845–1848

ARCTIC OCEAN

GREENLAND (Denmark)

ALASKA (1959) Purchased from Russia 1867

PACIFIC OCEAN

Hudson Bay

CANADA

United States claim ceded to Britain 1846

Ceded by Britain 1818

Disputed by United States and Britain 1783–1842

WASH. (1889)

British claim ceded 1846 OREGON (1859)

IDAHO (1890)

MONTANA (1889)

N.D. (1889)

S.D. (1889)

MINN. (1858)

WIS. (1848)

MICHIGAN (1837)

ME. (1820)

VT. (1791)

N.H. (1788)

N.Y. (1788)

MASS. (1788)

R.I. (1790)

CONN. (1788)

WYO. (1890)

IOWA (1846)

PA. (1787)

N.J. (1787)

OHIO (1803)

NEVADA (1864)

UTAH (1896)

COLO. (1876)

NEBRASKA (1867)

ILL. (1818)

IND. (1816)

W.VA. (1863)

VA. (1788)

DEL. (1787)

MD. (1788)

CALIF. (1850)

KANAS (1861)

MO. (1821)

KY. (1792)

N.C. (1789)

TENN. (1796)

ARIZONA (1912)

NEW MEXICO (1912)

OKLA. (1907)

ARK. (1836)

S.C. (1788)

TEXAS (1845)

MISS. (1817)

ALA. (1819)

GA. (1788)

ATLANTIC OCEAN

LA. (1812)

Annexed 1810

Annexed 1813

FLA. (1845)

BAHAMAS

MEXICO

Gulf of Mexico

PUERTO RICO (1898)

CUBA

0   200   400 mi

0   200   400 km

HAWAII (1959)

PACIFIC OCEAN

HAWAIIAN ISLANDS Annexed 1898

THE DECLARATION OF INDEPENDENCE

IN CONGRESS, JULY 4, 1776,

THE UNANIMOUS DECLARATION OF THE THIRTEEN UNITED STATES OF AMERICA

When, in the course of human events, it becomes necessary for one people to dissolve the political bands which have connected them with another, and to assume, among the powers of the earth, the separate and equal station to which the laws of nature and of nature's God entitle them, a decent respect to the opinions of mankind requires that they should declare the causes which impel them to the separation.

We hold these truths to be self-evident, that all men are created equal; that they are endowed by their Creator with certain unalienable rights; that among these, are life, liberty, and the pursuit of happiness. That, to secure these rights, governments are instituted among men, deriving their just powers from the consent of the governed; that, whenever any form of government becomes destructive of these ends, it is the right of the people to alter or to abolish it, and to institute a new government, laying its foundation on such principles, and organizing its powers in such form, as to them shall seem most likely to effect their safety and happiness. Prudence, indeed, will dictate that governments long established, should not be changed for light and transient causes; and, accordingly, all experience hath shown, that mankind are more disposed to suffer, while evils are sufferable, than to right themselves by abolishing the forms to which they are accustomed. But, when a long train of abuses and usurpations, pursuing invariably the same object, evinces a design to reduce them under absolute despotism, it is their right, it is their duty, to throw off such government and to provide new guards for their future security. Such has been the patient sufferance of these colonies, and such is now the necessity which constrains them to alter their former systems of government. The history of the present King of Great Britain is a history of repeated injuries and usurpations, all having, in direct object, the establishment of an absolute tyranny over these States. To prove this, let facts be submitted to a candid world:

He has refused his assent to laws the most wholesome and necessary for the public good.

He has forbidden his governors to pass laws of immediate and pressing importance, unless suspended in their operation till his assent should be obtained; and, when so suspended, he has utterly neglected to attend to them.

He has refused to pass other laws for the accommodation of large districts of people, unless those people would relinquish the right of representation in the legislature; a right inestimable to them, and formidable to tyrants only.

He has called together legislative bodies at places unusual, uncomfortable, and distant from the depository of their public records, for the sole purpose of fatiguing them into compliance with his measures.

He has dissolved representative houses repeatedly for opposing, with manly firmness, his invasions on the rights of the people.

He has refused, for a long time after such dissolutions, to cause others to be elected; whereby the legislative powers, incapable of annihilation, have returned to the people at large for their exercise; the state remaining, in the meantime, exposed to all the danger of invasion from without, and convulsions within.

He has endeavored to prevent the population of these States; for that purpose, obstructing the laws for naturalization of foreigners, refusing to pass others to encourage their migration hither, and raising the conditions of new appropriations of lands.

He has obstructed the administration of justice, by refusing his assent to laws for establishing judiciary powers.

He has made judges dependent on his will alone, for the tenure of their officers, and the amount and payment of their salaries.

He has erected a multitude of new offices, and sent hither swarms of officers to harass our people, and eat out their substance.

He has kept among us, in time of peace, standing armies, without the consent of our legislatures.

He has affected to render the military independent of, and superior to, the civil power.

He has combined, with others, to subject us to a jurisdiction foreign to our Constitution, and unacknowledged by our laws; giving his assent to their acts of pretended legislation:

For quartering large bodies of armed troops among us:

For protecting them by a mock trial, from punishment, for any murders which they should commit on the inhabitants of these States:

For cutting off our trade with all parts of the world:

For imposing taxes on us without our consent:

For depriving us, in many cases, of the benefit of trial by jury:

For transporting us beyond seas to be tried for pretended offences:

For abolishing the free system of English laws in a neighboring province, establishing therein an arbitrary government, and enlarging its boundaries, so as to render it at once an example and fit instrument for introducing the same absolute rule into these colonies:

For taking away our charters, abolishing our most valuable laws, and altering, fundamentally, the powers of our governments:

For suspending our own legislatures, and declaring themselves invested with power to legislate for use in all cases whatsoever.

He has abdicated government here, by declaring us out of his protection, and waging war against us.

He has plundered our seas, ravaged our coasts, burnt our towns, and destroyed the lives of our people.

He is, at this time, transporting large armies of foreign mercenaries to complete the works of death, desolation, and tyranny, already begun, with circumstances of cruelty and perfidy scarcely paralleled in the most barbarous ages, and totally unworthy the head of a civilized nation.

He has constrained our fellow citizens, taken captive on the high seas, to bear arms against their country, to become the executioners of their friends, and brethren, or to fall themselves by their hands.

He has excited domestic insurrections amongst us, and has endeavored to bring on the inhabitants of our frontiers, the merciless Indian savages, whose known rule of warfare is an undistinguished destruction of all ages, sexes, and conditions.

In every stage of these oppressions, we have petitioned for redress, in the most humble terms; our repeated petitions have been answered only by repeated injury. A prince, whose character is thus marked by every act which may define a tyrant, is unfit to be the ruler of a free people.

Nor have we been wanting in attention to our British brethren. We have warned them, from time to time, of attempts made by their legislature to extend an unwarrantable jurisdiction over us. We have reminded them of the circumstances of our emigration and settlement here. We have appealed to their native justice and magnanimity, and we have conjured them, by the ties of our common kindred, to disavow these usurpations, which would inevitably interrupt our connections and correspondence. They, too, have been deaf to the voice of justice and consanguinity. We must, therefore, acquiesce in the necessity, which denounces our separation, and hold them as we hold the rest of mankind, enemies in war, in peace, friends.

We, therefore, the representatives of the United States of America, in general Congress assembled, appealing to the Supreme Judge of the world for the rectitude of our intentions, do, in the name, and by the authority of the good people of these colonies, solemnly publish and declare, that these united colonies are, and of right ought to be, free and independent states: that they are absolved from all allegiance to the British Crown, and that all political connection between them and the state of Great Britain is, and ought to be, totally dissolved; and that, as free and independent states, they have full power to levy war, conclude peace, contract alliances, establish commerce, and to do all other acts and things which independent states may of right do. And, for the support of this declaration, with a firm reliance on the protection of Divine Providence, we mutually pledge to each other our lives, our fortunes, and our sacred honor.

The foregoing Declaration was, by order of Congress, engrossed, and signed by the following members:

JOHN HANCOCK

New Hampshire
Josiah Bartlett
William Whipple
Matthew Thornton

Massachusetts Bay
Samuel Adams
John Adams
Robert Treat Paine
Elbridge Gerry

Rhode Island
Stephen Hopkins
William Ellery

Connecticut
Robert Sherman
Samuel Huntington
William Williams
Oliver Wolcott

New York
William Floyd
Philip Livingston
Francis Lewis
Lewis Morris

New Jersey
Richard Stockton
John Witherspoon
Francis Hopkinson
John Hart
Abraham Clark

Pennsylvania
Robert Morris
Benjamin Rush
Benjamin Franklin
John Morton
George Clymer
James Smith
George Taylor
James Wilson
George Ross

Delaware
Caesar Rodney
George Read
Thomas McKean

Maryland
Samuel Chase
William Paca
Thomas Stone
Charles Carroll,
   of Carrollton

Virginia
George Wythe
Richard Henry Lee
Thomas Jefferson
Benjamin Harrison
Thomas Nelson, Jr.
Francis Lightfoot Lee
Carter Braxton

North Carolina
William Hooper
Joseph Hewes
John Penn

South Carolina
Edward Rutledge
Thomas Heyward, Jr.
Thomas Lynch, Jr.
Arthur Middleton

Georgia
Button Gwinnett
Lyman Hall
George Walton

Resolved, That copies of the Declaration be sent to the several assemblies, conventions, and committees, or councils of safety, and to the several commanding officers of the continental troops; that it be proclaimed in each of the United States, at the head of the army.

THE CONSTITUTION OF THE UNITED STATES OF AMERICA[1]

We the People of the United States, in Order to form a more perfect Union, establish Justice, insure domestic Tranquility, provide for the common defence, promote the general Welfare, and secure the Blessings of Liberty to ourselves and our Posterity, do ordain and establish this CONSTITUTION for the United States of America.

Article I

SECTION 1.

All legislative Powers herein granted shall be vested in a Congress of the United States, which shall consist of a Senate and House of Representatives.

SECTION 2.

The House of Representatives shall be composed of Members chosen every second Year by the People of the several States, and the Electors in each State shall have the Qualifications requisite for Electors of the most numerous Branch of the State Legislature.

No Person shall be a Representative who shall not have attained to the Age of twenty-five Years, and been seven Years a Citizen of the United States, and who shall not, when elected, be an Inhabitant of that State in which he shall be chosen.

[Representatives and direct Taxes[2] shall be apportioned among the several States which may be included within this Union, according to their respective Numbers, which shall be determined by adding to the whole Number of free Persons, including those bound to Service for a Term of Years, and excluding Indians not taxed, three fifths of all other Persons.][3] The actual Enumeration shall be made within three Years after the first Meeting of the Congress of the United States, and within every subsequent Term of ten Years, in such Manner as they shall by Law direct. The Number of Representatives shall not exceed one for every thirty Thousand, but each State shall have at Least one Representative; and until such enumeration shall be made, the State of New Hampshire shall be entitled to chuse three, Massachusetts eight, Rhode-Island and Providence Plantations one, Connecticut five, New York six, New Jersey four, Pennsylvania eight, Delaware one, Maryland six, Virginia ten, North Carolina five, South Carolina five, and Georgia three.

When vacancies happen in the Representation from any State, the Executive Authority thereof shall issue Writs of Election to fill such Vacancies.

The House of Representatives shall chuse their Speaker and other Officers; and shall have the sole Power of Impeachment.

SECTION 3.

The Senate of the United States shall be composed of two Senators from each State, chosen by the Legislature thereof, for six Years; and each Senator shall have one Vote.

Immediately after they shall be assembled in Consequence of the first Election, they shall be divided as equally as may be into three Classes. The Seats of the Senators of the first Class shall be vacated at the Expiration of the second Year, of the second Class at the Expiration of the fourth Year, and of the third Class at the Expiration of the sixth Year, so that one-third may be chosen every second Year; and if Vacancies happen by Resignation, or otherwise, during the Recess of the Legislature of any State, the Executive thereof may make temporary Appointments until the next Meeting of the Legislature, which shall then fill such Vacancies.

No Person shall be a Senator who shall not have attained to the Age of thirty Years, and been nine Years a Citizen of the United States, and who shall not, when elected, be an Inhabitant of that State for which he shall be chosen.

The Vice President of the United States shall be President of the Senate, but shall have no vote, unless they be equally divided.

The Senate shall chuse their other Officers, and also a President pro tempore, in the absence of the Vice President, or when he shall exercise the office of President of the United States.

The Senate shall have the sole Power to try all Impeachments. When sitting for that purpose they shall be on Oath or Affirmation. When the President of the United States is tried, the Chief Justice shall preside: And no person shall be convicted without the Concurrence of two thirds of the Members present.

Judgment in Cases of Impeachment shall not extend further than to removal from Office, and disqualification to hold and enjoy any Office of honor, Trust, or Profit under the United States: but the Party convicted shall nevertheless be liable and subject to Indictment, Trial, Judgment, and Punishment, according to Law.

SECTION 4.

The Times, Places and Manner of holding Elections for Senators and Representatives, shall be prescribed in each State by the Legislature thereof; but the Congress may at any time by Law make or alter such Regulations, except as to the Places of Chusing Senators.

The Congress shall assemble at least once in every Year, and such Meeting shall be on the first Monday in December, unless they shall by Law appoint a different day.

SECTION 5.

Each House shall be the Judge of the Elections, Returns and Qualifications of its own Members, and a Majority of each shall constitute a Quorum to do Business; but a smaller number may adjourn from day to day, and may be authorized to compel the Attendance of absent Members, in such Manner, and under such Penalties, as each House may provide.

---

[1]This version, which follows the original Constitution in capitalization and spelling, was published by the United States Department of the Interior, Office of Education, in 1935.

[2]Altered by the Sixteenth Amendment.

[3]Negated by the Fourteenth Amendment.

Each House may determine the Rules of its Proceedings, punish its Members for disorderly Behaviour, and, with the Concurrence of two thirds, expel a Member.

Each House shall keep a Journal of its Proceedings, and from time to time publish the same, excepting such Parts as may in their Judgment require Secrecy; and the Yeas and Nays of the Members of either House on any question shall, at the Desire of one fifth of those Present, be entered on the Journal.

Neither House, during the Session of Congress, shall, without the Consent of the other, adjourn for more than three days, nor to any other Place than that in which the two Houses shall be sitting.

SECTION 6.

The Senators and Representatives shall receive a Compensation for their Services, to be ascertained by Law, and paid out of the Treasury of the United States. They shall in all Cases, except Treason, Felony, and Breach of the Peace, be privileged from Arrest during their Attendance at the Session of their respective Houses, and in going to and returning from the same; and for any Speech or Debate in either House, they shall not be questioned in any other Place.

No Senator or Representative shall, during the Time for which he was elected, be appointed to any civil Office under the Authority of the United States, which shall have been created, or the Emoluments whereof shall have been increased, during such time; and no Person holding any Office under the United States shall be a Member of either House during his continuance in Office.

SECTION 7.

All Bills for raising Revenue shall originate in the House of Representatives; but the Senate may propose or concur with Amendments as on other bills.

Every Bill which shall have passed the House of Representatives and the Senate, shall, before it become a Law, be presented to the President of the United States; If he approve he shall sign it, but if not he shall return it, with his Objections, to that House in which it shall have originated, who shall enter the Objections at large on their Journal, and proceed to reconsider it. If after such Reconsideration two thirds of that House shall agree to pass the bill, it shall be sent, together with the objections, to the other House, by which it shall likewise be reconsidered, and if approved by two thirds of that House, it shall become a Law. But in all such Cases the Votes of both Houses shall be determined by Yeas and Nays, and the Names of the Persons voting for and against the Bill shall be entered on the Journal of each House respectively. If any Bill shall not be returned by the President within ten Days (Sundays excepted) after it shall have been presented to him, the Same shall be a Law, in like Manner as if he had signed it, unless the Congress by their Adjournment prevent its Return, in which Case it shall not be a Law.

Every Order, Resolution, or Vote to which the Concurrence of the Senate and House of Representatives may be necessary (except on a question of Adjournment) shall be presented to the President of the United States; and before the Same shall take Effect, shall be approved by him, or being disapproved by him, shall be repassed by two thirds of the Senate and House of Representatives, according to the Rules and Limitations prescribed in the Case of a Bill.

SECTION 8.

The Congress shall have Power To lay and collect Taxes, Duties, Imposts and Excises, to pay the Debts and provide for the common Defence and general Welfare of the United States; but all Duties, Imposts and Excises shall be uniform throughout the United States;

To borrow money on the credit of the United States;

To regulate Commerce with foreign Nations, and among the several States, and with the Indian Tribes;

To establish an uniform rule of Naturalization, and uniform Laws on the subject of Bankruptcies throughout the United States;

To coin Money, regulate the Value thereof, and of foreign Coin, and fix the Standard of Weights and Measures;

To provide for the Punishment of counterfeiting the Securities and current Coin of the United States;

To establish Post Offices and post Roads;

To promote the Progress of Science and useful Arts, by securing for limited Times to Authors and Inventors the exclusive Right to their respective Writings and Discoveries;

To constitute Tribunals inferior to the Supreme Court;

To define and punish Piracies and Felonies committed on the high Seas, and Offenses against the Law of Nations;

To declare War, grant Letters of Marque and Reprisal, and make Rules concerning Captures on Land and Water;

To raise and support Armies, but no Appropriation of Money to that Use shall be for a longer Term than two Years;

To provide and maintain a Navy;

To make Rules for the Government and Regulation of the land and naval forces;

To provide for calling forth the Militia to execute the Laws of the Union, suppress Insurrections and repel Invasions;

To provide for organizing, arming, and disciplining the Militia, and for governing such Part of them as may be employed in the Service of the United States, reserving to the States respectively, the Appointment of the Officers, and the Authority of training the Militia according to the discipline prescribed by Congress;

To exercise exclusive Legislation in all Cases whatsoever, over such District (not exceeding ten Miles square) as may, by Cession of particular States, and the acceptance of Congress, become the Seat of the Government of the United States, and to exercise like Authority over all Places purchased by the Consent of the Legislature of the State in which the Same shall be, for the Erection of Forts, Magazines, Arsenals, Dockyards, and other needful Buildings;–And

To make all Laws which shall be necessary and proper for carrying into Execution for foregoing Powers, and all other Powers vested by this Constitution in the Government of the United States, or in any Department or Officer thereof.

SECTION 9.

The Migration or Importation of such Persons as any of the States now existing shall think proper to admit, shall not be prohibited by the Congress prior to the Year one thousand eight hundred and eight, but a tax or duty may be imposed on such Importation, not exceeding ten dollars for each Person.

The privilege of the Writ of Habeas Corpus shall not be suspended, unless when in Cases of Rebellion or Invasion the public Safety may require it.

No bill of Attainder or ex post facto Law shall be passed.

No capitation, or other direct, Tax shall be laid unless in Proportion to the Census or Enumeration herein before directed to be taken.

No Tax or Duty shall be laid on Articles exported from any State.

No Preference shall be given by any Regulation of Commerce or Revenue to the Ports of one State over those of another: nor shall Vessels bound to, or from, one State, be obliged to enter, clear, or pay Duties in another.

No Money shall be drawn from the Treasury, but in Consequence of Appropriations made by Law; and a regular Statement and Account of the Receipts and Expenditures of all public Money shall be published from time to time.

No title of Nobility shall be granted by the United States: And no Person holding any Office of Profit or Trust under them, shall, without the Consent of the Congress, accept of any present, Emolument, Office, or title, of any kind whatever, from any King, Prince, or foreign State.

SECTION 10.

No State shall enter into any Treaty, Alliance, or Confederation; grant Letters of Marque and Reprisal; coin Money; emit Bills of Credit; make any Thing but gold and silver Coin a Tender in Payment of Debts; pass any Bill of Attainder, ex post facto Law, or Law impairing the Obligation of Contracts, or grant any title of Nobility.

No State shall, without the Consent of the Congress, lay any Imposts or Duties on Imports or Exports, except what may be absolutely necessary for executing its inspection Laws; and the net Produce of all Duties and Imposts, laid by any State on Imports or Exports, shall be for the use of the Treasury of the United States; and all such Laws shall be subject to the Revision and Control of the Congress.

No state shall, without the Consent of Congress, lay any duty of Tonnage, keep Troops, or Ships of War in time of Peace, enter into any Agreement or Compact with another State, or with a foreign Power, or engage in War, unless actually invaded, or in such imminent Danger as will not admit of delay.

Article II

SECTION 1.

The executive Power shall be vested in a President of the United States of America. He shall hold his Office during the Term of four years, and, together with the Vice President, chosen for the same Term, be elected, as follows:

Each State shall appoint, in such Manner as the Legislature thereof may direct, a Number of Electors, equal to the whole Number of Senators and Representatives to which the State may be entitled in the Congress: but no Senator or Representative, or Person holding an Office of Trust or Profit under the United States, shall be appointed an Elector.

[The Electors shall meet in their respective States, and vote by Ballot for two persons, of whom one at least shall not be an Inhabitant of the same State with themselves. And they shall make a List of all the Persons voted for, and of the Number of Votes for each; which List they shall sign and certify, and transmit sealed to the Seat of the Government of the United States, directed to the President of the Senate. The President of the Senate shall, in the Presence of the Senate and House of Representatives, open all the Certificates, and the Votes shall then be counted. The Person having the greatest Number of Votes shall be the President, if such Number be a Majority of the whole Number of Electors appointed; and if there be more than one who have such Majority, and have an equal Number of Votes, then the House of Representatives shall immediately chuse by Ballot one of them for President; and if no Person have a Majority, then from the five highest on the list the said House shall in like Manner chuse the President. But in chusing the President, the Votes shall be taken by States, the Representation from each State having one Vote; a quorum for this Purpose shall consist of a Member or Members from two-thirds of the States, and a Majority of all the States shall be necessary to a Choice. In every Case, after the Choice of the President, the Person having the greatest Number of Votes of the Electors shall be the Vice President. But if there should remain two or more who have equal votes, the Senate shall chuse from them by Ballot the Vice President.][4]

The Congress may determine the Time of chusing the Electors, and the Day on which they shall give their Votes; which Day shall be the same throughout the United States.

No person except a natural-born Citizen, or a Citizen of the United States, at the time of the Adoption of this Constitution, shall be eligible to the Office of President; neither shall any Person be eligible to that Office who shall not have attained to the Age of thirty-five years, and been fourteen Years a Resident within the United States.

In Case of the Removal of the President from Office, or of his Death, Resignation, or Inability to discharge the Powers and Duties of the said Office, the same shall devolve on the Vice President, and the Congress may by Law provide for the Case of Removal, Death, Resignation, or Inability, both of the President and Vice President, declaring what Officer shall then act as President, and such Officer shall act accordingly, until the disability be removed, or a President shall be elected.

The President shall, at stated Times, receive for his Services a Compensation, which shall neither be increased nor diminished during the Period for which he shall have been elected, and he shall not receive within that Period any other Emolument from the United States, or any of them.

Before he enter on the execution of his Office, he shall take the following Oath or Affirmation:—"I do solemnly swear (or affirm) that I will faithfully execute the Office of President of

[4]Revised by the Twelfth Amendment.

the United States, and will, to the best of my Ability, preserve, protect, and defend the Constitution of the United States."

SECTION 2.

The President shall be Commander in Chief of the Army and Navy of the United States, and of the Militia of the several States, when called into the actual Service of the United States; he may require the Opinion, in writing, of the principal Officer in each of the executive Departments, upon any subject relating to the Duties of their respective Offices, and he shall have Power to Grant Reprieves and Pardons for Offenses against the United States, except in Cases of Impeachment.

He shall have Power, by and with the Advice and Consent of the Senate, to make Treaties, provided two-thirds of the Senators present concur; and he shall nominate, and by and with the Advice and Consent of the Senate, shall appoint Ambassadors, other public Ministers and Consuls, Judges of the supreme Court, and all other Officers of the United States, whose Appointments are not herein otherwise provided for, and which shall be established by Law: but the Congress may by Law vest the Appointment of such inferior Officers, as they think proper, in the President alone, in the Courts of Law, or in the Heads of Departments.

The President shall have Power to fill up all Vacancies that may happen during the Recess of the Senate, by granting Commissions which shall expire at the End of their next Session.

SECTION 3.

He shall from time to time give to the Congress Information of the State of the Union, and recommend to their Consideration such Measures as he shall judge necessary and expedient; he may, on extraordinary occasions, convene both Houses, or either of them, and in Case of Disagreement between them, with respect to the Time of Adjournment, he may adjourn them to such Time as he shall think proper; he shall receive Ambassadors and other public Ministers; he shall take care that the Laws be faithfully executed, and shall Commission all the Officers of the United States.

SECTION 4.

The President, Vice President and all civil Officers of the United States, shall be removed from Office on Impeachment for, and Conviction of, Treason, Bribery, or other high Crimes and Misdemeanors.

Article III

SECTION 1.

The judicial Power of the United States, shall be vested in one supreme Court, and in such inferior Courts as the Congress may from time to time ordain and establish. The Judges, both of the supreme and inferior Courts, shall hold their Offices during good Behaviour, and shall, at stated Times, receive for their Services, a Compensation, which shall not be diminished during their Continuance in Office.

SECTION 2.

The judicial Power shall extend to all Cases, in Law and Equity, arising under this Constitution, the Laws of the United States,

and Treaties made, or which shall be made, under their Authority;–to all Cases affecting ambassadors, other public ministers and consuls;–to all cases of admiralty and maritime Jurisdiction;–to Controversies to which the United States shall be a Party;–to Controversies between two or more States;– between a State and Citizens of another State;[5]–between Citizens of different States–between Citizens of the same State claiming Lands under Grants of different States, and between a State, or the Citizens thereof, and foreign States, Citizens, or Subjects.

In all Cases affecting Ambassadors, other public Ministers and Consuls, and those in which a State shall be Party, the supreme Court shall have original Jurisdiction. In all the other Cases before mentioned, the supreme Court shall have appellate Jurisdiction, both as to Law and Fact, with such Exceptions, and under such Regulations as the Congress shall make.

The trial of all Crimes, except in Cases of Impeachment, shall be by Jury; and such Trial shall be held in the State where the said Crimes shall have been committed; but when not committed within any State, the Trial shall be at such Place or Places as the Congress may by Law have directed.

SECTION 3.

Treason against the United States, shall consist only in levying War against them, or in adhering to their Enemies, giving them Aid and Comfort. No Person shall be convicted of Treason unless on the Testimony of two Witnesses to the same overt Act, or on Confession in open Court.

The Congress shall have power to declare the Punishment of Treason, but no Attainder of Treason shall work Corruption of Blood, or Forfeiture except during the Life of the Person attained.

Article IV

SECTION 1.

Full Faith and Credit shall be given in each State to the public Acts, Records, and judicial Proceedings of every State. And the Congress may by general Laws prescribe the Manner in which such Acts, Records and Proceedings shall be proved, and the Effect thereof.

SECTION 2.

The Citizens of each State shall be entitled to all Privileges and Immunities of Citizens in the several States.

A Person charged in any State with Treason, Felony, or other Crime, who shall flee from Justice, and be found in another State, shall on demand of the executive Authority of the State from which he fled, be delivered up, to be removed to the State having Jurisdiction of the crime.

No Person held to Service or Labour in one State, under the Laws thereof, escaping into another, shall, in Consequence of any Law or Regulation therein, be discharged from such Service or Labour, but shall be delivered up on Claim of the Party to whom such Service or Labour may be due.

---

[5]Qualified by the Eleventh Amendment.

SECTION 3.

New States may be admitted by the Congress into this Union; but no new State shall be formed or erected within the Jurisdiction of any other State; nor any State be formed by the Junction of two or more States, or parts of States, without the Consent of the Legislatures of the States concerned as well as of the Congress.

The Congress shall have Power to dispose of and make all needful Rules and Regulations respecting the Territory or other Property belonging to the United States; and nothing in this Constitution shall be so construed as to Prejudice any Claims of the United States, or of any particular State.

SECTION 4.

The United States shall guarantee to every State in this Union a Republican Form of Government, and shall protect each of them against Invasion; and on Application of the Legislature, or of the Executive (when the Legislature cannot be convened) against domestic violence.

Article V

The Congress, whenever two-thirds of both Houses shall deem it necessary, shall propose Amendments to this Constitution, or, on the Application of the Legislatures of two-thirds of the several States, shall call a Convention for proposing Amendments, which, in either Case, shall be valid to all Intents and Purposes, as part of this Constitution, when ratified by the Legislatures of three-fourths of the several States, or by Conventions in three-fourths thereof, as the one or the other Mode of Ratification may be proposed by the Congress; Provided that no Amendment which may be made prior to the Year One thousand eight hundred and eight shall in any Manner affect the first and fourth Clauses in the Ninth Section of the first Article; and that no State, without its Consent, shall be deprived of its equal Suffrage in the Senate.

Article VI

All Debts contracted and Engagements entered into, before the Adoption of this Constitution, shall be as valid against the United States under this Constitution, as under the Confederation.

This Constitution, and the Laws of the United States which shall be made in Pursuance thereof; and all Treaties made, or which shall be made, under the Authority of the United States, shall be the supreme Law of the Land; and the Judges in every State shall be bound thereby, any Thing in the Constitution or Laws of any State to the Contrary not-withstanding.

The Senators and Representatives before mentioned, and the Members of the several State Legislatures, and all executive and judicial Officers, both of the United States and of the several States, shall be bound by Oath or Affirmation to support this Constitution; but no religious Tests shall ever be required as a qualification to any Office or public Trust under the United States.

Article VII

The Ratification of the Conventions of nine States shall be sufficient for the Establishment of this Constitution between the States so ratifying the same.

Done in convention by the Unanimous Consent of the States present the Seventeenth Day of September in the Year of our Lord one thousand seven hundred and Eighty seven, and of the Independence of the United States of America the Twelfth. In Witness whereof We have hereunto subscribed our Names.[6]

George Washington,
President and deputy from Virginia

New Hampshire
John Langdon
Nicholas Gilman

Massachusetts
Nathaniel Gorham
Rufus King

Connecticut
William Samuel Johnson
Roger Sherman

New York
Alexander Hamilton

Delaware
George Read
Gunning Beford, Jr.
John Dickinson
Richard Bassett
Jacob Broom

New Jersey
William Livingston
David Brearley
William Paterson
Jonathan Dayton

Pennsylvania
Benjamin Franklin
Thomas Mifflin
Robert Morris
George Clymer
Thomas FitzSimons
Jared Ingersoll
James Wilson
Gouverneur Morris

North Carolina
William Blount
Richard Dobbs Spaight
Hugh Williamson

Maryland
James McHenry
Daniel of St. Thomas
  Jenifer
Daniel Carroll

Virginia
John Blair
James Madison, Jr.

South Carolina
John Rutledge
Charles Cotesworth
  Pinckney
Charles Pinckney Pierce
  Butler

Georgia
William Few
Abraham Baldwin

Articles in Addition to, and Amendment of, the Constitution of the United States of America, Proposed by Congress, and Ratified by the Legislatures of the Several States, Pursuant to the Fifth Article of the Original Constitution[7]

---

[6]These are the full names of the signers, which in some cases are not the signatures on the document.

[7]This heading appears only in the joint resolution submitting the first ten amendments.

[Article I]

Congress shall make no law respecting an establishment of religion, or prohibiting the free exercise thereof; or abridging the freedom of speech, or of the press; or the right of the people peaceably to assemble, and to petition the Government for a redress of grievances.

[Article II]

A well regulated Militia, being necessary to the security of a free State, the right of the people to keep and bear Arms shall not be infringed.

[Article III]

No Soldier shall, in time of peace, be quartered in any house, without the consent of the Owner, nor in time of war, but in a manner to be prescribed by law.

[Article IV]

The right of the people to be secure in their persons, houses, papers, and effects, against unreasonable searches and seizures, shall not be violated, and no Warrants shall issue, but upon probable cause, supported by Oath or affirmation, and particularly describing the place to be searched, and the persons or things to be seized.

[Article V]

No person shall be held to answer for a capital or otherwise infamous crime, unless on a presentment or indictment of a Grand Jury, except in cases arising in the land or naval forces, or in the Militia, when in actual service in time of War or public danger; nor shall any person be subject for the same offence to be twice put in jeopardy of life or limb; nor shall be compelled in any criminal case to be a witness against himself, nor be deprived of life, liberty, or property, without due process of law; nor shall private property be taken for public use, without just compensation.

[Article VI]

In all criminal prosecutions, the accused shall enjoy the right to a speedy and public trial, by an impartial jury of the State and district wherein the crime shall have been committed, which district shall have been previously ascertained by law, and to be informed of the nature and cause of the accusation; to be confronted with the witnesses against him; to have compulsory process for obtaining witnesses in his favour, and to have the Assistance of Counsel for his defence.

[Article VII]

In suits at common law, where the value in controversy shall exceed twenty dollars, the right of trial by jury shall be preserved, and no fact tried by a jury, shall be otherwise reexamined in any Court of the United States, than according to the rules of the common law.

[Article VIII]

Excessive bail shall not be required, nor excessive fines imposed, nor cruel and unusual punishments inflicted.

[Article IX]

The enumeration in the Constitution, of certain rights, shall not be construed to deny or disparage others retained by the people.

[Article X]

The powers not delegated to the United States by the Constitution, nor prohibited by it to the States, are reserved to the States respectively, or to the people. [Amendments I–X, in force 1791.]

[Article XI][8]

The Judicial power of the United States shall not be construed to extend to any suit in law or equity, commenced or prosecuted against one of the United States by Citizens of another State, or by Citizens or Subjects of any Foreign State.

[Article XII][9]

The Electors shall meet in their respective States and vote by ballot for President and Vice-President, one of whom, at least, shall not be an inhabitant of the same State with themselves; they shall name in their ballots the person voted for as President, and in distinct ballots the person voted for as Vice-President, and they shall make distinct lists of all persons voted for as President, and of all persons voted for as Vice-President, and of the number of votes for each, which lists they shall sign and certify, and transmit sealed to the seal of the government of the United States, directed to the President of the Senate;–The President of the Senate shall, in the presence of the Senate and House of Representatives, open all the certificates and the votes shall then be counted;–The person having the greatest number of votes for President, shall be the President, if such number be a majority of the whole number of Electors appointed; and if no person have such majority, then from the persons having the highest numbers not exceeding three on the list of those voted for as President, the House of Representatives shall choose immediately, by ballot, the President. But in choosing the President, the votes shall be taken by states, the representation from each state having one vote; a quorum for this purpose shall consist of a member or members from two-thirds of the states, and a majority of all the states shall be necessary to a choice. And if the House of Representatives shall not choose a President whenever the right of choice shall devolve upon them, before the fourth day of March next following, then the Vice-President shall act as President, as in the case of the death or other constitutional disability of the President.–The person having the greatest

---

[8]Adopted in 1798.
[9]Adopted in 1804.

number of votes as Vice-President, shall be the Vice-President, if such number be a majority of the whole number of Electors appointed, and if no person have a majority, then from the two highest numbers on the list, the Senate shall choose the Vice-President; a quorum for the purpose shall consist of two-thirds of the whole number of Senators, and a majority of the whole number shall be necessary to a choice. But no person constitutionally ineligible to the office of President shall be eligible to that of Vice-President of the United States.

[Article XIII][10]

SECTION 1.

Neither slavery nor involuntary servitude, except as a punishment for crime whereof the party shall have been duly convicted, shall exist within the United States, or any place subject to their jurisdiction.

SECTION 2.

Congress shall have power to enforce this article by appropriate legislation.

[Article XIV][11]

SECTION 1.

All persons born or naturalized in the United States, and subject to the jurisdiction thereof, are citizens of the United States and of the State wherein they reside. No State shall make or enforce any law which shall abridge the privileges or immunities of citizens of the United States; nor shall any State deprive any person of life, liberty, or property, without due process of law; nor deny to any person within its jurisdiction the equal protection of the laws.

SECTION 2.

Representatives shall be apportioned among the several States according to their respective numbers, counting the whole number of persons in each State, excluding Indians not taxed. But when the right to vote at any election for the choice of electors for President and Vice-President of the United States, Representatives in Congress, the Executive and Judicial officers of a State, or the members of the Legislature thereof, is denied to any of the male inhabitants of such State, being twenty-one years of age, and citizens of the United States, or in any way abridged, except for participation in rebellion, or other crime, the basis of representation therein shall be reduced in the proportion which the number of such male citizens shall bear to the whole number of male citizens twenty-one years of age in such State.

SECTION 3.

No person shall be a Senator or Representative in Congress, or elector of President and Vice-President, or hold any office, civil or military, under the United States, or under any State, who, having previously taken an oath, as a member of Congress, or

as an officer of the United States, or as a member of any State legislature, or as an executive or judicial officer of any State, to support the Constitution of the United States, shall have engaged in insurrection or rebellion against the same, or given aid or comfort to the enemies thereof. But Congress may by a vote of two-thirds of each House, remove such disability.

SECTION 4.

The validity of the public debt of the United States, authorized by law, including debts incurred for payment of pensions and bounties for services in suppressing insurrection or rebellion, shall not be questioned. But neither the United States nor any State shall assume or pay any debts or obligation incurred in aid of insurrection or rebellion against the United States, or any claim for the loss or emancipation of any slave; but all such debts, obligations, and claims shall be held illegal and void.

SECTION 5.

The Congress shall have the power to enforce, by appropriate legislation, the provisions of this article.

[Article XV][12]

SECTION 1.

The right of citizens of the United States to vote shall not be denied or abridged by the United States or by any State on account of race, color, or previous condition of servitude–

SECTION 2.

The Congress shall have power to enforce this article by appropriate legislation.

[Article XVI][13]

The Congress shall have power to lay and collect taxes on incomes, from whatever source derived, without apportionment among the several States, and without regard to any census or enumeration.

[Article XVII][14]

The Senate of the United States shall be composed of two Senators from each State, elected by the people thereof, for six years; and each Senator shall have one vote. The electors in each State shall have the qualifications requisite for electors of the most numerous branch of the State legislatures.

When vacancies happen in the representation of any State in the Senate, the executive authority of such State shall issue writs of election to fill such vacancies: *Provided*, That the legislature of any State may empower the executive thereof to make temporary appointments until the people fill the vacancies by election as the legislature may direct.

This amendment shall not be so constructed as to affect the election or term of any Senator chosen before it becomes valid as part of the Constitution.

---

[10]Adopted in 1865.

[11]Adopted in 1868.

[12]Adopted in 1870.

[13]Adopted in 1913.

[14]Adopted in 1913.

[Article XVIII][15]

SECTION 1.
After one year from the ratification of this article the manufacture, sale, or transportation of intoxicating liquors within, the importation thereof into, or the exportation thereof from the United States and all territory subject to the jurisdiction thereof for beverage purposes is hereby prohibited.

SECTION 2.
The Congress and the several States shall have concurrent power to enforce this article by appropriate legislation.

SECTION 3.
This article shall be inoperative unless it shall have been ratified as an amendment to the Constitution by the legislatures of the several States, as provided in the Constitution, within seven years from the date of the submission hereof to the States by the Congress.

[Article XIX][16]

The right of citizens of the United States to vote shall not be denied or abridged by the United States or by any State on account of sex.

Congress shall have power to enforce this article by appropriate legislation.

[Article XX][17]

SECTION 1.
The terms of the President and Vice-President shall end at noon on the 20th day of January, and the terms of Senators and Representatives at noon on the 3d day of January, of the years in which such terms would have ended if this article had not been ratified; and the terms of their successors shall then begin.

SECTION 2.
The Congress shall assemble at least once in every year, and such meeting shall begin at noon on the 3d day of January, unless they shall by law appoint a different day.

SECTION 3.
If, at the time fixed for the beginning of the term of the President, the President elect shall have died, the Vice-President elect shall become President. If a President shall not have been chosen before the time fixed for the beginning of his term or if the President elect shall have failed to qualify, then the Vice-President elect shall act as President until a President shall have qualified; and the Congress may by law provide for the case wherein neither a President elect nor a Vice-President elect shall have qualified, declaring who shall then act as President, or the manner in which one who is to act shall be selected, and such person shall act accordingly until a President or Vice-President shall have qualified.

SECTION 4.
The Congress may by law provide for the case of the death of any of the persons from whom the House of Representatives may choose a President whenever the right of choice shall have developed upon them, and for the case of the death of any of the persons from whom the Senate may choose a Vice-President whenever the right of choice shall have developed upon them.

SECTION 5.
Sections 1 and 2 shall take effect on the 15th day of October following the ratification of this article.

SECTION 6.
This article shall be inoperative unless it shall have been ratified as an amendment to the Constitution by the legislatures of three-fourths of the several States within seven years from the date of its submission.

[Article XXI][18]

SECTION 1.
The eighteenth article of amendment to the Constitution of the United States is hereby repealed.

SECTION 2.
The transportation or importation into any State, Territory, or possession of the United States for delivery or use therein of intoxicating liquors, in violation of the laws thereof, is hereby prohibited.

SECTION 3.
This article shall be inoperative unless it shall have been ratified as an amendment to the Constitution by conventions in the several States, as provided in the Constitution, within seven years from the date of the submission hereof to the States by the Congress.

[Article XXII][19]

No person shall be elected to the office of the President more than twice, and no person who has held the office of President, or acted as President, for more than two years of a term to which some other person was elected President shall be elected to the office of the President more than once.

But this Article shall not apply to any person holding the office of President when this Article was proposed by the Congress, and shall not prevent any person who may be holding the office of President, or acting as President, during the term within which this Article becomes operative from holding the office of President or acting as President during the remainder of such term.

This article shall be inoperative unless it shall have been ratified as an amendment to the Constitution by the legislatures of three-fourths of the several states within seven years from the date of its submission to the states by the Congress.

[15]Adopted in 1918.
[16]Adopted in 1920.
[17]Adopted in 1933.
[18]Adopted in 1933.
[19]Adopted in 1961.

[Article XXIII][20]

SECTION 1.

The District constituting the seat of Government of the United States shall appoint in such manner as the Congress may direct:

A number of electors of President and Vice-President equal to the whole number of Senators and Representatives in Congress to which the District would be entitled if it were a State, but in no event more than the least populous State; they shall be in addition to those appointed by the States, but they shall be considered, for the purposes of the election of President and Vice-President, to be electors appointed by a State; and they shall meet in the District and perform such duties as provided by the twelfth article of amendment.

SECTION 2.

The Congress shall have power to enforce this article by appropriate legislation.

[Article XXIV][21]

SECTION 1.

The right of citizens of the United States to vote in any primary or other election for President or Vice President, for electors for President or Vice President, or for Senator or Representative in Congress, shall not be denied or abridged by the United States or any state by reason of failure to pay any poll tax or other tax.

SECTION 2.

The Congress shall have the power to enforce this article by appropriate legislation.

[Article XXV][22]

SECTION 1.

In case of the removal of the President from office or of his death or resignation, the Vice President shall become President.

SECTION 2.

Whenever there is a vacancy in the office of the Vice President, the President shall nominate a Vice President who shall take office upon confirmation by a majority vote of both Houses of Congress.

SECTION 3.

Whenever the President transmits to the President Pro Tempore of the Senate and the Speaker of the House of Representatives his written declaration that he is unable to discharge the powers and duties of his office, and until he transmits to them a written declaration to the contrary, such powers and duties shall be discharged by the Vice President as Acting President.

SECTION 4.

Whenever the Vice President and a majority of either the principal officers of the executive departments or of such other body as Congress may by law provide, transmit to the President Pro Tempore of the Senate and the Speaker of the House of Representatives their written declaration that the President is unable to discharge the powers and duties of his office, the Vice President shall immediately assume the powers and duties of the office as Acting President.

Thereafter, when the President transmits to the President Pro Tempore of the Senate and the Speaker of the House of Representatives his written declaration that no inability exists, he shall resume the powers and duties of his office unless the Vice President and a majority of either the principal officers of the executive departments or of such other body as Congress may by law provide, transmit within four days to the President Pro Tempore of the Senate and the Speaker of the House of Representatives their written declaration that the President is unable to discharge the powers and duties of his office. Thereupon Congress shall decide the issue, assembling within forty-eight hours for that purpose if not in session. If the Congress, within twenty-one days after receipt of the latter written declaration, or, if Congress is not in session, within twenty-one days after Congress is required to assemble, determines by two-thirds vote of both Houses that the President is unable to discharge the powers and duties of his office, the Vice President shall continue to discharge the same as Acting President; otherwise, the President shall resume the powers and duties of his office.

[Article XXVI][23]

SECTION 1.

The right of citizens of the United States, who are eighteen years of age or older, to vote shall not be denied or abridged by the United States or by any State on account of age.

SECTION 2.

The Congress shall have power to enforce this article by appropriate legislation.

[Article XXVII][24]

No law varying the compensation for the services of Senators and Representatives shall take effect until an election of Representatives shall have intervened.

---

[20]Adopted in 1961.

[21]Adopted in 1964.

[22]Adopted in 1967.

[23]Adopted in 1971.

[24]Adopted in 1992.

AP GLOSSARY OF AP TERMINOLOGY

American republic This political term refers to the United States of America and the idea that it protects individual civil liberties as well as represents the people's will.

African chattel Africans and their descendants were forced to work for masters in the English colonies without political or economic freedoms. Alt: slaves

American System An early 19th century vision of an economically self-sufficient America that would see government funded internal improvements paid for with higher protective tariffs.

Anglicization English political, religious and economic traits would transfer to the New World through trans-Atlantic print culture and Protestant evangelism.

Antebellum A period in American history prior to the Civil War which generally falls between 1800-1860. Alt: early 19th century or first half of 19th century

Assimilation Foreign born immigrants acquire the cultural traits of a society they have migrated to through this process. Alt: Acculturation

Baby boom Following WWII (1945-1965) there was a very large increase in the number of children born in America.

Backcountry culture This frontier American culture combined aspects of both the Eastern seaboard society with the unique aspects of the wilderness.

British Empire By the turn of the 20th century the island of Great Britain and her vast colonial holdings stretched from North and South America to the Pacific ports of China

Bonded labor People, either voluntarily (indentured servants) or involuntarily (slaves), legally tied to working for another person.

Capitalism This economic system is marked by private ownership of factories and resources and is based on free trade and competition whose formal principles were laid down in Adam Smith's *Wealth of Nations* (1776).

Central government This supreme political institution is invested with more power than the smaller regional or state governments that fall under its jurisdiction. Alt: Federal government

Centralized power A concept that refers to one government gathering nearly complete economic and political authority over a society.

Cereal crops Corn, oats and wheat are these types of crops that are grown to feed communities. Alt: Staple crops

Civil War Amendments Added to the Constitution in the five years following the end of the Civil War, the 13th, 14th and 15th amendments gave liberty, "equal protection" under the law and voting rights to the newly freed slaves.

Collective security This concept refers to several countries joining together in a defensive alliance for mutual protection against perceived enemies.

Colonial elites These wealthy individuals tended to be large plantation owners, merchants or shippers.

Colonization The process by which European powers settled their people in the western hemisphere during the 16th and 17th centuries and transplanted their economic, political and cultural features.

Columbian Exchange Plants, animals and material goods were transferred between the Western and Eastern Hemispheres because of the discovery of the New World by Christopher Columbus in 1492.

Conservatism A smaller federal government, low taxes, reduction of government funded social programs, a less regulated capitalist society and an adherence to traditional social mores define the general beliefs of this political philosophy.

Demographic This refers to the characteristics of population patterns and or changes.

Democratic Republicans This political party born in the 1790's followed the beliefs of Thomas Jefferson which included strict interpretation of the United States Constitution and a limited central government. Alt: Jeffersonians

Democrats Generally used in reference to a 20th century political party, this political group believes in broadening the powers of the federal government to regulate business and provide enlarged social programs for the underprivileged.

Détente, mutual coexistence During this period of relaxed tension between the United States and the Soviet Union in the early 1970's, the Cold War saw a reduction of armaments in the SALT I and ABM Treaties.

Encomienda system During Spanish colonization of the 16th and 17th century, Spain established this plantation-based agriculture system which included forced labor extracted from Native-Americans and later enslaved Africans. Alt: plantations

Enlightenment An intellectual movement that utilized human reason to question commonly accepted beliefs in political and religious practices of the late 17th and 18th century period.

European expansion, imperialism In the second half of the 19th century, European countries took economic and political control over foreign lands in Africa, Asia and the Middle East.

European Romanticism Emphasizing the emotional and intuitive over the rational, this intellectual movement of the early 19th century rejected many precepts of the Enlightenment.

Evangelism This religious concept refers to the spreading of a religious faith through proselytizing by its adherents and generally saw a surge during periods of religious revivalism such as the two Great Awakenings of the 18th and 19th centuries.

Federalism This principle embedded in the United States Constitution outlines the division of power between the state governments and the federal government.

Federalists These proponents of the ratification of the United States Constitution supported a stronger central government over state sovereignty in the late 18th century.

Feudalism Under this economic and cultural arrangement the mass of European population (serfs) exchanged their labor and service for protection provided by the nobles.

Free trade agreement An economic pact that reduces tariffs and economic restrictions between countries and is intended to stimulate economic activity; with the most notable attempt being the North American Free Trade Agreement (NAFTA).

Globalization, economic This growing network of international businesses has interests in many countries and is uniting the worldwide economy.

Great Society Lyndon Johnson's domestic social reform program, known as "The Great Society," featured the passage of Medicare and Medicaid and the addition of a new cabinet agency called the Department of Housing and Urban Development (HUD).

Hereditary privilege This cultural and legal system involves the passing down of property and social standing to one's heirs and thus enables wealthy families to maintain their social supremacy for generations.

Hierarchy Operating as a social class system, it artificially ranks people according to their economic and social standing.

Hispanics This contemporary term denotes someone from Central America with mixed Spanish and indigenous ancestry.

Holding companies These companies exist solely on paper and control the majority of stock in an actual company.

Homogeneous society A society, such as the Puritans of the 17th century, that enforces religious, cultural or racial conformity upon its inhabitants.

Ideology These beliefs or values define a person or a society.

Imperialism expansion of A mid-19th century movement by European countries designed to take over foreign lands for economic resources and markets.

Indentured servants Europeans who contracted out their labor for up to seven years in return for paid passage across the Atlantic to the New World.

Indian People native (indigenous) to North America prior to the arrival of the Europeans in the 16th century. Alt: American Indian, Native American

Intellectual This term tends to be used in regards to history that is conceptual or philosophical in its orientation. Alt: intellectual history

Intermarriage In reference to the mixing of two different ethnic groups through marriage, this term is generally used in reference to the relationships that developed between the Native-Americans and European groups during the colonization period. Alt: miscegenation

Laissez-faire This term refers to the economic concept in which the government does little to regulate big business or in other words keeps its "hands off" of businesses and is usually used in reference to the late 19th century industrialization period.

Latinos From Latin America (Central and South America), these people are linguistically connected (Spanish-speaking) and they are the largest growing minority group in contemporary America.

The Left In reference to the left side of the political spectrum, proponents support a more activist government that works to safeguard consumers against business abuses and provide social programs for the underprivileged.

Liberalism This economic-political ideology promotes more government involvement in the economy to correct social and economic inequalities.

Loyalist This person supported the king and Parliament during the American Revolution.

Maize cultivation Introduced to the Europeans by the Native-American peoples, this agricultural crop was the main staple crop that sustained both societies. Alt: corn

Market economy During the antebellum period, the agricultural interior of the United States (Ohio River Valley) was able to connect to the Northeast through transportation improvements, thus enabling the industrial north to sell its manufactured goods while receiving the raw materials of the Great Lakes Region.

Mercantilism A trade system between a mother country (European nation) and her colonies that uses the colonies both as a source of raw materials and as a market for manufactured goods.

Mexican-Americans Second generation Americans that emigrated from Mexico.

Middle class Based on socio-economic standing, people in this group have annual incomes that are above the poverty line which allows them have disposable income.

Military-industrial complex Businesses that manufacture armaments (planes, guns, ships, etc.) for the US military. Alt: defense industry

Mission settlements As the Spanish settled northward into North America in the 16th century they established Catholic churches (missions) which became the cultural and economic centers for the indigenous people.

Nationalism This cultural belief professes that one's own country is superior to other countries economically, culturally and/or politically. Alt: patriotism

Nativism A belief that a country should be composed of only original settlers (inhabitants) and should restrict emigration by foreigners.

Neoconservatism The resurgence of former conservative ideals following the implementation of the Great Society in the 1960's.

New World This 16th century European concept refers to the newly discovered lands to the west of Europe and across the Atlantic Ocean. Alt: Western Hemisphere

Nullification An antebellum belief that a state had the power to void a federal law if it was deemed oppressive.

Old World This is a reference to Europe and the Mediterranean regions following Columbus' voyage. Alt: Eastern Hemisphere

Partisan A person that supports a specific political ideology and works to actively advance it. Alt: party activist

Patriot A supporter of the independence of the American colonies from Great Britain during the American Revolution.

Peopling This geographic term refers to the movement of people to a particular area, region or country. Alt: Emigration or population shift

Plantation This large Southern farm during the pre-Civil War period employed slaves and grew cash crops such as cotton or tobacco.

Political machines A group of government officials associated with one party or political faction that control the government and who tend to rule in such a way as to favor themselves and their political benefactors.

Pueblo Revolt This 1680 revolt by Indians of the Southwestern part of the contemporary United States successfully removed Spanish control for twelve years.

Republican Party This political party born in the 1850's supports government encouragement of business growth through tax breaks or subsidies and a more conservative ideology in reference to maintaining the status quo.

Republicanism This ideology professes that a government's power is based upon the people's will and that the people's civil liberties should be protected.

The Right In reference to the right side of the political spectrum, proponents support a more limited government role in people's lives to protect individual liberties.

Second party system A political system which arose in the Jacksonian era that entails, it involves two partisan groups competing for the electorate's vote through campaigning for political office.

Shared labor market This concept refers to the sharing of labor between eastern and western hemispheres during the colonial period.

Segregation This cultural and legal term means the separation of public places and schools based on race.

Semisubsistence agriculture In the frontier regions due to terrain or climate the ability to farm was very limited and thus a farmer needed to hunt and gather as well as farm in order to survive.

Settlement houses These privately run organizations in the late 19th and early 20th century operated in urban areas and assisted immigrants with assimilating into the new world by providing education, housing and other vital services. Alt: Hull House Movement

Social justice This cultural belief states that lower socio-economic classes deserve equality in economic, political and social areas.

Social mobility Lower socio-economic groups have the opportunity to move upward in the social class structure.

Social safety net Government programs that aid the poor, indigent, elderly and disabled.

Staple crops Corn, oats and wheat are these types of crops that are grown to feed communities. Alt: Foodstuffs

States' rights These are state powers invested in a state according to the US Constitution and implied in the 10th amendment.

Tariff This is a tax imposed on foreign goods entering a country.

Trusts Usually associated with businesses during the Gilded Age and early 20th century, this term refers to large corporations that monopolize an industry Alt: business oligarchies

Utopianism The belief that society can be perfected and that through the correct application of political, religious or humanitarian precepts human misery can be eradicated.

Whigs A political party born in the 1830's in opposition to Andrew Jackson, it supported a stronger national government as proposed in the American System.

Worldview These perspectives reflect a person's ideas and beliefs concerning people and places that lie outside of their day-to-day lives.

Xenophobia Fear that a foreigner's beliefs or cultural values (communism, anarchy, Catholicism, etc.) will undermine and destroy the traditional fabric of the American society.

Geographic Terms

Asia Traditionally this region includes those countries that touch the Pacific Ocean on the east, the Indian Ocean to the south and the Arctic Ocean to the north and blends into Europe at the eastern edge of the Mediterranean Ocean.

Atlantic Seaboard Stretching from the southern tip of Newfoundland to the Florida Peninsula this geographic term tends to be used during the colonial period and would encompass New England, Middle and upper Southern colonies.

Atlantic World A reference to the African, European and American societies that border the Atlantic Ocean. This body of water touches the shores of Africa, Europe, North and South America.

Backcountry In U.S. history courses, this area is most commonly associated with western frontier Virginia and the Carolinas during the colonial era and the early republic; the focus is usually on conflict with the small-hold farmers of those areas and the coastal elite (i.e. Bacon's rebellion).

Caribbean Situated east of Central America, this area is composed of hundreds of islands from Cuba to the Bahamas that lie between North and South America and which is the land that the Spanish originally inhabited. Alt: West Indies

Central America The panhandle of North America, this geographic region refers to the isthmian countries South of Mexico and north of Columbia.

Great Basin This geographic region stretches between the Rocky Mountains on the eastern border to the Cascade and Sierra Nevada Mountains on the western side.

Great Plains Stretching between the Mississippi River and the Rocky Mountains these flat grasslands are composed of prairies and steppes.

Interior regions Generally used during the colonial period, this geographic terms refers to the middle part of contemporary United States east of the Mississippi River that ranges from the Great Lakes Region in the north to Louisiana.

Latin America This cultural term refers to the countries that stretch from Mexico to the Straits of Magellan.

Lower South This term is used in reference to the seven most southern states that seceded before Fort Sumter was fired upon in April of 1861.

Middle East Centered on the Arabian peninsula, this geographic region is bordered on the north by Turkey, the east by Afghanistan, the south by Yemen and the west by Egypt.

Midwest This region is composed of the twelve states that lie between North Dakota, Ohio and Kansas.

Northeast This region is composed of the nine states between Pennsylvania and Maine.

Northwest Territory South of the Great Lakes, east of the Mississippi and north of the Ohio River this area was the first area to see westward migration in order to find cheap farmland. The settlement of this area in the early 19th century led to the Market Revolution.

Old Northwest This region lies between the Great Lakes in the north, the Ohio River in the south and the Mississippi River on the west. Alt: Northwest Territory

The Pacific This historical term refers to the islands and archipelagos that stretch between China on the west to California on the east.

The Philippines Consisting of thousands of islands, this Southeast Asian country was taken over by the United States during the Spanish-American War.

Sun Belt Stretching from Virginia to Arizona, this southern region of the United States saw a tremendous growth in population following World War II because of its low tax rate, the invention of air-conditioning, and business-friendly environment.

Tidewater This most commonly refers to coastal areas of Virginia. In U.S. history it is often described as being wealthier, more established and more politically powerful than the backcountry areas (i.e. Bacon's rebellion).

Trans-Appalachian West Generally referred to as the lands west of the Appalachian Mountains which would include the Ohio River Valley and the lands of Kentucky during the late 18th and early 19th century.

Upper South Distinguished for its lower slave percentages than its southern brethren, this region was composed of those states that bordered northern states (Kentucky, Virginia, Delaware, Maryland)

West Indies Those islands that the Spanish, French and English colonized in the 15th and 16th century whose principal cash crop was sugar.

Western Hemisphere North and South America combined.

Terms with Multiple Labels

American Indian also known as Native American

American Revolution also known as Colonial War for Independence, War of Independence, The Revolutionary War

Central government also known as national government

Centralized power also known as federal power

Seven Years' War also known as the French and Indian War

Understanding Dates

Fifteenth century (15th century): 1400–1499

Sixteenth century (16th century): 1500–1599

Seventeenth century (17th century): 1600–1699

Eighteenth century (18th century): 1700–1799

Nineteenth century (19th century): 1800–1899

Twentieth century (20th century): 1900–1999

Twenty-first century (21st century): 2000–2099

FOR FURTHER READING

Chapter 1

Alvin M. Josephy, ed., *America in 1492: The World of the Indian Peoples Before the Arrival of Columbus* (1993) Brian M. Fagan, *The Great Journey: The Peopling of Ancient America* (1987) Annette Kolodny, *In Search of First Contact: The Vikings of Vinland, the Peoples of the Dawnland, and the Anglo-American Anxiety of Discovery* (2012), discusses the first known European literary narratives about contact with North America provide introductions to pre-Columbian history, as does Charles Mann, *1491: New Revelations of the Americas Before Columbus* (2005). William M. Denevan, ed., *The Native Population of the Americas in 1492* (1976) and Russell Thornton, *American Indian Holocaust and Survival: A Population History Since 1492* (1987) are important contributions to the debate over the size and character of the American population before Columbus. Alfred Crosby, *The Columbian Exchange: Biological and Cultural Consequences of 1492* (1972) explores the results of European-Indian contact in both the Americas and Europe. Gary Nash, *Red, White and Black: The Peoples of Early America* (1982) provides a brief, multiracial survey of colonial America. Philip Curtin, *The Atlantic Slave Trade: A Census* (1969) has become the indispensable starting point for understanding African forced migration to the Americas. John Thornton, *Africa and Africans in the Making of the Atlantic World* (1998) examines the impact of slavery and the slave trade on the entire Atlantic world from the fifteenth through the eighteenth centuries. *Columbus and the Age of Discovery* (1991) is a seven-part documentary film series on Christopher Columbus, his era, and his legacy.

Chapter 2

William Cronon, *Changes in the Land: Indians, Colonists, and the Ecology of New England* (1983) examines the social and environmental effects of English settlement in colonial America. Richard White, *The Middle Ground: Indians, Empires, and Republics in the Great Lakes Region, 1650-1815* (1991) is an important study of the accommodations that Indians and early European settlers made in the continental interior. Ann Kurt Keating, *Rising Up from the Indian Country: The Battle of Fort Dearborn and the Birth of Chicago* (2012), portrays the crucial period between 1795 and 1833 when Native Americans and white people interacted with violence and mutual reliance, resulting in the birth of Chicago. James H. Merrell, *The Indians' New World* (1991) and *Into the American Woods: Negotiators on the Pennsylvania Frontier* (1999) are among the best examinations of the impact of European settlement on eastern tribes. Nan Goodman, *Banished: Common Law and the Rhetoric of Social Exclusion in Early New England* (2012), analyzes the use of banishment by puritans as a means of social control by people who were themselves exiles. Nathaniel Philbrick, *Mayflower, A Story of Community, Courage, and War* (2006) is a vivid story of the Plymouth migration. Perry Miller, *The New England Mind: From Colony to Province* (1953) is a classic exposition of the Puritan intellectual milieu. David Hall, *Worlds of Wonder, Days of Judgment* (1990) is a good counterpoint to Miller. Ronald

Story, *Jonathan Edwards and the Gospel of Love* (2012) presents this puritan preacher as a profoundly social minister who preached a gospel of charity and community bound by love. Russell Shorto, *The Island at the Center of the World* (2003) is a portrait of Dutch Manhattan. Evan Haefeli, *New Netherland and the Dutch Origins of American Religious Liberty* (2012), offers a new reading of the way tolerance operated in colonial America. Edmund Morgan, *American Slavery, American Freedom* (1975) is a compelling narrative of political and social development in early Virginia. Richard S. Dunn, *Sugar and Slaves: The Rise of the Planter Class in the English West Indies, 1624-1713* (1972) is important for understanding the origins of British colonial slavery. David J. Weber, *The Spanish Frontier in North America* (1992) and James C. Brooks, *Captains and Cousins: Slavery, Kinship, and Community in the Southwest Borderlands* (2002) examine the northern peripheries of the Spanish Empire.

Chapter 3

Edward Countryman, *Americans: A Collision of Histories* (1996) includes a vivid picture of the many cultures that encountered one another in early America. Bernard Bailyn, *Voyagers to the West: A Passage in the Peopling of America on the Eve of the Revolution* (1986) reveals the complexity and scope of European emigration to North America. Bailyn's *The Origin of American Politics* (1968) is an introduction to colonial politics. Bernard Bailyn, *The Barbarous years: The Peopling of British North America* (2012) explores the first great transit of people from Britain, Europe and Africa to British North America. David Hackett Fischer, *Albion's Seed* (1989) suggests four major folkways for English migrants to America. Ira Berlin, *Many Thousands Gone: The First Two Centuries of Slavery in North America* (1998), Philip Morgan, *Slave Counterpoint: Black Culture in the Eighteenth-Century Chesapeake and Lowcountry* (1998). Robin Blackburn, *The Making of New World Slavery: From the Baroque to the Modern, 1492-1800* (1997) includes an important examination of the character of the institution in colonial America. Kathleen M. Brown, *Good Wives, Nasty Wenches, and Anxious Patriarchs: Gender, Race and Power in Colonial Virginia* (1996) places gender at the center of the development of slavery in the Chesapeake.

Chapter 4

Fred Anderson, *The Crucible of War: The Seven Years' War and the Fate of Empire in British North America, 1754-1766* (2000) is an account of the critical years in which the British Empire transformed itself through its colonial wars in America. David Armitage, *The Ideological Origins of the British Empire* (2000) examines the ideas of those who promoted and sought to justify Britain's imperial ambitions. Richard Bushman, *King and People in Colonial Massachusetts* (1987) traces the fracture between Massachusetts colonists and the imperial government. T. H. Breen, *The Marketplace of Revolution* (2004) argues that consumer politics played a major role in creating the Revolution. Jon Butler, *Becoming America: The Revolution Before*

1776 (2000) argues for the emergence of a distinctive American culture in the eighteenth century. Bernard Bailyn, *The Ideological Origins of the American Revolution* (1967) emphasizes the importance of English republican political thought for the revolutionary ideology of the American colonists.

Chapter 5

Robert Middlekauf, The Glorious Cause: The American Revolution, 1763–1789 (1985), a volume in the Oxford History of the United States, is a thorough, general history of the Revolution. Gordon Wood, *The Radicalism of the American Revolution* (1992) emphasizes the profound political change that the Revolution produced. David Hackett Fisher, *Washington's Crossing* (2004) uses this famous event to illuminate the meaning of the Revolution. Robert Gross, *The Minutemen and Their World* (1976) is an excellent social history of Revolutionary Concord. Mary Beth Norton, *Liberty's Daughters: The Revolutionary Experience of American Women, 1750–1800* (1980) demonstrates that the Revolution had a significant impact on the lives of American women as well. Eric Foner, *Tom Paine and Revolutionary America* (1976) connects the leading pamphleteer of the Revolution with urban radicalism in Philadelphia. Pauline Maier, *American Scripture* (1997) is a penetrating study of the making of the Declaration of Independence. Colin Calloway, *The American Revolution in Indian Country* (1995) is a study of an often-neglected aspect of the war. Alan Taylor, *The Divided Ground: Indians, Settlers, and the Northern Borderlands of the American Revolution* (2006) describes how the Iroquois nations tried to navigate the war to their advantage.

Chapter 6

Gordon Wood, *The Creation of the American Republic* (1969) is the leading analysis of the intellectual path from the Declaration of Independence to the American Constitution. Wood is also the author of *The Radicalism of the American Revolution* (1991) and *Empire of Liberty: A History of the Early Republic, 1789–1815* (2009). Stanley Elkins and Eric McKitrick, *The Age of Federalism* (1993) provides a detailed overview of political and economic development in the 1790s. Joyce Appleby, *Capitalism and a New Social Order: The Republican Vision of the 1790s* (1984) highlights liberal and capitalist impulses unleashed after the ratification of the Constitution. Joseph Ellis is the author of several books on the founders: *After the Revolution: Profiles of Early American Culture* (1979), which examines some of the framers of the new nation; *American Sphinx: The Character of Thomas Jefferson* (1997); Brian Steele, *Thomas Jefferson and the American Nationhood* (2012), emphasizes the centrality of nationhood to Thomas Jefferson's thought and politics. *Founding Brothers: The Revolutionary Generation* (2000); *Passionate Sage: The Character and Legacy of John Adams* (1993); and *American Creation* (2007), a portrait of the nation from Independence to the Louisiana Purchase. Ron Chernow, *Alexander Hamilton* (2004) and *George Washington* (2010) and Edmund Morgan, *Benjamin Franklin* (2002) are biographies of the founders.

Chapter 7

Joseph J. Ellis, *American Sphinx: The Character of Thomas Jefferson* (1997) is a perceptive study of the man, and his *After the Revolution: Profiles of Early American Culture* (2002) offers portraits of some of his allies and opponents. Henry Adams, *History of the United States During the Administration of Jefferson and Adams*, 9 vols. (1889–1891) is one of the great literary achievements of early American historiography. Frank Bergon, ed., *The Journals of Lewis and Clark* (1989) is a concise abridgment of these fascinating accounts of their explorations. James Ronda, *Lewis and Clark among the Indians* (1984) examines the exploration from a Native American perspective. Jeanne Boydston, *Home and Work: Housework, Wages, and the Ideology of Labor in the Early Republic* (1990) argues that the cultural status of women declined as the market revolution began to transform the American economy. Drew McCoy, *The Elusive Republic: Political Economy in Jeffersonian America* (1980) traces the Jeffersonian struggle to keep the United States free from European-style corruption and decay. Gary Wills, *James Madison* (2002) is an interpretive essay on this important early president. J. C. A. Stagg, *Mr. Madison's War: Politics, Diplomacy, and Warfare in the Early American Republic, 1783–1830* (1983) argues that James Madison led the United States to war against Great Britain in order to preserve vital American commercial interests, but that he underestimated New England opposition to the war.

Chapter 8

Daniel Walker Howe, *What Hath God Wrought: The Transformation of America, 1815–1848* (2007) is a study of the period following the War of 1812. Sean Wilentz, *The Rise of American Democracy: Jefferson to Lincoln* (2005) is a history of the rise of a "democratic creed" in early America. Frederick Jackson Turner, *The Frontier in American History* (1920) is the classic statement of American exceptionalism. John Mack Faragher, *Women and Men on the Overland Trail* (1979) was an early and influential book in the "new western history." Robert V. Remini, *Andrew Jackson and the Course of American Empire: 1767–1821* (1977) emphasizes Andrew Jackson's importance in American territorial expansion in the South prior to 1821 and in the development of American nationalism. Ernest R. May, *The Making of the Monroe Doctrine* (1975) presents the history of a leading principle of American foreign policy.

Chapter 9

Daniel Walker Howe, *What Hath God Wrought: The Transformation of America, 1815–1848* (2007) and Sean Wilentz, *The Rise of American Democracy: From Jefferson to Lincoln* (2005) are two important, broad studies. Arthur M. Schlesinger Jr., *The Age of Jackson* (1945), a classic study, represents Jacksonian politics as an eastern, urban democratic movement of working men and upper-class intellectuals. Bray Hammond, *Banks and Politics in America from the Revolution to the Civil War* (1957) challenges Schlesinger by arguing that the Bank War was essentially a struggle between different groups of capitalist elites.

Harry L. Watson, *Liberty and Power: The Politics of Jacksonian America* (1990) provides an important newer synthesis of Jacksonian politics. Richard Hofstadter, *The Idea of a Party System: The Rise of Legitimate Opposition in the United States, 1740-1840* (1969) traces the growing acceptance of the idea of partisan competition. William V. Freehling, *Prelude to Civil War: The Nullification Controversy in South Carolina* (1966) argues that South Carolina planters' anxiety over the fate of slavery was at the heart of the nullification crisis. Michael Rogin, *Fathers and Children: Andrew Jackson and the Destruction of American Indians* (1975) offers a more radical and idiosyncratic perspective on Jackson's career as an Indian fighter using the methods of psychoanalysis. Sean Wilentz, *Chants Democratic: New York City and the Rise of the American Working Class, 1788-1850* (1984) is an important study of the working-class during the Jacksonian period.

Chapter 10

Charles G. Sellers, *The Market Revolution: Jacksonian America, 1815-1846* (1991) demonstrates the overwhelming impact of the market revolution on American social and political development. Peter Bernstein, *The Wedding of the Waters* (2005) is an account of the creation of the Erie Canal. Christopher Clark, *The Roots of Rural Capitalism; Western Massachusetts, 1780-1860* (1990) is an examination of the impact of emerging capitalism on a rural area. David Hochfelder, *The Telegraph in America, 2832-1920* (2012), shows how the telegraph set the stage for today's information age. Paul Johnson, *A Shopkeeper's Millennium: Society and Revivals in Rochester, New York, 1815-1837* (1978) explores the changing character of class relations in upstate New York. Alice Kessler-Harris, *Out to Work: A History of Wage-Earning Women in the United States* (1982) is a broad history of women in the wage labor force. Thomas Dublin, *Transforming Women's Work: New England Lives in the Industrial Revolution* (1994) looks particularly at the mill towns of the Northeast. Christine Stansell, *City of Women: Sex and Class in New York, 1789-1860* (1983) explores the female world of antebellum New York City. Alan Taylor, *William Cooper's Town: Power and Persuasion on the Frontier in the Early American Republic* (1995) examines the early years of Cooperstown, New York, and the impact on it of the rise of the market and of democratic politics.

Chapter 11

Peter Kolchin, *American Slavery, 1619-1877* (1993) is a synthesis of the history of slavery in the United States from the settlement of Virginia through Reconstruction. Ira Berlin, *Many Thousands Gone* (2000) and *Generations of Captivity* (2003) are other histories of slavery. Walter Johnson, *Soul by Soul: Life Inside the Antebellum Slave Market* (2001) examines the slave trade. James Oakes, *Slavery and Freedom* (1990) provides an overview of southern politics and society in the antebellum period. Eugene Genovese's classic study, *Roll, Jordan, Roll: The World the Slaves Made* (1974) argues that masters and slaves forged a system of mutual obligations within a coercive social

system Genovese's *The Political Economy of Slavery* (1965) argues that slavery blocked southern economic development. James Oakes, *The Ruling Race: A History of American Slaveholders* (1982) argues that slaveowners were hardheaded businessmen and capitalists. Frederick Douglass's *Narrative of the Life of Frederick Douglass*, first published in 1845, is a classic autobiography. Elizabeth Fox-Genovese, *Within the Plantation Household* (1988) argues against the idea that black and white women shared a community of interests on southern plantations. Adam Rothman, *Slave Country* (2007) examines the expansion of the South, and of slavery within it. Charles C. Bolton, *Poor Whites of the Antebellum South: Tenants and Laborers in Central North and Northeast Mississippi* (1994) and Stephanic McCurry, *Masters of Small Worlds: Yeoman Households, Gender Relations, and the Political Culture of the Antebellum South Carolina Low Country* (1997) are good studies of neglected groups in the southern population. Steven Hahn, *The Roots of Southern Populism: Yeoman Farmers and the Transformation of the Georgia Upcountry, 1850-1890* (1983) argues that white farmers in upcountry regions of the antebellum South maintained economically self-sufficient communities on the periphery of the market.

Chapter 12

Steven Mintz, *Moralists and Moralizers: America's Pre-Civil War Reformers* (1995) and Ronald G. Walters, *American Reformers, 1815-1860* (1978) are overviews. David Reynolds, *Walt Whitman's America* (1995) is both a cultural biography of Whitman and an evocation of the society Whitman celebrated. Nancy F. Cott, *The Bonds of Womanhood: "Woman's Sphere" in New England, 1780-1835* (1977) argues that nineteenth-century feminism emerged from the separation of home and work in the early nineteenth-century. David Brion Davis, *The Problem of Slavery in the Age of Revolution, 1770-1823* (1975) is an influential study of the rise of antislavery sentiment in the Western world. Ronald G. Walters, *The Antislavery Appeal: American Abolitionists After 1830* (1976) emphasizes the religious motivations of antebellum abolitionism.

Chapter 13

Richard White, *It's Your Misfortune and None of My Own: A History of the American West* (1991) is a presentation of the social and economic history of the region. Anders Stephanson, *Manifest Destiny* (1995) briefly traces the origins of American expansion ideology. Ari Kelman, *A Misplaced Massacre: Struggling over the Memory of Sand Creek* (2013), probes the intersection of history and memory to explain the ways differing groups of Americans come to know a shared past. Paul D. Lack, *The Texas Revolutionary Experience: A Political and Social History, 1835-1836* (1992) chronicles Texas's route to independence from Mexico. Susan Lee Johnson, *Roaring Camp: The Social World of the Gold Rush* (2000) examines the experiences of men and women involved in the frenzy. William W. Freehling, *The Road to Disunion, Vol. 1: Secessionists at Bay, 1776-1854* (1990) and *Vol. 2: Secessionists Triumphant, 1854-1861*

(2007) explore the successful containment of sectionalism prior to the 1850s. David Potter, *The Impending Crisis, 1848-1861* (1976) is a thorough summary of a turbulent decade. Eric Foner, *Free Soil, Free Labor, Free Men* (1970) traces the emergence of the Republican Party. Michael Holt, *The Political Crisis of the 1850s* (1978) challenges Foner by emphasizing ethnic and religious alignment in northern politics. Manisha Sinha, *The Counterrevolution of Slavery* (2000) argues that South Carolina's apparently radical drive for secession was in fact a highly conservative effort in defense of slavery.

Chapter 14

James McPherson, *Battle Cry of Freedom* (1988) is a history of the Civil War. David Donald, *Lincoln* (1995) is a biography of the sixteenth president. James M. McPherson, *Abraham Lincoln and the Second American Revolution* (1990) offers reflections on the life and significance of Lincoln. Eric Foner, *The Fiery Trial* (2010) is a history of Lincoln and slavery. Doris Kearns Goodwin, *Team of Rivals* (2005) examines Lincoln's diverse and sometimes fractious Cabinet. John Burt, *Lincoln's Tragic Pragmatism: Lincoln, Douglas, and Moral Conflict* (2013), asks and analyzes the question: Can a liberal political system be used to mediate moral disputes? William McFeely, *Grant* (1981) are the leading biographies of the two most important Civil War generals. Iver Bernstein, *The New York City Draft Riots* (1990) examines an important event away from the battlefield. Jennifer L. Weber, *Copperheads* (2006) examines Northern opponents of the Civil War. Emory Thomas, *The Confederate Nation* (1979) is a one-volume history of the Confederacy. Drew Gilpin Faust is the author of *Mothers of Invention* (1996), which examines the lives of elite Southern women during the war, and *The Republic of Suffering: Death and the American Civil War* (2008). Ira Berlin et al., eds., *Free at last: A Documentary History of Slavery, Freedom and the Civil War* (1992) is a superb compilation of primary sources from slaves and slaveowners relating to the demise of slavery during the Civil War years. Ira Berlin et al., *Slaves No More: Three Essays on Emancipation and the Civil War* (1992), the companion volume to the documents in *Free at Last*, argues that slaves and freedmen played an active role in destroying slavery and redefining freedom. Edward L. Ayres, *In the Presence of Mine Enemies: War in the Heart of America* (2003) is a social history of two neighboring communities—one in the Union, the other in the Confederacy—at war. William Freehling, *The South vs. the South* (2001) notes the important role of pro-Union Southerners in determining the outcome of the war.

Chapter 15

Eric Foner, *Reconstruction: America's Unfinished Revolution, 1863-1877* (1988), a modern synthesis of Reconstruction scholarship, emphasizes the radicalism of Reconstruction and the role of freed people in the process of political and economic renovation. C. Vann Woodward, *Origins of the New South* (1951) is a classic work on the history of the South after Reconstruction and argues that a rising middle class defined the economic and political transformation of the New South. Nicholas Lemann, *Redemption: The Last Battle of the Civil War* (2006) reveals the determination of white southerners to regain control of their society. Edward Ayers, *The Promise of the New South* (1992) offers a portrait of social and cultural life in the New South. Leon Litwack, *Been in the Storm So Long: The Aftermath of Slavery* (1979) is a study of the experiences of freed slaves. Steven Hahn, *A Nation Under Our Feet: Black Political Struggles in the Rural South from Slavery to the Great Migration* (2003) is a wide-ranging history. C. Vann Woodward, *The Strange Career of Jim Crow* (rev. 1974) claims that segregation emerged only gradually across the South after Reconstruction. The "Woodward Thesis" has been challenged by, among others, Joel Williamson, *After Slavery: The Negro in South Carolina During Reconstruction* (1965); John W. Cell, *The Highest Stage of White Supremacy: The Origins of Segregation in South Africa and the American South* (1982); and Howard N. Rabinowitz, *Race Relations in the Urban South, 1865-1890* (1978).

Chapter 16

Frederick Jackson Turner's *The Frontier in American History* (1920) is a classic argument on the centrality of the frontier experience to American democracy. Patricia Nelson Limerick's *The Legacy of Conquest: The Unbroken Past of the American West* (1987) argues that the West was not a frontier but rather an inhabited place conquered by Anglo-Americans. Richard White. *"It's Your Misfortune and None of My Own": A History of the American West* (1991) is a general history of the region that revises many myths about the West. Jean Pfaelzer, *Driven Out: The Forgotten War Against Chinese Americans* (2007) illustrates anti-Chinese sentiment. John Mack Faragher, *Women and Men on the Overland Trail* (1979) examines the social experience of westering migrants, and Peggy Pascoe, *Relations of Rescue: The Search for Female Authority in the American West, 1874-1939* (1990) describes the female communities of the West. William Cronon, *Nature's Metropolis and the Great West* (1991) describes the relationships among economies and environments in the West. Robert Wooster, *The Military and United States Indian Policy, 1865-1902* (1988) and Sally Denton, *American Massacre: The Tragedy at Mountain Meadows, September 1857* (2003) examine the military campaigns against the Indians in the nineteenth century. Frederick E. Hoxie, *A Final Promise: The Campaign to Assimilate the Indians, 1880-1920* (1984) examines U.S. policies toward Native Americans. Richard Slotkin, *The Fatal Environment: The Myth of the Frontier in the Age of Industrialization* (1985) and *Gunfighter Nation* (1992) are provocative cultural studies of the idea of the West. Rebecca Solnit, *River of Shadows: Edward Muybridge and the Technological Wild West* (2003) considers the impact of photography on images of the West.

Chapter 17

Robert Wiebe's *The Search for Order, 1877-1920* (1968) is an analysis of America's evolution from a society to a national urban society. David Nasaw, *Andrew Carnegie* (2006) is a biography a famous industrial tycoon. Alfred D. Chandler Jr. describes the new business practices that made industrialization possible in *The Visible Hand: The Managerial Revolution in American Business* (1977) and *Scale and Scope: The Dynamics of Industrial Capitalism* (1990). Olivier Zunz analyzes the social underpinnings of the new corporate order in *Making America Corporate, 1870–1920* (1990) and *Why the American Century?* (1998). Daniel Rodgers, *The Work Ethic in Industrial America, 1850–1920* (1978) is an intellectual history of the way Americans viewed industrial workers. David Montgomery, *The Fall of the House of Labor: The Workplace, the State, and American Labor Activism, 1865–1925* (1987) analyzes the way industrialization shaped the workers. Alice Kessler-Harris documents the tremendous movement of women into the workforce in the period in *Out of Work: A History of Wage-Earning Women in the United States* (1982). John L. Thomas, *Alternative America: Henry George, Edward Bellamy, Henry Demarest Lloyd, and the Adversary Tradition* (1983) examines some important critics of corporate capitalism.

Chapter 18

John Bodnar provides a synthetic history of immigration in *The Transplanted: A History of Immigrants in America* (1985). The new urban mass culture of America's cities is the subject of William Leach, *Land of Desire: Merchants, Power, and the Rise of a New American Culture* (1993), and Kathy Peiss, *Cheap Amusements: Working Women and Leisure in Turn-of-the-Century New York* (1986). T. J. Jackson Lears, *No Place of Grace: Antimodernism and the Transformation of American Culture, 1880–1920* (1981) chronicles patterns of resistance to the new culture. Debby Applegate, *The Most Famous Man in America: The Biography of Henry Ward Beecher* (2006) examines a renowned clergyman. Roy Rosenzweig and Elizabeth Blackmar, *The Park and the People: A History of Central Park* (1992) studies the creation of America's most famous public park. Edwin G. Burrows and Mike Wallace, *Gotham: A History of New York City to 1898* (1998) is a thorough history of New York's remarkable growth. John F. Kasson, *Amusing the Millions: Coney Island at the Turn of the Century* (1978) is an illustrated history and interpretation of the amusement park's place in American culture. Jonathan Levy, *Freaks and Fortunes* (2012), shows the growth of capitalism and risk in the United States.

Chapter 19

A Government Out of Sight: The Mystery of National Authority in Nineteenth-Century America (2009) shows the growing public life. Two books charting the growing capacities of the American state during this period are Theda Skocpol, *Protecting Soldiers and Mothers: The Political Origins of Social Policy in the United States* (1992); and Stephen Skowronek, *Building a New American State: The Expansion of National Administrative Capacities, 1877–1920* (1982). Richard Hofstadter's *The Age of Reform: From Bryan to FDR* (1955) and Lawrence Goodwyn's *The Populist Moment* (1978) offer sharply contrasting characterizations of the populist and progressive reform movements of this time. Other important studies of populism include John D. Hicks, *The Populist Revolt* (1931), a classic account, and Steven Hahn, *The Roots of Southern Populism: Yeoman Farmers and the Transformation of the Georgia Upcountry* (1983). Michael Kazin, *The Populist Persuasion: An American History* (1995) places populist ideas in a broad historical context. David F. Healy, *U.S. Expansionism: Imperialist Urge in the 1890s* (1970) is a contrasting view. Walter LaFeber, *The Cambridge History of American Foreign Policy, Vol. 2: The Search for Opportunity, 1865–1913* (1993) is an overview. William Appleman Williams, *The Tragedy of American Diplomacy*, rev. ed. (1972), is a classic revisionist work on the origins and consequences of American imperialism, supplemented by his *Empire as a Way of Life: An Essay on the Causes and Character of America's Present Predicament* (1982). Anders Stephanson, *Manifest Destiny: American Expansionism and the Empire of Right* (1995) is a short history of Americans' ideology of expansionism. Warren Zimmermann, *First Great Triumph: How Five Americans Made Their Country a Great Power* (2002) describes a circle of powerful figures who together helped create an ideology of empire for the United States in the early twentieth century. Robert L. Beisner's *Twelve Against Empire* (1968) chronicles the careers of the leading opponents of imperial expansion. Emily S. Rosenberg, *Spreading the American Dream: American Economic and Cultural Expansion, 1890–1945* (1982) is a cultural interpretation. Gerald F. Linderman, *The Mirror of War: American Society and the Spanish-American War* (1974) examines the social meaning of the war within the United States. Stuart Creighton Miller, *"Benevolent Assimilation": The American Conquest of the Philippines, 1899–1903* (1982) describes the American war in the Philippines. Michael Hunt, *The Making of a Special Relationship: The United States and China to 1914* (1983) is an introduction to the subject.

Chapter 20

Richard Hofstadter, *The Age of Reform: From Bryan to FDR* (1955) is a classic. Robert Wiebe, *The Search for Order, 1877–1920* (1967) is an important interpretation of the era. Alan Dawley, *Struggles for Justice: Social Responsibility and the Liberal State* (1991) and Michael McGerr, *A Fierce Discontent: The Rise and Fall of the Progressive Movement in America, 1870–1920* (2003) are contrasting synthetic accounts of progressive movements and their ideas. For powerful insights into pragmatism, an important philosophical underpinning to much reform, see Robert Westbrook, *John Dewey and American Democracy* (1991) and Louis Menand, *The Metaphysical Club: A Story of Ideas* (2001). Richard Greenwald, *The Triangle Fire, the Protocols of Peace, and Industrial Democracy in Progressive Era New York* (2006) examines a critical event in stimulating reform.

Nancy Cott, *The Grounding of American Feminism* (1987) studies the shifting roles of women. Kathryn Kish Sklar, *Florence Kelley and the Nation's Work: The Rise of Women's Political Culture, 1830–1900* (1995) examines female reformers on the progressive movement. Glenda Gilmore, *Gender and Jim*

Crow: Women and the Politics of White Supremacy in North Carolina, 1896-1920 (1996) examines the role of gender in the construction of segregation. Louis Harlan, *Booker T. Washington: The Making of a Black Leader* (1956) and *Booker T. Washington: The Wizard of Tuskegee* (1983) are an outstanding multivolume biography, as are David Levering Lewis, *W. E. B. Du Bois: Biography of a Race* (1993) and *W. E. B. Du Bois: The Fight for Equality and the American Century* (2000).

John Milton Cooper Jr. compares the lives and ideas of the progressive movement's leading national politicians in *The Warrior and the Priest: Woodrow Wilson and Theodore Roosevelt* (1983). He is also the author of *Woodrow Wilson: A Biography* (2009). John Morton Blum, *The Republican Roosevelt* (1954) is a brief study. Donald E. Anderson, *William Howard Taft* (1973) is a useful account of this unhappy presidency. Arthur S. Link is Wilson's thorough biographer and the author of *Woodrow Wilson*, 5 vols. (1947-1965). Michael McGerr, *The Decline of Popular Politics* (1986) is the decline of public enthusiasm for parties in the North in the late nineteenth and early twentieth centuries. Stephen R. Fox, *The American Conservation Movement: John Muir and His Legacy* (1981) is another such study. John Opie, *Nature's Nation: An Environmental History of the United States* (1998) is an ambitious synthesis of environmental history.

Chapter 21

Ernest R. May, *The World War and American Isolation* (1959) is an authoritative account of the Great War. David Kennedy, *Over Here: The First World War and American Society* (1980) is a study of the domestic impact of the war. Robert D. Cuff, *The War Industries Board: Business-Government Relations During World War II* (1973) is an account of mobilization for war. Ronald Schaffer, *America in the Great War: The Rise of the War Welfare State* (1991) examines the ways in which mobilization for war created new public benefits for various groups, including labor. Maureen Greenwald, *Women, War, and Work* (1980) describes the impact of World War I on women workers. John Keegan, *The First World War* (1998) is a military history. Thomas Knock, *To End All Wars: Woodrow Wilson and the Quest for a New World Order* (1992) is a study of the battle for peace. Arno Mayer, *Wilson vs. Lenin* (1959) and *Politics and Diplomacy of Peacemaking: Containment and Counterrevolution* (1965) are revisionist accounts of the peacemaking process. Margaret MacMillan, *Paris 1919: Six Months That Changed the World* (2002) is an account of the Paris Peace Conference. World War I is captured by John Higham, *Strangers in the Land: Patterns of American Nativism* (1955). Paul L. Murphy, *World War I and the Origins of Civil Liberties* (1979) shows how wartime created new support for civil liberties. Beverly Gage, *The Day Wall Street Exploded* (2009) tells the story of postwar terrorism and the responses to it.

Chapter 22

Frederick Lewis Allen, *Only Yesterday* (1931) is a classic popular history of the 1920s. Ellis Hawley, *The Great War and the Search for a Modern Order* (1979) describes the effect of World War I on American ideas, culture, and society. William E. Leuchtenburg, *The Perils of Prosperity* (rev. ed. 1994) reveals the economic prosperity in the 1920s David Brody, *Workers in Industrial America* (1980) is a series of essays on welfare capitalism and other labor systems of the 1920s. David Nasaw, *The Patriarch: The Remarkable Life and Turbulent Times of Joseph P. Kennedy* (2012), relates the experiences of this powerful, yet flawed, man, his family, and the dangerous times in which they lived. T. J. Jackson Lears, *Fables of Abundance: A Cultural History of Advertising in America* (1994) and Roland Marchand, *Advertising the American Dream* (1985) are inquiries into the role of advertising in the new consumer culture. David Farber, *Sloan Rules: Alfred P. Sloan and the Triumph of General Motors* (2002) describes the consolidation of the giant automobile corporation. Alan Brinkley, *The Publisher: Henry Luce and His American Century* (2010) describes the rise of an important magazine empire. Robert Lynd and Helen Merrell Lynd, *Middletown* (1929) is a classic sociological study of how an American city encountered the consumer culture and economy of the 1920s. Ann Douglas's *Terrible Honesty: Mongrel Manhattan in the 1920s* (1995) examines the cultural and political history of the New Era in New York City. George Chauncey, *Gay New York: Gender, Urban Culture, and the Making of the Gay Male World, 1890-1940* (1994) is an excellent work in a relatively new field of history. The decline of the feminist movement in the 1920s is explored in Nancy Cott, *The Grounding of American Feminism* (1987). Gary Gerstle, *American Crucible* (2000) is an important study of the changing role of race and ethnicity in defining American nationhood in the twentieth century. George Marsden, *Fundamentalism and American Culture* (1980) is a study of some of the religious battles that came to a head in the 1920s. Edward J. Larson, *Summer for the Gods: The Scopes Trial and America's Continuing Debate over Science and Religion* (1997) is an analysis of the Scopes trial. Leonard Moore, *Citizen Klansmen: The Ku Klux Klan in Indiana, 1921-1928* (1991) is a view of the Klan. Kathleen M. Blee, *Women and the Klan: Racism and Gender in the 1920s* (1991) re-creates the female world of the Klan. Kevin Boyle, *Arc of Justice: A Saga of Race, Civil Rights, and Murder in the Jazz Age* (2004) is a portrait of New Era racial norms. Morton Keller, *Regulating a New Economy: Public Policy and Economic Change in America, 1900-1933* (1990) and *Regulating a New Society: Public Policy and Social Change in America, 1900-1933* (1994) are studies of New Era public policy.

Chapter 23

Donald Worster scathingly indicts agricultural capitalism for its destruction of the plains environment in *Dust Bowl: The Southern Plains in the 1930s* (1979). Timothy Egan, *The Worst Hard Time* (2006) is a portrait of the impact of the Dust Bowl. Richard Pells, *Radical Visions and American Dreams: Culture and Social Thought in the Depression Years* (1973) is an important survey of the cultural and intellectual history of the 1930s. Susan Ware analyzes the effect of the Great Depression on women in *Holding Their Own: American Women in the 1930s*

(1982). The Communist Party's most popular period in the United States is the subject of Harvey Klehr's *The Heyday of American Communism: The Depression Decade* (1984) and, from quite different viewpoints, Robin D. G. Kelley, *Hammer and Hoe: Alabama Communists during the Great Depression* (1990) and Michael Denning, *The Cultural Front: The Laboring of American Culture in the Twentieth Century* (1997). Joan Hoff Wilson, *Herbert Hoover: Forgotten Progressive* (1975) argues that President Hoover was in many ways a surprisingly progressive thinker about the American social order.

Chapter 24

William E. Leuchtenburg, *Franklin D. Roosevelt and the New Deal* (1963) is a history of the New Deal. Anthony Badger, *The New Deal: The Depression Years* (1989) is another overview. David Kennedy, *Freedom from Fear: The American People in Depression and War, 1929-1945* (1999) is a narrative history. Geoffrey Ward, *Before the Trumpet: Young Franklin Roosevelt, 1882-1905* (1985) and *A First-Class Temperament: The Emergence of Franklin Roosevelt* (1989) are biographical accounts of the pre-presidential FDR. Frank Freidel, *Franklin D. Roosevelt: A Rendezvous with Destiny* (1990) is a one-volume biography by one of FDR's most important biographers. Alan Brinkley, *Franklin Delano Roosevelt* (2009) is a short biography. Jonathan Alter, *The Defining Moment* (2006) and Anthony Badger, *FDR: The First Hundred Days* (2008) portray the first months of the New Deal. Ellis Hawley, *The New Deal and the Problem of Monopoly* (1967) is a classic examination of the economic policies of the Roosevelt administration in its first five years. Colin Gordon, *New Deals: Business, Labor, and Politics in America, 1920-1935* (1994) is a reinterpretation of the early New Deal years. The transformation of liberalism after 1937 is the subject of Alan Brinkley, *The End of Reform: New Deal Liberalism in Recession and War* (1995). Jennifer Klein, *For All These Rights: Business, Labor, and the Shaping of America's Public-Private Welfare State* (2003) sees the origin of the modern welfare state as a product in part of struggles between labor and capital. Linda Gordon, *Pitied but Not Entitled: Single Mothers and the History of Welfare* (1994) is a pioneering work on women as the recipients and also the authors of government welfare policies. Alice Kessler-Harris, *In Pursuit of Equity: Women, Men, and the Quest for Economic Citizenship in Twentieth-Century America* (2001) is a study of the intersection of gender and economic rights. The efforts of Chicago workers to protest and organize is the subject of Lizabeth Cohen, *Making a New Deal: Industrial Workers in Chicago, 1919-1939* (1990). Nelson Lichtenstein, *The Most Dangerous Man in Detroit: Walter Reuther and the Fate of American Labor* (1995) is a study of one of the early leaders of the CIO. Jordan Schwarz, *The New Dealers: Power Politics in the Age of Roosevelt* (1993) examines the proponents of state-funded economic development of the South and West. Alan Brinkley, *Voices of Protest: Huey Long, Father Coughlin, and the Great Depression* (1982) examines some of the most powerful challenges to the New Deal. Nancy J. Weiss, *Farewell to the Party of Lincoln: Black Politics in the Age of FDR* (1983) take contrasting positions on what the New Deal did for African Americans.

Chapter 25

Robert Dallek, *Franklin D. Roosevelt and American Foreign Policy, 1932-1945* (1979) is a comprehensive study of Roosevelt's foreign policy, Akira Iriye, *The Cambridge History of American Foreign Relations, Vol. 3: The Globalizing of America, 1913-1945* (1993) is another important study. James MacGregor Burns, *Roosevelt: The Soldier of Freedom* (1970) and Warren F. Kimball, *The Juggler: Franklin Roosevelt as Wartime Statesman* (1991) are two studies of the wartime president. A. Scott Berg, *Lindbergh* (1998) is a biography of the aviation hero who became a controversial figure in the 1930s. Akira Iriye, *The Origins of the Second World War in Asia and the Pacific* (1988) examines the conflict between China and Japan that preceded American intervention in the Pacific war. Gordon Prange, *At Dawn We Slept* (1981) examines the controversial attack on Pearl Harbor from both the Japanese and American sides.

Chapter 26

John Morton Blum, *V Was for Victory: Politics and American Culture During World War II* (1976) and Richard Polenberg, *War and Society* (1972) are studies of the home front during World War II. David Kennedy, *Freedom from Fear: The American People in Depression and War, 1929-1945* (1999) is a narrative of both the American military experience in the war and the war's impact on American politics and society. Alan Brinkley, *The End of Reform: New Deal Liberalism in Recession and War* (1995) examines the impact of the war on liberal ideology and political economy. Ira Katznelson, *Fear Itself: The New Deal and the Origins of Our Time* (2014), shows how the Great Depression and the World War II led to the power and affluence of the American state. Doris Kearns Goodwin, *No Ordinary Time: Franklin and Eleanor Roosevelt: The Home Front in World War II* (1994) is a portrait of the Roosevelts during the war. John W. Dower, *War Without Mercy: Race and Power in the Pacific War* (1986) examines the intense racism that shaped both sides of the war between the United States and Japan. John Keegan, *Six Armies in Normandy: From D-Day to the Liberation of Paris, June 6-August 25, 1944* (1982) is an account of the Normandy invasion. David S. Wyman, *The Abandonment of the Jews: America and the Holocaust, 1941-1945* (1984) is sharply critical of American policy toward the victims of the Holocaust. Richard Rhodes, *The Making of the Atomic Bomb* (1987) is an account of one of the scientific projects of the twentieth century. Gar Alperovitz, *The Decision to Use the Atomic Bomb and the Architecture of an American Myth* (1995) is an exhaustive and highly critical study of why the United States used atomic weapons in 1945.

Chapter 27

Several books by John Lewis Gaddis, *Strategies of Containment* (1982), *The United States and the Origins of the Cold War, 1941-1947* (1972), and *The Cold War: A New History* (2005), provide an introduction to Cold War history. Walter LaFeber, *America,*

Russia, and the Cold War, 1945-1967 is a survey of American-Soviet relations. Warren I. Cohen, *The Cambridge History of American Foreign Relations, Vol. 4: America in the Age of Soviet Power, 1945-1991* (1991) is a general history. Michael Hogan, *The Marshall Plan* (1987) is a provocative interpretation. David McCullough, *Truman* (1992) is a popular biography. Alonzo Hamby, *Man of the People: A Life of Harry S. Truman* (1995) is a scholarly one. Bruce Cumings, *The Origins of the Korean War* (1980) is a study of the context for America's first armed conflict of the Cold War. Ellen Schrecker, *Many Are the Crimes: McCarthyism in America* (1998) is an interpretation of McCarthyism, and David Oshinsky, *A Conspiracy So Immense: The World of Joe McCarthy* (1983) is a biography. Michael Ybarra, *Washington Gone Crazy: Senator Pat McCarran and the Great American Communist Hunt* (2004) is a study of another important figure in the Red Scare.

Chapter 28

James T. Patterson, *Grand Expectations: Postwar America, 1945-1974* (1996) is a history of the postwar era. John P. Diggins, *The Proud Decades: America in War and Peace, 1941-1960* (1989) and Godfrey Hodgson, *America in Our Time* (1976) are other important surveys. Kenneth T. Jackson, *The Crabgrass Frontier: The Suburbanization of the United States* (1985) is a classic history of a major social movement. Karal Ann Marling, *As Seen on TV: The Visual Culture of Everyday Life in the 1950s* (1995) is a study of the new medium. Lizabeth Cohen, *A Consumer's Republic: The Politics of Mass Consumption in Postwar America* (2003) examines the power of consumerism in postwar America. Elaine Tyler May, *Homeward Bound: American Families in the Cold War* (1988) is a challenging cultural history. Paul Boyer, *By the Bomb's Early Light: American Thought and Culture at the Dawn of the Atomic Age* (1985) examines the impact of the atomic bomb. Stephen Ambrose, *Eisenhower the President* (1984) is a good biography. Richard Kluger, *Simple Justice* (1975) is a classic history of the *Brown* decision, John Egerton, *Speak Now Against the Day: The Generation Before the Civil Rights Movement in the South* (1994) is a history of struggles over white supremacy in the first years after World War II. Michael Kazin, *American Dreamers: How the Left Changed a Nation* (2012), follows radicalism from the abolitionist movement of the antebellum period to the Occupy movement of the past decade.

Chapter 29

Allen J. Matusow, *The Unraveling of America: A History of Liberalism in the 1960s* (1984) is a history of this turbulent decade. Robert Dallek, *Lone Star Rising: Lyndon Johnson and His Times, 1908-1960* (1991), *Flawed Giant: Lyndon B. Johnson, 1960-1973* (1998), and *An Unfinished Life: John F. Kennedy, 1917-1963* (2003) are biographies. Raymond Arsenault, *Freedom Riders: 1961 and the Struggle for Justice* (2006) is a study of the civil rights movement. William Chafe, *Civilities and Civil Rights: Greensboro, North Carolina, and the Black Struggle for Freedom* (1980) examines the southern civil rights movement. Taylor Branch, *Parting the Waters: America in the*

King Years, 1959-63 (1988), *Pillar of Fire: America in the King Years, 1963-65*, and *At Canaan's Edge: America in the King Years, 1965-68* (2006) are good histories of the movement. Nicholas Lemann, *The Promised Land: The Great Black Migration and How It Changed America* (1991) is a study of the postwar African American migration to northern cities and of the Great Society's response to it. Ernest R. May and Philip D. Zelikow, *The Kennedy Tapes: Inside the White House During the Cuban Missile Crisis* (1997) provides the annotated transcripts of the taped meetings of Kennedy's inner circle. Sheldon Stern, *The Cuban Missile Crisis in American Memory: Myths vs. Reality* (2012), exposes the misconceptions and outright lies that have influenced our understanding of the Cuban Missile Crisis. Robert D. Schulzinger, *A Time for War: The United States and Vietnam, 1945-1975* (1997) is a general history of the war. Neil Sheehan, *A Bright Shining Lie: John Paul Vann and America in Vietnam* (1988) is a picture of the war as experienced by a significant military figure of the 1960s. Larry Berman, *Planning a Tragedy* (1982) and *Lyndon Johnson's War* (1989); and David Halberstam, *The Best and the Brightest* (1972) are interpretations of the American decision to intervene and stay in Vietnam. Dan T. Carter, *The Politics of Rage: George Wallace, the Origins of the New Conservatism, and the Transformation of American Politics* (1995) is a study of the career of George Wallace. Mark Kurlansky, *1968: The Year That Rocked the World* (2003) is a broader history of that turbulent year.

Chapter 30

John Morton Blum, *Years of Discord: American Politics and Society, 1961-1974* (1991) is an overview. Margaret Cruikshank, *The Rise of a Gay and Lesbian Liberation Movement* (1992) and David Eisenbach, *Gay Power: An American Revolution* (2006) recount another important struggle of the 1960s and beyond. Stephen Ambrose, *Nixon: The Triumph of a Politician, 1962-1972* (1989) and *Nixon, Ruin and Recovery, 1973-1990* (1992) provides a chronicle of this important presidency. Samuel Walker, *Presidents and Civil Liberties from Wilson to Obama* (2014), presents a history of the civil liberties records of American presidents from Wilson to Obama. Margaret MacMillan, *Nixon and Mao: The Week That Changed the World* (2007) examines Nixon's most famous diplomatic effort. David Greenberg, *Nixon's Shadow: The History of an Image* (2004), shows the complex nature of this influential president. David Greenberg, *Nixon's Shadow* (2003) is a perceptive examination of Nixon's place in American culture. Marilyn Young, *The Vietnam Wars, 1945-1990* (1991) provides. A full account of the last years of American involvement in Vietnam and of the conflicts in the region that followed the American withdrawal. Martha Biondi, *The Black Revolution on Campus* (2014), shows how black power was established in higher education in the late 1960s and early 1970s.

Chapter 31

Bruce J. Schulman, *The Seventies: The Great Shift in American Culture, Society, and Politics* (2001) and James T. Patterson,

Restless Giant: The United States from Watergate to Bush v. Gore (2005) are broad histories of the era. Yanek Mieczkowski, *Gerald Ford and the Challenges of the 1970s* (2005) is a scholarly study. Gaddis Smith, *Morality, Reason, and Power* (1986) examines the Carter foreign policy. Steven Gillon, *The Democrats' Dilemma: Walter Mondale and the Liberal Legacy* (1992) is a discussion of the travails of the Democrats in the 1970s. Sheldon Stern, *The Cuban Missile Crisis in American Memory: Myths vs. Reality* (2012), exposes the misconceptions and outright lies that have influenced our understanding of the Cuban Missile Crisis. Jerome L. Himmelstein, *To the Right: The Transformation of American Conservatism* (1990) and Godfrey Hodgson, *The World Turned Upside Down: A History of the Conservative Ascendancy in America* (1996) are introductions to the subject as is Kevin Kruse, *White Flight: Atlanta and the Making of Modern Conservatism* (2005). David R. Swartz, *Moral Minority: The Evangelical Left in an Age of Conservatism* (2014), is the first comprehensive study of the evangelical left. Lou Cannon, *President Reagan: The Role of a Lifetime* (1990) and Haynes Johnson, *Sleepwalking Through History* (1991) are accounts by journalists who covered the Reagan White House. Gill Troy, *Morning in America: How Ronald Reagan Invented the 1980s* (2005) is a scholarly study. John Lewis Gaddis, *The United States and the End of the Cold War* (1992) and *We Now Know: Rethinking Cold War History* (1997) examine the transformation of the world order after 1989. Richard Rhodes, *Arsenals of Folly* (2007) is a passionate account of the nuclear arms race. Herbert Parmet, *George Bush: The Life of a Lone Star Yankee* (1997) is the first major scholarly study of the 41st president.

Chapter 32

John Lewis Gaddis, *The United States and the End of the Cold War* (1992), *We Now Know: Rethinking Cold War History* (1997), and *Surprise, Security, and the American Experience* (2004) are early examinations of the post–Cold War transformation of the world order. Clinton's own memoir, *My Life* (2004) is a valuable account of his presidency. John F. Harris, *The Survivor: President Clinton and His Times* (2005) is a valuable overview of this presidency. David Halberstam, *War in a Time of Peace. Bush, Clinton, and the Generals* (2001) examines the foreign policy and military ventures of the Bush and Clinton years. Samantha Power, *"A Problem from Hell": America and the Age of Genocide* (2003) is a study of a major question in the United States. George Packer, *The Assassin's Gate: America in Iraq* (2006); Jane Mayer, *The Dark Side* (2007); Lawrence Wright, *The Looming Tower: Al-Qaeda and the Road to 9/11* (2006) are among the many studies of the post-9/11 years and the war in Iraq. William Julius Wilson, *The Truly Disadvantaged* (1987) and *When Work Disappears* (1996) are important studies of the inner-city poor from one of America's leading sociologists. David Boies and Theodore B. Olson, *Redeeming the Dream: The case for Marriage Equality* (2014), presents the story of two landmark Supreme Court cases in support of the right of gay people to marry. David A. Hollinger, *Postethnic America: Beyond Multiculturalism* (1995) is a comment on the debates over multiculturalism.

DESIGN ELEMENTS

FRONT MATTER CREDITS

INDEX

Page references followed by b indicate boxes; i, illustrations; m, maps.

Weapons–*Cont.*
  in Cold War
    nuclear age culture in, 744
    research of, 738
    types of, 760–761, 848–849
  colonial American, 48, 80
  G. W. Bush and assault, 860
  of urban national guard groups, 499
  in World War I, 583i, 592, 594
  in World War II, 695–699, 713–714, 727–730
"Weapons of mass destruction," 873, 874, 879
Weathermen (militants), 798b, 810
Weatherwise's Federal Almanack, 163i
Weaver, James B., 518, 523
Weaver, Robert, 680, 785
Weavers (vocal group), 798b
Webb, Walter Prescott, 447b
Webster-Ashburton Treaty (1842), 251
Webster, Daniel
  Bank of the United States and, 242
  as Congressman, 210
  on Dartmouth College, 224
  final portrait of, 237i
  on representation, 231
  as Secretary of State, 249
  as Senator, 236–237
  on slavery in territories, 353
  as Whig leader/candidate, 245–246, 246m
Webster-Hayne debate, 236–237
Webster, Noah, 184
Weems, Mason, 184
Weibe, Robert, 556b
Weimar Republic, 689
Weisbrot, Robert, 788b
Welch, Robert, 741
Welch, William H., 555
Weld, Theodore Dwight, 335
Welfare capitalism, 617
Welfare reform, 858
Welfare state, 684, 774–775
Welfare system; *see also* Government assistance; Public relief agencies
  Eisenhower and, 774
  L. Johnson's program of, 784
  Nixon and, 828
  in progressive reform, 555i
  in Reconstruction era, 415;
    see also Freedmen's Bureau
  Social Security insurance vs., 672
Welles, Orson, 651, 696i, 696–697b
Wellesley College, 511
Wells College, 511
Wells, H. G., 696b
Wells, Ida B., 425, 428
Wesley, Charles, 90
Wesley, John, 90, 185
West; *see also* Midwest; Northwest (midwest), Old; Southwest; Westward expansion

agriculture in, 270, 453–456
in American literature, 316
after American Revolution, 152m
Civil War in, 384–385, 388, 389m
conservation movement and, 574
conservative opposition in, 842
economy of Far, 438–443
education in, 325
farmers' organizations in, 523
Federalist government and, 172
free-soilers and, 335
Great Depression and, 645, 646
growth of, 257, 755
Jacksonian democracy and, 234, 234b
Native Americans moved in/to, 241, 447–453, 450m, 814m
New Deal and, 683
political parties of, 245
progressive reform in, 523
public land sales in, 170, 195, 344
railroads in, 266, 355
romance of Far, 443–447
settlement of, 281, 289
slavery abolished in, 372
societies of Far, 431–438
trade/trapping in, 219–220, 220i
voting rights in, 231
Webster-Hayne debate on, 236
workforce in, 523, 770
World War II and, 712
West Coast Hotel v. *Parrish*, 675
West Coast rap, 868b
West from Appomattox (Richardson), 417b
West Germany; *see* Federal Republic of Germany (West)
West, Nathanael, 654
West Point; *see* Military Academy at West Point, United States
West Roxbury, Massachusetts, 319
West Virginia, 388, 461
Westad, Arne, 737b
Western Conference, 504
Western culture and globalization, 870
Western Europe
  economic reconstruction of, 737–738
  as major world power, 827
  NATO and military capabilities of, 739–740
Western Federation of Miners, 597
Western Union Telegraph Company, 266
Westward expansion
  American Revolution and, 146–147
  British acts controlling, 109, 119
  Burr conspiracy against, 201–202
  colonial American, 40, 56–57
  Confederation on, 153–155, 154i
  conflicts over, 202–208, 342–344, 346–348
  crises between North/South on, 354–361
  European, to New World, 7–21, 58b
  French/Indian War and, 101, 107
  Lewis/Clark's exploration and, 200–201

Louisiana purchase and, 197–202
Manifest Destiny and, 340–341, 341m
Mexican War and, 348–350
migration trails of, 344i, 344–346, 345m
nationalism and, 218–220
Native Americans and, 155, 218, 220, 343, 345
sectional debate on slavery and, 351–354, 354m
War of 1812 and, 208–211
Westward Expansion (Billington), 446b
Weyler, Valeriano, 538–538
Wheeler, Burton, 698
Wheeler-Nicholson, Malcolm, 676b
Wheeler, United States v., 815
Wheelwright, John, 45
When Jesus Came, the Corn Mothers Went Away (Gutiérrez), 58b
Whiggery, 245
Whigs coalition, 109, 117
Whigs (party)
  anti-immigration sentiment and, 262
  birth of, 234, 244–246
  destruction of, 356
  in elections, 246m, 247–251, 248m, 347, 351, 354–355
Whirling Thunder, 239i
Whiskey Rebellion, 172, 173i
"Whiskey ring," 413
Whistler, James McNeil, 509
"White Citizens Councils" (1950s), 772
White-collar workers, 766
White House
  conference on football, 504
  in Jeffersonian era, 193, 194m
  Office of War Mobilization in, 713
  taping system of, 833
  in War of 1812, 208
White, Hugh Lawson, 246, 246m
White, John, 12i, 31
White Leagues, 414
"White Man's Burden" (Kipling), 534b
White Over Black (Jordan), 72b
White, Richard, 58b, 447b
White Tower (drive-in), 756b
White, Walter, 646
White, William Allen, 562b, 698
Whitefield, George, 22b, 90–91, 94i
Whiteman, Narcissa, 343–344
Whiteman, Paul, 628b
Whites
  anti-abolitionism by southern, 332–333
  Constitutional rights for, 166–167
  Indian affairs management by, 448
  Jacksonian democracy for, 234, 235b
  in New South, 422–424, 428
  in Reconstruction South, 407–412, 418–419
  society of, in old South, 298–303
Whitman, Marcus, 343–344
Whitman, Walt, 316–317, 817